Fundamentals of Computer Algorithms

SECOND EDITION

ELLIS HOROWITZ
University of Southern California

SARTAJ SAHNI
University of Florida

SANGUTHEVAR RAJASEKARAN
University of Connecticut

Universities Press

FUNDAMENTALS OF COMPUTER ALGORITHMS

UNIVERSITIES PRESS (INDIA) PRIVATE LIMITED

Registered Office
3-6-747/1/A and 3-6-754/1, Himayatnagar, Hyderabad 500 029, Telangana, India
info@universitiespress.com; www.universitiespress.com

Distributed by
Orient Blackswan Private Limited

Registered Office
3-6-752, Himayatnagar, Hyderabad 500 029, Telangana, India

Other Offices
Bengaluru, Chennai, Guwahati, Hyderabad, Kolkata,
Mumbai, New Delhi, Noida, Patna

502161

First published in India by
Universities Press (India) Private Limited 2008
Reprinted 2008 (6 times), 2009, 2010 (twice), 2012 (twice), 2013, 2014, 2015 (twice), 2016 (twice), 2017, 2018, 2019, 2022 (twice), 2023 (twice), 2025

ISBN 978 81 7371 612 6

Printed at
Navya Printers, Hyderabad 500 013

Published by
Universities Press (India) Private Limited
3-6-747/1/A and 3-6-754/1, Himayatnagar
Hyderabad 500 029, Telangana, India

To my nuclear family,

MARYANNE, *PIPI*, *CHANOCH*, *and IRA*

– Ellis Horowitz

To my children,

AGAM, *NEHA*, and *PARAM*

– Sartaj Sahni

To,

KEERAN, *KRISHNA*, *PANDI*, and *PONNUTHAI*

– Sanguthevar Rajasekaran

PREFACE

If we try to identify those contributions of computer science that will be long lasting, surely one of these will be the refinement of the concept called *algorithm*. Ever since man invented the idea of a machine which could perform basic mathematical operations, the study of what can be computed and how it can be done well was launched. This study, inspired by the computer, has led to the discovery of many important algorithms and design methods. The discipline called computer science has embraced the study of algorithms as its own. It is the purpose of this book to organize what is known about them in a coherent fashion so that students and practitioners can learn to devise and analyze new algorithms for themselves.

A book which contains every algorithm ever invented would be exceedingly large. Traditionally, algorithms books proceeded by examining only a small number of problem areas in depth. For each specific problem the most efficient algorithm for its solution is usually presented and analyzed. This approach has one major flaw. Though the student sees many fast algorithms and may master the tools of analysis, she/he remains unconfident about how to devise good algorithms in the first place.

The missing ingredient is a lack of emphasis on *design* techniques. A knowledge of design will certainly help one to create good algorithms, yet without the tools of analysis there is no way to determine the quality of the result. This observation that design should be taught on a par with analysis led us to a more promising line of approach: namely to organize this book around some fundamental strategies of algorithm design. The number of basic design strategies is reasonably small. Moreover all of the algorithms one would typically wish to study can easily be fit into these categories; for example, mergesort and quicksort are perfect examples of the divide-and-conquer strategy while Kruskal's minimum spanning tree algorithm and Dijkstra's single source shortest path algorithm are straight forward examples of the greedy strategy. An understanding of these strategies is an essential first step towards acquiring the skills of design.

Though we strongly feel that the emphasis on design as well as analysis is the appropriate way to organize the study of algorithms, a cautionary remark is in order. First, we have not included every known design principle. One example is linear programming which is one of the most successful techniques, but is often discussed in a course of its own. Secondly, the student should be inhibited from taking a cookbook approach to algorithm design by assuming that each algorithm must derive from only a single technique. This is not so.

A major portion of this book, Chapters 3 through 9, deal with the different design strategies. First each strategy is described in general terms. Typically a "program abstraction" is given which outlines the form that the computation will take if this strategy can be applied. Following this there are a succession of examples which reveal the intricacies and varieties of the general strategy. The examples are somewhat loosely ordered in terms of increasing complexity. The type of complexity may arise in several ways. Usually we begin with a problem which is very simple to understand and requires no data structures other than a one-dimensional array. For this problem it is usually obvious that the design strategy yields a correct solution. Later examples may require a proof that an algorithm based on this design technique does work. Or, the later algorithms may require more sophisticated data structures (e.g., trees or graphs) and their analyses may be more complex. The major goal of this organization is to emphasize the arts of synthesis and analysis of algorithms. Auxiliary goals are to expose the student to good program structure and to proofs of algorithm correctness.

The algorithms in this book are presented in a pseudocode that resembles C. Section 1.2.1 describes the pseudocode conventions. Most of the algorithms presented in this book are short and the language constructs used to describe them are simple enough that any one can understand.

Another special feature of this book is that we cover the area of randomized algorithms extensively. Many of the algorithms discussed in Chapters 13, 14, and 15 are randomized. Some randomized algorithms are presented in the other chapters as well. An introductory one quarter course on parallel algorithms might cover Chapters 13, 14, and 15 and perhaps some minimal additional material.

We have identified certain sections of the text (indicated with (*)) that are more suitable for advanced courses. We view the material presented in this book as ideal for a one semester or two quarter course given to juniors, seniors, or graduate students. It does require prior experience with programming in a higher level language but everything else is self-contained. Practically speaking, it seems that a course on data structures is helpful, if only for the fact that the students have greater programming maturity. For a school on the quarter system, the first quarter might cover the basic design techniques as given in Chapters 3 through 9: divide-and-conquer, the greedy method, dynamic programming, search and traversal, backtracking, branch-and-bound, and algebraic methods (see TABLE I). The second quarter would cover Chapters 10 through 15: lower bound theory, $\mathcal{NP}$-completeness and approximation methods, PRAM algorithms, Mesh algorithms and Hypercube algorithms (see TABLE II).

Week	Subject	Reading
1	Introduction	1.1 to 1.3
2	Introduction Data structures	1.4 2.1, 2.2
3	Data structures	2.3 to 2.6
4	Divide-and-conquer	Chapter 3 Assignment I due
5	The greedy method	Chapter 4 Exam I
6	Dynamic programming	Chapter 5
7	Search and traversal techniques	Chapter 6 Assignment II due
8	Backtracking	Chapter 7
9	Branch-and-bound	Chapter 8
10	Algebraic methods	Chapter 9 Assignment III due Exam II

TABLE I: FIRST QUARTER

For a semester schedule where the student has not been exposed to data structures and O-notation, Chapters 1 through 7, 11, and 13 is about the right amount of material (see TABLE III).

A more rigorous pace would cover Chapters 1 to 7, 11, 13, and 14 (see TABLE IV).

Week	Subject	Reading
1	Lower bound theory	10.1 to 10.3
2	Lower bound theory $\mathcal{NP}$-complete and $\mathcal{NP}$-hard problems	10.4 11.1, 11.2
3	$\mathcal{NP}$-complete and $\mathcal{NP}$-hard problems	11.3, 11.4
4	$\mathcal{NP}$-complete and $\mathcal{NP}$-hard problems Approximation algorithms	11.5, 11.6 12.1, 12.2 Assignment I due
5	Approximation algorithms	12.3 to 12.6 Exam I
6	PRAM algorithms	13.1 to 13.4
7	PRAM algorithms	13.5 to 13.9 Assignment II due
8	Mesh algorithms	14.1 to 14.5
9	Mesh algorithms Hypercube algorithms	14.6 to 14.8 15.1 to 15.3
10	Hypercube algorithms	15.4 to 15.8 Assignment III due Exam II

TABLE II: SECOND QUARTER

An advanced course, for those who have prior knowledge about data structures and O notation, might consist of Chapters 3 to 11, and 13 to 15 (see TABLE V).

Week	Subject	Reading
1	Introduction	1.1 to 1.3
2	Introduction Data structures	1.4 2.1, 2.2
3	Data structures	2.3 to 2.6
4	Divide-and-conquer	3.1 to 3.4 Assignment I due
5	Divide-and-conquer	3.5 to 3.7 Exam I
6	The greedy method	4.1 to 4.4
7	The greedy method	4.5 to 4.7 Assignment II due
8	Dynamic programming	5.1 to 5.5
9	Dynamic programming	5.6 to 5.10
10	Search and traversal	6.1 to 6.4 Assignment III due Exam II
11	Backtracking	7.1 to 7.3
12	Backtracking	7.4 to 7.6
13	$\mathcal{NP}$-complete and $\mathcal{NP}$-hard problems	11.1 to 11.3 Assignment IV due
14	$\mathcal{NP}$-complete and $\mathcal{NP}$-hard problems	11.4 to 11.6
15	PRAM algorithms	13.1 to 13.4
16	PRAM algorithms	13.5 to 13.9 Assignment V due Exam III

TABLE III: SEMESTER – Medium pace (no prior exposure)

Week	Subject	Reading
1	Introduction	1.1 to 1.3
2	Introduction Data structures	1.4 2.1, 2.2
3	Data structures	2.3 to 2.6
4	Divide-and-conquer	3.1 to 3.5 Assignment I due
5	Divide-and-conquer The greedy method	3.6 to 3.7 4.1 to 4.3 Exam I
6	The greedy method	4.4 to 4.7
7	Dynamic programming	5.1 to 5.7 Assignment II due
8	Dynamic programming Search and traversal techniques	5.8 to 5.10 6.1 to 6.2
9	Search and traversal techniques Backtracking	6.3, 6.4 7.1, 7.2
10	Backtracking	7.3 to 7.6 Assignment III due Exam II
11	$\mathcal{NP}$-hard and $\mathcal{NP}$-complete problems	11.1 to 11.3
12	$\mathcal{NP}$-hard and $\mathcal{NP}$-complete problems	11.4 to 11.6
13	PRAM algorithms	13.1 to 13.4 Assignment IV due
14	PRAM algorithms	13.5 to 13.9
15	Mesh algorithms	14.1 to 14.3
16	Mesh algorithms	14.4 to 14.8 Assignment V due Exam III

TABLE IV: SEMESTER – Rigorous pace (no prior exposure)

Week	Subject	Reading
1	Divide-and-conquer	3.1 to 3.5
2	Divide-and-conquer The greedy method	3.6, 3.7 4.1 to 4.3
3	The greedy method	4.4 to 4.7
4	Dynamic programming	Chapter 5 Assignment I due
5	Search and traversal techniques	Chapter 6 Exam I
6	Backtracking	Chapter 7
7	Branch-and-bound	Chapter 8 Assignment II due
8	Algebraic methods	Chapter 9
9	Lower bound theory	Chapter 10
10	$\mathcal{NP}$-complete and $\mathcal{NP}$-hard problems	11.1 to 11.3 Exam II Assignment III
11	$\mathcal{NP}$-complete and $\mathcal{NP}$-hard problems	11.4 to 11.6
12	PRAM algorithms	13.1 to 13.4
13	PRAM algorithms	13.5 to 13.9 Assignment IV due
14	Mesh algorithms	14.1 to 14.5
15	Mesh algorithms Hypercube algorithms	14.6 to 14.8 15.1 to 15.3
16	Hypercube algorithms	15.4 to 15.8 Assignment V due Exam III

TABLE V: SEMESTER – Advanced course (rigorous pace)

For homework there are numerous exercises at the end of each chapter. The most popular and instructive homework assignment we have found is one which requires the student to execute and time two programs using the same data sets. This requires the student to code the algorithm in a suitable programming language, devise suitable data sets, and write a main program which outputs the timing results. The timing results should agree with the asymptotic analysis that was done for the algorithm. This is a nontrivial task which can be both educational and fun. Most importantly it emphasizes an aspect of this field that is often neglected, that there is an experimental side to the practice of algorithms.

In this new edition, we have added many new examples and exercises, enhanced the treatment of amortized complexity, and updated the references and selected readings associated with each chapter.

Acknowledgments

We are grateful to Martin J. Biernat, Jeff Jenness, Saleem Khan, Ming-Yang Kao, Douglas M. Campbell, and Stephen P. Leach for their critical comments which have immensely enhanced our presentation. We are thankful to the students at UF for pointing out mistakes in earlier versions. We are also thankful to Teo Gonzalez, Danny Krizanc, and David Wei who carefully read portions of this book.

Ellis Horowitz
Sartaj Sahni
Sanguthevar Rajasekaran
October, 2007

Contents

Chapter 1

INTRODUCTION

1.1 WHAT IS AN ALGORITHM?

The word algorithm comes from the name of a Persian author, Abu Ja'far Mohammed ibn Musa al Khowarizmi (c. 825 A.D.), who wrote a textbook on mathematics. This word has taken on a special significance in computer science, where "algorithm" has come to refer to a method that can be used by a computer for the solution of a problem. This is what makes algorithm different from words such as process, technique, or method.

Definition 1.1 [Algorithm]: An *algorithm* is a finite set of instructions that, if followed, accomplishes a particular task. In addition, all algorithms must satisfy the following criteria:

1. **Input.** Zero or more quantities are externally supplied.
2. **Output.** At least one quantity is produced.
3. **Definiteness.** Each instruction is clear and unambiguous.
4. **Finiteness.** If we trace out the instructions of an algorithm, then for all cases, the algorithm terminates after a finite number of steps.
5. **Effectiveness.** Every instruction must be very basic so that it can be carried out, in principle, by a person using only pencil and paper. It is not enough that each operation be definite as in criterion 3; it also must be feasible. □

An algorithm is composed of a finite set of steps, each of which may require one or more operations. The possibility of a computer carrying out these operations necessitates that certain constraints be placed on the type of operations an algorithm can include.

Criteria 1 and 2 require that an algorithm produce one or more *outputs* and have zero or more *inputs* that are externally supplied. According to criterion 3, each operation must be *definite*, meaning that it must be perfectly clear what should be done. Directions such as "add 6 or 7 to x" or "compute 5/0" are not permitted because it is not clear which of the two possibilities should be done or what the result is.

The fourth criterion for algorithms we assume in this book is that they *terminate* after a finite number of operations. A related consideration is that the time for termination should be reasonably short. For example, an algorithm could be devised that decides whether any given position in the game of chess is a winning position. The algorithm works by examining all possible moves and counter moves that could be made from the starting position. The difficulty with this algorithm is that even using the most modern computers, it may take billions of years to make the decision. We must be very concerned with analyzing the efficiency of each of our algorithms.

Criterion 5 requires that each operation be *effective*; each step must be such that it can, at least in principle, be done by a person using pencil and paper in a finite amount of time. Performing arithmetic on integers is an example of an effective operation, but arithmetic with real numbers is not, since some values may be expressible only by infinitely long decimal expansion. Adding two such numbers would violate the effectiveness property.

Algorithms that are definite and effective are also called *computational procedures*. One important example of computational procedures is the operating system of a digital computer. This procedure is designed to control the execution of jobs, in such a way that when no jobs are available, it does not terminate but continues in a waiting state until a new job is entered. Though computational procedures include important examples such as this one, we restrict our study to computational procedures that always terminate.

To help us achieve the criterion of definiteness, algorithms are written in a programming language. Such languages are designed so that each legitimate sentence has a unique meaning. A *program* is the expression of an algorithm in a programming language. Sometimes words such as procedure, function, and subroutine are used synonymously for program. Most readers of this book have probably already programmed and run some algorithms on a computer. This is desirable because before you study a concept in general, it helps if you had some practical experience with it. Perhaps you had some difficulty getting started in formulating an initial solution to a problem, or perhaps you were unable to decide which of two algorithms was better. The goal of this book is to teach you how to make these decisions.

The study of algorithms includes many important and active areas of research. There are four distinct areas of study one can identify:

1. *How to devise algorithms* — Creating an algorithm is an art which may never be fully automated. A major goal of this book is to study vari-

ous design techniques that have proven to be useful in that they have often yielded good algorithms. By mastering these design strategies, it will become easier for you to devise new and useful algorithms. Many of the chapters of this book are organized around what we believe are the major methods of algorithm design. The reader may now wish to glance back at the table of contents to see what these methods are called. Some of these techniques may already be familiar, and some have been found to be so useful that books have been written about them. Dynamic programming is one such technique. Some of the techniques are especially useful in fields other than computer science such as operations research and electrical engineering. In this book we can only hope to give an introduction to these many approaches to algorithm formulation. All of the approaches we consider have applications in a variety of areas including computer science. But some important design techniques such as linear, nonlinear, and integer programming are not covered here as they are traditionally covered in other courses.

2. *How to validate algorithms* — Once an algorithm is devised, it is necessary to show that it computes the correct answer for all possible legal inputs. We refer to this process as *algorithm validation*. The algorithm need not as yet be expressed as a program. It is sufficient to state it in any precise way. The purpose of the validation is to assure us that this algorithm will work correctly independently of the issues concerning the programming language it will eventually be written in. Once the validity of the method has been shown, a program can be written and a second phase begins. This phase is referred to as *program proving* or sometimes as *program verification*. A proof of correctness requires that the solution be stated in two forms. One form is usually as a program which is annotated by a set of assertions about the input and output variables of the program. These assertions are often expressed in the predicate calculus. The second form is called a *specification*, and this may also be expressed in the predicate calculus. A proof consists of showing that these two forms are equivalent in that for every given legal input, they describe the same output. A complete proof of program correctness requires that each statement of the programming language be precisely defined and all basic operations be proved correct. All these details may cause a proof to be very much longer than the program.

3. *How to analyze algorithms* — This field of study is called analysis of algorithms. As an algorithm is executed, it uses the computer's central processing unit (CPU) to perform operations and its memory (both immediate and auxiliary) to hold the program and data. *Analysis of algorithms* or *performance analysis* refers to the task of determining how much computing time and storage an algorithm requires. This is a challenging area which sometimes requires great mathematical skill. An important result of this study is that it allows you to make quantitative judgments about the value of one algorithm over another. Another result is that it allows you to predict whether the software will meet any efficiency constraints that exist.

Questions such as how well does an algorithm perform in the best case, in the worst case, or on the average are typical. For each algorithm in the text, an analysis is also given. Analysis is more fully described in Section 1.3.2.

4. *How to test a program* — Testing a program consists of two phases: debugging and profiling (or performance measurement). *Debugging* is the process of executing programs on sample data sets to determine whether faulty results occur and, if so, to correct them. However, as E. Dijkstra has pointed out, "debugging can only point to the presence of errors, but not to their absence." In cases in which we cannot verify the correctness of output on sample data, the following strategy can be employed: let more than one programmer develop programs for the same problem, and compare the outputs produced by these programs. If the outputs match, then there is a good chance that they are correct. A proof of correctness is much more valuable than a thousand tests (if that proof is correct), since it guarantees that the program will work correctly for all possible inputs. *Profiling* or *performance measurement* is the process of executing a correct program on data sets and measuring the time and space it takes to compute the results. These timing figures are useful in that they may confirm a previously done analysis and point out logical places to perform useful optimization. A description of the measurement of timing complexity can be found in Section 1.3.6. For some of the algorithms presented here, we show how to devise a range of data sets that will be useful for debugging and profiling.

These four categories serve to outline the questions we ask about algorithms throughout this book. As we can't hope to cover all these subjects completely, we content ourselves with concentrating on design and analysis, spending less time on program construction and correctness.

EXERCISES

1. Look up the words algorism and algorithm in your dictionary and write down their meanings.

2. The name al-Khowarizmi (algorithm) literally means "from the town of Khowarazm." This city is now known as Khiva, and is located in Uzbekistan. See if you can find this country in an atlas.

3. Use the WEB to find out more about al-Khowarizmi, e.g., his dates, a picture, or a stamp.

4. Describe two applications for which it is highly undesirable that the corresponding computer program terminate after a finite number of steps.

1.2 ALGORITHM SPECIFICATION

1.2.1 Pseudocode Conventions

In computational theory, we distinguish between an algorithm and a program. The latter does not have to satisfy the finiteness condition. For example, we can think of an operating system that continues in a "wait" loop until more jobs are entered. Such a program does not terminate unless the system crashes. Since our programs always terminate, we use "algorithm" and "program" interchangeably in this text.

We can describe an algorithm in many ways. We can use a natural language like English, although if we select this option, we must make sure that the resulting instructions are definite. Graphic representations called *flowcharts* are another possibility, but they work well only if the algorithm is small and simple. In this text we present most of our algorithms using a pseudocode that resembles C.

1. Comments begin with // and continue until the end of line.

2. Blocks are indicated with matching braces: **{** and **}**. A compound statement (i.e., a collection of simple statements) can be represented as a block. The body of a procedure also forms a block. Statements are delimited by ;.

3. An identifier begins with a letter. The data types of variables are not explicitly declared. The types will be clear from the context. Whether a variable is global or local to a procedure will also be evident from the context. We assume simple data types such as integer, float, char, boolean, and so on. Compound data types can be formed with **records**. Here is an example:

   $$\begin{array}{lll} node = \textbf{record} & & \\ \{ & datatype\_1 & data\_1; \\ & \vdots & \\ & datatype\_n & data\_n; \\ & node & *link; \\ \} & & \end{array}$$

   In this example, *link* is a pointer to the record type *node*. Individual data items of a record can be accessed with $\rightarrow$ and period. For instance if p points to a record of type *node*, $p \rightarrow data\_1$ stands for the value of the first field in the record. On the other hand, if q is a record of type *node*, $q.data\_1$ will denote its first field.

4. Assignment of values to variables is done using the assignment statement

$\langle variable \rangle := \langle expression \rangle$;

5. There are two boolean values **true** and **false**. In order to produce these values, the logical operators **and**, **or**, and **not** and the relational operators $<, \leq, =, \neq, \geq$, and $>$ are provided.

6. Elements of multidimensional arrays are accessed using [and]. For example, if A is a two dimensional array, the (i, j)th element of the array is denoted as $A[i, j]$. Array indices start at zero.

7. The following looping statements are employed: **for**, **while**, and **repeat-until**. The **while** loop takes the following form:

   while ⟨*condition*⟩ **do**
   {
   ⟨*statement* 1⟩
   ⋮
   ⟨*statement n*⟩
   }

   As long as ⟨*condition*⟩ is **true**, the statements get executed. When ⟨*condition*⟩ becomes **false**, the loop is exited. The value of ⟨*condition*⟩ is evaluated at the top of the loop.

   The general form of a **for** loop is

   for *variable* := *value*1 **to** *value*2 **step** *step* **do**
   {
   ⟨*statement* 1⟩
   ⋮
   ⟨*statement n*⟩
   }

   Here *value*1, *value*2, and *step* are arithmetic expressions. A variable of type integer or real or a numerical constant is a simple form of an arithmetic expression. The clause "**step** *step*" is optional and taken as +1 if it does not occur. *step* could either be positive or negative. *variable* is tested for termination at the start of each iteration. The **for** loop can be implemented as a **while** loop as follows:

   variable := *value*1;
   fin := *value*2;
   incr := *step*;
   while $((variable - fin) * step \leq 0)$ **do**
   {

```
        ⟨statement 1⟩
              ⋮
        ⟨statement n⟩
        variable := variable + incr;
    }
```

A **repeat-until** statement is constructed as follows:

```
    repeat
        ⟨statement 1⟩
              ⋮
        ⟨statement n⟩
    until ⟨condition⟩
```

The statements are executed as long as ⟨*condition*⟩ is **false**. The value of ⟨*condition*⟩ is computed after executing the statements.

The instruction **break;** can be used within any of the above looping instructions to force exit. In case of nested loops, **break;** results in the exit of the innermost loop that it is a part of. A **return** statement within any of the above also will result in exiting the loops. A **return** statement results in the exit of the function itself.

8. A conditional statement has the following forms:

```
    if ⟨condition⟩ then ⟨statement⟩
    if ⟨condition⟩ then ⟨statement 1⟩ else ⟨statement 2⟩
```

Here ⟨*condition*⟩ is a boolean expression and ⟨*statement*⟩, ⟨*statement* 1⟩, and ⟨*statement* 2⟩ are arbitrary statements (simple or compound).

We also employ the following **case** statement:

```
    case
    {
        :⟨condition 1⟩: ⟨statement 1⟩
                  ⋮
        :⟨condition n⟩: ⟨statement n⟩
        :else: ⟨statement n + 1⟩
    }
```

Here ⟨*statement* 1⟩, ⟨*statement* 2⟩, etc. could be either simple statements or compound statements. A **case** statement is interpreted as follows. If ⟨*condition* 1⟩ is **true**, ⟨*statement* 1⟩ gets executed and the **case** statement is exited. If ⟨*statement* 1⟩ is **false**, ⟨*condition* 2⟩

is evaluated. If ⟨*condition* 2⟩ is **true**, ⟨*statement* 2⟩ gets executed and the **case** statement exited, and so on. If none of the conditions ⟨*condition* 1⟩, ... , ⟨*condition* n⟩ are true, ⟨*statement* $n+1$⟩ is executed and the **case** statement is exited. The **else** clause is optional.

9. Input and output are done using the instructions **read** and **write**. No format is used to specify the size of input or output quantities.

10. There is only one type of procedure: **Algorithm**. An algorithm consists of a heading and a body. The heading takes the form

    Algorithm *Name* (⟨*parameter list*⟩)

    where *Name* is the name of the procedure and (⟨*parameter list*⟩) is a listing of the procedure parameters. The body has one or more (simple or compound) statements enclosed within braces **{** and **}**. An algorithm may or may not return any values. Simple variables to procedures are passed by value. Arrays and records are passed by reference. An array name or a record name is treated as a pointer to the respective data type.

    As an example, the following algorithm finds and returns the maximum of n given numbers:

```
Algorithm Max(A, n)
// A is an array of size n.
{
    Result := A[1];
    for i := 2 to n do
        if A[i] > Result then Result := A[i];
    return Result;
}
```

    In this algorithm (named Max), A and n are procedure parameters. *Result* and i are local variables.

Next we present two examples to illustrate the process of translating a problem into an algorithm.

Example 1.1 [Selection sort] Suppose we must devise an algorithm that sorts a collection of $n \geq 1$ elements of arbitrary type. A simple solution is given by the following

> *From those elements that are currently unsorted, find the smallest and place it next in the sorted list.*

Although this statement adequately describes the sorting problem, it is not an algorithm because it leaves several questions unanswered. For example, it does not tell us where and how the elements are initially stored or where we should place the result. We assume that the elements are stored in an array a, such that the ith integer is stored in the ith position $a[i]$, $1 \leq i \leq n$. Algorithm 1.1 is our first attempt at deriving a solution.

```
for i := 1 to n do
{
    Examine a[i] to a[n] and suppose
    the smallest element is at a[j];
    Interchange a[i] and a[j];
}
```

Algorithm 1.1 Selection sort algorithm

To turn Algorithm 1.1 into a pseudocode program, two clearly defined subtasks remain: finding the smallest element (say $a[j]$) and interchanging it with $a[i]$. We can solve the latter problem using the code

$$t := a[i]; \; a[i] := a[j]; \; a[j] := t;$$

The first subtask can be solved by assuming the minimum is $a[i]$, checking $a[i]$ with $a[i+1], a[i+2], \ldots$, and, whenever a smaller element is found, regarding it as the new minimum. Eventually $a[n]$ is compared with the current minimum, and we are done. Putting all these observations together, we get the algorithm SelectionSort (Algorithm 1.2).

The obvious question to ask at this point is, Does SelectionSort work correctly? Throughout this text we use the notation $a[i:j]$ to denote the array elements $a[i]$ through $a[j]$.

Theorem 1.1 Algorithm SelectionSort(a, n) correctly sorts a set of $n \geq 1$ elements; the result remains in $a[1:n]$ such that $a[1] \leq a[2] \leq \cdots \leq a[n]$.

Proof: We first note that for any i, say $i = q$, following the execution of lines 6 to 9, it is the case that $a[q] \leq a[r]$, $q < r \leq n$. Also observe that when i becomes greater than q, $a[1:q]$ is unchanged. Hence, following the last execution of these lines (that is, $i = n$), we have $a[1] \leq a[2] \leq \cdots \leq a[n]$.

We observe at this point that the upper limit of the **for** loop in line 4 can be changed to $n-1$ without damaging the correctness of the algorithm.
□

```
Algorithm SelectionSort(a, n)
// Sort the array a[1 : n] into nondecreasing order.
{
    for i := 1 to n do
    {
        j := i;
        for k := i + 1 to n do
            if (a[k] < a[j]) then j := k;
        t := a[i]; a[i] := a[j]; a[j] := t;
    }
}
```

Algorithm 1.2 Selection sort

1.2.2 Recursive Algorithms

A recursive function is a function that is defined in terms of itself. Similarly, an algorithm is said to be recursive if the same algorithm is invoked in the body. An algorithm that calls itself is *direct recursive*. Algorithm $\mathcal{A}$ is said to be *indirect recursive* if it calls another algorithm which in turn calls $\mathcal{A}$. These recursive mechanisms are extremely powerful, but even more importantly, many times they can express an otherwise complex process very clearly. For these reasons we introduce recursion here.

Typically, beginning programmers view recursion as a somewhat mystical technique that is useful only for some very special class of problems (such as computing factorials or Ackermann's function). This is unfortunate because any algorithm that can be written using assignment, the **if-then-else** statement, and the **while** statement can also be written using assignment, the **if-then-else** statement, and recursion. Of course, this does not say that the resulting algorithm will necessarily be easier to understand. However, there are many instances when this will be the case. When is recursion an appropriate mechanism for algorithm exposition? One instance is when the problem itself is recursively defined. Factorial fits this category, as well as binomial coefficients, where

$$\binom{n}{m} = \binom{n-1}{m} + \binom{n-1}{m-1} = \frac{n!}{m!(n-m)!}$$

The following two examples show how to develop a recursive algorithm. In the first example, we consider the Towers of Hanoi problem, and in the second, we generate all possible permutations of a list of characters.

Example 1.2 [Towers of Hanoi] The Towers of Hanoi puzzle is fashioned after the ancient Tower of Brahma ritual (see Figure 1.1). According to legend, at the time the world was created, there was a diamond tower (labeled A) with 64 golden disks. The disks were of decreasing size and were stacked on the tower in decreasing order of size bottom to top. Besides this tower there were two other diamond towers (labeled B and C). Since the time of creation, Brahman priests have been attempting to move the disks from tower A to tower B using tower C for intermediate storage. As the disks are very heavy, they can be moved only one at a time. In addition, at no time can a disk be on top of a smaller disk. According to legend, the world will come to an end when the priests have completed their task.

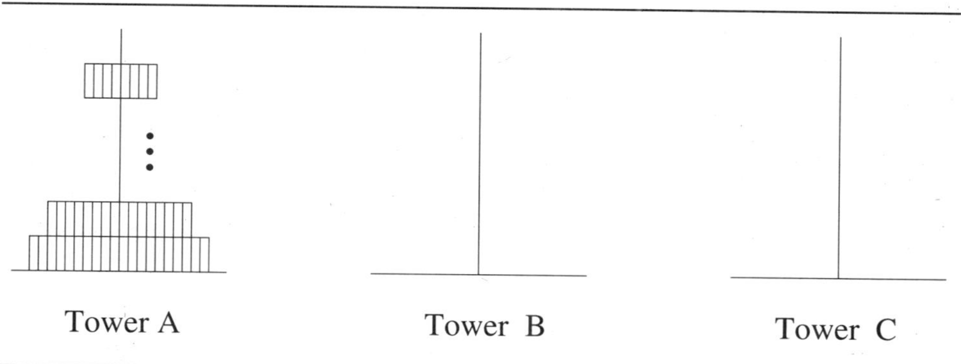

Figure 1.1 Towers of Hanoi

A very elegant solution results from the use of recursion. Assume that the number of disks is n. To get the largest disk to the bottom of tower B, we move the remaining $n-1$ disks to tower C and then move the largest to tower B. Now we are left with the task of moving the disks from tower C to tower B. To do this, we have towers A and B available. The fact that tower B has a disk on it can be ignored as the disk is larger than the disks being moved from tower C and so any disk can be placed on top of it. The recursive nature of the solution is apparent from Algorithm 1.3. This algorithm is invoked by TowersOfHanoi(n,A,B,C). Observe that our solution for an n-disk problem is formulated in terms of solutions to two $(n-1)$-disk problems. □

Example 1.3 [Permutation generator] Given a set of $n \geq 1$ elements, the problem is to print all possible permutations of this set. For example, if the set is $\{a, b, c\}$, then the set of permutations is $\{(a, b, c), (a, c, b), (b, a, c), (b, c, a), (c, a, b), (c, b, a)\}$. It is easy to see that given n elements, there are

```
Algorithm TowersOfHanoi(n, x, y, z)
// Move the top n disks from tower x to tower y.
{
    if (n ≥ 1) then
    {
        TowersOfHanoi(n − 1, x, z, y);
        write ("move top disk from tower", x,
        "to top of tower", y);
        TowersOfHanoi(n − 1, z, y, x);
    }
}
```

Algorithm 1.3 Towers of Hanoi

$n!$ different permutations. A simple algorithm can be obtained by looking at the case of four elements (a, b, c, d). The answer can be constructed by writing

1. a followed by all the permutations of (b, c, d)
2. b followed by all the permutations of (a, c, d)
3. c followed by all the permutations of (a, b, d)
4. d followed by all the permutations of (a, b, c)

The expression "followed by all the permutations" is the clue to recursion. It implies that we can solve the problem for a set with n elements if we have an algorithm that works on $n - 1$ elements. These considerations lead to Algorithm 1.4, which is invoked by Perm$(a, 1, n)$. Try this algorithm out on sets of length one, two, and three to ensure that you understand how it works. □

EXERCISES

1. Horner's rule is a means for evaluating a polynomial at a point x_0 using a minimum number of multiplications. If the polynomial is $A(x) = a_n x^n + a_{n-1} x^{n-1} + \cdots + a_1 x + a_0$, Horner's rule is

$$A(x_0) = (\cdots (a_n x_0 + a_{n-1}) x_0 + \cdots + a_1) x_0 + a_0$$

```
Algorithm Perm(a, k, n)
{
    if (k = n) then write (a[1 : n]); // Output permutation.
    else// a[k : n] has more than one permutation.
        // Generate these recursively.
        for i := k to n do
        {
            t := a[k]; a[k] := a[i]; a[i] := t;
            Perm(a, k + 1, n);
            // All permutations of a[k + 1 : n]
            t := a[k]; a[k] := a[i]; a[i] := t;
        }
}
```

Algorithm 1.4 Recursive permutation generator

(a) Use Horner's rule to evaluate the polynomial $3x^4 + 2x^3 + 8x^2 + 9x + 1$ at $x = 2$.

(b) Write an algorithm to evaluate a polynomial using Horner's rule.

2. Given n boolean variables $x_1, x_2, \ldots,$ and x_n, we wish to print all possible combinations of truth values they can assume. For instance, if $n = 2$, there are four possibilities: true, true; true, false; false, true; and false, false. Write an algorithm to accomplish this.

3. Devise an algorithm that inputs three integers and outputs them in nondecreasing order.

4. Present an algorithm that searches an unsorted array $a[1 : n]$ for the element x. If x occurs, then return a position in the array; else return zero.

5. The factorial function $n!$ has value 1 when $n \leq 1$ and value $n * (n-1)!$ when $n > 1$. Write both a recursive and an iterative algorithm to compute $n!$.

6. The Fibonacci numbers are defined as $f_0 = 0$, $f_1 = 1$, and $f_i = f_{i-1} + f_{i-2}$ for $i > 1$.

   (a) List the values of f_2 through f_7.

   (b) Write both a recursive and an iterative algorithm to compute f_i.

7. Give both a recursive and an iterative algorithm to compute the binomial coefficient $\binom{n}{m}$ as defined in Section 1.2.2, where $\binom{n}{0} = \binom{n}{n} = 1$.

8. Ackermann's function $A(m, n)$ is defined as follows:

$$A(m,n) = \begin{cases} n+1 & \text{if } m = 0 \\ A(m-1,\ 1) & \text{if } n = 0 \\ A(m-1,\ A(m,\ n-1)) & \text{otherwise} \end{cases}$$

   This function is studied because it grows very fast for small values of m and n. Write a recursive algorithm for computing this function. Then write a nonrecursive algorithm for computing it.

9. The *pigeonhole principle* states that if a function f has n distinct inputs but less than n distinct outputs, then there exist two inputs a and b such that $a \neq b$ and $f(a) = f(b)$. Present an algorithm to find a and b such that $f(a) = f(b)$. Assume that the function inputs are $1, 2, \ldots,$ and n.

10. Give an algorithm to solve the following problem: Given n, a positive integer, determine whether n is the sum of all of its divisors, that is, whether n is the sum of all t such that $1 \leq t < n$, and t divides n.

11. Consider the function $F(x)$ that is defined by "if x is even, then $F(x) = x/2$; else $F(x) = F(F(3x + 1))$." Prove that $F(x)$ terminates for all integers x. (*Hint:* Consider integers of the form $(2i + 1)2^k - 1$ and use induction.)

12. If S is a set of n elements, the *powerset* of S is the set of all possible subsets of S. For example, if $S = (a, b, c)$, then $powerset(S) = \{(\ ),$ (a), (b), (c), (a, b), (a, c), (b, c), $(a, b, c)\}$. Write a recursive algorithm to compute $powerset(S)$.

1.3 PERFORMANCE ANALYSIS

One goal of this book is to develop skills for making evaluative judgments about algorithms. There are many criteria upon which we can judge an algorithm. For instance:

1. Does it do what we want it to do?

2. Does it work correctly according to the original specifications of the task?

3. Is there documentation that describes how to use it and how it works?

4. Are procedures created in such a way that they perform logical subfunctions?

5. Is the code readable?

These criteria are all vitally important when it comes to writing software, most especially for large systems. Though we do not discuss how to reach these goals, we try to achieve them throughout this book with the pseudocode algorithms we write. Hopefully this more subtle approach will gradually infect your own program-writing habits so that you will automatically strive to achieve these goals.

There are other criteria for judging algorithms that have a more direct relationship to performance. These have to do with their computing time and storage requirements.

Definition 1.2 [Space/Time complexity] The *space complexity* of an algorithm is the amount of memory it needs to run to completion. The *time complexity* of an algorithm is the amount of computer time it needs to run to completion. □

Performance evaluation can be loosely divided into two major phases: (1) a priori estimates and (2) a posteriori testing. We refer to these as *performance analysis* and *performance measurement*, respectively.

1.3.1 Space Complexity

Algorithm abc (Algorithm 1.5) computes $a+b+b*c+(a+b-c)/(a+b)+4.0$; Algorithm Sum (Algorithm 1.6) computes $\sum_{i=1}^{n} a[i]$ iteratively, where the $a[i]$'s are real numbers; and RSum (Algorithm 1.7) is a recursive algorithm that computes $\sum_{i=1}^{n} a[i]$.

```
Algorithm abc(a, b, c)
{
    return a + b + b * c + (a + b - c)/(a + b) + 4.0;
}
```

Algorithm 1.5 Computes $a + b + b * c + (a + b - c)/(a + b) + 4.0$

The space needed by each of these algorithms is seen to be the sum of the following components:

```
Algorithm Sum(a, n)
{
    s := 0.0;
    for i := 1 to n do
        s := s + a[i];
    return s;
}
```

Algorithm 1.6 Iterative function for sum

```
Algorithm RSum(a, n)
{
    if (n ≤ 0) then return 0.0;
    else return RSum(a, n − 1) + a[n];
}
```

Algorithm 1.7 Recursive function for sum

1. A fixed part that is independent of the characteristics (e.g., number, size) of the inputs and outputs. This part typically includes the instruction space (i.e., space for the code), space for simple variables and fixed-size component variables (also called *aggregate*), space for constants, and so on.

2. A variable part that consists of the space needed by component variables whose size is dependent on the particular problem instance being solved, the space needed by referenced variables (to the extent that this depends on instance characteristics), and the recursion stack space (insofar as this space depends on the instance characteristics).

The space requirement $S(P)$ of any algorithm P may therefore be written as $S(P) = c + S_P$(instance characteristics), where c is a constant.

When analyzing the space complexity of an algorithm, we concentrate solely on estimating S_P(instance characteristics). For any given problem, we need first to determine which instance characteristics to use to measure the space requirements. This is very problem specific, and we resort to examples to illustrate the various possibilities. Generally speaking, our choices are limited to quantities related to the number and magnitude of the inputs to and outputs from the algorithm. At times, more complex measures of the interrelationships among the data items are used.

Example 1.4 For Algorithm 1.5, the problem instance is characterized by the specific values of a, b, and c. Making the assumption that one word is adequate to store the values of each of a, b, c, and the result, we see that the space needed by abc is independent of the instance characteristics. Consequently, S_P(instance characteristics) $= 0$. □

Example 1.5 The problem instances for Algorithm 1.6 are characterized by n, the number of elements to be summed. The space needed by n is one word, since it is of type *integer*. The space needed by a is the space needed by variables of type array of floating point numbers. This is at least n words, since a must be large enough to hold the n elements to be summed. So, we obtain $S_{\mathsf{Sum}}(n) \geq (n+3)$ (n for $a[\,]$, one each for n, i, and s). □

Example 1.6 Let us consider the algorithm RSum (Algorithm 1.7). As in the case of Sum, the instances are characterized by n. The recursion stack space includes space for the formal parameters, the local variables, and the return address. Assume that the return address requires only one word of memory. Each call to RSum requires at least three words (including space for the values of n, the return address, and a pointer to $a[\,]$). Since the depth of recursion is $n+1$, the recursion stack space needed is $\geq 3(n+1)$. □

1.3.2 Time Complexity

The time $T(P)$ taken by a program P is the sum of the compile time and the run (or execution) time. The compile time does not depend on the instance characteristics. Also, we may assume that a compiled program will be run several times without recompilation. Consequently, we concern ourselves with just the run time of a program. This run time is denoted by t_P(instance characteristics).

Because many of the factors t_P depends on are not known at the time a program is conceived, it is reasonable to attempt only to estimate t_P. If we knew the characteristics of the compiler to be used, we could proceed to determine the number of additions, subtractions, multiplications, divisions, compares, loads, stores, and so on, that would be made by the code for P. So, we could obtain an expression for $t_P(n)$ of the form

$$t_P(n) = c_a ADD(n) + c_s SUB(n) + c_m MUL(n) + c_d DIV(n) + \cdots$$

where n denotes the instance characteristics, and c_a, c_s, c_m, c_d, and so on, respectively, denote the time needed for an addition, subtraction, multiplication, division, and so on, and ADD, SUB, MUL, DIV, and so on, are functions whose values are the numbers of additions, subtractions, multiplications, divisions, and so on, that are performed when the code for P is used on an instance with characteristic n.

Obtaining such an exact formula is in itself an impossible task, since the time needed for an addition, subtraction, multiplication, and so on, often depends on the numbers being added, subtracted, multiplied, and so on. The value of $t_P(n)$ for any given n can be obtained only experimentally. The program is typed, compiled, and run on a particular machine. The execution time is physically clocked, and $t_P(n)$ obtained. Even with this experimental approach, one could face difficulties. In a multiuser system, the execution time depends on such factors as system load, the number of other programs running on the computer at the time program P is run, the characteristics of these other programs, and so on.

Given the minimal utility of determining the exact number of additions, subtractions, and so on, that are needed to solve a problem instance with characteristics given by n, we might as well lump all the operations together (provided that the time required by each is relatively independent of the instance characteristics) and obtain a count for the total number of operations. We can go one step further and count only the number of program steps.

A *program step* is loosely defined as a syntactically or semantically meaningful segment of a program that has an execution time that is independent of the instance characteristics. For example, the entire statement

$$\textbf{return } a + b + b * c + (a + b - c)/(a + b) + 4.0;$$

of Algorithm 1.5 could be regarded as a step since its execution time is independent of the instance characteristics (this statement is not strictly true, since the time for a multiply and divide generally depends on the numbers involved in the operation).

The number of steps any program statement is assigned depends on the kind of statement. For example, comments count as zero steps; an assignment statement which does not involve any calls to other algorithms is counted as one step; in an iterative statement such as the **for**, **while**, and **repeat-until** statements, we consider the step counts only for the control part of the statement. The control parts for **for** and **while** statements have the following forms:

$$\textbf{for } i := \langle expr \rangle \textbf{ to } \langle expr1 \rangle \textbf{ do}$$

$$\textbf{while } (\langle expr \rangle) \textbf{ do}$$

Each execution of the control part of a **while** statement is given a step count equal to the number of step counts assignable to $\langle expr \rangle$. The step count for each execution of the control part of a **for** statement is one, unless the counts attributable to $\langle expr \rangle$ and $\langle expr1 \rangle$ are functions of the instance characteristics. In this latter case, the first execution of the control part of the **for** has a step count equal to the sum of the counts for $\langle expr \rangle$ and $\langle expr1 \rangle$ (note that these expressions are computed only when the loop is started). Remaining executions of the **for** statement have a step count of one; and so on.

We can determine the number of steps needed by a program to solve a particular problem instance in one of two ways. In the first method, we introduce a new variable, *count*, into the program. This is a global variable with initial value 0. Statements to increment *count* by the appropriate amount are introduced into the program. This is done so that each time a statement in the original program is executed, *count* is incremented by the step count of that statement.

Example 1.7 When the statements to increment *count* are introduced into Algorithm 1.6, the result is Algorithm 1.8. The change in the value of *count* by the time this program terminates is the number of steps executed by Algorithm 1.6.

Since we are interested in determining only the change in the value of *count*, Algorithm 1.8 may be simplified to Algorithm 1.9. For every initial value of *count*, Algorithms 1.8 and 1.9 compute the same final value for *count*. It is easy to see that in the **for** loop, the value of *count* will increase by a total of $2n$. If *count* is zero to start with, then it will be $2n+3$ on termination. So each invocation of Sum (Algorithm 1.6) executes a total of $2n+3$ steps. □

Example 1.8 When the statements to increment *count* are introduced into Algorithm 1.7, Algorithm 1.10 is obtained. Let $t_{\mathsf{RSum}}(n)$ be the increase in the value of *count* when Algorithm 1.10 terminates. We see that $t_{\mathsf{RSum}}(0) = 2$. When $n > 0$, *count* increases by 2 plus whatever increase results from the invocation of RSum from within the **else** clause. From the definition of t_{RSum}, it follows that this additional increase is $t_{\mathsf{RSum}}(n-1)$. So, if the value of *count* is zero initially, its value at the time of termination is $2+t_{\mathsf{RSum}}(n-1)$, $n > 0$.

When analyzing a recursive program for its step count, we often obtain a recursive formula for the step count, for example,

$$t_{\mathsf{RSum}}(n) = \begin{cases} 2 & \text{if } n = 0 \\ 2 + t_{\mathsf{RSum}}(n-1) & \text{if } n > 0 \end{cases}$$

These recursive formulas are referred to as *recurrence relations*. One way of solving any such recurrence relation is to make repeated substitutions for each occurrence of the function t_{RSum} on the right-hand side until all such occurrences disappear:

```
Algorithm Sum(a, n)
{
    s := 0.0;
    count := count + 1; // count is global; it is initially zero.
    for i := 1 to n do
    {
        count := count + 1; // For for
        s := s + a[i]; count := count + 1; // For assignment
    }
    count := count + 1; // For last time of for
    count := count + 1; // For the return
    return s;
}
```

Algorithm 1.8 Algorithm 1.6 with count statements added

```
Algorithm Sum(a, n)
{
    for i := 1 to n do count := count + 2;
    count := count + 3;
}
```

Algorithm 1.9 Simplified version of Algorithm 1.8

$$
\begin{aligned}
t_{\mathsf{RSum}}(n) &= 2 + t_{\mathsf{RSum}}(n-1) \\
&= 2 + 2 + t_{\mathsf{RSum}}(n-2) \\
&= 2(2) + t_{\mathsf{RSum}}(n-2) \\
&\;\;\vdots \\
&= n(2) + t_{\mathsf{RSum}}(0) \\
&= 2n + 2, \qquad\qquad n \geq 0
\end{aligned}
$$

So the step count for RSum (Algorithm 1.7) is $2n + 2$. □

The step count is useful in that it tells us how the run time for a program changes with changes in the instance characteristics. From the step count for Sum, we see that if n is doubled, the run time also doubles (approximately);

```
Algorithm RSum(a, n)
{
    count := count + 1; // For the if conditional
    if (n ≤ 0) then
    {
        count := count + 1; // For the return
        return 0.0;
    }
    else
    {
        count := count + 1;  // For the addition, function
                             // invocation and return
        return RSum(a, n - 1) + a[n];
    }
}
```

Algorithm 1.10 Algorithm 1.7 with count statements added

if n increases by a factor of 10, the run time increases by a factor of 10; and so on. So, the run time grows *linearly* in n. We say that Sum is a linear time algorithm (the time complexity is linear in the instance characteristic n).

Definition 1.3 [Input size] One of the instance characteristics that is frequently used in the literature is the *input size*. The input size of any instance of a problem is defined to be the number of words (or the number of elements) needed to describe that instance. The input size for the problem of summing an array with n elements is $n + 1$, n for listing the n elements and 1 for the value of n (Algorithms 1.6 and 1.7). The problem tackled in Algorithm 1.5 has an input size of 3. If the input to any problem instance is a single element, the input size is normally taken to be the number of bits needed to specify that element. Run times for many of the algorithms presented in this text are expressed as functions of the corresponding input sizes. □

Example 1.9 [Matrix addition] Algorithm 1.11 is to add two $m \times n$ matrices a and b together. Introducing the *count*-incrementing statements leads to Algorithm 1.12. Algorithm 1.13 is a simplified version of Algorithm 1.12 that computes the same value for *count*. Examining Algorithm 1.13, we see that line 7 is executed n times for each value of i, or a total of mn times; line 5 is executed m times; and line 9 is executed once. If *count* is 0 to begin with, it will be $2mn + 2m + 1$ when Algorithm 1.13 terminates.

From this analysis we see that if $m > n$, then it is better to interchange the two **for** statements in Algorithm 1.11. If this is done, the step count becomes $2mn+2n+1$. Note that in this example the instance characteristics are given by m and n and the input size is $2mn + 2$. □

```
Algorithm Add(a, b, c, m, n)
{
    for i := 1 to m do
        for j := 1 to n do
            c[i, j] := a[i, j] + b[i, j];
}
```

Algorithm 1.11 Matrix addition

```
Algorithm Add(a, b, c, m, n)
{
    for i := 1 to m do
    {
        count := count + 1; // For 'for i'
        for j := 1 to n do
        {
            count := count + 1; // For 'for j'
            c[i, j] := a[i, j] + b[i, j];
            count := count + 1; // For the assignment
        }
        count := count + 1;// For loop initialization and
                           // last time of 'for j'
    }
    count := count + 1;    // For loop initialization and
                           // last time of 'for i'
}
```

Algorithm 1.12 Matrix addition with counting statements

The second method to determine the step count of an algorithm is to build a table in which we list the total number of steps contributed by each

```
Algorithm Add(a, b, c, m, n)
{
    for i := 1 to m do
    {
        count := count + 2;
        for j := 1 to n do
            count := count + 2;
    }
    count := count + 1;
}
```

Algorithm 1.13 Simplified algorithm with counting only

statement. This figure is often arrived at by first determining the number of steps per execution (s/e) of the statement and the total number of times (i.e., frequency) each statement is executed. *The s/e of a statement is the amount by which the count changes as a result of the execution of that statement.* By combining these two quantities, the total contribution of each statement is obtained. By adding the contributions of all statements, the step count for the entire algorithm is obtained.

In Table 1.1, the number of steps per execution and the frequency of each of the statements in Sum (Algorithm 1.6) have been listed. The total number of steps required by the algorithm is determined to be $2n + 3$. It is important to note that the frequency of the **for** statement is $n + 1$ and not n. This is so because i has to be incremented to $n + 1$ before the **for** loop can terminate.

Table 1.2 gives the step count for RSum (Algorithm 1.7). Notice that under the s/e (steps per execution) column, the **else** clause has been given a count of $1 + t_{\text{RSum}}(n - 1)$. This is the total cost of this line each time it is executed. It includes all the steps that get executed as a result of the invocation of RSum from the **else** clause. The frequency and total steps columns have been split into two parts: one for the case $n = 0$ and the other for the case $n > 0$. This is necessary because the frequency (and hence total steps) for some statements is different for each of these cases.

Table 1.3 corresponds to algorithm Add (Algorithm 1.11). Once again, note that the frequency of the first **for** loop is $m + 1$ and not m. This is so as i needs to be incremented up to $m + 1$ before the loop can terminate. Similarly, the frequency for the second **for** loop is $m(n + 1)$.

When you have obtained sufficient experience in computing step counts, you can avoid constructing the frequency table and obtain the step count as

Statement	s/e	frequency	total steps
Algorithm Sum(a, n)	0	–	0
{	0	–	0
$s := 0.0;$	1	1	1
for $i := 1$ **to** n **do**	1	$n+1$	$n+1$
$s := s + a[i];$	1	n	n
return s;	1	1	1
}	0	–	0
Total			$2n+3$

Table 1.1 Step table for Algorithm 1.6

Statement	s/e	frequency		total steps	
		$n=0$	$n>0$	$n=0$	$n>0$
Algorithm RSum(a, n)	0	–	–	0	0
{					
if $(n \leq 0)$ **then**	1	1	1	1	1
return 0.0;	1	1	0	1	0
else return					
RSum$(a, n-1) + a[n]$;	$1+x$	0	1	0	$1+x$
}	0	–	–	0	0
Total				2	$2+x$

$$x = t_{\mathsf{RSum}}(n-1)$$

Table 1.2 Step table for Algorithm 1.7

in the following example.

Example 1.10 [Fibonacci numbers] The Fibonacci sequence of numbers starts as

$$0, 1, 1, 2, 3, 5, 8, 13, 21, 34, 55, \ldots$$

Each new term is obtained by taking the sum of the two previous terms. If we call the first term of the sequence f_0, then $f_0 = 0,\ f_1 = 1$, and in general

$$f_n = f_{n-1} + f_{n-2}, \quad n \geq 2$$

Statement	s/e	frequency	total steps
1 **Algorithm** Add(a, b, c, m, n)	0	—	0
2 {	0	—	0
3 **for** $i := 1$ **to** m **do**	1	$m+1$	$m+1$
4 **for** $j := 1$ **to** n **do**	1	$m(n+1)$	$mn+m$
5 $c[i,j] := a[i,j] + b[i,j];$	1	mn	mn
6 }	0	—	0
Total			$2mn+2m+1$

Table 1.3 Step table for Algorithm 1.11

Fibonacci (Algorithm 1.14) takes as input any nonnegative integer n and prints the value f_n.

```
1   Algorithm Fibonacci(n)
2   // Compute the nth Fibonacci number.
3   {
4       if (n ≤ 1) then
5           write (n);
6       else
7       {
8           fnm2 := 0; fnm1 := 1;
9           for i := 2 to n do
10          {
11              fn := fnm1 + fnm2;
12              fnm2 := fnm1; fnm1 := fn;
13          }
14          write (fn);
15      }
16  }
```

Algorithm 1.14 Fibonacci numbers

To analyze the time complexity of this algorithm, we need to consider the two cases (1) $n = 0$ or 1 and (2) $n > 1$. When $n = 0$ or 1, lines 4 and 5 get executed once each. Since each line has an s/e of 1, the total step count for this case is 2. When $n > 1$, lines 4, 8, and 14 are each executed once.

Line 9 gets executed n times, and lines 11 and 12 get executed $n-1$ times each (note that the last time line 9 is executed, i is incremented to $n+1$, and the loop exited). Line 8 has an s/e of 2, line 12 has an s/e of 2, and line 13 has an s/e of 0. The remaining lines that get executed have s/e's of 1. The total steps for the case $n > 1$ is therefore $4n + 1$. □

Summary of Time Complexity

The time complexity of an algorithm is given by the number of steps taken by the algorithm to compute the function it was written for. The number of steps is itself a function of the instance characteristics. Although any specific instance may have several characteristics (e.g., the number of inputs, the number of outputs, the magnitudes of the inputs and outputs), the number of steps is computed as a function of some subset of these. Usually, we choose those characteristics that are of importance to us. For example, we might wish to know how the computing (or run) time (i.e., time complexity) increases as the number of inputs increase. In this case the number of steps will be computed as a function of the number of inputs alone. For a different algorithm, we might be interested in determining how the computing time increases as the magnitude of one of the inputs increases. In this case the number of steps will be computed as a function of the magnitude of this input alone. Thus, before the step count of an algorithm can be determined, we need to know exactly which characteristics of the problem instance are to be used. These define the variables in the expression for the step count. In the case of Sum, we chose to measure the time complexity as a function of the number n of elements being added. For algorithm Add, the choice of characteristics was the number m of rows and the number n of columns in the matrices being added.

Once the relevant characteristics $(n, m, p, q, r, \ldots)$ have been selected, we can define what a step is. A *step* is any computation unit that is independent of the characteristics $(n, m, p, q, r, \ldots)$. Thus, 10 additions can be one step; 100 multiplications can also be one step; but n additions cannot. Nor can $m/2$ additions, $p+q$ subtractions, and so on, be counted as one step.

A systematic way to assign step counts was also discussed. Once this has been done, the time complexity (i.e., the total step count) of an algorithm can be obtained using either of the two methods discussed.

The examples we have looked at so far were sufficiently simple that the time complexities were nice functions of fairly simple characteristics like the number of inputs and the number of rows and columns. For many algorithms, the time complexity is not dependent solely on the number of inputs or outputs or some other easily specified characteristic. For example, the searching algorithm you wrote for Exercise 4 in Section 1.2, may terminate in one step if x is the first element examined by your algorithm, or it may take two steps (this happens if x is the second element examined), and so on. In other words, knowing n alone is not enough to estimate the run time of your algorithm.

We can extricate ourselves from the difficulties resulting from situations when the chosen parameters are not adequate to determine the step count uniquely by defining three kinds of step counts: best case, worst case, and average. The *best-case step count* is the minimum number of steps that can be executed for the given parameters. The *worst-case step count* is the maximum number of steps that can be executed for the given parameters. The *average step count* is the average number of steps executed on instances with the given parameters.

Our motivation to determine step counts is to be able to compare the time complexities of two algorithms that compute the same function and also to predict the growth in run time as the instance characteristics change.

Determining the exact step count (best case, worst case, or average) of an algorithm can prove to be an exceedingly difficult task. Expending immense effort to determine the step count exactly is not a very worthwhile endeavor, since the notion of a step is itself inexact. (Both the instructions $x := y;$ and $x := y + z + (x/y) + (x * y * z - x/z);$ count as one step.) Because of the inexactness of what a step stands for, the exact step count is not very useful for comparative purposes. An exception to this is when the difference between the step counts of two algorithms is very large, as in $3n + 3$ versus $100n + 10$. We might feel quite safe in predicting that the algorithm with step count $3n+3$ will run in less time than the one with step count $100n+10$. But even in this case, it is not necessary to know that the exact step count is $100n + 10$. Something like, "it's about $80n$ or $85n$ or $75n$," is adequate to arrive at the same conclusion.

For most situations, it is adequate to be able to make a statement like $c_1n^2 \leq t_P(n) \leq c_2n^2$ or $t_Q(n, m) = c_1n + c_2m$, where c_1 and c_2 are nonnegative constants. This is so because if we have two algorithms with a complexity of $c_1n^2 + c_2n$ and c_3n respectively, then we know that the one with complexity c_3n will be faster than the one with complexity $c_1n^2 + c_2n$ for sufficiently large values of n. For small values of n, either algorithm could be faster (depending on c_1, c_2, and c_3). If $c_1 = 1$, $c_2 = 2$, and $c_3 = 100$, then $c_1n^2 + c_2n \leq c_3n$ for $n \leq 98$ and $c_1n^2 + c_2n > c_3n$ for $n > 98$. If $c_1 = 1$, $c_2 = 2$, and $c_3 = 1000$, then $c_1n^2 + c_2n \leq c_3n$ for $n \leq 998$.

No matter what the values of c_1, c_2, and c_3, there will be an n beyond which the algorithm with complexity c_3n will be faster than the one with complexity $c_1n^2 + c_2n$. This value of n will be called the *break-even point*. If the break-even point is zero, then the algorithm with complexity c_3n is always faster (or at least as fast). The exact break-even point cannot be determined analytically. The algorithms have to be run on a computer in order to determine the break-even point. To know that there is a break-even point, it is sufficient to know that one algorithm has complexity $c_1n^2 + c_2n$ and the other c_3n for some constants c_1, c_2, and c_3. There is little advantage in determining the exact values of c_1, c_2, and c_3.

1.3.3 Amortized Complexity

Suppose that a sequence I1, I2, D1, I3, I4, I5, I6, D2, I7 of insert and delete operations is performed on a set. Assume that the *actual cost* of each of the seven inserts is one. (We use the terms *cost* and *complexity* interchangeably.) By this, we mean that each insert takes one unit of time. Further, suppose that the delete operations D1 and D2 have an actual cost of eight and ten, respectively. So, the total cost of the sequence of operations is 25.

In an amortization scheme we charge some of the actual cost of an operation to other operations. This reduces the charged cost of some operations and increases that of others. The *amortized cost* of an operation is the total cost charged to it. The cost transferring (amortization) scheme is required to be such that the sum of the amortized costs of the operations is greater than or equal to the sum of their actual costs. If we charge one unit of the cost of a delete operation to each of the inserts since the last delete operation (if any), then two units of the cost of D1 get transferred to I1 and I2 (the charged cost of each increases by one), and four units of the cost of D2 get transferred to I3 to I6. The amortized cost of each of I1 to I6 becomes two, that of I7 becomes equal to its actual cost (that is, one), and that of each of D1 and D2 becomes 6. The sum of the amortized costs is 25, which is the same as the sum of the actual costs.

Now suppose we can prove that no matter what sequence of insert and delete operations is performed, we can charge costs in such a way that the amortized cost of each insertion is no more than two and that of each deletion is no more than six. This enables us to claim that the actual cost of any insert/delete sequence is no more than $2 * i + 6 * d$, where i and d are, respectively, the number of insert and delete operations in the sequence. Suppose that the actual cost of a deletion is no more than ten and that of an insertion is one. Using actual costs, we can conclude that the sequence cost is no more than $i + 10 * d$. Combining these two bounds, we obtain $\min\{2 * i + 6 * d,\ i + 10 * d\}$ as a bound on the sequence cost. Hence, using the notion of cost amortization, we can obtain tighter bounds on the complexity of a sequence of operations.

The amortized time complexity to perform insert, delete, and search operations in splay trees is $O(\log n)$. This amortization is over n operations. In other words, the total time taken for processing an arbitrary sequence of n operations is $O(n \log n)$. Some operations may take much longer than $O(\log n)$ time, but when amortized over n operations, each operation costs $O(\log n)$ time.

Unlike the actual, best-, average-, and worst-case complexities of an operation, which are closely related to the step count for that operation, the amortized complexity of an operation is an accounting artifact that often bears no direct relationship to the actual complexity of that operation. The amortized complexity of an operation could be anything. *The only requirement is that the sum of the amortized complexities of all operations in any sequence of operations be greater than or equal to their sum of the actual complexities.* That is

$$\sum_{1 \leq i \leq n} amortized(i) \geq \sum_{1 \leq i \leq n} actual(i) \tag{1.1}$$

where $amortized(i)$ and $actual(i)$, respectively, denote the amortized and actual complexities of the ith operation in a sequence of n operations. Because of this requirement on the sum of the amortized complexities of the operations in any sequence of operations, we may use the sum of the amortized complexities as an upper bound on the complexity of any sequence of operations.

You may view the amortized cost of an operation as being the amount you charge the operation rather than the amount the operation costs. You can charge an operation any amount you wish so long as the amount charged to all operations in the sequence is at least equal to the actual cost of the operation sequence.

Relative to the actual and amortized costs of each operation in a sequence of n operations, we define a *potential function* $P(i)$ as below.

$$P(i) = amortized(i) - actual(i) + P(i-1) \tag{1.2}$$

That is, the ith operation causes the potential function to change by the difference between the amortized and actual costs of that operation. If we sum Equation 1.2 for $1 \leq i \leq n$, we get

$$\sum_{1 \leq i \leq n} P(i) = \sum_{1 \leq i \leq n} (amortized(i) - actual(i) + P(i-1))$$

or

$$\sum_{1 \leq i \leq n} (P(i) - P(i-1)) = \sum_{1 \leq i \leq n} (amortized(i) - actual(i))$$

or

$$P(n) - P(0) = \sum_{1 \leq i \leq n} (amortized(i) - actual(i))$$

From Equation 1.1, it follows that

$$P(n) - P(0) \geq 0 \tag{1.3}$$

Under the assumption that $P(0) = 0$, the potential $P(i)$ is the amount by which the first i operations have been overcharged (i.e., they have been charged more than their actual cost).

Generally, when we analyze the complexity of a sequence of n operations, n can be any nonnegative integer. Therefore, Equation 1.3 must hold for all nonnegative integers.

Three popular methods to arrive at amortized costs for operations are:

1. **Aggregate Method:** In the aggregate method, we determine an upper bound $UpperBoundOnSumOfActualCosts(n)$ for the sum of the actual costs of the n operations. The amortized cost of each operation is set equal to $UpperBoundOnSumOfActualCosts(n)/n$. You may verify that this assignment of amortized costs satisfies Equation 1.1 and is, therefore, valid.

2. **Accounting Method:** In this method, we assign amortized costs to the operations (possibly by guessing what assignment will work), compute the $P(i)$s using Equation 1.2, and show that $P(n) - P(0) \geq 0$.

3. **Potential Method:** Here, we start with a potential function (again, possibly obtained using good guess work) that satisfies Equation 1.3, and compute the amortized complexities using Equation 1.2.

Although, at this time, you may feel most comfortable with the aggregate method. this method is often the hardest to use because it is often quite difficult to obtain a bound on the aggregate actual cost that is smaller than the bound obtained by using the worst-case cost of each operation in the sequence. The accounting method is intuitive (we simply verify that the sum of the amortized costs is at least equal to the sum of the actual costs) and often results in tight bounds on the complexity of a sequence of operations. The potential method is often the hardest to use (because of the difficulty of determining the proper potential function to use), but for some applications remains the only way to obtain tight complexity bounds.

Example 1.11 [Maintenance Contract] In January, you buy a new car from a dealer who offers you the following maintenance contract: \$50 each month other than March, June, September and December (this covers an oil change and general inspection), \$100 every March, June, and September (this covers an oil change, a minor tune-up, and a general inspection), and \$200 every December (this covers an oil change, a major tune-up, and a general inspection). We are to obtain an upper bound on the cost of this maintenance contract as a function of the number of months.

Worst-Case Method

We can bound the contract cost for the first n months by taking the product of n and the maximum cost incurred in any month (i.e., \$200). This would

month	1	2	3	4	5	6	7	8
actual cost	50	50	100	50	50	100	50	50
amortized cost	75	75	75	75	75	75	75	75
$P()$	25	50	25	50	75	50	75	100

month	9	10	11	12	13	14	15	16
actual cost	100	50	50	200	50	50	100	50
amortized	75	75	75	75	75	75	75	75
$P()$	75	100	125	0	25	50	25	50

Table 1.4 Maintenence contract example

be analagous to the traditional way to estimate the complexity–take the product of the number of operations and the worst-case complexity of an operation. Using this approach, we get \$200n as an upper bound on the contract cost. The upper bound is correct because the actual cost for n months does not exceed \$200n.

Aggregate Method

To use the aggregate method for amortized complexity, we first determine an upper bound on the sum of the costs for the first n months. As tight a bound as is possible is desired. The sum of the actual monthly costs of the contract for the first n months is

$$\begin{aligned}
& 200\lfloor n/12\rfloor + 100 * (\lfloor n/3\rfloor - \lfloor n/12\rfloor) + 50 * (n - \lfloor n/3\rfloor) \\
= \; & 100 * \lfloor n/12\rfloor + 50 * \lfloor n/3\rfloor + 50 * n \\
\le \; & 100 * n/12 + 50 * n/3 + 50 * n \\
= \; & 50n(1/6 + 1/3 + 1) \\
= \; & 50n(3/2) \\
= \; & 75n
\end{aligned}$$

The amortized cost for each month is set to \$75. Table 1.4 shows the actual costs, the amortized costs, and the potential function value (assuming $P(0) = 0$) for the first 16 months of the contract.

Notice that some months are charged more than their actual cost and others are charged less than their actual cost. The cumulative difference between what the operations are charged and their actual costs is given by the potential function. The potential function satisfies Equation 1.3 for all values of n. When we use the amortized cost of \$75 per month, we get \$75n as an upper bound on the contract cost for n months. This bound is tighter than the bound of \$200n obtained using the worst-case monthly cost.

Accounting Method

To use the accounting method, we must first assign an amortized cost for each month and then show that this assignment satisifes Equation 1.3. We have the option to assign a different amortized cost to each month. In our maintenance contract example, we know the actual cost by month and could use this actual cost as the amortized cost. It is, however, easier to work with an equal cost assignment for each month. When analyzing the complexity of operation sequences that consist of two or more types of operations (for example, when dealing with lists of elements, the operation sequence may be made up of search, insert, and delete operations) we often assign a different amortized cost to operations of different types. However, operations of the same type have the same amortized cost.

To get the best upper bound on the sum of the actual costs, we must set the amortized monthly cost to be the smallest number for which Equation 1.3 is satisifed for all n. From the above table, we see that using any cost less than \$75 will result in $P(n) - P(0) < 0$ for some values of n. Therefore, the smallest assignable amortized cost consistent with Equation 1.3 is \$75.

Generally, when the accounting method is used, we have not computed the aggregate cost. Therefore, we would not know that \$75 is the least assignable amortized cost. So we start by assigning an amortized cost (obtained by making an educated guess) to each of the different operation types and then proceed to show that this assignment of amortized costs satisfies Equation 1.3. Once we have shown this, we can obtain an upper bound on the cost of any operation sequence by computing

$$\sum_{1 \le i \le k} f(i) * amortized(i)$$

where k is the number of different operation types and $f(i)$ is the frequency of operation type i (i.e., the number of times operations of this type occur in the operation sequence).

For our maintenance contract example, we might try an amortized cost of \$70. When we use this amortized cost, we discover that Equation 1.3 is not satisifed for $n = 12$ (for example) and so \$70 is an invalid amortized cost assignment. We might next try \$80. By constructing a table such as the one above, we will observe that Equation 1.3 is satisfied for all months in the first 12 month cycle, and then conclude that the equation is satisifed for all n. Now, we can use \$80n as an upper bound on the contract cost for n months.

Potential Method

We first define a potential function for the analysis. The only guideline you have in defining this function is that the potential function represents the cumulative difference between the amortized and actual costs. So, if you have an amortized cost in mind, you may be able to use this knowledge to develop a potential function that satsifies Equation 1.3, and then use the potential function and the actual operation costs (or an upper bound on these actual costs) to verify the amortized costs.

If we are extremely experienced, we might start with the potential function

$$P(n) = \begin{cases} 0 & n \bmod 12 = 0 \\ 25 & n \bmod 12 = 1 \text{ or } 3 \\ 50 & n \bmod 12 = 2, 4 \text{ or } 6 \\ 75 & n \bmod 12 = 5, 7 \text{ or } 9 \\ 100 & n \bmod 12 = 8, \text{ or } 10 \\ 125 & n \bmod 12 = 11 \end{cases}$$

Without the aid of the table constructed for the aggregate method, it would take quite some ingenuity to come up with this potential function. Having formulated a potential function and verified that this potential function satisfies Equation 1.3 for all n, we proceed to use Equation 1.2 to determine the amortized costs.

From Equation 1.2, we obtain

$$amortized(i) = actual(i) + P(i) - P(i-1)$$

Therefore,

$$\begin{aligned} amortized(1) &= actual(1) + P(1) - P(0) = 50 + 25 - 0 = 75 \\ amortized(2) &= actual(2) + P(2) - P(1) = 50 + 50 - 25 = 75 \\ amortized(3) &= actual(3) + P(3) - P(2) = 100 + 25 - 50 = 75 \end{aligned}$$

and so on. Therefore, the amortized cost for each month is \$75. So, the actual cost for n months is at most \$75n. □

Example 1.12 [The McWidget Company] The famous McWidget company manufactures widgets. At its headquarters, the company has a large display that shows how many widgets have been manufactured so far. Each time a widget is manufactured, a maintenance person updates this display. The cost for this update is $\$c+dm$, where c is a fixed trip charge, d is a charge per display digit that is to be changed, and m is the number of digits that are to be changed. For example, when the display is changed from 1399 to 1400, the cost to the company is $\$c + 3d$ because 3 digits must be changed. The

McWidget company wishes to amortize the cost of maintaining the display over the widgets that are manufactured, charging the same amount to each widget. More precisely, we are looking for an amount $\$e = amortized(i)$ that should be leavied against each widget so that the sum of these charges equals or exceeds the actual cost of maintaining/updating the display ($\$e * n \geq$ actual total cost incurred for first n widgets for all $n \geq 1$). To keep the overall selling price of a widget low, we wish to find as small an e as possible. Clearly, $e > c+d$ because each time a widget is made, at least one digit (the least significant one) has to be changed.

Worst-Case Method

This method does not work well in this application because there is no finite worst-case cost for a single display update. As more and more widgets are manufactured, the number of digits that need to be changed increases. For example, when the 1000th widget is made, 4 digits are to be changed incurring a cost of $c+4d$, and when the $1,000,000$th widget is made, 7 digits are to be changed incurring a cost of $c+7d$. If we use the worst-case method, the amortized cost to each widget becomes infinity. We can, however, come up with a worst-case cost that is a function of the number, n, of widgets made so far. The number of digits in the display at this time is $\lfloor \log_{10} n \rfloor + 1$. So, in the worst-case, the number of digits of display that were changed upon manufacture of a single widget is $\lfloor \log_{10} n \rfloor + 1$. Using the worst-case method, the amortized cost to each widget is $\$c + (\lfloor \log_{10} n \rfloor + 1)d$. This doesn't really help the McWidget company determine how much o the display update cost to charge each widget as the company expects to manufacture widgets indefinitely. Fortunately, by using an amortized analysis as below, we can come up with a finite charge that is to be leavied each widget.

Aggregate Method

Let n be the number of widgets made so far. As noted earlier, the least significant digit of the display has been changed n times. The digit in the tens place changes once for every ten widgets made, that in the hundreds place changes once for evey hundred widgets made, that in the thousands place changes once for evey thousand widgets made, and so on. Thefore, the aggregate number of digits that have changed is bounded by

$$n(1 + 1/10 + 1/100 + 1/1000 + \cdots) = (1.11111\cdots)n$$

So, the amortized cost of updating the display is $c + d(1.11111\cdots)n/n < c + 1.12d$. If the McWidget company adds $\$c + 1.12d$ to the selling price of each widget, it will collect enough money to pay for the cost of maintaining the display. Each widget is charged the cost of changing 1.12 digits regardless of the number of digits that are actually changed. Table 1.5 shows the actual

widget	1	2	3	4	5	6	7	8
actual cost	1	1	1	1	1	1	1	1
amortized cost	1.12	1.12	1.12	1.12	1.12	1.12	1.12	1.12
$P()$	0.12	0.24	0.36	0.48	0.60	0.72	0.84	0.96

widget	9	10	11	12	13	14	15	16
actual cost	1	2	1	1	1	1	1	1
amortized cost	1.12	1.12	1.12	1.12	1.12	1.12	1.12	1.12
$P()$	1.08	0.20	0.32	0.44	0.56	0.68	0.80	0.92

widget	17	18	19	20	21	22	23	24
actual cost	1	1	1	2	1	1	1	1
amortized cost	1.12	1.12	1.12	1.12	1.12	1.12	1.12	1.12
P()	1.04	1.16	1.28	0.40	0.52	0.64	0.76	0.88

Table 1.5 McWidget example

cost, as measured by the number of digits that change, of maintaining the display, the amortized cost (i.e., 1.12 digits per widget), and the potential function. The potential function gives the difference between the sum of the amortized costs and the sum of the actual costs. Notice how the potential function builds up so that when it comes time to pay for changing two digits, the previous potential function value plus the current amortized cost exceeds 2. From our derivation of the amortized cost, it follows that the potential function is always nonnegative.

Accounting Method

We begin by assigning an amortized cost to the individual operations, and then we show that these assigned costs satsify Equation 1.3. Having already done an amortized analysis using the aggregate method, we see that Equation 1.3 is satisfied when we assign an amortized cost of $\$c + 1.12d$ to each display change. Typically, however, the use of the accounting method is not preceded by an application of the aggregate method and we start by guessing an amortized cost and then showing that this guess satisfies Equation 1.3.

Suppose we assign a guessed amortized cost of $\$c + 2d$ for each display change. Then,

$$\begin{aligned}
P(n) - P(0) &= \sum_{1 \le i \le n} (amortized(i) - actual(i)) \\
&= (c + 2d)n - \sum_{1 \le i \le n} actual(i) \\
&= (c + 2d)n - (c + (1 + 1/10 + 1/100 + \cdots)d)n \\
&\ge (c + 2d)n - (c + 1.12d)n \\
&\ge 0
\end{aligned}$$

This analysis also shows us that we can reduce the amortized cost of a widget to $\$c + 1.12d$.

An alternative proof method, called the *credit method*, that is useful in some analyses involves distributing the excess charge $P(i) - P(0)$ over various accounting entities, and using these stored excess charges (called *credits*) to establish $P(i+1) - P(0) \ge 0$. For our McWidget example, we use the display digits as the accounting entities. Initially, each digit is 0 and each digit has a credit of 0 dollars. Suppose we have guessed an amortized cost of $\$c + (1.111\cdots)d$. When the first widget is manufactured, $\$c + d$ of the amortized cost is used to pay for the update of the display and the remaining $\$(0.111\cdots)d$ of the amortized cost is retained as a credit by the least significant digit of the display. Similarly, when the second through ninth widgets are manufactured, $\$c + d$ of the amortized cost is used to pay for the update of the display and the remaining $\$(0.111\cdots)d$ of the amortized cost is retained as a credit by the least significant digit of the display. Following the manufacture of the ninth widget, the least significant digit of the display has a credit of $\$(0.999\cdots)d$ and the remaining digits have no credit. When the tenth widget is manufactured, $\$c + d$ of the amortized cost are used to pay for the trip charge and the cost of changing the least significant digit. The least significant digit now has a credit of $\$(1.111\cdots)d$. Of this credit, $\$d$ are used to pay for the change of the next least significant digit (i.e., the digit in the tens place), and the remaining $\$(0.111\cdots)d$ are transferred to the ten s digit as a credit. Continuing in this way, we see that when the display shows 99, the credit on the ten's digit is $\$(0.999\cdots)d$ and that on the one s digit (i.e., the least significant digit) is also $\$(0.999\cdots)d$. When the 100th widget is manufactured, $\$c + d$ of the amortized cost are used to pay for the trip charge and the cost of changing the least significant digit, and the credit on the least significant digit becomes $\$(1.111\cdots)d$. Of this credit, $\$d$ are used to pay for the change of the tens digit from 9 to 0, the remaining $\$(0.111\cdots)d$ credit on the one's digit is transferred to the ten's digit. The credit on the ten's digit now becomes $\$(1.111\cdots)d$. Of this credit, $\$d$ are used to pay for the change of the hundred's digit from 0 to 1, the remaining $\$(0.111\cdots)d$ credit on the ten's digit is transferred to the hundred's digit.

The above accounting scheme ensures that the credit on each digit of the display always equals $\$(0.111\cdots)dv$, where v is the value of the digit (e.g., when the display is 206 the credit on the one's digit is $\$(0.666\cdots)d$, the credit on the tens's digit is \$0, and that on the hundred's digit is $\$(0.222\cdots)d$.

From the preceding discussion, it follows that $P(n) - P(0)$ equals the sum of the digit credits and this sum is always nonnegative. Therefore, Equation 1.3 holds for all n.

Potential Method

We first postulate a potential function that satisfies Equation 1.3, and then use this function to obtain the amortized costs. From the credit method analysis used above, we see that we should use the potential function

$$P(n) = (0.111\cdots)d\sum_i v_i$$

where v_i is the value of the ith digit of the display. For example, when the display shows 206 (at this time $n = 206$), the potential function value is $(0.888\cdots)d$. This potential function satisifies Equation 1.3.

Let q be the number of 9s at the right end of j (i.e., when $j = 12903999$, $q = 3$). When the display changes from j to $j+1$, the potential change is $(0.111\cdots)d(1-9q)$ and the actual cost of updating the display is $\$c+(q+1)d$. From Equation 1.2, it follows that the amortized cost for the display change is

$$\begin{aligned}\text{actual cost} + \text{potential change} &= c + (q+1)d + (0.111\cdots)d(1-9q)\\ &= c + (1.111\cdots)d\end{aligned}$$

$\square$

Example 1.13 [Subset Generation] The subsets of a set of n elements are defined by the 2^n vectors $x[1:n]$, where each $x[i]$ is either 0 or 1. $x[i] = 1$ iff the ith element of the set is a member of the subset. The subsets of a set of three elements are given by the eight vectors $000, 100, 010, 110, 001, 101, 011, 111$, for example. Our subset enumeration strategy is to start with the subset $000\cdots000$ and generate the remaining subsets one at a time by invoking a function called $NextSubset$. This function scans the current subset vector from left to right changing 1s to 0s until the first 0 is encountered. This first 0 is changed to 1 and the function terminates. In case no 0 is encountered, there is no next subset. The described function was used to generate the sequence of subsets of 3 elements given earlier. We wish to determine how much time it takes to generate the first $m, 1 \leq m < 2^n$ subsets (excluding the starting subset $000\cdots000$.

Worst-Case Method

The complexity of $NextSubset$ is c, where c is the number of $x[i]$s that change. Since all n of the $x[i]$s could change in a single invocation of $NextSubset$, the worst-case complexity of $NextSubset$ is n. Using the worst-case method, the time required to generate the first m subsets is at most mn.

Aggregate Method

When $NextSubset$ is invoked m times, $x[n]$ changes m times; $x[n-1]$ changes $\lfloor m/2 \rfloor$ times; $x[n-2]$ changes $\lfloor m/4 \rfloor$ times; $x[n-3]$ changes $\lfloor m/8 \rfloor$ times; and so on. Therefore the sum of the actual costs of the first m invocations is

$$\sum_{0 \le i \le \lfloor \log_2 m \rfloor} \lfloor m/2^i \rfloor < 2m$$

Therefore, the complexity of generating the first m subsets is actually less than $2m$, a tighter bound than obtained using the worst-case method.

The amortized complexity of $NextSubset$ is (sum of actual costs)$/m < 2m/m = 2$.

Accounting Method

We first guess the amortized complexity of $NextSubset$, and then show that this amortized complexity satisfies Equation 1.3. Suppose we guess that the amortized complexity is 2. To verify this guess, we must show that $P(m) - P(0) \ge 0$ for all m.

We shall use the credit method used in the McWidget example. In this method, we distribute the excess charge $P(i) - P(0)$ over various accounting entities, and use these stored excess charges to establish $P(i+1) - P(0) \ge 0$. We use the $x[j]$s as the accounting entities. Initially, each $x[j]$ is 0 and has a credit of 0. When the first subset is generated, 1 unit of the amortized cost is used to pay for the single $x[j]$ that changes and the remaining 1 unit of the amortized cost is retained as a credit by $x[n]$, which is the $x[j]$ that has changed to 1. When the second subset is generated, the credit on $x[n]$ is used to pay for changing $x[n]$ to 0, 1 unit of the amortized cost is used to pay for changing $x[n-1]$ to 1, and the remaining 1 unit of the amortized cost is retained as a credit by $x[n-1]$, which is the $x[j]$ that has changed to 1. When the third subset is generated, 1 unit of the amortized cost is used to pay for changing $x[n]$ to 1, and the remaining 1 unit of the amortized cost is retained as a credit by $x[n]$, which is the $x[j]$ that has changed to 1. When the fourth subset is generated, the credit on $x[n]$ is used to pay for changing $x[n]$ to 0, the credit on $x[n-1]$ is used to pay for changing $x[n-1]$ to **0**, 1 unit of the amortized cost is used to pay for changing $x[n-2]$ to 1, and the remaining 1 unit of the amortized cost is retained as a credit by $x[n-2]$, which is the $x[j]$ that has changed to 1. Continuing in this way, we see that each $x[j]$ that is 1 has a credit of 1 unit on it. This credit is used to pay the actual cost of changing this $x[j]$ from 1 to 0. One unit of the amortized cost of $NextSubset$ is used to pay for the actual cost of changing an $x[j]$ to 1, and the remaining one unit of the amortized cost is retained as a credit by this $x[j]$.

The above accounting scheme ensures that the credit on each $x[j]$ that is 1 is exactly 1, and the credit on each $x[j]$ that is 0 is 0.

From the preceding discussion, it follows that $P(m) - P(0)$ equals the number of $x[j]$s that are 1. Since this number is always nonnegative, Equation 1.3 holds for all m.

Having established that the amortized complexity of $NextSubset$ is 2, we conclude that the complexity of generating the first m subsets is at most $m *$ amortized complexity $= 2m$.

Potential Method

We first postulate a potential function that satisfies Equation 1.3, and then use this function to obtain the amortized costs. Let $P(j)$ be the potential just after the jth subset is generated. From the proof used above for the accounting method, we can see that we should define $P(j) =$ number of $x[i]$s in the jth subset that are equal to 1.

By definition, the 0th subset has all $x[i]$ equal to 0. Since $P(0) = 0$ and $P(j) \geq 0$ for all j, this potential function P satisfies Equation 1.3.

Consider any subset $x[1:n]$. Let q be the number of 1s at the left end of $x[]$ (i.e., $x[0], x[1], \cdots,$ and $x[q-1]$ are all 1s). Assume that there is a next subset. So, $x[q] = 0$. When the next subset is generated, the potential change is $1-q$ because q 1s are replaced by 0 and a 0 is replaced by a 1. The actual cost of generating the next subset is $q+1$. From Equation 1.2, it follows that, when there is a next subset, the amortized cost for $NextSubset$ is

$$\text{actual cost} + \text{potential change} = q + 1 + 1 - q = 2$$

Consequently, the actual cost of generating the first m subsets is at most $2m$. □

1.3.4 Asymptotic Notation (O, Ω, Θ)

With the previous discussion as motivation, we introduce some terminology that enables us to make meaningful (but inexact) statements about the time and space complexities of an algorithm. In the remainder of this chapter, the functions f and g are nonnegative functions.

Definition 1.4 [Big "oh"] The function $f(n) = O(g(n))$ (read as "f of n is big oh of g of n") iff (if and only if) there exist positive constants c and n_0 such that $f(n) \leq c * g(n)$ for all n, $n \geq n_0$. □

Example 1.14 The function $3n + 2 = O(n)$ as $3n + 2 \leq 4n$ for all $n \geq 2$. $3n + 3 = O(n)$ as $3n + 3 \leq 4n$ for all $n \geq 3$. $100n + 6 = O(n)$ as $100n+6 \leq 101n$ for all $n \geq 6$. $10n^2+4n+2 = O(n^2)$ as $10n^2+4n+2 \leq 11n^2$ for all $n \geq 5$. $1000n^2 + 100n - 6 = O(n^2)$ as $1000n^2 + 100n - 6 \leq 1001n^2$ for $n \geq 100$. $6*2^n + n^2 = O(2^n)$ as $6*2^n + n^2 \leq 7*2^n$ for $n \geq 4$. $3n+3 = O(n^2)$ as $3n + 3 \leq 3n^2$ for $n \geq 2$. $10n^2 + 4n + 2 = O(n^4)$ as $10n^2 + 4n + 2 \leq 10n^4$ for $n \geq 2$. $3n + 2 \neq O(1)$ as $3n + 2$ is not less than or equal to c for any constant c and all $n \geq n_0$. $10n^2 + 4n + 2 \neq O(n)$. □

We write $O(1)$ to mean a computing time that is a constant. $O(n)$ is called *linear*, $O(n^2)$ is called *quadratic*, $O(n^3)$ is called *cubic*, and $O(2^n)$ is called *exponential*. If an algorithm takes time $O(\log n)$, it is faster, for sufficiently large n, than if it had taken $O(n)$. Similarly, $O(n \log n)$ is better than $O(n^2)$ but not as good as $O(n)$. These seven computing times–$O(1)$, $O(\log n)$, $O(n)$, $O(n \log n)$, $O(n^2)$, $O(n^3)$, and $O(2^n)$–are the ones we see most often in this book.

As illustrated by the previous example, the statement $f(n) = O(g(n))$ states only that $g(n)$ is an upper bound on the value of $f(n)$ for all n, $n \geq n_0$. It does not say anything about how good this bound is. Notice that $n = O(2^n)$, $n = O(n^{2.5})$, $n = O(n^3)$, $n = O(2^n)$, and so on. For the statement $f(n) = O(g(n))$ to be informative, $g(n)$ should be as small a function of n as one can come up with for which $f(n) = O(g(n))$. So, while we often say that $3n + 3 = O(n)$, we almost never say that $3n + 3 = O(n^2)$, even though this latter statement is correct.

From the definition of O, it should be clear that $f(n) = O(g(n))$ is not the same as $O(g(n)) = f(n)$. In fact, it is meaningless to say that $O(g(n)) = f(n)$. The use of the symbol $=$ is unfortunate because this symbol commonly denotes the equals relation. Some of the confusion that results from the use of this symbol (which is standard terminology) can be avoided by reading the symbol $=$ as "is" and not as "equals."

Theorem 1.2 obtains a very useful result concerning the order of $f(n)$ (that is, the $g(n)$ in $f(n) = O(g(n))$) when $f(n)$ is a polynomial in n.

Theorem 1.2 If $f(n) = a_m n^m + \cdots + a_1 n + a_0$, then $f(n) = O(n^m)$.

Proof:

$$\begin{aligned} f(n) &\leq \textstyle\sum_{i=0}^{m} |a_i| n^i \\ &\leq n^m \textstyle\sum_{i=0}^{m} |a_i| n^{i-m} \\ &\leq n^m \textstyle\sum_{i=0}^{m} |a_i| \qquad \text{for } n \geq 1 \end{aligned}$$

So, $f(n) = O(n^m)$ (assuming that m is fixed). □

Definition 1.5 [Omega] The function $f(n) = \Omega(g(n))$ (read as "f of n is omega of g of n") iff there exist positive constants c and n_0 such that $f(n) \geq c * g(n)$ for all n, $n \geq n_0$. □

Example 1.15 The function $3n + 2 = \Omega(n)$ as $3n + 2 \geq 3n$ for $n \geq 1$ (the inequality holds for $n \geq 0$, but the definition of Ω requires an $n_0 > 0$). $3n+3 = \Omega(n)$ as $3n+3 \geq 3n$ for $n \geq 1$. $100n+6 = \Omega(n)$ as $100n+6 \geq 100n$ for $n \geq 1$. $10n^2 + 4n + 2 = \Omega(n^2)$ as $10n^2 + 4n + 2 \geq n^2$ for $n \geq 1$. $6 * 2^n + n^2 = \Omega(2^n)$ as $6 * 2^n + n^2 \geq 2^n$ for $n \geq 1$. Observe also that $3n + 3 = \Omega(1)$, $10n^2 + 4n + 2 = \Omega(n)$, $10n^2 + 4n + 2 = \Omega(1)$, $6 * 2^n + n^2 = \Omega(n^{100})$, $6 * 2^n + n^2 = \Omega(n^{50.2})$, $6 * 2^n + n^2 = \Omega(n^2)$, $6 * 2^n + n^2 = \Omega(n)$, and $6 * 2^n + n^2 = \Omega(1)$. □

As in the case of the big oh notation, there are several functions $g(n)$ for which $f(n) = \Omega(g(n))$. The function $g(n)$ is only a lower bound on $f(n)$. For the statement $f(n) = \Omega(g(n))$ to be informative, $g(n)$ should be as large a function of n as possible for which the statement $f(n) = \Omega(g(n))$ is true. So, while we say that $3n + 3 = \Omega(n)$ and $6 * 2^n + n^2 = \Omega(2^n)$, we almost never say that $3n + 3 = \Omega(1)$ or $6 * 2^n + n^2 = \Omega(1)$, even though both of these statements are correct.

Theorem 1.3 is the analogue of Theorem 1.2 for the omega notation.

Theorem 1.3 If $f(n) = a_m n^m + \cdots + a_1 n + a_0$ and $a_m > 0$, then $f(n) = \Omega(n^m)$.

Proof: Left as an exercise. □

Definition 1.6 [Theta] The function $f(n) = \Theta(g(n))$ (read as "f of n is theta of g of n") iff there exist positive constants c_1, c_2, and n_0 such that $c_1 g(n) \leq f(n) \leq c_2 g(n)$ for all n, $n \geq n_0$. □

Example 1.16 The function $3n + 2 = \Theta(n)$ as $3n + 2 \geq 3n$ for all $n \geq 2$ and $3n + 2 \leq 4n$ for all $n \geq 2$, so $c_1 = 3$, $c_2 = 4$, and $n_0 = 2$. $3n + 3 = \Theta(n)$, $10n^2 + 4n + 2 = \Theta(n^2)$, $6 * 2^n + n^2 = \Theta(2^n)$, and $10 * \log n + 4 = \Theta(\log n)$. $3n+2 \neq \Theta(1)$, $3n+3 \neq \Theta(n^2)$, $10n^2+4n+2 \neq \Theta(n)$, $10n^2+4n+2 \neq \Theta(1)$, $6 * 2^n + n^2 \neq \Theta(n^2)$, $6 * 2^n + n^2 \neq \Theta(n^{100})$, and $6 * 2^n + n^2 \neq \Theta(1)$. □

The theta notation is more precise than both the the big oh and omega notations. The function $f(n) = \Theta(g(n))$ iff $g(n)$ is both an upper and lower bound on $f(n)$.

Notice that the coefficients in all of the $g(n)$'s used in the preceding three examples have been 1. This is in accordance with practice. We almost never find ourselves saying that $3n + 3 = O(3n)$, that $10 = O(100)$, that $10n^2 + 4n + 2 = \Omega(4n^2)$, that $6 * 2^n + n^2 = O(6 * 2^n)$, or that $6 * 2^n + n^2 = \Theta(4 * 2^n)$, even though each of these statements is true.

Theorem 1.4 If $f(n) = a_m n^m + \cdots + a_1 n + a_0$ and $a_m > 0$, then $f(n) = \Theta(n^m)$.

Proof: Left as an exercise. □

Definition 1.7 [Little "oh"] The function $f(n) = o(g(n))$ (read as "f of n is little oh of g of n") iff

$$\lim_{n\to\infty} \frac{f(n)}{g(n)} = 0$$

□

Example 1.17 The function $3n + 2 = o(n^2)$ since $\lim_{n\to\infty} \frac{3n+2}{n^2} = 0$. $3n + 2 = o(n \log n)$. $3n + 2 = o(n \log\log n)$. $6 * 2^n + n^2 = o(3^n)$. $6 * 2^n + n^2 = o(2^n \log n)$. $3n + 2 \neq o(n)$. $6 * 2^n + n^2 \neq o(2^n)$. □

Analogous to o is the notation ω defined as follows.

Definition 1.8 [Little omega] The function $f(n) = \omega(g(n))$ (read as "f of n is little omega of g of n") iff

$$\lim_{n\to\infty} \frac{g(n)}{f(n)} = 0$$

□

Example 1.18 Let us reexamine the time complexity analyses of the previous section. For the algorithm Sum (Algorithm 1.6) we determined that $t_{\mathsf{Sum}}(n) = 2n + 3$. So, $t_{\mathsf{Sum}}(n) = \Theta(n)$. For Algorithm 1.7, $t_{\mathsf{RSum}}(n) = 2n + 2 = \Theta(n)$. □

Although we might all see that the O, Ω, and Θ notations have been used correctly in the preceding paragraphs, we are still left with the question, Of what use are these notations if we have to first determine the step count exactly? The answer to this question is that the asymptotic complexity (i.e., the complexity in terms of O, Ω, and Θ) can be determined quite easily without determining the exact step count. This is usually done by first determining the asymptotic complexity of each statement (or group of statements) in the algorithm and then adding these complexities. Tables 1.6 through 1.8 do just this for Sum, RSum, and Add (Algorithms 1.6, 1.7, and 1.11).

Although the analyses of Tables 1.6 through 1.8 are carried out in terms of step counts, it is correct to interpret $t_P(n) = \Theta(g(n))$, $t_P(n) = \Omega(g(n))$, or $t_P(n) = O(g(n))$ as a statement about the computing time of algorithm P. This is so because each step takes only $\Theta(1)$ time to execute.

Statement	s/e	frequency	total steps
Algorithm Sum(a, n)	0	—	$\Theta(0)$
{	0	—	$\Theta(0)$
$s := 0.0$;	1	1	$\Theta(1)$
for $i := 1$ **to** n **do**	1	$n+1$	$\Theta(n)$
$s := s + a[i]$;	1	n	$\Theta(n)$
return s;	1	1	$\Theta(1)$
}	0	—	$\Theta(0)$
Total			$\Theta(n)$

Table 1.6 Asymptotic complexity of Sum (Algorithm 1.6)

Statement	s/e	frequency		total steps	
		$n=0$	$n>0$	$n=0$	$n>0$
Algorithm RSum(a, n)	0	—	—	0	$\Theta(0)$
{	0	—	—	0	$\Theta(0)$
if $(n \leq 0)$ **then**	1	1	1	1	$\Theta(1)$
return 0.0;	1	1	0	1	$\Theta(0)$
else return					
RSum$(a, n-1) + a[n])$;	$1+x$	0	1	0	$\Theta(1+x)$
}	0	—	—	0	$\Theta(0)$
Total				2	$\Theta(1+x)$

$$x = t_{\mathsf{RSum}}(n-1)$$

Table 1.7 Asymptotic complexity of RSum (Algorithm 1.7).

After you have had some experience using the table method, you will be in a position to arrive at the asymptotic complexity of an algorithm by taking a more global approach. We elaborate on this method in the following examples.

Example 1.19 [Permutation generator] Consider Perm (Algorithm 1.4). When $k = n$, we see that the time taken is $\Theta(n)$. When $k < n$, the **else** clause is entered. At this time, the second **for** loop is entered $n - k + 1$ times. Each iteration of this loop takes $\Theta(n + t_{\mathsf{Perm}}(k+1, n))$ time. So, $t_{\mathsf{Perm}}(k,\ n) =$

Statement	s/e	frequency	total steps
Algorithm Add(a, b, c, m, n)	0	–	$\Theta(0)$
{	0	–	$\Theta(0)$
for $i := 1$ **to** m **do**	1	$\Theta(m)$	$\Theta(m)$
for $i := 1$ **to** n **do**	1	$\Theta(mn)$	$\Theta(mn)$
$c[i, j] := a[i, j] + b[i, j]$;	1	$\Theta(mn)$	$\Theta(mn)$
}	0	–	$\Theta(0)$
Total			$\Theta(mn)$

Table 1.8 Asymptotic complexity of Add (Algorithm 1.11)

$\Theta((n-k+1)(n+t_{\mathsf{Perm}}(k+1,\ n)))$ when $k < n$. Since $t_{\mathsf{Perm}}(k+1,\ n)$ is at least n when $k+1 \leq n$, we get $t_{\mathsf{Perm}}(k,\ n) = \Theta((n-k+1)t_{\mathsf{Perm}}(k+1,\ n))$ for $k < n$. Using the substitution method, we obtain $t_{\mathsf{Perm}}(1, n) = \Theta(n(n!))$, $n \geq 1$. □

Example 1.20 [Magic square] The next example we consider is a problem from recreational mathematics. A magic square is an $n \times n$ matrix of the integers 1 to n^2 such that the sum of every row, column, and diagonal is the same. Figure 1.2 gives an example magic square for the case $n = 5$. In this example, the common sum is 65.

15	8	1	24	17
16	14	7	5	23
22	20	13	6	4
3	21	19	12	10
9	2	25	18	11

Figure 1.2 Example magic square

H. Coxeter has given the following simple rule for generating a magic square when n is odd:

> Start with 1 in the middle of the top row; then go up and left, assigning numbers in increasing order to empty squares; if you fall off the square imagine the same square as tiling the plane and continue; if a square is occupied, move down instead and continue.

The magic square of Figure 1.2 was formed using this rule. Algorithm 1.15 is for creating an $n \times n$ magic square for the case in which n is odd. This results from Coxeter's rule.

The magic square is represented using a two-dimensional array having n rows and n columns. For this application it is convenient to number the rows (and columns) from 0 to $n-1$ rather than from 1 to n. Thus, when the algorithm "falls off the square," the **mod** operator sets i and/or j back to 0 or $n-1$.

The time to initialize and output the square is $\Theta(n^2)$. The third **for** loop (in which *key* ranges over 2 through n^2) is iterated $n^2 - 1$ times and each iteration takes $\Theta(1)$ time. So, this **for** loop takes $\Theta(n^2)$ time. Hence the overall time complexity of Magic is $\Theta(n^2)$. Since there are n^2 positions in which the algorithm must place a number, we see that $\Theta(n^2)$ is the best bound an algorithm for the magic square problem can have. □

Example 1.21 [Computing x^n] Our final example is to compute x^n for any real number x and integer $n \geq 0$. A naive algorithm for solving this problem is to perform $n-1$ multiplications as follows:

```
power := x;
for i := 1 to n - 1 do power := power * x;
```

This algorithm takes $\Theta(n)$ time. A better approach is to employ the "repeated squaring" trick. Consider the special case in which n is an integral power of 2 (that is, in which n equals 2^k for some integer k). The following algorithm computes x^n.

```
power := x;
for i := 1 to k do power := power^2;
```

The value of *power* after q iterations of the **for** loop is x^{2^q}. Therefore, this algorithm takes only $\Theta(k) = \Theta(\log n)$ time, which is a significant improvement over the run time of the first algorithm.

Can the same algorithm be used when n is not an integral power of 2? Fortunately, the answer is yes. Let $b_k b_{k-1} \cdots b_1 b_0$ be the binary representation of the integer n. This means that $n = \sum_{q=0}^{k} b_q 2^q$. Now,

$$x^n = x^{\sum_{q=0}^{k} b_q 2^q} = (x)^{b_0} * (x^2)^{b_1} * (x^4)^{b_2} * \cdots * (x^{2^k})^{b_k}$$

```
Algorithm Magic(n)
// Create a magic square of size n, n being odd.
{
    if ((n mod 2) = 0) then
    {
        write ("n is even"); return;
    }
    else
    {
        for i := 0 to n - 1 do  // Initialize square to zero.
            for j := 0 to n - 1 do  square[i, j] := 0;
        square[0, (n - 1)/2] := 1; // Middle of first row
        // (i, j) is the current position.
        j := (n - 1)/2;
        for key := 2 to n^2 do
        {
            // Move up and left. The next two if statements
            // may be replaced by the mod operator if
            // -1 mod n has the value n - 1.
            if (i ≥ 1) then k := i - 1; else k := n - 1;
            if (j ≥ 1) then l := j - 1; else l := n - 1;
            if (square[k, l] ≥ 1) then i := (i + 1) mod n;
            else // square[k, l] is empty.
            {
                i := k; j := l;
            }
            square[i, j] := key;
        }
        // Output the magic square.
        for i := 0 to n - 1 do
            for j := 0 to n - 1 do write (square[i, j]);
    }
}
```

Algorithm 1.15 Magic square

Also observe that b_0 is nothing but n **mod** 2 and that $\lfloor n/2 \rfloor$ is $b_k b_{k-1} \cdots b_1$ in binary form. These observations lead us to Exponentiate (Algorithm 1.16) for computing x^n.

```
1   Algorithm Exponentiate(x, n)
2   // Return x^n for an integer n ≥ 0.
3   {
4       m := n; power := 1; z := x;
5       while (m > 0) do
6       {
7           while ((m mod 2) = 0) do
8           {
9               m := ⌊m/2⌋; z := z^2;
10          }
11          m := m - 1; power := power * z;
12      }
13      return power;
14  }
```

Algorithm 1.16 Computation of x^n

Proving the correctness of this algorithm is left as an exercise. The variable m starts with the value of n, and after every iteration of the innermost **while** loop (line 7), its value decreases by a factor of at least 2. Thus there will be only $\Theta(\log n)$ iterations of the **while** loop of line 7. Each such iteration takes $\Theta(1)$ time. Whenever control exits from the innermost **while** loop, the value of m is odd and the instructions $m := m - 1$; $power := power * z$; are executed once. After this execution, since m becomes even, either the innermost **while** loop is entered again or the outermost **while** loop (line 5) is exited (in case $m = 0$). Therefore the instructions $m := m - 1$; $power := power * z$; can only be executed $O(\log n)$ times. In summary, the overall run time of Exponentiate is $\Theta(\log n)$. □

1.3.5 Practical Complexities

We have seen that the time complexity of an algorithm is generally some function of the instance characteristics. This function is very useful in determining how the time requirements vary as the instance characteristics change. The complexity function can also be used to compare two algorithms P and Q that perform the same task. Assume that algorithm P has complexity $\Theta(n)$ and algorithm Q has complexity $\Theta(n^2)$. We can assert that algorithm P is faster than algorithm Q for sufficiently large n. To see the validity of this assertion, observe that the computing time of P is bounded from above by cn for some constant c and for all n, $n \geq n_1$, whereas that of Q is bounded from below by dn^2 for some constant d and all n, $n \geq n_2$. Since $cn \leq dn^2$ for $n \geq c/d$, algorithm P is faster than algorithm Q whenever $n \geq \max\{n_1, n_2, c/d\}$.

You should always be cautiously aware of the presence of the phrase "sufficiently large" in an assertion like that of the preceding discussion. When deciding which of the two algorithms to use, you must know whether the n you are dealing with is, in fact, sufficiently large. If algorithm P runs in $10^6 n$ milliseconds, whereas algorithm Q runs in n^2 milliseconds, and if you always have $n \leq 10^6$, then, other factors being equal, algorithm Q is the one to use.

To get a feel for how the various functions grow with n, you are advised to study Table 1.9 and Figure 1.3 very closely. It is evident from Table 1.9 and Figure 1.3 that the function 2^n grows very rapidly with n. In fact, if an algorithm needs 2^n steps for execution, then when $n = 40$, the number of steps needed is approximately $1.1 * 10^{12}$. On a computer performing one billion steps per second, this would require about 18.3 minutes. If $n = 50$, the same algorithm would run for about 13 days on this computer. When $n = 60$, about 310.56 years are required to execute the algorithm and when $n = 100$, about $4 * 10^{13}$ years are needed. So, we may conclude that the utility of algorithms with exponential complexity is limited to small n (typically $n \leq 40$).

$\log n$	n	$n \log n$	n^2	n^3	2^n
0	1	0	1	1	2
1	2	2	4	8	4
2	4	8	16	64	16
3	8	24	64	512	256
4	16	64	256	4,096	65,536
5	32	160	1,024	32,768	4,294,967,296

Table 1.9 Function values

Algorithms that have a complexity that is a polynomial of high degree are also of limited utility. For example, if an algorithm needs n^{10} steps, then using our 1-billion-steps-per-second computer, we need 10 seconds when $n = 10$, 3171 years when $n = 100$, and $3.17 * 10^{13}$ years when $n = 1000$. If the algorithm's complexity had been n^3 steps instead, then we would need one second when $n = 1000$, 110.67 minutes when $n = 10{,}000$, and 11.57 days when $n = 100{,}000$.

Table 1.10 gives the time needed by a one-billion-steps-per-second com-

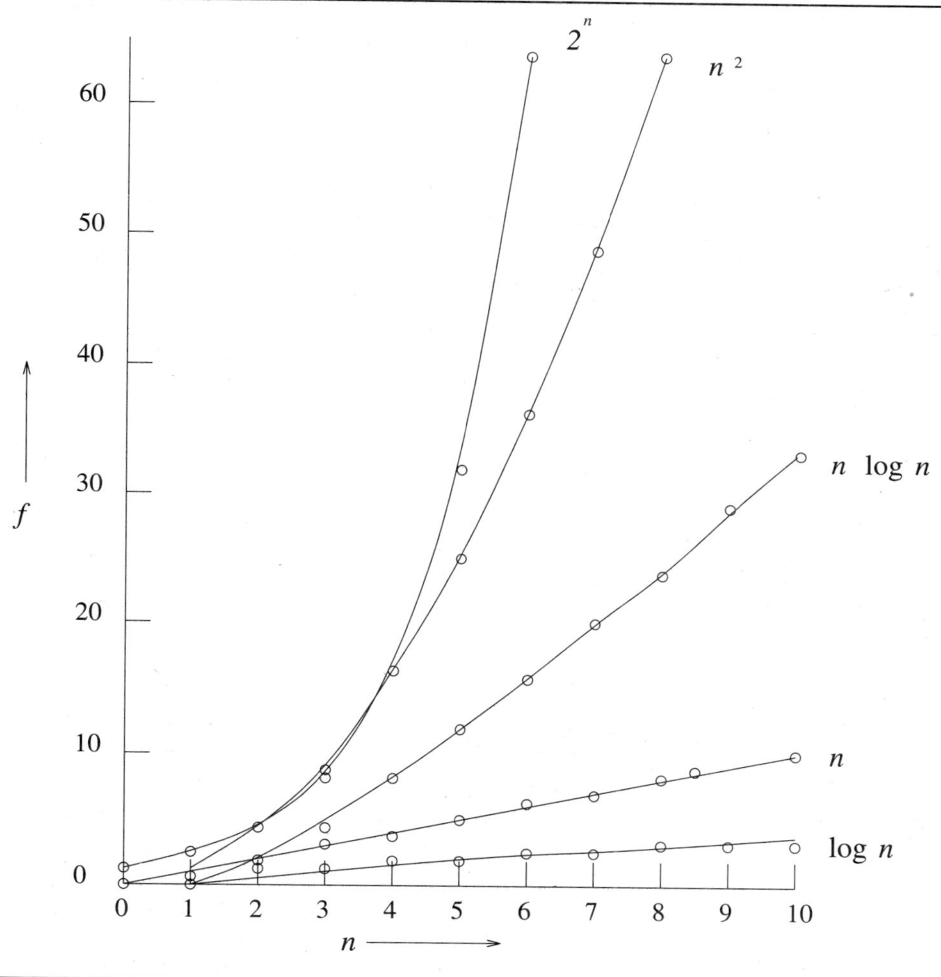

Figure 1.3 Plot of function values

puter to execute an algorithm of complexity $f(n)$ instructions. You should note that currently only the fastest computers can execute about 1 billion instructions per second. From a practical standpoint, it is evident that for reasonably large n (say $n > 100$), only algorithms of small complexity (such as n, $n \log n$, n^2, and n^3) are feasible. Further, this is the case even if you could build a computer capable of executing 10^{12} instructions per second. In this case, the computing times of Table 1.10 would decrease by a factor of 1000. Now, when $n = 100$, it would take 3.17 years to execute n^{10} instructions and $4 * 10^{10}$ years to execute 2^n instructions.

	$f(n)$						
n	n	$n \log_2 n$	n^2	n^3	n^4	n^{10}	2^n
10	.01 μs	.03 μs	.1 μs	1 μs	10 μs	10 s	1 μs
20	.02 μs	.09 μs	.4 μs	8 μs	160 μs	2.84 h	1 ms
30	.03 μs	.15 μs	.9 μs	27 μs	810 μs	6.83 d	1 s
40	.04 μs	.21 μs	1.6 μs	64 μs	2.56 ms	121 d	18 m
50	.05 μs	.28 μs	2.5 μs	125 μs	6.25 ms	3.1 y	13 d
100	.10 μs	.66 μs	10 μs	1 ms	100 ms	3171 y	$4 * 10^{13}$ y
10^3	1 μs	9.96 μs	1 ms	1 s	16.67 m	$3.17 * 10^{13}$ y	$32 * 10^{283}$ y
10^4	10 μs	130 μs	100 ms	16.67 m	115.7 d	$3.17 * 10^{23}$ y	
10^5	100 μs	1.66 ms	10 s	11.57 d	3171 y	$3.17 * 10^{33}$ y	
10^6	1 ms	19.92 ms	16.67 m	31.71 y	$3.17 * 10^7$ y	$3.17 * 10^{43}$ y	

μs = microsecond = 10^{-6} seconds; ms = milliseconds = 10^{-3} seconds
s = seconds; m = minutes; h = hours; d = days; y = years

Table 1.10 Times on a 1-billion-steps-per-second computer

1.3.6 Performance Measurement

Performance measurement is concerned with obtaining the space and time requirements of a particular algorithm. These quantities depend on the compiler and options used as well as on the computer on which the algorithm is run. Unless otherwise stated, all performance values provided in this book are obtained using the Gnu C++ compiler, the default compiler options, and the Sparc 10/30 computer workstation.

In keeping with the discussion of the preceding section, we do not concern ourselves with the space and time needed for compilation. We justify this by the assumption that each program (after it has been fully debugged) is compiled once and then executed several times. Certainly, the space and time needed for compilation are important during program testing, when more time is spent on this task than in running the compiled code.

We do not consider measuring the run-time space requirements of a program. Rather, we focus on measuring the computing time of a program. To obtain the computing (or run) time of a program, we need a clocking procedure. We assume the existence of a program GetTime() that returns the current time in milliseconds.

Suppose we wish to measure the worst-case performance of the sequential search algorithm (Algorithm 1.17). Before we can do this, we need to (1)

decide on the values of n for which the times are to be obtained and (2) determine, for each of the above values of n, the data that exhibit the worst-case behavior.

```
Algorithm SeqSearch(a, x, n)
// Search for x in a[1 : n]. a[0] is used as additional space.
{
    i := n; a[0] := x;
    while (a[i] ≠ x) do i := i − 1;
    return i;
}
```

Algorithm 1.17 Sequential search

The decision on which values of n to use is based on the amount of timing we wish to perform and also on what we expect to do with the times once they are obtained. Assume that for Algorithm 1.17, our intent is simply to predict how long it will take, in the worst case, to search for x, given the size n of a. An asymptotic analysis reveals that this time is $\Theta(n)$. So, we expect a plot of the times to be a straight line. Theoretically, if we know the times for any two values of n, the straight line is determined, and we can obtain the time for all other values of n from this line. In practice, we need the times for more than two values of n. This is so for the following reasons:

1. Asymptotic analysis tells us the behavior only for sufficiently large values of n. For smaller values of n, the run time may not follow the asymptotic curve. To determine the point beyond which the asymptotic curve is followed, we need to examine the times for several values of n.

2. Even in the region where the asymptotic behavior is exhibited, the times may not lie exactly on the predicted curve (straight line in the case of Algorithm 1.17) because of the effects of low-order terms that are discarded in the asymptotic analysis. For instance, an algorithm with asymptotic complexity $\Theta(n)$ can have time complexity $c_1 n + c_2 \log n + c_3$ or, for that matter, any other function of n in which the highest-order term is $c_1 n$ for some constant c_1, $c_1 > 0$.

It is reasonable to expect that the asymptotic behavior of Algorithm 1.17 begins for some n that is smaller than 100. So, for $n > 100$, we obtain the run time for just a few values. A reasonable choice is $n = 200, 300, 400, \ldots, 1000$. There is nothing magical about this choice of values. We can just as well use $n = 500, 1,000, 1,500, \ldots, 10,000$ or $n = 512,\ 1,024,\ 2,048, \ldots,$ 2^{15}. It costs us more in terms of computer time to use the latter choices, and we probably do not get any better information about the run time of Algorithm 1.17 using these choices.

For n in the range [0, 100] we carry out a more-refined measurement, since we are not quite sure where the asymptotic behavior begins. Of course, if our measurements show that the straight-line behavior does not begin in this range, we have to perform a more-detailed measurement in the range [100, 200], and so on, until the onset of this behavior is detected. Times in the range [0, 100] are obtained in steps of 10 beginning at $n = 0$.

Algorithm 1.17 exhibits its worst-case behavior when x is chosen such that it is not one of the $a[i]$'s. For definiteness, we set $a[i] = i$, $1 \leq i \leq n$, and $x = 0$. At this time, we envision using an algorithm such as Algorithm 1.18 to obtain the worst-case times.

```
Algorithm TimeSearch()
{
    for j := 1 to 1000 do  a[j] := j;
    for j := 1 to 10 do
    {
        n[j] := 10 * (j - 1); n[j + 10] := 100 * j;
    }
    for j := 1 to 20 do
    {
        h := GetTime();
        k := SeqSearch(a, 0, n[j]);
        h1 := GetTime();
        t := h1 - h;
        write (n[j], t);
    }
}
```

Algorithm 1.18 Algorithm to time Algorithm 1.17

The timing results of this algorithm is summarized in Table 1.11. The times obtained are too small to be of any use to us. Most of the times are zero; this indicates that the precision of our clock is inadequate. The nonzero times are just noise and are not representative of the time taken.

To time a short event, it is necessary to repeat it several times and divide the total time for the event by the number of repetitions.

n	time	n	time
0	0	100	0
10	0	200	0
20	0	300	1
30	0	400	0
40	0	500	1
50	0	600	0
60	0	700	0
70	0	800	1
80	0	900	0
90	0	1000	0

Table 1.11 Timing results of Algorithm 1.18. Times are in milliseconds.

Since our clock has an accuracy of about one-tenth of a second, we should not attempt to time any single event that takes less than about one second. With an event time of at least ten seconds, we can expect our observed times to be accurate to one percent.

The body of Algorithm 1.18 needs to be changed to that of Algorithm 1.19. In this algorithm, $r[i]$ is the number of times the search is to be repeated when the number of elements in the array is $n[i]$. Notice that rearranging the timing statements as in Algorithm 1.20 or 1.21 does not produce the desired results. For instance, from the data of Table 1.11, we expect that with the structure of Algorithm 1.20, the value output for $n = 0$ will still be 0. This is because there is a chance that in every iteration of the **for** loop, the clock does not change between the two times GetTime() is called. With the structure of Algorithm 1.21, we expect the algorithm never to exit the **while** loop when $n = 0$ (in reality, the loop will be exited because occasionally the measured time will turn out to be a few milliseconds).

Yet another alternative is shown in Algorithm 1.22. This approach can be expected to yield satisfactory times. It cannot be used when the timing procedure available gives us only the time since the last invocation of GetTime. Another difficulty is that the measured time includes the time needed to read the clock. For small n, this time may be larger than the time to run SeqSearch. This difficulty can be overcome by determining the time taken by the timing procedure and subtracting this time later.

Timing results of Algorithm 1.19, is given in Table 1.12. The times for n in the range [0, 1000] are plotted in Figure 1.4. Values in the range [10, 100] have not been plotted. The linear dependence of the worst-case time

```
Algorithm TimeSearch()
{
    // Repetition factors
    r[21] := {0, 200000, 200000, 150000, 100000, 100000, 100000,
        50000, 50000, 50000, 50000, 50000, 50000, 50000, 50000,
        50000, 50000, 25000, 25000, 25000, 25000};
    for j := 1 to 1000 do a[j] := j;
    for j := 1 to 10 do
    {
        n[j] := 10 * (j - 1); n[j + 10] := 100 * j;
    }
    for j := 1 to 20 do
    {
        h := GetTime();
        for i := 1 to r[j] do k := SeqSearch(a, 0, n[j]);
        h1 := GetTime();
        t1 := h1 - h;
        t := t1; t := t/r[j];
        write (n[j], t1, t);
    }
}
```

Algorithm 1.19 Timing algorithm

```
t := 0;
for i := 1 to r[j] do
{
    h := GetTime();
    k := SeqSearch(a, 0, n[j]);
    h1 := GetTime();
    t := t + h1 - h;
}
t := t/r[j];
```

Algorithm 1.20 Improper timing construct

```
t := 0;
while (t < DESIRED_TIME) do
{
    h := GetTime();
    k := SeqSearch(a, 0, n[j]);
    h1 := GetTime();
    t := t + h1 - h;
}
```

Algorithm 1.21 Another improper timing construct

```
h := GetTime(); t := 0;
while (t < DESIRED_TIME) do
{
    k := SeqSearch(a, 0, n[j]);
    h1 := GetTime();
    t := h1 - h;
}
```

Algorithm 1.22 An alternate timing construct

on n is apparent from this graph.

The graph of Figure 1.4 can be used to predict the run time for other values of n. We can go one step further and get the equation of the straight line. The equation of this line is $t = c + mn$, where m is the slope and c the value for $n = 0$. From the graph, we see that $c = 0.002$. Using the point $n = 600$ and $t = 0.186$, we obtain $m = (t - c)/n = 0.184/600 = 0.0003067$. So the line of Figure 1.4 has the equation $t = 0.002 + 0.0003067n$, where t is the time in milliseconds. From this, we expect that when $n = 1000$, the worst-case search time will be 0.3087 millisecond, and when $n = 500$, it will be 0.155 millisecond. Compared to the observed times of Table 1.12, we see that these figures are very accurate!

Summary of Running Time Calculation

To obtain the run time of a program, we need to plan the experiment. The following issues need to be addressed during the planning stage:

n	$t1$	t	n	$t1$	t
0	308	0.002	100	1683	0.034
10	923	0.005	200	3359	0.067
20	1181	0.008	300	4693	0.094
30	1087	0.011	400	6323	0.126
40	1384	0.014	500	7799	0.156
50	1691	0.017	600	9310	0.186
60	999	0.020	700	5419	0.217
70	1156	0.023	800	6201	0.248
80	1306	0.026	900	6994	0.280
90	1460	0.029	1000	7725	0.309

Times are in milliseconds

Table 1.12 Worst-case run times for Algorithm 1.17

1. What is the accuracy of the clock? How accurate do our results have to be? Once the desired accuracy is known, we can determine the length of the shortest event that should be timed.

2. For each instance size, a repetition factor needs to be determined. This is to be chosen such that the event time is at least the minimum time that can be clocked with the desired accuracy.

3. Are we measuring worst-case or average performance? Suitable test data need to be generated.

4. What is the purpose of the experiment? Are the times being obtained for comparative purposes, or are they to be used to predict run times? If the latter is the case, then contributions to the run time from such sources as the repetition loop and data generation need to be subtracted (in case they are included in the measured time). If the former is the case, then these times need not be subtracted (provided they are the same for all programs being compared).

5. In case the times are to be used to predict run times, then we need to fit a curve through the points. For this, the asymptotic complexity should be known. If the asymptotic complexity is linear, then a least-squares straight line can be fit; if it is quadratic, then a parabola can be used (that is, $t = a_0 + a_1 n + a_2 n^2$). If the complexity is $\Theta(n \log n)$, then a

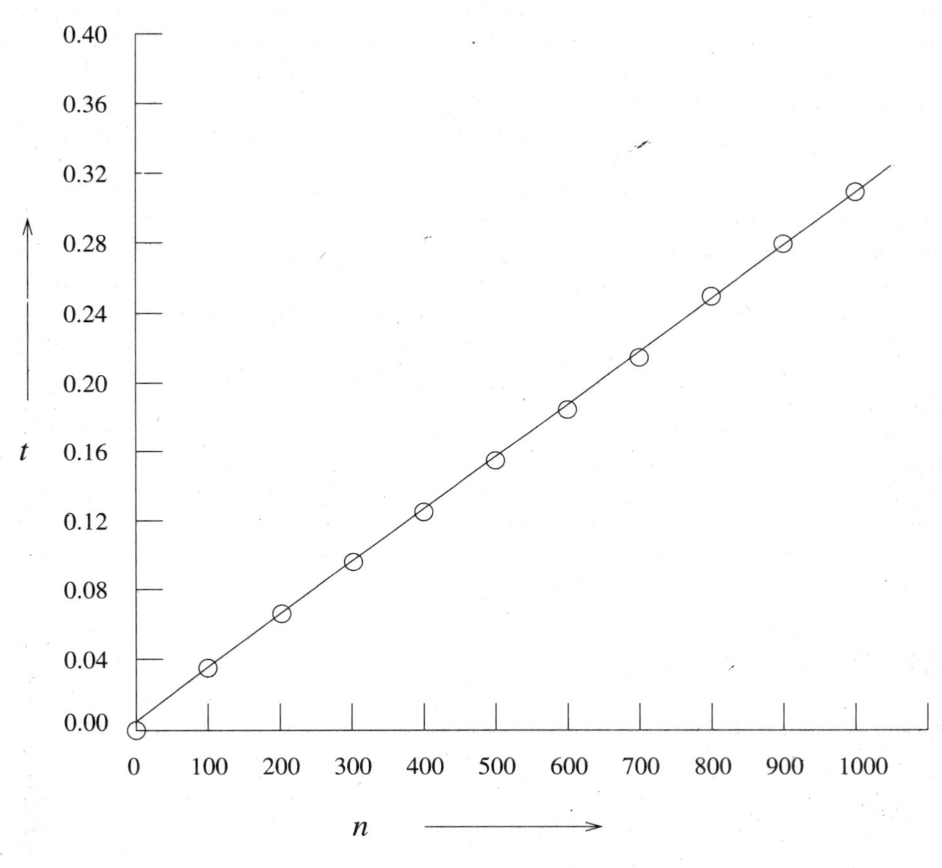

Figure 1.4 Plot of the data in Table 1.12

least-squares curve of the form $t = a_0 + a_1 n + a_2 n \log_2 n$ can be fit. When obtaining the least-squares approximation, one should discard data corresponding to small values of n, since the program does not exhibit its asymptotic behavior for these n.

Generating Test Data

Generating a data set that results in the worst-case performance of an algorithm is not always easy. In some cases, it is necessary to use a computer program to generate the worst-case data. In other cases, even this is very difficult. In these cases, another approach to estimating worst-case performance is taken. For each set of values of the instance characteristics of interest, we generate a suitably large number of random test data. The run times for each of these test data are obtained. The maximum of these times is used as an estimate of the worst-case time for this set of values of the instance characteristics.

To measure average-case times, it is usually not possible to average over all possible instances of a given characteristic. Although it is possible to do this for sequential search, it is not possible for a sort algorithm. If we assume that all keys are distinct, then for any given n, $n!$ different permutations need to be used to obtain the average time. Obtaining average-case data is usually much harder than obtaining worst-case data. So, we often adopt the strategy outlined above and simply obtain an estimate of the average time on a suitable set of test data.

Whether we are estimating worst-case or average time using random data, the number of instances that we can try is generally much smaller than the total number of such instances. Hence, it is desirable to analyze the algorithm being tested to determine classes of data that should be generated for the experiment. This is a very algorithm-specific task, and we do not go into it here.

EXERCISES

1. Compare the two functions n^2 and $2^n/4$ for various values of n. Determine when the second becomes larger than the first.

2. Prove by induction:

   (a) $\sum_{i=1}^{n} i = n(n+1)/2, \; n \geq 1$

   (b) $\sum_{i=1}^{n} i^2 = n(n+1)(2n+1)/6, \; n \geq 1$

   (c) $\sum_{i=0}^{n} x^i = (x^{n+1}-1)/(x-1), \; x \neq 1, \; n \geq 0$

3. Determine the frequency counts for all statements in the following two algorithm segments:

```
for i := 1 to n do
    for j := 1 to i do
        for k := 1 to j do
            x := x + 1;
```

(a)

```
i := 1;
while (i <= n) do
{
    x := x + 1;
    i := i + 1;
}
```

(b)

4. (a) Introduce statements to increment *count* at all appropriate points in Algorithm 1.23.

```
Algorithm D(x, n)
{
    i := 1;
    repeat
    {
        x[i] := x[i] + 2; i := i + 2;
    } until (i > n);
    i := 1;
    while (i ≤ ⌊n/2⌋) do
    {
        x[i] := x[i] + x[i + 1]; i := i + 1;
    }
}
```

Algorithm 1.23 Example algorithm

   (b) Simplify the resulting algorithm by eliminating statements. The simplified algorithm should compute the same value for *count* as computed by the algorithm of part (a).

   (c) What is the exact value of *count* when the algorithm terminates? You may assume that the initial value of *count* is 0.

   (d) Obtain the step count for Algorithm 1.23 using the frequency method. Clearly show the step count table.

5. Do Exercise 4 for Transpose (Algorithm 1.24).

6. Do Exercise 4 for Algorithm 1.25. This algorithm multiplies two $n \times n$ matrices a and b.

7. (a) Do Exercise 4 for Algorithm 1.26. This algorithm multiplies two matrices a and b, where a is an $m \times n$ matrix and b is an $n \times p$ matrix.

   (b) Under what conditions is it profitable to interchange the two outermost **for** loops?

8. What is the relationship between a correct assignment of amortized complexities to operations and the actual complexities of these operations?

9. How are potential function, amortized complexity, and actual complexity related?

```
Algorithm Transpose(a, n)
{
    for i := 1 to n - 1 do
        for j := i + 1 to n do
        {
            t := a[i, j]; a[i, j] := a[j, i]; a[j, i] := t;
        }
}
```

Algorithm 1.24 Matrix transpose

```
Algorithm Mult(a, b, c, n)
{
    for i := 1 to n do
        for j := 1 to n do
        {
            c[i, j] := 0;
            for k := 1 to n do
                c[i, j] := c[i, j] + a[i, k] * b[k, j];
        }
}
```

Algorithm 1.25 Matrix multiplication

```
Algorithm Mult(a, b, c, m, n, p)
{
    for i := 1 to m do
        for j := 1 to p do
        {
            c[i, j] := 0;
            for k := 1 to n do
                c[i, j] := c[i, j] + a[i, k] * b[k, j];
        }
}
```

Algorithm 1.26 Matrix multiplication

10. The McWidget company has been bought out by a computer manufacturer who insists that all displays be in binary. Rework the McWidget example using a binary display.

11. Suppose that a sequence of tasks is performed. The actual complexity of the ith task is 1 when i is not a power of 2. When i is a power of 2, the complexity of the ith task is i. Use each of the methods (a) aggregate, (b) accounting, and (c) potential function to show that the amortized complexity of a task is $O(1)$.

12. Imagine that a data structure is represented as an array whose initial length is 1. The data structure operations are *insert* and *delete*. An *insert* takes 1 time unit except when the number of elements in the data structure prior to the insert equals the array length n; at this time, the insert takes n time units because we double the array length. A *delete* takes 1 time unit except when the number of elements left in the array is less than (array length)/4. When the number of elements left in the array is less than (array length)/4, the array length is halved and the *delete* takes (array length)/2 time units. Use each of the methods (a) aggregate, (b) accounting, and (c) potential function to show that the amortized complexity of each data structure operation is $O(1)$.

13. Show that the following equalities are correct:

    (a) $5n^2 - 6n = \Theta(n^2)$
    (b) $n! = O(n^n)$
    (c) $2n^2 2^n + n \log n = \Theta(n^2 2^n)$
    (d) $\sum_{i=0}^{n} i^2 = \Theta(n^3)$
    (e) $\sum_{i=0}^{n} i^3 = \Theta(n^4)$.
    (f) $n^{2^n} + 6 * 2^n = \Theta(n^{2^n})$
    (g) $n^3 + 10^6 n^2 = \Theta(n^3)$
    (h) $6n^3/(\log n + 1) = O(n^3)$
    (i) $n^{1.001} + n \log n = \Theta(n^{1.001})$
    (j) $n^{k+\epsilon} + n^k \log n = \Theta(n^{k+\epsilon})$ for all fixed k and ϵ, $k \geq 0$ and $\epsilon > 0$
    (k) $10n^3 + 15n^4 + 100n^2 2^n = O(100n^2 2^n)$
    (l) $33n^3 + 4n^2 = \Omega(n^2)$
    (m) $33n^3 + 4n^2 = \Omega(n^3)$

14. Show that the following equalities are incorrect:

    (a) $10n^2 + 9 = O(n)$

(b) $n^2 \log n = \Theta(n^2)$
(c) $n^2/\log n = \Theta(n^2)$
(d) $n^3 2^n + 6n^2 3^n = O(n^3 2^n)$

15. Prove Theorems 1.3 and 1.4.

16. Analyze the computing time of SelectionSort (Algorithm 1.2).

17. Obtain worst-case run times for SelectionSort (Algorithm 1.2). Do this for suitable values of n in the range [0, 100]. Your report must include a plan for the experiment as well as the measured times. These times are to be provided both in a table and as a graph.

18. Consider the algorithm Add (Algorithm 1.11).
    (a) Obtain run times for $n = 1, 10, 20, \ldots, 100$.
    (b) Plot the times obtained in part (a).

19. Do the previous exercise for matrix multiplication (Algorithm 1.26).

20. A complex-valued matrix X is represented by a pair of matrices (A, B), where A and B contain real values. Write an algorithm that computes the product of two complex-valued matrices (A, B) and (C, D), where $(A, B) * (C, D) = (A + iB) * (C + iD) = (AC - BD) + i(AD + BC)$. Determine the number of additions and multiplications if the matrices are all $n \times n$.

1.4 RANDOMIZED ALGORITHMS

1.4.1 Basics of Probability Theory

Probability theory has the goal of characterizing the outcomes of natural or conceptual "experiments." Examples of such experiments include tossing a coin ten times, rolling a die three times, playing a lottery, gambling, picking a ball from an urn containing white and red balls, and so on.

Each possible outcome of an experiment is called a *sample point* and the set of all possible outcomes is known as the *sample space* S. In this text we assume that S is finite (such a sample space is called a *discrete sample space*). An *event* E is a subset of the sample space S. If the sample space consists of n sample points, then there are 2^n possible events.

Example 1.22 [Tossing three coins] When a coin is tossed, there are two possible outcomes: heads (H) and tails (T). Consider the experiment of throwing three coins. There are eight possible outcomes: HHH, HHT, HTH, HTT, THH, THT, TTH, and TTT. Each such outcome is a sample point. The sets $\{HHT, HTT, TTT\}$, $\{HHH, TTT\}$, and $\{ \}$ are three possible events. The third event has no sample points and is the empty set. For this experiment there are 2^8 possible events. □

Definition 1.9 [Probability] The probability of an event E is defined to be $\frac{|E|}{|S|}$, where S is the sample space. □

Example 1.23 [Tossing three coins] The probability of the event $\{HHT, HTT, TTT\}$ is $\frac{3}{8}$. The probability of the event $\{HHH, TTT\}$ is $\frac{2}{8}$ and that of the event $\{ \}$ is zero. □

Note that the probability of S, the sample space, is 1.

Example 1.24 [Rolling two dice] Let us look at the experiment of rolling two (six-faced) dice. There are 36 possible outcomes some of which are $(1,1), (1,2), (1,3), \ldots$. What is the probability that the sum of the two faces is 10? The event that the sum is 10 consists of the following sample points: $(4,6)$, $(5,5)$, and $(6,4)$. Therefore, the probability of this event is $\frac{3}{36} = \frac{1}{12}$. □

Definition 1.10 [Mutual exclusion] Two events E_1 and E_2 are said to be *mutually exclusive* if they do not have any common sample points, that is, if $E_1 \cap E_2 = \Phi$. □

Example 1.25 [Tossing three coins] When we toss three coins, let E_1 be the event that there are two H's and let E_2 be the event that there are at least two T's. These two events are mutually exclusive since there are no common sample points. On the other hand, if E_2' is defined to be the event that there is at least one T, then E_1 and E_2' will *not* be mutually exclusive since they will have THH, HTH, and HHT as common sample points. □

The probability of event E is denoted as $Prob.[E]$. The *complement* of E, denoted $\bar{E}$, is defined to be $S - E$. If E_1 and E_2 are two events, the probability of E_1 or E_2 or both happening is denoted as $Prob.[E_1 \cup E_2]$. The probability of both E_1 and E_2 occurring at the same time is denoted as $Prob.[E_1 \cap E_2]$. The corresponding event is $E_1 \cap E_2$.

Theorem 1.5

$$\begin{array}{rcl} 1.\ Prob.[\bar{E}] & = & 1 - Prob.[E]. \\ 2.\ Prob.[E_1 \cup E_2] & = & Prob.[E_1] + Prob.[E_2] - Prob.[E_1 \cap E_2] \\ & \leq & Prob.[E_1] + Prob.[E_2] \end{array}$$

Definition 1.11 [Conditional probability] Let E_1 and E_2 be any two events of an experiment. The *conditional probability of E_1 given E_2*, denoted by $Prob.[E_1|E_2]$, is defined as $\frac{Prob.[E_1 \cap E_2]}{Prob.[E_2]}$. □

Example 1.26 [Tossing four coins] Consider the experiment of tossing four coins. Let E_1 be the event that the number of H's is even and let E_2 be the event that there is at least one H. Then, E_2 is the complement of the event that there are no H's. The probability of no H's is $\frac{1}{16}$. Therefore, $Prob.[E_2] = 1 - \frac{1}{16} = \frac{15}{16}$. $Prob.[E_1 \cap E_2]$ is $\frac{7}{16}$ since the event $E_1 \cap E_2$ has the seven sample points $HHHH$, $HHTT$, $HTHT$, $HTTH$, $THHT$, $THTH$, and $TTHH$. Thus, $Prob.[E_1|E_2]$ is $\frac{7/16}{15/16} = \frac{7}{15}$. □

Definition 1.12 [Independence] Two events E_1 and E_2 are said to be *independent* if $Prob.[E_1 \cap E_2] = Prob.[E_1] * Prob.[E_2]$. □

Example 1.27 [Rolling a die twice] Intuitively, we say two events E_1 and E_2 are independent if the probability of one event happening is in no way affected by the occurrence of the other event. In other words, if $Prob.[E_1|E_2] = Prob.[E_1]$, these two events are independent. Suppose we roll a die twice. What is the probability that the outcome of the second roll is 5 (call this event E_1), given that the outcome of the first roll is 4 (call this event E_2)? The answer is $\frac{1}{6}$ no matter what the outcome of the first roll is. In this case E_1 and E_2 are independent. Therefore, $Prob.[E_1 \cap E_2] = \frac{1}{6} * \frac{1}{6} = \frac{1}{36}$. □

Example 1.28 [Flipping a coin 100 times] If a coin is flipped 100 times what is the probability that all of the outcomes are tails? The probability that the first outcome is T is $\frac{1}{2}$. Since the outcome of the second flip is independent of the outcome of the first flip, the probability that the first two outcomes are T's can be obtained by multiplying the corresponding probabilities to get $\frac{1}{4}$. Extending the argument to all 100 outcomes, we conclude that the probability of obtaining 100 T's is $\left(\frac{1}{2}\right)^{100}$. In this case we say the outcomes of the 100 coin flips are *mutually independent.* □

Definition 1.13 [Random variable] Let S be the sample space of an experiment. A *random variable* on S is a function that maps the elements of S to the set of real numbers. For any sample point $s \in S$, $X(s)$ denotes the image of s under this mapping. If the range of X, that is, the set of values X can take, is finite, we say X is *discrete.*

Let the range of a discrete random variable X be $\{r_1, r_2, \ldots, r_m\}$. Then, $Prob.[X = r_i]$, for any i, is defined to be the the number of sample points whose image is r_i divided by the number of sample points in S. In this text we are concerned mostly with discrete random variables. □

Example 1.29 We flip a coin four times. The sample space consists of 2^4 sample points. We can define a random variable X on S as the number of heads in the coin flips. For this random variable, then, $X(HTHH) = 3$, $X(HHHH) = 4$, and so on. The possible values that X can take are $0, 1, 2, 3$, and 4. Thus X is discrete. $Prob.[X = 0]$ is $\frac{1}{16}$, since the only sample point whose image is 0 is $TTTT$. $Prob.[X = 1]$ is $\frac{4}{16}$, since the four sample points $HTTT$, $THTT$, $TTHT$, and $TTTH$ have 1 as their image. □

Definition 1.14 [Expected value] If the sample space of an experiment is $S = \{s_1, s_2, \ldots, s_n\}$, the *expected value* or the *mean* of any random variable X is defined to be $\sum_{i=1}^{n} Prob.[s_i] * X(s_i) = \frac{1}{n}\sum_{i=1}^{n} X(s_i)$. □

Example 1.30 [Coin tosses] The sample space corresponding to the experiment of tossing three coins is $S = \{HHH, HHT, HTH, HTT, THH, THT, TTH, TTT\}$. If X is the number of heads in the coin flips, then the expected value of X is $\frac{1}{8}(3 + 2 + 2 + 1 + 2 + 1 + 1 + 0) = 1.5$. □

Definition 1.15 [Probability distribution] Let X be a discrete random variable defined over the sample space S. Let $\{r_1, r_2, \ldots, r_m\}$ be its range. Then, the *probability distribution* of X is the sequence $Prob.[X = r_1]$, $Prob.[X = r_2]$, ..., $Prob.[X = r_m]$. Notice that $\sum_{i=1}^{m} Prob.[X = r_i] = 1$. □

Example 1.31 [Coin tosses] If a coin is flipped three times and X is the number of heads, then X can take on four values, 0, 1, 2, and 3. The probability distribution of X is given by $Prob.[X = 0] = \frac{1}{8}$, $Prob.[X = 1] = \frac{3}{8}$, $Prob.[X = 2] = \frac{3}{8}$, and $Prob.[X = 3] = \frac{1}{8}$. □

Definition 1.16 [Binomial distribution] A *Bernoulli* trial is an experiment that has two possible outcomes, namely, *success* and *failure*. The probability of success is p. Consider the experiment of conducting the Bernoulli trial n times. This experiment has a sample space S with 2^n sample points. Let X be a random variable on S defined to be the numbers of successes in the n trials. The variable X is said to have a *binomial distribution* with parameters (n, p). The expected value of X is np. Also,

$$Prob.[X = i] = \binom{n}{i} p^i (1 - p)^{n-i}$$

□

In several applications, it is necessary to estimate the probabilities at the tail ends of probability distributions. One such estimate is provided by the following lemma.

Lemma 1.1 [Markov's inequality] If X is any nonnegative random variable whose mean is μ, then

$$Prob.[X \geq x] \ \leq \ \frac{\mu}{x}$$

□

Example 1.32 Let μ be the mean of a random variable X. We can use Markov's lemma (also called Markov's inequality) to make the following statement: "The probability that the value of X exceeds 2μ is $\leq \frac{1}{2}$." Consider the example: if we toss a coin 1000 times, what is the probability that the number of heads is ≥ 600? If X is the number of heads in 1000 tosses, then, the expected value of X, $E[X]$, is 500. Applying Markov's inequality with $x = 600$ and $\mu = 500$, we infer that $P[X \geq 600] \leq \frac{5}{6}$. □

Though Markov's inequality can be applied to any nonnegative random variable, it is rather weak. We can obtain tighter bounds for a number of important distributions including the binomial distribution. These bounds are due to Chernoff. Chernoff bounds as applied to the binomial distribution are employed in this text to analyze randomized algorithms.

Lemma 1.2 [Chernoff bounds] If X is a binomial with parameters $(n, \ p)$, and $m > np$ is an integer, then

$$Prob.(X \geq m) \ \leq \ \left(\frac{np}{m}\right)^m e^{(m-np)}. \tag{1.4}$$

$$\text{Also,} \ \ Prob.(X \leq \lfloor (1-\epsilon)pn \rfloor) \ \leq \ e^{(-\epsilon^2 np/2)} \tag{1.5}$$

$$\text{and} \ \ Prob.(X \geq \lceil (1+\epsilon)np \rceil) \ \leq \ e^{(-\epsilon^2 np/3)} \tag{1.6}$$

for all $0 < \epsilon < 1$. □

Example 1.33 Consider the experiment of tossing a coin 1000 times. We want to determine the probability that the number X of heads is ≥ 600. We can use Equation 1.6 to estimate this probability. The value for ϵ here is 0.2. Also, $n = 1000$ and $p = \frac{1}{2}$. Equation 1.6 now becomes

$$P[X \geq 600] \leq e^{[-(0.2)^2(500/3)]} = e^{-20/3} \leq 0.001273$$

This estimate is more precise than that given by Markov's inequality. □

1.4.2 Randomized Algorithms: An Informal Description

A randomized algorithm is one that makes use of a randomizer (such as a random number generator). Some of the decisions made in the algorithm depend on the output of the randomizer. Since the output of any randomizer might differ in an unpredictable way from run to run, the output of a randomized algorithm could also differ from run to run for the same input. The execution time of a randomized algorithm could also vary from run to run for the same input.

Randomized algorithms can be categorized into two classes: The first is algorithms that always produce the same (correct) output for the same input. These are called *Las Vegas* algorithms. The execution time of a Las Vegas algorithm depends on the output of the randomizer. If we are lucky, the algorithm might terminate fast, and if not, it might run for a longer period of time. In general the execution time of a Las Vegas algorithm is characterized as a random variable (see Section 1.4.1 for a definition). The second is algorithms whose outputs might differ from run to run (for the same input). These are called *Monte Carlo* algorithms. Consider any problem for which there are only two possible answers, say, yes and no. If a Monte Carlo algorithm is employed to solve such a problem, then the algorithm might give incorrect answers depending on the output of the randomizer. We require that the probability of an incorrect answer from a Monte Carlo algorithm be low. Typically, for a fixed input, a Monte Carlo algorithm does not display much variation in execution time between runs, whereas in the case of a Las Vegas algorithm this variation is significant.

We can think of a randomized algorithm with one possible randomizer output to be different from the same algorithm with a different possible randomizer output. Therefore, a randomized algorithm can be viewed as a family of algorithms. For a given input, some of the algorithms in this family may run for indefinitely long periods of time (or may give incorrect answers). The objective in the design of a randomized algorithm is to ensure that the number of such bad algorithms in the family is only a small fraction of the total number of algorithms. If for *any* input we can show that at least $1 - \epsilon$ (ϵ being very close to 0) fraction of algorithms in the family will run quickly (respectively give the correct answer) on that input, then clearly, a random algorithm in the family will run quickly (or output the correct answer) on any input with probability $\geq 1 - \epsilon$. In this case we say that this family of algorithms (or this randomized algorithm) runs quickly (respectively gives the correct answer) with probability at least $1 - \epsilon$, where ϵ is called the *error probability*.

Definition 1.17 [The $\widetilde{O}()$] Just like the $O()$ notation is used to characterize the run times of non randomized algorithms, $\widetilde{O}()$ is used for characterizing the run times of Las Vegas algorithms. We say a Las Vegas algorithm has a resource (time, space, and so on.) bound of $\widetilde{O}(g(n))$ if there exists a constant

c such that the amount of resource used by the algorithm (on any input of size n) is no more than $c\alpha g(n)$ with probability $\geq 1 - \frac{1}{n^\alpha}$. We shall refer to these bounds as *high probability* bounds.

Similar definitions apply also to such functions as $\widetilde{\Theta}()$, $\widetilde{\Omega}()$, $\widetilde{o}()$, etc. □

Definition 1.18 [High probability] By *high probability* we mean a probability of $\geq 1 - n^{-\alpha}$ for any fixed α. We call α the probability parameter. □

As mentioned above, the run time T of any Las Vegas algorithm is typically characterized as a random variable over a sample space S. The sample points of S are all possible outcomes for the randomizer used in the algorithm. Though it is desirable to obtain the distribution of T, often this is a challenging and unnecessary task. The expected value of T often suffices as a good indicator of the run time. We can do better than obtaining the mean of T but short of computing the exact distribution by obtaining the high probability bounds. The high probability bounds of our interest are of the form "With high probability the value of T will not exceed T_0," for some appropriate T_0.

Several results from probability theory can be employed to obtain high probability bounds on any random variable. Two of the more useful such results are Markov's inequality and Chernoff bounds.

Next we give two examples of randomized algorithms. The first is of the Las Vegas type and the second is of the Monte Carlo type. Other examples are presented throughout the text. We say a Monte Carlo (Las Vegas) algorithm has *failed* if it does not give a correct answer (terminate within a specified amount of time).

1.4.3 Identifying the Repeated Element

Consider an array $a[\ ]$ of n numbers that has $\frac{n}{2}$ distinct elements and $\frac{n}{2}$ copies of another element. The problem is to identify the repeated element.

Any deterministic algorithm for solving this problem will need at least $\frac{n}{2} + 2$ time steps in the worst case. This fact can be argued as follows: Consider an adversary who has perfect knowledge about the algorithm used and who is in charge of selecting the input for the algorithm. Such an adversary can make sure that the first $\frac{n}{2} + 1$ elements examined by the algorithm are all distinct. Even after having looked at $\frac{n}{2} + 1$ elements, the algorithm will not be in a position to infer the repeated element. It will have to examine at least $\frac{n}{2} + 2$ elements and hence take at least $\frac{n}{2} + 2$ time steps.

In contrast there is a simple and elegant randomized Las Vegas algorithm that takes only $\widetilde{O}(\log n)$ time. It randomly picks two array elements and checks whether they come from two different cells and have the same value. If they do, the repeated element has been found. If not, this basic step of sampling is repeated as many times as it takes to identify the repeated element.

In this algorithm, the sampling performed is with repetitions; that is, the first and second elements are randomly picked from out of the n elements (each element being equally likely to be picked). Thus there is a probability (equal to $\frac{1}{n}$) that the same array element is picked each time. If we just check for the equality of the two elements picked, our answer might be incorrect (in case the algorithm picked the same array index each time). Therefore, it is essential to make sure that the two array indices picked are different and the two array cells contain the same value.

```
RepeatedElement(a, n)
// Finds the repeated element from a[1 : n].
{
    while (true) do
    {
        i := Random() mod n + 1; j := Random() mod n + 1;
        // i and j are random numbers in the range [1, n].
        if ((i ≠ j) and (a[i] = a[j])) then return i;
    }
}
```

Algorithm 1.27 Identifying the repeated array number

This algorithm is given in Algorithm 1.27. The algorithm returns the array index of one of the copies of the repeated element. Now we prove that the run time of the above algorithm is $\widetilde{O}(\log n)$. Any iteration of the **while** loop will be successful in identifying the repeated number if i is any one the $\frac{n}{2}$ array indices corresponding to the repeated element and j is any one of the same $\frac{n}{2}$ indices other than i. In other words, the probability that the algorithm quits in any given iteration of the **while** loop is $P = \frac{n/2(n/2-1)}{n^2}$, which is $\geq \frac{1}{5}$ for all $n \geq 10$. This implies that the probability that the algorithm does not quit in a given iteration is $< \frac{4}{5}$.

Therefore, the probability that the algorithm does not quit in 10 iterations is $< \left(\frac{4}{5}\right)^{10} < .1074$. So, Algorithm 1.27 will terminate in 10 iterations or less with probability $\geq .8926$. The probability that the algorithm does not terminate in 100 iterations is $< \left(\frac{4}{5}\right)^{100} < 2.04 * 10^{-10}$. That is, almost certainly the algorithm will quit in 100 iterations or less. If n equals $2 * 10^6$, for example, any deterministic algorithm will have to spend at least one million time steps, as opposed to the 100 iterations of Algorithm 1.27!

In general, the probability that the algorithm does not quit in the first $c\alpha \log n$ (c is a constant to be fixed) iterations is

$$< (4/5)^{c\alpha \log n} = n^{-c\alpha \log (5/4)}$$

which will be $< n^{-\alpha}$ if we pick $c \geq \frac{1}{\log (5/4)}$.

Thus the algorithm terminates in $\frac{1}{\log (5/4)}\alpha \log n$ iterations or less with probability $\geq 1 - n^{-\alpha}$. Since each iteration of the **while** loop takes $O(1)$ time, the run time of the algorithm is $\widetilde{O}(\log n)$.

Note that this algorithm, if it terminates, will always output the correct answer and hence is of the Las Vegas type. The above analysis shows that the algorithm will terminate quickly with high probability.

The same problem of inferring the repeated element can be solved using many deterministic algorithms. For example, sorting the array is one way. But sorting takes $\Omega(n \log n)$ time (proved in Chapter 10). An alternative is to partition the array into $\lceil \frac{n}{3} \rceil$ parts, where each part (possibly except for one part) has three array elements, and to search the individual parts for the repeated element. At least one of the parts will have two copies of the repeated element. (Prove this!) The run time of this algorithm is $\Theta(n)$.

1.4.4 Primality Testing

Any integer greater than one is said to be a *prime* if its only divisors are 1 and the integer itself. By convention, we take 1 to be a nonprime. Then $2, 3, 5, 7, 11$, and 13 are the first six primes. Given an integer n, the problem of deciding whether n is a prime is known as *primality testing*. It has a number of applications including cryptology.

If a number n is composite (i.e., nonprime), it must have a divisor $\leq \lfloor \sqrt{n} \rfloor$. This observation leads to the following simple algorithm for primality testing: Consider each number ℓ in the interval $[2, \lfloor \sqrt{n} \rfloor]$ and check whether ℓ divides n. If none of these numbers divides n, then n is prime; otherwise it is composite.

Assuming that it takes $\Theta(1)$ time to determine whether one integer divides another, the naive primality testing algorithm has a run time of $O(\sqrt{n})$. The input size for this problem is $\lceil (\log n + 1) \rceil$, since n can be represented in binary form with these many bits. Thus the run time of this simple algorithm is exponential in the input size (notice that $\sqrt{n} = 2^{\frac{1}{2} \log n}$).

We can devise a Monte Carlo randomized algorithm for primality testing that runs in time $O((\log n)^2)$. The output of this algorithm is correct with high probability. If the input is prime, the algorithm never gives an incorrect answer. However, if the input number is composite (i.e., nonprime), then there is a small probability that the answer may be incorrect. Algorithms of this kind are said to have *one-sided error*.

Before presenting further details, we list two theorems from number theory that will serve as the backbone of the algorithm. The proofs of these theorems can be found in the references supplied at the end of this chapter

Theorem 1.6 [Fermat] If n is prime, then $a^{n-1} \equiv 1 \pmod{n}$ for any integer $a < n$. □

Theorem 1.7 The equation $x^2 \equiv 1 \pmod{n}$ has exactly two solutions, namely 1 and $n-1$, if n is prime. □

Corollary 1.1 If the equation $x^2 \equiv 1 \pmod{n}$ has roots other than 1 and $n-1$, then n is composite. □

Note: Any integer x which is neither 1 nor $n-1$ but which satisfies $x^2 \equiv 1 \pmod{n}$ is said to be a *nontrivial square root* of 1 modulo n.

Fermat's theorem suggests the following algorithm for primality testing: Randomly choose an $a < n$ and check whether $a^{n-1} \equiv 1 \pmod{n}$ (call this Fermat's equation). If Fermat's equation is not satisfied, n is composite. If the equation is satisfied, we try some more random a's. If on each a tried, Fermat's equation is satisfied, we output "n is prime"; otherwise we output "n is composite." In order to compute a^{n-1} **mod** n, we could employ Exponentiate (Algorithm 1.16) with some minor modifications. The resultant primality testing algorithm is given as Algorithm 1.28. Here *large* is a number sufficiently *large* that ensures a probability of correctness of $\geq 1 - n^{-\alpha}$.

If the input is prime, Algorithm 1.28 will never output an incorrect answer. If n is composite, will Fermat's equation never be satisfied for any a less than n and greater than one? If so, the above algorithm has to examine just one a before coming up with the correct answer. Unfortunately, the answer to this question is no. Even if n is composite, Fermat's equation may be satisfied depending on the a chosen.

Is it the case that for every n (that is composite) there will be some nonzero constant fraction of a's less than n that will not satisfy Fermat's equation? If the answer is yes and if the above algorithm tries a sufficiently large number of a's, there is a high probability that at least one a violating Fermat's equation will be found and hence the correct answer be output. Here again, the answer is no. There are composite numbers (known as Carmichael numbers) for which every a that is less than and relatively prime to n will satisfy Fermat's equation. (The number of a's that do not satisfy Fermat's equation need not be a constant fraction.) The numbers 561 and 1105 are examples of Carmichael numbers.

Fortunately, a slight modification of the above algorithm takes care of these problems. The modified primality testing algorithm (also known as Miller-Rabin's algorithm) is the same as Prime0 (Algorithm 1.28) except

```
Prime0(n, α)
// Returns true if n is a prime and false otherwise.
// α is the probability parameter.
{
    q := n − 1;
    for i := 1 to large do  // Specify large.
    {
        m := q; y := 1;
        a := Random() mod q + 1;
        // Choose a random number in the range [1, n − 1].
        z := a;
        // Compute a^(n−1) mod n.
        while (m > 0) do
        {
            while (m mod 2 = 0) do
            {
                z := z^2 mod n; m := ⌊m/2⌋;
            }
            m := m − 1; y := (y * z) mod n;
        }
        if (y ≠ 1) then return false;
        // If a^(n−1) mod n is not 1, n is not a prime.
    }
    return true;
}
```

Algorithm 1.28 Primality testing: first attempt

that within the body of Prime0, we also look for nontrivial square roots of n. The modified version is given in Algorithm 1.29. We assume that n is odd.

Miller-Rabin's algorithm will never give an incorrect answer if the input is prime, since Fermat's equation will always be satisfied and no nontrivial square root of 1 modulo n can be found. If n is composite, the above algorithm will detect the compositeness of n if the randomly chosen a either leads to the discovery of a nontrivial square root of 1 or violates Fermat's equation. Call any such a a *witness* to the compositeness of n. What is the probability that a randomly chosen a will be a witness to the compositeness of n? This question is answered by the following theorem (the proof can be found in the references at the end of this chapter).

```
Prime(n, α)
// Returns true if n is a prime and false otherwise.
// α is the probability parameter.
{
    q := n − 1;
    for i := 1 to α * log(n) do
    {
        m := q; y := 1;
        a := Random() mod q + 1;
        // Choose a random number in the range [1, n − 1].
        z := a;
        // Compute a^(n−1) mod n.
        while (m > 0) do
        {
            while (m mod 2 = 0) do
            {
                x := z; z := z^2 mod n;
                // If x is a nontrivial square
                // root of 1, n is not a prime.
                if ((z = 1) and (x ≠ 1) and (x ≠ q)) then
                    return false;
                m := ⌊m/2⌋;
            }
            m := m − 1; y := (y * z) mod n;
        }
        if (y ≠ 1) return false;
        // If a^(n−1) mod n is not 1, n is not a prime.
    }
    return true;
}
```

Algorithm 1.29 Miller-Rabin's primality testing algorithm

Theorem 1.8 There are at least $\frac{n-1}{2}$ witnesses to the compositeness of n if n is composite and odd. □

Assume that n is composite (since if n is prime, the algorithm will always be correct). The probability that a randomly chosen a will be a witness is $\geq \frac{n-1}{2n}$, which is very nearly equal to $\frac{1}{2}$. This means that a randomly chosen a will fail to be a witness with probability $\leq \frac{1}{2}$.

Therefore, the probability that none of the first $\alpha \log n$ a's chosen is a witness is $\leq \left(\frac{1}{2}\right)^{\alpha \log n} = n^{-\alpha}$. In other words, the algorithm Prime will give an incorrect answer with only probability $\leq n^{-\alpha}$.

The run time of the outermost **while** loop is nearly the same as that of Exponentiate (Algorithm 1.16) and equal to $O(\log n)$. Since this **while** loop is executed $O(\log n)$ times, the run time of the whole algorithm is $O(\log^2 n)$.

1.4.5 Advantages and Disadvantages

Two of the most important advantages of using randomized algorithms are their simplicity and efficiency. You may have already gotten a feel for this from the examples of repeated element identification and primality testing. A majority of the randomized algorithms found in the literature are simpler than the best deterministic algorithms for the same problems. Randomized algorithms have also been shown to yield better complexity bounds. As we have already seen, for the repeated element identification problem (Section 1.4.3), any deterministic algorithm will have to spend $\Omega(n)$ time, whereas a simple randomized algorithm can solve the same problem in $\widetilde{O}(\log n)$ time.

Not only do randomized algorithms yield superior asymptotic run-time bounds, but they also have been demonstrated to be competitive in practice.

A skeptical reader at this point might ask: How dependable are randomized algorithms in practice? After all there is a nonzero probability that they may fail. Most readers are also aware that there is a probability (however small it may be) that the hardware itself may fail. So, if we design a fast algorithm for a problem with an error probability much less than that of the hardware failure probability, then it is more likely for the machine to break down than for the algorithm to fail.

You are cautioned at this point that there are critical applications such as in a nuclear reactor where even a small probability of error (or a small probability of a longer run time) cannot be tolerated. Also, the use of a randomizer within an algorithm doesn't always result in better performance. Exercises 10 and 13 illustrate this.

EXERCISES

1. For the experiment of drawing 5 cards out of a deck of 52 cards, what is the sample space? If X is defined to be the number of hearts in the 5 cards drawn, what is the distribution of X? What is the mean of X?

2. A die is rolled twice. Let X be the sum of the two faces. Compute the sample space of the experiment, the distribution of X, and the expected value of X.

3. A coin is flipped n times. Estimate the probability that the number of heads is greater than or equal to $\lceil(1.02n)\rceil$. Do this first using Markov's inequality and then using Chernoff bounds. Compute these estimates for each of the following choices for n: 50, 500, 5,000, and 50,000.

4. Given a two-sided *biased* coin (i.e., the probability of a *head* is not 1/2). Using this coin how will you simulate an unbiased coin? (*Hint*: You may flip the biased coin many times to determine one outcome of the simulated unbiased coin.)

5. Given a 2-sided coin. Using this coin, how will you simulate an n-sided coin

   (a) when n is a power of 2?.

   (b) when n is not a power of 2?.

6. Compute the run time of the Las Vegas algorithm given in Algorithm 1.30 and express it using the $\widetilde{O}()$ notation.

```
LasVegas()
{
    while (true) do
    {
        i := Random() mod 2;
        if (i ≥ 1) then return;
    }
}
```

Algorithm 1.30 A Las Vegas algorithm

7. There are $\sqrt{n}$ copies of an element in the array c. Every other element of c occurs exactly once. If the algorithm RepeatedElement is used to identify the repeated element of c, will the run time still be $\widetilde{O}(\log n)$? If so, why? If not, what is the new run time?

8. What is the minimum number of times that an element should be repeated in an array (the other elements of the array occurring exactly once) so that it can be found using RepeatedElement in $\widetilde{O}(\log n)$ time?

9. An array a has $\frac{n}{4}$ copies of a particular unknown element x. Every other element in a has at most $\frac{n}{8}$ copies. Present an $O(\log n)$ time

Monte Carlo algorithm to identify x. The answer should be correct with high probability. Can you develop an $\widetilde{O}(\log n)$ time Las Vegas algorithm for the same problem?

10. Consider the naive Monte Carlo algorithm for primality testing presented in Algorithm 1.31. Here Power(x, y) computes x^y. What should be the value of t for the algorithm's output to be correct with high probability?

```
Prime1(n)
{
    // Specify t.
    for i := 1 to t do
    {
        m := Power(n, 0.5);
        j := Random() mod m + 2;
        if ((n mod j) = 0) then return false;
        // If j divides n, n is not prime.
    }
    return true;
}
```

Algorithm 1.31 Another primality testing algorithm

11. Let $\mathcal{A}$ be a Monte Carlo algorithm that solves a decision problem π in time T. The output of $\mathcal{A}$ is correct with probability c where c is a constant $> \frac{1}{2}$. Show how you can modify $\mathcal{A}$ so that its answer is correct with high probability. The modified version can take $O(T \log n)$ time.

12. In general a Las Vegas algorithm is preferable to a Monte Carlo algorithm, since the answer given by the former is guaranteed to be correct. There may be critical situations in which even a very small probability of an incorrect answer is unacceptable. Say there is a Monte Carlo algorithm for solving a problem π in T_1 time units whose output is correct with probability $\geq \frac{1}{2}$. Also assume that there is another algorithm that can check whether a given answer is valid for π in T_2 time units. Show how you use these two algorithms to arrive at a Las Vegas algorithm for solving π in time $\widetilde{O}((T_1 + T_2) \log n)$.

13. The problem considered here is that of searching for an element x in an array $a[1 : n]$. Algorithm 1.17 gives a deterministic $\Theta(n)$ time

algorithm for this problem. Show that any deterministic algorithm will have to take $\Omega(n)$ time in the worst case for this problem. In contrast a randomized Las Vegas algorithm that searches for x is given in Algorithm 1.32. This algorithm assumes that x is in $c[\,]$. What is the $\widetilde{O}()$ run time of this algorithm?

```
Algorithm RSearch(a, x, n)
// Searches for x in a[1 : n]. Assume that x is in a[ ].
{
    while (true) do
    {
        i := Random() mod n + 1;
        // i is random in the range [1, n].
        if (a[i] = x) then  return i;
    }
}
```

Algorithm 1.32 Randomized search

1.5 REFERENCES AND READINGS

For a more detailed discussion of performance analysis and measurement, see *Data Structures, Applications, and Applications in C++*, Second Edition, by S. Sahni, Silicon Press, 2005.

For more on amortized complexity, see
http://www.cise.ufl.edu/ sahni/dsaaj/enrich/c2/amortize.htm.

For a discussion on mathematical tools for analysis see *Concrete Mathematics: A Foundation for Computer Science*, by R. L. Graham, D. E. Knuth, and O. Patashnik, Addison-Wesley, 1989.

More details about the primality testing algorithm can be found in *Introduction to Algorithms*, by T. H. Cormen, C. E. Leiserson, R. L. Rivest, and C. Stein, Second Edition, MIT Press, 2001.

An excellent introductory text on probability theory is *Probability and Random Processes*, by G. R. Grimmet and D. R. Stirzaker, Oxford University Press, 1988. A proof of Lemma 1.1 can be found in this book. For a proof of Lemma 1.2 see *Queueing Systems*, Vol. I, by L. Kleinrock, John Wiley & Sons, 1975.

A formal treatment of randomized algorithms and several examples can be found in "Derivation of randomized algorithms for sorting and selection," by S. Rajasekaran and J. H. Reif, in *Parallel Algorithm Derivation and Program Transformation*, edited by R. Paige, J. H. Reif, and R. Wachter, Kluwer Academic Publishers, 1993, pp. 187–205. For more on randomized algorithms see *Randomized Algorithms* by R. Motwani and P. Raghavan, Cambridge University Press, 1995.

Chapter 2

ELEMENTARY DATA STRUCTURES

Now that we have examined the fundamental methods we need to express and analyze algorithms, we might feel all set to begin. But, alas, we need to make one last diversion, and that is a discussion of data structures. One of the basic techniques for improving algorithms is to structure the data in such a way that the resulting operations can be efficiently carried out. In this chapter, we review only the most basic and commonly used data structures. Many of these are used in subsequent chapters. We should be familiar with stacks and queues (Section 2.1), binary trees (Section 2.2), and graphs (Section 2.6) and be able to refer to the other structures as needed.

2.1 STACKS AND QUEUES

One of the most common forms of data organization in computer programs is the ordered or linear list, which is often written as $a = (a_1, a_2, \ldots, a_n)$. The a_i's are referred to as *atoms* and they are chosen from some set. The null or empty list has $n = 0$ elements. A *stack* is an ordered list in which all insertions and deletions are made at one end, called the *top*. A *queue* is an ordered list in which all insertions take place at one end, the *rear*, whereas all deletions take place at the other end, the *front*.

The operations of a stack imply that if the elements A, B, C, D, and E are inserted into a stack, in that order, then the first element to be removed (deleted) must be E. Equivalently we say that the last element to be inserted into the stack is the first to be removed. For this reason stacks are sometimes referred to as **L**ast **I**n **F**irst **O**ut (**LIFO**) lists. The operations of a queue require that the first element that is inserted into the queue is the first one to be removed. Thus queues are known as **F**irst **I**n **F**irst **O**ut (**FIFO**) lists. See Figure 2.1 for examples of a stack and a queue each containing the same

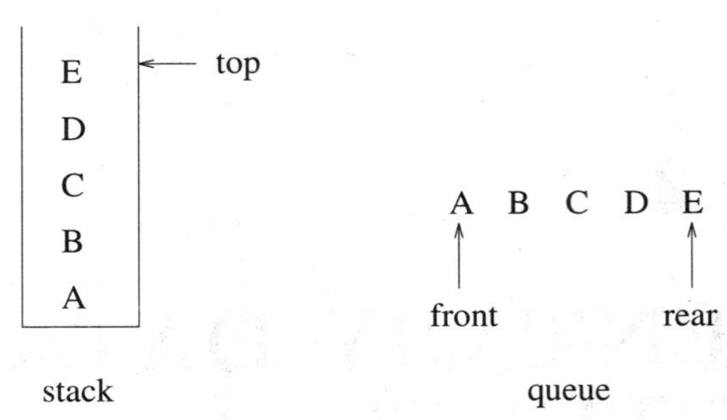

Figure 2.1 Example of a stack and a queue

five elements inserted in the same order. Note that the data object queue as defined here need not correspond to the concept of queue that is studied in queuing theory.

The simplest way to represent a stack is by using a one-dimensional array, say $stack[0 : n-1]$, where n is the maximum number of allowable entries. The first or bottom element in the stack is stored at $stack[0]$, the second at $stack[1]$, and the ith at $stack[i-1]$. Associated with the array is a variable, typically called *top*, which points to the top element in the stack. To test whether the stack is empty, we ask "**if** $(top < 0)$". If not, the topmost element is at $stack[top]$. Checking whether the stack is full can be done by asking "**if** $(top \geq n-1)$". Two more substantial operations are inserting and deleting elements. The corresponding algorithms are Add and Delete (Algorithm 2.1).

Each execution of Add or Delete takes a constant amount of time and is independent of the number of elements in the stack.

Another way to represent a stack is by using links (or pointers). A *node* is a collection of data and link information. A stack can be represented by using nodes with two fields, possibly called *data* and *link*. The data field of each node contains an item in the stack and the corresponding link field points to the node containing the next item in the stack. The link field of the last node is zero, for we assume that all nodes have an address greater than zero. For example, a stack with the items A, B, C, D, and E inserted in that order, looks as in Figure 2.2.

The variable *top* points to the topmost node (the last item inserted) in the list. The empty stack is represented by setting $top := 0$. Because of the way the links are pointing, insertion and deletion are easy to accomplish. See Algorithm 2.2.

In the case of Add, the statement $temp :=$ **new** *node*; assigns to the

```
Algorithm Add(item)
// Push an element onto the stack. Return true if successful;
// else return false. item is used as an input.
{
    if (top ≥ n − 1) then
    {
        write ("Stack is full!"); return false;
    }
    else
    {
        top := top + 1; stack[top] := item; return true;
    }
}
```

```
Algorithm Delete(item)
// Pop the top element from the stack. Return true if successful
// else return false. item is used as an output.
{
    if (top < 0) then
    {
        write ("Stack is empty!"); return false;
    }
    else
    {
        item := stack[top]; top := top − 1; return true;
    }
}
```

Algorithm 2.1 Operations on a stack

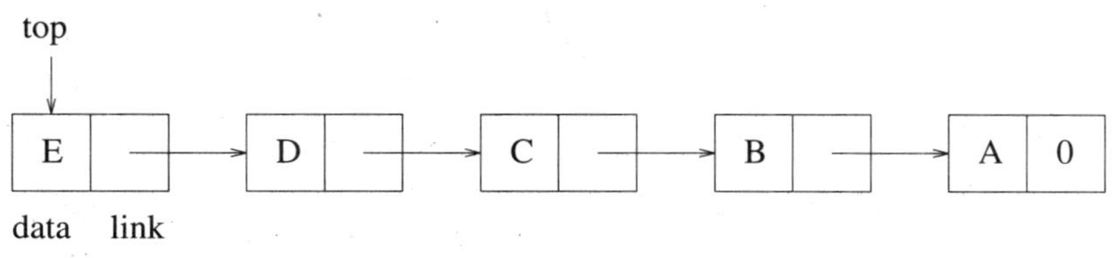

Figure 2.2 Example of a five-element, linked stack

```
// Type is the type of data.
node =record
{
    Type data; node *link;
}

Algorithm Add(item)
{
    // Get a new node.
    temp := new node;
    if (temp ≠ 0) then
    {
        (temp → data) := item; (temp → link) := top;
        top := temp; return true;
    }
    else
    {
        write ("Out of space!");
        return false;
    }
}

Algorithm Delete(item)
{
    if (top = 0) then
    {
        write ("Stack is empty!");
        return false;
    }
    else
    {
        item := (top → data); temp := top;
        top := (top → link);
        delete temp; return true;
    }
}
```

Algorithm 2.2 Linked representation of a stack

variable *temp* the address of an available node. If no more nodes exist, it returns 0. If a node exists, we store appropriate values into the two fields of the node. Then the variable *top* is updated to point to the new top element of the list. Finally, **true** is returned. If no more space exists, it prints an error message and returns **false**. Refering to Delete, if the stack is empty, then trying to delete an item produces the error message "Stack is empty!" and **false** is returned. Otherwise the top element is stored as the value of the variable *item*, a pointer to the first node is saved, and *top* is updated to point to the next node. The deleted node is returned for future use and finally **true** is returned.

The use of links to represent a stack requires more storage than the sequential array $stack[0 : n-1]$ does. However, there is greater flexibility when using links, for many structures can simultaneously use the same pool of available space. Most importantly the times for insertion and deletion using either representation are independent of the size of the stack.

An efficient queue representation can be obtained by taking an array $q[0 : n-1]$ and treating it as if it were circular. Elements are inserted by increasing the variable *rear* to the next free position. When $rear = n - 1$, the next element is entered at $q[0]$ in case that spot is free. The variable *front* always points one position counterclockwise from the first element in the queue. The variable $front = rear$ if and only if the queue is empty and we initially set $front := rear := 0$. Figure 2.3 illustrates two of the possible configurations for a circular queue containing the four elements J1 to J4 with $n > 4$.

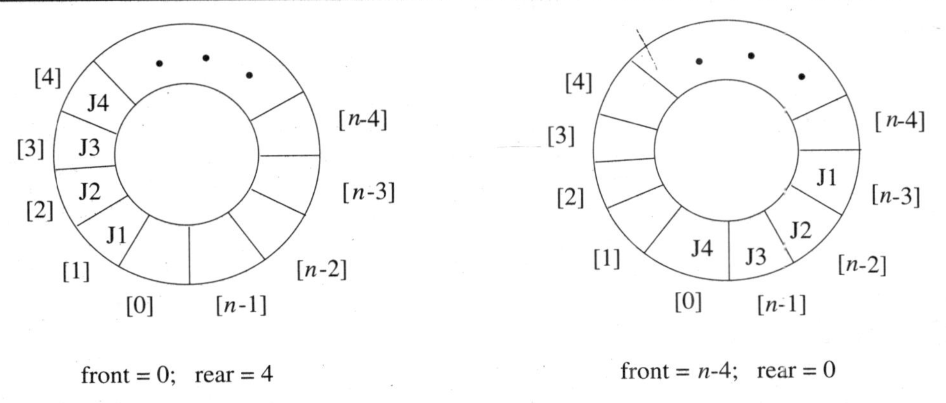

Figure 2.3 Circular queue of capacity $n - 1$ containing four elements J1, J2, J3, and J4

To insert an element, it is necessary to move *rear* one position clockwise.

This can be done using the code

if $(rear = n - 1)$ **then** $rear := 0$;
else $rear := rear + 1$;

A more elegant way to do this is to use the built-in modulo operator which computes remainders. Before doing an insert, we increase the rear pointer by saying $rear := (rear + 1)$ **mod** n;. Similarly, it is necessary to move $front$ one position clockwise each time a deletion is made. An examination of Algorithm 2.3(a) and (b) shows that by treating the array circularly, addition and deletion for queues can be carried out in a fixed amount of time or $O(1)$.

One surprising feature in these two algorithms is that the test for queue full in AddQ and the test for queue empty in DeleteQ are the same. In the case of AddQ, however, when $front = rear$, there is actually one space free, $q[rear]$, since the first element in the queue is not at $q[front]$ but is one position clockwise from this point. However, if we insert an item there, then we cannot distinguish between the cases full and empty, since this insertion leaves $front = rear$. To avoid this, we signal queue full and permit a maximum of $n - 1$ rather than n elements to be in the queue at any time. One way to use all n positions is to use another variable, tag, to distinguish between the two situations; that is, $tag = 0$ if and only if the queue is empty. This however slows down the two algorithms. Since the AddQ and DeleteQ algorithms are used many times in any problem involving queues, the loss of one queue position is more than made up by the reduction in computing time.

Another way to represent a queue is by using links. Figure 2.4 shows a queue with the four elements A, B, C, and D entered in that order. As with the linked stack example, each node of the queue is composed of the two fields *data* and *link*. A queue is pointed at by two variables, $front$ and $rear$. Deletions are made from the front, and insertions at the rear. Variable $front = 0$ signals an empty queue. The procedures for insertion and deletion in linked queues are left as exercises.

EXERCISES

1. Modify the array implementation of a stack (Algorithm /refpgm2.1.1) so that when we are to add an element to a full stack, an attempt is made to double the size of the array. For this, allocate a new array of twice the size and copy elements from the old array to the new one. The cost of array doubling is linear in the size of the new array.

   (a) Test the correctness of your modified stack class.

```
Algorithm AddQ(item)
// Insert item in the circular queue stored in q[0 : n - 1].
// rear points to the last item, and front is one
// position counterclockwise from the first item in q.
{
    rear := (rear + 1) mod n; // Advance rear clockwise.
    if (front = rear) then
    {
        write ("Queue is full!");
        if (front = 0) then rear := n - 1;
        else rear := rear - 1;
        // Move rear one position counterclockwise.
        return false;
    }
    else
    {
        q[rear] := item; // Insert new item.
        return true;
    }
}
```

(a) Addition of an element

```
Algorithm DeleteQ(item)
// Removes and returns the front element of the queue q[0 : n - 1].
{
    if (front = rear) then
    {
        write ("Queue is empty!");
        return false;
    }
    else
    {
        front := (front + 1) mod n; // Advance front clockwise.
        item := q[front]; // Set item to front of queue.
        return true;
    }
}
```

(b) Deletion of an element

Algorithm 2.3 Basic queue operations

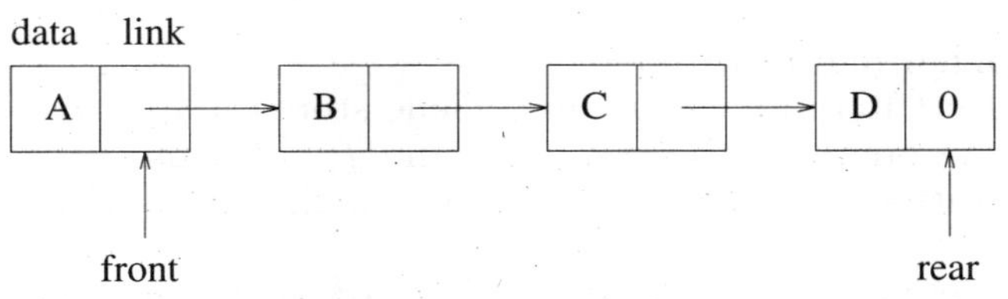

Figure 2.4 A linked queue with four elements

   (b) Show that while the complexity of an individual add is now $O(m)$, where m is the size of the stack, the complexity of performing a sequence of m adds (possibly with some deletes) is $O(m)$.

2. Do Exercise 1 for the array representation of a queue (Algorithm 2.3).

3. Write algorithms for AddQ and DeleteQ, assuming the queue is represented as a linked list.

4. A linear list is being maintained circularly in an array $c[0 : n-1]$ with f and r set up as for circular queues.

   (a) Obtain a formula in terms of f, r, and n for the number of elements in the list.
   (b) Write an algorithm to delete the kth element in the list.
   (c) Write an algorithm to insert an element y immediately after the kth element.

   What is the time complexity of your algorithms for parts (b) and (c)?

5. Let $X = (x_1, \ldots, x_n)$ and $Y = (y_1, \ldots, y_m)$ be two linked lists. Write an algorithm to merge the two lists to obtain the linked list $Z = (x_1, y_1, x_2, y_2, \ldots, x_m, y_m, x_{m+1}, \ldots, x_n)$ if $m \leq n$ or $Z = (x_1, y_1, x_2, y_2, \ldots, x_n, y_n, y_{n+1}, \ldots, y_m)$ if $m > n$.

6. A double-ended queue (deque) is a linear list for which insertions and deletions can occur at either end. Show how to represent a deque in a one-dimensional array and write algorithms that insert and delete at either end.

7. Consider the hypothetical data object $X2$. The object $X2$ is a linear list with the restriction that although additions to the list can be made at either end, deletions can be made from one end only. Design a linked list representation for $X2$. Specify initial and boundary conditions for your representation.

2.2 TREES

Definition 2.1 [Tree] A *tree* is a finite set of one or more nodes such that there is a specially designated node called the *root* and the remaining nodes are partitioned into $n \geq 0$ disjoint sets $T_1, \ldots, T_n$, where each of these sets is a tree. The sets $T_1, \ldots, T_n$ are called the *subtrees* of the root. □

2.2.1 Terminology

There are many terms that are often used when referring to trees. Consider the tree in Figure 2.5. This tree has 13 nodes, each data item of a node being a single letter for convenience. The root contains A (we usually say node A), and we normally draw trees with their roots at the top. The number of subtrees of a node is called its *degree*. The degree of A is 3, of C is 1, and of F is 0. Nodes that have degree zero are called *leaf* or *terminal* nodes. The set {K, L, F, G, M, I, J} is the set of leaf nodes of Figure 2.5. The other nodes are referred to as *nonterminals*. The roots of the subtrees of a node X are the *children* of X. The node X is the *parent* of its children. Thus the children of D are H, I, and J, and the parent of D is A.

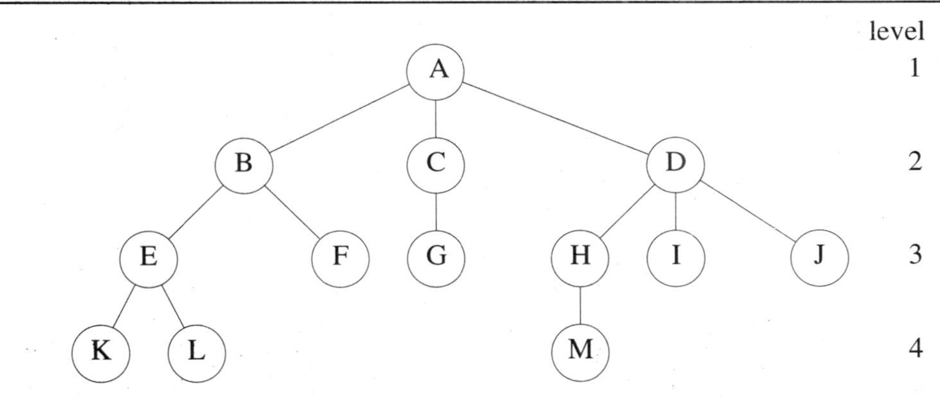

Figure 2.5 A sample tree

Children of the same parent are said to be *siblings*. For example H, I, and J are siblings. We can extend this terminology if we need to so that we can ask for the grandparent of M, which is D, and so on. The *degree* of a tree is the maximum degree of the nodes in the tree. The tree in Figure 2.5 has degree 3. The *ancestors* of a node are all the nodes along the path from the root to that node. The ancestors of M are A, D, and H.

The *level* of a node is defined by initially letting the root be at level one. If a node is at level p, then its children are at level $p+1$. Figure 2.5 shows the levels of all nodes in that tree. The *height* or *depth* of a tree is defined to be the maximum level of any node in the tree.

A *forest* is a set of $n \geq 0$ disjoint trees. The notion of a forest is very close to that of a tree because if we remove the root of a tree, we get a forest. For example, in Figure 2.5 if we remove A, we get a forest with three trees.

Now how do we represent a tree in a computer's memory? If we wish to use a linked list in which one node corresponds to one node in the tree, then a node must have a varying number of fields depending on the number of children. However, it is often simpler to write algorithms for a data representation in which the node size is fixed. We can represent a tree using a fixed node size list structure. Such a list representation for the tree of Figure 2.5 is given in Figure 2.6. In this figure nodes have three fields: *tag*, *data*, and *link*. Only two of these fields, *data* and *link*, are shown in Figure 2.6. The *tag* field of a node, which is not shown in the figure, is one if the node has a down-pointing arrow; otherwise it is zero. The fields *data* and *link* are used as before with the exception that when $tag = 1$, *data* contains a pointer to a list rather than a data item. A tree is represented by storing the root in the first node followed by nodes that point to sublists each of which contains one subtree of the root.

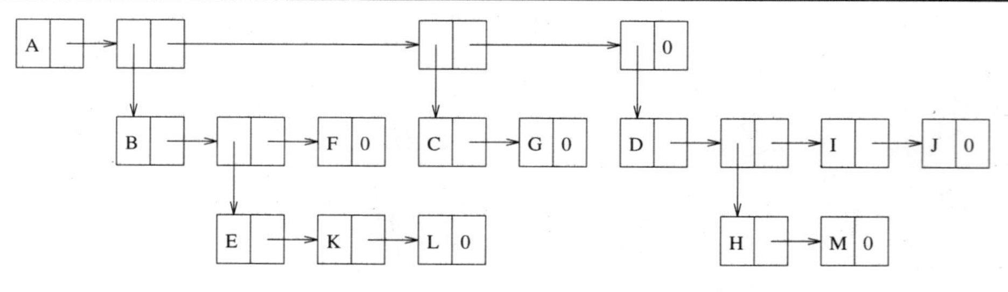

Figure 2.6 List representation for the tree of Figure 2.5

2.2.2 Binary Trees

A binary tree is an important type of tree structure that occurs very often. It is characterized by the fact that any node can have at most two children; that is, there is no node with degree greater than two. For binary trees we distinguish between the subtree on the left and that on the right, whereas for other trees the order of the subtrees is irrelevant. Furthermore a binary tree is allowed to have zero nodes whereas any other tree must have at least one node. Thus a binary tree is really a different kind of object than any other tree.

Definition 2.2 A *binary tree* is a finite set of nodes that is either empty or consists of a root and two disjoint binary trees called the *left* and *right* subtrees. □

Figure 2.7 shows two sample binary trees. These two trees are special kinds of binary trees. Figure 2.7(a) is a *skewed* tree, skewed to the left. There is a corresponding tree skewed to the right, which is not shown. The tree in Figure 2.7(b) is called a *complete* binary tree. This kind of tree is defined formally later on. Notice that for this tree all terminal nodes are on two adjacent levels. The terms that we introduced for trees, such as degree, level, height, leaf, parent, and child, all apply to binary trees in the same way.

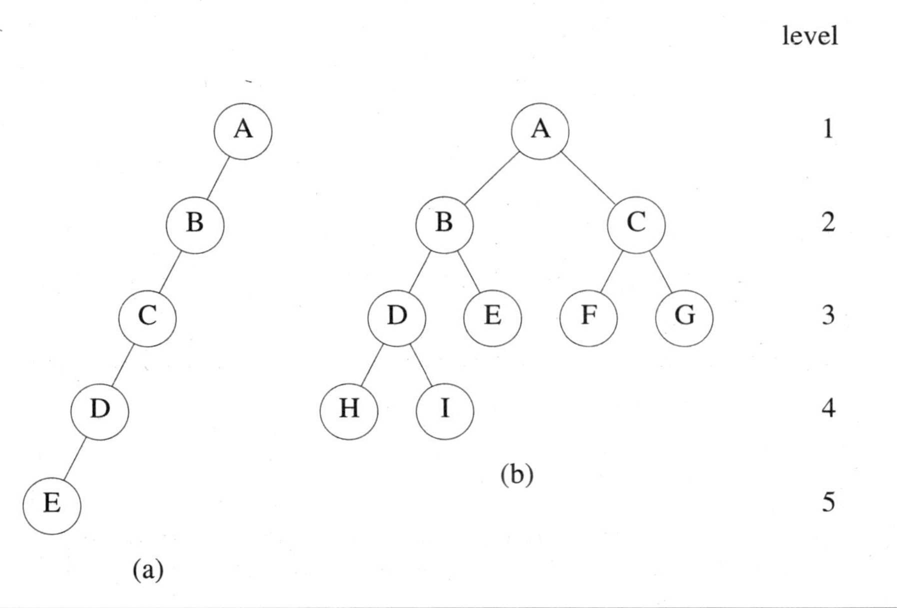

Figure 2.7 Two sample binary trees

Lemma 2.1 The maximum number of nodes on level i of a binary tree is 2^{i-1}. Also, the maximum number of nodes in a binary tree of depth k is $2^k - 1, k > 0$. □

The binary tree of depth k that has exactly $2^k - 1$ nodes is called a *full* binary tree of depth k. Figure 2.8 shows a full binary tree of depth 4. A very elegant sequential representation for full binary trees results from sequentially numbering the nodes, starting with the node on level one, then going to those on level two, and so on. Nodes on any level are numbered from left to right (see Figure 2.8). A binary tree with n nodes and depth k is *complete* iff its nodes correspond to the nodes that are numbered one to n in the full binary tree of depth k. A consequence of this definition is that in a complete tree, leaf nodes occur on at most two adjacent levels. The nodes of an n-node complete tree may be compactly stored in a one-dimensional array, $tree[1:n]$, with the node numbered i being stored in $tree[i]$. The next lemma shows how to easily determine the locations of the parent, left child, and right child of any node i in the binary tree without explicitly storing any link information.

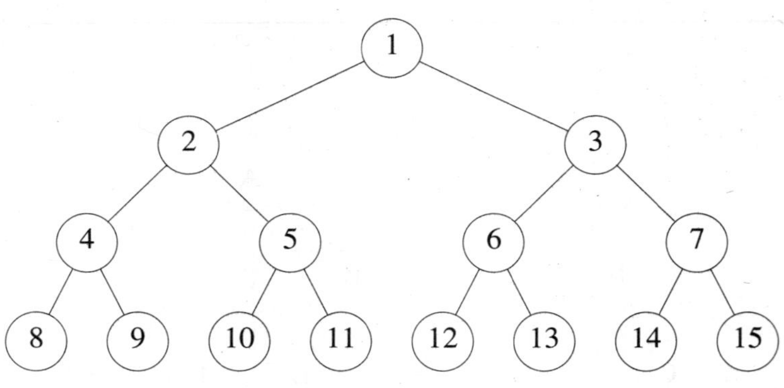

Figure 2.8 Full binary tree of depth 4

Lemma 2.2 If a complete binary tree with n nodes is represented sequentially as described before, then for any node with index i, $1 \leq i \leq n$, we have:

1. $parent(i)$ is at $\lfloor i/2 \rfloor$ if $i \neq 1$. When $i = 1, i$ is the root and has no parent.

2. $lchild(i)$ is at $2i$ if $2i \leq n$. If $2i > n$, i has no left child.

3. $rchild(i)$ is at $2i+1$ if $2i+1 \leq n$. If $2i+1 > n$, i has no right child. □

This representation can clearly be used for all binary trees though in most cases there is a lot of unutilized space. For complete binary trees the representation is ideal as no space is wasted. For the skewed tree of Figure 2.7, however, less than a third of the array is utilized. In the worst case a right-skewed tree of depth k requires $2^k - 1$ locations. Of these only k are occupied.

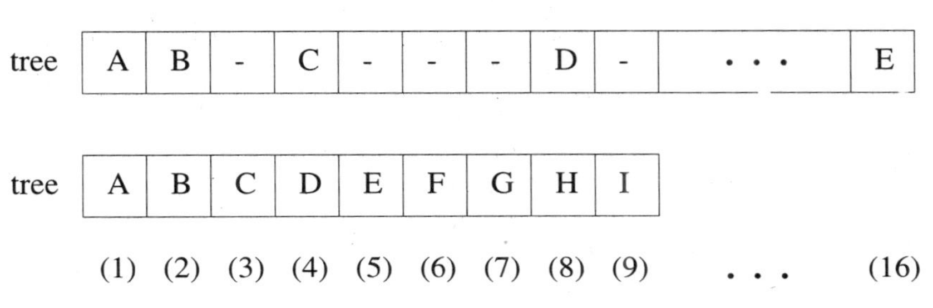

Figure 2.9 Sequential representation of the binary trees of Figure 2.7

Although the sequential representation, as in Figure 2.9, appears to be good for complete binary trees, it is wasteful for many other binary trees. In addition, the representation suffers from the general inadequacies of sequential representations. Insertion or deletion of nodes requires the movement of potentially many nodes to reflect the change in level number of the remaining nodes. These problems can be easily overcome through the use of a linked representation. Each node has three fields: *lchild*, *data*, and *rchild*. Although this node structure makes it difficult to determine the parent of a node, for most applications it is adequate. In case it is often necessary to be able to determine the parent of a node, then a fourth field, *parent*, can be included with the obvious interpretation. The representation of the binary trees of Figure 2.7 using a three-field structure is given in Figure 2.10.

EXERCISES

1. Show that the height of binary tree that has n, $n \geq 0$, nodes is at most n and at least $\lceil \log_2(n+1) \rceil$.

2. What is the maximum number of nodes in a binary tree that has m leaves?

3. In a k-ary tree, $k > 1$, each node may have up to k children. These

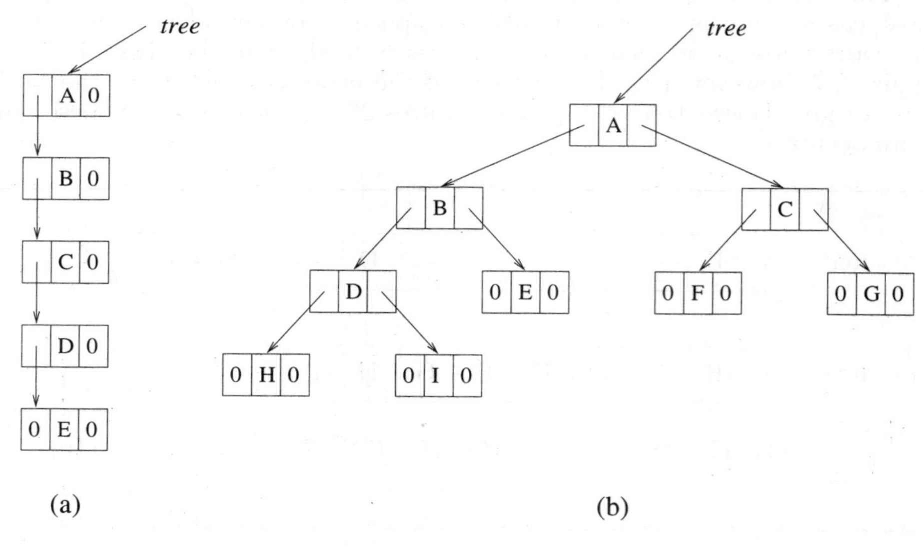

Figure 2.10 Linked representations for the binary trees of Figure 2.7

children are called, respectively, the first, second, $\cdots$, kth child of the node. A 2-ary tree is a binary tree.

(a) Determine the analogue of Lemma 2.1 for k-ary trees.

(b) Determine the analogue of Lemma 2.2 for k-ary trees.

2.3 DICTIONARIES

An abstract data type that supports the operations insert, delete, and search is called a *dictionary.* Dictionaries have found application in the design of numerous algorithms.

Example 2.1 Consider the database of books maintained in a library system. When a user wants to check whether a particular book is available, a *search* operation is called for. If the book is available and is issued to the user, a *delete* operation can be performed to remove this book from the set of available books. When the user returns the book, it can be *insert*ed back into the set. □

It is essential that we are able to support the above-mentioned operations as efficiently as possible since these operations are performed quite frequently. A number of data structures have been devised to realize a dictionary. At a very high level these can be categorized as comparison methods and direct access methods. Hashing is an example of the latter. We elaborate only on binary search trees which are an example of the former.

2.3.1 Binary Search Trees

Definition 2.3 [Binary search tree] A *binary search tree* is a binary tree. It may be empty. If it is not empty, then it satisfies the following properties:

1. Every element has a key and no two elements have the same key (i.e., the keys are distinct).

2. The keys (if any) in the left subtree are smaller than the key in the root.

3. The keys (if any) in the right subtree are larger than the key in the root.

4. The left and right subtrees are also binary search trees. □

A *binary search tree* can support the operations search, insert, and delete among others. In fact, with a binary search tree, we can search for a data element both by key value and by rank (i.e., find an element with key x, find the fifth-smallest element, delete the element with key x, delete the fifth-smallest element, insert an element and determine its rank, and so on).

There is some redundancy in the definition of a binary search tree. Properties 2, 3, and 4 together imply that the keys must be distinct. So, property 1 can be replaced by the property: The root has a key.

Some examples of binary trees in which the elements have distinct keys are shown in Figure 2.11. The tree of Figure 2.11(a) is not a binary search tree, despite the fact that it satisfies properties 1, 2, and 3. The right subtree fails to satisfy property 4. This subtree is not a binary search tree, as its right subtree has a key value (22) that is smaller than that in the subtree's root (25). The binary trees of Figure 2.11(b) and (c) are binary search trees.

Searching a Binary Search Tree

Since the definition of a binary search tree is recursive, it is easiest to describe a recursive search method. Suppose we wish to search for an element with key x. An element could in general be an arbitrary structure that has as one of its fields a *key*. We assume for simplicity that the element just consists of a *key* and use the terms element and key interchangeably. We begin at the root. If the root is 0, then the search tree contains no elements and the

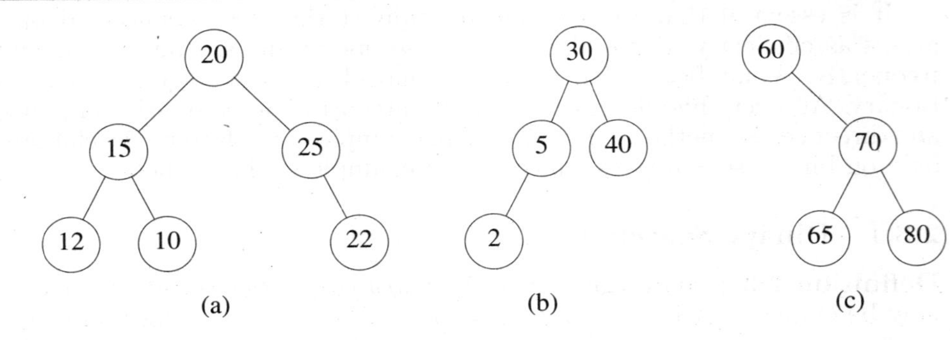

Figure 2.11 Binary trees

search is unsuccessful. Otherwise, we compare x with the key in the root. If x equals this key, then the search terminates successfully. If x is less than the key in the root, then no element in the right subtree can have key value x, and only the left subtree is to be searched. If x is larger than the key in the root, only the right subtree needs to be searched. The subtrees can be searched recursively as in Algorithm 2.4. This function assumes a linked representation for the search tree. Each node has the three fields *lchild*, *rchild*, and *data*. The recursion of Algorithm 2.4 is easily replaced by a **while** loop, as in Algorithm 2.5.

```
Algorithm Search(t, x)
{
    if (t = 0) then return 0;
    else if (x = t → data) then return t;
         else if (x < t → data) then
                   return Search(t → lchild, x);
              else return Search(t → rchild, x);
}
```

Algorithm 2.4 Recursive search of a binary search tree

If we wish to search by rank, each node should have an additional field *leftsize*, which is one plus the number of elements in the left subtree of the node. For the search tree of Figure 2.11(b), the nodes with keys 2, 5, 30, and 40, respectively, have *leftsize* equal to 1, 2, 3, and 1. Algorithm 2.6

```
Algorithm ISearch(x)
{
    found := false;
    t := tree;
    while ((t ≠ 0) and not found) do
    {
        if (x = (t → data)) then found := true;
        else if (x < (t → data)) then t := (t → lchild);
             else t := (t → rchild);
    }
    if (not found) then return 0;
    else return t;
}
```

Algorithm 2.5 Iterative search of a binary search tree

searches for the kth-smallest element.

```
Algorithm Searchk(k)
{
    found := false; t := tree;
    while ((t ≠ 0) and not found) do
    {
        if (k = (t → leftsize)) then found := true;
        else if (k < (t → leftsize)) then t := (t → lchild);
             else
             {
                 k := k − (t → leftsize);
                 t := (t → rchild);
             }
    }
    if (not found) then return 0;
    else return t;
}
```

Algorithm 2.6 Searching a binary search tree by rank

As can be seen, a binary search tree of height h can be searched by key as well as by rank in $O(h)$ time.

Insertion into a Binary Search Tree

To insert a new element x, we must first verify that its key is different from those of existing elements. To do this, a search is carried out. If the search is unsuccessful, then the element is inserted at the point the search terminated. For instance, to insert an element with key 80 into the tree of Figure 2.12(a), we first search for 80. This search terminates unsuccessfully, and the last node examined is the one with key 40. The new element is inserted as the right child of this node. The resulting search tree is shown in Figure 2.12(b). Figure 2.12(c) shows the result of inserting the key 35 into the search tree of Figure 2.12(b).

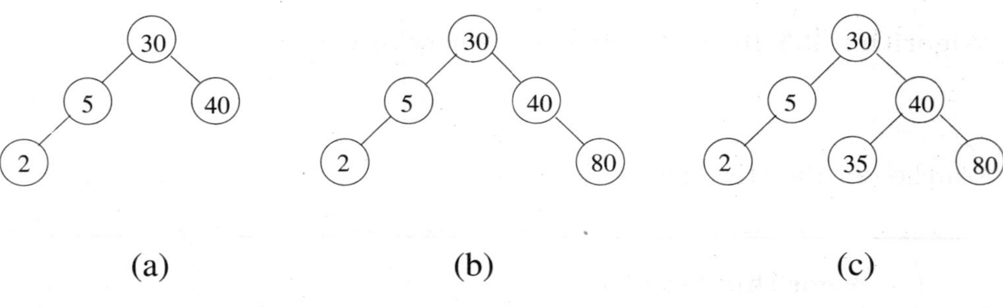

Figure 2.12 Inserting into a binary search tree

Algorithm 2.7 implements the insert strategy just described. If a node has a *leftsize* field, then this is updated too. Regardless, the insertion can be performed in $O(h)$ time, where h is the height of the search tree.

Deletion from a Binary Search Tree

Deletion of a leaf element is quite easy. For example, to delete 35 from the tree of Figure 2.12(c), the left-child field of its parent is set to 0 and the node disposed. This gives us the tree of Figure 2.12(b). To delete the 80 from this tree, the right-child field of 40 is set to 0; this gives the tree of Figure 2.12(a). Then the node containing 80 is disposed.

The deletion of a nonleaf element that has only one child is also easy. The node containing the element to be deleted is disposed, and the single child takes the place of the disposed node. So, to delete the element 5 from the tree of Figure 2.12(b), we simply change the pointer from the parent

```
Algorithm Insert(x)
// Insert x into the binary search tree.
{
    found := false;
    p := tree;
    // Search for x. q is the parent of p.
    while ((p ≠ 0) and not found) do
    {
        q := p; // Save p.
        if (x = (p → data)) then found := true;
        else  if (x < (p → data)) then p := (p → lchild);
              else p := (p → rchild);
    }

    // Perform insertion.
    if (not found) then
    {
        p := new TreeNode;
        (p → lchild) := 0; (p → rchild) := 0; (p → data) := x;
        if (tree ≠ 0) then
        {
            if (x < (q → data)) then (q → lchild) := p;
            else (q → rchild) := p;
        }
        else tree := p;
    }
}
```

Algorithm 2.7 Insertion into a binary search tree

node (i.e., the node containing 30) to the single-child node (i.e., the node containing 2).

When the element to be deleted is in a nonleaf node that has two children, the element is replaced by either the largest element in its left subtree or the smallest one in its right subtree. Then we proceed to delete this replacing element from the subtree from which it was taken. For instance, if we wish to delete the element with key 30 from the tree of Figure 2.13(a), then we replace it by either the largest element, 5, in its left subtree or the smallest element, 40, in its right subtree. Suppose we opt for the largest element in the left subtree. The 5 is moved into the root, and the tree of Figure 2.13(b) is obtained. Now we must delete the second 5. Since this node has only one child, the pointer from its parent is changed to point to this child. The tree of Figure 2.13(c) is obtained. We can verify that regardless of whether the replacing element is the largest in the left subtree or the smallest in the right subtree, it is originally in a node with a degree of at most one. So, deleting it from this node is quite easy. We leave the writing of the deletion procedure as an exercise. It should be evident that a deletion can be performed in $O(h)$ time if the search tree has a height of h.

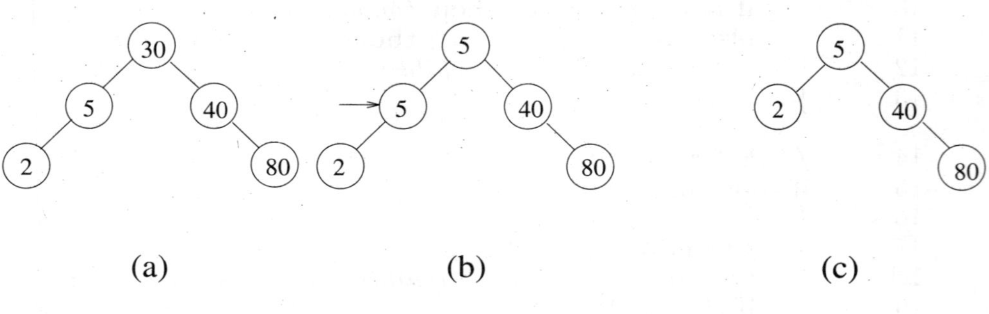

Figure 2.13 Deletion from a binary search tree

Height of a Binary Search Tree

Unless care is taken, the height of a binary search tree with n elements can become as large as n. This is the case, for instance, when Algorithm 2.7 is used to insert the keys $[1, 2, 3, \ldots, n]$, in this order, into an initially empty binary search tree. It can, however, be shown that when insertions and deletions are made at random using the procedures given here, the height of the binary search tree is $O(\log n)$ on the average.

Search trees with a worst-case height of $O(\log n)$ are called *balanced search trees.* Balanced search trees that permit searches, inserts, and deletes to be performed in $O(\log n)$ time are listed in Table 2.1. Examples include AVL trees, 2-3 trees, Red-Black trees, and B-trees. On the other hand splay trees take $O(\log n)$ time for each of these operations in the *amortized* sense. A description of these balanced trees can be found in the book by E. Horowitz, S. Sahni, and D. Mehta cited at the end of this chapter.

Data structure	search	insert	delete
Binary search tree	$O(n)$ (wc) $O(\log n)$ (av)	$O(n)$ (wc) $O(\log n)$ (av)	$O(n)$ (wc) $O(\log n)$ (av)
AVL tree	$O(\log n)$ (wc)	$O(\log n)$ (wc)	$O(\log n)$ (wc)
2-3 tree	$O(\log n)$ (wc)	$O(\log n)$ (wc)	$O(\log n)$ (wc)
Red-Black tree	$O(\log n)$ (wc)	$O(\log n)$ (wc)	$O(\log n)$ (wc)
B-tree	$O(\log n)$ (wc)	$O(\log n)$ (wc)	$O(\log n)$ (wc)
Splay tree	$O(\log n)$ (am)	$O(\log n)$ (am)	$O(\log n)$ (am)

Table 2.1 Summary of dictionary implementations. Here (wc) stands for worst case, (av) for average case, and (am) for amortized cost.

EXERCISES

1. Write an algorithm to delete an element x from a binary search tree t. What is the time complexity of your algorithm?

2. Present an algorithm to start with an initially empty binary search tree and make n random insertions. Use a uniform random number generator to obtain the values to be inserted. Measure the height of the resulting binary search tree and divide this height by $\log_2 n$. Do this for $n = 100, 500, 1,000, 2,000, 3,000, \ldots, 10,000$. Plot the ratio height$/\log_2 n$ as a function of n. The ratio should be approximately constant (around 2). Verify that this is so.

3. Suppose that each node in a binary search tree also has the field $leftsize$ as described in the text. Design an algorithm to insert an element x into such a binary search tree. The complexity of your algorithm should be $O(h)$, where h is the height of the search tree. Show that this is the case.

4. Do Exercise 3, but this time present an algorithm to delete the element with the kth-smallest key in the binary search tree.

5. Find an efficient data structure for representing a subset S of the integers from 1 to n. Operations we wish to perform on the set are

   - **INSERT**(i) to insert the integer i to the set S. If i is already in the set, this instruction must be ignored.
   - **DELETE** to delete an arbitrary member from the set.
   - **MEMBER**(i) to check whether i is a member of the set.

Your data structure should enable each one of the above operations in constant time (irrespective of the cardinality of S).

6. Any algorithm that merges two sorted lists of size n and m, respectively, must make at least $n + m - 1$ comparisons in the worst case. What implications does this have on the run time of any comparison-based algorithm that combines two binary search trees that have n and m elements, respectively?

7. It is known that every comparison-based algorithm to sort n elements must make $O(n \log n)$ comparisons in the worst case. What implications does this have on the complexity of initializing a binary search tree with n elements?

2.4 PRIORITY QUEUES

Any data structure that supports the operations of search min (or max), insert, and delete min (or max, respectively) is called a *priority queue.*

Example 2.2 Suppose that we are selling the services of a machine. Each user pays a fixed amount per use. However, the time needed by each user is different. We wish to maximize the returns from this machine under the assumption that the machine is not to be kept idle unless no user is available. This can be done by maintaining a priority queue of all persons waiting to use the machine. Whenever the machine becomes available, the user with the smallest time requirement is selected. Hence, a priority queue that supports delete min is required. When a new user requests the machine, his or her request is put into the priority queue.

If each user needs the same amount of time on the machine but people are willing to pay different amounts for the service, then a priority queue based on the amount of payment can be maintained. Whenever the machine becomes available, the user willing to pay the most is selected. This requires a delete max operation. □

Example 2.3 Suppose that we are simulating a large factory. This factory has many machines and many jobs that require processing on some of the machines. An *event* is said to occur whenever a machine completes the processing of a job. When an event occurs, the job has to be moved to the queue for the next machine (if any) that it needs. If this queue is empty, the job can be assigned to the machine immediately. Also, a new job can be scheduled on the machine that has become idle (provided that its queue is not empty).

To determine the occurrence of events, a priority queue is used. This queue contains the finish time of all jobs that are presently being worked on.

The next event occurs at the least time in the priority queue. So, a priority queue that supports delete min can be used in this application. □

The simplest way to represent a priority queue is as an unordered linear list. Suppose that we have n elements in this queue and the delete max operation is to be supported. If the list is represented sequentially, additions are most easily performed at the end of this list. Hence, the insert time is $\Theta(1)$. A deletion requires a search for the element with the largest key, followed by its deletion. Since it takes $\Theta(n)$ time to find the largest element in an n-element unordered list, the delete time is $\Theta(n)$. Each deletion takes $\Theta(n)$ time. An alternative is to use an ordered linear list. The elements are in nondecreasing order if a sequential representation is used. The delete time for each representation is $\Theta(1)$ and the insert time $O(n)$. When a *max heap* is used, both additions and deletions can be performed in $O(\log n)$ time.

2.4.1 Heaps

Definition 2.4 [Heap] A *max (min) heap* is a complete binary tree with the property that the value at each node is at least as large as (as small as) the values at its children (if they exist). Call this property the *heap property.* □

In this section we study in detail an efficient way of realizing a priority queue. We might first consider using a queue since inserting new elements would be very efficient. But finding the largest element would necessitate a scan of the entire queue. A second suggestion might be to use a sorted list that is stored sequentially. But an insertion could require moving all of the items in the list. What we want is a data structure that allows *both* operations to be done efficiently. One such data structure is the max heap.

The definition of a max heap implies that one of the largest elements is at the root of the heap. If the elements are distinct, then the root contains the largest item. A max heap can be implemented using an array $a[\,]$.

To insert an element into the heap, one adds it "at the bottom" of the heap and then compares it with its parent, grandparent, greatgrandparent, and so on, until it is less than or equal to one of these values. Algorithm Insert (Algorithm 2.8) describes this process in detail.

Figure 2.14 shows one example of how Insert would insert a new value into an existing heap of six elements. It is clear from Algorithm 2.8 and Figure 2.14 that the time for Insert can vary. In the best case the new element is correctly positioned initially and no values need to be rearranged. In the worst case the number of executions of the **while** loop is proportional to the number of levels in the heap. Thus if there are n elements in the heap, inserting a new element takes $\Theta(\log n)$ time in the worst case.

To delete the maximum key from the max heap, we use an algorithm called Adjust. Adjust takes as input the array $a[\,]$ and the integers i and n.

```
Algorithm Insert(a, n)
{
    // Inserts a[n] into the heap which is stored in a[1 : n − 1].
    i := n; item := a[n];
    while ((i > 1) and (a[⌊i/2⌋] < item)) do
    {
        a[i] := a[⌊i/2⌋]; i := ⌊i/2⌋;
    }
    a[i] := item; return true;
}
```

Algorithm 2.8 Insertion into a heap

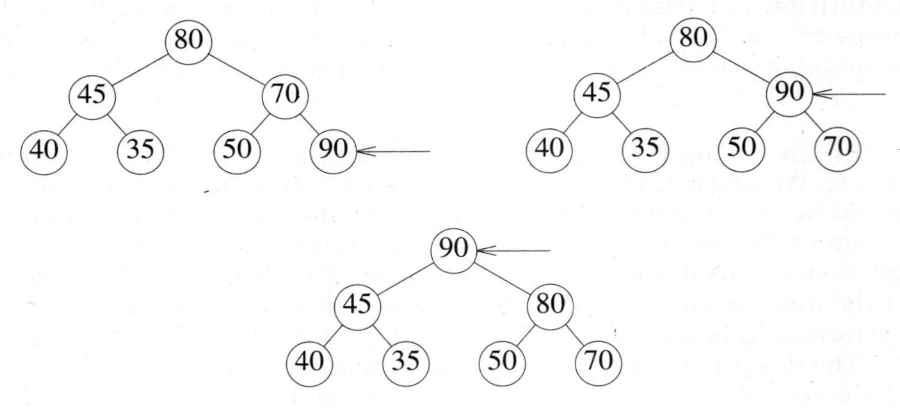

Figure 2.14 Action of Insert inserting 90 into an existing heap

It regards $a[1:n]$ as a complete binary tree. If the subtrees rooted at $2i$ and $2i+1$ are already max heaps, then Adjust will rearrange elements of $a[\,]$ such that the tree rooted at i is also a max heap. The maximum element from the max heap $a[1:n]$ can be deleted by deleting the root of the corresponding complete binary tree. The last element of the array, that is, $a[n]$, is copied to the root, and finally we call Adjust$(a, 1, n-1)$. Both Adjust and DelMax are described in Algorithm 2.9.

```
Algorithm Adjust(a, i, n)
// The complete binary trees with roots 2i and 2i + 1 are
// combined with node i to form a heap rooted at i. No
// node has an address greater than n or less than 1.
{
    j := 2i; item := a[i];
    while (j ≤ n) do
    {
        if ((j < n) and (a[j] < a[j + 1])) then j := j + 1;
            // Compare left and right child
            // and let j be the larger child.
        if (item ≥ a[j]) then break;
            // A position for item is found.
        a[⌊j/2⌋] := a[j]; j := 2j;
    }
    a[⌊j/2⌋] := item;
}
```

```
Algorithm DelMax(a, n, x)
// Delete the maximum from the heap a[1 : n] and store it in x.
{
    if (n = 0) then
    {
        write ("heap is empty"); return false;
    }
    x := a[1]; a[1] := a[n];
    Adjust(a, 1, n − 1); return true;
}
```

Algorithm 2.9 Deletion from a heap

Note that the worst-case run time of Adjust is also proportional to the height of the tree. Therefore, if there are n elements in a heap, deleting the maximum can be done in $O(\log n)$ time.

To sort n elements, it suffices to make n insertions followed by n deletions from a heap. Algorithm 2.10 has the details. Since insertion and deletion take $O(\log n)$ time each in the worst case, this sorting algorithm has a time complexity of $O(n \log n)$.

```
Algorithm Sort(a, n)
// Sort the elements a[1 : n].
{
    for i := 1 to n do Insert(a, i);
    for i := n to 1 step -1 do
    {
        DelMax(a, i, x); a[i] := x;
    }
}
```

Algorithm 2.10 A sorting algorithm

It turns out that we can insert n elements into a heap faster than we can apply Insert n times. Before getting into the details of the new algorithm, let us consider how the n inserts take place. Figure 2.15 shows how the data (40, 80, 35, 90, 45, 50, and 70) move around until a heap is created when using Insert. Trees to the left of any $\rightarrow$ represent the state of the array $a[1:i]$ before some call of Insert. Trees to the right of $\rightarrow$ show how the array was altered by Insert to produce a heap. The array is drawn as a complete binary tree for clarity.

The data set that causes the heap creation method using Insert to behave in the worst way is a set of elements in ascending order. Each new element rises to become the new root. There are at most 2^{i-1} nodes on level i of a complete binary tree, $1 \le i \le \lceil \log_2(n+1) \rceil$. For a node on level i the distance to the root is $i-1$. Thus the worst-case time for heap creation using Insert is

$$\sum_{1 \le i \le \lceil \log_2(n+1) \rceil} (i-1)2^{i-1} < \lceil \log_2(n+1) \rceil 2^{\lceil \log_2(n+1) \rceil} = O(n \log n)$$

A surprising fact about Insert is that its average behavior on n random inputs is asymptotically faster than its worst case, $O(n)$ rather than $O(n \log n)$. This implies that on the average each new value only rises a constant number of levels in the tree.

It is possible to devise an algorithm that can perform n inserts in $O(n)$ time rather than $O(n \log n)$. This reduction is achieved by an algorithm that regards any array $a[1:n]$ as a complete binary tree and works from the leaves up to the root, level by level. At each level, the left and right subtrees of any node are heaps. Only the value in the root node may violate the heap property.

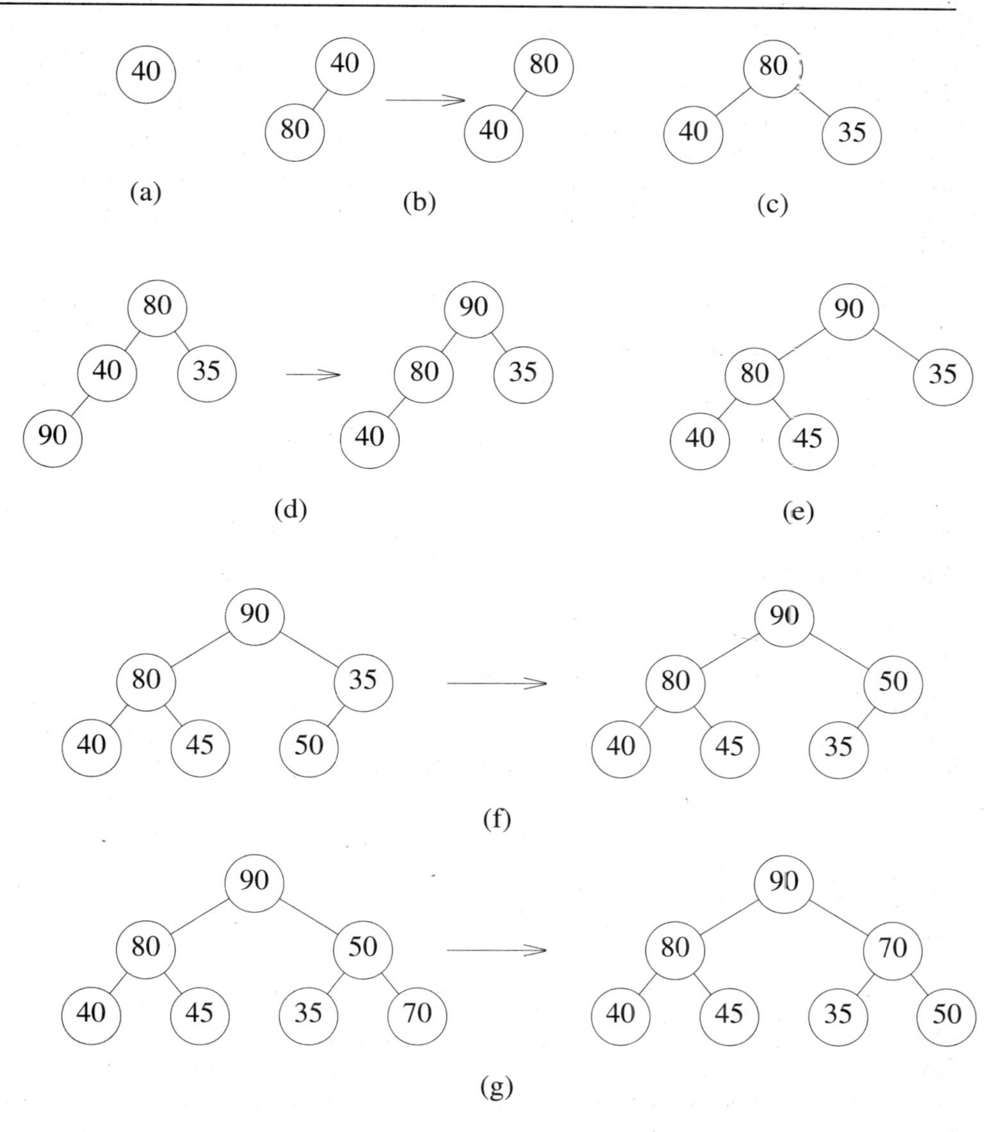

Figure 2.15 Forming a heap from the set $\{40, 80, 35, 90, 45, 50, 70\}$

Given n elements in $a[1:n]$, we can create a heap by applying Adjust. It is easy to see that leaf nodes are already heaps. So we can begin by calling Adjust for the parents of leaf nodes and then work our way up, level by level, until the root is reached. The resultant algorithm is Heapify (Algorithm 2.11). In Figure 2.16 we observe the action of Heapify as it creates a heap out of the given seven elements. The initial tree is drawn in Figure 2.16(a). Since $n = 7$, the first call to Adjust has $i = 3$. In Figure 2.16(b) the three elements 118, 151, and 132 are rearranged to form a heap. Subsequently Adjust is called with $i = 2$ and $i = 1$; this gives the trees in Figure 2.16(c) and (d).

```
Algorithm Heapify(a, n)
// Readjust the elements in a[1 : n] to form a heap.
{
    for i := ⌊n/2⌋ to 1 step −1 do Adjust(a, i, n);
}
```

Algorithm 2.11 Creating a heap out of n arbitrary elements

For the worst-case analysis of Heapify let $2^{k-1} \leq n < 2^k$, where $k = \lceil \log(n+1) \rceil$, and recall that the levels of the n-node complete binary tree are numbered 1 to k. The worst-case number of iterations for Adjust is $k - i$ for a node on level i. The total time for Heapify is proportional to

$$\sum_{1 \leq i \leq k} 2^{i-1}(k-i) = \sum_{1 \leq i \leq k-1} i2^{k-i-1} \leq n \sum_{1 \leq i \leq k-1} i/2^i \leq 2n = O(n) \quad (2.1)$$

Comparing Heapify with the repeated use of Insert, we see that the former is faster in the worst case, requiring $O(n)$ versus $O(n \log n)$ operations. However, Heapify requires that all the elements be available before heap creation begins. Using Insert, we can add a new element into the heap at any time.

Our discussion on insert, delete, and so on, so far has been with respect to a max heap. It should be easy to see that a parallel discussion could have been carried out with respect to a min heap. For a min heap it is possible to delete the smallest element in $O(\log n)$ time and also to insert an element in $O(\log n)$ time.

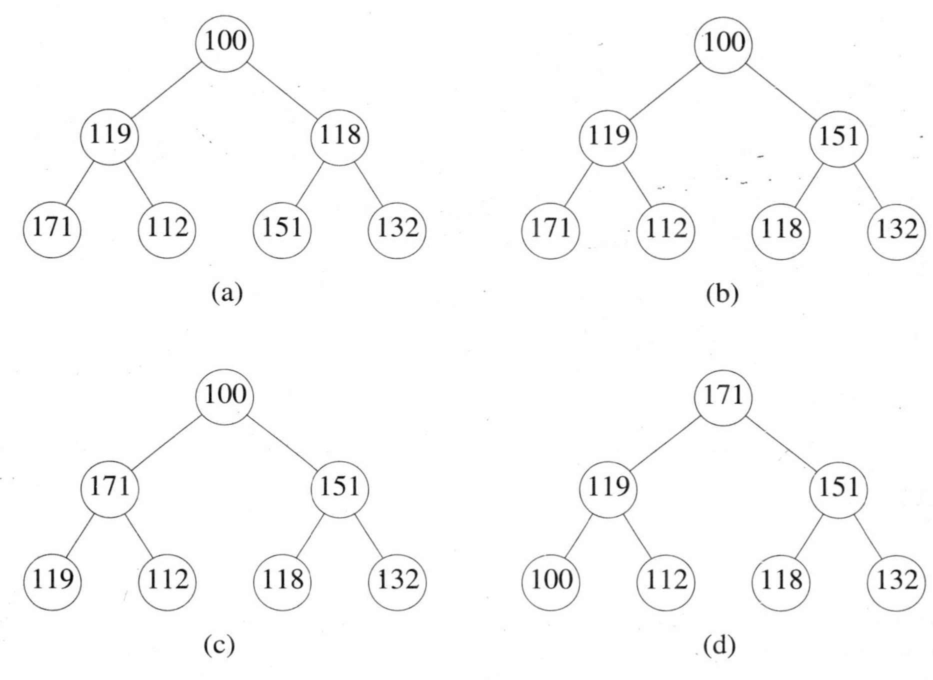

Figure 2.16 Action of Heapify$(a, 7)$ on the data (100, 119, 118, 171, 112, 151, and 132)

2.4.2 Heap Sort

The best-known example of the use of a heap arises in its application to sorting. A conceptually simple sorting strategy has been given before, in which the maximum value is continually removed from the remaining unsorted elements. A sorting algorithm that incorporates the fact that n elements can be inserted in $O(n)$ time is given in Algorithm 2.12.

Though the call of Heapify requires only $O(n)$ operations, Adjust possibly requires $O(\log n)$ operations for each invocation. Thus the worst-case time is $O(n \log n)$. Notice that the storage requirements, besides $a[1:n]$, are only for a few simple variables.

A number of other data structures can also be used to implement a priority queue. Examples include the binomial heap, deap, Fibonacci heap, and so on. A description of these can be found in the book by E. Horowitz, S. Sahni, and D. Mehta. Table 2.2 summarizes the performances of these data

```
Algorithm HeapSort(a, n)
// a[1 : n] contains n elements to be sorted. HeapSort
// rearranges them inplace into nondecreasing order.
{
    Heapify(a, n); // Transform the array into a heap.
    // Interchange the new maximum with the element
    // at the end of the array.
    for i := n to 2 step -1 do
    {
        t := a[i]; a[i] := a[1]; a[1] := t;
        Adjust(a, 1, i - 1);
    }
}
```

Algorithm 2.12 Heap sort

structures. Many of these data structures support the operations of deleting and searching for arbitrary elements (Red-Black tree being an example), in addition to the ones needed for a priority queue.

Data structure	insert	delete min
Min heap	$O(\log n)$ (wc)	$O(\log n)$ (wc)
Min-max heap	$O(\log n)$ (wc)	$O(\log n)$ (wc)
Deap	$O(\log n)$ (wc)	$O(\log n)$ (wc)
Leftist tree	$O(\log n)$ (wc)	$O(\log n)$ (wc)
Binomial heap	$O(\log n)$ (wc) $O(1)$ (am)	$O(\log n)$ (wc) $O(\log n)$ (am)
Fibonacci heap	$O(\log n)$ (wc) $O(1)$ (am)	$O(\log n)$ (wc) $O(\log n)$ (am)
2-3 tree	$O(\log n)$ (wc)	$O(\log n)$ (wc)
Red-Black tree	$O(\log n)$ (wc)	$O(\log n)$ (wc)

Table 2.2 Performances of different data structures when realizing a priority queue. Here (wc) stands for worst case and (am) denotes amortized cost.

EXERCISES

1. Consider the array [-, 3, 5, 6, 7, 20, 8, 2, 9, 12, 15, 30, 17].
   (a) Draw the corresponding complete binary tree.
   (b) Heapify the tree by using the method of Algorithm 2.11. Show the result in both tree and array format.
   (c) Now insert the elements 15, 20, and 45 (in this order) using the bubbling up process of Algorithm 2.8. Show the max heap following each insert.
   (d) Perform four delete max operations on the max heap of part (c). Use the method of Algorithm 2.9. Show the max heap following each delete.

2. Do Exercise 1 beginning with the array [-, 10, 2, 7, 6, 5, 9, 12, 35, 22, 15, 1, 3, 4].

3. Do Exercise 1 beginning with the array [-, 1, 2, 3, 4, 5, 6, 7, 8, 9, 10, 12, 15, 22, 35].

4. Do Exercise 1 under the assumption that you are to have a min heap. The initial array is [-, 30, 17, 20, 15, 10, 12, 5, 7, 8, 5, 2, 9]. For part (b) insert 1, 10, 6, and 4. For part (d) perform three remove min operations.

5. Verify for yourself that algorithm Insert (Algorithm 2.8) uses only a constant number of comparisons to insert a random element into a heap by performing an appropriate experiment.

6. (a) Equation 2.1 makes use of the fact that the sum $\sum_{i=1}^{\infty} \frac{i}{2^i}$ converges. Prove this fact.
   (b) Use induction to show that $\sum_{i=1}^{k} 2^{i-1}(k-i) = 2^k - k - 1, k \geq 1$.

7. Write an algorithm to delete the element in position i of a max heap. The complexity of your algorithm should be $O(\log n)$.

8. Program and run algorithm HeapSort (Algorithm 2.12) and compare its time with the time of any of the sorting algorithms discussed in Chapter 1.

9. Design a data structure that supports the following operations: INSERT and MIN. The worst-case run time should be $O(1)$ for each of these operations.

10. Notice that a binary search tree can be used to implement a priority queue.

(a) Present an algorithm to delete the largest element in a binary search tree. Your procedure should have complexity $O(h)$, where h is the height of the search tree. Since h is $O(\log n)$ on average, you can perform each of the priority queue operations in average time $O(\log n)$.

(b) Compare the performances of max heaps and binary search trees as data structures for priority queues. For this comparison, generate random sequences of insert and delete max operations and measure the total time taken for each sequence by each of these data structures.

11. Input is a sequence X of n keys with many duplications such that the number of distinct keys is d ($< n$). Present an $O(n \log d)$-time sorting algorithm for this input. (For example, if $X = 5, 6, 1, 18, 6, 4, 4, 1, 5, 17$, the number of distinct keys in X is six.)

2.5 SETS AND DISJOINT SET UNION

2.5.1 Introduction

In this section we study the use of forests in the representation of sets. We shall assume that the elements of the sets are the numbers $1, 2, 3, \ldots, n$. These numbers might, in practice, be indices into a symbol table in which the names of the elements are stored. We assume that the sets being represented are pairwise disjoint (that is, if S_i and S_j, $i \neq j$, are two sets, then there is no element that is in both S_i and S_j). For example, when $n = 10$, the elements can be partitioned into three disjoint sets, $S_1 = \{1, 7, 8, 9\}$, $S_2 = \{2, 5, 10\}$, and $S_3 = \{3, 4, 6\}$. Figure 2.17 shows one possible representation for these sets. In this representation, each set is represented as a tree. Notice that for each set we have linked the nodes from the children to the parent, rather than our usual method of linking from the parent to the children. The reason for this change in linkage becomes apparent when we discuss the implementation of set operations.

The operations we wish to perform on these sets are:

1. **Disjoint set union**. If S_i and S_j are two disjoint sets, then their union $S_i \cup S_j$ = all elements x such that x is in S_i or S_j. Thus, $S_1 \cup S_2 = \{1, 7, 8, 9, 2, 5, 10\}$. Since we have assumed that all sets are disjoint, we can assume that following the union of S_i and S_j, the sets S_i and S_j do not exist independently; that is, they are replaced by $S_i \cup S_j$ in the collection of sets.

2. **Find**(i). Given the element i, find the set containing i. Thus, 4 is in set S_3, and 9 is in set S_1.

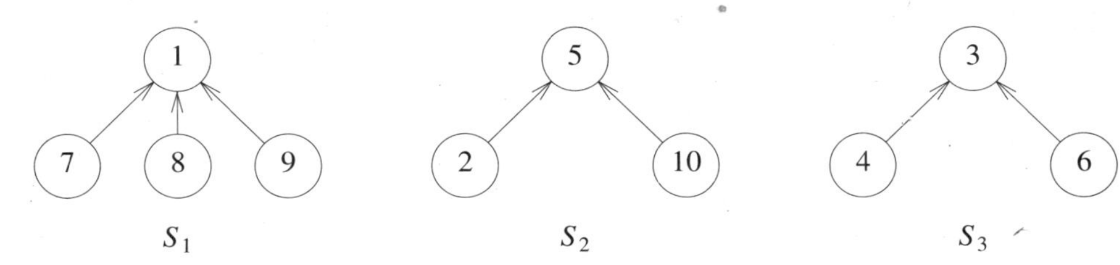

Figure 2.17 Possible tree representation of sets

2.5.2 Union and Find Operations

Let us consider the union operation first. Suppose that we wish to obtain the union of S_1 and S_2 (from Figure 2.17). Since we have linked the nodes from children to parent, we simply make one of the trees a subtree of the other. $S_1 \cup S_2$ could then have one of the representations of Figure 2.18.

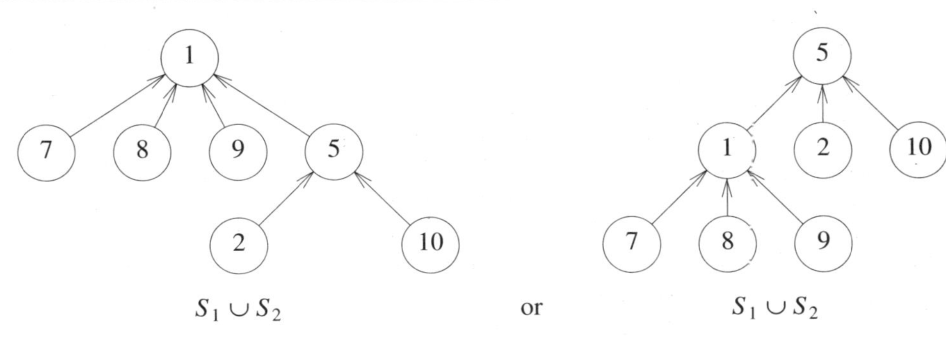

Figure 2.18 Possible representations of $S_1 \cup S_2$

To obtain the union of two sets, all that has to be done is to set the parent field of one of the roots to the other root. This can be accomplished easily if, with each set name, we keep a pointer to the root of the tree representing that set. If, in addition, each root has a pointer to the set name, then to determine which set an element is currently in, we follow parent links to the root of its tree and use the pointer to the set name. The data representation for S_1, S_2, and S_3 may then take the form shown in Figure 2.19.

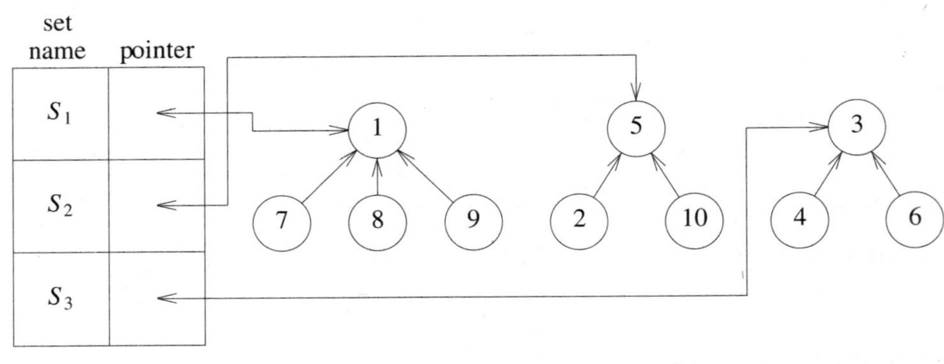

Figure 2.19 Data representation for S_1, S_2, and S_3

In presenting the union and find algorithms, we ignore the set names and identify sets just by the roots of the trees representing them. This simplifies the discussion. The transition to set names is easy. If we determine that element i is in a tree with root j, and j has a pointer to entry k in the set name table, then the set name is just $name[k]$. If we wish to unite sets S_i and S_j, then we wish to unite the trees with roots FindPointer(S_i) and FindPointer(S_j). Here FindPointer is a function that takes a set name and determines the root of the tree that represents it. This is done by an examination of the [set name, pointer] table. In many applications the set name is just the element at the root. The operation of $Find(i)$ now becomes: Determine the root of the tree containing element i. The function $Union(i, j)$ requires two trees with roots i and j be joined. Also to simplify, assume that the set elements are the numbers 1 through n.

Since the set elements are numbered 1 through n, we represent the tree nodes using an array $p[1 : n]$, where n is the maximum number of elements. The ith element of this array represents the tree node that contains element i. This array element gives the parent pointer of the corresponding tree node. Figure 2.20 shows this representation of the sets S_1, S_2, and S_3 of Figure 2.17. Notice that root nodes have a parent of -1.

We can now implement $Find(i)$ by following the indices, starting at i until we reach a node with parent value -1. For example, $Find(6)$ starts at 6 and then moves to 6's parent, 3. Since $p[3]$ is negative, we have reached the root. The operation $Union(i, j)$ is equally simple. We pass in two trees with roots i and j. Adopting the convention that the first tree becomes a subtree of the second, the statement $p[i] := j$; accomplishes the union.

i	[1]	[2]	[3]	[4]	[5]	[6]	[7]	[8]	[9]	[10]
p	-1	5	-1	3	-1	3	1	1	1	5

Figure 2.20 Array representation of S_1, S_2, and S_3 of Figure 2.17

```
Algorithm SimpleUnion(i, j)
{
    p[i] := j;
}

Algorithm SimpleFind(i)
{
    while (p[i] ≥ 0) do i := p[i];
    return i;
}
```

Algorithm 2.13 Simple algorithms for union and find

Algorithm 2.13 gives the descriptions of the union and find operations just discussed. Although these two algorithms are very easy to state, their performance characteristics are not very good. For instance, if we start with q elements each in a set of its own (that is, $S_i = \{i\}$, $1 \leq i \leq q$), then the initial configuration consists of a forest with q nodes, and $p[i] = 0$, $1 \leq i \leq q$. Now let us process the following sequence of *union-find* operations:

$$Union(1,2),\ Union(2,3),\ Union(3,4),\ Union(4,5), \ldots,\ Union(n-1,n)$$

$$Find(1),\ Find(2), \ldots,\ Find(n)$$

This sequence results in the degenerate tree of Figure 2.21.

Since the time taken for a union is constant, the $n-1$ unions can be processed in time $O(n)$. However, each find requires following a sequence of *parent* pointers from the element to be found to the root. Since the time required to process a find for an element at level i of a tree is $O(i)$, the total time needed to process the n finds is $O(\sum_{i=1}^{n} i) = O(n^2)$.

We can improve the performance of our union and find algorithms by avoiding the creation of degenerate trees. To accomplish this, we make use of a weighting rule for $Union(i, j)$.

Figure 2.21 Degenerate tree

Definition 2.5 [Weighting rule for *Union(i,j)*] If the number of nodes in the tree with root i is less than the number in the tree with root j, then make j the parent of i; otherwise make i the parent of j. □

When we use the weighting rule to perform the sequence of set unions given before, we obtain the trees of Figure 2.22. In this figure, the unions have been modified so that the input parameter values correspond to the roots of the trees to be combined.

To implement the weighting rule, we need to know how many nodes there are in every tree. To do this easily, we maintain a *count* field in the root of every tree. If i is a root node, then $count[i]$ equals the number of nodes in that tree. Since all nodes other than the roots of trees have a positive number in the p field, we can maintain the count in the p field of the roots as a negative number.

Using this convention, we obtain Algorithm 2.14. In this algorithm the time required to perform a union has increased somewhat but is still bounded by a constant (that is, it is $O(1)$). The find algorithm remains unchanged. The maximum time to perform a find is determined by Lemma 2.3.

Lemma 2.3 Assume that we start with a forest of trees, each having one node. Let T be a tree with m nodes created as a result of a sequence of unions each performed using WeightedUnion. The height of T is no greater than $\lfloor \log_2 m \rfloor + 1$.

Proof: The lemma is clearly true for $m = 1$. Assume it is true for all trees with i nodes, $i \leq m - 1$. We show that it is also true for $i = m$.

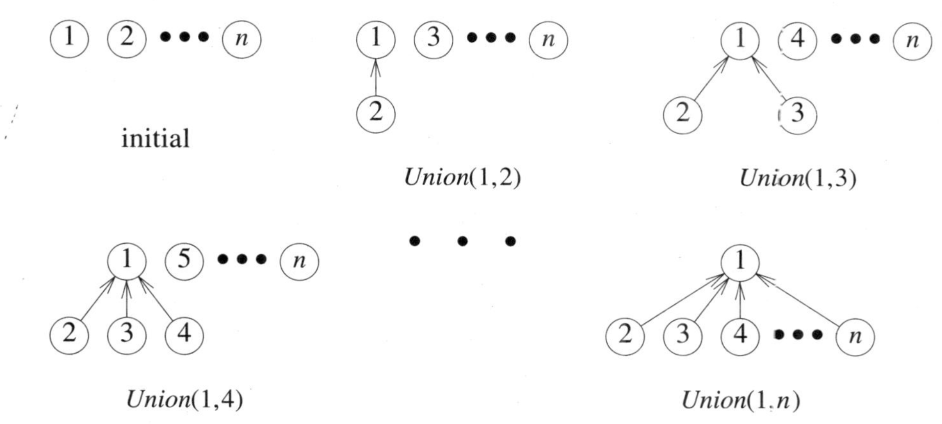

Figure 2.22 Trees obtained using the weighting rule

```
Algorithm WeightedUnion(i, j)
// Union sets with roots i and j, i ≠ j, using the
// weighting rule. p[i] = −count[i] and p[j] = −count[j].
{
    temp := p[i] + p[j];
    if (p[i] > p[j]) then
    { // i has fewer nodes.
        p[i] := j; p[j] := temp;
    }
    else
    { // j has fewer or equal nodes.
        p[j] := i; p[i] := temp;
    }
}
```

Algorithm 2.14 Union algorithm with weighting rule

Let T be a tree with m nodes created by WeightedUnion. Consider the last union operation performed, $Union(k, j)$. Let a be the number of nodes in tree j, and $m - a$ the number in k. Without loss of generality we can assume $1 \leq a \leq \frac{m}{2}$. Then the height of T is either the same as that of k or is one more than that of j. If the former is the case, the height of T is $\leq \lfloor \log_2 (m - a) \rfloor + 1 \leq \lfloor \log_2 m \rfloor + 1$. However, if the latter is the case, the height of T is $\leq \lfloor \log_2 a \rfloor + 2 \leq \lfloor \log_2 \frac{m}{2} \rfloor + 2 \leq \lfloor \log_2 m \rfloor + 1$. □

Example 2.4 shows that the bound of Lemma 2.3 is achievable for some sequence of unions.

Example 2.4 Consider the behavior of WeightedUnion on the following sequence of unions starting from the initial configuration $p[i] = -count[i] = -1$, $1 \leq i \leq 8 = n$:

$$Union(1, 2),\ Union(3, 4),\ Union(5, 6),\ Union(7, 8),$$
$$Union(1, 3),\ Union(5, 7),\ Union(1, 5)$$

The trees of Figure 2.23 are obtained. As is evident, the height of each tree with m nodes is $\lfloor \log_2 m \rfloor + 1$. □

From Lemma 2.3, it follows that the time to process a find is $O(\log m)$ if there are m elements in a tree. If an intermixed sequence of $u - 1$ union and f find operations is to be processed, the time becomes $O(u + f \log u)$, as no tree has more than u nodes in it. Of course, we need $O(n)$ additional time to initialize the n-tree forest.

Surprisingly, further improvement is possible. This time the modification is made in the find algorithm using the *collapsing rule.*

Definition 2.6 [Collapsing rule]: If j is a node on the path from i to its root and $p[i] \neq root[i]$, then set $p[j]$ to $root[i]$. □

CollapsingFind (Algorithm 2.15) incorporates the collapsing rule.

Example 2.5 Consider the tree created by WeightedUnion on the sequence of unions of Example 2.4. Now process the following eight finds:

$$Find(8),\ Find(8), \ldots,\ Find(8)$$

If SimpleFind is used, each $Find(8)$ requires going up three parent link fields for a total of 24 moves to process all eight finds. When CollapsingFind is used, the first $Find(8)$ requires going up three links and then resetting two links. Note that even though only two parent links need to be reset, CollapsingFind will reset three (the parent of 5 is reset to 1). Each of the remaining seven finds requires going up only one link field. The total cost is now only 13 moves. □

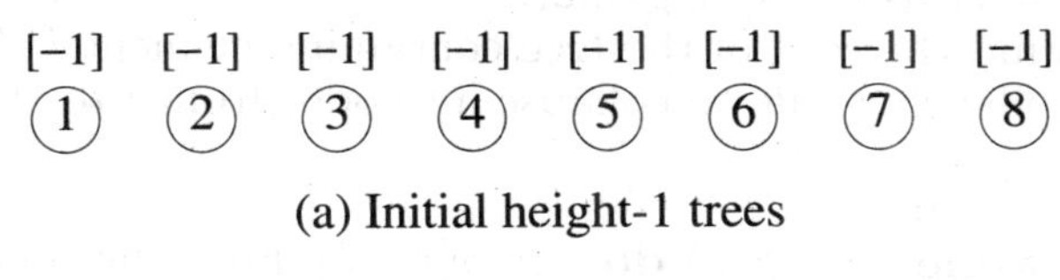

(a) Initial height-1 trees

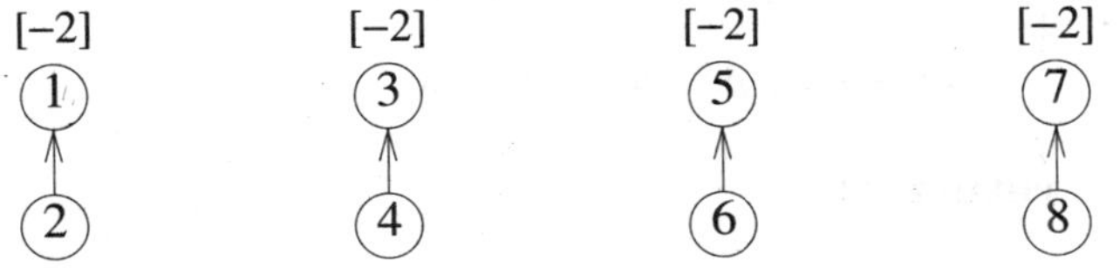

(b) Height-2 trees following *Union*(1,2), (3,4), (5,6), and (7,8)

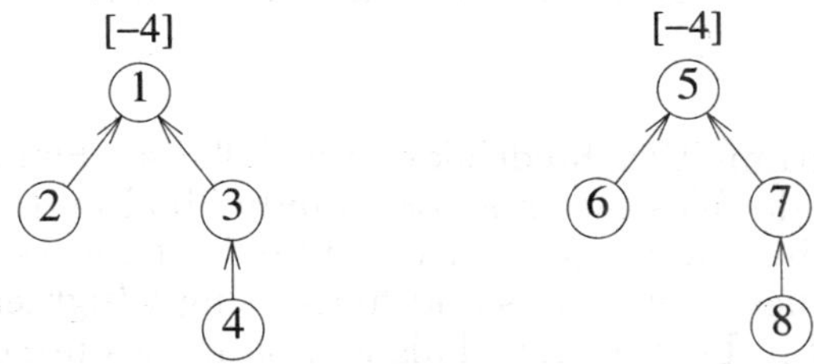

(c) Height-3 trees following *Union*(1,3) and (5,7)

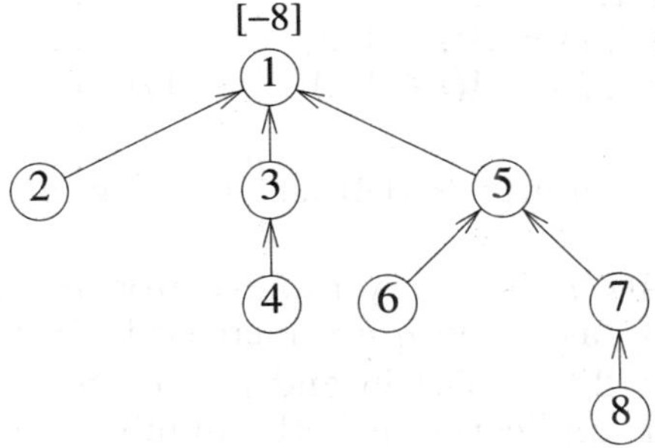

(d) Height-4 tree following *Union*(1,5)

Figure 2.23 Trees achieving worst-case bound

```
Algorithm CollapsingFind(i)
// Find the root of the tree containing element i. Use the
// collapsing rule to collapse all nodes from i to the root.
{
    r := i;
    while (p[r] > 0) do r := p[r]; // Find the root.
    while (i ≠ r) do  // Collapse nodes from i to root r.
    {
        s := p[i]; p[i] := r; i := s;
    }
    return r;
}
```

Algorithm 2.15 Find algorithm with collapsing rule

In the algorithms WeightedUnion and CollapsingFind, use of the collapsing rule roughly doubles the time for an individual find. However, it reduces the worst-case time over a sequence of finds. The worst-case complexity of processing a sequence of unions and finds using WeightedUnion and CollapsingFind is stated in Lemma 2.4. This lemma makes use of a function $\alpha(p,q)$ that is related to a functional inverse of Ackermann's function $A(i,j)$. These functions are defined as follows:

$$\begin{array}{ll} A(1,j) = 2^j & \text{for } j \geq 1 \\ A(i,1) = A(i-1,2) & \text{for } i \geq 2 \\ A(i,j) = A(i-1, A(i,j-1)) & \text{for } i,j \geq 2 \end{array}$$

$$\alpha(p,q) = \min\{z \geq 1 | A(z, \lfloor \frac{p}{q} \rfloor) > \log_2 q\}, \quad p \geq q \geq 1$$

The function $A(i,j)$ is a very rapidly growing function. Consequently, α grows very slowly as p and q are increased. In fact, since $A(3,1) = 16$, $\alpha(p,q) \leq 3$ for $q < 2^{16} = 65,536$ and $p \geq q$. Since $A(4,1)$ is a very large number and in our application q is the number n of set elements and p is $n + f$ (f is the number of finds), $\alpha(p,q) \leq 4$ for all practical purposes.

Lemma 2.4 [Tarjan and Van Leeuwen] Assume that we start with a forest of trees, each having one node. Let $T(f,u)$ be the maximum time required to process any intermixed sequence of f finds and u unions. Assume that $u \geq \frac{n}{2}$. Then

$$k_1[n + f\alpha(f+n,n)] \leq T(f,u) \leq k_2[n + f\alpha(f+n,n)]$$

for some positive constants k_1 and k_2. □

The requirement that $u \geq \frac{n}{2}$ in Lemma 2.4 is really not significant, as when $u < \frac{n}{2}$, some elements are involved in no union operation. These elements remain in singleton sets throughout the sequence of union and find operations and can be eliminated from consideration, as find operations that involve these can be done in $O(1)$ time each. Even though the function $\alpha(f, u)$ is a very slowly growing function, the complexity of our solution to the set representation problem is not linear in the number of unions and finds. The space requirements are one node for each element.

In the exercises, we explore alternatives to the weight rule and the collapsing rule that preserve the time bounds of Lemma 2.4.

EXERCISES

1. Suppose we start with n sets, each containing a distinct element.
   (a) Show that if u unions are performed, then no set contains more than $u + 1$ elements.
   (b) Show that at most $n - 1$ unions can be performed before the number of sets becomes 1.
   (c) Show that if fewer than $\lceil \frac{n}{2} \rceil$ unions are performed, then at least one set with a single element in it remains.
   (d) Show that if u unions are performed, then at least $\max\{n - 2u, 0\}$ singleton sets remain.
2. Experimentally compare the performance of SimpleUnion and SimpleFind (Algorithm 2.13) with WeightedUnion (Algorithm 2.14) and CollapsingFind (Algorithm 2.15). For this, generate a random sequence of union and find operations.
3. (a) Present an algorithm HeightUnion that uses the *height rule* for union operations instead of the weighting rule. This rule is defined below:

   Definition 2.7 [Height rule] If the height of tree i is less than that of tree j, then make j the parent of i; otherwise make i the parent of j. □

   Your algorithm must run in $O(1)$ time and should maintain the height of each tree as a negative number in the p field of the root.

   (b) Show that the height bound of Lemma 2.3 applies to trees constructed using the height rule.

(c) Give an example of a sequence of unions that start with n singleton sets and create trees whose heights equal the upper bounds given in Lemma 2.3. Assume that each union is performed using the height rule.

(d) Experiment with the algorithms WeightedUnion (Algorithm 2.14) and HeightUnion to determine which produces better results when used in conjunction with CollapsingFind (Algorithm 2.15).

4. (a) Write an algorithm SplittingFind that uses *path splitting*, defined below, for the find operations instead of path collapsing.

Definition 2.8 [Path splitting] The parent pointer in each node (except the root and its child) on the path from i to the root is changed to point to the node's grandparent. □

Note that when path splitting is used, a single pass from i to the root suffices. R. Tarjan and J. Van Leeuwen have shown that Lemma 2.4 holds when path splitting is used in conjunction with either the weight or the height rule for unions.

(b) Experiment with CollapsingFind (Algorithm 2.15) and SplittingFind to determine which produces better results when used in conjunction with WeightedUnion (Algorithm 2.14).

5. (a) Design an algorithm HalvingFind that uses *path halving*, defined below, for the find operations instead of path collapsing.

Definition 2.9 [Path halving] In path halving, the parent pointer of every other node (except the root and its child) on the path from i to the root is changed to point to the nodes grandparent. □

Note that path halving, like path splitting (Exercise 4), can be implemented with a single pass from i to the root. However, in path halving, only half as many pointers are changed as in path splitting. Tarjan and Van Leeuwen have shown that Lemma 2.4 holds when path halving is used in conjunction with either the weight or the height rule for unions.

(b) Experiment with CollapsingFind and HalvingFind to determine which produces better results when used in conjunction with WeightedUnion (Algorithm 2.14).

2.6 GRAPHS

2.6.1 Introduction

The first recorded evidence of the use of graphs dates back to 1736, when Leonhard Euler used them to solve the now classical Königsberg bridge problem. In the town of Königsberg (now Kaliningrad) the river Pregel (Pregolya) flows around the island Kneiphof and then divides into two. There are, therefore, four land areas that have this river on their borders (see Figure 2.24(a)). These land areas are interconnected by seven bridges, labeled a to g. The land areas themselves are labeled A to D. The Königsberg bridge problem is to determine whether, starting at one land area, it is possible to walk across all the bridges exactly once in returning to the starting land area. One possible walk: Starting from land area B, walk across bridge a to island A, take bridge e to area D, take bridge g to C, take bridge d to A, take bridge b to B, and take bridge f to D.

This walk does not go across all bridges exactly once, nor does it return to the starting land area B. Euler answered the Königsberg bridge problem in the negative: The people of Königsberg cannot walk across each bridge exactly once and return to the starting point. He solved the problem by representing the land areas as vertices and the bridges as edges in a graph (actually a multigraph) as in Figure 2.24(b). His solution is elegant and applies to all graphs. Defining the *degree* of a vertex to be the number of edges incident to it, Euler showed that there is a walk starting at any vertex, going through each edge exactly once and terminating at the start vertex if and only if the degree of each vertex is even. A walk that does this is called *Eulerian*. There is no Eulerian walk for the Königsberg bridge problem, as all four vertices are of odd degree.

Since this first application, graphs have been used in a wide variety of applications. Some of these applications are the analysis of electric circuits, finding shortest routes, project planning, identification of chemical compounds, statistical mechanics, genetics, cybernetics, linguistics, social sciences, and so on. Indeed, it might well be said that of all mathematical structures, graphs are the most widely used.

2.6.2 Definitions

A graph G consists of two sets V and E. The set V is a finite, nonempty set of *vertices*. The set E is a set of pairs of vertices; these pairs are called *edges*. The notations $V(G)$ and $E(G)$ represent the sets of vertices and edges, respectively, of graph G. We also write $G = (V, E)$ to represent a graph. In an *undirected graph* the pair of vertices representing any edge is unordered. Thus, the pairs (u, v) and (v, u) represent the same edge. In a *directed graph* each edge is represented by a directed pair $\langle u, v\rangle$; u is the *tail* and v the *head* of the edge. Therefore, $\langle v, u\rangle$ and $\langle u, v\rangle$ represent two different edges.

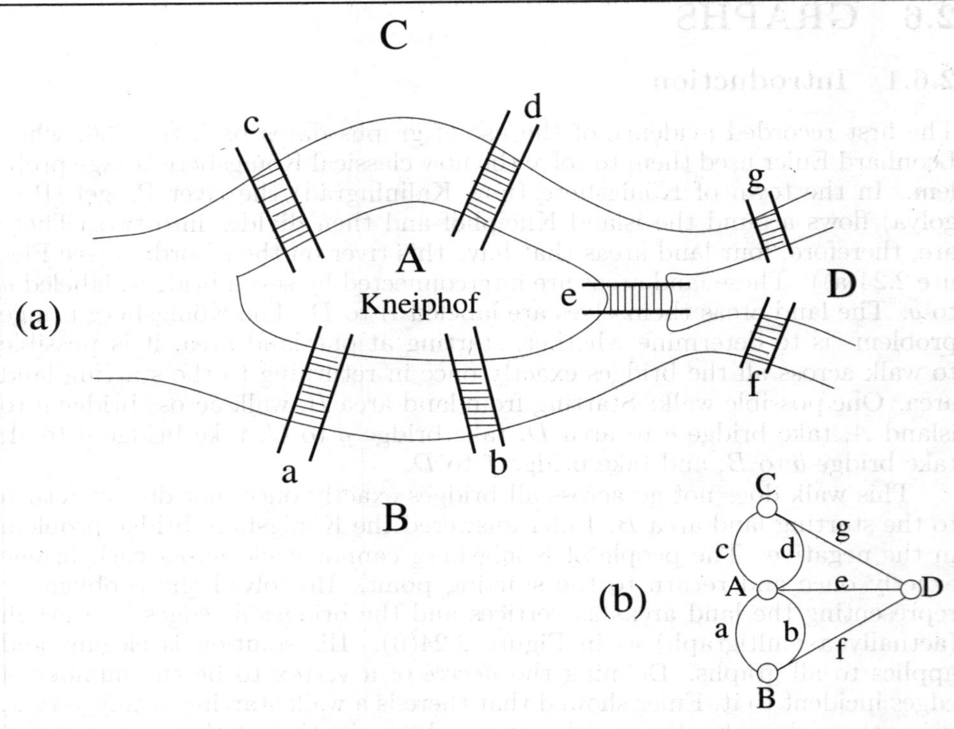

Figure 2.24 Section of the river Pregel in Königsberg and Euler's graph

Figure 2.25 shows three graphs: G_1, G_2, and G_3. The graphs G_1 and G_2 are undirected; G_3 is directed.

The set representations of these graphs are

$$
\begin{array}{ll}
V(G_1) = \{1,2,3,4\} & E(G_1) = \{(1,2),(1,3),(1,4),(2,3),(2,4),(3,4)\} \\
V(G_2) = \{1,2,3,4,5,6,7\} & E(G_2) = \{(1,2),(1,3),(2,4),(2,5),(3,6),(3,7)\} \\
V(G_3) = \{1,2,3\} & E(G_3) = \{\langle 1,2\rangle,\langle 2,1\rangle,\langle 2,3\rangle\}
\end{array}
$$

Notice that the edges of a directed graph are drawn with an arrow from the tail to the head. The graph G_2 is a tree; the graphs G_1 and G_3 are not.

Since we define the edges and vertices of a graph as sets, we impose the following restrictions on graphs:

1. A graph may not have an edge from a vertex v back to itself. That is, edges of the form (v, v) and $\langle v, v\rangle$ are not legal. Such edges are known as *self-edges* or *self-loops*. If we permit self-edges, we obtain a data

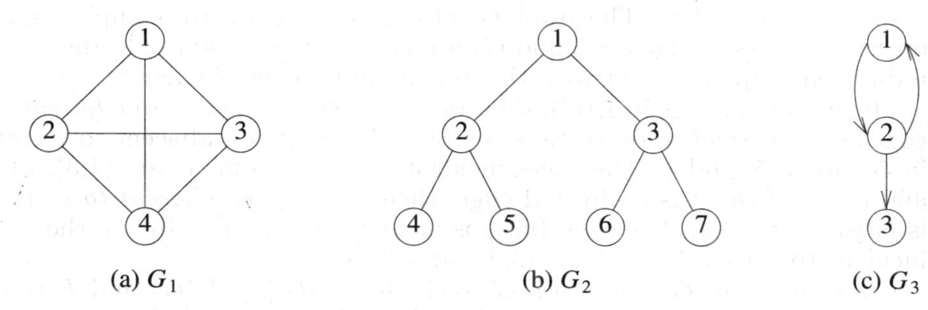

Figure 2.25 Three sample graphs

object referred to as a *graph with self-edges*. An example is shown in Figure 2.26(a).

2. A graph may not have multiple occurrences of the same edge. If we remove this restriction, we obtain a data object referred to as a *multigraph* (see Figure 2.26(b)).

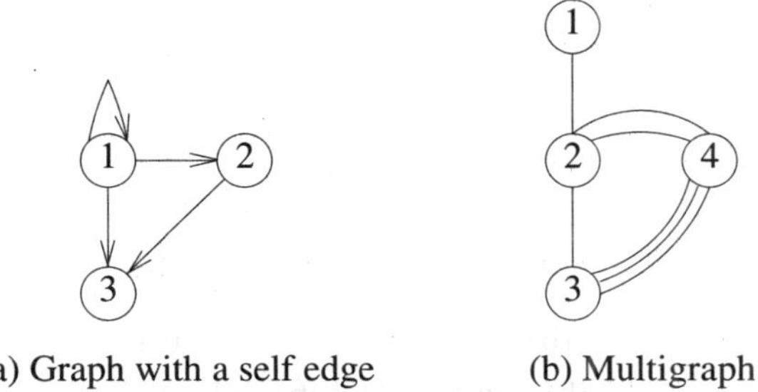

Figure 2.26 Examples of graphlike structures

The number of distinct unordered pairs (u, v) with $u \neq v$ in a graph with n vertices is $\frac{n(n-1)}{2}$. This is the maximum number of edges in any n-vertex, undirected graph. An n-vertex, undirected graph with exactly $\frac{n(n-1)}{2}$ edges is said to be *complete*. The graph G_1 of Figure 2.25(a) is the complete graph on four vertices, whereas G_2 and G_3 are not complete graphs. In the case of a directed graph on n vertices, the maximum number of edges is $n(n-1)$.

If (u, v) is an edge in $E(G)$, then we say vertices u and v are *adjacent* and edge (u, v) is *incident* on vertices u and v. The vertices adjacent to vertex 2 in G_2 are 4, 5, and 1. The edges incident on vertex 3 in G_2 are (1,3), (3,6), and (3,7). If $\langle u, v\rangle$ is a directed edge, then vertex u is *adjacent to* v, and v is *adjacent from* u. The edge $\langle u, v\rangle$ is incident to u and v. In G_3, the edges incident to vertex 2 are $\langle 1,2\rangle$, $\langle 2,1\rangle$, and $\langle 2,3\rangle$.

A *subgraph* of G is a graph G' such that $V(G') \subseteq V(G)$ and $E(G') \subseteq E(G)$. Figure 2.27 shows some of the subgraphs of G_1 and G_3.

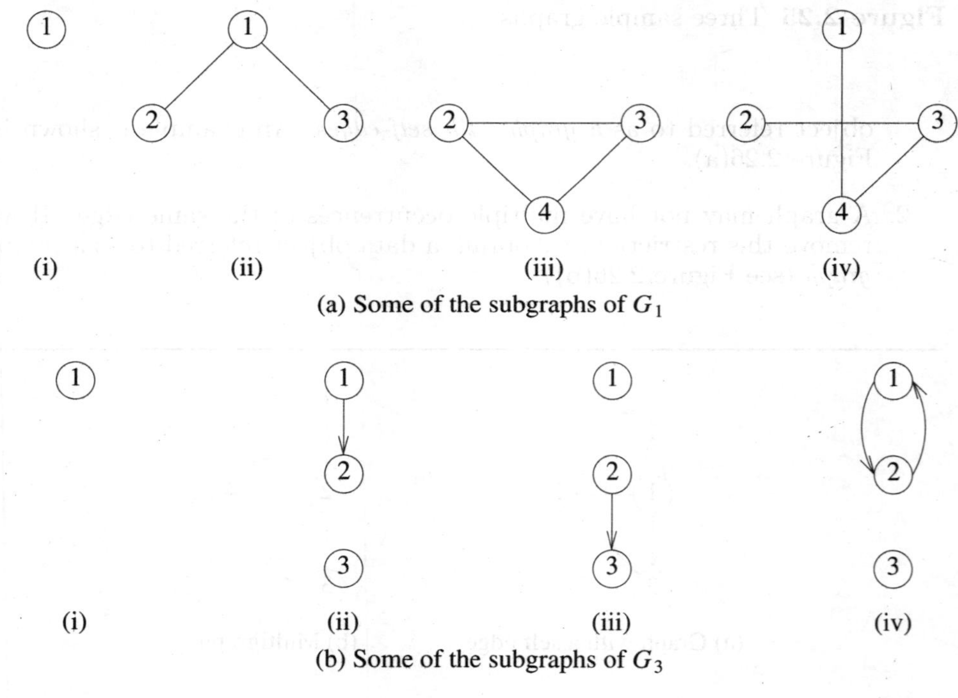

Figure 2.27 Some subgraphs

A *path* from vertex u to vertex v in graph G is a sequence of vertices $u, i_1, i_2, \ldots, i_k, v$, such that $(u, i_1), (i_1, i_2), \ldots, (i_k, v)$ are edges in $E(G)$. If G' is directed, then the path consists of the edges $\langle u, i_1\rangle, \langle i_1, i_2\rangle, \ldots, \langle i_k, v\rangle$

in $E(G')$. The *length* of a path is the number of edges on it. A *simple path* is a path in which all vertices except possibly the first and last are distinct. A path such as (1,2), (2,4), (4,3), is also written as 1, 2, 4, 3. Paths 1, 2, 4, 3 and 1, 2, 4, 2 of G_1 are both of length 3. The first is a simple path; the second is not. The path 1, 2, 3 is a simple directed path in G_3, but 1, 2, 3, 2 is not a path in G_3, as the edge $\langle 3, 2 \rangle$ is not in $E(G_3)$.

A *cycle* is a simple path in which the first and last vertices are the same. The path 1, 2, 3, 1 is a cycle in G_1 and 1, 2, 1 is a cycle in G_3. For directed graphs we normally add the prefix "directed" to the terms cycle and path.

In an undirected graph G, two vertices u and v are said to be *connected* iff there is a path in G from u to v (since G is undirected, this means there must also be a path from v to u). An undirected graph is said to be connected iff for every pair of distinct vertices u and v in $V(G)$, there is a path from u to v in G. Graphs G_1 and G_2 are connected, whereas G_4 of Figure 2.28 is not. A *connected component* (or simply a component) H of an undirected graph is a *maximal* connected subgraph. By "maximal," we mean that G contains no other subgraph that is both connected and properly contains H. G_4 has two components, H_1 and H_2 (see Figure 2.28).

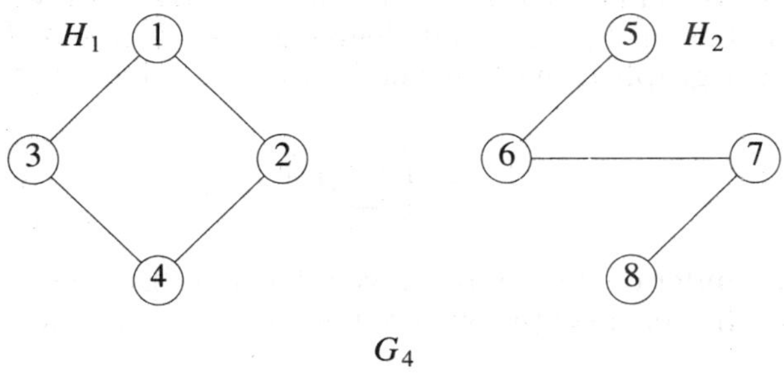

Figure 2.28 A graph with two connected components

A *tree* is a connected acyclic (i.e., has no cycles) graph. A directed graph G is said to be *strongly connected* iff for every pair of distinct vertices u and v in $V(G)$, there is a directed path from u to v and also from v to u. The graph G_3 (repeated in Figure 2.29(a)) is not strongly connected, as there is no path from vertex 3 to 2. A *strongly connected component* is a maximal subgraph that is strongly connected. The graph G_3 has two strongly connected components (see Figure 2.29(b)).

The degree of a vertex is the number of edges incident to that vertex. The degree of vertex 1 in G_1 is 3. If G is a directed graph, we define the

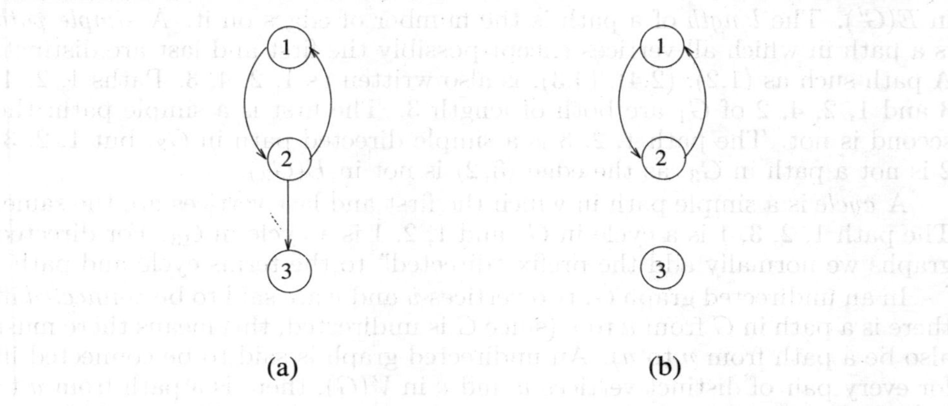

Figure 2.29 A graph and its strongly connected components

in-degree of a vertex v to be the number of edges for which v is the head. The *out-degree* is defined to be the number of edges for which v is the tail. Vertex 2 of G_3 has in-degree 1, out-degree 2, and degree 3. If d_i is the degree of vertex i in a graph G with n vertices and e edges, then the number of edges is

$$e = \left(\sum_{i=1}^{n} d_i \right) /2$$

In the remainder of this chapter, we refer to a directed graph as a *digraph*. When we use the term graph, we assume that it is an undirected graph.

2.6.3 Graph Representations

Although several representations for graphs are possible, we study only the three most commonly used: adjacency matrices, adjacency lists, and adjacency multilists. Once again, the choice of a particular representation depends on the application we have in mind and the functions we expect to perform on the graph.

Adjacency Matrix

Let $G = (V, E)$ be a graph with n vertices, $n \geq 1$. The adjacency matrix of G is a two-dimensional $n \times n$ array, say a, with the property that $a[i, j]$ = 1 iff the edge (i, j) ($\langle i, j \rangle$ for a directed graph) is in $E(G)$. The element $a[i, j] = 0$ if there is no such edge in G. The adjacency matrices for the graphs G_1, G_3, and G_4 are shown in Figure 2.30. The adjacency matrix for an undirected graph is symmetric, as the edge (i, j) is in $E(G)$ iff the edge (j, i) is also in $E(G)$. The adjacency matrix for a directed graph may not be symmetric (as is the case for G_3). The space needed to represent a graph using its adjacency matrix is n^2 bits. About half this space can be saved in the case of an undirected graph by storing only the upper or lower triangle of the matrix.

	1	2	3	4
1	0	1	1	1
2	1	0	1	1
3	1	1	0	1
4	1	1	1	0

(a) G_1

	1	2	3
1	0	1	0
2	1	0	1
3	0	0	0

(b) G_3

	1	2	3	4	5	6	7	8
1	0	1	1	0	0	0	0	0
2	1	0	0	1	0	0	0	0
3	1	0	0	1	0	0	0	0
4	0	1	1	0	0	0	0	0
5	0	0	0	0	0	1	0	0
6	0	0	0	0	1	0	1	0
7	0	0	0	0	0	1	0	1
8	0	0	0	0	0	0	1	0

(c) G_4

Figure 2.30 Adjacency matrices

From the adjacency matrix, we can readily determine whether there is an edge connecting any two vertices i and j. For an undirected graph the degree of any vertex i is its row sum:

$$\sum_{j=1}^{n} a[i, j]$$

For a directed graph the row sum is the out-degree, and the column sum is the in-degree.

Suppose we want to answer a nontrivial question about graphs, such as How many edges are there in G? or Is G connected? Adjacency matrices require at least n^2 time, as $n^2 - n$ entries of the matrix (diagonal entries are zero) have to be examined. When graphs are sparse (i.e., most of the terms in the adjacency matrix are zero), we would expect that the former question could be answered in significantly less time, say $O(e + n)$, where e is the number of edges in G, and $e < \frac{n^2}{2}$. Such a speedup is made possible through the use of a representation in which only the edges that are in G are explicitly stored. This leads to the next representation for graphs, adjacency lists.

Adjacency Lists

In this representation of graphs, the n rows of the adjacency matrix are represented as n linked lists. There is one list for each vertex in G. The nodes in list i represent the vertices that are adjacent from vertex i. Each node has at least two fields: *vertex* and *link*. The *vertex* field contains the indices of the vertices adjacent to vertex i. The adjacency lists for G_1, G_3, and G_4 are shown in Figure 2.31. Notice that the vertices in each list are not required to be ordered. Each list has a head node. The head nodes are sequential, and so provide easy random access to the adjacency list for any particular vertex.

For an undirected graph with n vertices and e edges, this representation requires n head nodes and $2e$ list nodes. Each list node has two fields. In terms of the number of bits of storage needed, this count should be multiplied by $\log n$ for the head nodes and $\log n + \log e$ for the list nodes, as it takes $O(\log m)$ bits to represent a number of value m. Often, you can sequentially pack the nodes on the adjacency lists, and thereby eliminate the use of pointers. In this case, an array *node* $[1 : n + 2e + 1]$ can be used. The *node*$[i]$ gives the starting point of the list for vertex i, $1 \leq i \leq n$, and *node*$[n + 1]$ is set to $n + 2e + 2$. The vertices adjacent from vertex i are stored in *node*$[i], \ldots,$ *node*$[i + 1] - 1$, $1 \leq i \leq n$. Figure 2.32 shows the sequential representation for the graph G_4 of Figure 2.28.

The degree of any vertex in an undirected graph can be determined by just counting the number of nodes in its adjacency list. So, the number of edges in G can be determined in $O(n + e)$ time.

For a digraph, the number of list nodes is only e. The out-degree of any vertex can be determined by counting the number of nodes on its adjacency list. Hence, the total number of edges in G can be determined in $O(n + e)$ time. Determining the in-degree of a vertex is a little more complex. If there is a need to access repeatedly all vertices adjacent to another vertex, then it may be worth the effort to keep another set of lists in addition to the adjacency lists. This set of lists, called *inverse adjacency lists*, contains one list for each vertex. Each list contains a node for each vertex adjacent to the vertex it represents (see Figure 2.33).

One can also adopt a simpler version of the list structure in which each node has four fields and represents one edge. The node structure is

tail	head	column link for head	row link for tail

Figure 2.34 shows the resulting structure for the graph G_3 of Figure 2.25(c). The head nodes are stored sequentially.

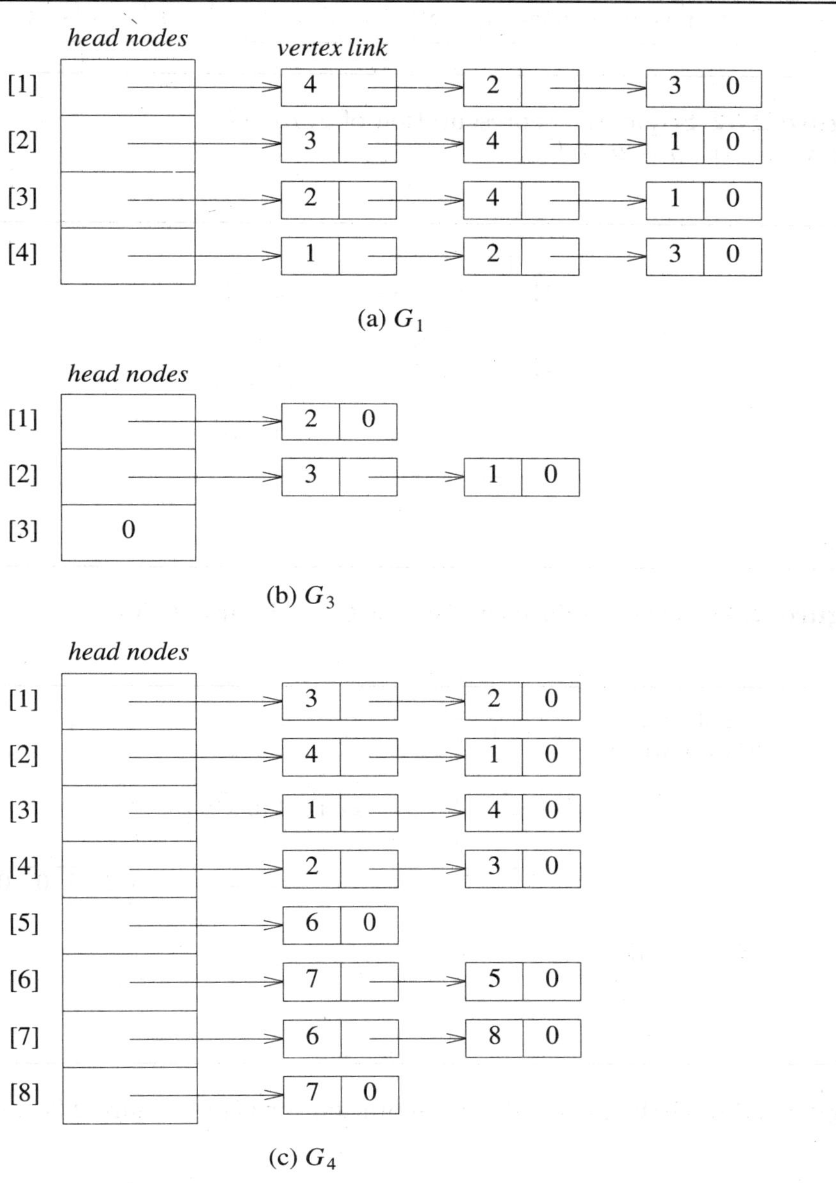

Figure 2.31 Adjacency lists

1	2	3	4	5	6	7	8	9	10	11	12	13	14	15	16	17	18	19	20	21	22	23
10	12	14	16	18	19	21	23	24	3	2	4	1	1	4	2	3	6	7	5	6	8	7

Figure 2.32 Sequential representation of graph G_4:
Array $node[1 : n + 2e + 1]$

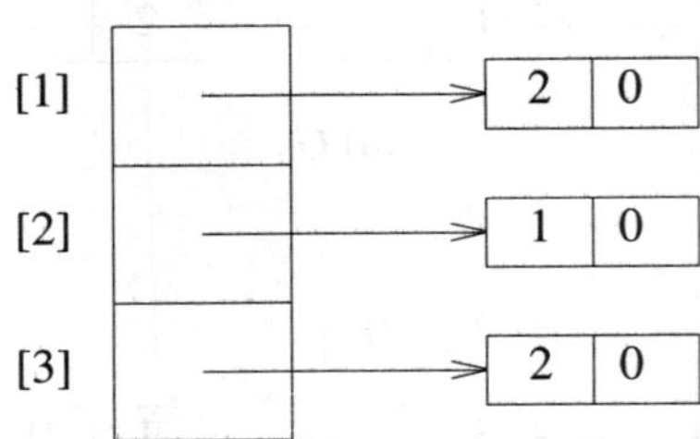

Figure 2.33 Inverse adjacency lists for G_3 of Figure 2.25(c)

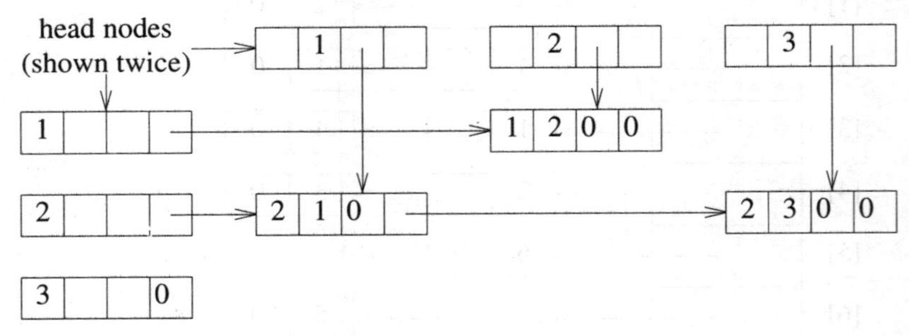

Figure 2.34 Orthogonal list representation for G_3 of Figure 2.25(c)

Adjacency Multilists

In the adjacency list representation of an undirected graph, each edge (u, v) is represented by two entries, one on the list for u and the other on the list for v. In some applications it is necessary to be able to determine the second entry for a particular edge and mark that edge as having been examined. This can be accomplished easily if the adjacency lists are maintained as multilists (i.e., lists in which nodes can be shared among several lists). For each edge there is exactly one node, but this node is in two lists (i.e., the adjacency lists for each of the two nodes to which it is incident). The new node structure is

m	$vertex1$	$vertex2$	$list1$	$list2$

where m is a one-bit mark field that can be used to indicate whether the edge has been examined. The storage requirements are the same as for normal adjacency lists, except for the addition of the mark bit m. Figure 2.35 shows the adjacency multilists for G_1 of Figure 2.25(a).

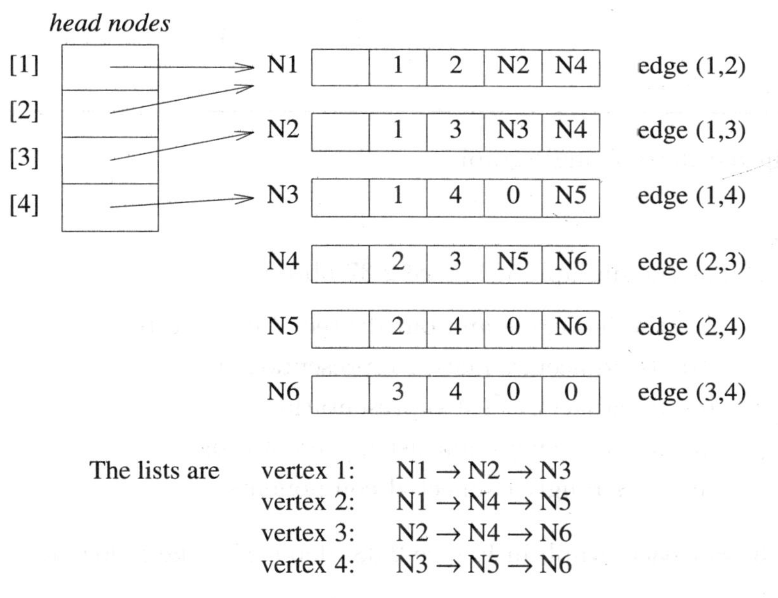

Figure 2.35 Adjacency multilists for G_1 of Figure 2.25(a)

Weighted Edges

In many applications, the edges of a graph have weights assigned to them. These weights may represent the distance from one vertex to another or the cost of going from one vertex to an adjacent vertex. In these applications, the adjacency matrix entries $a[i, j]$ keep this information too. When adjacency lists are used, the weight information can be kept in the list nodes by including an additional field, *weight*. A graph with weighted edges is called a *network*.

EXERCISES

1. Does the multigraph of Figure 2.36 have an Eulerian walk? If so, find one.

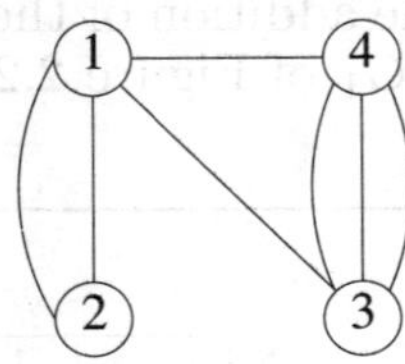

Figure 2.36 A multigraph

2. For the digraph of Figure 2.37 obtain
   (a) the in-degree and out-degree of each vertex
   (b) its adjacency-matrix representation
   (c) its adjacency-list representation
   (d) its adjacency-multilist representation
   (e) its strongly connected components

3. For each graph in Figure 2.38, determine the following:
   (a) The in-degree of each vertex.
   (b) The out-degree of each vertex.
   (c) The set of vertices adjacent from vertex 2.
   (d) The set of vertices adjacent to vertex 1.
   (e) The set of edges incident from vertex 3.
   (f) The set of edges incident to vertex 4.
   (g) All directed cycles and their lengths.

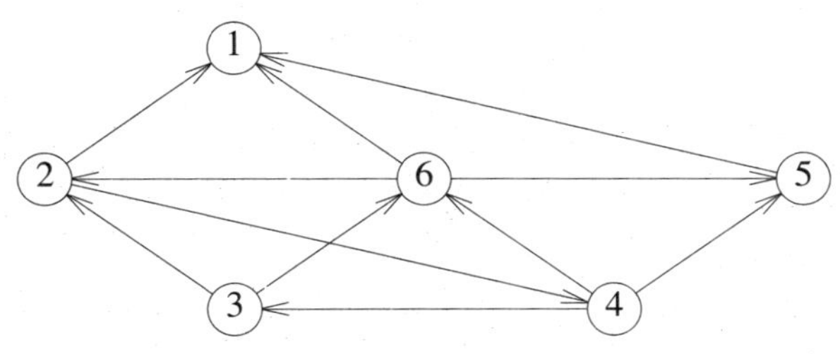

Figure 2.37 A digraph

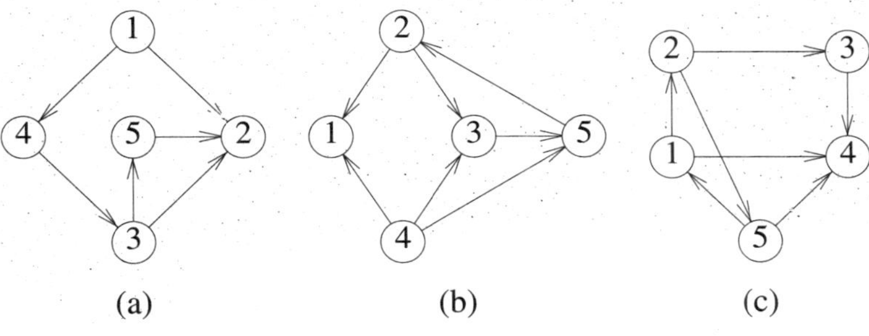

Figure 2.38 Digraphs

4. Draw the complete undirected graphs on one, two, three, four, and five vertices. Prove that the number of edges in an n-vertex complete graph is $\frac{n(n-1)}{2}$.

5. Let G be any undirected graph. Show that the number of vertices with odd degrees is even.

6. Is the directed graph of Figure 2.39 strongly connected? List all the simple paths.

7. Obtain the adjacency-matrix, adjacency-list, and adjacency-multilist representations of the graph of Figure 2.39.

8. Show that the sum of the degrees of the vertices of an undirected graph is twice the number of edges.

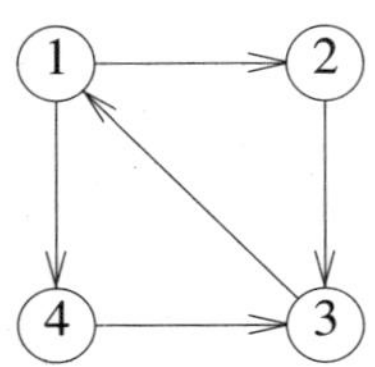

Figure 2.39 A directed graph

9. Prove or disprove:

   If $G(V, E)$ is a finite directed graph such that the out-degree of each vertex is at least one, then there is a directed cycle in G.

10. (a) Let G be a connected, undirected graph on n vertices. Show that G must have at least $n - 1$ edges and that all connected, undirected graphs with $n - 1$ edges are trees.

    (b) What is the minimum number of edges in a strongly connected digraph with n vertices? What form do such digraphs have?

11. For an undirected graph G with n vertices, prove that the following are equivalent:

    (a) G is a tree.

    (b) G is connected, but if any edge is removed, the resulting graph is not connected.

    (c) For any two distinct vertices $u \in V(G)$ and $v \in V(G)$, there is exactly one simple path from u to v.

    (d) G contains no cycles and has $n - 1$ edges.

12. Let $G = (V, E)$ be a connected graph with $|V| > 1$. Show that G contains either a vertex of degree 1 or a cycle (or both).

13. Let $G = (V, E)$ be a connected undirected graph that contains at least one cycle. Let $(i, j) \in E$ be an edge that is on at least one cycle of G. Show that the graph $H = (V,\ E - \{(i, j)\})$ is also connected.

14. Prove the following:

    (a) For every n there exists a connected undirected graph containing exactly $n - 1$ edges, $n \geq 1$.

(b) Every n-vertex connected undirected graph contains at least $n-1$ edges. You may use the results of the previous two exercises.

15. (a) Show that for every n, $n \geq 2$, there exists a strongly connected digraph that contains exactly n edges.

    (b) Show that every n vertex strongly connected digraph contains at least n edges, $n \geq 2$.

16. Write an algorithm to input the number of vertices in an undirected graph and its edges one by one and to set up the linked adjacency-list representation of the graph. You may assume that no edge is input twice. What is the run time of your procedure as a function of the number of vertices and the number of edges?

17. Do the preceding exercise but now set up the multilist representation.

18. Let G be an undirected, connected graph with at least one vertex of odd degree. Show that G contains no Eulerian walk.

19. Devise a suitable representation for graphs so that they can be stored on disk. Write an algorithm that reads in such a graph and creates its adjacency matrix. Write another algorithm that creates the adjacency lists from the disk input.

2.7 REFERENCES AND READINGS

A wide-ranging examination of data structures and their efficient implementation can be found in the following:
Fundamentals of Data Structures in C++, Second Edition, by E. Horowitz, S. Sahni, and D. Mehta, Silicon Press, 2007.
Handbook of Data Structures and Applications, by D. Mehta and S. Sahni (editors), Chapman-Hall/CRC, 2005.

Data Structures, Algorithms, and Applications in C++, by S. Sahni, Second Edition, Silicon Press, 2005.

A proof of Lemma 2.4 can be found in "Worst-case analysis of set union algorithms," by R. Tarjan and J. Van Leeuwen, *Journal of the ACM* 31; no. 2 (1984): 245–281.

Chapter 3

DIVIDE AND CONQUER

3.1 GENERAL METHOD

Given a function to compute on n inputs the *divide-and-conquer* strategy suggests splitting the inputs into k distinct subsets, $1 < k \leq n$, yielding k subproblems. These subproblems must be solved, and then a method must be found to combine subsolutions into a solution of the whole. If the subproblems are still relatively large, then the divide-and-conquer strategy can possibly be reapplied. Often the subproblems resulting from a divide-and-conquer design are of the *same* type as the original problem. For those cases the reapplication of the divide-and-conquer principle is naturally expressed by a recursive algorithm. Now smaller and smaller subproblems of the same kind are generated until eventually subproblems that are small enough to be solved without splitting are produced.

Example 3.1 [Detecting a Counterfeit Coin] You are given a bag with 16 coins and told that one of these coins may be counterfeit. Further, you are told that counterfeit coins are lighter than genuine ones. Your task is to determine whether the bag contains a counterfeit coin. To aid you in this task, you have a machine that compares the weights of two sets of coins and tells you which set is lighter or whether both sets have the same weight.

We can compare the weights of coins 1 and 2. If coin 1 is lighter than coin 2, then coin 1 is counterfeit and we are done with our task. If coin 2 is lighter than coin 1, then coin 2 is counterfeit. If both coins have the same weight, we compare coins 3 and 4. Again, if one coin is lighter, a counterfeit coin has been detected and we are done. If not, we compare coins 5 and 6. Proceeding in this way, we can determine whether the bag contains a counterfeit coin by making at most eight weight comparisons. This process also identifies the counterfeit coin.

Another approach is to use the divide-and-conquer methodology. Suppose that our 16-coin instance is considered a large instance. In step 1, we divide the original instance into two or more smaller instances. Let us divide our 16-coin instance into two 8-coin instances by arbitrarily selecting 8 coins for the first instance (say A) and the remaining 8 coins for the second instance B. In step 2, we need to determine whether A or B has a counterfeit coin. For this step we use our machine to compare the weights of the coin sets A and B. If both sets have the same weight, a counterfeit coin is not present in the 16-coin set. If A and B have different weights, a counterfeit coin is present and it is in the lighter set. Finally, in step 3 we take the results from step 2 and generate the answer for the original 16-coin instance. For the counterfeit-coin problem, step 3 is easy. The 16-coin instance has a counterfeit coin iff either A or B has one. So with just one weight comparison, we can complete the task of determining the presence of a counterfeit coin.

Now suppose we need to identify the counterfeit coin. We will define a "small" instance to be one with two or three coins. Note that if there is only one coin, we cannot tell whether it is counterfeit. All other instances are "large" instances. If we have a small instance, we may identify the counterfeit coin by comparing one of the coins with up to two other coins, performing at most two weight comparisons.

The 16-coin instance is a large instance. So it is divided into two 8-coin instances A and B as above. By comparing the weights of these two instances, we determine whether or not a counterfeit coin is present. If not, the algorithm terminates. Otherwise, we continue with the subinstance known to have the counterfeit coin. Suppose B is the lighter set. It is divided into two sets of four coins each. Call these sets $B1$ and $B2$. The two sets are compared. One set of coins must be lighter. If $B1$ is lighter, the counterfeit coin is in $B1$ and $B1$ is divided into two sets of two coins each. Call these sets $B1a$ and $B1b$. The two sets are compared, and we continue with the lighter set. Since the lighter set has only two coins, it is a small instance. Comparing the weights of the two coins in the lighter set, we can determine which is lighter. The lighter one is the counterfeit coin. □

To be more precise, suppose we consider the divide-and-conquer strategy when it splits the input into two subproblems of the same kind as the original problem. This splitting is typical of many of the problems we examine here. We can write a control abstraction that mirrors the way an algorithm based on divide-and-conquer will look. By a *control abstraction* we mean a procedure whose flow of control is clear but whose primary operations are specified by other procedures whose precise meanings are left undefined. DAndC (Algorithm 3.1) is initially invoked as DAndC(P), where P is the problem to be solved.

Small(P) is a Boolean-valued function that determines whether the input size is small enough that the answer can be computed without splitting. If this is so, the function S is invoked. Otherwise the problem P is divided into smaller subproblems. These subproblems $P_1, P_2, \ldots, P_k$ are solved by

```
Algorithm DAndC(P)
{
    if Small(P) then return S(P);
    else
    {
        divide P into smaller instances P_1, P_2, ..., P_k, k >= 1;
        Apply DAndC to each of these subproblems;
        return Combine(DAndC(P_1),DAndC(P_2),...,DAndC(P_k));
    }
}
```

Algorithm 3.1 Control abstraction for divide and conquer

recursive applications of DAndC. Combine is a function that determines the solution to P using the solutions to the k subproblems. If the size of P is n and the sizes of the k subproblems are $n_1, n_2, \ldots, n_k$, respectively, then the computing time of DAndC is described by the recurrence relation

$$T(n) = \begin{cases} g(n) & n \text{ small} \\ T(n_1) + T(n_2) + \cdots + T(n_k) \quad + \quad f(n) & \text{otherwise} \end{cases} \tag{3.1}$$

where $T(n)$ is the time for DAndC on any input of size n and $g(n)$ is the time to compute the answer directly for small inputs. The function $f(n)$ is the time for dividing P and combining the solutions to subproblems. For divide-and-conquer-based algorithms that produce subproblems of the same type as the original problem, it is very natural to first describe such algorithms using recursion.

The complexity of many divide-and-conquer algorithms is given by recurrences of the form

$$T(n) = \begin{cases} T(1) & n = 1 \\ aT(n/b) + f(n) & n > 1 \end{cases} \tag{3.2}$$

where a and b are known constants. We assume that $T(1)$ is known and n is a power of b (i.e., $n = b^k$).

One of the methods for solving any such recurrence relation is called the *substitution method.* This method repeatedly makes substitution for each occurrence of the function T in the right-hand side until all such occurrences disappear.

Example 3.2 Consider the case in which $a = 2$ and $b = 2$. Let $T(1) = 2$ and $f(n) = n$. We have

$$\begin{aligned} T(n) &= 2T(n/2) + n \\ &= 2[2T(n/4) + n/2] + n \\ &= 4T(n/4) + 2n \\ &= 4[2T(n/8) + n/4] + 2n \\ &= 8T(n/8) + 3n \\ &\vdots \end{aligned}$$

In general, we see that $T(n) = 2^iT(n/2^i) + in$, for any $\log_2 n \geq i \geq 1$. In particular, then, $T(n) = 2^{\log_2 n}T(n/2^{\log_2 n}) + n \log_2 n$, corresponding to the choice of $i = \log_2 n$. Thus, $T(n) = nT(1) + n \log_2 n = n \log_2 n + 2n$. □

Beginning with the recurrence (3.2) and using the substitution method, it can be shown that

$$T(n) = n^{\log_b a}[T(1) + u(n)]$$

where $u(n) = \sum_{j=1}^{k} h(b^j)$ and $h(n) = f(n)/n^{\log_b a}$. Table 3.1 tabulates the asymptotic value of $u(n)$ for various values of $h(n)$. This table allows one to easily obtain the asymptotic value of $T(n)$ for many of the recurrences one encounters when analyzing divide-and-conquer algorithms. Let us consider some examples using this table.

$h(n)$	$u(n)$
$O(n^r)$, $r < 0$	$O(1)$
$\Theta((\log n)^i)$, $i \geq 0$	$\Theta((\log n)^{i+1}/(i+1))$
$\Omega(n^r)$, $r > 0$	$\Theta(h(n))$

Table 3.1 $u(n)$ values for various $h(n)$ values

Example 3.3 Look at the following recurrence when n is a power of 2:

$$T(n) = \begin{cases} T(1) & n = 1 \\ T(n/2) + c & n > 1 \end{cases}$$

Comparing with (3.2), we see that $a = 1$, $b = 2$, and $f(n) = c$. So, $\log_b(a) = 0$ and $h(n) = f(n)/n^{\log_b a} = c = c(\log n)^0 = \Theta((\log n)^0)$. From Table 3.1, we obtain $u(n) = \Theta(\log n)$. So, $T(n) = n^{\log_b a}[c + \Theta(\log n)] = \Theta(\log n)$. □

Example 3.4 Next consider the case in which $a = 2$, $b = 2$, and $f(n) = cn$. For this recurrence, $\log_b a = 1$ and $h(n) = f(n)/n = c = \Theta((\log n)^0)$. Hence, $u(n) = \Theta(\log n)$ and $T(n) = n[T(1) + \Theta(\log n)] = \Theta(n \log n)$. □

Example 3.5 As another example, consider the recurrence $T(n) = 7T(n/2) + 18n^2$, $n \geq 2$ and a power of 2. We obtain $a = 7$, $b = 2$, and $f(n) = 18n^2$. So, $\log_b a = \log_2 7 \approx 2.81$ and $h(n) = 18n^2/n^{\log_2 7} = 18n^{2-\log_2 7} = O(n^r)$, where $r = 2 - \log_2 7 < 0$. So, $u(n) = O(1)$. The expression for $T(n)$ is

$$\begin{aligned} T(n) &= n^{\log_2 7}[T(1) + O(1)] \\ &= \Theta(n^{\log_2 7}) \end{aligned}$$

as $T(1)$ is assumed to be a constant. □

Example 3.6 As a final example, consider the recurrence $T(n) = 9T(n/3) + 4n^6$, $n \geq 3$ and a power of 3. Comparing with (3.2), we obtain $a = 9$, $b = 3$, and $f(n) = 4n^6$. So, $\log_b a = 2$ and $h(n) = 4n^6/n^2 = 4n^4 = \Omega(n^4)$. From Table 3.1, we see that $u(n) = \Theta(h(n)) = \Theta(n^4)$. So,

$$\begin{aligned} T(n) &= n^2[T(1) + \Theta(n^4)] \\ &= \Theta(n^6) \end{aligned}$$

as $T(1)$ can be assumed constant. □

EXERCISES

1. Extend the divide-and-conquer method of Example 3.1 to the case of $n > 1$ coins. How many weight comparisons are done?

2. Consider the counterfeit-coin problem of Example 3.1. Suppose that the information "counterfeit coins are lighter than genuine ones" is changed to "counterfeit coins and genuine coins do not have the same weight." Also assume that the coin bag contains n coins.

   (a) Formulate a divide-and-conquer algorithm that either outputs the message "there is no counterfeit coin" or identifies the counterfeit coin. Your algorithm should recursively divide large problem instances into two smaller ones. How many weight comparisons are needed to identify the counterfeit coin (in case such a coin exists)?

(b) Repeat part (a) with the requirement that large instances are divided into three smaller ones.

3. Solve the recurrence relation (3.2) for the following choices of a, b, and $f(n)$ (c being a constant):

(a) $a = 1,\ b = 2$, and $f(n) = cn$

(b) $a = 5,\ b = 4$, and $f(n) = cn^2$

(c) $a = 28,\ b = 3$, and $f(n) = cn^3$

4. Solve the following recurrence relations using the substitution method:

(a) All three recurrences of Exercise 3.

(b)

$$T(n) = \begin{cases} 1 & n \le 4 \\ T(\sqrt{n}) + c & n > 4 \end{cases}$$

(c)

$$T(n) = \begin{cases} 1 & n \le 4 \\ 2T(\sqrt{n}) + \log n & n > 4 \end{cases}$$

(d)

$$T(n) = \begin{cases} 1 & n \le 4 \\ 2T(\sqrt{n}) + \frac{\log n}{\log\log n} & n > 4 \end{cases}$$

3.2 DEFECTIVE CHESSBOARD

A **defective chessboard** is a $2^k \times 2^k$ board of squares with exactly one defective square. Figure 3.1 shows some of the possible defective chessboards for $k \le 2$. The defective square is shaded. Note that when $k = 0$, there is only one possible defective chessboard (Figure 3.1(a)). In fact, for any k there are exactly 2^{2k} different defective chessboards.

In the defective-chessboard problem, we are required to tile a defective chessboard using triominoes (Figure 3.2). In this tiling two triominoes may not overlap, triominoes should not cover the defective square, and triominoes must cover all other squares. With these constraints the number of triominoes to be used becomes $(2^{2k} - 1)/3$. We can verify that $(2^{2k} - 1)/3$ is an integer. A defective chessboard with $k = 0$ is easily tiled, as it has no nondefective squares. The number of triominoes used in the tiling is zero. When $k = 1$, there are exactly three nondefective squares and these squares are covered using a triomino in one of the orientations of Figure 3.2.

The divide-and-conquer method leads to an elegant solution to the defective-chessboard problem. The method suggests reducing the problem of tiling a

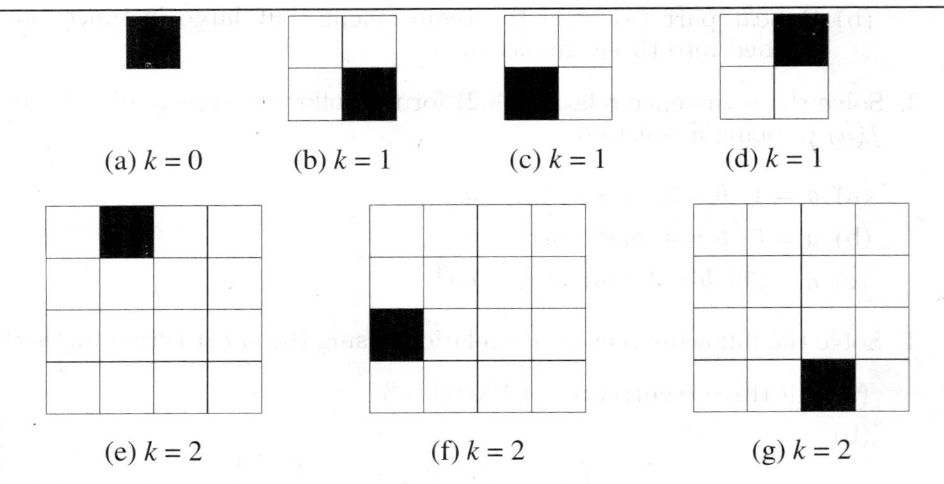

Figure 3.1 Defective chessboards

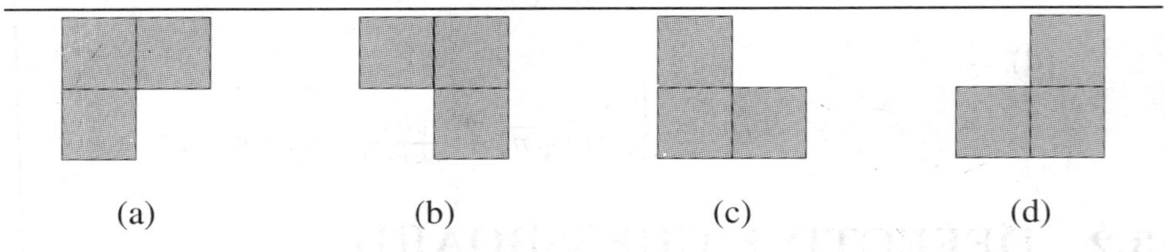

Figure 3.2 Triominoes with different orientations

$2^k \times 2^k$ defective chessboard to that of tiling smaller defective chessboards. A natural partitioning of a $2^k \times 2^k$ chessboard would be into four $2^{k-1} \times 2^{k-1}$ chessboards as in Figure 3.3(a). Notice that when such a partitioning is done, only one of the four smaller boards has a defect (as the original $2^k \times 2^k$ board had exactly one defective square). Tiling one of the four smaller boards corresponds to tiling a defective $2^{k-1} \times 2^{k-1}$ chessboard. To convert the remaining three boards to defective boards, we place a triomino at the corner formed by these three. Figure 3.3(b) shows this placement for the case when the defect in the original $2^k \times 2^k$ chessboard falls into the upper left $2^{k-1} \times 2^{k-1}$ board. We can use this partitioning technique recursively to tile the entire $2^k \times 2^k$ defective chessboard. The recursion terminates when the chessboard size has been reduced to 1×1. The chessboard's only square now has a

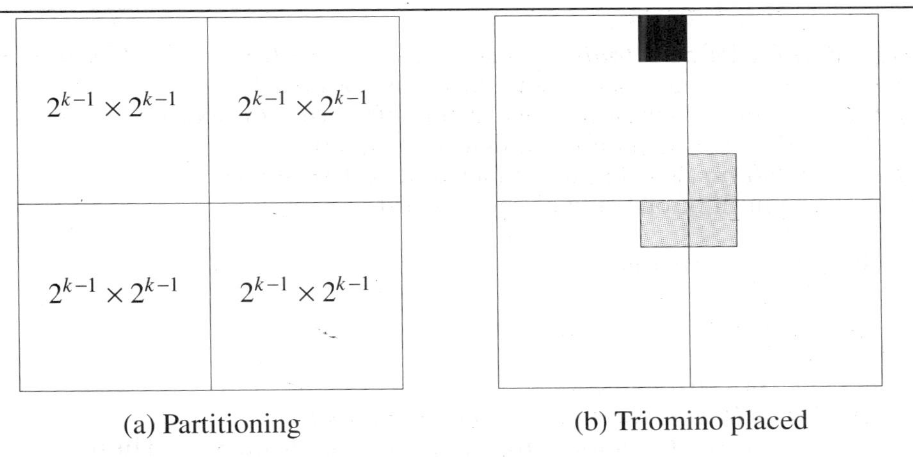

Figure 3.3 Partitioning a $2^k \times 2^k$ board

defect, and no triominoes are to be placed.

In terms of the terminology used in the divide-and-conquer control abstraction of Algorithm 3.1, `Small(P)` is true only when $k = 0$ (i.e., we are dealing with a 1×1 defective chessboard); dividing `P` into smaller instances is accomplished by dividing `P` into four instances of size $2^{k-1} \times 2^{k-1}$ and placing a triomino at the center of `P` so as to cover one square in each of the three smaller instances that does not have a defect; and combining the solutions obtained recursively for the four smaller instances requires no additional work.

Algorithm 3.2 gives the pseudocode for this divide-and-conquer strategy. This pseudocode employs two global variables *board* and *tile*. *board* is a two-dimensional array that represents the chessboard, and *board*[0][0] represents the top-left corner square of the chessboard; *tile*, an integer variable with initial value 1, gives the index of the next tile to use.

The initial invocation is `TileBoard(0,0,dRow,dCol,size)` where `size` $= 2^k$, and `dRow` and `dCol` give the row and column index of the defect. The number of tiles needed to tile the defective chessboard is $(\texttt{size}^2 - 1)/3$. Function `tileBoard` represents these tiles by the integers 1 through $(\texttt{size}^2 - 1)/3$ and labels each nondefective square of the chessboard with the number of the tile that covers it.

Let $t(k)$ denote the time taken by `TileBoard` to tile a $2^k \times 2^k$ defective chessboard. When $k = 0$, `size` equals 1 and a constant d amount of time is spent. When $k > 0$, four recursive calls are made. These calls take $4t(k-1)$ time. In addition to this time, time is spent testing the `if` conditionals and

```
Algorithm TileBoard(topRow, topColumn, defectRow, defectColumn, size)
// topRow is row number of top-left corner of board.
// topColumn is column number of top-left corner of board.
// defectRow is row number of defective square.
// defectColumn is column number of defective square.
// size is length of one side of chess board.
{
    if (size = 1) return ;
    tileToUse := tile++;
    quadrantSize := size/2;

    // tile top-left quadrant
    if (defectRow < topRow + quadrantSize&&
            defectColumn < topColumn + quadrantSize) then
        // defect is in this quadrant
        TileBoard(topRow, topColumn, defectRow, defectColumn,
            quadrantSize);
    else
    {
        // no defect in this quadrant
        // place a tile in bottom-right corner
        board[topRow + quadrantSize - 1][topColumn + quadrantSize - 1]
            := tileToUse;
        // tile the rest
        TileBoard(topRow, topColumn, topRow + quadrantSize - 1,
            topColumn + quadrantSize - 1, quadrantSize);
    }

    // code for remaining three quadrants is similar
}
```

Algorithm 3.2 Tiling a defective chessboard

tiling three nondefective squares. Let this time be denoted by the constant c. We obtain the following recurrence for t:

$$t(k) = \begin{cases} d & k = 0 \\ 4t(k-1) + c & k > 0 \end{cases} \tag{3.3}$$

We may solve this recurrence using the substitution method (see exercises) to obtain $t(k) = \Theta(4^k) = \Theta(\text{number of tiles needed})$. Since we must spend at least $\Theta(1)$ time placing each tile, we cannot obtain an asymptotically faster algorithm than divide and conquer.

EXERCISES

1. Consider an 8×8 defective chessboard with a defect in position (0,3). Show the tiling obtained by Algorithm 3.2.

2. Consider an 8×8 defective chessboard with a defect in position (2,2). Show the tiling obtained by Algorithm 3.2.

3. Write a complete program for the defective-chessboard problem. Include modules to welcome the user to the program; input the chessboard size and location of the defect; and output the tiled chessboard. The output is to be provided on a color monitor using colored tiles. No two tiles that share a common boundary should be colored the same. Since the chessboard is a planar figure, it is possible to color the tiles in this way using at most four colors. However, for this exercise, it is sufficient to devise a greedy coloring heuristic that attempts to use as few colors as possible.

4. Solve the recurrence of Equation 3.3 using the substitution method.

3.3 BINARY SEARCH

Let a_i, $1 \leq i \leq n$, be a list of elements that are sorted in nondecreasing order. Consider the problem of determining whether a given element x is present in the list. If x is present, we are to determine a value j such that $a_j = x$. If x is not in the list, then j is to be set to zero. Let $P = (n, a_i, \ldots, a_\ell, x)$ denote an arbitrary instance of this search problem (n is the number of elements in the list, $a_i, \ldots, a_\ell$ is the list of elements, and x is the element searched for).

Divide-and-conquer can be used to solve this problem. Let $\mathsf{Small}(P)$ be true if $n = 1$. In this case, $\mathsf{S}(P)$ will take the value i if $x = a_i$; otherwise it will take the value 0. Then $g(1) = \Theta(1)$. If P has more than one element, it can be divided (or reduced) into a new subproblem as follows. Pick an index q (in the range $[i, \ell]$) and compare x with a_q. There are three possibilities: (1) $x = a_q$: In this case the problem P is immediately solved. (2) $x < a_q$: In this case x has to be searched for only in the sublist $a_i, a_{i+1}, \ldots, a_{q-1}$. Therefore, P reduces to $(q - i, a_i, \ldots, a_{q-1}, x)$. (3) $x > a_q$: In this case the sublist to be searched is $a_{q+1}, \ldots, a_\ell$. P reduces to $(\ell - q, a_{q+1}, \ldots, a_\ell, x)$.

In this example, any given problem P gets divided (reduced) into one new subproblem. This division takes only $\Theta(1)$ time. After a comparison with a_q, the instance remaining to be solved (if any) can be solved by using this divide-and-conquer scheme again. If q is always chosen such that a_q is the middle element (that is, $q = \lfloor (n+1)/2 \rfloor$), then the resulting search algorithm is known as binary search. Note that the answer to the new subproblem is also the answer to the original problem P; there is no need for any combining. Algorithm 3.3 describes this binary search method, where BinSrch has four inputs $a[\,], i, l$, and x. It is initially invoked as BinSrch$(a, 1, n, x)$.

A nonrecursive version of BinSrch is given in Algorithm 3.4. BinSearch has three inputs a, n, and x. The **while** loop continues processing as long as there are more elements left to check. At the conclusion of the procedure 0 is returned if x is not present, or j is returned, such that $a[j] = x$.

```
Algorithm BinSrch(a, i, l, x)
// Given an array a[i : l] of elements in nondecreasing
// order, 1 ≤ i ≤ l, determine whether x is present, and
// if so, return j such that x = a[j]; else return 0.
{
    if (l = i) then // If Small(P)
    {
        if (x = a[i]) then return i;
        else return 0;
    }
    else
    { // Reduce P into a smaller subproblem.
        mid := ⌊(i + l)/2⌋;
        if (x = a[mid]) then return mid;
        else if (x < a[mid]) then
                 return BinSrch(a, i, mid − 1, x);
             else return BinSrch(a, mid + 1, l, x);
    }
}
```

Algorithm 3.3 Recursive binary search

Is BinSearch an algorithm? We must be sure that all of the operations such as comparisons between x and $a[mid]$ are well defined. The relational operators carry out the comparisons among elements of a correctly if these operators are appropriately defined. Does BinSearch terminate? We observe that *low* and *high* are integer variables such that each time through the loop either x is found or *low* is increased by at least one or *high* is decreased by at least one. Thus we have two sequences of integers approaching each other

```
Algorithm BinSearch(a, n, x)
// Given an array a[1 : n] of elements in nondecreasing
// order, n ≥ 0, determine whether x is present, and
// if so, return j such that x = a[j]; else return 0.
{
    low := 1; high := n;
    while (low ≤ high) do
    {
        mid := ⌊(low + high)/2⌋;
        if (x < a[mid]) then high := mid − 1;
        else if (x > a[mid]) then low := mid + 1;
             else return mid;
    }
    return 0;
}
```

Algorithm 3.4 Iterative binary search

and eventually *low* becomes greater than *high* and causes termination in a finite number of steps if x is not present.

Example 3.7 Let us select the 14 entries

$$-15, -6, 0, 7, 9, 23, 54, 82, 101, 112, 125, 131, 142, 151$$

place them in $a[1:14]$, and simulate the steps that BinSearch goes through as it searches for different values of x. Only the variables *low*, *high*, and *mid* need to be traced as we simulate the algorithm. We try the following values for x: 151, -14, and 9 for two successful searches and one unsuccessful search. Table 3.2 shows the traces of BinSearch on these three inputs. □

These examples may give us a little more confidence about Algorithm 3.4, but they by no means prove that it is correct. Proofs of algorithms are very useful because they establish the correctness of the algorithm for *all* possible inputs, whereas testing gives much less in the way of guarantees. Unfortunately, algorithm proving is a very difficult process and the complete proof of an algorithm can be many times longer than the algorithm itself. We content ourselves with an informal "proof" of BinSearch.

Theorem 3.1 Algorithm BinSearch(a, n, x) works correctly.

$x = 151$	*low*	*high*	*mid*
	1	14	7
	8	14	11
	12	14	13
	14	14	14
			found

$x = -14$	*low*	*high*	*mid*
	1	14	7
	1	6	3
	1	2	1
	2	2	2
	2	1	not found

$x = 9$	*low*	*high*	*mid*
	1	14	7
	1	6	3
	4	6	5
			found

Table 3.2 Three examples of binary search on 14 elements

Proof: We assume that all statements work as expected and that comparisons such as $x > a[mid]$ are appropriately carried out. Initially $low = 1$, $high = n$, $n \geq 0$, and $a[1] \leq a[2] \leq \cdots \leq a[n]$. If $n = 0$, the **while** loop is not entered and 0 is returned. Otherwise we observe that each time through the loop the possible elements to be checked for equality with x are $a[low]$, $a[low + 1]$, ..., $a[mid]$, ..., $a[high]$. If $x = a[mid]$, then the algorithm terminates successfully. Otherwise the range is narrowed by either increasing low to $mid + 1$ or decreasing $high$ to $mid - 1$. Clearly this narrowing of the range does not affect the outcome of the search. If low becomes greater than $high$, then x is not present and hence the loop is exited. □

Notice that to fully test binary search, we need not concern ourselves with the values of $a[1 : n]$. By varying x sufficiently, we can observe all possible computation sequences of BinSearch without devising different values for a. To test all successful searches, x must take on the n values in a. To test all unsuccessful searches, x need only take on $n + 1$ different values. Thus the complexity of testing BinSearch is $2n + 1$ for each n.

Now let's analyze the execution profile of BinSearch. The two relevant characteristics of this profile are the frequency counts and space required for the algorithm. For BinSearch, storage is required for the n elements of the array plus the variables $low, high, mid$, and x, or $n + 4$ locations. As for the time, there are three possibilities to consider: the best, average, and worst cases.

Suppose we begin by determining the time for BinSearch on the previous data set. We observe that the only operations in the algorithm are comparisons and some arithmetic and data movements. We concentrate on comparisons between x and the elements in $a[\ ]$, recognizing that the frequency count of all other operations is of the same order as that for these comparisons. Comparisons between x and elements of $a[\ ]$ are referred to as *element comparisons*. We assume that only one comparison is needed to determine which of the three possibilities of the **if** statement holds. The number of element comparisons needed to find each of the 14 elements is

a:	[1]	[2]	[3]	[4]	[5]	[6]	[7]	[8]	[9]	[10]	[11]	[12]	[13]	[14]
Elements:	−15	−6	0	7	9	23	54	82	101	112	125	131	142	151
Comparisons:	3	4	2	4	3	4	1	4	3	4	2	4	3	4

No element requires more than 4 comparisons to be found. The average is obtained by summing the comparisons needed to find all 14 items and dividing by 14; this yields 45/14, or approximately 3.21, comparisons per successful search on the average. There are 15 possible ways that an unsuccessful search may terminate depending on the value of x. If $x < a[1]$, the algorithm requires 3 element comparisons to determine that x is not present. For all the remaining possibilities, BinSearch requires 4 element comparisons. Thus the average number of element comparisons for an unsuccessful search is $(3 + 14 * 4)/15 = 59/15 \approx 3.93$.

The analysis just done applies to any sorted sequence containing 14 elements. But the result we would prefer is a formula for n elements. A good way to derive such a formula plus a better way to understand the algorithm is to consider the sequence of values for *mid* that are produced by BinSearch for all possible values of x. These values are nicely described using a binary decision tree in which the value in each node is the value of *mid*. For example, if $n = 14$, then Figure 3.4 contains a binary decision tree that traces the way in which these values are produced by BinSearch.

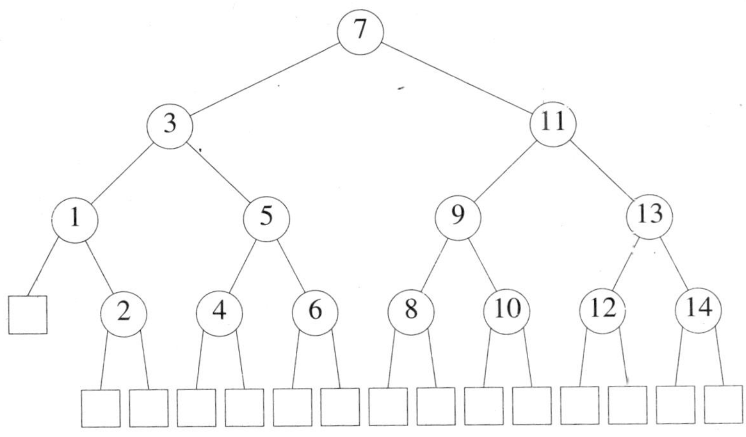

Figure 3.4 Binary decision tree for binary search, $n = 14$

The first comparison is x with $a[7]$. If $x < a[7]$, then the next comparison is with $a[3]$; similarly, if $x > a[7]$, then the next comparison is with $a[11]$. Each path through the tree represents a sequence of comparisons in the binary search method. If x is present, then the algorithm will end at one of the circular nodes that lists the index into the array where x was found. If x is not present, the algorithm will terminate at one of the square nodes. Circular nodes are called *internal* nodes, and square nodes are referred to as *external nodes.*

Theorem 3.2 If n is in the range $[2^{k-1}, 2^k)$, then BinSearch makes at most k element comparisons for a successful search and either $k-1$ or k comparisons for an unsuccessful search. (In other words the time for a successful search is $O(\log n)$ and for an unsuccessful search is $\Theta(\log n)$).

Proof: Consider the binary decision tree describing the action of BinSearch on n elements. All successful searches end at a circular node whereas all unsuccessful searches end at a square node. If $2^{k-1} \leq n < 2^k$, then all circular nodes are at levels $1, 2, \ldots, k$ whereas all square nodes are at levels k and $k+1$ (note that the root is at level 1). The number of element comparisons needed to terminate at a circular node on level i is i whereas the number of element comparisons needed to terminate at a square node at level i is only $i-1$. The theorem follows. □

Theorem 3.2 states the worst-case time for binary search. To determine the average behavior, we need to look more closely at the binary decision tree and equate its size to the number of element comparisons in the algorithm. The *distance* of a node from the root is one less than its level. The *internal path length* I is the sum of the distances of all internal nodes from the root. Analogously, the *external path length* E is the sum of the distances of all external nodes from the root. It is easy to show by induction that for any binary tree with n internal nodes, E and I are related by the formula

$$E = I + 2n$$

It turns out that there is a simple relationship between E, I, and the average number of comparisons in binary search. Let $A_s(n)$ be the average number of comparisons in a successful search, and $A_u(n)$ the average number of comparisons in an unsuccessful search. The number of comparisons needed to find an element represented by an internal node is one more than the distance of this node from the root. Hence,

$$A_s(n) = 1 + I/n$$

The number of comparisons on any path from the root to an external node is equal to the distance between the root and the external node. Since every binary tree with n internal nodes has $n+1$ external nodes, it follows that

$$A_u(n) = E/(n+1)$$

Using these three formulas for $E, A_s(n)$, and $A_u(n)$, we find that

$$A_s(n) = (1 + 1/n)A_u(n) - 1$$

From this formula we see that $A_s(n)$ and $A_u(n)$ are directly related. The minimum value of $A_s(n)$ (and hence $A_u(n)$) is achieved by an algorithm whose binary decision tree has minimum external and internal path length. This minimum is achieved by the binary tree all of whose external nodes are on adjacent levels, and this is precisely the tree that is produced by binary search. From Theorem 3.2 it follows that E is proportional to $n \log n$. Using this in the preceding formulas, we conclude that $A_s(n)$ and $A_u(n)$ are both proportional to log n. Thus we conclude that the average- and worst-case numbers of comparisons for binary search are the same to within a constant factor. The best-case analysis is easy. For a successful search only one element comparison is needed. For an unsuccessful search, Theorem 3.2 states that $\lfloor \log n \rfloor$ element comparisons are needed in the best case.

In conclusion we are now able to completely describe the computing time of binary search by giving formulas that describe the best, average, and worst cases:

successful searches			**unsuccessful searches**
$\Theta(1)$,	$\Theta(\log n)$,	$\Theta(\log n)$	$\Theta(\log n)$
best,	average,	worst	best, average, worst

Can we expect another searching algorithm to be significantly better than binary search in the worst case? This question is pursued rigorously in Chapter 10. But we can anticipate the answer here, which is no. The method for proving such an assertion is to view the binary decision tree as a general model for any searching algorithm that depends on comparisons of entire elements. Viewed in this way, we observe that the *longest* path to discover any element is minimized by binary search, and so any alternative algorithm is no better from this point of view.

Before we end this section, there is an interesting variation of binary search that makes only one comparison per iteration of the **while** loop. This variation appears as Algorithm 3.5. The correctness proof of this variation is left as an exercise.

BinSearch will sometimes make twice as many element comparisons as BinSearch1 (for example, when $x > a[n]$). However, for successful searches BinSearch1 may make $(\log n)/2$ more element comparisons than BinSearch (for example, when $x = a[mid]$). The analysis of BinSearch1 is left as an exercise. It should be easy to see that the best-, average-, and worst-case times for BinSearch1 are $\Theta(\log n)$ for both successful and unsuccessful searches.

```
Algorithm BinSearch1(a, n, x)
// Same specifications as BinSearch except n > 0
{
    low := 1; high := n + 1;
    // high is one more than possible.
    while (low < (high - 1)) do
    {
        mid := ⌊(low + high)/2⌋;
        if (x < a[mid]) then high := mid;
            // Only one comparison in the loop.
        else low := mid; // x ≥ a[mid]
    }
    if (x = a[low]) then return low; // x is present.
    else return 0; // x is not present.
}
```

Algorithm 3.5 Binary search using one comparison per cycle

Array sizes	5,000	10,000	15,000	20,000	25,000	30,000
successful searches						
BinSearch	51.30	67.95	67.72	73.85	76.77	73.40
BinSearch1	47.68	53.92	61.98	67.46	68.95	71.11
unsuccessful searches						
BinSearch	50.40	66.36	76.78	79.54	78.20	81.15
BinSearch1	41.93	52.65	63.33	66.86	69.22	72.26

Table 3.3 Computing times for two binary search algorithms; times are in microseconds

These two algorithms were run on a Sparc 10/30. The first two rows in Table 3.3 represent the average time for a successful search. The second set of two rows give the average times for all possible unsuccessful searches. For both successful and unsuccessful searches BinSearch1 did marginally better than BinSearch.

EXERCISES

1. Run the recursive and iterative versions of binary search and compare the times. For appropriate sizes of n, have each algorithm find every element in the set. Then try all $n+1$ possible unsuccessful searches.

2. Prove by induction the relationship $E = I + 2n$ for a binary tree with n internal nodes. The variables E and I are the external and internal path length, respectively.

3. In an infinite array, the first n cells contain integers in sorted order and the rest of the cells are filled with ∞. Present an algorithm that takes x as input and finds the position of x in the array in $\Theta(\log n)$ time. *You are not given the value of n.*

4. Devise a "binary" search algorithm that splits the set not into two sets of (almost) equal sizes but into two sets, one of which is twice the size of the other. How does this algorithm compare with binary search?

5. Devise a ternary search algorithm that first tests the element at position $n/3$ for equality with some value x, and then checks the element at $2n/3$ and either discovers x or reduces the set size to one-third the size of the original. Compare this with binary search.

6. (a) Prove that BinSearch1 works correctly.

   (b) Verify that the following algorithm segment functions correctly according to the specifications of binary search. Discuss its computing time.

```
low := 1; high := n;
repeat {
    mid := ⌊(low + high)/2⌋;
    if (x ≥ a[mid]) then low := mid;
    else high := mid;
} until ((low + 1) = high)
```

3.4 FINDING THE MAXIMUM AND MINIMUM

Let us consider another simple problem that can be solved by the divide-and-conquer technique. The problem is to find the maximum and minimum items in a set of n elements. Algorithm 3.6 is a straightforward algorithm to accomplish this.

In analyzing the time complexity of this algorithm, we once again concentrate on the number of element comparisons. The justification for this

```
Algorithm StraightMaxMin(a, n, max, min)
// Set max to the maximum and min to the minimum of a[1 : n].
{
    max := min := a[1];
    for i := 2 to n do
    {
        if (a[i] > max) then max := a[i];
        if (a[i] < min) then min := a[i];
    }
}
```

Algorithm 3.6 Straightforward maximum and minimum

is that the frequency count for other operations in this algorithm is of the same order as that for element comparisons. More importantly, when the elements in $a[1:n]$ are polynomials, vectors, very large numbers, or strings of characters, the cost of an element comparison is much higher than the cost of the other operations. Hence the time is determined mainly by the total cost of the element comparisons.

StraightMaxMin requires $2(n-1)$ element comparisons in the best, average, and worst cases. An immediate improvement is possible by realizing that the comparison $a[i] < min$ is necessary only when $a[i] > max$ is false. Hence we can replace the contents of the **for** loop by

```
if (a[i] > max) then max := a[i];
else if (a[i] < min) then min := a[i];
```

Now the best case occurs when the elements are in increasing order. The number of element comparisons is $n-1$. The worst case occurs when the elements are in decreasing order. In this case the number of element comparisons is $2(n-1)$.

A divide-and-conquer algorithm for this problem would proceed as follows: Let $P = (n, a[i], \ldots, a[j])$ denote an arbitrary instance of the problem. Here n is the number of elements in the list $a[i], \ldots, a[j]$ and we are interested in finding the maximum and minimum of this list. Let Small(P)/ be true when $n \leq 2$. In this case, the maximum and minimum are $a[i]$ if $n = 1$. If $n = 2$, the problem can be solved by making one comparison.

If the list has more than two elements, P has to be divided into smaller instances. For example, we might divide P into the two instances $P_1 =$

$(\lfloor n/2 \rfloor, a[1], \ldots, a[\lfloor n/2 \rfloor])$ and $P_2 = (n - \lfloor n/2 \rfloor, a[\lfloor n/2 \rfloor + 1], \ldots, a[n])$. After having divided P into two smaller subproblems, we can solve them by recursively invoking the same divide-and-conquer algorithm. How can we combine the solutions for P_1 and P_2 to obtain a solution for P? If MAX(P) and MIN(P) are the maximum and minimum of the elements in P, then MAX(P) is the larger of MAX(P_1) and MAX(P_2). Also, MIN(P) is the smaller of MIN(P_1) and MIN(P_2).

Algorithm 3.7 results from applying the strategy just described. MaxMin is a recursive algorithm that finds the maximum and minimum of the set of elements $\{a(i), a(i+1), \ldots, a(j)\}$. The situation of set sizes one ($i = j$) and two ($i = j - 1$) are handled separately. For sets containing more than two elements, the midpoint is determined (just as in binary search) and two new subproblems are generated. When the maxima and minima of these subproblems are determined, the two maxima are compared and the two minima are compared to achieve the solution for the entire set.

The procedure is initially invoked by the statement

$$\mathsf{MaxMin}(1, n, x, y)$$

Suppose we simulate MaxMin on the following nine elements:

a:	[1]	[2]	[3]	[4]	[5]	[6]	[7]	[8]	[9]
	22	13	−5	−8	15	60	17	31	47

A good way of keeping track of recursive calls is to build a tree by adding a node each time a new call is made. For this algorithm each node has four items of information: i, j, max, and min. On the array $a[\,]$ above, the tree of Figure 3.5 is produced.

Examining Figure 3.5, we see that the root node contains 1 and 9 as the values of i and j corresponding to the initial call to MaxMin. This execution produces two new calls to MaxMin, where i and j have the values 1, 5 and 6, 9, respectively, and thus split the set into two subsets of approximately the same size. From the tree we can immediately see that the maximum depth of recursion is four (including the first call). The circled numbers in the upper left corner of each node represent the orders in which max and min are assigned values.

Now what is the number of element comparisons needed for MaxMin? If $T(n)$ represents this number, then the resulting recurrence relation is

$$T(n) = \begin{cases} T(\lceil n/2 \rceil) + T(\lceil n/2 \rceil) + 2 & n > 2 \\ 1 & n = 2 \\ 0 & n = 1 \end{cases}$$

When n is a power of two, $n = 2^k$ for some positive integer k, then

```
Algorithm MaxMin(i, j, max, min)
// a[1 : n] is a global array. Parameters i and j are integers,
// 1 ≤ i ≤ j ≤ n. The effect is to set max and min to the
// largest and smallest values in a[i : j], respectively.
{
    if (i = j) then max := min := a[i]; // Small(P)
    else if (i = j - 1) then  // Another case of Small(P)
        {
            if (a[i] < a[j]) then
            {
                max := a[j]; min := a[i];
            }
            else
            {
                max := a[i]; min := a[j];
            }
        }
        else
        {   // If P is not small, divide P into subproblems.
            // Find where to split the set.
                mid := ⌊(i + j)/2⌋;
            // Solve the subproblems.
                MaxMin(i, mid, max, min);
                MaxMin(mid + 1, j, max1, min1);
            // Combine the solutions.
                if (max < max1) then max := max1;
                if (min > min1) then min := min1;
        }
}
```

Algorithm 3.7 Recursively finding the maximum and minimum

$$
\begin{aligned}
T(n) &= 2T(n/2) + 2 \\
&= 2(2T(n/4) + 2) + 2 \\
&= 4T(n/4) + 4 + 2 \\
&\vdots \\
&= 2^{k-1}T(2) + \textstyle\sum_{1 \le i \le k-1} 2^i \\
&= 2^{k-1} + 2^k - 2 = 3n/2 - 2
\end{aligned}
\qquad (3.4)
$$

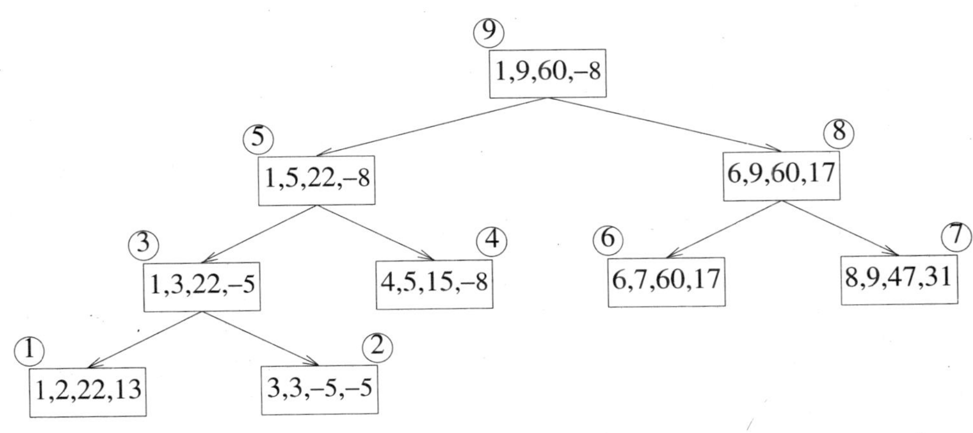

Figure 3.5 Trees of recursive calls of MaxMin

Note that $3n/2 - 2$ is the best-, average-, and worst-case number of comparisons when n is a power of two.

Compared with the $2n - 2$ comparisons for the straightforward method, this is a saving of 25% in comparisons. It can be shown that no algorithm based on comparisons uses less than $3n/2 - 2$ comparisons. So in this sense algorithm MaxMin is optimal (see Chapter 10 for more details). But does this imply that MaxMin is better in practice? Not necessarily. In terms of storage, MaxMin is worse than the straightforward algorithm because it requires stack space for i, j, $max, min, max1$, and $min1$. Given n elements, there will be $\lfloor \log_2 n \rfloor + 1$ levels of recursion and we need to save seven values for each recursive call (don't forget the return address is also needed).

Let us see what the count is when element comparisons have the same cost as comparisons between i and j. Let $C(n)$ be this number. First, we observe that lines 6 and 7 in Algorithm 3.7 can be replaced with

if $(i \geq j - 1)$ { // Small(P)

to achieve the same effect. Hence, a single comparison between i and $j - 1$ is adequate to implement the modified **if** statement. Assuming $n = 2^k$ for some positive integer k, we get

$$C(n) = \begin{cases} 2C(n/2) + 3 & n > 2 \\ 2 & n = 2 \end{cases}$$

Solving this equation, we obtain

$$\begin{aligned} C(n) &= 2C(n/2) + 3 \\ &= 4C(n/4) + 6 + 3 \\ &\vdots \\ &= 2^{k-1}C(2) + 3 \sum_0^{k-2} 2^i \\ &= 2^k + 3 * 2^{k-1} - 3 \\ &= 5n/2 - 3 \end{aligned} \tag{3.5}$$

The comparative figure for StraightMaxMin is $3(n-1)$ (including the comparison needed to implement the **for** loop). This is larger than $5n/2 - 3$. Despite this, MaxMin will be slower than StraightMaxMin because of the overhead of stacking i, j, max, and min for the recursion.

Algorithm 3.7 makes several points. If comparisons among the elements of $a[\,]$ are much more costly than comparisons of integer variables, then the divide-and-conquer technique has yielded a more efficient (actually an optimal) algorithm. On the other hand, if this assumption is not true, the technique yields a less-efficient algorithm. Thus the divide-and-conquer strategy is seen to be only a guide to better algorithm design which may not always succeed. Also we see that it is sometimes necessary to work out the constants associated with the computing time bound for an algorithm. Both MaxMin and StraightMaxMin are $\Theta(n)$, so the use of asymptotic notation is not enough of a discriminator in this situation. Finally, see the exercises for another way to find the maximum and minimum using only $3n/2 - 2$ comparisons.

Note: In the design of any divide-and-conquer algorithm, typically, it is a straightforward task to define Small(P) and S(P). So, from now on, we only discuss how to divide any given problem P and how to combine the solutions to subproblems.

EXERCISES

1. Translate algorithm MaxMin into a computationally equivalent procedure that uses no recursion.

2. Test your iterative version of MaxMin derived above against StraightMaxMin. Count all comparisons.

3. There is an iterative algorithm for finding the maximum and minimum which, though not a divide-and-conquer-based algorithm, is probably more efficient than MaxMin. It works by comparing consecutive pairs of elements and then comparing the larger one with the current maximum and the smaller one with the current minimum. Write out the algorithm completely and analyze the number of comparisons it requires.

4. In Algorithm 3.7, what happens if lines 7 to 17 are dropped? Does the resultant function still compute the maximum and minimum elements correctly?

3.5 MERGE SORT

As another example of divide and conquer, we investigate a sorting algorithm that has the nice property that in the worst case its complexity is $O(n \log n)$. This algorithm is called *merge sort*. We assume throughout that the elements are to be sorted in nondecreasing order. Given a sequence of n elements (also called keys) $a[1], \ldots, a[n]$, the general idea is to imagine them split into two sets $a[1], \ldots, a[\lfloor n/2 \rfloor]$ and $a[\lfloor n/2 \rfloor + 1], \ldots, a[n]$. Each set is individually sorted, and the resulting sorted sequences are merged to produce a single sorted sequence of n elements. Thus we have another ideal example of the divide-and-conquer strategy in which the splitting is into two equal-sized sets and the combining operation is the merging of two sorted sets into one.

MergeSort (Algorithm 3.8) describes this process very succinctly using recursion and a function Merge (Algorithm 3.9) which merges two sorted sets. Before executing MergeSort, the n elements should be placed in $a[1 : n]$. Then MergeSort(1,n) causes the keys to be rearranged into nondecreasing order in a.

Example 3.8 Consider the array of ten elements $a[1 : 10] = (310, 285, 179, 652, 351, 423, 861, 254, 450, 520)$. Algorithm MergeSort begins by splitting $a[\,]$ into two subarrays each of size five ($a[1 : 5]$ and $a[6 : 10]$). The elements in $a[1 : 5]$ are then split into two subarrays of size three ($a[1 : 3]$) and two ($a[4 : 5]$). Then the items in $a[1 : 3]$ are split into subarrays of size two ($a[1 : 2]$) and one ($a[3 : 3]$). The two values in $a[1 : 2]$ are split a final time into one-element subarrays, and now the merging begins. Note that no movement of data has yet taken place. A record of the subarrays is implicitly maintained by the recursive mechanism. Pictorially the file can now be viewed as

$$(310 \mid 285 \mid 179 \mid 652, 351 \mid 423, 861, 254, 450, 520)$$

where vertical bars indicate the boundaries of subarrays. Elements $a[1]$ and $a[2]$ are merged to yield

```
Algorithm MergeSort(low, high)
// a[low : high] is a global array to be sorted.
// Small(P) is true if there is only one element
// to sort. In this case the list is already sorted.
{
    if (low < high) then  // If there are more than one element
    {
        // Divide P into subproblems.
            // Find where to split the set.
                mid := ⌊(low + high)/2⌋;
        // Solve the subproblems.
            MergeSort(low, mid);
            MergeSort(mid + 1, high);
        // Combine the solutions.
            Merge(low, mid, high);
    }
}
```

Algorithm 3.8 Merge sort

$$(285, 310 \mid 179 \mid 652, 351 \mid 423, 861, 254, 450, 520)$$

Then $a[3]$ is merged with $a[1:2]$ and

$$(179, 285, 310 \mid 652, 351 \mid 423, 861, 254, 450, 520)$$

is produced. Next, elements $a[4]$ and $a[5]$ are merged:

$$(179, 285, 310 \mid 351, 652 \mid 423, 861, 254, 450, 520)$$

and then $a[1:3]$ and $a[4:5]$:

$$(179, 285, 310, 351, 652 \mid 423, 861, 254, 450, 520)$$

At this point the algorithm has returned to the first invocation of MergeSort and is about to process the second recursive call. Repeated recursive calls are invoked producing the following subarrays:

$$(179, 285, 310, 351, 652 \mid 423 \mid 861 \mid 254 \mid 450, 520)$$

Elements $a[6]$ and $a[7]$ are merged. Then $a[8]$ is merged with $a[6:7]$:

```
Algorithm Merge(low, mid, high)
// a[low : high] is a global array containing two sorted
// subsets in a[low : mid] and in a[mid + 1 : high]. The goal
// is to merge these two sets into a single set residing
// in a[low : high]. b[ ] is an auxiliary global array.
{
    h := low; i := low; j := mid + 1;
    while ((h ≤ mid) and (j ≤ high)) do
    {
        if (a[h] ≤ a[j]) then
        {
            b[i] := a[h];h := h + 1;
        }
        else
        {
            b[i] := a[j]; j := j + 1;
        }
        i := i + 1;
    }
    if (h > mid) then
        for k := j to high do
        {
            b[i] := a[k]; i := i + 1;
        }
    else
        for k := h to mid do
        {
            b[i] := a[k]; i := i + 1;
        }
    for k := low to high do a[k] := b[k];
}
```

Algorithm 3.9 Merging two sorted subarrays using auxiliary storage

$$(179,\ 285,\ 310,\ 351,\ 652 \mid 254,\ 423,\ 861 \mid 450,\ 520)$$

Next $a[9]$ and $a[10]$ are merged, and then $a[6:8]$ and $a[9:10]$:

$$(179,\ 285,\ 310,\ 351,\ 652 \mid 254,\ 423,\ 450,\ 520,\ 861)$$

At this point there are two sorted subarrays and the final merge produces the fully sorted result

(179, 254, 285, 310, 351, 423, 450, 520, 652, 861)

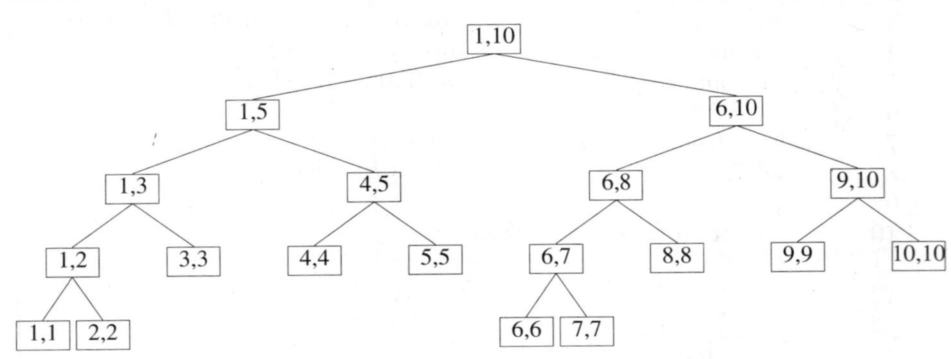

Figure 3.6 Tree of calls of MergeSort$(1, 10)$

Figure 3.6 is a tree that represents the sequence of recursive calls that are produced by MergeSort when it is applied to ten elements. The pair of values in each node are the values of the parameters *low* and *high*. Notice how the splitting continues until sets containing a single element are produced. Figure 3.7 is a tree representing the calls to procedure Merge by MergeSort. For example, the node containing 1, 2, and 3 represents the merging of $a[1:2]$ with $a[3]$. □

If the time for the merging operation is proportional to n, then the computing time for merge sort is described by the recurrence relation

$$T(n) = \begin{cases} a & n = 1, a \text{ a constant} \\ 2T(n/2) + cn & n > 1, c \text{ a constant} \end{cases}$$

When n is a power of 2, $n = 2^k$, we can solve this equation by successive substitutions:

$$\begin{aligned} T(n) &= 2(2T(n/4) + cn/2) + cn \\ &= 4T(n/4) + 2cn \\ &= 4(2T(n/8) + cn/4) + 2cn \\ &\vdots \\ &= 2^k T(1) + kcn \\ &= an + cn \log n \end{aligned}$$

It is easy to see that if $2^k < n \leq 2^{k+1}$, then $T(n) \leq T(2^{k+1})$. Therefore

$$T(n) = O(n \log n)$$

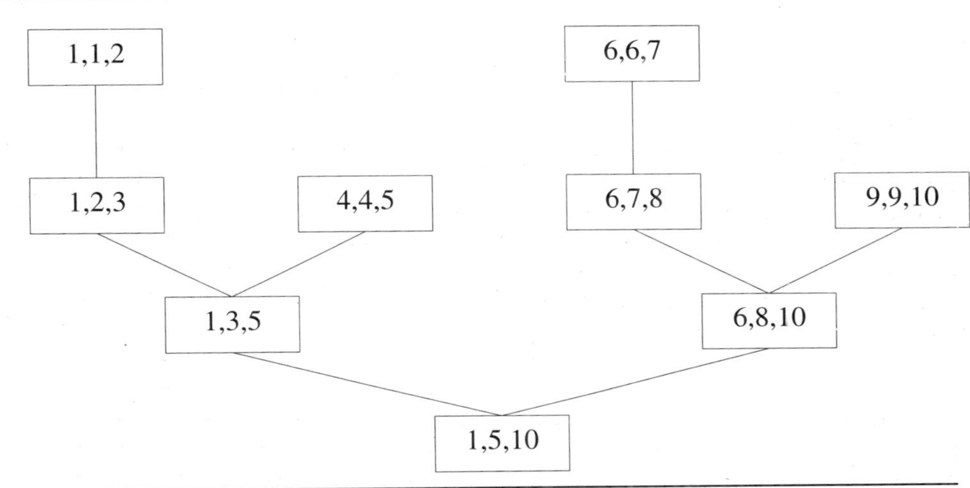

Figure 3.7 Tree of calls of Merge

Though Algorithm 3.8 nicely captures the divide-and-conquer nature of merge sort, there remain several inefficiencies that can and should be eliminated. We present these refinements in an attempt to produce a version of merge sort that is good enough to execute. Despite these improvements the algorithm's complexity remains $O(n \log n)$. We see in Chapter 10 that no sorting algorithm based on comparisons of entire keys can do better.

One complaint we might raise concerning merge sort is its use of $2n$ locations. The additional n locations were needed because we couldn't reasonably merge two sorted sets in place. But despite the use of this space the algorithm must still work hard and copy the result placed into $b[low : high]$ back into $a[low : high]$ on each call of Merge. An alternative to this copying is to associate a new field of information with each key. (The elements in $a[\ ]$ are called *keys*.) This field is used to link the keys and any associated information together in a sorted list (keys and related information are called *records*). Then the merging of the sorted lists proceeds by changing the link values, and no records need be moved at all. A field that contains only a link will generally be smaller than an entire record, so less space will be used.

Along with the original array $a[\ ]$, we define an auxiliary array $link[1 : n]$ that contains integers in the range $[0, n]$. These integers are interpreted as pointers to elements of $a[\ ]$. A list is a sequence of pointers ending with a zero. Below is one set of values for *link* that contains two lists: Q and R. The integer $Q = 2$ denotes the start of one list and $R = 5$ the start of the other.

link:	[1]	[2]	[3]	[4]	[5]	[6]	[7]	[8]
	6	4	7	1	3	0	8	0

The two lists are $Q = (2, 4, 1, 6)$ and $R = (5, 3, 7, 8)$. Interpreting these lists as describing sorted subsets of $a[1:8]$, we conclude that $a[2] \leq a[4] \leq a[1] \leq a[6]$ and $a[5] \leq a[3] \leq a[7] \leq a[8]$.

Another complaint we could raise about MergeSort is the stack space that is necessitated by the use of recursion. Since merge sort splits each set into two approximately equal-sized subsets, the maximum depth of the stack is proportional to $\log n$. The need for stack space seems indicated by the top-down manner in which this algorithm was devised. The need for stack space can be eliminated if we build an algorithm that works bottom-up; see the exercises for details.

As can be seen from function MergeSort and the previous example, even sets of size two will cause two recursive calls to be made. For small set sizes most of the time will be spent processing the recursion instead of sorting. This situation can be improved by not allowing the recursion to go to the lowest level. In terms of the divide-and-conquer control abstraction, we are suggesting that when Small is true for merge sort, more work should be done than simply returning with no action. We use a second sorting algorithm that works well on small-sized sets.

Insertion sort works exceedingly fast on arrays of less than, say, 16 elements, though for large n its computing time is $O(n^2)$. Its basic idea for sorting the items in $a[1:n]$ is as follows:

```
for j := 2 to n do {
    place a[j] in its correct position in the sorted set a[1 : j − 1];
}
```

Though all the elements in $a[1:j-1]$ may have to be moved to accommodate $a[j]$, for small values of n the algorithm works well. Algorithm 3.10 has the details.

The statements within the **while** loop can be executed zero up to a maximum of j times. Since j goes from 2 to n, the worst-case time of this procedure is bounded by

$$\sum_{2 \leq j \leq n} j = n(n+1)/2 - 1 = \Theta(n^2)$$

Its best-case computing time is $\Theta(n)$ under the assumption that the body of the **while** loop is never entered. This will be true when the data is already in sorted order.

```
Algorithm InsertionSort(a, n)
// Sort the array a[1 : n] into nondecreasing order, n ≥ 1.
{
    for j := 2 to n do
    {
        // a[1 : j − 1] is already sorted.
        item := a[j]; i := j − 1;
        while ((i ≥ 1) and (item < a[i])) do
        {
            a[i + 1] := a[i]; i := i − 1;
        }
        a[i + 1] := item;
    }
}
```

Algorithm 3.10 Insertion sort

```
Algorithm MergeSort1(low, high)
// The global array a[low : high] is sorted in nondecreasing order
// using the auxiliary array link[low : high]. The values in link
// represent a list of the indices low through high giving a[ ] in
// sorted order. A pointer to the beginning of the list is returned.
{
    if ((high − low) < 15) then
        return InsertionSort1(a, link, low, high);
    else
    {
        mid := ⌊(low + high)/2⌋;
        q := MergeSort1(low, mid);
        r := MergeSort1(mid + 1, high);
        return Merge1(q, r);
    }
}
```

Algorithm 3.11 Merge sort using links

We are now ready to present the revised version of merge sort with the inclusion of insertion sort and the links. Function MergeSort1 (Algorithm 3.11) is initially invoked by placing the keys of the records to be sorted in $a[1:n]$ and setting $link[1:n]$ to zero. Then one says MergeSort1$(1, n)$. A pointer to a list of indices that give the elements of $a[\ ]$ in sorted order is returned. Insertion sort is used whenever the number of items to be sorted is less than 16. The version of insertion sort as given by Algorithm 3.10 needs to be altered so that it sorts $a[low : high]$ into a linked list. Call the altered version InsertionSort1. The revised merging function, Merge1, is given in Algorithm 3.12.

```
Algorithm Merge1(q, r)
// q and r are pointers to lists contained in the global array
// link[0 : n]. link[0] is introduced only for convenience and need
// not be initialized. The lists pointed at by q and r are merged
// and a pointer to the beginning of the merged list is returned.
{
    i := q; j := r; k := 0;
    // The new list starts at link[0].
    while ((i ≠ 0) and (j ≠ 0)) do
    { // While both lists are nonempty do
        if (a[i] ≤ a[j]) then
        { // Find the smaller key.
            link[k] := i; k := i; i := link[i];
            // Add a new key to the list.
        }
        else
        {
            link[k] := j; k := j; j := link[j];
        }
    }
    if (i = 0) then link[k] := j;
    else link[k] := i;
    return link[0];
}
```

Algorithm 3.12 Merging linked lists of sorted elements

Example 3.9 As an aid to understanding this new version of merge sort, suppose we simulate the algorithm as it sorts the eight-element sequence (50,

10, 25, 30, 15, 70, 35, 55). We ignore the fact that less than 16 elements would normally be sorted using InsertionSort. The *link* array is initialized to zero. Table 3.4 shows how the *link* array changes after each call of MergeSort1 completes. On each row the value of p points to the list in *link* that was created by the last completion of Merge1. To the right are the subsets of sorted elements that are represented by these lists. For example, in the last row $p = 2$ which begins the list of links 2, 5, 3, 4, 7, 1, 8, and 6; this implies $a[2] \leq a[5] \leq a[3] \leq a[4] \leq a[7] \leq a[1] \leq a[8] \leq a[6]$. □

	(0)	(1)	(2)	(3)	(4)	(5)	(6)	(7)	(8)	
a:	-	50	10	25	30	15	70	35	55	
link:	0	0	0	0	0	0	0	0	0	
q r p										
1 2 2	2	0	1	0	0	0	0	0	0	(10, 50)
3 4 3	3	0	1	4	0	0	0	0	0	(10, 50), (25, 30)
2 3 2	2	0	3	4	1	0	0	0	0	(10, 25, 30, 50)
5 6 5	5	0	3	4	1	6	0	0	0	(10, 25, 30, 50), (15, 70)
7 8 7	7	0	3	4	1	6	0	8	0	(10, 25, 30, 50), (15, 70), (35, 55)
5 7 5	5	0	3	4	1	7	0	8	6	(10, 25, 30, 50) (15, 35, 55, 70)
2 5 2	2	8	5	4	7	3	0	1	6	(10, 15, 25, 30, 35, 50, 55, 70)

MergeSort1 applied to $a[1:8] = (50, 10, 25, 30, 15, 70, 35, 55)$

Table 3.4 Example of *link* array changes

EXERCISES

1. Why is it necessary to have the auxiliary array $b[low : high]$ in function Merge? Give an example that shows why in-place merging is inefficient.

2. The worst-case time of procedure MergeSort is $O(n \log n)$. What is its best-case time? Can we say that the time for MergeSort is $\Theta(n \log n)$?

3. A sorting method is said to be *stable* if at the end of the method, identical elements occur in the same order as in the original unsorted set. Is merge sort a stable sorting method?

4. Suppose $a[1 : m]$ and $b[1 : n]$ both contain sorted elements in non-decreasing order. Write an algorithm that merges these items into $c[1 : m + n]$. Your algorithm should be shorter than Algorithm 3.9 (Merge) since you can now place a large value in $a[m + 1]$ and $b[n + 1]$.

5. Given a file of n records that are partially sorted as $x_1 \leq x_2 \leq \cdots \leq x_m$ and $x_{m+1} \leq \cdots \leq x_n$, is it possible to sort the entire file in time $O(n)$ using only a small fixed amount of additional storage?

6. Another way to sort a file of n records is to scan the file, merge consecutive pairs of size one, then merge pairs of size two, and so on. Write an algorithm that carries out this process. Show how your algorithm works on the data set (100, 300, 150, 450, 250, 350, 200, 400, 500).

7. A version of insertion sort is used by Algorithm 3.11 to sort small subarrays. However, its parameters and intent are slightly different from the procedure InsertionSort of Algorithm 3.10. Write a version of insertion sort that will work as Algorithm 3.11 expects.

8. The sequences $X_1, X_2, \ldots, X_\ell$ are sorted sequences such that $\sum_{i=1}^{\ell} |X_i| = n$. Show how to merge these ℓ sequences in time $O(n \log \ell)$.

3.6 QUICK SORT

The divide-and-conquer approach can be used to arrive at an efficient sorting method different from merge sort. In merge sort, the file $a[1:n]$ was divided at its midpoint into subarrays which were independently sorted and later merged. In quick sort, the division into two subarrays is made so that the sorted subarrays do not need to be merged later. This is accomplished by rearranging the elements in $a[1:n]$ such that $a[i] \leq a[j]$ for all i between 1 and m and all j between $m+1$ and n for some m, $1 \leq m \leq n$. Thus, the elements in $a[1:m]$ and $a[m+1:n]$ can be independently sorted. No merge is needed. The rearrangement of the elements is accomplished by picking some element of $a[\ ]$, say $t = a[s]$, and then reordering the other elements so that all elements appearing before t in $a[1:n]$ are less than or equal to t and all elements appearing after t are greater than or equal to t. This rearranging is referred to as *partitioning*.

Function Partition of Algorithm 3.13 (due to C. A. R. Hoare) accomplishes an in-place partitioning of the elements of $a[m:p-1]$. It is assumed that $a[p] \geq a[m]$ and that $a[m]$ is the partitioning element. If $m = 1$ and $p-1 = n$, then $a[n+1]$ must be defined and must be greater than or equal to all elements in $a[1:n]$. The assumption that $a[m]$ is the partition element is merely for convenience; other choices for the partitioning element than the first item in the set are better in practice. The function Interchange(a, i, j) exchanges $a[i]$ with $a[j]$.

Example 3.10 As an example of how Partition works, consider the following array of nine elements. The function is initially invoked as Partition$(a, 1, 10)$. The ends of the horizontal line indicate those elements which were interchanged to produce the next row. The element $a[1] = 65$ is the partitioning

```
Algorithm Partition(a, m, p)
// Within a[m], a[m + 1], ..., a[p − 1] the elements are
// rearranged in such a manner that if initially t = a[m],
// then after completion a[q] = t for some q between m
// and p − 1, a[k] ≤ t for m ≤ k < q, and a[k] ≥ t
// for q < k < p. q is returned. Set a[p] = ∞.
{
    v := a[m]; i := m; j := p;
    repeat
    {
        repeat
            i := i + 1;
        until (a[i] ≥ v);

        repeat
            j := j − 1;
        until (a[j] ≤ v);

        if (i < j) then Interchange(a, i, j);

    } until (i ≥ j);

    a[m] := a[j]; a[j] := v; return j;
}
```

```
Algorithm Interchange(a, i, j)
// Exchange a[i] with a[j].
{
    p := a[i];
    a[i] := a[j]; a[j] := p;
}
```

Algorithm 3.13 Partition the array $a[m : p - 1]$ about $a[m]$

element and it is eventually (in the sixth row) determined to be the fifth smallest element of the set. Notice that the remaining elements are unsorted but partitioned about $a[5] = 65$. □

(1)	(2)	(3)	(4)	(5)	(6)	(7)	(8)	(9)	(10)	i	p
65	70	75	80	85	60	55	50	45	$+\infty$	2	9
65	45	75	80	85	60	55	50	70	$+\infty$	3	8
65	45	50	80	85	60	55	75	70	$+\infty$	4	7
65	45	50	55	85	60	80	75	70	$+\infty$	5	6
65	45	50	55	60	85	80	75	70	$+\infty$	6	5
60	45	50	55	65	85	80	75	70	$+\infty$		

Using Hoare's clever method of partitioning a set of elements about a chosen element, we can directly devise a divide-and-conquer method for completely sorting n elements. Following a call to the function Partition, two sets S_1 and S_2 are produced. All elements in S_1 are less than or equal to the elements in S_2. Hence S_1 and S_2 can be sorted independently. Each set is sorted by reusing the function Partition. Algorithm 3.14 describes the complete process.

```
Algorithm QuickSort(p, q)
// Sorts the elements a[p], ..., a[q] which reside in the global
// array a[1 : n] into ascending order; a[n + 1] is considered to
// be defined and must be ≥ all the elements in a[1 : n].
{
    if (p < q) then // If there are more than one element
    {
        // divide P into two subproblems.
            j := Partition(a, p, q + 1);
                // j is the position of the partitioning element.
        // Solve the subproblems.
            QuickSort(p, j - 1);
            QuickSort(j + 1, q);
        // There is no need for combining solutions.
    }
}
```

Algorithm 3.14 Sorting by partitioning

In analyzing QuickSort, we count only the number of element comparisons $C(n)$. It is easy to see that the frequency count of other operations is of the same order as $C(n)$. We make the following assumptions: the n elements to be sorted are distinct, and the input distribution is such that the partition element $v = a[m]$ in the call to Partition(a, m, p) has an equal probability of being the ith smallest element, $1 \le i \le p - m$, in $a[m : p - 1]$.

First, let us obtain the worst-case value $C_w(n)$ of $C(n)$. The number of element comparisons in each call of Partition is at most $p - m + 1$. Let r be the total number of elements in all the calls to Partition at any level of recursion. At level one only one call, Partition$(a, 1, n+1)$, is made and $r = n$; at level two at most two calls are made and $r = n - 1$; and so on. At each level of recursion, $O(r)$ element comparisons are made by Partition. At each level, r is at least one less than the r at the previous level as the partitioning elements of the previous level are eliminated. Hence $C_w(n)$ is the sum on r as r varies from 2 to n, or $O(n^2)$. Exercise 7 examines input data on which QuickSort uses $\Omega(n^2)$ comparisons.

The average value $C_A(n)$ of $C(n)$ is much less than $C_w(n)$. Under the assumptions made earlier, the partitioning element v has an equal probability of being the ith-smallest element, $1 \le i \le p - m$, in $a[m : p - 1]$. Hence the two subarrays remaining to be sorted are $a[m : j]$ and $a[j + 1 : p - 1]$ with probability $1/(p - m), m \le j < p$. From this we obtain the recurrence

$$C_A(n) = n + 1 + \frac{1}{n} \sum_{1 \le k \le n} [C_A(k - 1)) + C_A(n - k)] \tag{3.6}$$

The number of element comparisons required by Partition on its first call is $n + 1$. Note that $C_A(0) = C_A(1) = 0$. Multiplying both sides of (3.6) by n, we obtain

$$nC_A(n) = n(n + 1) + 2[C_A(0) + C_A(1) + \cdots + C_A(n - 1)] \tag{3.7}$$

Replacing n by $n - 1$ in (3.7) gives

$$(n - 1)C_A(n - 1) = n(n - 1) + 2[C_A(0) + \cdots + C_A(n - 2)]$$

Subtracting this from (3.7), we get

$$nC_A(n) - (n - 1)C_A(n - 1) \quad = \quad 2n + 2C_A(n - 1)$$

or

$$C_A(n)/(n + 1) \quad = \quad C_A(n - 1)/n + 2/(n + 1)$$

Repeatedly using this equation to substitute for $C_A(n - 1), C_A(n - 2), \ldots,$ we get

$$\begin{aligned}
\frac{C_A(n)}{n+1} &= \frac{C_A(n-2)}{n-1} + \frac{2}{n} + \frac{2}{n+1} \\
&= \frac{C_A(n-3)}{n-2} + \frac{2}{n-1} + \frac{2}{n} + \frac{2}{n+1} \\
&\vdots \\
&= \frac{C_A(1)}{2} + 2\sum_{3\le k\le n+1} \frac{1}{k} \\
&= 2\sum_{3\le k\le n+1} \frac{1}{k}
\end{aligned} \tag{3.8}$$

Since

$$\sum_{3\le k\le n+1} \frac{1}{k} \le \int_2^{n+1} \frac{1}{x}\, dx = \log_e(n+1) - \log_e 2$$

(3.8) yields

$$C_A(n) \le 2(n+1)[\log_e(n+2) - \log_e 2] = O(n \log n)$$

Even though the worst-case time is $O(n^2)$, the average time is only $O(n \log n)$. Let us now look at the stack space needed by the recursion. In the worst case the maximum depth of recursion may be $n-1$. This happens, for example, when the partition element on each call to Partition is the smallest value in $a[m : p-1]$. The amount of stack space needed can be reduced to $O(\log n)$ by using an iterative version of quick sort in which the smaller of the two subarrays $a[p : j-1]$ and $a[j+1 : q]$ is always sorted first. Also, the second recursive call can be replaced by some assignment statements and a jump to the beginning of the algorithm. With these changes, QuickSort takes the form of Algorithm 3.15.

We can now verify that the maximum stack space needed is $O(\log n)$. Let $S(n)$ be the maximum stack space needed. Then it follows that

$$S(n) \le \begin{cases} 2 + S(\lfloor (n-1)/2 \rfloor) & n > 1 \\ 0 & n \le 1 \end{cases}$$

which is less than $2 \log n$.

As remarked in Section 3.5, InsertionSort is exceedingly fast for n less than about 16. Hence InsertionSort can be used to speed up QuickSort2 whenever $q - p < 16$. The exercises explore various possibilities for selection of the partition element.

3.6.1 Performance Measurement

QuickSort and MergeSort were evaluated on a SUN workstation 10/30. In both cases the recursive versions were used. For QuickSort the Partition function was altered to carry out the median of three rule (i.e. the partitioning

```
Algorithm QuickSort2(p, q)
// Sorts the elements in a[p : q].
{
    // stack is a stack of size 2 log(n).
    repeat
    {
        while (p < q) do
        {
            j := Partition(a, p, q + 1);
            if ((j − p) < (q − j)) then
            {
                Add(j + 1); // Add j + 1 to stack.
                Add(q); q := j − 1; // Add q to stack
            }
            else
            {
                Add(p); // Add p to stack.
                Add(j − 1); p := j + 1; // Add j − 1 to stack
            }
        } // Sort the smaller subfile.
        if stack is empty then return;
        Delete(q); Delete(p); // Delete q and p from stack.
    } until (false);
}
```

Algorithm 3.15 Iterative version of QuickSort

element was the median of $a[m]$, $a[\lfloor (m+p-1)/2 \rfloor]$ and $a[p-1]$). Each data set consisted of random integers in the range (0, 1000). Tables 3.5 and 3.6 record the actual computing times in milliseconds. Table 3.5 displays the average computing times. For each n, 50 random data sets were used. Table 3.6 shows the worst-case computing times for the 50 data sets.

Scanning the tables, we immediately see that QuickSort is faster than MergeSort for all values. Even though both algorithms require $O(n \log n)$ time on the average, QuickSort usually performs well in practice. The exercises discuss other tests that would make useful comparisons.

n	1000	2000	3000	4000	5000
MergeSort	72.8	167.2	275.1	378.5	500.6
QuickSort	36.6	85.1	138.9	205.7	269.0
n	6000	7000	8000	9000	10000
MergeSort	607.6	723.4	811.5	949.2	1073.6
QuickSort	339.4	411.0	487.7	556.3	645.2

Table 3.5 Average computing times for two sorting algorithms on random inputs

n	1000	2000	3000	4000	5000
MergeSort	105.7	206.4	335.2	422.1	589.9
QuickSort	41.6	97.1	158.6	244.9	397.8
n	6000	7000	8000	9000	10000
MergeSort	691.3	794.8	889.5	1067.2	1167.6
QuickSort	383.8	497.3	569.9	616.2	738.1

Table 3.6 Worst-case computing times for two sorting algorithms on random inputs

3.6.2 Randomized Sorting Algorithms

Though algorithm QuickSort has an average time of $O(n \log n)$ on n elements, its worst-case time is $O(n^2)$. On the other hand it does not make use of any additional memory as does MergeSort. A possible input on which QuickSort displays worst-case behavior is one in which the elements are already in sorted order. In this case the partition will be such that there will be only one element in one part and the rest of the elements will fall in the other part. The performance of any divide-and-conquer algorithm will be good if the resultant subproblems are as evenly sized as possible. Can QuickSort be modified so that it performs well on every input? The answer is yes. Is the technique of using the median of the three elements $a[p]$, $a[\lfloor (q+p)/2 \rfloor]$, and

$a[q]$ the solution? Unfortunately it is possible to construct inputs for which even this method will take $\Omega(n^2)$ time, as is explored in the exercises.

The solution is the use of a randomizer. While sorting the array $a[p:q]$, instead of picking $a[m]$, pick a random element (from among $a[p], \ldots, a[q]$) as the partition element. The resultant randomized algorithm (RQuickSort) works on any input and runs in an expected $O(n \log n)$ time, where the expectation is over the space of all possible outcomes for the randomizer (rather than the space of all possible inputs). The code for RQuickSort is given in Algorithm 3.16. Note that this is a Las Vegas algorithm since it will always output the correct answer. Every call to the randomizer Random takes a certain amount of time. If there are only a very few elements to sort, the time taken by the randomizer may be comparable to the rest of the computation. For this reason, we invoke the randomizer only if $(q-p) > 5$. But 5 is not a magic number; in the machine employed, this seems to give the best results. In general this number should be determined empirically.

```
Algorithm RQuickSort(p, q)
// Sorts the elements a[p], ..., a[q] which reside in the global
// array a[1 : n] into ascending order. a[n + 1] is considered to
// be defined and must be ≥ all the elements in a[1 : n].
{
    if (p < q) then
    {
        if ((q − p) > 5) then
            Interchange(a, Random() mod (q − p + 1) + p, p);
        j := Partition(a, p, q + 1);
            // j is the position of the partitioning element.
        RQuickSort(p, j − 1);
        RQuickSort(j + 1, q);
    }
}
```

Algorithm 3.16 Randomized quick sort algorithm

The proof of the fact that RQuickSort has an expected $O(n \log n)$ time is the same as the proof of the average time of QuickSort. Let $A(n)$ be the average time of RQuickSort on *any input* of n elements. Then the number of elements in the second part will be $0, 1, 2, \ldots, n-2$, or $n-1$, all with an equal probability of $\frac{1}{n}$ (in the probability space of outcomes for the randomizer).

Thus the recurrence relation for $A(n)$ will be

$$A(n) = \frac{1}{n} \sum_{1\le k\le n} (A(k-1) + A(n-k)) + n + 1$$

This is the same as Equation 3.4, and hence its solution is $O(n \log n)$.

RQuickSort and QuickSort (without employing the median of three elements rule) were evaluated on a SUN 10/30 workstation. Table 3.7 displays the times for the two algorithms in milliseconds averaged over 100 runs. For each n, the input considered was the sequence of numbers $1, 2, \ldots, n$. As we can see from the table, RQuickSort performs much better than QuickSort. Note that the times shown in this table for QuickSort are much more than the corresponding entries in Tables 3.5 and 3.6. The reason is that QuickSort makes $\Theta(n^2)$ comparisons on inputs that are already in sorted order. However, on random inputs its average performance is very good.

n	1000	2000	3000	4000	5000
QuickSort	195.5	759.2	1728	3165	4829
RQuickSort	9.4	21.0	30.5	41.6	52.8

Table 3.7 Comparison of QuickSort and RQuickSort on the input $a[i] = i$, $1 \le i \le n$; times are in milliseconds.

The performance of RQuickSort can be improved in various ways. For example, we could pick a small number (say 11) of the elements in the array $a[\ ]$ randomly and use the median of these elements as the partition element. These randomly chosen elements form a random sample of the array elements. We would expect that the median of the sample would also be an approximate median of the array and hence result in an approximately even partitioning of the array.

An even more generalized version of the above random sampling technique is shown in Algorithm 3.17. Here we choose a random sample S of s elements (where s is a function of n) from the input sequence X and sort them using HeapSort, MergeSort, or any other sorting algorithm. Let $\ell_1, \ell_2, \ldots, \ell_s$ be the sorted sample. We partition X into $s+1$ parts using the sorted sample as partition keys. In particular $X_1 = \{x \in X | x \le \ell_1\}$; $X_i = \{x \in X | \ell_{i-1} < x \le \ell_i\}$, for $i = 2, 3, \ldots, s$; and $X_{s+1} = \{x \in X | x > \ell_s\}$. After having partitioned X into $s+1$ parts, we sort each part recursively. For a proper choice of s, the number of comparisons made in this algorithm is only $n \log n + \tilde{o}(n \log n)$. Note the constant 1 before $n \log n$. We see in Chapter 10 that this number is very close to the information theoretic lower bound for sorting.

```
Algorithm RSort(a, n)
// Sort the elements a[1 : n].
{
    Randomly sample s elements from a[ ];
    Sort this sample;
    Partition the input using the sorted sample as partition keys;
    Sort each part separately;
}
```

Algorithm 3.17 A randomized algorithm for sorting

Choose $s = \frac{n}{\log^2 n}$. The sample can be sorted in $O(s \log s) = O(\frac{n}{\log n})$ time and comparisons if we use HeapSort or MergeSort. If we store the sorted sample elements in an array, say $b[\,]$, for each $x \in X$, we can determine which part X_i it belongs to in $\leq \log n$ comparisons using binary search on $b[\,]$. Thus the partitioning process takes $n \log n + O(n)$ comparisons. In the exercises you are asked to show that with high probability the cardinality of each X_i is no more than $\tilde{O}(\frac{n}{s} \log n) = \tilde{O}(\log^3 n)$. Using HeapSort or MergeSort to sort each of the X_i's (without employing recursion on any of them), the total cost of sorting the X_i's is

$$\sum_{i=1}^{s+1} O(|X_i| \log |X_i|) = \max_{1 \leq i \leq s+1} \{\log |X_i|\} \sum_{i=1}^{s+1} O(|X_i|)$$

Since each $|X_i|$ is $\tilde{O}(\log^3 n)$, the cost of sorting the $s+1$ parts is $\tilde{O}(n \log \log n) = \tilde{o}(n \log n)$. In summary, the number of comparisons made in this randomized sorting algorithm is $n \log n + \tilde{o}(n \log n)$.

EXERCISES

1. Show how QuickSort sorts the following sequences of keys: 1, 1, 1, 1, 1, 1, 1 and 5, 5, 8, 3, 4, 3, 2.

2. QuickSort is not a stable sorting algorithm. However, if the key in $a[i]$ is changed to $a[i] * n + i - 1$, then the new keys are all distinct. After

sorting, which transformation will restore the keys to their original values?

3. In the function Partition, Algorithm 3.13, discuss the merits or demerits of altering the statement **if** $(i < j)$ to **if** $(i \leq j)$. Simulate both algorithms on the data set (5, 4, 3, 2, 5, 8, 9) to see the difference in how they work.

4. Function QuickSort uses the output of function Partition, which returns the position where the partition element is placed. If equal keys are present, then two elements can be properly placed instead of one. Show how you might change Partition so that QuickSort can take advantage of this situation.

5. In addition to Partition, there are many other ways to partition a set. Consider modifying Partition so that i is incremented while $a[i] \leq v$ instead of $a[i] < v$. Rewrite Partition making all of the necessary changes to it and then compare the new version with the original.

6. Compare the sorting methods MergeSort1 and QuickSort2 (Algorithm 3.11 and 3.15, respectively). Devise data sets that compare both the average- and worst-case times for these two algorithms.

7. (a) On which input data does the algorithm QuickSort exhibit its worst-case behavior?

   (b) Answer part (a) for the case in which the partitioning element is selected according to the median of three rule.

8. With MergeSort we included insertion sorting to eliminate the bookkeeping for small merges. How would you use this technique to improve QuickSort?

9. Take the iterative versions of MergeSort and QuickSort and compare them for the same-size data sets as used in Section 3.6.1.

10. Let S be a sample of s elements from X. If X is partitioned into $s+1$ parts as in Algorithm 3.17, show that the size of each part is $\widetilde{O}(\frac{n}{s}\log n)$.

3.7 SELECTION

The Partition algorithm of Section 3.6 can also be used to obtain an efficient solution for the selection problem. In this problem, we are given n elements $a[1:n]$ and are required to determine the kth-smallest element. If the partitioning element v is positioned at $a[j]$, then $j-1$ elements are less than or equal to $a[j]$ and $n-j$ elements are greater than or equal to $a[j]$. Hence if $k < j$, then the kth-smallest element is in $a[1:j-1]$; if $k = j$, then $a[j]$ is the kth-smallest element; and if $k > j$, then the kth-smallest element is the $(k-j)$th-smallest element in $a[j+1:n]$. The resulting algorithm is function Select1 (Algorithm 3.18). This function places the kth-smallest element into position $a[k]$ and partitions the remaining elements so that $a[i] \leq a[k]$, $1 \leq i < k$, and $a[i] \geq a[k]$, $k < i \leq n$.

```
Algorithm Select1(a, n, k)
// Selects the kth-smallest element in a[1 : n] and places it
// in the kth position of a[ ]. The remaining elements are
// rearranged such that a[m] ≤ a[k] for 1 ≤ m < k, and
// a[m] ≥ a[k] for k < m ≤ n.
{
    low := 1; up := n + 1;
    a[n + 1] := ∞; // a[n + 1] is set to infinity.
    repeat
    {
        // Each time the loop is entered,
        // 1 ≤ low ≤ k ≤ up ≤ n + 1.
        j := Partition(a, low, up);
             // j is such that a[j] is the jth-smallest value in a[ ].
        if (k = j) then return;
        else if (k < j) then up := j; // j is the new upper limit.
             else low := j + 1; // j + 1 is the new lower limit.
    } until (false);
}
```

Algorithm 3.18 Finding the kth-smallest element

Example 3.11 Let us simulate Select1 as it operates on the same array used to test Partition in Section 3.6. The array has the nine elements 65, 70, 75, 80, 85, 60, 55, 50, and 45, with $a[10] = \infty$. If $k = 5$, then the first call of Partition will be sufficient since 65 is placed into $a[5]$. Instead, assume that we are looking for the seventh-smallest element of a, that is, $k = 7$. The next invocation of Partition is Partition$(6, 10)$.

a:	(5)	(6)	(7)	(8)	(9)	(10)
	65	85	80	75	70	$+\infty$
	65	70	80	75	85	$+\infty$

This last call of Partition has uncovered the ninth-smallest element of a. The next invocation is Partition$(6, 9)$.

a:	(5)	(6)	(7)	(8)	(9)	(10)
	65	70	80	75	85	$+\infty$
	65	70	80	75	85	$+\infty$

This time, the sixth element has been found. Since $k \neq j$, another call to Partition is made, Partition$(7, 9)$.

a:	(5)	(6)	(7)	(8)	(9)	(10)
	65	70	80	75	85	$+\infty$
	65	70	75	80	85	$+\infty$

Now 80 is the partition value and is correctly placed at $a[8]$. However, Select1 has still not found the seventh-smallest element. It needs one more call to Partition, which is Partition$(7, 8)$. This performs only an interchange between $a[7]$ and $a[8]$ and returns, having found the correct value. □

In analyzing Select1, we make the same assumptions that were made for QuickSort:

1. The n elements are distinct.

2. The input distribution is such that the partition element can be the ith-smallest element of $a[m : p-1]$ with an equal probability for each i, $1 \leq i \leq p - m$.

Partition requires $O(p - m)$ time. On each successive call to Partition, either m increases by at least one or j decreases by at least one. Initially $m = 1$ and $j = n + 1$. Hence, at most n calls to Partition can be made. Thus, the worst-case complexity of Select1 is $O(n^2)$. The time is $\Omega(n^2)$, for example, when the input $a[1 : n]$ is such that the partitioning element on the ith call to Partition is the ith-smallest element and $k = n$. In this case, m increases by one following each call to Partition and j remains unchanged. Hence, n calls are made for a total cost of $O(\sum_1^n i) = O(n^2)$. The average computing time of Select1 is, however, only $O(n)$. Before proving this fact, we specify more precisely what we mean by the average time.

Let $T_A^k(n)$ be the average time to find the kth-smallest element in $a[1:n]$. This average is taken over all $n!$ different permutations of n distinct elements. Now define $T_A(n)$ and $R(n)$ as follows:

$$T_A(n) = \frac{1}{n} \sum_{1 \le k \le n} T_A^k(n)$$

and

$$R(n) = \max_k \; \{T_A^k(n)\}$$

$T_A(n)$ is the average computing time of Select1. It is easy to see that $T_A(n) \le R(n)$. We are now ready to show that $T_A(n) = O(n)$.

Theorem 3.3 The average computing time $T_A(n)$ of Select1 is $O(n)$.

Proof: On the first call to Partition, the partitioning element v is the ith-smallest element with probability $\frac{1}{n}, 1 \le i \le n$ (this follows from the assumption on the input distribution). The time required by Partition and the **if** statement in Select1 is $O(n)$. Hence, there is a constant $c, c > 0$, such that

$$\begin{aligned}
T_A^k(n) &\le cn + \frac{1}{n}[\sum_{1 \le i < k} T_A^{k-1}(n-i) + \sum_{k < i \le n} T_A^k(i-1)], \quad n \ge 2 \\
\text{So, } R(n) &\le cn + \frac{1}{n} \max_k \; \{\sum_{1 \le i < k} R(n-i) + \sum_{k < i \le n} R(i-1)\} \\
R(n) &\le cn + \frac{1}{n} \max_k \; \{\sum_{n-k+1}^{n-1} R(i) + \sum_{k}^{n-1} R(i)\}, \quad n \ge 2 \qquad (3.9)
\end{aligned}$$

We assume that c is chosen such that $R(1) \le c$ and show, by induction on n, that $R(n) \le 4cn$.
Induction Base: For $n = 2$, (3.9) gives

$$\begin{aligned}
R(n) &\le 2c + \frac{1}{2} \max \; \{R(1), R(1)\} \\
&\le 2.5c < 4cn
\end{aligned}$$

Induction Hypothesis: Assume $R(n) \le 4cn$ for all $n, 2 \le n < m$.
Induction Step: For $n = m$, (3.9) gives

$$R(m) \le cm + \frac{1}{m} \max_k \left\{ \sum_{m-k+1}^{m-1} R(i) + \sum_{k}^{m-1} R(i) \right\}$$

Since we know that $R(n)$ is a nondecreasing function of n, it follows that

$$\sum_{m-k+1}^{m-1} R(i) + \sum_{k}^{m-1} R(i)$$

is maximized if $k = \frac{m}{2}$ when m is even and $k = \frac{m+1}{2}$ when m is odd. Thus, if m is even, we obtain

$$\begin{aligned}
R(m) &\leq cm + \frac{2}{m}\sum_{m/2}^{m-1} R(i) \\
&\leq cm + \frac{8c}{m}\sum_{m/2}^{m-1} i \\
&< 4cm \\
\text{If } m \text{ is odd}, R(m) &\leq cm + \frac{2}{m}\sum_{(m+1)/2}^{m-1} R(i) \\
&\leq cm + \frac{8c}{m}\sum_{(m+1)/2}^{m-1} \\
&< 4cm
\end{aligned}$$

Since $T_A(n) \leq R(n)$, it follows that $T_A(n) \leq 4cn$, and so $T_A(n)$ is $O(n)$. □

The space needed by Select1 is $O(1)$.

Algorithm 3.16 is a randomized version of QuickSort in which the partition element is chosen from the array elements randomly with equal probability. The same technique can be applied to Select1 and the partition element can be chosen to be a random array element. The resulting randomized Las Vegas algorithm (call it RSelect) has an expected time of $O(n)$ (where the expectation is over the space of randomizer outputs) on *any input*. The proof of this expected time is the same as in Theorem 3.3.

3.7.1 A Worst-Case Optimal Algorithm

By choosing the partitioning element v more carefully, we can obtain a selection algorithm with worst-case complexity $O(n)$. To obtain such an algorithm, v must be chosen so that at least some fraction of the elements is smaller than v and at least some (other) fraction of elements is greater than v. Such a selection of v can be made using the median of medians (mm) rule. In this rule the n elements are divided into $\lfloor n/r \rfloor$ groups of r

elements each (for some $r, r > 1$). The remaining $n - r\lfloor n/r \rfloor$ elements are not used. The median m_i of each of these $\lfloor n/r \rfloor$ groups is found. Then, the median mm of the m_i's, $1 \le i \le \lfloor n/r \rfloor$, is found. The median mm is used as the partitioning element. Figure 3.8 illustrates the m_i's and mm when $n = 35$ and $r = 7$. The five groups of elements are $B_i, 1 \le i \le 5$. The seven elements in each group have been arranged into nondecreasing order down the column. The middle elements are the m_i's. The columns have been arranged in nondecreasing order of m_i. Hence, the m_i corresponding to column 3 is mm.

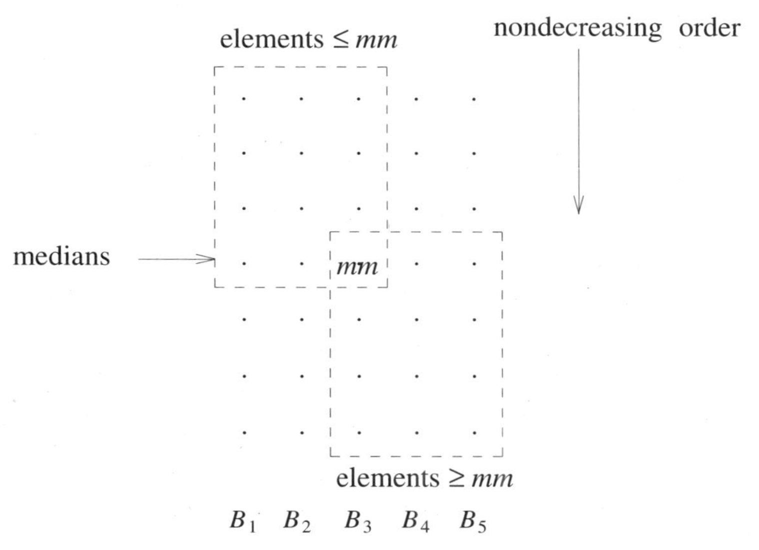

Figure 3.8 The median of medians when $r = 7$, $n = 35$

Since the median of r elements is the $\lceil r/2 \rceil$th-smallest element, it follows (see Figure 3.8) that at least $\lceil \lfloor n/r \rfloor /2 \rceil$ of the m_i's are less than or equal to mm and at least $\lfloor n/r \rfloor - \lceil \lfloor n/r \rfloor /2 \rceil + 1 \ge \lceil \lfloor n/r \rfloor /2 \rceil$ of the m_i's are greater than or equal to mm. Hence, at least $\lceil r/2 \rceil \lceil \lfloor n/r \rfloor /2 \rceil$ elements are less than or equal to (or greater than or equal to) mm. When $r = 5$, this quantity is at least $1.5 \lfloor n/5 \rfloor$. Thus, if we use the median of medians rule with $r = 5$ to select $v = mm$, we are assured that at least $1.5 \lfloor n/5 \rfloor$ elements will be greater than or equal to v. This in turn implies that at most $n - 1.5 \lfloor n/5 \rfloor \le .7n + 1.2$ elements are less than v. Also, at most $.7n + 1.2$ elements are greater than v. Thus, the median of medians rule satisfies our earlier requirement on v.

The algorithm to select the kth-smallest element uses the median of

```
1   Algorithm Select2(a, k, low, up)
2   // Find the k-th smallest in a[low : up].
3   {
4       n := up - low + 1;
5       if (n ≤ r) then sort a[low : up] and return the k-th element;
6       Divide a[low : up] into n/r subsets of size r each;
7       Ignore excess elements;
8       Let m[i], 1 ≤ i ≤ (n/r) be the set of medians of
9       the above n/r subsets.
10      v := Select2(m, ⌈(n/r)/2⌉, 1, n/r);
11      Partition a[low : up] using v as the partition element;
12      Assume that v is at position j;
13      if (k = (j - low + 1)) then return v;
14      elseif (k < (j - low + 1)) then
15              return Select2(a, k, low, j - 1);
16          else return Select2(a, k - (j - low + 1), j + 1, up);
17  }
```

Algorithm 3.19 Selection pseudocode using the median of medians rule

medians rule to determine a partitioning element. This element is computed by a recursive application of the selection algorithm. A high-level description of the new selection algorithm appears as Select2 (Algorithm 3.19). Select2 can now be analyzed for any given r. First, let us consider the case in which $r = 5$ and all elements in $a[\ ]$ are distinct. Let $T(n)$ be the worst-case time requirement of Select2 when invoked with $up - low + 1 = n$. Lines 4 to 9 and 11 to 12 require at most $O(n)$ time (note that since $r = 5$ is fixed, each $m[i]$ (lines 8 and 9) can be found in $O(1)$ time). The time for line 10 is $T(n/5)$. Let S and R, respectively, denote the elements $a[low : j-1]$ and $a[j+1 : up]$. We see that $|S|$ and $|R|$ are at most $.7n + 1.2$, which is no more than $3n/4$ for $n \geq 24$. So, the time for lines 13 to 16 is at most $T(3n/4)$ when $n \geq 24$. Hence, for $n \geq 24$, we obtain

$$T(n) \leq T(n/5) + T(3n/4) + cn \tag{3.10}$$

where c is chosen sufficiently large that

$$T(n) \leq cn \quad \text{for } n \leq 24$$

A proof by induction easily establishes that $T(n) \leq 20cn$ for $n \geq 1$. Algorithm Select2 with $r = 5$ is a linear time algorithm for the selection problem on distinct elements! The exercises examine other values of r that also yield this behavior. Let us now see what happens when the elements of $a[\,]$ are not all distinct. In this case, following a use of Partition (line 11), the size of S or R may be more than $.7n + 1.2$ as some elements equal to v may appear in both S and R. One way to handle the situation is to partition $a[\,]$ into three sets U, S, and R such that U contains all elements equal to v, S has all elements smaller than v, and R has the remainder. Lines 11 to 16 become:

```
Partition a[ ] into U, S, and R as above.
if (|S| ≥ k) then return Select2(a, k, low, low + |S| − 1);
else if ((|S| + |U|) ≥ k) then return v;
     else return Select2(a, k − |S| − |U|, low + |S| + |U|, up);
```

When this is done, the recurrence (3.10) is still valid as $|S|$ and $|R|$ are $\leq .7n + 1.2$. Hence, the new Select2 will be of linear complexity even when elements are not distinct.

Another way to handle the case of nondistinct elements is to use a different r. To see why a different r is needed, let us analyze Select2 with $r = 5$ and nondistinct elements. Consider the case when $.7n+1.2$ elements are less than v and the remaining elements are equal to v. An examination of Partition reveals that at most half the remaining elements may be in S. We can verify that this is the worst case. Hence, $|S| \leq .7n + 1.2 + (.3n - 1.2)/2 = .85n + .6$. Similarly, $|R| \leq .85n + .6$. Since, the total number of elements involved in the two recursive calls (in lines 10 and 15 or 16) is now $1.05n + .6 \geq n$, the complexity of Select2 is not $O(n)$. If we try $r = 9$, then at least $2.5\lfloor n/9 \rfloor$ elements will be less than or equal to v and at least this many will be greater than or equal to v. Hence, the size of S and R will be at most $n - 2.5\lfloor n/9 \rfloor + 1/2(2.5\lfloor n/9 \rfloor) = n - 1.25\lfloor n/9 \rfloor \leq 31/36n + 1.25 \leq 63n/72$ for $n \geq 90$. Hence, we obtain the recurrence

$$T(n) \leq \begin{cases} T(n/9) + T(63n/72) + c_1 n & n \geq 90 \\ c_1 n & n < 90 \end{cases}$$

where c_1 is a suitable constant. An inductive argument shows that $T(n) \leq 72c_1 n, n \geq 1$. Other suitable values of r are obtained in the exercises.

As far as the additional space needed by Select2 is concerned, we see that space is needed for the recursion stack. The recursive call from line 15 or 16 is easily eliminated as this call is the last statement executed in Select2. Hence, stack space is needed only for the recursion from line 10. The maximum depth of recursion is $\log n$. The recursion stack should be capable of handling this depth. In addition to this stack space, space is needed only for some simple variables.

3.7.2 Implementation of Select2

Before attempting to write a pseudocode algorithm implementing Select2, we need to decide how the median of a set of size r is to be found and where we are going to store the $\lfloor n/r \rfloor$ medians of lines 8 and 9. Since, we expect to be using a small r (say $r = 5$ or 9), an efficient way to find the median of r elements is to sort them using InsertionSort(a, i, j). This algorithm is a modification of Algorithm 3.10 to sort $a[i : j]$. The median is now the middle element in $a[i : j]$. A convenient place to store these medians is at the front of the array. Thus, if we are finding the kth-smallest element in $a[low : up]$, then the elements can be rearranged so that the medians are $a[low]$, $a[low+1]$, $a[low+2]$, and so on. This makes it easy to implement line 10 as a selection on consecutive elements of $a[\,]$. Function Select2 (Algorithm 3.20) results from the above discussion and the replacement of the recursive calls of lines 15 and 16 by equivalent code to restart the algorithm.

An alternative to moving the medians to the front of the array $a[low : up]$ (as in the Interchange statement within the **for** loop) is to delete this statement and use the fact that the medians are located at $low + (i-1)r + \lceil r/2 \rceil - 1, 1 \leq i \leq \lfloor n/r \rfloor$. Hence, Select2, Partition, and InsertionSort need to be rewritten to work on arrays for which the interelement distance is $b, b \geq 1$. At the start of the algorithm, all elements are a distance of one apart, i.e., $a[1], a[2], \ldots, a[n]$. On the first call of Select2 we wish to use only elements that are r apart starting with $a[\lceil r/2 \rceil]$. At the next level of recursion, the elements will be r^2 apart and so on. This idea is developed further in the exercises. We refer to arrays with an interelement distance of b as *b-spaced arrays.*

Algorithms Select1 (Algorithm 3.18) and Select2 (Algorithm 3.20) were implemented and run on a SUN Sparcstation 10/30. Table 3.8 summarizes the experimental results obtained. Times shown are in milliseconds. These algorithms were tested on random integers in the range [0, 1000] and the average execution times (over 500 input sets) were computed. Select1 outperforms Select2 on random inputs. But if the input is already sorted (or nearly sorted), Select2 can be expected to be superior to Select1.

EXERCISES

1. Rewrite Select2, Partition, and InsertionSort using b-spaced arrays.

2. (a) Assume that Select2 is to be used only when all elements in a are distinct. Which of the following values of r guarantee $O(n)$ worst-case performance: $r = 3, 5, 7, 9,$ and 11? Prove your answers.

   (b) Do you expect the computing time of Select2 to increase or decrease if a larger (but still eligible) choice for r is made? Why?

```
Algorithm Select2(a, k, low, up)
// Return i such that a[i] is the kth-smallest element in
// a[low : up]; r is a global variable as described in the text.
{
    repeat
    {
        n := up - low + 1; // Number of elements
        if (n ≤ r) then
        {
            InsertionSort(a, low, up);
            return low + k - 1;
        }
        for i := 1 to ⌊n/r⌋ do
        {
            InsertionSort(a, low + (i - 1) * r, low + i * r - 1);
            // Collect medians in the front part of a[low : up].
            Interchange(a, low + i - 1,
                low + (i - 1) * r + ⌈r/2⌉ - 1);
        }
        j := Select2(a, ⌈⌊n/r⌋/2⌉, low, low + ⌊n/r⌋ - 1); // mm
        Interchange(a, low, j);
        j := Partition(a, low, up + 1);
        if (k = (j - low + 1)) then return j;
        else if (k < (j - low + 1)) then up := j - 1;
            else
            {
                k := k - (j - low + 1); low := j + 1;
            }
    } until (false);
}
```

Algorithm 3.20 Algorithm Select2

3. Do Exercise 2 for the case in which a is not restricted to distinct elements. Let $r = 7, 9, 11, 13,$ and 15 in part (a).

4. Section 3.7 describes an alternative way to handle the situation when $a[\,]$ is not restricted to distinct elements. Using the partitioning element v, $a[\,]$ is divided into three subsets. Write algorithms corresponding to Select1 and Select2 using this idea. Using your new version of Select2 show that the worst-case computing time is $O(n)$ even when

n	1,000	2,000	3,000	4,000	5,000
Select1	7.42	23.50	30.44	39.24	52.36
Select2	49.54	104.02	174.54	233.56	288.64
n	6,000	7,000	8,000	9,000	10,000
Select1	70.88	83.14	95.00	101.32	111.92
Select2	341.34	414.06	476.98	532.30	604.40

Table 3.8 Comparison of Select1 and Select2 on random inputs

$r = 5$.

5. Determine optimal r values for worst-case and average performances of function Select2.

6. [Shamos] Let $x[1 : n]$ and $y[1 : n]$ contain two sets of integers, each sorted in nondecreasing order. Write an algorithm that finds the median of the $2n$ combined elements. What is the time complexity of your algorithm? (*Hint*: Use binary search.)

7. Let S be a (not necessarily sorted) sequence of n keys. A key k in S is said to be an *approximate median* of S if $|\{k' \in S : k' < k\}| \geq \frac{n}{4}$ and $|\{k' \in S : k' > k\}| \geq \frac{n}{4}$. Devise an $O(n)$ time algorithm to find all the approximate medians of S.

8. Input are a sequence S of n distinct keys, not necessarily in sorted order, and two integers m_1 and m_2 $(1 \leq m_1, m_2 \leq n)$. For any x in S, we define the *rank* of x in S to be $|\{k \in S : k \leq x\}|$. Show how to output all the keys of S whose ranks fall in the interval $[m_1, m_2]$ in $O(n)$ time.

9. The kth *quantiles* of an n-element set are the $k - 1$ elements from the set that divide the sorted set into k equal-sized sets. Give an $O(n \log k)$ time algorithm to list the kth quantiles of a set.

10. Input is a (not necessarily sorted) sequence $S = k_1, k_2, \ldots, k_n$ of n arbitrary numbers. Consider the collection C of n^2 numbers of the form $\min\{k_i, k_j\}$, for $1 \leq i, j \leq n$. Present an $O(n)$-time and $O(n)$-space algorithm to find the median of C.

11. Given two vectors $X = (x_1, \ldots, x_n)$ and $Y = (y_1, \ldots, y_n)$, $X < Y$ if there exists an $i, 1 \leq i \leq n$, such that $x_j = y_j$ for $1 \leq j < i$ and $x_i < y_i$. Given m vectors each of size n, write an algorithm that determines the minimum vector. Analyze the time complexity of your algorithm.

12. Present an $O(1)$ time Monte Carlo algorithm to find the median of an array of n numbers. The answer output should be correct with probability $\geq \frac{1}{n}$.

13. Input is an array $a[\ ]$ of n numbers. Present an $O(\log n)$ time Monte Carlo algorithm to output any member of $a[\ ]$ that is greater than or equal to the median. The answer should be correct with high probability. Provide a probability analysis.

14. Given a set X of n numbers, how will you find an element of X whose rank in X is at most $\frac{n}{f(n)}$, using a Monte Carlo algorithm? Your algorithm should run in time $O(f(n) \log n)$. Prove that the output will be correct with high probability.

15. In addition to Select1 and Select2, we can think of at least two more selection algorithms. The first of these is very straightforward and appears as Algorithm 3.21 (Algorithm Select3). The time complexity of Select3 is

$$O(n \min \{k, n - k + 1\})$$

Hence, it is very fast for values of k close to 1 or close to n. In the worst case, its complexity is $O(n^2)$. Its average complexity is also $O(n^2)$.

Another selection algorithm proceeds by first sorting the n elements into nondecreasing order and then picking out the kth element. A complete sort can be avoided by using a minheap. Now, only k elements need to be removed from the heap. The time to set up the heap is $O(n)$. An additional $O(k \log n)$ time is needed to make k deletions. The total complexity is $O(n + k \log n)$. This basic algorithm can be improved further by using a maxheap when $k > n/2$ and deleting $n - k + 1$ elements. The complexity is now $O(n + \log n \min \{k, n - k + 1\})$. Call the resulting algorithm Select4. Now that we have four plausible selection algorithms, we would like to know which is best. On the basis of the asymptotic analyses of the four selection algorithms, we can make the following qualitative statements about our expectations on the relative performance of the four algorithms.

- Because of the overhead involved in Select1, Select2, and Select4 and the relative simplicity of Select3, Select3 will be fastest both

```
Algorithm Select3(a, n, k)
// Rearrange a[ ] such that a[k] is the k-th smallest.
{
    if (k ≤ ⌊n/2⌋) then
        for i := 1 to k do
        {
            q := i; min := a[i];
            for j := i + 1 to n do
                if (a[j] < min) then
                {
                    q := j; min := a[j];
                }
            Interchange(a, q, i);
        }
    else
        for i := n to k step −1 do
        {
            q := i; max := a[i];
            for j := (i − 1) to 1 step −1 do
                if (a[j] > max) then
                {
                    q := j; max := a[j];
                }
            Interchange(a, q, i);
        }
}
```

Algorithm 3.21 Straightforward selection algorithm

on the average and in the worst case for small values of n. It will also be fastest for large n and very small or very large k, for example, $k = 1, 2, n$, or $n - 1$.

- For larger values of n, Select1 will have the best behavior on the average.
- As far as worst-case behavior is concerned, Select2 will out-perform the others when n is suitably large. However, there will probably be a range of n for which Select4 will be faster than both Select2 and Select3. We expect this because of the relatively large overhead in Select2 (i.e., the constant term in $O(n)$ is relatively large).

- As a result of the above assertions, it is desirable to obtain composite algorithms for good average and worst-case performances. The composite algorithm for good worst-case performance will have the form of function Select2 but will include the following after the first **if** statement.

  if $(n < c_1)$ **then return** Select3$(a,\ m,\ p,\ k)$;
  else if $(n < c_2)$ **then return** Select4$(a,\ m,\ p,\ k)$;

Since the overheads in Select1 and Select4 are about the same, the constants associated with the average computing times will be about the same. Hence, Select1 may always be better than Select4 or there may be a small c_3 such that Select4 is better than Select1 for $n < c_3$. In any case, we expect there is a $c_4, c_4 > 0$, such that Select3 is faster than Select1 on the average for $n < c_4$.

To verify the preceding statements and determine c_1, c_2, c_3, and c_4, it is necessary to program the four algorithms in some programming language and run the four corresponding programs on a computer. Once the programs have been written, test data are needed to determine average and worst-case computing times. So, let us now say something about the data needed to obtain computing times from which $c_i, 1 \leq i \leq 4$, can be determined. Since we would also like information regarding the average and worst-case computing times of the resulting composite algorithms, we need test data for this too. We limit our testing to the case of distinct elements.

To obtain worst-case computing times for Select1, we change the algorithm slightly. This change will not affect its worst-case computing time but will enable us to use a rather simple data set to determine this time for various values of n. We dispense with the random selection rule for Partition and instead use $a[m]$ as the partitioning element. It is easy to see that the worst-case time is obtained with $a[i] = i$, $1 \leq i \leq n$, and $k = n$. As far as the average time for any given n is concerned, it is not easy to arrive at one data set and a k that exhibits this time. On the other hand, trying out all $n!$ different input permutations and $k = 1, 2, \ldots, n$ for each of these is not a feasible way to find the average. An approximation to the average computing time can be obtained by trying out a few (say ten) random permutations of the numbers $1, 2, \ldots, n$ and for each of these using a few (say five) random values of k. The average of the times obtained can be used as an approximation to the average computing time. Of course, using more permutations and more k values results in a better approximation. However, the number of permutations and k values we can use is limited by the amount of computational resources (in terms of time) we have available.

For Select2, the average time can be obtained in the same way as for Select1. For the worst-case time we can either try to figure out an input permutation for which the number of elements less than the median of medians is always as large as possible and then use $k = 1$. A simpler approach is to find just an approximation to the worst-case time. This can be done by taking the max of the computing times for all the tests used to obtain the average computing time. Since the computing times for Select2 vary with r, it is first necessary to determine an r that yields optimum behavior. Note that the r's for optimum average and worst-case behaviors may be different.

We can verify that the worst-case data for Select3 are $a[i] = n + 1 - i$, for $1 \leq i \leq n$, and $k = \frac{n}{2}$. The computing time for Select3 is relatively insensitive to the input permutation. This permutation affects only the number of times the second **if** statement of Algorithm 3.21 is executed. On the average, this will be done about half the time. This can be achieved by using $a[i] = n + 1 - i$, $1 \leq i \leq n/2$, and $a[i] = n + 1$, $n/2 < i \leq n$. The k value needed to obtain the average computing time is readily seen to be $n/4$.

(a) What test data would you use to determine worst-case and average times for Select4?

(b) Use the ideas above to obtain a table of worst-case and average times for Select1, Select2, Select3, and Select4.

16. Program Select1 and Select3. Determine when algorithm Select1 becomes better than Select3 on the average and also when Select2 better than Select3 for worst-case performance.

17. [Project] Program the algorithms of Exercise 4 as well as Select3 and Select4. Carry out a complete test along the lines discussed in Exercise 15. Write a detailed report together with graphs explaining the data sets, test strategies, and determination of $c_1, \ldots, c_4$. Write the final composite algorithms and give tables of computing times for these algorithms.

3.8 STRASSEN'S MATRIX MULTIPLICATION

Let A and B be two $n \times n$ matrices. The product matrix $C = AB$ is also an $n \times n$ matrix whose i, jth element is formed by taking the elements in the ith row of A and the jth column of B and multiplying them to get

$$C(i,j) = \sum_{1 \leq k \leq n} A(i,k)B(k,j) \tag{3.11}$$

for all i and j between 1 and n. To compute $C(i, j)$ using this formula, we need n multiplications. As the matrix C has n^2 elements, the time for the resulting matrix multiplication algorithm, which we refer to as the conventional method is $\Theta(n^3)$.

The divide-and-conquer strategy suggests another way to compute the product of two $n \times n$ matrices. For simplicity we assume that n is a power of 2, that is, that there exists a nonnegative integer k such that $n = 2^k$. In case n is not a power of two, then enough rows and columns of zeros can be added to both A and B so that the resulting dimensions are a power of two (see the exercises for more on this subject). Imagine that A and B are each partitioned into four square submatrices, each submatrix having dimensions $\frac{n}{2} \times \frac{n}{2}$. Then the product AB can be computed by using the above formula for the product of 2×2 matrices: if AB is

$$\begin{bmatrix} A_{11} & A_{12} \\ A_{21} & A_{22} \end{bmatrix} \begin{bmatrix} B_{11} & B_{12} \\ B_{21} & B_{22} \end{bmatrix} = \begin{bmatrix} C_{11} & C_{12} \\ C_{21} & C_{22} \end{bmatrix} \tag{3.12}$$

then

$$\begin{aligned} C_{11} &= A_{11}B_{11} + A_{12}B_{21} \\ C_{12} &= A_{11}B_{12} + A_{12}B_{22} \\ C_{21} &= A_{21}B_{11} + A_{22}B_{21} \\ C_{22} &= A_{21}B_{12} + A_{22}B_{22} \end{aligned} \tag{3.13}$$

If $n = 2$, then formulas (3.12) and (3.13) are computed using a multiplication operation for the elements of A and B. These elements are typically floating point numbers. For $n > 2$, the elements of C can be computed using *matrix* multiplication and addition operations applied to matrices of size $n/2 \times n/2$. Since n is a power of 2, these matrix products can be recursively computed by the same algorithm we are using for the $n \times n$ case. This algorithm will continue applying itself to smaller-sized submatrices until n becomes suitably small ($n = 2$) so that the product is computed directly.

To compute AB using (3.13), we need to perform eight multiplications of $n/2 \times n/2$ matrices and four additions of $n/2 \times n/2$ matrices. Since two $n/2 \times n/2$ matrices can be added in time cn^2 for some constant c, the overall computing time $T(n)$ of the resulting divide-and-conquer algorithm is given by the recurrence

$$T(n) = \begin{cases} b & n \leq 2 \\ 8T(n/2) + cn^2 & n > 2 \end{cases}$$

where b and c are constants.

This recurrence can be solved in the same way as earlier recurrences to obtain $T(n) = O(n^3)$. Hence no improvement over the conventional method has been made. Since matrix multiplications are more expensive than matrix additions ($O(n^3)$ versus $O(n^2)$), we can attempt to reformulate the equations for C_{ij} so as to have fewer multiplications and possibly more additions. Volker Strassen has discovered a way to compute the C_{ij}'s of (3.13) using only 7 multiplications and 18 additions or subtractions. His method involves first computing the seven $n/2 \times n/2$ matrices P, Q, R, S, T, U, and V as in (3.14). Then the C_{ij}'s are computed using the formulas in (3.15). As can be seen, P, Q, R, S, T, U, and V can be computed using 7 matrix multiplications and 10 matrix additions or subtractions. The C_{ij}'s require an additional 8 additions or subtractions.

$$\begin{aligned}
P &= (A_{11} + A_{22})(B_{11} + B_{22}) \\
Q &= (A_{21} + A_{22})B_{11} \\
R &= A_{11}(B_{12} - B_{22}) \\
S &= A_{22}(B_{21} - B_{11}) \\
T &= (A_{11} + A_{12})B_{22} \\
U &= (A_{21} - A_{11})(B_{11} + B_{12}) \\
V &= (A_{12} - A_{22})(B_{21} + B_{22})
\end{aligned} \tag{3.14}$$

$$\begin{aligned}
C_{11} &= P + S - T + V \\
C_{12} &= R + T \\
C_{21} &= Q + S \\
C_{22} &= P + R - Q + U
\end{aligned} \tag{3.15}$$

The resulting recurrence relation for $T(n)$ is

$$T(n) = \begin{cases} b & n \leq 2 \\ 7T(n/2) + an^2 & n > 2 \end{cases} \tag{3.16}$$

where a and b are constants. Working with this formula, we get

$$\begin{aligned}
T(n) &= an^2[1 + 7/4 + (7/4)^2 + \cdots + (7/4)^{k-1}] + 7^k T(1) \\
&\leq cn^2(7/4)^{\log_2 n} + 7^{\log_2 n}, \ c \text{ a constant} \\
&= cn^{\log_2 4 + \log_2 7 - \log_2 4} + n^{\log_2 7} \\
&= O(n^{\log_2 7}) \approx O(n^{2.81})
\end{aligned}$$

EXERCISES

1. Verify by hand that Equations 3.14 and 3.15 yield the correct values for C_{11}, C_{12}, C_{21}, and C_{22}.

2. Write an algorithm that multiplies two $n \times n$ matrices using $O(n^3)$ operations. Determine the precise number of multiplications, additions, and array element accesses.

3. If k is a nonnegative constant, then prove that the recurrence

$$T(n) = \begin{cases} k & n = 1 \\ 3T(n/2) + kn & n > 1 \end{cases} \tag{3.17}$$

has the following solution (for n a power of 2):

$$T(n) = 3kn^{\log_2 3} - 2kn \tag{3.18}$$

4. Give a proof that shows that the recurrence relation $T(n) = mT(n/2)$ $+an^2$ is satisfied by $T(n) = O(n^{\log m})$ for $m > 4$.

5. Program Strassen's matrix multiplication algorithm as well as the classical $\Theta(n^3)$ one. Determine when Strassen's method outperforms the classical one.

6. Let u and v be two n-bit numbers, where for simplicity n is a power of 2. The traditional multiplication algorithm requires $O(n^2)$ operations. A divide-and-conquer based algorithm splits the numbers into two equal parts and computes the product as

$$\begin{aligned} uv &= (a2^{n/2} + b)(c2^{n/2} + d) \\ uv &= ac2^n + (ad + bc)2^{n/2} + bd \end{aligned} \tag{3.19}$$

The multiplications ac, ad, bc, and bd are done using this algorithm recursively.

   (a) Determine the computing time of the above algorithm.

   (b) What is the computing time if $ad + bc$ is computed as $(a + b)$ $(c + d) - ac - bd$?

7. It is possible to consider the product of matrices of size $n \times n$, where n is a power of 3. Using divide-and-conquer, the problem can be reduced to the multiplication of 3×3 matrices. The conventional method requires 27 multiplications. How many times must one be able to multiply 3×3 matrices so that the resultant computing time is smaller than $O(n^{2.81})$? How many times for 4×4 matrices?

8. For any even integer n, it is always possible to find integers m and k such that $n = m2^k$. To find the product of two $n \times n$ matrices, Strassen suggests partitioning them into $2^k \times 2^k$ submatrices each having $m \times m$ elements. Then start with Strassen's method to multiply the original matrices and uses the standard method for multiplying the required pairs of submatrices. Write a multiplication procedure for general n.

9. [Winograd] Let $n = 2p, V = (v_1, \ldots, v_n)$, and $W = (w_1, \ldots, w_n)$. Then we can compute the vector product VW by the formula

$$\sum_{1 \le i \le p} (v_{2i-1} + w_{2i})(v_{2i} + w_{2i-1}) - \sum_{1 \le i \le p} v_{2i-1}v_{2i} - \sum_{1 \le i \le p} w_{2i-1}w_{2i} \tag{3.20}$$

which requires $3n/2$ multiplications. Show how to use this formula for the multiplication of two $n \times n$ matrices employing only $n^3/2 + n^2$ multiplications rather than the usual n^3 multiplications.

10. [Fiduccia] The product of two 2×2 matrices can be rewritten as the matrix-vector product

$$\begin{bmatrix} a_{11} & a_{12} & 0 & 0 \\ a_{21} & a_{22} & 0 & 0 \\ 0 & 0 & a_{11} & a_{12} \\ 0 & 0 & a_{21} & a_{22} \end{bmatrix} \begin{bmatrix} b_{11} \\ b_{21} \\ b_{12} \\ b_{22} \end{bmatrix}$$

The above matrices can be further decomposed into a product of three matrices:

$$\begin{bmatrix} 1 & 1 & 0 & 0 & 0 & 0 & 0 \\ 0 & -1 & 1 & 0 & 0 & 1 & 1 \\ -1 & 0 & 0 & -1 & 1 & 0 & -1 \\ 0 & 0 & -1 & 1 & 0 & 0 & 0 \end{bmatrix}$$

$$\begin{bmatrix} a-b & 0 & 0 & 0 & 0 & 0 & 0 \\ 0 & b & 0 & 0 & 0 & 0 & 0 \\ 0 & 0 & c-d & 0 & 0 & 0 & 0 \\ 0 & 0 & 0 & c & 0 & 0 & 0 \\ 0 & 0 & 0 & 0 & a+c & 0 & 0 \\ 0 & 0 & 0 & 0 & 0 & b+d & 0 \\ 0 & 0 & 0 & 0 & 0 & 0 & b+c \end{bmatrix} \begin{bmatrix} 1 & 0 & 0 & 0 \\ 1 & 1 & 0 & 0 \\ 0 & 0 & 0 & 1 \\ 0 & 0 & 1 & 1 \\ 1 & 0 & 1 & 0 \\ 0 & 1 & 0 & 1 \\ 1 & 0 & 0 & -1 \end{bmatrix}$$

Resolve the seven-multiplication scheme implied by this matrix decomposition. Is it different from the one given in Section 3.8?

3.9 CONVEX HULL

A convex hull is an important structure in geometry that can be used in the construction of many other geometric structures. The convex hull of a set S of points in the plane is defined to be the smallest convex polygon containing all the points of S. [A polygon is defined to be convex if for any two points p_1 and p_2 inside the polygon, the directed line segment from p_1 to p_2 (denoted $\langle p_1, p_2 \rangle$) is fully contained in the polygon.] See Figure 3.9 for an example.

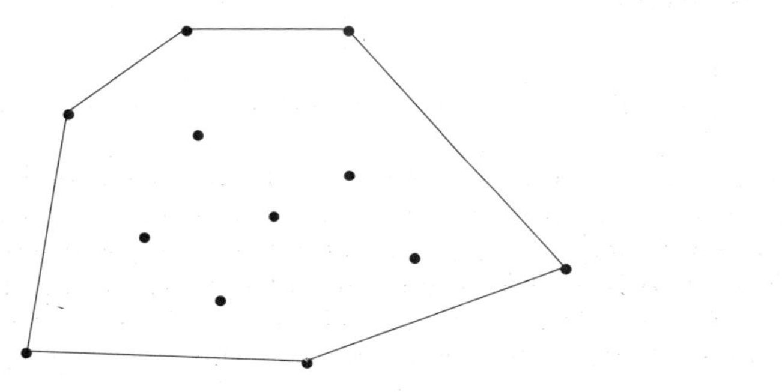

Figure 3.9 Convex hull: an example

The vertices of the convex hull of a set S of points form a (not necessarily proper) subset of S. There are two variants of the convex hull problem: (1) obtain the vertices of the convex hull (these vertices are also called *extreme points*), and (2) obtain the vertices of the convex hull in some order (clockwise, for example).

Here is a simple algorithm for obtaining the extreme points of a given set S of points in the plane. To check whether a particular point $p \in S$ is extreme, look at each possible triplet of points and see whether p lies in the triangle formed by these three points. If p lies in any such triangle, it is not extreme; otherwise it is. Testing whether p lies in a given triangle can be done in $\Theta(1)$ time (using the methods described in Section 3.8.1). Since there are $\Theta(n^3)$ possible triangles, it takes $\Theta(n^3)$ time to determine whether a given point is an extreme point or not. Since there are n points, this algorithm runs in a total of $\Theta(n^4)$ time.

Using divide-and-conquer, we can solve both versions of the convex hull problem in $\Theta(n \log n)$ time. We develop three algorithms for the convex hull in this section. The first has a worst-case time of $\Theta(n^2)$ whereas its average time is $\Theta(n \log n)$. This algorithm has a divide-and-conquer structure similar to that of QuickSort. The second has a worst-case time complexity of $\Theta(n \log n)$ and is not based on divide-and-conquer. The third algorithm is based on divide-and-conquer and has a time complexity of $\Theta(n \log n)$ in the worst case. Before giving further details, we digress to discuss some primitive geometric methods that are used in the convex hull algorithms.

3.9.1 Some Geometric Primitives

Let A be an $n \times n$ matrix whose elements are $\{a_{ij}\}$, $1 \leq i,\ j \leq n$. The ijth *minor* of A, denoted as A_{ij}, is defined to be the submatrix of A obtained by deleting the ith row and jth column. The *determinant* of A, denoted $\det(A)$, is given by

$$\det(A) = \begin{cases} a_{11} & n = 1 \\ a_{11}\det(A_{11}) - a_{12}\det(A_{12}) + \cdots + (-1)^{n-1}\det(A_{1n}) & n > 1 \end{cases}$$

Consider the directed line segment $\langle p_1, p_2 \rangle$ from some point $p_1 = (x_1, y_1)$ to some other point $p_2 = (x_2, y_2)$. If $q = (x_3, y_3)$ is another point, we say q *is to the left (right) of* $\langle p_1, p_2 \rangle$ if the angle $p_1 p_2 q$ is a left (right) turn. [An angle is said to be a left (right) turn if it is less than or equal to (greater than or equal to) 180°.] We can check whether q is to the left (right) of $\langle p_1, p_2 \rangle$ by evaluating the determinant of the following matrix:

$$\begin{bmatrix} x_1 & x_2 & x_3 \\ y_1 & y_2 & y_3 \\ 1 & 1 & 1 \end{bmatrix}$$

If this determinant is positive (negative), then q is to the left (right) of $\langle p_1, p_2 \rangle$. If this determinant is zero, the three points are colinear. This test can be used, for example, to check whether a given point p is within a triangle formed by three points, say p_1, p_2, and p_3 (in clockwise order). The point p is within the triangle iff p is to the right of the line segments $\langle p_1, p_2 \rangle$, $\langle p_2, p_3 \rangle$, and $\langle p_3, p_1 \rangle$.

Also, for any three points $(x_1, y_1), (x_2, y_2)$, and (x_3, y_3), the *signed area* formed by the corresponding triangle is given by one-half of the above determinant.

Let $p_1, p_2, \ldots, p_n$ be the vertices of the convex polygon Q in clockwise order. Let p be any other point. It is desired to check whether p lies in the interior of Q or outside. Consider a horizontal line h that extends from $-\infty$ to ∞ and goes through p. There are two possibilities: (1) h does not intersect any of the edges of Q, (2) h intersects some of the edges of Q. If case (1) is true, then, p is outside Q. In case (2), there can be at most two points of intersection. If h intersects Q at a single point, it is counted as two. Count the number of points of intersections that are to the left of p. If this number is even, then p is external to Q; otherwise it is internal to Q. This method of checking whether p is interior to Q takes $\Theta(n)$ time.

3.9.2 The QuickHull Algorithm

An algorithm that is similar to QuickSort can be devised to compute the convex hull of a set X of n points in the plane. This algorithm, called QuickHull, first identifies the two points (call them p_1 and p_2) of X with the smallest and largest x-coordinate values. Assume now that there are no ties. Later we see how to handle ties. Both p_1 and p_2 are extreme points and part of the convex hull. The set X is divided into X_1 and X_2 so that X_1 has all the points to the left of the line segment $\langle p_1, p_2 \rangle$ and X_2 has all the points to the right of $\langle p_1, p_2 \rangle$. Both X_1 and X_2 include the two points p_1 and p_2. Then, the convex hulls of X_1 and X_2 (called the *upper hull* and *lower hull*, respectively) are computed using a divide-and-conquer algorithm called Hull. The union of these two convex hulls is the overall convex hull.

If there is more than one point with the smallest x-coordinate, let p_1' and p_1'' be the points from among these with the least and largest y-coordinates, respectively. Similarly define p_2' and p_2'' for the points with the largest x-coordinate values. Now X_1 will be all the points to the left of $\langle p_1'', p_2'' \rangle$ (including p_1'' and p_2'') and X_2 will be all the points to the right of $\langle p_1', p_2' \rangle$ (including p_1' and p_2'). In the rest of the discussion we assume for simplicity that there are no ties for p_1 and p_2. Appropriate modifications are needed in the event of ties.

We now describe how Hull computes the convex hull of X_1. We determine a point of X_1 that belongs to the convex hull of X_1 and use it to partition the problem into two independent subproblems. Such a point is obtained by computing the area formed by p_1, p, and p_2 for each p in X_1 and picking the one with the largest (absolute) area. Ties are broken by picking the point p for which the angle pp_1p_2 is maximum. Let p_3 be that point.

Now X_1 is divided into two parts; the first part contains all the points of X_1 that are to the left of $\langle p_1, p_3 \rangle$ (including p_1 and p_3), and the second part contains all the points of X_1 that are to the left of $\langle p_3, p_2 \rangle$ (including p_3 and p_2) (see Figure 3.10). There cannot be any point of X_1 that is to the left of both $\langle p_1, p_3 \rangle$ and $\langle p_3, p_2 \rangle$. Also, all the other points are interior points and can be dropped from future consideration. The convex hull of each part is computed recursively, and the two convex hulls are merged easily by placing one next to the other in the right order.

If there are m points in X_1, we can identify the point of division p_3 in time $O(m)$. Partitioning X_1 into two parts can also be done in $O(m)$ time. Merging the two convex hulls can be done in time $O(1)$. Let $T(m)$ stand for the run time of Hull on a list of m points and let m_1 and m_2 denote the sizes of the two resultant parts. Note that $m_1 + m_2 \leq m$. The recurrence relation for $T(m)$ is $T(m) = T(m_1) + T(m_2) + O(m)$, which is similar to the one for the run time of QuickSort. The worst-case run time is thus $O(m^2)$ on an input of m points. This happens when the partitioning at each level of recursion is highly uneven.

If the partitioning is nearly even at each level of recursion, then the run

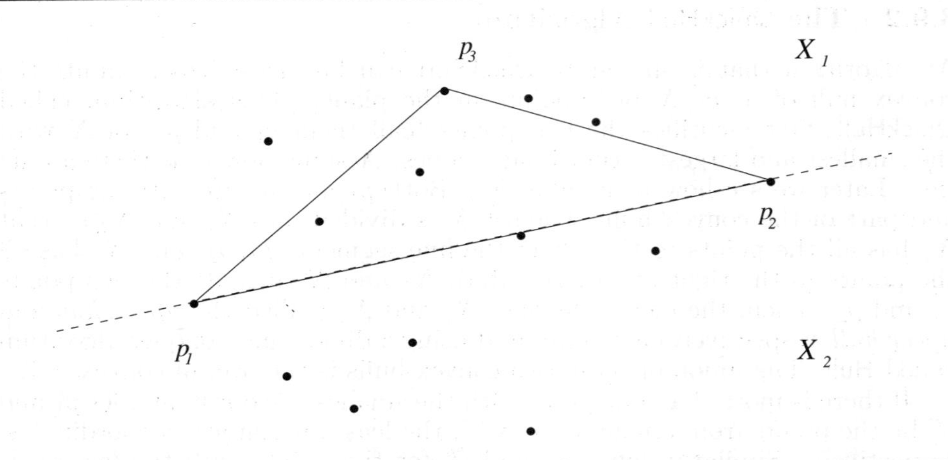

Figure 3.10 Identifying a point on the convex hull of X_1

time will equal $O(m \log m)$ as in the case of QuickSort. Thus the average run time of QuickHull is $O(n \log n)$, on an input of size n, under appropriate assumptions on the input distribution.

3.9.3 Graham's Scan

If S is a set of points in the plane, Graham's scan algorithm identifies the point p from S with the lowest y-coordinate value (ties are broken by picking the leftmost among these). It then sorts the points of S according to the angle subtended by the points and p with the positive x-axis. Figure 3.11 gives an example. After having sorted the points, if we scan through the sorted list starting at p, every three successive points will form a left turn if all of these points lie on the hull. On the other hand if there are three successive points, say p_1, p_2, and p_3, that form a right turn, then we can immediately eliminate p_2 since it cannot lie on the convex hull. Notice that it will be an internal point because it lies within the triangle formed by p, p_1, and p_3.

We can eliminate all the interior points using the above procedure. Starting from p, we consider three successive points p_1, p_2, and p_3 at a time. To begin with, $p_1 = p$. If these points form a left turn, we move to the next point in the list (that is, we set $p_1 = p_2$, and so on). If these three points form a right turn, then p_2 is deleted since it is an interior point. We move one point behind in the list by setting p_1 equal to its predecessor. This process of scanning ends when we reach the point p again.

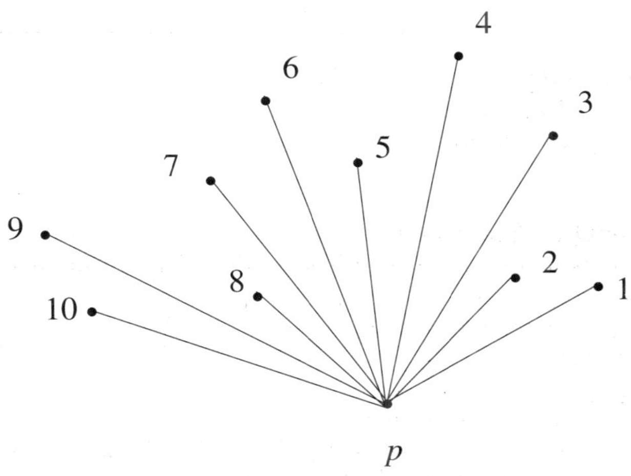

Figure 3.11 Graham's scan algorithm sorts the points first

Example 3.12 In Figure 3.11, the first three points looked at are $p, 1$, and 2. Since these form a left turn, we move to $1, 2$, and 3. These form a right turn and hence 2 is deleted. Next, the three points $p, 1$, and 3 are considered. These form a left turn and hence the pointer is moved to point 1. The points $1, 3$, and 4 also form a left turn, and the scan proceeds to $3, 4$, and 5 and then to $4, 5$, and 6. Now point 5 gets deleted. The triplets $3, 4, 6$; $4, 6, 7$; and $6, 7, 8$ form left turns whereas the next triplet $7, 8, 9$ forms a right turn. Therefore, 8 gets deleted and in the next round 7 also gets eliminated. The next three triplets examined are $4, 6, 9$; $6, 9, 10$; and $9, 10, p$, all of which are left turns. The final hull obtained is $p, 1, 3, 4, 6, 9$, and 10, which are points on the hull in counterclockwise (ccw) order. □

This scan process is given in Algorithm 3.22. In this algorithm the set of points is realized as a doubly linked list *ptslist*. Function Scan runs in $O(n)$ time since for each triplet examined, either the scan moves one node ahead or one point gets removed. In the latter case, the scan moves one node back. Also note that for each triplet, the test as to whether a left or right turn is formed can be done in $O(1)$ time. Function Area computes the signed area formed by three points. The major work in the algorithm is in sorting the points. Since sorting takes $O(n \log n)$ time, the total time of Graham's scan algorithm is $O(n \log n)$.

```
point = record{
    float x; float y;
    point *prev; point *next;
};

Algorithm Scan(list)
// list is a pointer to the first node in the input list.
{
    *p := list; *p1 := list;
    repeat
    {
        p2 := (p1 → next);
        if ((p2 → next) ≠ 0) then p3 := (p2 → next);
        else return; // End of the list
        temp := Area((p1 → x), (p1 → y), (p2 → x),
            (p2 → y), (p3 → x), (p3 → y));
        if (temp ≥ 0.0) then p1 := (p1 → next);
        // If p1, p2, p3 form a left turn, move one point ahead;
        // If not, delete p2 and move back.
        else
        {
            (p1 → next) := p3; (p3 → prev) := p1; delete p2;
            p1 := (p1 → prev);
        }
    } until (false);
}

Algorithm ConvexHull(ptslist)
{
    // ptslist is a pointer to the first item of the input list. Find
    // the point p in ptslist of lowest y-coordinate. Sort the
    // points according to the angle made with p and the x-axis.

    Sort(ptslist); Scan(ptslist); PrintList(ptslist);
}
```

Algorithm 3.22 Graham's scan algorithm

3.9.4 An $O(n \log n)$ Divide-and-Conquer Algorithm

In this section we present a simple divide-and-conquer algorithm, called DCHull, which also takes $O(n \log n)$ time and computes the convex hull in clockwise order.

Given a set X of n points, like that in the case of QuickHull, the problem is reduced to finding the upper hull and the lower hull separately and then putting them together. Since the computations of the upper and lower hulls are very similar, we restrict our discussion to computing the upper hull. The divide-and-conquer algorithm for computing the upper hull partitions X into two nearly equal halves. Partitioning is done according to the x-coordinate values of points using the median x-coordinate as the splitter (see Section 3.7 for a discussion on median finding). Upper hulls are recursively computed for the two halves. These two hulls are then merged by finding the *line of tangent* (i.e., a straight line connecting a point each from the two halves, such that all the points of X are on one side of the line) (see Figure 3.12).

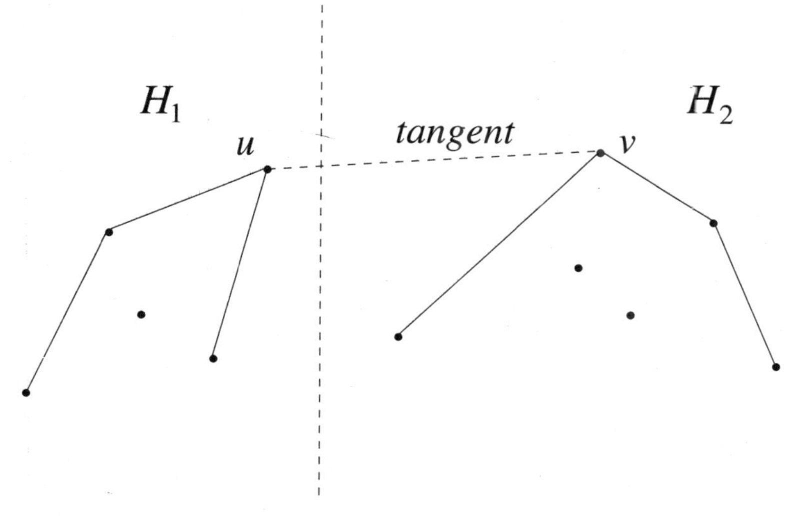

Figure 3.12 Divide and conquer to compute the convex hull

To begin with, the points p_1 and p_2 are identified [where p_1 (p_2) is the point with the least (largest) x-coordinate value]. This can be done in $O(n)$ time. Ties can be handled in exactly the same manner as in QuickHull. So, assume that there are no ties. All the points that are to the left of the line segment $\langle p_1, p_2 \rangle$ are separated from those that are to the right. This separation also can be done in $O(n)$ time. From here on, by "input" and "X" we mean all the points that are to the left of the line segment $\langle p_1, p_2 \rangle$. Also let $|X| = N$.

Sort the input points according to their x-coordinate values. Sorting can be done in $O(N \log N)$ time. This sorting is done only once in the computation of the upper hull. Let $q_1, q_2, \ldots, q_N$ be the sorted order of these points. Now partition the input into two equal halves with $q_1, q_2, \ldots, q_{N/2}$ in the first half and $q_{N/2+1}, q_{N/2+2}, \ldots, q_N$ in the second half. The upper hull of each half is computed recursively. Let H_1 and H_2 be the upper hulls. Upper hulls are maintained as linked lists in clockwise order. We refer to the first element in the list as the leftmost point and the last element as the rightmost point.

The line of tangent is then found in $O(\log^2 N)$ time. If (u, v) is the line of tangent, then all the points of H_1 that are to the right of u are dropped. Similarly, all the points that are to the left of v in H_2 are dropped. The remaining part of H_1, the line of tangent, and the remaining part of H_2 form the upper hull of the given input set.

If $T(N)$ is the run time of the above recursive algorithm for the upper hull on an input of N points, then we have

$$T(N) \;=\; 2T(N/2) + O(N)$$

which solves to $T(N) = O(N \log N)$. Thus the run time is dominated by the initial sorting step.

The only part of the algorithm that remains to be specified is how to find the line of tangent $\langle u, v \rangle$ in $O(\log^2 N)$ time. The way to find the tangent is to start from the middle point, call it p, of H_1. Here the middle point refers to the middle element of the corresponding list. Find the tangent of p with H_2. Let $\langle p, q \rangle$ be the tangent. Using $\langle p, q \rangle$, we can determine whether u is to the left of, equal to, or to the right of p in H_1. A binary search in this fashion on the points of H_1 reveals u. Use a similar procedure to isolate v.

Lemma 3.1 Let H_1 and H_2 be two upper hulls with at most m points each. If p is any point of H_1, its point q of tangency with H_2 can be found in $O(\log m)$ time.

Proof. If q' is any point in H_2, we can check whether q' is to the left of, equal to, or to the right of q in $O(1)$ time (see Figure 3.13). In Figure 3.13, x and y are the left and right neighbors of q' in H_2, respectively. If $\angle pq'x$ is a right turn and $\angle pq'y$ is a left turn, then q is to the right of q' (see case 1 of Figure 3.13). If $\angle pq'x$ and $\angle pq'y$ are both right turns, then $q' = q$ (see case 2 of Figure 3.13); otherwise q is to the left of q' (see case 3 of Figure 3.13). Thus we can perform a binary search on the points of H_2 and identify q in $O(\log m)$ time. □

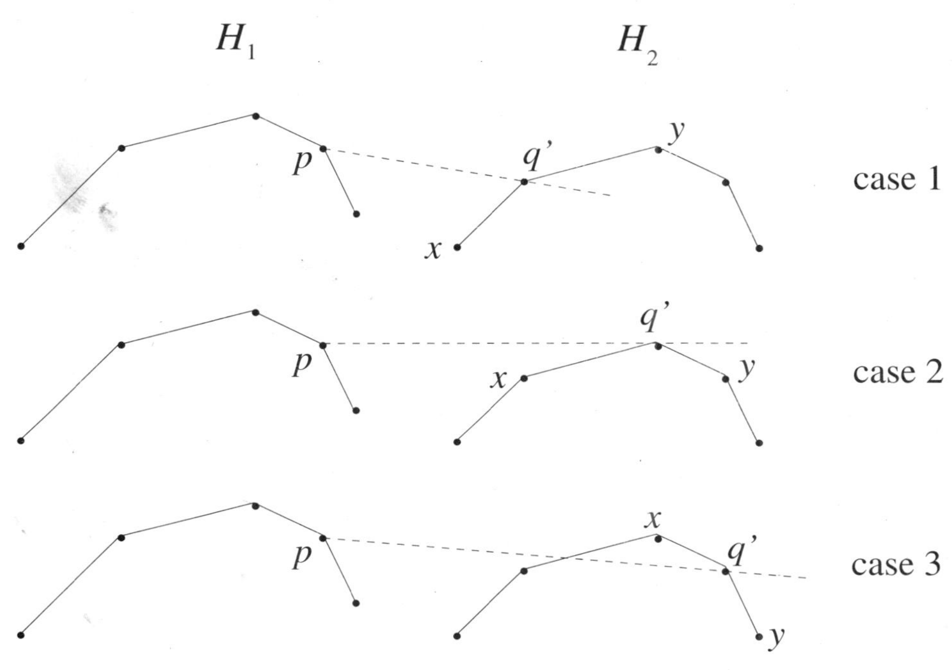

Figure 3.13 Proof of Lemma 3.1

Lemma 3.2 If H_1 and H_2 are two upper hulls with at most m points each, their common tangent can be computed in $O(\log^2 m)$ time.

Proof. Let $u \in H_1$ and $v \in H_2$ be such that $\langle u, v \rangle$ is the line of tangent. Also let p be an arbitrary point of H_1 and let $q \in H_2$ be such that $\langle p, q \rangle$ is a tangent of H_2. Given p and q, we can check in $O(1)$ time whether u is to the left of, equal to, or to the right of p (see Figure 3.14). Here x and y are left and right neighbors, respectively, of p in H_1. If $\langle p, q \rangle$ is also tangential to H_1, then $p = u$. If $\angle xpq$ is a left turn, then u is to the left of p; otherwise u is to the right of p. This suggests a binary search for u. For each point p of H_1 chosen, we have to determine the tangent from p to H_2 and then decide the relative positioning of p with respect to u. We can do this computation in $O(\log m \times \log m) = O(\log^2 m)$ time. □

In summary, given two upper hulls with $\frac{N}{2}$ points each, the line of tangent can be computed in $O(\log^2 N)$ time.

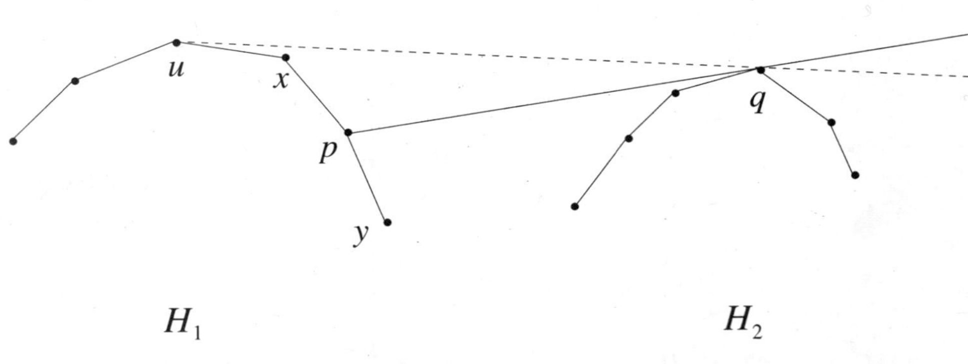

Figure 3.14 Proof of Lemma 3.2

Theorem 3.4 A convex hull of n points in the plane can be computed in $O(n \log n)$ time. □

EXERCISES

1. Write an algorithm in pseudocode that implements QuickHull and test it using suitable data.

2. Code the divide-and-conquer algorithm DCHull and test it using appropriate data.

3. Run the three algorithms for convex hull discussed in this section on various random inputs and compare their performances.

4. Algorithm DCHull can be modified as follows: Instead of using the median as the splitter, we could use a randomly chosen point as the splitter. Then X is partitioned into two around this point. The rest of the function DCHull is the same. Write code for this modified algorithm and compare it with DCHull empirically.

5. Let S be a set of n points in the plane. It is given that there is only a constant (say c) number of points on the hull of S. Can you devise a convex hull algorithm for S that runs in time $o(n \log n)$? Conceive of special algorithms for $c = 3$ and $c = 4$ first and then generalize.

3.10 REFERENCES AND READINGS

Algorithm MaxMin (Algorithm 3.6) is due to I. Pohl and the quick sort algorithm (Algorithm 3.13) is due to C. A. R. Hoare. The randomized sorting algorithm in Algorithm 3.16 is due to W. D. Frazer and A. C. McKeller and the selection algorithm of Algorithm 3.19 is due to M. Blum, R. Floyd, V. Pratt, R. Rivest and R. E. Tarjan.

For more on randomized sorting and selection see:
"Expected time bounds for selection," by R. Floyd and R. Rivest, *Communications of the ACM* 18, no. 3 (1975): 165–172.
"Samplesort: A Sampling Approach to Minimal Storage Tree Sorting," by W. D. Frazer and A. C. McKeller, *Journal of the ACM* 17, no. 3 (1970): 496–507.
"Derivation of Randomized Sorting and Selection Algorithms," by S. Rajasekaran and J. H. Reif, in *Parallel Algorithm Derivation and Program Transformation*, edited by R. Paige, J. H. Reif, and R. Wachter, Kluwer Academic Publishers, 1993, pp. 187–205.

The matrix multiplication algorithm in Section 3.7 is due to V. Strassen. For more information on the matrix multiplication problem see "Matrix multiplication via arithmetic progressions," by D. Coppersmith and S. Winograd, *Journal of Symbolic Computation* 9 (1990): 251–280. A complex $O(n^{2.376})$ time algorithm for multiplying two $n \times n$ matrices is given in this paper.

For more applications of divide-and-conquer see:
Computational Geometry, by F. Preparata and M. I. Shamos, Springer-Verlag, 1985.
Computational Geometry: An Introduction Through Randomized Algorithms by K. Mulmuley, Prentice-Hall, 1994.
Introduction to Algorithms: A Creative Approach, by U. Manber, Addison-Wesley, 1989.

3.11 ADDITIONAL EXERCISES

1. What happens to the worst-case run time of quick sort if we use the median of the given keys as the splitter key? (Assume that the selection algorithm of Section 3.6 is employed to determine the median).

2. The sets A and B have n elements each given in the form of sorted arrays. Present an $O(n)$ time algorithm to compute $A \cup B$ and $A \cap B$.

3. The sets A and B have m and n elements (respectively) from a linear order. These sets are not necessarily sorted. Also assume that $m \leq n$.

Show how to compute $A \cup B$ and $A \cap B$ in $O(n \log m)$ time.

4. Consider the problem of sorting a sequence X of n keys where each key is either zero or one (i.e., each key is a bit). One way of sorting X is to start with two empty lists L_0 and L_1. Let $X = k_1, k_2, \ldots, k_n$. For each $1 \leq i \leq n$ do: If $k_i = 0$, then append k_i to L_0. If $k_i = 1$, then append k_i to L_1. After processing all the keys of X in this manner, output the list L_0 followed by the list L_1.

   The above idea of sorting can be extended to the case in which each key is of length more than one bit. In particular, if the keys are integers in the range $[0, m-1]$, then we start with m empty lists, $L_0, L_1, \ldots, L_{m-1}$, one list (or *bucket*) for each possible value that a key can take. Then the keys are processed in a similar fashion. In particular, if a key has a value ℓ, then it will be appended to the ℓth list.

   Write an algorithm that employs this idea to sort n keys assuming that each key is in the range $[0, m-1]$. Show that the run time of your algorithm is $O(n+m)$. This algorithm is known as the *bucket sort.*

5. Consider the problem of sorting n two-digit integers. The idea of *radix sort* can be employed. We first sort the numbers only with respect to their least significant digits (LSDs). Followed by this, we apply a sort with respect to their second LSDs. More generally, d-digit numbers can be sorted in d phases, where in the ith phase ($1 \leq i \leq d$) we sort the keys only with respect to their ith LSDs. Will this algorithm always work?

   As an example, let the input be $k_1 = 12, k_2 = 45, k_3 = 23, k_4 = 14, k_5 = 32$, and $k_6 = 57$. After sorting these keys with respect to their LSDs, we end up with: $k_5 = 32, k_1 = 12, k_3 = 23, k_4 = 14, k_2 = 45$, and $k_6 = 57$. When we sort the resultant sequence with respect to the keys' second LSDs (i.e., the next-most significant digits), we get $k_1 = 12, k_4 = 14, k_3 = 23, k_5 = 32, k_2 = 45$, and $k_6 = 57$, which is the correct answer!

   But note that in the second phase of the algorithm, $k_4 = 14, k_1 = 12, k_3 = 23, k_5 = 32, k_2 = 45, k_6 = 57$ is also a valid sort with respect to the second LSDs. The result in any phase of radix sorting can be forced to be correct by enforcing the following condition on the sorting algorithm to be used. "Keys with equal values should remain in the same relative order in the output as they were in the input." Any sorting algorithm that satisfies this is called a *stable sort.*

   Note that in the above example, if the algorithm used to sort the keys in the second phase is stable, then the output will be correct. In summary, radix sort can be employed to sort d-digit numbers in d phases such that the sort applied in each phase (except the first phase) is stable.

More generally, radix sort can be used to sort integers of arbitrary length. As usual, the algorithm will consist of phases in each of which the keys are sorted only with respect to certain parts of their keys. The parts used in each phase could be single bits, single digits, or more generally, ℓ bits, for some appropriate ℓ.

In Exercise 4, you showed that n integers in the range $[0, m-1]$ can be sorted in $O(n+m)$ time. Is your algorithm stable? If not, make it stable. As a special case, your algorithm can sort n integers in the range $[0, n-1]$ in $O(n)$ time. Use this algorithm together with the idea of radix sorting to develop an algorithm that can sort n integers in the range $[0, n^c - 1]$ (for any fixed c) in $O(n)$ time.

6. Two sets A and B have n elements each. Assume that each element is an integer in the range $[0, n^{100}]$. These sets are not necessarily sorted. Show how to check whether these two sets are disjoint in $O(n)$ time. Your algorithm should use $O(n)$ space.

7. Input are the sets $S_1, S_2, \ldots,$ and S_ℓ (where $\ell \le n$). Elements of these sets are integers in the range $[0, n^c - 1]$ (for some fixed c). Also let $\sum_{i=1}^{\ell} |S_i| = n$. The goal is to output S_1 in sorted order, then S_2 in sorted order, and so on. Present an $O(n)$ time algorithm for this problem.

8. Input is an array of n numbers where each number is an integer in the range $[0, N]$ (for some $N >> n$). Present an algorithm that runs in the worst case in time $O\left(n \frac{\log N}{\log n}\right)$ and checks whether all these n numbers are distinct. Your algorithm should use only $O(n)$ space.

9. Let S be a sequence of n^2 integers in the range $[1, n]$. Let $R(i)$ be the number of i's in the sequence (for $i = 1, 2, \ldots, n$). Given S, we have to compute an approximate value of $R(i)$ for each i. If $N(i)$ is an approximation to $R(i), i = 1, \ldots, n$, it should be the case that (with high probability) $N(i) \ge R(i)$ for each i and $\sum_{i=1}^{n} N(i) = O(n^2)$. Of course we can do this computation in deterministic $O(n^2)$ time. Design a randomized algorithm for this problem that runs in time $O(n \log^{O(1)} n)$.

Chapter 4

THE GREEDY METHOD

4.1 THE GENERAL METHOD

The greedy method is perhaps the most straightforward design technique we consider in this text, and what's more it can be applied to a wide variety of problems. Most, though not all, of these problems have n inputs and require us to obtain a subset that satisfies some constraints. Any subset that satisfies these constraints is called a *feasible* solution. We need to find a feasible solution that either maximizes or minimizes a given *objective function*. A feasible solution that does this is called an *optimal solution*. There is usually an obvious way to determine a feasible solution but not necessarily an optimal solution.

The greedy method suggests that one can devise an algorithm that works in stages, considering one input at a time. At each stage, a decision is made regarding whether a particular input is in an optimal solution. This is done by considering the inputs in an order determined by some selection procedure. If the inclusion of the next input into the partially constructed optimal solution will result in an infeasible solution, then this input is not added to the partial solution. Otherwise, it is added. The selection procedure itself is based on some optimization measure. This measure may be the objective function. In fact, several different optimization measures may be plausible for a given problem. Most of these, however, will result in algorithms that generate suboptimal solutions. This version of the greedy technique is called the *subset paradigm*.

We can describe the subset paradigm abstractly, but more precisely than above, by considering the control abstraction in Algorithm 4.1.

The function Select selects an input from $a[\,]$ and removes it. The selected input's value is assigned to x. Feasible is a Boolean-valued function that determines whether x can be included into the solution vector. The function Union combines x with the solution and updates the objective function. The function Greedy describes the essential way that a greedy algorithm will look,

```
Algorithm Greedy(a, n)
// a[1 : n] contains the n inputs.
{
    solution := ∅; // Initialize the solution.
    for i := 1 to n do
    {
        x := Select(a);
        if Feasible(solution, x) then
            solution := Union(solution, x);
    }
    return solution;
}
```

Algorithm 4.1 Greedy method control abstraction for the subset paradigm

once a particular problem is chosen and the functions Select, Feasible, and Union are properly implemented.

For problems that do not call for the selection of an optimal subset, in the greedy method we make decisions by considering the inputs in some order. Each decision is made using an optimization criterion that can be computed using decisions already made. Call this version of the greedy method the *ordering paradigm.* Sections 4.1 through 4.6 consider problems that fit the subset paradigm, and Sections 4.7 through 4.9 consider problems that fit the ordering paradigm.

Example 4.1 [Change Making] A child buys candy valued at less than $1 and gives a $1 bill to the cashier. The cashier wishes to return change using the fewest number of coins. Assume that an unlimited supply of quarters, dimes, nickels, and pennies is available. The cashier constructs the change in stages. In each stage a coin is added to the change. This coin is selected using the greedy criterion: *At each stage increase the total amount of change constructed by as much as possible.* To assure feasibility (i.e., the change given exactly equals the desired amount) of the solution, the selected coin should not cause the total amount of change given so far to exceed the final desired amount.

Suppose that 67 cents in change is due the child. The first two coins selected are quarters. A quarter cannot be selected for the third coin because such a selection results in an infeasible selection of coins (change exceeds 67 cents). The third coin selected is a dime, then a nickel is selected, and finally two pennies are added to the change.

The greedy method has intuitive appeal in that we construct the change by using a strategy that our intuition tells us should result in the fewest (or at least close to the fewest) number of coins being given out. We can actually prove that the greedy algorithm just described does indeed generate change with the fewest number of coins (see Exercise 2). □

Example 4.2 [Machine Scheduling] You are given n tasks and an infinite supply of machines on which these tasks can be performed. Each task has a start time s_i and a finish time f_i, $s_i < f_i$. $[s_i, f_i]$ is the processing interval for task i. Two tasks i and j overlap iff their processing intervals overlap at a point other than the interval start or end. For example, the interval [1, 4] overlaps with [2, 4], but not with [4, 7]. A **feasible** task-to-machine assignment is an assignment in which no machine is assigned two overlapping tasks. Therefore, in a feasible assignment each machine works on at most one task at any time. An **optimal assignment** is a feasible assignment that utilizes the fewest number of machines.

Suppose we have $n = 7$ tasks labeled a through g and that their start and finish times are as shown in Figure 4.1(a). The following task-to-machine assignment is a feasible assignment that utilizes seven machines: Assign task a to machine $M1$, task b to machine $M2$, $\cdots$, task g to machine $M7$. This assignment is not an optimal assignment because other assignments use fewer machines. For example, we can assign tasks a, b, and d to the same machine, reducing the number of utilized machines to five.

A greedy way to obtain an optimal task assignment is to assign the tasks in stages, one task per stage and in nondecreasing order of task start times. Call a machine **old** if at least one task has been assigned to it. If a machine is not old, it is **new**. For machine selection, use the greedy criterion: *If an old machine becomes available by the start time of the task to be assigned, assign the task to this machine; if not, assign it to a new machine.*

For the data of Figure 4.1(a), the tasks in nondecreasing order of task start time are a, f, b, c, g, e, d. The greedy algorithm assigns tasks to machines in this order. The algorithm has $n = 7$ stages, and in each stage one task is assigned to a machine. Stage 1 has no old machines, so a is assigned to a new machine (say, $M1$). This machine is now busy from time 0 to time 2 (see Figure 4.1(b)). In stage 2 task f is considered. Since the only old machine is busy when task f is to start, it is assigned to a new machine (say, $M2$). When task b is considered in stage 3, we find that the old machine $M1$ is free at time $s_b = 3$, so b is assigned to $M1$. The availability time for $M1$ becomes $f_b = 7$, and that for M_2 is $f_f = 5$. In stage 4 task c is considered. Since neither of the old machines is available at time $s_c = 4$, task c is assigned to a new machine (say, $M3$). The availability time of this machine becomes $f_c = 7$. Task g is considered in stage 5 and assigned to machine $M2$, which is the first to become available. Task e is assigned in stage 6 to machine $M1$ or $M3$ (assume it is assigned to $M1$), and finally, in stage 7, task d is assigned to machine $M2$ or $M3$ (Figure 4.1(b) assumes

task	a	b	c	d	e	f	g
start	0	3	4	9	7	1	6
finish	2	7	7	11	10	5	8

(a) Seven tasks

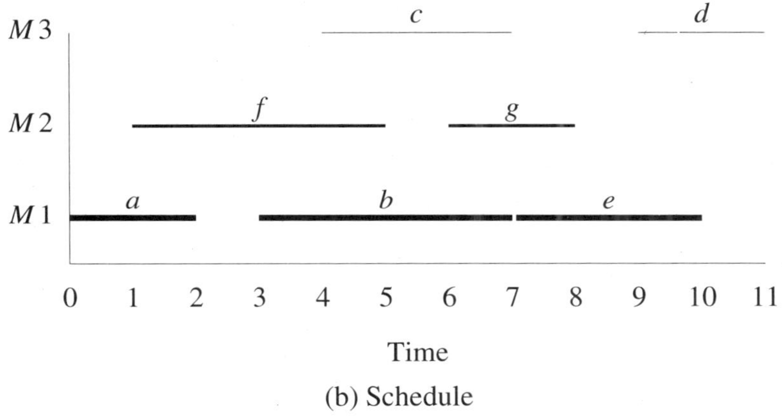

(b) Schedule

Figure 4.1 Tasks and a three-machine schedule

task d is assigned to $M3$).

The proof that the described greedy algorithm generates optimal assignments is left as an exercise (Exercise 8). The algorithm may be implemented to have complexity $O(n \log n)$ by sorting the tasks in nondecreasing order of s_i, using an $O(n \log n)$ sort (such as heap sort) and then using a min heap of availability times for the old machines. □

EXERCISES

1. Write a control abstraction for the ordering paradigm.

2. Show that the greedy algorithm for the change-making problem (Example 4.1) generates change with the fewest number of coins when the cashier has an unlimited supply of quarters, dimes, nickels, and pennies.

3. Consider the change-making problem of Example 4.1. Suppose that the cashier has only a limited number of quarters, dimes, nickels, and pennies. Formulate a greedy solution to the change-making problem. Does your algorithm always use the fewest number of coins? Prove your result.

4. Extend the algorithm of Example 4.1 to the case when the cashier has \$100, \$50, \$20, \$10, \$5, and \$1 bills in addition to coins and a customer gives u dollars and v cents as payment toward a purchase of x dollars and y cents. Does your algorithm always generate change with the fewest total number of bills and coins? Prove this.

5. Write a program implementing the change-making solution of Example 4.1. Assume that the cashier has bills in the denominations \$100, \$50, \$20, \$10, \$5, and \$1 in addition to coins. Your program should include a method to input the purchase amount and the amount given by the customer as well as a method to output the amount of change and a breakdown by denomination.

6. Suppose that some country has coins in the denominations 14, 12, 5, and 1 cents. Will the greedy method of Example 4.1 always generate change with the fewest number of coins? Prove your answer.

7. (a) Show that the greedy algorithm of Example 4.2 always finds an optimal task assignment.

   (b) Program your algorithm so that its complexity is $O(n \log n)$; n is the number of tasks.

8. Consider the machine-scheduling problem of Example 4.2. Assume that only one machine is available and that we are to select the largest number of tasks that can be scheduled on this machine. For the example, the largest task selection is $\{a, b, e\}$. A greedy algorithm for this task-selection problem would select the tasks in stages. In each stage one task is selected using the following criterion: *From the remaining tasks, select the one that has the least finish time and does not overlap with any of the already selected tasks.*

   (a) Show that this greedy algorithm obtains optimal selections.

   (b) Develop an $O(n \log n)$ implementation of this algorithm. (*Hint:* Use a min heap of finish times.)

4.2 CONTAINER LOADING

A large ship is to be loaded with cargo. The cargo is containerized, and all containers are the same size. Different containers may have different weights.

Let w_i be the weight of the ith container, $1 \le i \le n$. The cargo capacity of the ship is c. We wish to load the ship with the maximum number of containers.

This problem can be formulated as an optimization problem in the following way: Let x_i be a variable whose value can be either 0 or 1. If we set x_i to 0, then container i is not to be loaded. If x_i is 1, then the container is to be loaded. We wish to assign values to the x_is that satisfy the constraints $\sum_{i=1}^{n} w_i x_i \le c$ and $x_i \in \{0,1\}$, $1 \le i \le n$. The optimization function is $\sum_{i=1}^{n} x_i$.

Every set of x_is that satisfies the constraints is a feasible solution. Every feasible solution that maximizes $\sum_{i=1}^{n} x_i$ is an optimal solution.

The ship may be loaded in stages; one container per stage. At each stage we need to select a container to load. For this decision we may use the greedy criterion: *From the remaining containers, select the one with least weight.* This order of selection will keep the total weight of the selected containers minimum and hence leave maximum capacity for loading more containers. Using the greedy algorithm just outlined, we first select the container that has least weight, then the one with the next smallest weight, and so on until either all containers have been loaded or there isn't enough capacity for the next one.

Example 4.3 Suppose that $n = 8$, $[w_1, \cdots, w_8] = [100, 200, 50, 90, 150, 50, 20, 80]$, and $c = 400$. When the greedy algorithm is used, the containers are considered for loading in the order 7, 3, 6, 8, 4, 1, 5, 2. Containers 7, 3, 6, 8, 4, and 1 together weigh 390 units and are loaded. The available capacity is now 10 units, which is inadequate for any of the remaining containers. In the greedy solution we have $[x_1, \cdots, x_8] = [1, 0, 1, 1, 0, 1, 1, 1]$ and $\sum x_i = 6$. □

Algorithm 4.2 gives the pseudocode for the greedy container-loading method. This code utilizes the fact that the greedy method loads containers in increasing order of their weight. Each element of the array c has two components–*id*, which is an identifier in the range 1 through number of containers (*id* is a container identifier) and *weight*, which is the weight of the container.

Algorithm 4.2 begins by sorting the containers by weights using a sort algorithm such as heap sort or merge sort. Following the sort, containers are loaded in increasing order of weight. The sort takes $O(n \log n)$ time, where n is the number of containers. Since the remainder of the algorithm takes $O(n)$ time, the overall time complexity of Algorithm 4.2 is $O(n \log n)$.

Theorem 4.1 *The greedy algorithm generates optimal loadings.*

Proof: Let $x = [x_1, \cdots, x_n]$ be the solution produced by the greedy algorithm and let $y = [y_1, \cdots, y_n]$ be any feasible solution. We will show that

```
Algorithm ContainerLoading(c, capacity, numberOfContainers, x)
// Greedy algorithm for container loading.
// Set x[i] = 1 iff container c[i], i ≥ 1 is loaded.
{
    // sort into increasing order of weight
    Sort(c, numberOfContainers);

    n := numberOfContainers;

    // initialize x
    for i := 1 to n do
        x[i] := 0;

    // select containers in order of weight
    i := 1;
    while (i ≤ n && c[i].weight ≤ capacity)
    {
        // enough capacity for container c[i].id
        x[c[i].id] := 1;
        capacity− = c[i].weight; // remaining capacity
        i++;
    }
}
```

Algorithm 4.2 Loading containers

$\sum_{i=1}^{n} x_i \geq \sum_{i=1}^{n} y_i$. Without loss of generality we may assume that the containers have been ordered so that $w_i \leq w_{i+1}$, $1 \leq i < n$. From the way the greedy algorithm works, we know that there is a k, $0 \leq k \leq n$ such that $x_i = 1$, $i \leq k$, and $x_i = 0$, $i > k$.

We use induction on the number p of positions i such that $x_i \neq y_i$. For the induction base, we see that when $p = 0$, x and y are the same. So $\sum_{i=1}^{n} x_i \geq \sum_{i=1}^{n} y_i$. For the induction hypothesis, let m be an arbitrary natural number and assume that $\sum_{i=1}^{n} x_i \geq \sum_{i=1}^{n} y_i$ whenever $p \leq m$.

In the induction step, we show that $\sum_{i=1}^{n} x_i \geq \sum_{i=1}^{n} y_i$ when $p = m + 1$. Find the least integer j, $1 \leq j \leq n$, such that $x_j \neq y_j$. Since $p \neq 0$, such a j exists. Also, $j \leq k$, as otherwise y is not a feasible solution. Since $x_j \neq y_j$ and $x_j = 1$, $y_j = 0$. Set y_j to 1.

If the resulting y is a feasible solution, let z denote the resulting y. If the resulting y denotes an infeasible solution, there must be an l in the range

$[k+1, n]$ for which $y_l = 1$. Set y_l to 0. Let z denote the resulting y. As $w_j \leq w_l$, z is a feasible loading.

In either case, $\sum_{i=1}^{n} z_i \geq \sum_{i=1}^{n} y_i$, and z differs from x in at most $p-1 = m$ positions. From the induction hypothesis, it follows that $\sum_{i=1}^{n} x_i \geq \sum_{i=1}^{n} z_i, \geq \sum_{i=1}^{n} y_i$. □

EXERCISES

1. Suppose you have 6 containers whose weights are 50, 10, 30, 20, 60, and 5 and a ship whose capacity is 100. Use Algorithm 4.2 to find an optimal solution to this instance of the container loading problem.

2. Extend the greedy solution for the container loading problem to the case when there are two ships. Does your algorithm always generate optimal solutions?

3. We are given n tasks to perform in sequence. Suppose that task i needs t_i units of time. If the tasks are done in the order 1, 2, $\cdots$, n, then task i completes at time $c_i = \sum_{j=1}^{i} t_j$. The average completion time (ACT) is $\frac{1}{n} \sum_{i=1}^{n} c_i$.

   (a) Consider the case of four tasks with task times (4, 2, 8, 1). What is the ACT when the task order is 1, 2, 3, 4?

   (b) What is the ACT when the task order is 2, 1, 4, 3?

   (c) The following method constructs a task order that tries to minimize the ACT: *Construct the order in n stages; in each stage select from the remaining tasks one with least task time.* For the example of part (a), this strategy results in the task order 4, 2, 1, 3. What is the ACT for this greedy order?

   (d) Write an algorithm that implements the greedy strategy of (c). The complexity of your algorithm should be $O(n \log n)$. Show that this is so.

   (e) Show that the greedy strategy of (c) results in task orders that have minimum ACT.

4. If two people perform the n tasks of Exercise 3, we need an assignment of tasks to each and an order in which each person is to perform his/her assigned tasks. The task completion times and ACT are defined as in Exercise 3. A possible greedy method that aims to minimize the ACT is as follows: *The two workers select tasks alternately and one at a time; from the remaining tasks, one with least task time is selected; each person does his/her tasks in the order selected.* For the example of Exercise 3(a), if person 1 begins the selection process, he/she selects

task 4, person 2 selects task 2, person 1 selects task 1, and finally person 2 selects task 3.

(a) Write an algorithm to implement this strategy. What is its time complexity?

(b) Does the outlined greedy strategy always minimize the ACT? Prove your answer.

5. (a) Extend the greedy algorithm of Exercise 4 to the case when m persons are available to do the tasks.

(b) Does your algorithm guarantee optimal solutions? Prove your answer.

(c) What is the time complexity of your algorithm?

4.3 KNAPSACK PROBLEM

Let us try to apply the greedy method to solve the knapsack problem. We are given n objects and a knapsack or bag. Object i has a weight w_i and the knapsack has a capacity m. If a fraction x_i, $0 \leq x_i \leq 1$, of object i is placed into the knapsack, then a profit of $p_i x_i$ is earned. The objective is to obtain a filling of the knapsack that maximizes the total profit earned. Since the knapsack capacity is m, we require the total weight of all chosen objects to be at most m. Formally, the problem can be stated as

$$\text{maximize} \sum_{1 \leq i \leq n} p_i x_i \tag{4.1}$$

$$\text{subject to} \sum_{1 \leq i \leq n} w_i x_i \leq m \tag{4.2}$$

$$\text{and } 0 \leq x_i \leq 1, \quad 1 \leq i \leq n \tag{4.3}$$

The profits and weights are positive numbers.

A feasible solution (or filling) is any set $(x_1, \ldots, x_n)$ satisfying (4.2) and (4.3) above. An optimal solution is a feasible solution for which (4.1) is maximized.

Example 4.4 Consider the following instance of the knapsack problem: $n = 3, m = 20, (p_1, p_2, p_3) = (25, 24, 15)$, and $(w_1, w_2, w_3) = (18, 15, 10)$. Four feasible solutions are:

	(x_1, x_2, x_3)	$\sum w_i x_i$	$\sum p_i x_i$
1.	(1/2, 1/3, 1/4)	16.5	24.25
2.	(1, 2/15, 0)	20	28.2
3.	(0, 2/3, 1)	20	31
4.	(0, 1, 1/2)	20	31.5

Of these four feasible solutions, solution 4 yields the maximum profit. As we shall soon see, this solution is optimal for the given problem instance. □

Lemma 4.1 In case the sum of all the weights is $\leq m$, then $x_i = 1$, $1 \leq i \leq n$ is an optimal solution. □

So let us assume the sum of weights exceeds m. Now all the x_i's cannot be 1. Another observation to make is:

Lemma 4.2 All optimal solutions will fill the knapsack exactly. □

Lemma 4.2 is true because we can always increase the contribution of some object i by a fractional amount until the total weight is exactly m.

Note that the knapsack problem calls for selecting a subset of the objects and hence fits the subset paradigm. In addition to selecting a subset, the knapsack problem also involves the selection of an x_i for each object. Several simple greedy strategies to obtain feasible solutions whose sums are identically m suggest themselves. First, we can try to fill the knapsack by including next the object with largest profit. If an object under consideration doesn't fit, then a fraction of it is included to fill the knapsack. Thus each time an object is included (except possibly when the last object is included) into the knapsack, we obtain the largest possible increase in profit value. Note that if only a fraction of the last object is included, then it may be possible to get a bigger increase by using a different object. For example, if we have two units of space left and two objects with $(p_i = 4,\ w_i = 4)$ and $(p_j = 3, w_j = 2)$ remaining, then using j is better than using half of i. Let us use this selection strategy on the data of Example 4.4.

Object one has the largest profit value $(p_1 = 25)$. So it is placed into the knapsack first. Then $x_1 = 1$ and a profit of 25 is earned. Only 2 units of knapsack capacity are left. Object two has the next largest profit $(p_2 = 24)$. However, $w_2 = 15$ and it doesn't fit into the knapsack. Using $x_2 = 2/15$ fills the knapsack exactly with part of object 2 and the value of the resulting solution is 28.2. This is solution 2 and it is readily seen to be suboptimal. The method used to obtain this solution is termed a greedy method because at each step (except possibly the last one) we chose to introduce that object which would increase the objective function value the most. However, this greedy method did not yield an optimal solution. Note that even if we change the above strategy so that in the last step the objective function increases by as much as possible, an optimal solution is not obtained for Example 4.4.

We can formulate at least two other greedy approaches attempting to obtain optimal solutions. From the preceding example, we note that considering objects in order of nonincreasing profit values does not yield an optimal solution because even though the objective function value takes on large increases at each step, the number of steps is few as the knapsack capacity is

```
Algorithm GreedyKnapsack(m, n)
// p[1 : n] and w[1 : n] contain the profits and weights respectively
// of the n objects ordered such that p[i]/w[i] ≥ p[i + 1]/w[i + 1].
// m is the knapsack size and x[1 : n] is the solution vector.
{
    for i := 1 to n do x[i] := 0.0; // Initialize x.
    U := m;
    for i := 1 to n do
    {
        if (w[i] > U) then break;
        x[i] := 1.0; U := U − w[i];
    }
    if (i ≤ n) then x[i] := U/w[i];
}
```

Algorithm 4.3 Algorithm for greedy strategies for the knapsack problem

used up at a rapid rate. So, let us try to be greedy with capacity and use it up as slowly as possible. This requires us to consider the objects in order of nondecreasing weights w_i. Using Example 4.4, solution 3 results. This too is suboptimal. This time, even though capacity is used slowly, profits aren't coming in rapidly enough.

Thus, our next attempt is an algorithm that strives to achieve a balance between the rate at which profit increases and the rate at which capacity is used. At each step we include that object which has the maximum profit per unit of capacity used. This means that objects are considered in order of the ratio p_i/w_i. Solution 4 of Example 4.4 is produced by this strategy. If the objects have already been sorted into nonincreasing order of p_i/w_i, then function GreedyKnapsack (Algorithm 4.3) obtains solutions corresponding to this strategy. Note that solutions corresponding to the first two strategies can be obtained using this algorithm if the objects are initially in the appropriate order. Disregarding the time to initially sort the objects, each of the three strategies outlined above requires only $O(n)$ time.

We have seen that when one applies the greedy method to the solution of the knapsack problem, there are at least three different measures one can attempt to optimize when determining which object to include next. These measures are total profit, capacity used, and the ratio of accumulated profit to capacity used. Once an optimization measure has been chosen, the greedy method suggests choosing objects for inclusion into the solution in such a way that each choice optimizes the measure at that time. Thus a greedy method using profit as its measure will at each step choose an object that increases the profit the most. If the capacity measure is used, the next object included will increase this the least. Although greedy-based algorithms using the first two measures do not guarantee optimal solutions for the knapsack problem, Theorem 4.2 shows that a greedy algorithm using strategy 3 always obtains an optimal solution. This theorem is proved using the following technique:

> *Compare the greedy solution with any optimal solution. If the two solutions differ, then find the first x_i at which they differ. Next, it is shown how to make the x_i in the optimal solution equal to that in the greedy solution without any loss in total value. Repeated use of this transformation shows that the greedy solution is optimal.*

This technique of proving solutions optimal is used often in this text. Hence, you should master it at this time.

Theorem 4.2 If $p_1/w_1 \geq p_2/w_2 \geq \cdots \geq p_n/w_n$, then GreedyKnapsack generates an optimal solution to the given instance of the knapsack problem.

Proof: Let $x = (x_1, \ldots, x_n)$ be the solution generated by GreedyKnapsack. If all the x_i equal one, then clearly the solution is optimal. So, let j be the least index such that $x_j \neq 1$. From the algorithm it follows that $x_i = 1$ for $1 \leq i < j$, $x_i = 0$ for $j < i \leq n$, and $0 \leq x_j < 1$. Let $y = (y_1, \ldots, y_n)$ be an optimal solution. From Lemma 4.2, we can assume that $\sum w_i y_i = m$. Let k be the least index such that $y_k \neq x_k$. Clearly, such a k must exist. It also follows that $y_k < x_k$. To see this, consider the three possibilities $k < j$, $k = j$, or $k > j$.

1. If $k < j$, then $x_k = 1$. But, $y_k \neq x_k$, and so $y_k < x_k$.
2. If $k = j$, then since $\sum w_i x_i = m$ and $y_i = x_i$ for $1 \leq i < j$, it follows that either $y_k < x_k$ or $\sum w_i y_i > m$.
3. If $k > j$, then $\sum w_i y_i > m$, and this is not possible.

Now suppose we increase y_k to x_k and decrease as many of $(y_{k+1}, \ldots, y_n)$ as necessary so that the total capacity used is still m. This results in a new solution $z = (z_1, \ldots, z_n)$ with $z_i = x_i$, $1 \leq i \leq k$, and $\sum_{k<i\leq n} w_i(y_i - z_i) = w_k(z_k - y_k)$. Then, for z we have

$$\begin{aligned}
\sum_{1\leq i\leq n} p_i z_i &= \sum_{1\leq i\leq n} p_i y_i + (z_k - y_k) w_k \frac{p_k}{w_k} - \sum_{k<i\leq n} (y_i - z_i) w_i \frac{p_i}{w_i} \\
&\geq \sum_{1\leq i\leq n} p_i y_i + \left[(z_k - y_k) w_k - \sum_{k<i\leq n} (y_i - z_i) w_i \right] \frac{p_k}{w_k} \\
&= \sum_{1\leq i\leq n} p_i y_i
\end{aligned}$$

If $\sum p_i z_i > \sum p_i y_i$, then y could not have been an optimal solution. If these sums are equal, then either $z = x$ and x is optimal, or $z \neq x$. In the latter case, repeated use of the above argument will either show that y is not optimal, or transform y into x and thus show that x too is optimal. □

EXERCISES

1. (a) Find an optimal solution to the knapsack instance $n = 7, m = 15$, $(p_1, p_2, \ldots, p_7) = (10, 5, 15, 7, 6, 18, 3)$, and $(w_1, w_2, \ldots, w_7) = (2, 3, 5, 7, 1, 4, 1)$.

   (b) Let $\hat{F}(I)$ be the value of the solution generated on problem instance I by GreedyKnapsack when the objects are input in nonincreasing order of the p_i's. Let $F^*(I)$ be the value of an optimal solution for this instance. How large can the ratio $F^*(I) \,/\, \hat{F}(I)$ get?

   (c) Answer (b) for the case in which the input is in nondecreasing order of the w_i's.

2. [0/1 Knapsack] Consider the knapsack problem discussed in this section. We add the requirement that $x_i = 1$ or $x_i = 0$, $1 \leq i \leq n$; that is, an object is either included or not included into the knapsack. We wish to solve the problem

$$\max \sum_1^n p_i x_i$$

$$\text{subject to} \sum_1^n w_i x_i \leq m$$

$$\text{and} \;\; x_i = 0 \text{ or } 1, \;\; 1 \leq i \leq n$$

   One greedy strategy is to consider the objects in order of nonincreasing density p_i/w_i and add the object into the knapsack if it fits. Show that this strategy doesn't necessarily yield an optimal solution.

4.4 TREE VERTEX SPLITTING

Consider a directed binary tree each edge of which is labeled with a real number (called its *weight*). Trees with edge weights are called *weighted trees*. A weighted tree can be used, for example, to model a distribution network in which electric signals or commodities such as oil are transmitted. Nodes in the tree correspond to receiving stations and edges correspond to transmission lines. It is conceivable that in the process of transmission some loss occurs (drop in voltage in the case of electric signals or drop in pressure in the case of oil). Each edge in the tree is labeled with the loss that occurs in traversing that edge. The network may not be able to tolerate losses beyond a certain level. In places where the loss exceeds the tolerance level, boosters have to be placed. Given a network and a loss tolerance level, the *Tree Vertex Splitting Problem (TVSP)* is to determine an optimal placement of boosters. It is assumed that the boosters can only be placed in the nodes of the tree.

The TVSP can be specified more precisely as follows: Let $T = (V, E, w)$ be a weighted directed tree, where V is the vertex set, E is the edge set, and w is the weight function for the edges. In particular, $w(i,j)$ is the weight of the edge $\langle i,j \rangle \in E$. The weight $w(i,j)$ is undefined for any $\langle i,j \rangle \notin E$. A *source vertex* is a vertex with in-degree zero, and a *sink vertex* is a vertex with out-degree zero. For any path P in the tree, its *delay*, $d(P)$, is defined to be the sum of the weights on that path. The delay of the tree T, $d(T)$, is the maximum of all the path delays.

Let T/X be the forest that results when each vertex u in X is split into two nodes u^i and u^o such that all the edges $\langle u,j \rangle \in E$ ($\langle j,u \rangle \in E$) are replaced by edges of the form $\langle u^o, j \rangle$ ($\langle j, u^i \rangle$). In other words, outbound edges from u now leave from u^o and inbound edges to u now enter at u^i. Figure 4.2 shows a tree before and after splitting the node 3. A node that gets split corresponds to a booster station. The TVSP is to identify a set $X \subseteq V$ of minimum cardinality for which $d(T/X) \leq \delta$, for some specified tolerance limit δ. Note that the TVSP has a solution only if the maximum edge weight is $\leq \delta$. Also note that the TVSP naturally fits the subset paradigm.

Given a weighted tree $T(V,E,w)$ and a tolerance limit δ, any subset X of V is a feasible solution if $d(T/X) \leq \delta$. Given an X, we can compute $d(T/X)$ in $O(|V|)$ time. A trivial way of solving the TVSP is to compute $d(T/X)$ for each possible subset X of V. But there are $2^{|V|}$ such subsets! A better algorithm can be obtained using the greedy method.

For the TVSP, the quantity that is optimized (minimized) is the number of nodes in X. A greedy approach to solving this problem is to compute for each node $u \in V$, the maximum delay $d(u)$ from u to any other node in its subtree. If u has a parent v such that $d(u) + w(v,u) > \delta$, then the node u gets split and $d(u)$ is set to zero. Computation proceeds from the leaves toward the root.

In the tree of Figure 4.3, let $\delta = 5$. For each of the leaf nodes $7, 8, 5, 9$, and 10 the delay is zero. The delay for any node is computed only after the delays for its children have been determined. Let u be any node and $C(u)$ be the set of all children of u. Then $d(u)$ is given by

$$d(u) = \max_{v \in C(u)} \{d(v) + w(u,v)\}$$

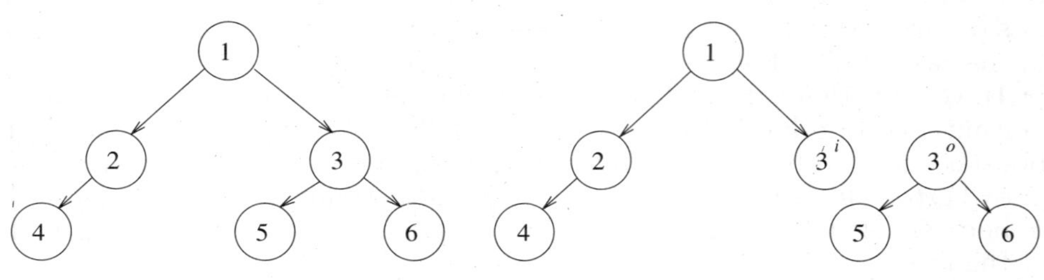

Figure 4.2 A tree before and after splitting the node 3

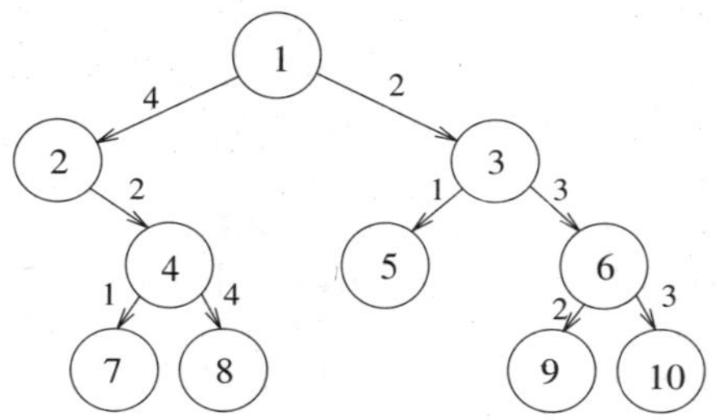

Figure 4.3 An example tree

Using the above formula, for the tree of Figure 4.3, $d(4) = 4$. Since $d(4) + w(2, 4) = 6 > \delta$, node 4 gets split. We set $d(4) = 0$. Now $d(2)$ can be computed and is equal to 2. Since $d(2) + w(1, 2)$ exceeds δ, node 2 gets split and $d(2)$ is set to zero. Then $d(6)$ is equal to 3. Also, since $d(6) + w(3, 6) > \delta$, node 6 has to be split. Set $d(6)$ to zero. Now $d(3)$ is computed as 3. Finally, $d(1)$ is computed as 5.

Figure 4.4 shows the final tree that results after splitting the nodes 2, 4, and 6. This algorithm is described in Algorithm 4.4, which is invoked as $\mathsf{TVS}(root, \delta)$, *root* being the root of the tree. The order in which TVS visits (i.e., computes the delay values of) the nodes of the tree is called the *post order* and is studied again in Chapter 6.

Algorithm TVS takes $\Theta(n)$ time, where n is the number of nodes in the tree. This can be seen as follows: When TVS is called on any node T, only

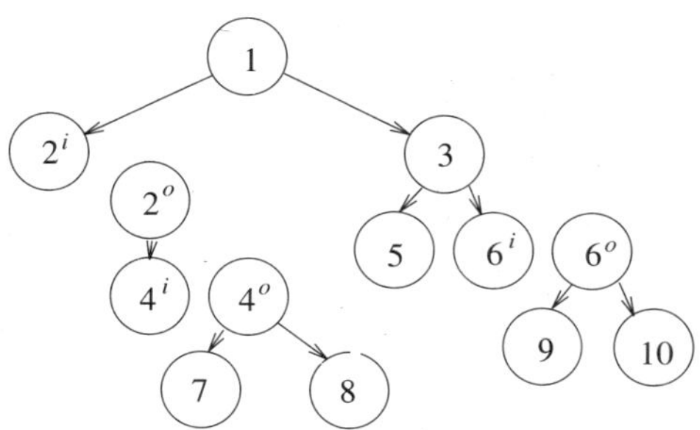

Figure 4.4 The final tree after splitting the nodes 2, 4, and 6

a constant number of operations are performed (excluding the time taken for the recursive calls). Also, TVS is called only once on each node T in the tree.

Algorithm 4.5 is a revised version of Algorithm 4.4 for the special case of directed binary trees. A sequential representation of the tree (see Section 2.2) has been employed. The tree is stored in the array *tree*[ ] with the root at *tree*[1]. Edge weights are stored in the array *weight*[ ]. If *tree*[*i*] has a tree node, the weight of the incoming edge from its parent is stored in *weight*[*i*]. The delay of node i is stored in $d[i]$. The array $d[\ ]$ is initialized to zero at the beginning. Entries in the arrays *tree*[ ] and *weight*[ ] corresponding to nonexistent nodes will be zero. As an example, for the tree of Figure 4.3, *tree*[ ] will be set to $\{1, 2, 3, 0, 4, 5, 6, 0, 0, 7, 8, 0, 0, 9, 10\}$ starting at cell 1. Also, *weight*[ ] will be set to $\{0, 4, 2, 0, 2, 1, 3, 0, 0, 1, 4, 0, 0, 2, 3\}$ at the beginning, starting from cell 1. The algorithm is invoked as TVS$(1, \delta)$. Now we show that TVS (Algorithm 4.4) will always split a minimal number of nodes.

Theorem 4.3 Algorithm TVS outputs a minimum cardinality set U such that $d(T/U) \leq \delta$ on any tree T, provided no edge of T has weight $> \delta$.

Proof: The proof is by induction on the number of nodes in the tree. If the tree has a single node, the theorem is true. Assume the theorem for all trees of size $\leq n$. We prove it for trees of size $n + 1$ also.

Let T be any tree of size $n + 1$ and let U be the set of nodes split by TVS. Also let W be a minimum cardinality set such that $d(T/W) \leq \delta$. We have to show that $|U| \leq |W|$. If $|U| = 0$, this is true. Otherwise, let x be the first vertex split by TVS. Let T_x be the subtree rooted at x. Let T' be the

```
Algorithm TVS(T, δ)
// Determine and output the nodes to be split.
// w() is the weighting function for the edges.
{
    if (T ≠ 0) then
    {
        d[T] := 0;
        for each child v of T do
        {
            TVS(v, δ);
            d[T] := max{d[T], d[v] + w(T, v)};
        }
        if ((T is not the root) and
                (d[T] + w(parent(T), T) > δ)) then
        {
            write (T); d[T] := 0;
        }
    }
}
```

Algorithm 4.4 The tree vertex splitting algorithm

tree obtained from T by deleting T_x except for x. Note that W has to have at least one node, say y, from T_x. Let $W' = W - \{y\}$. If there is a W^* such that $|W^*| < |W'|$ and $d(T'/W^*) \leq \delta$, then since $d(T/(W^* + \{x\})) \leq \delta$, W is not a minimum cardinality split set for T. Thus, W' has to be a minimum cardinality split set such that $d(T'/W') \leq \delta$.

If algorithm TVS is run on tree T', the set of split nodes output is $U - \{x\}$. Since T' has $\leq n$ nodes, $U - \{x\}$ is a minimum cardinality split set for T'. This in turn means that $|W'| \geq |U| - 1$. In other words, $|W| \geq |U|$. □

EXERCISES

1. For the tree of Figure 4.3 solve the TVSP when (a) $\delta = 4$ and (b) $\delta = 6$.

2. Rewrite TVS (Algorithm 4.4) for general trees. Make use of pointers.

```
Algorithm TVS(i, δ)
// Determine and output a minimum cardinality split set.
// The tree is realized using the sequential representation.
// Root is at tree[1]. N is the largest number such that
// tree[N] has a tree node.
{
    if (tree[i] ≠ 0) then // If the tree is not empty
        if (2i > N) then d[i] := 0; // i is a leaf.
        else
        {
            TVS(2i, δ);
            d[i] := max(d[i], d[2i] + weight[2i]);
            if (2i + 1 ≤ N) then
            {
                TVS(2i + 1, δ);
                d[i] := max(d[i], d[2i + 1] + weight[2i + 1]);
            }
        }
        if ((tree[i] ≠ 1) and (d[i] + weight[i] > δ)) then
        {
            write (tree[i]); d[i] := 0;
        }
}
```

Algorithm 4.5 TVS for the special case of binary trees

4.5 JOB SEQUENCING WITH DEADLINES

We are given a set of n jobs. Associated with job i is an integer deadline $d_i \geq 0$ and a profit $p_i > 0$. For any job i the profit p_i is earned iff the job is completed by its deadline. To complete a job, one has to process the job on a machine for one unit of time. Only one machine is available for processing jobs. A feasible solution for this problem is a subset J of jobs such that each job in this subset can be completed by its deadline. The value of a feasible solution J is the sum of the profits of the jobs in J, or $\sum_{i \in J} p_i$. An optimal solution is a feasible solution with maximum value. Here again, since the problem involves the identification of a subset, it fits the subset paradigm.

Example 4.5 Let $n = 4$, $(p_1, p_2, p_3, p_4) = (100, 10, 15, 27)$ and $(d_1, d_2, d_3, d_4) = (2, 1, 2, 1)$. The feasible solutions and their values are:

	feasible solution	processing sequence	value
1.	(1, 2)	2, 1	110
2.	(1, 3)	1, 3 or 3, 1	115
3.	(1, 4)	4, 1	127
4.	(2, 3)	2, 3	25
5.	(3, 4)	4, 3	42
6.	(1)	1	100
7.	(2)	2	10
8.	(3)	3	15
9.	(4)	4	27

Solution 3 is optimal. In this solution only jobs 1 and 4 are processed and the value is 127. These jobs must be processed in the order job 4 followed by job 1. Thus the processing of job 4 begins at time zero and that of job 1 is completed at time 2. □

To formulate a greedy algorithm to obtain an optimal solution, we must formulate an optimization measure to determine how the next job is chosen. As a first attempt we can choose the objective function $\sum_{i \in J} p_i$ as our optimization measure. Using this measure, the next job to include is the one that increases $\sum_{i \in J} p_i$ the most, subject to the constraint that the resulting J is a feasible solution. This requires us to consider jobs in nonincreasing order of the p_i's. Let us apply this criterion to the data of Example 4.5. We begin with $J = \emptyset$ and $\sum_{i \in J} p_i = 0$. Job 1 is added to J as it has the largest profit and $J = \{1\}$ is a feasible solution. Next, job 4 is considered. The solution $J = \{1, 4\}$ is also feasible. Next, job 3 is considered and discarded as $J = \{1, 3, 4\}$ is not feasible. Finally, job 2 is considered for inclusion into J. It is discarded as $J = \{1, 2, 4\}$ is not feasible. Hence, we are left with the solution $J = \{1, 4\}$ with value 127. This is the optimal solution for the given problem instance. Theorem 4.5 proves that the greedy algorithm just described always obtains an optimal solution to this sequencing problem.

Before attempting the proof, let us see how we can determine whether a given J is a feasible solution. One obvious way is to try out all possible permutations of the jobs in J and check whether the jobs in J can be processed in any one of these permutations (sequences) without violating the deadlines. For a given permutation $\sigma = i_1, i_2, i_3, \ldots, i_k$, this is easy to do, since the earliest time job $i_q, 1 \leq q \leq k$, will be completed is q. If $q > d_{i_q}$, then using σ, at least job i_q will not be completed by its deadline. However, if $|J| = i$, this requires checking $i!$ permutations. Actually, the feasibility of a set J can be determined by checking only one permutation of the jobs in J. This permutation is any one of the permutations in which jobs are ordered in nondecreasing order of deadlines.

Theorem 4.4 Let J be a set of k jobs and $\sigma = i_1, i_2, \ldots, i_k$ a permutation of jobs in J such that $d_{i_1} \leq d_{i_2} \leq \cdots \leq d_{i_k}$. Then J is a feasible solution iff the jobs in J can be processed in the order σ without violating any deadline.

Proof: Clearly, if the jobs in J can be processed in the order σ without violating any deadline, then J is a feasible solution. So, we have only to show that if J is feasible, then σ represents a possible order in which the jobs can be processed. If J is feasible, then there exists $\sigma' = r_1, r_2, \ldots, r_k$ such that $d_{r_q} \geq q$, $1 \leq q \leq k$. Assume $\sigma' \neq \sigma$. Then let a be the least index such that $r_a \neq i_a$. Let $r_b = i_a$. Clearly, $b > a$. In σ' we can interchange r_a and r_b. Since $d_{r_a} \geq d_{r_b}$, the resulting permutation $\sigma'' = s_1, s_2, \ldots, s_k$ represents an order in which the jobs can be processed without violating a deadline. Continuing in this way, σ' can be transformed into σ without violating any deadline. Hence, the theorem is proved. □

Theorem 4.4 is true even if the jobs have different processing times $t_i \geq 0$ (see the exercises).

Theorem 4.5 The greedy method described above always obtains an optimal solution to the job sequencing problem.

Proof: Let $(p_i, d_i), 1 \leq i \leq n$, define any instance of the job sequencing problem. Let I be the set of jobs selected by the greedy method. Let J be the set of jobs in an optimal solution. We now show that both I and J have the same profit values and so I is also optimal. We can assume $I \neq J$ as otherwise we have nothing to prove. Note that if $J \subset I$, then J cannot be optimal. Also, the case $I \subset J$ is ruled out by the greedy method. So, there exist jobs a and b such that $a \in I$, $a \notin J$, $b \in J$, and $b \notin I$. Let a be a highest-profit job such that $a \in I$ and $a \notin J$. It follows from the greedy method that $p_a \geq p_b$ for all jobs b that are in J but not in I. To see this, note that if $p_b > p_a$, then the greedy method would consider job b before job a and include it into I.

Now, consider feasible schedules S_I and S_J for I and J respectively. Let i be a job such that $i \in I$ and $i \in J$. Let i be scheduled from t to $t+1$ in S_I and t' to $t'+1$ in S_J. If $t < t'$, then we can interchange the job (if any) scheduled in $[t', t'+1]$ in S_I with i. If no job is scheduled in $[t', t'+1]$ in I, then i is moved to $[t', t'+1]$. The resulting schedule is also feasible. If $t' < t$, then a similar transformation can be made in S_J. In this way, we can obtain schedules S'_I and S'_J with the property that all jobs common to I and J are scheduled at the same time. Consider the interval $[t_a, t_a + 1]$ in S'_I in which the job a (defined above) is scheduled. Let b be the job (if any) scheduled in S'_J in this interval. From the choice of $a, p_a \geq p_b$. Scheduling a from t_a to $t_a + 1$ in S'_J and discarding job b gives us a feasible schedule for job set $J' = J - \{b\} \cup \{a\}$. Clearly, J' has a profit value no less than that of J and differs from I in one less job than J does.

By repeatedly using the transformation just described, J can be transformed into I with no decrease in profit value. So I must be optimal. □

A high-level description of the greedy algorithm just discussed appears as Algorithm 4.6. This algorithm constructs an optimal set J of jobs that

```
1   Algorithm GreedyJob(d, J, n)
2   // J is a set of jobs that can be completed by their deadlines.
3   {
4       J := {1};
5       for i := 2 to n do
6       {
7           if (all jobs in J ∪ {i} can be completed
8               by their deadlines) then J := J ∪ {i};
9       }
10  }
```

Algorithm 4.6 High-level description of job sequencing algorithm

can be processed by their due times. The selected jobs can be processed in the order given by Theorem 4.4.

Now, let us see how to represent the set J and how to carry out the test of lines 7 and 8 in Algorithm 4.6. Theorem 4.4 tells us how to determine whether all jobs in $J \cup \{i\}$ can be completed by their deadlines. We can avoid sorting the jobs in J each time by keeping the jobs in J ordered by deadlines. We can use an array $d[1:n]$ to store the deadlines of the jobs in the order of their p-values. The set J itself can be represented by a one-dimensional array $J[1:k]$ such that $J[r]$, $1 \leq r \leq k$ are the jobs in J and $d[J[1]] \leq d[J[2]] \leq \cdots \leq d[J[k]]$. To test whether $J \cup \{i\}$ is feasible, we have just to insert i into J preserving the deadline ordering and then verify that $d[J[r]] \leq r$, $1 \leq r \leq k+1$. The insertion of i into J is simplified by the use of a fictitious job 0 with $d[0] = 0$ and $J[0] = 0$. Note also that if job i is to be inserted at position q, then only the positions of jobs $J[q]$, $J[q+1]$, ..., $J[k]$ are changed after the insertion. Hence, it is necessary to verify only that these jobs (and also job i) do not violate their deadlines following the insertion. The algorithm that results from this discussion is function JS (Algorithm 4.7). The algorithm assumes that the jobs are already sorted such that $p_1 \geq p_2 \geq \cdots \geq p_n$. Further it assumes that $n \geq 1$ and the deadline $d[i]$ of job i is at least 1. Note that no job with $d[i] < 1$ can ever be finished by its deadline. Theorem 4.6 proves that JS is a correct implementation of the greedy strategy.

Theorem 4.6 Function JS is a correct implementation of the greedy-based method described above.

Proof: Since $d[i] \geq 1$, the job with the largest p_i will always be in the greedy solution. As the jobs are in nonincreasing order of the p_i's, line

```
1   Algorithm JS(d, j, n)
2   // d[i] ≥ 1, 1 ≤ i ≤ n are the deadlines, n ≥ 1. The jobs
3   // are ordered such that p[1] ≥ p[2] ≥ ··· ≥ p[n]. J[i]
4   // is the ith job in the optimal solution, 1 ≤ i ≤ k.
5   // Also, at termination d[J[i]] ≤ d[J[i + 1]], 1 ≤ i < k.
6   {
7       d[0] := J[0] := 0; // Initialize.
8       J[1] := 1; // Include job 1.
9       k := 1;
10      for i := 2 to n do
11      {
12          // Consider jobs in nonincreasing order of p[i]. Find
13          // position for i and check feasibility of insertion.
14          r := k;
15          while ((d[J[r]] > d[i]) and (d[J[r]] ≠ r)) do r := r - 1;
16          if ((d[J[r]] ≤ d[i]) and (d[i] > r)) then
17          {
18              // Insert i into J[ ].
19              for q := k to (r + 1) step -1 do J[q + 1] := J[q];
20              J[r + 1] := i; k := k + 1;
21          }
22      }
23      return k;
24  }
```

Algorithm 4.7 Greedy algorithm for sequencing unit time jobs with deadlines and profits

8 in Algorithm 4.7 includes the job with largest p_i. The **for** loop of line 10 considers the remaining jobs in the order required by the greedy method described earlier. At all times, the set of jobs already included in the solution is maintained in J. If $J[i]$, $1 \leq i \leq k$, is the set already included, then J is such that $d[J[i]] \leq d[J[i+1]]$, $1 \leq i < k$. This allows for easy application of the feasibility test of Theorem 4.4. When job i is being considered, the **while** loop of line 15 determines where in J this job has to be inserted. The use of a fictitious job 0 (line 7) allows easy insertion into position 1. Let w be such that $d[J[w]] \leq d[i]$ and $d[J[q]] > d[i]$, $w < q \leq k$. If job i is included into J, then jobs $J[q]$, $w < q \leq k$, have to be moved one position up in J (line 19). From Theorem 4.4, it follows that such a move retains feasibility of J iff $d[J[q]] \neq q$, $w < q \leq k$. This condition is verified in line 15. In

addition, i can be inserted at position $w+1$ iff $d[i] > w$. This is verified in line 16 (note $r = w$ on exit from the **while** loop if $d[J[q]] \neq q$, $w < q \leq k$). The correctness of JS follows from these observations. □

For JS there are two possible parameters in terms of which its complexity can be measured. We can use n, the number of jobs, and s, the number of jobs included in the solution J. The **while** loop of line 15 in Algorithm 4.7 is iterated at most k times. Each iteration takes $\Theta(1)$ time. If the conditional of line 16 is true, then lines 19 and 20 are executed. These lines require $\Theta(k-r)$ time to insert job i. Hence, the total time for each iteration of the **for** loop of line 10 is $\Theta(k)$. This loop is iterated $n-1$ times. If s is the final value of k, that is, s is the number of jobs in the final solution, then the total time needed by algorithm JS is $\Theta(sn)$. Since $s \leq n$, the worst-case time, as a function of n alone is $\Theta(n^2)$. If we consider the job set $p_i = d_i = n - i + 1$, $1 \leq i \leq n$, then algorithm JS takes $\Theta(n^2)$ time to determine J. Hence, the worst-case computing time for JS is $\Theta(n^2)$. In addition to the space needed for d, JS needs $\Theta(s)$ amount of space for J. Note that the profit values are not needed by JS. It is sufficient to know that $p_i \geq p_{i+1}$, $1 \leq i < n$.

The computing time of JS can be reduced from $O(n^2)$ to nearly $O(n)$ by using the disjoint set union and find algorithms (see Section 2.5) and a different method to determine the feasibility of a partial solution. If J is a feasible subset of jobs, then we can determine the processing times for each of the jobs using the rule: if job i hasn't been assigned a processing time, then assign it to the slot $[\alpha-1, \alpha]$, where α is the largest integer r such that $1 \leq r \leq d_i$ and the slot $[\alpha-1, \alpha]$ is free. This rule simply delays the processing of job i as much as possible. Consequently, when J is being built up job by job, jobs already in J do not have to be moved from their assigned slots to accommodate the new job. If for the new job being considered there is no α as defined above, then it cannot be included in J. The proof of the validity of this statement is left as an exercise.

Example 4.6 Let $n = 5, (p_1, \ldots, p_5) = (20, 15, 10, 5, 1)$ and $(d_1, \ldots, d_5) = (2, 2, 1, 3, 3)$. Using the above feasibility rule, we have

J	assigned slots	job considered	action	profit
$\emptyset$	none	1	assign to [1, 2]	0
{1}	[1, 2]	2	assign to [0, 1]	20
{1, 2}	[0, 1], [1, 2]	3	cannot fit; reject	35
{1, 2}	[0, 1], [1, 2]	4	assign to [2, 3]	35
{1, 2, 4}	[0, 1], [1, 2], [2, 3]	5	reject	40

The optimal solution is $J = \{1, 2, 4\}$ with a profit of 40. □

Since there are only n jobs and each job takes one unit of time, it is necessary only to consider the time slots $[i-1, i]$, $1 \leq i \leq b$, such that $b = \min\{n, \max\{d_i\}\}$. One way to implement the above scheduling rule is to partition the time slots $[i-1, i]$, $1 \leq i \leq b$, into sets. We use i to represent the time slots $[i-1, i]$. For any slot i, let n_i be the largest integer such that $n_i \leq i$ and slot n_i is free. To avoid end conditions, we introduce a fictitious slot $[-1, 0]$ which is always free. Two slots i and j are in the same set iff $n_i = n_j$. Clearly, if i and j, $i < j$, are in the same set, then $i, i+1, i+2, \ldots, j$ are in the same set. Associated with each set k of slots is a value $f(k)$. Then $f(k) = n_i$ for all slots i in set k. Using the set representation of Section 2.5, each set is represented as a tree. The root node identifies the set. The function f is defined only for root nodes. Initially, all slots are free and we have $b+1$ sets corresponding to the $b+1$ slots $[i-1, i]$, $0 \leq i \leq b$. At this time $f(i) = i$, $0 \leq i \leq b$. We use $p(i)$ to link slot i into its set tree. With the conventions for the union and find algorithms of Section 2.5, $p(i) = -1$, $0 \leq i \leq b$, initially. If a job with deadline d is to be scheduled, then we need to find the root of the tree containing the slot $\min\{n, d\}$. If this root is j, then $f(j)$ is the nearest free slot, provided $f(j) \neq 0$. Having used this slot, the set with root j should be combined with the set containing slot $f(j) - 1$.

Example 4.7 The trees defined by the $p(i)$'s for the first three iterations in Example 4.6 are shown in Figure 4.5. □

The fast algorithm appears as FJS (Algorithm 4.8). Its computing time is readily observed to be $O(n\alpha(2n, n))$ (recall that $\alpha(2n, n)$ is the inverse of Ackermann's function defined in Section 2.5). It needs an additional $2n$ words of space for f and p.

EXERCISES

1. You are given a set of n jobs. Associated with each job i is a processing time t_i and a deadline d_i by which it must be completed. A feasible schedule is a permutation of the jobs such that if the jobs are processed in that order, then each job finishes by its deadline. Define a greedy schedule to be one in which the jobs are processed in nondecreasing order of deadlines. Show that if there exists a feasible schedule, then all greedy schedules are feasible.

2. [Optimal assignment] Assume there are n workers and n jobs. Let v_{ij} be the value of assigning worker i to job j. An assignment of workers to jobs corresponds to the assignment of 0 or 1 to the variables x_{ij}, $1 \leq i$, $j \leq n$. Then $x_{ij} = 1$ means worker i is assigned to job j, and $x_{ij} = 0$ means that worker i is not assigned to job j. A valid assignment is one in which each worker is assigned to exactly one job and exactly

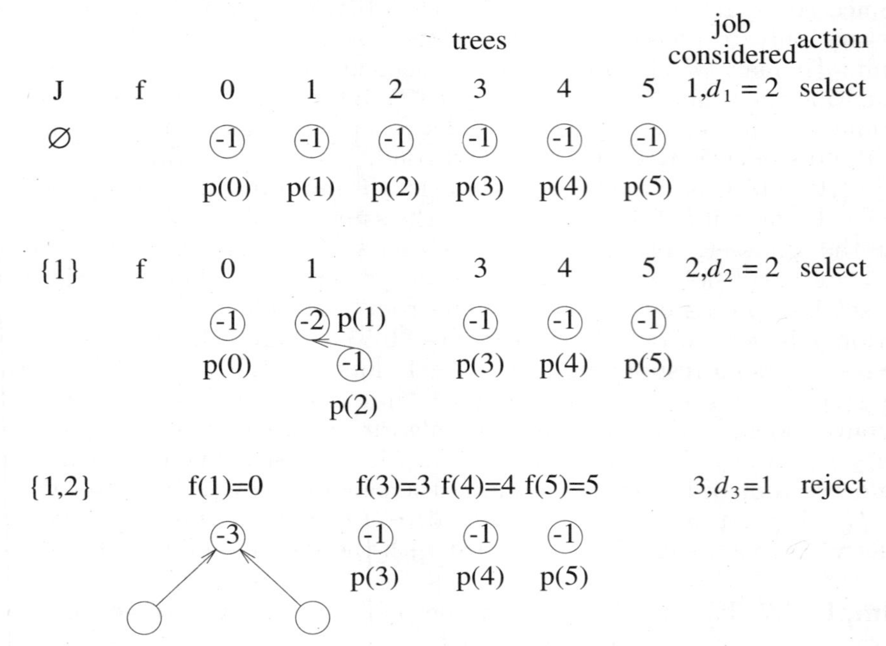

Figure 4.5 Fast job scheduling

one worker is assigned to any one job. The value of an assignment is $\sum_i \sum_j v_{ij} x_{ij}$.

For example, assume there are three workers w_1, w_2, and w_3 and three jobs j_1, j_2, and j_3. Let the values of assignment be $v_{11} = 11$, $v_{12} = 5$, $v_{13} = 8$, $v_{21} = 3$, $v_{22} = 7$, $v_{23} = 15$, $v_{31} = 8$, $v_{32} = 12$, and $v_{33} = 9$. Then, a valid assignment is $x_{12} = 1$, $x_{23} = 1$, and $x_{31} = 1$. The rest of the x_{ij}'s are zeros. The value of this assignment is $5 + 15 + 8 = 28$.

An optimal assignment is a valid assignment of maximum value. Write algorithms for two different greedy assignment schemes. One of these assigns a worker to the best possible job. The other assigns to a job the best possible worker. Show that neither of these schemes is guaranteed to yield optimal assignments. Is either scheme always better than the other? Assume $v_{ij} > 0$.

```
1   Algorithm FJS(d, n, b, j)
2   // Find an optimal solution J[1 : k]. It is assumed that
3   // p[1] ≥ p[2] ≥ ··· ≥ p[n] and that b = min{n, max_i(d[i])}.
4   {
5       // Initially there are b + 1 single node trees.
6       for i := 0 to b do f[i] := i;
7       k := 0; // Initialize.
8       for i := 1 to n do
9       { // Use greedy rule.
10          q := CollapsingFind(min(n, d[i]));
11          if (f[q] ≠ 0) then
12          {
13              k := k + 1; J[k] := i; // Select job i.
14              m := CollapsingFind(f[q] − 1);
15              WeightedUnion(m, q);
16              f[q] := f[m]; // q may be new root.
17          }
18      }
19  }
```

Algorithm 4.8 Faster algorithm for job sequencing

3. (a) What is the solution generated by the function JS when $n = 7$, $(p_1, p_2, \ldots, p_7) = (3, 5, 20, 18, 1, 6, 30)$, and $(d_1, d_2, \ldots, d_7) = (1, 3, 4, 3, 2, 1, 2)$?
   (b) Show that Theorem 4.4 is true even if jobs have different processing requirements. Associated with job i is a profit $p_i > 0$, a time requirement $t_i > 0$, and a deadline $d_i \geq t_i$.
   (c) Show that for the situation of part (a), the greedy method of this section doesn't necessarily yield an optimal solution.

4. (a) For the job sequencing problem of this section, show that the subset J represents a feasible solution iff the jobs in J can be processed according to the rule: if job i in J hasn't been assigned a processing time, then assign it to the slot $[\alpha - 1, \alpha]$, where α is the least integer r such that $1 \leq r \leq d_i$ and the slot $[\alpha - 1, \alpha]$ is free.
   (b) For the problem instance of Exercise 3(a) draw the trees and give the values of $f(i), 0 \leq i \leq n$, after each iteration of the **for** loop of line 8 of Algorithm 4.8.

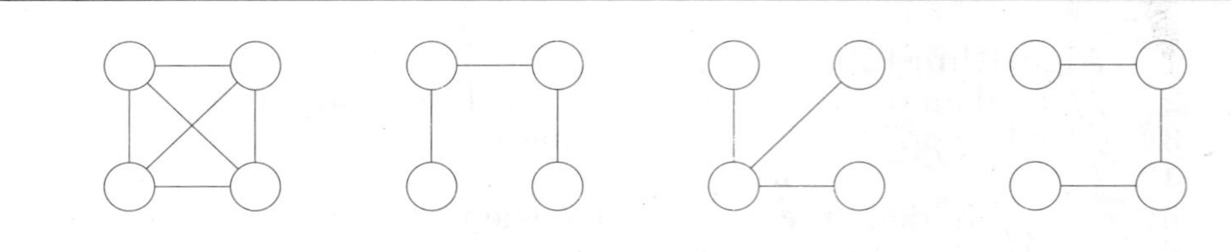

Figure 4.6 An undirected graph and three of its spanning trees

4.6 MINIMUM-COST SPANNING TREES

Definition 4.1 Let $G = (V, E)$ be an undirected connected graph. A subgraph $t = (V, E')$ of G is a *spanning tree* of G iff t is a tree. □

Example 4.8 Figure 4.6 shows the complete graph on four nodes together with three of its spanning trees. □

Spanning trees have many applications. For example, they can be used to obtain an independent set of circuit equations for an electric network. First, a spanning tree for the electric network is obtained. Let B be the set of network edges not in the spanning tree. Adding an edge from B to the spanning tree creates a cycle. Kirchoff's second law is used on each cycle to obtain a circuit equation. The cycles obtained in this way are independent (i.e., none of these cycles can be obtained by taking a linear combination of the remaining cycles) as each contains an edge from B that is not contained in any other cycle. Hence, the circuit equations so obtained are also independent. In fact, it can be shown that the cycles obtained by introducing the edges of B one at a time into the resulting spanning tree form a cycle basis, and so all other cycles in the graph can be constructed by taking a linear combination of the cycles in the basis.

Another application of spanning trees arises from the property that a spanning tree is a minimal subgraph G' of G such that $V(G') = V(G)$ and G' is connected. (A minimal subgraph is one with the fewest number of edges.) Any connected graph with n vertices must have at least $n - 1$ edges and all connected graphs with $n - 1$ edges are trees. If the nodes of G represent cities and the edges represent possible communication links connecting two cities, then the minimum number of links needed to connect the n cities is $n - 1$. The spanning trees of G represent all feasible choices.

In practical situations, the edges have weights assigned to them. These weights may represent the cost of construction, the length of the link, and so on. Given such a weighted graph, one would then wish to select cities to have minimum total cost or minimum total length. In either case the links

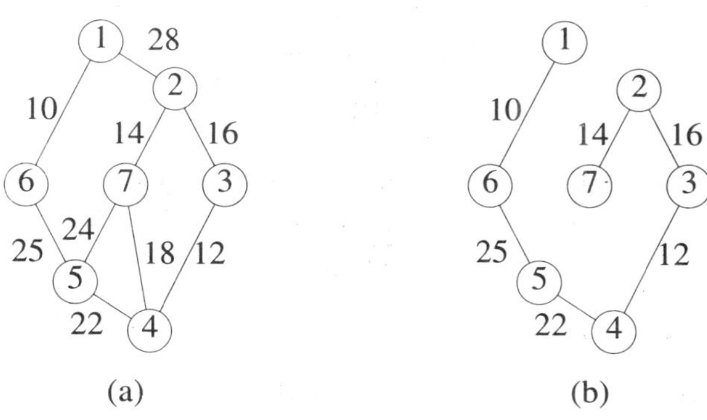

Figure 4.7 A graph and its minimum cost spanning tree

selected have to form a tree (assuming all weights are positive). If this is not so, then the selection of links contains a cycle. Removal of any one of the links on this cycle results in a link selection of less cost connecting all cities. We are therefore interested in finding a spanning tree of G with minimum cost. (The cost of a spanning tree is the sum of the costs of the edges in that tree.) Figure 4.7 shows a graph and one of its minimum-cost spanning trees. Since the identification of a minimum-cost spanning tree involves the selection of a subset of the edges, this problem fits the subset paradigm.

4.6.1 Prim's Algorithm

A greedy method to obtain a minimum-cost spanning tree builds this tree edge by edge. The next edge to include is chosen according to some optimization criterion. The simplest such criterion is to choose an edge that results in a minimum increase in the sum of the costs of the edges so far included. There are two possible ways to interpret this criterion. In the first, the set of edges so far selected form a tree. Thus, if A is the set of edges selected so far, then A forms a tree. The next edge (u, v) to be included in A is a minimum-cost edge not in A with the property that $A \cup \{(u, v)\}$ is also a tree. Exercise 2 shows that this selection criterion results in a minimum-cost spanning tree. The corresponding algorithm is known as Prim's algorithm.

Example 4.9 Figure 4.8 shows the working of Prim's method on the graph of Figure 4.7(a). The spanning tree obtained is shown in Figure 4.7(b) and has a cost of 99. □

Having seen how Prim's method works, let us obtain a pseudocode algorithm to find a minimum-cost spanning tree using this method. The algo-

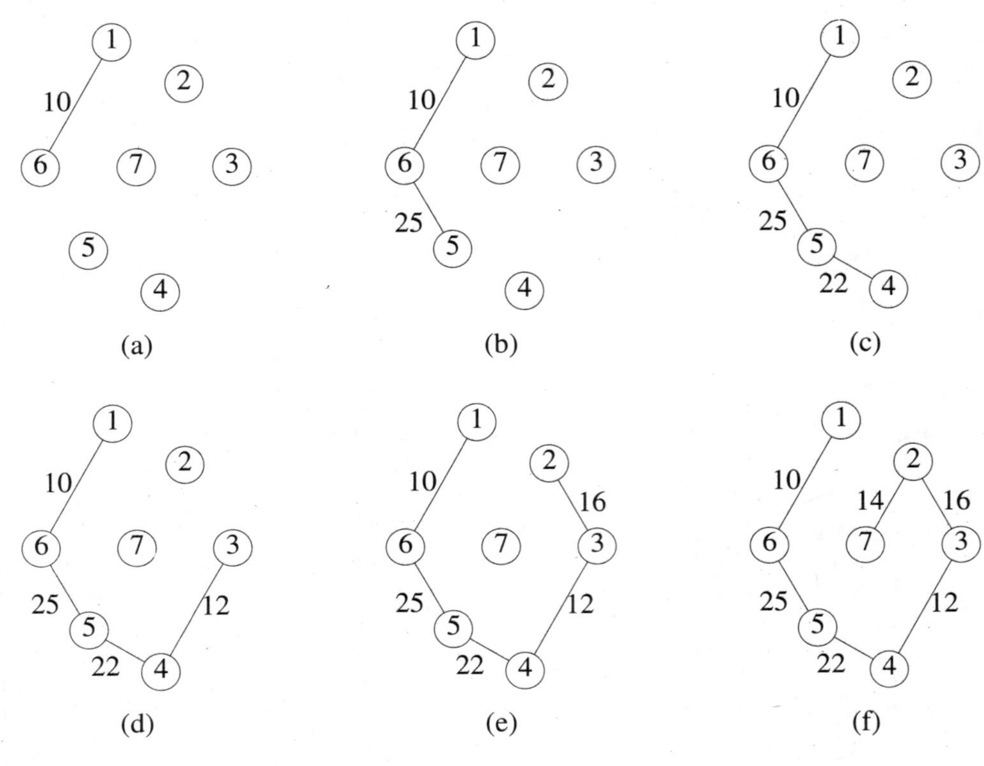

Figure 4.8 Stages in Prim's algorithm

rithm will start with a tree that includes only a minimum-cost edge of G. Then, edges are added to this tree one by one. The next edge (i, j) to be added is such that i is a vertex already included in the tree, j is a vertex not yet included, and the cost of (i, j), $cost[i, j]$, is minimum among all edges (k, l) such that vertex k is in the tree and vertex l is not in the tree. To determine this edge (i, j) efficiently, we associate with each vertex j not yet included in the tree a value $near[j]$. The value $near[j]$ is a vertex in the tree such that $cost[j, near[j]]$ is minimum among all choices for $near[j]$. We define $near[j] = 0$ for all vertices j that are already in the tree. The next edge to include is defined by the vertex j such that $near[j] \neq 0$ (j not already in the tree) and $cost[j, near[j]]$ is minimum.

In function Prim (Algorithm 4.9), line 9 selects a minimum-cost edge. Lines 10 to 15 initialize the variables so as to represent a tree comprising only the edge (k, l). In the **for** loop of line 16 the remainder of the spanning tree is built up edge by edge. Lines 18 and 19 select $(j, near[j])$ as the next edge to include. Lines 23 to 25 update $near[\ ]$.

The time required by algorithm Prim is $O(n^2)$, where n is the number of vertices in the graph G. To see this, note that line 9 takes $O(|E|)$ time and line 10 takes $\Theta(1)$ time. The **for** loop of line 12 takes $\Theta(n)$ time. Lines 18 and 19 and the **for** loop of line 23 require $O(n)$ time. So, each iteration of the **for** loop of line 16 takes $O(n)$ time. The total time for the **for** loop of line 16 is therefore $O(n^2)$. Hence, Prim runs in $O(n^2)$ time.

If we store the nodes not yet included in the tree as a red-black tree (see Section 2.4.2), lines 18 and 19 take $O(\log n)$ time. Note that a red-black tree supports the following operations in $O(\log n)$ time: insert, delete (an arbitrary element), find-min, and search (for an arbitrary element). The **for** loop of line 23 has to examine only the nodes adjacent to j. Thus its overall frequency is $O(|E|)$. Updating in lines 24 and 25 also takes $O(\log n)$ time (since an update can be done using a delete and an insertion into the red-black tree). Thus the overall run time is $O((n + |E|) \log n)$.

The algorithm can be speeded a bit by making the observation that a minimum-cost spanning tree includes for each vertex v a minimum-cost edge incident to v. To see this, suppose t is a minimum-cost spanning tree for $G = (V, E)$. Let v be any vertex in t. Let (v, w) be an edge with minimum cost among all edges incident to v. Assume that $(v, w) \notin E(t)$ and $cost[v, w] < cost[v, x]$ for all edges $(v, x) \in E(t)$. The inclusion of (v, w) into t creates a unique cycle. This cycle must include an edge (v, x), $x \neq w$. Removing (v, x) from $E(t) \cup \{(v, w)\}$ breaks this cycle without disconnecting the graph $(V, E(t) \cup \{(v, w)\})$. Hence, $(V, E(t) \cup \{(v, w)\} - \{(v, x)\})$ is also a spanning tree. Since $cost[v, w] < cost[v, x]$, this spanning tree has lower cost than t. This contradicts the assumption that t is a minimum-cost spanning tree of G. So, t includes minimum-cost edges as stated above.

From this observation it follows that we can start the algorithm with a tree consisting of any arbitrary vertex and no edge. Then edges can be added one by one. The changes needed are to lines 9 to 17. These lines can be replaced by the lines

```
9'        mincost := 0;
10'       for i := 2 to n do near[i] := 1;
11'           // Vertex 1 is initially in t.
12'       near[1] := 0;
13'-16'   for i := 1 to n - 1 do
17'       { // Find n - 1 edges for t.
```

4.6.2 Kruskal's Algorithm

There is a second possible interpretation of the optimization criteria mentioned earlier in which the edges of the graph are considered in nondecreasing

```
Algorithm Prim(E, cost, n, t)
// E is the set of edges in G. cost[1 : n, 1 : n] is the cost
// adjacency matrix of an n vertex graph such that cost[i, j] is
// either a positive real number or ∞ if no edge (i, j) exists.
// A minimum spanning tree is computed and stored as a set of
// edges in the array t[1 : n − 1, 1 : 2]. (t[i, 1], t[i, 2]) is an edge in
// the minimum-cost spanning tree. The final cost is returned.
{
    Let (k, l) be an edge of minimum cost in E;
    mincost := cost[k, l];
    t[1, 1] := k; t[1, 2] := l;
    for i := 1 to n do // Initialize near.
        if (cost[i, l] < cost[i, k]) then near[i] := l;
        else near[i] := k;
    near[k] := near[l] := 0;
    for i := 2 to n − 1 do
    { // Find n − 2 additional edges for t.
        Let j be an index such that near[j] ≠ 0 and
        cost[j, near[j]] is minimum;
        t[i, 1] := j; t[i, 2] := near[j];
        mincost := mincost + cost[j, near[j]];
        near[j] := 0;
        for k := 1 to n do // Update near[ ].
            if ((near[k] ≠ 0) and (cost[k, near[k]] > cost[k, j]))
                then near[k] := j;
    }
    return mincost;
}
```

Algorithm 4.9 Prim's minimum-cost spanning tree algorithm

order of cost. This interpretation is that the set t of edges so far selected for the spanning tree be such that it is possible to *complete* t into a tree. Thus t may not be a tree at all stages in the algorithm. In fact, it will generally only be a forest since the set of edges t can be completed into a tree iff there are no cycles in t. We show in Theorem 4.7 that this interpretation of the greedy method also results in a minimum-cost spanning tree. This method is due to Kruskal.

Example 4.10 Consider the graph of Figure 4.7(a). We begin with no edges selected. Figure 4.9(a) shows the current graph with no edges selected. Edge

(1, 6) is the first edge considered. It is included in the spanning tree being built. This yields the graph of Figure 4.9(b). Next, the edge (3, 4) is selected and included in the tree (Figure 4.9(c)). The next edge to be considered is (2, 7). Its inclusion in the tree being built does not create a cycle, so we get the graph of Figure 4.9(d). Edge (2, 3) is considered next and included in the tree Figure 4.9(e). Of the edges not yet considered, (7, 4) has the least cost. It is considered next. Its inclusion in the tree results in a cycle, so this edge is discarded. Edge (5, 4) is the next edge to be added to the tree being built. This results in the configuration of Figure 4.9(f). The next edge to be considered is the edge (7, 5). It is discarded, as its inclusion creates a cycle. Finally, edge (6, 5) is considered and included in the tree being built. This completes the spanning tree. The resulting tree (Figure 4.7(b)) has cost 99. □

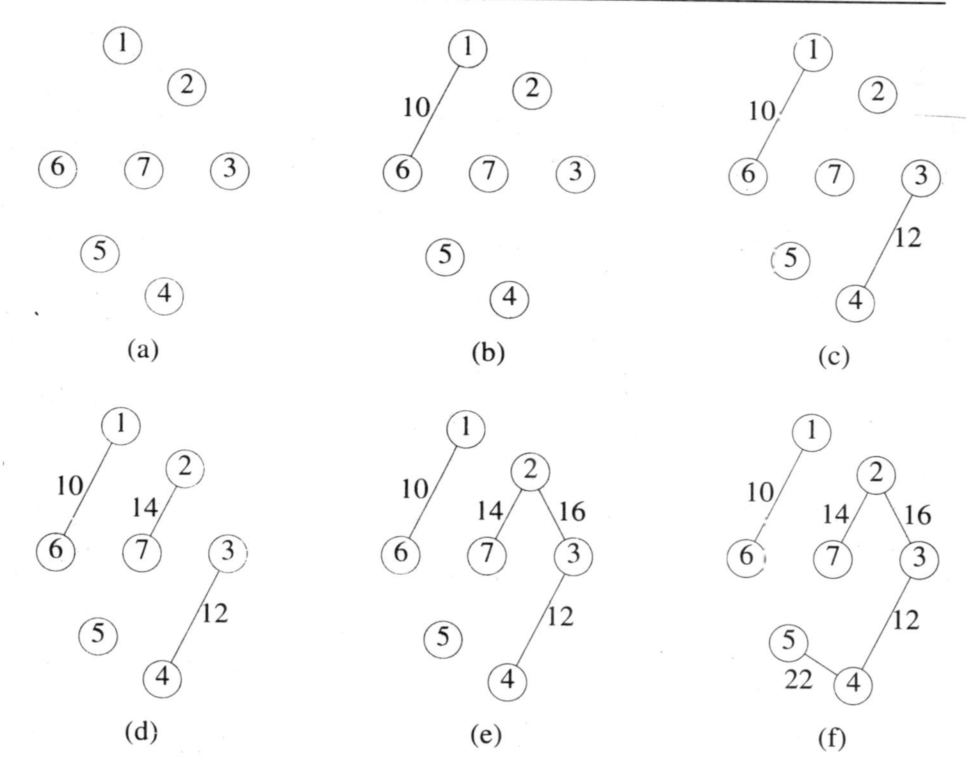

Figure 4.9 Stages in Kruskal's algorithm

```
1   t := ∅;
2   while ((t has less than n − 1 edges) and (E ≠ ∅)) do
3   {
4        Choose an edge (v, w) from E of lowest cost;
5        Delete (v, w) from E;
6        if (v, w) does not create a cycle in t then add (v, w) to t;
7        else discard (v, w);
8   }
```

Algorithm 4.10 Early form of minimum-cost spanning tree algorithm due to Kruskal

For clarity, Kruskal's method is written out more formally in Algorithm 4.10. Initially E is the set of all edges in G. The only functions we wish to perform on this set are (1) determine an edge with minimum cost (line 4) and (2) delete this edge (line 5). Both these functions can be performed efficiently if the edges in E are maintained as a sorted sequential list. It is not essential to sort all the edges so long as the next edge for line 4 can be determined easily. If the edges are maintained as a minheap, then the next edge to consider can be obtained in $O(\log |E|)$ time. The construction of the heap itself takes $O(|E|)$ time.

To be able to perform step 6 efficiently, the vertices in G should be grouped together in such a way that one can easily determine whether the vertices v and w are already connected by the earlier selection of edges. If they are, then the edge (v, w) is to be discarded. If they are not, then (v, w) is to be added to t. One possible grouping is to place all vertices in the same connected component of t into a set (all connected components of t will also be trees). Then, two vertices v and w are connected in t iff they are in the same set. For example, when the edge $(2, 6)$ is to be considered, the sets are $\{1, 2\}, \{3, 4, 6\}$, and $\{5\}$. Vertices 2 and 6 are in different sets so these sets are combined to give $\{1, 2, 3, 4, 6\}$ and $\{5\}$. The next edge to be considered is $(1, 4)$. Since vertices 1 and 4 are in the same set, the edge is rejected. The edge $(3, 5)$ connects vertices in different sets and results in the final spanning tree. Using the set representation and the union and find algorithms of Section 2.5, we can obtain an efficient (almost linear) implementation of line 6. The computing time is, therefore, determined by the time for lines 4 and 5, which in the worst case is $O(|E| \log |E|)$.

If the representations discussed above are used, then the pseudocode of Algorithm 4.11 results. In line 6 an initial heap of edges is constructed. In line 7 each vertex is assigned to a distinct set (and hence to a distinct tree).

```
1   Algorithm Kruskal(E, cost, n, t)
2   // E is the set of edges in G. G has n vertices. cost[u, v] is the
3   // cost of edge (u, v). t is the set of edges in the minimum-cost
4   // spanning tree. The final cost is returned.
5   {
6       Construct a heap out of the edge costs using Heapify;
7       for i := 1 to n do parent[i] := -1;
8       // Each vertex is in a different set.
9       i := 0; mincost := 0.0;
10      while ((i < n - 1) and (heap not empty)) do
11      {
12          Delete a minimum cost edge (u, v) from the heap
13          and reheapify using Adjust;
14          j := Find(u); k := Find(v);
15          if (j ≠ k) then
16          {
17              i := i + 1;
18              t[i, 1] := u; t[i, 2] := v;
19              mincost := mincost + cost[u, v];
20              Union(j, k);
21          }
22      }
23      if (i ≠ n - 1) then write ("No spanning tree");
24      else return mincost;
25  }
```

Algorithm 4.11 Kruskal's algorithm

The set t is the set of edges to be included in the minimum-cost spanning tree and i is the number of edges in t. The set t can be represented as a sequential list using a two-dimensional array $t[1 : n-1, 1 : 2]$. Edge (u, v) can be added to t by the assignments $t[i, 1] := u$; and $t[i, 2] := v$;. In the **while** loop of line 10, edges are removed from the heap one by one in nondecreasing order of cost. Line 14 determines the sets containing u and v. If $j \neq k$, then vertices u and v are in different sets (and so in different trees) and edge (u, v) is included into t. The sets containing u and v are combined (line 20). If $u = v$, the edge (u, v) is discarded as its inclusion into t would create a cycle. Line 23 determines whether a spanning tree was found. It follows that $i \neq n - 1$ iff the graph G is not connected. One can verify that the computing time is $O(|E| \log |E|)$, where E is the edge set of G.

Theorem 4.7 Kruskal's algorithm generates a minimum-cost spanning tree for every connected undirected graph G.

Proof: Let G be any undirected connected graph. Let t be the spanning tree for G generated by Kruskal's algorithm. Let t' be a minimum-cost spanning tree for G. We show that both t and t' have the same cost.

Let $E(t)$ and $E(t')$ respectively be the edges in t and t'. If n is the number of vertices in G, then both t and t' have $n-1$ edges. If $E(t) = E(t')$, then t is clearly of minimum cost. If $E(t) \neq E(t')$, then let q be a minimum-cost edge such that $q \in E(t)$ and $q \notin E(t')$. Clearly, such a q must exist. The inclusion of q into t' creates a unique cycle (Exercise 5). Let $q, e_1, e_2, \ldots, e_k$ be this unique cycle. At least one of the e_i's, $1 \leq i \leq k$, is not in $E(t)$ as otherwise t would also contain the cycle $q, e_1, e_2, \ldots, e_k$. Let e_j be an edge on this cycle such that $e_j \notin E(t)$. If e_j is of lower cost than q, then Kruskal's algorithm will consider e_j before q and include e_j into t. To see this, note that all edges in $E(t)$ of cost less than the cost of q are also in $E(t')$ and do not form a cycle with e_j. So $cost(e_j) \geq cost(q)$.

Now, reconsider the graph with edge set $E(t') \cup \{q\}$. Removal of any edge on the cycle $q, e_1, e_2, \ldots, e_k$ will leave behind a tree t'' (Exercise 5). In particular, if we delete the edge e_j, then the resulting tree t'' will have a cost no more than the cost of t' (as $cost(e_j) \geq cost(e)$). Hence, t'' is also a minimum-cost tree.

By repeatedly using the transformation described above, tree t' can be transformed into the spanning tree t without any increase in cost. Hence, t is a minimum-cost spanning tree. □

4.6.3 An Optimal Randomized Algorithm (∗)

Any algorithm for finding the minimum-cost spanning tree of a given graph $G(V, E)$ will have to spend $\Omega(|V| + |E|)$ time in the worst case, since it has to examine each node and each edge at least once before determining the correct answer. A randomized Las Vegas algorithm that runs in time $\widetilde{O}(|V| + |E|)$ can be devised as follows: (1) Randomly sample m edges from G (for some suitable m). (2) Let G' be the induced subgraph; that is, G' has V as its node set and the sampled edges in its edge set. The subgraph G' need not be connected. Recursively find a minimum-cost spanning tree for each component of G'. Let F be the resultant *minimum-cost spanning forest* of G'. (3) Using F, eliminate certain edges (called the *F-heavy edges*) of G that cannot possibly be in a minimum-cost spanning tree. Let G'' be the graph that results from G after elimination of the F-heavy edges. (4) Recursively find a minimum-cost spanning tree for G''. This will also be a minimum-cost spanning tree for G.

Steps 1 to 3 are useful in reducing the number of edges in G. The algorithm can be speeded up further if we can reduce the number of nodes in the input graph as well. Such a node elimination can be effected using the *Borůvka steps.* In a Borůvka step, for each node, an incident edge with minimum weight is chosen. For example in Figure 4.10(a), the edge $(1, 3)$ is chosen for node 1, the edge $(6, 7)$ is chosen for node 7, and so on. All the chosen edges are shown with thick lines. The connected components of the induced graph are found. In the example of Figure 4.10(a), the nodes 1, 2, and 3 form one component, the nodes 4 and 5 form a second component, and the nodes 6 and 7 form another component. Replace each component with a single node. The component with nodes 1, 2, and 3 is replaced with the node a. The other two components are replaced with the nodes b and c, respectively. Edges within the individual components are thrown away. The resultant graph is shown in Figure 4.10(b). In this graph keep only an edge of minimum weight between any two nodes. Delete any isolated nodes.

Since an edge is chosen for every node, the number of nodes after one Borůvka step reduces by a factor of at least two. A minimum-cost spanning tree for the reduced graph can be extended easily to get a minimum-cost spanning tree for the original graph. If E' is the set of edges in the minimum-cost spanning tree of the reduced graph, we simply include into E' the edges chosen in the Borůvka step to obtain the minimum-cost spanning tree edges for the original graph. In the example of Figure 4.10, a minimum-cost spanning tree for (c) will consist of the edges (a, b) and (b, c). Thus a minimum-cost spanning tree for the graph of (a) will have the edges: $(1, 3), (3, 2), (4, 5), (6, 7), (3, 4)$, and $(2, 6)$. More details of the algorithms are given below.

Definition 4.2 Let F be a forest that forms a subgraph of a given weighted graph $G(V, E)$. If u and v are any two nodes in F, let $F(u, v)$ denote the path (if any) connecting u and v in F and let $Fcost(u, v)$ denote the maximum weight of any edge in the path $F(u, v)$. If there is no path between u and v in F, $Fcost(u, v)$ is taken to be ∞. Any edge (x, y) of G is said to be F-heavy if $cost[x, y] > Fcost(x, y)$ and F-light otherwise. □

Note that all the edges of F are F-light. Also, any F-heavy edge cannot belong to a minimum-cost spanning tree of G. The proof of this is left as an exercise. The randomized algorithm applies two Borůvka steps to reduce the number of nodes in the input graph. Next, it samples the edges of G and processes them to eliminate a constant fraction of them. A minimum-cost spanning tree for the resultant reduced graph is recursively computed. From this tree, a spanning tree for G is obtained. A detailed description of the algorithm appears as Algorithm 4.12.

Lemma 4.3 states that Step 4 can be completed in time $O(|V| + |E|)$. The proof of this can be found in the references supplied at the end of this chapter. Step 1 takes $O(|V| + |E|)$ time and step 2 takes $O(|E|)$ time. Step 6 takes $O(|E|)$ time as well. The time taken in all the recursive calls in steps 3 and 5 can be shown to be $O(|V| + |E|)$. For a proof, see the references at the end of the chapter. A crucial fact that is used in the proof is that both the

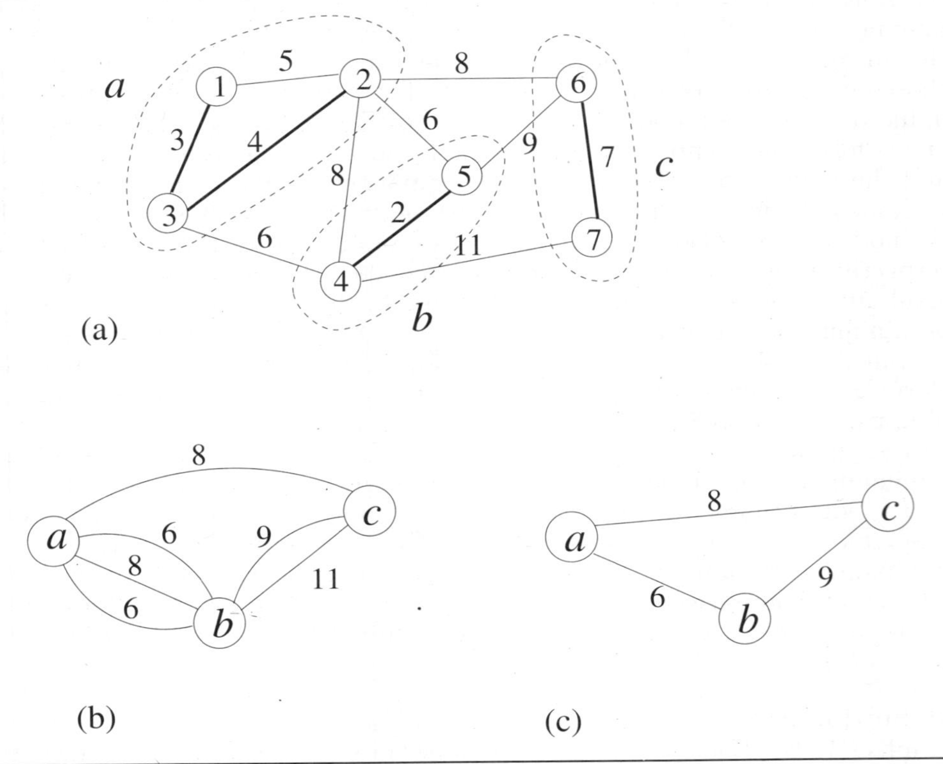

Figure 4.10 A Borůvka step

number of nodes and the number of edges are reduced by a constant factor, with high probability, in each level of recursion.

Lemma 4.3 Let $G(V, E)$ be any weighted graph and let F be a subgraph of G that forms a forest. Then, all the F-heavy edges of G can be identified in time $O(|V| + |E|)$. □

Theorem 4.8 A minimum-weight spanning tree for any given weighted graph can be computed in time $\widetilde{O}(|V| + |E|)$. □

EXERCISES

1. Compute a minimum cost spanning tree for the graph of Figure 4.11 using (a) Prim's algorithm and (b) Kruskal's algorithm.

Step 1. Apply two Borůvka steps. At the end, the number of nodes will have decreased by a factor at least 4. Let the resultant graph be $\widetilde{G}(\widetilde{V}, \widetilde{E})$.

Step 2. Form a subgraph $G'(V', E')$ of $\widetilde{G}$, where each edge of $\widetilde{G}$ is chosen randomly to be in E' with probability $\frac{1}{2}$. The expected number of edges in E' is $\frac{|\widetilde{E}|}{2}$.

Step 3. Recursively find a minimum-cost spanning forest F for G'.

Step 4. Eliminate all the F-heavy edges from $\widetilde{G}$. With high probability, at least a constant fraction of the edges of $\widetilde{G}$ will be eliminated. Let G'' be the resultant graph.

Step 5. Compute a minimum-cost spanning tree (call it T'') for G'' recursively. The tree T'' will also be a minimum-cost spanning tree for $\widetilde{G}$.

Step 6. Return the edges of T'' together with the edges chosen in the Borůvka steps of step 1. These are the edges of a minimum-cost spanning tree for G.

Algorithm 4.12 An optimal randomized algorithm

2. Prove that Prim's method of this section generates minimum-cost spanning trees.
3. (a) Rewrite Prim's algorithm under the assumption that the graphs are represented by adjacency lists.
   (b) Program and run the above version of Prim's algorithm against Algorithm 4.10. Compare the two on a representative set of graphs.
   (c) Analyze precisely the computing time and space requirements of your new version of Prim's algorithm using adjacency lists.
4. Program and run Kruskal's algorithm, described in Algorithm 4.11. You will have to modify functions Heapify and Adjust of Chapter 2. Use the same test data you devised to test Prim's algorithm in Exercise 3.

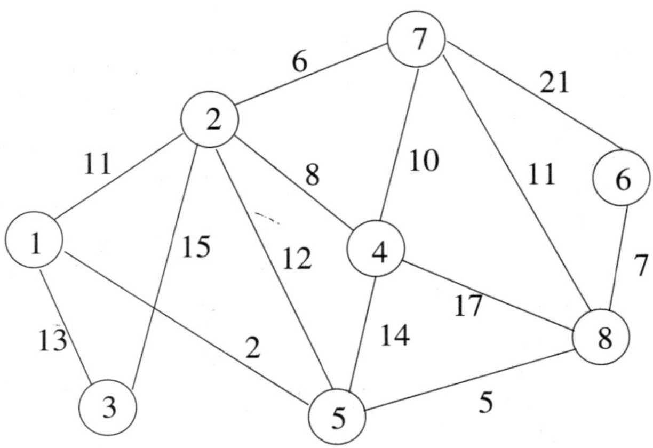

Figure 4.11 Graph for Exercise 1

5. (a) Show that if t is a spanning tree for the undirected graph G, then the addition of an edge q, $q \notin E(t)$ and $q \in E(G)$, to t creates a unique cycle.

   (b) Show that if any of the edges on this unique cycle is deleted from $E(t) \cup \{q\}$, then the remaining edges form a spanning tree of G.

6. In Figure 4.10, find a minimum-cost spanning tree for the graph of part (c) and extend the tree to obtain a minimum cost spanning tree for the graph of part (a). Verify the correctness of your answer by applying either Prim's algorithm or Kruskal's algorithm on the graph of part (a).

7. Let $G(V, E)$ be any weighted connected graph.

   (a) If C is any cycle of G, then show that the heaviest edge of C cannot belong to a minimum-cost spanning tree of G.

   (b) Assume that F is a forest that is a subgraph of G. Show that any F-heavy edge of G cannot belong to a minimum-cost spanning tree of G.

8. By considering the complete graph with n vertices, show that the number of spanning trees in an n vertex graph can be greater than $2^{n-1} - 2$.

4.7 OPTIMAL STORAGE ON TAPES

There are n programs that are to be stored on a computer tape of length l. Associated with each program i is a length $l_i, 1 \leq i \leq n$. Clearly, all programs can be stored on the tape if and only if the sum of the lengths of the programs is at most l. We assume that whenever a program is to be retrieved from this tape, the tape is initially positioned at the front. Hence, if the programs are stored in the order $I = i_1, i_2, \ldots, i_n$, the time t_j needed to retrieve program i_j is proportional to $\sum_{1 \leq k \leq j} l_{i_k}$. If all programs are retrieved equally often, then the expected or *mean retrieval time* (MRT) is $(1/n) \sum_{1 \leq j \leq n} t_j$. In the optimal storage on tape problem, we are required to find a permutation for the n programs so that when they are stored on the tape in this order the MRT is minimized. This problem fits the ordering paradigm. Minimizing the MRT is equivalent to minimizing $d(I) = \sum_{1 \leq j \leq n} \sum_{1 \leq k \leq j} l_{i_k}$.

Example 4.11 Let $n = 3$ and $(l_1, l_2, l_3) = (5, 10, 3)$. There are $n! = 6$ possible orderings. These orderings and their respective d values are:

ordering I	$d(I)$		
1, 2, 3	5 + 5 + 10 + 5 + 10 + 3	=	38
1, 3, 2	5 + 5 + 3 + 5 + 3 + 10	=	31
2, 1, 3	10 + 10 + 5 + 10 + 5 + 3	=	43
2, 3, 1	10 + 10 + 3 + 10 + 3 + 5	=	41
3, 1, 2	3 + 3 + 5 + 3 + 5 + 10	=	29
3, 2, 1	3 + 3 + 10 + 3 + 10 + 5	=	34

The optimal ordering is 3, 1, 2. □

A greedy approach to building the required permutation would choose the next program on the basis of some optimization measure. One possible measure would be the d value of the permutation constructed so far. The next program to be stored on the tape would be one that minimizes the increase in d. If we have already constructed the permutation $i_1, i_2, \ldots, i_r$, then appending program j gives the permutation $i_1, i_2, \ldots, i_r, i_{r+1} = j$. This increases the d value by $\sum_{1 \leq k \leq r} l_{i_k} + l_j$. Since $\sum_{1 \leq k \leq r} l_{i_k}$ is fixed and independent of j, we trivially observe that the increase in d is minimized if the next program chosen is the one with the least length from among the remaining programs.

The greedy algorithm resulting from the above discussion is so simple that we won't bother to write it out. The greedy method simply requires us to store the programs in nondecreasing order of their lengths. This ordering can be carried out in $O(n \log n)$ time using an efficient sorting algorithm (e.g., heap sort from Chapter 2). For the programs of Example 4.11, note that the permutation that yields an optimal solution is the one in which the programs are in nondecreasing order of their lengths. Theorem 4.9 shows that the MRT is minimized when programs are stored in this order.

Theorem 4.9 If $l_1 \leq l_2 \leq \cdots \leq l_n$, then the ordering $i_j = j, 1 \leq j \leq n$, minimizes

$$\sum_{k=1}^{n} \sum_{j=1}^{k} l_{i_j}$$

over all possible permutations of the i_j.

Proof: Let $I = i_1, i_2, \ldots, i_n$ be any permutation of the index set $\{1, 2, \ldots, n\}$. Then

$$d(I) = \sum_{k=1}^{n} \sum_{j=1}^{k} l_{i_j} = \sum_{k=1}^{n} (n-k+1) l_{i_k}$$

If there exist a and b such that $a < b$ and $l_{i_a} > l_{i_b}$, then interchanging i_a and i_b results in a permutation I' with

$$d(I') = \left[\sum_{\substack{k \\ k \neq a \\ k \neq b}} (n-k+1) l_{i_k} \right] + (n-a+1) l_{i_b} + (n-b+1) l_{i_a}$$

Subtracting $d(I')$ from $d(I)$, we obtain

$$\begin{aligned} d(I) - d(I') &= (n-a+1)(l_{i_a} - l_{i_b}) + (n-b+1)(l_{i_b} - l_{i_a}) \\ &= (b-a)(l_{i_a} - l_{i_b}) \\ &> 0 \end{aligned}$$

Hence, no permutation that is not in nondecreasing order of the l_i's can have minimum d. It is easy to see that all permutations in nondecreasing order of the l_i's have the same d value. Hence, the ordering defined by $i_j = j, 1 \leq j \leq n$, minimizes the d value. □

The tape storage problem can be extended to several tapes. If there are $m > 1$ tapes, $T_0, \ldots, T_{m-1}$, then the programs are to be distributed over these tapes. For each tape a storage permutation is to be provided. If I_j is the storage permutation for the subset of programs on tape j, then $d(I_j)$ is as defined earlier. The *total retrieval time* (TD) is $\sum_{0 \leq j \leq m-1} d(I_j)$. The objective is to store the programs in such a way as to minimize TD.

```
Algorithm Store(n, m)
// n is the number of programs and m the number of tapes.
{
    j := 0; // Next tape to store on
    for i := 1 to n do
    {
        write ("append program", i,
            "to permutation for tape", j);
        j := (j + 1) mod m;
    }
}
```

Algorithm 4.13 Assigning programs to tapes

The obvious generalization of the solution for the one-tape case is to consider the programs in nondecreasing order of l_i's. The program currently being considered is placed on the tape that results in the minimum increase in TD. This tape will be the one with the least amount of tape used so far. If there is more than one tape with this property, then the one with the smallest index can be used. If the jobs are initially ordered so that $l_1 \leq l_2 \leq \cdots \leq l_n$, then the first m programs are assigned to tapes $T_0, \ldots, T_{m-1}$ respectively. The next m programs will be assigned to tapes $T_0, \ldots, T_{m-1}$ respectively. The general rule is that program i is stored on tape $T_{i \bmod m}$. On any given tape the programs are stored in nondecreasing order of their lengths. Algorithm 4.13 presents this rule in pseudocode. It assumes that the programs are ordered as above. It has a computing time of $\Theta(n)$ and does not need to know the program lengths. Theorem 4.10 proves that the resulting storage pattern is optimal.

Theorem 4.10 If $l_1 \leq l_2 \leq \cdots \leq l_n$, then Algorithm 4.13 generates an optimal storage pattern for m tapes.

Proof: In any storage pattern for m tapes, let r_i be one greater than the number of programs following program i on its tape. Then the total retrieval time TD is given by

$$TD = \sum_{i=1}^{n} r_i l_i$$

In any given storage pattern, for any given n, there can be at most m programs for which $r_i = j$. From Theorem 4.9 it follows that TD is minimized if the m longest programs have $r_i = 1$, the next m longest programs have $r_i = 2$, and so on. When programs are ordered by length, that is, $l_1 \le l_2 \le \cdots \le l_n$, then this minimization criteria is satisfied if $r_i = \lceil (n-i+1)/m \rceil$. Observe that Algorithm 4.13 results in a storage pattern with these r_i's. □

The proof of Theorem 4.10 shows that there are many storage patterns that minimize TD. If we compute $r_i = \lceil (n-i+1)/m \rceil$ for each program i, then so long as all programs with the same r_i are stored on different tapes and have $r_i - 1$ programs following them, TD is the same. If n is a multiple of m, then there are at least $(m!)^{n/m}$ storage patterns that minimize TD. Algorithm 4.13 produces one of these.

EXERCISES

1. Find an optimal placement for 13 programs on three tapes T_0, T_1, and T_2, where the programs are of lengths $12, 5, 8, 32, 7, 5, 18, 26, 4, 3, 11, 10$, and 6.

2. Show that replacing the code of Algorithm 4.13 by

```
for i := 1 to n do
    write ("append program", i, "to permutation for
        tape", (i - 1) mod m);
```

   does not affect the output.

3. Let $P_1, P_2, \ldots, P_n$ be a set of n programs that are to be stored on a tape of length l. Program P_i requires a_i amount of tape. If $\sum a_i \le l$, then clearly all the programs can be stored on the tape. So, assume $\sum a_i > l$. The problem is to select a maximum subset Q of the programs for storage on the tape. (A maximum subset is one with the maximum number of programs in it). A greedy algorithm for this problem would build the subset Q by including programs in nondecreasing order of a_i.

   (a) Assume the P_i are ordered such that $a_1 \le a_2 \le \cdots \le a_n$. Write a function for the above strategy. Your function should output an array $s[1:n]$ such that $s[i] = 1$ if P_i is in Q and $s[i] = 0$ otherwise.

   (b) Show that this strategy always finds a maximum subset Q such that $\sum_{P_i \in Q} a_i \le l$.

   (c) Let Q be the subset obtained using the above greedy strategy. How small can the tape utilization ratio $(\sum_{P_i \in Q} a_i)/l$ get?

(d) Suppose the objective now is to determine a subset of programs that maximizes the tape utilization ratio. A greedy approach would be to consider programs in nonincreasing order of a_i. If there is enough space left on the tape for P_i, then it is included in Q. Assume the programs are ordered so that $a_1 \geq a_2 \geq \cdots \geq a_n$. Write a function incorporating this strategy. What is its time and space complexity?

(e) Show that the strategy of part (d) doesn't necessarily yield a subset that maximizes $(\sum_{P_i \in Q} a_i)/l$. How small can this ratio get? Prove your bound.

4. Assume n programs of lengths $l_1, l_2, \ldots, l_n$ are to be stored on a tape. Program i is to be retrieved with frequency f_i. If the programs are stored in the order $i_1, i_2, \ldots, i_n$, the *expected retrieval time* (ERT) is

$$\left[\sum_j (f_{i_j} \sum_{k=1}^{j} l_{i_k})\right] / \sum f_i$$

(a) Show that storing the programs in nondecreasing order of l_i does not necessarily minimize the ERT.

(b) Show that storing the programs in nonincreasing order of f_i does not necessarily minimize the ERT.

(c) Show that the ERT is minimized when the programs are stored in nonincreasing order of f_i/l_i.

5. Consider the tape storage problem of this section. Assume that two tapes $T1$ and $T2$, are available and we wish to distribute n given programs of lengths $l_1, l_2, \ldots, l_n$ onto these two tapes in such a manner that the maximum retrieval time is minimized. That is, if A and B are the sets of programs on the tapes $T1$ and $T2$ respectively, then we wish to choose A and B such that max $\{ \sum_{i \in A} l_i, \sum_{i \in B} l_i \}$ is minimized. A possible greedy approach to obtaining A and B would be to start with A and B initially empty. Then consider the programs one at a time. The program currently being considered is assigned to set A if $\sum_{i \in A} l_i$ $=$ min $\{ \sum_{i \in A} l_i, \sum_{i \in B} l_i \}$; otherwise it is assigned to B. Show that this does not guarantee optimal solutions even if $l_1 \leq l_2 \leq \cdots \leq l_n$. Show that the same is true if we require $l_1 \geq l_2 \geq \cdots \geq l_n$.

4.8 OPTIMAL MERGE PATTERNS

In Section 3.5 we saw that two sorted files containing n and m records respectively could be merged together to obtain one sorted file in time $O(n+$

m). When more than two sorted files are to be merged together, the merge can be accomplished by repeatedly merging sorted files in pairs. Thus, if files x_1, x_2, x_3, and x_4 are to be merged, we could first merge x_1 and x_2 to get a file y_1. Then we could merge y_1 and x_3 to get y_2. Finally, we could merge y_2 and x_4 to get the desired sorted file. Alternatively, we could first merge x_1 and x_2 getting y_1, then merge x_3 and x_4 and get y_2, and finally merge y_1 and y_2 and get the desired sorted file. Given n sorted files, there are many ways in which to pairwise merge them into a single sorted file. Different pairings require differing amounts of computing time. The problem we address ourselves to now is that of determining an optimal way (one requiring the fewest comparisons) to pairwise merge n sorted files. Since this problem calls for an ordering among the pairs to be merged, it fits the ordering paradigm.

Example 4.12 The files x_1, x_2, and x_3 are three sorted files of length $30, 20$, and 10 records each. Merging x_1 and x_2 requires 50 record moves. Merging the result with x_3 requires another 60 moves. The total number of record moves required to merge the three files this way is 110. If, instead, we first merge x_2 and x_3 (taking 30 moves) and then x_1 (taking 60 moves), the total record moves made is only 90. Hence, the second merge pattern is faster than the first. □

A greedy attempt to obtain an optimal merge pattern is easy to formulate. Since merging an n-record file and an m-record file requires possibly $n + m$ record moves, the obvious choice for a selection criterion is: at each step merge the two smallest size files together. Thus, if we have five files $(x_1, \ldots, x_5)$ with sizes $(20, 30, 10, 5, 30)$, our greedy rule would generate the following merge pattern: merge x_4 and x_3 to get z_1 ($|z_1| = 15$), merge z_1 and x_1 to get z_2 ($|z_2| = 35$), merge x_2 and x_5 to get z_3 ($|z_3| = 60$), and merge z_2 and z_3 to get the answer z_4. The total number of record moves is 205. One can verify that this is an optimal merge pattern for the given problem instance.

The merge pattern such as the one just described will be referred to as a *two-way merge pattern* (each merge step involves the merging of two files). The two-way merge patterns can be represented by binary merge trees. Figure 4.12 shows a binary merge tree representing the optimal merge pattern obtained for the above five files. The leaf nodes are drawn as squares and represent the given five files. These nodes are called *external nodes.* The remaining nodes are drawn as circles and are called *internal nodes.* Each internal node has exactly two children, and it represents the file obtained by merging the files represented by its two children. The number in each node is the length (i.e., the number of records) of the file represented by that node.

The external node x_4 is at a distance of 3 from the root node z_4 (a node at level i is at a distance of $i - 1$ from the root). Hence, the records of file

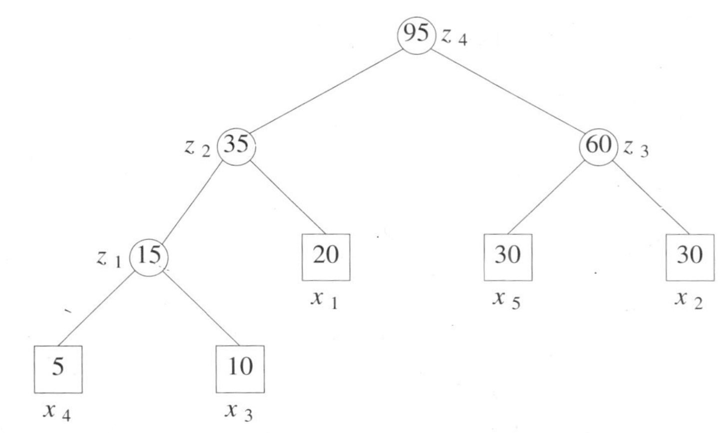

Figure 4.12 Binary merge tree representing a merge pattern

x_4 are moved three times, once to get z_1, once again to get z_2, and finally one more time to get z_4. If d_i is the distance from the root to the external node for file x_i and q_i, the length of x_i is then the total number of record moves for this binary merge tree is

$$\sum_{i=1}^{n} d_i q_i$$

This sum is called the *weighted external path length* of the tree.

An optimal two-way merge pattern corresponds to a binary merge tree with minimum weighted external path length. The function Tree of Algorithm 4.14 uses the greedy rule stated earlier to obtain a two-way merge tree for n files. The algorithm has as input a list *list* of n trees. Each node in a tree has three fields, *lchild*, *rchild*, and *weight*. Initially, each tree in *list* has exactly one node. This node is an external node and has *lchild* and *rchild* fields zero whereas *weight* is the length of one of the n files to be merged. During the course of the algorithm, for any tree in *list* with root node t, $t \rightarrow weight$ is the length of the merged file it represents ($t \rightarrow weight$ equals the sum of the lengths of the external nodes in tree t). Function Tree uses two functions, Least($list$) and Insert($list, t$). Least($list$) finds a tree in *list* whose root has least *weight* and returns a pointer to this tree. This tree is removed from *list*. Insert($list, t$) inserts the tree with root t into *list*. Theorem 4.11 shows that Tree (Algorithm 4.14) generates an optimal two-way merge tree.

```
    treenode = record {
        treenode * lchild; treenode * rchild;
        integer weight;
    };

1   Algorithm Tree(n)
2   // list is a global list of n single node
3   // binary trees as described above.
4   {
5       for i := 1 to n - 1 do
6       {
7           pt := new treenode; // Get a new tree node.
8           (pt → lchild) := Least(list); // Merge two trees with
9           (pt → rchild) := Least(list); // smallest lengths.
10          (pt → weight) := ((pt → lchild) → weight)
11                  +((pt → rchild) → weight);
12          Insert(list, pt);
13      }
14      return Least(list); // Tree left in list is the merge tree.
15  }
```

Algorithm 4.14 Algorithm to generate a two-way merge tree

Example 4.13 Let us see how algorithm Tree works when *list* initially represents six files with lengths $(2, 3, 5, 7, 9, 13)$. Figure 4.13 shows *list* at the end of each iteration of the **for** loop. The binary merge tree that results at the end of the algorithm can be used to determine which files are merged. Merging is performed on those files which are lowest (have the greatest depth) in the tree. □

The main **for** loop in Algorithm 4.14 is executed $n - 1$ times. If *list* is kept in nondecreasing order according to the *weight* value in the roots, then Least$(list)$ requires only $O(1)$ time and Insert$(list, t)$ can be done in $O(n)$ time. Hence the total time taken is $O(n^2)$. In case *list* is represented as a minheap in which the root value is less than or equal to the values of its children (Section 2.4), then Least$(list)$ and Insert$(list, t)$ can be done in $O(\log n)$ time. In this case the computing time for Tree is $O(n \log n)$. Some speedup may be obtained by combining the Insert of line 12 with the Least of line 9.

Theorem 4.11 If *list* initially contains $n \geq 1$ single node trees with *weight* values $(q_1, q_2, \ldots, q_n)$, then algorithm Tree generates an optimal two-way merge tree for n files with these lengths.

Proof: The proof is by induction on n. For $n = 1$, a tree with no internal nodes is returned and this tree is clearly optimal. For the induction hypothesis, assume the algorithm generates an optimal two-way merge tree for all $(q_1, q_2, \ldots, q_m)$, $1 \leq m < n$. We show that the algorithm also generates optimal trees for all $(q_1, q_2, \ldots, q_n)$. Without loss of generality, we can assume that $q_1 \leq q_2 \leq \cdots \leq q_n$ and q_1 and q_2 are the values of the *weight* fields of the trees found by algorithm Least in lines 8 and 9 during the first iteration of the **for** loop. Now, the subtree T of Figure 4.14 is created. Let T' be an optimal two-way merge tree for $(q_1, q_2, \ldots, q_n)$. Let p be an internal node of maximum distance from the root. If the children of p are not q_1 and q_2, then we can interchange the present children with q_1 and q_2 without increasing the weighted external path length of T'. Hence, T is also a subtree in an optimal merge tree. If we replace T in T' by an external node with weight $q_1 + q_2$, then the resulting tree T'' is an optimal merge tree for $(q_1 + q_2, q_3, \ldots, q_n)$. From the induction hypothesis, after replacing T by the external node with value $q_1 + q_2$, function Tree proceeds to find an optimal merge tree for $(q_1 + q_2, q_3, \ldots, q_n)$. Hence, Tree generates an optimal merge tree for $(q_1, q_2, \ldots, q_n)$. □

The greedy method to generate merge trees also works for the case of k-ary merging. In this case the corresponding merge tree is a k-ary tree. Since all internal nodes must have degree k, for certain values of n there is no corresponding k-ary merge tree. For example, when $k = 3$, there is no k-ary merge tree with $n = 2$ external nodes. Hence, it is necessary to introduce a certain number of dummy external nodes. Each dummy node is assigned a q_i of zero. This dummy value does not affect the weighted external path length of the resulting k-ary tree. Exercise 2 shows that a k-ary tree with all internal nodes having degree k exists only when the number of external nodes n satisfies the equality $n \bmod (k-1) = 1$. Hence, at most $k-2$ dummy nodes have to be added. The greedy rule to generate optimal merge trees is: at each step choose k subtrees with least length for merging. Exercise 3 proves the optimality of this rule.

Huffman Codes

Another application of binary trees with minimal weighted external path length is to obtain an optimal set of codes for messages $M_1, \ldots, M_{n+1}$. Each code is a binary string that is used for transmission of the corresponding message. At the receiving end the code is decoded using a decode tree. A decode tree is a binary tree in which external nodes represent messages.

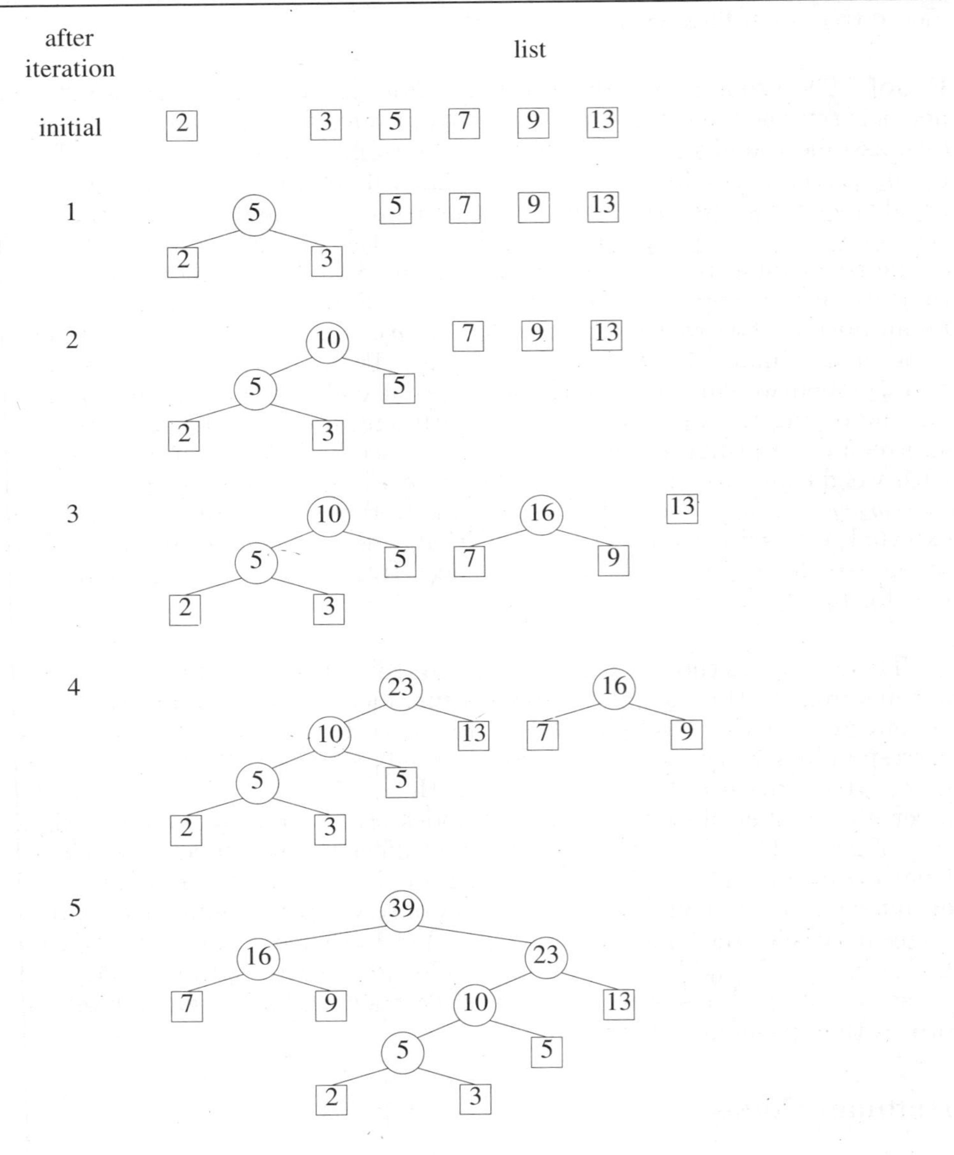

Figure 4.13 Trees in *list* of Tree for Example 4.13

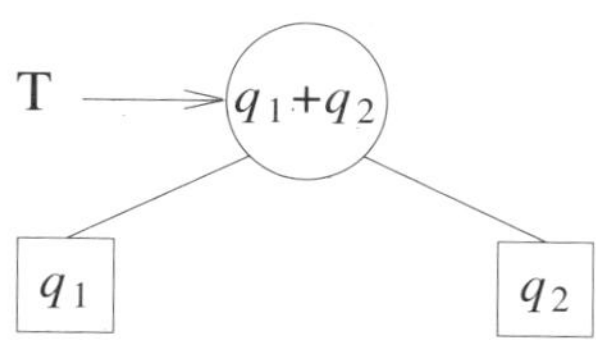

Figure 4.14 The simplest binary merge tree

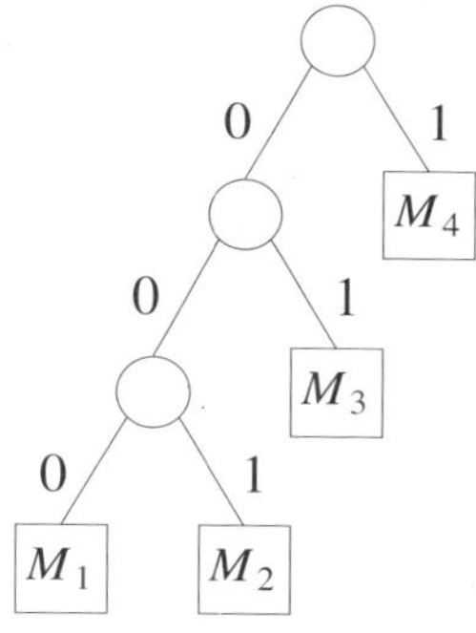

Figure 4.15 Huffman codes

The binary bits in the code word for a message determine the branching needed at each level of the decode tree to reach the correct external node. For example, if we interpret a zero as a left branch and a one as a right branch, then the decode tree of Figure 4.15 corresponds to codes 000, 001, 01, and 1 for messages M_1, M_2, M_3, and M_4 respectively. These codes are called Huffman codes. The cost of decoding a code word is proportional to the number of bits in the code. This number is equal to the distance of the corresponding external node from the root node. If q_i is the relative frequency with which message M_i will be transmitted, then the expected decode time is $\sum_{1\le i\le n+1} q_i d_i$, where d_i is the distance of the external node for message M_i from the root node. The expected decode time is minimized by choosing code words resulting in a decode tree with minimal weighted external path length! Note that $\sum_{1\le i\le n+1} q_i d_i$ is also the expected length of a transmitted message. Hence the code that minimizes expected decode time also minimizes the expected length of a message.

EXERCISES

1. Find an optimal binary merge pattern for ten files whose lengths are 28, 32, 12, 5, 84, 53, 91, 35, 3, and 11.

2. (a) Show that if all internal nodes in a tree have degree k, then the number n of external nodes is such that $n \bmod (k-1) = 1$.
   (b) Show that for every n such that $n \bmod (k-1) = 1$, there exists a k-ary tree T with n external nodes (in a k-ary tree all nodes have degree at most k). Also show that all internal nodes of T have degree k.

3. (a) Show that if $n \bmod (k-1) = 1$, then the greedy rule described following Theorem 4.11 generates an optimal k-ary merge tree for all $(q_1, q_2, \ldots, q_n)$.
   (b) Draw the optimal three-way merge tree obtained using this rule when $(q_1, q_2, \ldots, q_{11}) = (3, 7, 8, 9, 15, 16, 18, 20, 23, 25, 28)$.

4. Obtain a set of optimal Huffman codes for the messages $(M_1, \ldots, M_7)$ with relative frequencies $(q_1, \ldots, q_7) = (4, 5, 7, 8, 10, 12, 20)$. Draw the decode tree for this set of codes.

5. Let T be a decode tree. An optimal decode tree minimizes $\sum q_i d_i$. For a given set of q's, let D denote all the optimal decode trees. For any tree $T \in D$, let $L(T) = \max\ \{d_i\}$ and let $SL(T) = \sum d_i$. Schwartz has shown that there exists a tree $T^* \in D$ such that $L(T^*) = \min_{T \in D}\ \{L(T)\}$ and $SL(T^*) = \min_{T \in D}\ \{SL(T)\}$.

   (a) For $(q_1, \ldots, q_8) = (1, 1, 2, 2, 4, 4, 4, 4)$ obtain trees $T1$ and $T2$ such that $L(T1) > L(T2)$.
   (b) Using the data of a, obtain $T1$ and $T2 \in D$ such that $L(T1) = L(T2)$ but $SL(T1) > SL(T2)$.
   (c) Show that if the subalgorithm Least used in algorithm Tree is such that in case of a tie it returns the tree with least depth, then Tree generates a tree with the properties of T^*.

4.9 SINGLE-SOURCE SHORTEST PATHS

Graphs can be used to represent the highway structure of a state or country with vertices representing cities and edges representing sections of highway. The edges can then be assigned weights which may be either the distance between the two cities connected by the edge or the average time to drive along that section of highway. A motorist wishing to drive from city A to B would be interested in answers to the following questions:

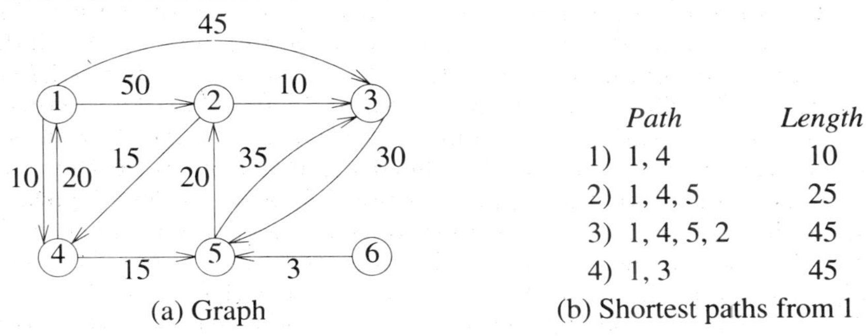

	Path	Length
1)	1, 4	10
2)	1, 4, 5	25
3)	1, 4, 5, 2	45
4)	1, 3	45

Figure 4.16 Graph and shortest paths from vertex 1 to all destinations

- Is there a path from A to B?
- If there is more than one path from A to B, which is the shortest path?

The problems defined by these questions are special cases of the path problem we study in this section. The length of a path is now defined to be the sum of the weights of the edges on that path. The starting vertex of the path is referred to as the *source*, and the last vertex the *destination*. The graphs are digraphs to allow for one-way streets. In the problem we consider, we are given a directed graph $G = (V, E)$, a weighting function *cost* for the edges of G, and a source vertex v_0. The problem is to determine the shortest paths from v_0 to *all* the remaining vertices of G. It is assumed that all the weights are positive. The shortest path between v_0 and some other node v is an ordering among a subset of the edges. Hence this problem fits the ordering paradigm.

Example 4.14 Consider the directed graph of Figure 4.16(a). The numbers on the edges are the weights. If node 1 is the source vertex, then the shortest path from 1 to 2 is $1, 4, 5, 2$. The length of this path is $10 + 15 + 20 = 45$. Even though there are three edges on this path, it is shorter than the path $1, 2$ which is of length 50. There is no path from 1 to 6. Figure 4.16(b) lists the shortest paths from node 1 to nodes $4, 5, 2$, and 3, respectively. The paths have been listed in nondecreasing order of path length. □

To formulate a greedy-based algorithm to generate the shortest paths, we must conceive of a multistage solution to the problem and also of an optimization measure. One possibility is to build the shortest paths one by one. As an optimization measure we can use the sum of the lengths of all paths so far generated. For this measure to be minimized, each individual path must be of minimum length. If we have already constructed i shortest paths, then using this optimization measure, the next path to be constructed should be the next shortest minimum length path. The greedy way (and also a systematic way) to generate the shortest paths from v_0 to the remaining vertices is to generate these paths in nondecreasing order of path length. First, a shortest path to the nearest vertex is generated. Then a shortest path to the second nearest vertex is generated, and so on. For the graph of Figure 4.16(a) the nearest vertex to $v_0 = 1$ is 4 ($cost[1,4] = 10$). The path $1, 4$ is the first path generated. The second nearest vertex to node 1 is 5 and the distance between 1 and 5 is 25. The path $1, 4, 5$ is the next path generated. In order to generate the shortest paths in this order, we need to be able to determine (1) the next vertex to which a shortest path must be generated and (2) a shortest path to this vertex. Let S denote the set of vertices (including v_0) to which the shortest paths have already been generated. For w not in S, let $dist[w]$ be the length of the shortest path starting from v_0, going through only those vertices that are in S, and ending at w. We observe that:

1. If the next shortest path is to vertex u, then the path begins at v_0, ends at u, and goes through only those vertices that are in S. To prove this, we must show that all the intermediate vertices on the shortest path to u are in S. Assume there is a vertex w on this path that is not in S. Then, the v_0 to u path also contains a path from v_0 to w that is of length less than the v_0 to u path. By assumption the shortest paths are being generated in nondecreasing order of path length, and so the shorter path v_0 to w must already have been generated. Hence, there can be no intermediate vertex that is not in S.

2. The destination of the next path generated must be that of vertex u which has the minimum distance, $dist[u]$, among all vertices not in S. This follows from the definition of $dist$ and observation 1. In case there are several vertices not in S with the same $dist$, then any of these may be selected.

3. Having selected a vertex u as in observation 2 and generated the shortest v_0 to u path, vertex u becomes a member of S. At this point the length of the shortest paths starting at v_0, going though vertices only in S, and ending at a vertex w not in S may decrease; that is, the value of $dist[w]$ may change. If it does change, then it must be due to a shorter path starting at v_0 and going to u and then to w. The intermediate vertices on the v_0 to u path and the u to w path must all be in S. Further, the v_0 to u path must be the shortest such path; otherwise $dist[w]$ is not defined properly. Also, the u to w path can

be chosen so as not to contain any intermediate vertices. Therefore, we can conclude that if $dist[w]$ is to change (i.e., decrease), then it is because of a path from v_0 to u to w, where the path from v_0 to u is the shortest such path and the path from u to w is the edge $\langle u, w \rangle$. The length of this path is $dist[u] + cost[u, w]$.

The above observations lead to a simple Algorithm 4.15 for the single-source shortest path problem. This algorithm (known as Dijkstra's algorithm) only determines the lengths of the shortest paths from v_0 to all other vertices in G. The generation of the paths requires a minor extension to this algorithm and is left as an exercise. In the function ShortestPaths (Algorithm 4.15) it is assumed that the n vertices of G are numbered 1 through n. The set S is maintained as a bit array with $S[i] = 0$ if vertex i is not in S and $S[i] = 1$ if it is. It is assumed that the graph itself is represented by its cost adjacency matrix with $cost[i, j]$'s being the weight of the edge $\langle i, j \rangle$. The weight $cost[i, j]$ is set to some large number, ∞, in case the edge $\langle i, j \rangle$ is not in $E(G)$. For $i = j$, $cost[i, j]$ can be set to any nonnegative number without affecting the outcome of the algorithm.

From our earlier discussion, it is easy to see that the algorithm is correct. The time taken by the algorithm on a graph with n vertices is $O(n^2)$. To see this, note that the **for** loop of line 7 in Algorithm 4.15 takes $\Theta(n)$ time. The **for** loop of line 12 is executed $n - 2$ times. Each execution of this loop requires $O(n)$ time at lines 15 and 16 to select the next vertex and again at the **for** loop of line 18 to update $dist$. So the total time for this loop is $O(n^2)$. In case a list t of vertices currently not in s is maintained, then the number of nodes on this list would at any time be $n - num$. This would speed up lines 15 and 16 and the **for** loop of line 18, but the asymptotic time would remain $O(n^2)$. This and other variations of the algorithm are explored in the exercises.

Any shortest path algorithm must examine each edge in the graph at least once since any of the edges could be in a shortest path. Hence, the minimum possible time for such an algorithm would be $\Omega(|E|)$. Since cost adjacency matrices were used to represent the graph, it takes $O(n^2)$ time just to determine which edges are in G, and so any shortest path algorithm using this representation must take $\Omega(n^2)$ time. For this representation then, algorithm ShortestPaths is optimal to within a constant factor. If a change to adjacency lists is made, the overall frequency of the **for** loop of line 18 can be brought down to $O(|E|)$ (since $dist$ can change only for vertices adjacent from u). If $V - S$ is maintained as a red-black tree (see Section 2.4.2), each execution of lines 15 and 16 takes $O(\log n)$ time. Note that a red-black tree supports the following operations in $O(\log n)$ time: insert, delete (an arbitrary element), find-min, and search (for an arbitrary element). Each update in line 21 takes $O(\log n)$ time as well (since an update can be done using a delete and an insertion into the red-black tree). Thus the overall run time is $O((n + |E|) \log n)$.

```
1   Algorithm ShortestPaths(v, cost, dist, n)
2   // dist[j], 1 ≤ j ≤ n, is set to the length of the shortest
3   // path from vertex v to vertex j in a digraph G with n
4   // vertices. dist[v] is set to zero. G is represented by its
5   // cost adjacency matrix cost[1 : n, 1 : n].
6   {
7       for i := 1 to n do
8       { // Initialize S.
9           S[i] := false; dist[i] := cost[v, i];
10      }
11      S[v] := true; dist[v] := 0.0; // Put v in S.
12      for num := 2 to n do
13      {
14          // Determine n − 1 paths from v.
15          Choose u from among those vertices not
16          in S such that dist[u] is minimum;
17          S[u] := true; // Put u in S.
18          for (each w adjacent to u with S[w] = false) do
19              // Update distances.
20              if (dist[w] > dist[u] + cost[u, w])) then
21                      dist[w] := dist[u] + cost[u, w];
22      }
23  }
```

Algorithm 4.15 Greedy algorithm to generate shortest paths

Example 4.15 Consider the eight vertex digraph of Figure 4.17(a) with cost adjacency matrix as in Figure 4.17(b). The values of *dist* and the vertices selected at each iteration of the **for** loop of line 12 in Algorithm 4.15 for finding all the shortest paths from Boston are shown in Figure 4.18. To begin with, S contains only Boston. In the first iteration of the **for** loop (that is, for $num = 2$), the city u that is not in S and whose $dist[u]$ is minimum is identified to be New York. New York enters the set S. Also the $dist[\,]$ values of Chicago, Miami, and New Orleans get altered since there are shorter paths to these cities via New York. In the next iteration of the **for** loop, the city that enters S is Miami since it has the smallest $dist[\,]$ value from among all the nodes not in S. None of the $dist[\,]$ values are altered. The algorithm continues in a similar fashion and terminates when only seven of the eight vertices are in S. By the definition of *dist*, the distance of the last vertex, in this case Los Angeles, is correct as the shortest path from

Boston to Los Angeles can go through only the remaining six vertices. □

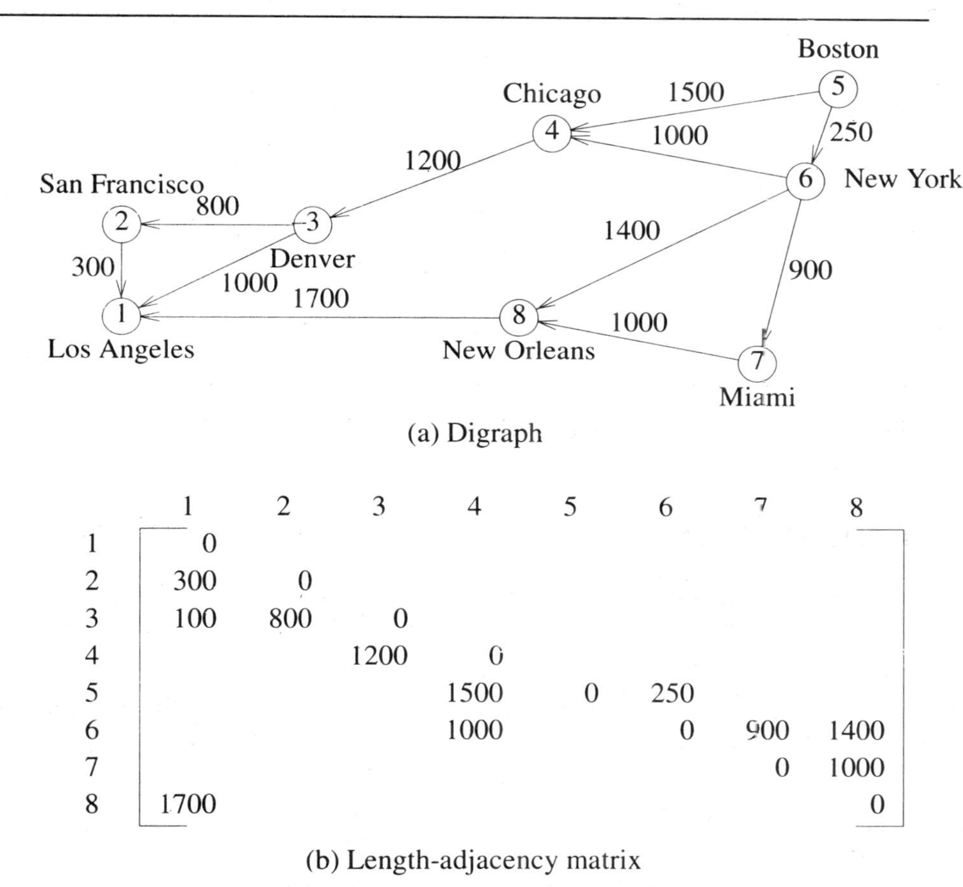

(a) Digraph

	1	2	3	4	5	6	7	8
1	0							
2	300	0						
3	100	800	0					
4			1200	0				
5				1500	0	250		
6				1000		0	900	1400
7							0	1000
8	1700							0

(b) Length-adjacency matrix

Figure 4.17 Figures for Example 4.15

One can easily verify that the edges on the shortest paths from a vertex v to all remaining vertices in a connected undirected graph G form a spanning tree of G. This spanning tree is called a *shortest-path spanning tree.* Clearly, this spanning tree may be different for different root vertices v. Figure 4.19 shows a graph G, its minimum-cost spanning tree, and a shortest-path spanning tree from vertex 1.

Iteration	S	Vertex selected	Distance							
			LA [1]	SF [2]	DEN [3]	CHI [4]	BOST [5]	NY [6]	MIA [7]	NO [8]
Initial	--	----	+∞	+∞	+∞	1500	0	250	+∞	+∞
1	{5}	6	+∞	+∞	+∞	1250	0	250	1150	1650
2	{5,6}	7	+∞	+∞	+∞	1250	0	250	1150	1650
3	{5,6,7}	4	+∞	+∞	2450	1250	0	250	1150	1650
4	{5,6,7,4}	8	3350	+∞	2450	1250	0	250	1150	1650
5	{5,6,7,4,8}	3	3350	3250	2450	1250	0	250	1150	1650
6	{5,6,7,4,8,3}	2	3350	3250	2450	1250	0	250	1150	1650
	{5,6,7,4,8,3,2}									

Figure 4.18 Action of ShortestPaths

EXERCISES

1. Use algorithm ShortestPaths to obtain in nondecreasing order the lengths of the shortest paths from vertex 1 to all remaining vertices in the digraph of Figure 4.20.

2. Using the directed graph of Figure 4.21 explain why ShortestPaths will not work properly. What is the shortest path between vertices v_1 and v_7 ?

3. Rewrite algorithm ShortestPaths under the following assumptions:

   (a) G is represented by its adjacency lists. The head nodes are HEAD(1),..., HEAD(n) and each list node has three fields: VERTEX, COST, and LINK. COST is the length of the corresponding edge and n the number of vertices in G.

   (b) Instead of representing S, the set of vertices to which the shortest paths have already been found, the set $T = V(G) - S$ is represented using a linked list. What can you say about the computing time of your new algorithm relative to that of ShortestPaths?

4. Modify algorithm ShortestPaths so that it obtains the shortest paths in addition to the lengths of these paths. What is the computing time of your algorithm?

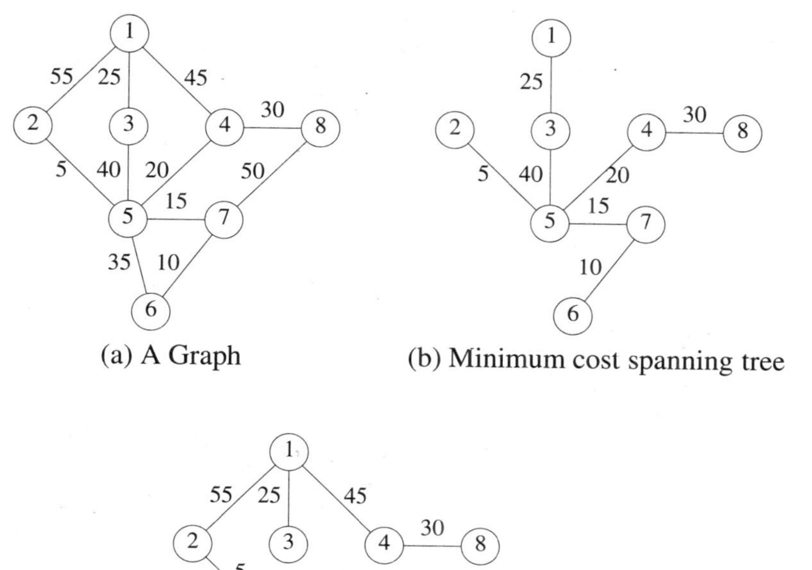

Figure 4.19 Graphs and spanning trees

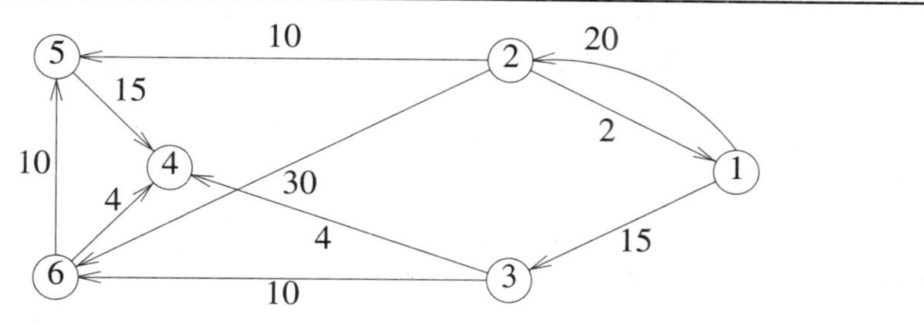

Figure 4.20 Directed graph

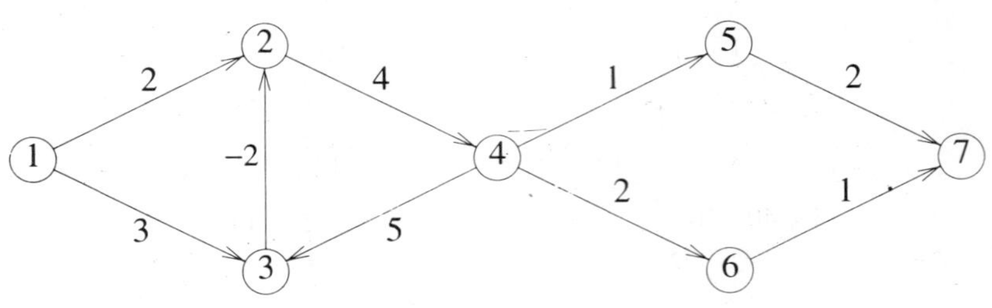

Figure 4.21 Another directed graph

4.10 REFERENCES AND READINGS

The linear time algorithm in Section 4.4 for the tree vertex splitting problem can be found in "Vertex upgrading problems for VLSI," by D. Paik, Ph.D. thesis, Department of Computer Science, University of Minnesota, October 1991.

The two greedy methods for obtaining minimum-cost spanning trees are due to R. C. Prim and J. B. Kruskal, respectively.

An $O(e \log \log v)$ time spanning tree algorithm has been given by A. C. Yao.

The optimal randomized algorithm for minimum-cost spanning trees presented in this chapter appears in "A randomized linear-time algorithm for finding minimum spanning trees," by P. N. Klein and R. E. Tarjan, in *Proceedings of the 26th Annual Symposium on Theory of Computing*, 1994, pp. 9–15. See also "A randomized linear-time algorithm to find minimum spanning trees," by D. R. Karger, P. N. Klein, and R. E. Tarjan, *Journal of the ACM* 42, no. 2 (1995): 321–328.

Proof of Lemma 4.3 can be found in "Verification and sensitivity analysis of minimum spanning trees in linear time," by B. Dixon, M. Rauch, and R. E. Tarjan, *SIAM Journal on Computing* 21 (1992): 1184–1192, and in "A simple minimum spanning tree verification algorithm," by V. King, *Proceedings of the Workshop on Algorithms and Data Structures*, 1995.

A very nearly linear time algorithm for minimum-cost spanning trees appears in "Efficient algorithms for finding minimum spanning trees in undirected and directed graphs," by H. N. Gabow, Z. Galil, T. Spencer, and R. E. Tarjan, *Combinatorica* 6 (1986): 109–122.

A linear time algorithm for minimum-cost spanning trees on a stronger model where the edge weights can be manipulated in their binary form is given in "Trans-dichotomous algorithms for minimum spanning trees and shortest paths," by M. Fredman and D. E. Willard, in *Proceedings of the 31st Annual Symposium on Foundations of Computer Science*, 1990, pp. 719–725.

The greedy method developed here to optimally store programs on tapes was first devised for a machine scheduling problem. In this problem n jobs have to be scheduled on m processors. Job i takes t_i amount of time. The time at which a job finishes is the sum of the job times for all jobs preceding and including job i. The average finish time corresponds to the mean access time for programs on tapes. The $(m!)^{n/m}$ schedules referred to in Theorem 4.10 are known as SPT (shortest processing time) schedules. The rule to generate SPT schedules as well as the rule of Exercise 4 (Section 4.7) are due to W. E. Smith.

The greedy algorithm for generating optimal merge trees is due to D. Huffman.

For a given set $\{q_1, \ldots, q_n\}$ there are many sets of Huffman codes minimizing $\sum q_i d_i$. From amongst these code sets there is one that has minimum $\sum d_i$ and minimum max $\{d_i\}$. An algorithm to obtain this code set was given by E. S. Schwartz.

The shortest-path algorithm of the text is due to E. W. Dijkstra.

For planar graphs, the shortest-path problem can be solved in linear time as has been shown in "Faster shortest-path algorithms for planar graphs," by P. Klein, S. Rao, and M. Rauch, in *Proceedings of the ACM Symposium on Theory of Computing*, 1994.

The relationship between greedy methods and matroids is discussed in *Combinatorial Optimization*, by E. Lawler, Holt, Rinehart and Winston, 1976.

4.11 ADDITIONAL EXERCISES

1. [Coin changing] Let $A_n = \{a_1, a_2, \ldots, a_n\}$ be a finite set of distinct coin types (for example, $a_1 = 50¢$, $a_2 = 25¢$, $a_3 = 10¢$, and so on.) We can assume each a_i is an integer and $a_1 > a_2 > \cdots > a_n$. Each type is available in unlimited quantity. The coin-changing problem is to make up an exact amount C using a minimum total number of coins. C is an integer > 0.

   (a) Show that if $a_n \neq 1$, then there exists a finite set of coin types and a C for which there is no solution to the coin-changing problem.

(b) Show that there is always a solution when $a_n = 1$.

(c) When $a_n = 1$, a greedy solution to the problem makes change by using the coin types in the order $a_1, a_2, \ldots, a_n$. When coin type a_i is being considered, as many coins of this type as possible are given. Write an algorithm based on this strategy. Show that this algorithm doesn't necessarily generate solutions that use the minimum total number of coins.

(d) Show that if $A_n = \{k^{n-1}, k^{n-2}, \ldots, k^0\}$ for some $k > 1$, then the greedy method of part (c) always yields solutions with a minimum number of coins.

2. [Set cover] You are given a family S of m sets $S_i, 1 \leq i \leq m$. Denote by $|A|$ the size of set A. Let $|S_i| = j_i$; that is, $S_i = \{s_1, s_2, \ldots, s_{j_i}\}$. A subset $T = \{T_1, T_2, \ldots, T_k\}$ of S is a family of sets such that for each $i, 1 \leq i \leq k$, $T_i = S_r$ for some $r, 1 \leq r \leq m$. The subset T is a *cover* of S iff $\cup T_i = \cup S_i$. The size of T, $|T|$, is the number of sets in T. A minimum cover of S is a cover of smallest size. Consider the following greedy strategy: build T iteratively, at the kth iteration $T = \{T_1, \ldots, T_{k-1}\}$, now add to T a set S_j from S that contains the largest number of elements not already in T, and stop when $\cup T_i = \cup S_i$.

(a) Assume that $\cup S_i = \{1, 2, \ldots, n\}$ and $m < n$. Using the strategy outlined above, write an algorithm to obtain set covers. How much time and space does your algorithm require?

(b) Show that the greedy strategy above doesn't necessarily obtain a minimum set cover.

(c) Suppose now that a minimum cover is defined to be one for which $\sum_{i=1}^{k} |T_i|$ is minimum. Does the above strategy always find a minimum cover?

3. [Node cover] Let $G = (V, E)$ be an undirected graph. A node cover of G is a subset U of the vertex set V such that every edge in E is incident to at least one vertex in U. A minimum node cover is one with the fewest number of vertices. Consider the following greedy algorithm for this problem:

```
Algorithm Cover(V, E)
{
    U := ∅;
    repeat
    {
        Let q be a vertex from V of maximum degree;
```

```
            Add q to U; Eliminate q from V;
            E := E − {(x, y) such that x = q or y = q};
        } until (E = ∅); // U is the node cover.
}
```

Does this algorithm always generate a minimum node cover?

4. [Traveling salesperson] Let G be a directed graph with n vertices. Let $length(u, v)$ be the length of the edge $\langle u, v\rangle$. A path starting at a given vertex v_0, going through every other vertex exactly once, and finally returning to v_0 is called a *tour*. The length of a tour is the sum of the lengths of the edges on the path defining the tour. We are concerned with finding a tour of minimum length. A greedy way to construct such a tour is: let (P, v) represent the path so far constructed; it starts at v_0 and ends at v. Initially P is empty and $v = v_0$, if all vertices in G are on P, then include the edge $\langle v, v_0\rangle$ and stop; otherwise include an edge $\langle v, w\rangle$ of minimum length among all edges from v to a vertex w not on P. Show that this greedy method doesn't necessarily generate a minimum-length tour.

Chapter 5

DYNAMIC PROGRAMMING

5.1 THE GENERAL METHOD

Dynamic programming is an algorithm design method that can be used when the solution to a problem can be viewed as the result of a sequence of decisions. In earlier chapters we saw many problems that can be viewed this way. Here are some examples:

Example 5.1 [Knapsack] The solution to the knapsack problem (Section 4.3) can be viewed as the result of a sequence of decisions. We have to decide the values of $x_i, 1 \leq i \leq n$. First we make a decision on x_1, then on x_2, then on x_3, and so on. An optimal sequence of decisions maximizes the objective function $\sum p_i x_i$. (It also satisfies the constraints $\sum w_i x_i \leq m$ and $0 \leq x_i \leq 1$.) □

Example 5.2 [Optimal merge patterns] This problem was discussed in Section 4.8. An optimal merge pattern tells us which pair of files should be merged at each step. As a decision sequence, the problem calls for us to decide which pair of files should be merged first, which pair second, which pair third, and so on. An optimal sequence of decisions is a least-cost sequence. □

Example 5.3 [Shortest path] One way to find a shortest path from vertex i to vertex j in a directed graph G is to decide which vertex should be the second vertex, which the third, which the fourth, and so on, until vertex j is reached. An optimal sequence of decisions is one that results in a path of least length. □

For some of the problems that may be viewed in this way, an optimal sequence of decisions can be found by making the decisions one at a time and never making an erroneous decision. This is true for all problems solvable by the greedy method. For many other problems, it is not possible to make stepwise decisions (based only on local information) in such a manner that the sequence of decisions made is optimal.

Example 5.4 [Shortest path] Suppose we wish to find a shortest path from vertex i to vertex j. Let A_i be the vertices adjacent from vertex i. Which of the vertices in A_i should be the second vertex on the path? There is no way to make a decision at this time and guarantee that future decisions leading to an optimal sequence can be made. If on the other hand we wish to find a shortest path from vertex i to all other vertices in G, then at each step, a correct decision can be made (see Section 4.9). □

One way to solve problems for which it is not possible to make a sequence of stepwise decisions leading to an optimal decision sequence is to try all possible decision sequences. We could enumerate all decision sequences and then pick out the best. But the time and space requirements may be prohibitive. Dynamic programming often drastically reduces the amount of enumeration by avoiding the enumeration of some decision sequences that cannot possibly be optimal. In dynamic programming an optimal sequence of decisions is obtained by making explicit appeal to the *principle of optimality*.

Definition 5.1 [Principle of optimality] The principle of optimality states that an optimal sequence of decisions has the property that whatever the initial state and decision are, the remaining decisions must constitute an optimal decision sequence with regard to the state resulting from the first decision. □

Thus, the essential difference between the greedy method and dynamic programming is that in the greedy method only one decision sequence is ever generated. In dynamic programming, many decision sequences may be generated. However, sequences containing suboptimal subsequences cannot be optimal (if the principle of optimality holds) and so will not (as far as possible) be generated.

Example 5.5 [Shortest path] Consider the shortest-path problem of Example 5.3. Assume that $i, i_1, i_2, \ldots, i_k, j$ is a shortest path from i to j. Starting with the initial vertex i, a decision has been made to go to vertex i_1. Following this decision, the problem state is defined by vertex i_1 and we need to find a path from i_1 to j. It is clear that the sequence $i_1, i_2, \ldots, i_k, j$ must constitute a shortest i_1 to j path. If not, let $i_1, r_1, r_2, \ldots, r_q, j$ be a shortest i_1 to j path. Then $i, i_1, r_1, \cdots, r_q, j$ is an i to j path that is shorter than the path $i, i_1, i_2, \ldots, i_k, j$. Therefore the principle of optimality applies for this problem. □

Example 5.6 [0/1 knapsack] The 0/1 knapsack problem is similar to the knapsack problem of Section 4.3 except that the x_i's are restricted to have a value of either 0 or 1. Using KNAP(l, j, y) to represent the problem

$$\begin{array}{c} \text{maximize} \sum_{l \le i \le j} p_i x_i \\ \text{subject to} \sum_{l \le i \le j} w_i x_i \le y \\ x_i = 0 \text{ or } 1, \; l \le i \le j \end{array} \tag{5.1}$$

the knapsack problem is KNAP$(1, n, m)$. Let $y_1, y_2, \ldots, y_n$ be an optimal sequence of 0/1 values for $x_1, x_2, \ldots, x_n$, respectively. If $y_1 = 0$, then $y_2, y_3, \ldots, y_n$ must constitute an optimal sequence for the problem KNAP(2, n, m). If it does not, then $y_1, y_2, \ldots, y_n$ is not an optimal sequence for KNAP$(1, n, m)$. If $y_1 = 1$, then $y_2, \ldots, y_n$ must be an optimal sequence for the problem KNAP$(2, n, m - w_1)$. If it isn't, then there is another 0/1 sequence $z_2, z_3, \ldots, z_n$ such that $\sum_{2 \le i \le n} w_i z_i \le m - w_1$ and $\sum_{2 \le i \le n} p_i z_i > \sum_{2 \le i \le n} p_i y_i$. Hence, the sequence $y_1, z_2, z_3, \ldots, z_n$ is a sequence for (5.1) with greater value. Again the principle of optimality applies. □

Let S_0 be the initial problem state. Assume that n decisions d_i, $1 \le i \le n$, have to be made. Let $D_1 = \{r_1, r_2, \ldots, r_j\}$ be the set of possible decision values for d_1. Let S_i be the problem state following the choice of decision r_i, $1 \le i \le j$. Let Γ_i be an optimal sequence of decisions with respect to the problem state S_i. Then, when the principle of optimality holds, an optimal sequence of decisions with respect to S_0 is the best of the decision sequences r_i, Γ_i, $1 \le i \le j$.

Example 5.7 [Shortest path] Let A_i be the set of vertices adjacent to vertex i. For each vertex $k \in A_i$, let Γ_k be a shortest path from k to j. Then, a shortest i to j path is the shortest of the paths $\{i, \Gamma_k | k \in A_i\}$. □

Example 5.8 [0/1 knapsack] Let $g_j(y)$ be the value of an optimal solution to KNAP$(j+1, n, y)$. Clearly, $g_0(m)$ is the value of an optimal solution to KNAP$(1, n, m)$. The possible decisions for x_1 are 0 and 1 ($D_1 = \{0, 1\}$). From the principle of optimality it follows that

$$g_0(m) = \max \; \{g_1(m), \; g_1(m - w_1) + p_1\} \tag{5.2}$$

□

While the principle of optimality has been stated only with respect to the initial state and decision, it can be applied equally well to intermediate states and decisions. The next two examples show how this can be done.

Example 5.9 [Shortest path] Let k be an intermediate vertex on a shortest i to j path $i, i_1, i_2, \ldots, k, p_1, p_2, \ldots, j$. The paths $i, i_1, \ldots, k$ and $k, p_1, \ldots, j$ must, respectively, be shortest i to k and k to j paths. □

Example 5.10 [0/1 knapsack] Let $y_1, y_2, \ldots, y_n$ be an optimal solution to KNAP$(1, n, m)$. Then, for each j, $1 \le j \le n$, $y_1, \ldots, y_j$, and $y_{j+1}, \ldots, y_n$ must be optimal solutions to the problems KNAP$(1, j, \sum_{1 \le i \le j} w_i y_i)$ and KNAP$(j+1, n, m - \sum_{1 \le i \le j} w_i y_i)$ respectively. This observation allows us to generalize (5.2) to

$$g_i(y) = \max \ \{g_{i+1}(y),\ g_{i+1}(y - w_{i+1}) + p_{i+1}\} \tag{5.3}$$

□

The recursive application of the optimality principle results in a recurrence equation of type (5.3). Dynamic programming algorithms solve this recurrence to obtain a solution to the given problem instance. The recurrence (5.3) can be solved using the knowledge $g_n(y) = 0$ for all $y \ge 0$ and $g_n(y) = -\infty$ for $y < 0$. From $g_n(y)$, one can obtain $g_{n-1}(y)$ using (5.3) with $i = n - 1$. Then, using $g_{n-1}(y)$, one can obtain $g_{n-2}(y)$. Repeating in this way, one can determine $g_1(y)$ and finally $g_0(m)$ using (5.3) with $i = 0$.

Example 5.11 [0/1 knapsack] Consider the case in which $n = 3$, $w_1 = 2, w_2 = 3, w_3 = 4$, $p_1 = 1, p_2 = 2, p_3 = 5$, and $m = 6$. We have to compute $g_0(6)$. The value of $g_0(6) = \max \ \{g_1(6),\ g_1(4) + 1\}$.

In turn, $g_1(6) = \max \ \{g_2(6),\ g_2(3)+2\}$. But $g_2(6) = \max \ \{g_3(6),\ g_3(2)+5\} = \max \ \{0, 5\} = 5$. Also, $g_2(3) = \max \ \{g_3(3),\ g_3(3 - 4) + 5\} = \max \ \{0, -\infty\} = 0$. Thus, $g_1(6) = \max \ \{5, 2\} = 5$.

Similarly, $g_1(4) = \max \ \{g_2(4),\ g_2(4 - 3) + 2\}$. But $g_2(4) = \max \ \{g_3(4),\ g_3(4 - 4) + 5\} = \max \ \{0, 5\} = 5$. The value of $g_2(1) = \max \ \{g_3(1),\ g_3(1 - 4) + 5\} = \max \ \{0, -\infty\} = 0$. Thus, $g_1(4) = \max \ \{5, 0\} = 5$.

Therefore, $g_0(6) = \max \ \{5, 5 + 1\} = 6$. □

Example 5.12 [Shortest path] Let P_j be the set of vertices adjacent to vertex j (that is, $k \in P_j$ iff $\langle k, j \rangle \in E(G)$). For each $k \in P_j$, let Γ_k be a shortest i to k path. The principle of optimality holds and a shortest i to j path is the shortest of the paths $\{\Gamma_k, j | k \in P_j\}$.

To obtain this formulation, we started at vertex j and looked at the last decision made. The last decision was to use one of the edges $\langle k, j \rangle$, $k \in P_j$. In a sense, we are looking backward on the i to j path. □

Example 5.13 [0/1 knapsack] Looking backward on the sequence of decisions $x_1, x_2, \ldots, x_n$, we see that

$$f_j(y) = \max \ \{f_{j-1}(y),\ f_{j-1}(y - w_j) + p_j\} \tag{5.4}$$

where $f_j(y)$ is the value of an optimal solution to KNAP$(1, j, y)$.

The value of an optimal solution to KNAP$(1, n, m)$ is $f_n(m)$. Equation 5.4 can be solved by beginning with $f_0(y) = 0$ for all y, $y \ge 0$, and $f_0(y) = -\infty$, for all y, $y < 0$. From this, $f_1, f_2, \ldots, f_n$ can be successively obtained.
□

The solution method outlined in Examples 5.12 and 5.13 may indicate that one has to look at all possible decision sequences to obtain an optimal decision sequence using dynamic programming. This is not the case. Because of the use of the principle of optimality, decision sequences containing subsequences that are suboptimal are *not* considered. Although the total number of different decision sequences is exponential in the number of decisions (if there are d choices for each of the n decisions to be made then there are d^n possible decision sequences), dynamic programming algorithms often have a polynomial complexity.

Another important feature of the dynamic programming approach is that optimal solutions to subproblems are retained so as to avoid recomputing their values. The use of these tabulated values makes it natural to recast the recursive equations into an iterative algorithm. Most of the dynamic programming algorithms in this chapter are expressed in this way.

The remaining sections of this chapter apply dynamic programming to a variety of problems. These examples should help you understand the method better and also realize the advantage of dynamic programming over explicitly enumerating all decision sequences.

EXERCISES

1. The principle of optimality does not hold for every problem whose solution can be viewed as the result of a sequence of decisions. Find two problems for which the principle does not hold. Explain why the principle does not hold for these problems.

2. For the graph of Figure 5.1, find the shortest path between the nodes 1 and 2. Use the recurrence relations derived in Examples 5.10 and 5.13.

5.2 MULTISTAGE GRAPHS

A multistage graph $G = (V, E)$ is a directed graph in which the vertices are partitioned into $k \geq 2$ disjoint sets V_i, $1 \leq i \leq k$. In addition, if $\langle u, v \rangle$ is an edge in E, then $u \in V_i$ and $v \in V_{i+1}$ for some $i, 1 \leq i < k$. The sets V_1 and V_k are such that $|V_1| = |V_k| = 1$. Let s and t, respectively, be the vertices in V_1 and V_k. The vertex s is the *source*, and t the *sink*. Let $c(i, j)$ be the cost of edge $\langle i, j \rangle$. The cost of a path from s to t is the sum of the costs of the edges on the path. The *multistage graph problem* is to find a minimum-cost path from s to t. Each set V_i defines a stage in the graph. Because of the constraints on E, every path from s to t starts in stage 1, goes to stage 2, then to stage 3, then to stage 4, and so on, and eventually terminates in stage k. Figure 5.2 shows a five-stage graph. A minimum-cost s to t path is indicated by the broken edges.

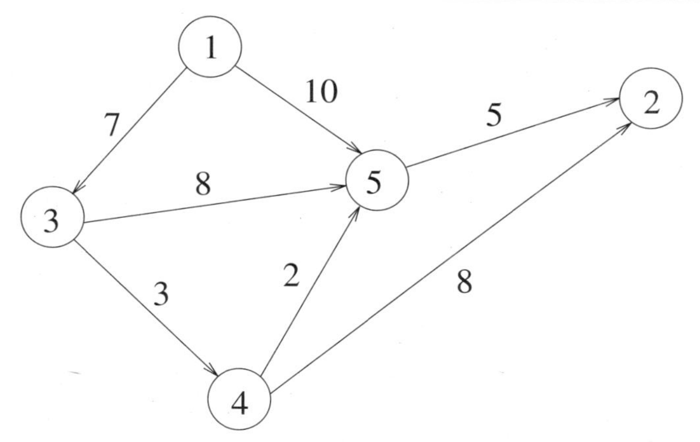

Figure 5.1 Graph for Exercise 2 (Section 5.1)

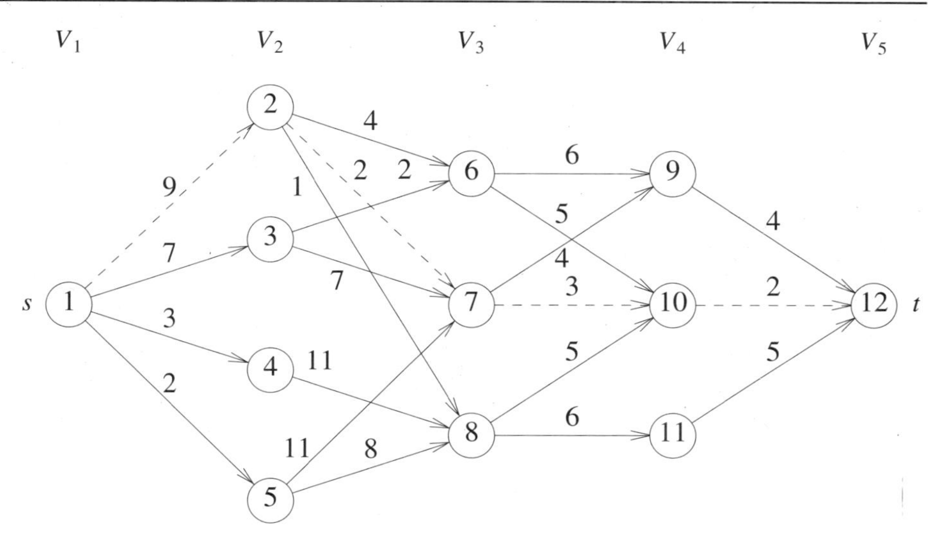

Figure 5.2 Five-stage graph

Many problems can be formulated as multistage graph problems. We give only one example. Consider a resource allocation problem in which n units of resource are to be allocated to r projects. If j, $0 \leq j \leq n$, units of the resource are allocated to project i, then the resulting net profit is $N(i,j)$. The problem is to allocate the resource to the r projects in such a way as to maximize total net profit. This problem can be formulated as an $r+1$ stage graph problem as follows. Stage i, $1 \leq i \leq r$, represents project i. There are $n+1$ vertices $V(i,j)$, $0 \leq j \leq n$, associated with stage i, $2 \leq i \leq r$. Stages 1 and $r+1$ each have one vertex, $V(1,0) = s$ and $V(r+1,n) = t$, respectively. Vertex $V(i,j)$, $2 \leq i \leq r$, represents the state in which a total of j units of resource have been allocated to projects $1, 2, \ldots, i-1$. The edges in G are of the form $\langle V(i,j), V(i+1,l) \rangle$ for all $j \leq l$ and $1 \leq i < r$. The edge $\langle V(i,j), V(i+1,l) \rangle$, $j \leq l$, is assigned a weight or cost of $N(i, l-j)$ and corresponds to allocating $l-j$ units of resource to project i, $1 \leq i < r$. In addition, G has edges of the type $\langle V(r,j), V(r+1,n) \rangle$. Each such edge is assigned a weight of $\max_{0 \leq p \leq n-j}\{N(r,p)\}$. The resulting graph for a three-project problem with $n = 4$ is shown in Figure 5.3. It should be easy to see that an optimal allocation of resources is defined by a maximum cost s to t path. This is easily converted into a minimum-cost problem by changing the sign of all the edge costs.

A dynamic programming formulation for a k-stage graph problem is obtained by first noticing that every s to t path is the result of a sequence of $k-2$ decisions. The ith decision involves determining which vertex in V_{i+1}, $1 \leq i \leq k-2$, is to be on the path. It is easy to see that the principle of optimality holds. Let $p(i,j)$ be a minimum-cost path from vertex j in V_i to vertex t. Let $cost(i,j)$ be the cost of this path. Then, using the forward approach, we obtain

$$cost(i,j) = \min_{\substack{l \in V_{i+1} \\ \langle j,l \rangle \in E}} \{c(j,l) + cost(i+1,l)\} \tag{5.5}$$

Since, $cost(k-1,j) = c(j,t)$ if $\langle j,t \rangle \in E$ and $cost(k-1,j) = \infty$ if $\langle j,t \rangle \notin E$, (5.5) may be solved for $cost(1,s)$ by first computing $cost(k-2,j)$ for all $j \in V_{k-2}$, then $cost(k-3,j)$ for all $j \in V_{k-3}$, and so on, and finally $cost(1,s)$. Trying this out on the graph of Figure 5.2, we obtain

$$\begin{aligned}
cost(3,6) &= \min\ \{6 + cost(4,9), 5 + cost(4,10)\} \\
&= 7 \\
cost(3,7) &= \min\ \{4 + cost(4,9), 3 + cost(4,10)\} \\
&= 5 \\
cost(3,8) &= 7 \\
cost(2,2) &= \min\ \{4 + cost(3,6), 2 + cost(3,7), 1 + cost(3,8)\} \\
&= 7 \\
cost(2,3) &= 9 \\
cost(2,4) &= 18
\end{aligned}$$

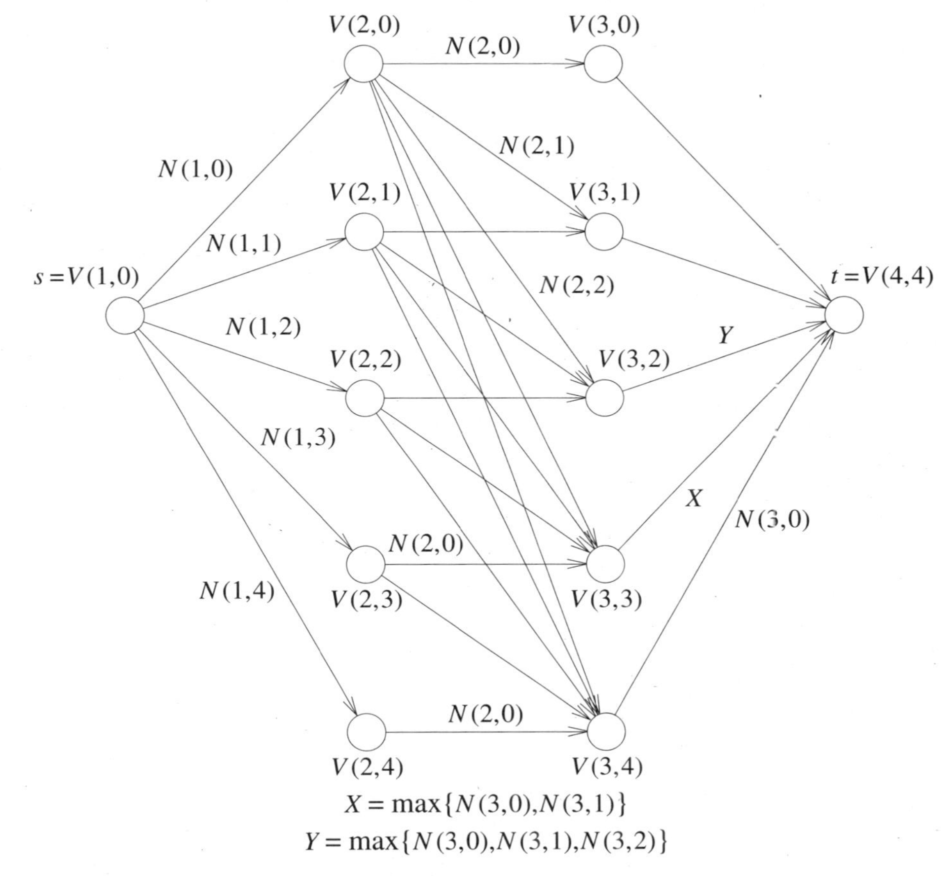

Figure 5.3 Four-stage graph corresponding to a three-project problem

$$
\begin{aligned}
cost(2,5) &= 15 \\
cost(1,1) &= \min\ \{9 + cost(2,2), 7 + cost(2,3), 3 + cost(2,4), \\
&\qquad\qquad 2 + cost(2,5)\} \\
&= 16
\end{aligned}
$$

Note that in the calculation of $cost(2,2)$, we have reused the values of $cost(3,6), cost(3,7)$, and $cost(3,8)$ and so avoided their reccmputation. A minimum cost s to t path has a cost of 16. This path can be determined easily if we record the decision made at each state (vertex). Let $d(i,j)$ be the value of l (where l is a node) that minimizes $c(j,l) + cost(i+1,l)$ (see Equation 5.5). For Figure 5.2 we obtain

$$\begin{array}{lllllllllll} d(3,6) & = & 10; & d(3,7) & = & 10; & d(3,8) & = & 10; & & \\ d(2,2) & = & 7; & d(2,3) & = & 6; & d(2,4) & = & 8; & d(2,5) & = 8; \\ d(1,1) & = & 2 & & & & & & & & \end{array}$$

Let the minimum-cost path be $s = 1, v_2, v_3, \ldots, v_{k-1}, t$. It is easy to see that $v_2 = d(1,1) = 2$, $v_3 = d(2, d(1,1)) = 7$, and $v_4 = d(3, d(2, d(1,1))) = d(3,7) = 10$.

Before writing an algorithm to solve (5.5) for a general k-stage graph, let us impose an ordering on the vertices in V. This ordering makes it easier to write the algorithm. We require that the n vertices in V are indexed 1 through n. Indices are assigned in order of stages. First, s is assigned index 1, then vertices in V_2 are assigned indices, then vertices from V_3, and so on. Vertex t has index n. Hence, indices assigned to vertices in V_{i+1} are bigger than those assigned to vertices in V_i (see Figure 5.2). As a result of this indexing scheme, *cost* and d can be computed in the order $n-1, n-2, \ldots, 1$. The first subscript in *cost*, p, and d only identifies the stage number and is omitted in the algorithm. The resulting algorithm, in pseudocode, is FGraph (Algorithm 5.1).

The complexity analysis of the function FGraph is fairly straightforward. If G is represented by its adjacency lists, then r in line 9 of Algorithm 5.1 can be found in time proportional to the degree of vertex j. Hence, if G has $|E|$ edges, then the time for the **for** loop of line 7 is $\Theta(|V| + |E|)$. The time for the **for** loop of line 16 is $\Theta(k)$. Hence, the total time is $\Theta(|V| + |E|)$. In addition to the space needed for the input, space is needed for *cost*[ ], *d*[ ], and *p*[ ].

The multistage graph problem can also be solved using the backward approach. Let $bp(i,j)$ be a minimum-cost path from vertex s to a vertex j in V_i. Let $bcost(i,j)$ be the cost of $bp(i,j)$. From the backward approach we obtain

$$bcost(i,j) = \min_{\substack{l \in V_{i-1} \\ \langle l,j \rangle \in E}} \{bcost(i-1,l) + c(l,j)\} \tag{5.6}$$

Since $bcost(2,j) = c(1,j)$ if $\langle 1,j \rangle \in E$ and $bcost(2,j) = \infty$ if $\langle 1,j \rangle \notin E$, $bcost(i,j)$ can be computed using (5.6) by first computing *bcost* for $i = 3$, then for $i = 4$, and so on. For the graph of Figure 5.2, we obtain

$$\begin{aligned} bcost(3,6) &= \min\,\{bcost(2,2) + c(2,6), bcost(2,3) + c(3,6)\} \\ &= \min\,\{9+4, 7+2\} \\ &= 9 \end{aligned}$$

```
Algorithm FGraph(G, k, n, p)
// The input is a k-stage graph G = (V, E) with n vertices
// indexed in order of stages. E is a set of edges and c[i, j]
// is the cost of ⟨i, j⟩. p[1 : k] is a minimum-cost path.
{
    cost[n] := 0.0;
    for j := n - 1 to 1 step -1 do
    { // Compute cost[j].
        Let r be a vertex such that ⟨j, r⟩ is an edge
        of G and c[j, r] + cost[r] is minimum;
        cost[j] := c[j, r] + cost[r];
        d[j] := r;
    }
    // Find a minimum-cost path.
    p[1] := 1; p[k] := n;
    for j := 2 to k - 1 do p[j] := d[p[j - 1]];
}
```

Algorithm 5.1 Multistage graph pseudocode corresponding to the forward approach

$$\begin{aligned} bcost(3,7) &= 11 \\ bcost(3,8) &= 10 \\ bcost(4,9) &= 15 \\ bcost(4,10) &= 14 \\ bcost(4,11) &= 16 \\ bcost(5,12) &= 16 \end{aligned}$$

The corresponding algorithm, in pseudocode, to obtain a minimum-cost $s - t$ path is BGraph (Algorithm 5.2). The first subscript on $bcost$, p, and d are omitted for the same reasons as before. This algorithm has the same complexity as FGraph provided G is now represented by its inverse adjacency lists (i.e., for each vertex v we have a list of vertices w such that $\langle w, v \rangle \in E$).

It should be easy to see that both FGraph and BGraph work correctly even on a more generalized version of multistage graphs. In this generalization, the graph is permitted to have edges $\langle u, v \rangle$ such that $u \in V_i, v \in V_j$, and $i < j$.

Note: In the pseudocodes FGraph and BGraph, $bcost(i, j)$ is set to ∞ for any $\langle i, j \rangle \notin E$. When programming these pseudocodes, one could use the maximum allowable floating point number for ∞. If the weight of any such

```
Algorithm BGraph(G, k, n, p)
// Same function as FGraph
{
    bcost[1] := 0.0;
    for j := 2 to n do
    { // Compute bcost[j].
        Let r be such that ⟨r, j⟩ is an edge of
        G and bcost[r] + c[r, j] is minimum;
        bcost[j] := bcost[r] + c[r, j];
        d[j] := r;
    }
    // Find a minimum-cost path.
    p[1] := 1; p[k] := n;
    for j := k - 1 to 2 do p[j] := d[p[j + 1]];
}
```

Algorithm 5.2 Multistage graph pseudocode corresponding to backward approach

edge is added to some other costs, a floating point overflow might occur. Care should be taken to avoid such overflows.

EXERCISES

1. Find a minimum-cost path from s to t in the multistage graph of Figure 5.4. Do this first using the forward approach and then using the backward approach.

2. Refine Algorithm 5.1 into a program. Assume that G is represented by its adjacency lists. Test the correctness of your code using suitable graphs.

3. Program Algorithm 5.1. Assume that G is an array $G[1 : e, 1 : 3]$. Each edge $\langle i, j \rangle$, $i < j$, of G is stored in $G[q]$, for some q and $G[q, 1] = i$, $G[q, 2] = j$, and $G[q, 3] =$ cost of edge $\langle i, j \rangle$. Assume that $G[q, 1] \leq G[q + 1, 1]$ for $1 \leq q < e$, where e is the number of edges in the multistage graph. Test the correctness of your function using suitable multistage graphs. What is the time complexity of your function?

4. Program Algorithm 5.2 for the multistage graph problem using the

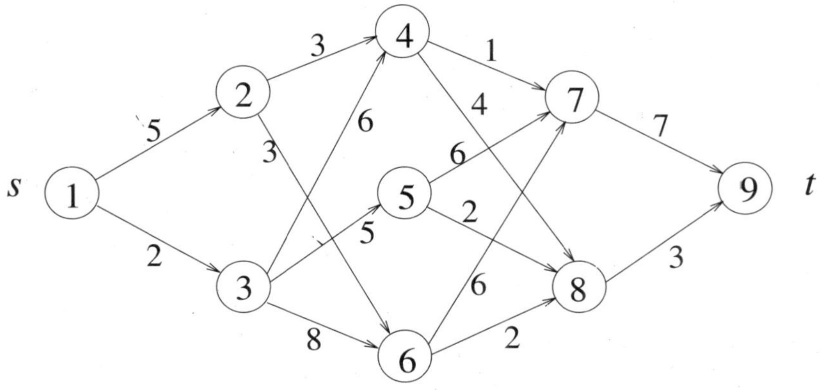

Figure 5.4 Multistage graph for Exercise 1

backward approach. Assume that the graph is represented using inverse adjacency lists. Test its correctness. What is its complexity?

5. Do Exercise 4 using the graph representation of Exercise 3. This time, however, assume that $G[q, 2] \le G[q+1, 2]$ for $1 \le q < e$.

6. Extend the discussion of this section to directed acyclic graphs (dags). Suppose the vertices of a dag are numbered so that all edges have the form $\langle i, j \rangle$, $i < j$. What changes, if any, need to be made to Algorithm 5.1 to find the length of the longest path from vertex 1 to vertex n?

7. [W. Miller] Show that BGraph1 computes shortest paths for directed acyclic graphs represented by adjacency lists (instead of inverse adjacency lists as in BGraph).

```
Algorithm BGraph1(G, n)
{
    bcost[1] := 0.0;
    for j := 2 to n do bcost[j] := ∞;
    for j := 1 to n − 1 do
        for each r such that ⟨j, r⟩ is an edge of G do
            bcost[r] := min(bcost[r], bcost[j] + c[j, r]);
}
```

Note: There is a possibility of a floating point overflow in this function. In such cases the program should be suitably modified.

5.3 ALL-PAIRS SHORTEST PATHS

Let $G = (V, E)$ be a directed graph with n vertices. Let *cost* be a cost adjacency matrix for G such that $cost(i,i) = 0$, $1 \le i \le n$. Then $cost(i,j)$ is the length (or cost) of edge $\langle i,j \rangle$ if $\langle i,j \rangle \in E(G)$ and $cost(i,j) = \infty$ if $i \ne j$ and $\langle i,j \rangle \notin E(G)$. The *all-pairs shortest-path problem* is to determine a matrix A such that $A(i,j)$ is the length of a shortest path from i to j. The matrix A can be obtained by solving n single-source problems using the algorithm ShortestPaths of Section 4.9. Since each application of this procedure requires $O(n^2)$ time, the matrix A can be obtained in $O(n^3)$ time. We obtain an alternate $O(n^3)$ solution to this problem using the principle of optimality. Our alternate solution requires a weaker restriction on edge costs than required by ShortestPaths. Rather than require $cost(i,j) \ge 0$, for every edge $\langle i,j \rangle$, we only require that G have no cycles with negative length. Note that if we allow G to contain a cycle of negative length, then the shortest path between any two vertices on this cycle has length $-\infty$.

Let us examine a shortest i to j path in G, $i \ne j$. This path originates at vertex i and goes through some intermediate vertices (possibly none) and terminates at vertex j. We can assume that this path contains no cycles for if there is a cycle, then this can be deleted without increasing the path length (no cycle has negative length). If k is an intermediate vertex on this shortest path, then the subpaths from i to k and from k to j must be shortest paths from i to k and k to j, respectively. Otherwise, the i to j path is not of minimum length. So, the principle of optimality holds. This alerts us to the prospect of using dynamic programming. If k is the intermediate vertex with highest index, then the i to k path is a shortest i to k path in G going through no vertex with index greater than $k-1$. Similarly the k to j path is a shortest k to j path in G going through no vertex of index greater than $k-1$. We can regard the construction of a shortest i to j path as first requiring a decision as to which is the highest indexed intermediate vertex k. Once this decision has been made, we need to find two shortest paths, one from i to k and the other from k to j. Neither of these may go through a vertex with index greater than $k-1$. Using $A^k(i,j)$ to represent the length of a shortest path from i to j going through no vertex of index greater than k, we obtain

$$A(i,j) = \min \, \{ \min_{1 \le k \le n} \{A^{k-1}(i,k) + A^{k-1}(k,j)\}, cost(i,j)\} \tag{5.7}$$

Clearly, $A^0(i,j) = cost(i,j)$, $1 \le i \le n$, $1 \le j \le n$. We can obtain a recurrence for $A^k(i,j)$ using an argument similar to that used before. A shortest path from i to j going through no vertex higher than k either goes through vertex k or it does not. If it does, $A^k(i,j) = A^{k-1}(i,k) + A^{k-1}(k,j)$. If it does not, then no intermediate vertex has index greater than $k-1$. Hence $A^k(i,j) = A^{k-1}(i,j)$. Combining, we get

$$A^k(i,j) = \min\ \{A^{k-1}(i,j),\ A^{k-1}(i,k) + A^{k-1}(k,j)\},\quad k \geq 1 \qquad (5.8)$$

The following example shows that (5.8) is not true for graphs with cycles of negative length.

Example 5.14 Figure 5.5 shows a digraph together with its matrix A^0. For this graph $A^2(1,3) \neq \min\{A^1(1,3),\ A^1(1,2) + A^1(2,3)\} = 2$. Instead we see that $A^2(1,3) = -\infty$. The length of the path

$$1, 2, 1, 2, 1, 2, \ldots, 1, 2, 3$$

can be made arbitrarily small. This is so because of the presence of the cycle 1 2 1 which has a length of -1. □

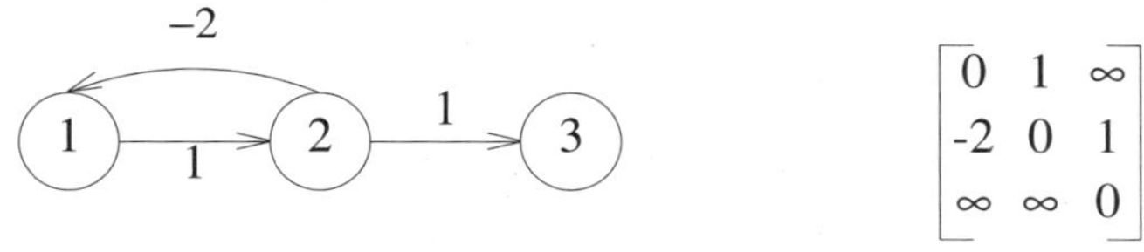

Figure 5.5 Graph with negative cycle

Recurrence (5.8) can be solved for A^n by first computing A^1, then A^2, then A^3, and so on. Since there is no vertex in G with index greater than n, $A(i,j) = A^n(i,j)$. Function AllPaths computes $A^n(i,j)$. The computation is done inplace so the superscript on A is not needed. The reason this computation can be carried out in-place is that $A^k(i,k) = A^{k-1}(i,k)$ and $A^k(k,j) = A^{k-1}(k,j)$. Hence, when A^k is formed, the kth column and row do not change. Consequently, when $A^k(i,j)$ is computed in line 11 of Algorithm 5.3, $A(i,k) = A^{k-1}(i,k) = A^k(i,k)$ and $A(k,j) = A^{k-1}(k,j) = A^k(k,j)$. So, the old values on which the new values are based do not change on this iteration.

Example 5.15 The graph of Figure 5.6(a) has the cost matrix of Figure 5.6(b). The initial A matrix, $A^{(0)}$, plus its values after 3 iterations $A^{(1)}$, $A^{(2)}$, and $A^{(3)}$ are given in Figure 5.6. □

```
Algorithm AllPaths(cost, A, n)
// cost[1 : n, 1 : n] is the cost adjacency matrix of a graph with
// n vertices; A[i, j] is the cost of a shortest path from vertex
// i to vertex j. cost[i, i] = 0.0, for 1 ≤ i ≤ n.
{
    for i := 1 to n do
        for j := 1 to n do
            A[i, j] := cost[i, j]; // Copy cost into A.
    for k := 1 to n do
        for i := 1 to n do
            for j := 1 to n do
                A[i, j] := min(A[i, j], A[i, k] + A[k, j]);
}
```

Algorithm 5.3 Function to compute lengths of shortest paths

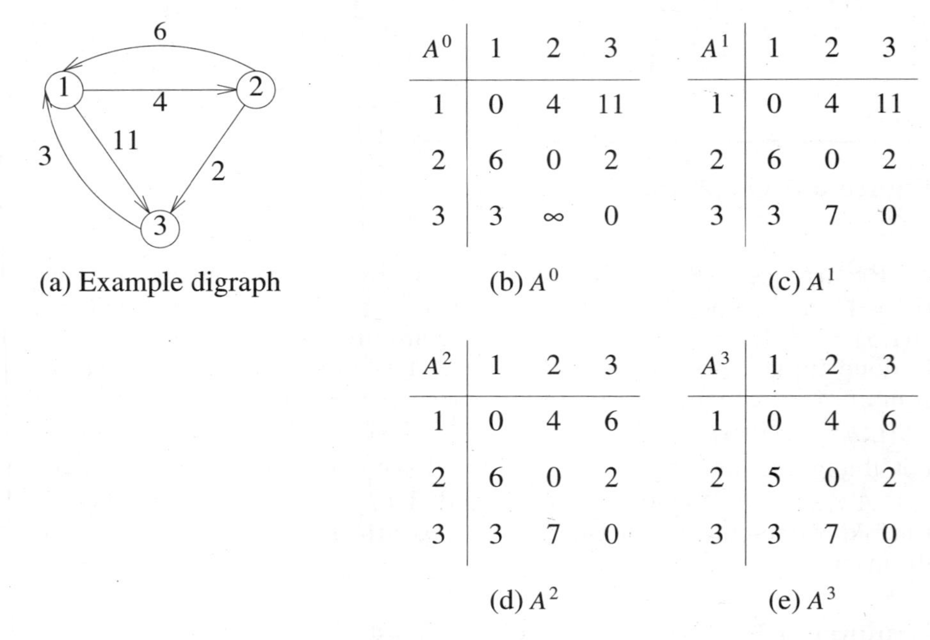

(a) Example digraph

A^0	1	2	3
1	0	4	11
2	6	0	2
3	3	∞	0

(b) A^0

A^1	1	2	3
1	0	4	11
2	6	0	2
3	3	7	0

(c) A^1

A^2	1	2	3
1	0	4	6
2	6	0	2
3	3	7	0

(d) A^2

A^3	1	2	3
1	0	4	6
2	5	0	2
3	3	7	0

(e) A^3

Figure 5.6 Directed graph and associated matrices

Let $M = \max\ \{cost(i,j)|\langle i,j\rangle \in E(G)\}$. It is easy to see that $A^n(ij) \leq (n-1)M$. From the working of AllPaths, it is clear that if $\langle i,j\rangle \notin E(G)$ and $i \neq j$, then we can initialize $cost(i,j)$ to any number greater than $(n-1)M$ (rather than the maximum allowable floating point number). If, at termination, $A(i,j) > (n-1)M$, then there is no directed path from i to j in G. Even for this choice of ∞, care should be taken to avoid any floating point overflows.

The time needed by AllPaths (Algorithm 5.3) is especially easy to determine because the looping is independent of the data in the matrix A. Line 11 is iterated n^3 times, and so the time for AllPaths is $\Theta(n^3)$. An exercise examines the extensions needed to obtain the i to j paths with these lengths. Some speedup can be obtained by noticing that the innermost **for** loop need be executed only when $A(i,k)$ and $A(k,j)$ are not equal to ∞.

EXERCISES

1. (a) Does the recurrence (5.8) hold for the graph of Figure 5.7? Why?

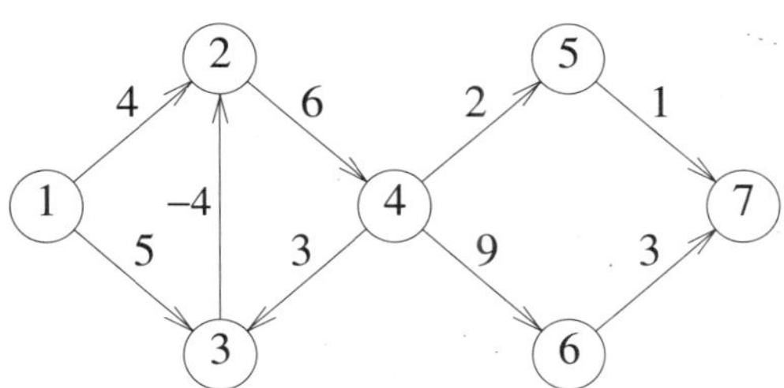

Figure 5.7 Graph for Exercise 1

   (b) Why does Equation 5.8 not hold for graphs with cycles of negative length?

2. Modify the function AllPaths so that a shortest path is output for each pair of vertices (i, j). What are the time and space complexities of the new algorithm?

3. Let A be the adjacency matrix of a directed graph G. Define the transitive closure A^+ of A to be a matrix with the property $A^+(i,j) = 1$ iff G has a directed path, containing at least one edge, from vertex i to vertex j. $A^+(i,j) = 0$ otherwise. The reflexive transitive closure A^* is a matrix with the property $A^*(i,j) = 1$ iff G has a path, containing zero or more edges, from i to j. $A^*(i,j) = 0$ otherwise.

   (a) Obtain A^+ and A^* for the directed graph of Figure 5.8.

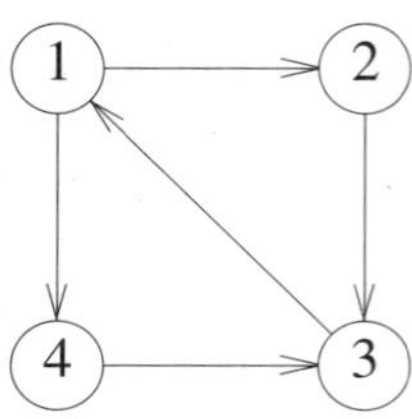

Figure 5.8 Graph for Exercise 3

(b) Let $A^k(i,j) = 1$ iff there is a path with zero or more edges from i to j going through no vertex of index greater than k. Define A^0 in terms of the adjacency matrix A.

(c) Obtain a recurrence between A^k and A^{k-1} similar to (5.8). Use the logical operators **or** and **and** rather than **min** and +.

(d) Write an algorithm, using the recurrence of part (c), to find A^*. Your algorithm can use only $O(n^2)$ space. What is its time complexity?

(e) Show that $A^+ = A \times A^*$, where matrix multiplication is defined as $A^+(i,j) = \vee_{k=1}^{n}(A(i,k) \wedge A^*(k,j))$. The operation $\vee$ is the logical **or** operation, and $\wedge$ the logical **and** operation. Hence A^+ may be computed from A^*.

5.4 SINGLE-SOURCE SHORTEST PATHS: GENERAL WEIGHTS

We now consider the single-source shortest path problem discussed in Section 4.9 when some or all of the edges of the directed graph G may have negative length. ShortestPaths (Algorithm 4.14) does not necessarily give the correct results on such graphs. To see this, consider the graph of Figure 5.9. Let $v = 1$ be the source vertex. Referring back to Algorithm 4.14, since $n = 3$, the loop of lines 12 to 22 is iterated just once. Also $u = 3$ in lines 15 and 16, and so no changes are made to $dist[\ ]$. The algorithm terminates with $dist[2] = 7$ and $dist[3] = 5$. The shortest path from 1 to 3 is 1, 2, 3. This path has length 2, which is less than the computed value of $dist[3]$.

When negative edge lengths are permitted, we require that the graph have no cycles of negative length. This is necessary to ensure that shortest paths consist of a finite number of edges. For example, in the graph of Figure 5.5, the length of the shortest path from vertex 1 to vertex 3 is $-\infty$. The

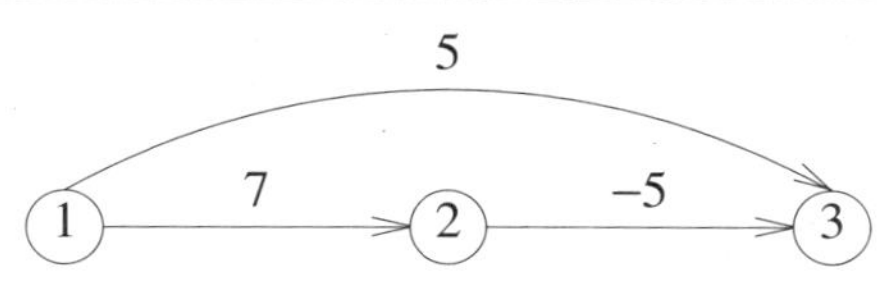

Figure 5.9 Directed graph with a negative-length edge

length of the path

$$1, 2, 1, 2, 1, 2, \cdots, 1, 2, 3$$

can be made arbitrarily small as was shown in Example 5.14.

When there are no cycles of negative length, there is a shortest path between any two vertices of an n-vertex graph that has at most $n-1$ edges on it. To see this, note that a path that has more than $n-1$ edges must repeat at least one vertex and hence must contain a cycle. Elimination of the cycles from the path results in another path with the same source and destination. This path is cycle-free and has a length that is no more than that of the original path, as the length of the eliminated cycles was at least zero. We can use this observation on the maximum number of edges on a cycle-free shortest path to obtain an algorithm to determine a shortest path from a source vertex to all remaining vertices in the graph. As in the case of ShortestPaths (Algorithm 4.14), we compute only the length, $dist[u]$, of the shortest path from the source vertex v to u. An exercise examines the extension needed to construct the shortest paths.

Let $dist^\ell[u]$ be the length of a shortest path from the source vertex v to vertex u under the constraint that the shortest path contains at most ℓ edges. Then, $dist^1[u] = cost[v, u]$, $1 \leq u \leq n$. As noted earlier, when there are no cycles of negative length, we can limit our search for shortest paths to paths with at most $n-1$ edges. Hence, $dist^{n-1}[u]$ is the length of an unrestricted shortest path from v to u.

Our goal then is to compute $dist^{n-1}[u]$ for all u. This can be done using the dynamic programming methodology. First, we make the following observations:

1. If the shortest path from v to u with at most k, $k > 1$, edges has no more than $k-1$ edges, then $dist^k[u] = dist^{k-1}[u]$.

2. If the shortest path from v to u with at most k, $k > 1$, edges has exactly k edges, then it is made up of a shortest path from v to some vertex j followed by the edge $\langle j, u\rangle$. The path from v to j has $k-1$ edges, and its length is $dist^{k-1}[j]$. All vertices i such that the edge

$\langle i, u \rangle$ is in the graph are candidates for j. Since we are interested in a shortest path, the i that minimizes $dist^{k-1}[i] + cost[i, u]$ is the correct value for j.

These observations result in the following recurrence for *dist*:

$$dist^k[u] = \min \{dist^{k-1}[u], \min_i \{dist^{k-1}[i] + cost[i, u]\}\}$$

This recurrence can be used to compute $dist^k$ from $dist^{k-1}$, for $k = 2, 3, \ldots, n-1$.

Example 5.16 Figure 5.10 gives a seven-vertex graph, together with the arrays $dist^k$, $k = 1, \ldots, 6$. These arrays were computed using the equation just given. For instance, $dist^k[1] = 0$ for all k since 1 is the source node. Also, $dist^1[2] = 6, dist^1[3] = 5$, and $dist^1[4] = 5$, since there are edges from 1 to these nodes. The distance $dist^1[]$ is ∞ for the nodes 5, 6, and 7 since there are no edges to these from 1.

$$\begin{aligned} dist^2[2] &= \min \{dist^1[2], \min_i dist^1[i] + cost[i, 2]\} \\ &= \min \{6, 0+6, 5-2, 5+\infty, \infty+\infty, \infty+\infty, \infty+\infty\} = 3 \end{aligned}$$

Here the terms $0+6, 5-2, 5+\infty, \infty+\infty, \infty+\infty$, and $\infty+\infty$ correspond to a choice of $i = 1, 3, 4, 5, 6$, and 7, respectively. The rest of the entries are computed in an analogous manner. □

An exercise shows that if we use the same memory location $dist[u]$ for $dist^k[u]$, $k = 1, \ldots, n-1$, then the final value of $dist[u]$ is still $dist^{n-1}[u]$. Using this fact and the recurrence for *dist* shown above, we arrive at the pseudocode of Algorithm 5.4 to compute the length of the shortest path from vertex v to each other vertex of the graph. This algorithm is referred to as the Bellman and Ford algorithm.

Each iteration of the **for** loop of lines 7 to 12 takes $O(n^2)$ time if adjacency matrices are used and $O(e)$ time if adjacency lists are used. Here e is the number of edges in the graph. The overall complexity is $O(n^3)$ when adjacency matrices are used and $O(ne)$ when adjacency lists are used. The observed complexity of the shortest-path algorithm can be reduced by noting that if none of the *dist* values change on one iteration of the **for** loop of lines 7 to 12, then none will change on successive iterations. So, this loop can be rewritten to terminate either after $n-1$ iterations or after the first iteration in which no *dist* values are changed, whichever occurs first. Another possibility is to maintain a queue of vertices i whose *dist* values changed on the previous iteration of the **for** loop. These are the only values for i that need to be considered in line 10 during the next iteration. When

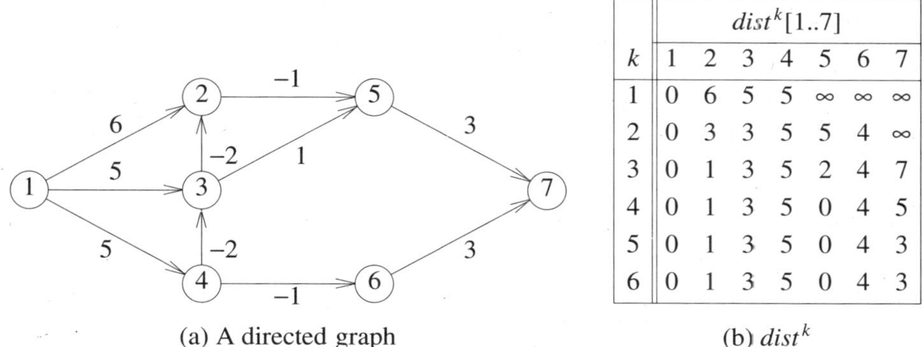

(a) A directed graph

k	$dist^k[1..7]$						
	1	2	3	4	5	6	7
1	0	6	5	5	∞	∞	∞
2	0	3	3	5	5	4	∞
3	0	1	3	5	2	4	7
4	0	1	3	5	0	4	5
5	0	1	3	5	0	4	3
6	0	1	3	5	0	4	3

(b) $dist^k$

Figure 5.10 Shortest paths with negative edge lengths

```
1   Algorithm BellmanFord(v, cost, dist, n)
2   // Single-source/all-destinations shortest
3   // paths with negative edge costs
4   {
5       for i := 1 to n do // Initialize dist.
6           dist[i] := cost[v, i];
7       for k := 2 to n − 1 do
8           for each u such that u ≠ v and u has
9                   at least one incoming edge do
10              for each ⟨i, u⟩ in the graph do
11                  if dist[u] > dist[i] + cost[i, u] then
12                      dist[u] := dist[i] + cost[i, u];
13  }
```

Algorithm 5.4 Bellman and Ford algorithm to compute shortest paths

a queue of these values is maintained, we can rewrite the loop of lines 7 to 12 so that on each iteration, a vertex i is removed from the queue, and the *dist* values of all vertices adjacent from i are updated as in lines 11 and 12. Vertices whose *dist* values decrease as a result of this are added to the end of the queue unless they are already on it. The loop terminates when the queue becomes empty. These two strategies to improve the performance of BellmanFord are considered in the exercises. Other strategies for improving performance are discussed in References and Readings. □

EXERCISES

1. Find the shortest paths from node 1 to every other node in the graph of Figure 5.11 using the Bellman and Ford algorithm.

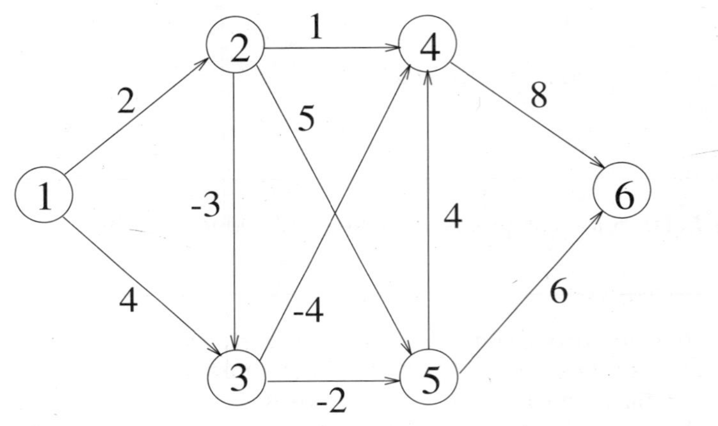

Figure 5.11 Graph for Exercise 1

2. Prove the correctness of BellmanFord (Algorithm 5.4). Note that this algorithm does not faithfully implement the computation of the recurrence for $dist^k$. In fact, for $k < n-1$, the $dist$ values following iteration k of the **for** loop of lines 7 to 12 may not be $dist^k$.

3. Transform BellmanFord into a program. Assume that graphs are represented using adjacency lists in which each node has an additional field called *cost* that gives the length of the edge represented by that node. As a result of this, there is no cost adjacency matrix. Generate some test graphs and test the correctness of your program.

4. Rewrite the algorithm BellmanFord so that the loop of lines 7 to 12 terminates either after $n-1$ iterations or after the first iteration in which no $dist$ values are changed, whichever occurs first.

5. Rewrite BellmanFord by replacing the loop of lines 7 to 12 with code that uses a queue of vertices that may potentially result in a reduction

of other *dist* vertices. This queue initially contains all vertices that are adjacent from the source vertex v. On each successive iteration of the new loop, a vertex i is removed from the queue (unless the queue is empty), and the *dist* values to vertices adjacent from i are updated as in lines 11 and 12 of Algorithm 5.4. When the *dist* value of a vertex is reduced because of this, it is added to the queue unless it is already on the queue.

(a) Prove that the new algorithm produces the same results as the original one.

(b) Show that the complexity of the new algorithm is no more than that of the original one.

6. Compare the run-time performance of the Bellman and Ford algorithms of the preceding two exercises and that of Algorithm 5.4. For this, generate test graphs that will expose the relative performances of the three algorithms.

7. Modify algorithm BellmanFord so that it obtains the shortest paths, in addition to the lengths of these paths. What is the computing time of your algorithm?

5.5 OPTIMAL BINARY SEARCH TREES (*)

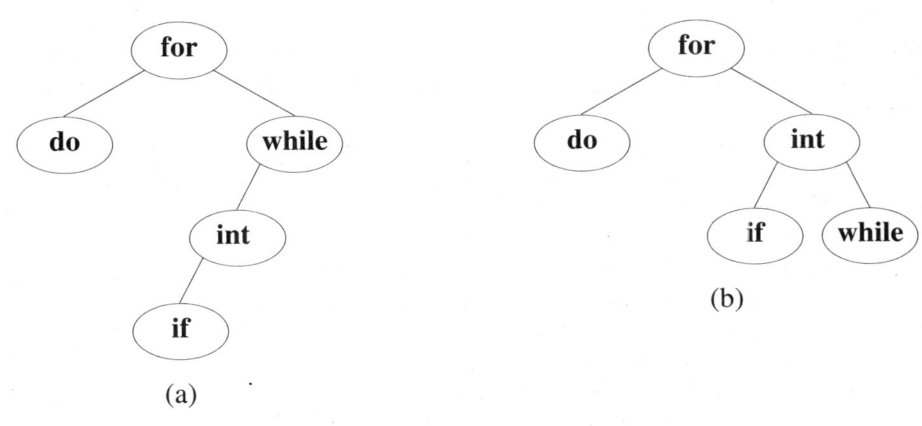

Figure 5.12 Two possible binary search trees

Given a fixed set of identifiers, we wish to create a binary search tree (see Section 2.3) organization. We may expect different binary search trees for the same identifier set to have different performance characteristics. The tree of Figure 5.12(a), in the worst case, requires four comparisons to find an identifier, whereas the tree of Figure 5.12(b) requires only three. On the average the two trees need 12/5 and 11/5 comparisons, respectively. For example, in the case of tree (a), it takes $1, 2, 2, 3$, and 4 comparisons, respectively, to find the identifiers **for, do, while, int,** and **if**. Thus the average number of comparisons is $\frac{1+2+2+3+4}{5} = \frac{12}{5}$. This calculation assumes that each identifier is searched for with equal probability and that no unsuccessful searches (i.e., searches for identifiers not in the tree) are made.

In a general situation, we can expect different identifiers to be searched for with different frequencies (or probabilities). In addition, we can expect unsuccessful searches also to be made. Let us assume that the given set of identifiers is $\{a_1, a_2, \ldots, a_n\}$ with $a_1 < a_2 < \cdots < a_n$. Let $p(i)$ be the probability with which we search for a_i. Let $q(i)$ be the probability that the identifier x being searched for is such that $a_i < x < a_{i+1}$, $0 \le i \le n$ (assume $a_0 = -\infty$ and $a_{n+1} = +\infty$). Then, $\sum_{0 \le i \le n} q(i)$ is the probability of an unsuccessful search. Clearly, $\sum_{1 \le i \le n} p(i) + \sum_{0 \le i \le n} q(i) = 1$. Given this data, we wish to construct an optimal binary search tree for $\{a_1, a_2, \ldots, a_n\}$. First, of course, we must be precise about what we mean by an optimal binary search tree.

In obtaining a cost function for binary search trees, it is useful to add a fictitious node in place of every empty subtree in the search tree. Such nodes, called external nodes, are drawn square in Figure 5.13. All other nodes are internal nodes. If a binary search tree represents n identifiers, then there will be exactly n internal nodes and $n + 1$ (fictitious) external nodes. Every internal node represents a point where a successful search may terminate. Every external node represents a point where an unsuccessful search may terminate.

If a successful search terminates at an internal node at level l, then l iterations of the **while** loop of Algorithm 2.5 are needed. Hence, the expected cost contribution from the internal node for a_i is $p(i) * \text{level}(a_i)$.

Unsuccessful searches terminate with $t = 0$ (i.e., at an external node) in algorithm ISearch (Algorithm 2.5). The identifiers not in the binary search tree can be partitioned into $n + 1$ equivalence classes $E_i, 0 \le i \le n$. The class E_0 contains all identifiers x such that $x < a_1$. The class E_i contains all identifiers x such that $a_i < x < a_{i+1}$, $1 \le i < n$. The class E_n contains all identifiers x, $x > a_n$. It is easy to see that for all identifiers in the same class E_i, the search terminates at the same external node. For identifiers in different E_i the search terminates at different external nodes. If the failure node for E_i is at level l, then only $l - 1$ iterations of the **while** loop are made. Hence, the cost contribution of this node is $q(i) * (level(E_i) - 1)$.

The preceding discussion leads to the following formula for the expected

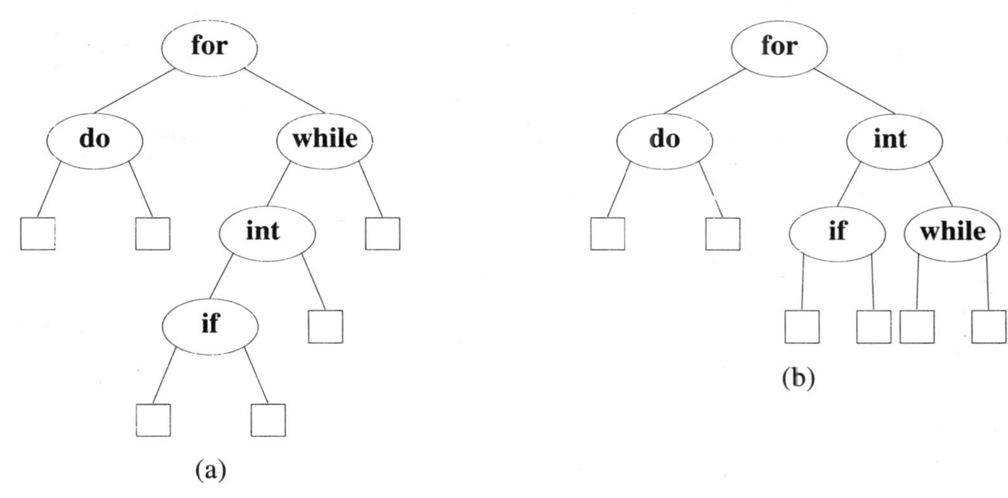

Figure 5.13 Binary search trees of Figure 5.12 with external nodes added

cost of a binary search tree:

$$\sum_{1 \le i \le n} p(i) * level(a_i) + \sum_{0 \le i \le n} q(i) * (level(E_i) - 1) \tag{5.9}$$

We define an optimal binary search tree for the identifier set $\{a_1, a_2, \ldots, a_n\}$ to be a binary search tree for which (5.9) is minimum.

Example 5.17 The possible binary search trees for the identifier set (a_1, a_2, a_3) = (**do, if, while**) are given if Figure 5.14. With equal probabilities $p(i) = q(i) = 1/7$ for all i, we have

$$\begin{array}{rclrcl} cost(\text{tree a}) & = & 15/7 & cost(\text{tree b}) & = & 13/7 \\ cost(\text{tree c}) & = & 15/7 & cost(\text{tree d}) & = & 15/7 \\ cost(\text{tree e}) & = & 15/7 & & & \end{array}$$

As expected, tree b is optimal. With $p(1) = .5$, $p(2) = .1$, $p(3) = .05$, $q(0) = .15$, $q(1) = .1$, $q(2) = .05$ and $q(3) = .05$ we have

$$\begin{array}{rclrcl} cost(\text{tree a}) & = & 2.65 & cost(\text{tree b}) & = & 1.9 \\ cost(\text{tree c}) & = & 1.5 & cost(\text{tree d}) & = & 2.05 \\ cost(\text{tree e}) & = & 1.6 & & & \end{array}$$

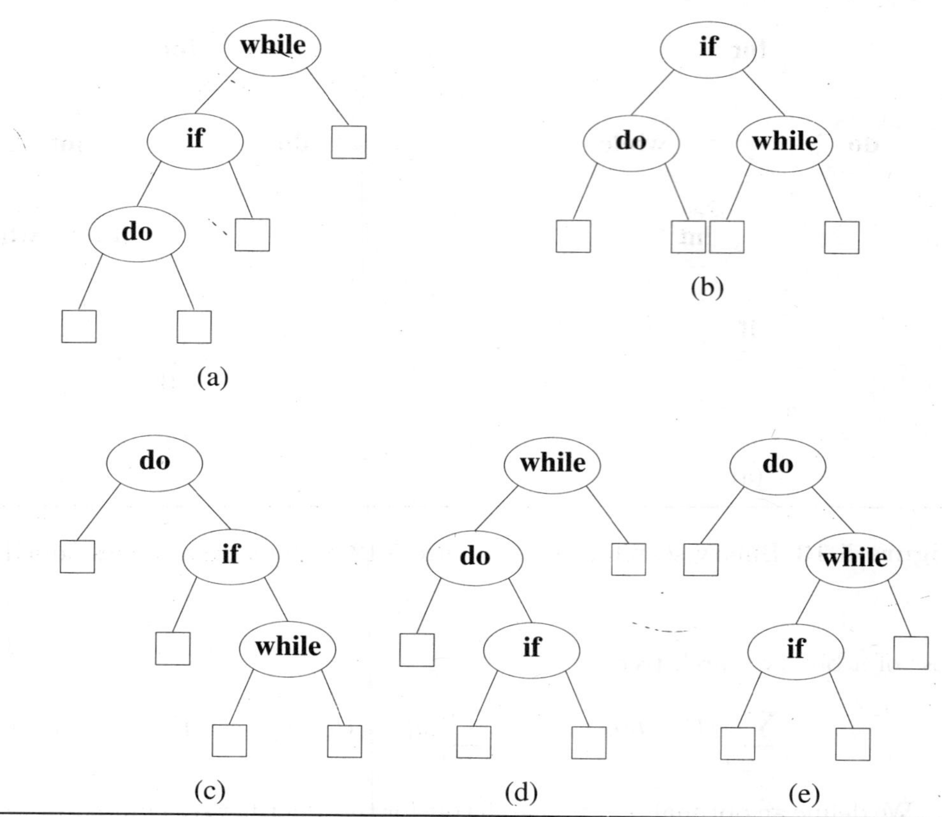

Figure 5.14 Possible binary search trees for the identifier set {**do**, **if**, **while**}

For instance, $cost$(tree a) can be computed as follows. The contribution from successful searches is $3*0.5+2*0.1+0.05 = 1.75$ and the contribution from unsuccessful searches is $3*0.15+3*0.1+2*0.05+0.05 = 0.90$. All the other costs can also be calculated in a similar manner. Tree c is optimal with this assignment of p's and q's. □

To apply dynamic programming to the problem of obtaining an optimal binary search tree, we need to view the construction of such a tree as the result of a sequence of decisions and then observe that the principle of optimality holds when applied to the problem state resulting from a decision. A possible approach to this would be to make a decision as to which of the a_i's should be assigned to the root node of the tree. If we choose a_k, then it is clear that the internal nodes for $a_1, a_2, \ldots, a_{k-1}$ as well as the external nodes for the classes $E_0, E_1, \ldots, E_{k-1}$ will lie in the left subtree l of the root. The remaining nodes will be in the right subtree r. Define

$$cost(l) = \sum_{1 \le i < k} p(i) * \text{level}(a_i) + \sum_{0 \le i < k} q(i) * (\text{level}(E_i) - 1)$$

and

$$cost(r) = \sum_{k < i \le n} p(i) * \text{level}(a_i) + \sum_{k < i \le n} q(i) * (\text{level}(E_i) - 1)$$

In both cases the level is measured by regarding the root of the respective subtree to be at level 1.

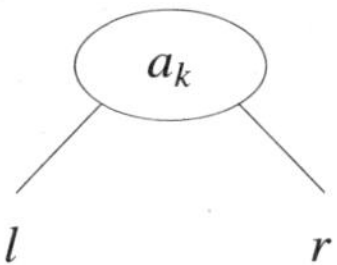

Figure 5.15 An optimal binary search tree with root a_k

Using $w(i,j)$ to represent the sum $q(i) + \sum_{l=i+1}^{j}(q(l) + p(l))$, we obtain the following as the expected cost of the search tree (Figure 5.15):

$$p(k) + cost(l) + cost(r) + w(0, k-1) + w(k, n) \tag{5.10}$$

If the tree is optimal, then (5.10) must be minimum. Hence, $cost(l)$ must be minimum over all binary search trees containing $a_1, a_2, \ldots, a_{k-1}$ and $E_0, E_1, \ldots, E_{k-1}$. Similarly $cost(r)$ must be minimum. If we use $c(i,j)$ to represent the cost of an optimal binary search tree t_{ij} containing $a_{i+1}, \ldots, a_j$ and $E_i, \ldots, E_j$, then for the tree to be optimal, we must have $cost(l) = c(0, k-1)$ and $cost(r) = c(k, n)$. In addition, k must be chosen such that

$$p(k) + c(0, k-1) + c(k, n) + w(0, k-1) + w(k, n)$$

is minimum. Hence, for $c(0, n)$ we obtain

$$c(0,n) = \min_{1 \le k \le n} \{c(0, k-1) + c(k, n) + p(k) + w(0, k-1) + w(k, n)\} \tag{5.11}$$

We can generalize (5.11) to obtain for any $c(i,j)$

$$c(i,j) = \min_{i<k\leq j} \{c(i,k-1) + c(k,j) + p(k) + w(i,k-1) + w(k,j)\}$$

$$c(i,j) = \min_{i<k\leq j} \{c(i,k-1) + c(k,j)\} + w(i,j) \tag{5.12}$$

Equation 5.12 can be solved for $c(0,n)$ by first computing all $c(i,j)$ such that $j-i=1$ (note $c(i,i)=0$ and $w(i,i)=q(i)$, $0 \leq i \leq n$). Next we can compute all $c(i,j)$ such that $j-i=2$, then all $c(i,j)$ with $j-i=3$, and so on. If during this computation we record the root $r(i,j)$ of each tree t_{ij}, then an optimal binary search tree can be constructed from these $r(i,j)$. Note that $r(i,j)$ is the value of k that minimizes (5.12).

Example 5.18 Let $n=4$ and $(a_1,a_2,a_3,a_4) =$ (**do, if, int, while**). Let $p(1:4) = (3,3,1,1)$ and $q(0:4) = (2,3,1,1,1)$. The p's and q's have been multiplied by 16 for convenience. Initially, we have $w(i,i) = q(i), c(i,i) = 0$ and $r(i,i) = 0$, $0 \leq i \leq 4$. Using Equation 5.12 and the observation $w(i,j) = p(j) + q(j) + w(i,j-1)$, we get

$$\begin{aligned}
w(0,1) &= p(1) + q(1) + w(0,0) = 8 \\
c(0,1) &= w(0,1) + \min\{c(0,0) + c(1,1)\} \quad = \quad 8 \\
r(0,1) &= 1 \\
w(1,2) &= p(2) + q(2) + w(1,1) \quad = \quad 7 \\
c(1,2) &= w(1,2) + \min \ \{c(1,1) + c(2,2)\} \quad = \quad 7 \\
r(0,2) &= 2 \\
w(2,3) &= p(3) + q(3) + w(2,2) \quad = \quad 3 \\
c(2,3) &= w(2,3) + \min \ \{c(2,2) + c(3,3)\} \quad = \quad 3 \\
r(2,3) &= 3 \\
w(3,4) &= p(4) + q(4) + w(3,3) \quad = \quad 3 \\
c(3,4) &= w(3,4) + \min \ \{c(3,3) + c(4,4)\} \quad = \quad 3 \\
r(3,4) &= 4
\end{aligned}$$

Knowing $w(i,i+1)$ and $c(i,i+1)$, $0 \leq i < 4$, we can again use Equation 5.12 to compute $w(i,i+2)$, $c(i,i+2)$, and $r(i,i+2)$, $0 \leq i < 3$. This process can be repeated until $w(0,4)$, $c(0,4)$, and $r(0,4)$ are obtained. The table of Figure 5.16 shows the results of this computation. The box in row i and column j shows the values of $w(j,j+i)$, $c(j,j+i)$ and $r(j,j+i)$ respectively.

The computation is carried out by row from row 0 to row 4. From the table we see that $c(0,4) = 32$ is the minimum cost of a binary search tree for (a_1, a_2, a_3, a_4). The root of tree t_{04} is a_2. Hence, the left subtree is t_{01} and the right subtree t_{24}. Tree t_{01} has root a_1 and subtrees t_{00} and t_{11}. Tree t_{24} has root a_3; its left subtree is t_{22} and its right subtree t_{34}. Thus, with the data in the table it is possible to reconstruct t_{04}. Figure 5.17 shows t_{04}. □

	0	1	2	3	4
0	$w_{00} = 2$ $c_{00} = 0$ $r_{00} = 0$	$w_{11} = 3$ $c_{11} = 0$ $r_{11} = 0$	$w_{22} = 1$ $c_{22} = 0$ $r_{22} = 0$	$w_{33} = 1$ $c_{33} = 0$ $r_{33} = 0$	$w_{44} = 1$ $c_{44} = 0$ $r_{44} = 0$
1	$w_{01} = 8$ $c_{01} = 8$ $r_{01} = 1$	$w_{12} = 7$ $c_{12} = 7$ $r_{12} = 2$	$w_{23} = 3$ $c_{23} = 3$ $r_{23} = 3$	$w_{34} = 3$ $c_{34} = 3$ $r_{34} = 4$	
2	$w_{02} = 12$ $c_{02} = 19$ $r_{02} = 1$	$w_{13} = 9$ $c_{13} = 12$ $r_{13} = 2$	$w_{24} = 5$ $c_{24} = 8$ $r_{24} = 3$		
3	$w_{03} = 14$ $c_{03} = 25$ $r_{03} = 2$	$w_{14} = 11$ $c_{14} = 19$ $r_{14} = 2$			
4	$w_{04} = 16$ $c_{04} = 32$ $r_{04} = 2$				

Figure 5.16 Computation of $c(0,4)$, $w(0,4)$, and $r(0,4)$

The above example illustrates how Equation 5.12 can be used to determine the c's and r's and also how to reconstruct t_{0n} knowing the r's. Let us examine the complexity of this procedure to evaluate the c's and r's. The evaluation procedure described in the above example requires us to compute $c(i,j)$ for $(j-i) = 1, 2, \ldots, n$ in that order. When $j - i = m$, there are $n - m + 1$ $c(i,j)$'s to compute. The computation of each of these $c(i,j)$'s requires us to find the minimum of m quantities (see Equation 5.12). Hence, each such $c(i,j)$ can be computed in time $O(m)$. The total time for all $c(i,j)$'s with $j - i = m$ is therefore $O(nm - m^2)$. The total time to evaluate all the $c(i,j)$'s and $r(i,j)$'s is therefore

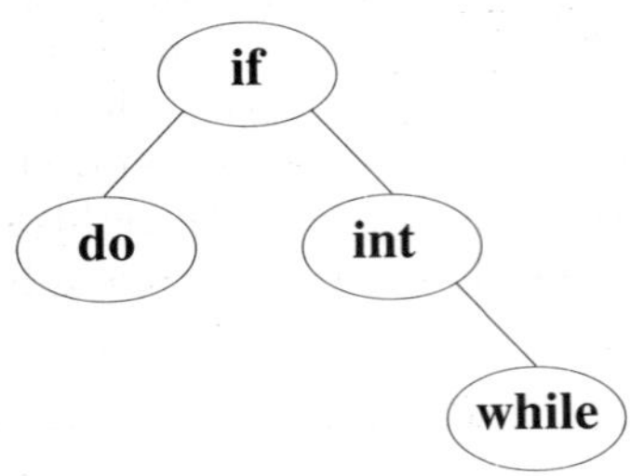

Figure 5.17 Optimal search tree for Example 5.18

$$\sum_{1 \le m \le n} (nm - m^2) = O(n^3)$$

We can do better than this using a result due to D. E. Knuth which shows that the optimal k in Equation 5.12 can be found by limiting the search to the range $r(i, j-1) \le k \le r(i+1, j)$. In this case the computing time becomes $O(n^2)$ (see the exercises). The function OBST (Algorithm 5.5) uses this result to obtain the values of $w(i,j)$, $r(i,j)$, and $c(i,j)$, $0 \le i \le j \le n$, in $O(n^2)$ time. The tree t_{0n} can be constructed from the values of $r(i,j)$ in $O(n)$ time. The algorithm for this is left as an exercise.

EXERCISES

1. Use function OBST (Algorithm 5.5) to compute $w(i,j)$, $r(i,j)$, and $c(i,j)$, $0 \le i < j \le 4$, for the identifier set (a_1, a_2, a_3, a_4) = (**cout, float, if, while**) with $p(1) = 1/20$, $p(2) = 1/5$, $p(3) = 1/10$, $p(4) = 1/20$, $q(0) = 1/5$, $q(1) = 1/10$, $q(2) = 1/5$, $q(3) = 1/20$, and $q(4) = 1/20$. Using the $r(i,j)$'s, construct the optimal binary search tree.

2. (a) Show that the computing time of function OBST (Algorithm 5.5) is $O(n^2)$.

   (b) Write an algorithm to construct the optimal binary search tree given the roots $r(i,j), 0 \le i < j \le n$. Show that this can be done in time $O(n)$.

3. Since often only the approximate values of the p's and q's are known, it is perhaps just as meaningful to find a binary search tree that is nearly

```
Algorithm OBST(p, q, n)
// Given n distinct identifiers a_1 < a_2 < ··· < a_n and probabilities
// p[i], 1 ≤ i ≤ n, and q[i], 0 ≤ i ≤ n, this algorithm computes
// the cost c[i, j] of optimal binary search trees t_ij for identifiers
// a_{i+1}, ..., a_j. It also computes r[i, j], the root of t_ij.
// w[i, j] is the weight of t_ij.
{
    for i := 0 to n − 1 do
    {
        // Initialize.
        w[i, i] := q[i]; r[i, i] := 0; c[i, i] := 0.0;
        // Optimal trees with one node
        w[i, i + 1] := q[i] + q[i + 1] + p[i + 1];
        r[i, i + 1] := i + 1;
        c[i, i + 1] := q[i] + q[i + 1] + p[i + 1];
    }
    w[n, n] := q[n]; r[n, n] := 0; c[n, n] := 0.0;
    for m := 2 to n do // Find optimal trees with m nodes.
        for i := 0 to n − m do
        {
            j := i + m;
            w[i, j] := w[i, j − 1] + p[j] + q[j];
            // Solve 5.12 using Knuth's result.
            k := Find(c, r, i, j);
                // A value of l in the range r[i, j − 1] ≤ l
                // ≤ r[i + 1, j] that minimizes c[i, l − 1] + c[l, j];
            c[i, j] := w[i, j] + c[i, k − 1] + c[k, j];
            r[i, j] := k;
        }
    write (c[0, n], w[0, n], r[0, n]);
}
```

```
Algorithm Find(c, r, i, j)
{
    min := ∞;
    for m := r[i, j − 1] to r[i + 1, j] do
        if (c[i, m − 1] + c[m, j]) < min then
        {
            min := c[i, m − 1] + c[m, j]; l := m;
        }
    return l;
}
```

Algorithm 5.5 Finding a minimum-cost binary search tree

optimal. That is, its cost, Equation 5.9, is almost minimal for the given p's and q's. This exercise explores an $O(n \log n)$ algorithm that results in nearly optimal binary search trees. The search tree heuristic we use is

> *Choose the root k such that $|w(0, k-1) - w(k, n)|$ is as small as possible. Repeat this procedure to find the left and right subtrees of the root.*

(a) Using this heuristic, obtain the resulting binary search tree for the data of Exercise 1. What is its cost?

(b) Write an algorithm implementing the above heuristic. Your algorithm should have time complexity $O(n \log n)$.

5.6 STRING EDITING

We are given two strings $X = x_1, x_2, \ldots, x_n$ and $Y = y_1, y_2, \ldots, y_m$, where x_i, $1 \leq i \leq n$, and y_j, $1 \leq j \leq m$, are members of a finite set of symbols known as the *alphabet.* We want to transform X into Y using a sequence of *edit operations* on X. The permissible edit operations are insert, delete, and change (a symbol of X into another), and there is a cost associated with performing each. The cost of a sequence of operations is the sum of the costs of the individual operations in the sequence. The problem of string editing is to identify a minimum-cost sequence of edit operations that will transform X into Y.

Let $D(x_i)$ be the cost of deleting the symbol x_i from X, $I(y_j)$ be the cost of inserting the symbol y_j into X, and $C(x_i, y_j)$ be the cost of changing the symbol x_i of X into y_j.

Example 5.19 Consider the sequences $X = x_1, x_2, x_3, x_4, x_5 = a, a, b, a, b$ and $Y = y_1, y_2, y_3, y_4 = b, a, b, b$. Let the cost associated with each insertion and deletion be 1 (for any symbol). Also let the cost of changing any symbol to any other symbol be 2. One possible way of transforming X into Y is delete each $x_i, 1 \leq i \leq 5$, and insert each $y_j, 1 \leq j \leq 4$. The total cost of this edit sequence is 9. Another possible edit sequence is delete x_1 and x_2 and insert y_4 at the end of string X. The total cost is only 3. □

A solution to the string editing problem consists of a sequence of decisions, one for each edit operation. Let $\mathcal{E}$ be a minimum-cost edit sequence for transforming X into Y. The first operation, O, in $\mathcal{E}$ is delete, insert, or change. If $\mathcal{E}' = \mathcal{E} - \{O\}$ and X' is the result of applying O on X, then $\mathcal{E}'$ should be a minimum-cost edit sequence that transforms X' into Y. Thus the principle of optimality holds for this problem. A dynamic programming solution for this problem can be obtained as follows. Define $cost(i, j)$ to be the minimum cost of any edit sequence for transforming $x_1, x_2, \ldots, x_i$ into $y_1, y_2, \ldots, y_j$ (for $0 \le i \le n$ and $0 \le j \le m$). Compute $cost(i, j)$ for each i and j. Then $cost(n, m)$ is the cost of an optimal edit sequence.

For $i = j = 0$, $cost(i, j) = 0$, since the two sequences are identical (and empty). Also, if $j = 0$ and $i > 0$, we can transform X into Y by a sequence of deletes. Thus, $cost(i, 0) = cost(i-1, 0) + D(x_i)$. Similarly, if $i = 0$ and $j > 0$, we get $cost(0, j) = cost(0, j-1) + I(y_j)$. If $i \ne 0$ and $j \ne 0$, $x_1, x_2, \ldots, x_i$ can be transformed into $y_1, y_2, \ldots, y_j$ in one of three ways:

1. Transform $x_1, x_2, \ldots, x_{i-1}$ into $y_1, y_2, \ldots, y_j$ using a minimum-cost edit sequence and then delete x_i. The corresponding cost is $cost(i-1, j) + D(x_i)$.

2. Transform $x_1, x_2, \ldots, x_{i-1}$ into $y_1, y_2, \ldots, y_{j-1}$ using a minimum-cost edit sequence and then change the symbol x_i to y_j. The associated cost is $cost(i-1, j-1) + C(x_i, y_j)$.

3. Transform $x_1, x_2, \ldots, x_i$ into $y_1, y_2, \ldots, y_{j-1}$ using a minimum-cost edit sequence and then insert y_j. This corresponds to a cost of $cost(i, j-1) + I(y_j)$.

The minimum cost of any edit sequence that transforms $x_1, x_2, \ldots, x_i$ into $y_1, y_2, \ldots, y_j$ (for $i > 0$ and $j > 0$) is the minimum of the above three costs, according to the principle of optimality. Therefore, we arrive at the following recurrence equation for $cost(i, j)$:

$$cost(i, j) = \begin{cases} 0 & i = j = 0 \\ cost(i-1, 0) + D(x_i) & j = 0,\ i > 0 \\ cost(0, j-1) + I(y_j) & i = 0,\ j > 0 \\ cost'(i, j) & i > 0,\ j > 0 \end{cases} \tag{5.13}$$

$$\text{where } cost'(i, j) = \min \{ \begin{array}{l} cost(i-1, j) + D(x_i), \\ cost(i-1, j-1) + C(x_i, y_j), \\ cost(i, j-1) + I(y_j) \; \} \end{array}$$

We have to compute $cost(i, j)$ for all possibles values of i and j ($0 \le i \le n$ and $0 \le j \le m$). There are $(n+1)(m+1)$ such values. These values can be computed in the form of a table, M, where each row of M corresponds to a particular value of i and each column of M corresponds to a specific value of j. $M(i, j)$ stores the value $cost(i, j)$. The zeroth row can be computed first since it corresponds to performing a series of insertions. Likewise the zeroth column can also be computed. After this, one could compute the entries of M in row-major order, starting from the first row. Rows should be processed in the order $1, 2, \ldots, n$. Entries in any row are computed in increasing order of column number.

The entries of M can also be computed in column-major order, starting from the first column. Looking at Equation 5.13, we see that each entry of M takes only $O(1)$ time to compute. Therefore the whole algorithm takes $O(mn)$ time. The value $cost(n, m)$ is the final answer we are interested in. Having computed all the entries of M, a minimum edit sequence can be obtained by a simple backward trace from $cost(n, m)$. This backward trace is enabled by recording which of the three options for $i > 0, j > 0$ yielded the minimum cost for each i and j.

Example 5.20 Consider the string editing problem of Example 5.19. $X = a, a, b, a, b$ and $Y = b, a, b, b$. Each insertion and deletion has a unit cost and a change costs 2 units. For the cases $i = 0, j > 1$, and $j = 0, i > 1$, $cost(i, j)$ can be computed first (Figure 5.18). Let us compute the rest of the entries in row-major order. The next entry to be computed is $cost(1, 1)$.

$$\begin{aligned} cost(1,1) &= \min \{cost(0,1) + D(x_1), cost(0,0) + C(x_1, y_1), cost(1,0) + I(y_1)\} \\ &= \min \{2, 2, 2\} = 2 \end{aligned}$$

Next is computed $cost(1, 2)$.

$$\begin{aligned} cost(1,2) &= \min \{cost(0,2) + D(x_1), cost(0,1) + C(x_1, y_2), cost(1,1) + I(y_2)\} \\ &= \min \{3, 1, 3\} = 1 \end{aligned}$$

The rest of the entries are computed similarly. Figure 5.18 displays the whole table. The value $cost(5, 4) = 3$. One possible minimum-cost edit sequence is delete x_1, delete x_2, and insert y_4. Another possible minimum cost edit sequence is change x_1 to y_2 and delete x_4. □

EXERCISES

1. Let $X = a, a, b, a, a, b, a, b, a, a$ and $Y = b, a, b, a, a, b, a, b$. Find a minimum-cost edit sequence that transforms X into Y.

2. Present a pseudocode algorithm that implements the string editing algorithm discussed in this section. Program it and test its correctness using suitable data.

3. Modify the above program not only to compute $cost(n, m)$ but also to output a minimum-cost edit sequence. What is the time complexity of your program?

4. Given a sequence X of symbols, a subsequence of X is defined to be any contiguous portion of X. For example, if $X = x_1, x_2, x_3, x_4, x_5$, x_2, x_3 and x_1, x_2, x_3 are subsequences of X. Given two sequences X and Y, present an algorithm that will identify the longest subsequence that

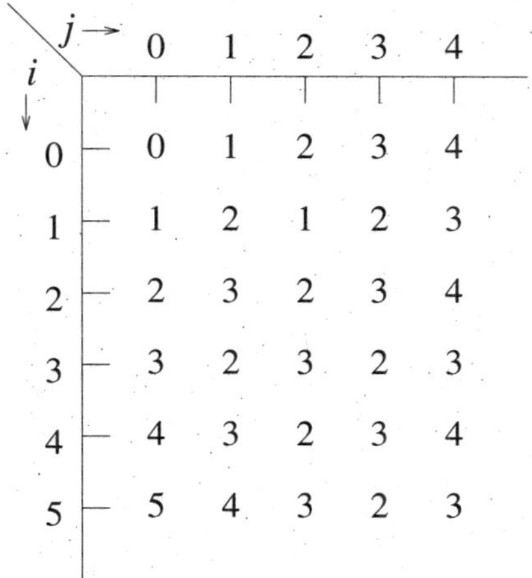

$i \downarrow$ \ $j \rightarrow$	0	1	2	3	4
0	0	1	2	3	4
1	1	2	1	2	3
2	2	3	2	3	4
3	3	2	3	2	3
4	4	3	2	3	4
5	5	4	3	2	3

Figure 5.18 Cost table for Example 5.20

is common to both X and Y. This problem is known as *the longest common subsequence problem.* What is the time complexity of your algorithm?

5.7 0/1 KNAPSACK

The terminology and notation used in this section is the same as that in Section 5.1. A solution to the knapsack problem can be obtained by making a sequence of decisions on the variables $x_1, x_2, \ldots, x_n$. A decision on variable x_i involves determining which of the values 0 or 1 is to be assigned to it. Let us assume that decisions on the x_i are made in the order $x_n, x_{n-1}, \ldots, x_1$. Following a decision on x_n, we may be in one of two possible states: the capacity remaining in the knapsack is m and no profit has accrued or the capacity remaining is $m - w_n$ and a profit of p_n has accrued. It is clear that the remaining decisions $x_{n-1}, \ldots, x_1$ must be optimal with respect to the problem state resulting from the decision on x_n. Otherwise, $x_n, \ldots, x_1$ will not be optimal. Hence, the principle of optimality holds.

Let $f_j(y)$ be the value of an optimal solution to KNAP$(1, j, y)$. Since the principle of optimality holds, we obtain

$$f_n(m) = \max \{f_{n-1}(m), f_{n-1}(m - w_n) + p_n\} \tag{5.14}$$

For arbitrary $f_i(y)$, $i > 0$, Equation 5.14 generalizes to

$$f_i(y) = \max\ \{f_{i-1}(y), f_{i-1}(y - w_i) + p_i\} \qquad (5.15)$$

Equation 5.15 can be solved for $f_n(m)$ by beginning with the knowledge $f_0(y) = 0$ for all non-negative y and $f_i(y) = -\infty, y < 0$. Then $f_1, f_2, \ldots, f_n$ can be successively computed using (5.15).

When the w_i's are integer, we need to compute $f_i(y)$ for integer y, $0 \le y \le m$. Since $f_i(y) = -\infty$ for $y < 0$, these function values need not be computed explicitly. Since each f_i can be computed from f_{i-1} in $\Theta(m)$ time, it takes $\Theta(mn)$ time to compute f_n. When the w_i's are real numbers, $f_i(y)$ is needed for real numbers y such that $0 \le y \le m$. So, f_i cannot be explicitly computed for all y in this range. Even when the w_i's are integer, the explicit $\Theta(mn)$ computation of f_n may not be the most efficient computation. So, we explore an alternative method for both cases.

Notice that $f_i(y)$ is an ascending step function; i.e., there are a finite number of y's, $0 = y_1 < y_2 < \cdots < y_k$, such that $f_i(y_1) < f_i(y_2) < \cdots < f_i(y_k)$; $f_i(y) = -\infty$, $y < y_1$; $f_i(y) = f_i(y_k)$, $y \ge y_k$; and $f_i(y) = f_i(y_j)$, $y_j \le y < y_{j+1}$. So, we need to compute only $f_i(y_j)$, $1 \le j \le k$. We use the ordered set $S^i = \{(f(y_j), y_j) | 1 \le j \le k\}$ to represent $f_i(y)$. Each member of S^i is a pair (P, W), where $P = f_i(y_j)$ and $W = y_j$. Notice that $S^0 = \{(0, 0)\}$. We can compute S^{i+1} from S^i by first computing

$$S_1^i = \{(P, W) | (P - p_{i+1}, W - w_{i+1}) \in S^i\} \qquad (5.16)$$

Now, S^{i+1} can be computed by merging the pairs in S^i and S_1^i together. Note that if S^{i+1} contains two pairs (P_j, W_j) and (P_k, W_k) with the property that $P_j \le P_k$ and $W_j \ge W_k$, then the pair (P_j, W_j) can be discarded because of (5.15). Discarding or purging rules such as this one are also known as *dominance rules*. Dominated tuples get purged. In the above, (P_k, W_k) dominates (P_j, W_j).

Interestingly, the strategy we have come up with can also be derived by attempting to solve the knapsack problem via a systematic examination of the up to 2^n possibilities for $x_1, x_2, \ldots, x_n$. Let S^i represent the possible states resulting from the 2^i decision sequences for $x_1, \ldots, x_i$. A state refers to a pair (P_j, W_j), W_j being the total weight of objects included in the knapsack and P_j being the corresponding profit. To obtain S^{i+1}, we note that the possibilities for x_{i+1} are $x_{i+1} = 0$ or $x_{i+1} = 1$. When $x_{i+1} = 0$, the resulting states are the same as for S^i. When $x_{i+1} = 1$, the resulting states are obtained by adding (p_{i+1}, w_{i+1}) to each state in S^i. Call the set of these additional states S_1^i. The S_1^i is the same as in Equation 5.16. Now, S^{i+1} can be computed by merging the states in S^i and S_1^i together.

Example 5.21 Consider the knapsack instance $n = 3, (w_1, w_2, w_3) = (2, 3, 4)$, $(p_1, p_2, p_3) = (1, 2, 5)$, and $m = 6$. For these data we have

$$\begin{aligned} S^0 &= \{(0,0)\}; S_1^0 = \{(1,2)\} \\ S^1 &= \{(0,0),(1,2)\}; S_1^1 = \{(2,3),(3,5)\} \\ S^2 &= \{(0,0),(1,2),(2,3),(3,5)\}; S_1^2 = \{(5,4),(6,6),(7,7),(8,9)\} \\ S^3 &= \{(0,0),(1,2),(2,3),(5,4),(6,6),(7,7),(8,9)\} \end{aligned}$$

Note that the pair (3, 5) has been eliminated from S^3 as a result of the purging rule stated above. □

When generating the S^i's, we can also purge all pairs (P, W) with $W > m$ as these pairs determine the value of $f_n(x)$ only for $x > m$. Since the knapsack capacity is m, we are not interested in the behavior of f_n for $x > m$. When all pairs (P_j, W_j) with $W_j > m$ are purged from the S^i's, $f_n(m)$ is given by the P value of the last pair in S^n (note that the S^i's are ordered sets). Note also that by computing S^n, we can find the solutions to all the knapsack problems KNAP$(1, n, x)$, $0 \leq x \leq m$, and not just KNAP$(1, n, m)$. Since, we want only a solution to KNAP$(1, n, m)$, we can dispense with the computation of S^n. The last pair in S^n is either the last one in S^{n-1} or it is $(P_j + p_n, W_j + w_n)$, where $(P_j, W_j) \in S^{n-1}$ such that $W_j + w_n \leq m$ and W_j is maximum.

If $(P1, W1)$ is the last tuple in S^n, a set of 0/1 values for the x_i's such that $\sum p_i x_i = P1$ and $\sum w_i x_i = W1$ can be determined by carrying out a search through the S^is. We can set $x_n = 0$ if $(P1, W1) \in S^{n-1}$. If $(P1, W1) \notin S^{n-1}$, then $(P1 - p_n, W1 - w_n) \in S^{n-1}$ and we can set $x_n = 1$. This leaves us to determine how either $(P1, W1)$ or $(P1 - p_n, W1 - w_n)$ was obtained in S^{n-1}. This can be done recursively.

Example 5.22 With $m = 6$, the value of $f_3(6)$ is given by the tuple (6, 6) in S^3 (Example 5.21). The tuple (6, 6) $\notin S^2$, and so we must set $x_3 = 1$. The pair (6, 6) came from the pair $(6 - p_3, 6 - w_3) = (1, 2)$. Hence (1, 2) $\in S^2$. Since $(1, 2) \in S^1$, we can set $x_2 = 0$. Since (1, 2) $\notin S^0$, we obtain $x_1 = 1$. Hence an optimal solution is $(x_1, x_2, x_3) = (1, 0, 1)$. □

We can sum up all we have said so far in the form of an informal algorithm DKP (Algorithm 5.6). To evaluate the complexity of the algorithm, we need to specify how the sets S^i and S_1^i are to be represented; provide an algorithm to merge S^i and S_1^i; and specify an algorithm that will trace through $S^{n-1}, \ldots, S^1$ and determine a set of 0/1 values for $x_n, \ldots, x_1$.

We can use an array *pair*[ ] to represent all the pairs (P, W). The P values are stored in *pair*[ ]*.p* and the W values in *pair*[ ]*.w*. Sets $S^0, S^1, \ldots, S^{n-1}$

```
Algorithm DKP(p, w, n, m)
{
    S^0 := {(0,0)};
    for i := 1 to n - 1 do
    {
        S_1^{i-1} := {(P,W)|(P - p_i, W - w_i) ∈ S^{i-1} and W ≤ m};
        S^i := MergePurge(S^{i-1}, S_1^{i-1});
    }
    (PX, WX) :=last pair in S^{n-1};
    (PY, WY) := (P' + p_n, W' + w_n) where W' is the largest W in
        any pair in S^{n-1} such that W + w_n ≤ m;
    // Trace back for x_n, x_{n-1}, ..., x_1.
    if (PX > PY) then x_n := 0;
    else x_n := 1;
    TraceBackFor(x_{n-1}, ..., x_1);
}
```

Algorithm 5.6 Informal knapsack algorithm

can be stored adjacent to each other. This requires the use of pointers $b[i]$, $0 \le i \le n$, where $b[i]$ is the location of the first element in S^i, $0 \le i < n$, and $b[n]$ is one more than the location of the last element in S^{n-1}.

Example 5.23 Using the representation above, the sets S^0, S^1, and S^2 of Example 5.21 appear as

	1	2	3	4	5	6	7	
pair[ ].*p*	0	0	1	0	1	2	3	
pair[ ].*w*	0	0	2	0	2	3	5	
	↑ $b[0]$	↑ $b[1]$		↑ $b[2]$				↑ $b[3]$

□

The merging and purging of S^{i-1} and S_1^{i-1} can be carried out at the same time that S_1^{i-1} is generated. Since the pairs in S^{i-1} are in increasing order of P and W, the pairs for S^i are generated in this order. If the next pair generated for S_1^{i-1} is (PQ, WQ), then we can merge into S^i all pairs from S^{i-1} with W value $\leq WQ$. The purging rule can be used to decide whether any pairs get purged. Hence, no additional space is needed in which to store S_1^{i-1}.

DKnap (Algorithm 5.7) generates S^i from S^{i-1} in this way. The S^i's are generated in the **for** loop of lines 7 to 42 of Algorithm 5.7. At the start of each iteration $t = b[i-1]$ and h is the index of the last pair in S^{i-1}. The variable k points to the next tuple in S^{i-1} that has to be merged into S^i. In line 10, the function Largest determines the largest q, $t \leq q \leq h$, for which $pair[q].w + w[i] \leq m$. This can be done by performing a binary search. The code for this function is left as an exercise. Since u is set such that for all $W_j, h \geq j > u$, $W_j + w_i > m$, the pairs for S_1^{i-1} are $(P(j) + p_i, W(j) + w_i)$, $1 \leq j \leq u$. The **for** loop of lines 11 to 33 generates these pairs. Each time a pair (pp, ww) is generated, all pairs (P, W) in S^{i-1} with $W < ww$ not yet purged or merged into S^i are merged into S^i. Note that none of these may be purged. Lines 21 to 25 handle the case when the next pair in S^{i-1} has a W value equal to ww. In this case the pair with lesser P value gets purged. In case $pp > P(next-1)$, then the pair (pp, ww) gets purged. Otherwise, (pp, ww) is added to S^i. The **while** loop of lines 31 and 32 purges all unmerged pairs in S^{i-1} that can be purged at this time. Finally, following the merging of S_1^{i-1} into S^i, there may be pairs remaining in S^{i-1} to be merged into S^i. This is taken care of in the **while** loop of lines 35 to 39. Note that because of lines 31 and 32, none of these pairs can be purged. Function TraceBack (line 43) implements the **if** statement and trace-back step of the function DKP (Algorithm 5.6). This is left as an exercise.

If $|S^i|$ is the number of pairs in S^i, then the array $pair$ should have a minimum dimension of $d = \sum_{0 \leq i \leq n-1} |S^i|$. Since it is not possible to predict the exact space needed, it is necessary to test for $next > d$ each time $next$ is incremented. Since each S^i, $i > 0$, is obtained by merging S^{i-1} and S_1^{i-1} and $|S_1^{i-1}| \leq |S^{i-1}|$, it follows that $|S^i| \leq 2|S^{i-1}|$. In the worst case no pairs will get purged and

$$\sum_{0 \leq i \leq n-1} |S^i| = \sum_{0 \leq i \leq n-1} 2^i = 2^n - 1$$

The time needed to generate S^i from S^{i-1} is $\Theta(|S^{i-1}|)$. Hence, the time needed to compute all the S^i's, $0 \leq i < n$, is $\Theta(\sum |S^{i-1}|)$. Since $|S^i| \leq 2^i$, the time needed to compute all the S^i's is $O(2^n)$. If the p_j's are integers, then each pair (P, W) in S^i has an integer P and $P \leq \sum_{1 \leq j \leq i} p_j$. Similarly, if the w_j's are integers, each W is an integer and $W \leq m$. In any S^i the pairs have distinct W values and also distinct P values. Hence,

```
PW = record {float p; float w; }

Algorithm DKnap(p, w, x, n, m)
{
    // pair[ ] is an array of PW's.
    b[0] := 1; pair[1].p := pair[1].w := 0.0; // S^0
    t := 1; h := 1; // Start and end of S^0
    b[1] := next := 2; // Next free spot in pair[ ]
    for i := 1 to n - 1 do
    { // Generate S^i.
        k := t;
        u := Largest(pair, w, t, h, i, m);
        for j := t to u do
        { // Generate S_1^{i-1} and merge.
            pp := pair[j].p + p[i]; ww := pair[j].w + w[i];
                // (pp, ww) is the next element in S_1^{i-1}.
            while ((k ≤ h) and (pair[k].w ≤ ww)) do
            {
                pair[next].p := pair[k].p;
                pair[next].w := pair[k].w;
                next := next + 1; k := k + 1;
            }
            if ((k ≤ h) and (pair[k].w = ww)) then
            {
                if pp < pair[k].p then pp := pair[k].p;
                k := k + 1;
            }
            if pp > pair[next - 1].p then
            {
                pair[next].p := pp; pair[next].w := ww;
                next := next + 1 ;
            }
            while ((k ≤ h) and (pair[k].p ≤ pair[next - 1].p))
                do k := k + 1;
        }
        // Merge in remaining terms from S^{i-1}.
        while (k ≤ h) do
        {
            pair[next].p := pair[k].p; pair[next].w := pair[k].w;
            next := next + 1; k := k + 1;
        }
        // Initialize for S^{i+1}.
        t := h + 1; h := next - 1; b[i + 1] := next;
    }
    TraceBack(p, w, pair, x, m, n);
}
```

$$|S^i| \leq 1 + \sum_{1 \leq j \leq i} p_j$$

when the p_j's are integers and

$$|S^i| \leq 1 + \min \; \{ \sum_{1 \leq j \leq i} w_j, m\}$$

when the w_j's are integers. When both the p_j's and w_j's are integers, the time and space complexity of DKnap (excluding the time for TraceBack) is $O(\min\{2^n,\, n\sum_{1\leq i\leq n} p_i, nm\})$. In this bound $\sum_{1\leq i\leq n} p_i$ can be replaced by $\sum_{1\leq i\leq n} p_i/\gcd\,(p_1,\ldots,p_n)$ and m by

$$1 + \min\{\sum_{j=1}^{i} w_j, m\}/\gcd(w_1, w_2, \ldots, w_n, m)$$

(see the exercises). The exercises indicate how TraceBack may be implemented so as to have a space complexity $O(1)$ and a time complexity $O(n^2)$.

Although the above analysis may seem to indicate that DKnap requires too much computational resource to be practical for large n, in practice many instances of this problem can be solved in a reasonable amount of time. This happens because usually, all the p's and w's are integers and m is much smaller than 2^n. The purging rule is effective in purging most of the pairs that would otherwise remain in the S^i's.

Algorithm DKnap can be speeded up by the use of heuristics. Let L be an estimate on the value of an optimal solution such that $f_n(m) \geq L$. Let PLEFT$(i) = \sum_{i<j\leq n} p_j$. If S^i contains a tuple (P, W) such that $P +$ PLEFT$(i) < L$, then (P, W) can be purged from S^i. To see this, observe that (P, W) can contribute at best the pair $(P + \sum_{i<j\leq n} p_j, W + \sum_{i<j\leq n} w)$ to S_1^{n-1}. Since $P + \sum_{i<j\leq n} p_j = P +$ PLEFT$(i) < L$, it follows that this pair cannot lead to a pair with value at least L and so cannot determine an optimal solution. A simple way to estimate L such that $L \leq f_n(m)$ is to consider the last pair (P, W) in S^i. Then, $P \leq f_n(m)$. A better estimate is obtained by adding some of the remaining objects to (P, W). Example 5.24 illustrates this. Heuristics for the knapsack problem are discussed in greater detail in the chapter on branch-and-bound. The exercises explore a divide-and-conquer approach to speed up DKnap so that the worst case time is $O(2^{n/2})$.

Example 5.24 Consider the following instance of the knapsack problem: $n = 6, (p_1, p_2, p_3, p_4, p_5, p_6) = (w_1, w_2, w_3, w_4, w_5, w_6) = (100, 50, 20, 10, 7, 3)$, and $m = 165$. Attempting to fill the knapsack using objects in the order 1, 2, 3, 4, 5, and 6, we see that objects 1, 2, 4, and 6 fit in and yield a profit of 163 and a capacity utilization of 163. We can thus begin with $L = 163$ as a value with the property $L \leq f_n(m)$. Since $p_i = w_i$, every pair $(P, W) \in S^i$, $0 \leq i \leq 6$ has $P = W$. Hence, each pair can be replaced by the singleton P or W. PLEFT(0) = 190, PLEFT(1) = 90, PLEFT(2) = 40, PLEFT(3) = 20, PLEFT(4) = 10, PLEFT(5) = 3, and PLEFT(6) = 0. Eliminating from each S^i any singleton P such that $P+$ PLEFT(i) $< L$, we obtain

$$\begin{aligned} S^0 = \{0\};\; S_1^0 = \{100\} \\ S^1 = \{100\};\; S_1^1 = \{150\} \\ S^2 = \{150\};\; S_1^2 = \phi \\ S^3 = \{150\};\; S_1^3 = \{160\} \\ S^4 = \{160\};\; S_1^4 = \phi \\ S^5 = \{160\} \end{aligned}$$

The singleton 0 is deleted from S^1 as 0 + PLEFT(1)< 163. The set S_1^2 does not contain the singleton 150 + 20 = 170 as $m < 170$. S^3 does not contain the 100 or the 120 as each is less than L − PLEFT(3). And so on. The value $f_6(165)$ can be determined from S^5. In this example, the value of L did not change. In general, L will change if a better estimate is obtained as a result of the computation of some S^i. If the heuristic wasn't used, then the computation would have proceeded as

$$\begin{aligned} S^0 &= \{0\} \\ S^1 &= \{0, 100\} \\ S^2 &= \{0, 50, 100, 150\} \\ S^3 &= \{0, 20, 50, 70, 100, 120, 150\} \\ S^4 &= \{0, 10, 20, 30, 50, 60, 70, 80, 100, 110, 120, 130, 150, 160\} \\ S^5 &= \{0, 7, 10, 17, 20, 27, 30, 37, 50, 57, 60, 67, 70, 77, 80, 87, 100, \\ &\quad 107, 110, 117, 120, 127, 130, 137, 150, 157, 160\} \end{aligned}$$

The value $f_6(165)$ can now be determined from S^5, using the knowledge $(p_6, w_6) = (3, 3)$. □

EXERCISES

1. Generate the sets $S^i, 0 \leq i \leq 4$ (Equation 5.16), when $(w_1, w_2, w_3, w_4) = (10, 15, 6, 9)$ and $(p_1, p_2, p_3, p_4) = (2, 5, 8, 1)$.

2. Write a function Largest$(pair, w, t, h, i, m)$ that uses binary search to determine the largest q, $t \leq q \leq h$, such that $pair[q].w + w[i] \leq m$.

3. Write a function TraceBack to determine an optimal solution $x_1, x_2, \ldots, x_n$ to the knapsack problem. Assume that $S^i, 0 \leq i < n$, have already been computed as in function DKnap. Knowing $b(i)$ and $b(i+1)$, you can use a binary search to determine whether $(P', W') \in S^i$. Hence, the time complexity of your algorithm should be no more than $O(n \max_i \{\log |S^i|\}) = O(n^2)$.

4. Give an example of a set of knapsack instances for which $|S^i| = 2^i$, $0 \leq i \leq n$. Your set should include one instance for each n.

5. (a) Show that if the p_j's are integers, then the size of each S^i, $|S^i|$, in the knapsack problem is no more than $1+\sum_{1 \leq i \leq j} p_j / gcd(p_1, p_2, \ldots, p_n)$, where $gcd(p_1, p_2, \ldots, p_n)$ is the greatest common divisor of the p_i's.
   (b) Show that when the w_j's are integer, then $|S^i| \leq 1 + \min\{\sum_{1 \leq j \leq i} w_j, m\} / gcd(w_1, w_2, \ldots, w_n, m)$.

6. (a) Using a divide-and-conquer approach coupled with the set generation approach of the text, show how to obtain an $O(2^{n/2})$ algorithm for the 0/1 knapsack problem.
   (b) Develop an algorithm that uses this approach to solve the 0/1 knapsack problem.
   (c) Compare the run time and storage requirements of this approach with those of Algorithm 5.7. Use suitable test data.

7. [0/1/2 Knapsack] Define the 0/1/2 knapsack problem to be

$$\text{maximize } \sum_{i=1}^{n} p_i x_i$$

subject to the constraints

$$\sum_{i=1}^{n} w_i x_i \leq c \text{ and } x_i \in \{0, 1, 2\}, \ 1 \leq i \leq n$$

Let f be as defined for the 0/1 knapsack problem.

(a) Determine equations similar to Equations 5.14 and 5.15 as well as an equation for f_0 for the 0/1/2 knapsack problem.

(b) Assume that the ws are integer. Write a function to compute f as a two-dimensional array and then to determine an optimal assignment of values for x.

(c) What is the complexity of your function?

8. [Two-dimensional Knapsack] The two-dimensional 0/1 knapsack problem is defined as

$$\text{maximize} \sum_{i=1}^{n} p_i x_i$$

subject to the constraints

$$\sum_{i=1}^{n} v_i x_i \leq c, \sum_{i=1}^{n} w_i x_i \leq d, \text{ and } x_i \in \{0, 1\}, \ 1 \leq i \leq n$$

Let $f(i, y, z)$ denote the value of an optimal solution to the two-dimensional knapsack problem with objects i through n, $c = y$, and $d = z$.

(a) Determine equations similar to Equations 5.14 and 5.15 for $f(n, y, z)$ and $f(i, y, z)$.

(b) Assume that the vs and ws are integer. Write a function to compute f as a three-dimensional array and then to determine an optimal assignment of values for x.

(c) What is the complexity of your function?

9. Consider the integer knapsack problem obtained by replacing the 0/1 constraint in (5.2) by $x_i \geq 0$ and integer. Generalize $f_i(x)$ to this problem in the obvious way.

(a) Obtain the dynamic programming recurrence relation corresponding to (5.15).

(b) Show how to transform this problem into a 0/1 knapsack problem. (*Hint*: Introduce new 0/1 variables for each x_i. If $0 \leq x_i < 2^j$, then introduce j variables, one for each bit in the binary representation of x_i.)

5.8 RELIABILITY DESIGN

In this section we look at an example of how to use dynamic programming to solve a problem with a multiplicative optimization function. The problem is to design a system that is composed of several devices connected in series (Figure 5.19). Let r_i be the reliability of device D_i (that is, r_i is the probability that device i will function properly). Then, the reliability of the entire system is Πr_i. Even if the individual devices are very reliable (the r_i's are very close to one), the reliability of the system may not be very good. For example, if $n = 10$ and $r_i = .99$, $1 \leq i \leq 10$, then $\Pi r_i = .904$. Hence, it is desirable to duplicate devices. Multiple copies of the same device type are connected in parallel (Figure 5.20) through the use of switching circuits. The switching circuits determine which devices in any given group are functioning properly. They then make use of one such device at each stage.

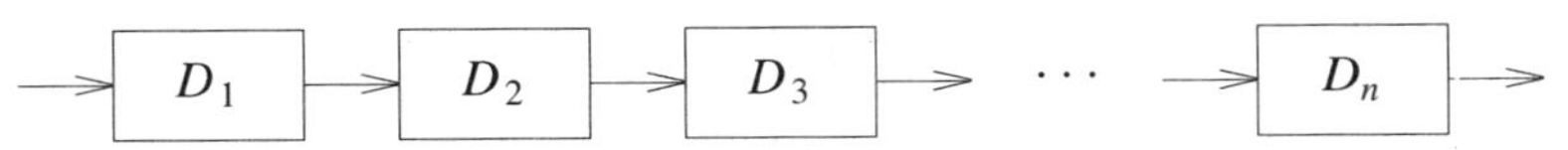

Figure 5.19 n devices D_i, $1 \leq i \leq n$, connected in series

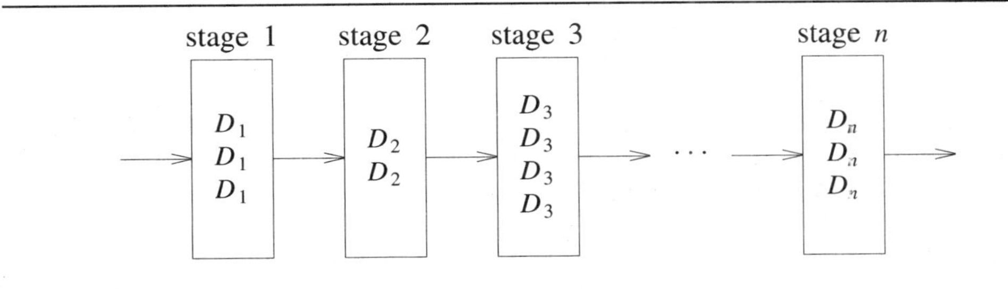

Figure 5.20 Multiple devices connected in parallel in each stage

If stage i contains m_i copies of device D_i, then the probability that all m_i have a malfunction is $(1 - r_i)^{m_i}$. Hence the reliability of stage i becomes $1 - (1 - r_i)^{m_i}$. Thus, if $r_i = .99$ and $m_i = 2$, the stage reliability becomes .9999. In any practical situation, the stage reliability is a little less than

$1-(1-r_i)^{m_i}$ because the switching circuits themselves are not fully reliable. Also, failures of copies of the same device may not be fully independent (e.g., if failure is due to design defect). Let us assume that the reliability of stage i is given by a function $\phi_i(m_i)$, $1 \leq n$. (It is quite conceivable that $\phi_i(m_i)$ may decrease after a certain value of m_i.) The reliability of the system of stages is $\Pi_{1\leq i\leq n}\phi_i(m_i)$.

Our problem is to use device duplication to maximize reliability. This maximization is to be carried out under a cost constraint. Let c_i be the cost of each unit of device i and let c be the maximum allowable cost of the system being designed. We wish to solve the following maximization problem:

$$\text{maximize } \Pi_{1\leq i\leq n}\ \phi_i(m_i)$$

$$\text{subject to } \sum_{1\leq i\leq n} c_i m_i \leq c \tag{5.17}$$

$$m_i \geq 1 \text{ and integer, } 1 \leq i \leq n$$

A dynamic programming solution can be obtained in a manner similar to that used for the knapsack problem. Since, we can assume each $c_i > 0$, each m_i must be in the range $1 \leq m_i \leq u_i$, where

$$u_i = \left\lfloor (c + c_i - \sum_{1}^{n} c_j)/c_i \right\rfloor$$

The upper bound u_i follows from the observation that $m_j \geq 1$. An optimal solution $m_1, m_2, \ldots, m_n$ is the result of a sequence of decisions, one decision for each m_i. Let $f_i(x)$ represent the maximum value of $\Pi_{1\leq j\leq i}\ \phi(m_j)$ subject to the constraints $\sum_{1\leq j\leq i} c_j m_j \leq x$ and $1 \leq m_j \leq u_j$, $1 \leq j \leq i$. Then, the value of an optimal solution is $f_n(c)$. The last decision made requires one to choose m_n from $\{1, 2, 3, \ldots, u_n\}$. Once a value for m_n has been chosen, the remaining decisions must be such as to use the remaining funds $c - c_n m_n$ in an optimal way. The principal of optimality holds and

$$f_n(c) = \max_{1\leq m_n\leq u_n} \{\phi_n(m_n) f_{n-1}(c - c_n m_n)\} \tag{5.18}$$

For any $f_i(x)$, $i \geq 1$, this equation generalizes to

$$f_i(x) = \max_{1\leq m_i\leq u_i} \{\phi_i(m_i) f_{i-1}(x - c_i m_i)\} \tag{5.19}$$

Clearly, $f_0(x) = 1$ for all x, $0 \leq x \leq c$. Hence, (5.19) can be solved using an approach similar to that used for the knapsack problem. Let S^i consist of tuples of the form (f, x), where $f = f_i(x)$. There is at most one tuple for each different x that results from a sequence of decisions on $m_1, m_2, \ldots, m_n$. The dominance rule (f_1, x_1) dominates (f_2, x_2) iff $f_1 \geq f_2$ and $x_1 \leq x_2$ holds for this problem too. Hence, dominated tuples can be discarded from S^i.

Example 5.25 We are to design a three stage system with device types D_1, D_2, and D_3. The costs are \$30, \$15, and \$20 respectively. The cost of the system is to be no more than \$105. The reliability of each device type is .9, .8 and .5 respectively. We assume that if stage i has m_i devices of type i in parallel, then $\phi_i(m_i) = 1-(1-r_i)^{m_i}$. In terms of the notation used earlier, $c_1 = 30$, $c_2 = 15$, $c_3 = 20$, $c = 105$, $r_1 = .9$, $r_2 = .8$, $r_3 = .5, u_1 = 2, u_2 = 3$, and $u_3 = 3$.

We use S^i to represent the set of all undominated tuples (f, x) that may result from the various decision sequences for $m_1, m_2, \ldots, m_i$. Hence, $f(x) = f_i(x)$. Beginning with $S^0 = \{(1, 0)\}$, we can obtain each S^i from S^{i-1} by trying out all possible values for m_i and combining the resulting tuples together. Using S_j^i to represent all tuples obtainable from S^{i-1} by choosing $m_i = j$, we obtain $S_1^1 = \{(.9,\ 30)\}$ and $S_2^1 = \{(.9,\ 30), (.99, 60)\}$. The set $S_1^2 = \{(.72, 45), (.792, 75)\}$; $S_2^2 = \{(.864,\ 60)\}$. Note that the tuple (.9504, 90) which comes from (.99, 60) has been eliminated from S_2^2 as this leaves only \$10. This is not enough to allow $m_3 = 1$. The set $S_3^2 = \{(.8928, 75)\}$. Combining, we get $S^2 = \{(.72, 45), (.864, 60), (.8928, 75)\}$ as the tuple (.792, 75) is dominated by (.864, 60). The set $S_1^3 = \{(.36, 65), (.432, 80), (.4464, 95)\}$, $S_2^3 = \{(.54, 85), (.648, 100)\}$, and $S_3^3 = \{(.63, 105)\}$. Combining, we get $S^3 = \{(.36, 65), (.432,\ 80), (.54,\ 85), (.648, 100)\}$.

The best design has a reliability of .648 and a cost of 100. Tracing back through the S^i's, we determine that $m_1 = 1, m_2 = 2$, and $m_3 = 2$. □

As in the case of the knapsack problem, a complete dynamic programming algorithm for the reliability problem will use heuristics to reduce the size of the S^i's. There is no need to retain any tuple (f, x) in S^i with x value greater that $c - \sum_{i \leq j \leq n} c_j$ as such a tuple will not leave adequate funds to complete the system. In addition, we can devise a simple heuristic to determine the best reliability obtainable by completing a tuple (f, x) in S^i. If this is less than a heuristically determined lower bound on the optimal system reliability, then (f, x) can be eliminated from S^i.

EXERCISE

1. (a) Present an algorithm similar to DKnap to solve the recurrence (5.19).

(b) What are the time and space requirements of your algorithm?

(c) Test the correctness of your algorithm using suitable test data.

5.9 THE TRAVELING SALESPERSON PROBLEM

We have seen how to apply dynamic programming to a subset selection problem (0/1 knapsack). Now we turn our attention to a permutation problem. Note that permutation problems usually are much harder to solve than subset problems as there are $n!$ different permutations of n objects whereas there are only 2^n different subsets of n objects ($n! > 2^n$). Let $G = (V, E)$ be a directed graph with edge costs c_{ij}. The variable c_{ij} is defined such that $c_{ij} > 0$ for all i and j and $c_{ij} = \infty$ if $\langle i, j\rangle \notin E$. Let $|V| = n$ and assume $n > 1$. A *tour* of G is a directed simple cycle that includes every vertex in V. The cost of a tour is the sum of the cost of the edges on the tour. The *traveling salesperson problem* is to find a tour of minimum cost.

The traveling salesperson problem finds application in a variety of situations. Suppose we have to route a postal van to pick up mail from mail boxes located at n different sites. An $n + 1$ vertex graph can be used to represent the situation. One vertex represents the post office from which the postal van starts and to which it must return. Edge $\langle i, j\rangle$ is assigned a cost equal to the distance from site i to site j. The route taken by the postal van is a tour, and we are interested in finding a tour of minimum length.

As a second example, suppose we wish to use a robot arm to tighten the nuts on some piece of machinery on an assembly line. The arm will start from its initial position (which is over the first nut to be tightened), successively move to each of the remaining nuts, and return to the initial position. The path of the arm is clearly a tour on a graph in which vertices represent the nuts. A minimum-cost tour will minimize the time needed for the arm to complete its task (note that only the total arm movement time is variable; the nut tightening time is independent of the tour).

Our final example is from a production environment in which several commodities are manufactured on the same set of machines. The manufacture proceeds in cycles. In each production cycle, n different commodities are produced. When the machines are changed from production of commodity i to commodity j, a change over cost c_{ij} is incurred. It is desired to find a sequence in which to manufacture these commodities. This sequence should minimize the sum of change over costs (the remaining production costs are sequence independent). Since the manufacture proceeds cyclically, it is necessary to include the cost of starting the next cycle. This is just the change over cost from the last to the first commodity. Hence, this problem can be regarded as a traveling salesperson problem on an n vertex graph with edge cost c_{ij}'s being the changeover cost from commodity i to commodity j.

In the following discussion we shall, without loss of generality, regard a tour to be a simple path that starts and ends at vertex 1. Every tour consists of an edge $\langle 1, k \rangle$ for some $k \in V - \{1\}$ and a path from vertex k to vertex 1. The path from vertex k to vertex 1 goes through each vertex in $V - \{1, k\}$ exactly once. It is easy to see that if the tour is optimal, then the path from k to 1 must be a shortest k to 1 path going through all vertices in $V - \{1, k\}$. Hence, the principle of optimality holds. Let $g(i, S)$ be the length of a shortest path starting at vertex i, going through all vertices in S, and terminating at vertex 1. The function $g(1, V - \{1\})$ is the length of an optimal salesperson tour. From the principal of optimality it follows that

$$g(1, V - \{1\}) = \min_{2 \le k \le n} \{c_{1k} + g(k, V - \{1, k\})\} \tag{5.20}$$

Generalizing (5.20), we obtain (for $i \notin S$)

$$g(i, S) = \min_{j \in S} \{c_{ij} + g(j, S - \{j\})\} \tag{5.21}$$

Equation 5.20 can be solved for $g(1, V - \{1\})$ if we know $g(k, V - \{1, k\})$ for all choices of k. The g values can be obtained by using (5.21). Clearly, $g(i, \phi) = c_{i1}$, $1 \le i \le n$. Hence, we can use (5.21) to obtain $g(i, S)$ for all S of size 1. Then we can obtain $g(i, S)$ for S with $|S| = 2$, and so on. When $|S| < n - 1$, the values of i and S for which $g(i, S)$ is needed are such that $i \neq 1$, $1 \notin S$, and $i \notin S$.

Example 5.26 Consider the directed graph of Figure 5.21(a). The edge lengths are given by matrix c of Figure 5.21(b).

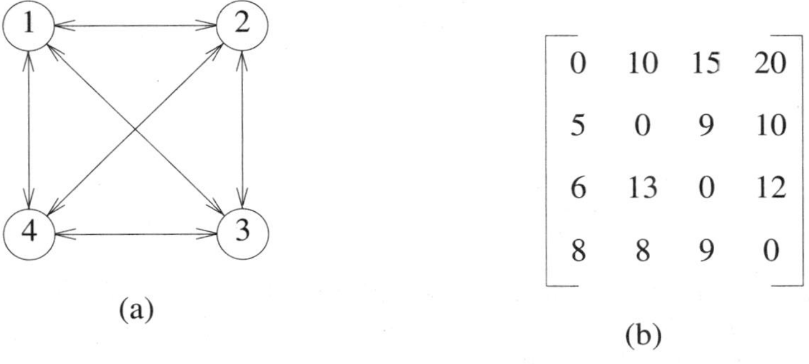

Figure 5.21 Directed graph and edge length matrix c

Thus $g(2, \phi) = c_{21} = 5, g(3, \phi) = c_{31} = 6$, and $g(4, \phi) = c_{41} = 8$. Using (5.21), we obtain

$$\begin{array}{lllllll} g(2,\{3\}) & = & c_{23} + g(3,\phi) & = & 15 & g(2,\{4\}) & = & 18 \\ g(3,\{2\}) & = & 18 & & & g(3,\{4\}) & = & 20 \\ g(4,\{2\}) & = & 13 & & & g(4,\{3\}) & = & 15 \end{array}$$

Next, we compute $g(i, S)$ with $|S| = 2$, $i \neq 1$, $1 \notin S$ and $i \notin S$.

$$\begin{array}{lllll} g(2,\{3,4\}) & = & \min\ \{c_{23} + g(3,\{4\}), c_{24} + g(4,\{3\})\} & = & 25 \\ g(3,\{2,4\}) & = & \min\ \{c_{32} + g(2,\{4\}), c_{34} + g(4,\{2\})\} & = & 25 \\ g(4,\{2,3\}) & = & \min\ \{c_{42} + g(2,\{3\}), c_{43} + g(3,\{2\})\} & = & 23 \end{array}$$

Finally, from (5.20) we obtain

$$\begin{array}{lll} g(1,\{2,3,4\}) & = & \min\{c_{12} + g(2,\{3,4\}), c_{13} + g(3,\{2,4\}), c_{14} + g(4,\{2,3\})\} \\ & = & \min\{35, 40, 43\} \\ & = & 35 \end{array}$$

An optimal tour of the graph of Figure 5.21(a) has length 35. A tour of this length can be constructed if we retain with each $g(i, S)$ the value of j that minimizes the right-hand side of (5.21). Let $J(i, S)$ be this value. Then, $J(1, \{2, 3, 4\}) = 2$. Thus the tour starts from 1 and goes to 2. The remaining tour can be obtained from $g(2, \{3, 4\})$. So $J(2, \{3, 4\}) = 4$. Thus the next edge is $\langle 2, 4 \rangle$. The remaining tour is for $g(4, \{3\})$. So $J(4, \{3\}) = 3$. The optimal tour is 1, 2, 4, 3, 1. □

Let N be the number of $g(i, S)$'s that have to be computed before (5.20) can be used to compute $g(1, V - \{1\})$. For each value of $|S|$ there are $n - 1$ choices for i. The number of distinct sets S of size k not including 1 and i is $\binom{n-2}{k}$. Hence

$$N = \sum_{k=0}^{n-2} (n - k - 1) \binom{n-2}{k} = (n - 1)2^{n-2}$$

An algorithm that proceeds to find an optimal tour by using (5.20) and (5.21) will require $\Theta(n^2 2^n)$ time as the computation of $g(i, S)$ with $|S| = k$ requires $k - 1$ comparisons when solving (5.21). This is better than enumerating all $n!$ different tours to find the best one. The most serious drawback of this dynamic programming solution is the space needed, $O(n2^n)$. This is too large even for modest values of n.

EXERCISE

1. (a) Obtain a data representation for the values $g(i, S)$ of the traveling salesperson problem. Your representation should allow for easy access to the value of $g(i, S)$, given i and S. (i) How much space does your representation need for an n vertex graph? (ii) How much time is needed to retrieve or update the value of $g(i, S)$?

   (b) Using the representation of (a), develop an algorithm corresponding to the dynamic programming solution of the traveling salesperson problem.

   (c) Test the correctness of your algorithm using suitable test data.

5.10 FLOW SHOP SCHEDULING

Often the processing of a job requires the performance of several distinct tasks. Computer programs run in a multiprogramming environment are input and then executed. Following the execution, the job is queued for output and the output eventually printed. In a general flow shop we may have n jobs each requiring m tasks $T_{1i}, T_{2i}, \ldots, T_{mi}$, $1 \leq i \leq n$, to be performed. Task T_{ji} is to be performed on processor P_j, $1 \leq j \leq m$. The time required to complete task T_{ji} is t_{ji}. A schedule for the n jobs is an assignment of tasks to time intervals on the processors. Task T_{ji} must be assigned to processor P_j. No processor may have more than one task assigned to it in any time interval. Additionally, for any job i the processing of task T_{ji}, $j > 1$, cannot be started until task $T_{j-1,i}$ has been completed.

Example 5.27 Two jobs have to be scheduled on three processors. The task times are given by the matrix $\mathcal{J}$

$$\mathcal{J} = \begin{bmatrix} 2 & 0 \\ 3 & 3 \\ 5 & 2 \end{bmatrix}$$

Two possible schedules for the jobs are shown in Figure 5.22. □

A *nonpreemptive* schedule is a schedule in which the processing of a task on any processor is not terminated until the task is complete. A schedule for which this need not be true is called *preemptive*. The schedule of Figure 5.22(a) is a preemptive schedule. Figure 5.22(b) shows a nonpreemptive schedule. The *finish time* $f_i(S)$ of job i is the time at which all tasks of job i have been completed in schedule S. In Figure 5.22(a), $f_1(S) = 10$ and $f_2(S) = 12$. In Figure 5.22(b), $f_1(S) = 11$ and $f_2(S) = 5$. The finish time $F(S)$ of a schedule S is given by

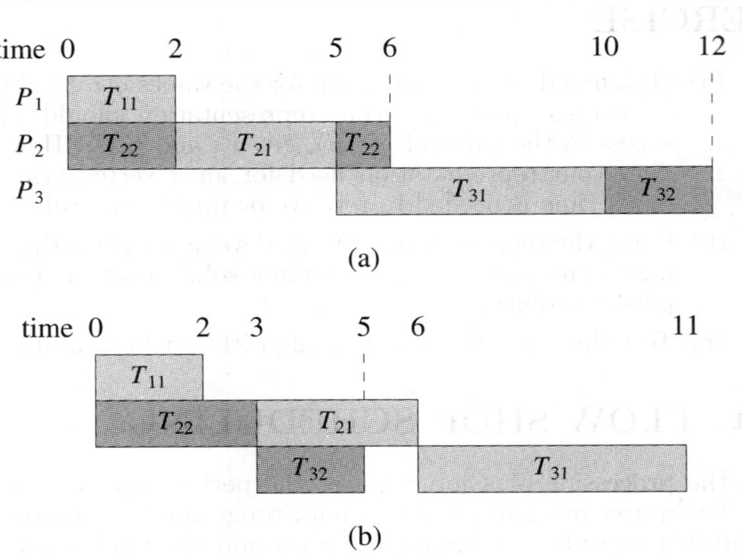

Figure 5.22 Two possible schedules for Example 5.27

$$F(S) = \max_{1 \le i \le n} \{f_i(S)\} \tag{5.22}$$

The *mean flow time* MFT(S) is defined to be

$$\text{MFT}(S) = \frac{1}{n} \sum_{1 \le i \le n} f_i(S) \tag{5.23}$$

An optimal finish time (OFT) schedule for a given set of jobs is a nonpreemptive schedule S for which $F(S)$ is minimum over all nonpreemptive schedules S. A preemptive optimal finish time (POFT) schedule, optimal mean finish time schedule (OMFT), and preemptive optimal mean finish (POMFT) schedule are defined in the obvious way.

Although the general problem of obtaining OFT and POFT schedules for $m > 2$ and of obtaining OMFT schedules is computationally difficult (see Chapter 11), dynamic programming leads to an efficient algorithm to obtain OFT schedules for the case $m = 2$. In this section we consider this special case.

For convenience, we shall use a_i to represent t_{1i}, and b_i to represent t_{2i}. For the two-processor case, one can readily verify that nothing is to be gained by using different processing orders on the two processors (this is not true for $m > 2$). Hence, a schedule is completely specified by providing a permutation of the jobs. Jobs will be executed on each processor in this order. Each task will be started at the earliest possible time. The schedule of Figure 5.23 is completely specified by the permutation (5, 1, 3, 2, 4). We make the simplifying assumption that $a_i \neq 0$, $1 \leq i \leq n$. Note that if jobs with $a_i = 0$ are allowed, then an optimal schedule can be constructed by first finding an optimal permutation for all jobs with $a_i \neq 0$ and then adding all jobs with $a_i = 0$ (in any order) in front of this permutation (see the exercises).

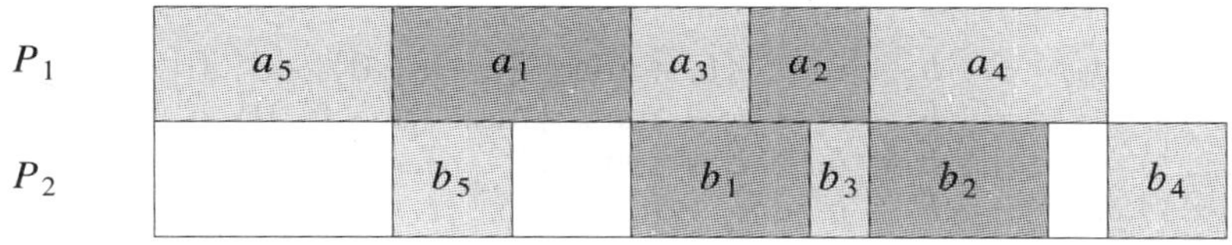

P_1	a_5	a_1		a_3	a_2	a_4			
P_2		b_5		b_1	b_3	b_2		b_4	

Figure 5.23 A schedule

It is easy to see that an optimal permutation (schedule) has the property that given the first job in the permutation, the remaining permutation is optimal with respect to the state the two processors are in following the completion of the first job. Let $\sigma_1, \sigma_2, \ldots, \sigma_k$ be a permutation prefix defining a schedule for jobs $T_1, T_2, \ldots, T_k$. For this schedule let f_1 and f_2 be the times at which the processing of jobs $T_1, T_2, \ldots, T_k$ is completed on processors P_1 and P_2 respectively. Let $t = f_2 - f_1$. The state of the processors following the sequence of decisions $T_1, T_2, \ldots, T_k$ is completely characterized by t. Let $g(S, t)$ be the length of an optimal schedule for the subset of jobs S under the assumption that processor 2 is not available until time t. The length of an optimal schedule for the job set $\{1, 2, \ldots, n\}$ is $g(\{1, 2, \ldots, n\}, 0)$.

Since the principle of optimality holds, we obtain

$$g(\{1, 2, \cdots, n\}, 0) = \min_{1 \leq i \leq n} \{a_i + g(\{1, 2, \cdots, n\} - \{i\}, b_i)\} \tag{5.24}$$

Equation 5.24 generalizes to (5.25) for arbitrary S and t. This generalization requires that $g(\phi, t) = \max\{t, 0\}$ and that $a_i \neq 0$, $1 \leq i \leq n$.

$$g(S, t) = \min_{i \in S} \{a_i + g(S - \{i\}, b_i + \max\{t - a_i, 0\})\} \tag{5.25}$$

The term max $\{t-a_i,0\}$ comes into (5.25) as task T_{2i} cannot start until $\max\{a_i,t\}$ (P_2 is not available until time t). Hence $f_2-f_1=b_i+\max\{a_i,t\}-a_i=b_i+\max\{t-a_i,0\}$. We can solve for $g(S,t)$ using an approach similar to that used to solve (5.21). However, it turns out that (5.25) can be solved algebraically and a very simple rule to generate an optimal schedule obtained.

Consider any schedule R for a subset of jobs S. Assume that P_2 is not available until time t. Let i and j be the first two jobs in this schedule. Then, from (5.25) we obtain

$$\begin{aligned} g(S,t) &= a_i+g(S-\{i\},b_i+\max\ \{t-a_i,0\}) \\ g(S,t) &= a_i+a_j+g(S-\{i,j\},b_j+\max\ \{b_i+\max\ \{t-a_i,0\}-a_j,0\}) \end{aligned} \tag{5.26}$$

Equation 5.26 can be simplified using the following result:

$$\begin{aligned} t_{ij} &= b_j+\max\ \{b_i+\max\ \{t-a_i,0\}-a_j,0\} \\ &= b_j+b_i-a_j+\max\ \{\max\ \{t-a_i,0\},a_j-b_i\} \\ &= b_j+b_i-a_j+\max\ \{t-a_i,a_j-b_i,0\} \\ t_{ij} &= b_j+b_i-a_j-a_i+\max\ \{t,a_i+a_j-b_i,a_i\} \end{aligned} \tag{5.27}$$

If jobs i and j are interchanged in R, then the finish time $g'(S,t)$ is

$$g'(S,t) \quad = \quad a_i+a_j+g(S-\{i,j\},t_{ji})$$

$$\text{where } t_{ji} \quad = \quad b_j+b_i-a_j-a_i+\max\ \{t,a_i+a_j-b_j,a_j\}$$

Comparing $g(S,t)$ and $g'(S,t)$, we see that if (5.28) below holds, then $g(S,t)\le g'(S,t)$.

$$\max\ \{t,a_i+a_j-b_i,a_i\}\le \max\ \{t,a_i+a_j-b_j,a_j\} \tag{5.28}$$

In order for (5.28) to hold for all values of t, we need

$$\max\ \{a_i+a_j-b_i,a_i\}\le \max\ \{a_i+a_j-b_j,a_j\}$$

$$\text{or}\ \ a_i+a_j+\max\ \{-b_i,-a_j\}\le a_i+a_j+\max\ \{-b_j,-a_i\}$$

$$\text{or}\ \ \min\ \{b_i,a_j\}\ge \min\ \{b_j,a_i\} \tag{5.29}$$

From (5.29) we can conclude that there exists an optimal schedule in which for every pair (i,j) of adjacent jobs, $\min\{b_i,a_j\}\ge\min\{b_j,a_i\}$. Exercise 4 shows that all schedules with this property have the same length.

Hence, it suffices to generate any schedule for which (5.29) holds for every pair of adjacent jobs. We can obtain a schedule with this property by making the following observations from (5.29). If $\min\{a_1, a_2, \ldots, a_n, b_1, b_2, \ldots, b_n\}$ is a_i, then job i should be the first job in an optimal schedule. If $\min\{a_1, a_2, \ldots, a_n, b_1, b_2, \ldots, b_n\}$ is b_j, then job j should be the last job in an optimal schedule. This enables us to make a decision as to the positioning of one of the n jobs. Equation 5.29 can now be used on the remaining $n - 1$ jobs to correctly position another job, and so on. The scheduling rule resulting from (5.29) is therefore:

1. Sort all the a_i's and b_j's into nondecreasing order.

2. Consider this sequence in this order. If the next number in the sequence is a_j and job j hasn't yet been scheduled, schedule job j at the leftmost available spot. If the next number is b_j and job j hasn't yet been scheduled, schedule job j at the rightmost available spot. If j has already been scheduled, go to the next number in the sequence.

Note that the above rule also correctly positions jobs with $a_i = 0$. Hence, these jobs need not be considered separately.

Example 5.28 Let $n = 4, (a_1, a_2, a_3, a_4) = (3, 4, 8, 10)$, and $(b_1, b_2, b_3, b_4) = (6, 2, 9, 15)$. The sorted sequence of a's and b's is $(b_2, a_1, a_2, b_1, a_3, b_3, a_4, b_4) = (2, 3, 4, 6, 8, 9, 10, 15)$. Let $\sigma_1, \sigma_2, \sigma_3$, and σ_4 be the optimal schedule. Since the smallest number is b_2, we set $\sigma_4 = 2$. The next number is a_1 and we set $\sigma_1 = a_1$. The next smallest number is a_2. Job 2 has already been scheduled. The next number is b_1. Job 1 has already been scheduled. The next is a_3 and we set σ_3. This leaves σ_3 free and job 4 unscheduled. Thus, $\sigma_3 = 4$. □

The scheduling rule above can be implemented to run in time $O(n \log n)$ (see exercises). Solving (5.24) and (5.25) directly for $g(1, 2, \ldots, n, 0)$ for the optimal schedule will take $\Omega(2^n)$ time as there are these many different S's for which $g(S, t)$ will be computed.

EXERCISES

1. N jobs are to be processed. Two machines A and B are available. If job i is processed on machine A, then a_i units of processing time are needed. If it is processed on machine B, then b_i units of processing time are needed. Because of the peculiarities of the jobs and the machines, it is quite possible that $a_i \geq b_i$ for some i while $a_j < b_j$ for some j, $j \neq i$. Obtain a dynamic programming formulation to determine the minimum time needed to process all the jobs. Note that jobs cannot

be split between machines. Indicate how you would go about solving the recurrence relation obtained. Do this on an example of your choice. Also indicate how you would determine an optimal assignment of jobs to machines.

2. N jobs have to be scheduled for processing on one machine. Associated with job i is a 3-tuple (p_i, t_i, d_i). The variable t_i is the processing time needed to complete job i. If job i is completed by its deadline d_i, then a profit p_i is earned. If not, then nothing is earned. From Section 4.5 we know that J is a subset of jobs that can all be completed by their deadlines iff the jobs in J can be processed in nondecreasing order of deadlines without violating any deadline. Assume $d_i \leq d_{i+1}$, $1 \leq i < n$. Let $f_i(x)$ be the maximum profit that can be earned from a subset J of jobs when $n = i$. Here $f_n(d_n)$ is the value of an optimal selection of jobs J. Let $f_0(x) = 0$. Show that for $x \leq t_i$,

$$f_i(x) = \max \ \{f_{i-1}(x),\ f_{i-1}(x - t_i) + p_i\}$$

3. Let I be any instance of the two-processor flow shop problem.

   (a) Show that the length of every POFT schedule for I is the same as the length of every OFT schedule for I. Hence, the algorithm of Section 5.10 also generates a POFT schedule.

   (b) Show that there exists an OFT schedule for I in which jobs are processed in the same order on both processors.

   (c) Show that there exists an OFT schedule for I defined by some permutation σ of the jobs (see part (b)) such that all jobs with $a_i = 0$ are at the front of this permutation. Further, show that the order in which these jobs appear at the front of the permutation is not important.

4. Let I be any instance of the two-processor flow shop problem. Let $\sigma = \sigma_1\sigma_2 \cdots \sigma_n$ be a permutation defining an OFT schedule for I.

   (a) Use (5.29) to argue that there exists an OFT σ such that $\min\ \{b_i, a_j) \geq \min\ \{b_j, a_i\}$ for every i and j such that $i = \sigma_k$ and $j = \sigma_{k+1}$ (that is, i and j are adjacent).

   (b) For a σ satisfying the conditions of part (a), show that $\min\{b_i, a_j\} \geq \min\{b_j, a_i\}$ for every i and j such that $i = \sigma_k$ and $j = \sigma_r, k < r$.

   (c) Show that all schedules corresponding to σ's satisfying the conditions of part (a) have the same finish time. (*Hint*: use part (b) to transform one of two different schedules satisfying (a) into the other without increasing the finish time.)

5.11 REFERENCES AND READINGS

Two references on dynamic programming are:
Dynamic Programming by R. E. Bellman, Dover Publications, 2003.

Dynamic Programming, by E. V. Denardo, Dover Publications, 2003.

The dynamic programming formulation for the shortest-paths problem was given by R. Floyd.

Bellman and Ford's algorithm for the single-source shortest-path problem (with general edge weights) can be found in the above mentioned book by R. E. Bellman.

The construction of optimal binary search trees using dynamic programming is described in *The Art of Programming: Sorting and Searching*, Vol. 3, by D. E. Knuth, Second Edition, Addison Wesley, 1998.

The string editing algorithm discussed in this chapter is in "The string-to-string correction problem," by R. A. Wagner and M. J. Fischer, *Journal of the ACM* 21, no. 1 (1974): 168–173.

The set generation approach to solving the 0/1 knapsack problem was formulated by G. Nemhauser and Z. Ullman, and E. Horowitz and S. Sahni.

Exercise 6 in Section 5.7 is due to E. Horowitz and S. Sahni.

The dynamic programming formulation for the traveling salesperson problem was given by M. Held and R. Karp.

The dynamic programming solution to the matrix product chain problem (Exercises 1 and 2 in Additional Exercises) is due to S. Godbole.

5.12 ADDITIONAL EXERCISES

1. [Matrix product chains] Let A, B, and C be three matrices such that $C = A \times B$. Let the dimensions of A, B, and C respectively be $m \times n, n \times p$, and $m \times p$. From the definition of matrix multiplication,

$$C(i,j) = \sum_{k=1}^{n} A(i,k)B(k,j)$$

   (a) Write an algorithm to compute C directly using the above formula. Show that the number of multiplications needed by your algorithm is mnp.

(b) Let $M_1 \times M_2 \times \cdots \times M_r$ be a chain of matrix products. This chain may be evaluated in several different ways. Two possibilities are $(\cdots((M_1 \times M_2) \times M_3) \times M_4) \times \cdots) \times M_r$ and $(M_1 \times (M_2 \times (\cdots \times (M_{r-1} \times M_r)\cdots)$. The cost of any computation of $M_1 \times M_2 \times \cdots \times M_r$ is the number of multiplications used. Consider the case $r = 4$ and matrices M_1 through M_4 with dimensions $100 \times 1, 1 \times 100, 100 \times 1$, and 1×100 respectively. What is the cost of each of the five ways to compute $M_1 \times M_2 \times M_3 \times M_4$? Show that the optimal way has a cost of 10,200 and the worst way has a cost of 1,020,000. Assume that all matrix products are computed using the algorithm of part (a).

(c) Let M_{ij} denote the matrix product $M_i \times M_{i+1} \times \cdots \times M_j$. Thus, $M_{ii} = M_i$, $1 \leq i \leq r$. $S = P_1, P_2, \ldots, P_{r-1}$ is a *product sequence* computing M_{1r} iff each product P_k is of the form $M_{ij} \times M_{j+1,q}$, where M_{ij} and $M_{j+1,q}$ have been computed either by an earlier product $P_l, l < k$, or represent an input matrix M_{tt}. Note that $M_{ij} \times M_{j+1,q} = M_{iq}$. Also note that every valid computation of M_{1r} using only pairwise matrix products at each step is defined by a product sequence. Two product sequences $S_1 = P_1, P_2, \ldots, P_{r-1}$ and $S_2 = U_1, U_2, \ldots, U_{r-1}$ are *different* if $P_i \neq U_i$ for some i. Show that the number of different product sequences if $(r-1)!$

(d) Although there are $(r-1)!$ different product sequences, many of these are essentially the same in the sense that the same pairs of matrices are multiplied. For example, the sequences $S_1 = (M_1 \times M_2), (M_3 \times M_4), (M_{12} \times M_{34})$ and $S_2 = (M_3 \times M_4), (M_1 \times M_2), (M_{12} \times M_{34})$ are different under the definition of part (c). However, the same pairs of matrices are multiplied in both S_1 and S_2. Show that if we consider only those product sequences that differ from each other in at least one matrix product, then the number of different sequences is equal to the number of different binary trees having exactly $r-1$ nodes.

(e) Show that the number of different binary trees with n nodes is

$$\frac{1}{n+1}\binom{2n}{n}$$

2. [Matrix product chains] In the preceding exercise it was established that the number of different ways to evaluate a matrix product chain is very large even when r is relatively small (say 10 or 20). In this exercise we shall develop an $O(r^3)$ algorithm to find an optimal product sequence (that is, one of minimum cost). Let $D(i), 0 \leq i \leq r$, represent the dimensions of the matrices; that is, M_i has $D(i-1)$ rows and $D(i)$

columns. Let $C(i,j)$ be the cost of computing M_{ij} using an optimal product sequence for M_{ij}. Observe that $C(i,i) = 0, 1 \leq i \leq r$, and that $C(i,i+1) = D(i-1)D(i)D(i+1), 1 \leq i \leq r$.

(a) Obtain a recurrence relation for $C(i,j), j > i$. This recurrence relation will be similar to Equation 5.14.

(b) Write an algorithm to solve the recurrence relation of part (a) for $C(1,r)$. Your algorithm should be of complexity $O(r^3)$.

(c) What changes are needed in the algorithm of part (b) to determine an optimal product sequence. Write an algorithm to determine such a sequence. Show that the overall complexity of your algorithm remains $O(r^3)$.

(d) Work through your algorithm (by hand) for the product chain of part (b) of the previous exercise. What are the values of $C(i,j), 1 \leq i \leq r$ and $j \geq i$? What is an optimal way to compute M_{14}?

3. There are two warehouses W_1 and W_2 from which supplies are to be shipped to destinations $D_i, 1 \leq i \leq n$. Let d_i be the demand at D_i and let r_i be the inventory at W_i. Assume $r_1 + r_2 = \sum d_i$. Let $c_{ij}(x_{ij})$ be the cost of shipping x_{ij} units from warehouse W_i to destination D_j. The warehouse problem is to find nonnegative integers $x_{ij}, 1 \leq i \leq 2$ and $1 \leq j \leq n$, such that $x_{1j} + x_{2j} = d_j$, $1 \leq j \leq n$, and $\sum_{i,j} c_{ij}(x_{ij})$ is minimized. Let $g_i(x)$ be the cost incurred when W_1 has an inventory of x and supplies are sent to $D_j, 1 \leq j \leq i$, in an optimal manner (the inventory at W_2 is $\sum_{1 \leq j \leq i} d_j - x$). The cost of an optimal solution to the warehouse problem is $g_n(r_1)$.

(a) Use the optimality principle to obtain a recurrence relation for $g_i(x)$.

(b) Write an algorithm to solve this recurrence and obtain an optimal sequence of values for $x_{ij}, 1 \leq i \leq 2, 1 \leq j \leq n$.

4. Given a warehouse with a storage capacity of B units and an initial stock of v units, let y_i be the quantity sold in each month, $i, 1 \leq i \leq n$. Let P_i be the per-unit selling price in month i, and x_i the quantity purchased in month i. The buying price is c_i per unit. At the end of each month, the stock in hand must be no more than B. That is,

$$v + \sum_{1 \leq i \leq j} (x_i - y_i) \leq B, \quad 1 \leq j \leq n$$

The amount sold in each month cannot be more than the stock at the end of the previous month (new stock arrives only at the end of a month). That is,

$$y_i \leq v + \sum_{1 \leq j < i} (x_j - y_j), \quad 1 \leq i \leq n$$

Also, we require x_i and y_i to be nonnegative integers. The total profit derived is

$$P_n = \sum_{j=1}^{n} (p_j y_j - c_j x_j)$$

The problem is to determine x_j and y_j such that P_n is maximized. Let $f_i(v_i)$ represent the maximum profit that can be earned in months $i+1, i+2, \ldots, n$, starting with v_i units of stock at the end of month i. Then $f_0(v)$ is the maximum value of P_n.

(a) Obtain the dynamic programming recurrence for $f_i(v_i)$ in terms of $f_{i+1}(v_i)$.

(b) What is $f_n(v_i)$?

(c) Solve part (a) analytically to obtain the formula

$$f_i(v_i) = a_i x_i + b_i v_i$$

for some constants a_i and b_i.

(d) Show that an optimal P_n is obtained by using the following strategy:

i. $p_i \geq c_i$

A. If $b_{i+1} \geq c_i$, then $y_i = v_i$ and $x_i = B$.

B. If $b_{i+1} \leq c_i$, then $y_i = v_i$ and $x_i = 0$.

ii. $c_i \geq p_i$

A. If $b_{i+1} \geq c_i$, then $y_i = 0$ and $x_i = B - v_i$.

B. If $b_{i+1} \leq p_i$, then $y_i = v_i$ and $x_i = 0$.

C. If $p_i \leq b_{i+1} \leq c_i$, then $y_i = 0$ and $x_i = 0$.

(e) Use the p_i and c_i in Figure 5.24 and obtain an optimal decision sequence from part (d).

Assume the warehouse capacity to be 100 and the initial stock to be 60.

i	1	2	3	4	5	6	7	8
p_i	8	8	2	3	4	3	2	5
c_i	3	6	7	1	4	5	1	3

Figure 5.24 p_i and c_i for Exercise 4

(f) From part (d) conclude that an optimal set of values for x_i and y_i will always lead to the following policy: Do no buying or selling for the first k months (k may be zero) and then oscillate between a full and an empty warehouse for the remaining months.

5. Assume that n programs are to be stored on two tapes. Let l_i be the length of tape needed to store the ith program. Assume that $\sum l_i \leq L$, where L is the length of each tape. A program can be stored on either of the two tapes. If S_1 is the set of programs on tape 1, then the worst-case access time for a program is proportional to $\max\{\sum_{i \in S_1} l_i, \sum_{i \notin S_1} l_i\}$. An optimal assignment of programs to tapes minimizes the worst-case access times. Formulate a dynamic programming approach to determine the worst-case access time of an optimal assignment. Write an algorithm to determine this time. What is the complexity of your algorithm?

6. Redo Exercise 5 making the assumption that programs will be stored on tape 2 using a different tape density than that used on tape 1. If l_i is the tape length needed by program i when stored on tape 1, then al_i is the tape length needed on tape 2.

7. [Longest Common Subsequence] String s is a subsequence of string a if s can be obtained from a by deleting some of the characters in a. The string "onion" is a subsequence of "recognition." s is a common subsequence of a and b iff it is a subsequence of both a and b. The length of s is its number of characters. Develop a dynamic-programming algorithm to find a longest common subsequence of the strings a and b. (*Hint:* Let $a = a_1 a_2 \cdots a_n$ and $b = b_1 b_2 \cdots b_m$. Define $l(i, j)$ to be the length of a longest common subsequence of the strings $a_i \cdots a_n$ and $b_j \cdots b_m$.) What is the complexity of your algorithm?

8. Do Exercise 7 but this time define $l(i, j)$ to be the length of a longest common subsequence of the strings $a_1 \cdots a_i$ and $b_1 \cdots b_j$.

9. Let $x_1, x_2, \cdots$, be a sequence of integers. Let $sum(i, j) = \sum_i^j x_k$, $i \leq j$. Write an algorithm to find i and j for which $sum(i, j)$ is maximum. What is the complexity of your algorithm?

10. Let L be an array of n distinct integers. Give an efficient algorithm to find the length of a longest increasing subsequence of entries in L. For example, if the entries are $11, 17, 5, 8, 6, 4, 7, 12, 3$, a longest increasing subsequence is $5, 6, 7, 12$. What is the run time of your algorithm?

Chapter 6

BASIC TRAVERSAL AND SEARCH TECHNIQUES

The techniques to be discussed in this chapter are divided into two categories. The first category includes techniques applicable only to binary trees. As described, these techniques involve examining every node in the given data object instance. Hence, these techniques are referred to as *traversal methods.* The second category includes techniques applicable to graphs (and hence also to trees and binary trees). These may not examine all vertices and so are referred to only as *search methods.* During a traversal or search the fields of a node may be used several times. It may be necessary to distinguish certain uses of the fields of a node. During these uses, the node is said to be *visited.* Visiting a node may involve printing out its data field, evaluating the operation specified by the node in the case of a binary tree representing an expression, setting a mark bit to one or zero, and so on. Since we are describing traversals and searches of trees and graphs independently of their application, we use the term "visited" rather than the term for the specific function performed on the node at this time.

6.1 TECHNIQUES FOR BINARY TREES

The solution to many problems involves the manipulation of binary trees, trees, or graphs. Often this manipulation requires us to determine a vertex (node) or a subset of vertices in the given data object that satisfies a given property. For example, we may wish to find all vertices in a binary tree with a data value less than x or we may wish to find all vertices in a given graph G that can be reached from another given vertex v. The determination of this subset of vertices satisfying a given property can be carried out by systematically examining the vertices of the given data object. This often takes the form of a search in the data object. When the search necessarily

```
treenode = record
{
    Type data; // Type is the data type of data.
    treenode *lchild; treenode *rchild;
}
```

```
Algorithm InOrder(t)
// t is a binary tree. Each node of t has
// three fields: lchild, data, and rchild.
{
    if t ≠ 0 then
    {
        InOrder(t → lchild);
        Visit(t);
        InOrder(t → rchild);
    }
}
```

Algorithm 6.1 Recursive formulation of inorder traversal

involves the examination of every vertex in the object being searched, it is called a *traversal*.

We have already seen an example of a problem whose solution required a search of a binary tree. In Section 5.5 we presented an algorithm to search a binary search tree for an identifier x. This algorithm is not a traversal algorithm as it does not examine every vertex in the search tree. Sometimes, we may wish to traverse a binary search tree (e.g., when we wish to list out all the identifiers in the tree). Algorithms for this are studied in this chapter.

There are many operations that we want to perform on binary trees. One that arises frequently is traversing a tree, or visiting each node in the tree exactly once. A traversal produces a linear order for the information in a tree. This linear order may be familiar and useful. When traversing a binary tree, we want to treat each node and its subtrees in the same fashion. If we let L, D, and R stand for moving left, printing the data, and moving right when at a node, then there are six possible combinations of traversal: *LDR, LRD, DLR, DRL, RDL*, and *RLD*. If we adopt the convention that we traverse left before right, then only three traversals remain: *LDR, LRD*, and *DLR*. To these we assign the names *inorder*, *postorder*, and *preorder*. Recursive functions for these three traversals are given in Algorithms 6.1 and 6.2.

```
Algorithm PreOrder(t)
// t is a binary tree. Each node of t has
// three fields: lchild, data, and rchild.
{
    if t ≠ 0 then
    {
        Visit(t);
        PreOrder(t → lchild);
        PreOrder(t → rchild);
    }
}
```

```
Algorithm PostOrder(t)
// t is a binary tree. Each node of t has
// three fields: lchild, data, and rchild.
{
    if t ≠ 0 then
    {
        PostOrder(t → lchild);
        PostOrder(t → rchild);
        Visit(t);
    }
}
```

Algorithm 6.2 Preorder and postorder traversals

Figure 6.1 shows a binary tree and Figure 6.2 traces how InOrder works on it. This trace assumes that visiting a node requires only the printing of its *data* field. The output resulting from this traversal is FDHGIBEAC. With Visit(t) replaced by a printing statement, the application of Algorithm 6.2 to the binary tree of Figure 6.1 results in the outputs ABDFGHIEC and FHIGDEBCA, respectively.

Theorem 6.1 Let $T(n)$ and $S(n)$, respectively, represent the time and space needed by any one of the traversal algorithms when the input tree t has $n \geq 0$ nodes. If the time and space needed to visit a node are $\Theta(1)$, then $T(n) = \Theta(n)$ and $S(n) = O(n)$.

Proof: Each traversal can be regarded as a walk through the binary tree. During this walk, each node is reached three times: once from its parent (or

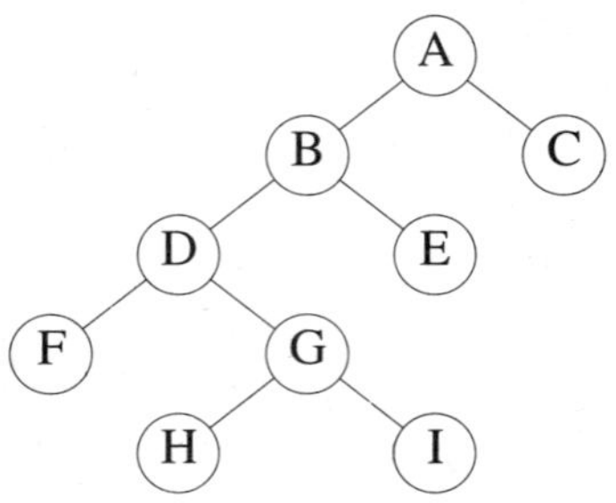

Figure 6.1 A binary tree

call of InOrder	value in root	action
main	A	
1	B	
2	D	
3	F	
4	—	print ('F')
4	—	print ('D')
3	G	
4	H	
5	—	print ('H')
5	—	print ('G')
4	I	
5	—	print ('I')
5	—	print ('B')
2	E	
3	—	print ('E')
3	—	print ('A')
1	C	
2	—	print ('C')
2	—	

Figure 6.2 Inorder traversal of the binary tree of Figure 6.1

as the start node in case the node is the root), once on returning from its left subtree, and once on returning from its right subtree. In each of these three times a constant amount of work is done. So, the total time taken by the traversal is $\Theta(n)$. The only additional space needed is that for the recursion stack. If t has depth d, then this space is $\Theta(d)$. For an n-node binary tree, $d \leq n$ and so $S(n) = O(n)$. □

EXERCISES

Unless otherwise stated, all binary trees are represented using nodes with three fields: *lchild*, *data*, and *rchild*.

1. Give an algorithm to count the number of leaf nodes in a binary tree t. What is its computing time?

2. Write an algorithm SwapTree(t) that takes a binary tree and swaps the left and right children of every node. An example is given in Figure 6.3. Use one of the three traversal methods discussed in Section 6.1.

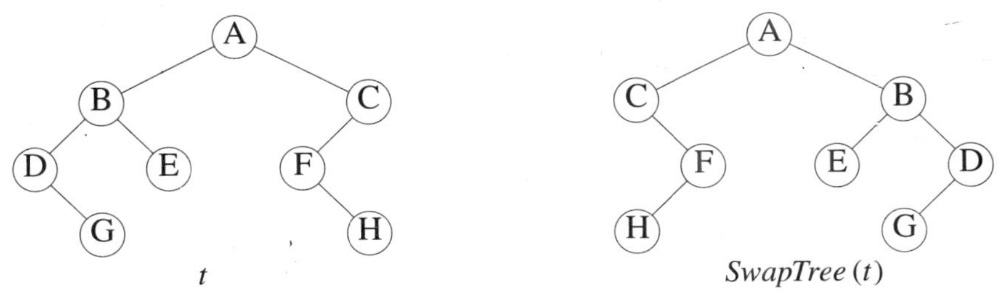

Figure 6.3 Swapping left and right children

3. Use one of the three traversal methods discussed in Section 6.1 to obtain an algorithm Equiv(t, u) that determines whether the binary trees t and u are equivalent. Two binary trees t and u are equivalent if and only if they are structurally equivalent and if the data in the corresponding nodes of t and u are the same.

4. Show the following:

   (a) Inorder and postorder sequences of a binary tree uniquely define the binary tree.

(b) Inorder and preorder sequences of a binary tree uniquely define the binary tree.

(c) Preorder and postorder sequences of a binary tree do not uniquely define the binary tree.

5. In the proof of Theorem 6.1, show, using induction, that $T(n) \leq c_2 n + c_1$ (where c_2 is a constant $\geq 2c_1$).

6. Write a function to construct the binary tree with a given inorder sequence I and a given postorder sequence P. What is the complexity of your function?

7. Do Exercise 6 for a given inorder and preorder sequence.

8. Write a nonrecursive algorithm for the preorder traversal of a binary tree t. Your algorithm may use a stack. What are the time and space requirements of your algorithm?

9. Do Exercise 8 for postorder as well as inorder traversals.

10. [Triple-order traversal] A triple-order traversal of a binary tree t is defined recursively by Algorithm 6.3. A very simple nonrecursive algorithm for such a traversal is given in Algorithm 6.4. In this algorithm p, q, and r point, respectively, to the present node, previously visited node, and next node to visit. The algorithm assumes that $t \neq 0$ and that an empty subtree of node p is represented by a link to p rather than a zero. Prove that Algorithm 6.4 is correct. (*Hint*: Three links, $lchild$, $rchild$, and one from its parent, are associated with each node s. Each time s is visited, the links are rotated counterclockwise, and so after three visits they are restored to the original configuration and the algorithm backs up the tree.)

11. [Level-order traversal] In a level order traversal of a binary tree t all nodes on level i are visited before any node on level $i + 1$ is visited. Within a level, nodes are visited left to right. In level-order the nodes of the tree of Figure 6.1 are visited in the order ABCDEFGHI. Write an algorithm Level(t) to traverse the binary tree t in level order. How much time and space are needed by your algorithm?

6.2 TECHNIQUES FOR GRAPHS

A fundamental problem concerning graphs is the reachability problem. In its simplest form it requires us to determine whether there exists a path in the given graph $G = (V, E)$ such that this path starts at vertex v and ends at vertex u. A more general form is to determine for a given starting vertex

```
Algorithm Triple(t)
{
    if t ≠ 0 then
    {
        Visit(t);
        Triple(t → lchild);
        Visit(t);
        Triple(t → rchild);
        Visit(t);
    }
}
```

Algorithm 6.3 Triple-order traversal for Exercise 10

```
Algorithm Trip(t);
// It is assumed that lchild and rchild fields are > 0.
{
    p := t; q := -1;
    while (p ≠ -1) do
    {
        Visit(p);
        r := (p → lchild); (p → lchild) := (p → rchild);
        (p → rchild) := q; q := p; p := r;
    }
}
```

Algorithm 6.4 A nonrecursive algorithm for the triple-order traversal for Exercise 10

$v \in V$ all vertices u such that there is a path from v to u. This latter problem can be solved by starting at vertex v and systematically searching the graph G for vertices that can be reached from v. We describe two search methods for this.

6.2.1 Breadth First Search and Traversal

In breadth first search we start at a vertex v and mark it as having been reached (visited). The vertex v is at this time said to be unexplored. A vertex is said to have been explored by an algorithm when the algorithm has visited all vertices adjacent from it. All unvisited vertices adjacent from v are visited next. These are new unexplored vertices. Vertex v has now been explored. The newly visited vertices haven't been explored and are put onto the end of a list of unexplored vertices. The first vertex on this list is the next to be explored. Exploration continues until no unexplored vertex is left. The list of unexplored vertices operates as a queue and can be represented using any of the standard queue representations (see Section 2.1). BFS (Algorithm 6.5) describes, in pseudocode, the details of the search. It makes use of the queue representation given in Section 2.1 (Algorithm 2.3).

Example 6.1 Let us try out the algorithm on the undirected graph of Figure 6.4(a). If the graph is represented by its adjacency lists as in Figure 6.4(c), then the vertices get visited in the order 1, 2, 3, 4, 5, 6, 7, 8. A breadth first search of the directed graph of Figure 6.4(b) starting at vertex 1 results in only the vertices 1, 2, and 3 being visited. Vertex 4 cannot be reached from 1. □

Theorem 6.2 Algorithm BFS visits all vertices reachable from v.

Proof: Let $G = (V, E)$ be a graph (directed or undirected) and let $v \in V$. We prove the theorem by induction on the length of the shortest path from v to every reachable vertex $w \in V$. The length (i.e., number of edges) of the shortest path from v to a reachable vertex w is denoted by $d(v, w)$.

Basis Step. Clearly, all vertices w with $d(v, w) \leq 1$ get visited.

Induction Hypothesis. Assume that all vertices w with $d(v, w) \leq r$ get visited.

Induction Step. We now show that all vertices w with $d(v, w) = r + 1$ also get visited.

Let w be a vertex in V such that $d(v, w) = r + 1$. Let u be a vertex that immediately precedes w on a shortest v to w path. Then $d(v, u) = r$ and so u gets visited by BFS. We can assume $u \neq v$ and $r \geq 1$. Hence, immediately before u gets visited, it is placed on the queue q of unexplored vertices. The algorithm doesn't terminate until q becomes empty. Hence, u is removed from q at some time and all unvisited vertices adjacent from it get visited in the **for** loop of line 11 of Algorithm 6.5. Hence, w gets visited. □

Theorem 6.3 Let $T(n, e)$ and $S(n, e)$ be the maximum time and maximum additional space taken by algorithm BFS on any graph G with n vertices

```
1   Algorithm BFS(v)
2   // A breadth first search of G is carried out beginning
3   // at vertex v. For any node i, visited[i] = 1 if i has
4   // already been visited. The graph G and array visited[ ]
5   // are global; visited[ ] is initialized to zero.
6   {
7       u := v; // q is a queue of unexplored vertices.
8       visited[v] := 1;
9       repeat
10      {
11          for all vertices w adjacent from u do
12          {
13              if (visited[w] = 0) then
14              {
15                  Add w to q; // w is unexplored.
16                  visited[w] := 1;
17              }
18          }
19          if q is empty then return; // No unexplored vertex.
20          Delete the next element, u, from q;
21                                  // Get first unexplored vertex.
22      } until(false);
23  }
```

Algorithm 6.5 Pseudocode for breadth first search

and e edges. $T(n,e) = \Theta(n+e)$ and $S(n,e) = \Theta(n)$ if G is represented by its adjacency lists. If G is represented by its adjacency matrix, then $T(n,e) = \Theta(n^2)$ and $S(n,e) = \Theta(n)$.

Proof: Vertices get added to the queue only in line 15 of Algorithm 6.5. A vertex w can get onto the queue only if $visited[w] = 0$. Immediately following w's addition to the queue, $visited[w]$ is set to 1 (line 16). Hence, each vertex can get onto the queue at most once. Vertex v never gets onto the queue and so at most $n-1$ additions are made. The queue space needed is at most $n-1$. The remaining variables take $O(1)$ space. Hence, $S(n,e) = O(n)$. If G is an n-vertex graph with v connected to the remaining $n-1$ vertices, then all $n-1$ vertices adjacent from v are on the queue at the same time. Furthermore, $\Theta(n)$ space is needed for the array *visited*. Hence $S(n,e) = \Theta(n)$. This result is independent of whether adjacency matrices or lists are used.

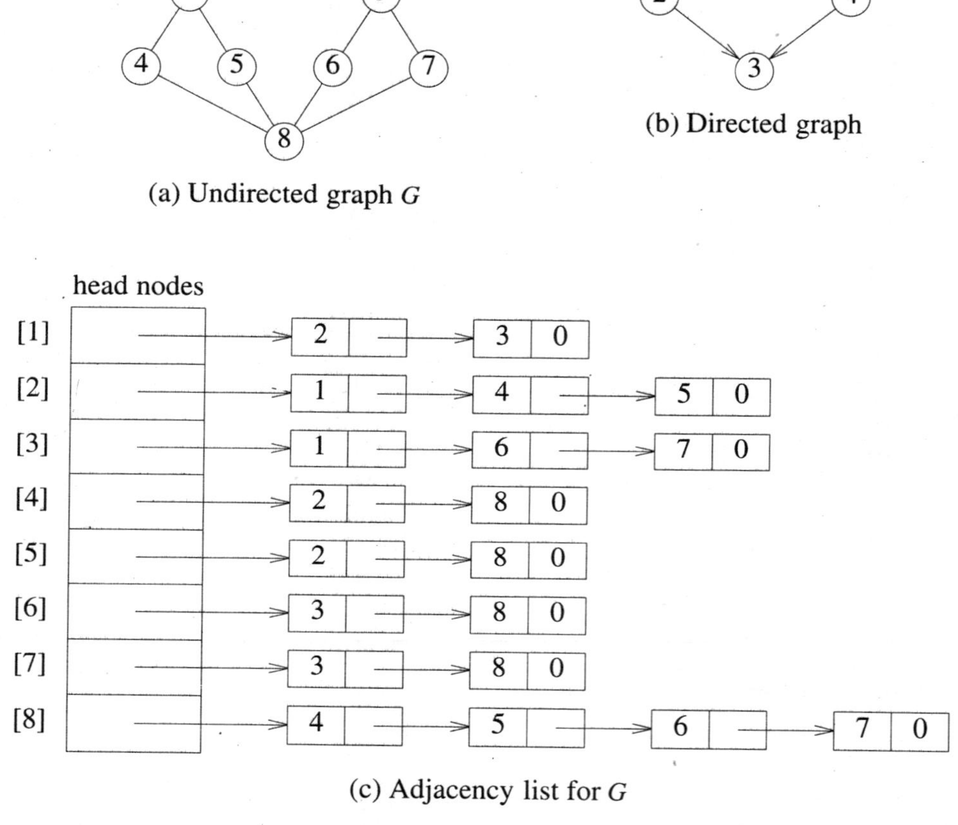

Figure 6.4 Example graphs and adjacency lists

If adjacency lists are used, then all vertices adjacent from u can be determined in time $d(u)$, where $d(u)$ is the degree of u if G is undirected and $d(u)$ is the out-degree of u if G is directed. Hence, when vertex u is being explored, the time for the **for** loop of line 11 of Algorithm 6.5 is $\Theta(d(u))$. Since each vertex in G can be explored at most once, the total time for the **repeat** loop of line 9 is $O(\sum d(u)) = O(e)$. Then $visited[i]$ has to be initialized to 0, $1 \leq i \leq n$. This takes $O(n)$ time. The total time is there-

```
Algorithm BFT(G, n)
// Breadth first traversal of G
{
    for i := 1 to n do // Mark all vertices unvisited.
        visited[i] := 0;
    for i := 1 to n do
        if (visited[i] = 0) then BFS(i);
}
```

Algorithm 6.6 Breadth first graph traversal

fore $O(n+e)$. If adjacency matrices are used, then it takes $\Theta(n)$ time to determine all vertices adjacent from u and the time becomes $O(n^2)$. If G is a graph such that all vertices are reachable from v, then all vertices get explored and the time is at least $O(n+e)$ and $O(n^2)$, respectively. Hence, $T(n,e) = \Theta(n+e)$ when adjacency lists are used, and $T(n,e) = \Theta(n^2)$ when adjacency matrices are used. □

If BFS is used on a connected undirected graph G, then all vertices in G get visited and the graph is traversed. However, if G is not connected, then at least one vertex of G is not visited. A complete traversal of the graph can be made by repeatedly calling BFS each time with a new unvisited starting vertex. The resulting traversal algorithm is known as breadth first traversal (BFT) (see Algorithm 6.6). The proof of Theorem 6.3 can be used for BFT too to show that the time and additional space required by BFT on an n-vertex e-edge graph are $\Theta(n+e)$ and $\Theta(n)$ respectively if adjacency lists are used. If adjacency matrices are used, then the bounds are $\Theta(n^2)$ and $\Theta(n)$, respectively.

6.2.2 Depth First Search and Traversal

A depth first search of a graph differs from a breadth first search in that the exploration of a vertex v is suspended as soon as a new vertex is reached. At this time the exploration of the new vertex u begins. When this new vertex has been explored, the exploration of v continues. The search terminates when all reached vertices have been fully explored. This search process is best described recursively as in Algorithm 6.7.

Example 6.2 A depth first search of the graph of Figure 6.4(a) starting at vertex 1 and using the adjacency lists of Figure 6.4(c) results in the vertices being visited in the order 1, 2, 4, 8, 5, 6, 3, 7. □

```
Algorithm DFS(v)
// Given an undirected (directed) graph G = (V, E) with
// n vertices and an array visited[ ] initially set
// to zero, this algorithm visits all vertices
// reachable from v. G and visited[ ] are global.
{
    visited[v] := 1;
    for each vertex w adjacent from v do
    {
        if (visited[w] = 0) then DFS(w);
    }
}
```

Algorithm 6.7 Depth first search of a graph

One can easily prove that DFS visits all vertices reachable from vertex v. If $T(n, e)$ and $S(n, e)$ represent the maximum time and maximum additional space taken by DFS for an n-vertex e-edge graph, then $S(n, e) = \Theta(n)$ and $T(n, e) = \Theta(n + e)$ if adjacency lists are used and $T(n, e) = \Theta(n^2)$ if adjacency matrices are used (see the exercises).

A depth first traversal of a graph is carried out by repeatedly calling DFS, with a new unvisited starting vertex each time. The algorithm for this (DFT) differs from BFT only in that the call to BFS(i) is replaced by a call to DFS(i). The exercises contain some problems that are solved best by BFS and others that are solved best by DFS. Later sections of this chapter also discuss graph problems solved best by DFS.

BFS and DFS are two fundamentally different search methods. In BFS a node is fully explored before the exploration of any other node begins. The next node to explore is the first unexplored node remaining. The exercises examine a search technique (D-search) that differs from BFS only in that the next node to explore is the most recently reached unexplored node. In DFS the exploration of a node is suspended as soon as a new unexplored node is reached. The exploration of this new node is immediately begun.

EXERCISES

1. Devise an algorithm using the idea of BFS to find a shortest (directed) cycle containing a given vertex v. Prove that your algorithm finds

a shortest cycle. What are the time and space requirements of your algorithm?

2. Show that DFS visits all vertices in G reachable from v.

3. Prove that the bounds of Theorem 6.3 hold for DFS.

4. It is easy to see that for any graph G, both DFS and BFS will take almost the same amount of time. However, the space requirements may be considerably different.

   (a) Give an example of an n-vertex graph for which the depth of recursion of DFS starting from a particular vertex v is $n-1$ whereas the queue of BFS has at most one vertex at any given time if BFS is started from the same vertex v.

   (b) Give an example of an n-vertex graph for which the queue of BFS has $n-1$ vertices at one time whereas the depth of recursion of DFS is at most one. Both searches are started from the same vertex.

5. Another way to search a graph is D-search. This method differs from BFS in that the next vertex to explore is the vertex most recently added to the list of unexplored vertices. Hence, this list operates as a stack rather than a queue.

   (a) Write an algorithm for D-search.

   (b) Show that D-search starting from vertex v visits all vertices reachable from v.

   (c) What are the time and space requirements of your algorithm?

6.3 CONNECTED COMPONENTS AND SPANNING TREES

If G is a connected undirected graph, then all vertices of G will get visited on the first call to BFS (Algorithm 6.5). If G is not connected, then at least two calls to BFS will be needed. Hence, BFS can be used to determine whether G is connected. Furthermore, all newly visited vertices on a call to BFS from BFT represent the vertices in a connected component of G. Hence the connected components of a graph can be obtained using BFT. For this, BFS can be modified so that all newly visited vertices are put onto a list. Then the subgraph formed by the vertices on this list make up a connected component. Hence, if adjacency lists are used, a breadth first traversal will obtain the connected components in $\Theta(n+e)$ time.

BFT can also be used to obtain the reflexive transitive closure matrix of an undirected graph G. If A^* is this matrix, then $A^*(i,j) = 1$ iff either $i = j$ or $i \neq j$ and i and j are in the same connected component. We can set up in $\Theta(n+e)$ time an array *connec* such that *connec*$[i]$ is the index of the connected component containing vertex i, $1 \leq i \leq n$. Hence, we can determine whether $A^*(i,j)$, $i \neq j$, is 1 or 0 by simply seeing whether *connec*$[i]$ = *connec*$[j]$. The reflexive transitive closure matrix of an undirected graph G with n vertices and e edges can therefore be computed in $\Theta(n^2)$ time and $\Theta(n)$ space using either adjacency lists or matrices (the space count does not include the space needed for A^* itself).

As a final application of breadth first search, consider the problem of obtaining a spanning tree for an undirected graph G. The graph G has a spanning tree iff G is connected. Hence, BFS easily determines the existence of a spanning tree. Furthermore, consider the set of edges (u, w) used in the **for** loop of line 11 of algorithm BFS to reach unvisited vertices w. These edges are called *forward edges.* Let t denote the set of these forward edges. We claim that if G is connected, then t is a spanning tree of G. For the graph of Figure 6.4(a) the set of edges t will be all edges in G except $(5,8)$, $(6,8)$, and $(7,8)$ (see Figure 6.5(b)). Spanning trees obtained using a breadth first search are called *breadth first spanning trees.*

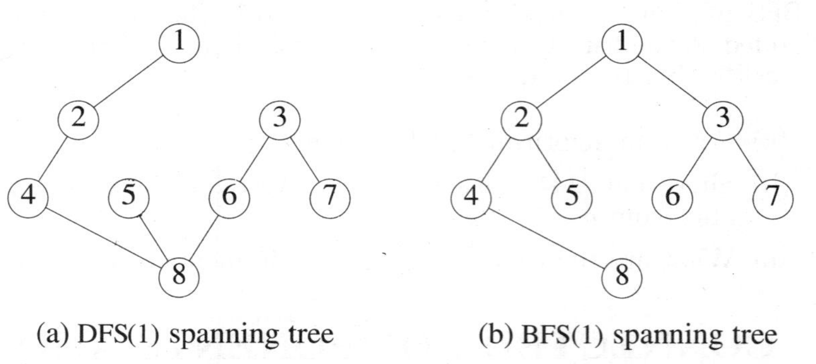

Figure 6.5 DFS and BFS spanning trees for the graph of Figure 6.4(a)

Theorem 6.4 Modify algorithm BFS by adding on the statements $t := \emptyset$; and $t := t \cup \{(u,w)\}$; to lines 8 and 16, respectively. Call the resulting algorithm BFS*. If BFS* is called so that v is any vertex in a connected undirected graph G, then on termination, the edges in t form a spanning tree of G.

Proof: We have already seen that if G is a connected graph on n vertices, then all n vertices will get visited. Also, each of these, except the start vertex

v, will get onto the queue once (line 15). Hence, t will contain exactly $n-1$ edges. All these edges are distinct. The $n-1$ edges in t will therefore define an undirected graph on n vertices. This graph will be connected since it contains a path from the start vertex v to every other vertex (and so there is a path between each two vertices). A simple proof by induction shows that every connected graph on n vertices with exactly $n-1$ edges is a tree. Hence t is a spanning tree of G. □

As in the case of BFT, the connected components of a graph can be obtained using DFT. Similarly, the reflexive transitive closure matrix of an undirected graph can be found using DFT. If DFS (Algorithm 6.7) is modified by adding $t := \emptyset$; and $t := t \cup \{(v, w)\}$; to line 7 and the **if** statement of line 10, respectively, then when DFS terminates, the edges in t define a spanning tree for the undirected graph G if G is connected. A spanning tree obtained in this manner is called a *depth first spanning tree.* For the graph of Figure 6.4(a) the spanning tree obtained will include all edges in G except for $(2,5)$, $(8,7)$, and $(1,3)$ (see Figure 6.5(a)). Hence, DFS and BFS are equally powerful for the search problems discussed so far.

EXERCISES

1. Show that for any undirected graph $G = (V, E)$, a call to BFS(v) with $v \in V$ results in visiting all the vertices in the connected component containing v.

2. Rewrite BFS and BFT so that all the connected components of the undirected graph G get printed out. Assume that G is input in adjacency list form.

3. Prove that if G is a connected undirected graph with n vertices and $n-1$ edges, then G is a tree.

4. Present a D-search-based algorithm that produces a spanning tree for an undirected connected graph.

5. (a) The *radius* of a tree is its depth. Show that the forward edges used in BFS(v) define a spanning tree with root v having minimum radius among all spanning trees, for the undirected connected graph G having root v.

   (b) Using the result of part (a), write an algorithm to find a minimum-radius spanning tree for G. What are the time and space requirements of your algorithm?

6. The *diameter* of a tree is the maximum distance between any two vertices. Let d be the diameter of a minimum-diameter spanning tree for

an undirected connected graph G. Let r be the radius of a minimum-radius spanning tree for G.

(a) Show that $2r - 1 \leq d \leq 2r$.

(b) Write an algorithm to find a minimum-diameter spanning tree for G. (*Hint*: Use breadth-first search followed by some local modification.)

(c) Prove that your algorithm is correct.

(d) What are the time and space requirements of your algorithm?

7. A *bipartite graph* $G = (V, E)$ is an undirected graph whose vertices can be partitioned into two disjoint sets V_1 and $V_2 = V - V_1$ with the properties that no two vertices in V_1 are adjacent in G and no two vertices in V_2 are adjacent in G. The graph G of Figure 6.4(a) is bipartite. A possible partitioning of V is $V_1 = \{1, 4, 5, 6, 7\}$ and $V_2 = \{2, 3, 8\}$. Write an algorithm to determine whether a graph G is bipartite. If G is bipartite, your algorithm should obtain a partitioning of the vertices into two disjoint sets V_1 and V_2 satisfying the properties above. Show that if G is represented by its adjacency lists, then this algorithm can be made to work in time $O(n + e)$, where $n = |V|$ and $e = |E|$.

8. Write an algorithm to find the reflexive transitive closure matrix A^* of a directed graph G. Show that if G has n vertices and e edges and is represented by its adjacency lists, then this can be done in time $\Theta(n^2 + ne)$. How much space does your algorithm take in addition to that needed for G and A^*? (*Hint*: Use either BFS or DFS.)

9. Input is an undirected connected graph $G(V, E)$ each one of whose edges has the same weight w (w being a real number). Give an $O(|E|)$ time algorithm to find a minimum-cost spanning tree for G. What is the weight of this tree?

10. Given are a directed graph $G(V, E)$ and a node $v \in V$. Write an efficient algorithm to decide whether there is a directed path from v to every other node in the graph. What is the worst-case run time of your algorithm?

11. Design an algorithm to decide whether a given undirected graph $G(V, E)$ contains a cycle of length 4. The running time of the algorithm should be $O(|V|^3)$.

12. Let $G(V, E)$ be a binary tree with n nodes. The *distance* between two vertices in G is the length of the path connecting these two vertices.

The problem is to construct an $n \times n$ matrix whose ijth entry is the distance between v_i and v_j. Design an $O(n^2)$ time algorithm to construct such a matrix. Assume that the tree is given in the adjacency-list representation.

13. Present an $O(|V|)$ time algorithm to check whether a given undirected graph $G(V, E)$ is a tree. The graph G is given in the form of an adjacency list.

6.4 BICONNECTED COMPONENTS AND DFS

In this section, by "graph" we always mean an undirected graph. A vertex v in a connected graph G is an *articulation point* if and only if the deletion of vertex v together with all edges incident to v disconnects the graph into two or more nonempty components.

Example 6.3 In the connected graph of Figure 6.6(a) vertex 2 is an articulation point as the deletion of vertex 2 and edges $(1,2), (2,3), (2,5), (2,7)$, and $(2,8)$ leaves behind two disconnected nonempty components (Figure 6.6(b)). Graph G of Figure 6.6(a) has only two other articulation points: vertex 5 and vertex 3. Note that if any of the remaining vertices is deleted from G, then exactly one component remains. □

A graph G is *biconnected* if and only if it contains no articulation points. The graph of Figure 6.6(a) is not biconnected. The graph of Figure 6.7 is biconnected. The presence of articulation points in a connected graph can be an undesirable feature in many cases. For example, if G represents a communication network with the vertices representing communication stations and the edges communication lines, then the failure of a communication station i that is an articulation point would result in the loss of communication to points other than i too. On the other hand, if G has no articulation point, then if any station i fails, we can still communicate between every two stations not including station i.

In this section we develop an efficient algorithm to test whether a connected graph is biconnected. For the case of graphs that are not biconnected, this algorithm will identify all the articulation points. Once it has been determined that a connected graph G is not biconnected, it may be desirable to determine a set of edges whose inclusion makes the graph biconnected. Determining such a set of edges is facilitated if we know the maximal subgraphs of G that are biconnected. $G' = (V', E')$ is a maximal biconnected subgraph of G if and only if G has no biconnected subgraph $G'' = (V'', E'')$ such that $V' \subseteq V''$ and $E' \subset E''$. A maximal biconnected subgraph is a *biconnected component*.

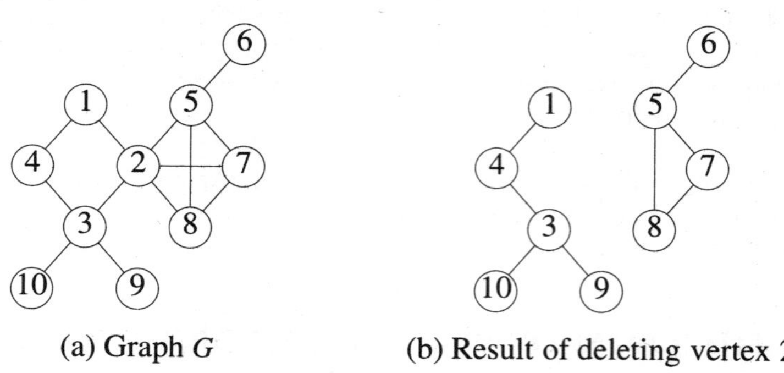

Figure 6.6 An example graph

The graph of Figure 6.7 has only one biconnected component (i.e., the entire graph). The biconnected components of the graph of Figure 6.6(a) are shown in Figure 6.8.

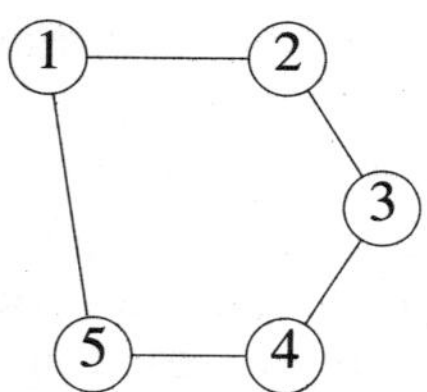

Figure 6.7 A biconnected graph

It is relatively easy to show that

Lemma 6.1 Two biconnected components can have at most one vertex in common and this vertex is an articulation point. □

Hence, no edge can be in two different biconnected components (as this would require two common vertices). The graph G can be transformed into a biconnected graph by using the edge addition scheme of Algorithm 6.8.

Since every biconnected component of a connected graph G contains at least two vertices (unless G itself has only one vertex), it follows that the v_i of line 5 exists.

Example 6.4 Using the above scheme to transform the graph of Figure 6.6(a) into a biconnected graph requires us to add edges $(4, 10)$ and $(10, 9)$ (corresponding to the articulation point 3), edge $(1, 5)$ (corresponding to the articulation point 2), and edge $(6, 7)$ (corresponding to point 5). □

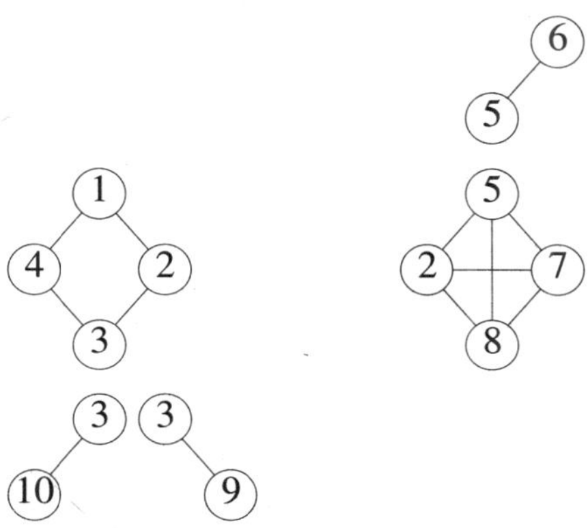

Figure 6.8 Biconnected components of graph of Figure 6.6(a)

Note that once the edges (v_i, v_{i+1}) of line 6 (Algorithm 6.8) are added, vertex a is no longer an articulation point. Hence following the addition of the edges corresponding to all articulation points, G has no articulation points and so is biconnected. If G has p articulation points and b biconnected components, then the scheme of Algorithm 6.8 introduces exactly $b - p$ new edges into G. One can show that this scheme may use more

```
1   for each articulation point a do
2   {
3       Let B_1, B_2, ..., B_k be the biconnected
4       components containing vertex a;
5       Let v_i, v_i ≠ a, be a vertex in B_i, 1 ≤ i ≤ k;
6       Add to G the edges (v_i, v_{i+1}), 1 ≤ i < k;
7   }
```

Algorithm 6.8 Scheme to construct a biconnected graph

than the minimum number of edges needed to make G biconnected (see the exercises).

Now, let us attack the problem of identifying the articulation points and biconnected components of a connected graph G with $n \geq 2$ vertices. The problem is efficiently solved by considering a depth first spanning tree of G.

Figure 6.9(a) and (b) shows a depth first spanning tree of the graph of Figure 6.6(a). In each figure there is a number outside each vertex. These numbers correspond to the order in which a depth first search visits these vertices and are referred to as the *depth first numbers (dfns)* of the vertex. Thus, $dfn[1] = 1$, $dfn[4] = 2$, $dfn[6] = 8$, and so on. In Figure 6.9(b) solid edges form the depth first spanning tree. These edges are called *tree edges*. Broken edges (i.e., all the remaining edges) are called *back edges*.

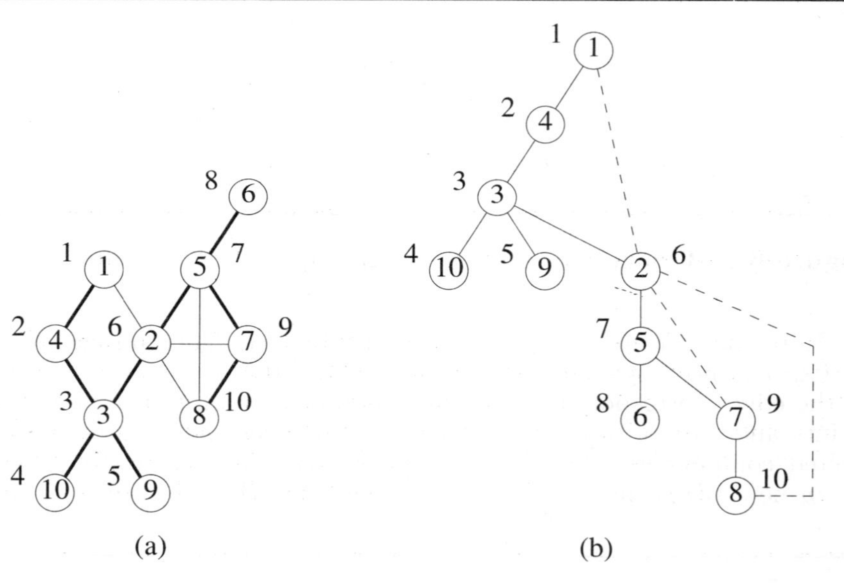

Figure 6.9 A depth first spanning tree of the graph of Figure 6.6(a)

Depth first spanning trees have a property that is very useful in identifying articulation points and biconnected components

Lemma 6.2 If (u, v) is any edge in G, then relative to the depth first spanning tree t, either u is an ancestor of v or v is an ancestor of u. So, there are no cross edges relative to a depth first spanning tree ((u, v) is a *cross* edge relative to t if and only if u is not an ancestor of v and v is not an ancestor of u).

Proof: To see this, assume that $(u, v) \in E(G)$ and (u, v) is a cross edge. Then (u, v) cannot be a tree edge as otherwise u is the parent of v or vice versa. So, (u, v) must be a back edge. Without loss of generality, we can assume $dfn[u] < dfn[v]$. Since vertex u is visited first, its exploration cannot be complete until vertex v is visited. From the definition of depth first search, it follows that u is an ancestor of all the vertices visited until u is completely explored. Hence u is an ancestor of v in t and (u, v) cannot be a cross edge. □

We make the following observation

Lemma 6.3 The root node of a depth first spanning tree is an articulation point iff it has at least two children. Furthermore, if u is any other vertex, then it is not an articulation point iff from every child w of u it is possible to reach an ancestor of u using only a path made up of descendents of w and a back edge. □

Note that if this cannot be done for some child w of u, then the deletion of vertex u leaves behind at least two nonempty components (one containing the root and the other containing vertex w). This observation leads to a simple rule to identify articulation points. For each vertex u, define $L[u]$ as follows:

$$L[u] = \min \{dfn[u],\ \min \{L[w] \mid w \text{ is a child of } u\},\ \min \{dfn[w] \mid (u, w) \text{ is a back edge}\}\}$$

It should be clear that $L[u]$ is the lowest depth first number that can be reached from u using a path of descendents followed by at most one back edge. From the preceding discussion it follows that if u is not the root, then u is an articulation point iff u has a child w such that $L[w] \geq dfn[u]$.

Example 6.5 For the spanning tree of Figure 6.9(b) the L values are $L[1 : 10] = \{1, 1, 1, 1, 6, 8, 6, 6, 5, 4\}$. Vertex 3 is an articulation point as child 10 has $L[10] = 4$ and $dfn[3] = 3$. Vertex 2 is an articulation point as child 5 has $L[5] = 6$ and $dfn[2] = 6$. The only other articulation point is vertex 5; child 6 has $L[6] = 8$ and $dfn[5] = 7$. □

$L[u]$ can be easily computed if the vertices of the depth first spanning tree are visited in postorder. Thus, to determine the articulation points, it is necessary to perform a depth first search of the graph G and visit the nodes in the resulting depth first spanning tree in postorder. It is possible to do both these functions in parallel. Pseudocode Art (Algorithm 6.9) carries out a depth first search of G. During this search each newly visited vertex gets assigned its depth first number. At the same time, $L[i]$ is computed for each vertex in the tree. This algorithm assumes that the connected graph G and the arrays dfn and L are global. In addition, it is assumed that the variable num is also global. It is clear from the algorithm that when vertex u has been explored and a return made from the function, then $L[u]$ has been correctly computed. Note that in the **else** clause of line 15, if $w \neq v$, then either (u, w) is a back edge or $dfn[w] > dfn[u] \geq L[u]$. In either case, $L[u]$ is correctly updated. The initial call to Art is Art(1, 0). Note dfn is initialized to zero before invoking Art.

```
1    Algorithm Art(u, v)
2    // u is a start vertex for depth first search. v is its parent if any
3    // in the depth first spanning tree. It is assumed that the global
4    // array dfn is initialized to zero and that the global variable
5    // num is initialized to 1. n is the number of vertices in G.
6    {
7        dfn[u] := num; L[u] := num; num := num + 1;
8        for each vertex w adjacent from u do
9        {
10           if (dfn[w] = 0) then
11           {
12               Art(w, u); // w is unvisited.
13               L[u] := min(L[u], L[w]);
14           }
15           else if (w ≠ v) then L[u] := min(L[u], dfn[w]);
16       }
17   }
```

Algorithm 6.9 Pseudocode to compute dfn and L

Once $L[1:n]$ has been computed, the articulation points can be identified in $O(e)$ time. Since Art has a complexity $O(n+e)$, where e is the number of edges in G, the articulation points of G can be determined in $O(n+e)$ time.

Now, what needs to be done to determine the biconnected components of G? If following the call to Art (line 12) $L[w] \geq dfn[u]$, then we know that u is either the root or an articulation point. Regardless of whether u is not the root or is the root and has one or more children, the edge (u, w) together with all edges (both tree and back) encountered during this call to Art (except for edges in other biconnected components contained in subtree w) forms a biconnected component. A formal proof of this statement appears in the proof of Theorem 6.5. The modified algorithm appears as Algorithm 6.10.

One can verify that the computing time of Algorithm 6.10 remains $O(n+e)$. The following theorem establishes the correctness of the algorithm. Note

```
Algorithm BiComp(u, v)
// u is a start vertex for depth first search. v is its parent if
// any in the depth first spanning tree. It is assumed that the
// global array dfn is initially zero and that the global variable
// num is initialized to 1. n is the number of vertices in G.
{
    dfn[u] := num; L[u] := num; num := num + 1;
    for each vertex w adjacent from u do
    {
        if ((v ≠ w) and (dfn[w] < dfn[u]))then
            add (u, w) to the top of a stack s;
        if (dfn[w] = 0) then
        {
            if (L[w] ≥ dfn[u]) then
            {
                write ("New bicomponent");
                repeat
                {
                    Delete an edge from the top of stack s;
                    Let this edge be (x, y);
                    write (x, y);
                } until (((x, y) = (u, w)) or ((x, y) = (w, u)));
            }
            BiComp(w, u); // w is unvisited.
            L[u] := min(L[u], L[w]);
        }
        else if (w ≠ v) then L[u] := min(L[u], dfn[w]);
    }
}
```

Algorithm 6.10 Pseudocode to determine bicomponents

that when G has only one vertex, it has no edges so the algorithm generates no output. In this case G does have a biconnected component, namely its single vertex. This case can be handled separately.

Theorem 6.5 Algorithm 6.10 correctly generates the biconnected components of the connected graph G when G has at least two vertices.

Proof: This can be shown by induction on the number of biconnected components in G. Clearly, for all biconnected graphs G, the root u of the depth first spanning tree has only one child w. Furthermore, w is the only vertex for which $L[w] \geq dfn[u]$ in line 11.1 of Algorithm 6.10. By the time w has been explored, all edges in G have been output as one biconnected component.

Now assume the algorithm works correctly for all connected graphs G with at most m biconnected components. We show that it also works correctly for all connected graphs with $m+1$ biconnected components. Let G be any such graph. Consider the first time that $L[w] \geq dfn[u]$ in line 11.1. At this time no edges have been output and so all edges in G incident to the descendents of w are on the stack and are above the edge (u, w). Since none of the descendents of u is an articulation point and u is, it follows that the set of edges above (u, w) on the stack forms a biconnected component together with the edge (u, w). Once these edges have been deleted from the stack and output, the algorithm behaves essentially as it would on the graph G', obtained by deleting from G the biconnected component just output. The behavior of the algorithm on G differs from that on G' only in that during the completion of the exploration of vertex u, some edges (u, r) such that (u, r) is in the component just output may be considered. However, for all such edges, $dfn[r] \neq 0$ and $dfn[r] > dfn[u] \geq L[u]$. Hence, these edges only result in a vacuous iteration of the **for** loop of line 8 and do not materially affect the algorithm.

One can easily establish that G' has at least two vertices. Since in addition G' has exactly m biconnected components, it follows from the induction hypothesis that the remaining components are correctly generated. □

It should be noted that the algorithm described above will work with any spanning tree relative to which the given graph has no cross edges. Unfortunately, graphs can have cross edges relative to breadth first spanning trees. Hence, algorithm Art cannot be adapted to BFS.

EXERCISES

1. For the graphs of Figure 6.10 identify the articulation points and draw the biconnected components.

2. Show that if G is a connected undirected graph, then no edge of G can be in two different biconnected components.

3. Let $G_i = (V_i, E_i), 1 \leq i \leq k$, be the biconnected components of a connected graph G. Show that

   (a) If $i \neq j$, then $V_i \cap V_j$ contains at most one vertex.

   (b) Vertex v is an articulation point of G iff $\{v\} = V_i \cap V_j$ for some i and j, $i \neq j$.

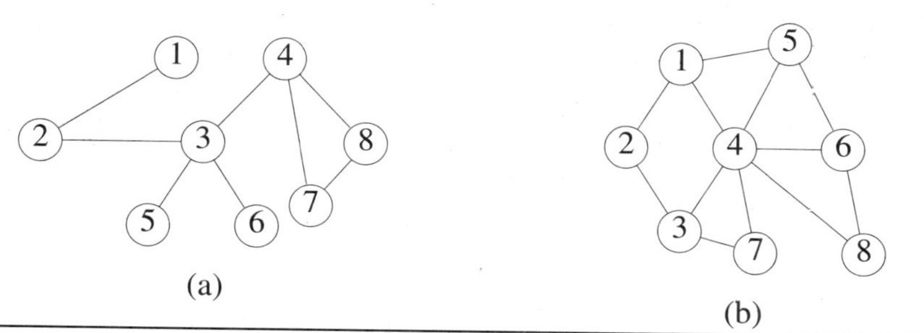

Figure 6.10 Graphs for Exercise 1

4. Show that the scheme of Algorithm 6.8 may use more than the minimum number of edges needed to make G biconnected.

5. Let G be a connected undirected graph. Write an algorithm to find the minimum number of edges that have to be added to G so that G becomes biconnected. Your algorithm should output such a set of edges. What are the time and space requirements of your algorithm?

6. Show that if t is a breadth first spanning tree for an undirected connected graph G, then G may have cross edges relative to t.

7. Prove that a nonroot vertex u is an articulation point iff $L[w] \geq dfn[u]$ for some child w of u.

8. Prove that in BiComp (Algorithm 6.10) if either $v = w$ or $dfn[w] > dfn[u]$, then edge (u, w) is either already on the stack of edges or has been output as part of a biconnected component.

9. Let $G(V, E)$ be any connected undirected graph. A *bridge* of G is defined to be an edge of G which when removed from G, will make it disconnected. Present an $O(|E|)$ time algorithm to find all the bridges of G.

10. Let $S(V, T)$ be any DFS tree for a given connected undirected graph $G(V, E)$. Prove that a leaf of S can not be an articulation point of G.

11. Prove or disprove: "An undirected graph $G(V, E)$ is biconnected if and only if for each pair of distinct vertices v and w in V there are two distinct paths from v to w that have no vertices in common except v and w."

6.5 REFERENCES AND READINGS

Several applications of depth first search to graph problems are given in "Depth first search and linear graph algorithms," by R. Tarjan, *SIAM Journal on Computing* 1, no. 2 (1972): 146–160.

The $O(n+e)$ depth first algorithm for biconnected components is due to R. Tarjan and appears in the preceding paper. This paper also contains an $O(n+e)$ algorithm to find the strongly connected components of a directed graph.

An $O(n+e)$ algorithm to find a smallest set of edges that, when added to a graph G, produces a biconnected graph has been given by A. Rosenthal and A. Goldner.

For an extensive coverage on graph algorithms see:

Data Structures and Network Algorithms, by R. E. Tarjan, Society for Industrial and Applied Mathematics, 1983.

Algorithmic Graph Theory, by A. Gibbons, Cambridge University Press, 1985.

Algorithmic Graph Theory and Perfect Graphs, by M. Golumbic, Academic Press, 1980.

Chapter 7

BACKTRACKING

7.1 THE GENERAL METHOD

In the search for fundamental principles of algorithm design, backtracking represents one of the most general techniques. Many problems which deal with searching for a set of solutions or which ask for an optimal solution satisfying some constraints can be solved using the backtracking formulation. The name backtrack was first coined by D. H. Lehmer in the 1950s. Early workers who studied the process were R. J. Walker, who gave an algorithmic account of it in 1960, and S. Golomb and L. Baumert who presented a very general description of it as well as a variety of applications.

In many applications of the backtrack method, the desired solution is expressible as an n-tuple $(x_1, \ldots, x_n)$, where the x_i are chosen from some finite set S_i. Often the problem to be solved calls for finding one vector that maximizes (or minimizes or satisfies) a *criterion function* $P(x_1, \ldots, x_n)$. Sometimes it seeks all vectors that satisfy P. For example, sorting the array of integers in $a[1:n]$ is a problem whose solution is expressible by an n-tuple, where x_i is the index in a of the ith smallest element. The criterion function P is the inequality $a[x_i] \leq a[x_{i+1}]$ for $1 \leq i < n$. The set S_i is finite and includes the integers 1 through n. Though sorting is not usually one of the problems solved by backtracking, it is one example of a familiar problem whose solution can be formulated as an n-tuple. In this chapter we study a collection of problems whose solutions are best done using backtracking.

Suppose m_i is the size of set S_i. Then there are $m = m_1 m_2 \cdots m_n$ n-tuples that are possible candidates for satisfying the function P. The *brute force approach* would be to form all these n-tuples, evaluate each one with P, and save those which yield the optimum. The backtrack algorithm has as its virtue the ability to yield the same answer with far fewer than m trials. Its basic idea is to build up the solution vector one component at a time and to use modified criterion functions $P_i(x_1, \ldots, x_i)$ (sometimes called bounding functions) to test whether the vector being formed has any chance of success. The major advantage of this method is this: if it is realized that the partial vector $(x_1, x_2, \ldots, x_i)$ can in no way lead to an optimal solution, then $m_{i+1} \cdots m_n$ possible test vectors can be ignored entirely.

Many of the problems we solve using backtracking require that all the solutions satisfy a complex set of constraints. For any problem these constraints can be divided into two categories: *explicit* and *implicit*.

Definition 7.1 Explicit constraints are rules that restrict each x_i to take on values only from a given set. □

Common examples of explicit constraints are

$$\begin{array}{rcrcl} x_i \geq 0 & \text{or} & S_i & = & \{\text{all nonnegative real numbers}\} \\ x_i = 0 \text{ or } 1 & \text{or} & S_i & = & \{0, 1\} \\ l_i \leq x_i \leq u_i & \text{or} & S_i & = & \{a : l_i \leq a \leq u_i\} \end{array}$$

The explicit constraints depend on the particular instance I of the problem being solved. All tuples that satisfy the explicit constraints define a possible *solution space* for I.

Definition 7.2 The implicit constraints are rules that determine which of the tuples in the solution space of I satisfy the criterion function. Thus implicit constraints describe the way in which the x_i must relate to each other. □

Example 7.1 [8-queens] A classic combinatorial problem is to place eight queens on an 8×8 chessboard so that no two "attack," that is, so that no two of them are on the same row, column, or diagonal. Let us number the rows and columns of the chessboard 1 through 8 (Figure 7.1). The queens can also be numbered 1 through 8. Since each queen must be on a different row, we can without loss of generality assume queen i is to be placed on row i. All solutions to the 8-queens problem can therefore be represented as 8-tuples $(x_1, \ldots, x_8)$, where x_i is the column on which queen i is placed. The explicit constraints using this formulation are $S_i = \{1, 2, 3, 4, 5, 6, 7, 8\}$, $1 \leq i \leq 8$. Therefore the solution space consists of 8^8 8-tuples. The implicit constraints for this problem are that no two x_i's can be the same (i.e., all queens must be on different columns) and no two queens can be on the same diagonal. The first of these two constraints implies that all solutions are permutations of the 8-tuple (1, 2, 3, 4, 5, 6, 7, 8). This realization reduces the size of the solution space from 8^8 tuples to 8! tuples. We see later how to formulate the second constraint in terms of the x_i. Expressed as an 8-tuple, the solution in Figure 7.1 is (4, 6, 8, 2, 7, 1, 3, 5). □

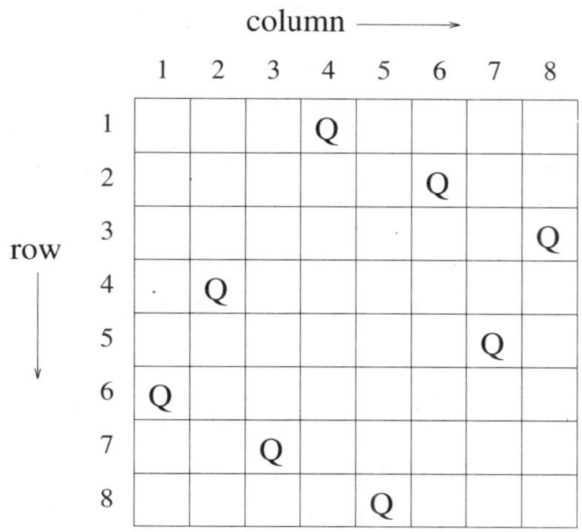

Figure 7.1 One solution to the 8-queens problem

Example 7.2 [Sum of subsets] Given positive numbers w_i, $1 \leq i \leq n$, and m, this problem calls for finding all subsets of the w_i whose sums are m. For example, if $n = 4$, $(w_1, w_2, w_3, w_4) = (11, 13, 24, 7)$, and $m = 31$, then the desired subsets are (11, 13, 7) and (24, 7). Rather than represent the solution vector by the w_i which sum to m, we could represent the solution vector by giving the indices of these w_i. Now the two solutions are described by the vectors (1, 2, 4) and (3, 4). In general, all solutions are k-tuples $(x_1, x_2, \ldots, x_k)$, $1 \leq k \leq n$, and different solutions may have different-sized tuples. The explicit constraints require $x_i \in \{j \mid j \text{ is an integer and } 1 \leq j \leq n\}$. The implicit constraints require that no two be the same and that the sum of the corresponding w_i's be m. Since we wish to avoid generating multiple instances of the same subset (e.g., (1, 2, 4) and (1, 4, 2) represent the same subset), another implicit constraint that is imposed is that $x_i < x_{i+1}$, $1 \leq i < k$.

In another formulation of the sum of subsets problem, each solution subset is represented by an n-tuple $(x_1, x_2, \ldots, x_n)$ such that $x_i \in \{0, 1\}$, $1 \leq i \leq n$. Then $x_i = 0$ if w_i is not chosen and $x_i = 1$ if w_i is chosen. The solutions to the above instance are (1, 1, 0, 1) and (0, 0, 1, 1). This formulation expresses all solutions using a fixed-sized tuple. Thus we conclude that there may be several ways to formulate a problem so that all solutions are tuples that satisfy some constraints. One can verify that for both of the above formulations, the solution space consists of 2^n distinct tuples. □

Backtracking algorithms determine problem solutions by systematically searching the solution space for the given problem instance. This search is facilitated by using a *tree organization* for the solution space. For a given solution space many tree organizations may be possible. The next two examples examine some of the ways to organize a solution into a tree.

Example 7.3 [n-queens] The n-queens problem is a generalization of the 8-queens problem of Example 7.1. Now n queens are to be placed on an $n \times n$ chessboard so that no two attack; that is, no two queens are on the same row, column, or diagonal. Generalizing our earlier discussion, the solution space consists of all $n!$ permutations of the n-tuple $(1, 2, \ldots, n)$. Figure 7.2 shows a possible tree organization for the case $n = 4$. A tree such as this is called a *permutation tree.* The edges are labeled by possible values of x_i. Edges from level 1 to level 2 nodes specify the values for x_1. Thus, the leftmost subtree contains all solutions with $x_1 = 1$; its leftmost subtree contains all solutions with $x_1 = 1$ and $x_2 = 2$, and so on. Edges from level i to level $i+1$ are labeled with the values of x_i. The solution space is defined by all paths from the root node to a leaf node. There are $4! = 24$ leaf nodes in the tree of Figure 7.2. □

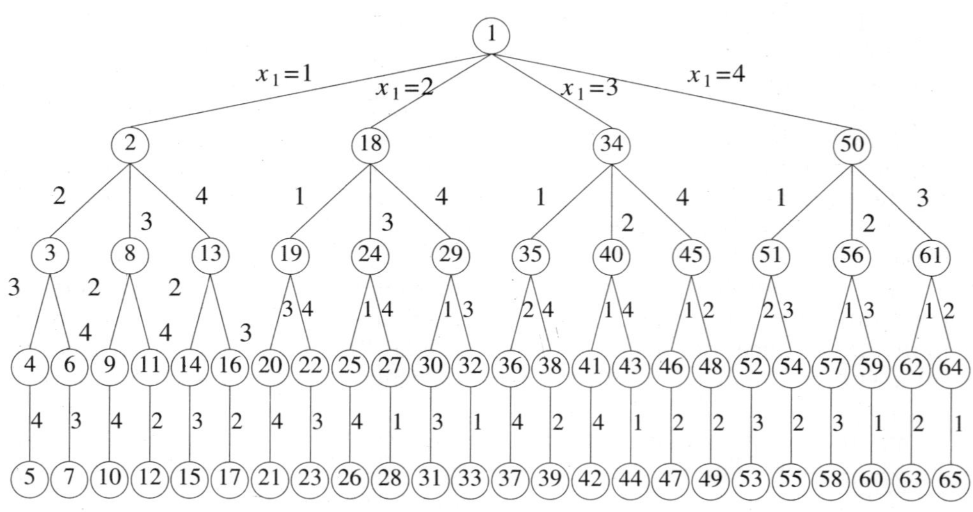

Figure 7.2 Tree organization of the 4-queens solution space. Nodes are numbered as in depth first search.

Example 7.4 [Sum of subsets] In Example 7.2 we gave two possible formulations of the solution space for the sum of subsets problem. Figures 7.3 and 7.4 show a possible tree organization for each of these formulations for the case $n = 4$. The tree of Figure 7.3 corresponds to the variable tuple size formulation. The edges are labeled such that an edge from a level i node to a level $i+1$ node represents a value for x_i. At each node, the solution space is partitioned into subsolution spaces. The solution space is defined by all paths from the root node to any node in the tree, since any such path corresponds to a subset satisfying the explicit constraints. The possible paths are () (this corresponds to the empty path from the root to itself), (1), (1, 2), (1, 2, 3), (1, 2, 3, 4), (1, 2, 4), (1, 3, 4), (2), (2, 3), and so on. Thus, the leftmost subtree defines all subsets containing w_1, the next subtree defines all subsets containing w_2 but not w_1, and so on.

The tree of Figure 7.4 corresponds to the fixed tuple size formulation. Edges from level i nodes to level $i + 1$ nodes are labeled with the value of x_i, which is either zero or one. All paths from the root to a leaf node define the solution space. The left subtree of the root defines all subsets containing w_1, the right subtree defines all subsets not containing w_1, and so on. Now there are 2^4 leaf nodes which represent 16 possible tuples. □

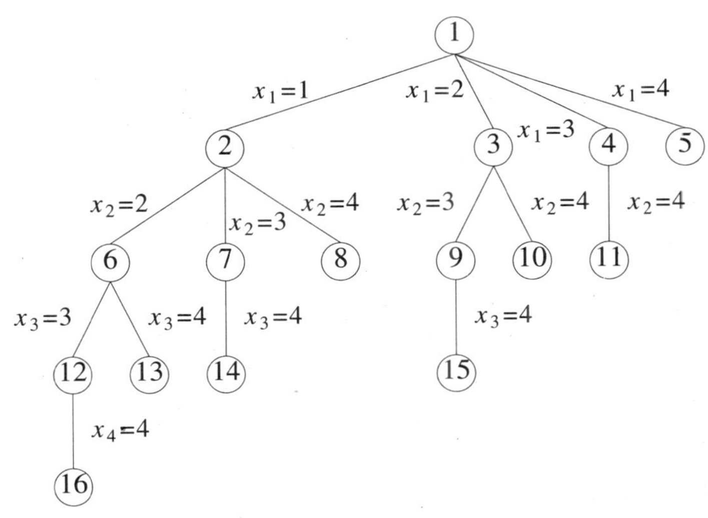

Figure 7.3 A possible solution space organization for the sum of subsets problem. Nodes are numbered as in breadth-first search.

At this point it is useful to develop some terminology regarding tree organizations of solution spaces. Each node in this tree defines a *problem state*. All paths from the root to other nodes define the *state space* of the problem. *Solution states* are those problem states s for which the path from the root to s defines a tuple in the solution space. In the tree of Figure 7.3 all nodes are solution states whereas in the tree of Figure 7.4 only leaf nodes are solution states. *Answer states* are those solution states s for which the path from the root to s defines a tuple that is a member of the set of solutions (i.e., it satisfies the implicit constraints) of the problem. The tree organization of the solution space is referred to as the *state space tree*.

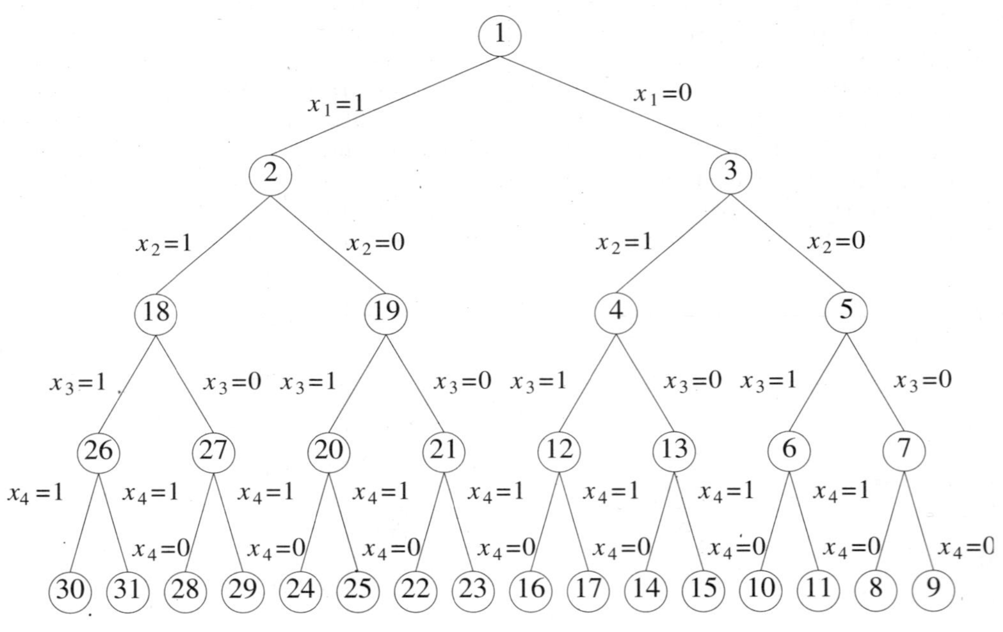

Figure 7.4 Another possible organization for the sum of subsets problems. Nodes are numbered as in D-search.

At each internal node in the space tree of Examples 7.3 and 7.4 the solution space is partitioned into disjoint sub-solution spaces. For example, at node 1 of Figure 7.2 the solution space is partitioned into four disjoint sets. Subtrees 2, 18, 34, and 50 respectively represent all elements of the solution space with $x_1 = 1$, 2, 3, and 4. At node 2 the sub-solution space with $x_1 = 1$ is further partitioned into three disjoint sets. Subtree 3 represents all solution space elements with $x_1 = 1$ and $x_2 = 2$. For all the state space trees we study in this chapter, the solution space is partitioned into disjoint sub-solution spaces at each internal node. It should be noted that this is not a requirement on a state space tree. The only requirement is that every element of the solution space be represented by at least one node in the state space tree.

The state space tree organizations described in Example 7.4 are called *static trees.* This terminology follows from the observation that the tree organizations are independent of the problem instance being solved. For some problems it is advantageous to use different tree organizations for different problem instances. In this case the tree organization is determined dynamically as the solution space is being searched. Tree organizations that are problem instance dependent are called *dynamic trees.* As an example, consider the fixed tuple size formulation for the sum of subsets problem (Example 7.4). Using a dynamic tree organization, one problem instance with $n = 4$ can be solved by means of the organization given in Figure 7.4. Another problem instance with $n = 4$ can be solved by means of a tree in which at level 1 the partitioning corresponds to $x_2 = 1$ and $x_2 = 0$. At level 2 the partitioning could correspond to $x_1 = 1$ and $x_1 = 0$, at level 3 it could correspond to $x_3 = 1$ and $x_3 = 0$, and so on. We see more of dynamic trees in Sections 7.6 and 8.3.

Once a state space tree has been conceived of for any problem, this problem can be solved by systematically generating the problem states, determining which of these are solution states, and finally determining which solution states are answer states. There are two fundamentally different ways to generate the problem states. Both of these begin with the root node and generate other nodes. A node which has been generated and all of whose children have not yet been generated is called a *live node*. The live node whose children are currently being generated is called the E-node (node being expanded). A *dead node* is a generated node which is not to be expanded further or all of whose children have been generated. In both methods of generating problem states, we have a list of live nodes. In the first of these two methods as soon as a new child C of the current E-node R is generated, this child will become the new E-node. Then R will become the E-node again when the subtree C has been fully explored. This corresponds to a depth first generation of the problem states. In the second state generation method, the E-node remains the E-node until it is dead. In both methods, *bounding functions* are used to kill live nodes without generating all their children. This is done carefully enough that at the conclusion of the process at least one answer node is always generated or all answer nodes are generated if the problem requires us to find all solutions. Depth first node generation with bounding functions is called *backtracking.* State generation methods in which the E-node remains the E-node until it is dead lead to *branch-and-bound* methods. The branch-and-bound technique is discussed in Chapter 8.

The nodes of Figure 7.2 have been numbered in the order they would be generated in a depth first generation process. The nodes in Figures 7.3 and 7.4 have been numbered according to two generation methods in which the E-node remains the E-node until it is dead. In Figure 7.3 each new node is placed into a queue. When all the children of the current E-node have been generated, the next node at the front of the queue becomes the new E-node. In Figure 7.4 new nodes are placed into a stack instead of a queue. Current terminology is not uniform in referring to these two alternatives. Typically the queue method is called breadth first generation and the stack method is called D-search (depth search).

Example 7.5 [4-queens] Let us see how backtracking works on the 4-queens problem of Example 7.3. As a bounding function, we use the obvious criteria that if $(x_1, x_2, \ldots, x_i)$ is the path to the current E-node, then all children nodes with parent-child labelings x_{i+1} are such that $(x_1, \ldots, x_{i+1})$ represents a chessboard configuration in which no two queens are attacking. We start with the root node as the only live node. This becomes the E-node and the path is (). We generate one child. Let us assume that the children are generated in ascending order. Thus, node number 2 of Figure 7.2 is generated and the path is now (1). This corresponds to placing queen 1 on column 1. Node 2 becomes the E-node. Node 3 is generated and immediately killed. The next node generated is node 8 and the path becomes (1, 3). Node 8 becomes the E-node. However, it gets killed as all its children represent board configurations that cannot lead to an answer node. We backtrack to node 2 and generate another child, node 13. The path is now (1, 4). Figure 7.5 shows the board configurations as backtracking proceeds. Figure 7.5 shows graphically the steps that the backtracking algorithm goes through as it tries to find a solution. The dots indicate placements of a queen which were tried and rejected because another queen was attacking. In Figure 7.5(b) the second queen is placed on columns 1 and 2 and finally settles on column 3. In Figure 7.5(c) the algorithm tries all four columns and is unable to place the next queen on a square. Backtracking now takes place. In Figure 7.5(d) the second queen is moved to the next possible column, column 4 and the third queen is placed on column 2. The boards in Figure 7.5 (e), (f), (g), and (h) show the remaining steps that the algorithm goes through until a solution is found.

Figure 7.6 shows the part of the tree of Figure 7.2 that is generated. Nodes are numbered in the order in which they are generated. A node that gets killed as a result of the bounding function has a B under it. Contrast this tree with Figure 7.2 which contains 31 nodes. □

With this example completed, we are now ready to present a precise formulation of the backtracking process. We continue to treat backtracking in a general way. We assume that all answer nodes are to be found and not just one. Let $(x_1, x_2, \ldots, x_i)$ be a path from the root to a node in a state space

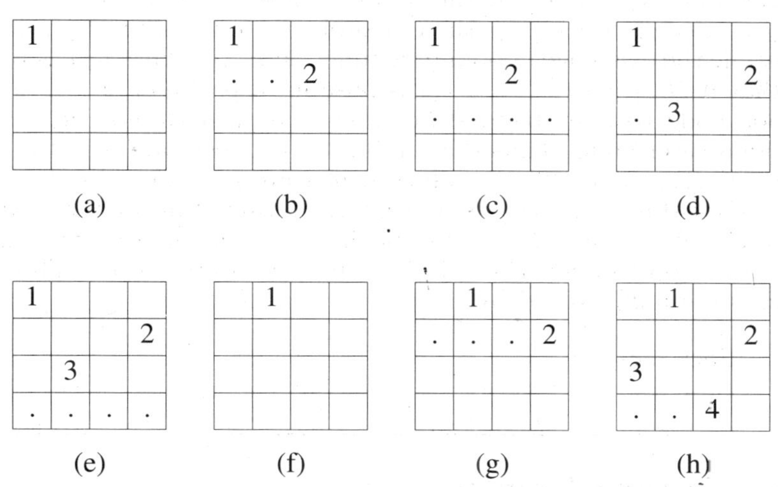

Figure 7.5 Example of a backtrack solution to the 4-queens problem

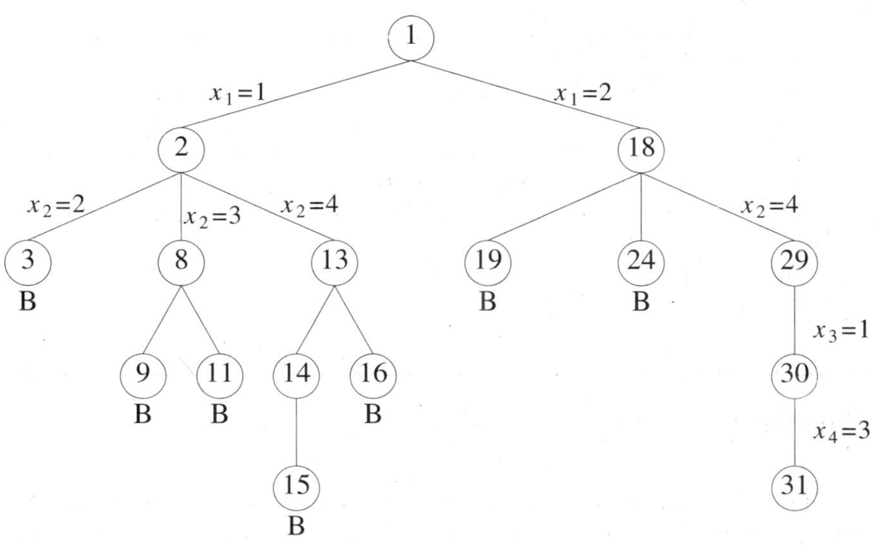

Figure 7.6 Portion of the tree of Figure 7.2 that is generated during backtracking

tree. Let $T(x_1, x_2, \ldots, x_i)$ be the set of all possible values for x_{i+1} such that $(x_1, x_2, \ldots, x_{i+1})$ is also a path to a problem state. $T(x_1, x_2, \ldots, x_n) = \emptyset$. We assume the existence of bounding function B_{i+1} (expressed as predicates) such that if $B_{i+1}(x_1, x_2, \ldots, x_{i+1})$ is false for a path $(x_1, x_2, \ldots, x_{i+1})$ from the root node to a problem state, then the path cannot be extended to reach an answer node. Thus the candidates for position $i+1$ of the solution vector $(x_1, \ldots, x_n)$ are those values which are generated by T and satisfy B_{i+1}. Algorithm 7.1 presents a recursive formulation of the backtracking technique. It is natural to describe backtracking in this way since it is essentially a postorder traversal of a tree (see Section 6.1). This recursive version is initially invoked by

```
Backtrack(1);
```

```
1   Algorithm Backtrack(k)
2   // This schema describes the backtracking process using
3   // recursion. On entering, the first k - 1 values
4   // x[1], x[2], ..., x[k - 1] of the solution vector
5   // x[1 : n] have been assigned. x[ ] and n are global.
6   {
7       for (each x[k] ∈ T(x[1], ..., x[k - 1]) do
8       {
9           if (B_k(x[1], x[2], ..., x[k]) ≠ 0) then
10          {
11              if (x[1], x[2], ..., x[k] is a path to an answer node)
12                  then write (x[1 : k]);
13              if (k < n) then Backtrack(k + 1);
14          }
15      }
16  }
```

Algorithm 7.1 Recursive backtracking algorithm

The solution vector $(x_1, \ldots, x_n)$, is treated as a global array $x[1:n]$. All the possible elements for the kth position of the tuple that satisfy B_k are generated, one by one, and adjoined to the current vector $(x_1, \ldots, x_{k-1})$. Each time x_k is attached, a check is made to determine whether a solution has been found. Then the algorithm is recursively invoked. When the **for** loop of line 7 is exited, no more values for x_k exist and the current copy of Backtrack ends. The last unresolved call now resumes, namely, the one that continues to examine the remaining elements assuming only $k - 2$ values have been set.

Note that this algorithm causes *all* solutions to be printed and assumes that tuples of various sizes may make up a solution. If only a single solution is desired, then a flag can be added as a parameter to indicate the first occurrence of success.

```
Algorithm IBacktrack(n)
// This schema describes the backtracking process.
// All solutions are generated in x[1 : n] and printed
// as soon as they are determined.
{
    k := 1;
    while (k ≠ 0) do
    {
        if (there remains an untried x[k] ∈ T(x[1], x[2], ...,
            x[k − 1]) and B_k(x[1], ..., x[k]) is true) then
        {
                if (x[1], ..., x[k] is a path to an answer node)
                    then write (x[1 : k]);
                k := k + 1; // Consider the next set.
        }
        else k := k − 1; // Backtrack to the previous set.
    }
}
```

Algorithm 7.2 General iterative backtracking method

An iterative version of Algorithm 7.1 appears in Algorithm 7.2. Note that $T()$ will yield the set of all possible values that can be placed as the first component x_1 of the solution vector. The component x_1 will take on those values for which the bounding function $B_1(x_1)$ is true. Also note how the elements are generated in a depth first manner. The variable k is continually incremented and a solution vector is grown until either a solution is found or no untried value of x_k remains. When k is decremented, the algorithm must resume the generation of possible elements for the kth position that have not yet been tried. Therefore one must develop a procedure that generates these values in some order. If only one solution is desired, replacing **write** $(x[1:k])$; with **{write** $(x[1:k])$; **return;}** suffices.

The efficiency of both the backtracking algorithms we've just seen depends very much on four factors: (1) the time to generate the next x_k, (2) the number of x_k satisfying the explicit constraints, (3) the time for the bounding functions B_k, and (4) the number of x_k satisfying the B_k. Bounding functions are regarded as good if they substantially reduce the number of nodes that are generated. However, there is usually a trade-off in that bounding functions that are good also take more time to evaluate. What is desired is a reduction in the overall computing time and not just a reduction in the number of nodes generated. For many problems, the size of the state space tree is too large to permit the generation of all nodes. Bounding functions must be used and hopefully at least one solution is found in a reasonable time span. Yet for many problems (e.g., n-queens) no sophisticated bounding methods are known.

One general principle of efficient searching is called *rearrangement.* For many problems the sets S_i can be taken in any order. This suggests that all other things being equal, it is more efficient to make the next choice from the set with the fewest elements. This strategy doesn't pay off for the n-queens problem, and examples can be constructed that prove this principle won't always work. The potential value of this heuristic is exhibited in Figure 7.7 by the two backtracking search trees for the same problem. If we are able to remove a node on level two of Figure 7.7(a), then we are effectively removing 12 possible 4-tuples from consideration. If we remove a node from level two of the tree in Figure 7.7(b), then only eight tuples are eliminated. More sophisticated rearrangement strategies are studied in conjunction with dynamic state space trees.

As stated previously, there are four factors that determine the time required by a backtracking algorithm. Once a state space tree organization is selected, the first three of these are relatively independent of the problem instance being solved. Only the fourth, the number of nodes generated, varies from one problem instance to another. A backtracking algorithm on one problem instance might generate only $O(n)$ nodes whereas on a different (and even closely related) instance it might generate almost all the nodes in the state space tree. If the number of nodes in the solution space is 2^n or $n!$, the worst-case time for a backtracking algorithm will generally be $O(p(n)\ 2^n)$ or $O(q(n)\ n!)$ respectively. The $p(n)$ and $q(n)$ are polynomials in n. The importance of backtracking lies in its ability to solve some instances with large n in a very small amount of time. The only difficulty is in predicting the behavior of a backtracking algorithm for the problem instance we wish to solve.

We can estimate the number of nodes that will be generated by a backtracking algorithm working on a certain instance by using Monte Carlo methods. The general idea in the estimation method is to generate a random path in the state space tree. Let X be a node on this random path. Assume that X is at level i of the state space tree. The bounding functions are used at node X to determine the number m_i of its children that do not get bounded. The next node on the path is obtained by randomly selecting one of these

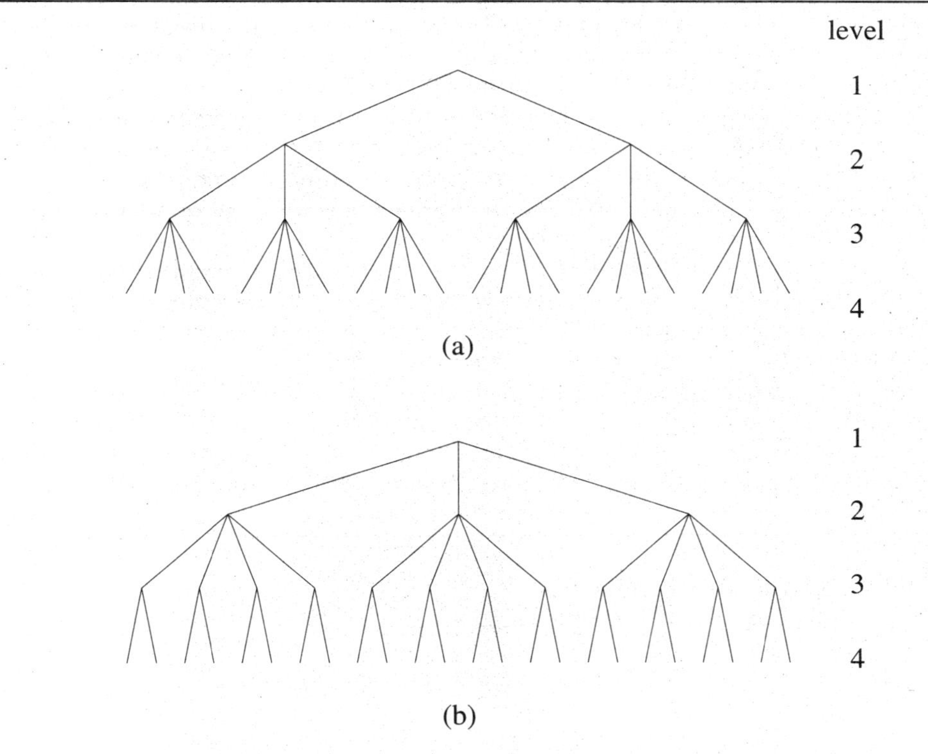

Figure 7.7 Rearrangement

m_i children that do not get bounded. The path generation terminates at a node which is a leaf or all of whose children get bounded. Using these m_i's. we can estimate the total number m of nodes in the state space tree that will not get bounded. This number is particularly useful when all answer nodes are to be searched for. In this case all unbounded nodes need to be generated. When only a single solution is desired, m may nct be such a good estimate for the number of nodes generated as the backtracking algorithm may arrive at a solution by generating only a small fraction of the m nodes. To estimate m from the m_i's, we need to make an assumption on the bounding functions. We shall assume that these functions are static; that is, the backtracking algorithm does not change its bounding functions as it gathers information during its execution. Moreover, exactly the same function is used for all nodes on the same level of the state space tree. This assumption is not true of most backtracking algorithms. In most cases the bounding functions get stronger as the search proceeds. In these cases our estimate for m is higher than one that could be obtained if the change in the bounding functions were taken into consideration.

Continuing with the assumption of static bounding functions, we see that the number of unbounded nodes on level 2 is m_1. If the search tree is such that nodes on the same level have the same degree, then we would expect each level 2 node to have on the average m_2 unbounded children. This yields a total of $m_1 m_2$ nodes on level 3. The expected number of unbounded nodes on level 4 is $m_1 m_2 m_3$. In general, the expected number of nodes on level $i+1$ is $m_1 m_2 \cdots m_i$. Hence, the estimated number m of unbounded nodes that will be generated in solving the given problem instance I is $m = 1 + m_1 + m_1 m_2 + m_1 m_2 m_3 + \cdots$.

Function Estimate (Algorithm 7.3) determines the value m. It selects a random path from the root of the state space tree. The function Size returns the size of the set T_k. The function Choose makes a random choice of an element in T_k. The desired sum is built using the variables m and r.

```
Algorithm Estimate()
// This algorithm follows a random path
// in a state space tree and produces an
// estimate of the number of nodes in the tree.
{
    k := 1; m := 1; r := 1;
    repeat
    {
        T_k := {x[k] | x[k] ∈ T(x[1], x[2], ..., x[k − 1])
                and B_k(x[1], ..., x[k]) is true};
        if (Size(T_k) = 0) then return m;
        r := r * Size(T_k); m := m + r;
        x[k] := Choose(T_k); k := k + 1;
    } until (false);
}
```

Algorithm 7.3 Estimating the efficiency of backtracking

We use this estimator in later sections (such as Section 7.2) as we examine backtracking solutions to various problems. A better estimate of the number of unbounded nodes that will be generated by a backtracking algorithm can be obtained by selecting several different random paths (typically no more than 20) and determining the average of these values.

EXERCISE

1. Change the two backtracking control abstractions, Algorithms 7.1 and 7.2, so that they find only a single solution rather than all solutions.

7.2 THE 8-QUEENS PROBLEM

Now we are ready to tackle the 8-queens problem via a backtracking solution. In fact we trivially generalize the problem and consider an $n \times n$ chessboard and try to find all ways to place n nonattacking queens. We observed from the 4-queens problem that we can let $(x_1, \ldots, x_n)$ represent a solution in which x_i is the column of the ith row where the ith queen is placed. The x_i's will all be distinct since no two queens can be placed in the same column. Now how do we test whether two queens are on the same diagonal?

If we imagine the chessboard squares being numbered as the indices of the two-dimensional array $a[1:n, 1:n]$, then we observe that every element on the same diagonal that runs from the upper left to the lower right has the same row−column value. For example, in Figure 7.1, consider the queen at $a[4,2]$. The squares that are diagonal to this queen (running from the upper left to the lower right) are $a[3,1]$, $a[5,3]$, $a[6,4]$, $a[7,5]$, and $a[8,6]$. All these squares have a row−column value of 2. Also, every element on the same diagonal that goes from the upper right to the lower left has the same row+column value. Suppose two queens are placed at positions (i,j) and (k,l). Then by the above they are on the same diagonal only if

$$i - j = k - l \quad \text{or} \quad i + j = k + l$$

The first equation implies

$$j - l = i - k$$

The second implies

$$j - l = k - i$$

Therefore two queens lie on the same diagonal if and only if $|j - l| = |i - k|$.

Place(k, i) (Algorithm 7.4) returns a boolean value that is **true** if the kth queen can be placed in column i. It tests both whether i is distinct from all previous values $x[1], \ldots, x[k-1]$ and whether there is no other queen on the same diagonal. Its computing time is $O(k-1)$.

Using Place, we can refine the general backtracking method as given by Algorithm 7.1 and give a precise solution to the n-queens problem (Algorithm 7.5). The array $x[\,]$ is global. The algorithm is invoked by NQueens$(1, n)$;.

```
Algorithm Place(k, i)
// Returns true if a queen can be placed in kth row and
// ith column. Otherwise it returns false. x[ ] is a
// global array whose first (k − 1) values have been set.
// Abs(r) returns the absolute value of r.
{
    for j := 1 to k − 1 do
        if ((x[j] = i) // Two in the same column
             or (Abs(x[j] − i) = Abs(j − k)))
                // or in the same diagonal
            then return false;
    return true;
}
```

Algorithm 7.4 Can a new queen be placed?

```
Algorithm NQueens(k, n)
// Using backtracking, this procedure prints all
// possible placements of n queens on an n × n
// chessboard so that they are nonattacking.
{
    for i := 1 to n do
    {
        if Place(k, i) then
        {
            x[k] := i;
            if (k = n) then write (x[1 : n]);
            else NQueens(k + 1, n);
        }
    }
}
```

Algorithm 7.5 All solutions to the n-queens problem

At this point we might wonder how effective function NQueens is over the brute force approach. For an 8×8 chessboard there are $\binom{64}{8}$ possible ways to place 8 pieces, or approximately 4.4 billion 8-tuples to examine. However, by allowing only placements of queens on distinct rows and columns, we require the examination of at most 8!, or only 40,320 8-tuples.

We can use Estimate to estimate the number of nodes that will be generated by NQueens. Note that the assumptions that are needed for Estimate do hold for NQueens. The bounding function is static. No change is made to the function as the search proceeds. In addition, all nodes on the same level of the state space tree have the same degree. In Figure 7.8 we see five 8×8 chessboards that were created using Estimate.

As required, the placement of each queen on the chessboard was chosen randomly. With each choice we kept track of the number of columns a queen could legitimately be placed on. These numbers are listed in the vector beneath each chessboard. The number following the vector represents the value that function Estimate would produce from these sizes. The average of these five trials is 1625. The total number of nodes in the 8-queens state space tree is

$$1 + \sum_{j=0}^{7} \left[\Pi_{i=0}^{j} (8 - i) \right] = 69,281$$

So the estimated number of unbounded nodes is only about 2.34% of the total number of nodes in the 8-queens state space tree. (See the exercises for more ideas about the efficiency of NQueens.)

EXERCISES

1. Algorithm NQueens can be made more efficient by redefining the function Place(k, i) so that it either returns the next legitimate column on which to place the kth queen or an illegal value. Rewrite both functions (Algorithms 7.4 and 7.5) so they implement this alternate strategy.

2. For the n-queens problem we observe that some solutions are simply reflections or rotations of others. For example, when $n = 4$, the two solutions given in Figure 7.9 are equivalent under reflection.

   Observe that for finding inequivalent solutions the algorithm need only set $x[1] = 2, 3, \ldots, \lceil n/2 \rceil$.

   (a) Modify NQueens so that only inequivalent solutions are computed.

   (b) Run the n-queens program devised above for $n = 8$, 9, and 10. Tabulate the number of solutions your program finds for each value of n.

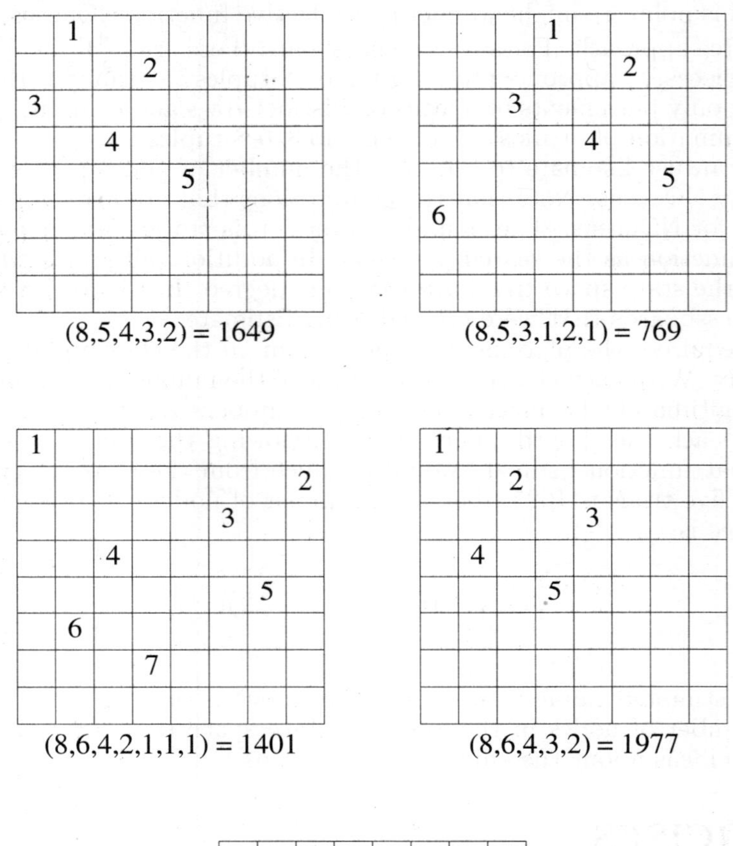

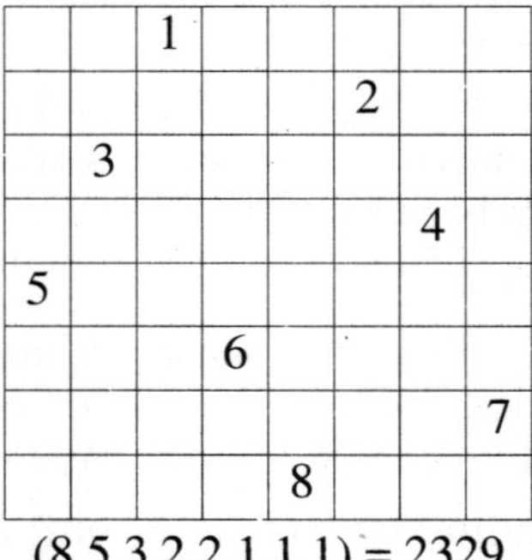

Figure 7.8 Five walks through the 8-queens problem plus estimates of the tree size

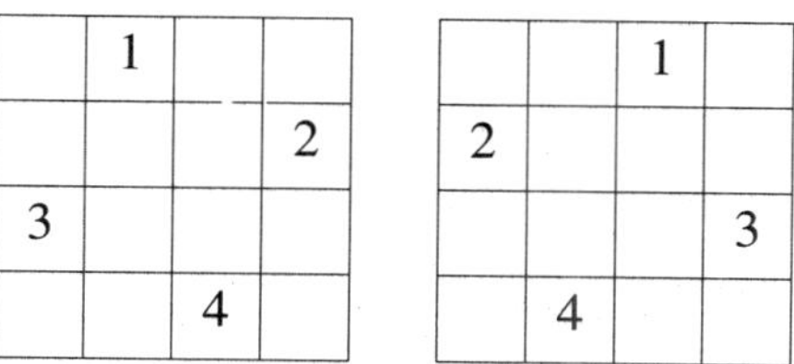

Figure 7.9 Equivalent solutions to the 4-queens problem

3. Given an $n \times n$ chessboard, a knight is placed on an arbitrary square with coordinates (x, y). The problem is to determine $n^2 - 1$ knight moves such that every square of the board is visited once if such a sequence of moves exists. Present an algorithm to solve this problem.

7.3 SUM OF SUBSETS

Suppose we are given n distinct positive numbers (usually called weights) and we desire to find all combinations of these numbers whose sums are m. This is called the *sum of subsets* problem. Examples 7.2 and 7.4 showed how we could formulate this problem using either fixed- or variable-sized tuples. We consider a backtracking solution using the fixed tuple size strategy. In this case the element x_i of the solution vector is either one or zero depending on whether the weight w_i is included or not.

The children of any node in Figure 7.4 are easily generated. For a node at level i the left child corresponds to $x_i = 1$ and the right to $x_i = 0$.

A simple choice for the bounding functions is $B_k(x_1, \ldots, x_k) =$ true iff

$$\sum_{i=1}^{k} w_i x_i + \sum_{i=k+1}^{n} w_i \geq m$$

Clearly $x_1, \ldots, x_k$ cannot lead to an answer node if this condition is not satisfied. The bounding functions can be strengthened if we assume the w_i's are initially in nondecreasing order. In this case $x_1, \ldots, x_k$ cannot lead to an answer node if

$$\sum_{i=1}^{k} w_i x_i + w_{k+1} > m$$

The bounding functions we use are therefore

$$B_k(x_1, \ldots, x_k) = \mathit{true} \text{ iff } \sum_{i=1}^{k} w_i x_i + \sum_{i=k+1}^{n} w_i \geq m$$

$$\text{and } \sum_{i=1}^{k} w_i x_i + w_{k+1} \leq m \tag{7.1}$$

Since our algorithm will not make use of B_n, we need not be concerned by the appearance of w_{n+1} in this function. Although we have now specified all that is needed to directly use either of the backtracking schemas, a simpler algorithm results if we tailor either of these schemas to the problem at hand. This simplification results from the realization that if $x_k = 1$, then

$$\sum_{i=1}^{k} w_i x_i + \sum_{i=k+1}^{n} w_i > m$$

For simplicity we refine the recursive schema. The resulting algorithm is SumOfSub (Algorithm 7.6).

Algorithm SumOfSub avoids computing $\sum_{i=1}^{k} w_i x_i$ and $\sum_{i=k+1}^{n} w_i$ each time by keeping these values in variables s and r respectively. *The algorithm assumes* $w_1 \leq m$ *and* $\sum_{i=1}^{n} w_i \geq m$. The initial call is SumOfSub$(0, 1, \sum_{i=1}^{n} w_i)$. It is interesting to note that the algorithm does not explicitly use the test $k > n$ to terminate the recursion. This test is not needed as on entry to the algorithm, $s \neq m$ and $s + r \geq m$. Hence, $r \neq 0$ and so k can be no greater than n. Also note that in the **else if** statement (line 11), since $s + w_k < m$ and $s + r \geq m$, it follows that $r \neq w_k$ and hence $k + 1 \leq n$. Observe also that if $s + w_k = m$ (line 9), then $x_{k+1}, \ldots, x_n$ must be zero. These zeros are omitted from the output of line 9. In line 11 we do not test for $\sum_{i=1}^{k} w_i x_i + \sum_{i=k+1}^{n} w_i \geq m$, as we already know $s + r \geq m$ and $x_k = 1$.

Example 7.6 Figure 7.10 shows the portion of the state space tree generated by function SumOfSub while working on the instance $n = 6$, $m = 30$, and $w[1:6] = \{5, 10, 12, 13, 15, 18\}$. The rectangular nodes list the values of s, k, and r on each of the calls to SumOfSub. Circular nodes represent points at which subsets with sums m are printed out. At nodes A, B, and C the output is respectively (1, 1, 0, 0, 1), (1, 0, 1, 1), and (0, 0, 1, 0, 0, 1). Note that the tree of Figure 7.10 contains only 23 rectangular nodes. The full state space tree for $n = 6$ contains $2^6 - 1 = 63$ nodes from which calls could be made (this count excludes the 64 leaf nodes as no call need be made from a leaf). □

```
Algorithm SumOfSub(s, k, r)
// Find all subsets of w[1 : n] that sum to m. The values of x[j],
// 1 ≤ j < k, have already been determined. s = Σ_{j=1}^{k-1} w[j] * x[j]
// and r = Σ_{j=k}^{n} w[j]. The w[j]'s are in nondecreasing order.
// It is assumed that w[1] ≤ m and Σ_{i=1}^{n} w[i] ≥ m.
{
    // Generate left child. Note: s + w[k] ≤ m since B_{k-1} is true.
    x[k] := 1;
    if (s + w[k] = m) then write (x[1 : k]); // Subset found
        // There is no recursive call here as w[j] > 0, 1 ≤ j ≤ n.
    else if (s + w[k] + w[k + 1] ≤ m)
            then SumOfSub(s + w[k], k + 1, r − w[k]);
    // Generate right child and evaluate B_k.
    if ((s + r − w[k] ≥ m) and (s + w[k + 1] ≤ m)) then
    {
        x[k] := 0;
        SumOfSub(s, k + 1, r − w[k]);
    }
}
```

Algorithm 7.6 Recursive backtracking algorithm for sum of subsets problem

EXERCISES

1. Prove that the size of the set of all subsets of n elements is 2^n.

2. Let $w = \{5, 7, 10, 12, 15, 18, 20\}$ and $m = 35$. Find all possible subsets of w that sum to m. Do this using SumOfSub. Draw the portion of the state space tree that is generated.

3. With $m = 35$, run SumOfSub on the data (a) $w = \{5, 7, 10, 12, 15, 18, 20\}$, (b) $w = \{20, 18, 15, 12, 10, 7, 5\}$, and (c) $w = \{15, 7, 20, 5, 18, 10, 12\}$. Are there any discernible differences in the computing times?

4. Write a backtracking algorithm for the sum of subsets problem using the state space tree corresponding to the variable tuple size formulation.

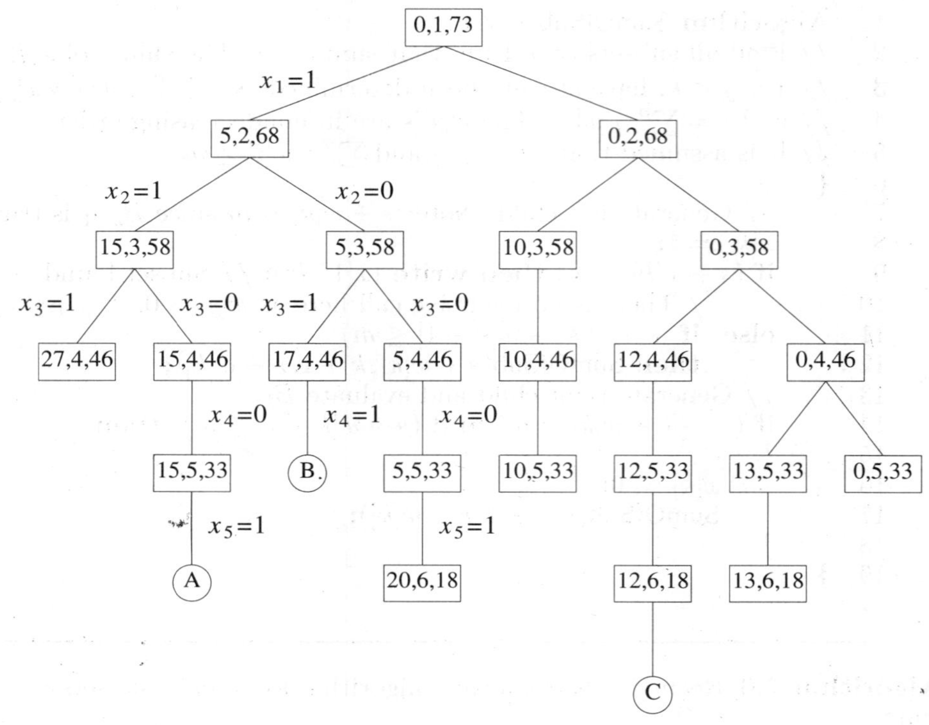

Figure 7.10 Portion of state space tree generated by SumOfSub

7.4 GRAPH COLORING

Let G be a graph and m be a given positive integer. We want to discover whether the nodes of G can be colored in such a way that no two adjacent nodes have the same color yet only m colors are used. This is termed the *m-colorability decision* problem and it is discussed again in Chapter 11. Note that if d is the degree of the given graph, then it can be colored with $d+1$ colors. The *m-colorability optimization* problem asks for the smallest integer m for which the graph G can be colored. This integer is referred to as the *chromatic number* of the graph. For example, the graph of Figure 7.11 can be colored with three colors $1, 2,$ and 3. The color of each node is indicated next to it. It can also be seen that three colors are needed to color this graph and hence this graph's chromatic number is 3.

A graph is said to be *planar* iff it can be drawn in a plane in such a

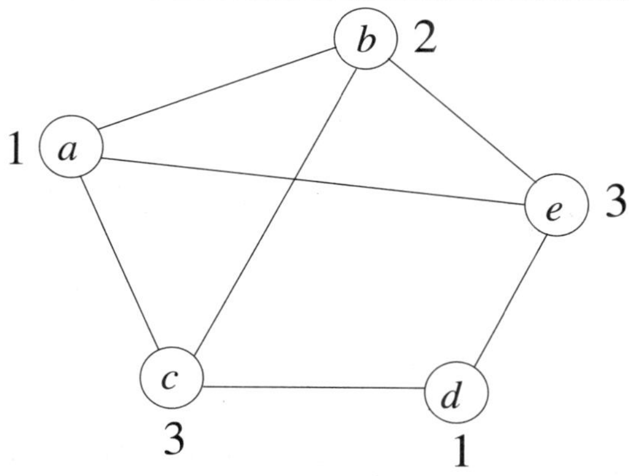

Figure 7.11 An example graph and its coloring

way that no two edges cross each other. A famous special case of the m-colorability decision problem is the 4-color problem for planar graphs. This problem asks the following question: given any map, can the regions be colored in such a way that no two adjacent regions have the same color yet only four colors are needed? This turns out to be a problem for which graphs are very useful, because a map can easily be transformed into a graph. Each region of the map becomes a node, and if two regions are adjacent, then the corresponding nodes are joined by an edge. Figure 7.12 shows a map with five regions and its corresponding graph. This map requires four colors. For many years it was known that five colors were sufficient to color any map, but no map that required more than four colors had ever been found. After several hundred years, this problem was solved by a group of mathematicians with the help of a computer. They showed that in fact four colors are sufficient. In this section we consider not only graphs that are produced from maps but all graphs. We are interested in determining all the different ways in which a given graph can be colored using at most m colors.

Suppose we represent a graph by its adjacency matrix $G[1 : n, 1 : n]$, where $G[i, j] = 1$ if (i, j) is an edge of G, and $G[i, j] = 0$ otherwise. The colors are represented by the integers $1, 2, \ldots, m$ and the solutions are given by the n-tuple $(x_1, \ldots, x_n)$, where x_i is the color of node i. Using the recursive backtracking formulation as given in Algorithm 7.1, the resulting algorithm is mColoring (Algorithm 7.7). The underlying state space tree used is a tree of degree m and height $n + 1$. Each node at level i has m children corresponding to the m possible assignments to x_i, $1 \leq i \leq n$. Nodes at level $n + 1$ are leaf nodes. Figure 7.13 shows the state space tree when $n =$

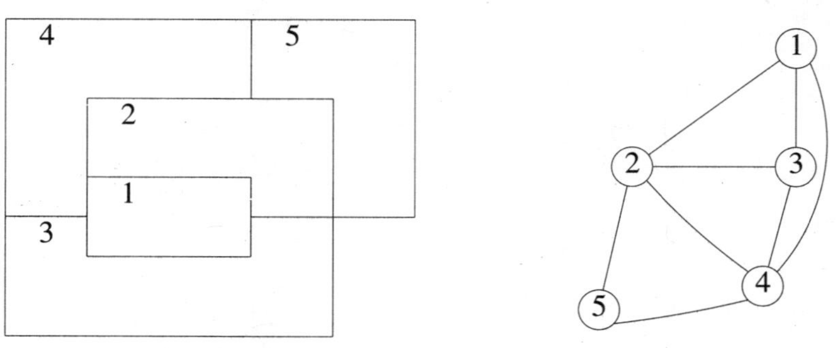

Figure 7.12 A map and its planar graph representation

3 and $m = 3$.

Function mColoring is begun by first assigning the graph to its adjacency matrix, *setting the array* $x[\,]$ *to zero*, and then invoking the statement mColoring(1);.

Notice the similarity between this algorithm and the general form of the recursive backtracking schema of Algorithm 7.1. Function NextValue (Algorithm 7.8) produces the possible colors for x_k after x_1 through x_{k-1} have been defined. The main loop of mColoring repeatedly picks an element from the set of possibilities, assigns it to x_k, and then calls mColoring recursively. For instance, Figure 7.14 shows a simple graph containing four nodes. Below that is the tree that is generated by mColoring. Each path to a leaf represents a coloring using at most three colors. Note that only 12 solutions exist with *exactly* three colors. In this tree, after choosing $x_1 = 2$ and $x_2 = 1$, the possible choices for x_3 are 2 and 3. After choosing $x_1 = 2$, $x_2 = 1$, and $x_3 = 2$, possible values for x_4 are 1 and 3. And so on.

An upper bound on the computing time of mColoring can be arrived at by noticing that the number of internal nodes in the state space tree is $\sum_{i=0}^{n-1} m^i$. At each internal node, $O(mn)$ time is spent by NextValue to determine the children corresponding to legal colorings. Hence the total time is bounded by $\sum_{i=0}^{n-1} m^{i+1}n = \sum_{i=1}^{n} m^i n = n(m^{n+1} - 2)/(m - 1) = O(nm^n)$.

EXERCISE

1. Program and run mColoring (Algorithm 7.7) using as data the complete graphs of size n = 2, 3, 4, 5, 6, and 7. Let the desired number of colors be $k = n$ and $k = n/2$. Tabulate the computing times for each value

```
Algorithm mColoring(k)
// This algorithm was formed using the recursive backtracking
// schema. The graph is represented by its boolean adjacency
// matrix G[1 : n, 1 : n]. All assignments of 1, 2, ..., m to the
// vertices of the graph such that adjacent vertices are
// assigned distinct integers are printed. k is the index
// of the next vertex to color.
{
    repeat
    {// Generate all legal assignments for x[k].
        NextValue(k); // Assign to x[k] a legal color.
        if (x[k] = 0) then return; // No new color possible
        if (k = n) then      // At most m colors have been
                             // used to color the n vertices.
            write (x[1 : n]);
        else mColoring(k + 1);
    } until (false);
}
```

Algorithm 7.7 Finding all m-colorings of a graph

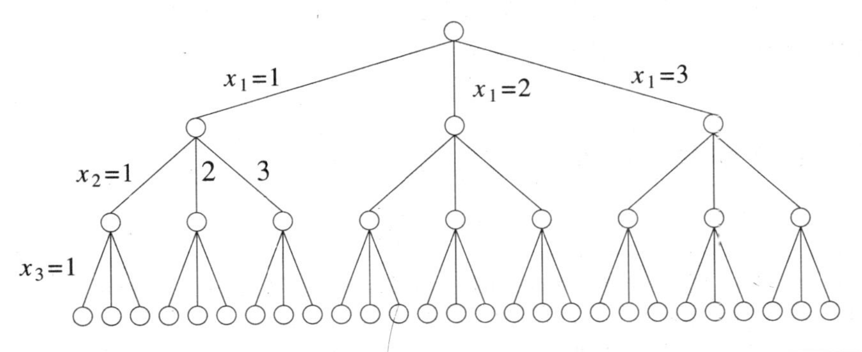

Figure 7.13 State space tree for mColoring when n =3 and m = 3

of n and k.

```
Algorithm NextValue(k)
// x[1],...,x[k-1] have been assigned integer values in
// the range [1,m] such that adjacent vertices have distinct
// integers. A value for x[k] is determined in the range
// [0,m]. x[k] is assigned the next highest numbered color
// while maintaining distinctness from the adjacent vertices
// of vertex k. If no such color exists, then x[k] is 0.
{
    repeat
    {
        x[k] := (x[k] + 1) mod (m + 1); // Next highest color.
        if (x[k] = 0) then return; // All colors have been used.
        for j := 1 to n do
        {   // Check if this color is
            // distinct from adjacent colors.
            if ((G[k,j] ≠ 0) and (x[k] = x[j]))
            // If (k,j) is and edge and if adj.
            // vertices have the same color.
                then break;
        }
        if (j = n + 1) then return; // New color found
    } until (false); // Otherwise try to find another color.
}
```

Algorithm 7.8 Generating a next color

7.5 HAMILTONIAN CYCLES

Let $G = (V, E)$ be a connected graph with n vertices. A Hamiltonian cycle (suggested by Sir William Hamilton) is a round-trip path along n edges of G that visits every vertex once and returns to its starting position. In other words if a Hamiltonian cycle begins at some vertex $v_1 \in G$ and the vertices of G are visited in the order $v_1, v_2, \ldots, v_{n+1}$, then the edges (v_i, v_{i+1}) are in E, $1 \leq i \leq n$, and the v_i are distinct except for v_1 and v_{n+1}, which are equal.

The graph $G1$ of Figure 7.15 contains the Hamiltonian cycle 1, 2, 8, 7, 6, 5, 4, 3, 1. The graph $G2$ of Figure 7.15 contains no Hamiltonian cycle. There is no known easy way to determine whether a given graph contains a Hamiltonian cycle. We now look at a backtracking algorithm that finds all the Hamiltonian cycles in a graph. The graph may be directed or undirected. Only distinct cycles are output.

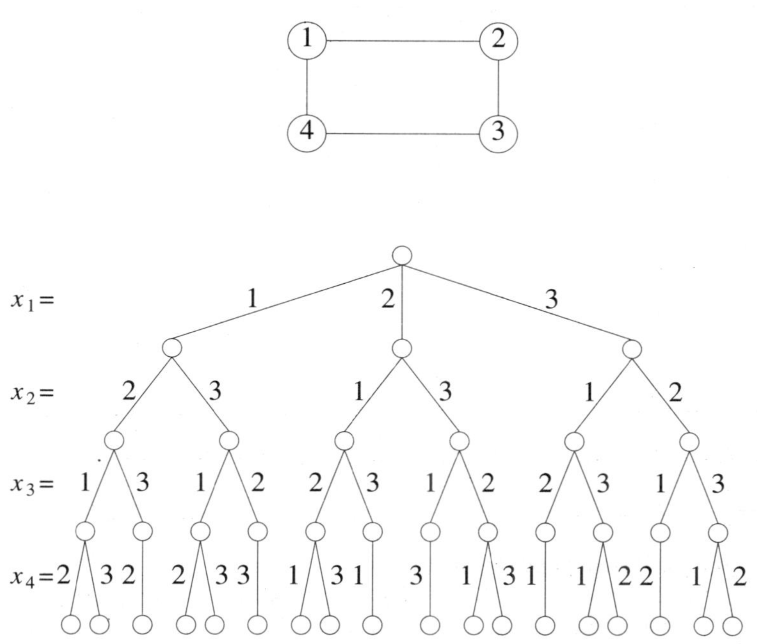

Figure 7.14 A 4-node graph and all possible 3-colorings

The backtracking solution vector $(x_1, \ldots, x_n)$ is defined so that x_i represents the ith visited vertex of the proposed cycle. Now all we need do is determine how to compute the set of possible vertices for x_k if $x_1, \ldots, x_{k-1}$ have already been chosen. If $k = 1$, then x_1 can be any of the n vertices. To avoid printing the same cycle n times, we require that $x_1 = 1$. If $1 < k < n$, then x_k can be any vertex v that is distinct from $x_1, x_2, \ldots, x_{k-1}$ and v is connected by an edge to x_{k-1}. The vertex x_n can only be the one remaining vertex and it must be connected to both x_{n-1} and x_1. We begin by presenting function NextValue(k) (Algorithm 7.9), which determines a possible next vertex for the proposed cycle.

Using NextValue we can particularize the recursive backtracking schema to find all Hamiltonian cycles (Algorithm 7.10). This algorithm is started by first initializing the adjacency matrix $G[1:n, 1:n]$, then setting $x[2:n]$ to zero and $x[1]$ to 1, and then executing Hamiltonian(2).

Recall from Section 5.9 the traveling salesperson problem which asked for a tour that has minimum cost. This tour is a Hamiltonian cycle. For the simple case of a graph all of whose edge costs are identical, Hamiltonian will

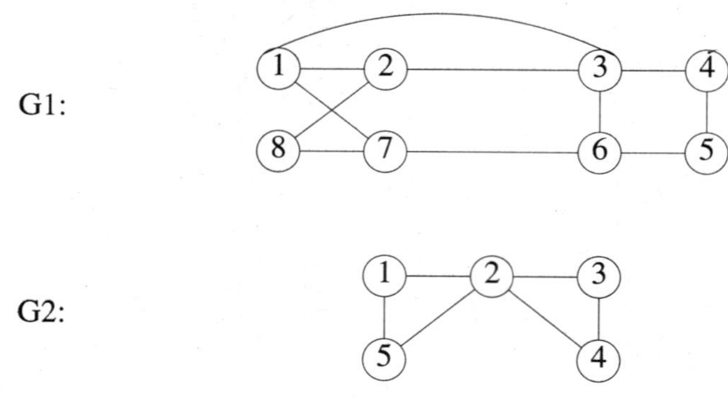

Figure 7.15 Two graphs, one containing a Hamiltonian cycle

```
Algorithm NextValue(k)
// x[1 : k − 1] is a path of k − 1 distinct vertices. If x[k] = 0, then
// no vertex has as yet been assigned to x[k]. After execution,
// x[k] is assigned to the next highest numbered vertex which
// does not already appear in x[1 : k − 1] and is connected by
// an edge to x[k − 1]. Otherwise x[k] = 0. If k = n, then
// in addition x[k] is connected to x[1].
{
    repeat
    {
        x[k] := (x[k] + 1) mod (n + 1); // Next vertex.
        if (x[k] = 0) then return;
        if (G[x[k − 1], x[k]] ≠ 0) then
        { // Is there an edge?
            for j := 1 to k − 1 do if (x[j] = x[k]) then break;
                        // Check for distinctness.
            if (j = k) then // If true, then the vertex is distinct.
                if ((k < n) or ((k = n) and G[x[n], x[1]] ≠ 0))
                    then return;
        }
    } until (false);
}
```

Algorithm 7.9 Generating a next vertex

```
Algorithm Hamiltonian(k)
// This algorithm uses the recursive formulation of
// backtracking to find all the Hamiltonian cycles
// of a graph. The graph is stored as an adjacency
// matrix G[1 : n, 1 : n]. All cycles begin at node 1.
{
    repeat
    { // Generate values for x[k].
        NextValue(k); // Assign a legal next value to x[k].
        if (x[k] = 0) then return;
        if (k = n) then write (x[1 : n]);
        else Hamiltonian(k + 1);
    } until (false);
}
```

Algorithm 7.10 Finding all Hamiltonian cycles

find a minimum-cost tour if a tour exists. If the common edge cost is c, the cost of a tour is cn since there are n edges in a Hamiltonian cycle.

EXERCISES

1. Determine the order of magnitude of the worst-case computing time for the backtracking procedure that finds all Hamiltonian cycles.

2. Draw the portion of the state space tree generated by Algorithm 7.10 for the graph $G1$ of Figure 7.15.

3. Generalize Hamiltonian so that it processes a graph whose edges have costs associated with them and finds a Hamiltonian cycle with minimum cost. You can assume that all edge costs are positive.

7.6 KNAPSACK PROBLEM

In this section we reconsider a problem that was defined and solved by a dynamic programming algorithm in Chapter 5, the 0/1 knapsack optimization problem. Given n positive weights w_i, n positive profits p_i, and a positive number m that is the knapsack capacity, this problem calls for choosing a subset of the weights such that

$$\sum_{1\le i\le n} w_i x_i \le m \text{ and } \sum_{1\le i\le n} p_i x_i \text{ is maximized} \tag{7.2}$$

The x_i's constitute a zero-one-valued vector.

The solution space for this problem consists of the 2^n distinct ways to assign zero or one values to the x_i's. Thus the solution space is the same as that for the sum of subsets problem. Two possible tree organizations are possible. One corresponds to the fixed tuple size formulation (Figure 7.4) and the other to the variable tuple size formulation (Figure 7.3). Backtracking algorithms for the knapsack problem can be arrived at using either of these two state space trees. Regardless of which is used, bounding functions are needed to help kill some live nodes without expanding them. A good bounding function for this problem is obtained by using an upper bound on the value of the best feasible solution obtainable by expanding the given live node and any of its descendants. If this upper bound is not higher than the value of the best solution determined so far, then that live node can be killed.

We continue the discussion using the fixed tuple size formulation. If at node Z the values of x_i, $1 \le i \le k$, have already been determined, then an upper bound for Z can be obtained by relaxing the requirement $x_i = 0$ or 1 to $0 \le x_i \le 1$ for $k+1 \le i \le n$ and using the greedy algorithm of Section 4.3 to solve the relaxed problem. Function Bound(cp, cw, k) (Algorithm 7.11) determines an upper bound on the best solution obtainable by expanding any node Z at level $k+1$ of the state space tree. The object weights and profits are $w[i]$ and $p[i]$. It is assumed that $p[i]/w[i] \ge p[i+1]/w[i+1]$, $1 \le i < n$.

From Bound it follows that the bound for a feasible left child of a node Z is the same as that for Z. Hence, the bounding function need not be used whenever the backtracking algorithm makes a move to the left child of a node. The resulting algorithm is BKnap (Algorithm 7.12). It was obtained from the recursive backtracking schema. Initially set $fp := -1$;. This algorithm is invoked as

BKnap$(1, 0, 0)$;

When $fp \ne -1$, $x[i]$, $1 \le i \le n$, is such that $\sum_{i=1}^{n} p[i]x[i] = fp$. In lines 8 to 18 left children are generated. In line 20, Bound is used to test whether a right child should be generated. The path $y[i]$, $1 \le i \le k$, is the path to the current node. The current weight $cw = \sum_{i=1}^{k-1} w[i]y[i]$ and $cp = \sum_{i=1}^{k-1} p[i]y[i]$. In lines 13 to 17 and 23 to 27 the solution vector is updated if need be.

So far, all our backtracking algorithms have worked on a static state space tree. We now see how a dynamic state space tree can be used for the

```
Algorithm Bound(cp, cw, k)
// cp is the current profit total, cw is the current
// weight total; k is the index of the last removed
// item; and m is the knapsack size.
{
    b := cp; c := cw;
    for i := k + 1 to n do
    {
        c := c + w[i];
        if (c < m) then b := b + p[i];
        else return b + (1 - (c - m)/w[i]) * p[i];
    }
    return b;
}
```

Algorithm 7.11 A bounding function

knapsack problem. One method for dynamically partitioning the solution space is based on trying to obtain an optimal solution using the greedy algorithm of Section 4.3. We first replace the integer constraint $x_i = 0$ or 1 by the constraint $0 \leq x_i \leq 1$. This yields the relaxed problem

$$\max \sum_{1 \leq i \leq n} p_i x_i \text{ subject to } \sum_{1 \leq i \leq n} w_i x_i \leq m \tag{7.3}$$

$$0 \leq x_i \leq 1, \qquad 1 \leq i \leq n$$

If the solution generated by the greedy method has all x_i's equal to zero or one, then it is also an optimal solution to the original 0/1 knapsack problem. If this is not the case, then exactly one x_i will be such that $0 < x_i < 1$. We partition the solution space of (7.2) into two subspaces. In one $x_i = 0$ and in the other $x_i = 1$. Thus the left subtree of the state space tree will correspond to $x_i = 0$ and the right to $x_i = 1$. In general, at each node Z of the state space tree the greedy algorithm is used to solve (7.3) under the added restrictions corresponding to the assignments already made along the path from the root to this node. In case the solution is all integer, then an optimal solution for this node has been found. If not, then there is exactly one x_i such that $0 < x_i < 1$. The left child of Z corresponds to $x_i = 0$, and the right to $x_i = 1$.

```
Algorithm BKnap(k, cp, cw)
// m is the size of the knapsack; n is the number of weights
// and profits. w[ ] and p[ ] are the weights and profits.
// p[i]/w[i] ≥ p[i + 1]/w[i + 1]. fw is the final weight of
// knapsack; fp is the final maximum profit. x[k] = 0 if w[k]
// is not in the knapsack; else x[k] = 1.
{
    // Generate left child.
    if (cw + w[k] ≤ m) then
    {
        y[k] := 1;
        if (k < n) then BKnap(k + 1, cp + p[k], cw + w[k]);
        if ((cp + p[k] > fp) and (k = n)) then
        {
            fp := cp + p[k]; fw := cw + w[k];
            for j := 1 to k do x[j] := y[j];
        }
    }
    // Generate right child.
    if (Bound(cp, cw, k) ≥ fp) then
    {
        y[k] := 0; if (k < n) then BKnap(k + 1, cp, cw);
        if ((cp > fp) and (k = n)) then
        {
            fp := cp; fw := cw;
            for j := 1 to k do x[j] := y[j];
        }
    }
}
```

Algorithm 7.12 Backtracking solution to the 0/1 knapsack problem

The justification for this partitioning scheme is that the noninteger x_i is what prevents the greedy solution from being a feasible solution to the 0/1 knapsack problem. So, we would expect to reach a feasible greedy solution quickly by forcing this x_i to be integer. Choosing left branches to correspond to $x_i = 0$ rather than $x_i = 1$ is also justifiable. Since the greedy algorithm requires $p_j/w_j \geq p_{j+1}/w_{j+1}$, we would expect most objects with low index (i.e., small j and hence high density) to be in an optimal filling of the knapsack. When x_i is set to zero, we are not preventing the greedy algorithm from using any of the objects with $j < i$ (unless x_j has already been set to zero). On the other hand, when x_i is set to one, some of the x_j's with $j < i$ will not be able to get into the knapsack. Therefore we expect to arrive at an optimal solution with $x_i = 0$. So we wish the backtracking algorithm to try this alternative first. Hence the left subtree corresponds to $x_i = 0$.

Example 7.7 Let us try out a backtracking algorithm and the above dynamic partitioning scheme on the following data: $p = \{11, 21, 31, 33, 43, 53, 55, 65\}$, $w = \{1, 11, 21, 23, 33, 43, 45, 55\}$, $m = 110$, and $n = 8$. The greedy solution corresponding to the root node (i.e., Equation (7.3)) is $x = \{1, 1, 1, 1, 1, 21/45, 0, 0\}$. Its value is 164.88. The two subtrees of the root correspond to $x_6 = 0$ and $x_6 = 1$, respectively (Figure 7.16). The greedy solution at node 2 is $x = \{1, 1, 1, 1, 1, 0, 21/45, 0\}$. Its value is 164.66. The solution space at node 2 is partitioned using $x_7 = 0$ and $x_7 = 1$. The next E-node is node 3. The solution here has $x_8 = 21/55$. The partitioning now is with $x_8 = 0$ and $x_8 = 1$. The solution at node 4 is all integer so there is no need to expand this node further. The best solution found so far has value 139 and $x = \{1, 1, 1, 1, 1, 0, 0, 0\}$. Node 5 is the next E-node. The greedy solution for this node is $x = \{1, 1, 1, 22/23, 0, 0, 0, 1\}$. Its value is 159.56. The partitioning is now with $x_4 = 0$ and $x_4 = 1$. The greedy solution at node 6 has value 156.66 and $x_5 = 2/3$. Next, node 7 becomes the E-node. The solution here is $\{1, 1, 1, 0, 0, 0, 0, 1\}$. Its value is 128. Node 7 is not expanded as the greedy solution here is all integer. At node 8 the greedy solution has value 157.71 and $x_3 = 4/7$. The solution at node 9 is all integer and has value 140. The greedy solution at node 10 is $\{1, 0, 1, 0, 1, 0, 0, 1\}$. Its value is 150. The next E-node is 11. Its value is 159.52 and $x_3 = 20/21$. The partitioning is now on $x_3 = 0$ and $x_3 = 1$. The remainder of the backtracking process on this knapsack instance is left as an exercise. □

Experimental work due to E. Horowitz and S. Sahni, cited in the references, indicates that backtracking algorithms for the knapsack problem generally work in less time when using a static tree than when using a dynamic tree. The dynamic partitioning scheme is, however, useful in the solution of integer linear programs. The general integer linear program is mathematically stated in (7.4).

$$\begin{array}{ll} \text{minimize} & \sum_{1 \le j \le n} c_j \, x_j \\ \text{subject to} & \sum_{1 \le j \le n} a_{ij} \, x_j \le b_i, \quad 1 \le i \le m \\ & x_j' s \text{ are nonnegative integers} \end{array} \tag{7.4}$$

If the integer constraints on the x_i's in (7.4) are replaced by the constraint $x_i \ge 0$, then we obtain a linear program whose optimal solution has a value at least as large as the value of an optimal solution to (7.4). Linear programs can be solved using the simplex methods (see the references). If the solution is not all integer, then a noninteger x_i is chosen to partition the solution space. Let us assume that the value of x_i in the optimal solution to the linear program corresponding to any node Z in the state space is v and v is not an integer. The left child of Z corresponds to $x_i \leq \lfloor v \rfloor$ whereas the right child of Z correspond to $x_i \geq \lceil v \rceil$. Since the resulting state space tree has a potentially infinite depth (note that on the path from the root to a node Z the solution space can be partitioned on one x_i many times as each x_i can have as value any nonnegative integer), it is almost always searched using a branch-and-bound method (see Chapter 8).

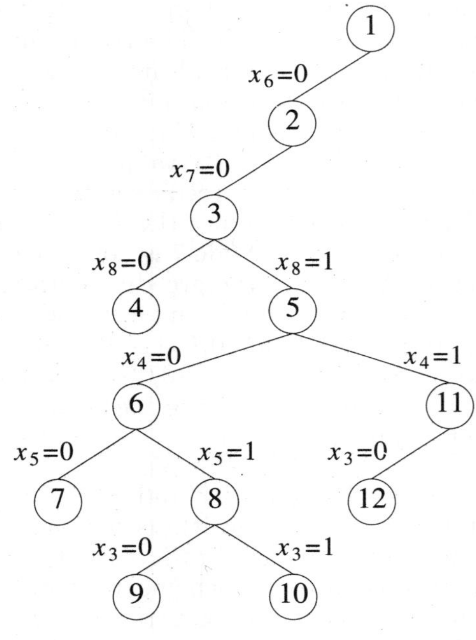

Figure 7.16 Part of the dynamic state space tree generated in Example 7.7

EXERCISES

1. (a) Present a backtracking algorithm for solving the knapsack optimization problem using the variable tuple size formulation.

(b) Draw the portion of the state space tree your algorithm will generate when solving the knapsack instance of Example 7.7.

2. Complete the state space tree of Figure 7.16.

3. Give a backtracking algorithm for the knapsack problem using the dynamic state space tree discussed in this section.

4. [Programming project] (a) Program the algorithms of Exercises 1 and 3. Run these two programs and BKnap using the following data: $p = \{11, 21, 31, 33, 43, 53, 55, 65\}$, $w = \{1, 11, 21, 23, 33, 43, 45, 55\}$, $m = 110$, and $n = 8$. Which algorithm do you expect to perform best?

   (b) Now program the dynamic programming algorithm of Section 5.7 for the knapsack problem. Use the heuristics suggested at the end of Section 5.7. Obtain computing times and compare this program with the backtracking programs.

5. (a) Obtain a knapsack instance for which more nodes are generated by the backtracking algorithm using a dynamic tree than using a static tree.

   (b) Obtain a knapsack instance for which more nodes are generated by the backtracking algorithm using a static tree than using a dynamic tree.

   (c) Strengthen the backtracking algorithms with the following heuristic: Build an array $minw[\ ]$ with the property that $minw[i]$ is the index of the object that has least weight among objects $i, i+1, \ldots, n$. Now any E-node at which decisions for $x_1, \ldots, x_{i-1}$ have been made and at which the unutilized knapsack capacity is less than $w[minw[i]]$ can be terminated provided the profit earned up to this node is no more than the maximum determined so far. Incorporate this into your programs of Exercise 4(a). Rerun the new programs on the same data sets and see what (if any) improvements result.

7.7 REFERENCES AND READINGS

An early modern account of backtracking was given by R. J. Walker. The technique for estimating the efficiency of a backtrack program was first proposed by M. Hall and D. E. Knuth and the dynamic partitioning scheme for the 0/1 knapsack problem was proposed by H. Greenberg and R. Hegerich. Experimental results showing static trees to be superior for this problem can be found in "Computing partitions with applications to the knapsack problem," by E. Horowitz and S. Sahni, *Journal of the ACM* 21, no. 2 (1974): 277–292.

Data presented in the above paper shows that the divide-and-conquer dynamic programming algorithm for the knapsack problem is superior to BKnap.

For a proof of the four-color theorem see *Every Planar Map is Four Colorable*, by K. I. Appel, American Mathematical Society, Providence, RI, 1989.

A discussion of the simplex method for solving linear programs may be found in:
Linear Programming: Methods and Applications, by S. Gass, 5th Edition, Dover Publications, 2003.
Linear Optimization and Extensions, by M. Padberg, Springer-Verlag, 1995.

7.8 ADDITIONAL EXERCISES

1. Suppose you are given n men and n women and two $n \times n$ arrays P and Q such that $P(i, j)$ is the preference of man i for woman j and $Q(i, j)$ is the preference of woman i for man j. Given an algorithm that finds a pairing of men and women such that the sum of the product of the preferences is maximized.

2. Let $A(1 : n, 1 : n)$ be an $n \times n$ matrix. The *determinant* of A is the number

$$\det(A) = \sum_s \mathrm{sgn}(s) a_{1,s(1)} a_{2,s(2)} \cdots a_{n,s(n)}$$

   where the sum is taken over all permutations $s(1), \ldots, s(n)$ of $\{1, 2, \ldots, n\}$ and sgn(s) is $+\,1$ or -1 according to whether s is an even or odd permutation. The *permanent* of A is defined as

$$\mathrm{per}(A) = \sum_s a_{1,s(1)} a_{2,s(2)} \cdots a_{n,s(n)}$$

   The determinant can be computed as a by-product of Gaussian elimination requiring $O(n^3)$ operations, but no polynomial time algorithm is known for computing permanents. Write an algorithm that computes the permanent of a matrix by generating the elements of s using backtracking. Analyze the time of your algorithm.

3. Let MAZE$(1 : n, 1 : n)$ be a zero- or one-valued, two-dimensional array that represents a maze. A one means a blocked path whereas a zero stands for an open position. You are to develop an algorithm that

begins at MAZE(1, 1) and tries to find a path to position MAZE(n, n). Once again backtracking is necessary here. See if you can analyze the time complexity of your algorithm.

4. The *assignment problem* is usually stated this way: There are n people to be assigned to n jobs. The cost of assigning the ith person to the jth job is $cost(i, j)$. You are to develop an algorithm that assigns every job to a person and at the same time minimizes the total cost of the assignment.

5. This problem is called the postage stamp problem. Envision a country that issues n different denominations of stamps but allows no more than m stamps on a single letter. For given values of m and n, write an algorithm that computes the greatest consecutive range of postage values, from one on up, and all possible sets of denominations that realize that range. For example, for $n = 4$ and $m = 5$, the stamps with values (1, 4, 12, 21) allow the postage values 1 through 71. Are there any other sets of four denominations that have the same range?

6. Here is a game called Hi-Q. Thirty-two pieces are arranged on a board as shown in Figure 7.17. Only the center position is unoccupied. A piece is only allowed to move by jumping over one of its neighbors into an empty space. Diagonal jumps are not permitted. When a piece is jumped, it is removed from the board. Write an algorithm that determines a series of jumps so that all the pieces except one are eventually removed and that final piece ends up at the center position.

7. Imagine a set of 12 plane figures each composed of five equal-size squares. Each figure differs in shape from the others, but together they can be arranged to make different-sized rectangles. In Figure 7.18 there is a picture of 12 pentominoes that are joined to create a 6×10 rectangle. Write an algorithm that finds all possible ways to place the pentominoes so that a 6×10 rectangle is formed.

8. Suppose a set of electric components such as transistors are to be placed on a circuit board. We are given a connection matrix CONN, where CONN(i, j) equals the number of connections between component i and component j, and a matrix DIST, where DIST (r, s) is the distance between position r and position s on the circuit board. The wiring of the board consists of placing each of n components at some location. The cost of a wiring is the sum of the products of $CONN(i, j) * DIST(r, s)$, where component i is placed at location r and component j is placed at location s. Compose an algorithm that finds an assignment of components to locations that minimizes the total cost of the wiring.

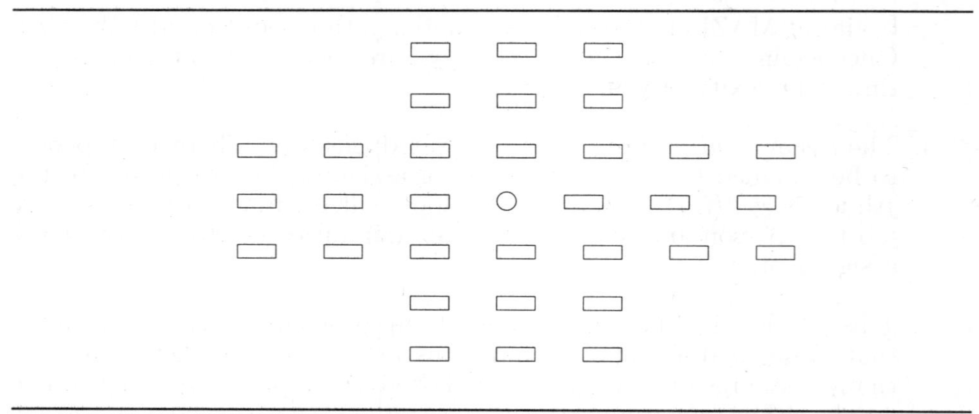

Figure 7.17 A Hi-Q board in its initial state

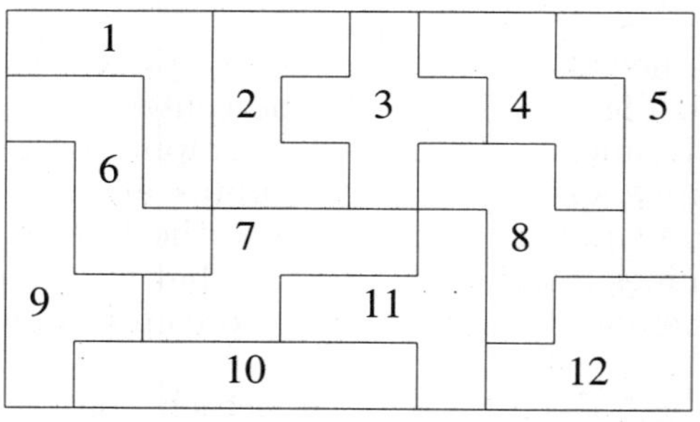

Figure 7.18 A pentomino configuration

9. Suppose there are n jobs to be executed but only k processors that can work in parallel. The time required by job i is t_i. Write an algorithm that determines which jobs are to be run on which processors and the order in which they should be run so that the finish time of the last job is minimized.

10. Two graphs $G(V, E)$ and $H(A, B)$ are called *isomorphic* if there is a one-to-one onto correspondence of the vertices that preserves the adjacency relationships. More formally if f is a function from V to A and (v, w) is an edge in E, then $(f(v), f(w))$ is an edge in H. Figure 7.19 shows two directed graphs that are isomorphic under the mapping that

1, 2, 3, 4, and 5 and go to a, b, c, d, and e. A brute force algorithm to test two graphs for isomorphism would try out all $n!$ possible correspondences and then test to see whether adjacency was preserved. A backtracking algorithm can do better than this by applying some obvious pruning to the resultant state space tree. First of all we know that for a correspondence to exist between two vertices, they must have the same degree. So we can select at an early stage vertices of degree k for which the second graph has the fewest number of vertices of degree k. This exercise calls for devising an isomorphism algorithm that is based on backtracking and makes use of these ideas.

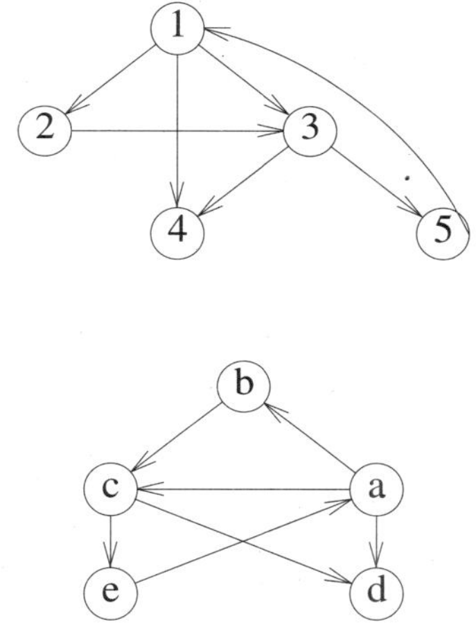

Figure 7.19 Two isomorphic graphs (Exercise 10)

11. A graph is called *complete* if all its vertices are connected to all the other vertices in the graph. A maximal complete subgraph of a graph is called a *clique*. By "maximal" we mean that this subgraph is contained within no other subgraph that is also complete. A clique of size k has $\binom{k}{i}$ subcliques of size i, $1 \le i \le k$. This implies that any algorithm that looks for a maximal clique must be careful to generate each subclique the fewest number of times possible. One way to generate the clique is to extend a clique of size m to size $m + 1$ and to continue this process by trying out all possible vertices. But this strategy generates the same clique many times; this can be avoided as follows. Given a clique X, suppose node v is the first node that is added to produce a clique of size one greater. After the backtracking process examines all possible

cliques that are produced from X and v, then no vertex adjacent to v need be added to X and examined. Let X and Y be cliques and let X be properly contained in Y. If all cliques containing X and vertex v have been generated, then all cliques with Y and v can be ignored. Write a backtracking algorithm that generates the maximal cliques of an undirected graph and makes use of these last rules for pruning the state space tree.

Chapter 8

BRANCH AND BOUND

8.1 THE METHOD

This chapter makes extensive use of terminology defined in Section 7.1. The reader is urged to review this section before proceeding.

The term branch and bound refers to all state space search methods in which all children of the E-node are generated before any other live node can become the E-node. We have already seen (in Section 7.1) two graph search strategies, BFS and D-search, in which the exploration of a new node cannot begin until the node currently being explored is fully explored. Both of these generalize to branch-and-bound strategies. In branch-and-bound terminology, a BFS-like state space search will be called FIFO (**F**irst **I**n **F**irst **O**ut) search as the list of live nodes is a first-in-first-out list (or queue). A D-search-like state space search will be called LIFO (**L**ast **I**n **F**irst **O**ut) search as the list of live nodes is a last-in-first-out list (or stack). As in the case of backtracking, bounding functions are used to help avoid the generation of subtrees that do not contain an answer node.

Example 8.1 [4-queens] Let us see how a FIFO branch-and-bound algorithm would search the state space tree (Figure 7.2) for the 4-queens problem. Initially, there is only one live node, node 1. This represents the case in which no queen has been placed on the chessboard. This node becomes the E-node. It is expanded and its children, nodes 2, 18, 34, and 50, are generated. These nodes represent a chessboard with queen 1 in row 1 and columns 1, 2, 3, and 4 respectively. The only live nodes now are nodes 2, 18, 34, and 50. If the nodes are generated in this order, then the next E-node is node 2. It is expanded and nodes 3, 8, and 13 are generated. Node 3 is immediately killed using the bounding function of Example 7.5. Nodes 8 and 13 are added to the queue of live nodes. Node 18 becomes the next E-node. Nodes 19, 24, and 29 are generated. Nodes 19 and 24 are killed as a result of the bounding functions. Node 29 is added to the queue of live nodes. The E-node is node 34. Figure 8.1 shows the portion of the tree of Figure 7.2 that is generated by a FIFO branch-and-bound search. Nodes that are killed as a result of the bounding functions have a "B" under them. Numbers inside the nodes correspond to the numbers in Figure 7.2. Numbers outside the nodes give the order in which the nodes are generated by FIFO branch and bound. At the time the answer node, node 31, is reached, the only live nodes remaining are nodes 38 and 54. A comparison of Figures 7.6 and 8.1 indicates that backtracking is a superior search method for this problem. □

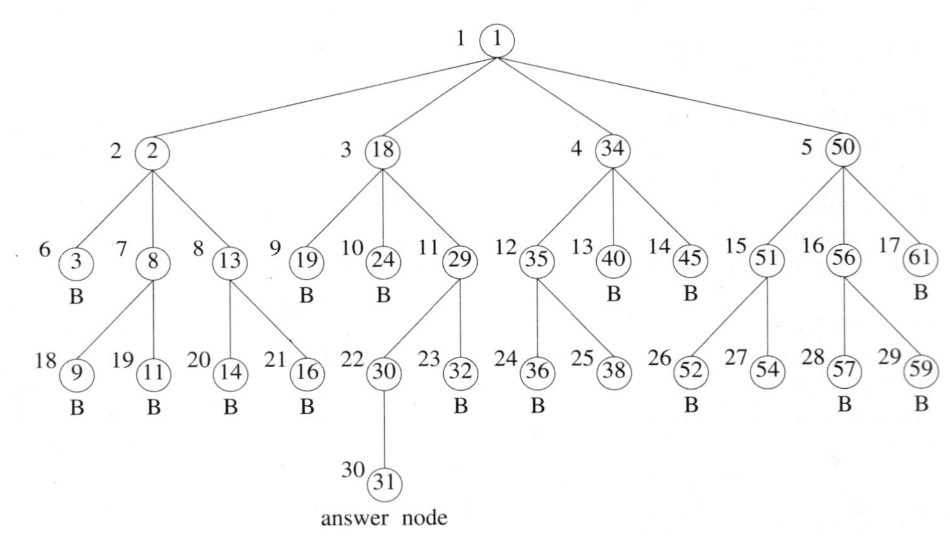

Figure 8.1 Portion of 4-queens state space tree generated by FIFO branch and bound

8.1.1 Least Cost (LC) Search

In both LIFO and FIFO branch and bound the selection rule for the next E-node is rather rigid and in a sense blind. The selection rule for the next E-node does not give any preference to a node that has a very good chance of getting the search to an answer node quickly. Thus, in Example 8.1, when node 30 is generated, it should have become obvious to the search algorithm that this node will lead to an answer node in one move. However, the rigid FIFO rule first requires the expansion of all live nodes generated before node 30 was expanded.

The search for an answer node can often be speeded by using an "intelligent" ranking function $\hat{c}(\cdot)$ for live nodes. The next E-node is selected on the basis of this ranking function. If in the 4-queens example we use a ranking function that assigns node 30 a better rank than all other live nodes, then node 30 will become the E-node following node 29. The remaining live nodes will never become E-nodes as the expansion of node 30 results in the generation of an answer node (node 31).

The ideal way to assign ranks would be on the basis of the additional computational effort (or cost) needed to reach an answer node from the live node. For any node x, this cost could be (1) the number of nodes in the subtree x that need to be generated before an answer node is generated or, more simply, (2) the number of levels the nearest answer node (in the subtree x) is from x. Using cost measure 2, the cost of the root of the tree of Figure 8.1 is 4 (node 31 is four levels from node 1). The costs of nodes 18 and 34, 29 and 35, and 30 and 38 are respectively 3, 2, and 1. The costs of all remaining nodes on levels 2, 3, and 4 are respectively greater than 3, 2, and 1. Using these costs as a basis to select the next E-node, the E-nodes are nodes 1, 18, 29, and 30 (in that order). The only other nodes to get generated are nodes 2, 34, 50, 19, 24, 32, and 31. It should be easy to see that if cost measure 1 is used, then the search would always generate the minimum number of nodes every branch-and-bound type algorithm must generate. If cost measure 2 is used, then the only nodes to become E-nodes are the nodes on the path from the root to the nearest answer node. The difficulty with using either of these ideal cost functions is that computing the cost of a node usually involves a search of the subtree x for an answer node. Hence, by the time the cost of a node is determined, that subtree has been searched and there is no need to explore x again. For this reason, search algorithms usually rank nodes only on the basis of an estimate $\hat{g}(\cdot)$ of their cost.

Let $\hat{g}(x)$ be an estimate of the additional effort needed to reach an answer node from x. Node x is assigned a rank using a function $\hat{c}(\cdot)$ such that $\hat{c}(x) = f(h(x)) + \hat{g}(x)$, where $h(x)$ is the cost of reaching x from the root and $f(\cdot)$ is any nondecreasing function. At first, we may doubt the usefulness of using an $f(\cdot)$ other than $f(h(x)) = 0$ for all $h(x)$. We can justify such an $f(\cdot)$ on the grounds that the effort already expended in reaching the live nodes cannot be reduced and all we are concerned with now is minimizing the additional effort we spend to find an answer node. Hence, the effort already expended need not be considered.

Using $f(\cdot) \equiv 0$ usually biases the search algorithm to make deep probes into the search tree. To see this, note that we would normally expect $\hat{g}(y) \leq \hat{g}(x)$ for y, a child of x. Hence, following x, y will become the E-node, then one of y's children will become the E-node, next one of y's grandchildren will become the E-node, and so on. Nodes in subtrees other than the subtree x will not get generated until the subtree x is fully searched. This would not be a cause for concern if $\hat{g}(x)$ were the true cost of x. Then, we would not wish to explore the remaining subtrees in any case (as x is guaranteed to get us to an answer node quicker than any other existing live node). However, $\hat{g}(x)$ is only an estimate of the true cost. So, it is quite possible that for two nodes w and z, $\hat{g}(w) < \hat{g}(z)$ and z is much closer to an answer node than w. It is therefore desirable not to overbias the search algorithm in favor of deep probes. By using $f(\cdot) \not\equiv 0$, we can force the search algorithm to favor a node z close to the root over a node w which is many levels below z. This would reduce the possibility of deep and fruitless searches into the tree.

A search strategy that uses a cost function $\hat{c}(x) = f(h(x)) + \hat{g}(x)$ to select the next E-node would always choose for its next E-node a live node with least $\hat{c}(\cdot)$. Hence, such a search strategy is called an LC-search (**L**east **C**ost search). It is interesting to note that BFS and D-search are special cases of LC-search. If we use $\hat{g}(x) \equiv 0$ and $f(h(x)) =$ level of node x, then a LC-search generates nodes by levels. This is essentially the same as a BFS. If $f(h(x)) \equiv 0$ and $\hat{g}(x) \geq \hat{g}(y)$ whenever y is a child of x, then the search is essentially a D-search. An LC-search coupled with bounding functions is called an LC branch-and-bound search.

In discussing LC-searches, we sometimes make reference to a cost function $c(\cdot)$ defined as follows: if x is an answer node, then $c(x)$ is the cost (level, computational difficulty, etc.) of reaching x from the root of the state space tree. If x is not an answer node, then $c(x) = \infty$ providing the subtree x contains no answer node; otherwise $c(x)$ equals the cost of a minimum-cost answer node in the subtree x. It should be easy to see that $\hat{c}(\cdot)$ with $f(h(x)) = h(x)$ is an approximation to $c(\cdot)$. From now on $c(x)$ is referred to as the cost of x.

8.1.2 The 15-puzzle: An Example

The 15-puzzle (invented by Sam Loyd in 1878) consists of 15 numbered tiles on a square frame with a capacity of 16 tiles (Figure 8.2). We are given an initial arrangement of the tiles, and the objective is to transform this arrangement into the goal arrangement of Figure 8.2(b) through a series of legal moves. The only legal moves are ones in which a tile adjacent to the empty spot (ES) is moved to ES. Thus from the initial arrangement of Figure 8.2(a), four moves are possible. We can move any one of the tiles numbered 2, 3, 5, or 6 to the empty spot. Following this move, other moves can be made. Each move creates a new arrangement of the tiles. These arrangements are called the *states* of the puzzle. The initial and goal arrangements are called the initial and goal states. A state is reachable from the initial state iff there is a sequence of legal moves from the initial state to this state. The state space of an initial state consists of all states that can be reached from the initial state. The most straightforward way to solve the puzzle would be to search the state space for the goal state and use the path from the initial state to the goal state as the answer. It is easy to see that there are 16! ($16! \approx 20.9 \times 10^{12}$) different arrangements of the tiles on the frame. Of these only one-half are reachable from any given initial state. Indeed, the state space for the problem is very large. Before attempting to search this state space for the goal state, it would be worthwhile to determine whether the goal state is reachable from the initial state. There is a very simple way to do this. Let us number the frame positions 1 to 16. Position i is the frame position containing tile numbered i in the goal arrangement of Figure 8.2(b). Position 16 is the empty spot. Let $position(i)$ be the position number in the initial state of the tile numbered i. Then $position(16)$ will denote the position of the empty spot.

1	3	4	15
2		5	12
7	6	11	14
8	9	10	13

(a) An arrangement

1	2	3	4
5	6	7	8
9	10	11	12
13	14	15	

(b) Goal arrangement

	shaded		shaded
shaded		shaded	
	shaded		shaded
shaded		shaded	

(c)

Figure 8.2 15-puzzle arrangements

For any state let $less(i)$ be the number of tiles j such that $j < i$ and $position(j) > position(i)$. For the state of Figure 8.2(a) we have, for example, $less(1) = 0$, $less(4) = 1$, and $less(12) = 6$. Let $x = 1$ if in the initial state the empty spot is at one of the shaded positions of Figure 8.2(c) and $x = 0$ if it is at one of the remaining positions. Then, we have the following theorem:

Theorem 8.1 The goal state of Figure 8.2(b) is reachable from the initial state iff $\sum_{i=1}^{16} less(i) + x$ is even.

Proof: Left as an exercise. □

Theorem 8.1 can be used to determine whether the goal state is in the state space of the initial state. If it is, then we can proceed to determine a sequence of moves leading to the goal state. To carry out this search, the state space can be organized into a tree. The children of each node x in this tree represent the states reachable from state x by one legal move. It is convenient to think of a move as involving a move of the empty space rather than a move of a tile. The empty space, on each move, moves either up, right, down, or left. Figure 8.3 shows the first three levels of the state space tree of the 15-puzzle beginning with the initial state shown in the root. Parts of levels 4 and 5 of the tree are also shown. The tree has been pruned a little. *No node p has a child state that is the same as p's parent.* The subtree eliminated in this way is already present in the tree and has root *parent*(p). As can be seen, there is an answer node at level 4.

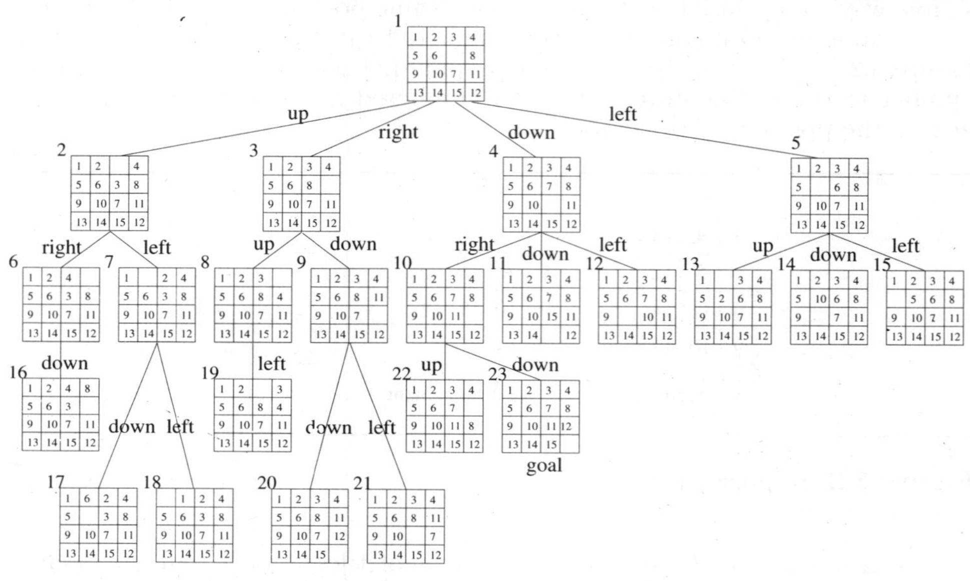

Figure 8.3 Part of the state space tree for the 15-puzzle

A depth first state space tree generation will result in the subtree of Figure 8.4 when the next moves are attempted in the order: move the empty space up, right, down, and left. Successive board configurations reveal that each move gets us farther from the goal rather than closer. The search of the state space tree is blind. It will take the leftmost path from the root regardless of the starting configuration. As a result, an answer node may never be found (unless the leftmost path ends in such a node). In a FIFO search of the tree of Figure 8.3, the nodes will be generated in the order numbered. A breadth first search will always find a goal node nearest to the root. However, such a search is also blind in the sense that no matter what the initial configuration, the algorithm attempts to make the same sequence of moves. A FIFO search always generates the state space tree by levels.

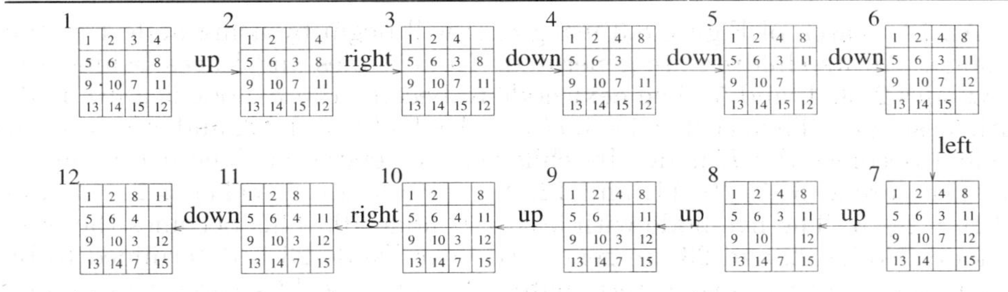

Figure 8.4 First ten steps in a depth first search

What we would like, is a more "intelligent" search method, one that seeks out an answer node and adapts the path it takes through the state space tree to the specific problem instance being solved. We can associate a cost $c(x)$ with each node x in the state space tree. The cost $c(x)$ is the length of a path from the root to a nearest goal node (if any) in the subtree with root x. Thus, in Figure 8.3, $c(1) = c(4) = c(10) = c(23) = 3$. When such a cost function is available, a very efficient search can be carried out. We begin with the root as the E-node and generate a child node with $c()$-value the same as the root. Thus children nodes 2, 3, and 5 are eliminated and only node 4 becomes a live node. This becomes the next E-node. Its first child, node 10, has $c(10) = c(4) = 3$. The remaining children are not generated. Node 4 dies and node 10 becomes the E-node. In generating node 10's children, node 22 is killed immediately as $c(22) > 3$. Node 23 is generated next. It is a goal node and the search terminates. In this search strategy, the only nodes to become E-nodes are nodes on the path from the root to a nearest goal node. Unfortunately, this is an impractical strategy as it is not possible to easily compute the function $c(\cdot)$ specified above.

We can arrive at an easy to compute estimate $\hat{c}(x)$ of $c(x)$. We can write $\hat{c}(x) = f(x) + \hat{g}(x)$, where $f(x)$ is the length of the path from the root to node x and $\hat{g}(x)$ is an estimate of the length of a shortest path from x to a goal node in the subtree with root x. One possible choice for $\hat{g}(x)$ is

$$\hat{g}(x) = \text{number of nonblank tiles not in their goal position}$$

Clearly, at least $\hat{g}(x)$ moves have to be made to transform state x to a goal state. More than $\hat{g}(x)$ moves may be needed to achieve this. To see this, examine the problem state of Figure 8.5. There $\hat{g}(x) = 1$ as only tile 7 is not in its final spot (the count for $\hat{g}(x)$ excludes the blank tile). However, the number of moves needed to reach the goal state is many more than $\hat{g}(x)$. So $\hat{c}(x)$ is a *lower bound* on the value of $c(x)$.

An LC-search of Figure 8.3 using $\hat{c}(x)$ will begin by using node 1 as the E-node. All its children are generated. Node 1 dies and leaves behind the live nodes 2, 3, 4, and 5. The next node to become the E-node is a live node with least $\hat{c}(x)$. Then $\hat{c}(2) = 1+4$, $\hat{c}(3) = 1+4$, $\hat{c}(4) = 1+2$, and $\hat{c}(5) = 1+4$. Node 4 becomes the E-node. Its children are generated. The live nodes at this time are 2, 3, 5, 10, 11, and 12. So $\hat{c}(10) = 2+1$, $\hat{c}(11) = 2+3$, and $\hat{c}(12) = 2+3$. The live node with least $\hat{c}$ is node 10. This becomes the next E-node. Nodes 22 and 23 are generated next. Node 23 is determined to be a goal node and the search terminates. In this case LC-search was almost as efficient as using the exact function $c()$. It should be noted that with a suitable choice for $\hat{c}()$, an LC-search will be far more selective than any of the other search methods we have discussed.

1	2	3	4
5	6		8
9	10	11	12
13	14	15	7

Figure 8.5 Problem state

8.1.3 Control Abstractions for LC-Search

Let t be a state space tree and $c()$ a cost function for the nodes in t. If x is a node in t, then $c(x)$ is the minimum cost of any answer node in the subtree with root x. Thus, $c(t)$ is the cost of a minimum-cost answer node in t. As remarked earlier, it is usually not possible to find an easily computable function $c()$ as defined above. Instead, a heuristic $\hat{c}$ that estimates $c()$ is used. This heuristic should be easy to compute and generally has the property that if x is either an answer node or a leaf node, then $c(x) = \hat{c}(x)$. LCSearch (Algorithm 8.1) uses $\hat{c}$ to find an answer node. The algorithm uses two functions Least() and Add(x) to delete and add a live node from or to the list of live nodes, respectively. Least() finds a live node with least $\hat{c}()$. This node is deleted from the list of live nodes and returned. Add(x) adds the new live node x to the list of live nodes. The list of live nodes will usually be implemented as a min-heap (Section 2.4). Algorithm LCSearch outputs the path from the answer node it finds to the root node t. This is easy to do if with each node x that becomes live, we associate a field *parent* which gives the parent of node x. When an answer node g is found, the path from

g to t can be determined by following a sequence of *parent* values starting from the current E-node (which is the parent of g) and ending at node t.

```
    listnode = record {
        listnode *next, *parent; float cost;
    }

1   Algorithm LCSearch(t)
2   // Search t for an answer node.
3   {
4       if *t is an answer node then output *t and return;
5       E := t; // E-node.
6       Initialize the list of live nodes to be empty;
7       repeat
8       {
9           for each child x of E do
10          {
11              if x is an answer node then output the path
12                  from x to t and return;
13              Add(x); // x is a new live node.
14              (x -> parent) := E; // Pointer for path to root.
15          }
16          if there are no more live nodes then
17          {
18              write ("No answer node"); return;
19          }
20          E := Least();
21      } until (false);
22  }
```

Algorithm 8.1 LC-search

The correctness of algorithm LCSearch is easy to establish. Variable E always points to the current E-node. By the definition of LC-search, the root node is the first E-node (line 5). Line 6 initializes the list of live nodes. At any time during the execution of LCSearch, this list contains all live nodes except the E-node. Thus, initially this list should be empty (line 6). The **for** loop of line 9 examines all the children of the E-node. If one of the children is an answer node, then the algorithm outputs the path from x to t and terminates. If a child of E is not an answer node, then it becomes a live node. It is added to the list of live nodes (line 13) and its *parent* field set to

E (line 14). When all the children of E have been generated, E becomes a dead node and line 16 is reached. This happens only if none of E's children is an answer node. So, the search must continue further. If there are no live nodes left, then the entire state space tree has been searched and no answer nodes found. The algorithm terminates in line 18. Otherwise, Least(), by definition, correctly chooses the next E-node and the search continues from here.

From the preceding discussion, it is clear that LCSearch terminates only when either an answer node is found or the entire state space tree has been generated and searched. Thus, termination is guaranteed only for finite state space trees. Termination can also be guaranteed for infinite state space trees that have at least one answer node provided a "proper" choice for the cost function $\hat{c}()$ is made. This is the case, for example, when $\hat{c}(x) > \hat{c}(y)$ for every pair of nodes x and y such that the level number of x is "sufficiently" higher than that of y. For infinite state space trees with no answer nodes, LCSearch will not terminate. Thus, it is advisable to restrict the search to find answer nodes with a cost no more than a given bound C.

One should note the similarity between algorithm LCSearch and algorithms for a breadth first search and D-search of a state space tree. If the list of live nodes is implemented as a queue with Least() and Add(x) being algorithms to delete an element from and add an element to the queue, then LCSearch will be transformed to a FIFO search schema. If the list of live nodes is implemented as a stack with Least() and Add(x) being algorithms to delete and add elements to the stack, then LCSearch will carry out a LIFO search of the state space tree. Thus, the algorithms for LC, FIFO, and LIFO search are essentially the same. The only difference is in the implementation of the list of live nodes. This is to be expected as the three search methods differ only in the selection rule used to obtain the next E-node.

8.1.4 Bounding

A branch-and-bound method searches a state space tree using any search mechanism in which all the children of the E-node are generated before another node becomes the E-node. We assume that each answer node x has a cost $c(x)$ associated with it and that a minimum-cost answer node is to be found. Three common search strategies are FIFO, LIFO, and LC. (Another method, heuristic search, is discussed in the exercises.) A cost function $\hat{c}(\cdot)$ such that $\hat{c}(x) \leq c(x)$ is used to provide lower bounds on solutions obtainable from any node x. If *upper* is an upper bound on the cost of a minimum-cost solution, then all live nodes x with $\hat{c}(x) > upper$ may be killed as all answer nodes reachable from x have cost $c(x) \geq \hat{c}(x) > upper$. The starting value for *upper* can be obtained by some heuristic or can be set to ∞. Clearly, so long as the initial value for *upper* is no less than the cost of a minimum-cost answer node, the above rules to kill live nodes will not result in the killing of a live node that can reach a minimum-cost answer node. Each time a new answer node is found, the value of *upper* can be updated.

Let us see how these ideas can be used to arrive at branch-and-bound algorithms for optimization problems. In this section we deal directly only with minimization problems. A maximization problem is easily converted to a minimization problem by changing the sign of the objective function. We need to be able to formulate the search for an optimal solution as a search for a least-cost answer node in a state space tree. To do this, it is necessary to define the cost function $c(\cdot)$ such that $c(x)$ is minimum for all nodes representing an optimal solution. The easiest way to do this is to use the objective function itself for $c(\cdot)$. For nodes representing feasible solutions, $c(x)$ is the value of the objective function for that feasible solution. For nodes representing infeasible solutions, $c(x) = \infty$. For nodes representing partial solutions, $c(x)$ is the cost of the minimum-cost node in the subtree with root x. Since $c(x)$ is in general as hard to compute as the original optimization problem is to solve, the branch-and-bound algorithm will use an estimate $\hat{c}(x)$ such that $\hat{c}(x) \leq c(x)$ for all x. In general then, the $\hat{c}(\cdot)$ function used in a branch-and-bound solution to optimization functions will estimate the objective function value and not the computational difficulty of reaching an answer node. In addition, to be consistent with the terminology used in connection with the 15-puzzle, any node representing a feasible solution (a solution node) will be an answer node. However, only minimum-cost answer nodes will correspond to an optimal solution. Thus, answer nodes and solution nodes are indistinguishable.

As an example optimization problem, consider the job sequencing with deadlines problem introduced in Section 4.5. We generalize this problem to allow jobs with different processing times. We are given n jobs and one processor. Each job i has associated with it a three tuple (p_i, d_i, t_i). Job i requires t_i units of processing time. If its processing is not completed by the deadline d_i, then a penalty p_i is incurred. The objective is to select a subset J of the n jobs such that all jobs in J can be completed by their deadlines. Hence, a penalty can be incurred only on those jobs not in J. The subset J should be such that the penalty incurred is minimum among all possible subsets J. Such a J is optimal.

Consider the following instance: $n = 4$, $(p_1, d_1, t_1) = (5, 1, 1)$, $(p_2, d_2, t_2) = (10, 3, 2)$, $(p_3, d_3, t_3) = (6, 2, 1)$, and $(p_4, d_4, t_4) = (3, 1, 1)$. The solution space for this instance consists of all possible subsets of the job index set $\{1, 2, 3, 4\}$. The solution space can be organized into a tree by means of either of the two formulations used for the sum of subsets problem (Example 7.2). Figure 8.6 corresponds to the variable tuple size formulation while Figure 8.7 corresponds to the fixed tuple size formulation. In both figures square nodes represent infeasible subsets. In Figure 8.6 all nonsquare nodes are answer nodes. Node 9 represents an optimal solution and is the only minimum-cost answer node. For this node $J = \{2, 3\}$ and the penalty (cost) is 8. In Figure 8.7 only nonsquare leaf nodes are answer nodes. Node 25 represents the optimal solution and is also a minimum-cost answer node. This node corresponds to $J = \{2, 3\}$ and a penalty of 8. The costs of the answer nodes of Figure 8.7 are given below the nodes.

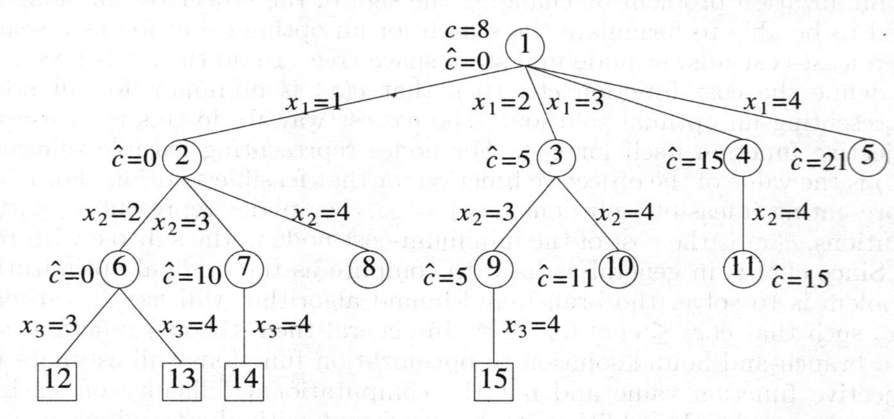

Figure 8.6 State space tree corresponding to variable tuple size formulation

We can define a cost function $c()$ for the state space formulations of Figures 8.6 and 8.7. For any circular node x, $c(x)$ is the minimum penalty corresponding to any node in the subtree with root x. The value of $c(x) = \infty$ for a square node. In the tree of Figure 8.6, $c(3) = 8$, $c(2) = 9$, and $c(1) = 8$. In the tree of Figure 8.7, $c(1) = 8$, $c(2) = 9$, $c(5) = 13$, and $c(6) = 8$. Clearly, $c(1)$ is the penalty corresponding to an optimal selection J.

A bound $\hat{c}(x)$ such that $\hat{c}(x) \leq c(x)$ for all x is easy to obtain. Let S_x be the subset of jobs selected for J at node x. If $m = \max\ \{i | i \in S_x\}$, then $\hat{c}(x) = \sum_{\substack{i<m \\ i \notin S_x}} p_i$ is an estimate for $c(x)$ with the property $\hat{c}(x) \leq c(x)$. For each circular node x in Figures 8.6 and 8.7, the value of $\hat{c}(x)$ is the number outside node x. For a square node, $\hat{c}(x) = \infty$. For example, in Figure 8.6 for node 6, $S_6 = \{1, 2\}$ and hence $m = 2$. Also, $\sum_{\substack{i<2 \\ i \notin S_2}} p_i = 0$. For node 7, $S_7 = \{1, 3\}$ and $m = 3$. Therefore, $\sum_{\substack{i<2 \\ i \notin S_2}} p_i = p_2 = 10$. And so on. In Figure 8.7, node 12 corresponds to the omission of job 1 and hence a penalty of 5; node 13 corresponds to the omission of jobs 1 and 3 and hence a penalty of 11; and so on.

A simple upper bound $u(x)$ on the cost of a minimum-cost answer node in the subtree x is $u(x) = \sum_{i \notin S_x} p_i$. Note that $u(x)$ is the cost of the solution S_x corresponding to node x.

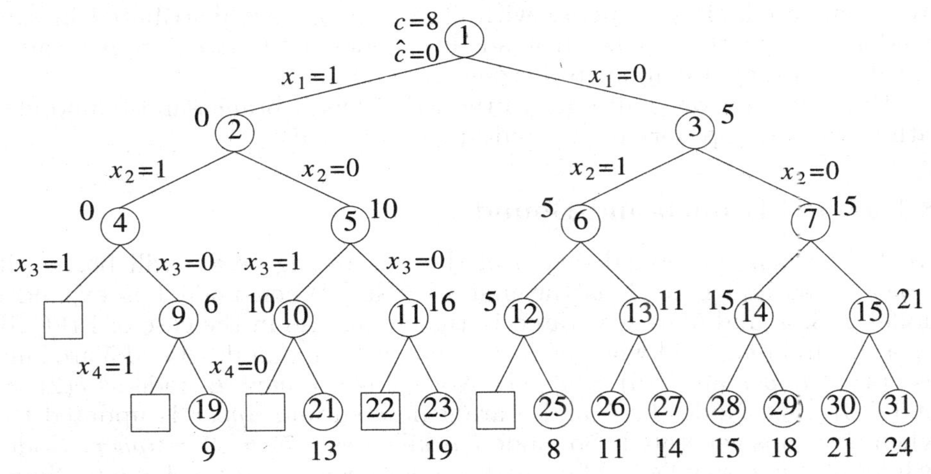

Figure 8.7 State space tree corresponding to fixed tuple size formulation

8.1.5 FIFO Branch-and-Bound

A FIFO branch-and-bound algorithm for the job sequencing problem can begin with *upper* $= \infty$ (or *upper* $= \sum_{1 \le i \le n} p_i$) as an upper bound on the cost of a minimum-cost answer node. Starting with node 1 as the E-node and using the variable tuple size formulation of Figure 8.6, nodes 2, 3, 4, and 5 are generated (in that order). Then $u(2) = 19$, $u(3) = 14$, $u(4) = 18$, and $u(5) = 21$. For example, node 2 corresponds to the inclusion of job 1. Thus $u(2)$ is obtained by summing the penalties of all the other jobs. The variable *upper* is updated to 14 when node 3 is generated. Since $\hat{c}(4)$ and $\hat{c}(5)$ are greater than *upper*, nodes 4 and 5 get killed (or bounded). Only nodes 2 and 3 remain alive. Node 2 becomes the next E-node. Its children, nodes 6, 7, and 8 are generated. Then $u(6) = 9$ and so *upper* is updated to 9. The cost $\hat{c}(7) = 10 >$ *upper* and node 7 gets killed. Node 8 is infeasible and so it is killed. Next, node 3 becomes the E-node. Nodes 9 and 10 are now generated. Then $u(9) = 8$ and so *upper* becomes 8. The cost $\hat{c}(10) = 11 >$ *upper*, and this node is killed. The next E-node is node 6. Both its children are infeasible. Node 9's only child is also infeasible. The minimum-cost answer node is node 9. It has a cost of 8.

When implementing a FIFO branch-and-bound algorithm, it is not economical to kill live nodes with $\hat{c}(x) >$ *upper* each time *upper* is updated. This is so because live nodes are in the queue in the order in which they were generated. Hence, nodes with $\hat{c}(x) > upper$ are distributed in some random way in the queue. Instead, live nodes with $\hat{c}(x) > upper$ can be killed when they are about to become E-nodes.

From here on we shall refer to the FIFO-based branch-and-bound algorithm with an appropriate $\hat{c}(.)$ and $u(.)$ as FIFOBB.

8.1.6 LC Branch-and-Bound

An LC branch-and-bound search of the tree of Figure 8.6 will begin with $upper = \infty$ and node 1 as the first E-node. When node 1 is expanded, nodes 2, 3, 4, and 5 are generated in that order. As in the case of FIFOBB, *upper* is updated to 14 when node 3 is generated and nodes 4 and 5 are killed as $\hat{c}(4) > upper$ and $\hat{c}(5) > upper$. Node 2 is the next E-node as $\hat{c}(2) = 0$ and $\hat{c}(3) = 5$. Nodes 6, 7, and 8 are generated and *upper* is updated to 9 when node 6 is generated. So, node 7 is killed as $\hat{c}(7) = 10 > upper$. Node 8 is infeasible and so killed. The only live nodes now are nodes 3 and 6. Node 6 is the next E-node as $\hat{c}(6) = 0 < \hat{c}(3)$. Both its children are infeasible. Node 3 becomes the next E-node. When node 9 is generated, *upper* is updated to 8 as $u(9) = 8$. So, node 10 with $\hat{c}(10) = 11$ is killed on generation. Node 9 becomes the next E-node. Its only child is infeasible. No live nodes remain. The search terminates with node 9 representing the minimum-cost answer node.

From here on we refer to the LC(LIFO)-based branch-and-bound algorithm with an appropriate $\hat{c}(.)$ and $u(.)$ as LCBB (LIFOBB).

EXERCISES

1. Prove Theorem 8.1.

2. Present an algorithm schema FifoBB for a FIFO branch-and-bound search for a least-cost answer node.

3. Give an algorithm schema LcBB for a LC branch-and-bound search for a least-cost answer node.

4. Write an algorithm schema LifoBB, for a LIFO branch-and-bound search for a least-cost answer node.

5. Draw the portion of the state space tree generated by FIFOBB, LCBB, and LIFOBB for the job sequencing with deadlines instance $n = 5$, $(p_1, p_2, \ldots, p_5) = (6, 3, 4, 8, 5)$, $(t_1, t_2, \ldots, t_5) = (2, 1, 2, 1, 1)$, and $(d_1, d_2, \ldots, d_5) = (3, 1, 4, 2, 4)$. What is the penalty corresponding to an optimal solution? Use a variable tuple size formulation and $\hat{c}(\cdot)$ and $u(\cdot)$ as in Section 8.1.

6. Write a branch-and-bound algorithm for the job sequencing with deadlines problem. Use the fixed tuple size formulation.

7. (a) Write a branch-and-bound algorithm for the job sequencing with deadlines problem using a dominance rule (see Section 5.7). Your algorithm should work with a fixed tuple size formulation and should generate nodes by levels. Nodes on each level should be kept in an order permitting easy use of your dominance rule.

   (b) Convert your algorithm into a program and, using randomly generated problem instances, determine the worth of the dominance rule as well as the bounding functions. To do this, you will have to run four versions of your program: ProgA$\cdots$ bounding functions and dominance rules are removed, ProgB$\cdots$ dominance rule is removed, ProgC$\cdots$ bounding function is removed, and ProgD$\cdots$ bounding functions and dominance rules are included. Determine computing time figures as well as the number of nodes generated.

8.2 0/1 KNAPSACK PROBLEM

To use the branch-and-bound technique to solve any problem, it is first necessary to conceive of a state space tree for the problem. We have already seen two possible state space tree organizations for the knapsack problem (Section 7.6). Still, we cannot directly apply the techniques of Section 8.1 since these were discussed with respect to minimization problems whereas the knapsack problem is a maximization problem. This difficulty is easily overcome by replacing the objective function $\sum p_i x_i$ by the function $-\sum p_i x_i$. Clearly, $\sum p_i x_i$ is maximized iff $-\sum p_i x_i$ is minimized. This modified knapsack problem is stated as (8.1).

$$\text{minimize} \quad -\sum_{i=1}^{n} p_i x_i$$

$$\text{subject to} \quad \sum_{i=1}^{n} w_i x_i \leq m \tag{8.1}$$

$$x_i = 0 \text{ or } 1, \quad 1 \leq i \leq n$$

We continue the discussion assuming a fixed tuple size formulation for the solution space. The discussion is easily extended to the variable tuple size formulation. Every leaf node in the state space tree representing an assignment for which $\sum_{1 \leq i \leq n} w_i x_i \leq m$ is an answer (or solution) node. All other leaf nodes are infeasible. For a minimum-cost answer node to correspond to any optimal solution, we need to define $c(x) = -\sum_{1 \leq i \leq n} p_i x_i$ for every answer node x. The cost $c(x) = \infty$ for infeasible leaf nodes. For nonleaf nodes, $c(x)$ is recursively defined to be min $\{c(lchild(x)), c(rchild(x))\}$.

We now need two functions $\hat{c}(x)$ and $u(x)$ such that $\hat{c}(x) \le c(x) \le u(x)$ for every node x. The cost $\hat{c}(\cdot)$ and $u(\cdot)$ satisfying this requirement may be obtained as follows. Let x be a node at level j, $1 \le j \le n+1$. At node x assignments have already been made to x_i, $1 \le i < j$. The cost of these assignments is $-\sum_{1\le i<j} p_i x_i$. So, $c(x) \le -\sum_{1\le i<j} p_i x_i$ and we may use $u(x) = -\sum_{1\le i<j} p_i x_i$. If $q = -\sum_{1\le i<j} p_i x_i$, then an improved upper bound function $u(x)$ is $u(x) = \mathsf{UBound}(q, \sum_{1\le i<j} w_i x_i, j-1, m)$, where UBound is defined in Algorithm 8.2. As for $c(x)$, it is clear that $\mathsf{Bound}(-q, \sum_{1\le i<j} w_i x_i, j-1) \le c(x)$, where Bound is as given in Algorithm 7.11.

```
Algorithm UBound(cp, cw, k, m)
// cp, cw, k, and m have the same meanings as in
// Algorithm 7.11. w[i] and p[i] are respectively
// the weight and profit of the ith object.
{
    b := cp; c := cw;
    for i := k + 1 to n do
    {
        if (c + w[i] ≤ m) then
        {
            c := c + w[i]; b := b − p[i];
        }
    }
    return b;
}
```

Algorithm 8.2 Function $u(\cdot)$ for knapsack problem

8.2.1 LC Branch-and-Bound Solution

Example 8.2 [LCBB] Consider the knapsack instance $n = 4$, $(p_1, p_2, p_3, p_4) = (10, 10, 12, 18)$, $(w_1, w_2, w_3, w_4) = (2, 4, 6, 9)$, and $m = 15$. Let us trace the working of an LC branch-and-bound search using $\hat{c}(\cdot)$ and $u(\cdot)$ as defined previously. We continue to use the fixed tuple size formulation. The search begins with the root as the E-node. For this node, node 1 of Figure 8.8, we have $\hat{c}(1) = -38$ and $u(1) = -32$.

The computation of $u(1)$ and $\hat{c}(1)$ is done as follows. The bound $u(1)$

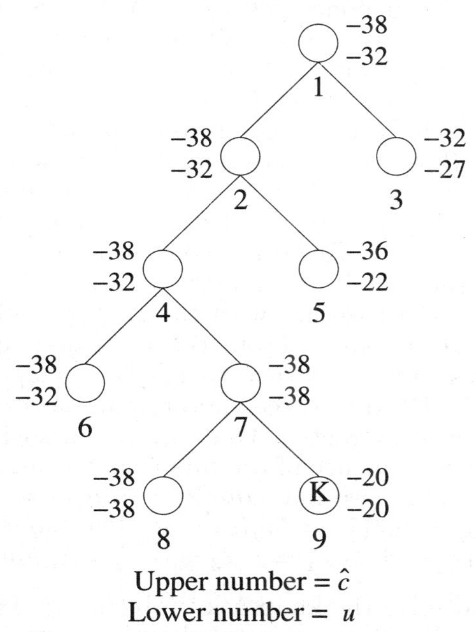

Figure 8.8 LC branch-and-bound tree for Example 8.2

has a value UBound(0, 0, 0, 15). UBound scans through the objects from left to right starting from j; it adds these objects into the knapsack until the first object that doesn't fit is encountered. At this time, the negation of the total profit of all the objects in the knapsack plus cw is returned. In Function UBound, c and b start with a value of zero. For $i = 1, 2$, and 3, c gets incremented by 2, 4, and 6, respectively. The variable b also gets decremented by 10, 10, and 12, respectively. When $i = 4$, the test $(c + w[i] \leq m)$ fails and hence the value returned is -32. Function Bound is similar to UBound, except that it also considers a fraction of the first object that doesn't fit the knapsack. For example, in computing $\hat{c}(1)$, the first object that doesn't fit is 4 whose weight is 9. The total weight of the objects 1, 2, and 3 is 12. So, Bound considers a fraction $\frac{3}{9}$ of the object 4 and hence returns $-32 - \frac{3}{9} * 18 = -38$.

Since node 1 is not a solution node, LCBB sets $ans = 0$ and $upper = -32$ (ans being a variable to store intermediate answer nodes). The E-node is expanded and its two children, nodes 2 and 3, generated. The cost $\hat{c}(2) = -38$, $\hat{c}(3) = -32$, $u(2) = -32$, and $u(3) = -27$. Both nodes are put onto the list of live nodes. Node 2 is the next E-node. It is expanded and nodes

4 and 5 generated. Both nodes get added to the list of live nodes. Node 4 is the live node with least $\hat{c}$ value and becomes the next E-node. Nodes 6 and 7 are generated. Assuming node 6 is generated first, it is added to the list of live nodes. Next, node 7 joins this list and *upper* is updated to -38. The next E-node will be one of nodes 6 and 7. Let us assume it is node 7. Its two children are nodes 8 and 9. Node 8 is a solution node. Then *upper* is updated to -38 and node 8 is put onto the live nodes list. Node 9 has $\hat{c}(9) > upper$ and is killed immediately. Nodes 6 and 8 are two live nodes with least $\hat{c}$. Regardless of which becomes the next E-node, $\hat{c}(E) \geq upper$ and the search terminates with node 8 the answer node. At this time, the value -38 together with the path 8, 7, 4, 2, 1 is printed out and the algorithm terminates. From the path one cannot figure out the assignment of values to the x_i's such that $\sum p_i x_i = upper$. Hence, a proper implementation of LCBB has to keep additional information from which the values of the x_i's can be extracted. One way is to associate with each node a one bit field, *tag*. The sequence of *tag* bits from the answer node to the root give the x_i values. Thus, we have $tag(2) = tag(4) = tag(6) = tag(8) = 1$ and $tag(3) = tag(5) = tag(7) = tag(9) = 0$. The *tag* sequence for the path 8, 7, 4, 2, 1 is 1 0 1 1 and so $x_4 = 1, x_3 = 0, x_2 = 1$, and $x_1 = 1$. □

To use LCBB to solve the knapsack problem, we need to specify (1) the structure of nodes in the state space tree being searched, (2) how to generate the children of a given node, (3) how to recognize a solution node, and (4) a representation of the list of live nodes and a mechanism for adding a node into the list as well as identifying the least-cost node. The node structure needed depends on which of the two formulations for the state space tree is being used. Let us continue with a fixed size tuple formulation. Each node x that is generated and put onto the list of live nodes must have a *parent* field. In addition, as noted in Example 8.2, each node should have a one bit *tag* field. This field is needed to output the x_i values corresponding to an optimal solution. To generate x's children, we need to know the level of node x in the state space tree. For this we shall use a field *level*. The left child of x is chosen by setting $x_{level(x)} = 1$ and the right child by setting $x_{level(x)} = 0$. To determine the feasibility of the left child, we need to know the amount of knapsack space available at node x. This can be determined either by following the path from node x to the root or by explicitly retaining this value in the node. Say we choose to retain this value in a field *cu* (capacity unused). The evaluation of $\hat{c}(x)$ and $u(x)$ requires knowledge of the profit $\sum_{1 \leq i < level(x)} p_i x_i$ earned by the filling corresponding to node x. This can be computed by following the path from x to the root. Alternatively, this value can be explicitly retained in a field *pe*. Finally, in order to determine the live node with least $\hat{c}$ value or to insert nodes properly into the list of live nodes, we need to know $\hat{c}(x)$. Again, we have a choice. The value $\hat{c}(x)$ may be stored explicitly in a field *ub* or may be computed when needed. Assuming all information is kept explicitly, we need nodes with six fields each: *parent*, *level*, *tag*, *cu*, *pe*, and *ub*.

Using this six-field node structure, the children of any live node x can be easily determined. The left child y is feasible iff $cu(x) \geq w_{level(x)}$. In this case, $parent(y) = x$, $level(y) = level(x) + 1$, $cu(y) = cu(x) - w_{level(x)}$, $pe(y) = pe(x) + p_{level(x)}$, $tag(y) = 1$, and $ub(y) = ub(x)$. The right child can be generated similarly. Solution nodes are easily recognized too. Node x is a solution node iff $level(x) = n + 1$.

We are now left with the task of specifying the representation of the list of live nodes. The functions we wish to perform on this list are (1) test if the list is empty, (2) add nodes, and (3) delete a node with least *ub*. We have seen a data structure that allows us to perform these three functions efficiently: a min-heap. If there are m live nodes, then function (1) can be carried out in $\Theta(1)$ time, whereas functions (2) and (3) require only $O(\log m)$ time.

8.2.2 FIFO Branch-and-Bound Solution

Example 8.3 Now, let us trace through the FIFOBB algorithm using the same knapsack instance as in Example 8.2. Initially the root node, node 1 of Figure 8.9, is the E-node and the queue of live nodes is empty. Since this is not a solution node, *upper* is initialized to $u(1) = -32$.

We assume the children of a node are generated left to right. Nodes 2 and 3 are generated and added to the queue (in that order). The value of *upper* remains unchanged. Node 2 becomes the next E-node. Its children, nodes 4 and 5, are generated and added to the queue. Node 3, the next E-node, is expanded. Its children nodes are generated. Node 6 gets added to the queue. Node 7 is immediately killed as $\hat{c}(7) >$ *upper*. Node 4 is expanded next. Nodes 8 and 9 are generated and added to the queue. Then *upper* is updated to $u(9) = -38$. Nodes 5 and 6 are the next two nodes to become E-nodes. Neither is expanded as for each, $\hat{c}() >$ *upper*. Node 8 is the next E-node. Nodes 10 and 11 are generated. Node 10 is infeasible and so killed. Node 11 has $\hat{c}(11) >$ *upper* and so is also killed. Node 9 is expanded next. When node 12 is generated, *upper* and *ans* are updated to -38 and 12 respectively. Node 12 joins the queue of live nodes. Node 13 is killed before it can get onto the queue of live nodes as $\hat{c}(13) >$ *upper*. The only remaining live node is node 12. It has no children and the search terminates. The value of *upper* and the path from node 12 to the root is output. As in the case of Example 8.2, additional information is needed to determine the x_i values on this path. □

At first we may be tempted to discard FIFOBB in favor of LCBB in solving knapsack. Our intuition leads us to believe that LCBB will examine fewer nodes in its quest for an optimal solution. However, we should keep in mind that insertions into and deletions from a heap are far more expensive

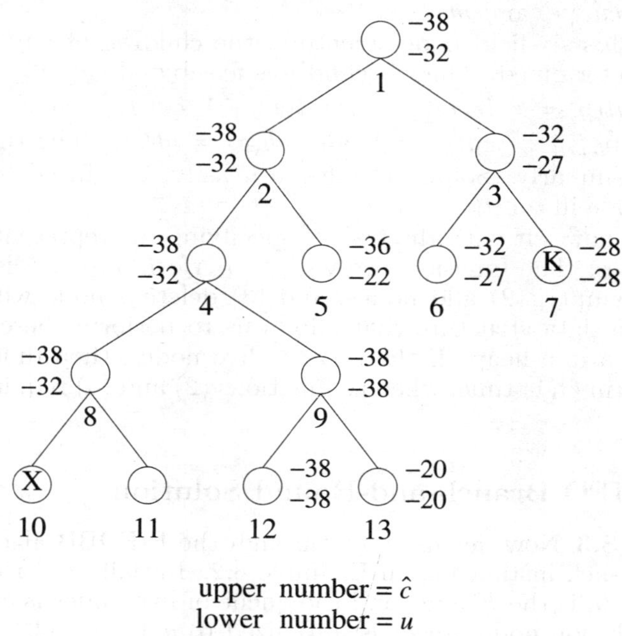

Figure 8.9 FIFO branch-and-bound tree for Example 8.3

(proportional to the logarithm of the heap size) than the corresponding operations on a queue ($\Theta(1)$). Consequently, the work done for each E-node is more in LCBB than in FIFOBB. Unless LCBB uses far fewer E-nodes than FIFOBB, FIFOBB will outperform (in terms of real computation time) LCBB.

We have now seen four different approaches to solving the knapsack problem: dynamic programming, backtracking, LCBB, and FIFOBB. If we compare the dynamic programming algorithm DKnap (Algorithm 5.7) and FIFOBB, we see that there is a correspondence between generating the $S^{(i)}$'s and generating nodes by levels. $S^{(i)}$ contains all pairs (P, W) corresponding to nodes on level $i+1$, $0 \leq i \leq n$. Hence, both algorithms generate the state space tree by levels. The dynamic programming algorithm, however, keeps the nodes on each level ordered by their profit earned (P) and capacity used (W) values. No two tuples have the same P or W value. In FIFOBB we may have many nodes on the same level with the same P or W value. It is not easy to implement the dominance rule of Section 5.7 into FIFOBB as nodes on a level are not ordered by their P or W values. However, the bounding rules can easily be incorporated into DKnap. Toward the end of Section 5.7 we discussed some simple heuristics to determine whether a pair $(P,\ W) \in S^{(i)}$ should be killed. These heuristics are readily seen to be bounding functions of the type discussed here. Let the algorithm resulting from the inclusion of the bounding functions into DKnap be DKnap1. DKnap1 is expected to be superior to FIFOBB as it uses the dominance rule in addition to the bounding functions. In addition, the overhead incurred each time a node is generated is less.

To determine which of the knapsack algorithms is best, it is necessary to program them and obtain real computing times for different data sets. Since the effectiveness of the bounding functions and the dominance rule is highly data dependent, we expect a wide variation in the computing time for different problem instances having the same number of objects n. To get representative times, it is necessary to generate many problem instances for a fixed n and obtain computing times for these instances. The generation of these data sets and the problem of conducting the tests is discussed in a programming project at the end of this section. The results of some tests can be found in the references to this chapter.

Before closing our discussion of the knapsack problem, we briefly discuss a very effective heuristic to reduce a knapsack instance with large n to an equivalent one with smaller n. This heuristic, Reduce, uses some of the ideas developed for the branch-and-bound algorithm. It classifies the objects $\{1, 2, \ldots, n\}$ into one of three categories $I1, I2$, and $I3$. $I1$ is a set of objects for which x_i must be 1 in every optimal solution. $I2$ is a set for which x_i must be 0. $I3$ is $\{1, 2, \ldots, n\} - I1 - I2$. Once $I1$, $I2$, and $I3$ have been determined, we need to solve only the reduced knapsack instance

$$\text{maximize} \sum_{i \in I3} p_i x_i$$

$$\text{subject to} \sum_{i \in I3} w_i x_i \leq m - \sum_{i \in I1} w_i x_i \tag{8.2}$$

$$x_i = 0 \text{ or } 1$$

From the solution to (8.2) an optimal solution to the original knapsack instance is obtained by setting $x_i = 1$ if $i \in I1$ and $x_i = 0$ if $i \in I2$.

Function Reduce (Algorithm 8.3) makes use of two functions Ubb and Lbb. The bound Ubb($I1$, $I2$) is an upper bound on the value of an optimal solution to the given knapsack instance with added constraints $x_i = 1$ if $i \in I1$ and $x_i = 0$ if $i \in I2$. The bound Lbb($I1$, $I2$) is a lower bound under the constraints of $I1$ and $I2$. Algorithm Reduce needs no further explanation. It should be clear that $I1$ and $I2$ are such that from an optimal solution to

```
Algorithm Reduce(p, w, n, m, I1, I2)
// Variables are as described in the discussion.
// p[i]/w[i] ≥ p[i+1]/w[i+1], 1 ≤ i < n.
{
    I1 := I2 := ∅;
    q := Lbb(∅, ∅);
    k := largest j such that w[1] + ··· + w[j] < m;
    for i := 1 to k do
    {
        if (Ubb(∅, {i}) < q) then I1 := I1 ∪ {i};
        else if (Lbb(∅, {i}) > q) then q := Lbb(∅, {i});
    }
    for i := k + 1 to n do
    {
        if (Ubb({i}, ∅) < q) then I2 := I2 ∪ {i};
        else if (Lbb({i}, ∅) > q) then q := Lbb({i}, ∅);
    }
}
```

Algorithm 8.3 Reduction pseudocode for knapsack problem

(8.2), we can easily obtain an optimal solution to the original knapsack problem.

The time complexity of Reduce is $O(n^2)$. Because the reduction procedure is very much like the heuristics used in DKnap1 and the knapsack algorithms of this chapter, the use of Reduce does not decrease the overall computing time by as much as may be expected by the reduction in the number of objects. These algorithms do dynamically what Reduce does. The exercises explore the value of Reduce further.

EXERCISES

1. Work out Example 8.2 using the variable tuple size formulation.

2. Work out Example 8.3 using the variable tuple size formulation.

3. Draw the portion of the state space tree generated by LCBB for the following knapsack instances:

(a) $n = 5$, $(p_1, p_2, \ldots, p_5) = (10,\ 15,\ 6,\ 8,\ 4)$, $(w_1, w_2, \ldots, w_5) = (4,\ 6,\ 3,\ 4,\ 2)$, and $m = 12$.

(b) $n = 5$, $(p_1, p_2, p_3, p_4, p_5) = (w_1, w_2, w_3, w_4, w_5) = (4,\ 4,\ 5,\ 8,\ 9)$ and $m = 15$.

4. Do Exercise 3 using LCBB on a dynamic state space tree (see Section 7.6). Use the fixed tuple size formulation.

5. Write a LCBB algorithm for the knapsack problem using the ideas given in Example 8.2.

6. Write a LCBB algorithm for the knapsack problem using the fixed tuple size formulation and the dynamic state space tree of Section 7.6.

7. [Programming project] Program the algorithms DKnap (Algorithm 5.7), DKnap1 (page 419), LCBB for knapsack, and Bknap (Algorithm 7.12). Compare these programs empirically using randomly generated data as below:

   (a) Random w_i and p_i, $w_i \in [1, 100]$, $p_i \in [1, 100]$, and $m = \sum_1^n w_i/2$.
   (b) Random w_i and p_i, $w_i \in [1, 100]$, $p_i \in [1, 100]$, and $m = 2\ \max\ \{w_i\}$.
   (c) Random w_i, $w_i \in [1, 100]$, $p_i = w_i + 10$, and $m = \sum_1^n w_i/2$.
   (d) Same as (c) except $m = 2\ \max\ \{w_i\}$.
   (e) Random p_i, $p_i \in [1, 100]$, $w_i = p_i + 10$, and $m = \sum_1^n w_i/2$.
   (f) Same as (e) except $m = 2\ \max\ \{w_i\}$.

   Obtain computing times for $n = 5, 10, 20, 30, 40, \ldots$. For each n, generate (say) ten problem instances from each of the above data sets. Report average and worst-case computing times for each of the above data sets. From these times can you say anything about the expected behavior of these algorithms?

   Now, generate problem instances with $p_i = w_i$, $1 \le i \le n$, $m = \sum w_i/2$, and $\sum w_i x_i \neq m$ for any 0, 1 assignment to the x_i's. Obtain computing times for your four programs for $n =$ 10, 20, and 30. Now study the effect of changing the range to [1, 1000] in data sets (a) through (f). In sets (c) to (f) replace $p_i = w_i + 10$ by $p_i = w_i + 100$ and $w_i = p_i + 10$ by $w_i = p_i + 100$.

8. [Programming project]

   (a) Program the reduction heuristic Reduce of Section 8.2. Generate several problem instances from the data sets of Exercise 7 and determine the size of the reduced problem instances. Use $n =$ 100, 200, 500, and 1000.

(b) Program DKnap and the backtracking algorithm Bknap for the knapsack problem. Compare the effectiveness of Reduce by running several problem instances (as in Exercise 7). Obtain average and worst-case computing times for DKnap and Bknap for the generated problem instances and also for the reduced instances. To the times for the reduced problem instances, add the time required by Reduce. What conclusion can you draw from your experiments?

8.3 TRAVELING SALESPERSON (*)

An $O(n^2 2^n)$ dynamic programming algorithm for the traveling salesperson problem was arrived at in Section 5.9. We now investigate branch-and-bound algorithms for this problem. Although the worst-case complexity of these algorithms will not be any better than $O(n^2 2^n)$, the use of good bounding functions will enable these branch-and-bound algorithms to solve some problem instances in much less time than required by the dynamic programming algorithm.

Let $G = (V, E)$ be a directed graph defining an instance of the traveling salesperson problem. Let c_{ij} equal the cost of edge $\langle i, j \rangle$, $c_{ij} = \infty$ if $\langle i, j \rangle \notin E$, and let $|V| = n$. Without loss of generality, we can assume that every tour starts and ends at vertex 1. So, the solution space S is given by $S = \{1, \pi, 1 | \pi$ is a permutation of $(2, 3, \ldots, n)\}$. Then $|S| = (n-1)!$. The size of S can be reduced by restricting S so that $(1, i_1, i_2, \ldots, i_{n-1}, 1) \in S$ iff $\langle i_j, i_{j+1} \rangle \in E$, $0 \le j \le n-1$, and $i_0 = i_n = 1$. S can be organized into a state space tree similar to that for the n-queens problem (see Figure 7.2). Figure 8.10 shows the tree organization for the case of a complete graph with $|V| = 4$. Each leaf node L is a solution node and represents the tour defined by the path from the root to L. Node 14 represents the tour $i_0 = 1, i_1 = 3, i_2 = 4, i_3 = 2$, and $i_4 = 1$.

To use LCBB to search the traveling salesperson state space tree, we need to define a cost function $c(\cdot)$ and two other functions $\hat{c}(\cdot)$ and $u(\cdot)$ such that $\hat{c}(r) \le c(r) \le u(r)$ for all nodes r. The cost $c(\cdot)$ is such that the solution node with least $c(\cdot)$ corresponds to a shortest tour in G. One choice for $c(\cdot)$ is

$$c(A) = \begin{cases} \text{length of tour defined by the path from the root to } A, & \text{if } A \text{ is a leaf} \\ \text{cost of a minimum-cost leaf in the subtree } A, & \text{if } A \text{ is not a leaf} \end{cases}$$

A simple $\hat{c}(\cdot)$ such that $\hat{c}(A) \le c(A)$ for all A is obtained by defining $\hat{c}(A)$ to be the length of the path defined at node A. For example, the path defined at node 6 of Figure 8.10 is $i_0, i_1, i_2 = 1, 2, 4$. It consists of the edges $\langle 1, 2 \rangle$ and $\langle 2, 4 \rangle$. A better $\hat{c}(\cdot)$ can be obtained by using the reduced cost matrix corresponding to G. A row (column) is said to be *reduced* iff it contains at

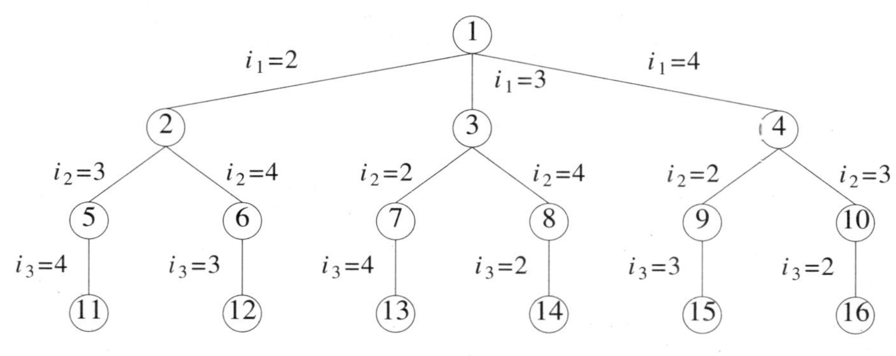

Figure 8.10 State space tree for the traveling salesperson problem with $n = 4$ and $i_0 = i_4 = 1$

least one zero and all remaining entries are non-negative. A matrix is *reduced* iff every row and column is reduced. As an example of how to reduce the cost matrix of a given graph G, consider the matrix of Figure 8.11(a). This corresponds to a graph with five vertices. Since every tour on this graph includes exactly one edge $\langle i, j \rangle$ with $i = k$, $1 \leq k \leq 5$, and exactly one edge $\langle i, j \rangle$ with $j = k$, $1 \leq k \leq 5$, subtracting a constant t from every entry in one column or one row of the cost matrix reduces the length of every tour by exactly t. A minimum-cost tour remains a minimum-cost tour following this subtraction operation. If t is chosen to be the minimum entry in row i (column j), then subtracting it from all entries in row i (column j) introduces a zero into row i (column j). Repeating this as often as needed, the cost matrix can be reduced. The total amount subtracted from the columns and rows is a lower bound on the length of a minimum-cost tour and can be used as the $\hat{c}$ value for the root of the state space tree. Subtracting 10, 2, 2, 3, 4, 1, and 3 from rows 1, 2, 3, 4, and 5 and columns 1 and 3 respectively of the matrix of Figure 8.11(a) yields the reduced matrix of Figure 8.11(b). The total amount subtracted is 25. Hence, all tours in the original graph have a length at least 25.

We can associate a reduced cost matrix with every node in the traveling salesperson state space tree. Let A be the reduced cost matrix for node R. Let S be a child of R such that the tree edge (R, S) corresponds to including edge $\langle i, j \rangle$ in the tour. If S is not a leaf, then the reduced cost matrix for S may be obtained as follows: (1) Change all entries in row i and column j of A to ∞. This prevents the use of any more edges leaving vertex i or entering vertex j. (2) Set $A(j, 1)$ to ∞. This prevents the use of edge $\langle j, 1 \rangle$. (3) Reduce all rows and columns in the resulting matrix except for rows and columns containing only ∞. Let the resulting matrix be B. Steps (1) and (2) are valid as no tour in the subtree s can contain edges of the type $\langle i, k\rangle$ or $\langle k, j\rangle$ or $\langle j, 1\rangle$ (except for edge $\langle i, j\rangle$). If r is the total amount subtracted in step (3) then $\hat{c}(S) = \hat{c}(R) + A(i, j) + r$. For leaf nodes, $\hat{c}(\cdot) = c()$ is easily computed as each leaf defines a unique tour. For the upper bound function u, we can use $u(R) = \infty$ for all nodes R.

$$\begin{bmatrix} \infty & 20 & 30 & 10 & 11 \\ 15 & \infty & 16 & 4 & 2 \\ 3 & 5 & \infty & 2 & 4 \\ 19 & 6 & 18 & \infty & 3 \\ 16 & 4 & 7 & 16 & \infty \end{bmatrix}$$

(a) Cost matrix

$$\begin{bmatrix} \infty & 10 & 17 & 0 & 1 \\ 12 & \infty & 11 & 2 & 0 \\ 0 & 3 & \infty & 0 & 2 \\ 15 & 3 & 12 & \infty & 0 \\ 11 & 0 & 0 & 12 & \infty \end{bmatrix}$$

(b) Reduced cost matrix
L = 25

Figure 8.11 An example

Let us now trace the progress of the LCBB algorithm on the problem instance of Figure 8.11(a). We use $\hat{c}$ and u as above. The initial reduced matrix is that of Figure 8.11(b) and *upper* $= \infty$. The portion of the state space tree that gets generated is shown in Figure 8.12. Starting with the root node as the E-node, nodes 2, 3, 4, and 5 are generated (in that order). The reduced matrices corresponding to these nodes are shown in Figure 8.13. The matrix of Figure 8.13(b) is obtained from that of 8.11(b) by (1) setting all entries in row 1 and column 3 to ∞, (2) setting the element at position (3, 1) to ∞, and (3) reducing column 1 by subtracting by 11. The $\hat{c}$ for node 3 is therefore 25 + 17 (the cost of edge $\langle 1, 3\rangle$ in the reduced matrix) + 11 = 53. The matrices and $\hat{c}$ value for nodes 2, 4, and 5 are obtained similarly. The value of *upper* is unchanged and node 4 becomes the next E-node. Its children 6, 7, and 8 are generated. The live nodes at this time are nodes 2, 3, 5, 6, 7, and 8. Node 6 has least $\hat{c}$ value and becomes the next E-node. Nodes 9 and 10 are generated. Node 10 is the next E-node. The solution node, node 11, is generated. The tour length for this node is $\hat{c}(11) = 28$ and *upper* is updated to 28. For the next E-node, node 5, $\hat{c}(5) = 31 >$ *upper*. Hence, LCBB terminates with 1, 4, 2, 5, 3, 1 as the shortest length tour.

An exercise examines the implementation considerations for the LCBB algorithm. A different LCBB algorithm can be arrived at by considering a different tree organization for the solution space. This organization is reached by regarding a tour as a collection of n edges. If $G = (V, E)$ has e edges, then every tour contains exactly n of the e edges. However, for each $i, 1 \leq i \leq n$, there is exactly one edge of the form $\langle i, j\rangle$ and one of the form $\langle k, i\rangle$ in every tour. A possible organization for the state space is a binary

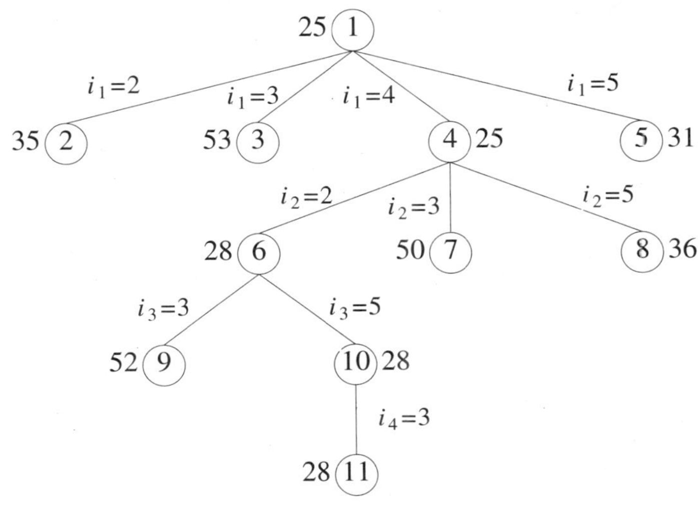

Figure 8.12 State space tree generated by procedure LCBB

tree in which a left branch represents the inclusion of a particular edge while the right branch represents the exclusion of that edge. Figure 8.14(b) and (c) represents the first two levels of two possible state space trees for the three vertex graph of Figure 8.14(a). As is true of all problems, many state space trees are possible for a given problem formulation. Different trees differ in the order in which decisions are made. Thus, in Figure 8.14(c) we first decide the fate of edge $\langle 1, 2 \rangle$. Rather than use a static state space tree, we now consider a dynamic state space tree (see Section 7.1). This is also a binary tree. However, the order in which edges are considered depends on the particular problem instance being solved. We compute $\hat{c}$ in the same way as we did using the earlier state space tree formulation.

As an example of how LCBB would work on the dynamic binary tree formulation, consider the cost matrix of Figure 8.11(a). Since a total of 25 needs to be subtracted from the rows and columns of this matrix to obtain the reduced matrix of Figure 8.11(b), all tours have a length at least 25. This fact is represented by the root of the state space tree of Figure 8.15. Now, we must decide which edge to use to partition the solution space into two subsets. If edge $\langle i, j \rangle$ is used, then the left subtree of the root represents all tours including edge $\langle i, j \rangle$ and the right subtree represents all tours that

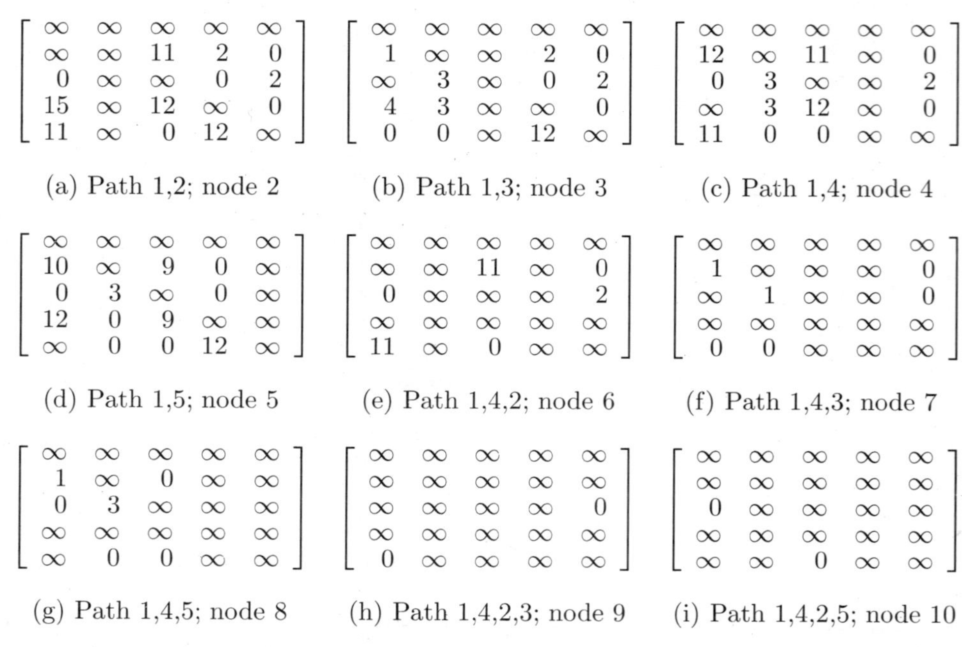

Figure 8.13 Reduced cost matrices corresponding to nodes in Figure 8.12

do not include edge $\langle i, j \rangle$. If an optimal tour is included in the left subtree, then only $n - 1$ edges remain to be selected. If all optimal tours lie in the right subtree, then we have still to select n edges. Since the left subtree selects fewer edges, it should be easier to find an optimal solution in it than to find one in the right subtree. Consequently, we would like to choose as the partitioning edge an edge $\langle i, j \rangle$ that has the highest probability of being in an optimal tour. Several heuristics for determining such an edge can be formulated. A selection rule that is commonly used is select that edge which results in a right subtree that has highest $\hat{c}$ value. The logic behind this is that we soon have right subtrees (perhaps at lower levels) for which the $\hat{c}$ value is higher than the length of an optimal tour. Another possibility is to choose an edge such that the difference in the $\hat{c}$ values for the left and right subtrees is maximum. Other selection rules are also possible.

When LCBB is used with the first of the two selection rules stated above and the cost matrix of Figure 8.11(a), the tree of Figure 8.15 is generated. At the root node, we have to determine an edge $\langle i, j \rangle$ that will maximize the $\hat{c}$ value of the right subtree. If we select an edge $\langle i, j \rangle$ whose cost in the reduced matrix (Figure 8.11(b)) is positive, then the $\hat{c}$ value of the right

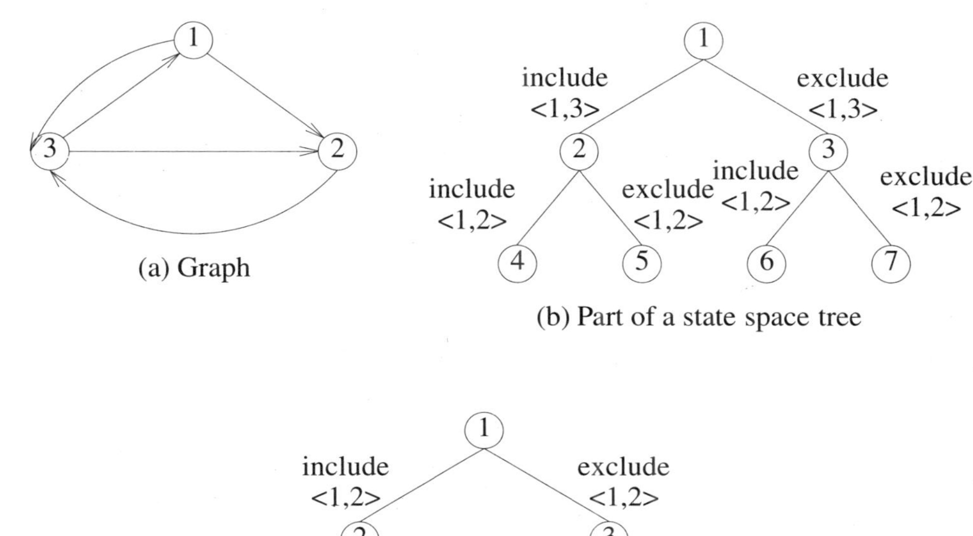

(a) Graph

(b) Part of a state space tree

(c) Part of a state space tree

Figure 8.14 An example

subtree will remain 25. This is so as the reduced matrix for the right subtree will have $B(i, j) = \infty$ and all other entries will be identical to those in Figure 8.11(b). Hence B will be reduced and $\hat{c}$ cannot increase. So, we must choose an edge with reduced cost 0. If we choose $\langle 1, 4\rangle$, then $B(1, 4) = \infty$ and we need to subtract 1 from row 1 to obtain a reduced matrix. In this case $\hat{c}$ will be 26. If $\langle 3, 1\rangle$ is selected, then 11 needs to be subtracted from column 1 to obtain the reduced matrix for the right subtree. So, $\hat{c}$ will be 36. If A is the reduced cost matrix for node R, then the selection of edge $\langle i, j\rangle$ $(A(i, j) = 0)$ as the next partitioning edge will increase the $\hat{c}$ of the right subtree by $\triangle = \min_{k \neq j}\{A(i, k)\} + \min_{k \neq i}\{A(k, j)\}$ as this much needs to be subtracted from row i and column j to introduce a zero into both.

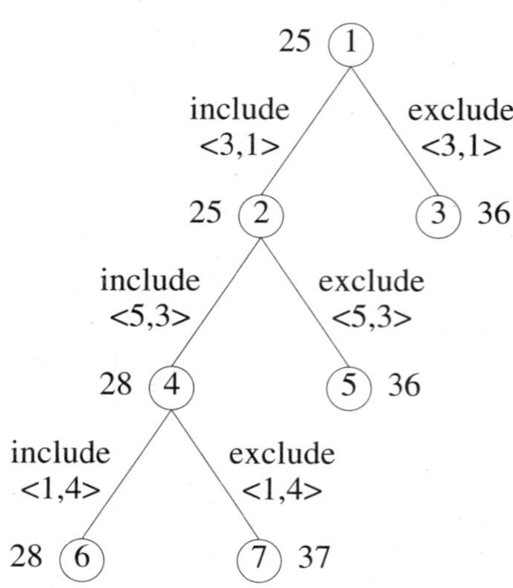

Figure 8.15 State space tree for Figure 8.11(a)

For edges $\langle 1,4\rangle, \langle 2,5\rangle, \langle 3,1\rangle$ $\langle 3,4\rangle, \langle 4,5\rangle, \langle 5,2\rangle$, and $\langle 5,3\rangle, \triangle = 1$, 2, 11, 0, 3, 3, and 11 respectively. So, either of the edges $\langle 3,1\rangle$ or $\langle 5,3\rangle$ can be used. Let us assume that LCBB selects edge $\langle 3,1\rangle$. The $\hat{c}(2)$ (Figure 8.15) can be computed in a manner similar to that for the state space tree of Figure 8.12. In the corresponding reduced cost matrix all entries in row 3 and column 1 will be ∞. Moreover the entry (1, 3) will also be ∞ as inclusion of this edge will result in a cycle. The reduced matrices corresponding to nodes 2 and 3 are given in Figure 8.16(a) and (b). The $\hat{c}$ values for nodes 2 and 3 (as well as for all other nodes) appear outside the respective nodes.

Node 2 is the next E-node. For edges $\langle 1,4\rangle, \langle 2,5\rangle, \langle 4,5\rangle, \langle 5,2\rangle$, and $\langle 5,3\rangle$, $\triangle = 3, 2, 3, 3$, and 11 respectively. Edge $\langle 5,3\rangle$ is selected and nodes 4 and 5 generated. The corresponding reduced matrices are given in Figure 8.16(c) and (d). Then $\hat{c}(4)$ becomes 28 as we need to subtract 3 from column 2 to reduce this column. Note that entry (1, 5) has been set to ∞ in Figure 8.16(c). This is necessary as the inclusion of edge $\langle 1,5\rangle$ to the collection $\{\langle 3,1\rangle, \langle 5,3\rangle\}$ will result in a cycle. In addition, entries in column 3 and row 5 are set to ∞. Node 4 is the next E-node. The $\triangle$ values corresponding to edges $\langle 1,4\rangle, \langle 2,5\rangle$, and $\langle 4,2\rangle$ are 9, 2, and 0 respectively. Edge $\langle 1,4\rangle$ is selected and nodes 6 and 7 generated. The edge selection at node 6 is $\{\langle 3,1\rangle, \langle 5,3\rangle, \langle 1,4\rangle\}$. This corresponds to the path 5, 3, 1, 4. So, entry (4,

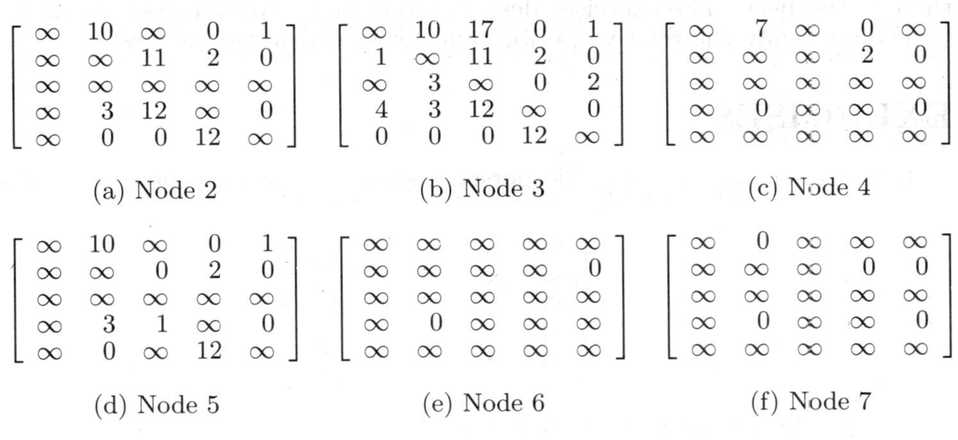

Figure 8.16 Reduced cost matrices for Figure 8.15

5) is set to ∞ in Figure 8.16(e). In general if edge $\langle i, j\rangle$ is selected, then the entries in row i and column j are set to ∞ in the left subtree. In addition, one more entry needs to be set to ∞. This is an entry whose inclusion in the set of edges would create a cycle (Exercise 4 examines how to determine this). The next E-node is node 6. At this time three of the five edges have already been selected. The remaining two may be selected directly. The only possibility is $\{\langle 4,2\rangle, \langle 2,5\rangle\}$. This gives the path $5, 3, 1, 4, 2, 5$ with length 28. So *upper* is updated to 28. Node 3 is the next E-node. Now LCBB terminates as $\hat{c}(3) = 36 > upper$.

In the preceding example, LCBB was modified slightly to handle nodes close to a solution node differently from other nodes. Node 6 is only two levels from a solution node. Rather than evaluate $\hat{c}$ at the children of 6 and then obtain their grandchildren, we just obtained an optimal solution for that subtree by a complete search with no bounding. We could have done something similar when generating the tree of Figure 8.12. Since node 6 is only two levels from the leaf nodes, we can simply skip computing $\hat{c}$ for the children and grandchildren of 6, generate all of them, and pick the best. This works out to be quite efficient as it is easier to generate a subtree with a small number of nodes and evaluate all the solution nodes in it than it is to compute $\hat{c}$ for one of the children of 6. This latter statement is true of many applications of branch-and-bound. Branch-and-bound is used on large subtrees. Once a small subtree is reached (say one with 4 or 6 nodes in it), then that subtree is fully evaluated without using the bounding functions.

We have now seen several branch-and-bound strategies for the traveling salesperson problem. It is not possible to determine analytically which of these is the best. The exercises describe computer experiments that determine empirically the relative performance of the strategies suggested.

EXERCISES

1. Consider the traveling salesperson instance defined by the cost matrix

$$\begin{bmatrix} \infty & 7 & 3 & 12 & 8 \\ 3 & \infty & 6 & 14 & 9 \\ 5 & 8 & \infty & 6 & 18 \\ 9 & 3 & 5 & \infty & 11 \\ 18 & 14 & 9 & 8 & \infty \end{bmatrix}$$

   (a) Obtain the reduced cost matrix

   (b) Using a state space tree formulation similar to that of Figure 8.10 and $\hat{c}$ as described in Section 8.3, obtain the portion of the state space tree that will be generated by LCBB. Label each node by its $\hat{c}$ value. Write out the reduced matrices corresponding to each of these nodes.

   (c) Do part (b) using the reduced matrix method and the dynamic state space tree approach discussed in Section 8.3.

2. Do Exercise 1 using the following traveling salesperson cost matrix:

$$\begin{bmatrix} \infty & 11 & 10 & 9 & 6 \\ 8 & \infty & 7 & 3 & 4 \\ 8 & 4 & \infty & 4 & 8 \\ 11 & 10 & 5 & \infty & 5 \\ 6 & 9 & 5 & 5 & \infty \end{bmatrix}$$

3. (a) Describe an efficient implementation for a LCBB traveling salesperson algorithm using the reduced cost matrix approach and (i) a dynamic state space tree and (ii) a static tree as in Figure 8.10.

   (b) Are there any problem instances for which the LCBB will generate fewer nodes using a static tree than using a dynamic tree? Prove your answer.

4. Consider the LCBB traveling salesperson algorithm described using the dynamic state space tree formulation. Let A and B be nodes. Let B be a child of A. If the edge (A, B) represents the inclusion of edge $\langle i, j \rangle$ in the tour, then in the reduced matrix for B all entries in row i and column j are set to ∞. In addition, one more entry is set to ∞. Obtain an efficient way to determine this entry.

5. [Programming project] Write computer programs for the following traveling salesperson algorithms:

   (a) The dynamic programming algorithm of Chapter 5

   (b) A backtracking algorithm using the static tree formulation of Section 8.3

   (c) A backtracking algorithm using the dynamic tree formulation of Section 8.3

   (d) A LCBB algorithm corresponding to (b)

   (e) A LCBB algorithm corresponding to (c)

   Design data sets to be used to compare the efficiency of the above algorithms. Randomly generate problem instances from these data sets and obtain computing times for your programs. What conclusions can you draw from your computing times?

8.4 EFFICIENCY CONSIDERATIONS

One can pose several questions concerning the performance characteristics of branch-and-bound algorithms that find least-cost answer nodes. We might ask questions such as:

1. Does the use of a better starting value for *upper* always decrease the number of nodes generated?

2. Is it possible to decrease the number of nodes generated by expanding some nodes with $\hat{c}() > upper$?

3. Does the use of a better $\hat{c}$ always result in a decrease in (or at least not an increase in) the number of nodes generated? (A $\hat{c}_2$ is better than $\hat{c}_1$ iff $\hat{c}_1(x) \le \hat{c}_2(x) \le c(x)$ for all nodes x.)

4. Does the use of dominance relations ever result in the generation of more nodes than would otherwise be generated?

In this section we answer these questions. Although the answers to most of the questions examined agree with our intuition, the answers to others are contrary to intuition. However, even in cases in which the answer does not agree with intuition, we can expect the performance of the algorithm to generally agree with the intuitive expectations. All the following theorems assume that the branch-and-bound algorithm is to find a minimum-cost solution node. Consequently, $c(x)$ = cost of minimum-cost solution node in subtree x.

Theorem 8.2 Let t be a state space tree. The number of nodes of t generated by FIFO, LIFO, and LC branch-and-bound algorithms cannot be decreased by the expansion of any node x with $\hat{c}(x) \geq upper$, where *upper* is the current upper bound on the cost of a minimum-cost solution node in the tree t.

Proof: The theorem follows from the observation that the value of *upper* cannot be decreased by expanding x (as $\hat{c}(x) \geq upper$). Hence, such an expansion cannot affect the operation of the algorithm on the remainder of the tree. □

Theorem 8.3 Let U_1 and $U_2, U_1 < U_2$, be two initial upper bounds on the cost of a minimum-cost solution node in the state space tree t. Then FIFO, LIFO, and LC branch-and-bound algorithms beginning with U_1 will generate no more nodes than they would if they started with U_2 as the initial upper bound.

Proof: Left as an exercise. □

Theorem 8.4 The use of a better $\hat{c}$ function in conjunction with FIFO and LIFO branch-and-bound algorithms does not increase the number of nodes generated.

Proof: Left as an exercise. □

Theorem 8.5 If a better $\hat{c}$ function is used in a LC branch-and-bound algorithm, the number of nodes generated may increase.

Proof: Consider the state space tree of Figure 8.17. All leaf nodes are solution nodes. The value outside each leaf is its cost. From these values it follows that $c(1) = c(3) = 3$ and $c(2) = 4$. Outside each of nodes 1, 2, and 3 is a pair of numbers $\binom{\hat{c}_1}{\hat{c}_2}$. Clearly, $\hat{c}_2$ is a better function than $\hat{c}_1$. However, if $\hat{c}_2$ is used, node 2 can become the E-node before node 3, as $\hat{c}_2(2) = \hat{c}_2(3)$. In this case all nine nodes of the tree will get generated. When $\hat{c}_1$ is used, nodes 4, 5, and 6 are not generated. □

Now, let us look at the effect of dominance relations. Formally, a dominance relation D is given by a set of tuples, $D = \{(i_1, i_2), (i_3, i_4), (i_5, i_6), \ldots\}$. If $(i, j) \in D$, then node i is said to dominate node j. By this we mean that subtree i contains a solution node with cost no more than the cost of a minimum-cost solution node in subtree j. Dominated nodes can be killed without expansion.

Since every node dominates itself, $(i, i) \in D$ for all i and D. The relation (i, i) should not result in the killing of node i. In addition, it is quite possible for D to contain tuples (i_1, i_2), $(i_2, i_3), (i_3, i_4), \ldots, (i_n, i_1)$. In this

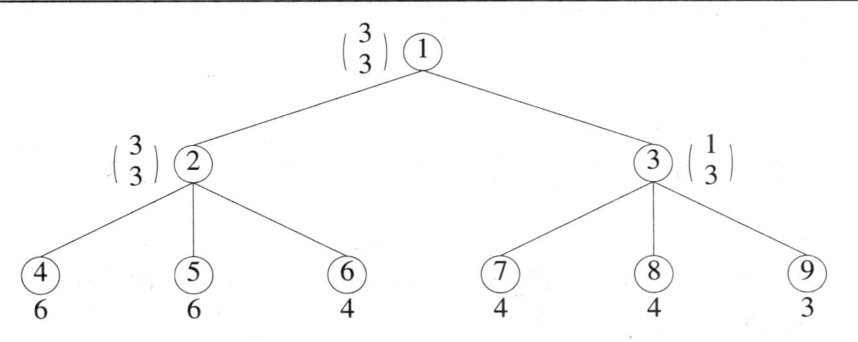

Figure 8.17 Example tree for Theorem 8.5

case, the transitivity of D implies that each node i_k dominates all nodes $i_j, 1 \leq j \leq n$. Care should be taken to leave at least one of the i_j's alive. A dominance relation D_2 is said to be *stronger* than another dominance relation D_1 iff $D_1 \subset D_2$. In the following theorems I denotes the identity relation $\{(i,i)|1 \leq i \leq n\}$.

Theorem 8.6 The number of nodes generated during a FIFO or LIFO branch-and-bound search for a least-cost solution node may increase when a stronger dominance relation is used.

Proof: Consider the state space tree of Figure 8.18. The only solution nodes are leaf nodes. Their cost is written outside the node. For the remaining nodes the number outside each node is its $\hat{c}$ value. The two dominance relations to use are $D_1 = I$ and $D_2 = I \cup \{(5,2),(5,8)\}$. Clearly, D_2 is stronger than D_1 and fewer nodes are generated using D_1 rather than D_2. □

Theorem 8.7 Let D_1 and D_2 be two dominance relations. Let D_2 be stronger than D_1 and such that $(i,j) \in D_2, i \neq j$, implies $\hat{c}(i) < \hat{c}(j)$. An LC branch-and-bound using D_1 generates at least as many nodes as one using D_2.

Proof: Left as an exercise. □

Theorem 8.8 If the condition $\hat{c}(i) < \hat{c}(j)$ in Theorem 8.7 is removed then an LC branch-and-bound using the relation D_1 may generate fewer nodes than one using D_2.

Proof: Left as an exercise. □

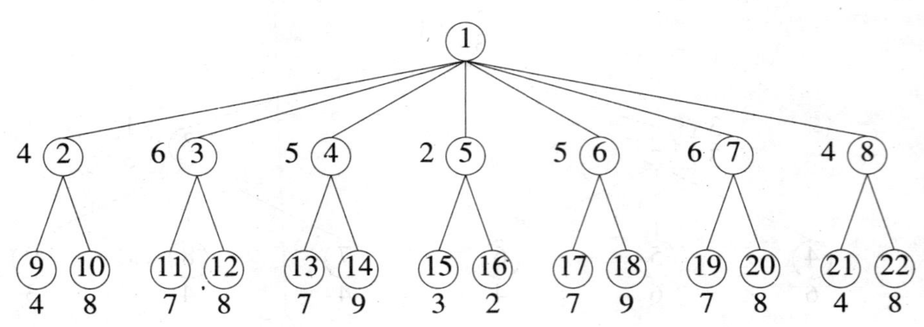

Figure 8.18 Example tree for Theorem 8.6

EXERCISES

1. Prove Theorem 8.3.

2. Prove Theorem 8.4.

3. Prove Theorem 8.7.

4. Prove Theorem 8.8.

5. [Heuristic search] Heuristic search is a generalization of FIFO, LIFO, and LC searches. A heuristic function $h(\cdot)$ is used to evaluate all live nodes. The next E-node is the live node with least $h(\cdot)$. Discuss the advantages of using a heuristic function $h(\cdot)$ different from $\hat{c}(\cdot)$ in the search for a least-cost answer node. Consider the knapsack and traveling salesperson problems as two example problems. Also consider any other problems you wish. For these problems devise reasonable functions $h(\cdot)$ (different from $\hat{c}(\cdot)$). Obtain problem instances on which heuristic search performs better than LC-search.

8.5 REFERENCES AND READINGS

LC branch-and-bound algorithms have been extensively studied by researchers in areas such as artificial intelligence and operations research.

Branch-and-bound algorithms using dominance relations in a manner similar to that suggested by FIFOKNAP (resulting in DKnap1) were given by M. Held and R. Karp.

The reduction technique for the knapsack problem is due to G. Ingargiola and J. Korsh.

The reduced matrix technique to compute $\hat{c}$ is due to J. Little, K. Murty, D. Sweeny, and C. Karel. They employed the dynamic state space tree approach.

The results of Section 8.4 are based on the work of W. Kohler, K. Steiglitz, and T. Ibaraki.

The application of branch-and-bound and other techniques to the knapsack and related problems is discussed extensively in *Knapsack Problems: Algorithms and Computer Implementations*, by S. Martello and P. Toth, John Wiley and Sons, 1990.

Chapter 9

ALGEBRAIC PROBLEMS

9.1 THE GENERAL METHOD

In this chapter we shift our attention away from the problems we've dealt with previously to concentrate on methods for dealing with numbers and polynomials. Though computers have the ability already built-in to manipulate integers and reals, they are not directly equipped to manipulate symbolic mathematical expressions such as polynomials. One must determine a way to represent them and then write procedures that perform the desired operations. A system that allows for the manipulation of mathematical expressions (usually including arbitrary precision integers, polynomials, and rational functions) is called a *mathematical symbol manipulation system.* These systems have been fruitfully used to solve a variety of scientific problems for many years. The techniques we study here have often led to efficient ways to implement the operations offered by these systems.

The first design technique we present is called *algebraic transformation.* Assume we have an input I that is a member of set S_1 and a function $f(I)$ that describes what must be computed. Usually the output $f(I)$ is also a member of S_1. Though a method may exist for computing $f(I)$ using operations on elements in S_1, this method may be inefficient. The algebraic transformation technique suggests that we alter the input into another form to produce a member of set S_2. The set S_2 contains exactly the same elements as S_1 except it assumes a different representation for them. Why would we transform the input into another form? Because it may be easier to compute the function f for elements of S_2 than for elements of S_1. Once the answer in S_2 is computed, an *inverse transformation* is performed to yield the result in set S_1.

Example 9.1 Let S_1 be the set of integers represented using decimal notation, and S_2 the set of integers using binary notation. Given two integers from set S_1, plus any arithmetic operations to carry out on these numbers, today's computers can transform the numbers into elements of set S_2, perform the operations, and transform the result back into decimal form. The algorithms for transforming the numbers are familiar to most students of computer science. To go from elements of set S_1 to set S_2, repeated division by 2 is used, and from set S_2 to set S_1, repeated multiplication is used. The value of binary representation is the simplification that results in the internal circuitry of a computer. □

Example 9.2 Let S_1 be the set of n-degree polynomials ($n \geq 0$) with integer coefficients represented by a list of their coefficients; e.g.,

$$A(x) = a_n x^n + \cdots + a_1 x + a_0$$

The set S_2 consists of exactly the same set of polynomials but is represented by their values at $2n+1$ points; that is, the $2n+1$ pairs $(x_i,\ A(x_i))$, $1 \leq i \leq 2n+1$, would represent the polynomial A. (At this stage we won't worry about what the values of x_i are, but for now you can consider them consecutive integers.) The function f to be computed is the one that determines the product of two polynomials $A(x)$ and $B(x)$, assuming the set S_1 representation to start with. Rather than forming the product directly using the conventional method (which requires $O(n^2)$ operations, where n is the degree of A and B and any possible growth in the size of the coefficients is ignored), we could transform the two polynomials into elements of the set S_2. We do this by *evaluating* $A(x)$ and $B(x)$ at $2n+1$ points. The product can now be computed simply, by multiplying the corresponding points together. The representation of $A(x)B(x)$ in set S_2 is given by the tuples $(x_i,\ A(x_i)B(x_i))$, $1 \leq i \leq 2n+1$, and requires only $O(n)$ operations to compute. We can determine the product of $A(x)B(x)$ in coefficient form by finding the polynomial that *interpolates* (or satisfies) these $2n+1$ points. It is easy to show that there is a unique polynomial of degree $\leq 2n$ that goes through $2n+1$ points.

Figure 9.1 describes these transformations in a graphical form indicating the two paths one can take to reach the coefficient product domain, either directly by conventional multiplication or indirectly by algebraic transformation. The transformation in one direction is effected by evaluation whereas the inverse transformation is accomplished by interpolation. The value of the scheme rests entirely on whether these transformations can be carried out efficiently.

For instance, if $A(x) = 3x^2 + 4x + 1$ and $B(x) = x^2 + 2x + 5$, these can be represented by the pairs $(0,1), (1,8), (2,21), (3,40)$, and $(4,65)$ and $(0,5), (1,8),\ (2,13), (3,20)$, and $(4,29)$, respectively. Then $A(x)B(x)$ in S_2 takes the form $(0,5),\ (1,64), (2,273), (3,800)$, and $(4,1885)$. □

The world of algebraic algorithms is so broad that we only attempt to cover a few of the interesting topics. In Section 9.2 we discuss the question

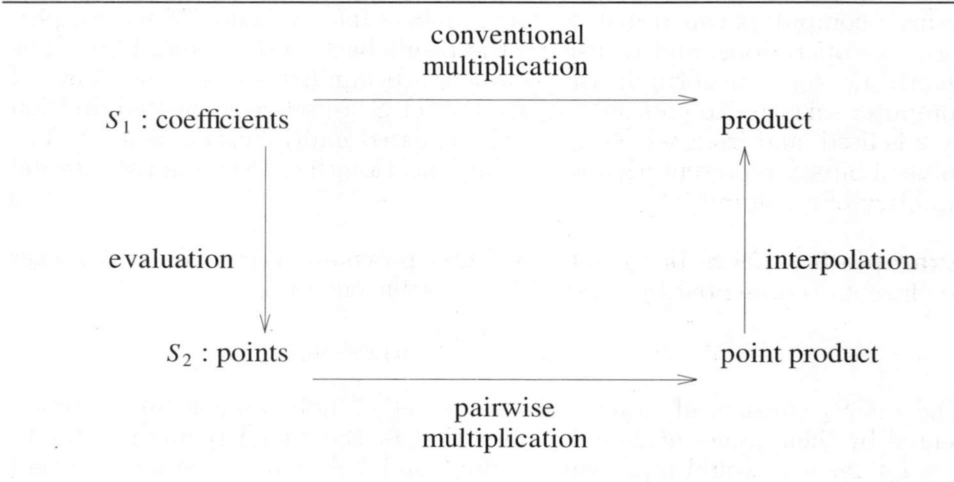

Figure 9.1 Transformation technique for polynomial products

of polynomial evaluation at one or more points and the inverse operation of polynomial interpolation at n points. Then in Section 9.3 we discuss the same problems as in Section 9.2 but this time assuming the n points are nth roots of unity. This is shown to be equivalent to computing the Fourier transform. We also show how the divide-and-conquer strategy leads to the *fast* Fourier transform algorithm. In Section 9.4 we shift our attention to integer problems, in this case the processes of modular arithmetic. Modular arithmetic can be viewed as a transformation scheme that is useful for speeding up large precision integer arithmetic operations. Moreover we see that transformation into and out of modular form is a special case of evaluation and interpolation. Thus there is an algebraic unity to Sections 9.2, 9.3, and 9.4. Finally, in Section 9.5 we present asymptotically efficient algorithms for n-point evaluation and interpolation.

EXERCISES

1. Devise an algorithm that accepts a number in decimal and produces the equivalent number in binary.

2. Devise an algorithm that performs the inverse transformation of Exercise 1.

3. Show the tuples that would result by representing the polynomials

$5x^2 + 3x + 10$ and $7x + 4$ at the values $x = 0, 1, 2, 3, 4, 5,$ and 6. What set of tuples is sufficient to represent the product of these two polynomials?

4. If $A(x) = a_n x^n + \cdots + a_1 x + a_0$, then the derivative of $A(x)$, $A'(x) = n a_n x^{n-1} + \cdots + a_1$. Devise an algorithm that produces the value of a polynomial and its derivative at a point $x = v$. Determine the number of required arithmetic operations.

9.2 EVALUATION AND INTERPOLATION

In this section we examine the operations on polynomials of evaluation and interpolation. As we search for efficient algorithms, we see examples of another design strategy called *algebraic simplification*. When applied to algebraic problems, algebraic simplification refers to the process of reexpressing computational formulas so that the required number of operations to compute these formulas is minimized. One issue we ignore here is the numerical stability of the resulting algorithms. Though this is often an important consideration, it is too far from our purposes.

A *univariate polynomial* is generally written as

$$A(x) = a_n x^n + a_{n-1} x^{n-1} + \cdots + a_1 x + a_0$$

where x is an indeterminate and the a_i may be integers, floating point numbers, or more generally elements of a commutative ring or a field. If $a_n \neq 0$, then n is called the *degree* of A.

When considering the representation of a polynomial by its coefficients, there are at least two alternatives. The first calls for storing the degree followed by degree + 1 coefficients:

$$(n, a_n, a_{n-1}, \ldots, a_1, a_0)$$

This is termed the *dense* representation because it explicitly stores all coefficients whether or not they are zero. We observe that for a polynomial such as $x^{1000} + 1$ the dense representation is wasteful since it requires 1002 locations although there are only two nonzero terms.

The second representation calls for storing only each *nonzero* coefficient and its corresponding exponent; for example, if all the a_i are nonzero, then the polynomial is stored as

$$(n, a_n, n-1, a_{n-1}, \ldots, 1, a_1,\ 0, a_0).$$

This is termed the *sparse* representation because the storage depends directly on the number of nonzero terms and not on the degree. For a polynomial of degree n, all of whose coefficients are nonzero, this second representation requires roughly twice the storage of the first. However, that is the

```
Algorithm StraightEval(A, n, v)
{
    r := 1; s := a_0;
    for i := 1 to n do
    {
        r := r * v;
        s := s + a_i * r;
    }
    return s;
}
```

Algorithm 9.1 Straightforward evaluation

worst case. For high-degree polynomials with few nonzero terms, the second representation is many times better than the first.

Secondarily we note that the terms of a polynomial will often be linked together rather than sequentially stored. However, we will avoid this complication in the following algorithms and assume that we can access the ith coefficient by writing a_i.

Suppose we are given the polynomial $A(x) = a_n x^n + \cdots + a_0$ and we wish to evaluate it at a point v, that is, compute $A(v)$. The straightforward or right-to-left method adds $a_1 v$ to a_0 and $a_2 v^2$ to this sum and continues as described in Algorithm 9.1. The analysis of this algorithm is quite simple: $2n$ multiplications, n additions, and $2n+2$ assignments are made (excluding the **for** loop).

An improvement to this procedure was devised by Isaac Newton in 1711. The same improvement was used by W. G. Horner in 1819 to evaluate the coefficients of $A(x+c)$. The method came to be known as Horner's rule. They rewrote the polynomial as

$$A(x) = (\cdots((a_n x + a_{n-1})x + a_{n-2})x + \cdots + a_1)x + a_0$$

This is our first and perhaps most famous example of algebraic simplification. The function for evaluation that is based on this formula is given in Algorithm 9.2.

Horner's rule requires n multiplications, n additions, and $n+1$ assignments (excluding the **for** loop). Thus we see that it is an improvement over the straightforward method by a factor of 2. In fact in Chapter 10 we see that Horner's rule yields the optimal way to evaluate an nth-degree polynomial.

```
Algorithm Horner(A, n, v)
{
    s := a_n;
    for i := n - 1 to 0 step -1 do
    {
        s := s * v + a_i;
    }
    return s;
}
```

Algorithm 9.2 Horner's rule

Now suppose we consider the sparse representation of a polynomial, $A(x) = a_m x^{e_m} + \cdots + a_1 x^{e_1}$, where the $a_i \neq 0$ and $e_m > e_{m-1} > \cdots > e_1 \geq 0$. The straightforward algorithm (Algorithm 9.1), when generalized to this sparse case, is given in Algorithm 9.3.

```
Algorithm SStraightEval(A, m, v)
// Sparse straightforward evaluation.
// m is number of nonzero terms.
{
    s := 0;
    for i := 1 to m do
    {
        s := s + a_i * Power(v, e_i);
    }
    return s;
}
```

Algorithm 9.3 Sparse evaluation

Power(v, e) returns v^e. Assuming that v^e is computed by repeated multiplication with v, this operation requires $e - 1$ multiplications and Algorithm 9.3 requires $e_m + e_{m-1} + \cdots + e_1$ multiplications, m additions, and $m + 1$ assignments. This is horribly inefficient and can easily be improved by an algorithm based on computing

```
Algorithm NStraightEval(A, m, v)
{
    s := e_0 := 0; t := 1;
    for i := 1 to m do
    {
        r := Power(v, e_i - e_{i-1});
        t := t * r;
        s := s + a_i * t;
    }
    return s;
}
```

Algorithm 9.4 Evaluating a polynomial represented in coefficient-exponent form

```
Algorithm SHorner(A, m, v)
{
    s := e_0 := 0;
    for i := m to 1 step -1 do
    {
        s := (s + a_i) * Power(v, e_i - e_{i-1});
    }
    return s;
}
```

Algorithm 9.5 Horner's rule for a sparse representation

$$v^{e1}, v^{e2-e1}v^{e1}, v^{e3-e2}v^{e2}, \ldots$$

Algorithm 9.4 requires $e_m + m$ multiplications, $3m + 3$ assignments, m additions, and m subtractions.

A more clever scheme is to generalize Horner's strategy in the revised formula

$$A(x) = (\cdots((a_m x^{e_m - e_{m-1}} + a_{m-1})x^{e_{m-1}-e_{m-2}} + \cdots + a_2)x^{e_2 - e_1} + a_1)x^{e_1}$$

The function of Algorithm 9.5 is based on this formula. The number of multiplications required is

$$(e_m - e_{m-1} - 1) + \cdots + (e_1 - e_0 - 1) + m = e_m$$

which is the degree of A. In addition there are m additions, m subtractions, and $m+2$ assignments. Thus we see that Horner's rule is easily adapted to either the sparse or the dense polynomial model and in both cases the number of operations is bounded and linear in the degree. With a little more work one can find an even better method, assuming a sparse representation, which requires only $m + \log_2 e_m$ multiplications. (See the exercises for a hint.)

Given n points (x_i, y_i), the *interpolation* problem is to find the coefficients of the unique polynomial $A(x)$ of degree $\leq n-1$ that goes through these n points. Mathematically the answer to this problem was given by Lagrange:

$$A(x) = \sum_{1 \leq i \leq n} \left(\prod_{\substack{i \neq j \\ 1 \leq j \leq n}} \frac{(x - x_j)}{(x_i - x_j)} \right) y_i \tag{9.1}$$

To verify that $A(x)$ does satisfy the n points, we observe that

$$A(x_i) = \left(\prod_{\substack{i \neq j \\ 1 \leq j \leq n}} \frac{(x_i - x_j)}{(x_i - x_j)} \right) y_i = y_i \tag{9.2}$$

since every other term becomes zero. The numerator of each term is a product of $n-1$ factors and hence the degree of A is $\leq n-1$.

Example 9.3 Consider the input $(0,5), (1,10)$, and $(2,21)$. Using Equation 9.1, we get

$$\begin{aligned} A(x) &= \tfrac{(x-1)}{(0-1)}\tfrac{(x-2)}{(0-2)}5 + \tfrac{(x-0)}{(1-0)}\tfrac{(x-2)}{(1-2)}10 + \tfrac{(x-0)}{(2-0)}\tfrac{(x-1)}{(2-1)}21 \\ &= \tfrac{5}{2}(x^2 - 3x + 2) - 10(x^2 - 2x) + \tfrac{21}{2}(x^2 - x) \\ &= 3x^2 + 2x + 5 \end{aligned}$$

We can verify that $A(0) = 5$, $A(1) = 10$, and $A(2) = 21$. □

We now give an algorithm (Algorithm 9.6) that produces the coefficients of $A(x)$ using Equation 9.1. We need to perform some addition and multiplication of polynomials. So we assume that the operators $+, *, /$, and $=$ have been overloaded to take polynomials as operands.

```
Algorithm Lagrange(X, Y, n, A)
// X and Y are one-dimensional arrays containing
// n points (x_i, y_i), 1 ≤ i ≤ n. A is a
// polynomial that interpolates these points.
{
    // poly is a polynomial.
    A := 0;
    for i := 1 to n do
    {
        poly := 1; denom := 1;
        for j := 1 to n do
            if (i ≠ j) then
            {
                poly := poly * (x − X[j]);
                    // x − X[j] is a degree one polynomial in x.
                denom := denom * (X[i] − X[j]);
            }
        A := A + (poly * Y[i]/denom);
    }
}
```

Algorithm 9.6 Lagrange interpolation

An analysis of the computing time of Lagrange is instructive. The **if** statement is executed n^2 times. The time to compute each new value of *denom* is one subtraction and one multiplication, but the execution of $*$ (as applied to polynomials) requires more than constant time per call. Since the degree of $x - X[j]$ is one, the time for one execution of $*$ is proportional to the degree of *poly*, which is at most $j-1$ on the jth iteration.

Therefore the total cost of the polynomial multiplication step is

$$\sum_{1\le i\le n}\sum_{1\le j\le n}(j-1) = \sum_{1\le i\le n}\left(\frac{n(n+1)}{2}-n\right)$$

$$= n^2(n+1)/2 - n^2$$

$$\text{Thus} \sum_{1\le i\le n}\sum_{1\le j\le n}(j-1) = O(n^3) \tag{9.3}$$

This result is discouraging because it is so high. Perhaps we should search for a better method. Suppose we already have an interpolating polynomial $A(x)$ such that $A(x_i) = y_i$ for $1 \le i \le n$ and we want to add just one more point (x_{n+1}, y_{n+1}). How would we compute this new interpolating polynomial given the fact that $A(x)$ was already available? If we could solve this problem efficiently, then we could apply our solution n times to get an n-point interpolating polynomial.

Let $G_{j-1}(x)$ interpolate $j-1$ points (x_k, y_k), $1 \le k < j$, so that $G_{j-1}(x_k) = y_k$. Also let $D_{j-1}(x) = (x - x_1)\cdots(x - x_{j-1})$. Then we can compute $G_j(x)$ by the formula

$$G_j(x) = [y_j - G_{j-1}(x_j)]\frac{D_{j-1}(x)}{D_{j-1}(x_j)} + G_{j-1}(x) \tag{9.4}$$

We observe that

$$G_j(x_k) = [y_j - G_{j-1}(x_j)]\frac{D_{j-1}(x_k)}{D_{j-1}(x_j)} + G_{j-1}(x_k)$$

but $D_{j-1}(x_k) = 0$ for $1 \le k < j$. So

$$G_j(x_k) = G_{j-1}(x_k) = y_k$$

Also we observe that

$$\begin{aligned} G_j(x_j) &= [y_j - G_{j-1}(x_j)]\frac{D_{j-1}(x_j)}{D_{j-1}(x_j)} + G_{j-1}(x_j) \\ &= y_j - G_{j-1}(x_j) + G_{j-1}(x_j) \\ &= y_j \end{aligned}$$

Example 9.4 Consider again the input $(0,5), (1,10)$, and $(2,21)$. Here $G_1(x) = 5$ and $D_1(x) = (x - x_1) = x$.

$$G_2(x) = [y_2 - G_1(x_2)]\frac{D_1(x)}{D_1(x_2)} + G_1(x) = (10-5)\frac{x}{1} + 5 = 5x + 5$$

Also, $D_2(x) = (x - x_1)(x - x_2) = (x-0)(x-1) = x^2 - x$. Finally,

$$\begin{aligned} G_3(x) &= [y_3 - G_2(x_3)]\frac{D_2(x)}{D_2(x_3)} + G_2(x) \\ &= [21 - 15]\frac{x^2 - x}{2} + (5x+5) = 3x^2 + 2x + 5 \quad \square \end{aligned}$$

Having verified that this formula is correct, we present an algorithm (Algorithm 9.7) for computing the interpolating polynomial that is based on Equation 9.4. Notice that from the equation, two applications of Horner's rule are required, one for evaluating $G_{j-1}(x)$ at x_j and the other for evaluating $D_{j-1}(x)$ at x_j.

```
Algorithm Interpolate(X, Y, n, G)
// Assume n ≥ 2. X[1 : n] and Y[1 : n] are the
// n pairs of points. The unique interpolating
// polynomial of degree < n is returned in G.
{
    // D is a polynomial.
    G := Y[1]; // G begins as a constant.
    D := x − X[1]; // D is a linear polynomial.
    for j := 2 to n do
    {
        denom := Horner(D, j − 1, X[j]); // Evaluate D at X[j].
        num := Horner(G, j − 2, X[j]); // Evaluate G at X[j].
            G := G + (D * (Y[j] − num)/denom);
        D := D * (x − X[j]);
    }
}
```

Algorithm 9.7 Newtonian interpolation

On the jth iteration D has degree $j-1$ and G has degree $j-2$. Therefore the invocations of Horner require

$$\sum_{1\le j\le n-1} (j-1+j-2) = n(n-1) - 3(n-1) = n^2 - 4n + 3 \tag{9.5}$$

multiplications in total. The term $(Y[j] - num)/denom$ in Algorithm 9.7 is a constant. Multiplying this constant by D requires j multiplications and multiplying D by $x - X[j]$ requires j multiplications. The addition with G requires zero multiplications. Thus the remaining steps require

$$\sum_{1\le j\le n-1} (2j) = n(n-1) \tag{9.6}$$

operations, so the entire algorithm Interpolate requires $O(n^2)$ operations.

In conclusion we observe that for a dense polynomial of degree n, evaluation can be accomplished using $O(n)$ operations or, for a sparse polynomial with m nonzero terms and degree n, evaluation can be done using at most $O(m+n) = O(n)$ operations. Also, given n points, we can produce the interpolating polynomial in $O(n^2)$ time. In Chapter 10 we discuss the question of the optimality of Horner's rule for evaluation. Section 9.5 presents an even faster way to perform the interpolation of n points as well as the evaluation of a polynomial at n points.

EXERCISES

1. Devise a divide-and-conquer algorithm to evaluate a polynomial at a point. Analyze carefully the time for your algorithm. How does it compare to Horner's rule?

2. Present algorithms for overloading the operators + and $*$ in the case of polynomials.

3. Assume that polynomials such as $A(x) = a_n x^n + \cdots + a_0$ are represented using the dense form. Present an algorithm that overloads the operators + and = to perform the instruction $r = s + t;$, where r, s, and t are arbitrary polynomials.

4. Using the same assumptions as for Exercise 3, write an algorithm to perform $r = s * t;$.

5. Let $A(x) = a_n x^n + \cdots + a_0$, $p = n/2$ and $q = \lceil n/2 \rceil$. Then a variation of Horner's rule states that

$$\begin{aligned} A(x) &= (\cdots(a_{2p}x^2 + a_{2p-2})x^2 + \cdots)x^2 + a_0 \\ &\quad +((\cdots(a_{2q-1}x^2 + a_{2q-3})x^2 + \cdots)x^2 + a_1)x \end{aligned}$$

   Show how to use this formula to evaluate $A(x)$ at $x = v$ and $x = -v$.

6. Given the polynomial $A(x)$ in Exercise 5 devise an algorithm that computes the coefficients of polynomial $A(x+c)$ for some constant c.

7. Suppose the polynomial $A(x)$ has real coefficients but we wish to evaluate A at the complex number $x = u + iv$, u and v being real. Develop an algorithm to do this.

8. Suppose the polynomial $A(x) = a_m x^{e_m} + \cdots + a_1 x^{e_1}$, where $a_i \neq 0$ and $e_m > e_{m-1} > \cdots > e_1 \geq 0$, is represented using the sparse form. Write a function PAdd(r, s, t) that computes the sum of two such polynomials r and s and stores the result in t.

9. Using the same assumptions as in Exercise 8, write a function PMult(r, s, t) that computes the product of the polynomials r and s and places the result in t. What is the computing time of your function?

10. Determine the polynomial of smallest degree that interpolates the points (0, 1), (1, 2), and (2, 3).

11. Given n points $(x_i,\ y_i)$, $1 \leq i \leq n$, devise an algorithm that computes both the interpolating polynomial $A(x)$ and its derivative at the same time. How efficient is your algorithm?

12. Prove that the polynomial of degree $\leq n$ that interpolates $n+1$ points is unique.

13. The binary method for exponentiation uses the binary expansion of the exponent n to determine when to square the temporary result and when to multiply it by x. Since there are $\lfloor \log n \rfloor + 1$ bits in n, the algorithm requires $O(\log n)$ operations; this algorithm is an order of magnitude faster than iteration. The method appears as Algorithm 1.20. Show how to use the binary method to evaluate a sparse polynomial in time $m + \log e_m$.

14. Suppose you are given the real and imaginary parts of two complex numbers. Show that the real and imaginary parts of their product can be computed using only three multiplications.

15. (a) Show that the polynomials $ax + b$ and $cx + d$ can be multiplied using only three scalar multiplications.
    (b) Employ the above algorithm to devise a divide-and-conquer algorithm to multiply two given nth degree polynomials in time $\Theta(n^{\log_2 3})$.

16. The Fibonacci sequence is defined as $f_0 = 0,\ f_1 = 1$, and $f_n = f_{n-1} + f_{n-2}$ for $n \geq 2$. Give an $O(\log n)$ algorithm to compute f_n. (*Hint*:

$$\begin{bmatrix} f_{n-1} \\ f_n \end{bmatrix} = \begin{bmatrix} 0 & 1 \\ 1 & 1 \end{bmatrix} \begin{bmatrix} f_{n-2} \\ f_{n-1} \end{bmatrix}.)$$

9.3 THE FAST FOURIER TRANSFORM

If one is able to devise an algorithm that is an order of magnitude faster than any previous method, that is a worthy accomplishment. When the improvement is for a process that has many applications, then that accomplishment has a significant impact on researchers and practitioners. This is the case of the fast Fourier transform. No algorithm improvement has had a greater impact in the recent past than this one. The Fourier transform is used by electrical engineers in a variety of ways including speech transmission, coding theory, and image processing. But before this fast algorithm was developed, the use of this transform was considered impractical.

The Fourier transform of a continuous function $a(t)$ is given by

$$A(f) = \int_{-\infty}^{\infty} a(t)e^{2\pi ift}\, dt \tag{9.7}$$

whereas the inverse transform of $A(f)$ is

$$a(t) = \frac{1}{2\pi}\int_{-\infty}^{\infty} A(f)e^{-2\pi ift}\, df \tag{9.8}$$

The i in the above two equations stands for the square root of -1. The constant e is the base of the natural logarithm. The variable t is often regarded as time, and f is taken to mean frequency. Then the Fourier transform is interpreted as taking a function of time into a function of frequency.

Corresponding to this continuous Fourier transform is the *discrete* Fourier transform which handles sample points of $a(t)$, namely, $a_0, a_1, \ldots, a_{N-1}$. The discrete Fourier transform is defined by

$$A_j = \sum_{0\le k\le N-1} a_k e^{2\pi ijk/N}, \quad 0 \le j \le N-1 \tag{9.9}$$

and the inverse is

$$a_k = \frac{1}{N}\sum_{0\le j\le N-1} A_j e^{-2\pi ijk/N}, \quad 0 \le k \le N-1 \tag{9.10}$$

In the discrete case a set of N sample points is given and a resulting set of N points is produced. An important fact to observe is the close connection between the discrete Fourier transform and polynomial evaluation. If we imagine the polynomial

$$a(x) = a_{N-1}x^{N-1} + a_{N-2}x^{N-2} + \cdots + a_1x + a_0$$

then the Fourier element A_j is the value of $a(x)$ at $x = w^j$, where $w = e^{2\pi i/N}$. Similarly for the inverse Fourier transform if we imagine the polynomial with the Fourier coefficients

$$A(x) = A_{N-1}x^{N-1} + A_{N-2}x^{N-2} + \cdots + A_1x + A_0$$

then each a_k is the value of $A(x)/N$ at $x = (w^{-1})^k$, where $w = e^{2\pi i/N}$. Thus, the *discrete Fourier transform* corresponds exactly to the evaluation of a polynomial at N points: $w^0, w^1, \ldots, w^{N-1}$.

From the preceding section we know that we can evaluate an Nth-degree polynomial at N points using $O(N^2)$ operations. We apply Horner's rule once for each point. The *fast Fourier transform* (abbreviated FFT) is an algorithm for computing these N values using only $O(N \log N)$ operations. This algorithm was popularized by J. M. Cooley and J. W. Tukey in 1965, and the long history of this method was traced by J. M. Cooley, P. A. Lewis and P. D. Welch.

A hint that the Fourier transform can be computed faster than by Horner's rule comes from observing that the evaluation points are not arbitrary but are in fact very special. They are the N powers w^j for $0 \le j \le N-1$, where $w = e^{2\pi i/N}$. The point w is a primitive Nth root of unity in the complex plane.

Definition 9.1 An element w in a commutative ring is called a *primitive* Nth *root of unity* if

1. $w \neq 1$
2. $w^N = 1$
3. $\sum_{0 \le p \le N-1} w^{jp} = 0,\ 1 \le j \le N-1$ □

Example 9.5 Let $N = 4$. Then, $w = e^{\pi i/2} = cos(\pi/2) + i\ sin(\pi/2) = i$. Thus, $w \neq 1$, and $w^4 = i^4 = 1$. Also, $\sum_{0 \le p \le 3} w^{jp} = 1 + i^j + i^{2j} + i^{3j} = 0$. □

We now present two simple properties of Nth roots from which we can see how the FFT algorithm can easily be understood.

Theorem 9.1 Let $N = 2n$ and suppose w is a primitive Nth root of unity. Then $-w^j = w^{j+n}$.

Proof: Here $(w^{j+n})^2 = (w^j)^2(w^n)^2 = (w^j)^2(w^{2n}) = (w^j)^2$ since $w^n = 1$. Since the w^j are distinct, we know that $w^j \neq w^{j+n}$, so we can conclude that $w^{j+n} = -w^j$. □

Theorem 9.2 Let $N = 2n$ and w a primitive Nth root of unity. Then w^2 is a primitive nth root of unity.

Proof: Since $w^N = w^{2n} = 1$, $(w^2)^n = 1$; this implies w^2 is an nth root of unity. In addition we observe that $(w^2)^j \neq 1$ for $1 \le j \le n-1$ since otherwise we would have $w^k = 1$ for $1 \le k < 2n = N$ which would contradict the fact that w is a primitive Nth root of unity. Therefore w^2 is a primitive nth root of unity. □

From this theorem we can conclude that if w^j, $0 < j \leq N-1$, are the primitive Nth roots of unity and $N = 2n$, then w^{2j}, $0 < j \leq n-1$, are primitive nth roots of unity. Using these two theorems, we are ready to show how to derive a divide-and-conquer algorithm for the Fourier transform. The complexity of the algorithm is $O(N \log N)$, an order of magnitude faster than the $O(N^2)$ of the conventional algorithm which uses polynomial evaluation.

Again let $a_{N-1}, \ldots, a_0$ be the coefficients to be transformed and let $a(x) = a_{N-1}x^{N-1} + \cdots + a_1 x + a_0$. We break $a(x)$ into two parts, one of which contains even-numbered exponents and the other odd-numbered exponents.

$$\begin{aligned} a(x) &= (a_{N-1}x^{N-1} + a_{N-3}x^{N-3} + \cdots + a_1 x) \\ &\quad + (a_{N-2}x^{N-2} + \cdots + a_2 x^2 + a_0) \end{aligned}$$

Letting $y = x^2$, we can rewrite $a(x)$ as a sum of two polynomials.

$$\begin{aligned} a(x) &= (a_{N-1}y^{n-1} + a_{N-3}y^{n-2} + \cdots + a_1)x \\ &\quad + (a_{N-2}y^{n-1} + a_{N-4}y^{n-2} + \cdots + a_0) \\ &= c(y)x + b(y) \end{aligned}$$

Recall that the values of the Fourier transform are $a(w^j)$, $0 \leq j \leq N-1$. Therefore the values of $a(x)$ at the points w^j, $0 \leq j \leq n-1$, are now expressible as

$$\begin{aligned} a(w^j) &= c(w^{2j})w^j + b(w^{2j}) \\ a(w^{j+n}) &= -c(w^{2j})w^j + b(w^{2j}) \end{aligned}$$

These two formulas are computationally valuable in that they reveal how to take a problem of size N and transform it into two identical problems of size $n = N/2$. These subproblems are the evaluation of $b(y)$ and $c(y)$, each of degree $n-1$, at the points $(w^2)^j$, $0 \leq j \leq n-1$, and these points are primitive nth roots. This is an example of divide-and-conquer, and we can apply the divide-and-conquer strategy again as long as the number of points remains even. This leads us to always choose N as a power of 2, $N = 2^m$, for then we can continue to carry out the splitting procedure until a trivial problem is reached, namely, evaluating a constant polynomial.

FFT (Algorithm 9.8) combines all these ideas into a recursive version of the fast Fourier transform algorithm. Dense representation for polynomials

```
Algorithm FFT(N, a(x), w, A)
// N = 2^m, a(x) = a_{N-1}x^{N-1} + ··· + a_0, and w is a
// primitive Nth root of unity. A[0 : N - 1] is set to
// the values a(w^j), 0 ≤ j ≤ N - 1.
{
    // b and c are polynomials.
    // B, C, and wp are complex arrays.
    if N = 1 then A[0] := a_0;
    else
    {
        n := N/2;
        b(x) := a_{N-2}x^{n-1} + ··· + a_2x + a_0;
        c(x) := a_{N-1}x^{n-1} + ··· + a_3x + a_1;
        FFT(n, b(x), w^2, B);
        FFT(n, c(x), w^2, C);
        wp[-1] := 1/w;
        for j := 0 to n - 1 do
        {
            wp[j] := w * wp[j - 1];
            A[j] := B[j] + wp[j] * C[j];
            A[j + n] := B[j] - wp[j] * C[j];
        }
    }
}
```

Algorithm 9.8 Recursive fast Fourier transform

is assumed. We overload the operators $+$, $-$, $*$, and $=$ with regard to complex numbers.

Now let us derive the computing time of FFT. Let $T(N)$ be the time for the algorithm applied to N inputs. Then we have

$$T(N) = 2T(N/2) + DN$$

where D is a constant and DN is a bound on the time needed to form $b(x)$, $c(x)$, and A. Since $T(1) = d$, where d is another constant, we can repeatedly simplify this recurrence relation to get

$$T(2^m) = 2T(2^{m-1}) + D2^m$$

$$
\begin{aligned}
&= \\
&\vdots \\
&= Dm2^m + T(1)2^m \\
&= DN\log_2 N + dN \\
&= O(N\log_2 N)
\end{aligned}
$$

Suppose we return briefly to the problem considered at the beginning of this chapter, the multiplication of polynomials. The transformation technique calls for evaluating $A(x)$ and $B(x)$ at $2N+1$ points (where N is the degree of A and B), computing the $2N+1$ products $A(x_i)B(x_i)$, and then finding the product $A(x)B(x)$ in coefficient form by computing the interpolating polynomial that satisfies these points. In Section 9.2 we saw that N-point evaluation and interpolation required $O(N^2)$ operations, so that no asymptotic improvement is gained by using this transformation over the conventional multiplication algorithm. However, in this section we have seen that if the points are chosen to be the $N = 2^m$ distinct powers of a primitive Nth root of unity, then evaluation and interpolation can be done using at most $O(N \log N)$ operations. Therefore by using the fast Fourier transform algorithm, we can multiply two N-degree polynomials in $O(N \log N)$ operations.

The divide-and-conquer strategy plus some simple properties of primitive Nth roots of unity leads to a very nice conceptual framework for understanding the FFT. The above analysis shows that asymptotically it is better than the direct method by an order of magnitude. However the version we have produced uses auxiliary space for b, c, B, and C. We need to study this algorithm more closely to eliminate this overhead.

Example 9.6 Consider the case in which $a(x) = a_3x^3 + a_2x^2 + a_1x + a_0$. Let us walk through the execution of Algorithm 9.8 on this input. Here $N = 4, n = 2$, and $w = i$. The polynomials b and c are constructed as $b(x) = a_2x + a_0$ and $c(x) = a_3x + a_1$. Function FFT is invoked on $b(x)$ and $c(x)$ to get $B[0] = a_0 + a_2$, $B[1] = a_0 + a_2w^2$, $C[0] = a_1 + a_3$, and $C[1] = a_1 + a_3w^2$.

In the **for** loop, the array $A[\ ]$ is modified. When $j = 0$, $wp[0] = 1$. Thus, $A[0] = B[0] + C[0] = a_0 + a_1 + a_2 + a_3$ and $A[2] = B[0] - C[0] = a_0 + a_2 - a_1 - a_3 = a_0 + a_1w^2 + a_2w^4 + a_3w^6$ (since $w^2 = -1, w^4 = 1$, and $w^6 = -1$). When $j = 1$, $wp[1] = w$. Then $A[1] = B[1] + wC[1] = a_0 + a_2w^2 + w(a_1 + a_3w^2) = a_0 + a_1w + a_2w^2 + a_3w^3$ and $A[3] = B[1] - wC[1] = a_0 + a_2w^2 - w(a_1 + a_3w^2) = a_0 - a_1w + a_2w^2 - a_3w^3 = a_0 + a_1w^3 + a_2w^6 + a_3w^9$ (since $w^2 = -1, w^4 = 1$, and $w^6 = -1$). □

9.3.1 An In-place Version of the FFT

Recall that if we view the elements of the vector $(a_0, \ldots, a_{N-1})$ to be transformed as coefficients of a polynomial $a(x)$, then the Fourier transform is the same as computing $a(w^j)$ for $0 \leq j < N$. This transformation is also equivalent to computing the remainder when $a(x)$ is divided by the linear polynomial $x - w^j$, for if $q(x)$ and c are the quotient and remainder such that

$$a(x) = (x - w^j)q(x) + c$$

then $a(w^j) = 0 * q(x) + c = c$. We could divide $a(x)$ by these N linear polynomials, but that would require $O(N^2)$ operations. Instead we make use of the principle called *balancing* and compute these remainders with the help of a process that is structured like a binary tree.

Consider the product of the linear factors $(x - w^0)(x - w^1) \cdots (x - w^7) = x^8 - w^0$. All the intermediate terms cancel and leave only the exponents eight and zero with nonzero coefficients. If we select out from this product the even- and odd-degree terms, a similar phenomenon occurs: $(x - w^0)(x - w^2)(x - w^4)(x - w^6) = (x^4 - w^0)$ and $(x - w^1)(x - w^3)\ (x - w^5)(x - w^7) = (x^4 - w^4)$. Continuing in a similar fashion, we see in Figure 9.2 that the selected products have only two nonzero terms and we can continue this splitting until only linear factors are present.

Now suppose we want to compute the remainders of $a(x)$ by eight linear factors $(x - w^0), \ldots, (x - w^7)$. We begin by computing the remainder of $a(x)$ divided by the product $d(x) = (x - w^0) \cdots (x - w^7)$. If $a(x) = q(x)d(x) + r(x)$, then $a(w^j) = r(w^j)$, $0 \leq j \leq 7$, since $d(w^j) = 0$ and the degree of $r(x)$ is less than the degree of $d(x)$ which equals 8. Now we divide $r(x)$ by $x^4 - w^0$ and obtain $s(x)$, and by $x^4 - w^4$ and obtain $t(x)$. Then $a(w^j) = r(w^j) = s(w^j)$ for $j = 0, 2, 4$, and 6 and $a(w^j) = r(w^j) = t(w^j)$ for $j = 1, 3, 5$, and 7 and degrees of s and t are less than 4. Next we divide $s(x)$ by $x^2 - w^0$ and $x^2 - w^4$ and obtain remainders $u(x)$ and $v(x)$, where $a(w^j) = u(w^j)$ for $j = 0$ and 4 and $a(w^j) = v(w^j)$ for $j = 2$ and 6. Notice how each divisor has only two nonzero terms and so the division process will be fast. Continuing in this way, we eventually conclude with the eight values $a(x) \bmod (x - w^i)$ for $j = 0, 1, \ldots, 7$.

By carrying out successive divisions down the binary tree of Figure 9.2, we eventually arrive at the appropriate coefficients of the Fourier transform. The order of these coefficients is permuted in the same way the $x - w^i$ appear at the bottom of the tree, but this can be corrected at the end of the algorithm. Since this permutation caused the polynomials at each node of the tree to have such a simple form, the division at each stage is simple and the resulting computation time for the entire transform reduces to $O(N \log N)$. One can see this in a simple way by observing that the tree

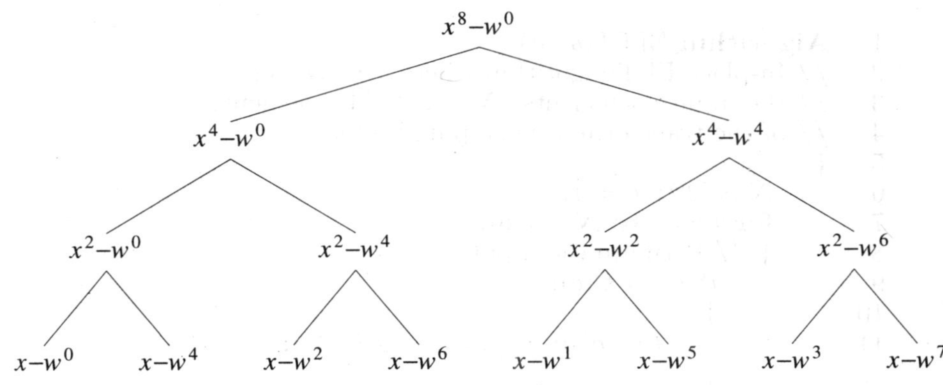

Figure 9.2 Divisors in the FFT algorithm of size eight

has $\log N$ levels and 2^i nodes on each level, where a dividend polynomial on level i has at most 2^{m-i} terms. Thus the work on the ith level is proportional to $2^i 2^{m-i} = 2^m = N$ and hence $O(N \log N)$ bounds the time for the entire algorithm. Algorithm 9.9 uses this point of view to produce an FFT algorithm that is iterative in nature.

The NFFT is an in-place, iterative version of the fast Fourier transform. Note that the elements of the vector to be transformed are initially stored in the array $a[1 : N]$. The NFFT begins by rearranging the input so that at the end of the algorithm the correct values are in their proper positions. Complex arithmetic is assumed, and $w = e^{2\pi i/N}$ is expressed in terms of sines and cosines. To verify that the complexity of the NFFT is truly $O(N \log N)$, assume $N = 2^m$ and examine the triply nested **for** loops. The statements contained in the innermost **for** loop require no more than constant time for each iteration. The innermost **for** loop is executed no more than $\lceil N/2^i \rceil < 2^{m-i+1}$ times. This implies that the total time of NFFT is bounded by

$$\sum_{1 \le i \le m} \sum_{1 \le j \le 2^{i-1}} c2^{m-i+1} = \sum_{1 \le i \le m} c2^m = c2^m m = O(N \log N)$$

Example 9.7 Now suppose we simulate the algorithm as it works on the particular case $N = 4$. We assume as inputs the symbolic quantities $a[1] = a_0$, $a[2] = a_1$, $a[3] = a_2$, and $a[4] = a_3$. Initially $m = 2$ and $N = 4$. After the first **for** loop is completed, the array contains the elements permuted as $a[1] = a_0$, $a[2] = a_2$, $a[3] = a_1$, and $a[4] = a_3$. The main **for** loop is executed for $i = 1$ and $i = 2$. After the $i = 1$ pass is completed, the array contains

```
Algorithm NFFT(a, m)
// In-place FFT algorithm where a[1 : N] has
// the input coefficients. N = 2^m. The elements
// of the transform are computed inplace.
{
    N := 2^m; j := 1;
    for i := 1 to N - 1 do
    { // Permute the input.
        if i < j then
        {
            t := a[j]; a[j] := a[i]; a[i] := t;
        }
        q := ⌊N/2⌋;
        while (q < j) do
        {
            j := j - q; q := ⌊q/2⌋;
        }
        j := j + q;
    }
    for i := 1 to m do
    {
        pow := ⌊2^i/2⌋;
        r := 1;
        s := cos(π/pow) + i sin(π/pow);
            // An Nth root of unity.
        for j := 1 to pow do
        {
            for q := j to N  step 2^i do
            {
                t := a[q + pow] * r;
                a[q + pow] := a[q] - t;
                // Compute the next pair.
                a[q] := a[q] + t;
            }
            r := r * s;
        }
    }
}
```

Algorithm 9.9 In-place nonrecursive FFT

$a[1] = a_0 + a_2$, $a[2] = a_0 - a_2$, $a[3] = a_1 + a_3$, and $a[4] = a_1 - a_3$. At this point we observe that in general that $w^{N/2} = -1$ and in this case $w^2 = -1$ and the complex number expressed as the 2-tuple $\cos\pi + i\ \sin\pi)$ is equal to w. At the end of the algorithm the final values in the array a are $a[1] = a_0+a_1+a_2+a_3$, $a[2] = a_0+wa_1+w^2a_2+w^3a_3$, $a[3] = a_0+w^2a_1+a_2+w^2a_3$, and $a[4] = a_0 + w^3a_1 + w^2a_2 + wa_3$. □

9.3.2 Some Remaining Points

Up to now we have been treating the value w as $e^{2\pi i/N}$. This is a complex number (it has an imaginary part) and its value cannot be represented exactly in a digital computer. Thus the arithmetic operations performed in the Fourier transform algorithm were assumed to be operations on complex numbers, and this implies they are approximations to the actual values. When the inputs to be transformed are readings from a continuous signal, approximations of w do not cause any significant loss in accuracy. However, there are occasions when we would prefer an exact result, for instance, when we are using the FFT for polynomial multiplication in a mathematical symbol manipulation system. It is possible to circumvent the need for approximate, complex arithmetic by working in a finite field.

Let p be chosen such that it is a prime that is less than your computer's word size and such that the integers $0, 1, \cdots, p-1$ contain a primitive nth root of unity. By doing all the arithmetic of the fast Fourier transform modulo p, all the results are single precision. By choosing p to be a prime, the integers $0, 1, \ldots, p-1$ form a field and all arithmetic operations including division can be performed. If all values during the computation are bounded by $p-1$, then the exact answer is formed since $x \bmod p = x$ if $0 \leq x < p$. However, if one or more values exceed $p-1$, the exact answer can still be produced by repeating the transform using several different primes followed by the Chinese Remainder Theorem as described in the next section. So the question that remains is, given an N, can one find a sufficient number of primes of a certain size that contain Nth roots? From finite field theory $\{0, 1, \ldots, p-1\}$ contains a primitive Nth root if and only if N divides $p-1$. Therefore, to transform a sequence of size $N = 2^m$, primes of the form $p = 2^e k + 1$, where $m \leq e$, must be found. Call such a number a *Fourier* prime. J. Lipson has shown that there are more than $x/(2^{e-1}\ \ln\, x)$ Fourier primes less than x with exponent e, and hence there are more than enough for any reasonable application. For example, if the word size is 32 bits, let $x = 2^{31}$ and $e = 20$. Then there are approximately 182 primes of the form $2^f k+1$, where $f \geq 20$. Any of these Fourier primes would suffice to compute the FFT of a sequence of at most 2^{20}. See the exercises for more details.

EXERCISES

1. A polynomial of degree $n > 0$ has n derivatives, each one obtained by taking the derivative of the previous one. Devise an algorithm that produces the values of a polynomial and its n derivatives.

2. Show the result of applying the Fourier transform to the sequence $(a_0, \ldots, a_7)$.

3. The Fourier transform can be generalized to k dimensions. For example, the two-dimensional transform takes the matrix $a(0 : n-1, 0 : n-1)$ and yields the transformed matrix

$$A(i,j) = \sum_{0 \le k \le n-1} \sum_{0 \le l \le n-1} a_{k,l} w^{-(ik+jl)/n} \tag{9.11}$$

for an $n \times n$ matrix with elements in $GF(p)$. The inverse transformation is

$$a(i,j) = \frac{1}{n^2} \sum_{0 \le k \le n-1} \sum_{0 \le l \le n-1} A(k,l) w^{-(ik+jl)/n} \tag{9.12}$$

Define the two-dimensional convolution $C(i,j) = A(i,j)B(i,j)$ and derive an efficient algorithm for computing it.

4. Present an $O(n)$ time algorithm to compute the coefficients of the polynomial $(1+x)^n$. How much time is needed if you use the FFT algorithm to solve this problem?

5. An $n \times n$ *Toeplitz* matrix is a matrix A with the property that $A[i,j] = A[i-1, j-1]$, $2 \le i, j \le n$. Give an $O(n \log n)$ algorithm to multiply a Toeplitz matrix with an arbitrary $(n \times 1)$ column vector.

9.4 MODULAR ARITHMETIC

Another example of a useful set of transformations is modular arithmetic. Modular arithmetic is useful in one context because it allows the reformulation of the way addition, subtraction, and multiplication are performed. This reformulation is one that exploits parallelism whereas the normal methods for doing arithmetic are serial. The growth of special computers that make it desirable to perform parallel computation make modular arithmetic attractive. A second use of modular arithmetic is with systems that allow symbolic mathematical computation. These software packages usually provide operations that permit arbitrarily large integers and rational numbers as operands. Modular arithmetic has been found to yield efficient algorithms for the manipulation of large numbers. Finally there is an intrinsic interest in finite field arithmetic (the integers $0, 1, \ldots, p-1$, where p is a prime form a field) by number theorists and electrical engineers specializing in communications and coding theory. In this section we study this subject from a computer scientist's point of view, namely, the development of efficient algorithms for the required operations.

The mod operator is defined as

$$\begin{aligned} x \bmod y &= x - y \lfloor x/y \rfloor, \qquad \text{if } y \neq 0 \\ x \bmod 0 &= x \end{aligned}$$

Note that $\frac{x}{y}$ corresponds to fixed point integer division which is commonly found on most current-day computers.

We denote the set of integers $\{0, 1, \ldots, p-1\}$, where p is a prime, by GF(p) (the Galois field with p elements), named after the mathematician E. Galois who studied and characterized the properties of these fields. Also we assume that p is a single precision number for the computer you plan to execute on. It is, in fact, true that the set GF(p) forms a field under the following definitions of addition, subtraction, multiplication, and division, where $a, b \in \text{GF}(p)$:

$$\begin{aligned} (a+b) \bmod p &= \begin{cases} a+b & \text{if } a+b < p \\ a+b-p & \text{if } a+b \geq p \end{cases} \\ (a-b) \bmod p &= \begin{cases} a-b & \text{if } a-b \geq 0 \\ a-b+p & \text{if } a-b < 0 \end{cases} \end{aligned}$$

$(ab) \bmod p = r$ such that r is the remainder when the product ab is divided by p; $ab = qp + r$, where $0 \leq r < p$.

$(a/b) \bmod p = (ab^{-1}) \bmod p = r$, the unique remainder when ab^{-1} is divided by p; $ab^{-1} = qp + r,\ 0 \leq r < p$.

The factor b^{-1} is the *multiplicative inverse* of b in GF(p). For every element b in GF(p) except zero, there exists a unique element called b^{-1} such that $bb^{-1} \bmod p = 1$.

Now what are the computing times of these operations? We have assumed that p is a single precision integer; this implies that all $a, b \in \text{GF}(p)$ are also single precision integers. The time for addition, subtraction, and multiplication mod p, given the formulas above, is easily seen to be $O(1)$. But before we can determine the time for division, we must develop an algorithm to compute the multiplicative inverse of an element $b \in \text{GF}(p)$.

By definition we know that to find $x = b^{-1}$, there must exist an integer k, $0 \leq k < p$, such that $bx = kp + 1$. For example, if $p = 7$,

b :	1	2	3	4	5	6	(element)
b^{-1} :	1	4	5	2	3	6	(inverse)
k :	0	1	2	1	2	5	

An algorithm for computing the inverse of b in GF(p) is provided by generalizing Euclid's algorithm for the computation of greatest common divisors (gcds). Given two nonnegative integers a and b, Euclid's algorithm computes their gcd. The essential step that guarantees the validity of his method consists of showing that the greatest common divisor of a and b ($a > b \geq 0$) is equal to a if b is zero and is equal to the greatest common divisor of b and the remainder of a divided by b if b is nonzero.

Example 9.8

$$\gcd(22,8) = \gcd(8,6) = \gcd(6,2) = \gcd(2,0) = 2$$

$$\text{and } \gcd(21,13) = \gcd(13,8) = \gcd(8,5) = \gcd(5,3) = \gcd(3,2) = \gcd(2,1) = \gcd(1,0) = 1 \ \square$$

Expressing this process as a recursive function gives Algorithm 9.10.

```
Algorithm GCD(a, b)
// Assume a > b ≥ 0.
{
    if b ≠ 0 then return GCD(b, a mod b);
    else return a;
}
```

Algorithm 9.10 Algorithm to compute the gcd of two numbers

Using Euclid's algorithm, it is also possible to compute two more integers x and y such that $ax + by = \gcd(a, b)$. Letting a be a prime p and $b \in$ GF(p), the gcd(p, b) $= 1$ (since the only divisors of a prime are itself and one), and Euclid's generalization reduces to finding integers x and y such that $px + by = 1$. This implies that y is the multiplicative inverse of b mod p.

A close examination of ExEuclid (Algorithm 9.11) shows that Euclid's gcd algorithm is carried out by the steps $q := \lfloor c/d \rfloor$;, $e := c - d * q$;, $c := d$;, and

```
Algorithm ExEuclid(b, p)
// b is in GF(p), p being a prime. ExEuclid is a function
// whose result is the integer x such that bx + kp = 1.
{
    c := p; d := b; x := 0; y := 1;
    while (d ≠ 1) do
    {
        q := ⌊c/d⌋;
        e := c − d * q;
        w := x − y * q;
        c := d; d := e; x := y; y := w;
    }
    if y < 0 then y := y + p;
    return y;
}
```

Algorithm 9.11 Extended Euclidean algorithm

$d := e$;. The only other steps are the updatings of x and y as the algorithm proceeds. To analyze the time for ExEuclid, we need to know the number of divisions Euclid's algorithm may require. This was answered in the worst case by G. Lamé in 1845.

Theorem 9.3 [G. Lamé, 1845] For $n \geq 1$, let a and b be integers $a > b > 0$, such that Euclid's algorithm applied to a and b requires n division steps. Then $n \leq 5 \log_{10} b$. □

Thus the **while** loop is executed no more than $O(\text{iog}_{10} p)$ times, and this is the computing time for the extended Euclidean algorithm and hence for modular division. By *modular arithmetic* we mean the operations of addition, subtraction, multiplication, and division modulo p as previously defined.

Now let's see how we can use modular arithmetic as a transformation technique to help us work with integers. We begin by looking at how we can represent integers using a set of moduli, then how we perform arithmetic on this representation, and finally how we can produce the proper integer result.

Let a and b be integers and suppose that a is represented by the r-tuple $(a_1, \ldots, a_r)$, where $a_i = a \bmod p_i$, and b is represented by $(b_1, \ldots, b_r)$, where $b_i = b \bmod p_i$. The p_i are typically single precision primes. This is called a *mixed radix* representation which contrasts with the conventional representation of integers using a single radix such as 10 (decimal) or 2 (binary). The rules for addition, subtraction, and multiplication using a mixed radix representation are as follows:

$$\begin{aligned}(a_1,\ldots,a_r)+(b_1,\ldots,b_r) &= ((a_1+b_1) \bmod p_1,\ldots,(a_r+b_r) \bmod p_r)\\ (a_1,\ldots,a_r)(b_1,\ldots,b_r) &= ((a_1b_1) \bmod p_1,\ldots,(a_rb_r) \bmod p_r)\end{aligned}$$

Example 9.9 For example, let the moduli be $p_1 = 3$, $p_2 = 5$, and $p_3 = 7$ and suppose we start with the integers 10 and 15.

$$\begin{aligned}10 &= (10 \bmod 3, 10 \bmod 5, 10 \bmod 7) = (1,0,3)\\ 15 &= (15 \bmod 3, 15 \bmod 5, 15 \bmod 7) = (0,0,1)\end{aligned}$$

Then

$$\begin{aligned}10+15 &= (25 \bmod 3, 25 \bmod 5, 25 \bmod 7) = (1,0,4)\\ &= (1+0 \bmod 3, 0+0 \bmod 5, 3+1 \bmod 7) = (1,0,4)\end{aligned}$$

$$\begin{aligned}\text{Also } 15-10 &= (5 \bmod 3, 5 \bmod 5, 5 \bmod 7) = (2,0,5)\\ &= (0-1 \bmod 3, 0-0 \bmod 5, 1-3 \bmod 7) = (2,0,5)\end{aligned}$$

$$\begin{aligned}\text{Also } 10*15 &= (150 \bmod 3, 150 \bmod 5, 150 \bmod 7) = (0,0,3)\\ &= (1*0 \bmod 3, 0*0 \bmod 5, 3*1 \bmod 7) = (0,0,3) \ \square\end{aligned}$$

After we have performed some desired sequence of arithmetic operations using these r-tuples, we are left with some r-tuple $(c_1,\ldots,c_r)$. We now need some way of transforming back from modular form with the assurance that the resulting integer is the correct one. The ability to do this is guaranteed by the following theorem which was first proven in full generality by L. Euler in 1734.

Theorem 9.4 [Chinese Remainder Theorem] Let $p_1,\ldots,p_r$ be positive integers that are pairwise relatively prime (no two integers have a common factor). Let $p = p_1 \cdots p_r$ and let $b, a_1,\ldots,a_r$ be integers. Then, there is exactly one integer a that satisfies the conditions

$$b \le a < b+p \quad \text{and} \quad a = a_i \bmod p_i \quad \text{for } 1 \le i \le r$$

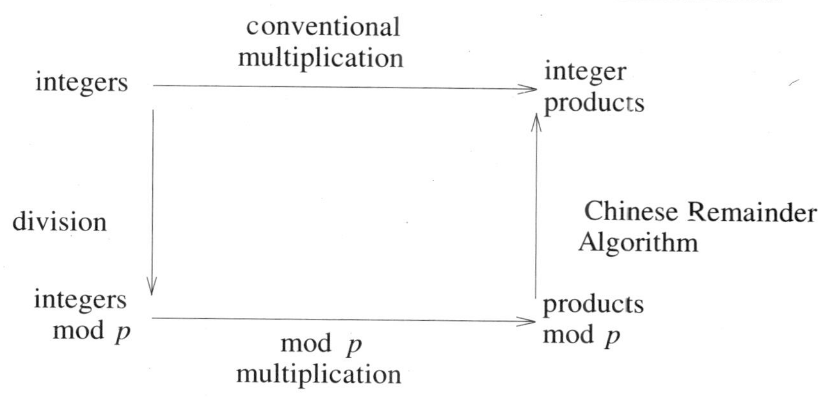

Figure 9.3 Integer multiplication by mod p transformations

Proof: Let x be another integer, different from a, such that $a = x \bmod p_i$ for $1 \leq i \leq r$. Then $a - x$ is a multiple of p_i for all i. Since the p_i are pairwise relatively prime, it follows that $a - x$ is a multiple of p. Thus, there can be only one solution that satisfies these relations. We show how to construct this value in a moment. □

A pictorial view of these transformations when applied to integer multiplication is given in Figure 9.3. Instead of using conventional multiplication, which requires $O((\log a)^2)$ operations ($a = \max(a, b)$), we choose a set of primes $p_1, \ldots, p_r$ and compute $a_i = a \bmod p_i, b_i = b \bmod p_i$, and then $c_i = a_i b_i \bmod p_i$. These are all single precision operations and so they require $O(r)$ steps. The r must be sufficiently large so that $ab < p_1 \cdots p_r$. The precision of a is proportional to log a and hence the precision of ab is no more than 2 log $a = O(\log a)$. Thus $r = O(\log a)$ and the time for transformation into modular form and computing the r products is $O(\log a)$. Therefore the value of this method rests on how fast we can perform the inverse transformation by the Chinese Remainder Algorithm.

Suppose we consider how to compute the value in the Chinese Remainder Theorem for only two moduli: Given $a \bmod p$ and $b \bmod q$, we wish to determine the unique c such that $c \bmod p = a$ and $c \bmod q = b$. The value for c that satisfies these two constraints is easily seen to be

$$c = (b - a)sp + a$$

where s is the multiplicative reciprocal of $p \bmod q$; that is, s satisfies $ps \bmod q = 1$. To show that this is correct, we note that

```
Algorithm OneStepCRA(a, p, b, q)
// a and b are in GF(p); gcd(p, q) = 1. This function
// returns a c such that c mod p = a and c mod q = b.
{
    t := a mod q; pb := p mod q; s := ExEuclid(pb, q);
    u := ((b - t) * s) mod q; if (u < 0) then u := u + q;
    t := u * p + a; return t;
}
```

Algorithm 9.12 One-step Chinese Remainder Algorithm

$$((b-a)sp + a) \bmod p = a$$

since the term $(b-a)sp$ has p as a factor. Secondly

$$\begin{aligned} ((b-a)sp + a) \bmod q &= (b-a)sp \bmod q + a \bmod q \\ &= (b-a) \bmod q + a \bmod q \\ &= (b-a+a) \bmod q \\ &= b \end{aligned}$$

OneStepCRA (Algorithm 9.12) uses ExEuclid and arithmetic modulo p to compute the formula we have just described. The computing time is dominated by the call to ExEuclid which requires $O(\log q)$ operations.

The simplest way to use this procedure to implement the Chinese Remainder Theorem for r moduli is to apply it $r-1$ times in the following way. Given a set of congruences $a_i \bmod p_i$, $1 \le i \le r$, we let OneStepCRA be called $r-1$ times with the following set of values for the parameters.

	a	p	b	q	output
First time	a_1	p_1	a_2	p_2	c_1
Second time	c_1	p_1p_2	a_3	p_3	c_2
Third time	c_2	$p_1p_2p_3$	a_4	p_4	c_3
...	...	...	.	.	...
$(r-1)$st time	c_{r-2}	$p_1p_2\cdots p_{r-1}$	a_r	p_r	c_{r-1}

The final result c_{r-1} is an integer such that $c_{r-1} \bmod p_i = a_i$ for $1 \le i \le r$ and $c_{r-1} < p_1 \cdots p_r$. The total computing time is $O(r \log q) = O(r^2)$.

Example 9.10 Suppose we wish to take 4, 6, and 8 and compute $4 + 8 * 6 = 52$. Let $p_1 = 7$, and $p_2 = 11$.

$$\begin{array}{lcllcl} 4 & = & (4 \bmod 7, 4 \bmod 11) & = & (4,4) \\ 6 & = & (6 \bmod 7, 6 \bmod 11) & = & (6,6) \\ 8 & = & (8 \bmod 7, 8 \bmod 11) & = & (1,8) \\ 8*6 & = & (6*1 \bmod 7, 8*6 \bmod 11) & = & (6,4) \\ 4+8*6 & = & (4+6 \bmod 7, 4+4 \bmod 11) & = & (3,8) \end{array}$$

So, we must convert the 2-tuple (3, 8) back to integer notation. Using OneStepCRA with $a = 3, b = 8, p = 7$, and $q = 11$, we get

$t = a \bmod q = 3 \bmod 11 = 3$
$pb = p \bmod q = 7 \bmod 11 = 7$
$s = \mathsf{ExEuclid}(pb,\ q) = 8;\ k = 5$
$u = ((b - t)s) \bmod q = (8 - 3)8 \bmod 11 = 40 \bmod 11 = 7$
return $(u * p + a) = 7 * 7 + 3 = 52$ □

In conclusion we review the computing times for modular arithmetic. If $a, b \in \mathrm{GF}(p)$, where p is single precision, then

operation	computing time
$a + b$	$O(1)$
ab	$O(1)$
a/b	$O(\log p)$
$c := (c_1, \ldots, c_r)$	$O(r \log c)$
$c_i = c \bmod\ p_i$	
$c := (c_1, \ldots, c_r)$	$O(r^2)$

EXERCISES

1. Given the finite field $A = \{0, 1, \ldots, p-1\}$, one of these elements x is such that $x^0, x, x^2, \ldots, x^{p-2}$ are equal to all the nonzero elements of A. The element x is called a primitive element. If x is a primitive element and n divides $p - 1$, then $x^{(p-1)/n}$ is a primitive nth root of unity. To find such a value x, we use the fact that $x^{(p-1)/q} \neq 1$ for each prime factor q of $p - 1$. Use this fact to write an algorithm that, when given a, b, and e, finds the a largest Fourier prime less than or equal to b of the form $2^f k + 1$ with $f \geq e$. For example, if $a = 10, b = 2^{31}$, and $e = 20$, the answer is:

p	f	least primitive element
2130706433	24	3
2114977793	20	3
2113929217	25	5
2099249153	21	3
2095054849	21	11
2088763393	23	5
2077229057	20	3
2070937601	20	6
2047868929	20	13
2035286017	20	10

2. [Diffie, Hellman, Rivest, Shamir, Adelman] Some people are connected to a computer network. They need a mechanism with which they can send messages to one another that can't be decoded by a third party (security) and in addition can prove any particular message to have been sent by a given person (a signature). In short each person needs an encoding mechanism E and a decoding mechanism D such that $D(E(M)) = M$ for any message M. A signature feature is possible if the sender A first decodes her or his message and sends it and it is encoded by the receiver using A's encoding scheme E ($E(D(M)) = M$). The E for all users is published in a public directory. The scheme to implement D and E proposed by Rivest, Shamir, and Adelman relies on the difficulty of factoring versus the simplicity of determining several large (100 digit) primes. Using modular arithmetic, see whether you can construct an encoding function that is invertible but only if the factors of a number are known.

9.5 EVEN FASTER EVALUATION AND INTERPOLATION

In this section we study four problems:

1. From an n-precision integer compute its residues modulo n single precision primes.

2. From an n-degree polynomial compute its values at n points.

3. From n single precision residues compute the unique n-precision integer that is congruent to the residues.

4. From n points compute the unique interpolating polynomial through those points.

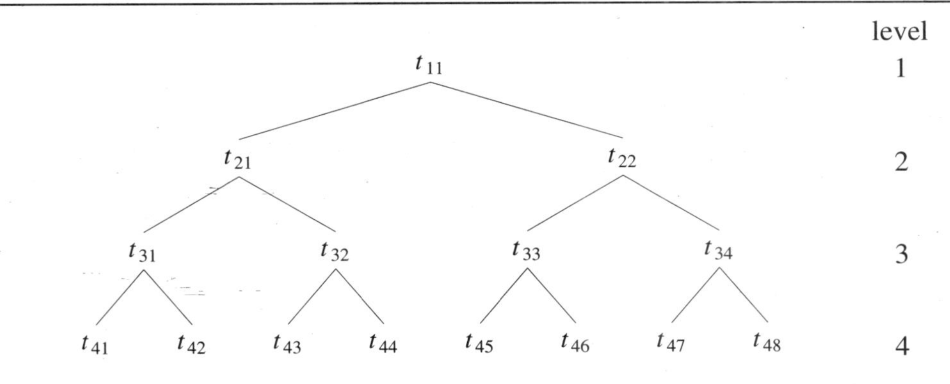

Figure 9.4 A binary tree

We saw in Sections 9.2 and 9.4 that the classical methods for problems 1 to 4 take $O(n^2)$ operations. Here we show how to use the fast Fourier transform to speed up all four problems. In particular we derive algorithms for problems 1 and 2 whose times are $O(n(\log n)^2)$ and for problems 3 and 4 whose times are $O(n(\log n)^3)$. These algorithms rely on the fast Fourier transform as it is used to perform n-precision integer multiplication in time $O(n \log n \log \log n)$. This algorithm, developed by A. Schonhage and V. Strassen, is the fastest known way to multiply. Because this algorithm is complex to describe and already appears in several places (see, e.g., D. E. Knuth cited in References and Readings at the end of this chapter), we simply assume its existence here. Moreover to simplify things somewhat, we assume that for n-precision integers and for n-degree polynomials the time to add or subtract is $O(n)$ and the time to multiply or divide is $O(n \log n)$. In addition we assume that an extended gcd algorithm is available (see Algorithm 9.11) for integers or polynomials whose computing times are $O(n(\log n)^2)$.

Now consider the binary tree as shown in Figure 9.4. As we go down the tree, the level numbers increase, while the root of the tree is at the top at level 1. The ith level has 2^{i-1} nodes and a tree with m levels has a total of $2^m - 1$ nodes. We are interested in computing different functions at every node of such a binary tree. Algorithm 9.13 is an algorithm for moving up the tree.

Subsequently we are concerned about the cost of the operation $*$, which is denoted by $C(*)$. Given the value of $C(*)$ on the ith level (call it $C_i(*)$) and Algorithm 9.13, the total time needed to compute every node in a tree is

```
Algorithm MoveUpATree(t, n)
// n = 2^(m-1) values are stored in t[1 : m, 1 : n] in locations
// t[m, 1 : n]. The algorithm causes the nodes of a binary tree
// to be visited so that at each node an abstract binary operation
// denoted by * is performed. The resulting values are stored
// in the array as indicated in Figure 9.4.
{
    for i := m - 1 to 1  step -1 do
    {
        p := 1;
        for j := 1 to 2^(i-1) do
        {
            t[i, j] := t[i + 1, p] * t[i + 1, p + 1];
            p := p + 2;
        }
    }
}
```

Algorithm 9.13 Moving up a tree

$$\sum_{1 \le i \le m-1} 2^{i-1} C_i(*) \tag{9.13}$$

Similarly Algorithm 9.14 is an algorithm that computes elements as we go down the tree. We now proceed to the specific problems.

Problem 1 Let u be an n-precision integer and $p_1, \ldots, p_n$ be single precision primes. We wish to compute the n residues $u_i = u \bmod p_i$ that give the mixed radix representation for u. We consider the binary tree in Figure 9.5. Starting from the leaves of the tree, we move up the tree, computing the products indicated at each node of the tree.

If $n = 2^{m-1}$, then products on the ith level have precision 2^{m-i}, $1 \le i \le m$. Using our fast integer multiplication algorithm, we can compute the elements going up the tree. Therefore $C_i(*)$ is $2^{m-i-1}(m-i-1)$ and the total time to complete the tree is

$$\begin{aligned} & \textstyle\sum_{1 \le i \le m-1} 2^{i-1} 2^{m-i-1}(m-i-1) \\ = \;& 2^{m-2}\left(\frac{(m-1)(m-2)}{2}\right) \;=\; O(n(\log n)^2) \end{aligned} \tag{9.14}$$

```
Algorithm MoveDownATree(s, t, m)
// n = 2^(m-1) and t[1,1] is given. Also, s[1 : m, 1 : n] is given
// containing a binary tree of values. The algorithm produces
// elements and stores them in the array t[1 : m, 1 : n] at the
// positions that correspond to the nodes of the binary tree
// in Figure 9.4.
{
    for i := 2 to m do
    {
        p := 1;
        for j := 1 to 2^(i-1) step 2 do
        {
            t[i, j] := s[i, j] * t[i - 1, p];
            t[i, j + 1] := s[i, j + 1] * t[i - 1, p];
            p := p + 1;
        }
    }
}
```

Algorithm 9.14 Moving down a tree

Now to compute the n residues $u_i = u \bmod p_i$, we reverse direction and proceed to compute functions down the tree. Since u is n-precision and the primes are all near the maximum size of a single precision number, we first compute $u \bmod p_1 \cdots p_n = ub$. Then the algorithm continues by computing

$$u_{2,1} \;=\; ub \bmod p_1 \cdots p_{n/2} \quad \text{and} \quad u_{2,2} \;=\; ub \bmod p_{n/2+1} \cdots p_n$$

Then we compute

$$u_{3,1} = u_{2,1} \bmod p_1 \cdots p_{n/4}, \qquad u_{3,2} = u_{2,1} \bmod p_{n/4+1} \cdots p_{n/2}$$
$$u_{3,3} = u_{2,2} \bmod p_{n/2+1} \cdots p_{3n/4}, \qquad u_{3,4} = u_{2,2} \bmod p_{3n/4+1} \cdots p_n$$

and so on down the tree until we have

$$u_{m,1} = u_1, \quad u_{m,2} = u_2, \quad \ldots \quad , \; u_{m,2^{(m-1)}} = u_n$$

A node on level i is computed using the previously computed product of primes at that position plus the element $u_{j,i-1}$ at the descendant node. The

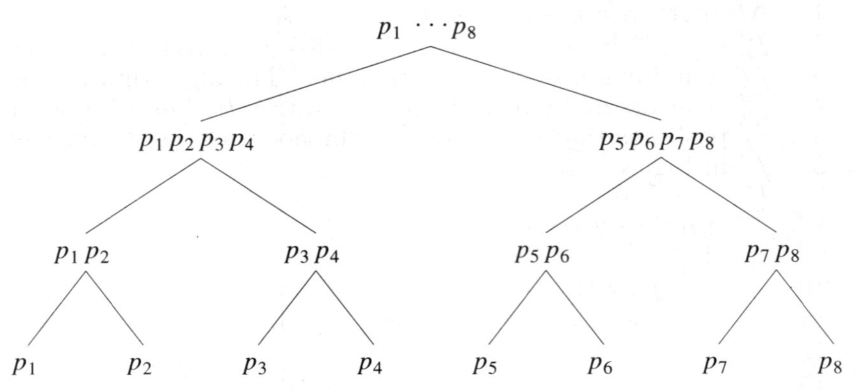

Figure 9.5 Binary tree with moduli

computation requires a division operation so $C_i(*)$ is $2^{m-i+1}(m-i+1)$ and the total time for problem 1 is

$$\begin{aligned} &\textstyle\sum_{1\le i\le m} 2^{i-1}2^{m-i+1}(m-i+1) \\ &= 2^m\left(m^2 - \tfrac{m(m-1)}{2}\right) = O(n(\log n)^2) \end{aligned} \tag{9.15}$$

Problem 2 Let $P(x)$ be an n-degree polynomial and $x_1, \ldots, x_n$ be n single precision points. We wish to compute the n values $P(x_i)$, $1 \le i \le n$. We can use the binary tree in Figure 9.6 to perform this computation.

First, we move up the tree and compute the products indicated at each node of the tree. If $n = 2^{m-1}$, the products on the ith level have degree 2^{m-i}. Using fast polynomial multiplication, we compute the elements going up the tree. Therefore $C_i(*)$ is $2^{m-i-1}(m-i-1)$ and the total time to complete the tree is

$$\begin{aligned} &\textstyle\sum_{1\le i\le m-1} 2^{i-1}2^{m-i-1}(m-i-1) \\ &= 2^{m-2}\left(\tfrac{(m-1)(m-2)}{2}\right) = O(n(\log n)^2) \end{aligned} \tag{9.16}$$

Now to compute the n values $P(x_i)$, we reverse direction and proceed to compute functions down the tree. If $D(x) = (x - x_1)\cdots(x - x_n)$, then we can divide $P(x)$ by $D(x)$ and obtain the quotient and remainder

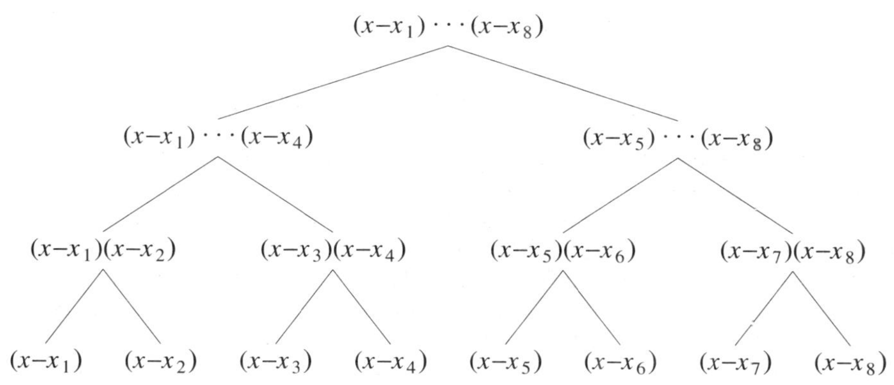

Figure 9.6 A binary tree with linear moduli

$$P(x) = D(x)Q(x) + R_{11}(x)$$

where the degree of R_{11} is less than the degree of D. By substitution it follows that

$$P(x_i) = R_{11}(x_i), \qquad 1 \le i \le n$$

The algorithm would continue by dividing $R_{11}(x)$ by the first $n/2$ factors of $D(x)$ and then by the second $n/2$ factors. Calling these polynomials $D_1(x)$ and $D_2(x)$, we get the quotients and remainders

$$\begin{aligned} R_{11}(x) &= D_1(x)Q_1(x) + R_{21}(x) \\ R_{11}(x) &= D_2(x)Q_2(x) + R_{22}(x) \end{aligned}$$

By the same argument we see that

$$P(x_i) = \begin{cases} R_{21}(x_i), & 1 \le i \le n/2 \\ R_{22}(x_i), & n/2+1 \le i \le n \end{cases} \tag{9.17}$$

Eventually we arrive at constants $R_{m,1}, \ldots, R_{m,2^{(m-1)}}$, where $P(x_i) = R_{m,i}$ for $1 \le i \le n$. Since the time for multiplication and division of polynomials is the same, $C_i(*)$ is $2^{m-i}(m-i)$ and the total for problem 2 is

$$\begin{aligned} & \textstyle\sum_{1\le i\le m} 2^{i-1}2^{m-i}(m-i) \\ = \; & 2^{m-1}\left(m^2 - \frac{m(m+1)}{2}\right) \; = \; O(n(\log n)^2) \end{aligned} \tag{9.18}$$

Problem 3 Given n residues u_i of n single precision primes p_i, we wish to find the unique n-precision integer u such that $u \bmod p_i = u_i$, $1 \le i \le n$. It follows from the Chinese Remainder Theorem, Theorem 9.4, that this integer exists and is unique. For this problem, as for problem 1, we assume the binary tree in Figure 9.5 has already been computed. What we need to do is go up the tree and at each node compute a new integer that is congruent to the product of the integers at the children nodes. For example, at the first level let $u_i = u_{m,i}$, $1 \le i \le n = 2^{m-1}$. Then for i odd, we compute from $u_{m,i} \bmod p_i$ and $u_{m,i+1} \bmod p_{i+1}$ the unique integer $u_{m-1,i} = u_{m,i} \bmod p_i$ and $u_{m-1,i} = u_{m,i+1} \bmod p_{i+1}$. Thus $u_{m-1,i}$ lies in the range $[0,\ p_i p_{i+1})$. Repeating this process up the tree, we eventually produce the integer u in the interval $[0,\ p_1 \cdots p_n)$. So we need to develop an algorithm that proceeds from level i to $i-1$. But we already have such an algorithm, the one-step Chinese Remainder Algorithm OneStepCRA. The time for this algorithm was shown to be dominated by the time for ExEuclid. Using our assumption that ExEuclid can be done in $O(n(\log n)^2)$ operations, where n is the maximum precision of the moduli, then this is also the time for OneStepCRA. Note the difference between its use in this section and in Section 9.4. In Section 9.4 only one of the moduli was growing.

We now apply this one-step algorithm to an algorithm that proceeds up the tree of Figure 9.5. The total time for problem 3 is seen to be

$$\begin{aligned} & \textstyle\sum_{1\le i\le m-1} 2^{i-1}2^{m-i-1}(m-i-1)^2 \\ = \; & 2^{m-2}\textstyle\sum_{1\le i\le m-1}(m-i-1)^2 \; = \; O(n(\log n)^3) \end{aligned} \tag{9.19}$$

Problem 4 Given n values $y_1, \ldots, y_n$ at $n = 2^{m-1}$ points $(x_1, \ldots, x_n)$, we wish to compute the unique interpolating polynomial $P(x)$ of degree $\le n-1$ such that $P(x_i) = y_i$. For this problem, as for problem 2, we assume that the binary tree in Figure 9.6 has already been computed. Again we need an algorithm that goes up the tree and at each node computes a new interpolating polynomial from its two children. For example, at level m we compute polynomials $R_{m1}(x), \ldots, R_{mn}(x)$ such that $R_{mi}(x_i) = y_i, 1 \le i \le n$. Then at level $m-1$ we compute $R_{m-1,1}, \ldots, R_{m-1,n/2}$ such that, for $1 \le i \le n/2$,

$$\begin{aligned} R_{m-1,i}(x_{2i-1}) &= y_{2i-1} \\ R_{m-1,i}(x_{2i}) &= y_{2i}. \end{aligned}$$

```
1   Algorithm BalancedInterp(U1, U2, Q1, Q2, k)
2   // U1, U2, Q1, and Q2 are all polynomials in x. U1 interpolates
3   // the first k/2 points and U2 interpolates the next k/2 points.
4   {
5       P1 := U1 mod Q2;
6           // a mod b computes the poly. reminder of a(x)/b(x).
7       P2 := Q1 mod Q2;
8       P3 := ExEuclid(P2, Q2);
9           // The extended Euclidean alg. for polynomials.
10      P4 := P3 mod Q2;
11      return U1 + (U2 - P1) * P4 * Q1;
12  }
```

Algorithm 9.15 Balanced interpolation

and so on, until $R_{11}(x) = P(x)$. Therefore we need an algorithm that combines two interpolating polynomials to give a third that interpolates at both sets of points. This requires a generalization, Algorithm 9.15, of algorithm Interpolate, Algorithm 9.7. In this algorithm, the operators $+$, $-$, $*$, and **mod** have been overloaded to take polynomial operands. Also, $Q1(x) = (x - x_1)(x - x_2) \cdots (x - x_{k/2})$ and $Q2(x) = (x - x_{k/2+1}) \cdots (x - x_k)$ with $\gcd(Q1, Q2) = 1$. BalancedInterp returns a polynomial A such that $A(x_i) = U1(x_i)$ for $1 \le i \le k/2$ and $A(x_i) = U2(x_i)$ for $k/2 + 1 \le i \le k$. The degree of A is $\le k - 1$.

We note that lines 5, 7, and 8 of Algorithm 9.15 imply that there exist quotients $C1, C2$, and $C3$ such that

$$\begin{aligned} U1 &= Q2 * C1 + P1, \quad \deg(P1) < \deg(Q2) \quad \text{(a)} \\ Q1 &= Q2 * C2 + P2, \quad \deg(P2) < \deg(Q2) \quad \text{(b)} \\ P4 * P2 + C3 * Q2 &= 1, \quad \deg(P4) < \deg(Q2) \quad \text{(c)} \end{aligned}$$

$P4$ is the multiplicative inverse of $P2$ **mod** $Q2$. Therefore

$$\begin{aligned} A &= U1 + (U2 - P1) * P4 * Q1 \quad \text{(i)} \\ A &= U1 + (U2 + Q2 * C1 - U1)((1 - C3 * Q2)/P2) * Q1 \quad \text{(ii)} \end{aligned}$$

using (a) and (c). By (i), $A(x_i) = U1(x_i)$ for $1 \le i \le k/2$ since $Q1(x)$ evaluated at those points is zero. By (ii), it is easy to see that $A(x) = U2(x)$

at points $x_{k/2+1}, \ldots, x_k$.

Now lines 5 and 7 take $O(k \log k)$ operations. To compute the multiplicative inverse of $P2$, we use the extended gcd algorithm for polynomials which takes $O(k(\log k)^2)$ operations. The time for line 10 is no more than $O(k \log k)$ so the total time for one-step interpolation is $O(k(\log k)^2)$.

Applying this one-step algorithm as we proceed up the tree gives a total computing time for problem 4 of

$$\sum_{1 \le i \le m-1} 2^{i-1} 2^{m-i-1} (m-i-1)^2 = O(n(\log n)^3) \tag{9.20}$$

The exercises show how one can further reduce the time for problems 3 and 4 using preconditioning.

EXERCISES

1. Investigate the problem of evaluating an nth-degree polynomial $a(x)$ at the n points 2^i, $0 \le i \le n-1$. Note that $a(2^i)$ requires no multiplications, only n additions and n shifts.

2. Given the n points $(2^i, y_i)$, $0 \le i \le n-1$, where y_i is an integer, design an algorithm that produces the unique interpolating polynomial of degree $\le n$. Try to minimize the number of multiplications.

3. In Section 9.5 the time for the n-value Chinese Remainder Algorithm and n-point interpolation is shown to be $O(n(\log n)^3)$. However, it is possible to get modified algorithms whose complexities are $O(n(\log n)^2)$ if we allow certain values to be computed in advance without cost. Assuming the moduli and the points are so known, what should be computed in advance to lower the complexity of these two problems?

9.6 REFERENCES AND READINGS

The fast Fourier transform algorithm was popularized by J. M. Cooley and J. W. Tukey. For more details on the FFT see:

The Fast Fourier Transform and Its Applications, by O. Brigham, Prentice Hall, 1988.

Numerical Recipes: The Art of Scientific Computing, by W. H. Press, B. P. Flannery, and S. A. Teukolsky, Cambridge University Press, 1986.

Numerical Recipes in C, by W. H. Press, B. P. Flannery, S. A. Teukolsky, and W. T. Vetterling, Cambridge University Press, 1988.

For an interesting collection of papers that deal with evaluation, interpolation, and modular arithmetic see *The Computational Complexity of Algebraic and Numeric Problems*, by A. B. Borodin and I. Munro, American Elsevier, 1975.

For a survey on the gcd and related number theoretic algorithms see "Number-Theoretic Algorithms," by E. Bach, *Annual Review of Computer Science* 4 (1990): 119–172.

The use of the FFT plus modular arithmetic for multiplying large precision integers was originally given by A. Schonhage and V. Strassen.

English accounts of the method, which requires $O(n \log n \log\log n)$ operations to multiply two n bit integers, can be found in:
The Design and Analysis of Computer Algorithms, by A. V. Aho, J. E. Hopcroft, and J. D. Ullman, Addison-Wesley, 1974.
The Art of Computer Programming: Semi-Numerical Algorithms, by D. E. Knuth, Vol. II, Addison-Wesley, 1969.

Chapter 10

LOWER BOUND THEORY

In the previous nine chapters we surveyed a broad range of problems and their algorithmic solution. Our main task for each problem was to obtain a correct and efficient solution. If two algorithms for solving the same problem were discovered and their times differed by an order of magnitude, then the one with the smaller order was generally regarded as superior. But still we are left with the question: is there a faster method? The purpose of this chapter is to expose you to some techniques that have been used to establish that a given algorithm is the most efficient possible. The way this is done is by discovering a function $g(n)$ that is a lower bound on the time that *any* algorithm must take to solve the given problem. If we have an algorithm whose computing time is the same order as $g(n)$, then we know that asymptotically we can do no better.

Recall from Chapter 1 that there is a mathematical notation for expressing lower bounds. If $f(n)$ is the time for some algorithm, then we write $f(n) = \Omega(g(n))$ to mean that $g(n)$ is a lower bound for $f(n)$. Formally this equation can be written if there exist positive constants c and n_0 such that $|f(n)| \geq c|g(n)|$ for all $n > n_0$. In addition to developing lower bounds to within a constant factor, we are also concerned with determining more exact bounds whenever this is possible.

Deriving good lower bounds is often more difficult than devising efficient algorithms. Perhaps this is because a lower bound states a fact about *all* possible algorithms for solving a problem. Usually we cannot enumerate and analyze all these algorithms, so lower bound proofs are often hard to obtain.

However, for many problems it is possible to easily observe that a lower bound identical to n exists, where n is the number of inputs (or possibly outputs) to the problem. For example, consider all algorithms that find the maximum of an unordered set of n integers. Clearly every integer must be examined at least once, so $\Omega(n)$ is a lower bound for any algorithm that solves this problem. Or, suppose we wish to find an algorithm that efficiently multiplies two $n \times n$ matrices. Then $\Omega(n^2)$ is a lower bound on any such algorithm since there are $2n^2$ inputs that must be examined and n^2 outputs that must be computed. Bounds such as these are often referred to as *trivial* lower bounds because they are so easy to obtain. We know how to find the maximum of n elements by an algorithm that uses only $n-1$ comparisons so there is no gap between the upper and lower bounds for this problem. But for matrix multiplication the best-known algorithm requires $O(n^{2+\epsilon})$ operations ($\epsilon > 0$), and so there is no reason to believe that a better method cannot be found.[1]

In Section 10.1 we present the computational model called *comparison trees*. These are useful for determining lower bounds for sorting and searching problems. In Section 10.2 we examine a technique for establishing lower bounds called an *oracle* and study a closely related method called an *adversary argument*. Deriving lower bounds with the technique of reductions is introduced in Section 10.3. In Section 10.4 we study some arguments that have been used to find lower bounds for the arithmetic and algebraic problems discussed in Chapter 9.

10.1 COMPARISON TREES

In this section we study the use of comparison trees for deriving lower bounds on problems that are collectively called *sorting and searching*. We see how these trees are especially useful for modeling the way in which a large number of sorting and searching algorithms work. By appealing to some elementary facts about trees, the lower bounds are obtained.

Suppose that we are given a set S of distinct values on which an ordering relation $<$ holds. The *sorting problem* calls for determining a permutation of the integers 1 to n, say $p(1)$ to $p(n)$, such that the n distinct values from S stored in $A[1:n]$ satisfy $A[p(1)] < A[p(2)] < \cdots < A[p(n)]$. The *ordered searching problem* asks whether a given element $x \in S$ occurs within the elements in $A[1:n]$ that are ordered so that $A[1] < \cdots < A[n]$. If x is in $A[1:n]$, then we are to determine an i between 1 and n such that $A[i] = x$. The *merging problem* assumes that two ordered sets of distinct inputs from S are given in $A[1:m]$ and $B[1:n]$ such that $A[1] < \cdots < A[m]$ and $B[1] < \cdots < B[n]$; these $m+n$ values are to be rearranged into an array $C[1:m+n]$ so that $C[1] < \cdots < C[m+n]$. For all these problems we restrict the class of algorithms we are considering to those which work solely by making comparisons between elements. No arithmetic involving elements is permitted, though it is possible for the algorithm to move elements around. These algorithms are referred to as *comparison-based* algorithms. We rule out algorithms such as radix sort that decompose the values into subparts.

---

[1]See Chapter 3 for more details.

10.1.1 Ordered Searching

In obtaining the lower bound for the ordered searching problem, we consider only those comparison-based algorithms in which every comparison between two elements of S is of the type "compare x and $A[i]$." The progress of any searching algorithm that satisfies this restriction can be described by a path in a binary tree. Each internal node in this tree represents a comparison between x and an $A[i]$. There are three possible outcomes of this comparison: $x < A[i]$, $x = A[i]$, or $x > A[i]$. We can assume that if $x = A[i]$, the algorithm terminates. The left branch is taken if $x < A[i]$, and the right branch is taken if $x > A[i]$. If the algorithm terminates following a left or right branch (but before another comparison between x and an element of $A[\,]$), then no i has been found such that $x = A[i]$ and the algorithm must declare the search unsuccessful.

Figure 10.1 shows two comparison trees, one modeling a linear search algorithm and the other a binary search (see Algorithm 3.2). It should be easy to see that the comparison tree for any search algorithm must contain at least n internal nodes corresponding to the n different values of i for which $x = A[i]$ and at least one external node corresponding to an unsuccessful search.

Theorem 10.1 Let $A[1:n]$, $n \geq 1$, contain n distinct elements, ordered so that $A[1] < \cdots < A[n]$. Let FIND(n) be the minimum number of comparisons needed, in the worst case, by any comparison-based algorithm to recognize whether $x \in A[1:n]$. Then FIND$(n) \geq \lceil \log(n+1) \rceil$.

Proof: Consider all possible comparison trees that model algorithms to solve the searching problem. The value of FIND(n) is bounded below by the distance of the longest path from the root to a leaf in such a tree. There must be n internal nodes in all these trees corresponding to the n possible successful occurrences of x in A. If all internal nodes of a binary tree are at levels less than or equal to k, then there are at most $2^k - 1$ internal nodes. Thus $n \leq 2^k - 1$ and FIND$(n) = k \geq \lceil \log(n+1) \rceil$. □

From Theorem 10.1 and Theorem 3.2 we can conclude that binary search is an optimal worst-case algorithm for solving the searching problem.

10.1.2 Sorting

Now let's consider the sorting problem. We can describe any sorting algorithm that satisfies the restrictions of the comparison tree model by a binary tree. Consider the case in which the n numbers $A[1:n]$ to be sorted are distinct. Now, any comparison between $A[i]$ and $A[j]$ must result in one of two possibilities: either $A[i] < A[j]$ or $A[i] > A[j]$. So, the comparison tree is a binary tree in which each internal node is labeled by the pair $i:j$ which represents the comparison of $A[i]$ with $A[j]$. If $A[i]$ is less than $A[j]$,

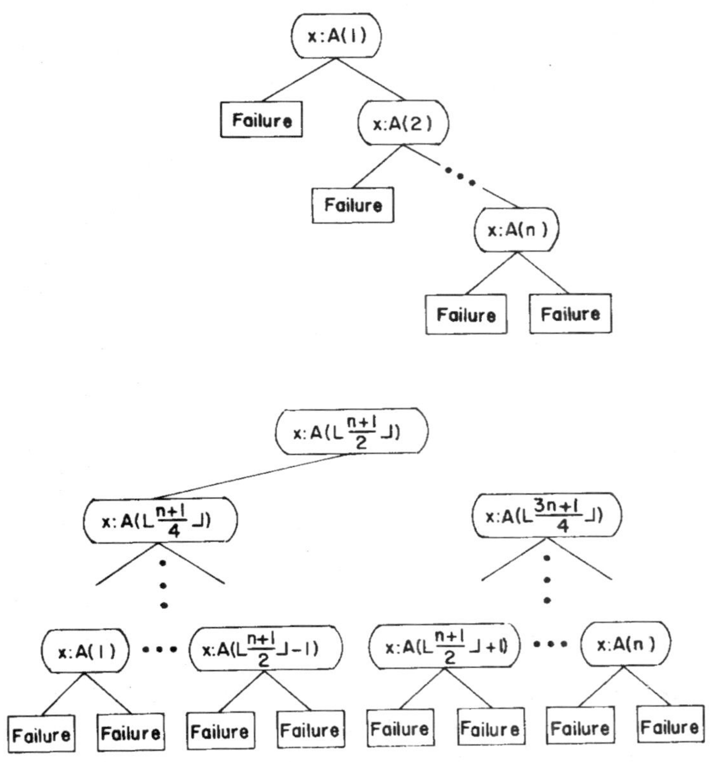

Figure 10.1 Comparison trees for two searching algorithms

then the algorithm proceeds down the left branch of the tree; otherwise it proceeds down the right branch. The external nodes represent termination of the algorithm. Associated with every path from the root to an external node is a unique permutation. To see that this permutation is unique, note that the algorithms we allow are only permitted to move data and make comparisons. The data movement on any path from the root to an external node is the same no matter what the initial input values are. As there are $n!$ different possible permutations of n items, and any one of these might legitimately be the only correct answer for the sorting problem on a given instance, the comparison tree must have at least $n!$ external nodes.

Figure 10.2 shows a comparison tree for sorting three items. The first comparison is $A[1] : A[2]$. If $A[1]$ is less than $A[2]$, then the next comparison is $A[2]$ with $A[3]$. If $A[2]$ is less than $A[3]$, then the left branch leads to an external node containing $1, 2, 3$. This implies that the original set was already sorted for $A[1] < A[2] < A[3]$. The other five external nodes correspond to the other possible orderings that could yield a sorted set.

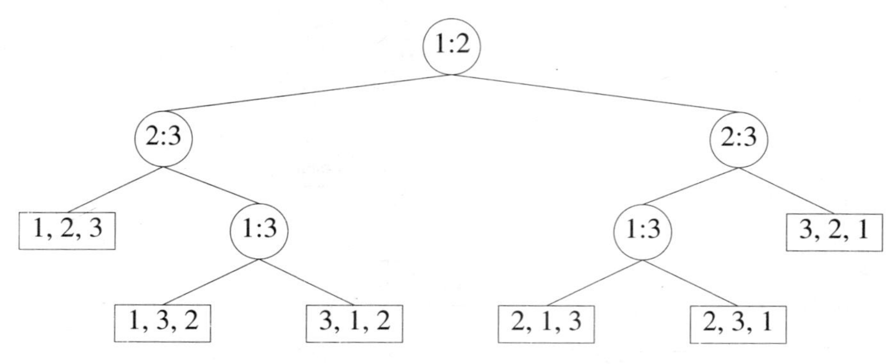

Figure 10.2 A comparison tree for sorting three items

Example 10.1 Let $A[1] = 21, A[2] = 13$, and $A[3] = 18$. At the root of the comparison tree (in Figure 10.2), 21 and 13 are compared, and as a result, the computation proceeds to the right subtree. Now, 13 and 18 are compared and the computation proceeds to the left subtree. Then $A[1]$ and $A[3]$ are compared and the computation proceeds to the right subtree to yield the permutation $A[2], A[3], A[1]$. □

We consider the worst case for all comparison-based sorting algorithms. Let $T(n)$ be the minimum number of comparisons that are sufficient to sort n items in the worst case. Using our knowledge of binary trees once again, if all internal nodes are at levels less than k, then there are at most 2^k external nodes (one more than the number of internal nodes). Therefore, if we let $k = T(n)$

$$n! \leq 2^{T(n)}$$

Since $T(n)$ is an integer, we get the lower bound

$$T(n) \geq \lceil \log n! \rceil$$

By Stirling's approximation (see Exercise 7) it follows that

n	1	2	3	4	5	6	7	8	9	10	11	12	13
$\lceil \log n! \rceil$	0	1	3	5	7	10	13	16	19	22	26	29	33
BISORT(n)	0	1	3	5	8	11	14	17	21	25	29	33	37

Table 10.1 Bounds for minimum comparison sorting

$$\lceil \log n! \rceil = n \log n - n/\ln 2 + (1/2)\log n + O(1)$$

where ln 2 refers to the natural logarithm of 2 whereas $\log n$ is the logarithm to the base 2 of n. This formula shows that $T(n)$ is of the order $n \log n$. *Hence we say that any comparison-based sorting algorithm needs* $\Omega(n \log n)$ *time.* (This bound can be shown to hold even when operations more complex than comparisons are allowed, for example, operations such as addition, subtraction, and in some cases arbitrary analytic functions.)

How close do the known sorting methods get to this lower bound of $T(n)$? Consider the bottom-up version of merge sort which first orders consecutive pairs of elements and then merges adjacent groups of size $2, 4, 8, \ldots$ until the entire sorted set is produced. The worst-case number of comparisons required by this algorithm is bounded by

$$\sum_{1 \le i \le k} (n/2^i)(2^i - 1) \le n \log n - O(n) \tag{10.1}$$

Thus we know at least one algorithm that requires slightly less than $n \log n$ comparisons. Is there still a better method?

The sorting strategy called *binary insertion sorting* works in the following way. The next unsorted item is chosen and a binary search (see Algorithm 3.2) is performed on the sorted set to determine where to place this new item. Then the sorted items are moved to make room for the new value. This algorithm requires $O(n^2)$ data movements to sort the entire set but far fewer comparisons. Let BISORT(n) be the number of comparisons it requires. Then by the results of Section 3.3

$$\text{BISORT}(n) = \sum_{1 \le k \le n} \lceil \log_2 k \rceil \tag{10.2}$$

which is equal to

$$n \lceil \log n \rceil - 2^{\lceil \log n \rceil} + 1$$

Now suppose we compare BISORT(n) with the theoretical lower bound. This is done in Table 10.1. Scanning Table 10.1, we observe that for $n =$

1, 2, 3, and 4, the values are the same so binary insertion is optimal. But for $n = 5$, there is a difference of one and so we are left with the question of whether 7 or 8 is the minimum number of comparisons in the worst case needed to sort five items. This question has been answered by L. Ford, Jr., and S. Johnson, who presented a sorting algorithm that requires even fewer comparisons than the binary insertion method. In fact their method requires exactly $T(n)$ comparisons for $1 \le n \le 11$ and $20 \le n \le 21$.

To see how the Ford-Johnson method works, we consider the sorting of 17 items that originally reside in $SORTED[1:17]$. We begin by comparing consecutive pairs $SORTED[1] : SORTED[2]$, $SORTED[3] : SORTED[4]$, ... , $SORTED[15] : SORTED[16]$ and placing the larger items into the array $HIGH$ and the smaller items into the array LOW. The item $LOW[9]$ gets $SORTED[17]$. Then we sort the array $HIGH$ using this algorithm recursively in nonincreasing order, so that $HIGH[1]$ has the largest element. Permute the array LOW also according to this permutation. When this is done, we have $LOW[1] < HIGH[1] < HIGH[2] < \cdots < HIGH[8]$. Though $LOW[2]$ through $LOW[9]$ remain unsorted, we do know that $LOW[i] \le HIGH[i]$ for $2 \le i \le 8$. Now inserting $LOW[2]$ into the sorted set possibly requires two comparisons and at the same time causes the insertion of $LOW[3]$ to possibly require three more comparisons for a total of five. A better approach is to insert first $LOW[3]$ among the items $LOW[1]$, $HIGH[1]$, and $HIGH[2]$ using binary insertion and then insert $LOW[2]$. Each insertion requires only two comparisons and the merged elements are stored back into the array $SORTED$. This gives us the new relationships $SORTED[1] < SORTED[2] < \cdots < SORTED[6] < HIGH[4] < HIGH[5] < HIGH[6] < HIGH[7] < HIGH[8]$ and $LOW[i] \le HIGH[i]$, for $4 \le i \le 8$. Eleven items are now sorted and six remain to be merged. If we insert $LOW[4]$ followed by $LOW[5]$, three and four comparisons may be needed respectively. Once again it is more economical to first insert $LOW[5]$ and then $LOW[4]$; each insertion requires at most three comparisons. This gives us the new situation $SORTED[1] < \cdots < SORTED[10] < HIGH[6] < HIGH[7] < HIGH[8]$ and $LOW[i] < HIGH[i]$ for $6 \le i \le 8$. Inserting $LOW[7]$ requires only four comparisons, and then inserting $LOW[8]$ requires five comparisons. However if we insert $LOW[9]$ and then $LOW[8]$, $LOW[7]$, and $LOW[6]$, then each item requires at most four comparisons. We do the insertions in the order $LOW[9]$ to $LOW[6]$ and get the completely sorted set of 17 items.

A count of the total number of comparisons needed to sort the 17 items is 8 to compare $SORTED[i] : SORTED[i+1]$, 16 to sort $HIGH[1:8]$ using merge insertion recursively, 4 to insert $LOW[3]$ and $LOW[2]$, 6 to insert $LOW[5]$ and $LOW[4]$, and 16 to insert $LOW[9]$ to $LOW[6]$ – a total of 50. The value of $\lceil \log n! \rceil$ for $n = 17$ is 49, and so merge insertion requires only one more comparison than the theoretical lower bound.

In general, merge insertion can be summarized as follows: Let the items to be sorted be $SORTED[1:n]$. Make pairwise comparisons of $SORTED[i]$ and $SORTED[i+1]$; place the larger items into an array $HIGH$ and the smaller items into array LOW. If n is odd, then the last item of $SORTED$ is appended to LOW. Now apply merge insertion to the elements of $HIGH$. Permute LOW using the same permutation. Then we know that $HIGH[1] < HIGH[2] < \cdots < HIGH[\lfloor n/2 \rfloor]$ and $LOW[i] < HIGH[i]$ for $1 \leq i \leq \lfloor n/2 \rfloor$. Now we insert the items of LOW into the $HIGH$ array using binary insertion. However, the order in which we insert the LOWs is important. We want to select the maximum number of items in LOW so that the number of comparisons required to insert each one into the already sorted list is a constant j. As we have seen from our example, the insertion proceeds in the order $LOW(t_j)$, $LOW(t_j - 1)$, ... , $LOW(t_{j-1}+1)$, where the t_j are a set of increasing integers. In fact t_j has the form $t_j = 2^j - t_{j-1}$, and in the exercises it is shown that this recurrence relation can be solved to give the formula $t_j = (2^{j+1} + (-1)^j)/3$. Thus items are inserted in the order $LOW[3]$, $LOW[2]$; $LOW[5]$, $LOW[4]$; $LOW[11]$, $LOW[10]$, $LOW[9]$, $LOW[8]$, $LOW[7]$, $LOW[6]$; and so on.

It can be shown that the time for this algorithm is

$$\sum_{1 \leq k \leq n} \left\lceil \log_2 \frac{3k}{4} \right\rceil \tag{10.3}$$

For $n = 1$ to 21, the values of this sum are

$$0, 1, 3, 5, 7, 10, 13, 16, 19, 22, 26, 30, 34, 38, 42, 46, 50, 54, 58, 62, 66$$

Comparing these values with $\lceil \log n! \rceil$, we see that merge insertion is truly optimal for $1 \leq n \leq 11$ and $n =$ 20, 21.

10.1.3 Selection

From our previous discussion it should be clear that any comparison tree that models comparison-based algorithms for finding the maximum of n elements has at least 2^{n-1} external nodes since each path from the root to an external node must contain at least $n-1$ internal nodes. This implies at least $n-1$ comparisons for otherwise at least two of the input items never lose a comparison and the largest is not yet found.

Now suppose we let $L_k(n)$ denote a lower bound for the number of comparisons necessary for a comparison-based algorithm to determine the largest, second largest, ... , kth largest out of n elements, in the worst case. $L_1(n) = n-1$ as previously. Since the comparison tree must contain enough external nodes to allow for any possible permutation of the input, it follows immediately that $L_k(n) \geq \lceil \log n(n-1) \cdots (n-k+1) \rceil$.

Theorem 10.2 $L_k(n) \geq n-k+\lceil \log n(n-1)\cdots(n-k+2)\rceil$ for all integers k and n, where $1 \leq k \leq n$.

Proof: As before internal nodes of the comparison tree contain integers of the form $i : j$ that imply a comparison between the input items $A[i]$ and $A[j]$. If $A[i] < A[j]$, then the algorithm proceeds down the left branch; otherwise it proceeds down the right branch. Now consider the set of all possible inputs and place inputs into the same equivalence class if their $k-1$ largest values appear in the same positions. There will be $n(n-1)\cdots(n-k+2)$ equivalence classes which we denote by E_i, $i = 1, 2, \ldots$. Now consider the external nodes for the set of inputs in the equivalence class E_i (for some i). The external nodes of the entire tree are also partitioned into classes called X_i. For all external nodes in X_i the positions of the largest, ..., $k-1$st-largest elements are identical. If we examine the subtree of the original comparison tree that defines the class X_i, then we observe that all comparisons are made on the position of the $n-k+1$ smallest elements; in essence we are trying to determine the kth-largest element. Therefore this subtree can be viewed as a comparison tree for finding the largest of $n-k+1$ elements and it has at least 2^{n-k} external nodes.

Hence the original tree contains at least $n(n-1)\cdots(n-k+2)2^{n-k}$ external nodes and the theorem follows. □

EXERCISES

1. Draw the comparison tree for sorting four elements.

2. Draw the comparison tree for sorting four elements that is produced by the binary insertion method.

3. When equality between keys is permitted, there are 13 possible permutations when sorting three elements. What are they?

4. When keys are allowed to be equal, a comparison can have one of three results: $A[i] < A[j]$, $A[i] = A[j]$, or $A[i] > A[j]$. Sorting algorithms can therefore be represented by extended ternary comparison trees. Draw an extended ternary tree for sorting three elements when equality is allowed.

5. Let $TE(n)$ be the minimum number of comparisons needed to sort n items and to determine all equalities between them. It is clear that $TE(n) \geq T(n)$ since the n items could be distinct. Show that $TE(n) = T(n)$.

6. Find a comparison tree for sorting six elements that has all external nodes on levels 10 and 11.

7. Stirling's approximation is $n! \sim \sqrt{2\pi n}(n/e)^n e^{1/(12n)}$. Show how this approximation is used to demonstrate that $\lceil \log n! \rceil = n \log n - n/(\ln 2) + (1/2)\log n + O(1)$.

8. Prove that the closed form for $\text{BISORT}(n) = n\lceil \log n \rceil - 2^{\lceil \log n \rceil} + 1$ is correct.

9. Show that $\log(n!)$ is approximately equal to $n \log n - n \log e + O(1)$ by using the fact that the function $\log k$ is monotonic and bounded below by $\int_{k-1}^{k} \log x \, dx$.

10. Show that the sum $2^k - 2^{k-1} + 2^{k-2} + \cdots + (-1)^k 2^0 = (2^{k+1} + (-1)^k)/3$.

11. A *partial ordering* is a binary relation, denoted by $\leq$, such that if $x \leq y$ and $y \leq z$, $x \leq z$ and if $x \leq y$ and $y \leq x$, $x = y$. A *total ordering* is a partial ordering such that for all x and y, either $x \leq y$ or $y \leq x$. How can a directed graph be used to model a partial ordering or a total ordering?

12. Let $A[1:n]$ and $B[1:n]$ each contain n unordered elements. Show that if comparisons between pairs of elements of A or B are not allowed, then $\Omega(n^2)$ operations are required to test whether the elements of A are identical (though possibly a permutation) of the elements of B.

13. In the derivation of the Ford-Johnson sorting algorithm, the sequence t_j must be determined. Explain why $t_j + t_{j-1} = 2^j$. Then show how to derive the formula $t_j = (2^{j+1} + (-1)^j)/3$.

10.2 ORACLES AND ADVERSARY ARGUMENTS

One of the proof techniques that is useful for obtaining lower bounds consists of making use of an oracle. The most famous oracle in history was called the Delphic oracle, located in Delphi, Greece. This oracle can still be found, situated in the side of a hill embedded in some rocks. In olden times people would approach the oracle and ask it a question. After some period of time elapsed, the oracle would reply and a caretaker would interpret the oracle's answer.

A similar phenomenon takes place when we use an oracle to establish a lower bound. Given some model of computation such as comparison trees, the oracle tells us the outcome of each comparison. To derive a good lower bound, the oracle tries its best to cause the algorithm to work as hard as it can. It does this by choosing as the outcome of the next test, the result that causes the most work to be required to determine the final answer. And by keeping track of the work that is done, a worst-case lower bound for the problem can be derived.

10.2.1 Merging

Now we consider the merging problem. Given the sets $A[1:m]$ and $B[1:n]$, where the items in A and the items in B are sorted, we investigate lower bounds for algorithms that merge these two sets to give a single sorted set. As was the case for sorting, we assume that all the $m+n$ elements are distinct and that $A[1] < A[2] < \cdots < A[m]$ and $B[1] < B[2] < \cdots < B[n]$. It is possible that after these two sets are merged, the n elements of B can be interleaved within A in every possible way. Elementary combinatorics tells us that there are $\binom{m+n}{m}$ ways that the A's and B's can merge together while preserving the ordering within A and B. For example, if $m = 3, n = 2$, $A[1] = x, A[2] = y, A[3] = z$, $B[1] = u$, and $B[2] = v$, there are $\binom{3+2}{3} =$ 10 ways in which A and B can merge: u, v, x, y, z; u, x, v, y, z; u, x, y, v, z; u, x, y, z, v; x, u, v, y, z; x, u, y, v, z; x, u, y, z, v; x, y, u, v, z; x, y, u, z, v; and x, y, z, u, v.

Thus if we use comparison trees as our model for merging algorithms, then there will be $\binom{m+n}{m}$ external nodes, and therefore at least

$$\left\lceil \log \binom{m+n}{n} \right\rceil$$

comparisons are required by any comparison-based merging algorithm. The conventional merging algorithm that was given in Section 3.5 (Algorithm 3.9) takes $m+n-1$ comparisons. If we let MERGE(m, n) be the minimum number of comparisons needed to merge m items with n items, then we have the inequality

$$\left\lceil \log \binom{m+n}{n} \right\rceil \leq \text{MERGE}(m, n) \leq m+n-1$$

The exercises show that these upper and lower bounds can get arbitrarily far apart as m gets much smaller than n. This should not be a surprise because the conventional algorithm is designed to work best when m and n are approximately equal. In the extreme case when $m = 1$, we observe that binary insertion would require the fewest number of comparisons needed to merge $A[1]$ into $B[1], \ldots, B[n]$.

When m and n are equal, the lower bound given by the comparison tree model is too low and the number of comparisons for the conventional merging algorithm can be shown to be optimal.

Theorem 10.3 MERGE$(m, m) = 2m - 1$, for $m \geq 1$.

Proof: Consider any algorithm that merges the two sets $A[1] < \cdots < A[m]$ and $B[1] < \cdots < B[m]$. We already have an algorithm that requires $2m - 1$ comparisons. If we can show that MERGE$(m, m) \geq 2m - 1$, then the theorem follows. Consider any comparison-based algorithm for solving the merging problem and an instance for which the final result is $B[1] < A[1] < B[2] < A[2] < \cdots < B[m] < A[m]$, that is, for which the B's and A's alternate. Any merging algorithm must make each of the $2m - 1$ comparisons $B[1] : A[1]$, $A[1] : B[2]$, $B[2] : A[2]$, ... ,$B[m] : A[m]$ while merging the given inputs. To see this, suppose that a comparison of type $B[i] : A[i]$ is not made for some i. Then the algorithm cannot distinguish between the previous ordering and the one in which

$$B[1] < A[1] < \cdots < A[i-1] < A[i] < B[i] < B[i+1] < \cdots < B[m] < A[m]$$

So the algorithm will not necessarily merge the A's and B's properly. If a comparison of type $A[i] : B[i+1]$ is not made, then the algorithm will not be able to distinguish between the cases in which $B[1] < A[1] < B[2] < \cdots < B[m] < A[m]$ and in which $B[1] < A[1] < B[2] < A[2] < \cdots < A[i-1] < B[i] < B[i+1] < A[i] < A[i+1] < \cdots < B[m] < A[m]$. So any algorithm must make all $2m - 1$ comparisons to produce this final result. The theorem follows. □

10.2.2 Largest and Second Largest

For another example that we can solve using oracles, consider the problem of finding the largest and the second largest elements out of a set of n. What is a lower bound on the number of comparisons required by any algorithm that finds these two quantities? Theorem 10.2 has already provided us with an answer using comparison trees. An algorithm that makes $n - 1$ comparisons to find the largest and then $n-2$ to find the second largest gives an immediate upper bound of $2n - 3$. So a large gap still remains.

This problem was originally stated in terms of a tennis tournament in which the values are called players and the largest value is interpreted as the winner, and the second largest as the runner-up. Figure 10.3 shows a sample tournament among eight players. The winner of each match (which is the larger of the two values being compared) is promoted up the tree until the final round, which in this case, determines McMahon as the winner. Now, who are the candidates for second place? The runner-up must be someone who lost to McMahon but who did not lose to anyone else. In Figure 10.3 that means that either Guttag, Rosen, or Francez are the possible candidates for second place.

Figure 10.3 leads us to another algorithm for determining the runner-up once the winner of a tournament has been found. The players who have lost to the winner play a second tournament to determine the runner-up. This second tournament need only be replayed along the path that the winner, in

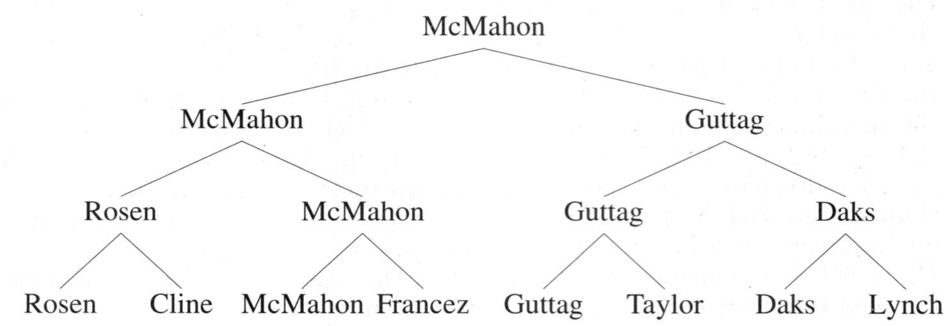

Figure 10.3 A tennis tournament

this case McMahon, followed as he rose through the tree. For a tournament with n players, there are $\lceil \log n \rceil$ levels, and hence only $\lceil \log n \rceil - 1$ comparisons are required for this second tournament. This new algorithm, which was first suggested by J. Schreier in 1932, requires a total of $n - 2 + \lceil \log n \rceil$ comparisons. Therefore we have an identical agreement between the known upper and lower bounds for this problem.

Now we show how the same lower bound can be derived using an oracle.

Theorem 10.4 Any comparison-based algorithm that computes the largest and second largest of a set of n unordered elements requires $n - 2 + \lceil \log n \rceil$ comparisons.

Proof: Assume that a tournament has been played and the largest element and the second-largest element obtained by some method. Since we cannot determine the second-largest element without having determined the largest element, we see that at least $n - 1$ comparisons are necessary. Therefore all we need to show is that there is always some sequence of comparisons that forces the second largest to be found in $\lceil \log n \rceil - 1$ additional comparisons.

Suppose that the winner of the tournament has played x matches. Then there are x people who are candidates for the runner-up position. The runner-up has lost only once, to the winner, and the other $x - 1$ candidates must have lost to one other person. Therefore we produce an oracle that decides the results of matches in such a way that the winner plays $\lceil \log n \rceil$ other people.

In a match between a and b the oracle declares a the winner if a is previously undefeated and b has lost at least once or if both a and b are undefeated but a has won more matches than b. In any other case the oracle can decide arbitrarily as long as it remains consistent.

Now, consider a tournament in which the outcome of each match is determined by the above oracle. Imagine drawing a directed graph with n vertices corresponding to this tournament. Each vertex corresponds to one of the n players. Draw a directed edge from vertex b to $a, b \neq a$, if and only if either player a has defeated b or a has defeated another player who has defeated b. It is easy to see by induction that any player who has played and won only x matches can have at most 2^{x-1} edges pointing into her or his corresponding node. Since for the overall winner there must be an edge from each of the remaining $n-1$ vertices, it follows that the winner must have played at least $\lceil \log n \rceil$ matches. □

10.2.3 State Space Method

Another technique for establishing lower bounds that is related to oracles is the state space description method. Often it is possible to describe any algorithm for solving a given problem by a set of n-tuples. A *state space description* is a set of rules that show the possible states (n-tuples) that an algorithm can assume from a given state and a single comparison. Once the state transitions are given, it is possible to derive lower bounds by arguing that the finish state cannot be reached using any fewer transitions. As an example of the state space description method, we consider a problem originally defined and solved in Section 3.4: given n distinct items, find the maximum and the minimum. Recall that the divide-and-conquer-based solution required $\lceil 3n/2 \rceil - 2$ comparisons. We would like to show that this algorithm is indeed optimal.

Theorem 10.5 Any algorithm that computes the largest and smallest elements of a set of n unordered elements requires $\lceil 3n/2 \rceil - 2$ comparisons.

Proof: The technique we use to establish a lower bound is to define an oracle by a state table. We consider the state of a comparison-based algorithm as being described by a 4-tuple (a, b, c, d), where a is the number of items that have never been compared, b is the number of items that have won but never lost, c is the number of items that have lost but never won, and d is the number of items that have both won and lost. Originally the algorithm is in state $(n, 0, 0, 0)$ and concludes with $(0, 1, 1, n-2)$. Then, after each comparison the tuple (a, b, c, d) can make progress only if it assumes one of the five possible states shown in Figure 10.4.

To get the state $(0, 1, 1, n-2)$ from the state $(n, 0, 0, 0)$, $\lceil 3n/2 \rceil - 2$ comparisons are needed. To see this, observe that the quickest way to get the a component to zero requires $n/2$ state changes yielding the tuple $(0, n/2, n/2, 0)$. Next the b and c components are reduced; this requires an additional $n-2$ state changes. □

$(a-2, b+1, c+1, d)$	if $a \geq 2$	//Two items from a //are compared.
$(a-1, b, c+1, d)$ or $(a-1, b+1, c, d)$ or $(a-1, b, c, d+1)$	if $a \geq 1$	//An item from a //is compared with //one from b or c.
$(a, b-1, c, d+1)$	if $b \geq 2$	//Two items from b //are compared.
$(a, b, c-1, d+1)$	if $c \geq 2$	//Two items from c //are compared.

Figure 10.4 States for max-min problem

10.2.4 Selection

We end this section by deriving another lower bound on the selection problem. We originally studied this problem in Chapter 3 where we presented several solutions. One of the algorithms presented there has a worst-case complexity of $O(n)$ no matter what value is being selected. Therefore we know that asymptotically any selection algorithm requires $\Theta(n)$ time. Let $\text{SEL}_k(n)$ be the minimum number of comparisons needed for finding the kth element of an unordered set of size n. We have already seen that for $k = 1$, $\text{SEL}_1(n) = n - 1$ and, for $k = 2$, $\text{SEL}_2(n) = n - 2 + \lceil \log n \rceil$. In the following paragraphs we present a state table that shows that $n-k+(k-1)\left\lceil \log \frac{n}{2(k-1)} \right\rceil \leq \text{SEL}_k(n)$. We continue to use the terminology that refers to an element of the set as a player and to a comparison between two players as a match that must be won by one of the players. A procedure for selecting the kth-largest element is referred to as a tournament that finds the kth-best player.

To derive this lower bound on the selection problem, an oracle is constructed in the form of a state transition table that will cause any comparison-based algorithm to make at least $n-k+(k-1)\left\lceil \log \frac{n}{2(k-1)} \right\rceil$ comparisons. The tuple size for states in this case is two, (it was four for the max-min problem), and the components of a tuple, say (Map, Set), are Map, a mapping from the integers $1, 2, \ldots, n$ onto itself, and Set, an ordered subset of the input. The initial state is the identity mapping (that is, $Map(i) = 1, 1 \leq i \leq n$) and the empty set. Intuitively, at any given time, the players in Set are the top players (from among all). In particular, the ith player that enters Set is the ith-best player. Candidates for entering Set are chosen according to their Map values. At any time period t the oracle is assumed to be given two unordered elements from the input, say a and b, and the oracle acts as follows:

1. If a and b are both in Set at time t, then a wins iff $a > b$. The tuple (Map, Set) remains unchanged.

2. If a is in Set and b is not in Set, then a wins and the tuple (Map, Set) remains unchanged.

3. If a and b are both not in Set and if $Map(a) > Map(b)$ at time t, then a wins. If $Map(a) = Map(b)$, then it doesn't matter who wins as long as no inconsistency with any previous decision is made. In either case, if $Map(a) + Map(b) \geq n/(k-1)$ at time t, then Map is unchanged and the winner is inserted into Set as a new member. If $Map(a)+Map(b) < n/(k-1)$, Set stays the same and we set Map(the loser):= 0 at time $t+1$ and Map(the winner) := $Map(a) + Map(b)$ at time $t+1$ and, for all items $w, w \neq a, w \neq b$, $Map(w)$ stays the same.

Lemma 10.1 Using the oracle just defined, the $k-1$ best players will have played at least $(k-1)\left\lceil \log \frac{n}{2(k-1)} \right\rceil$ matches when the tournament is completed.

Proof: At time t the number of matches won by any player x is greater than or equal to $\lceil \log Map(x) \rceil$. The elements in Set are ordered so that $x_1 < \cdots < x_j$. Now for all w in the input $\sum_w Map(w) = n$. Let $W = \{y : y$ is not in Set but Map$(y) > 0\}$. Since for all w in the input $Map(w) < n/(k-1)$, it follows that the size of Set plus the size of W is greater than $k-1$. However, since the elements y in W can only be less than some x_i in Set, if the size of Set is less than $k-1$ at the end of the tournament, then any player in Set or W is a candidate to be one of the $k-1$ best players. This is a contradiction, so it follows that at the end of the tournament $|Set| \geq k-1$.

Let x be any element of Set. If it has entered Set by defeating y, it can only be because $Map(x) + Map(y) \geq n/(k-1)$ and $Map(x) \geq Map(y)$. This in turn means that $Map(x) \geq \frac{n}{2(k-1)}$ implying that x has played at least $\left\lceil \log \frac{n}{2(k-1)} \right\rceil$ matches. This is true for every member of Set and $|Set| \geq (k-1)$. □

We are now in a position to establish the main theorem.

Theorem 10.6 [Hayfil] The function $\text{SEL}_k(n)$ satisfies

$$\text{SEL}_k(n) \;\geq\; n - k + (k-1)\left\lceil \log \frac{n}{2(k-1)} \right\rceil$$

Proof: According to Lemma 10.1, the $k-1$ best players have played at least $(k-1)\left\lceil \log \frac{n}{2(k-1)} \right\rceil$ matches. Any player who is not among the k best players has lost at least one match against a player who is not among the

$k-1$ best. Thus there are $n-k$ additional matches that were not included in the count of the matches played by the $k-1$ top players. The theorem follows. □

EXERCISES

1. Let $m = \alpha n$. Then by Stirling's approximation $\log \binom{\alpha n+n}{\alpha n} = n[(1+\alpha)\log(1+\alpha) - \alpha\log\alpha] - \frac{1}{2}\log n + O(1)$. Show that as $\alpha \to 0$, the difference between this formula and $m+n-1$ gets arbitrarily large.

2. Let $F(n)$ be the minimum number of comparisons, in the worst case, needed to insert $B[1]$ into the ordered set $A[1] < A[2] < \cdots < A[n]$. Prove by induction that $F(n) \geq \lceil \log n + 1 \rceil$.

3. A search program is a finite sequence of instructions of three types: (1) **if** $(f(x)\ r\ 0)$ **goto** L1; **else goto** L2;, where r is either $<$, $>$, or $=$ and x is a vector; (2) **accept**; and (3) **reject**. The sum of subsets problem asks for a subset I of the integers $1, 2, \ldots, n$ for the inputs $w_1, \ldots, w_n$ such that $\sum_{i\in I}(w_i) = b$, where b is a given number. Consider search programs for which the function f is restricted so that it can only make comparisons of the form

$$\sum_{i\in I}(w_i) = b \tag{10.4}$$

   Using the adversary technique D. Dobkin and R. Lipton have shown that $\Omega(2^n)$ such operations are required to solve the sum of subsets problem $(w_1, \ldots, w_n, b)$. See if you can derive their proof.

4. [W. Miller]

   (a) Let (N, R) denote the reflexive transitive closure of a directed graph (N, E). Thus $\langle u, v\rangle$ is an edge in R if there is a path from u to v using zero or more edges in E. Show that R is a partial order on N iff (N, E) is acyclic.

   (b) Prove that $(N, E \cup \langle u, v\rangle)$ is acyclic iff (N, E) is acyclic and there is no path from v to u using edges in E.

   (c) Prove that if (N, E) is acyclic and u and v are distinct elements of N, then $(N, E \cup \langle u, v\rangle)$ or $(N, E \cup \langle v, u\rangle))$ is acyclic.

   (d) Show that it is natural to think of an oracle as constructing an acyclic digraph on the set N of players. Interpret (b) and (c) as rules governing how the oracle may resolve matches.

10.3 LOWER BOUNDS THROUGH REDUCTIONS

Here we discuss a very important technique that can be used to derive lower bounds. This technique calls for *reducing* a problem for which a lower bound is already known to the given problem.

Definition 10.1 Let P_1 and P_2 be any two problems. We say P_1 *reduces* to P_2 (also written $P_1 \propto P_2$) in time $\tau(n)$ if an instance of P_1 can be converted into an instance of P_2 and a solution for P_1 can be obtained from a solution for P_2 in time $\leq \tau(n)$. □

Example 10.2 Let P_1 be the problem of selection (discussed in Section 3.7) and P_2 be the problem of sorting. Let the input have n numbers. If the numbers are sorted, say in an array $A[\ ]$, the ith-smallest element of the input can be obtained as $A[i]$. Thus P_1 reduces to P_2 in $O(1)$ time. □

Example 10.3 Let S_1 and S_2 be two sets with m elements each. The problem P_1 is to check whether the two sets are *disjoint*, that is, whether $S_1 \cap S_2 = \emptyset$. P_2 is the sorting problem. We can show that $P_1 \propto P_2$ in $O(m)$ time as follows.

Let $S_1 = \{k_1, k_2, \ldots, k_m\}$ and $S_2 = \{\ell_1, \ell_2, \ldots, \ell_m\}$. The instance of P_2 to be created has $n = 2m$ and the sequence of keys to be sorted is $X = (k_1, 1), (k_2, 1), \ldots, (k_m, 1), (\ell_1, 2), (\ell_2, 2), \ldots, (\ell_m, 2)$. In other words, each key in X is a tuple and the sorting has to be done in lexicographic order. The conversion of P_1 to P_2 takes $O(m)$ time, since it involves the creation of $2m$ tuples.

Now we have to show that a solution to P_1 is obtainable from the solution to P_2 in $O(m)$ time. Let X' be X in sorted order. Once X' has been computed, what remains to be done is to sequentially go though the elements of X' from left to right and check whether there are two successive elements $(x, 1)$ and $(y, 2)$ such that $x = y$. If there are no such elements, then S_1 and S_2 are disjoint; otherwise they are not. □

Note: If P_1 reduces to P_2 in $\tau(n)$ time and if $T(n)$ is a lower bound on the solution time of P_1, then, clearly, $T(n) - \tau(n)$ is a lower bound on the solution time of P_2. In Example 10.3, we can infer that P_2 has a lower bound of $T(n) - O(n)$, where $T(n)$ is a lower bound for the solution of P_1 on two sets with $m = n/2$ elements each. In Chapter 11 we revisit the notion of reduction in the context of $\mathcal{NP}$-hard problems.

Now we present several examples to illustrate the above technique of reduction in deriving lower bounds. The first problem is that of computing the convex hull of points in the plane (see Section 3.9) and the second problem is P_2 of Example 10.3.

10.3.1 Finding the Convex Hull

Given n points in the plane, recall that the convex hull problem is to identify the vertices of the hull in some order (clockwise or counterclockwise). We now show that any algorithm for this problem takes $\Omega(n \log n)$ time. If we call the convex hull problem P_2 and the problem of sorting P_1, then this lower bound is obtained by showing that P_1 reduces to P_2 in $O(n)$ time. Since sorting of n points needs $\Omega(n \log n)$ time (see Section 10.1), the result readily follows.

Let P_1 be the problem of sorting the sequence of numbers $K = k_1, k_2, \ldots, k_n$. P_2 takes as input points in the plane. We convert the n numbers into the n points $(k_1, k_1^2), (k_2, k_2^2), \ldots, (k_n, k_n^2)$. Construction of these points takes $O(n)$ time. These points lie on the parabola $y = x^2$.

The convex hull of these points has all the n points as vertices and moreover they are ordered according to their x-coordinate values (that is, k_i values). If $X = (\ell_1, \ell_1^2), (\ell_2, \ell_2^2), \ldots, (\ell_n, \ell_n^2)$ is the output (in counterclockwise order) for P_2, we can identify the point of X with the least x-coordinate in $O(n)$ time. If $(\ell', {\ell'}^2)$ is this point, the sorted order of K is the x-coordinates of points in X starting from ℓ' and moving counterclockwise. Thus determining the output for P_1 also takes $O(n)$ time.

Example 10.4 Consider the problem of sorting the numbers $2, 3, 1$, and 4. The four points created are $(2, 4), (3, 9), (1, 1)$, and $(4, 16)$. The convex hull of these points is shown in Figure 10.5. All the four points are on the hull. A counterclockwise ordering of the hull is $(3, 9), (4, 16), (1, 1)$, and $(2, 4)$, from which the sorted order of the points can be retrieved. □

Therefore we arrive at the following lemma.

Lemma 10.2 Computing the convex hull of n given points in the plane needs $\Omega(n \log n)$ time. □

10.3.2 Disjoint Sets Problem

In Example 10.3 we showed a reduction from the problem P_1 of deciding whether two given sets are disjoint to the problem P_2 of sorting. This reduction can then be used to derive a lower bound on the solution time of P_2, making use of any known lower bounds for the solution of P_1. But the only lower bound we have proved so far is for P_2 and not for P_1. Now we would like to derive a lower bound for P_1.

Lemma 10.3 Any algorithm for solving P_1, when the sets are of size n each, needs $\Omega(n \log n)$ time.

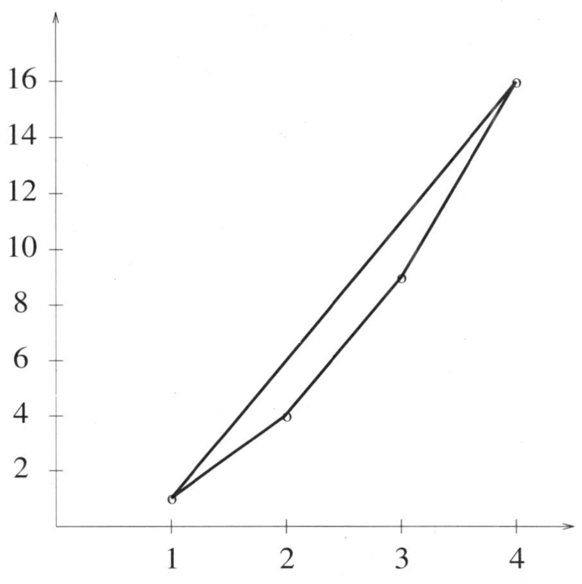

Figure 10.5 Sorting numbers using the convex hull reduction

Proof: We show that $P_2 \propto P_1$ in $O(n)$ time. Let $K = k_1, k_2, \ldots, k_n$ be any sequence of n numbers that we want to sort. Also let $X = x_1, x_2, \ldots, x_n$ be the sorted order of the sequence K. To construct an instance of P_1, we let $S_1 = \{(k_1, 0), (k_2, 0), \ldots, (k_n, 0)\}$ and $S_2 = \{(k_1, 1), (k_2, 1), \ldots, (k_n, 1)\}$.

Any algorithm for P_1 must compare $(x_i, 1)$ with $(x_{i+1}, 0)$ for each i, $1 \leq i \leq n-1$. If not, we can replace $(x_i, 1)$ in S_2 with $(x_{i+1}, 0)$ and force the algorithm to output an incorrect answer. Replacing $(x_i, 1)$ with $(x_{i+1}, 0)$ does not in any way alter the outcomes of other comparisons made by the algorithm.

Our claim is that the above comparisons are sufficient to sort K. The sorted order of K can be obtained by constructing a graph $G(V, E)$ as follows: $V = \{k_1, k_2, \ldots, k_n\}$ and there is a directed edge from k_i to k_j if the algorithm for P_1 has determined that $k_i < k_j$ (for any $1 \leq i, j \leq n$). This graph is constructible in $O(n + T(n))$ time, where $T(n)$ is the run time of the algorithm for P_1. To obtain the elements of K in sorted order, find the smallest element x_1 in $O(n)$ time. Find the smallest among all the neighbors of x_1 in G; this will be x_2. Then find the smallest among all the neighbors of x_2 in G; this will be x_3. And so on. The total time spent is clearly $O(n + |V| + |E|) = O(n + T(n))$. □

10.3.3 On-line Median Finding

In this problem, at every time step we are given a new key. We are required to compute the median of all the given keys before the next key is given. So, if n keys are given in all, we have to compute n medians.

Example 10.5 Let $n = 7$. Say the first key input is 7. We output the median as 7. After this we are given the second key, say 15. The median is either 7 or 15. Say the next 5 keys input are $3, 17, 8, 11$, and 5, in this order. The corresponding medians output will be $7, 7$ or $15, 8, 8$ or 11, and 8, respectively. □

Lemma 10.4 The on-line median finding problem (call it P_2) requires $\Omega(n \log n)$ time for its solution, where n is the total number of keys input.

Proof: The lemma is proved by reducing P_1 to P_2, where P_1 is the problem of sorting. Let P_1 be the problem of sorting the sequence of keys $K = k_1, k_2, \ldots, k_n$. The instance of P_2 should be such that each key of K is an on-line median. Also, the smallest key of K should be output before the second-smallest key, which in turn should be output before the third smallest key, and so on. Such an instance of P_2 is created by extending the sequence K with $-\infty$s and ∞s as follows:

$$-\infty, -\infty, \ldots, -\infty, k_1, k_2, \ldots, k_n, \infty, \infty, \infty, \infty, \ldots, \infty\infty$$

That is, the input consists of n $-\infty$s followed by K and then $2n$ ∞s. This instance of P_2 can be generated in $O(n)$ time. The solution to P_2 consists of $4n$ medians. Note that when the first ∞ is input, the median of all given keys is the smallest key of K. Also, when the third ∞ is input, the median is the second-largest key of K. And so on. In other words the sorted order of K is nothing but the $2n+1$st median, the $2n+3$rd median, ..., the $4n-1$st median output by any algorithm for P_2. Therefore, P_1 can be solved given a solution to P_2, and hence P_1 reduces to P_2 in $O(n)$ time.

If $S(n)$ is the time needed to sort n keys and $M(m)$ is the solution time of P_2 on a total of m keys, then the above reduction shows that $S(n) \leq M(4n) + O(n)$. But we know that $S(n) \geq cn \log n$ for some constant c. Therefore, $M(4n) \geq cn \log n - O(n)$. That is, $M(n) \geq c\frac{n}{4} \log \frac{n}{4} - O(\frac{n}{4})$; this implies that $M(n) = \Omega(n \log n)$. □

10.3.4 Multiplying Triangular Matrices

An $n \times n$ matrix A whose elements are $\{a_{ij}\}$, $1 \leq i, j \leq n$, is said to be *upper triangular* if $a_{ij} = 0$ whenever $i > j$. It is said to be *lower triangular* if $a_{ij} = 0$ for $i < j$. A matrix that is either upper triangular or lower triangular is said to be *triangular.*

We are interested in deriving lower bounds for the problem of multiplying two triangular matrices. We restrict our discussion to lower triangular matrices. But the results to be derived hold for upper triangular matrices also. Let A and B be two $n \times n$ lower triangular matrices. If $M(n)$ is the time needed to multiply two $n \times n$ full matrices (call this problem P_1) and $M_t(n)$ is the time needed to multiply two lower triangular matrices (call this problem P_2), then clearly $M(n) \geq M_t(n)$. More interestingly, it turns out that $M_t(n) = \Omega(M(n))$; that is, the problem of multiplying two triangular matrices is asymptotically no easier than multiplying two full matrices of the same dimensions.

Lemma 10.5 $M_t(n) = \Omega(M(n))$.

Proof: We show that P_1 reduces to P_2 in $O(n^2)$ time. Note that $M(n) = \Omega(n^2)$ since there are $2n^2$ elements in the input and n^2 in the output. Let the two matrices to be multiplied be A and B and of size $n \times n$ each. The instance of P_2 to be created is the following:

$$A' = \begin{bmatrix} O & O & O \\ O & O & O \\ O & A & O \end{bmatrix} \qquad B' = \begin{bmatrix} O & O & O \\ B & O & O \\ O & O & O \end{bmatrix}$$

Here O stands for the *zero matrix*, that is, an $n \times n$ matrix all of whose entries are zeros. Both A' and B' are of size $3n \times 3n$ each. Multiplying the two matrices, we get

$$A'B' = \begin{bmatrix} O & O & O \\ O & O & O \\ AB & O & O \end{bmatrix}$$

Thus the product AB is easily obtainable from the product $A'B'$. Problem P_1 reduces to P_2 in $O(n^2)$ time. This reduction implies that $M(n) \leq M_t(3n) + O(n^2)$; this in turn means $M_t(n) \geq M(\frac{n}{3}) - O(n^2)$. Since $M(n) = \Omega(n^2)$, $M(\frac{n}{3}) = \Omega(M(n))$. Hence, $M_t(n) = \Omega(M(n))$. □

Note that the above lemma also implies that $M_t(n) = \Theta(M(n))$.

10.3.5 Inverting a Lower Triangular Matrix

Let A be an $n \times n$ matrix. Also, let I be the $n \times n$ *identity matrix*, that is, the matrix for which $i_{kk} = 1$, for $1 \leq k \leq n$, and whose every other element is zero. The elements a_{kk} of any matrix A are called the *diagonal elements* of A. Every element of I is zero except for the diagonal elements which are all ones. If there exists an $n \times n$ matrix B such that $AB = I$, then we say B is the *inverse* of A and A is said to be *invertible*. The inverse of A is also denoted as A^{-1}. Not every matrix is invertible. For example, the zero matrix has no inverse.

In this section we concentrate on obtaining a lower bound on the inversion time of a lower triangular matrix. It can be shown that a triangular matrix is invertible if and only if all its diagonal elements are nonzero. Let P_1 be the problem of multiplying two full matrices and P_2 be the problem of inverting a lower triangular matrix. Let $M(n)$ and $I_t(n)$ be the corresponding time complexities. We show that $M(n) = \Theta(I_t(n))$.

Lemma 10.6 $M(n) = O(I_t(n))$.

Proof: The claim is that P_1 reduces to P_2 in $O(n^2)$ time, from which the lemma follows. Let A and B be the two $n \times n$ full matrices to be multiplied. We construct the following lower triangular matrix in $O(n^2)$ time:

$$C = \begin{bmatrix} I & O & O \\ B & I & O \\ O & A & I \end{bmatrix}$$

where the O's and I's are $n \times n$ zero matrices and identity matrices, respectively. C is a $3n \times 3n$ matrix. The inverse of C is

$$C^{-1} = \begin{bmatrix} I & O & O \\ -B & I & O \\ AB & -A & I \end{bmatrix}$$

where $-A$ refers to A with all the elements negated. Here also we see that the product AB is obtainable easily from the inverse of C. Thus we get $M(n) \le I_t(3n) + O(n^2)$, and hence $M(n) = O(I_t(n))$. □

Lemma 10.7 $I_t(n) = O(M(n))$.

Proof: Let A be the $n \times n$ lower triangular matrix to be inverted. Partition A into four submatrices of size $\frac{n}{2} \times \frac{n}{2}$ each as follows:

$$A = \begin{bmatrix} A_{11} & O \\ A_{21} & A_{22} \end{bmatrix}$$

Both A_{11} and A_{22} are lower triangular matrices and A_{21} could possibly be a full matrix. The inverse of A can be verified to be

$$A^{-1} = \begin{bmatrix} A_{11}^{-1} & O \\ -A_{22}^{-1}A_{21}A_{11}^{-1} & A_{22}^{-1} \end{bmatrix}$$

The above equation suggests a divide-and-conquer algorithm for inverting A. To invert A which is of size $n \times n$, it suffices to invert two lower triangular matrices (A_{11} and A_{22}) of size $\frac{n}{2} \times \frac{n}{2}$ each and perform two matrix multiplications (i.e., compute D=$A_{22}^{-1}(A_{21}A_{11}^{-1})$) and negate a matrix ($D$). D can be negated in $\frac{n^2}{4}$ time. The run time of such a divide-and-conquer algorithm satisfies the following recurrence relation:

$$I_t(n) \leq 2I_t\left(\frac{n}{2}\right) + 2M\left(\frac{n}{2}\right) + \frac{n^2}{4}$$

Using repeated substitution, we get

$$I_t(n) \leq 2M\left(\frac{n}{2}\right) + 2^2M\left(\frac{n}{2^2}\right) + \cdots + O(n^2)$$

Since $M(n) = \Omega(n^2)$, the above simplifies to

$$I_t(n) = O(M(n) + n^2) = O(M(n)).\square$$

Lemmas 10.6 and 10.7 together imply that $I_t(n) = \Theta(M(n))$.

10.3.6 Computing the Transitive Closure

Let G be a directed graph whose adjacency matrix is A. Recall that the reflexive transitive closure (or simply the transitive closure) of G, denoted A^*, is a matrix such that $A^*(i,j) = 1$ if and only if there is a directed path of length zero or more from node i to node j in G. In this section we wish to compute lower bounds on the computing time of A^* given A.

In the following discussion we assume that all the diagonal elements of A are zeros. There is an interesting relationship between the different powers of A and A^* captured in the following lemma

Lemma 10.8 Let A be the adjacency matrix of a given directed graph G. Then, $A^k(i,j) = 1$ if and only if there is a path from node i to node j of length exactly equal to k, for any $0 \leq k \leq n$. Here the matrix products are interpreted as follows: Scalar addition corresponds to boolean or and scalar multiplication corresponds to boolean and.

Proof: We prove the lemma by induction on k. When $k = 0$, A^0 is the identity matrix and the lemma holds, since there is a path of length zero from every node to itself. When $k = 1$, the lemma is also true, since $A(i,j) = 1$ if and only if there is an edge from i to j. Assume that the lemma is true for all path lengths up to $k-1$, $k > 1$. We prove it for a path length of k.

If there is a path of length k from node i to node j, this path consists of an edge from node i to some other node q and then a path from q to j of length $k-1$. In other words, using the induction hypothesis, there exists a q such that $A(i,q) = 1$ and $A^{k-1}(q,j) = 1$. If there is such a q, then $A^k(i,j) = (A * A^{k-1})(i,j)$ is surely 1.

Conversely, if $A^k(i,j) = 1$, then since $A^k = A * A^{k-1}$, there exists a q such that $A(i,q) = 1$ and $A^{k-1}(q,j) = 1$. This means that there is a path from node i to node j of length k. □

If there is a path at all from node i to node j in G, the shortest such path will be of length $\leq (n-1)$, n being the number of nodes in G.

Lemma 10.9 $A^* = I + A + A^2 + \cdots + A^{n-1}$. □

Lemma 10.9 gives another algorithm for computing A^*. (We saw search-based algorithms in Section 6.3.) Let $T(n)$ be the time needed to compute the transitive closure of an n-node graph.

Lemma 10.10 $M(n) \leq T(3n) + O(n^2)$, and hence $M(n) = O(T(n))$.

Proof: If A and B are the given $n \times n$ matrices to be multiplied, form the following $3n \times 3n$ matrix C in $O(n^2)$ time:

$$C = \begin{bmatrix} O & A & O \\ O & O & B \\ O & O & O \end{bmatrix}$$

C^2 is given by

$$C^2 = \begin{bmatrix} O & O & AB \\ O & O & O \\ O & O & O \end{bmatrix}$$

Also, $C^k = O$ for $k \geq 3$. Therefore, using Lemma 10.9,

$$C^* = I + C + C^2 + \cdots + C^{n-1} = I + C + C^2 = \begin{bmatrix} I & A & AB \\ O & I & B \\ O & O & I \end{bmatrix}$$

Given C^*, it is easy to obtain the product AB. □

Lemma 10.11 $T(n) = O(M(n))$.

Proof: The proof is analogous to that of Lemma 10.7. Let $G(V,E)$ be the graph under consideration and A its adjacency matrix. The matrix A is partitioned into four submatrices of size $\frac{n}{2} \times \frac{n}{2}$ each:

$$A = \begin{bmatrix} A_{11} & A_{12} \\ A_{21} & A_{22} \end{bmatrix}$$

Recall that row i of A corresponds to edges going out of node i. Let V_1 be the set of nodes corresponding to rows $1, 2, \ldots, \frac{n}{2}$ of A and V_2 be the set of nodes corresponding to the rest of the rows.

The entry $A_{11}^*(i, j) = 1$ if and only if there is a path from node $i \in V_1$ to node $j \in V_1$ all of whose intermediate nodes are also from V_1. A similar property holds for A_{22}^*.

Let $D = A_{12}A_{21}$ and let u and $v \in V_1$. Then, $D(u, v) = 1$ if and only if there exists a $w \in V_2$ such that $\langle u, w \rangle$ and $\langle w, v \rangle$ are in E. A similar statement holds for $A_{21}A_{12}$.

Let the transitive closure of G be given by

$$A^* = \begin{bmatrix} C_{11} & C_{12} \\ C_{21} & C_{22} \end{bmatrix}$$

Our goal is to derive a divide-and-conquer algorithm for computing A^*. Therefore, we should find a way of computing C_{11}, C_{12}, C_{21}, and C_{22} from A_{11}^* and A_{22}^*.

First we consider the computation of C_{11}. Note that C_{11} corresponds to paths from i to j, where i and j are in V_1. Of course the intermediate nodes in such paths could as well be from V_2. Any such path from i to j can have several segments, where each segment starts from a node, say u_q, from V_1, goes to $w_q \in V_2$ through an edge, goes to x_q of V_2 through a path of arbitrary length, and goes to $y_q \in V_1$ through an edge (see Figure 10.6). Any such segment corresponds to $A_{11} + A_{12}A_{22}^*A_{21}$. Since there could be an arbitrary number of such segments, we get

$$C_{11} = (A_{11} + A_{12}A_{22}^*A_{21})^*$$

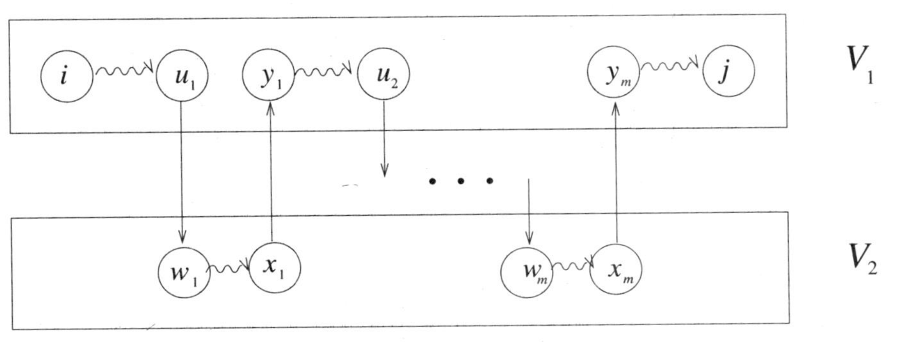

Figure 10.6 A possible path in C_{11}

Using similar reasoning, the rest of A^* can also be determined: $C_{12} = C_{11}A_{12}A_{22}^*$, $C_{21} = A_{22}^*A_{21}C_{11}$, and $C_{22} = A_{22}^* + A_{22}^*A_{21}C_{11}A_{12}A_{22}^*$.

Thus the above divide-and-conquer algorithm for computing A^* performs two transitive closures on matrices of size $\frac{n}{2} \times \frac{n}{2}$ each (A_{22}^* and $(A_{11} + A_{12}A_{22}^*A_{21})^*$), six matrix multiplications, and two matrix additions on matrices of size $\frac{n}{2} \times \frac{n}{2}$ each. Therefore we get

$$T(n) \leq 2T\left(\frac{n}{2}\right) + 6M\left(\frac{n}{2}\right) + O(n^2)$$

Repeated substitution yields

$$T(n) \leq \left[6M\left(\frac{n}{2}\right) + 12M\left(\frac{n}{4}\right) + 24M\left(\frac{n}{8}\right) + \cdots\right] + O(n^2)$$

But, $M(n) \geq n^2$, and hence $M(n/2) \leq 4M(n)$. Using this fact, we see that $T(n) = O(M(n) + n^2) = O(M(n))$. □

Lemmas 10.10 and 10.11 show that $T(n) = \Theta(M(n))$.

EXERCISES

1. In Section 3.9 we stated two variants of the convex hull problem. Lemma 10.2 proves a lower bound for one version of the problem. In the other version, we are only supposed to find the vertices of the hull (not necessarily in any order). Will Lemma 10.2 hold even for this version?

2. If $M(n)$ is the time needed to multiply two $n \times n$ matrices, and $S(n)$ is the time needed to square an $n \times n$ matrix, show that $M(n) = \Theta(S(n))$ (i.e., show that multiplying and squaring matrices have essentially the same difficulty).

3. Consider the disjoint sets problem of Example 10.3. Say the elements of S_1 as well as those of S_2 are integers from the range $[0, m^c]$ for some constant c, where $|S_1| = |S_2| = m$. Will a lower bound of $\Omega(m \log m)$ still hold? If yes, why? If not, present an algorithm with $o(m \log m)$ run time.

4. In the disjoint sets problem, if $|S_1| = m$ and $|S_2| = O(1)$, will a lower bound of $\Omega(m \log m)$ hold? Prove your answer.

5. The *distinct elements* problem is to take as input n numbers and decide whether these numbers are distinct (i.e., no number is repeated). Show that any algorithm for the solution of the distinct elements problem needs $\Omega(n \log n)$ time.

10.4 TECHNIQUES FOR ALGEBRAIC PROBLEMS (*)

In this section we examine two methods, substitution and linear independence, for deriving lower bounds on arithmetic and algebraic problems. The algebraic problems we consider here are operations on integers, polynomials, and rational functions. Solutions to these problems were presented in Chapter 9. In addition we also include matrix multiplication and related operations which were discussed in Chapter 3.

The model of computation we use is called a *straight-line program*. It is called this because there are no branching instructions allowed. This implies that if we know a way of solving a problem for n inputs, then a *set* of straight-line programs, one each for solving a different size n, can be given. The only statement in a straight-line program is the assignment which has the form $S := p$ **op** q;. Here S, p, and q are variables of bounded size and **op** is typically one of the arithmetic operations: addition, subtraction, multiplication, or division. Moreover p and q are either constants, input variables, or variables that have already appeared on the left of an assignment statement. For example, one possible straight-line program that computes the value of a degree-two polynomial $a_2x^2 + a_1x + a_0$ has the form

$$\begin{array}{lcl} v1 & := & a_2 * x; \\ v1 & := & v1 + a_1; \\ v1 & := & v1 * x; \\ ans & := & v1 + a_0; \end{array}$$

To determine the complexity of a straight-line program, we assume that each instruction takes one unit of time and requires one unit of space. Then the time complexity of a straight-line program is its number of assignments or its length. A more realistic assumption takes into account the fact that an integer n requires $\lfloor \log n \rfloor + 1$ bits to represent it. But in this section we assume that all operands are small enough to occupy a fixed-sized register, and hence the unit-cost assumption is appropriate.

Now we need to consider the class of constants we intend to allow. This requires some elementary definitions from algebra.

Definition 10.2 A *ring* is an algebraic structure containing a set of elements S and two binary operations denoted by $+$ and $*$. For each $a, b \in S, a + b$ and $a * b$ are also in S. Also the following properties hold:

$$\begin{array}{rcll}(a+b)+c &=& a+(b+c) \text{ and} & \\ (a*b)*c &=& a*(b*c) & \text{(associativity)} \\ a+b &=& b+a & \text{(commutativity)} \\ (a+b)*c &=& a*c+b*c \text{ and} & \\ a*(b+c) &=& a*b+a*c & \text{(distributivity)} \\ a+0 &=& 0+a=a & \text{(additive identity, } 0 \in S) \\ a*1 &=& 1*a=a & \text{(multiplicative identity, } 1 \in S)\end{array}$$

For each $a \in S$, there is an additive inverse denoted by $-a$ such that $a + (-a) = (-a) + a = 0$. If multiplication is also commutative, then the ring is called commutative. □

Definition 10.3 A *field* is a commutative ring such that for each element $a \in S$ (other than 0), there is a multiplicative inverse denoted by $a^{-1} \in S$ that satisfies the equation $a * a^{-1} = 1$. □

Example 10.6 The real numbers form a field under the regular operations of addition and multiplication. Similarly for the complex numbers. However, the integers with operations $+$ and $*$ do not form a field since only plus or minus one has a multiplicative inverse. Another field is the set of integers modulo a prime as discussed in Chapter 9. It forms a finite field consisting of the integers $\{0, 1, \ldots, p-1\}$. □

Definition 10.4 An *indeterminate* over an algebraic system S is a symbol that does not occur in S. The *extension* of S by the indeterminates $x_1, \ldots, x_n$ is the smallest commutative ring that contains all combinations of the elements of S and the indeterminates. Such an extension is denoted by $S[x_1, \ldots, x_n]$. When an extension is made to a field that allows for quotients of combinations of elements of S and indeterminates, then that is denoted by $S(x_1, \ldots, x_n)$. □

The elements in an extension $S[x_1, \ldots, x_n]$ can be viewed as polynomials in the variables x_i with coefficients from the set S. The elements in an extension $S(x_1, \cdots, x_n)$ should be viewed as rational functions of the variables x_i with coefficients that are from S. The indeterminates are independent in the sense that no one can be expressed by the others, and hence two such polynomials or rational functions are equal only if one can be transformed into the other using the laws of the ring or field.

The field of constants can make an important difference in the complexity of the algorithms for some problems. For example, if we wish to examine programs for computing $x^2 + y^2$, where the field is the reals, then two multiplications are required. However if the field is the complex numbers, then only one complex multiplication is needed, namely $(x + iy)(x - iy)$.

Theorem 10.7 Every algorithm for computing the value of a general nth-degree polynomial that uses only $+$, $-$, and $*$ requires n additions or subtractions.

Proof: Any straight-line program that computes the value of $a_n x^n + \cdots + a_0$ can be transformed into a program to compute $a_n + \cdots + a_0$ given some field of constants F and a vector $A = (a_n, \ldots, a_0)$ of indeterminates. This new program is produced by inserting the statement $s := 1$; at the beginning and then replacing every occurrence of x by s. We now prove by induction that $a_n + \cdots + a_0$ requires n additions or subtractions. For $n = 1$, we need to compute $a_1 + a_0$ *as an element in* $F[a_1, a_0]$. If we disallow additions or subtractions, then by the definition of extension only products of the a_i multiplied by constants from the field can be produced. Thus $a_1 + a_0$ requires one addition. Now suppose we have computed a sum or difference of at least two terms, where each term is possibly a product of elements from the vector A and possibly a field element. Without loss of generality assume that a_n appears in one of these terms. If we substitute zero for a_n, then this eliminates the need for this first addition or subtraction since one of the arguments is zero. We are now computing $a_{n-1} + \cdots + a_0$ which by the induction hypotheses requires $n-1$ additions or subtractions. Thus the theorem follows. □

The basic idea of this proof is the substitution argument. Using the same technique, one can derive a not much more complicated theorem that shows that Horner's rule is optimal with respect to multiplications or divisions.

Definition 10.5 Suppose F and G are two fields such that F is contained in G and we are computing in $G(a_1, \ldots, a_n)$. The operation f **op** g, where **op** is $*$ or $/$, is said to be *inactive* if one of the following holds: (1) $g \in F$, (2) $f \in F$ and the operation is multiplication, or (3) $f \in G$ and $g \in G$. □

Any multiplication or division that is not inactive is called *active*. So, for example, operations such as $x * x$ or $15 * a_i$ are inactive whereas operations such as $x * a_i$ or $a_1 * a_2$ or $15/a_i$ are active.

Definition 10.6 Let $A = (a_0, \ldots, a_n)$. Then $p_1(A), \ldots, p_u(A)$ is *linearly independent* if there does not exist a nontrivial set of constants $c_1, \ldots, c_n$ such that $\sum c_i p_i =$ a constant. □

The polynomial $P(A, x)$ can be thought of as a general polynomial in the sense that it is a function not only of x but also of the inputs A. We can write $P(A, x)$ as $\sum(p_i(A)x^i) + r(x)$, where u of the p_i are linearly independent.

Theorem 10.8 [Borodin, Munro] If u active $*$ or $/$ are required to compute $P(A, x)$, then n active $*$ or $/$ are required to evaluate a general nth-degree polynomial.

Proof: The proof proceeds by induction on u. Suppose $u = 1$. If there is no active $*$ or $/$, then it is only possible to form $p_i(A) + r(x)$ for some i. Now suppose $(p_i(A) + r_1(x)) * (p_j(A) + r_2(x))$ is the first active multiplication in a straight-line program that computes $P(A, x)$. Without loss of generality assume that $p_j(A) \neq$ a constant. Then, in the straight-line program let $p_j(A) + r_2(x)$ be replaced by a constant d such that no illegal division by zero is caused. This can always be done for if p_j is a linear combination of constants c_i times a_i and since there must exist a $j : c_j \neq 0$, then by setting

$$a_j = -\frac{1}{c_j}\left(\sum_{i,i\neq j} c_i a_i + r_2(x) - d\right) \tag{10.5}$$

it follows that $(p_j(A) + r_2(x)) = d$. Now consider $P(A, x)$, where the substitution of a_j has been made. The polynomial P can be rewritten in the form

$$\sum_{0\leq i\leq n} P_i'(x)x^i + r'(x) \tag{10.6}$$

Therefore by making the one replacement, we can remove one active multiplication or division and we are now computing a new expression. If it can be shown that there are $u-1$ linearly independent p_j, then by the induction hypothesis there are at least $u - 1$ remaining active $*$ or $/$ and the theorem follows. Proof of this can be found in the exercises. □

Corollary 10.1 Horner's rule is an optimal algorithm with respect to the number of multiplications and divisions necessary to evaluate a polynomial.

Proof: From the previous theorem, the result in the exercises that under substitution $u - 1$ linearly independent combinations remain, and the fact that Horner's rule requires only n multiplications, the corollary follows. □

Another method of proof for deriving lower bounds for algebraic problems is to consider these problems in a matrix setting. Returning to polynomial evaluation, we can express this problem in the following way: compute the $1 \times (n + 1)$ by $(n + 1) \times 1$ matrix product

$$\begin{bmatrix}1 \; x \; x^2 \; \ldots \; x^n\end{bmatrix} \begin{bmatrix} a_0 \\ a_1 \\ \vdots \\ a_n \end{bmatrix} \tag{10.7}$$

which is the product of two vectors.

Another problem is complex number multiplication. The product of $(a+ib)(c+id) = ac - bd + (bc+ad)i$ can be written in terms of matrices as

$$\begin{bmatrix} a & -b \\ b & a \end{bmatrix} \begin{bmatrix} c \\ d \end{bmatrix} = \begin{bmatrix} ac - bd \\ bc + ad \end{bmatrix} \tag{10.8}$$

In more general terms we wish to consider problems that can be formulated as the product of a matrix times a vector:

$$\begin{bmatrix} a_{11}, & \cdots, & a_{1n} \\ \vdots & & \\ a_{m1}, & \cdots, & a_{mn} \end{bmatrix} \begin{bmatrix} x_1 \\ \vdots \\ x_n \end{bmatrix} \tag{10.9}$$

Definition 10.7 Let F be a field and $x_1, \ldots, x_n$ be indeterminates. Let $F^m[x_1, \ldots, x_n]$ stand for the m-dimensional space of vectors with components from $F[x_1, \ldots, x_n]$ and F^m stand for the m-dimensional space of vectors with components from F. A set of vectors $v_1, \ldots, v_k$ from $F^m[x_1, \ldots, x_n]$ is *linearly independent modulo* F^m if for $u_1, \ldots, u_k$ in F the sum $\sum_{i=1}^{k}(u_i v_i) = 0$ in F^m implies the u_i are all zero. If the v_i are not linearly independent, then they are called linearly *dependent* modulo F^m. The *row rank* of a matrix A modulo F^r is the number of linearly independent rows modulo F^r. The *column rank* is the number of linearly independent columns. □

We now state the main theorem of this section.

Theorem 10.9 Let A be an $r \times s$ matrix with elements from the extension field $F[x_1, \ldots, x_n]$ and $y = [y_1, \ldots, y_s]$ a column vector containing s indeterminates.

1. If the row rank of A is v, then any computation of Ay requires at least v active multiplications.

2. If the column rank of A is w, then any computation of Ay requires at least w active multiplications.

3. If A contains a submatrix B of size $v \times w$ such that for any vectors $p \in F^v$ and $q \in F^w$, $p^T Bq \in F$ iff $p = 0$ or $q = 0$, then any computation of Ay requires $v + w - 1$ multiplications.

Proof: For a proof of part (1) see the paper by S. Winograd. For a proof of parts (2) and (3) see the papers by C. Fiduccia. Also see A. V. Aho, J. E. Hopcroft and J. D. Ullman. □

Example 10.7 Reconsider the problem of multiplying two 2×2 matrices

$$\begin{bmatrix} a & b \\ c & d \end{bmatrix} \begin{bmatrix} e & f \\ g & h \end{bmatrix} = \begin{bmatrix} ae+bg & af+bh \\ ce+dg & cf+dh \end{bmatrix}$$

which by definition seemingly requires eight multiplications. We can rephrase this computation in terms of a matrix-vector product as shown in Figure 10.7. The first 2×2 matrix, say A, has been expanded as the 4×4 matrix

$$\begin{bmatrix} A & O \\ O & A \end{bmatrix}$$

$$\begin{bmatrix} a & b & 0 & 0 \\ c & d & 0 & 0 \\ 0 & 0 & a & b \\ 0 & 0 & c & d \end{bmatrix} \begin{bmatrix} e \\ g \\ f \\ h \end{bmatrix} = \left(\begin{bmatrix} a-b & 0 & 0 & 0 \\ 0 & 0 & 0 & 0 \\ a+b & 0 & 0 & 0 \\ 0 & 0 & 0 & 0 \end{bmatrix} \right.$$

$$+ \begin{bmatrix} b & b & 0 & 0 \\ -b & -b & 0 & 0 \\ 0 & 0 & 0 & 0 \\ 0 & 0 & 0 & 0 \end{bmatrix} + \begin{bmatrix} 0 & 0 & 0 & 0 \\ 0 & 0 & 0 & c-d \\ 0 & 0 & 0 & 0 \\ 0 & 0 & 0 & -c+d \end{bmatrix}$$

$$+ \begin{bmatrix} 0 & 0 & 0 & 0 \\ 0 & 0 & 0 & 0 \\ 0 & 0 & -c & -c \\ 0 & 0 & c & c \end{bmatrix} + \begin{bmatrix} 0 & 0 & 0 & 0 \\ 0 & 0 & 0 & 0 \\ a+c & 0 & a+c & 0 \\ 0 & 0 & 0 & 0 \end{bmatrix}$$

$$\left. + \begin{bmatrix} 0 & 0 & 0 & 0 \\ 0 & b+d & 0 & b+d \\ 0 & 0 & 0 & 0 \\ 0 & 0 & 0 & 0 \end{bmatrix} + \begin{bmatrix} 0 & 0 & 0 & 0 \\ b+c & 0 & 0 & -b-c \\ -b-c & 0 & 0 & b+c \\ 0 & 0 & 0 & 0 \end{bmatrix} \right) \begin{bmatrix} e \\ g \\ f \\ h \end{bmatrix}$$

Figure 10.7 Multiplying two 2×2 matrices

This matrix is then decomposed into a sum of seven matrices, each of size 4×4. Both the row rank and the column rank of each matrix is one and hence by Theorem 10.9 we see that seven multiplications are necessary. □

Example 10.8 Given two complex numbers $a + ib$ and $c + id$, the product $(a + ib)(c + id) = ac - bd + i(ad + bc)$ can be described by the matrix-vector computation

$$\begin{bmatrix} a & -b \\ b & a \end{bmatrix} \begin{bmatrix} c \\ d \end{bmatrix} = \begin{bmatrix} ac - bd \\ bc + cd \end{bmatrix} \tag{10.10}$$

which seemingly requires 4 multiplications, but it can also be written as

$$\left(\begin{bmatrix} a+b & 0 \\ 0 & a-b \end{bmatrix} + \begin{bmatrix} -b & -b \\ b & b \end{bmatrix} \right) \begin{bmatrix} c \\ d \end{bmatrix} \tag{10.11}$$

The row and column rank of the first matrix is two whereas the row and column rank of the second matrix is 1. Thus three multiplications are necessary. The product can be computed as:

1. $a(d - c)$
2. $(a + b)c$
3. $b(c + d)$

Then (2) − (3) $= ac - bd$ and (1) + (2) $= ad + bc$. □

Example 10.9 Equation 10.7 phrases the evaluation of an nth-degree polynomial in terms of a matrix-vector product. The matrix has n linearly independent columns modulo the constant field F, and thus by Theorem 10.9, n multiplications are necessary. □

In this section we've already seen that any algorithm that evaluates a general nth-degree polynomial requires n multiplications or divisions and n additions or subtractions. This assertion was based on the assumption that the input into any algorithm was both the value of x plus the coefficients of the polynomial. We might take another view and consider how well we can do if the coefficients of the polynomial are known in advance and functions of these coefficients can be computed without cost before evaluation begins. This process of computing functions of the coefficients is referred to as *preconditioning.*

Suppose we begin by considering the general fourth-degree polynomial $A(x) = a_4x^4 + a_3x^3 + a_2x^2 + a_1x + a_0x^0$ and the scheme

$$y := (x + c_0)x + c_1; \qquad A(x) := ((y + x + c_2)y + c_3)c_4;$$

Only three multiplications and five additions are required if we can determine the values of the c_i in terms of the a_i. Expanding $A(x)$ in terms of x and the c_i, we get

$$A(x) = c_4x^4 + (2c_0c_4 + c_4)x^3 + (c_0^2 + 2c_1 + c_0c_4 + c_2c_4)x^2 + (2c_0c_1c_4 + c_1c_4 + c_0c_2c_4)x + (c_1^2c_4 + c_1c_2c_4 + c_3c_4)$$

and equating the above coefficients with the a_i, we get

$c_4 = a_4$; $\quad c_0 = (a_3/a_4 - 1)/2$
$b = a_2/a_4 - c_0(c_0 + 1)$
$c_1 = a_1/a_4 - c_0b$; $\quad c_2 = b - 2c_1$; $\quad c_3 = a_0/a_4 - c_1(c_1 + c_2)$

Example 10.10 Applying the above method to the polynomial $A(x) = -x^4 + 3x^3 - 2x^2 + 2x + 1$ yields the straight-line program

$q := x - 2;$
$r := q * x;$
$y := r - 2;$
$s := y + x;$
$t := s + 4;$
$u := t * y;$
$v := u + 3;$
$p := -1 * v;$

which evaluates to $A(x)$ in just three multiplications. □

In fact it can be shown that for any polynomial $A(x)$ of degree $n \geq 3$, there exist real numbers c, d_i, and e_i for $0 \leq i \leq \lceil n/2 \rceil - 1 = m$ such that $A(x)$ can be evaluated in $\lfloor n/2 \rfloor + 2$ multiplications and n additions by the following scheme:

$y := x + c;\ w := y * y;$
$z := (a_n * y + d_0) * y + e_0$ (n even); $z := a_n * y + e_0$ (n odd);
$z := z * (w - d_i) + e_i$; **for** $i = 1, 2, \ldots, m$;
$answer := z;$

Now that we have a scheme that reduces the number of required multiplications by about one-half, it is natural to ask how close we have come to the optimal. The lower bound we are about to present follows from the fact that any straight-line program can be put into a normal form involving a limited number of constants. We restrict our arguments here to programs without division, leaving the extension to interested readers.

Lemma 10.12 [Motzkin 1954] For any straight line program with k multiplications and a single input variable x, there exists an equivalent program using at most $2k$ constants.

Proof: Let s_i, $0 \le i \le k$, denote the result of the ith multiplication. We can rewrite the program as

$s_0 := x$;
$s_i := L_i * R_i$; **for** $1 \le i \le k$
$A(x) := L_{k+1}$;

where each L_i and R_i is a certain sum of a constant (which may accumulate other constants from the original program) and an earlier s_j (an s_j may appear several times in this sum). The first product $s_1 = (c_1 + m_1x)(c_2 + m_2x)$ can be replaced by $s_1 = mx(x + c)$, where $m = m_1m_2$ and $c = m_1c_2 + m_2c_1$, provided that later constants are suitably altered. □

Lemma 10.13 [Belaga 1958] For any straight-line program with k addition-subtractions and a single input variable x, there exists an equivalent program using at most $k + 1$ constants.

Proof: Let s_i, $0 \le i \le k$, be the result of the kth addition-subtraction. As in the previous proof, we can rewrite the program as

$s_0 := x$;
$s_i := c_i * p_i + d_i * q_i$; $1 \le i \le k$
$A(x) := c_{k+1} * p_{k+1}$;

where each p_i and q_i is a product of earlier s_j. For $k = 1, 2, \ldots$, replace s_i by $s_i = (c_i d_i^{-1})p_i + q_i$ simultaneously replacing subsequent references to s_i by $d_i s_i$. □

Theorem 10.10 [Motzkin, Belaga] A randomly selected polynomial of degree n has probability zero of being computable either with less than $\lceil (n+1) /2 \rceil$ multiplications-divisions or with less than n addition-subtractions.

Proof sketch: If a given straight-line program with the single input variable x has only a few operations, then we can assume that it has at most n constants. Each time these constants are set, they determine a set of coefficients of the polynomial computed by the last operation of the program. Given $A(x)$ of degree n, the probability is zero that the program's n or fewer constants can be adjusted to align the computed polynomial with all $n + 1$ of the given polynomial coefficients. A formal proof here relies on showing that the subset of $(n + 1)$-dimensional space that can be so represented has Lebesque measure zero. It follows (because the set of straight-line programs is enumerable if we identify programs differing only in their constants) that the constants of any such short program can be set so as to evaluate the polynomial with only zero probability. □

The above theorem shows that the preconditioning method previously given comes very close to being optimal, but some room for improvement remains.

EXERCISES

1. Let A be an $n \times n$ symmetric matrix $A(i,j) = A(j,i)$ for $1 \leq i,j \leq n$. Show that if p is the number of nonzero entries of $A(i,j), i < j$, then $n+p$ multiplications are sufficient to compute Ax.

2. Show how an $n \times n$ matrix can be multiplied by two $n \times 1$ vectors using $(3n^2 + 5n)/2$ multiplications.

3. [Borodin, Munro] This exercise completes the proof of Theorem 10.9. Let $p_1(a_1 \ \ldots \ a_s), \ldots, p_u(a_1 \ldots a_s)$ be u linearly independent functions of $a_1, \ldots, a_s$. Let $a_1 = p(a_2 \cdots a_s)$. Then show that there are at least $u-1$ linearly independent $p_i^{'} = p_i$, where a_1 is replaced by p.

4. [W. Miller] Show that the inner product of two n-vectors can be computed in $\lceil n/2 \rceil$ multiplications if separate preconditioning of the vector elements is not counted.

5. Consider the problem of determining a lower bound for the problem of multiplying an $m \times n$ matrix A by an $n \times 1$ vector. Show how to reexpress this problem using a different matrix formulation so that Theorem 10.9 can be applied and yield the lower bound of mn multiplications.

6. Write an exponentiation procedure which computes x^n using the low-order to the high-order bits of n.

10.5 REFERENCES AND READINGS

For a detailed account of lower bounds for sorting, merging, and selecting, see Sections 5.3, 5.3.1, 5.3.2, and 5.3.3 in *The Art of Computer Programming*, Vol. III Sorting and Searching, by D. E. Knuth, Second Edition, Addison-Wesley, 1998.

The sorting algorithm that requires the fewest known number of comparisons was originally presented by L. Ford, Jr. and S. Johnson.

The lower bound on the selection problem can be found in "Bounds for selection," by L. Hyafil, *SIAM Journal on Computing* 5, no. 1 (March 1976): 109–114.

Exercise 3 (Section 10.2) is due to D. Dobkin and R. Lipton.

The proof of Lemma 10.3 is from "A lower bound result for the common element problem and its implication for reflexive reasoning," by P. Dietz, D. Krizanc, S. Rajasekaran, and L. Shastri, manuscript, 1993.

Many of the algebraic lower bounds can be found in the following two books:
The Computation Complexity of Algebraic and Numeric Problems, by A. Borodin and I. Munro, American Elsevier, 1975.
The Design and Analysis of Computer Algorithms by A. V. Aho, J. E. Hopcroft and J. D. Ullman, Addison-Wesley, 1974.

Theorem 10.9 was proven by S. Winograd and Fiduccia. See:
"On the number of multiplications necessary to compute certain functions" by S. Winograd, *Comm. Pure and Applied Math.* 23 (1970): 165–179.
"On obtaining upper bounds on the complexity of matrix multiplication" by C. Fiduccia, *Proc. IBM Symposium on complexity of computer computations*, March 1972.

"Fast matrix multiplication" by C. Fiduccia, *Proc. 3rd Annual ACM symposium on theory of computing*, (1971): 45–49.

Chapter 11

$\mathcal{NP}$-HARD AND $\mathcal{NP}$-COMPLETE PROBLEMS

11.1 BASIC CONCEPTS

In this chapter we are concerned with the distinction between problems that can be solved by a polynomial time algorithm and problems for which no polynomial time algorithm is known. It is an unexplained phenomenon that for many of the problems we know and study, the best algorithms for their solutions have computing times that cluster into two groups. The first group consists of problems whose solution times are bounded by polynomials of small degree. Examples we have seen in this book include ordered searching, which is $O(\log n)$, polynomial evaluation which is $O(n)$, sorting which is $O(n \log n)$, and string editing which is $O(mn)$.

The second group is made up of problems whose best-known algorithms are nonpolynomial. Examples we have seen include the traveling salesperson and the knapsack problems for which the best algorithms given in this text have complexities $O(n^2 2^n)$ and $O(2^{n/2})$ respectively. In the quest to develop efficient algorithms, no one has been able to develop a polynomial time algorithm for any problem in the second group. This is very important because algorithms whose computing times are greater than polynomial (typically the time is exponential) very quickly require such vast amounts of time to execute that even moderate-size problems cannot be solved (see Section 1.3 for more details).

The theory of $\mathcal{NP}$-completeness which we present here does not provide a method of obtaining polynomial time algorithms for problems in the second group. Nor does it say that algorithms of this complexity do not exist. Instead, what we do is show that many of the problems for which there are no known polynomial time algorithms are computationally related. In fact, we establish two classes of problems. These are given the names $\mathcal{NP}$-hard and $\mathcal{NP}$-complete. A problem that is $\mathcal{NP}$-complete has the property that it can be solved in polynomial time if and only if all other $\mathcal{NP}$-complete problems can also be solved in polynomial time. If an $\mathcal{NP}$-hard problem can be solved in polynomial time, then all $\mathcal{NP}$-complete problems can be solved in polynomial time. All $\mathcal{NP}$-complete problems are $\mathcal{NP}$-hard, but some $\mathcal{NP}$-hard problems are not known to be $\mathcal{NP}$-complete.

Although one can define many distinct problem classes having the properties stated above for the $\mathcal{NP}$-hard and $\mathcal{NP}$-complete classes, the classes we study are related to nondeterministic computations (to be defined later). The relationship of these classes to nondeterministic computations together with the apparent power of nondeterminism leads to the intuitive (though as yet unproved) conclusion that no $\mathcal{NP}$-complete or $\mathcal{NP}$-hard problem is polynomially solvable.

We see that the class of $\mathcal{NP}$-hard problems (and the subclass of $\mathcal{NP}$-complete problems) is very rich as it contains many interesting problems from a wide variety of disciplines. First, we formalize the preceding discussion of the classes.

11.1.1 Nondeterministic Algorithms

Up to now the notion of algorithm that we have been using has the property that the result of every operation is uniquely defined. Algorithms with this property are termed *deterministic algorithms*. Such algorithms agree with the way programs are executed on a computer. In a theoretical framework we can remove this restriction on the outcome of every operation. We can allow algorithms to contain operations whose outcomes are not uniquely defined but are limited to specified sets of possibilities. The machine executing such operations is allowed to choose any one of these outcomes subject to a termination condition to be defined later. This leads to the concept of a *nondeterministic algorithm*. To specify such algorithms, we introduce three new functions:

1. Choice(S) arbitrarily chooses one of the elements of set S.

2. Failure() signals an unsuccessful completion.

3. Success() signals a successful completion.

The assignment statement $x :=$ Choice($1, n$) could result in x being assigned any one of the integers in the range $[1, n]$. There is no rule specifying how this choice is to be made. The Failure() and Success() signals are used to define a computation of the algorithm. These statements cannot be used to effect a **return**. Whenever there is a set of choices that leads to a successful completion, then one such set of choices is always made and the algorithm terminates successfully. *A nondeterministic algorithm terminates unsuccessfully if and only if there exists no set of choices leading to a success signal.* The computing times for Choice, Success, and Failure are taken to be $O(1)$. A machine capable of executing a nondeterministic algorithm in this way is called a *nondeterministic machine.* Although nondeterministic machines (as defined here) do not exist in practice, we see that they provide strong intuitive reasons to conclude that certain problems cannot be solved by fast deterministic algorithms.

Example 11.1 Consider the problem of searching for an element x in a given set of elements $A[1:n]$, $n \geq 1$. We are required to determine an index j such that $A[j] = x$ or $j = 0$ if x is not in A. A nondeterministic algorithm for this is Algorithm 11.1.

```
j := Choice(1, n);
if A[j] = x then {write (j); Success();}
write (0); Failure();
```

Algorithm 11.1 Nondeterministic search

From the way a nondeterministic computation is defined, it follows that the number 0 can be output if and only if there is no j such that $A[j] = x$. Algorithm 11.1 is of nondeterministic complexity $O(1)$. Note that since A is not ordered, every deterministic search algorithm is of complexity $\Omega(n)$. □

Example 11.2 [Sorting] Let $A[i]$, $1 \leq i \leq n$, be an unsorted array of positive integers. The nondeterministic algorithm NSort(A, n) (Algorithm 11.2) sorts the numbers into nondecreasing order and then outputs them in this order. An auxiliary array $B[1:n]$ is used for convenience. Line 4 initializes B to zero though any value different from all the $A[i]$ will do. In the **for** loop of lines 5 to 10, each $A[i]$ is assigned to a position in B. Line 7 nondeterministically determines this position. Line 8 ascertains that $B[j]$ has not already been used. Thus, the order of the numbers in B is some permutation of the initial order in A. The **for** loop of lines 11 and 12 verifies that B is sorted in nondecreasing order. A successful completion is achieved if and only if the numbers are output in nondecreasing order. Since there is always a set of choices at line 7 for such an output order, algorithm NSort is a sorting algorithm. Its complexity is $O(n)$. Recall that all deterministic sorting algorithms must have a complexity $\Omega(n \log n)$. □

```
Algorithm NSort(A, n)
// Sort n positive integers.
{
    for i := 1 to n do B[i] := 0; // Initialize B[ ].
    for i := 1 to n do
    {
        j := Choice(1, n);
        if B[j] ≠ 0 then Failure();
        B[j] := A[i];
    }
    for i := 1 to n − 1 do  // Verify order.
        if B[i] > B[i + 1] then Failure();
    write (B[1 : n]);
    Success();
}
```

Algorithm 11.2 Nondeterministic sorting

A deterministic interpretation of a nondeterministic algorithm can be made by allowing unbounded parallelism in computation. In theory, each time a choice is to be made, the algorithm makes several copies of itself. One copy is made for each of the possible choices. Thus, many copies are executing at the same time. The first copy to reach a successful completion terminates all other computations. If a copy reaches a failure completion, then only that copy of the algorithm terminates. Although this interpretation may enable one to better understand nondeterministic algorithms, it is important to remember that a nondeterministic machine does not make any copies of an algorithm every time a choice is to be made. Instead, it has the ability to select a "correct" element from the set of allowable choices (if such an element exists) every time a choice is to be made. A correct element is defined relative to a shortest sequence of choices that leads to a successful termination. In case there is no sequence of choices leading to a successful termination, we assume that the algorithm terminates in one unit of time with output "unsuccessful computation." Whenever successful termination is possible, a nondeterministic machine makes a sequence of choices that is a shortest sequence leading to a successful termination. Since, the machine we are defining is fictitious, it is not necessary for us to concern ourselves with how the machine can make a correct choice at each step.

Definition 11.1 Any problem for which the answer is either zero or one is called a *decision problem.* An algorithm for a decision problem is termed a *decision algorithm.* Any problem that involves the identification of an optimal (either minimum or maximum) value of a given cost function is known as an *optimization problem.* An *optimization algorithm* is used to solve an optimization problem. □

It is possible to construct nondeterministic algorithms for which many different choice sequences lead to successful completions. Algorithm NSort of Example 11.2 is one such algorithm. If the numbers $A[i]$ are not distinct, then many different permutations will result in a sorted sequence. If NSort were written to output the permutation used rather than the $A[i]$'s in sorted order, then its output would not be uniquely defined. We concern ourselves only with those nondeterministic algorithms that generate unique outputs. In particular we consider only nondeterministic decision algorithms. A successful completion is made if and only if the output is 1. A 0 is output if and only if there is no sequence of choices leading to a successful completion. The output statement is implicit in the signals Success and Failure. No explicit output statements are permitted in a decision algorithm. Clearly, our earlier definition of a nondeterministic computation implies that the output from a decision algorithm is uniquely defined by the input parameters and algorithm specification.

Although the idea of a decision algorithm may appear very restrictive at this time, many optimization problems can be recast into decision problems with the property that the decision problem can be solved in polynomial time if and only if the corresponding optimization problem can. In other cases, we can at least make the statement that if the decision problem cannot be solved in polynomial time, then the optimization problem cannot either.

Example 11.3 [Maximum clique] A maximal complete subgraph of a graph $G = (V, E)$ is a *clique.* The size of the clique is the number of vertices in it. The *max clique problem* is an optimization problem that has to determine the size of a largest clique in G. The corresponding decision problem is to determine whether G has a clique of size at least k for some given k. Let DClique(G, k) be a deterministic decision algorithm for the clique decision problem. If the number of vertices in G is n, the size of a max clique in G can be found by making several applications of DClique. DClique is used once for each k, $k = n, n-1, n-2, \ldots$, until the output from DClique is 1. If the time complexity of DClique is $f(n)$, then the size of a max clique can be found in time $\leq n\ f(n)$. Also, if the size of a max clique can be determined in time $g(n)$, then the decision problem can be solved in time $g(n)$. Hence, the max clique problem can be solved in polynomial time if and only if the clique decision problem can be solved in polynomial time. □

Example 11.4 [0/1 knapsack] The knapsack decision problem is to determine whether there is a 0/1 assignment of values to x_i, $1 \leq i \leq n$, such that

$\sum p_i x_i \geq r$ and $\sum w_i x_i \leq m$. The r is a given number. The p_i's and w_i's are nonnegative numbers. If the knapsack decision problem cannot be solved in deterministic polynomial time, then the optimization problem cannot either. □

Before proceeding further, it is necessary to arrive at a uniform parameter n to measure complexity. We assume that n is the length of the input to the algorithm (that is, n is the input size). We also assume that all inputs are integer. Rational inputs can be provided by specifying pairs of integers. Generally, the length of an input is measured assuming a binary representation; that is, if the number 10 is to be input, then in binary it is represented as 1010. Its length is 4. In general, a positive integer k has a length of $\lfloor \log_2 k \rfloor + 1$ bits when represented in binary. The length of the binary representation of 0 is 1. The size, or length, n of the input to an algorithm is the sum of the lengths of the individual numbers being input. In case the input is given using a different representation (say radix r), then the length of a positive number k is $\lfloor \log_r k \rfloor + 1$. Thus, in decimal notation, $r = 10$ and the number 100 has a length $\log_{10} 100 + 1 = 3$. Since $\log_r k = \log_2 k / \log_2 r$, the length of any input using radix r ($r > 1$) representation is $c(r)n$, where n is the length using a binary representation and $c(r)$ is a number that is fixed for a given r.

When inputs are given using the radix $r = 1$, we say the input is in *unary form*. In unary form, the number 5 is input as 11111. Thus, the length of a positive integer k is k. It is important to observe that the length of a unary input is exponentially related to the length of the corresponding r-ary input for radix r, $r > 1$.

Example 11.5 [Max clique] The input to the max clique decision problem can be provided as a sequence of edges and an integer k. Each edge in $E(G)$ is a pair of numbers (i, j). The size of the input for each edge (i, j) is $\lfloor \log_2 i \rfloor + \lfloor \log_2 j \rfloor + 2$ if a binary representation is assumed. The input size of any instance is

$$n = \sum_{\substack{(i,j) \in E(G) \\ i<j}} (\lfloor \log_2 i \rfloor + \lfloor \log_2 j \rfloor + 2) + \lfloor \log_2 k \rfloor + 1$$

Note that if G has only one connected component, then $n \geq |V|$. Thus, if this decision problem cannot be solved by an algorithm of complexity $p(n)$ for some polynomial $p()$, then it cannot be solved by an algorithm of complexity $p(|V|)$. □

Example 11.6 [0/1 knapsack] Assuming p_i, w_i, m, and r are all integers, the input size for the knapsack decision problem is

$$q = \sum_{1 \le i \le n} (\lfloor \log_2 p_i \rfloor + \lfloor \log_2 w_i \rfloor) + 2n + \lfloor \log_2 m \rfloor + \lfloor \log_2 r \rfloor + 2$$

Note that $q > n$. If the input is given in unary notation, then the input size s is $\sum p_i + \sum w_i + m + r$. Note that the knapsack decision and optimization problems can be solved in time $p(s)$ for some polynomial $p()$ (see the dynamic programming algorithm). However, there is no known algorithm with complexity $O(p(n))$ for some polynomial $p()$. □

We are now ready to formally define the complexity of a nondeterministic algorithm.

Definition 11.2 The *time required by a nondeterministic algorithm* performing on any given input is the minimum number of steps needed to reach a successful completion if there exists a sequence of choices leading to such a completion. In case successful completion is not possible, then the time required is $O(1)$. A nondeterministic algorithm is of complexity $O(f(n))$ if for all inputs of size n, $n \ge n_0$, that result in a successful completion, the time required is at most $cf(n)$ for some constants c and n_0. □

In Definition 11.2 we assume that each computation step is of a fixed cost. In word-oriented computers this is guaranteed by the finiteness of each word. When each step is not of a fixed cost, it is necessary to consider the cost of individual instructions. Thus, the addition of two m-bit numbers takes $O(m)$ time, their multiplication takes $O(m^2)$ time (using classical multiplication), and so on. To see the necessity of this, consider the algorithm Sum (Algorithm 11.3). This is a deterministic algorithm for the sum of subsets decision problem. It uses an $(m+1)$-bit word s. The ith bit in s is zero if and only if no subset of the integers $A[j]$, $1 \le j \le n$, sums to i. Bit 0 of s is always 1 and the bits are numbered $0, 1, 2, \ldots, m$ right to left. The function Shift shifts the bits in s to the left by $A[i]$ bits. The total number of steps for this algorithm is only $O(n)$. However, each step moves $m+1$ bits of data and would take $O(m)$ time on a conventional computer. Assuming one unit of time is needed for each basic operation for a fixed word size, the complexity is $O(nm)$ and not $O(n)$.

The virtue of conceiving of nondeterministic algorithms is that often what would be very complex to write deterministically is very easy to write nondeterministically. In fact, it is very easy to obtain polynomial time nondeterministic algorithms for many problems that can be deterministically solved by a systematic search of a solution space of exponential size.

Example 11.7 [Knapsack decision problem] DKP (Algorithm 11.4) is a nondeterministic polynomial time algorithm for the knapsack decision problem.

```
Algorithm Sum(A, n, m)
{
    s := 1;
        // s is an (m + 1)-bit word. Bit zero is 1.
    for i := 1 to n do
        s := s or Shift(s, A[i]);
    if the mth bit in s is 1 then
        write ("A subset sums to m.");
    else write ("No subset sums to m.");
}
```

Algorithm 11.3 Deterministic sum of subsets

```
1   Algorithm DKP(p, w, n, m, r, x)
2   {
3       W := 0; P := 0;
4       for i := 1 to n do
5       {
6           x[i] := Choice(0, 1);
7           W := W + x[i] * w[i]; P := P + x[i] * p[i];
8       }
9       if ((W > m) or (P < r)) then Failure();
10      else Success();
11  }
```

Algorithm 11.4 Nondeterministic knapsack algorithm

The **for** loop of lines 4 to 8 assigns 0/1 values to $x[i]$, $1 \leq i \leq n$. It also computes the total weight and profit corresponding to this choice of $x[\,]$. Line 9 checks to see whether this assignment is feasible and whether the resulting profit is at least r. A successful termination is possible iff the answer to the decision problem is yes. The time complexity is $O(n)$. If q is the input length using a binary representation, the time is $O(q)$. □

Example 11.8 [Max clique] Algorithm DCK (Algorithm 11.5) is a nondeterministic algorithm for the clique decision problem. The algorithm begins by trying to form a set of k distinct vertices. Then it tests to see whether these vertices form a complete subgraph. If G is given by its adjacency matrix and $|V| = n$, the input length m is $n^2 + \lfloor \log_2 k \rfloor + \lfloor \log_2 n \rfloor + 2$. The **for** loop of lines 4 to 9 can easily be implemented to run in nondeterministic time $O(n)$. The time for the **for** loop of lines 11 and 12 is $O(k^2)$. Hence the overall nondeterministic time is $O(n + k^2) = O(n^2) = O(m)$. There is no known polynomial time deterministic algorithm for this problem. □

```
1   Algorithm DCK(G, n, k)
2   {
3       S := ∅; // S is an initially empty set.
4       for i := 1 to k do
5       {
6           t := Choice(1, n);
7           if t ∈ S then Failure();
8           S := S ∪ {t} // Add t to set S.
9       }
10      // At this point S contains k distinct vertex indices.
11      for all pairs (i, j) such that i ∈ S, j ∈ S, and i ≠ j do
12          if (i, j) is not an edge of G then Failure();
13      Success();
14  }
```

Algorithm 11.5 Nondeterministic clique pseudocode

Example 11.9 [Satisfiability] Let $x_1, x_2, \ldots$ denote boolean variables (their value is either true or false). Let $\bar{x_i}$ denote the negation of x_i. A *literal* is either a variable or its negation. A formula in the propositional calculus is an expression that can be constructed using literals and the operations **and** and **or**. Examples of such formulas are $(x_1 \wedge x_2) \vee (x_3 \wedge \bar{x_4})$ and $(x_3 \vee \bar{x_4}) \wedge (x_1 \vee \bar{x_2})$. The symbol $\vee$ denotes **or** and $\wedge$ denotes **and**. A formula is in *conjunctive normal form* (CNF) if and only if it is represented as $\wedge_{i=1}^{k} c_i$, where the c_i are clauses each represented as $\vee l_{ij}$. The l_{ij} are literals. It is in *disjunctive normal form* (DNF) if and only if it is represented as $\vee_{i=1}^{k} c_i$ and each clause c_i is represented as $\wedge l_{ij}$. Thus $(x_1 \wedge x_2) \vee (x_3 \wedge \bar{x_4})$ is in DNF whereas $(x_3 \vee \bar{x_4}) \wedge (x_1 \vee \bar{x_2})$ is in CNF. The **satisfiability** problem is to determine whether a formula is true for some assignment of truth values to the variables. *CNF-satisfiability* is the satisfiability problem for CNF formulas.

It is easy to obtain a polynomial time nondeterministic algorithm that terminates successfully if and only if a given propositional formula $E(x_1, \ldots, x_n)$ is satisfiable. Such an algorithm could proceed by simply choosing (nondeterministically) one of the 2^n possible assignments of truth values to $(x_1, \ldots, x_n)$ and verifying that $E(x_1, \ldots, x_n)$ is true for that assignment.

Eval (Algorithm 11.6) does this. The nondeterministic time required by the algorithm is $O(n)$ to choose the value of $(x_1, \ldots, x_n)$ plus the time needed to deterministically evaluate E for that assignment. This time is proportional to the length of E. □

```
Algorithm Eval(E, n)
// Determine whether the propositional formula E is
// satisfiable. The variables are x1, x2, ..., xn.
{
    for i := 1 to n do  // Choose a truth value assignment.
        xi := Choice(false, true);
    if E(x1, ..., xn) then Success();
    else Failure();
}
```

Algorithm 11.6 Nondeterministic satisfiability

11.1.2 The Classes $\mathcal{NP}$-hard and $\mathcal{NP}$-complete

In measuring the complexity of an algorithm, we use the input length as the parameter. An algorithm A is of *polynomial complexity* if there exists a polynomial $p()$ such that the computing time of A is $O(p(n))$ for every input of size n.

Definition 11.3 $\mathcal{P}$ is the set of all decision problems solvable by deterministic algorithms in polynomial time. $\mathcal{NP}$ is the set of all decision problems solvable by nondeterministic algorithms in polynomial time. □

Since deterministic algorithms are just a special case of nondeterministic ones, we conclude that $\mathcal{P} \subseteq \mathcal{NP}$. What we do not know, and what has become perhaps the most famous unsolved problem in computer science, is whether $\mathcal{P} = \mathcal{NP}$ or $\mathcal{P} \neq \mathcal{NP}$.

Is it possible that for all the problems in $\mathcal{NP}$, there exist polynomial time deterministic algorithms that have remained undiscovered? This seems unlikely, at least because of the tremendous effort that has already been expended by so many people on these problems. Nevertheless, a proof that $\mathcal{P} \neq \mathcal{NP}$ is just as elusive and seems to require as yet undiscovered techniques. But as with many famous unsolved problems, they serve to generate other useful results, and the question of whether $\mathcal{NP} \subseteq \mathcal{P}$ is no exception. Figure 11.1 displays the relationship between $\mathcal{P}$ and $\mathcal{NP}$ assuming that $\mathcal{P} \neq \mathcal{NP}$.

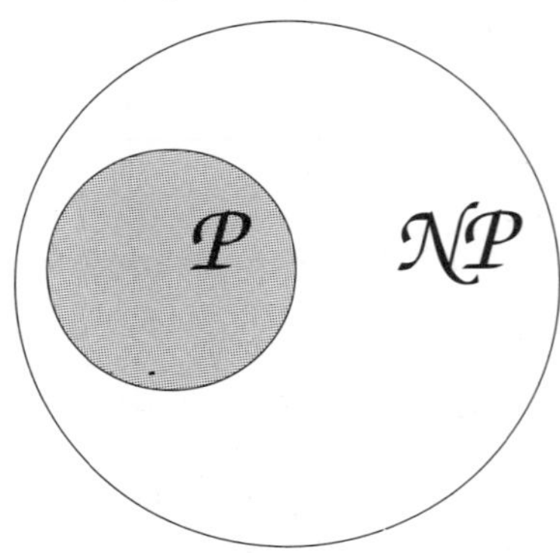

Figure 11.1 Commonly believed relationship between $\mathcal{P}$ and $\mathcal{NP}$

S. Cook formulated the following question: Is there any single problem in $\mathcal{NP}$ such that if we showed it to be in $\mathcal{P}$, then that would imply that $\mathcal{P} = \mathcal{NP}$? Cook answered his own question in the affirmative with the following theorem.

Theorem 11.1 [Cook] Satisfiability is in $\mathcal{P}$ if and only if $\mathcal{P} = \mathcal{NP}$.

Proof: See Section 11.2. □

We are now ready to define the $\mathcal{NP}$-hard and $\mathcal{NP}$-complete classes of problems. First we define the notion of reducibility. Note that this definition is similar to the one made in Section 10.3.

Definition 11.4 Let L_1 and L_2 be problems. Problem L_1 *reduces* to L_2 (also written $L_1 \propto L_2$) if and only if there is a way to solve L_1 by a deterministic polynomial time algorithm using a deterministic algorithm that solves L_2 in polynomial time. □

This definition implies that if we have a polynomial time algorithm for L_2, then we can solve L_1 in polynomial time. One can readily verify that $\propto$ is a transitive relation (that is, if $L_1 \propto L_2$ and $L_2 \propto L_3$, then $L_1 \propto L_3$).

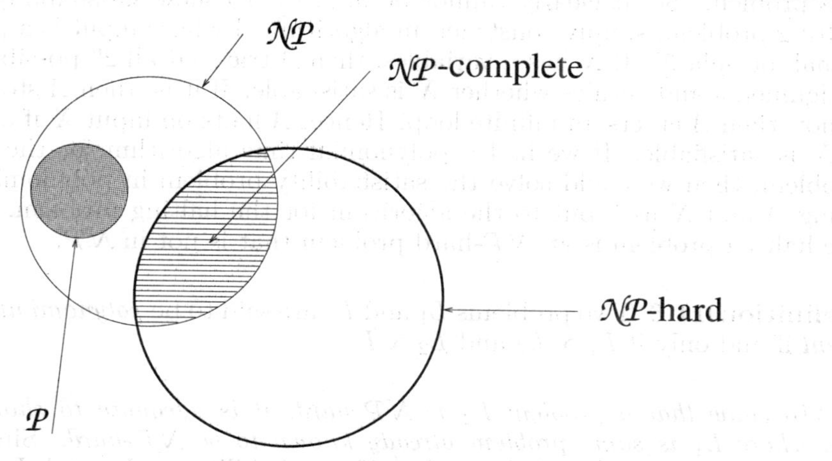

Figure 11.2 Commonly believed relationship among $\mathcal{P}$, $\mathcal{NP}$, $\mathcal{NP}$-complete, and $\mathcal{NP}$-hard problems

Definition 11.5 A problem L is $\mathcal{NP}$-hard if and only if satisfiability reduces to L (satisfiability $\propto L$). A problem L is $\mathcal{NP}$-complete if and only if L is $\mathcal{NP}$-hard and $L \in \mathcal{NP}$. □

It is easy to see that there are $\mathcal{NP}$-hard problems that are not $\mathcal{NP}$-complete. Only a decision problem can be $\mathcal{NP}$-complete. However, an optimization problem may be $\mathcal{NP}$-hard. Furthermore if L_1 is a decision problem and L_2 an optimization problem, it is quite possible that $L_1 \propto L_2$. One can trivially show that the knapsack decision problem reduces to the knapsack optimization problem. For the clique problem one can easily show that the clique decision problem reduces to the clique optimization problem. In fact, one can also show that these optimization problems reduce to their corresponding decision problems (see the exercises). Yet, optimization problems cannot be $\mathcal{NP}$-complete whereas decision problems can. There also exist $\mathcal{NP}$-hard decision problems that are not $\mathcal{NP}$-complete. Figure 11.2 shows the relationship among these classes.

Example 11.10 As an extreme example of an $\mathcal{NP}$-hard decision problem that is not $\mathcal{NP}$-complete consider the halting problem for deterministic algorithms. The *halting problem* is to determine for an arbitrary deterministic algorithm A and an input I whether algorithm A with input I ever terminates (or enters an infinite loop). It is well known that this problem is undecidable. Hence, there exists no algorithm (of any complexity) to solve this problem. So, it clearly cannot be in $\mathcal{NP}$. To show satisfiability $\propto$ the halting problem, simply construct an algorithm A whose input is a propositional formula X. If X has n variables, then A tries out all 2^n possible truth assignments and verifies whether X is satisfiable. If it is, then A stops. If it is not, then A enters an infinite loop. Hence, A halts on input X if and only if X is satisfiable. If we had a polynomial time algorithm for the halting problem, then we could solve the satisfiability problem in polynomial time using A and X as input to the algorithm for the halting problem. Hence, the halting problem is an $\mathcal{NP}$-hard problem that is not in $\mathcal{NP}$. □

Definition 11.6 Two problems L_1 and L_2 are said to be *polynomially equivalent* if and only if $L_1 \propto L_2$ and $L_2 \propto L_1$. □

To show that a problem L_2 is $\mathcal{NP}$-hard, it is adequate to show $L_1 \propto L_2$, where L_1 is some problem already known to be $\mathcal{NP}$-hard. Since $\propto$ is a transitive relation, it follows that if satisfiability $\propto L_1$ and $L_1 \propto L_2$, then satisfiability $\propto L_2$. *To show that an $\mathcal{NP}$-hard decision problem is $\mathcal{NP}$-complete, we have just to exhibit a polynomial time nondeterministic algorithm for it.*

Later sections show many problems to be $\mathcal{NP}$-hard. Although we restrict ourselves to decision problems, it should be clear that the corresponding optimization problems are also $\mathcal{NP}$-hard. The $\mathcal{NP}$-completeness proofs are left as exercises (for those problems that are $\mathcal{NP}$-complete).

EXERCISES

1. Given two sets S_1 and S_2, the disjoint sets problem is to check whether the sets have a common element (see Section 10.3.2). Present an $O(1)$ time nondeterministic algorithm for this problem.

2. Given a sequence of n numbers, the distinct elements problem is to check if there are equal numbers (see Section 10.3, Exercise 5). Give an $O(1)$ time nondeterministic algorithm for this problem.

3. Obtain a nondeterministic algorithm of complexity $O(n)$ to determine whether there is a subset of n numbers a_i, $1 \leq i \leq n$, that sums to m.

4. (a) Show that the knapsack optimization problem reduces to the knapsack decision problem when all the p's, w's, and m are integer and the complexity is measured as a function of input length. (*Hint*: If the input length is q, then $\sum p_i \leq n2^q$, where n is the number of objects. Use a binary search to determine the optimal solution value.)

(b) Let DK be an algorithm for the knapsack decision problem. Let r be the value of an optimal solution to the knapsack optimization problem. Show how to obtain a 0/1 assignment for the x_i, $1 \leq i \leq n$, such that $\sum p_i x_i = r$ and $\sum w_i x_i \leq m$ by making n applications of DK.

5. Show that the clique optimization problem reduces to the clique decision problem.
6. Let Sat(E) be an algorithm to determine whether a propositional formula E in CNF is satisfiable. Show that if E is satisfiable and has n variables $x_1, x_2, \ldots, x_n$, then using Sat(E) n times, one can determine a truth value assignment for the x_i's for which E is true.
7. Let π_2 be a problem for which there exists a deterministic algorithm that runs in time $2^{\sqrt{n}}$ (where n is the input size). Prove or disprove:

   If π_1 is another problem such that π_1 is polynomially reducible to π_2, then π_1 can be solved in deterministic $O(2^{\sqrt{n}})$ time on any input of size n.

11.2 COOK'S THEOREM (*)

Cook's theorem (Theorem 11.1) states that satisfiability is in $\mathcal{P}$ if and only if $\mathcal{P} = \mathcal{NP}$. We now prove this important theorem. We have already seen that satisfiability is in $\mathcal{NP}$ (Example 11.9). Hence, if $\mathcal{P} = \mathcal{NP}$, then satisfiability is in $\mathcal{P}$. It remains to be shown that if satisfiability is in $\mathcal{P}$, then $\mathcal{P} = \mathcal{NP}$. To do this, we show how to obtain from any polynomial time nondeterministic decision algorithm A and input I a formula $Q(A, I)$ such that Q is satisfiable iff A has a successful termination with input I. If the length of I is n and the time complexity of A is $p(n)$ for some polynomial $p()$, then the length of Q is $O(p^3(n) \log n) = O(p^4(n))$. The time needed to construct Q is also $O(p^3(n) \log n)$. A deterministic algorithm Z to determine the outcome of A on any input I can be easily obtained. Algorithm Z simply computes Q and then uses a deterministic algorithm for the satisfiability problem to determine whether Q is satisfiable. If $O(q(m))$ is the time needed to determine whether a formula of length m is satisfiable, then the complexity of Z is $O(p^3(n) \log n + q(p^3(n) \log n))$. If satisfiability is in $\mathcal{P}$, then $q(m)$ is a polynomial function of m and the complexity of Z becomes $O(r(n))$ for some polynomial $r()$. Hence, if satisfiability is in $\mathcal{P}$, then for every nondeterministic algorithm A in $\mathcal{NP}$ we can obtain a deterministic Z in $\mathcal{P}$. So, the above construction shows that if satisfiability is in $\mathcal{P}$, then $\mathcal{P} = \mathcal{NP}$.

Before going into the construction of Q from A and I, we make some simplifying assumptions on our nondeterministic machine model and on the form of A. These assumptions do not in any way alter the class of decision problems in $\mathcal{NP}$ or $\mathcal{P}$. The simplifying assumptions are as follows.

1. The machine on which A is to be executed is word oriented. Each word is w bits long. Multiplication, addition, subtraction, and so on, between numbers one word long take one unit of time. If numbers are longer than a word, then the corresponding operations take at least as many units as the number of words making up the longest number.

2. A *simple expression* is an expression that contains at most one operator and all operands are simple variables (i.e., no array variables are used). Some sample simple expression are $-B, B+C, D$ **or** E, and F. We assume that all assignments in A are in one of the following forms:

   (a) ⟨simple variable⟩ := ⟨simple expression⟩

   (b) ⟨array variable⟩ := ⟨simple variable⟩

   (c) ⟨simple variable⟩ := ⟨array variable⟩

   (d) ⟨simple variable⟩ := Choice(S), where S is a finite set $\{S_1, S_2, \ldots, S_k\}$ or l,u. In the latter case the function chooses an integer in the range $[l : u]$.

   Indexing within an array is done using a simple integer variable and all index values are positive. Only one-dimensional arrays are allowed. Clearly, all assignment statements not falling into one of the above categories can be replaced by a set of statements of these types. Hence, this restriction does not alter the class $\mathcal{NP}$.

3. All variables in A are of type integer or boolean.

4. Algorithm A contains no **read** or **write** statements. The only input to A is via its parameters. At the time A is invoked, all variables (other than the parameters) have value zero (or **false** if boolean).

5. Algorithm A contains no constants. Clearly, all constants in any algorithm can be replaced by new variables. These new variables can be added to the parameter list of A and the constants associated with them can be part of the input.

6. In addition to simple assignment statements, A is allowed to contain only the following types of statements:

   (a) The statement **goto** k, where k is an instruction number.

   (b) The statement **if** c **then goto** a;. Variable c is a simple boolean variable (i.e., not an array) and a is an instruction number.

(c) Success(), Failure().

(d) Algorithm A may contain type declaration and dimension statements. These are not used during execution of A and so need not be translated into Q. The dimension information is used to allocate array space. It is assumed that successive elements in an array are assigned to consecutive words in memory.

It is assumed that the instructions in A are numbered sequentially from 1 to ℓ (if A has ℓ instructions). Every statement in A has a number. The **goto** instructions in (a) and (b) use this numbering scheme to effect a branch. It should be easy to see how to rewrite **repeat-until**, **for**, and so on, statements in terms of **goto** and **if** c **then goto** a statements. Also, note that the **goto** k statement can be replaced by the statement **if true then goto** k. So, this may also be eliminated.

7. Let $p(n)$ be a polynomial such that A takes no more than $p(n)$ time units on any input of length n. Because of the complexity assumption of 1), A cannot change or use more than $p(n)$ words of memory. We assume that A uses some subset of the words indexed 1, 2, 3, $\ldots, p(n)$. This assumption does not restrict the class of decision problems in $\mathcal{NP}$. To see this, let $f(1), f(2), \ldots, f(k)$, $1 \leq k \leq p(n)$, be the distinct words used by A while working on input I. We can construct another polynomial time nondeterministic algorithm A' that uses $2p(n)$ words indexed $1, 2, \ldots, 2p(n)$ and solves the same decision problem as A does. A' simulates the behavior of A. However, A' maps the addresses $f(1), f(2), \ldots, f(k)$ onto the set $\{1, 2, \ldots, k\}$. The mapping function used is determined dynamically and is stored as a table in words $p(n) + 1$ through $2p(n)$. If the entry at word $p(n) + i$ is j, then A' uses word i to hold the same value that A stored in word j. The simulation of A proceeds as follows: Let k be the number of distinct words referenced by A up to this time. Let j be a word referenced by A in the current step. A' searches its table to find word $p(n) + i$, $1 \leq i \leq k$, such that the contents of this word is j. If no such i exists, then A' sets $k := k + 1$; $i := k$; and word $p(n) + k$ is given the value j. A' makes use of the word i to do whatever A would have done with word j. Clearly, A' and A solve the same decision problem. The complexity of A' is $O(p^2(n))$ as it takes A' $p(n)$ time to search its table and simulate a step of A. Since $p^2(n)$ is also a polynomial in n, restricting our algorithms to use only consecutive words does not alter the classes $\mathcal{P}$ and $\mathcal{NP}$.

Formula Q makes use of several boolean variables. We state the semantics of two sets of variables used in Q:

1. $B(i, j, t)$, $1 \leq i \leq p(n)$, $1 \leq j \leq w$, $0 \leq t < p(n)$

$B(i,j,t)$ represents the status of bit j of word i following t steps (or time units) of computation. The bits in a word are numbered from right to left. The rightmost bit is numbered 1. Q is constructed so that in any truth assignment for which Q is true, $B(i,j,t)$ is true if and only if the corresponding bit has value 1 following t steps of some successful computation of A on input I.

2. $S(j,t)$, $1 \leq j \leq \ell$, $1 \leq t \leq p(n)$

   Recall that ℓ is the number of instructions in A. $S(j,t)$ represents the instruction to be executed at time t. Q is constructed so that in any truth assignment for which Q is true, $S(j,t)$ is true if and only if the instruction executed by A at time t is instruction j.

Q is made up of six subformulas, C, D, E, F, G, and H. $Q = C \wedge D \wedge E \wedge F \wedge G \wedge H$. These subformulas make the following assertions:

C: The initial status of the $p(n)$ words represents the input I. All non-input variables are zero.

D: Instruction 1 is the first instruction to execute.

E: At the end of the ith step, there can be only one next instruction to execute. Hence, for any fixed i, exactly one of the $S(j,i)$, $1 \leq j \leq \ell$, can be true.

F: If $S(j,i)$ is true, then $S(j,i+1)$ is also true if instruction j is a Success or Failure statement. $S(j+1,i+1)$ is true if j is an assignment statement. If j is a **goto** k statement, then $S(k,i+1)$ is true. The last possibility for j is the **if** c **then** a; statement. In this case $S(a,i+1)$ is true if c is true and $S(j+1,i+1)$ is true if c is false.

G: If the instruction executed at step t is not an assignment statement, then the $B(i,j,t)$'s are unchanged. If this instruction is an assignment and the variable on the left-hand side is X, then only X may change. This change is determined by the right-hand side of the instruction.

H: The instruction to be executed at time $p(n)$ is a Success instruction. Hence the computation terminates successfully.

Clearly, if C through H make the above assertions, then $Q = C \wedge D \wedge E \wedge F \wedge G \wedge H$ is satisfiable if and only if there is a successful computation of A on input I. We now give the formulas C through H. While presenting these formulas, we also indicate how each may be transformed into CNF. This transformation increases the length of Q by an amount independent of n (but dependent on w and ℓ). This enables us to show that CNF-satisfiability is $\mathcal{NP}$-complete.

1. Formula C describes the input I. We have

$$C = \bigwedge_{\substack{1\le i\le p(n)\\ 1\le j\le w}} T(i,j,0)$$

$T(i,j,0)$ is $B(i,j,0)$ if the input calls for bit $B(i,j,0)$ (i.e., bit j of word i) to be 1. $T(i,j,0)$ is $\bar{B}(i,j,0)$ otherwise. Thus, if there is no input, then

$$C = \bigwedge_{\substack{1\le i\le p(n)\\ 1\le j\le w}} \bar{B}(i,j,0)$$

Clearly, C is uniquely determined by I and is in CNF. Also, C is satisfiable only by a truth assignment representing the initial values of all variables in A.

2. $D = S(1,1) \wedge \bar{S}(2,1) \wedge \bar{S}(3,1) \wedge \cdots \wedge \bar{S}(\ell,1)$

Clearly, D is satisfiable only by the assignment $S(1,1)$ = true and $S(i,1)$ = false, $2 \le i \le \ell$. Using our interpretation of $S(i,1)$, this means that D is true if and only if instruction 1 is the first to be executed. Note that D is in CNF.

3. $E = \bigwedge_{1<t\le p(n)} E_t$

Each E_t will assert that there is a unique instruction for step t. We can define E_t to be

$$E_t = (S(1,t) \vee (S(2,t) \vee \cdots \vee S(\ell,t)) \wedge (\bigwedge_{\substack{1\le j\le \ell\\ 1\le k\le \ell\\ j\ne k}} (\bar{S}(j,t) \vee \bar{S}(k,t))$$

One can verify that E_t is true iff exactly one of the $S(j,t)$'s, $1 \le j \le \ell$, is true. Also, note that E is in CNF.

4. $F = \bigwedge_{\substack{1\le i\le \ell\\ 1\le t<p(n)}} F_{i,t}$

Each $F_{i,t}$ asserts that either instruction i is not the one to be executed at time t or, if it is, then the instruction to be executed at time $t+1$ is correctly determined by instruction i. Formally, we have

$$F_{i,t} = \bar{S}(i,t) \vee L$$

where L is defined as follows:

(a) If instruction i is Success or Failure, then L is $S(i, t+1)$. Hence the program cannot leave such an instruction.
(b) If instruction i is **goto** k, then L is $S(k, t+1)$.
(c) If instruction i is **if** X **then goto** k and variable X is represented by word j, then L is $((B(j,1,t-1) \wedge S(k,t+1)) \vee (\bar{B}(j,1,t-1) \wedge S(i+1,t+1)))$. This assumes that bit 1 of X is 1 if and only if X is true.
(d) If instruction i is not any of the above, then L is $S(i+1, t+1)$.

The $F_{i,t}$'s defined in cases (a), (b), and (d) are in CNF. The $F_{i,t}$ in case (c) can be transformed into CNF using the boolean identity $a \vee (b \wedge c) \vee (d \wedge e) \equiv (a \vee b \vee d) \wedge (a \vee c \vee d) \wedge (a \vee b \vee e) \wedge (a \vee c \vee e)$.

5. $G = \bigwedge_{\substack{1 \le i \le \ell \\ 1 \le t < p(n)}} G_{i,t}$

Each $G_{i,t}$ asserts that at time t either instruction i is not executed or it is and the status of the $p(n)$ words after step t is correct with respect to the status before step t and the changes resulting from instruction i. Formally, we have

$$G_{i,t} = \bar{S}(i,t) \vee M$$

where M is defined as follows:

(a) If instruction i is a **goto**, **if-then-goto-**, Success, or Failure statement, then M asserts that the status of the $p(n)$ words is unchanged; that is, $B(k,j,t-1) = B(k,j,t)$, $1 \le k \le p(n)$, $1 \le j \le w$.

$$M = \bigwedge_{\substack{1 \le k \le p(n) \\ 1 \le j \le w}} ((B(k,j,t-1) \wedge B(k,j,t)) \vee (\bar{B}(k,j,t-1) \wedge (\bar{B}(k,j,t))$$

In this case, $G_{i,t}$ can be written as

$$G_{i,t} = \bigwedge_{\substack{1 \le k \le p(n) \\ 1 \le j \le w}} (\bar{S}(i,t) \vee (B(k,j,t-1) \wedge B(k,j,t)) \vee (\bar{B}(k,j,t-1) \wedge (\bar{B}(k,j,t)))$$

Each clause in $G_{i,t}$ is of the form $z \vee (x \wedge s) \vee (\bar{x} \wedge \bar{s})$, where z is $\bar{S}(i,t)$, x represents a $B(,,t-1)$, and s represents a $B(,,t)$. Note that $z \vee (x \wedge s) \vee (\bar{x} \wedge \bar{s})$ is equivalent to $(x \vee \bar{s} \vee z) \wedge (\bar{x} \vee s \vee z)$. Hence, $G_{i,t}$ can be transformed into CNF easily.

(b) If i is an assignment statement of type 2(a), then M depends on the operator (if any) on the right-hand side. We first describe the form of M for the case in which instruction i is of type $Y := V+Z$. Let Y, V, and Z be respectively represented in words y, v, and z. We make the simplifying assumption that all numbers are nonnegative. The exercises examine the case in which negative numbers are allowed and 1's complement arithmetic is used. To get a formula asserting that the bits $B(y, j, t)$, $1 \le j \le w$, represent the sum of $B(v, j, t-1)$ and $B(z, j, t-1)$, $1 \le j \le w$, we have to make use of w additional bits $C(j, t)$, $1 \le j \le w$. $C(j, t)$ represents the carry from the addition of the bits $B(v, j, t-1), B(z, j, t-1)$, and $C(j-1, t)$, $1 < j \le w$. $C(1, t)$ is the carry from the addition of $B(v, 1, t-1)$ and $B(z, 1, t-1)$. Recall that a bit is 1 iff the corresponding variable is true. Performing a bitwise addition of V and Z, we obtain $C(1, t) = B(v, 1, t-1) \wedge B(z, 1, t-1)$ and $B(y, 1, t) = B(v, 1, t-1) \oplus B(z, 1, t-1)$, where $\oplus$ is the **exclusive or** operation ($a \oplus b$ is true iff exactly one of a and b is true). Note that $a \oplus b \equiv (a \vee b) \wedge (\overline{a \wedge b}) \equiv (a \vee b) \wedge (\bar{a} \vee \bar{b})$. Hence, the right-hand side of the expression for $B(y, 1, t)$ can be transformed into CNF using this identity. For the other bits of Y, one can verify that

$$B(y, j, t) = B(v, j, t-1) \oplus (B(z, j, t-1) \oplus C(j-1, t)) \quad \text{and}$$

$$\begin{aligned} C(j, t) \quad = \quad & (B(v, j, t-1) \wedge B(z, j, t-1)) \vee (B(v, j, t-1) \\ & \wedge C(j-1, t)) \\ & \vee (B(z, j, t-1) \wedge C(j-1, t)) \end{aligned}$$

Finally, we require that $C(w, t) =$ false (i.e., there is no overflow). Let M' be the **and** of all the equations for $B(y, j, t)$ and $C(j, t)$, $1 \le j \le w$. M is given by

$$\begin{aligned} M \quad = \quad (& \bigwedge_{\substack{1 \le k \le p(n) \\ k \ne y \\ 1 \le j \le w}} ((B(k, j, t-1) \wedge B(k, j, t)) \\ & \wedge (\bar{B}(k, j, t-1) \wedge \bar{B}(k, j, t))) \wedge M' \end{aligned}$$

$G_{i,t}$ can be converted into CNF using the idea of 5(a). This transformation increases the length of $G_{i,t}$ by a constant factor independent of n. We leave it to the reader to figure out what M is when instruction i is either of the forms $Y := V$; and $Y := V \odot Z$;, for $\odot$ one of $-, /, *, <, >, \leq, =$, and so on.

When i is an assignment statement of type 2(b) or 2(c), then it is necessary to select the correct array element. Consider an instruction of type 2(b): $R[m] := X$;. In this case formula M can be written as

$$M = W \wedge (\bigwedge_{1 \leq j \leq u} M_j)$$

where u is the dimension of R. Note that because of restriction (7) on algorithm A, $u \leq p(n)$. W asserts that $1 \leq m \leq u$. The specification of W is left as an exercise. Each M_j asserts that either $m \neq j$ or $m = j$ and only the jth element of R changes. Let us assume that the values of X and m are respectively stored in words x and m and that $R(1 : u)$ is stored in words $\alpha, \alpha + 1, \ldots, \alpha + u - 1$. M_j is given by

$$M_j = \bigvee_{1 \leq k \leq w} T(m, k, t-1) \vee Z$$

where T is B if the kth bit in the binary representation of j is 0 and T is $\bar{B}$ otherwise. Z is defined as

$$\begin{aligned} Z = \bigwedge_{\substack{1 \leq k \leq w \\ 1 \leq r \leq p(n) \\ r \neq \alpha + j - 1}} & ((B(r, k, t-1) \wedge B(r, k, t)) \vee (\bar{B}(r, k, t-1) \\ & \wedge \bar{B}(r, k, t-1))) \\ & \bigwedge_{1 \leq k \leq w} ((B(\alpha + j - 1, k, t) \wedge B(x, k, t-1)) \\ & \vee (\bar{B}(\alpha + j - 1, k, t) \wedge \bar{B}(x, k, t-1))) \end{aligned}$$

Note that the number of literals in M is $O(p^2(n))$. Since j is w bits long, it can represent only numbers smaller than 2^w. Hence, for $u \geq 2^w$, we need a different indexing scheme. A simple generalization is to allow multiprecision arithmetic. The index variable j can then use as many words as needed. The number of words used depends on u. At most $\log(p(n))$ words are needed. This calls for a slight change in M_j, but the number of literals in M remains $O(p^2(n))$. There is no need to explicitly incorporate multiprecision arithmetic as by giving the program access to individual words in a multiprecision index j, we can require the program to simulate multiprecision arithmetic.

When i is an instruction of type 2(c), the form of M is similar to that obtained for instructions of type 2(b). Next, we describe how to construct M for the case in which i is of the form $Y :=$ Choice(S);, where S is either a set of the form $S = \{S_1, S_2, \ldots, S_k\}$ or S is of the form r, u. Assume Y is represented by word y. If S is a set, then we define

$$M = \bigvee_{1 \le j \le k} M_j$$

M_j asserts that Y is S_j. This is easily done by choosing $M_j = a_1 \wedge a_2 \wedge \cdots \wedge a_w$, where $a_\ell = B(y, \ell, t)$ if bit ℓ is 1 in S_ℓ and $a_\ell = \bar{B}(y, \ell, t)$ if bit ℓ is zero in S_ℓ. If S is of the form r, u, then M is just the formula that asserts $r \le Y \le u$. This is left as an exercise. In both cases, $G_{i,t}$ can be transformed into CNF and the length of $G_{i,t}$ increased by at most a constant amount.

6. Let $i_1, i_2, \ldots, i_k$ be the statement numbers corresponding to success statements in A. H is given by

$$H = S(i_1, p(n)) \vee S(i_2, p(n)) \vee \cdots \vee S(i_k, p(n))$$

One can readily verify that $Q = C \wedge D \wedge E \wedge F \wedge G \wedge H$ is satisfiable if and only if the computation of algorithm A with input I terminates successfully. Further, Q can be transformed into CNF as described above. Formula C contains $wp(n)$ literals, D contains ℓ literals, E contains $O(\ell^2 p(n))$ literals, F contains $O(\ell p(n))$ literals, G contains $O(\ell w p^3(n))$ literals, and H contains at most ℓ literals. The total number of literals appearing in Q is $O(\ell w p^3(n)) = O(p^3(n))$ as ℓw is constant. Since there are $O(wp^2(n) + \ell p(n))$ distinct literals in Q, each literal can be written using $O(\log(wp^2(n) + \ell p(n))) = O(\log n)$ bits. The length of Q is therefore $O(p^3(n) \log n) = O(p^4(n))$ as $p(n)$ is at least n. The time to construct Q from A and I is also $O(p^3(n) \log n)$.

The preceding construction shows that every problem in $\mathcal{NP}$ reduces to satisfiability and also to CNF-satisfiability. Hence, if either of these two problems is in $\mathcal{P}$, then $\mathcal{NP} \subseteq \mathcal{P}$ and so $\mathcal{P} = \mathcal{NP}$. Also, since satisfiability is in $\mathcal{NP}$, the construction of a CNF formula Q shows that satisfiability $\propto$ CNF-satisfiability. This together with the knowledge that CNF-satisfiability is in $\mathcal{NP}$ implies that CNF-satisfiability is $\mathcal{NP}$-complete. Note that satisfiability is also $\mathcal{NP}$-complete as satisfiability $\propto$ satisfiability and satisfiability is in $\mathcal{NP}$.

EXERCISES

1. In conjunction with formula G in the proof of Cook's theorem (Section 11.2), obtain M for the following cases for instruction i. Note that

M can contain at most $O(p(n))$ literals (as a function of n). Obtain M under the assumption that negative numbers are represented in ones complement. Show how the corresponding $G_{i,t}$'s can be transformed into CNF. The length of $G_{i,t}$ must increase by no more than a constant factor (say w^2) during this transformation.

(a) $Y := Z;$
(b) $Y := V - Z;$
(c) $Y := V + Z;$
(d) $Y := V * Z;$
(e) $Y :=$ Choice(0,1);
(f) $Y :=$ Choice(r, u);, where r and u are variables

2. Show how to encode the following instructions as CNF formulas: (a) **for** and (b) **while**.

3. Prove or disprove: If there exists a polynomial time algorithm to convert a boolean formula in CNF into an equivalent formula in DNF, then $\mathcal{P} = \mathcal{NP}$.

11.3 $\mathcal{NP}$-HARD GRAPH PROBLEMS

The strategy we adopt to show that a problem L_2 is $\mathcal{NP}$-hard is:

1. Pick a problem L_1 already known to be $\mathcal{NP}$-hard.

2. Show how to obtain (in polynomial deterministic time) an instance I' of L_2 from any instance I of L_1 such that from the solution of I' we can determine (in polynomial deterministic time) the solution to instance I of L_1 (see Figure 11.3).

3. Conclude from step (2) that $L_1 \propto L_2$.

4. Conclude from steps (1) and (3) and the transitivity of $\propto$ that L_2 is $\mathcal{NP}$-hard.

For the first few proofs we go through all the above steps. Later proofs explicitly deal only with steps (1) and (2). An $\mathcal{NP}$-hard decision problem L_2 can be shown to be $\mathcal{NP}$-complete by exhibiting a polynomial time nondeterministic algorithm for L_2. All the $\mathcal{NP}$-hard decision problems we deal with here are $\mathcal{NP}$-complete. The construction of polynomial time nondeterministic algorithms for these problems is left as an exercise.

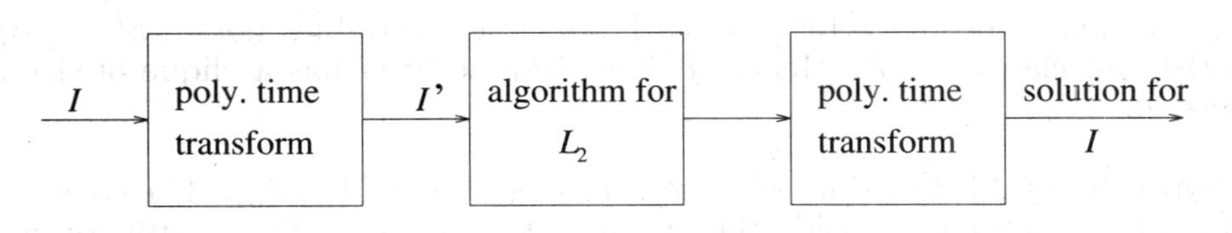

Figure 11.3 Reduction of L_1 to L_2

11.3.1 Clique Decision Problem (CDP)

The clique decision problem was introduced in Section 11.1. We show in Theorem 11.2 that CNF-satisfiability $\propto$ CDP. Using this result, the transitivity of $\propto$, and the knowledge that satisfiability $\propto$ CNF-satisfiability (Section 11.2), we can readily establish that satisfiability $\propto$ CDP. Hence, CDP is $\mathcal{NP}$-hard. Since, CDP $\in \mathcal{NP}$, CDP is also $\mathcal{NP}$-complete.

Theorem 11.2 CNF-satisfiability $\propto$ clique decision problem.

Proof: Let $F = \bigwedge_{1 \leq i \leq k} C_i$ be a propositional formula in CNF. Let x_i, $1 \leq i \leq n$, be the variables in F. We show how to construct from F a graph $G = (V, E)$ such that G has a clique of size at least k if and only if F is satisfiable. If the length of F is m, then G is obtainable from F in $O(m)$ time. Hence, if we have a polynomial time algorithm for CDP, then we can obtain a polynomial time algorithm for CNF-satisfiability using this construction.

For any F, $G = (V, E)$ is defined as follows: $V = \{\langle \sigma, i \rangle | \sigma$ is a literal in clause $C_i\}$ and $E = \{(\langle \sigma, i \rangle, \langle \delta, j \rangle) \mid i \neq j \text{ and } \sigma \neq \bar{\delta}\}$. A sample construction is given in Example 11.11.

Claim: F is satisfiable if and only if G has a clique of size $\geq k$.

Proof of Claim: If F is satisfiable, then there is a set of truth values for x_i, $1 \leq i \leq n$, such that each clause is true with this assignment. Thus, with this assignment there is at least one literal σ in each C_i such that σ is true. Let $S = \{\langle \sigma, i \rangle \mid \sigma \text{ is true in } C_i\}$ be a set containing exactly one $\langle \sigma, i \rangle$ for each i. Between any two nodes $\langle \sigma, i \rangle$ and $\langle \delta, j \rangle$ in S there is an edge in G, since $i \neq j$ and both σ and δ have the value true. Thus, S forms a clique in G of size k.

Similarly, if G has a clique $K = (V', E')$ of size at least k, then let $S = \{\langle \sigma, i \rangle \mid \langle \sigma, i \rangle \in V'\}$. Clearly, $|S| = k$ as G has no clique of size more than k. Furthermore, if $S' = \{\sigma \mid \langle \sigma, i \rangle \in S \text{ for some } i\}$, then S' cannot contain both a literal δ and its complement $\bar{\delta}$ as there is no edge connecting $\langle \delta, i \rangle$ and $\langle \bar{\delta}, j \rangle$ in G. Hence by setting x_i = true if $x_i \in S'$ and x_i = false if

$\bar{x}_i \in S'$ and choosing arbitrary truth values for variables not in S', we can satisfy all clauses in F. Hence, F is satisfiable iff G has a clique of size at least k. □

Example 11.11 Consider $F = (x_1 \vee x_2 \vee x_3) \wedge (\bar{x}_1 \vee \bar{x}_2 \vee \bar{x}_3)$. The construction of Theorem 11.2 yields the graph of Figure 11.4. This graph contains six cliques of size two. Consider the clique with vertices $\{\langle x_1, 1\rangle, \langle \bar{x}_2, 2\rangle\}$. By setting x_1 = true and $\bar{x}_2$ = true (that is, x_2 = false), F is satisfied. The x_3 may be set either to true or false. □

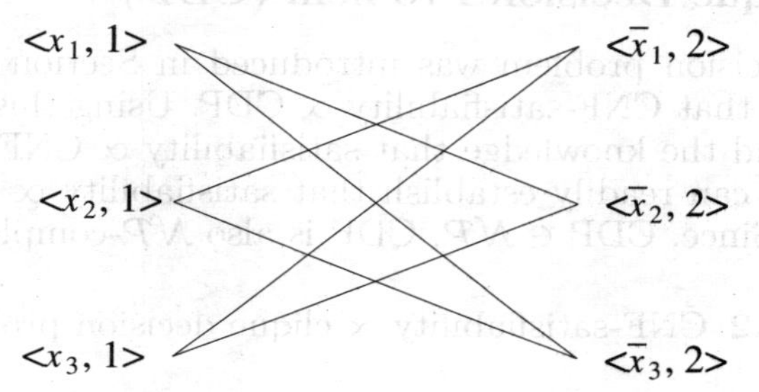

Figure 11.4 A sample graph and satisfiability

11.3.2 Node Cover Decision Problem (NCDP)

A set $S \subseteq V$ is a *node cover* for a graph $G = (V, E)$ if and only if all edges in E are incident to at least one vertex in S. The size $|S|$ of the cover is the number of vertices in S.

Example 11.12 Consider the graph of Figure 11.5. $S = \{2, 4\}$ is a node cover of size 2. $S = \{1, 3, 5\}$ is a node cover of size 3. □

In the node cover decision problem we are given a graph G and an integer k. We are required to determine whether G has a node cover of size at most k.

Theorem 11.3 The clique decision problem $\propto$ the node cover decision problem.

Proof: Let $G = (V, E)$ and k define an instance of CDP. Assume that $|V| = n$. We construct a graph G' such that G' has a node cover of size at

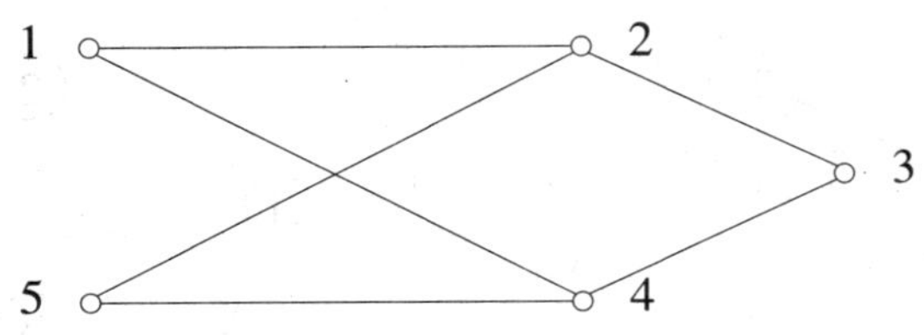

Figure 11.5 A sample graph and node cover

most $n - k$ if and only if G has a clique of size at least k. Graph G' is given by $G' = (V, \bar{E})$, where $\bar{E} = \{(u, v) \mid u \in V, v \in V \text{ and } (u, v) \notin E\}$. The set G' is known as the *complement* of G.

Now, we show that G has a clique of size at least k if and only if G' has a node cover of size at most $n - k$. Let K be any clique in G. Since there are no edges in $\bar{E}$ connecting vertices in K, the remaining $n - |K|$ vertices in G' must cover all edges in $\bar{E}$. Similarly, if S is a node cover of G', then $V - S$ must form a complete subgraph in G.

Since G' can be obtained from G in polynomial time, CDP can be solved in polynomial deterministic time if we have a polynomial time deterministic algorithm for NCDP. □

Example 11.13 Figure 11.6 shows a graph G and its complement G'. In this figure, G' has a node cover of $\{4, 5\}$, since every edge of G' is incident either on the node 4 or on the node 5. Thus, G has a clique of size $5 - 2 = 3$ consisting of the nodes $1, 2,$ and 3. □

Note that since CNF-satisfiability $\propto$ CDP, CDP $\propto$ NCDP and $\propto$ is transitive, it follows that NCDP is $\mathcal{NP}$-hard. NCDP is also in $\mathcal{NP}$ because we can nondeterministically choose a subset $C \subseteq V$ of size k and verify in polynomial time that C is a cover of G. So NCDP is $\mathcal{NP}$-complete.

11.3.3 Chromatic Number Decision Problem (CNDP)

A coloring of a graph $G = (V, E)$ is a function $f : V \rightarrow \{1, 2, \ldots, k\}$ defined for all $i \in V$. If $(u, v) \in E$, then $f(u) \neq f(v)$. The *chromatic number decision problem* is to determine whether G has a coloring for a given k.

Example 11.14 A possible 2-coloring of the graph of Figure 11.5 is $f(1) = f(3) = f(5) = 1$ and $f(2) = f(4) = 2$. Clearly, this graph has no 1-coloring. □

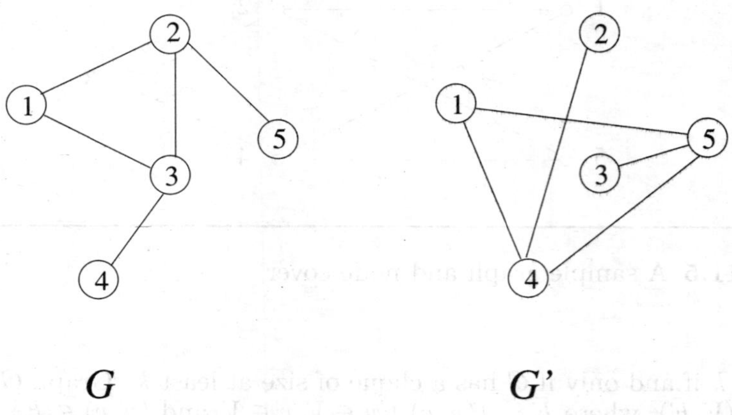

Figure 11.6 A graph and its complement

In proving CNDP to be $\mathcal{NP}$-hard, we shall make use of the $\mathcal{NP}$-hard problem SATY. This is the CNF-satisfiability problem with the restriction that each clause has at most three literals. The reduction CNF-satisfiability $\propto$ SATY is left as an exercise.

Theorem 11.4 Satisfiability with at most three literals per clause $\propto$ chromatic number decision problem.

Proof: Let F be a CNF formula having at most three literals per clause and having r clauses $C_1, C_2, \ldots, C_r$. Let x_i, $1 \leq i \leq n$, be the n variables in F. We can assume $n \geq 4$. If $n < 4$, then we can determine whether F is satisfiable by trying out all eight possible truth value assignments to x_1, x_2, and x_3. We construct, in polynomial time, a graph G that is $n+1$ colorable if and only if F is satisfiable. The graph $G = (V, E)$ is defined by

$$V = \{x_1, x_2, \ldots, x_n\} \cup \{\bar{x}_1, \bar{x}_2, \ldots, \bar{x}_n\} \cup \{y_1, y_2, \ldots, y_n\} \cup \{C_1, C_2, \ldots, C_r\}$$

where $y_1, y_2, \ldots, y_n$ are new variables, and

$$E = \{(x_i,\ \bar{x}_i), 1 \leq i \leq n\} \cup \{(y_i, y_j)|i \neq j\} \cup \{(y_i, x_j)|i \neq j\}$$
$$\cup \{(y_i, \bar{x}_j)|i \neq j\} \cup \{(x_i, C_j)|x_i \notin C_j\} \cup \{\bar{x}_i, C_j)|\bar{x}_i \notin C_j\}$$

To see that G is $n+1$ colorable if and only if F is satisfiable, we first observe that the y_i's form a complete subgraph on n vertices. Hence, each y_i

must be assigned a distinct color. Without loss of generality we can assume that in any coloring of G, y_i is given the color i. Since y_i is also connected to all the x_j's and $\bar{x}_j$'s except x_i and $\bar{x}_i$, the color i can be assigned to only x_i and $\bar{x}_i$. However, $(x_i, \bar{x}_i) \in E$ and so a new color, $n+1$, is needed for one of these vertices. The vertex that is assigned the new color $n+1$ is called a *false vertex.* The other vertex is a *true* vertex. The only way to color G using $n+1$ colors is to assign color $n+1$ to one of $\{x_i, \bar{x}_i\}$ for each i, $1 \leq i \leq n$.

Under what conditions can the remaining vertices be colored using no new colors? Since $n \geq 4$ and each clause has at most three literals, each C_i is adjacent to a pair of vertices $x_j, \bar{x}_j$ for at least one j. Consequently, no C_i can be assigned the color $n+1$. Also, no C_i can be assigned a color corresponding to an x_j or $\bar{x}_j$ not in clause C_i. The last two statements imply that the only colors that can be assigned to C_i correspond to vertices x_j or $\bar{x}_j$ that are in clause C_i and are true vertices. Hence, G is $n+1$ colorable if and only if there is a true vertex corresponding to each C_i. So, G is $n+1$ colorable iff F is satisfiable. □

11.3.4 Directed Hamiltonian Cycle (DHC) (*)

A directed Hamiltonian cycle in a directed graph $G = (V, E)$ is a directed cycle of length $n = |V|$. So, the cycle goes through every vertex exactly once and then returns to the starting vertex. The DHC problem is to determine whether G has a directed Hamiltonian cycle.

Example 11.15 1, 2, 3, 4, 5, 1 is a directed Hamiltonian cycle in the graph of Figure 11.7. If the edge $\langle 5, 1\rangle$ is deleted from this graph, then it has no directed Hamiltonian cycle. □

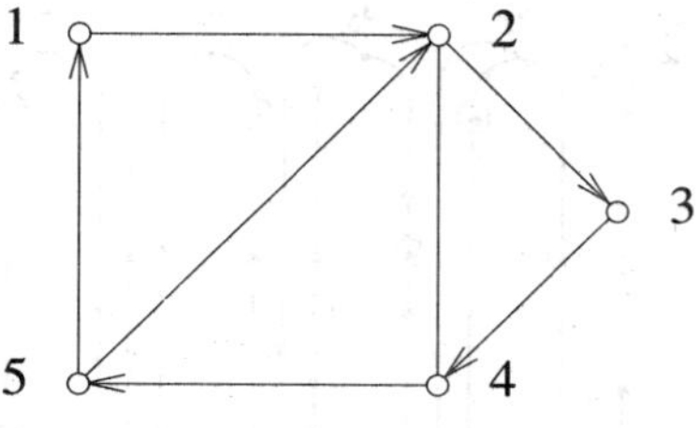

Figure 11.7 A sample graph and Hamiltonian cycle

Theorem 11.5 CNF-satisfiability $\propto$ directed Hamiltonian cycle.

Proof: Let F be a propositional formula in CNF. We show how to construct a directed graph G such that F is satisfiable if and only if G has a directed Hamiltonian cycle. Since this construction can be carried out in time polynomial in the size of F, it will follow that CNF-satisfiability $\propto$ DHC. Understanding the construction of G is greatly facilitated by the use of an example. The example we use is $F = C_1 \wedge C_2 \wedge C_3 \wedge C_4$, where

$$\begin{aligned} C_1 &= x_1 \vee \bar{x}_2 \vee x_4 \vee \bar{x}_5 \\ C_2 &= \bar{x}_1 \vee x_2 \vee x_3 \\ C_3 &= \bar{x}_1 \vee \bar{x}_3 \vee x_5 \\ C_4 &= \bar{x}_1 \vee \bar{x}_2 \vee \bar{x}_3 \vee x_4 \vee \bar{x}_5 \end{aligned}$$

Assume that F has r clauses $C_1, C_2, \ldots, C_r$ and n variables $x_1, x_2, \ldots, x_n$. Draw an array with r rows and $2n$ columns. Row i denotes clause C_i. Each variable x_i is represented by two adjacent columns, one for each of the literals x_i and $\bar{x}_i$. Figure 11.8 shows the array for the example formula. Insert a $\odot$ into column x_i and row C_j if and only if x_i is a literal in C_j. Insert a $\odot$ into column $\bar{x}_i$ and row C_j if and only if $\bar{x}_i$ is a literal in C_j. Between each pair of columns x_i and $\bar{x}_i$ introduce two vertices u_i and v_i, u_i at the top and v_i at the bottom of the column. For each i, draw two chains of edges upward from v_i to u_i, one connecting together all $\odot$s in column x_i and the other connecting all $\odot$s in column $\bar{x}_i$ (see Figure 11.8). Now, draw edges $\langle u_i, v_{i+1}\rangle$, $1 \le i < n$. Introduce a box $\boxed{\text{i}}$ at the right end of each row C_i, $1 \le i < r$. Draw the edges $\langle u_n, \boxed{1}\rangle$ and $\langle \boxed{\text{r}}, v_1\rangle$. Draw edges $\langle \boxed{\text{i}}, \boxed{\text{i+1}}\rangle$, $1 \le i < r$ (see Figure 11.8).

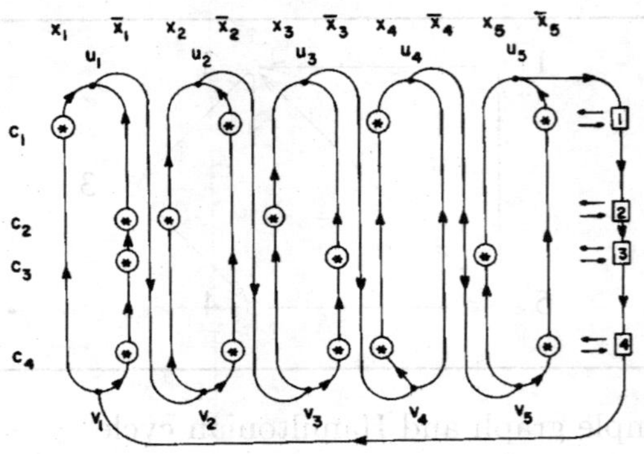

Figure 11.8 Array structure for the formula in Theorem 11.5

To complete the graph, we replace each $\odot$ and $\boxed{i}$ by a subgraph. Each $\odot$ is replaced by the subgraph of Figure 11.9(a) (of course, unique vertex labelings are needed for each copy of the subgraph). Each box $\boxed{i}$ is replaced by the subgraph of Figure 11.10. In this subgraph A_i is an entrance node and B_i an exit node. The edges $\langle \boxed{i}, \boxed{i+1} \rangle$ referred to earlier are really $\langle B_i, A_{i+1}\rangle$. Edge $\langle u_n, \boxed{1} \rangle$ is $\langle u_n, A_1\rangle$ and $\langle \boxed{r}, v_1\rangle$ is $\langle B_r, v_1\rangle$. The variable j_i is the number of literals in clause C_i. In the subgraph of Figure 11.10 an edge of the type shown in Figure 11.11 indicates a connection to a $\odot$ subgraph in row C_i. $R_{i,a}$ is connected to the 1 vertex of the $\odot$ and $R_{i,a+1}$ (or $R_{i,1}$ if $a = j_i$) is entered from the 3 vertex.

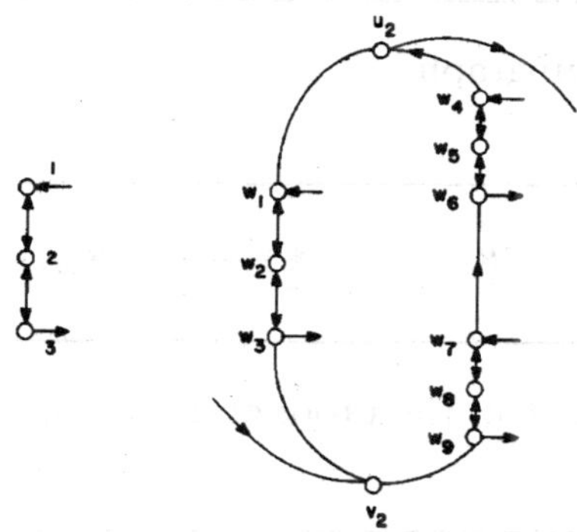

Figure 11.9 The $\odot$ subgraph and its insertion into column 2

Thus in the $\odot$ subgraph (shown in Figure 11.12) of Figure 11.9(b) w_1 and w_3 are the 1 and 3 vertices respectively. The incoming edge is $\langle R_{i,1}, w_1\rangle$ and the outgoing edge is $\langle w_3, R_{i,2}\rangle$. This completes the construction of G.

If F is satisfiable, then let S be an assignment of truth values for which F is true. A Hamiltonian cycle for G can start at v_1 and go to u_1, then to v_2, then to u_2, then to v_3, then to $u_3, \ldots$, and then to u_n. In going from v_i to u_i, this cycle uses the column corresponding to x_i if x_i is true in S. Otherwise it goes up the column corresponding to $\bar{x}_i$. From u_n this cycle goes to A_1 and then through $R_{1,1}, R_{1,2}, R_{1,3}, \ldots, R_{1,j_i}$, and B_1 to A_2 to $\cdots$ to v_1. In going from $R_{i,a}$ to $R_{i,a+1}$ in any subgraph $\boxed{i}$, a diversion is made to a $\odot$ subgraph in row i if and only if the vertices of that $\odot$ subgraph are not already on the path from v_i to $R_{i,a}$. Note that if C_i has i_j literals, then the construction of $\boxed{i}$ allows a diversion to at most $i_j - 1$ $\odot$ subgraphs. This is adequate as at least one $\odot$ subgraph must already have been traversed

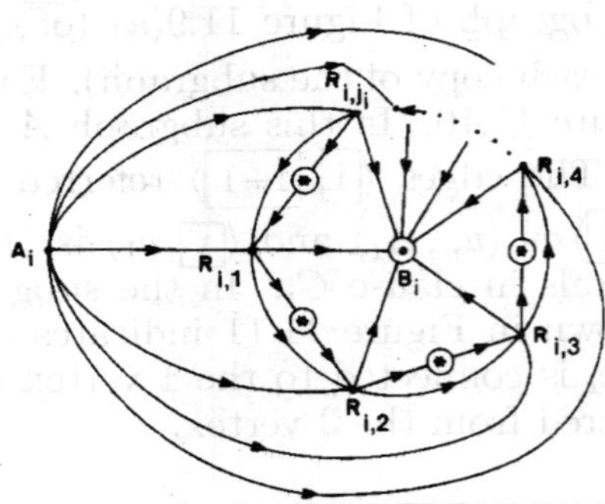

Figure 11.10 The H_i subgraph

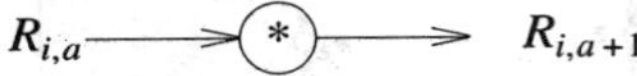

Figure 11.11 A construct in the proof of Theorem 11.5

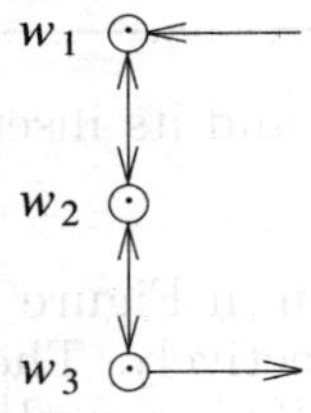

Figure 11.12 Another construct in the proof of Theorem 11.5

in row C_i (because at least one such subgraph must correspond to a true literal). So, if F is satisfiable, then G has a directed Hamiltonian cycle.

It remains to show that if G has a directed Hamiltonian cycle, then F is satisfiable. This can be seen by starting at vertex v_1 on any Hamiltonian cycle for G. Because of the construction of the $\odot$ and $\boxed{\text{i}}$ subgraphs, such a cycle must proceed by going up exactly one column of each pair $(x_i, \bar{x}_i)$.

In addition, this part of the cycle must traverse at least one $\odot$ subgraph in each row. Hence the columns used in going from v_i to u_i, $1 \leq i \leq n$, define a truth assignment for which F is true.

We conclude that F is satisfiable if and only if G has a Hamiltonian cycle. The theorem now follows from the observation that G can be obtained from F in polynomial time. □

11.3.5 Traveling Salesperson Decision Problem (TSP)

The traveling salesperson problem was introduced in Chapter 5. The corresponding decision problem is to determine whether a complete directed graph $G = (V, E)$ with edge costs $c(u, v)$ has a tour of cost at most M.

Theorem 11.6 Directed Hamiltonian cycle (DHC) $\propto$ the traveling salesperson decision problem (TSP).

Proof: From the directed graph $G = (V, E)$ construct the complete directed graph $G' = (V, E')$, $E' = \{\langle i, j \rangle \mid i \neq j\}$ and $c(i, j) = 1$ if $\langle i, j \rangle \in E$; $c(i, j) = 2$ if $i \neq j$ and $\langle i, j \rangle \notin E$. Clearly, G' has a tour of cost at most n iff G has a directed Hamiltonian cycle. □

11.3.6 AND/OR Graph Decision Problem (AOG)

Many complex problems can be broken down into a series of subproblems such that the solution of all or some of these results in the solution of the original problem. These subproblems can be broken down further into sub-subproblems, and so on, until the only problems remaining are sufficiently primitive as to be trivially solvable. This breaking down of a complex problem into several subproblems can be represented by a directed graphlike structure in which nodes represent problems and descendents of nodes represent the subproblems associated with them.

Example 11.16 The graph of Figure 11.13(a) represents a problem A that can be solved by solving either both the subproblems B and C or the single subproblem D or E. □

Groups of subproblems that must be solved in order to imply a solution to the parent node are joined together by an arc going across the respective edges (as the arc across the edges $\langle A, B\rangle$ and $\langle A, C\rangle$). By introducing dummy nodes in Figure 11.13(b), all nodes can be made to be such that their solution requires either all descendents to be solved or only one descendent to be solved. Nodes of the first type are called AND nodes and those of the latter type OR nodes. Nodes A and A'' of Figure 11.13(b) are OR nodes whereas node A' is an AND node. The AND nodes are drawn with an arc across all edges leaving the node. Nodes with no descendents are called *terminal*.

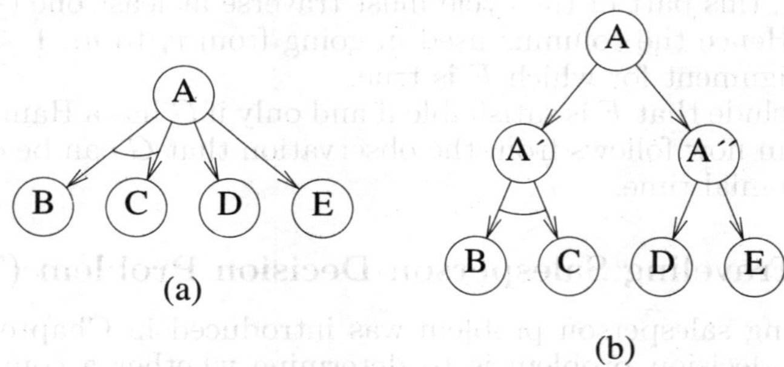

Figure 11.13 Graphs representing problems

Terminal nodes represent primitive problems and are marked either solvable or not solvable. Solvable terminal nodes are represented by rectangles. An AND/OR graph need not always be a tree.

Breaking down a problem into several subproblems is known as *problem reduction*. Problem reduction has been used on such problems as theorem proving, symbolic integration, and analysis of industrial schedules. When problem reduction is used, two different problems may generate a common subproblem. In this case it may be desirable to have only one node representing the subproblem (this would imply that the subproblem is to be solved only once). Figure 11.14 shows two AND/OR graphs for cases in which this is done.

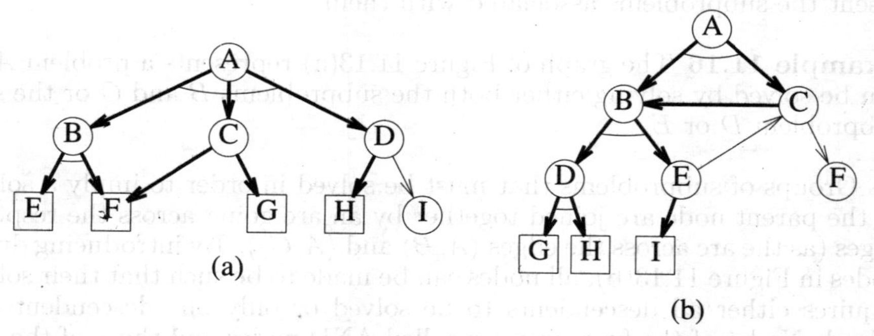

Figure 11.14 Two AND/OR graphs that are not trees

Note that the graph is no longer a tree. Furthermore, such graphs may have directed cycles as in Figure 11.14(b). The presence of a directed cycle does not in itself imply the unsolvability of the problem. In fact, problem A of Figure 11.14(b) can be solved by solving the primitive problems G, H, and I. This leads to the solution of D and E and hence of B and C. A *solution graph* is a subgraph of solvable nodes that shows that the problem is solved. Possible solution graphs for the graphs of Figure 11.14 are shown by heavy edges.

Let us assume that there is a cost associated with each edge in the AND/OR graph. The *cost* of a solution graph H of an AND/OR graph G is the sum of the costs of the edges in H. The *AND/OR graph decision problem* (AOG) is to determine whether G has a solution graph of cost at most k, for k a given input.

Example 11.17 Consider the directed graph of Figure 11.15. The problem to be solved is P_1. To do this, one can solve node P_2, P_3, or P_7, as P_1 is an OR node. The cost incurred is then either 2, 2, or 8 (i.e., cost in addition to that of solving one of P_2, P_3, or P_7). To solve P_2, both P_4 and P_5 have to be solved, as P_2 is an AND node. The total cost to do this is 2. To solve P_3, we can solve either P_5 or P_6. The minimum cost to do this is 1. Node P_7 is free. In this example, then, the optimal way to solve P_1 is to solve P_6 first, then P_3, and finally P_1. The total cost for this solution is 3. □

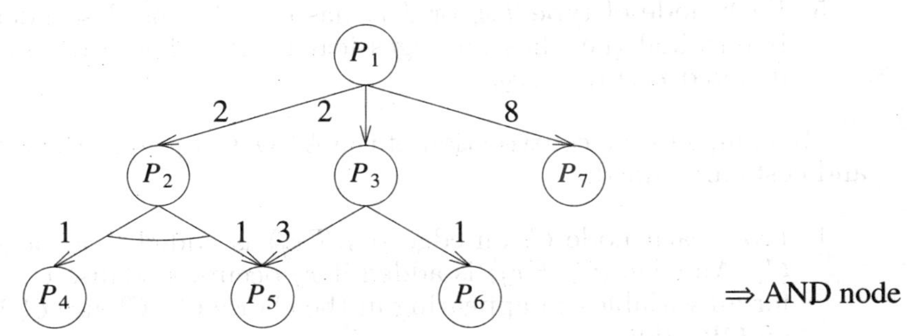

Figure 11.15 AND/OR graph

Theorem 11.7 CNF-satisfiability $\propto$ the AND/OR graph decision problem.

Proof: Let P be a propositional formula in CNF. We show how to transform a formula P in CNF into an AND/OR graph such that the AND/OR graph so obtained has a certain minimum cost solution if and only if P is satisfiable. Let

$$P = \bigwedge_{i=1}^{k} C_i, \quad C_i = \bigvee l_j$$

where the l_j's are literals. The variables of P, $V(P)$ are $x_1, x_2, \ldots, x_n$. The AND/OR graph will have nodes as follows:

1. There is a special node S with no incoming arcs. This node represents the problem to be solved.

2. The node S is an AND node with descendent nodes $P, x_1, x_2, \ldots, x_n$.

3. Each node x_i represents the corresponding variable x_i in the formula P. Each x_i is an OR node with two descendents denoted Tx_i and Fx_i respectively. If Tx_i is solved, then this will correspond to assigning a truth value of true to the variable x_i. Solving node Fx_i will correspond to assigning a truth value of false to x_i.

4. The node P represents the formula P and is an AND node. It has k descendents $C_1, C_2, \ldots, C_k$. Node C_i corresponds to the clause C_i in the formula P. The nodes C_i are OR nodes.

5. Each node of type Tx_i or Fx_i has exactly one descendent node that is terminal (i.e., has no edges leaving it). These terminal nodes are denoted $v_1, v_2, \ldots, v_{2n}$.

To complete the construction of the AND/OR graph, the following edges and costs are added:

1. From each node C_i an edge $\langle C_i, Tx_j \rangle$ is added if x_j occurs in clause C_i. An edge $\langle C_i, Fx_j \rangle$ is added if $\bar{x}_j$ occurs in clause C_i. This is done for all variables x_j appearing in the clause C_i. Clause C_i is designated an OR node.

2. Edges from nodes of type Tx_i or Fx_i to their respective terminal nodes are assigned a weight, or cost of 1.

3. All other edges have a cost of 0.

In order to solve S, each of the nodes $P, x_1, x_2, \ldots, x_n$ must be solved. Solving nodes $x_1, x_2, \cdots, x_n$ costs n. To solve P, we must solve all the nodes $C_1, C_2, \ldots, C_k$. The cost of a node C_i is at most 1. However, if one of its descendent nodes was solved while solving the nodes $x_1, x_2, \ldots, x_n$, then the additional cost to solve C_i is 0, as the edges to its descendent nodes have cost 0 and one of its descendents has already been solved. That is, a node C_i can be solved at no cost if one of the literals occurring in the clause C_i has been assigned a value of true. From this it follows that the entire graph (that is, node S) can be solved at a cost n if there is some assignment of truth values to the x_i's such that at least one literal in each clause is true under that assignment, i.e., if the formula P is satisfiable. If P is not satisfiable, then the cost is more than n.

We have now shown how to construct an AND/OR graph from a formula P such that the AND/OR graph so constructed has a solution of cost n if and only if P is satisfiable. Otherwise the cost is more than n. The construction clearly takes only polynomial time. This completes the proof. □

Example 11.18 Consider the formula

$$P = (x_1 \vee x_2 \vee x_3) \wedge (\bar{x}_1 \vee \bar{x}_2 \vee x_3) \wedge (\bar{x}_1 \vee x_2); \quad V(P) = x_1, x_2, x_3; \quad n = 3$$

Figure 11.16 shows the AND/OR graph obtained by applying the construction of Theorem 11.7.

The nodes Tx_1, Tx_2, and Tx_3 can be solved at a total cost of 3. The node P costs nothing extra. The node S can then be solved by solving all its descendent nodes and the nodes Tx_1, Tx_2, and Tx_3. The total cost for this solution is 3 (which is n). Assigning the truth value of true to the variables of P results in P's being true. □

EXERCISES

1. Let SATY be the problem of determining whether a propositional formula in CNF having at most three literals per clause is satisfiable. Show that CNF-satisfiability $\propto$ SATY. *Hint*: Show how to write a clause with more than three literals as the **and** of several clauses each containing at most three literals. For this you have to introduce some new variables. Any assignment that satisfies the original clause must satisfy all the new clauses created.

2. Let SAT3 be similar to SATY (Exercise 1) except that each clause has exactly three literals. Show that SATY $\propto$ SAT3.

3. Let F be a propositional formula in CNF. Two literals x and y in F are *compatible* if and only if they are not in the same clause and $x \neq \bar{y}$. The literals x and y are *incompatible* if and only if x and y are not compatible. Let SATINC be the problem of determining whether a formula F in which each literal is incompatible with at most three other literals is satisfiable. Show that SAT3 $\propto$ SATINC.

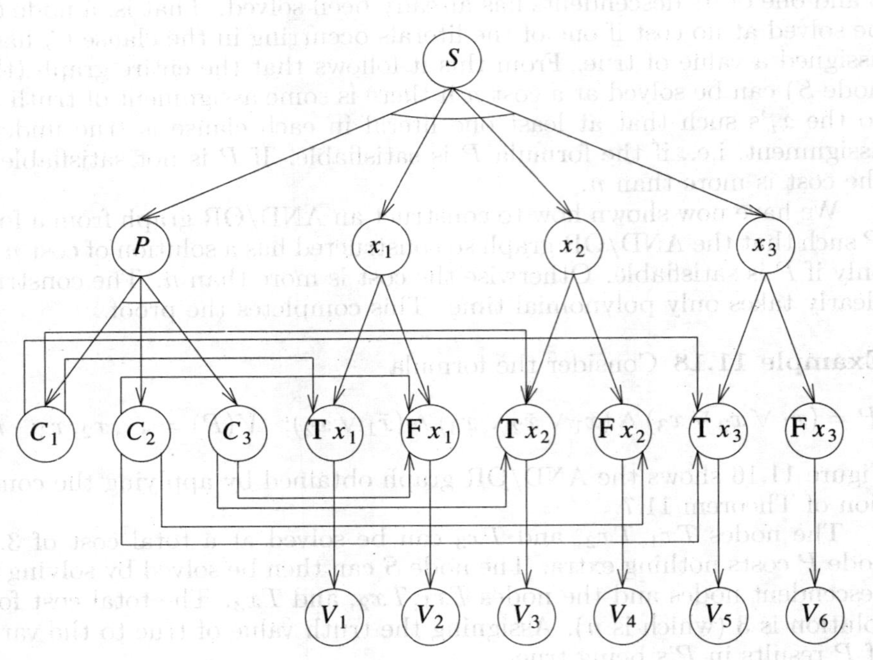

Figure 11.16 AND/OR graph for Example 11.18

4. Let 3-NODE COVER be the node cover decision problem of Section 11.3 restricted to graphs of degree 3. Show that SATINC $\propto$ 3-NODE COVER (see Exercise 3).

5. [Feedback node set]

   (a) Let $G = (V, E)$ be a directed graph. Let $S \subseteq V$ be a subset of vertices such that the deletion of S and all edges incident to vertices in S results in a graph G' with no directed cycles. Such an

S is a feedback node set. The size of S is the number of vertices in S. The feedback node set decision problem (FNS) is to determine for a given input k whether G has a feedback node set of size at most k. Show that the node cover decision problem $\propto$ FNS.

(b) Write a polynomial time nondeterministic algorithm for FNS.

6. [Feedback arc set] Let $G = (V, E)$ be a directed graph. $S \subseteq E$ is a feed back arc set of G if and only if every directed cycle in G contains an edge in S. The feedback arc set decision problem (FAS) is to determine whether G has a feedback arc set of size at most k.

   (a) Show that the node cover decision problem $\propto$ FAS.

   (b) Write a polynomial time nondeterministic algorithm for FAS.

7. The feedback node set optimization problem is to find a minimum feedback node set (see Exercise 5). Show that this problem reduces to FNS.

8. Show that the feedback arc set minimization problem reduces to FAS (Exercise 6).

9. [Hamiltonian cycle] Let UHC be the problem of determining whether in any given undirected graph G, there exists an undirected cycle going through each vertex exactly once and returning to the start vertex. Show that DHC $\propto$ UHC (DHC is defined in Section 11.3).

10. Show UHC $\propto$ CNF-satisfiability.

11. Show DHC $\propto$ CNF-satisfiability.

12. [Hamiltonian path] An i to j Hamiltonian path in graph G is a path from vertex i to vertex j that includes each vertex exactly once. Show that UHC is reducible to the problem of determining whether G has an i to j Hamiltonian path.

13. [Minimum equivalent graph] A directed graph $G = (V, E)$ is an equivalent graph of the directed graph $G' = (V, E')$ if and only if $E \subseteq E'$ and the transitive closures of G and G' are the same. G is a minimum equivalent graph if and only if $|E|$ is minimum among all equivalent graphs of G'. The minimum equivalent graph decision problem (MEG) is to determine whether G' has a minimum equivalent graph with $|E| \leq k$, where k is some given input.

    (a) Show that DHC $\propto$ MEG.

    (b) Write a nondeterministic polynomial time algorithm for MEG.

14. [Clique cover] The clique cover decision problem (CC) is to determine whether G is the union of l or fewer cliques. Show that the chromatic number decision problem $\propto$ CC.

15. [Set cover] Let $F = \{S_j\}$ be a finite family of sets. Let $T \subseteq F$ be a subset of F. T is a cover of F iff

$$\bigcup_{S_i \in T} S_i = \bigcup_{S_i \in F} S_i$$

The set cover decision problem is to determine whether F has a cover T containing no more than k sets. Show that the node cover decision problem is reducible to this problem.

16. [Exact cover] Let $F = \{S_j\}$ be as in Exercise 15. $T \subseteq F$ is an exact cover of F iff T is a cover of F and the sets in T are pairwise disjoint. Show that the chromatic number decision problem reduces to the problem of determining whether F has an exact cover.

17. Show that SAT3 $\propto$ EXACT COVER (see Exercise 16).

18. [Hitting set] Let F be as in Exercise 16. The hitting set problem is to determine whether there exists a set H such that $|H \cap S_j| = 1$ for all $S_j \in F$. Show that exact cover $\propto$ hitting set.

19. [Tautology] A propositional formula is a tautology if and only if it is true for all possible truth assignments to its variables. The tautology problem is to determine whether a DNF formula is a tautology.

    (a) Show that CNF-satisfiability $\propto$ DNF tautology.

    (b) Write a polynomial time nondeterministic algorithm TAUT(F) that terminates successfully if and only if F is not a tautology.

20. [Minimum boolean form] Let the length of a propositional formula be equal to the sum of the number of literals in each clause. Two formulas F and G on variables $x_1, \ldots, x_n$ are equivalent if for all assignments to $x_1, \ldots, x_n$, F is true if and only if G is true. Show that deciding whether F has an equivalent formula of length no more than k is $\mathcal{NP}$-hard. (*Hint*: Show DNF tautology reduces to this problem.)

11.4 $\mathcal{NP}$-HARD SCHEDULING PROBLEMS

To prove the results of this section, we need to use the $\mathcal{NP}$-hard problem called *partition*. This problem requires us to decide whether a given multiset $A = \{a_1, a_2, \ldots, a_n\}$ of n positive integers has a partition P such that $\sum_{i \in P} a_i = \sum_{i \notin P} a_i$. We can show this problem is $\mathcal{NP}$-hard by first showing the sum of subsets problem (Chapter 7) to be $\mathcal{NP}$-hard. Recall that in the sum of subsets problem we have to determine whether $A = \{a_1, a_2, \ldots, a_n\}$ has a subset S that sums to a given integer M.

Theorem 11.8 Exact cover $\propto$ sum of subsets.

Proof: The exact cover problem is shown $\mathcal{NP}$-hard in Section 11.3, Exercise 16. In this problem we are given a family of sets $F = \{S_1, S_2, \ldots, S_k\}$ and are required to determine whether there is a subset $T \subseteq F$ of disjoint sets such that

$$\bigcup_{S_i \in T} S_i = \bigcup_{S_i \in F} S_i = \{u_1, u_2, \ldots, u_n\}$$

From any given instance of this problem, construct the sum of subsets problem $A = \{a_1, \ldots, a_k\}$ with $a_j = \sum_{1 \le i \le n} \epsilon_{ji}(k+1)^{i-1}$, where $\epsilon_{ji} = 1$ if $u_i \in S_j$ and $\epsilon_{ji} = 0$ otherwise, and $M = \sum_{0 \le i < n}(k+1)^i = ((k+1)^n - 1)/k$. Clearly, F has an exact cover if and only if $A = \{a_1, \ldots, a_k\}$ has a subset with sum M. Since A and M can be constructed from F in polynomial time, exact cover $\propto$ sum of subsets. □

Theorem 11.9 Sum of subsets $\propto$ partition.

Proof: Let $A = \{a_1, \ldots, a_n\}$ and M define an instance of the sum of subsets problem. Construct the set $B = \{b_1, b_2 \ldots, b_{n+2}\}$ with $b_i = a_i$, $1 \le i \le n$, $b_{n+1} = M + 1$, and $b_{n+2} = (\sum_{1 \le i \le n} a_i) + 1 - M$. B has a partition if and only if A has a subset with sum M. Since B can be obtained from A and M in polynomial time, sum of subsets $\propto$ partition. □

One can easily show partition $\propto$ 0/1-knapsack and partition $\propto$ job sequencing with deadlines. Hence, these problems are also $\mathcal{NP}$-hard.

11.4.1 Scheduling Identical Processors

Let P_i, $1 \le i \le m$, be m identical processors (or machines). The P_i could, for example, be line printers in a computer output room. Let J_i, $1 \le i \le n$, be n jobs. Job J_i requires t_i processing time. A schedule S is an assignment of jobs to processors. For each job J_i, S specifies the time intervals and the processor(s) on which this job is to be processed. A job cannot be processed by more than one processor at any given time. Let f_i be the time at which the processing of job J_i is completed. The *mean finish time* (MFT) of schedule S is

$$\text{MFT}(S) = \frac{1}{n} \sum_{1 \le i \le n} f_i$$

Let w_i be a weight associated with each job J_i. The *weighted mean finish time* (WMFT) of schedule S is

$$\text{WMFT}(S) = \frac{1}{n} \sum_{1 \le i \le n} w_i f_i$$

Let T_i be the time at which P_i finishes processing all jobs (or job segments) assigned to it. The *finish time* (FT) of S is

$$\text{FT}(S) = \max_{1 \le i \le m} \{T_i\}$$

Schedule S is a *nonpreemptive schedule* if and only if each job J_i is processed continuously from start to finish on the same processor. In a *preemptive* schedule each job need not be processed continuously to completion on one processor.

At this point it is worth noting the similarity between the optimal tape storage problem of Section 4.7 and nonpreemptive schedules. Mean retrieval time, weighted mean retrieval time, and maximum retrieval time respectively correspond to mean finish time, weighted mean finish time, and finish time. Minimum finish time schedules can therefore be obtained using the algorithm developed in Section 4.7. Obtaining minimum weighted mean finish time and minimum finish time nonpreemptive schedules is $\mathcal{NP}$-hard.

Theorem 11.10 Partition $\propto$ minimum finish time nonpreemptive schedule.

Proof: We prove this for $m = 2$. The extension to $m > 2$ is trivial. Let a_i, $1 \le i \le n$, be an instance of the partition problem. Define n jobs with processing requirements $t_i = a_i$, $1 \le i \le n$. There is a nonpreemptive schedule for this set of jobs on two processors with finish time at most $\sum t_i/2$ iff there is a partition of the a_i's. □

Example 11.19 Consider the following input to the partition problem: $a_1 = 2, a_2 = 5, a_3 = 6, a_4 = 7$, and $a_5 = 10$. The corresponding minimum finish time nonpreemptive schedule problem has the input $t_1 = 2, t_2 = 5, t_3 = 6, t_4 = 7$, and $t_5 = 10$. There is a nonpreemptive schedule for this set of jobs with finish time 15: P_1 takes the jobs t_2 and t_5; P_2 takes the jobs t_1, t_3, and t_4. This solution yields a solution for the partition problem also: $\{a_2, a_5\}, \{a_1, a_3, a_4\}$. □

Theorem 11.11 Partition $\propto$ minimum WMFT nonpreemptive schedule.

Proof: Once again we prove this for $m = 2$ only. The extension to $m > 2$ is trivial. Let a_i, $1 \le i \le n$, define an instance of the partition problem. Construct a two-processor scheduling problem with n jobs and $w_i = t_i = a_i$,

$1 \leq i \leq n$. For this set of jobs there is a nonpreemptive schedule S with weighted mean flow time at most $1/2\sum a_i^2 + 1/4(\sum a_i)^2$ if and only if the a_i's have a partition. To see this, let the weights and times of jobs on P_1 be $(\bar{w}_1, \bar{t}_1), \ldots, (\bar{w}_k, \bar{t}_k)$ and on P_2 be $(\bar{\bar{w}}_1, \bar{\bar{t}}_1), \ldots, (\bar{\bar{w}}_l, \bar{\bar{t}}_l)$. Assume this is the order in which the jobs are processed on their respective processors. Then, for this schedule S we have

$$\begin{aligned} n * \text{WMFT}(S) &= \bar{w}_1\bar{t}_1 + \bar{w}_2(\bar{t}_1 + \bar{t}_2) + \cdots + \bar{w}_k(\bar{t}_1 + \cdots \bar{t}_k) \\ &\quad + \bar{\bar{w}}_1\bar{\bar{t}}_1 + \bar{\bar{w}}_2(\bar{\bar{t}}_1 + \bar{\bar{t}}_2) + \cdots + \bar{\bar{w}}_l(\bar{\bar{t}}_1 + \cdots \bar{\bar{t}}_l) \\ &= \tfrac{1}{2}\sum w_i^2 + \tfrac{1}{2}(\sum \bar{w}_i)^2 + \tfrac{1}{2}(\sum w_i - \sum \bar{w}_i)^2 \end{aligned}$$

Thus, $n * \text{WMFT}(S) \geq (1/2)\sum w_i^2 + (1/4)(\sum w_i)^2$. This value is obtainable iff the w_i's (and so also the a_i's) have a partition. □

Example 11.20 Consider again the partition problem $a_1 = 2, a_2 = 5, a_3 = 6, a_4 = 7$, and $a_5 = 10$. Here, $\frac{1}{2}\sum a_i^2 = \frac{1}{2}(2^2 + 5^2 + 6^2 + 7^2 + 10^2) = 107$, $\sum a_i = 30$, and $\frac{1}{4}(\sum a_i)^2 = 225$. Thus, $1/2\sum a_i^2 + 1/4(\sum a_i)^2 = 107 + 225 = 332$. The corresponding minimum WMFT nonpreemptive schedule problem has the input $w_i = t_i = a_i$ for $1 \leq i \leq 5$. If we assign the jobs t_2 and t_5 to P_1 and the remaining jobs to P_2,

$$n * \text{WFMT}(S) = 5 * 5 + 10(5 + 10) + 2 * 2 + 6(2 + 6) + 7(2 + 6 + 7) = 332$$

The same also yields a solution to the partition problem. □

11.4.2 Flow Shop Scheduling

We shall use the flow shop terminology developed in Section 5.10. When $m = 2$, minimum finish time schedules can be obtained in $O(n \log n)$ time if n jobs are to be scheduled. When $m = 3$, obtaining minimum finish time schedules (whether preemptive or nonpreemptive) is $\mathcal{NP}$-hard. For the case of nonpreemptive schedules this is easy to see (Exercise 2). We prove the result for preemptive schedules. The proof we give is also valid for the nonpreemptive case. However, a much simpler proof exists for the nonpreemptive case.

Theorem 11.12 Partition $\propto$ the minimum finish time preemptive flow shop schedule ($m > 2$).

Proof: We use only three processors. Let $A = \{a_1, a_2, \ldots, a_n\}$ define an instance of the partition problem. Construct the following preemptive flow shop instance FS, with $n+2$ jobs, $m = 3$ machines, and at most 2 nonzero tasks per job:

$$t_{1,i} = a_i; \quad t_{2,i} = 0; \quad t_{3,i} = a_i, 1 \le i \le n$$

$$t_{1,n+1} = T/2; \quad t_{2,n+1} = T; \quad t_{3,n+1} = 0$$

$$t_{1,n+2} = 0; \quad t_{2,n+2} = T; \quad t_{3,n+2} = T/2$$

$$\text{where } T = \sum_{1}^{n} a_i$$

We now show that the preceding flow shop instance has a preemptive schedule with finish time at most $2T$ if and only if A has a partition.

1. If A has a partition u, then there is a nonpreemptive schedule with finish time $2T$. One such schedule is shown in Figure 11.17.
2. If A has no partition, then all preemptive schedules for FS must have a finish time greater than $2T$. This can be shown by contradiction. Assume that there is preemptive schedule for FS with finish time at most $2T$. We make the following observations regarding this schedule:
   (a) Task $t_{1,n+1}$ must finish by time T as $t_{2,n+1} = T$ and cannot start until $t_{1,n+1}$ finishes.
   (b) Task $t_{3,n+2}$ cannot start before T units of time have elapsed as $t_{2,n+2} = T$.

Observation (a) implies that only $T/2$ of the first T time units are free on processor one. Let V be the set of indices of tasks completed on processor 1 by time T (excluding task $t_{1,n+1}$). Then,

$$\sum_{i \in V} t_{1,i} < T/2$$

as A has no partition. Hence

$$\sum_{\substack{i \notin V \\ 1 \le i \le n}} t_{3,i} > T/2$$

The processing of jobs not included in V cannot commence on processor 3 until after time T since their processor 1 processing is not completed until after T. This together with observation (b) implies that the total amount of processing left for processor 3 at time T is

$$t_{3,n+2} + \sum_{\substack{i \notin V \\ 1 \le i \le n}} t_{3,i} > T$$

The schedule length must therefore be more than $2T$. □

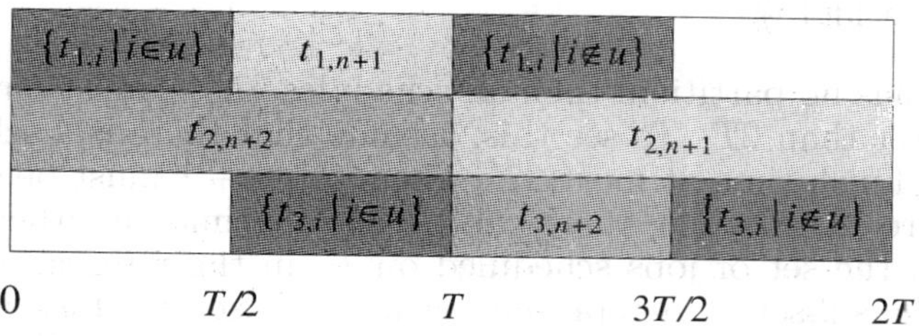

Figure 11.17 A possible schedule

11.4.3 Job Shop Scheduling

A job shop, like a flow shop, has m different processors. The n jobs to be scheduled require the completion of several tasks. The time of the jth task for job J_i is $t_{k,i,j}$. Task j is to be performed on processor P_k. The tasks for any job J_i are to be carried out in the order $1, 2, 3, \ldots$, and so on. Task j cannot begin until task $j-1$ (if $j > 1$) has been completed. Note that it is quite possible for a job to have many tasks that are to be performed on the same processor. In a nonpreemptive schedule, a task once begun is processed without interruption until it is completed. The definitions of FT(S) and MFT(S) extend to this problem in a natural way. Obtaining either a minimum finish time preemptive schedule or a minimum finish time nonpreemptive schedule is $\mathcal{NP}$-hard even when $m = 2$. The proof for the nonpreemptive case is very simple (use partition). We present the proof for the preemptive case. This proof will also be valid for the nonpreemptive case but will not be the simplest proof for this case.

Theorem 11.13 Partition $\propto$ minimum finish time preemptive job shop schedule ($m > 1$).

Proof: We use only two processors. Let $A = \{a_1, a_2, \ldots, a_n\}$ define an instance of the partition problem. Construct the following job shop instance JS, with $n+1$ jobs and $m = 2$ processors.

$$\begin{array}{ll} \text{Jobs } 1, \ldots, n: & t_{1,i,1} = t_{2,i,2} = a_i \ \text{ for } 1 \le i \le n \\ \text{Job } n+1: & t_{2,n+1,1} = t_{1,n+1,2} = t_{2,n+1,3} = t_{1,n+1,4} = T/2 \end{array}$$

$$\text{where } T = \sum_{1}^{n} a_i$$

We show that the job shop problem has a preemptive schedule with finish time at most $2T$ if and only if S has a partition.

1. If A has a partition, u then there is a schedule with finish time $2T$ (see Figure 11.18).

2. If A has no partition, then all schedules for JS must have a finish time greater than $2T$. To see this, assume that there is a schedule S for JS with finish time at most $2T$. Then, job $n+1$ must be scheduled as in Figure 11.18. Also, there can be no idle time on either P_1 or P_2. Let R be the set of jobs scheduled on P_1 in the interval $[0, T/2]$. Let R' be the subset of R representing jobs whose first task is completed on P_1 in this interval. Since the a_i's have no partition, $\sum_{j \in R'} t_{i,j,1} < T/2$. Consequently, $\sum_{j \in R'} t_{2,j,2} < T/2$. Since only the second tasks of jobs in R' can be scheduled on P_2 in the interval $[T/2, T]$, it follows that there is some idle time on P_2 in this interval. Hence, S must have finish time greater than $2T$. □

$\{t_{1,i,1} \mid i \in u\}$	$t_{1,n+1,2}$	$\{t_{1,i,1} \mid i \notin u\}$	$t_{1,n+1,4}$
$t_{2,n+1,1}$	$\{t_{2,i,2} \mid i \in u\}$	$t_{2,n+1,3}$	$\{t_{2,i,2} \mid i \notin u\}$

0 $T/2$ T $3T/2$ $2T$

Figure 11.18 Another schedule

EXERCISES

1. [Job sequencing] Show that the job sequencing with deadlines problem (Section 8.1.4) is $\mathcal{NP}$-hard.

2. Show that partition $\propto$ the minimum finish time nonpreemptive three-processor flow shop schedule. Use only one job that has three nonzero tasks. All other jobs have only one nonzero task.

3. Show that partition $\propto$ the minimum finish time nonpreemptive two-processor job shop schedule. Use only one job that has three nonzero tasks. All other jobs have only one nonzero task.

4. Let $J_1, \ldots, J_n$ be n jobs. Job i has a processing time t_i and a deadline d_i. Job i is not available for processing until time r_i. Show that

deciding whether all n jobs can be processed on one machine without violating any deadline is $\mathcal{NP}$-hard. (*Hint*: Use partition.)

5. Let J_i, $1 \le i \le n$, be n jobs as in Exercise 4. Assume $r_i = 0$, $1 \le i \le n$. Let f_i be the finish time of J_i in a one-processor schedule S. The *tardiness* T_i of J_i is max $\{0, f_i - d_i\}$. Let w_i, $1 \le i \le n$, be nonnegative weights associated with the J_i's. The total weighted tardiness is $\sum w_i T_i$. Show that finding a schedule minimizing $\sum w_i T_i$ is $\mathcal{NP}$-hard. (*Hint*: Use partition).

6. Let J_i, $1 \le i \le n$, be n jobs. Job J_i has a processing time of t_i. Its processing cannot begin until time r_i. Let w_i be a weight associated with J_i. Let f_i be the finish time of J_i in a one-processor schedule S. Show that finding a one-processor schedule that minimizes $\sum w_i f_i$ is $\mathcal{NP}$-hard.

7. Show that the problem of obtaining optimal finish time preemptive schedules for a two-processor flow shop is $\mathcal{NP}$-hard when jobs are released at two different times R_1 and R_2. Jobs released at R_i cannot be scheduled before R_i.

11.5 $\mathcal{NP}$-HARD CODE GENERATION PROBLEMS

The function of a compiler is to translate programs written in some source language into an equivalent assembly language or machine language program. Thus, the C++ compiler on the Sparc 10 translates C++ programs into the machine language of this machine. We look at the problem of translating arithmetic expressions in a language such as C++ into assembly language code. The translation clearly depends on the particular assembly language (and hence machine) being used. To begin, we assume a very simple machine model. We call this model machine A. This machine has only one register called the *accumulator*. All arithmetic has to be performed in this register. If $\odot$ represents a binary operator such as $+, -, *$, and $/$, then the left operand of $\odot$ must be in the accumulator. For simplicity, we restrict ourselves to these four operators. The discussion easily generalizes to other operators. The relevant assembly language instructions are:

LOAD X load accumulator with contents of memory location X.
STORE X store contents of accumulator into memory location X.
OP X OP may be ADD, SUB, MPY, or DIV.

The instruction OP X computes the operator OP using the contents of the accumulator as the left operand and that of memory location X as the right operand. As an example, consider the arithmetic expression $(a +$

$b)/(c+d)$. Two possible assembly language versions of this expression are given in Figure 11.19. $T1$ and $T2$ are temporary storage areas in memory. In both cases the result is left in the accumulator. Code (a) is two instructions longer than code (b). If each instruction takes the same amount of time, then code (b) will take 25% less time than code (a). For the expressions $(a+b)/(c+d)$ and the given machine A, it is easy to see that code (b) is optimal.

```
LOAD   a        LOAD   c
ADD    b        ADD    d
STORE  T1       STORE  T1
LOAD   c        LOAD   a
ADD    d        ADD    b
STORE  T2       DIV    T1
LOAD   T1
DIV    T2

  (a)             (b)
```

Figure 11.19 Two possible codes for $(a+b)/(c+d)$

Definition 11.7 A *translation* of an expression E into the machine or assembly language of a given machine is *optimal* if and only if it has a minimum number of instructions. □

Definition 11.8 A binary operator $\odot$ is *commutative* in the domain D iff $a \odot b = b \odot a$ for all a and b in D. □

Machine A can be generalized to another machine B. Machine B has $N \geq 1$ registers in which arithmetic can be performed. There are four types of machine instructions for B:

1. LOAD M, R
2. STORE M, R
3. OP $R1, M, R2$
4. OP $R1, R2, R3$

These four instruction types perform the following functions:

1. LOAD M, R places the contents of memory location M into register $R, 1 \leq R \leq N$.

2. STORE M, R stores the contents of register $R, 1 \leq R \leq N$, into memory location M.

3. OP $R1$, M, $R2$ computes contents($R1$) OP contents(M) and places the result in register $R2$. OP is any binary operator (for example, $+$, $-$, $*$, or $/$); $R1$ and $R2$ are registers; $R1$ may equal $R2$; M is a memory location.

4. OP $R1, R2, R3$ is similar to instruction type (3). Here $R1, R2$, and $R3$ are registers. Some or all of these registers may be the same.

In comparing the two machine models A and B, we note that when $N = 1$, instructions of types (1), (2) and (3) for model B are the same as the corresponding instructions for model A. Instructions of type (4) only allow trivial operations like $a + a, a - a, a * a$, and a/a to be performed without an additional memory access. This does not change the number of instructions in the optimal codes for A and B when $N = 1$. Hence, model A is in a sense identical to model B when $N = 1$. For model B, we see that the optimal code for a given expression E may be different for different values of N. Figure 11.20 shows the optimal code for the expression $(a + b)/(c * d)$. Two cases are considered, $N = 1$ and $N = 2$. Note that when $N = 1$, one store has to be made whereas when $N = 2$, no stores are needed. The registers are labeled $R1$ and $R2$. Register $T1$ is a temporary storage location in memory.

(a) $N = 1$		(b) $N = 2$	
LOAD	$c, R1$	LOAD	$c, R1$
MPY	$R1, d, R1$	MPY	$R1, d, R1$
STORE	$R1, T1$	LOAD	$a, R2$
LOAD	$a, R1$	ADD	$R2, b, R2$
ADD	$R1, b, R1$	DIV	$R2, R1, R1$
DIV	$R1, T1, R1$		

Figure 11.20 Optimal codes for $N = 1$ and $N = 2$

Given an expression E, the first question we ask is: can E be evaluated without any STOREs? A closely related question is: what is the minimum number of registers needed to evaluate E without any stores? We show that this problem is $\mathcal{NP}$-hard.

11.5.1 Code Generation with Common Subexpressions

When arithmetic expressions have common subexpressions, they can be represented by a directed acyclic graph (dag). Every internal node (node with nonzero out-degree) in the dag represents an operator. Assuming the expression contains only binary operators, each internal node P has out-degree two. The two nodes adjacent from P are called the left and right children of P respectively. The children of P are the roots of the dags for the left and right operands of P. Node P is the parent of its children. Figure 11.21 shows some expressions and their dag representations.

Definition 11.9 A *leaf* is a node with out-degree zero. A *level-one* node is a node both of whose children are leaves. A *shared node* is a node with more than one parent. A *leaf dag* is a dag in which all shared nodes are leaves. A *level-one* dag is a dag in which all shared nodes are level-one nodes. □

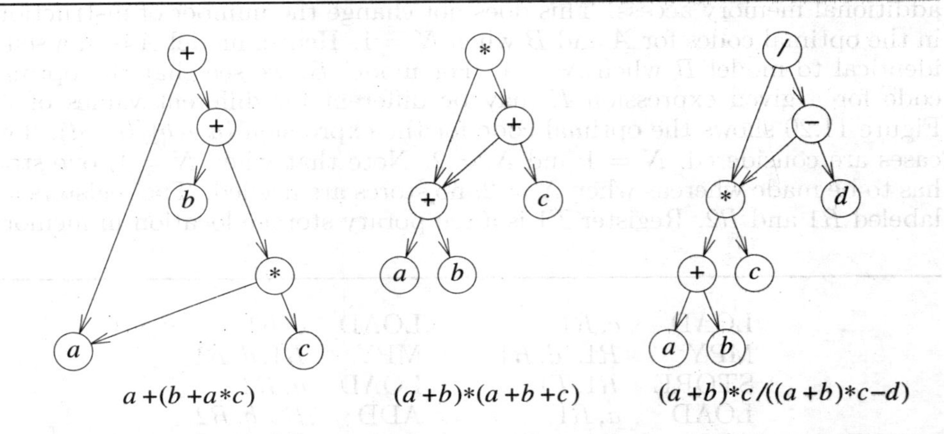

Figure 11.21 Expressions and their dags

Example 11.21 The dag of Figure 11.21(a) is a leaf dag. Figure 11.21(b) is a level-one dag. Figure 11.21(c) is neither a leaf dag nor a level-one dag. □

A leaf dag results from an arithmetic expression in which the only common subexpressions are simple variables or constants. A level-one dag results from an expression in which the only common subexpressions are of the form a $\odot$ b, where a and b are simple variables or constants and $\odot$ is an operator.

The problem of generating optimal code for level-one dags is $\mathcal{NP}$-hard even when the machine for which code is being generated has only one register. Determining the minimum number of registers needed to evaluate a dag with no STOREs is also $\mathcal{NP}$-hard.

Example 11.22 The optimal codes for the dag of Figure 11.21(b) for one- and two-register machines is given in Figure 11.22.

The minimum number of registers needed to evaluate this dag without any STOREs is two. □

```
LOAD    a,R1              LOAD   a,R1
ADD     R1,b,R1           ADD    R1,b,R1
STORE   T1,R1             ADD    R1,c,R2
ADD     R1,c,R1           MUL    R1,R2,R1
STORE   T2,R1
LOAD    T1,R1
MUL     R1,T2, R1

        (a)                      (b)
```

Figure 11.22 Optimal codes for one- and two-register machines

To prove the above statements, we use the feedback node set (FNS) problem that is shown to be $\mathcal{NP}$-hard in Exercise 5 (Section 11.3).

FNS: Given a directed graph $G = (V, E)$ and an integer k, determine whether there exists a subset V' of vertices $V' \subseteq V$ and $|V'| \leq k$ such that the graph $H = (V - V', E - \{\langle u, v\rangle | u \in V' \text{ or } v \in V'\})$ obtained from G by deleting all vertices in V' and all edges incident to a vertex in V' contains no directed cycles.

We explicitly prove only that generating optimal code is $\mathcal{NP}$-hard. Using the construction of this proof, we can also show that determining the minimum number of registers needed to evaluate a dag with no STOREs is $\mathcal{NP}$-hard as well. The proof assumes that expressions can contain commutative operators and that shared nodes may be computed only once. It is easily extended to allow recomputation of shared nodes. Using an idea due to R. Sethi, the proof is easily extended to the case in which only noncommutative operations are allowed (see Exercise 1).

Theorem 11.14 FNS $\propto$ the optimal code generation for level-one dags on a one-register machine.

Proof: Let G, k be an instance of FNS. Let n be the number of vertices in G. We construct a dag A with the property that the optimal code for the expression corresponding to A has at most $n + k$ LOADs if and only if G has a feedback node set of size at most R.

The dag A consists of three kinds of nodes: leaf nodes, chain nodes, and tree nodes. All chain and tree nodes are internal nodes representing commutative operators (for example, +). Leaf nodes represent distinct variables. We use d_v to denote the out-degree of vertex v of G. Corresponding to each vertex v of G, there is a directed chain of chain nodes $v_1, v_2, \ldots, v_{d_v+1}$ in A. Node v_{d_v+1} is the *head node* of the chain for v and is the parent of two leaf nodes v_L and v_R (see Example 11.23 and Figure 11.23). Vertex v_1 is the *tail* of the chain. From each of the chain nodes corresponding to vertex v, except the head node, there is one directed edge to the head node of one of the chains corresponding to a vertex w such that $\langle v, w\rangle$ is an edge in G. Each such edge goes to a distinct head. Note that as a result of the addition of these edges, each chain node now has out-degree two. Since each chain node represents a commutative operator, it does not matter which of its two children is regarded as the left child.

At this point we have a dag in which the tail of every chain has in-degree zero. We now introduce tree nodes to combine all the tails so that we are left with only one node (the root) with in-degree zero. Since G has n vertices, we need $n-1$ tree nodes (note that every binary tree with $n-1$ internal nodes has n external nodes). These $n-1$ nodes are connected together to form a binary tree (any binary tree with $n-1$ nodes will do). In place of the external nodes we connect the tails of the n chains (see Figure 11.23(b)). This yields a dag A corresponding to an arithmetic expression.

It is easy to see that every optimal code for A will have exactly n LOADs of leaf nodes. Also, there will be exactly one instruction of type $\odot$ for every chain node and tree node (we assume that a shared node is computed only once). Hence, the only variable is the number of LOADs and STOREs of chain and tree nodes. If G has no directed cycles, then its vertices can be arranged in topological order (vertex u precedes vertex v in a topological ordering only if there is no directed path from u to v in G). Let $v_1, v_2, \ldots, v_n$ be a topological ordering of the vertices in G. The expression A can be computed using no LOADs of chain and tree nodes by first computing all nodes on the chain for v_n and storing the result of the tail node. Next, all nodes on the chain for v_{n-1} can be computed. In addition, we can compute any nodes on the path from the tail for v_{n-1} to the root for which both operands are available. Finally, one result needs to be stored. Next, the chain for v_{n-2} can be computed. Again, we can compute all nodes on the path from this chain tail to the root for which both operands are available. Continuing in this way, the entire expression can be computed.

If G contains at least one cycle $v_1, v_2, \ldots, v_i, v_1$, then every code for A must contain at least one LOAD of a chain node on a chain for one of $v_1, v_2, \ldots, v_i$. Further, if none of these vertices is on any other cycle, then all their chain nodes can be computed using only one load of a chain node. This argument is readily generalized to show that if the size of a minimum feedback node set is p, then every optimal code for A contains exactly $n + p$ LOADs. The p LOADs correspond to a combination of tail nodes corresponding to a minimum feedback node set and the siblings of these tail nodes. If we had used noncommutative operators for chain nodes and made each successor on a chain the left child of its parent, then the p LOADs would correspond to the tails of the chains of any minimum feedback set. Furthermore, if the optimal code contains p LOADs of chain nodes, then G has a feedback node set of size p. □

Example 11.23 Figure 11.23(b) shows the dag A corresponding to the graph G of Figure 11.23(a). The set $\{r, s\}$ is a minimum feedback node set for G. The operator in each chain and tree node can be assumed to be $+$. Each code for A has a load corresponding to one of $(p_L, p_R), (q_L, q_R), \ldots,$ and (u_L, u_R). The expression A can be computed using only two additional LOADs by computing nodes in the order r_4, s_2, q_2, q_1, p_2, p_1, c, u_3, u_2, u_1, t_2, t_1, e, s_1, r_3, r_2, r_1, d, b, and a. Note that a LOAD is needed to compute s_1 and also to compute r_3. □

11.5.2 Implementing Parallel Assignment Instructions

A *parallel assignment instruction* has the format $(v_1, v_2, \ldots, v_n) := (e_1, e_2;, \ldots, e_n)$ where the v_i's are distinct variable names and the e_i's are expressions. The semantics of this statement is that the value of v_i is updated to be the value of the expression e_i, $1 \leq i \leq n$. The value of the expression e_i is to be computed using the values the variables in e_i have before this instruction is executed.

Example 11.24 1. $(A, B) := (B, C)$; is equivalent to $A := B$; $B := C$;.

2. $(A, B) := (B, A)$; is equivalent to $T := A$; $A := B$; $B := T$;.

3. $(A, B) := (A + B, A - B)$; is equivalent to $T1 := A$; $T2 := B$; $A := T1 + T2$; $B := T1 - T2$; and also to $T1 := A$; $A := A + B$; $B := T1 - B$;. □

As the above example indicates, it may be necessary to store some of the v_i's in temporary locations when executing a parallel assignment. These stores are needed only when some of the v_i's appear in the expressions e_j, $1 \leq j \leq n$. A variable v_i is *referenced* by expression e_i if and only if v_i appears in e_j. It should be clear that only referenced variables need to be copied into temporary locations. Further, parts (2) and (3) of Example 11.24 show that not all referenced variables need to copied.

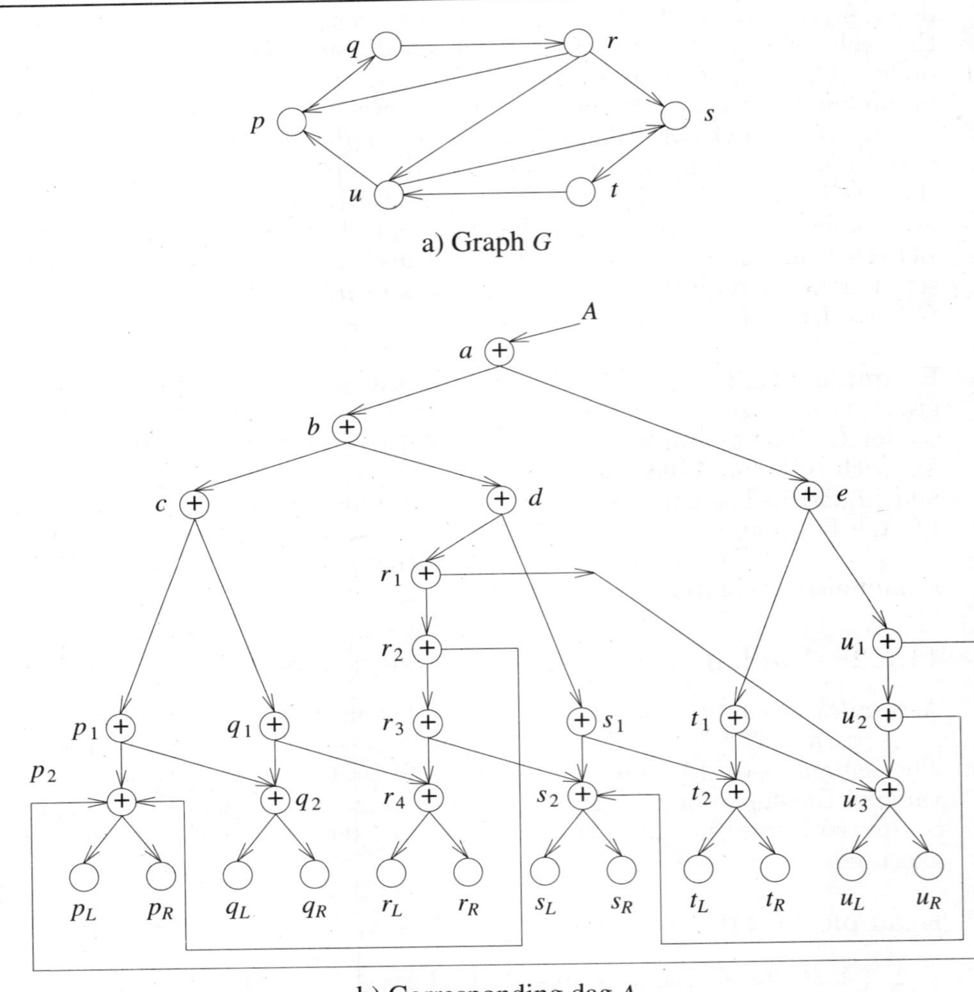

Figure 11.23 A graph and its corresponding dag

An implementation of a parallel assignment statement is a sequence of instructions of types $T_j = v_i$ and $v_i = e'_i$, where e'_i is obtained from e_i by replacing all occurrences of a v_i that have already been updated with references to the temporary locations in which the old values of v_i has been saved. Let $R = (\tau(1), \ldots, \tau(n))$ be a permutation of $(1, 2, \ldots, n)$. Then R

is a *realization* of an assignment statement. It specifies the order in which statements of type $v_i = e'_i$ appear in an implementation of a parallel assignment statement. The order is $v_{\tau(1)} = e'_{\tau(1)}, v_{\tau(2)} = e'_{\tau(2)}$, and so on. The implementation also has statements of type $T_j = v_i$ interspersed. Without loss of generality we can assume that the statement $T_j = v_i$ (if it appears in the implementation) immediately precedes the statement $v_i = e'_i$. Hence, a realization completely characterizes an implementation. The minimum number of instructions of type $T_j = v_i$ for any given realization is easy to determine. This number is the cost of the realization. The *cost* $C(R)$ of a realization R is the number of v_i that are referenced by an e_j that corresponds to an instruction $v_j = e'_j$ that appears after the instruction $v_i = e'_i$.

Example 11.25 Consider the statement $(A, B, C) := (D, A + B, A - B)$;. The 3! $= 6$ different realizations and their costs are given in Figure 11.24. The realization 3, 2, 1 corresponding to the implementation $C = A - B; B = A + B; A = D$; needs no temporary stores ($C(R) = 0$). □

R	$C(R)$
1, 2, 3	2
1, 3, 2	2
2, 1 3	2
2, 3, 1	1
3, 1, 2	1
3, 2, 1	0

Figure 11.24 Realization for Example 11.25

An optimal realization for a parallel assignment statement is one with minimum cost. When the expressions e_i are all variable names or constants, an optimal realization can be found in linear time ($O(n)$). When the e_i are allowed to be expressions with operators then finding an optimal realization is $\mathcal{NP}$-Hard. We prove this statement using the feedback node set problem.

Theorem 11.15 FNS $\propto$ the minimum-cost realization.

Proof: Let $G = (V, E)$ be any n-vertex directed graph. Construct the parallel assignment statement $P : (v_1, v_2, \ldots, v_n) := (e_1, e_2, \ldots, e_n)$, where the v_i's correspond to the n vertices in V and e_i is the expression $v_{i_1} + v_{i_2} + \cdots + v_{i_j}$. The set $\{v_{i_1}, v_{i_2}, \ldots, v_{i_j}\}$ is the set of vertices adjacent from v_i (that is, $\langle v_i, v_{i_l}\rangle \in E(G)$, $1 \le l \le j$). This construction requires at most $O(n^2)$ time.

Let U be any feedback node set for G. Let $G' = (V', E') = (V - U, E - \{\langle x, y\rangle | x \in U \text{ or } y \in U\})$ be the graph obtained by deleting vertex set U and all edges incident to vertices in U. From the definition of a feedback node set, it follows that G' is acyclic. So, the vertices in $V - U$ can be arranged in a sequence $s_1, s_2, \ldots, s_m$, where $m = |V - U|$ and E' contains no edge $\langle s_j, s_i\rangle$ for any i and j, $1 \le i < j \le m$. Hence, an implementation of P in which variables corresponding to vertices in U are first stored in temporary locations followed by the instructions $v_i = e'_i$ corresponding to $v_i \in U$, followed by the corresponding instructions for $s_1, s_2, \ldots, s_m$ (in that order), will be a correct implementation. (Note that e'_i is e_i with all occurrences of $v_i \in U$ replaced by the corresponding temporary location.) The realization R corresponding to this implementation has $C(R) = |U|$. Hence, if G has a feedback node set of size at most k, then P has an optimal realization of cost at most k.

Suppose P has a realization R of cost k. Let U be the set of k variables that have to be stored in temporary locations and let $R = (q_1, q_2, \ldots, q_n)$. From the definition of $C(R)$ it follows that no e_{q_i} references a v_{q_j} with $j < i$ unless $v_{q_j} \in U$. Hence, the deletion of vertices in U from G leaves G acyclic. Thus, U defines a feedback node set of size k for G.

G has a feedback node set of size at most k if and only if P has a realization of cost at most k. Thus we can solve the feedback node set problem in polynomial time if we have a polynomial time algorithm that determines a minimum-cost realization. □

EXERCISES

1. (a) How should the proof of Theorem 11.14 be modified to permit recomputation of shared nodes?

   (b) [R. Sethi] Modify the proof of Theorem 11.14 so that it holds for level-one dags representing expressions in which all operators are noncommutative. (*Hint*: Designate the successor vertex on a chain to be the left child of its predecessor vertex and use the $n+1$ node binary tree of Figure 11.25 to connect together the tail nodes of the n chains.)

   (c) Show that optimal code generation is $\mathcal{NP}$-hard for leaf dags on an infinite register machine. (*Hint*: Use FNS.)

11.6 SOME SIMPLIFIED $\mathcal{NP}$-HARD PROBLEMS

Once we have shown a problem L to be $\mathcal{NP}$-hard, we would be inclined to dismiss the possibility that L can be solved in deterministic polynomial

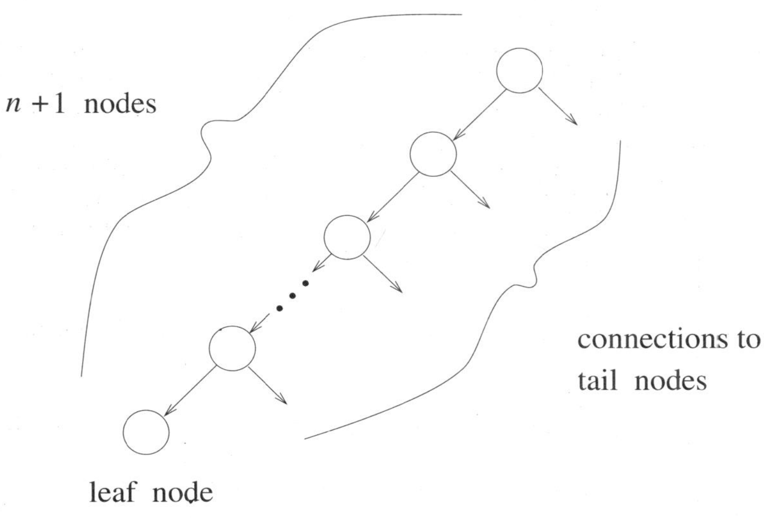

Figure 11.25 Figure for Exercise 1

time. At this point, however, we can naturally ask the question: Can a suitably restricted version (i.e., some subclass) of an $\mathcal{NP}$-hard problem be solved in deterministic polynomial time? It should be easy to see that by placing enough restrictions on any $\mathcal{NP}$-hard problem (or by defining a sufficiently small subclass), we can arrive at a polynomially solvable problem. As examples, consider the following:

1. CNF-satisfiability with at most three literals per clause is $\mathcal{NP}$-hard. If each clause is restricted to have at most two literals, then CNF-satisfiability is polynomially solvable.

2. Generating optimal code for a parallel assignment statement is $\mathcal{NP}$-hard. However, if the expressions e_i are restricted to be simple variables, then optimal code can be generated in polynomial time.

3. Generating optimal code for level-one dags is $\mathcal{NP}$-hard, but optimal code for trees can be generated in polynomial time.

4. Determining whether a planar graph is three colorable is $\mathcal{NP}$-hard. To determine whether it is two colorable, we only have to see whether it is bipartite.

Since it is very unlikely that $\mathcal{NP}$-hard problems are polynomially solvable, it is important to determine the weakest restrictions under which we can solve a problem in polynomial time.

To narrow the gap between subclasses for which polynomial time algorithms are known and those for which such algorithms are not known, it is desirable to obtain as strong a set of restrictions under which a problem remains $\mathcal{NP}$-hard or $\mathcal{NP}$-complete.

We state without proof the severest restrictions under which certain problems are known to be $\mathcal{NP}$-hard or $\mathcal{NP}$-complete. We state these simplified or restricted problems as decision problems. For each problem we specify only the input and the decision to be made.

Theorem 11.16 The following decision problems are $\mathcal{NP}$-complete.

1. **Node cover**
   Input: An undirected graph G with node degree at most 3 and an integer k.
   Decision: Does G have a node cover of size at most k?

2. **Planar Node Cover**
   Input: A planar undirected graph G with node degree at most 6 and an integer k.
   Decision: Does G have a node cover of size at most k?

3. **Colorability**
   Input: A planar undirected graph G with node degree at most four.
   Decision: Is G three colorable?

4. **Undirected Hamiltonian Cycle**
   Input: An undirected graph G with node degree at most three.
   Decision: Does G have a Hamiltonian cycle?

5. **Planar Undirected Hamiltonian Cycle**
   Input: A planar undirected graph.
   Decision: Does G have a Hamiltonian cycle?

6. **Planar Directed Hamiltonian Path**
   Input: A planar directed graph G with in-degree at most 3 and out-degree at most 4.
   Decision: Does G have a directed Hamiltonian path?

7. **Unary Input Partition**
   Input: Positive integers a_i, $1 \leq i \leq m$, n, and B such that

$$\sum_{1 \leq i \leq m} a_i = nB, \quad \frac{B}{4} < a_i < \frac{B}{2}, \quad 1 \leq i \leq m, \quad m = 3n$$

Input is in unary notation.
Decision: Is there a partition $\{A_1, \ldots, A_n\}$ of the a_i's such that each A_i contains three elements and

$$\sum_{a \in A_i} a = B, \quad 1 \le i \le n$$

8. **Unary Flow Show**
Input: Task times in unary notation and an integer T.
Decision: Is there a two-processor nonpreemptive schedule with mean finish time at most T?

9. **Simple Max Cut**
Input: A graph $G = (V, E)$ and an integer k.
Decision: Does V have a subset V_1 such that there are at least k edges $(u, v) \in E$ with $u \in V_1$ and $v \notin V_1$?

10. **SAT2**
Input: A propositional formula F in CNF. Each clause in F has at most two literals. An integer k.
Decision: Can at least k clauses of F be satisfied?

11. **Minimum Edge Deletion Bipartite Subgraph**
Input: An undirected graph G and an integer k.
Decision: Can G be made bipartite by the deletion of at most k edges?

12. **Minimum Node Deletion Bipartite Subgraph**
Input: An undirected graph G and an integer k.
Decision: Can G be made bipartite by the deletion of at most k vertices

13. **Minimum Cut into Equal-Sized Subsets**
Input: An undirected graph $G = (V, E)$, two distinguished vertices s and t, and a positive integer W.
Decision: Is there a partition $V = V_1 \cup V_2$, $V_1 \cap V_2 = \phi$, $|V_1| = |V_2|$, $s \in V_1, t \in V_2$, and $|\{(u, v)|u \in V_1, v \in V_2 \text{ and } (u, v) \in E\}| \le W$?

14. **Simple Optimal Linear Arrangement**
Input: An undirected graph $G = (V, E)$ and an integer k. $|V| = n$.
Decision: Is there a one-to-one function $f : V \to \{1, 2, \ldots, n\}$ such that

$$\sum_{(u,v) \in E} |f(u) - f(v)| \le k$$

11.7 REFERENCES AND READINGS

A comprehensive treatment of $\mathcal{NP}$-hard and $\mathcal{NP}$-complete problems can be found in *Computers and intractability: A Guide to the Theory of NP-Completeness*, by M. Garey and D. Johnson, W. H. Freeman, 1979.

Our proof satisfiability $\propto$ directed Hamiltonian cycle is due to P. Hermann. The proof satisfiability $\propto$ AND/OR Graphs and the proof used in the text for Theorem 11.11 were given by S. Sahni. Theorem 11.11 is due to J. Bruno, E. G. Coffman, Jr., and R. Sethi.

Theorems 11.12 and 11.13 are due to T. Gonzalez and S. Sahni. The proof of Theorem 11.13 is due to D. Nassimi. The proof of Theorem 11.14 is due to A. Aho, S. Johnson, and J. Ullman.

The fact that the code generation problem for one-register machines is $\mathcal{NP}$-hard was first proved by J. Bruno and R. Sethi. The result in their paper is stronger than Theorem 11.14 as it applies even to expressions containing no commutative operators. Theorem 11.15 is due to R. Sethi.

The results stated in Section 11.6 were presented by D. Johnson and L. Stockmeyer.

For additional material on complexity theory see *Complexity Theory*, by C. H. Papadimitriou, Addison-Wesley, 1994.

11.8 ADDITIONAL EXERCISES

1. [Circuit realization] Let C be a circuit made up of **and, or,** and **not** gates. Let $x_1, \ldots, x_n$ be the inputs and f the output. Show that deciding whether $f(x_1, \ldots, x_n) = F(x_1, \ldots, x_n)$, where F is a propositional formula, is $\mathcal{NP}$-hard.

2. Show that determining whether C is a minimum circuit (i.e., has a minimum number of gates, see Exercise 1) realizing a formula F is $\mathcal{NP}$-hard.

3. [0/1 knapsack] Show that Partition $\propto$ the 0/1 knapsack decision problem.

4. [Quadratic programming] Show that finding the maximum of a function $f(x_1, \ldots, x_n)$ subject to the linear constraints $\sum_{1leqj \leq n} a_{ij}x_j \leq b_i, 1 \leq i \leq n$, and $x_i \geq 0,\ 1 \leq i \leq n$ is $\mathcal{NP}$-hard. The function f is restricted to be of the form $\sum c_i x_i^2 + \sum d_i x_i$.

5. Let $G = (V, E)$ be a graph. Let $w(i, j)$ be a weighting function for the edges of G. A *cut* of G is a subset $S \subseteq V$. The *weight* of a cut is

$$\sum_{i \in S, j \notin S} w(i, j)$$

A *max-cut* is a cut of maximum weight. Show that the problem of determining the weight of a max-cut is $\mathcal{NP}$-hard.

6. [Plant location] Let S_i, $1 \le i \le n$, be n possible sites at which plants can be located. At each site at most one plant can be located. If a plant is located at site S_i, then a fixed cost F_i is incurred. This is the cost of setting up the plant. A plant located at S_i has a maximum production capacity of C_i. There are n destinations $D_i, 1 \le i \le m$, to which products have to be shipped. The demand at D_i is $d_i, 1 \le i \le m$. The per-unit cost of shipping a product from site i to destination j is c_{ij}. A destination can be supplied from many plants. Define $y_i = 0$ if no plant is located at site i and $y_i = 1$ otherwise. Let x_{ij} be the number of units of the product shipped from S_i to D_j. Then, the total cost is

$$\sum_i F_i y_i + \sum_i \sum_j c_{ij} x_{ij}, \ \ \sum_i x_{ij} = d_j, \ \text{ and } \ \sum_j x_{ij} \le C_i y_i$$

All x_{ij} are nonnegative integers. We assume that $\sum C_{ij} \ge \sum d_i$. Show that finding y_i and x_{ij} so that the total cost is minimized is $\mathcal{NP}$-hard.

7. [Concentrator location] This problem is very similar to the plant location problem (Exercise 6). The only difference is that each destination may be supplied by only one plant. When this restriction is imposed, the plant location problem becomes the concentrator location problem arising in computer network design. The destinations represent computer terminals. The plants represent the concentration of information from the terminals which they supply. Show that the concentrator location problem is $\mathcal{NP}$-hard under each of the following conditions:

   (a) $n = 2, C_1 = C_2$, and $F_1 = F_2$. (*Hint*: Use Partition.)

   (b) $F_i/C_i = F_{i+1}/C_{i+1}, 1 \le i < n$, and $d_i = 1$. (*Hint*: Use exact cover.)

8. [Steiner trees] Let T be a tree and R a subset of the vertices in T. Let $w(i, j)$ be the weight of edge (i, j) in T. If (i, j) is not an edge in T, then $w(i, j) = \infty$. A Steiner tree is a subtree of T that includes the vertex set R. It may include other vertices too. Its cost is the sum of the weights of the edges in it. Show that finding a minimum-cost Steiner tree is $\mathcal{NP}$-hard.

9. Assume that P is a parallel assignment statement $(v_1, \ldots, v_n) := (e_1, \ldots, e_n)$;, where each e_i is a simple variable and the v_i's are distinct. For convenience, assume that the distinct variables in P are $(v_1, \ldots, v_m)$ with $m \geq n$ and that $E = (i_1, i_2, \ldots, i_n)$ is a set of indices such that $e_{i_j} = v_{i_j}$. Then write an $O(n)$ time algorithm to find an optimal realization for P.

10. Let $F = \{S_j\}$ be a finite family of sets. Let $T \leq F$ be a subfamily of F. The size of $T, |T|$, is the number of sets in T. Let S_i and S_j be two sets in T. Also S_i and S_j are disjoint if and only if $S_i \cap S_j = \phi$. T is a disjoint subset of F if and only if every two sets in T are disjoint. The set packing problem is to determine a disjoint subfamily T of maximum size. Show that clique $\propto$ set packing.

11. Show that the following decision problem is $\mathcal{NP}$-complete.
Input: Positive integer $n; w_i, 1 \leq i < n$, and M.
Decision: Do there exist nonnegative integers $x_i \geq 0, 1 \leq i \leq n$; such that
$$\sum_{1 \leq i \leq n} w_i x_i = M$$

12. An *independent set* in an undirected graph $G(V, E)$ is a set of vertices no two of which are connected. Given a graph G and an integer k, the problem is to determine whether G has an independent set of size k. Show that this problem is $\mathcal{NP}$-complete.

13. Given an undirected graph $G(V, E)$ and an integer k, the goal is to determine whether G has a clique of size k **and** an independent set of size k. Show that this problem is $\mathcal{NP}$-complete.

14. Is the following problem in $\mathcal{P}$? If yes, give a polynomial time algorithm; if not, show it is $\mathcal{NP}$-complete.

    Input are an undirected graph $G = (V, E)$ of degree 1000 and an integer $k(\leq |V|)$. Decide whether G has a clique of size k.

15. Given an integer $m \times n$ matrix A and an integer $m \times 1$ vector b, the *0-1 integer programming problem* asks whether there is an integer $n \times 1$ vector x with elements in the the set $\{0, 1\}$ such that $Ax \leq b$. Prove that 0-1 integer programming is $\mathcal{NP}$-complete.

16. Input are finite sets $A_1, A_2, \ldots, A_m$ and $B_1, B_2, \ldots, B_n$. The *set intersection problem* is to decide whether there is a set T such that $|T \cap A_i| \geq 1$ for $i = 1, 2, \ldots, m$, and $|T \cap B_j| \leq 1$ for $j = 1, 2, \ldots, n$. Show that the set intersection problem is $\mathcal{NP}$-complete.

17. We say an undirected graph $G(V, E)$ is k colorable if each node of G can be labeled with an integer in the range $[1, k]$, such that no two nodes connected by an edge have the same label. Is the following problem in $\mathcal{P}$? If yes, present a polynomial time algorithm for its solution. If not, show that it is $\mathcal{NP}$-complete.

    Given an undirected acyclic graph $G(V, E)$ and an integer k, decide whether G is k colorable.

18. Is the following problem in $\mathcal{P}$? If yes, present a polynomial time algorithm; if not, show that it is $\mathcal{NP}$-complete.

    Input are an undirected graph $G(V, E)$ and an integer $1 \leq k \leq |V|$. Also, assume that the degree of each node in G is $|V| - O(1)$. The problem is to check whether G has a vertex cover of size k.

19. Assume that there is a polynomial time algorithm CLQ to solve the CLIQUE decision problem.

    (a) Show how to use CLQ to determine the maximum clique size of a given graph in polynomial time.

    (b) Show how to use CLQ to find a maximum clique in polynomial time.

Chapter 12

APPROXIMATION ALGORITHMS

12.1 INTRODUCTION

In the preceding chapter we saw strong evidence to support the claim that no $\mathcal{NP}$-hard problem can be solved in polynomial time. Yet, many $\mathcal{NP}$-hard optimization problems have great practical importance and it is desirable to solve large instances of these problems in a reasonable amount of time. The best-known algorithms for $\mathcal{NP}$-hard problems have a worst-case complexity that is exponential in the number of inputs. Although the results of the last chapter may favor abandoning the quest for polynomial time algorithms, there is still plenty of room for improvement in an exponential algorithm. We can look for algorithms with subexponential complexity, say $2^{n/c}$ (for $c > 1$), $2^{\sqrt{n}}$, or $n^{\log n}$. In the exercises of Section 5.7 an $O(2^{n/2})$ algorithm for the knapsack problem was developed. This algorithm can also be used for the partition, sum of subsets, and exact cover problems. $O(2^{n/3})$ time algorithms for the max-clique, max-independent set, and minimum node cover problems are known (see the references at the end of this chapter). The discovery of a subexponential algorithm for an $\mathcal{NP}$-hard problem increases the maximum problem size that can be solved. However, for large problem instances, even an $O(n^4)$ algorithm requires too much computational effort. Clearly, what is needed is an algorithm of low polynomial complexity (say $O(n)$ or $O(n^2)$).

The use of heuristics in an existing algorithm may enable it to quickly solve a large instance of a problem provided the heuristic works on that instance. This was clearly demonstrated in the chapters on backtracking and branch-and-bound. A heuristic, however, does not work equally effectively on all problem instances. Exponential time algorithms, even coupled with heuristics, still show exponential behavior on some set of inputs. If we are to produce an algorithm of low polynomial complexity to solve an $\mathcal{NP}$-hard optimization problem, then it is necessary to relax the meaning of "solve." In this chapter we discuss two relaxations of the meaning of "solve." In the first we remove the requirement that the algorithm that solves the optimization problem P must always generate an optimal solution. This requirement is replaced by the requirement that the algorithm for P must always generate a feasible solution with value close to the value of an optimal solution. A feasible solution with value close to the value of an optimal solution is called an *approximate solution.* An *approximation algorithm* for P is an algorithm that generates approximate solutions for P.

Although at first one may discount the virtue of an approximate solution, one should bear in mind that often, the data for the problem instance being solved is only known approximately. Hence, an approximate solution (provided its value is sufficiently close to that of an exact solution) may be no less meaningful than an exact solution. In the case of $\mathcal{NP}$-hard problems, approximate solutions have added importance as exact solutions (i.e., optimal solutions) may not be obtainable in a feasible amount of computing time. An approximate solution may be all one can get using a reasonable amount of computing time.

In the second relaxation we look for an algorithm for P that *almost always* generates optimal solutions. Algorithms with this property are called *probabilistically good* algorithms. These are considered in Section 12.6. In the remainder of this section we develop the terminology to be used in discussing approximation algorithms.

Let P be a problem such as the knapsack or the traveling salesperson problem. Let I be an instance of problem P and let $F^*(I)$ be the value of an optimal solution to I. An approximation algorithm generally produces a feasible solution to I whose value $\hat{F}(I)$ is less than (greater than) $F^*(I)$ if P is a maximization (minimization) problem. Several categories of approximation algorithms can be defined.

Let A be an algorithm that generates a feasible solution to every instance I of a problem P. Let $F^*(I)$ be the value of an optimal solution to I and let $\hat{F}(I)$ be the value of the feasible solution generated by A.

Definition 12.1 A is an *absolute approximation* algorithm for problem P if and only if for every instance I of P, $|F^*(I) - \hat{F}(I)| \leq k$ for some constant k. □

Definition 12.2 A is an $f(n)$-*approximate* algorithm if and only if for every instance I of size n, $|F^*(I) - \hat{F}(I)|/F^*(I) \leq f(n)$ for $F^*(I) > 0$. □

Definition 12.3 An ϵ-*approximate* algorithm is an $f(n)$-approximate algorithm for which $f(n) \leq \epsilon$ for some constant ϵ. □

Note that for maximization problems, $|F^*(I) - \hat{F}(I)|/F^*(I) \leq 1$ for every feasible solution to I. Hence, for maximization problems we normally require $\epsilon < 1$ for an algorithm to be judged ϵ-approximate. In the next few definitions we consider algorithms $A(\epsilon)$ with ϵ an input to A.

Definition 12.4 $A(\epsilon)$ is an *approximation scheme* if and only if for every given $\epsilon > 0$ and problem instance I, $A(\epsilon)$ generates a feasible solution such that $|F^*(I) - \hat{F}(I)|/F^*(I) \leq \epsilon$. Again, we assume $F^*(I) > 0$. □

Definition 12.5 An approximation scheme is a *polynomial time approximation scheme* if and only if for every fixed $\epsilon > 0$, it has a computing time that is polynomial in the problem size. □

Definition 12.6 An approximation scheme whose computing time is a polynomial both in the problem size and in $1/\epsilon$ is a *fully polynomial time approximation scheme.* □

Clearly, the most desirable kind of approximation algorithm is an absolute approximation algorithm. Unfortunately, for most $\mathcal{NP}$-hard problems it can be shown that fast algorithms of this type exist only if $\mathcal{P} = \mathcal{NP}$. Surprisingly, this statement is true even for the existence of $f(n)$-approximate algorithms for certain $\mathcal{NP}$-hard problems.

Example 12.1 Consider the knapsack instance $n = 3$, $m = 100$, $\{p_1, p_2, p_3\} = \{20, 10, 19\}$, and $\{w_1, w_2, w_3\} = \{65, 20, 35\}$. The solution $(x_1, x_2, x_3) = (1, 1, 1)$ is not a feasible solution as $\sum w_i x_i > m$. The solution $(x_1, x_2, x_3) = (1,0,1)$ is an optimal solution. Its value, $\sum p_i x_i$, is 39. Hence, $F^*(I) = 39$ for this instance. The solution $(x_1, x_2, x_3) = (1, 1, 0)$ is suboptimal. Its value is $\sum p_i x_i = 30$. This is a candidate for a possible output from an approximation algorithm. In fact, every feasible solution (in this case all three-element 0/1 vectors other than $(1, 1, 1)$ are feasible) is a candidate for output by an approximation algorithm. If the solution (1, 1, 0) is generated by an approximation algorithm on this instance, then $\hat{F}(I) = 30$, $|F^*(I) - \hat{F}(I)| = 9$, and $F^*(I) - \hat{F}(I)|/F^*(I) = 0.3$. □

Example 12.2 Consider the following approximation algorithm for the 0/1 knapsack problem: assume the objects are in nonincreasing order of p_i/w_i. If object i fits, then set $x_i = 1$; otherwise set $x_i = 0$. When this algorithm is used on the instance $(p_1, p_2) = (100, 20), (w_1, w_2) = (4, 1)$, and $m = 4$, the objects are considered in the order 1, 2 and the result is $(x_1, x_2) = (1, 0)$ which is optimal. Now, consider the instance $n = 2$, $(p_1, p_2) = (2, r), (w_1, w_2) = (1, r)$, and $m = r$. When $r > 2$, the optimal solution is $(x_1, x_2) = (0, 1)$. Its value, $F^*(I)$, is r. The solution generated by the approximation algorithm is $(x_1, x_2) = (1, 0)$. Its value, $\hat{F}(I)$, is 2. Hence, $|F^*(I) -$

$\hat{F}(I)| = r - 2$. Our approximation algorithm is not an absolute approximation algorithm as there exists no constant k such that $|F^*(I) - \hat{F}(I)| \leq k$ for all instances I. Furthermore, note that $|F^*(I) - \hat{F}(I)|/F^*(I) = 1 - 2/r$. This approaches 1 as r becomes large. $|F^*(I) - \hat{F}(I)|/F^*(I) \leq 1$ for every feasible solution to every knapsack instance. Since the above algorithm always generates a feasible solution, it is a 1-approximate algorithm. It is, however, not an ϵ-approximate algorithm for any ϵ, $\epsilon < 1$. □

Corresponding to the notions of an absolute approximation algorithm and $f(n)$-approximate algorithm, we can define approximation problems in the obvious way. So, we can speak of k-absolute approximate problems and $f(n)$-approximate problems. The .5-approximate knapsack problem is to find any 0/1 feasible solution with $|F^*(I) - \hat{F}(I)|/F^*(I) \leq .5$.

Approximation algorithms are usually just heuristics or rules that on the surface look like they might solve the optimization problem exactly. However, they do not. Instead, they only guarantee to generate feasible solutions with values within some constant or some factor of the optimal value. Being heuristic in nature, these algorithms are very much dependent on the individual problem being solved.

EXERCISE

1. The following $\mathcal{NP}$-hard problems were defined in Chapter 11. For those defined in Chapter 11, the exercise numbers appear in parentheses. For each of these problems, clearly state the corresponding absolute approximation problem. (Some of the problems listed below were defined as decision problems. For these, there correspond obvious optimization problems that are also $\mathcal{NP}$-hard. Define the absolute approximation problem relative to the corresponding optimization problem.) Also, show that the corresponding absolute approximation problem is $\mathcal{NP}$-hard.

   (a) Node cover

   (b) Set cover (Section 11.3 Problem 15)

   (c) Set packing (Chapter 11, Additional Exercise 10)

   (d) Feedback node set

   (e) Feedback arc set (Section 11.3, Exercise 6)

   (f) Chromatic number

   (g) Clique cover (Section 11.3, Exercise 14)

   (h) Max-independent set (see Section 12.6)

```
Algorithm AColor(V, E)
// Determine an approximation to the minimum number of colors.
{
    if V = ∅ then return 0;
    else if E = ∅ then return 1;
        else if G is bipartite then return 2;
            else return 4;
}
```

Algorithm 12.1 Approximate coloring

(i) Nonpreemptive scheduling of independent tasks to minimize finish time on $m > 1$ processors (Section 12.3)

(j) Flow shop scheduling to minimize finish time ($m > 2$)

(k) Job shop scheduling to minimize finish time ($m > 1$)

12.2 ABSOLUTE APPROXIMATIONS

12.2.1 Planar Graph Coloring

There are very few $\mathcal{NP}$-hard optimization problems for which polynomial time absolute approximation algorithms are known. One problem is that of determining the minimum number of colors needed to color a planar graph $G = (V, E)$. It is known that every planar graph is four colorable. One can easily determine whether a graph is zero, one, or two colorable. It is zero colorable iff $V = \emptyset$. It is one colorable iff $E = \emptyset$. It is two colorable iff it is bipartite (see Section 6.3, Exercise 7). Determining whether a planar graph is three colorable is $\mathcal{NP}$-hard. However, all planar graphs are four colorable. An absolute approximation algorithm with $|F^*(I) - \hat{F}(I)| \leq 1$ is easy to obtain. Algorithm 12.1 is such an algorithm. It finds an exact answer when the graph can be colored using at most two colors. Since we can determine whether a graph is bipartite in time $O(|V| + |E|)$, the complexity of the algorithm is $O(|V| + |E|)$.

12.2.2 Maximum Programs Stored Problem

Assume that we have n programs and two storage devices (say disks or tapes). We assume the devices are disks. Our discussion applies to any

```
Algorithm PStore(l, n, L)
// Assume that l[i] ≤ l[i + 1], 1 ≤ i < n.
{
    i := 1;
    for j := 1 to 2 do
    {
        sum := 0; // Amount of disk j already assigned
        while (sum + l[i]) ≤ L do
        {
            write ("Store program", i, "on disk", j);
            sum := sum + l[i]; i := i + 1;
            if i > n then return;
        }
    }
}
```

Algorithm 12.2 Approximation algorithm to store programs

kind of storage device. Let l_i be the amount of storage needed to store the ith program. Let L be the storage capacity of each disk. Determining the maximum number of these n programs that can be stored on the two disks (without splitting a program over the disks) is $\mathcal{NP}$-hard.

Theorem 12.1 Partition $\propto$ maximum programs stored.

Proof: Let $\{a_1, a_2, \ldots, a_n\}$ define an instance of the partition problem. We can assume $\sum a_i = 2T$. Define an instance of the maximum programs stored problem as follows: $L = T$ and $l_i = a_i$, $1 \leq i \leq n$. Clearly, $\{a_1, \ldots, a_n\}$ has a partition if and only if all n programs can be stored on the two disks. □

By considering programs in order of nondecreasing storage requirement l_i, we can obtain a polynomial time absolute approximation algorithm. Function PStore (Algorithm 12.2) assumes $l_1 \leq l_2 \leq \cdots \leq l_n$ and assigns programs to disk 1 so long as enough space remains on this tape. Then it begins assigning programs to disk 2. In addition to the time needed to initially sort the programs into nondecreasing order of l_i, $O(n)$ time is needed to obtain the storage assignment.

Example 12.3 Let $L = 10$, $n = 4$, and $(l_1, l_2, l_3, l_4) = (2, 4, 5, 6)$. Function PStore will store programs 1 and 2 on disk 1 and only program 3 on disk 2. An optimal storage scheme stores all four programs. One way to do this is to store programs 1 and 4 on disk 1 and the other two on disk 2. □

Theorem 12.2 Let I be any instance of the maximum programs stored problem. Let $F^*(I)$ be the maximum number of programs that can be stored on two disks each of length L. Let $\hat{F}(I)$ be the number of programs stored using the function PStore. Then $|F^*(I) - \hat{F}(I)| \leq 1$.

Proof: Assume that k programs are stored when PStore is used. Then, $\hat{F}(I) = k$. Consider the program storage problem when only one disk of capacity $2L$ is available. In this case, considering programs in order of the nondecreasing storage requirement maximizes the number of programs stored. Assume that p programs get stored when this strategy is used on a single disk of length $2L$. Clearly, $p \geq F^*(I)$ and $\sum_1^p l_i \leq 2L$. Let j be the largest index such that $\sum_1^j l_i \leq L$. It is easy to verify that $j \leq p$ and that PStore assigns the first j programs to disk 1. Also,

$$\sum_{i=j+1}^{p-1} l_i \leq \sum_{i=j+2}^{p} l_i \leq L$$

Hence, PStore assigns at least programs $j+1, j+2, \ldots, p-1$ to disk 2. So, $\hat{F}(I) \geq p-1$ and $|F^*(I) - \hat{F}(I)| \leq 1$. □

Function PStore can be extended in the obvious way to obtain a $k-1$ absolute approximation algorithm for the case of k disks.

12.2.3 $\mathcal{NP}$-hard Absolute Approximations

The absolute approximation algorithms for the planar graph coloring and the maximum program storage problems are very simple and straightforward. Thus, one may expect that polynomial time absolute approximation algorithms exist for most other $\mathcal{NP}$-hard problems. Unfortunately, for the majority of $\mathcal{NP}$-hard problems one can provide very simple proofs to show that a polynomial time absolute approximation algorithm exists if and only if a polynomial time exact algorithm does. Let us look at some sample proofs.

Theorem 12.3 The absolute approximate knapsack problem is $\mathcal{NP}$-hard.

Proof: We show that the 0/1 knapsack problem with integer profits reduces to the absolute approximate knapsack problem. The theorem then follows from the observation that the knapsack problem with integer profits is $\mathcal{NP}$-hard. Assume there is a polynomial time algorithm A that guarantees feasible solutions such that $|F^*(I) - \hat{F}(I)| \leq k$ for every instance I and a fixed k. Let (p_i, w_i), $1 \leq i \leq n$, and m define an instance of the knapsack problem. Assume the p_i are integer. Let I' be the instance defined by

$((k+1)\, p_i, w_i)$, $1 \leq i \leq n$, and m. Clearly, I and I' have the same set of feasible solutions. Further, $F^*(I') = (k+1)F^*(I)$, and I and I' have the same optimal solutions. Also, since all the p_i are integer, it follows that all feasible solutions to I' either have value $F^*(I')$ or value at most $F^*(I') - (k+1)$. If $\hat{F}(I')$ is the value of the solution generated by A, for instance I', then $F^*(I') - \hat{F}(I')$ is either 0 or at least $k+1$. Hence if $F^*(I') - \hat{F}(I') \leq k$, then $F^*(I') = \hat{F}(I')$. So, A can be used to obtain an optimal solution for I' and hence I. Since the length of I' is at most $(\log k)$(length of I), it follows that using the above construction, we can obtain a polynomial time algorithm for the knapsack problem with integer profits. □

Example 12.4 Consider the knapsack instance $n = 3$, $m = 100$, $(p_1, p_2, p_3) = (1, 2, 3)$, and $(w_1, w_2, w_3) = (50, 60, 30)$. The feasible solutions are (1, 0, 0), (0, 1, 0), (0, 0, 1), (1, 0, 1), and (0, 1, 1). The values of these solutions are 1, 2, 3, 4, and 5 respectively. If we multiply the p's by 5, then $(\hat{p_1}, \hat{p_2}, \hat{p_3}) = (5, 10, 15)$. The feasible solutions are unchanged. Their values are now 5, 10, 15, 20, and 25 respectively. If we had an absolute approximation algorithm for $k = 4$, then this algorithm would have to output the solution (0, 1, 1) as no other solution would be within 4 of the optimal solution value. □

Now, consider the problem of obtaining a maximum clique of an undirected graph. The following theorem shows that obtaining a polynomial time absolute approximation algorithm for this problem is as hard as obtaining a polynomial time algorithm for the exact problem.

Theorem 12.4 Max clique $\propto$ absolute approximation max clique.

Proof: Assume that the algorithm for the absolute approximation problem finds solutions such that $|F^*(I) - \hat{F}(I)| \leq k$. From any given graph $G = (V, E)$, we construct another graph $G' = (V', E')$ so that G' consists of $k+1$ copies of G connected together such that there is an edge between every two vertices in distinct copies of G. That is, if $V = \{v_1, v_2, \ldots, v_n\}$, then

$$\begin{aligned} V' &= \cup_{i=1}^{k+1}\{v_1^i, v_2^i, \ldots, v_n^i\} \\ \text{and } E' &= (\cup_{i=1}^{k+1}\{(v_p^i, v_r^i) | (v_p, v_r) \in E\}) \cup \{(v_p^i, v_r^j) | i \neq j\} \end{aligned}$$

Clearly, the maximum clique size in G is q if and only if the maximum clique size in G' is $(k+1)q$. Further, any clique in G' that is within k of the optimal clique size in G' must contain a subclique of size q, which is a clique of size q in G. Hence, we can obtain a maximum clique for G from a k-absolute approximate maximum clique for G'. □

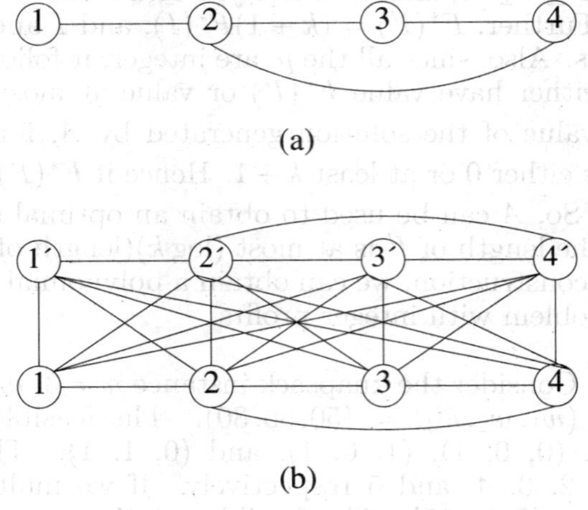

Figure 12.1 Graphs for Example 12.5

Example 12.5 Figure 12.1 (b) shows the graph G' that results when the construction of Theorem 12.4 is applied to the graph of Figure 12.1(a). We have assumed $k = 1$. The graph of Figure 12.1(a) has two cliques. One consists of the vertex set $\{1,2\}$, and the other $\{2,3,4\}$. Thus, an absolute approximation algorithm for $k = 1$ could output either of the two as a solution clique. In the graph of Figure 12.1(b), however, the two cliques are $\{1,2,1',2'\}$ and $\{2,3,4,2',3',4'\}$. Only the latter can be output. Hence, an absolute approximation algorithm with $k = 1$ outputs the maximum clique. □

12.3 ϵ-APPROXIMATIONS

12.3.1 Scheduling Independent Tasks

Obtaining minimum finish time schedules on m, $m \geq 2$, identical processors is $\mathcal{NP}$-hard. There exists a very simple scheduling rule that generates schedules with a finish time very close to that of an optimal schedule. An instance I of the scheduling problem is defined by a set of n task times t_i, $1 \leq i \leq n$, and m, the number of processors. The scheduling rule we are about to describe is known as the LPT (longest processing time) rule. An LPT schedule is a schedule that results from this rule.

Definition 12.7 An *LPT schedule* is one that is the result of an algorithm that, whenever a processor becomes free, assigns to that processor a task whose time is the largest of those tasks not yet assigned. Ties are broken in an arbitrary manner. □

Example 12.6 Let $m = 3, n = 6$, and $(t_1, t_2, t_3, t_4, t_5, t_6) = (8, 7, 6, 5, 4\ , 3)$. In an LPT schedule, tasks 1, 2, and 3 are assigned to processors 1, 2, and 3 respectively. Tasks 4, 5, and 6 are respectively assigned to processors 3, 2, and 1. Figure 12.2 shows this LPT schedule. The finish time is 11. Since $\sum t_i/3 = 11$, the schedule is also optimal. □

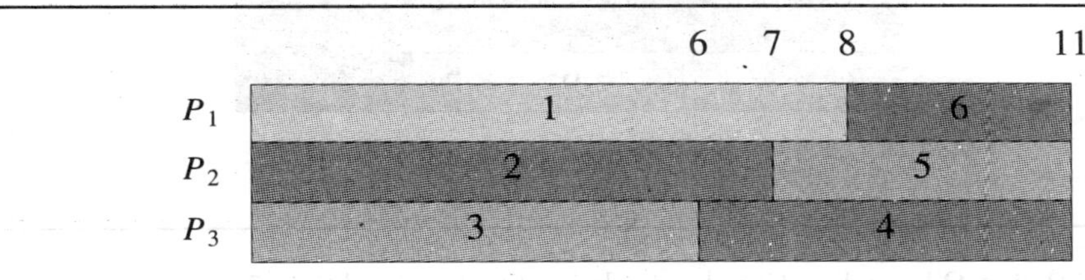

Figure 12.2 LPT schedule for Example 12.6

Example 12.7 Let $m = 3$, $n = 7$, and $(t_1, t_2, t_3, t_4, t_5, t_6, t_7) = (5, 5, 4, 4, 3, 3, 3)$. Figure 12.3(a) shows the LPT schedule. This has a finish time of 11. Figure 12.3(b) shows an optimal schedule. Its finish time is 9. Hence, for this instance $|F^*(I) - \hat{F}(I)|/F^*(I) = (11 - 9)/9 = 2/9$. □

It is possible to implement the LPT rule so that at most $O(n \log n)$ time is needed to generate an LPT schedule for n tasks on m processors. An exercise examines this. The preceding examples show that although the LPT rule may generate optimal schedules for some problem instances, it does not do so for all instances. How bad can LPT schedules be relative to optimal schedules? This question is answered by the following theorem.

Theorem 12.5 [Graham] Let $F^*(I)$ be the finish time of an optimal m-processor schedule for instance I of the task scheduling problem. Let $\hat{F}(I)$ be the finish time of an LPT schedule for the same instance. Then,

$$\frac{|F^*(I) - \hat{F}(I)|}{|F^*(I)|} \leq \frac{1}{3} - \frac{1}{3m}$$

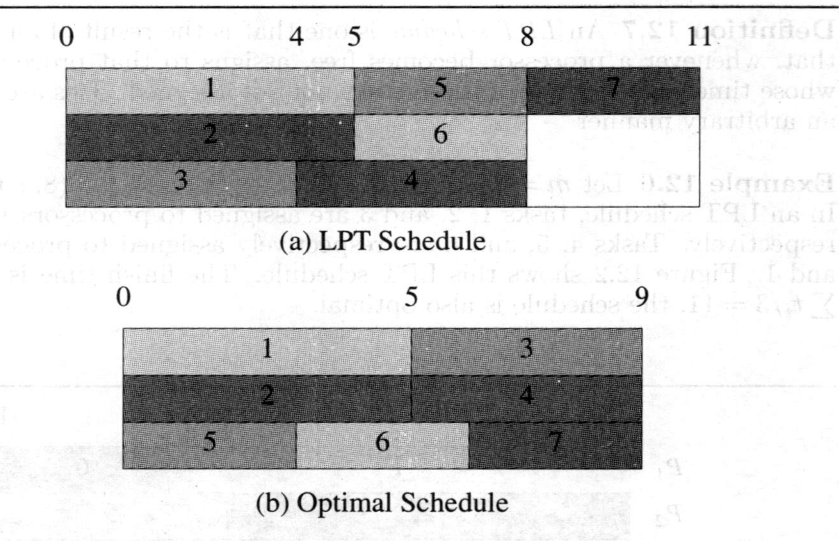

Figure 12.3 LPT and optimal schedules for Example 12.7

Proof: The theorem is clearly true for $m = 1$. So assume $m \geq 2$. Assume that for some m, $m > 1$, there exists a set of tasks for which the theorem is not true. Then, let $(t_1, t_2, \ldots, t_n)$ define an instance I with the fewest number of tasks for which the theorem is violated. We may assume that $t_1 \geq t_2 \geq \cdots \geq t_n$ and that an LPT schedule is obtained by assigning tasks in the order $1, 2, 3, \ldots, n$.

Let S be the LPT schedule obtained by assigning these n tasks in this order. Let $\hat{F}(I)$ be its finish time. Let k be the index of a task with latest completion time. Then, $k = n$. To see this, suppose $k < n$. Then, the finish time $\hat{f}$ of the LPT schedule for tasks $1,2,\ldots,k$ is also $\hat{F}(I)$. The finish time f^* of an optimal schedule for these k tasks is no more than $F^*(I)$. Hence, $|f^* - \hat{f}|/f^* \geq |F^*(I) - \hat{F}(I)|/F^*(I) > 1/3 - 1/(3m)$. (The latter inequality follows from the assumption on I.) Then $|f^* - \hat{f}|/f^* > 1/3 - 1/(3m)$ contradicts the assumption that I is the smallest m-processor instance for which the theorem does not hold. Hence, $k = n$.

Now, we show that in no optimal schedule for I can more than two tasks be assigned to any processor. Hence, $n \leq 2m$. Since task n has the latest completion time in the LPT schedule for I, it follows that this task is started at time $\hat{F}(I) - t_n$ in this schedule. Further, no processor can have any idle time until this time. Hence, we obtain

$$\begin{aligned}
\hat{F}(I) - t_n &\leq \tfrac{1}{m}\textstyle\sum_1^{n-1} t_i \\
\text{So, } \hat{F}(I) &\leq \tfrac{1}{m}\textstyle\sum_1^{n} t_i + \tfrac{m-1}{m} t_n \\
\text{Since } F^*(I) &\geq \tfrac{1}{m}\textstyle\sum_1^{n} t_i
\end{aligned}$$

we can conclude that

$$\begin{aligned}
\hat{F}(I) - F^*(I) &\leq \tfrac{m-1}{m} t_n \\
\text{or } \tfrac{|F^*(I) - \hat{F}(I)|}{F^*(I)} &\leq \tfrac{m-1}{m} \tfrac{t_n}{F^*(I)}
\end{aligned}$$

But, from the assumption on I, the left-hand side of the above inequality is greater than $1/3 - 1/(3m)$. So,

$$\begin{aligned}
\tfrac{1}{3} - \tfrac{1}{3m} &< \tfrac{m-1}{m} \tfrac{t_n}{F^*(I)} \\
\text{or } m - 1 &< \tfrac{3(m-1)t_n}{F^*(I)} \\
\text{or } F^*(I) &< 3t_n
\end{aligned}$$

Hence, in an optimal schedule for I, no more than two tasks can be assigned to any processor. When the optimal schedule contains at most two tasks on any processor, then it can be shown that the LPT schedule is also optimal. We leave this part of the proof as an exercise. Hence, $|F^*(I) - \hat{F}(I)|/F^*(I) = 0$ for this case. This contradicts the assumption on I. So, there can be no I that violates the theorem. □

Theorem 12.5 establishes the LPT rule as a $(1/3 - 1/(3m))$-approximate rule for task scheduling. As remarked earlier, this rule can be implemented to have complexity $O(n \log n)$. The following example shows that $1/3 - 1/(3m)$ is a tight bound on the worst-case performance of the LPT rule.

Example 12.8 Let $n = 2m+1$, $t_i = 2m - \lfloor (i+1)/2 \rfloor$, $i = 1, 2, \ldots, 2m$, and $t_{2m+1} = m$. Figure 12.4(a) shows the LPT schedule. This has a finish time of $4m - 1$. Figure 12.4(b) shows an optimal schedule. Its finish time is $3m$. Hence, $|F^*(I) - \hat{F}(I)|/F^*(I) = 1/3 - 1/(3m)$. □

For LPT schedules, the worst-case error bound of $1/3 - 1/(3m)$ is not very indicative of the expected closeness of LPT finish times to optimal finish times. When $m = 10$, the worst-case error bound is .3. Efficient ϵ-approximate algorithms exist for many scheduling problems. The references at the end of this chapter point to some of the better-known ϵ-approximate

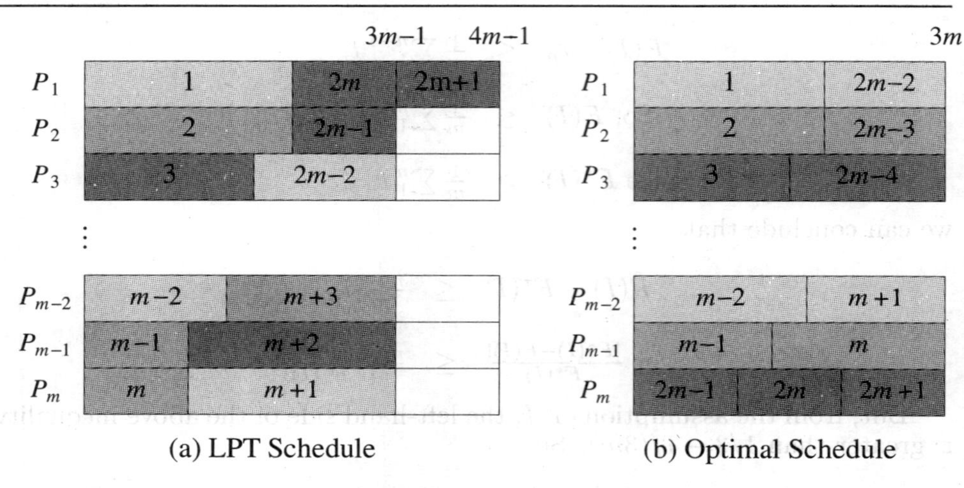

Figure 12.4 Schedules for Example 12.8

scheduling algorithms. Some of these algorithms are also discussed in the exercises.

12.3.2 Bin Packing

In this problem we are given n objects that have to be placed in bins of equal capacity L. Object i requires l_i units of bin capacity. The objective is to determine the minimum number of bins needed to accommodate all n objects. No object may be placed partly in one bin and partly in another.

Example 12.9 Let $L = 10$, $n = 6$, and $(l_1, l_2, l_3, l_4, l_5, l_6) = (5, 6, 3, 1, 2, 4)$. Figure 12.5 shows a packing of the six objects using only three bins. Numbers in bins are object indices. Obviously, at least three bins are needed. □

The bin packing problem can be regarded as a variation of the scheduling problem considered earlier. The bins represent processors and L is the time by which all tasks must be completed. The variable l_i is the processing requirement of task i. The problem is to determine the minimum number of processors needed to accomplish this. An alternative interpretation is to regard the bins as tapes. The variable L is the length of a tape, and l_i the tape length needed to store program i. The problem is to determine the minimum number of tapes needed to store all n programs. Clearly, many interpretations exist for this problem.

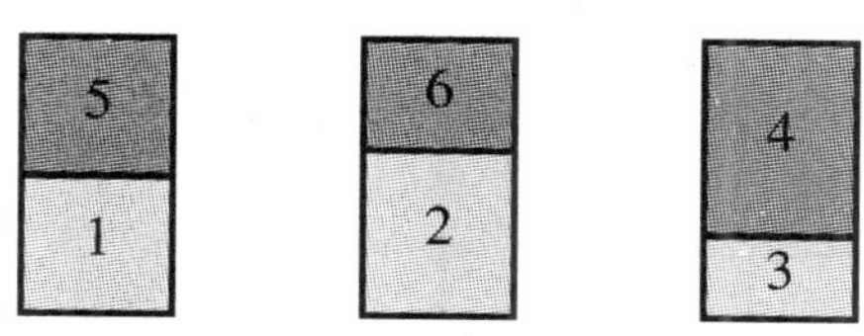

Figure 12.5 Optimal packing for Example 12.9

Theorem 12.6 The bin packing problem is $\mathcal{NP}$-hard.

Proof: To see this, consider the partition problem. Let $\{a_1, a_2, \ldots, a_n\}$ be an instance of the partition problem. Define an instance of the bin packing problem as $l_i = a_i$, $1 \leq i \leq n$, and $L = \sum a_i/2$. Clearly, the minimum number of bins needed is two if and only if there is a partition for $\{a_1, a_2, \ldots, a_n\}$. □

One can devise many simple heuristics for the bin packing problem. These will not, in general, obtain optimal packings. They will, however, obtain packings that use only a small fraction of bins more than an optimal packing. Four simple heuristics are:

1. First Fit (FF): Index the bins $1, 2, 3, \ldots$. All bins are initially filled to level zero. Objects are considered for packing in the order $1, 2, \ldots, n$. To pack object i, find the least index j such that bin j is filled to a level r, $r \leq L - l_i$. Pack i into bin j. Bin j is now filled to level $r + l_i$.

2. Best Fit (BF): The initial conditions on the bins and objects are the same as for FF. When object i is being considered, find the least j such that bin j is filled to a level r, $r \leq L - l_i$ and as large as possible. Pack i into bin j. Bin j is now filled to level $r + l_i$.

3. First Fit Decreasing (FFD): Reorder the objects so that $l_i \geq l_{i+1}$, $1 \leq i < n$. Now use FF to pack the objects.

4. Best Fit Decreasing (BFD): Reorder the objects so that $l_i \geq l_{i+1}$, $1 \leq i < n$. Now use BF to pack the objects.

Example 12.10 Consider the problem instance of Example 12.9. Figure 12.6 shows the packings resulting when each of the four packing heuristics is used. For FFD and BFD the six objects are considered in the order $4, 2, 1, 5, 6, 3$. As is evident from the figure, FFD and BFD do better than either FF or BF on this instance. Although FFD and BFD obtain optimal packings on this instance, they do not in general obtain such packings. □

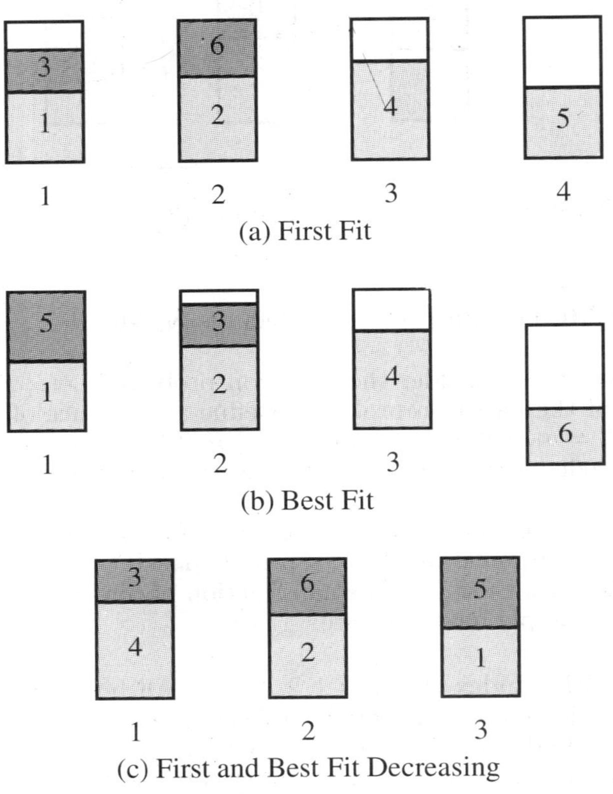

Figure 12.6 Packings resulting from the four heuristics

Theorem 12.7 Let I be an instance of the bin packing problem and $F^*(I)$ be the minimum number of bins needed for this instance. The packing generated by either FF or BF uses no more than $(17/10)F^*(I)+2$ bins. The packing generated by either FFD or BFD uses no more than $(11/9)F^*(I)+4$ bins. These bounds are the best possible for the respective algorithms.

Proof: The proof of this theorem is rather long and complex. It may be found in the paper "Worst-Case Performance Bounds For Simple One-Dimensional Packing Algorithms," by D. Johnson, A. Demers, J. Ullman, M. Garey, and R. Graham, *SIAM Journal on Computing* 3, no. 4, 1974:

299-325. □

12.3.3 $\mathcal{NP}$-hard ϵ-approximation Problems

As in the case of absolute approximations, there exist many $\mathcal{NP}$-hard optimization problems for which the corresponding ϵ-approximation problems are also $\mathcal{NP}$-hard. Let us look at some of these. To begin, consider the traveling salesperson problem.

Theorem 12.8 Hamiltonian cycle $\propto$ ϵ-approximate traveling salesperson.

Proof: Let $G(N, A)$ be any graph. Construct the complete graph $G_1(V, E)$ such that $V = N$ and $E = \{(u, v) | u, v \in V \text{ and } u \neq v\}$. Define the edge weighting function w to be

$$w(u, v) = \begin{cases} 1 & \text{if } (u, v) \in A \\ k & \text{otherwise} \end{cases}$$

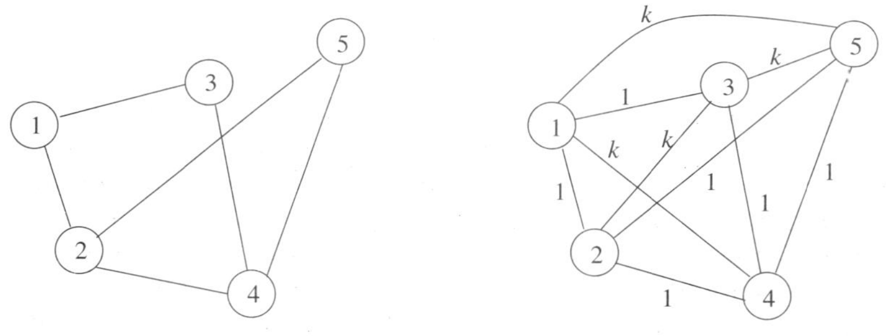

Figure 12.7 An example graph G and its G_1

Figure 12.7 shows an example graph G and the corresponding G_1. Let $n = |N|$. For $k > 1$, the traveling salesperson problem on G_1 has a solution of length n if and only if G has a Hamiltonian cycle. Otherwise, all solutions to G_1 have length $\geq k + n - 1$. If we choose $k \geq (1 + \epsilon)n$, then the only solutions approximating a solution with value n (if there was a Hamiltonian cycle in G_1) also have length n. Consequently, if the ϵ-approximate solution has length $\leq (1+\epsilon)n$, then it must be of length n. If it has length $> (1+\epsilon)n$, then G has no Hamiltonian cycle. □

Another $\mathcal{NP}$-hard ϵ-approximation problem is the 0/1 integer programming problem. In the optimization version of this problem we are provided with a linear optimization function $f(x) = \sum p_i x_i + p_0$. We are required to find a 0/1 vector $(x_1, x_2, \ldots, x_n)$ such that $f(x)$ is optimized (either maximized or minimized) subject to the constraints that $\sum a_{ij}x_j \leq b_i$, $1 \leq i \leq k$. The parameter k is the number of constraints. Note that the 0/1-knapsack problem is a special case of the 0/1 integer programming problem just described. Hence, the integer programming problem is also $\mathcal{NP}$-hard. We shall now show that the corresponding ϵ-approximation problem is $\mathcal{NP}$-hard for all ϵ, $\epsilon > 0$. This is true even when there is only one constraint (that is, $k = 1$).

Theorem 12.9 Partition $\propto$ ϵ-approximate integer programming.

Proof: Let $(a_1, a_2, \ldots, a_n)$ be an instance of the partition problem. Construct the 0/1 integer program

$$\begin{aligned} \text{minimize } 1 + k(m - \textstyle\sum a_i x_i) \\ \text{subject to } \textstyle\sum a_i x_i \leq m \\ x_i = 0 \text{ or } 1, \quad 1 \leq i \leq n \\ m = \textstyle\sum a_i/2 \end{aligned}$$

The value of an optimal solution is 1 if and only if the a_i's have a partition. If they don't, then every optimal solution has a value at least $1 + k$. Suppose there is a polynomial time ϵ-approximate algorithm for the 0/1 integer programming problem for some ϵ, $\epsilon > 0$. Then, by choosing $k > \epsilon$ and using the above construction, this approximation algorithm can be used to solve, in polynomial time, the partition problem. The given partition instance has a partition if and only if the ϵ-approximate algorithm generates a solution with value 1. All other solutions have value $\hat{F}(I)$ such that $|F^*(I) - \hat{F}(I)|/F^*(I) \geq k > \epsilon$. □

As a final example of an ϵ-approximation problem that is $\mathcal{NP}$-hard for all ϵ, $\epsilon > 0$, consider the quadratic assignment problem. In one interpretation this problem is concerned with optimally locating m plants. There are n possible sites for these plants, $n \geq m$. At most one plant may be located in any of these n sites. We use $x_{i,k}$, $1 \leq i \leq n$, $1 \leq k \leq m$, as mn 0/1 variables. The variable $x_{i,k} = 1$ if and only if plant k is to be located at site i. The location of the plants is to be chosen so as to minimize the total cost of transporting goods between plants. Let $d_{k,l}$ be the amount of goods to be transported from plant k to plant l. We have $d_{k,k} = 0$, $1 \leq k \leq m$. Let $c_{i,j}$ be the cost of transporting one unit of the goods from site i to site j. Then $c_{i,i} = 0$, $1 \leq i \leq n$. The *quadratic assignment problem* has the following mathematical formulation

$$\text{minimize } f(x) = \sum_{i,j=1}^{n} \sum_{k,l=1}^{m} c_{i,j} d_{k,l} x_{i,k} x_{j,l}$$

$$\begin{aligned} \text{subject to } \textstyle\sum_{k=1}^{m} x_{i,k} &\leq 1,\ 1 \leq i \leq n \\ \textstyle\sum_{i=1}^{n} x_{i,k} &= 1,\ 1 \leq k \leq m \\ x_{i,k} &= 0, 1, \text{ for all } i, k \\ c_{i,j}, d_{k,l} &\geq 0,\ 1 \leq i, j \leq n,\ 1 \leq k, l \leq m \end{aligned}$$

The first condition ensures that at most one plant is located at any site. The second condition ensures that every plant is located at exactly one site. The function $f(x)$ is the total transportation cost.

Example 12.11 Assume two plants are to be located ($m = 2$) and there are three possible sites ($n = 3$). Assume

$$\begin{bmatrix} d_{11} & d_{12} \\ d_{21} & d_{22} \end{bmatrix} = \begin{bmatrix} 0 & 4 \\ 10 & 0 \end{bmatrix}$$

$$\text{and } \begin{bmatrix} c_{11} & c_{12} & c_{13} \\ c_{21} & c_{22} & c_{23} \\ c_{31} & c_{32} & c_{33} \end{bmatrix} = \begin{bmatrix} 0 & 9 & 3 \\ 5 & 0 & 10 \\ 2 & 6 & 0 \end{bmatrix}$$

If plant 1 is located at site 1 and plant 2 at site 2, then the transportation cost $f(x)$ is $9*4+5*10 = 86$. If plant 1 is located at site 3 and plant 2 at site 1, then the cost $f(x)$ is $2*4 + 3*10 = 38$. The optimal locations are plant 1 at site 1 and plant 2 at site 3. The cost $f(x)$ is $3*4 + 2*10 = 32$. □

Theorem 12.10 Hamiltonian cycle $\propto$ ϵ-approximate quadratic assignment.

Proof: Let $G(N, A)$ be an undirected graph with $m = |N|$. The following quadratic assignment instance is constructed from G:

$$\begin{aligned} n &= m \\ c_{j,i} &= \begin{cases} 1 & \text{if } i = (j \bmod m) + 1,\ 1 \leq i, j \leq m \\ 0 & \text{otherwise} \end{cases} \\ d_{k,l} &= \begin{cases} 1 & \text{if } (k, l) \in A,\ 1 \leq k, l \leq m \\ \omega & \text{otherwise} \end{cases} \end{aligned}$$

The total cost $f(\gamma)$ of an assignment γ of plants to locations is $\sum_{i=1}^{n} c_{i,j}\ d_{\gamma(i)\gamma(j)}$, where $j = (i \bmod m) + 1$ and $\gamma(i)$ is the index of the plant assigned to location i. If G has a Hamiltonian cycle $i_1, i_2, \ldots, i_n, i_1$, then the assignment $\gamma(j) = i_j$ has a cost $f(\gamma) = m$. If G has no Hamiltonian cycle, then at least one of the values $d_{\gamma(i),\ \gamma(i \bmod m+1)}$ must be ω and so the cost becomes $\geq m + \omega - 1$. Choosing $\omega > (1+\epsilon)m$ results in optimal solutions with a value of m if G has a Hamiltonian cycle, and value $> (1+\epsilon)m$ if G has no Hamiltonian cycle. Thus, from an ϵ-approximate solution, it can be determined whether G has a Hamiltonian cycle. □

Many other ϵ-approximation problems are known to be $\mathcal{NP}$-hard. Some of these are examined in the exercises. Although the three problems just discussed were $\mathcal{NP}$-hard for ϵ, $\epsilon > 0$, it is quite possible for an ϵ-approximation problem to be $\mathcal{NP}$-hard only for ϵ in some range, say $0 < \epsilon \leq r$. For $\epsilon > r$, there may exist simple polynomial time approximation algorithms.

EXERCISES

1. Obtain an $O(n \log n)$ algorithm that implements the LPT scheduling rule.

2. Show that LPT schedules are optimal for all task sets that have optimal schedules in which no more than two tasks are assigned to any processor.

3. A uniform processor system is a set of $m \geq 1$ processors. Processor i operates at a speed s_i, $s_i > 0$. If task i requires t_i units of processing, then it may be completed in t_i/s_i units of real time on processor p_i. When $s_i = 1$, $1 \leq i \leq m$, we have a system of identical processors (Section 12.3). An MLPT schedule is defined to be any schedule obtained by assigning tasks to processors in order of nonincreasing processing times. When a task is being considered for assignment to a processor, it is assigned to that processor on which its finishing time will be earliest. Ties are broken by assigning the task to a processor with least index.

   (a) Let $m = 3$, $s_1 = 1, s_2 = 2$, and $s_3 = 3$. Let the number n of tasks be 6. Let $(t_1, t_2, t_3, t_4, t_5, t_6) = (9, 6, 3, 3, 2, 2)$. Obtain the MLPT schedule for this set of tasks. Is this an optimal schedule? If not, obtain an optimal schedule.

   (b) Show that there exists a two processor system and a set I for which $|F^*(I) - \hat{F}(I)|/F^*(I) > 1/3 - 1/(3m)$. The time $\hat{F}(I)$ is the finish time of the MLPT schedule. Note that $1/3 - 1/(3m)$ is the bound for LPT schedules on identical processors.

   (c) Write an algorithm to obtain MLPT schedules. What is the time complexity of your algorithm?

4. Let I be any instance of the uniform processor scheduling problem. Let $\hat{F}(I)$ and $F^*(I)$ respectively be the finish times of MLPT and optimal schedules. Show that $\hat{F}(I)/F^*(I) \leq 2m/(m+1)$ (see Exercise 3).

5. For a uniform processor system (see Exercises 3 and 4), show that when $m = 2$, $\hat{F}(I)/F^*(I) \leq (1 + \sqrt{17})/4$. Show that this is the best possible bound for $m = 2$.

6. Let $P_1, \ldots, P_m$ be a set of processors. Let t_{ij}, $t_{ij} > 0$, be the time needed to process task i if its processing is carried out on processor P_j, $1 \leq i \leq n$, $1 \leq j \leq m$. For a uniform processor system, $t_{ij}/t_{ik} = s_k/s_j$, where s_k and s_j are the speeds of P_k and P_j respectively. In a system of *nonidentical processors*, such a relation need not exist. As an example, consider $n = 2$, $m = 2$, and

$$\begin{bmatrix} t_{11} & t_{12} \\ t_{21} & t_{22} \end{bmatrix} = \begin{bmatrix} 1 & 2 \\ 3 & 2 \end{bmatrix}$$

If task 1 is processed on P_2 and task 2 on P_1, then the finish time is 3. If task 1 is processed on P_1 and task 2 on P_2, the finish time is 2. Show that if a schedule is constructed by assigning task i to processor j so that $t_{ij} \leq t_{ik}$, $1 \leq k \leq m$, then $\hat{F}(I)/F^*(I) \leq m$. The times $\hat{F}(I)$ and $F^*(I)$ are the finish times of the schedule constructed and of an optimal schedule, respectively. Show that this bound is best possible for this algorithm.

7. For the scheduling problem of Exercise 6, define function Schedule as in Algorithm 12.3. Then $f[j]$ is the current finish time on processor j. So, $\hat{F}(I) = \max_j \{f[j]\}$. Show that $\hat{F}(I)/F^*(I) \leq m$ and this bound is best possible.

8. In Exercise 7, first order the tasks so that $\min_j \{t_{i,j}\} \geq \min_j \{t_{i+1,j}\}$, $1 \leq i < n$. Then use function `Schedule`. Show that $\hat{F}(I)/F^*(I) \leq m$ and this bound is best possible.

9. Show that the results of Exercise 7 hold even if the initial ordering is such that $\max_j \{t_{i,j}\} \geq \max_j \{t_{i+1,j}\}$, $1 \leq i < n$.

10. Consider the following heuristic for the max clique problem: delete from G a vertex that is not connected to every other vertex and repeat until the remaining graph is a clique. Show that this heuristic does not result in an ϵ-approximate algorithm for the max clique problem for any ϵ, $0 < \epsilon < 1$.

```
Algorithm Schedule(f, t)
{
    for j := 1 to m do f[j] := 0;
    for i := 1 to n do
    {
        k :=least j such that
            f[j] + t[i, j] ≤ f[l] + t[i, l], 1 ≤ l ≤ m;
        f[k] := f[k] + t[i, k];
    }
}
```

Algorithm 12.3 Scheduling

11. For the max clique problem, consider the following heuristic: Let $S = \emptyset$. Add to S a vertex not in S that is connected to all vertices in S. If there is no such vertex, then stop with S the approximate max clique; otherwise repeat. Show that the algorithm resulting from this heuristic in not an ϵ-approximate algorithm for the max-clique problem for any ϵ, $\epsilon < 1$.

12. Show the function Color (Algorithm 12.4) is not an ϵ-approximate coloring algorithm for the minimum colorability problem for any ϵ, $\epsilon > 0$.

13. Consider any tour for the traveling salesperson problem. Let city i_1 be the starting point. Assume the n cities appear in the tour in the order $i_1, i_2, i_3, \ldots, i_n, i_{n+1} = i_1$. Let $l(i_j, i_{j+1})$ be the length of edge $\langle i_j, i_{j+1} \rangle$. The arrival time Y_k at city i_k is

$$Y_k = \sum_{j=1}^{k-1} l(i_j, i_{j+1}), \quad 1 < k \leq n+1$$

The mean arrival time $\overline{Y}$ is

$$\overline{Y} = \frac{1}{n} \sum_{k=2}^{n+1} Y_k$$

Show that the ϵ-approximate minimum mean arrival time problem is $\mathcal{NP}$-hard for all ϵ, $\epsilon > 0$.

```
Algorithm Color(G)
// G = (V, E) is a graph with |V| = n vertices. col[i]
// is the color to use for vertex i, 1 ≤ i ≤ n.
{
    i := 1; // Next color to use
    j := 0; // Number of vertices colored
    while j ≠ n do
    {
        S := ∅; // Vertices colored with i
        while there is an uncolored vertex, v,
            not adjacent to a vertex in S do
        {
            col[v] := i; S := S ∪ {v}; j := j + 1;
        }
        i := i + 1;
    }
}
```

Algorithm 12.4 Function for Exercise 12

14. Let Y_k and $\overline{Y}$ be as in Exercise 13. The variance σ in arrival times is

$$\frac{1}{n}\sum_{2}^{n+1}(Y_k - \overline{Y})^2$$

Show that the ϵ-approximate minimum variance time problem is $\mathcal{NP}$-hard for all ϵ, $\epsilon > 0$.

12.4 POLYNOMIAL TIME APPROXIMATION SCHEMES

12.4.1 Scheduling Independent Tasks

We have seen that the LPT rule leads to a $(1/3 - 1/(3m))$-approximate algorithm for the problem of obtaining an m processor schedule for n tasks. A polynomial time approximation scheme is also known for this problem. This scheme relies on the following scheduling rule: Let k be some specified and fixed integer. Obtain an optimal schedule for the k longest tasks. Schedule the remaining $n - k$ tasks using the LPT rule.

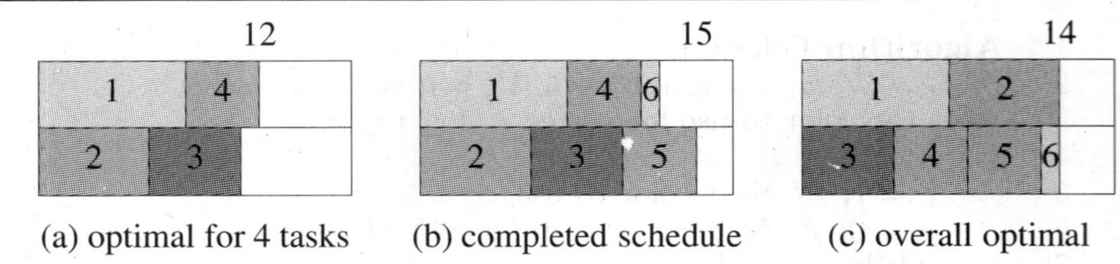

(a) optimal for 4 tasks (b) completed schedule (c) overall optimal

Figure 12.8 Using the approximation schedule with $k = 4$

Example 12.12 Let $m = 2$, $n = 6$, $(t_1, t_2, t_3, t_4, t_5, t_6) = (8, 6, 5, 4, 4, 1)$, and $k = 4$. The four longest tasks have task times 8, 6, 5, and 4 respectively. An optimal schedule for these has finish time 12 (Figure 12.8(a)). When the remaining two tasks are scheduled using the LPT rule, the schedule of Figure 12.8(b) results. This has finish time 15. Figure 12.8(c) shows an optimal schedule. This has finish time 14. □

Theorem 12.11 [Graham] Let I be an m-processor instance of the scheduling problem. Let $F^*(I)$ be the finish time of an optimal schedule for I and let $\hat{F}(I)$ be the length of the schedule generated by the above scheduling rule. Then,

$$\frac{|F^*(I) - \hat{F}(I)|}{F^*(I)} \leq \frac{1 - 1/m}{1 + \lfloor k/m \rfloor}$$

Proof: Let r be the finish time of an optimal schedule for the k longest tasks. If $\hat{F}(I) = r$, then $F^*(I) = \hat{F}(I)$ and the theorem is proved. So, assume $\hat{F}(I) > r$. Let t_i, $1 \leq i \leq n$, be the task times of the n tasks of I. Without loss of generality, we can assume $t_i \geq t_{i+1}$, $1 \leq i < n$, and $n > k$. Also, we can assume $n > m$. Let j, $j > k$, be such that task j has finish time $\hat{F}(I)$. Then, no processor is idle in the interval $[0, \hat{F}(I) - t_j]$. Since $t_{k+1} \geq t_j$, it follows that no processor is idle in the interval $[0, \hat{F}(I) - t_{k+1}]$. Hence,

$$\begin{aligned} \textstyle\sum_{i=1}^{n} t_i &\geq m(\hat{F}(I) - t_{k+1}) + t_{k+1} \\ \text{and so, } F^*(I) &\geq \tfrac{1}{m}\textstyle\sum_1^n t_i \geq \hat{F}(I) - \tfrac{m-1}{m} t_{k+1} \\ \text{or } |F^*(I) - \hat{F}(I)| &\leq \tfrac{m-1}{m} t_{k+1} \end{aligned}$$

Since $t_i \geq t_{k+1}$, $1 \leq i \leq k+1$, and at least one processor must execute at least $1 + \lfloor k/m \rfloor$ of these $k+1$ tasks, it follows that

$$F^*(I) \geq (1 + \lfloor k/m \rfloor) t_{k+1}$$

Combining these two inequalities, we obtain

$$\frac{|F^*(I) - \hat{F}(I)|}{F^*(I)} \leq \frac{(m-1)/m}{1 + \lfloor k/m \rfloor} = \frac{1 - 1/m}{1 + \lfloor k/m \rfloor} \qquad \square$$

Using the result of Theorem 12.11, we can construct a polynomial time ϵ-approximation scheme for the scheduling problem. This scheme has ϵ as an input variable. For any input ϵ, it computes an integer k such that $\epsilon \leq (1 - 1/m)/(1 + \lfloor k/m \rfloor)$. This defines the k to be used in the scheduling rule described above. Solving for k, we obtain that any integer k, $k > (m-1)/\epsilon - m$, guarantees ϵ-approximate schedules. The time required to obtain such schedules, however, depends mainly on the time needed to obtain an optimal schedule for k tasks on m machines. Using a branch-and-bound algorithm, this time is $O(m^k)$. The time needed to arrange the tasks so that $t_i \geq t_{i+1}$ and also to obtain the LPT schedule for the remaining $n - k$ tasks is $O(n \log n)$. Hence the total time needed by the ϵ-approximate scheme is $O(n \log n + m^k) = O(n \log n + m^{\lceil (m-1)/\epsilon - m \rceil})$. Since this time is not polynomial in $1/\epsilon$ (it is exponential in $1/\epsilon$), this approximation scheme is not a fully polynomial time approximation scheme. It is a polynomial time approximation scheme (for any fixed m) as the computing time is polynomial in the number of tasks n.

12.4.2 0/1 Knapsack

The 0/1 knapsack heuristic proposed in Example 12.2 does not result in an ϵ-approximate algorithm for any ϵ, $0 < \epsilon < 1$. Suppose we try the heuristic described by function EpsilonApprox (Algorithm 12.5). In this function $p[\ ]$ and $w[\ ]$ are the sets of profits and weights respectively. It is assumed that $p_i/w_i \geq p_{i+1}/w_{i+1}$, $1 \leq i < n$. The variable m is the knapsack capacity and k a nonnegative integer. In the **for** loop of lines 8 to 12, all $\sum_{i=0}^{k} \binom{n}{i}$ different subsets I consisting of at most k of the n objects are generated. If the currently generated subset I is such that $\sum_{i \in I} w_i > m$, it is discarded (as it is infeasible). Otherwise, the space remaining in the knapsack (that is, $m - \sum_{i \in I} w_i$) is filled using the heuristic described in Example 12.2. This heuristic is stated more formally as function LBound (Algorithm 12.6).

Example 12.13 Consider the knapsack problem instance with $n = 8$ objects, size of knapsack $= m = 110$, $p = \{11, 21, 31, 33, 43, 53, 55, 65\}$, and $w = \{1, 11, 21, 23, 33, 43, 45, 55\}$.

```
Algorithm EpsilonApprox(p, w, m, n, k)
// The size of a combination is the number of objects in it.
// The weight of a combination is the sum of the weights
// of the objects in that combination; k is a nonnegative
// integer that defines the order of the algorithm.
{
    Pmax := 0;
    for all combinations I of size ≤ k and weight ≤ m do
    {
        P_I := Σ_{i∈I} p_i;
        Pmax := max(Pmax, P_I + LBound(I, p, w, m, n));
    }
    return Pmax;
}
```

Algorithm 12.5 Heuristic algorithm for knapsack problem

```
Algorithm LBound(I, p, w, m, n)
{
    s := 0;
    t := m − Σ_{i∈I} w_i;
    for i := 1 to n do
        if (i ∉ I) and (w[i] ≤ t) then
        {
            s := s + p[i]; t := t − w[i];
        }
    return s;
}
```

Algorithm 12.6 Subalgorithm for function EpsilonApprox

The optimal solution is obtained by putting objects 1, 2, 3, 5, and 6 into the knapsack. This results in an optimal profit p^* of 159 and a weight of 109.

We obtain the following approximations for different k:

1. $k = 0$. $Pmax$ is just the lower bound solution $\mathsf{LBound}(\phi, p, w, m, n) = 139$, $x = (1, 1, 1, 1, 1, 0, 0, 0)$, $w = \sum_i x_i w_i = 89$, and $(p^* - Pmax)/P^* =$

$20/159 = .126$.

2. $k = 1$. $Pmax = 151$, $x = (1, 1, 1, 1, 0, 0, 1, 0)$, $w = 101$, and $(p^* - Pmax)/p^* = 8/159 = .05$.

3. $k = 2$. $Pmax = p^* = 159$, $x = (1, 1, 1, 0, 1, 1, 0, 0)$, and $w = 109$.

Table 12.1 gives the details for $k = 1$. It is interesting to note that the combinations $I = \{1\}$, $\{2\}$, $\{3\}$, $\{4\}$, $\{5\}$ need not be tried since for $I = \emptyset$, x_6 is the first x_i, which is 0, and so these combinations yield the same $Pmax$. This is true for all combinations I that include only objects for which x_i was 1 in the solution for $I = \emptyset$. □

Theorem 12.12 [Sahni] Let J be an instance of the knapsack problem. Let n, m, p and w be as defined for function EpsilonApprox. Let p^* be the value of an optimal solution for J. Let $Pmax$ be as defined by function EpsilonApprox on termination. Then,

$$|p^* - Pmax|/p^* < 1/(k + 1)$$

I	$Pmax$	P_I	R_I	LBound	$PMAX = \max\{Pmax, P_I + \text{LBound}\}$	$x_{optimal}$
$\emptyset$	0	11	1	128	139	(1,1,1,1,1,0,0,0)
6	139	53	43	96	149	(1,1,1,1,0,1,0,0)
7	149	55	45	9	151	(1,1,1,1,0,0,1,0)
8	151	65	55	63	151	(1,1,1,1,0,0,1,0)

* Note that rather than update $x_{optimal}$, it is easier to update the optimal I and recompute $x_{optimal}$ at the end.

Table 12.1 Expansion of Example 12.13 for $k = 1$

Proof: Let R be the set of objects included in the knapsack in some optimal solution. So, $\sum_{i \in R} p_i = p^*$ and $\sum_{i \in R} w_i \leq m$. If the number of objects in R, $|R|$, is such that $|R| \leq k$, then at some time in the execution of function EpsilonApprox, $I = R$ and so $Pmax = p^*$. Therefore, assume $|R| > k$. Let $(\hat{p}_i, \hat{w}_i)$, $1 \leq i \leq |R|$, be the profits and weights of the objects in R. Assume these have been indexed so that $\hat{p}_i, \ldots, \hat{p}_k$ are the k largest profits in R, and $\hat{p}_i/\hat{w}_i \geq \hat{p}_{i+1}/\hat{w}_{i+1}$, $k < i < |R|$. From the first of these assumptions, it follows that $\hat{p}_{k+q} \leq p^*/(k + 1)$, $1 \leq q \leq |R| - k$. Since the **for** loop of lines 8 to 11 tries out all combinations of size at most k, it follows that in some iteration, I corresponds to the set of k largest profits in R. Hence, $P_I = \sum_{i \in I} p_i = \sum_{i=1}^{k} \hat{p}_i$. Consider the computation of line 10 in this iteration. In the computation of LBound(I, p, w, m, n), let j be the least index such that $j \notin I, w_j > t$, and $j \in R$. Thus, object j corresponds to one of the objects $(\hat{p}_r, \hat{w}_r)$, $k < r \leq |R|$, and j is not included in the knapsack by function LBound. Let object j correspond to $(\hat{p}_q, \hat{w}_q)$.

At the time object j is considered, $t < w_j = \hat{w}_q$. The amount of space filled by function LBound is $m - \sum_{i \in I} w_i - t$, and this is larger than $\sum_{i=k+1}^{q-1} w_i$ (as $\sum_1^q \hat{w}_i \leq m$). Since this amount of space is filled by considering objects in nondecreasing order of p_i/w_i, it follows that the profit s added by LBound is no less than

$$\sum_{i=k+1}^{q-1} \hat{p}_i + \frac{\hat{p}_q}{\hat{w}_q} \triangle$$

$$\text{where } \triangle \;=\; m - t - \textstyle\sum_1^{q-1} \hat{w}_i$$

$$\text{Also, } \textstyle\sum_{i=q}^{|R|} \hat{p}_i \;\leq\; \frac{\hat{p}_q}{\hat{w}_q}(m - \sum_1^{q-1} \hat{w}_i)$$

From these two inequalities, we obtain

$$\begin{aligned} p^* &= P_I + \textstyle\sum_{k+1}^{|R|} \hat{p}_i \\ &\leq P_I + s - \frac{\hat{p}_q}{\hat{w}_q} \triangle + \frac{\hat{p}_q}{\hat{w}_q}(m - \sum_1^{q-1} \hat{w}_i) \\ &= P_I + s + \hat{p}_q(t/\hat{w}_q) \\ &< P_I + s + \hat{p}_q \end{aligned}$$

Since, $Pmax \geq P_I + s$ and $\hat{p}_q \leq p^*/(k+1)$, it follows that

$$\frac{|p^* - Pmax|}{p^*} < \frac{\hat{p}_q}{p^*} \leq \frac{1}{k+1}$$

This completes the proof. □

The time required by Algorithm 12.5 is $O(n^{k+1})$. To see this, note that the total number of subsets tried is

$$\sum_{i=0}^{k} \binom{n}{i} \text{ and } \sum_{i=0}^{k} \binom{n}{i} \leq \sum_{i=0}^{k} n^i = \frac{n^{k+1} - 1}{n - 1} = O(n^k)$$

Function LBound has complexity $O(n)$. So, the total time is $O(n^{k+1})$.

Function EpsilonApprox can be used as a polynomial time approximation scheme. For any given ϵ, $0 < \epsilon < 1$, we can choose k to be the least integer greater than or equal to $(1/\epsilon) - 1$. This will guarantee a fractional error in the solution value of at most ϵ. The computing time is $O(n^{1/\epsilon})$.

Although Theorem 12.12 provides an upper bound on $|p^* - Pmax|/p^*$, it does not say anything about how good this bound is. Nor does it say anything about the kind of performance we can expect in practice. Let us now address these two problems.

Theorem 12.13 [Sahni] For every k there exist knapsack instances for which $|(p^* - Pmax)/p^*|$ gets as close to $1/(k+1)$ as desired.

Proof: For any k, the simplest examples approaching the lower bound are obtained by setting $n = k+2$; $w_1 = 1$; $p_1 = 2$; $p_i, w_i = r$, $2 \leq i \leq k+2$, $r > 2$; and $m = (k+1)r$. Then $p^* = (k+1)r$. The $Pmax$ given by EpsilonApprox for this k is $kr + 2$ and therefore $|(p^* - Pmax)/p^*| = (1 - 2/r)/(k+1)$. By choosing r increasingly large, one can get as close to $1/(k+1)$ as desired. □

Another upper bound on the value of $|(p^* - Pmax)/p^*|$ can be obtained from the proof of Theorem 12.12. We know that $p^* - Pmax < \hat{p}_q$ and $p^* \geq Pmax$. Also since $\hat{p}_q$ is one of $\hat{p}_{k+1}, \ldots, \hat{p}_{|R|}$, it follows that $\hat{p}_q \leq \bar{p}$, where $\bar{p}$ is the $(k+1)$st largest p. Hence $|(p^* - Pmax)/p^*| < \min\{1/(k+1),\ \bar{p}/Pmax\}$. In most cases $\bar{p}/Pmax$ will be smaller than $1/(k+1)$ and so will give a better estimate of closeness in cases in which the optimal is not known. We note that $\bar{p}$ is easy to compute.

Theorem 12.14 [Sahni] The deviation of the solution $Pmax$ obtained from the ϵ-approximate algorithm from the true optimal p^* is bounded by $|(p^* - Pmax)/p^*| < \min\ \{1/(k+1),\ \bar{p}/Pmax\}$. □

EXERCISES

1. Show that if line 11 of Algorithm 12.5 is changed to $Pmax = \max$ {Pmax,LBound(I, p, w, m, n)} and the fourth line of function LBound replaced by the line $t := m$;, then the resulting algorithm is not ϵ-approximate for any ϵ, $0 < \epsilon < 1$. Note that the new heuristic constrains I to be outside the knapsack. The original heuristic constrains I to be inside the knapsack.

2. Let $G = (V, E)$ be an undirected graph. Assume that the vertices represent documents. The edges are weighted so that $w(i, j)$ is the dissimilarity between documents i and j. It is desired to partition the vertices into $k \geq 3$ disjoint clusters such that

$$\sum_{i=1}^{k} \sum_{\substack{(u,v) \in E \\ u,v \in C_i}} w(u, v)$$

is minimized. The set C_i is the set of documents in cluster i. Show that the ϵ-approximate version of this problem is $\mathcal{NP}$-hard for all ϵ, $\epsilon > 0$. Note that k is a fixed integer provided with each problem instance and may be different for different instances.

3. Show that if we change the optimization function of Exercise 2 to maximize

$$\sum_{\substack{u \in C_i \\ v \notin C_1 \\ (u,v) \in E}} w(u,v)$$

then there is a polynomial time ϵ-approximation algorithm for some ϵ, $0 < \epsilon < 1$.

12.5 FULLY POLYNOMIAL TIME APPROXIMATION SCHEMES

The approximation algorithms and schemes we have seen so far are particular to the problem considered. There is no set of well-defined techniques that we can use to obtain such algorithms. The heuristics used depend very much on the particular problem being solved. For the case of fully polynomial time approximation schemes, we can identify three underlying techniques. These techniques apply to a variety of optimization problems. We discuss these three techniques in terms of maximization problems. We assume the maximization problem to be of the form

$$\max \sum_{i=1}^{n} p_i x_i$$

$$\text{subject to } \sum_{i=1}^{n} a_{ij} x_i \le b_j, \ 1 \le j \le m$$

$$x_i = 0 \text{ or } 1, \quad 1 \le i \le n \tag{12.1}$$

$$p_i, \ a_{ij} \ge 0$$

Without loss of generality, we assume that $a_{ij} \le b_j$, $1 \le i \le n$ and $1 \le j \le m$.

If $1 \le k \le n$, then the assignment $x_i = y_i$, is said to be a *feasible assignment* if and only if there exists at least one feasible solution to (12.1) with $x_i = y_i$, $1 \le i \le k$. A *completion* of a feasible assignment $x_i = y_i$ is any feasible solution to (12.1) with $x_i = y_i$, $1 \le i \le k$. Let $x_i = y_i$ and $x_i = z_i$, $1 \le i \le k$, be two feasible assignments such that for at least one j, $1 \leq j \leq k$, $y_i \neq z_j$. Let $\sum_{i=1}^{k} p_i y_i = \sum_{i=1}^{k} p_i z_i$. We say that $y_1, \ldots, y_k$ *dominates* $z_1, \ldots, z_k$ if and only if there exists a completion $y_1, \ldots, y_k, y_{k+1}, \ldots, y_n$ such that $\sum_{i=1}^{n} p_i y_i$ is greater than or equal to $\sum_{1 \leq i \leq n} p_i z_i$ for all completions $z_1, \ldots, z_n$ of $z_1, \ldots, z_k$. The approximation techniques to be discussed apply to those problems that can be formulated as (12.1) and for which simple rules can be found to determine when one feasible assignment dominates another. Such rules exist, for example, for problems solvable by the dynamic programming technique. Some such problems are 0/1 knapsack, job sequencing with deadlines, job sequencing to minimize finish time, and job sequencing to minimize weighted mean finish time.

One way to solve problems stated as above is to systematically generate all feasible assignments starting from the null assignment. Let $S^{(i)}$ represent the set of all feasible assignments for $x_1, x_2, \ldots, x_i$. Then $S^{(0)}$ represents the null assignment and $S^{(n)}$ the set of all completions. The answer to our problem is an assignment in $S^{(n)}$ that maximizes the objective function. The solution approach is then to generate $S^{(i+1)}$ from $S^{(i)}, 1 \leq i < n$. If an $S^{(i)}$ contains two feasible assignments $y_1, \ldots, y_i$ and $z_1, \ldots, z_i$ such that $\sum_{j=1}^{i} p_j y_j = \sum_{j=1}^{i} p_j z_j$, then use of the dominance rules enables us to discard or kill that assignment which is dominated. In some cases the dominance rules may permit the discarding or killing of a feasible assignment even when $\sum p_j y_j \neq \sum p_j z_j$. This happens, for instance, in the knapsack problem (see Section 5.7). Following the use of the dominance rules, it is the case that for each feasible assignment in $S^{(i)}$, $\sum_{j=1}^{i} p_j x_j$ is distinct. However, despite this, it is possible for each $S^{(i)}$ to contain twice as many feasible assignments as in $S^{(i-1)}$. This results in a worst-case computing time that is exponential in n. Note that this solution approach is identical to the dynamic programming solution methodology for the knapsack problem (Section 5.7) and also to the branch-and-bound algorithm later developed for this problem (Section 8.2).

The approximation methods we discuss are called *rounding, interval partitioning*, and *separation*. These methods restrict the number of distinct $\sum_{j=1}^{i} p_j x_j$ to only a polynomial function of n. The error introduced is within some prespecified bound.

12.5.1 Rounding

The aim of rounding is to start from a problem instance I that is formulated as in (12.1) and to transform it to another problem instance I' that is easier to solve. This transformation is carried out in such a way that the optimal solution value of I' is close to the optimal solution value of I. In particular, if we are provided with a bound ϵ on the fractional difference between the exact and approximate solution values, then we require that $|F^*(I) - F^*(I')/F^*(I)| \leq \epsilon$, where $F^*(I)$ and $F^*(I')$ represent the optimal solution values of I and I' respectively.

Problem instance I' is obtained from I by changing the objective function to $\max \sum q_i x_i$. Since I and I' have the same constraints, they have the same feasible solutions. Hence, if the p_i's and q_i's differ by only a small amount, the value of an optimal solution to I' will be close to the value of an optimal solution to I.

For example, if the p_i in I have the values $(p_1, p_2, p_3, p_4) = (1.1, 2.1, 1001.6, 1002.3)$ and we construct I' with $(q_1, q_2, q_3, q_4) = (0, 0, 1000, 1000)$, it is easy to see that the value of any solution in I is at most 7.1 more than the value of the same solution in I'. This worst-case difference is achieved only when $x_i = 1$, $1 \le i \le 4$, is a feasible solution for I (and hence also for I'). Since $a_{ij} \le b_j$, $1 \le i \le n$ and $1 \le j \le m$, it follows that $F^*(I) \ge 1002.3$ (as one feasible solution is $x_1 = x_2 = x_3 = 0$ and $x_4 = 1$). But $F^*(I) - F^*(I') \le 7.1$ and so $(F^*(I) - F^*(I'))/F^*(I) \le 0.007$. Solving I using the procedure outlined above, the feasible assignments in $S^{(i)}$ could have the following distinct profit values:

$$\begin{array}{ll} S^{(0)} & \{0\} \\ S^{(1)} & \{0, 1.1\} \\ S^{(2)} & \{0, 1.1, 2.1, 3.2\} \\ S^{(3)} & \{0, 1.1, 2.1, 3.2, 1001.6, 1002.7, 1003.7, 1004.8\} \\ S^{(4)} & \{0, 1.1, 2.1, 3.2, 1001.6, 1002.3, 1002.7, 1003.4, 1003.7, \\ & \quad 1004.4, 1004.8, 1005.5, 2003.9, 2005, 2006, 2007.1\} \end{array}$$

Thus, barring any elimination of feasible assignments resulting from the dominance rules or from any heuristic, the solution of I using the procedure outlined requires the computation of $\sum_{0 \le i \le n} |S^{(i)}| = 31$ feasible assignments.

The feasible assignments for I' have the following values:

$$\begin{array}{ll} S^{(0)} & \{0\} \\ S^{(1)} & \{0\} \\ S^{(2)} & \{0\} \\ S^{(3)} & \{0, 1000\} \\ S^{(4)} & \{0, 1000, 2000\} \end{array}$$

Note that $\sum_{i=0}^{n} |S^{(i)}|$ is only 8. Hence I' can be solved in about one-fourth the time needed for I. An inaccuracy of at most .7% is introduced.

Given the p_i's and an ϵ, what should the q_i's be so that

$$|F^*(I) - F^*(I')|/F^*(I) \le \epsilon \text{ and } \sum_{i=0}^{n} |S^{(i)}| \le u(n, 1/\epsilon)$$

where u is a polynomial in n and $1/\epsilon$? Once we figure this out, we have a fully polynomial approximation scheme for our problem since it is possible to go from $S^{(i-1)}$ to $S^{(i)}$ in time proportional to $O(S^{(i-1)})$ (see the knapsack algorithm of Section 5.7).

Let LB be an estimate for $F^*(I)$ such that $F^*(I) \geq$ LB. Clearly, we can assume LB $\geq \max\{p_i\}$. If

$$\sum_{i=1}^{n} |p_i - q_i| \leq \epsilon F^*(I)$$

then it is clear that $[F^*(I) - F^*(I')]/F^*(I) \leq \epsilon$. Define $q_i = p_i - \text{rem}(p_i, (\text{LB}\cdot\epsilon)/n)$, where rem$(a, b)$ is the remainder of a/b, that is, $a - \lfloor a/b \rfloor b$ (for example, rem(7, 6) = 1/6 and rem(2.2, 1.3) = .9). Since rem$(p_i, \text{LB}\cdot\epsilon/n) < \text{LB}\cdot\epsilon/n$, it follows that $\sum |p_i - q_i| < \text{LB}\cdot\epsilon \leq F^*\cdot\epsilon$. Hence, if an optimal solution to I' is used as an optimal solution for I, the fractional error is less than ϵ.

To determine the time required to solve I' exactly, it is useful to introduce another problem I'' with s_i, $1 \leq i \leq n$, as its objective function coefficients. Define $s_i = \lfloor (p_i \cdot n)/(\text{LB}\cdot\epsilon) \rfloor$, $1 \leq i \leq n$. It is easy to see that $s_i = (q_i \cdot n)/(\text{LB}\cdot\epsilon)$. Clearly, the $S^{(i)}$'s corresponding to the solutions of I' and I'' will have the same number of tuples. The (r, t) is a tuple in an $S^{(i)}$ for I' if and only if $((r\cdot n)/(\text{LB}\cdot\epsilon), t)$ is a tuple in the $S^{(i)}$ for I''. Hence, the time needed to solve I' is the same as that needed to solve I''. Since $p_i \leq$ LB, it follows that $s_i \leq \lfloor n/\epsilon \rfloor$. Hence

$$|S^{(i)}| \leq 1 + \textstyle\sum_{j=1}^{i} s_j \quad \leq \quad 1 + i\lfloor n/\epsilon \rfloor$$

$$\text{and so } \textstyle\sum_{i=0}^{n-1} |S^{(i)}| \quad \leq \quad n + \sum_{i=0}^{n-1} i\lfloor n/\epsilon \rfloor = O(n^3/\epsilon)$$

Thus, if we can go from $S^{(i-1)}$ to $S^{(i)}$ in $O(|S^{(i-1)}|)$ time, then I'' and hence I' can be solved in $O(n^3/\epsilon)$ time. Moreover, the solution for I' will be an ϵ-approximate solution for I and we thus have a fully polynomial time approximation scheme. When using rounding, we solve I'' and use the resulting optimal solution as the solution to I.

Example 12.14 Consider the 0/1 knapsack problem of Section 5.7. While solving this problem by successively generating $S^{(0)}, S^{(1)}, \ldots, S^{(n)}$, the feasible assignments for $S^{(i)}$ can be represented by tuples of the form (r, t), where

$$r = \sum_{j=1}^{i} p_j x_j \text{ and } t = \sum_{j=1}^{i} w_j x_j$$

The dominance rule developed in Section 5.7 for this problem is (r_1, t_1) dominates (r_2, t_2) iff $t_1 \leq t_2$ and $r_1 \geq r_2$.

Let us solve the following instance of the 0/1 knapsack problem: $n = 5$, $m = 1112$, and $(p_1, p_2, p_3, p_4, p_5) = (w_1, w_2, w_3, w_4, w_5) = \{1, 2, 10, 100, 1000\}$. Since $p_i = w_i$, $1 \leq i \leq 5$, the tuples (r, t) in $S^{(i)}$, $0 \leq i \leq 5$, have $r = t$. Consequently, it is necessary to retain only one of the two coordinates r and t. The $S^{(i)}$ obtained for this instance are $S^{(0)} = \{0\}$, $S^{(1)} = \{0, 1\}$, $S^{(2)} = \{0, 1, 2, 3\}$, $S^{(3)} = \{0, 1, 2, 3, 10, 11, 12, 13\}$, $S^{(4)} = \{0, 1, 2, 3, 10, 11, 12, 13, 100, 101, 102, 103, 110, 111, 112, 113\}$, and $S^{(5)} = \{0, 1, 2, 3, 10, 11, 12, 13, 100, 101, 102, 103, 110, 111, 112, 113, 1000, 1001, 1002, 1003, 1010, 1011, 1012, 1013, 1100, 1101, 1102, 1103, 1110, 1111, 1112\}$.

The optimal solution has value $\sum p_i x_i = 1112$.

Now, let us use rounding on this problem instance to find an approximate solution with value at most 10% less than the optimal value. We thus have $\epsilon = 1/10$. Also, we know that $F^*(I) \geq \text{LB} \geq \max \{p_i\} = 1000$. The problem I'' to be solved is $n = 5$, $m = 1112$, $(s_1, s_2, s_3, s_4, s_5) = (0, 0, 0, 5, 50)$, and $(w_1, w_2, w_3, w_4, w_5) = (1, 2, 10, 100, 1000)$. Hence, $S^{(0)} = S^{(1)} = S^{(2)} = S^{(3)} = \{(0, 0)\}$, $S^{(4)} = \{(0, 0), (5, 100)\}$, and $S^{(5)} = \{(0, 0), (5, 100), (50, 1000), (55, 1100)\}$.

The optimal solution is $(x_1, x_2, x_3, x_4, x_5) = (0, 0, 0, 1, 1)$. Its value in I'' is 55, and in the original problem 1100. The error $(F^*(I) - \hat{F}(I))/F^*(I)$ is therefore $12/1112 < 0.011 < \epsilon$. At this time we see that the solution can be improved by setting either $x_1 = 1$ or $x_3 = 1$. □

Rounding as described in its full generality results in $O(n^3/\epsilon)$ time approximation schemes. It is possible to specialize this technique to the specific problem being solved. In particular, we can obtain specialized and asymptotically faster polynomial time approximation schemes for the knapsack problem as well as for the problem of scheduling tasks on two processors to minimize finish time. The complexity of the resulting algorithms is $O(n(\log n + 1/\epsilon^2))$.

Let us investigate the specialized rounding scheme for the 0/1 knapsack problem. Let I be an instance of this problem and let ϵ be the desired accuracy. Let $P^*(I)$ be the value of an optimal solution. First, a good estimate UB for $P^*(I)$ is obtained. This is done by ordering the n objects in I so that $p_i/w_i \geq p_{i+1}/w_{i+1}$, $1 \leq i < n$. Next, we find the largest j such that $\sum_1^j w_i \leq m$. If $j = n$, then the optimal solution is $x_i = 1$, $1 \leq i \leq n$, and $P^*(I) = \sum p_i$. So, assume $j < n$. Define $\text{UB} = \sum_1^{j+1} p_i$. We can show $\frac{1}{2}\,\text{UB} \leq P^*(I) <$UB. The inequality $P^*(I) < \text{UB}$ follows from the ordering on p_i/w_i. The inequality $\frac{1}{2}\,\text{UB} \leq P^*(I)$ follows from the observation that

$$P^*(I) \geq \sum_{i=1}^{j} p_i \text{ and } P^*(I) \geq \max\left\{\sum_{i}^{j} p_i, p_{j+1}\right\}$$

Hence, $2P^*(I) \geq \sum_1^{j+1} p_i = \text{UB}$.

Now, let $\delta = \text{UB}\epsilon^2/9$. Divide the n objects into two classes, BIG and SMALL. BIG includes all objects with $p_i > \epsilon\text{UB}/3$. SMALL includes all other objects. Let the number of objects in BIG be r. Replace each p_i in BIG by q_i such that $q_i = \lfloor p_i/\delta \rfloor$ (this is the rounding step). The knapsack problem is solved exactly using these r objects and the q_i's.

Let $S^{(r)}$ be the set of tuples resulting from the dynamic programming algorithm. For each tuple $(x, y) \in S^{(r)}$, fill the remaining space $m - y$ by considering the objects in SMALL in nondecreasing order of p_i/w_i. Use the filling that has maximum value as the answer.

Example 12.15 Consider the problem instance of Example 12.14: $n = 5$, $(p_1, p_2, p_3, p_4, p_5) = (w_1, w_2, w_3, w_4, w_5) = (1, 2, 10, 100, 1000)$, $m = 1112$, and $\epsilon = 1/10$. The objects are already in nonincreasing order of p_i/w_i. For this instance, $\text{UB} = \sum_1^5 p_i = 1113$. Hence, $\delta = 3.71/3$ and $\epsilon.\text{UB}/3 = 37.1$. SMALL, therefore, includes objects 1, 2, and 3. BIG $= \{4, 5\}$. So $q_4 = \lfloor p_4/\delta \rfloor = 94$ and $q_5 = \lfloor p_5/\delta \rfloor = 946$. Solving the knapsack instance $n = 2$, $m = 1112$, $(q_4, w_4) = (94, 100)$, and $(q_5, w_5) = (946, 1000)$, we obtain $S^{(0)} = \{(0, 0)\}$, $S^{(1)} = \{(0, 0), (94, 100)\}$, and $S^{(2)} = \{(0, 0), (94, 100), (946, 1000), (1040, 1100)\}$. Filling (0, 0) from SMALL, we get the tuple (13, 13). Filling (94, 100), (946, 1000), and (1040, 1100) yields the tuples (107, 113), (959, 1013), and (1043, 1100) respectively. The answer is given by the tuple (1043, 1100). This corresponds to $(x_1, x_2, x_3, x_4, x_5) = (1, 1, 0, 1, 1)$ and $\sum p_i x_i = 1103$. □

An exercise explores a modification to the basic rounding scheme illustrated in Example 12.15. This modification results in better solutions.

Theorem 12.15 [Ibarra and Kim] The algorithm just described is an ϵ approximate algorithm for the 0/1-knapsack problem. □

The time needed to initially sort according to p_i/w_i is $O(n \log n)$. So UB can be computed in $O(n)$ time. Since $P^*(I) \leq \text{UB}$, there are at most $\text{UB}/\delta = 9/\epsilon^2$ tuples in any $S^{(i)}$ in the solution of BIG. The time to obtain $S^{(r)}$ is therefore $O(r/\epsilon^2) \leq O(n/\epsilon^2)$. Filling each tuple in $S^{(r)}$ with objects from SMALL takes $O(|\text{SMALL}|)$ time. Since $|S^{(r)}| \leq 9/\epsilon^2$, the total time for this step is at most $O(n/\epsilon^2)$. The total time for the algorithm is therefore $O(n(\log n + 1/\epsilon^2))$. A faster approximation scheme for the knapsack problem has been obtained by G. Lawler. His scheme also uses rounding.

12.5.2 Interval Partitioning

Unlike rounding, interval partitioning does not transform the original problem instance into one that is easier to solve. Instead, an attempt is made to solve the problem instance I by generating a restricted class of the feasible assignments for $S^{(0)}, S^{(1)}, \ldots, S^{(n)}$. Let P_i be the maximum $\sum_{j=1}^{i} p_j x_j$ among all feasible assignments generated for $S^{(i)}$. Then the profit interval $[0, P_i]$ is divided into subintervals each of size $P_i\epsilon/(n-1)$ (except possibly the last interval which may be a little smaller). All feasible assignments in $S^{(i)}$ with $\sum_{j=1}^{i} p_j x_j$ in the same subinterval are regarded as having the same $\sum_{j=1}^{i} p_j x_j$ and the dominance rules are used to discard all but one of them. The $S^{(i)}$ resulting from this elimination are used in the generation of the $S^{(i+1)}$. Since the number of subintervals for each $S^{(i)}$ is at most $\lceil n/\epsilon \rceil + 1$, $|S^{(i)}| \leq \lceil n/\epsilon \rceil + 1$. Hence, $\sum_1^n |S^{(i)}| = O(n^2/\epsilon)$.

The error introduced in each feasible assignment due to this elimination in $S^{(i)}$ is less than the subinterval length. This error may, however, propagate from $S^{(1)}$ up through $S^{(n)}$. However, the error is additive. Let $\hat{F}(I)$ be the value of the optimal generated using interval partitioning, and $F^*(I)$ the value of a true optimal. It follows that

$$F^*(I) - \hat{F}(I) \leq (\epsilon \sum_{i=1}^{n-1} P_i)/(n-1)$$

Since $P_i \leq F^*(I)$, it follows that $[F^*(I) - \hat{F}(I)/F^*(I)] \leq \epsilon$, as desired.

In many cases the algorithm can be speeded by starting with a good estimate LB for $F^*(I)$ such that $F^*(I) \geq \text{LB}$. The subinterval size is then $\text{LB}\epsilon/(n-1)$ rather than $P_i\epsilon/(n-1)$. When a feasible assignment with value greater than LB is discovered, the subinterval size can also be chosen as described.

Example 12.16 Consider the same instance of the 0/1 knapsack problem as in Example 12.14. Then $\epsilon = 1/10$ and $F^*(I) \geq \text{LB} \geq 1000$. We can start with a subinterval size of $\text{LB}.\epsilon/(n-1) = 1000/40 = 25$. Since all tuples (p, t) in $S^{(i)}$ have $p = t$, only p is explicitly retained. The intervals are $[0, 25), [25, 50), \ldots$, and so on. Using interval partitioning, we obtain $S^{(0)} = S^{(1)} = S^{(2)} = S^{(3)} = \{0\}, S^{(4)} = \{0, 100\}$, and $S^{(5)} = \{0,\ 100,\ 1000,\ 1100\}$.

The best solution generated using interval partitioning is $(x_1, x_2, x_3, x_4, x_5) = (0, 0, 0, 1, 1)$ and its value $\hat{F}(I)$ is 1100. Then $[F^*(I) - \hat{F}(I)]/F^*(I) = 12/1112 < 0.011 < \epsilon$. Again, the solution value can be improved by using a heuristic to change some of the x_i's from 0 to 1. □

12.5.3 Separation

Assume that in solving a problem instance I, we have obtained an $S^{(i)}$ with feasible solutions having $\sum_{i \leq j \leq i} p_j x_j$: 0, 3.9, 4.1, 7.8, 8.2, 11.9, 12.1. Further assume that the interval size $P_i\epsilon/(n-1)$ is 2. Then the subintervals

```
    J := assignment corresponding to a_0; XP := a_0;
    for j := 1 to r do
        if a_j > XP + P_i ϵ/(n − 1) then
        {
            put assignment corresponding to a_j into J;
            XP := a_j;
        }
```

Algorithm 12.7 Separation method

are $[0,2)$, $[2,4)$, $[4,6)$, $[6,8)$, $[8,10)$, $[10,12)$, and $[12,14)$. Each feasible solution value falls in a different subinterval and so no feasible assignments are eliminated. However, there are three pairs of assignments with values within $P_i\epsilon/(n-1)$. If the dominance rules are used for each pair, only four assignments remain. The error introduced is at most $P_i\epsilon/(n-1)$. More formally, let a_0, a_1, a_2, $\ldots$, a_r be the distinct values of $\sum_{j=1}^{i} p_j x_j$ in $S^{(i)}$. Let us assume $a_0 < a_1 < a_2 < \cdots < a_r$. We construct a new set J from $S^{(i)}$ by making a left to right scan and retaining a tuple only if its value exceeds the value of the last tuple in J by more than $P_i\epsilon/(n-1)$. This is described by Algorithm 12.7. This algorithm assumes that the assignment with less profit dominates the one with more profit if we regard both assignments as yielding the same profit $\sum p_j x_j$. If the reverse is true, the algorithm can start with a_r and work downward. The analysis for this strategy is the same as that for interval partitioning. The same comments regarding the use of a good estimate for $F^*(I)$ hold here too.

Intuitively one may expect separation to always work better than interval partitioning. The following example illustrates that this need not be the case. However, empirical studies with one problem indicate interval partitioning to be inferior in practice.

Example 12.17 Using separation on the data of Example 12.14 yields the same $S^{(i)}$ as obtained using interval partitioning. We have already seen an instance in which separation performs better than interval partitioning. Now, we see an example in which interval partitioning does better than separation. Assume that the subinterval size LB.$\epsilon/(n-1)$ is 2. Then the intervals are $[0,2)$, $[2,4)$, $[4,6), \ldots$, and so on. Assume further that $(p_1,\ p_2,\ p_3,\ p_4,\ p_5) = (3,\ 1,\ 5.1,\ 5.1,\ 5.1)$. Then, following the use of interval partitioning, we have $S^{(0)}=\{0\}$, $S^{(1)}=\{0,3\}$, $S^{(2)}=\{0,3,4\}$, $S^{(3)} = \{0,3,4,8.1\}$, $S^{(4)} = \{0,3,4,8.1,13.2\}$, and $S^{(5)} = \{0,3,4,8.1,13.2,18.3\}$.

Using separation with LB.$\epsilon/(n-1) = 2$, we have $S^{(0)} = \{0\}$, $S^{(1)} = \{0,$

3}, $S^{(2)} = \{0, 3\}$, $S^{(3)} = \{0, 3, 5.1, 8.1\}$, $S^{(4)} = \{0, 3, 5.1, 8.1, 10.2, 13.2\}$, and $S^{(5)} = \{0, 3, 5.1, 8.1, 10.2, 13.2, 15.3, 18.3\}$. □

The exercises examine some of the other problems to which these techniques apply. It is interesting to note that one can couple existing heuristics to the approximation schemes that result from these three techniques. This is because of the similarity in solution procedures for the exact and approximate problems. In the approximation algorithms of Sections 12.2 to 12.4 it is usually not possible to use existing heuristics.

At this point, one might well ask what kind of $\mathcal{NP}$-hard problems can have fully polynomial time approximation schemes? No $\mathcal{NP}$-hard ϵ-approximation problem can have such a scheme unless $\mathcal{P} = \mathcal{NP}$. A stronger result can be proven. This stronger result is that the only $\mathcal{NP}$-hard problems that can have fully polynomial time approximation schemes (unless $\mathcal{P} = \mathcal{NP}$) are those which are polynomially solvable if restricted to problem instances in which all numbers are bounded by a fixed polynomial in n. Examples of such problems are the knapsack and job sequencing with deadlines problems.

Definition 12.8 [Garey and Johnson] Let L be some problem. Let I be an instance of L and let LENGTH(I) be the number of bits in the representation of I. Let MAX(I) be the magnitude of the largest number in I. Without loss of generality, we can assume that all numbers in I are integer. For some fixed polynomial p, let L_p be problem L restricted to those instances I for which MAX(I) $\leq p$(LENGTH(I)). Problem L is *strongly $\mathcal{NP}$-hard* if and only if there exists a polynomial p such that L_p is $\mathcal{NP}$-hard. □

Examples of problems that are strongly $\mathcal{NP}$-hard are Hamiltonian cycle, node cover, feedback arc set, traveling salesperson, max clique, and so on. The 0/1 knapsack problem is probably not strongly $\mathcal{NP}$-hard (note that there is no known way to show that a problem is not strongly $\mathcal{NP}$-hard) as when MAX(I) $\leq p$(LENGTH(I)), I can be solved in time O(LENGTH$(I)^2$ p(LENGTH(I)) using the dynamic programming algorithm of Section 5.7.

Theorem 12.16 [Garey and Johnson] Let L be an optimization problem such that all feasible solutions to all possible instances have a value that is a positive integer. Further, assume that for all instances I of L, the optimal value $F^*(I)$ is bounded by a polynomial function p in the variables LENGTH(I) and MAX(I); that is, $0 < F^*(I) < p$(LENGTH(I), MAX(I)) and $F^*(I)$ is an integer. If L has a fully polynomial time approximation scheme, then L has an exact algorithm of complexity a polynomial in LENGTH(I) and MAX(I).

Proof: Suppose L has a fully polynomial time approximation scheme. We show how to obtain optimal solutions to L in polynomial time. Let I be any instance of L. Define $\epsilon = 1/p(\text{LENGTH}(I),\ \text{MAX}(I))$. With this ϵ, the approximation scheme is forced to generate an optimal solution. To see this, let $\hat{F}(I)$ be the value of the solution generated. Then,

$$|F^*(I) - \hat{F}(I)| \le \epsilon F^*(I) \le F^*(I)/p(\text{LENGTH}(I), \text{MAX}(I)) < 1$$

Since, by assumption, all feasible solutions are integer valued, $F^*(I) = \hat{F}(I)$. Therefore, with this ϵ, the approximation scheme becomes an exact algorithm.

The complexity of the resulting exact algorithm is easy to obtain. Let $q(\text{LENGTH}(I), 1/\epsilon)$ be a polynomial such that the complexity of the approximation scheme is $O(q(\text{LENGTH}(I), 1/\epsilon))$. The complexity of this scheme when ϵ is chosen as above is $O(q(\text{LENGTH}(I),\ p(\text{LENGTH}(I),\ \text{MAX}(I))))$, which is $O(q'(\text{LENGTH}(I),\ \text{MAX}(I)))$ for some polynomial q'. □

When Theorem 12.16 is applied to integer-valued problems that are $\mathcal{NP}$-hard in the strong sense, we see that no such problem can have a fully polynomial time approximation scheme unless $\mathcal{P} = \mathcal{NP}$. The above theorem also tells us something about the kind of exact algorithms obtainable for strongly $\mathcal{NP}$-hard problems. A *pseudo-polynomial* time algorithm is one whose complexity is a polynomial in LENGTH(I) and MAX(I). The dynamic programming algorithm for the knapsack problem (Section 5.7) is a pseudo-polynomial time algorithm. No strongly $\mathcal{NP}$-hard problem can have a pseudo-polynomial time algorithm unless $\mathcal{P} = \mathcal{NP}$.

EXERCISES

1. Consider the $O(n(\log n + 1/\epsilon^2))$ rounding algorithm for the 0/1 knapsack problem. Let $S^{(r)}$ be the final set of tuples in the solution of BIG. Show that no more than $(9/\epsilon^2)/q_i$ objects with rounded profit value q_i can contribute to any tuple in $S^{(r)}$. From this, conclude that BIG can have at most $(9/\epsilon^2)/q_i$ objects with rounded profit value q_i. Hence, $r \le \sum (9/\epsilon^2)/q_i$, where q_i is in the range $[3/\epsilon, 9/\epsilon^2]$. Now, show that the time needed to obtain $S^{(r)}$ is $O(81/\epsilon^4 \ln(3/\epsilon))$. Use the relation

$$\sum_{3/\epsilon}^{9/\epsilon^2} \frac{9/\epsilon^2}{q_i} \simeq \int_{3/\epsilon}^{9/\epsilon^2} \frac{9}{\epsilon^2} \frac{dq_i}{q_i} = \frac{9}{\epsilon^2} \ln \frac{3}{\epsilon}$$

2. Write an algorithm for the $O(n(\log n + 1/\epsilon^2))$ rounding scheme discussed in Section 12.5. When solving BIG, use three tuples (P, Q, W)

such that $P = \sum p_i x_i$, $Q = \sum q_i x_i$, and $W = \sum w_i x_i$. Tuple (P_1, Q_1, W_1) dominates (P_2, Q_2, W_2) if and only if $Q_1 \geq Q_2$ and $W_1 \leq W_2$. In case $Q_1 = Q_2$ and $W_1 = W_2$, then an additional dominance criteria can be used. In this case the tuple (P_1, Q_1, W_1) dominates (P_2, Q_2, W_2) if and only if $P_1 > P_2$. Otherwise, (P_2, Q_2, W_2) dominates (P_1, Q_1, W_1). Show that your algorithm is of time complexity $O(n(\log n + 1/\epsilon^2))$.

3. Use separation to obtain a fully polynomial time approximation scheme for the independent task scheduling problem when $m = 2$ (see Section 12.4).

4. Do Exercise 3 for the case in which the two processors operate at speeds s_1 and $s_2, s_1 \neq s_2$ (see Exercise 3).

5. Do Exercise 3 for the case when the two processors are nonidentical (see Exercise 4).

6. Use separation to obtain a fully polynomial time approximation algorithm for the job sequencing with deadlines problem.

7. Use separation to obtain a fully polynomial time approximation scheme for the problem of obtaining two processor schedules with minimum mean weighted finish time (see Section 11.4). Assume that the two processors are identical.

8. Do Exercise 7 for the case in which a minimum mean finish time schedule that has minimum finish time among all minimum mean finish time schedules is desired. Again, assume two identical processors.

9. Do Exercise 3 using rounding.

10. Do Exercise 4 using rounding.

11. Do Exercise 5 using rounding.

12. Do Exercise 6 using rounding.

13. Do Exercise 7 using rounding.

14. Do Exercise 8 using rounding.

15. Show that the following problems are strongly $\mathcal{NP}$-hard:

    (a) Max clique
    (b) Set cover
    (c) Node cover
    (d) Set packing

(e) Feedback node set
(f) Feedback arc set
(g) Chromatic number
(h) Clique cover

12.6 PROBABILISTICALLY GOOD ALGORITHMS (*)

The approximation algorithms of the preceding sections had the nice property that their worst-case performance could be bounded by some constants (k in the case of an absolute approximation and ϵ in the case of an ϵ-approximation). The requirement of bounded performance tends to categorize other algorithms that usually work well as being bad. Some algorithms with unbounded performance may in fact almost always either solve the problem exactly or generate a solution that is exceedingly close in value to the value of an optimal solution. Such algorithms are good in a probabilistic sense. If we pick a problem instance I at random, then there is a very high probability that the algorithm will generate a very good approximate solution. In this section we consider two algorithms with this property. Both algorithms are for $\mathcal{NP}$-hard problems.

First, since we carry out a probabilistic analysis of the algorithms, we need to define a sample space of inputs. The sample space is set up by first defining a sample space S_n for each problem size n. Problem instances of size n are drawn from S_n. Then, the overall sample space is the infinite Cartesian product $S_1 \times S_2 \times S_3 \times \cdots \times S_n \cdots$. An element of the sample space is a sequence $X = x_1, x_2, \ldots, x_n, \ldots$ such that x_i is drawn from S_i.

Definition 12.9 [Karp] An algorithm A solves a problem L *almost everywhere* (abbreviated *a.e.*) if, when $X = x_1, x_2, \ldots, x_n, \ldots$ is drawn from the sample space $S_1 \times S_2 \times S_3 \times \cdots \times S_n \cdots$, the number of x_i on which the algorithm fails to solve L is finite with probability 1. □

Since both the algorithms we discuss are for $\mathcal{NP}$-hard graph problems, we first describe the sample space for which the probabilistic analysis is carried out. Let $p(n)$ be a function such that $0 \leq p(n) \leq 1$ for all $n \geq 0$. A random n vertex graph is constructed by including edge (i, j), $i \neq j$, with probability $p(n)$.

The first algorithm we consider is an algorithm to find a Hamiltonian cycle in an undirected graph. Informally, this algorithm proceeds as follows. First, an arbitrary vertex (say vertex 1) is chosen as the start vertex. The algorithm maintains a simple path P starting from vertex 1 and ending at vertex k. Initially P is a trivial path with $k = 1$; that is, there are no edges in P. At each iteration of the algorithm an attempt is made to increase the length of P. This is done by considering an edge (k, j) incident to the end point k of P. When edge (k, j) is being considered, one of three possibilities exist:

1. $j = 1$ and path P includes all the vertices of the graph. In this case a Hamiltonian cycle has been found and the algorithm terminates.

2. j is not on the path P. In this case the length of path P is increased by adding (k, j) to it. Then j becomes the new endpoint of P.

3. j is already on path P. Now there is a unique edge $e = (j, m)$ in P such that the deletion of e from and the inclusion of (k, j) to P result in a simple path. Then e is deleted and (k, j) is added to P. P is now a simple path with endpoint m.

The algorithm is constrained so that case 3 does not generate two paths of the same length having the same endpoint. With a proper choice of data representations, this algorithm can be implemented to run in time $O(n^2)$, where n is the number of vertices in graph G. It is easy to see that this algorithm does not always find a Hamiltonian cycle in a graph that contains such a cycle.

Theorem 12.17 [Posa] If $p(n) \approx (\alpha \ln n/n)$, $\alpha > 1$, then the preceding algorithm finds a Hamiltonian cycle (a.e.). □

Example 12.18 Let us try out the above algorithm on the five-vertex graph of Figure 12.9. The path P initially consists of vertex 1 only. Assume edge (1, 4) is chosen. This represents case 2 and P is expanded to $\{1, 4\}$. Assume edge (4, 5) is chosen next. Path P now becomes $\{1, 4, 5\}$. Edge (1, 5) is the only possibility for the next edge. This results in case 3 and P becomes $\{1, 5, 4\}$. Now assume edges (4, 3) and (3, 2) are considered. Path P becomes $\{1, 5, 4, 3, 2\}$. If edge (1, 2) is next considered, a Hamiltonian cycle is found and the algorithm terminates. □

The next probabilistically good algorithm we look at is for the maximum independent set problem. A subset of vertices N of graph $G(V, E)$ is said to be independent if and only if no two vertices in N are adjacent in G. Indep (Algorithm 12.8) is a greedy algorithm to construct a maximum independent set.

One can easily construct examples of n vertex graphs for which Indep generates independent sets of size 1 when in fact a maximum independent set contains $n - 1$ vertices. However, for certain probability distributions it can be shown that Indep generates good approximations almost everywhere. If $F^*(I)$ and $\hat{F}(I)$ represent the size of a maximum independent set and one generated by algorithm Indep, respectively, then the following theorem is obtained.

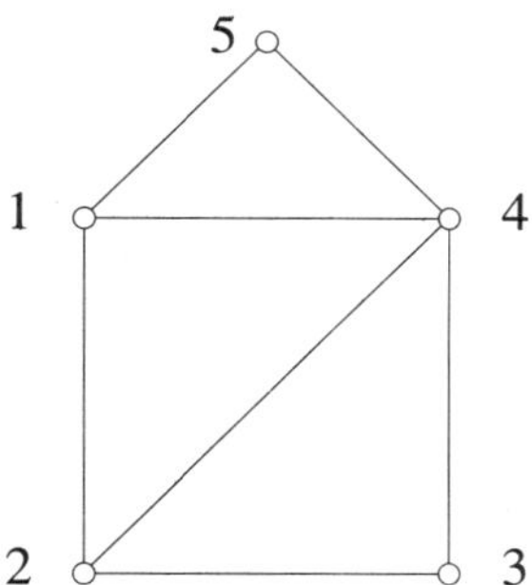

Figure 12.9 Graph for Example 12.18

```
Algorithm Indep(V, E)
{
    N := ∅;
    while there is a v ∈ (V − N) and
              v not adjacent to any vertex in N do
        N := N ∪ {v};
    return N;
}
```

Algorithm 12.8 Finding an independent set

Theorem 12.18 [Karp] If $p(n) = c$, for some constant c, then for every $\epsilon > 0$, we have

$$[F^*(I) - \hat{F}(I)]/F^*(I) \leq .5 + \epsilon \quad \text{(a.e.)} \quad \square$$

Algorithm Indep can easily be implemented to have polynomial complexity. Some other $\mathcal{NP}$-hard problems for which probabilistically good algorithms are known are the Euclidean traveling salesperson, minimal coloring of graphs, set covering, maximum weighted clique, and partition.

EXERCISE

1. Show that function Indep is not an ϵ-approximate algorithm for the maximum independent set problem for any ϵ, $0 < \epsilon < 1$.

12.7 REFERENCES AND READINGS

An authoritative refernce on approximation algorithms is *Handbook of Approximation Algorithms and Metaheuristics*, by T. Gonzalez (editor), Chapman & Hall/CRC, 2007.

The terms approximation scheme, polynomial time approximation scheme, and fully polynomial time approximation scheme were coined by M. Garey and D. Johnson. S. Sahni pointed out that for the 0/1 knapsack problem the corresponding absolute approximation problem is also $\mathcal{NP}$-hard. The polynomial time approximation scheme for the 0/1 knapsack problem discussed in Section 12.4 is also due to S. Sahni.

The analysis of the LPT rule of Section 12.3 is due to R. Graham. The polynomial time approximation scheme for scheduling independent tasks that was discussed in Section 12.4 is also due to him.

An excellent bibliography on approximation algorithms is "Approximation algorithms for combinatorial problems: an annotated bibliography," by M. Garey and D. Johnson, in *Algorithms and Complexity: Recent Results and New Directions*, J. Traub, ed., Academic Press, 1976.

The approximation algorithm MSat2 (Exercise 2) was given by K. Lieberherr. S. Sahni and T. Gonzalez were the first to show the existence of $\mathcal{NP}$-hard ϵ-approximate problems. Garey and Johnson have shown that the ϵ-approximate graph coloring problem is $\mathcal{NP}$-hard for $\epsilon < 1$. O. Ibarra and C. Kim were the first to discover the existence of fully polynomial time approximation schemes for $\mathcal{NP}$-hard problems.

Our discussion of the general techniques rounding, interval partitioning, and separation is based on the work of Sahni. The notion of strongly $\mathcal{NP}$-hard is due to Garey and Johnson. Theorem 12.16 is also due to them.

The discussion of probabilistically good algorithms is based on the work of R. Karp. Theorem 12.17 is due to L. Posa.

12.8 ADDITIONAL EXERCISES

1. The satisfiability problem was introduced in Chapter 11. Define maximum satisfiability to be the problem of determining a maximum subset of clauses that can be satisfied simultaneously. If a formula has p clauses, then all p clauses can be simultaneously satisfied if and only if the formula is satisfiable. For function MSat (Algorithm 12.9), show that for every instance i, $|F^*(i) - \hat{F}(i)|/F^*(i) \leq 1/(k+1)$. Then k is the minimum number of literals in any clause of i. Show that this bound is best possible for this algorithm.

2. Show that if function MSat2 (Algorithm 12.10) is used for the maximum satisfiability problem of Exercise 1, then $|F^*(i) - \hat{F}(i)|/F^*(i) \leq 1/2^k$, where $k, \hat{F}$, and F^* are as in Exercise 1.

```
Algorithm MSat(I)
// Approximation algorithm for maximum satisfiability.
// I is a formula. Let x[1 : n] be the variables in I
// and let C_i, 1 ≤ i ≤ p be the clauses.
{
    CL := ∅; // Set of clauses simultaneously satisfiable
    Left := {C_i | 1 ≤ i ≤ p}; // Remaining clauses
    Lit := {x_i, x̄_i | 1 ≤ i ≤ n}; // Set of all literals
    while Lit contains a literal occurring in a clause in Left do
    {
        Let y be a literal in Lit that is in
            the most clauses of Left;
        Let R be the subset of clauses in Left that contains y;
        CL := CL ∪ R; Left := Left − R;
        Lit := Lit − {y, ȳ};
    }
    return CL;
}
```

Algorithm 12.9 Function for Exercise 1

3. Consider the set cover problem of Section 11.3, Exercise 15. Show that if the function SetCover (Algorithm 12.11) is used for the optimization version of this problem, then

$$\frac{\hat{F}(I)}{F^*(I)} \leq \sum_{1}^{k} \frac{1}{j}$$

where k is the maximum number of elements in any set. Show that this bound is best possible.

4. Consider a modified set cover problem (MSC) in which we are required to find a cover T such that $\sum_{s \in T} |s|$ is minimum.

   (a) Show that exact cover $\propto$ MSC (see Section 11.3, Exercise 16).

   (b) Show that the function MSC (Algorithm 12.12) is not an ϵ-approximate algorithm for this problem for any $\epsilon, \epsilon > 0$.

```
Algorithm MSat2(I)
// Same function as MSat
{
    w[i] := 2^(-|C_i|), 1 <= i <= p;
        // Weighting function |C_i| = number of literals in C_i.
    CL := ∅; Left := {C_i | 1 <= i <= p};
    Lit := {x_i, x̄_i | 1 <= i <= n};
    while Lit contains a literal occurring in a clause in Left do
    {
        Let y ∈ Lit be such that y occurs in a clause in Left;
        Let R be the subset of clauses in Left containing y;
        Let S be the subset of clauses in Left containing ȳ;
        if Σ_{C_i ∈ R} w[i] >= Σ_{C_i ∈ S} w[i] then
        {
            CL := CL ∪ R;
            Left := Left − R;
            w[i] := 2 * w[i] for each C_i ∈ S;
        }
        else
        {
            CL := CL ∪ S;
            Left := Left − S;
            w[i] := 2 * w[i] for each C_i ∈ R;
        }
        Lit := Lit − {y, ȳ};
    }
    return CL;
}
```

Algorithm 12.10 Function for Exercise 2

5. An edge disjoint cycle cover of an undirected graph G is a set of edge disjoint cycles such that every vertex is included in at least one cycle. The size of such a cycle cover is the number of cycles in it.

   (a) Show that finding a minimum cycle cover of this type is $\mathcal{NP}$-hard.

   (b) Show that the ϵ-approximation version of this problem is $\mathcal{NP}$-hard for all ϵ, $\epsilon > 0$.

6. Show that if the cycles in Exercise 5 are constrained to be vertex disjoint, then the problem remains $\mathcal{NP}$-hard. Show that the ϵ-approximate

```
Algorithm SetCover(F)
// S_i, 1 ≤ i ≤ m are the sets in F. |S_i| is the
// number of elements in S_i. |∪ S_i| = n.
{
    G := ∪S_i;
    for i := 1 to m do R_i := S_i;
    cov := ∅; // Elements covered
    T := ∅; // Cover being constructed
    while cov ≠ G do
    {
        Let R_j be such that |R_j| ≥ |R_q|, 1 ≤ q ≤ m;
        cov := cov ∪ R_j; T := T ∪ S_j;
        for i := 1 to m do R_i := R_i − R_j;
    }
    return T;
}
```

Algorithm 12.11 Function for Exercise 3

```
Algorithm MSC(F)
// Same variables as in SetCover
{
    T := ∅; Left := {S_i|1 ≤ i ≤ m}; G := ∪S_i;
    while G ≠ ∅ do
    {
        Let S_j be a set in Left such that
        |S_j − G|/|S_j ∩ G| ≤ |S_q − G|/|S_q ∩ G| for all S_q in Left;
        T := T ∪ S_j; G := G − S_j; Left := Left − S_j;
    }
    return T;
}
```

Algorithm 12.12 Function for Exercise 4

version is $\mathcal{NP}$-hard for all ϵ, $\epsilon > 0$.

7. Let $G = (V, E)$ be an undirected graph. Let $f : E \to Z$ be an edge

weighting function and let $w : V \rightarrow Z$ be a vertex weighting function. Let k be a fixed integer, $k \geq 2$. The problem is to obtain k disjoint sets $S_1, \ldots, S_k$ such that:

(a) $\cup S_i = V$

(b) $S_i \cap S_j = \phi \quad \text{for} \quad i \neq j$

(c) $\sum_{j \in S_i} w(j) \leq W; \qquad 1 \leq i \leq k$

(d) $\sum_{i=1}^{k} \sum_{\substack{(u,v) \in E \\ u,v \in S_i}} f(u,v)$ is maximized

W is a number that may vary from instance to instance. This partitioning problem finds application in the minimization of the cost of interpage references between subroutines of a program. Show that the ϵ-approximate version of this problem is $\mathcal{NP}$-hard for all ϵ, $0 < \epsilon < 1$.

8. In one interpretation of the generalized assignment problem, we have m agents who have to perform n tasks. If agent i is assigned to perform task j, then cost c_{ij} is incurred. When agent i performs task j, r_{ij} units of her or his resources are used. Agent i has a total of b_i units of resource. The objective is to find an assignment of agents to tasks such that the total cost of the assignment is minimized and no agent requires more than her or his total available resource to complete the tasks she or he is assigned to. Only one agent may be assigned to a task.

   Using x_{ij} as a 0/1 variable such that $x_{ij} = 1$ if agent i is assigned to task j and $x_{ij} = 0$ otherwise, the generalized assignment problem can be formulated mathematically as

$$\begin{array}{rll} \text{minimize} & \sum_{i=1}^{m} \sum_{j=1}^{n} c_{ij} x_{ij} & \\ \text{subject to} & \sum_{j=1}^{n} r_{ij} x_{ij} \leq b_i, & 1 \leq i \leq m \\ & \sum_{i=1}^{m} x_{ij} = 1, & 1 \leq j \leq n \\ & x_{ij} = 0 \text{ or } 1, & \text{for all } i \text{ and } j \end{array}$$

   The constraints $\sum x_{ij} = 1$ ensure that exactly one agent is assigned to each task. Many other interpretations are possible for this problem.

   Show that the corresponding ϵ-approximation problem is $\mathcal{NP}$-hard for all ϵ, $\epsilon > 0$.

Chapter 13

PRAM ALGORITHMS

13.1 INTRODUCTION

So far our discussion of algorithms has been confined to single-processor computers. In this chapter we study algorithms for parallel machines (i.e., computers with more than one processor). There are many applications in day-to-day life that demand real-time solutions to problems. For example, weather forecasting has to be done in a timely fashion. In the case of severe hurricanes or snowstorms, evacuation has to be done in a short period of time. If an expert system is used to aid a physician in surgical procedures, decisions have to be made within seconds. And so on. Programs written for such applications have to perform an enormous amount of computation. In the forecasting example, large-sized matrices have to be operated on. In the medical example, thousands of rules have to be tried. Even the fastest single-processor machines may not be able to come up with solutions within tolerable time limits. Parallel machines offer the potential of decreasing the solution times enormously.

Example 13.1 Assume that you have 5 loads of clothes to wash. Also assume that it takes 25 minutes to wash one load in a washing machine. Then, it will take 125 minutes to wash all the clothes using a single machine. On the other hand, if you had 5 machines, washing could be completed in just 25 minutes! In this example, if there are p washing machines and p loads of clothes, then the washing time can be cut down by a factor of p compared to having a single machine. Here we have assumed that every machine takes exactly the same time to wash. If this assumption is invalid, then the washing time will be dictated by the slowest machine. □

Example 13.2 As another example, say there are 100 numbers to be added and there are two persons A and B. Person A can add the first 50 numbers. At the same time B can add the next 50 numbers. When they are done, one of them can add the two individual sums to get the finaı answer. So, two people can add the 100 numbers in almost half the time required by one. □

The idea of parallel computing is very similar. Given a problem to solve, we partition the problem into many subproblems; let each processor work on a subproblem; and when all the processors are done, the partial solutions are combined to arrive at the final answer. If there are p processors, then potentially we can cut down the solution time by a factor of p. We refer to any algorithm designed for a single-processor machine as a *sequential algorithm* and any designed for a multiprocessor machine as a *parallel algorithm.*

Definition 13.1 Let π be a given problem for which the best-known sequential algorithm has a run time of $S'(n)$, where n is the problem size. If a parallel algorithm on a p-processor machine runs in time $T'(n,p)$, then the *speedup* of the parallel algorithm is defined to be $\frac{S'(n)}{T'(n,p)}$.

If the best-known sequential algorithm for π has an asymptotic run time of $S(n)$ and if $T(n,p)$ is the asymptotic run time of a parallel algorithm, then the *asymptotic speedup* of the parallel algorithm is defined to be $\frac{S(n)}{T(n,p)}$. If $\frac{S(n)}{T(n,p)} = \Theta(p)$, then the algorithm is said to have *linear speedup.* □

Note: In this book we use the terms "speedup" and "asymptotic speedup" interchangeably. Which one is meant is clear from the context.

Example 13.3 For the problem of Example 13.2, the 100 numbers can be added sequentially in 99 units of time. Person A can add 50 numbers in 49 units of time. At the same time, B can add the other 50 numbers. In another unit of time, the two partial sums can be added; this means the parallel run time is 50. So the speedup of this parallel algorithm is $\frac{99}{50} = 1.98$, which is very nearly equal to 2! □

Example 13.4 There are many sequential sorting algorithms such as heap sort (Section 2.4.2) that are optimal and run in time $\Theta(n \log n)$, n being the number of keys to be sorted. Let $\mathcal{A}$ be an n-processor parallel algorithm that sorts n keys in $\Theta(\log n)$ time and let $\mathcal{B}$ be an n^2-processor algorithm that also sorts n keys in $\Theta(\log n)$ time.

Then, the speedup of $\mathcal{A}$ is $\frac{\Theta(n \log n)}{\Theta(\log n)} = \Theta(n)$. On the other hand, the speedup of $\mathcal{B}$ is also $\frac{\Theta(n \log n)}{\Theta(\log n)} = \Theta(n)$. Algorithm $\mathcal{A}$ has linear speedup, whereas $\mathcal{B}$ does not have a linear speedup. □

Definition 13.2 If a p-processor parallel algorithm for a given problem runs in time $T(n,p)$, the *total work done* by this algorithm is defined to be $pT(n,p)$. The *efficiency* of the algorithm is defined to be $\frac{S(n)}{pT(n,p)}$, where

$S(n)$ is the asymptotic run time of the best known sequential algorithm for solving the same problem. Also, the parallel algorithm is said to be *work-optimal* if $pT(n, p) = O(S(n))$. □

Note: A parallel algorithm is work-optimal if and only if it has linear speedup. Also, the efficiency of a work-optimal parallel algorithm is $\Theta(1)$.

Example 13.5 Let w be the time needed to wash one load of clothes on a single machine in Example 13.1. Also let n be the total number of loads to wash. A single machine will take time nw. If there are p machines, the washing time is $\lceil \frac{n}{p} \rceil w$. Thus the speedup is $n/\lceil \frac{n}{p} \rceil$. This speedup is $> \frac{p}{2}$ if $n \geq p$. So, the asymptotic speedup is $\Omega(p)$ and hence the parallel algorithm has linear speedup and is work-optimal. Also, the efficiency is $\frac{nw}{p\lceil \frac{n}{p} \rceil w}$. This is $\Theta(1)$ if $n \geq p$. □

Example 13.6 For the algorithm $\mathcal{A}$ of Example 13.4, the total work done is $n\Theta(\log n) = \Theta(n \log n)$. Its efficiency is $\frac{\Theta(n \log n)}{\Theta(n \log n)} = \Theta(1)$. Thus, $\mathcal{A}$ is work-optimal and has a linear speedup. The total work done by algorithm $\mathcal{B}$ is $n^2\Theta(\log n) = \Theta(n^2 \log n)$ and its efficiency is $\frac{\Theta(n \log n)}{\Theta(n^2 \log n)} = \Theta(\frac{1}{n})$. As a result, $\mathcal{B}$ is not work-optimal! □

Is it possible to get a speedup of more than p for any problem on a p-processor machine? Assume that it is possible (such a speedup is called a *superlinear speedup*). In particular, let π be the problem under consideration and S be the best-known sequential run time. If there is a parallel algorithm on a p-processor machine whose speedup is better than p, it means that the parallel run time T satisfies $T < \frac{S}{p}$; that is, $pT < S$. Note that a single step of the parallel algorithm can be simulated on a single processor in time $\leq p$. Thus the whole parallel algorithm can be simulated sequentially in time $\leq pT < S$. This is a contradiction since by assumption S is the run time of the best-known sequential algorithm for solving π!

The preceding discussion is valid only when we consider asymptotic speedups. When the speedup is defined with respect to the actual run times on the sequential and parallel machines, it is possible to obtain superlinear speedup. Two of the possible reasons for such an anomaly are (1) p processors have more aggregate memory than one and (2) the cache-hit frequency may be better for the parallel machine as the p-processors may have more aggregate cache than does one processor.

One way of solving a given problem in parallel is to explore many techniques (i.e., algorithms) and identify the one that is the most parallelizable. To achieve a good speedup, it is necessary to parallelize every component of the underlying technique. If a fraction f of the technique cannot be parallelized (i.e., has to be run serially), then the maximum speedup that can be obtained is limited by f. Amdahl's law (proof of which is left as an exercise) relates the maximum speedup achievable with f and p (the number of processors used) as follows.

Lemma 13.1 Maximum speedup $= \frac{1}{f+\frac{1-f}{p}}$. □

Example 13.7 Consider some technique for solving a problem π. Assume that $p = 10$. If $f = 0.5$ for this technique, then the maximum speedup that can be obtained is $\frac{1}{0.5+\frac{1-0.5}{10}} = \frac{20}{11}$, which is less than 2! If $f = 0.1$, then the maximum speedup is $\frac{10}{1.9}$, which is slightly more than 5! Finally, if $f = 0.01$, then the maximum speedup is $\frac{10}{1.09}$, which is slightly more than 9! □

EXERCISES

1. Algorithms $\mathcal{A}$ and $\mathcal{B}$ are parallel algorithms for solving the selection problem (Section 3.7). Algorithm $\mathcal{A}$ uses $n^{0.5}$ processors and runs in time $\Theta(n^{0.5})$. Algorithm $\mathcal{B}$ uses n processors and runs in $\Theta(\log n)$ time. Compute the works done, speedups, and efficiencies of these two algorithms. Are these algorithms work-optimal?

2. Mr. Ultrasmart claims to have found an algorithm for selection that runs in time $\Theta(\log n)$ using $n^{3/4}$ processors. Is this possible?

3. Prove Amdahl's law.

13.2 COMPUTATIONAL MODEL

The sequential computational model we have employed so far is the RAM (random access machine). In the RAM model we assume that any of the following operations can be performed in one unit of time: addition, subtraction, multiplication, division, comparison, memory access, assignment, and so on. This model has been widely accepted as a valid sequential model. On the other hand when it comes to parallel computing, numerous models have been proposed and algorithms have been designed for each such model.

An important feature of parallel computing that is absent in sequential computing is the need for interprocessor communication. For example, given any problem, the processors have to communicate among themselves and agree on the subproblems each will work on. Also, they need to communicate to see whether every one has finished its task, and so on. Each machine or processor in a parallel computer can be assumed to be a RAM. Various parallel models differ in the way they support interprocessor communication. Parallel models can be broadly categorized into two: fixed connection machines and shared memory machines.

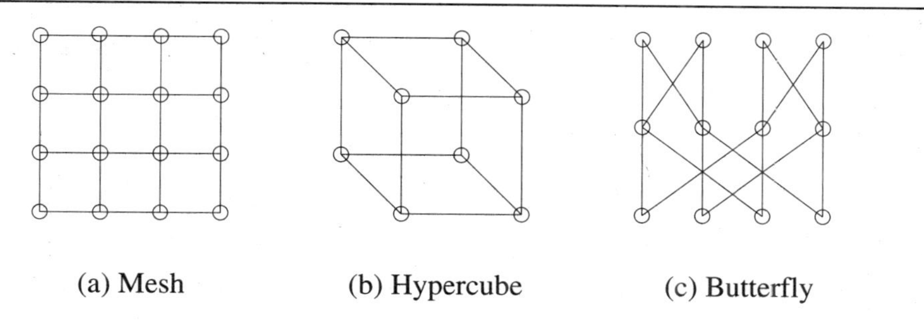

Figure 13.1 Examples of fixed connection machines

A fixed connection network is a graph $G(V, E)$ whose nodes represent processors and whose edges represent communication links between processors. Usually we assume that the degree of each node is either a constant or a slowly increasing function of the number of nodes in the graph. Examples include the mesh, hypercube, butterfly, and so on (see Figure 13.1). Interprocessor communication is done through the communication links. Any two processors connected by an edge in G can communicate in one step. In general two processors can communicate through any of the paths connecting them. The communication time depends on the lengths of these paths (at least for small packets). More details of these models are provided in Chapters 14 and 15.

In shared memory models [also called PRAMs (Parallel Random Access Machines)], a number (say p) of processors work synchronously. They communicate with each other using a common block of global memory that is accessible by all. This global memory is also called *common* or *shared* memory (see Figure 13.2). Communication is performed by writing to and/or reading from the common memory. Any two processors i and j can communicate in two steps. In the first step, processor i writes its message into memory cell j, and in the second step, processor j reads from this cell. In contrast, in a fixed connection machine, the communication time depends on the lengths of the paths connecting the communicating processors.

Each processor in a PRAM is a RAM with some local memory. A single step of a PRAM algorithm can be one of the following: arithmetic operation (such as addition, division, and so on.), comparison, memory access (local or global), assignment, etc. The number (m) of cells in the global memory is typically assumed to be the same as p. But this need not always be the case. In fact we present algorithms for which m is much larger or smaller than p. We also assume that the input is given in the global memory and there is space for the output and for storing intermediate results. Since the global

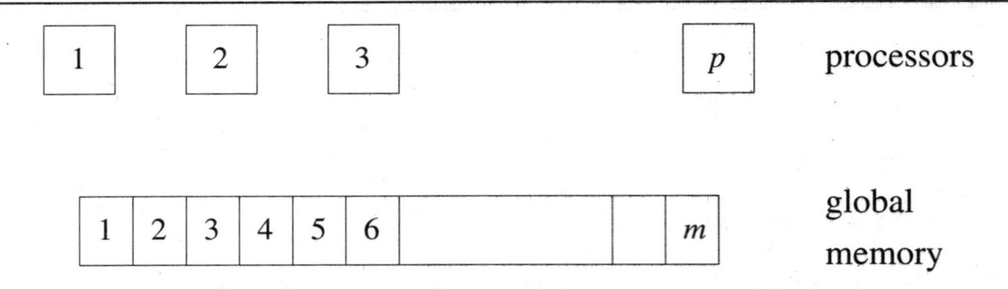

Figure 13.2 A parallel random access machine

memory is accessible by all processors, access conflicts may arise. What happens if more than one processor tries to access the same global memory cell (for the purpose of reading from or writing into)? There are several ways of resolving read and write conflicts. Accordingly, several variants of the PRAM arise.

EREW (Exclusive Read and Exclusive Write) PRAM is the shared memory model in which no concurrent read or write is allowed on any cell of the global memory. Note that ER or EW does not preclude different processors simultaneously accessing different memory cells. For example, at a given time step, processor one might access cell five and at the same time processor two might access cell 12, and so on. But processors one and two cannot access memory cell ten, for example, at the same time. CREW (Concurrent Read and Exclusive Write) PRAM is a variation that permits concurrent reads but not concurrent writes. Similarly one could also define the ERCW model. Finally, the CRCW PRAM model allows both concurrent reads and concurrent writes.

In a CREW or CRCW PRAM, if more than one processor tries to read from the same cell, clearly, they will read the same information. But in a CRCW PRAM, if more than one processor tries to write in the same cell, then possibly they may have different messages to write. Thus there has to be an additional mechanism to determine which message gets to be written. Accordingly, several variants of the CRCW PRAM can be derived. In a *common* CRCW PRAM, concurrent writes are permitted in any cell only if all the processors conflicting for this cell have the same message to write. In an *arbitrary* CRCW PRAM, if there is a conflict for writing, one of the processors will succeed in writing and we don't know which one. Any algorithms designed for this model should work no matter which processors succeed in the event of conflicts. The *priority* CRCW PRAM lets the processor with the highest priority succeed in the case of conflicts. Typically each processor is assigned a (static) priority to begin with.

Example 13.8 Consider a 4-processor machine and also consider an operation in which each processor has to read from the global cell $M[1]$. This operation can be denoted as

Processor i (**in parallel for** $1 \leq i \leq 4$) **does**:

Read $M[1]$;

This concurrent read operation can be performed in one unit of time on the CRCW as well as on the CREW PRAMs. But on the EREW PRAM, concurrent reads are prohibited. Still, we can perform this operation on the EREW PRAM making sure that at any given time no two processors attempt to read from the same memory cell. One way of performing this is as follows: processor 1 reads $M[1]$ at the first time unit; processor 2 reads $M[1]$ at the second time unit; and processors 3 and 4 read $M[1]$ at the third and fourth time units, respectively. The total run time is four. Better algorithms for general cases are considered in later sections (see Section 13.6, Exercise 11).

Now consider the operation in which each processor has to access $M[1]$ for writing at the same time. Since only one message can be written to $M[1]$, one has to assume some scheme for resolving contentions. This operation can be denoted as

Processor i (**in parallel for** $1 \leq i \leq 4$) **does**:

Write $M[1]$;

Again, on the CRCW PRAM, this operation can be completed in one unit of time. On the CREW and EREW PRAMs, concurrent writes are prohibited. However, these models can simulate the effects of a concurrent write. Consider our simple example of four processors trying to write in $M[1]$. Simulating a common CRCW PRAM requires the four processors to verify that all wish to write the same value. Following this, processor 1 can do the writing. Simulating a priority CRCW PRAM requires the four processors to first determine which has the highest priority, and then the one with this priority does the write. Other models may be similarly simulated. Exercise 12 of Section 13.6 deals with more general concurrent writes. □

Note that any algorithm that runs on a p-processor EREW PRAM in time $T(n, p)$, where n is the problem size, can also run on a p-processor CREW PRAM or a CRCW PRAM within the same time. But a CRCW PRAM algorithm or a CREW PRAM algorithm may not be implementable on an EREW PRAM preserving the asymptotic run time. In Example 13.8, we saw that the implementation of a single concurrent write or concurrent read step takes much more time on the EREW PRAM. Likewise, a

---

Processor i (**in parallel for** $1 \leq i \leq n$) **does:**

if $(A[i] = 1)$ **then** $A[0] := A[i]$;

Algorithm 13.1 Computing the boolean OR in $O(1)$ time

p-processor CRCW PRAM algorithm may not be implementable on a p-processor CREW PRAM preserving the asymptotic run time. It turns out that there is a strict hierarchy among the variants of the PRAM in terms of their computational power. For example, a CREW PRAM is strictly more powerful than an EREW PRAM. This means that there is at least one problem that can be solved in asymptotically less time on a CREW PRAM than on an EREW PRAM, given the same number of processors. Also, any version of the CRCW PRAM is more powerful than a CREW PRAM as is demonstrated by Example 13.9.

Example 13.9 $A[0] = A[1]||A[2]|| \cdots ||A[n]$ is the Boolean (or logical) OR of the n bits $A[1:n]$. $A[0]$ is easily computed in $O(n)$ time on a RAM. Algorithm 13.1 shows how $A[0]$ can be computed in $\Theta(1)$ time using an n-processor CRCW PRAM.

Assume that $A[0]$ is zero to begin with. In the first time step, processor i, for $1 \leq i \leq n$, reads memory location $A[i]$ and proceeds to write a 1 in memory location $A[0]$ if $A[i]$ is a 1. Since several of the $A[i]$'s may be 1, several processors may write to $A[0]$ concurrently. Hence the algorithm cannot be run (as such) on an EREW or CREW PRAM. In fact, for these two models, it is known that the parallel complexity of the Boolean OR problem is $\Omega(\log n)$ no matter how many processors are used. Note that the algorithm of Algorithm 13.1 works on all three varieties of the CRCW PRAM. □

Theorem 13.1 The boolean OR of n bits can be computed in $O(1)$ time on an n-processor common CRCW PRAM. □

There exists a hierarchy among the different versions of the CRCW PRAM also. Common, arbitrary, and priority form an increasing hierarchy of computing power. Let EREW$(p, T(n,p))$ denote the set of all problems that can be solved using a p-processor EREW PRAM in time $T(n,p)$ (n being the problem size). Similarly define CREW$(p, T(n,p))$ and CRCW$(p, T(n,p))$. Then,

$$\text{EREW}(p, T(n,p)) \subset \text{CREW}(p, T(n,p)) \subset \text{Common CRCW}(p, T(n,p))$$

$$\subset \text{Arbitrary CRCW}(p, T(n,p)) \subset \text{Priority CRCW}(p, T(n,p))$$

All the algorithms developed in this chapter for the PRAM model assume some relationship between the problem size n and the number of processors p. For example, the CRCW PRAM algorithm of Algorithm 13.1 solves a problem of size n using n processors. In practice, however, a problem of size n is solved on a computer with a constant number p of processors. All the algorithms designed under some assumptions about the relationship between n and p can also be used when fewer processors are available as there is a general slow-down lemma for the PRAM model.

Let $\mathcal{A}$ be a parallel algorithm for solving problem π that runs in time T using p processors. The slow-down lemma concerns the simulation of the same algorithm on a p'-processor machine (for $p' < p$).

Each step of algorithm $\mathcal{A}$ can be simulated on the p'-processor machine (call it $\mathcal{M}$) in time $\leq \lceil \frac{p}{p'} \rceil$, since a processor of $\mathcal{M}$ can be in charge of simulating $\lceil \frac{p}{p'} \rceil$ processors of the original machine. Thus, the simulation time on $\mathcal{M}$ is $\leq T \lceil \frac{p}{p'} \rceil$. Therefore, the total work done on $\mathcal{M}$ is $\leq p'T \lceil \frac{p}{p'} \rceil$ $\leq pT + p'T = O(pT)$. This results in the following lemma.

Lemma 13.2 [Slow-down lemma] Any parallel algorithm that runs on a p-processor machine in time T can be run on a p'-processor machine in time $O\left(\frac{pT}{p'}\right)$, for any $p' < p$. □

Since no such slow-down lemma is known for the models of Chapters 14 and 15, we need to develop different algorithms when the number of processors changes relative to the problem size. So, in Chapters 14 and 15 we develop algorithms under different assumptions about the relationship between n and p.

Example 13.10 Algorithm 13.1 runs in $\Theta(1)$ time using n processors. Using the slow-down lemma, the same algorithm also runs in $\Theta(\log n)$ time using $\frac{n}{\log n}$ processors; it also runs in $\Theta(\sqrt{n})$ time using $\sqrt{n}$ processors; and so on. When $p = 1$, the algorithm runs in time $\Theta(n)$, which is the same as the run time of the best sequential algorithm! □

Note: In Chapters one through nine we presented various algorithm design techniques and demonstrated how they can be applied to solve several specific problems. In the domain of parallel algorithms also some common ideas have been repeatedly employed to design algorithms over a wide variety of models. In Chapters 13, 14, and 15 we consider the PRAM, mesh, and hypercube models, respectively. In particular, we study the following problems: prefix computation, list ranking, selection, merging, sorting, some basic graph problems, and convex hull. For each of these problems a common theme is used to solve it on the three different models. In Chapter 13 we present full details of these common themes. In Chapters 14 and 15 we only point out the differences in implementation.

EXERCISES

1. Present an $O(1)$ time n-processor common CRCW PRAM algorithm for computing the boolean AND of n bits.

2. Input is an array of n elements. Give an $O(1)$ time, n-processor common CRCW PRAM algorithm to check whether the array is in sorted order.

3. Solve the boolean OR and AND problems on the CREW and EREW PRAMs. What are the time and processor bounds of your algorithms?

4. The array A is an array of n keys, where each key is an integer in the range $[1, n]$. The problem is to decide whether there are any repeated elements in A. Show how you do this in $O(1)$ time on an n-processor CRCW PRAM. Which version of the CRCW PRAM are you using?

5. Can Exercise 4 be solved in $O(1)$ time using n processors on any of the PRAMs if the keys are arbitrary? How about if there are n^2 processors?

6. The string matching problem takes as input a text t and a pattern p, where t and p are strings from an alphabet Σ. The problem is to determine all the occurrences of p in t. Present an $O(1)$ time PRAM algorithm for string matching. Which PRAM are you using and what is the processor bound of your algorithm?

7. The algorithm $\mathcal{A}$ is a parallel algorithm that has two components. The first component runs in $\Theta(\log\log n)$ time using $\frac{n}{\log\log n}$ EREW PRAM processors. The second component runs in $\Theta(\log n)$ time using $\frac{n}{\log n}$ CREW PRAM processors. Show that the whole algorithm can be run in $\Theta(\log n)$ time using $\frac{n}{\log n}$ CREW PRAM processors.

13.3 FUNDAMENTAL TECHNIQUES AND ALGORITHMS

In this section we introduce two basic problems that arise in the parallel solution of numerous problems. The first problem is known as the *prefix computation problem* and the second one is called the *list ranking problem.*

13.3.1 Prefix Computation

Let Σ be any domain in which the binary *associative* operator $\oplus$ is defined. An operator $\oplus$ is said to be associative if for any three elements x, y, and z from Σ, $((x \oplus y) \oplus z) = (x \oplus (y \oplus z))$; that is, the order in which the operation $\oplus$ is performed does not matter. It is also assumed that $\oplus$ is unit time computable and that Σ is closed under this operation; that is, for any $x, y \in \Sigma$, $x \oplus y \in \Sigma$. The prefix computation problem on Σ has as input n elements from Σ, say, $x_1, x_2, \ldots, x_n$. The problem is to compute the n elements $x_1, x_1 \oplus x_2, \ldots, x_1 \oplus x_2 \oplus x_3 \oplus \cdots \oplus x_n$. The output elements are often referred to as the *prefixes*.

Example 13.11 Let Σ be the set of integers and $\oplus$ be the usual addition operation. If the input to the prefix computation problem is $3, -5, 8, 2, 5, 4$, the output is $3, -2, 6, 8, 13, 17$. As another example, let Σ be the set of integers and $\oplus$ be the multiplication operation. If $2, 3, 1, -2, -4$ is the input, the output is $2, 6, 6, -12, 48$. □

Example 13.12 Let Σ be the set of all integers and $\oplus$ be the minimum operator. Note that the minimum operator is associative. If the input to the prefix computation problem is $5, 8, -2, 7, -11, 12$, the output is $5, 5, -2, -2, -11, -11$. In particular, the last element output is the minimum among all the input elements. □

The prefix computation problem can be solved in $O(n)$ time sequentially. Any sequential algorithm for this problem needs $\Omega(n)$ time. Fortunately, work-optimal algorithms are known for the prefix computation problem on many models of parallel computing. We present a CREW PRAM algorithm that uses $\frac{n}{\log n}$ processors and runs in $O(\log n)$ time. Note that the work done by such an algorithm is $O(n)$ and hence the algorithm has an efficiency of $\Theta(1)$ and is work-optimal. Also, the speedup of this algorithm is $\Theta(n/\log n)$.

We employ the divide-and-conquer strategy to devise the prefix algorithm. Let the input be $x_1, x_2, \ldots, x_n$. Without loss of generality assume that n is an integral power of 2. We first present an n-processor and $O(\log n)$ time algorithm (Algorithm 13.2).

Example 13.13 Let $n = 8$ and $p = 8$. Let the input to the prefix computation problem be $12, 3, 6, 8, 11, 4, 5, 7$ and let $\oplus$ be addition. In step 1, processors 1 to 4 compute the prefix sums of $12, 3, 6, 8$ to arrive at $12, 15, 21, 29$. At the same time processors 5 to 8 compute the prefix sums of $11, 4, 5, 7$ to obtain $11, 15, 20, 27$. In step 2, processors 1 to 4 don't do anything. Processors 5 to 8 update their results by adding 29 to every prefix sum and get $40, 44, 49, 56$. □

What is the time complexity of Algorithm 13.2? Let $T(n)$ be the run time of Algorithm 13.2 on any input of size n using n processors. Step 1 takes

---

Step 0. If $n = 1$, one processor outputs x_1.

Step 1. Let the first $n/2$ processors recursively compute the prefixes of $x_1, x_2, \ldots, x_{n/2}$ and let $y_1, y_2, \ldots, y_{n/2}$ be the result. At the same time let the rest of the processors recursively compute the prefixes of $x_{n/2+1}, x_{n/2+2}, \ldots, x_n$ and let $y_{n/2+1}, y_{n/2+2}, \ldots, y_n$ be the output.

Step 2. Note that the first half of the final answer is the same as $y_1, y_2, \ldots, y_{n/2}$. The second half of the final answer is $y_{n/2} \oplus y_{n/2+1}, y_{n/2} \oplus y_{n/2+2}, \ldots, y_{n/2} \oplus y_n$.
Let the second half of the processors read $y_{n/2}$ concurrently from the global memory and update their answers. This step takes $O(1)$ time.

Algorithm 13.2 Prefix computation in $O(\log n)$ time

$T(\frac{n}{2})$ time and step 2 takes $O(1)$ time. So, we get the following recurrence relation for $T(n)$:

$$T(n) \;=\; T\left(\frac{n}{2}\right) + O(1), \;\; T(1) = 1$$

This solves to $T(n) = O(\log n)$. Note that in defining the run time of a parallel divide-and-conquer algorithm, it is essential to quantify it with the number of processors used.

Algorithm 13.2 is not work-optimal for the prefix computation problem since the total work done by this algorithm is $\Theta(n \log n)$, whereas the run time of the best-known sequential algorithm is $\Theta(n)$. A work-optimal algorithm can be obtained by decreasing the number of processors used to $\frac{n}{\log n}$, while keeping the asymptotic run time the same. The number of processors used can be decreased to $\frac{n}{\log n}$ as follows. We first reduce the number of inputs to $\frac{n}{\log n}$, apply the non-work-optimal Algorithm 13.2 to compute the prefixes of the reduced input, and then finally compute all the n prefixes. Every processor will be in charge of computing $\log n$ final answers. If the input is $x_1, x_2, \ldots, x_n$ and the output is $y_1, y_2, \ldots, y_n$, let processor i be in charge of the outputs $y_{(i-1)\log n+1}, y_{(i-1)\log n+2}, \ldots, y_{i \log n}$, for $i = 1, 2, \ldots, \frac{n}{\log n}$. The detailed algorithm appears as Algorithm 13.3. The correctness of the algorithm is clear. Step 1 takes $O(\log n)$ time. Step 2

Step 1. Processor i $(i = 1, 2, \ldots, \frac{n}{\log n})$ in parallel computes the prefixes of its $\log n$ assigned elements $x_{(i-1)\log n+1}, x_{(i-1)\log n+2}, \ldots, x_{i \log n}$. This takes $O(\log n)$ time. Let the results be $z_{(i-1)\log n+1}, z_{(i-1)\log n+2}, \ldots, z_{i \log n}$.

Step 2. A total of $\frac{n}{\log n}$ processors collectively employ Algorithm 13.2 to compute the prefixes of the $\frac{n}{\log n}$ elements $z_{\log n}, z_{2\log n}, z_{3\log n}, \ldots, z_n$. Let $w_{\log n}, w_{2\log n}, w_{3\log n}, \ldots, w_n$ be the result.

Step 3. Each processor updates the prefixes it computed in step 1 as follows. Processor i computes and outputs $w_{(i-1)\log n} \oplus z_{(i-1)\log n+1}, w_{(i-1)\log n} \oplus z_{(i-1)\log n+2}, \ldots, w_{(i-1)\log n} \oplus z_{i\log n}$, for $i = 2, 3, \ldots, \frac{n}{\log n}$. Processor 1 outputs $z_1, z_2, \ldots, z_{\log n}$ without any modifications.

Algorithm 13.3 Work-optimal logarithmic time prefix computation

takes $O(\log(\frac{n}{\log n})) = O(\log n)$ time (using Algorithm 13.2). Finally, step 3 also takes $O(\log n)$ time. Thus we get the following theorem.

Theorem 13.2 Prefix computation on an n-element input can be performed in $O(\log n)$ time using $\frac{n}{\log n}$ CREW PRAM processors. □

Example 13.14 Let the input to the prefix computation be 5, 12, 8, 6, 3, 9, 11, 12, 1, 5, 6, 7, 10, 4, 3, 5 and let $\oplus$ stand for addition. Here $n = 16$ and $\log n = 4$. Thus in step 1, each of the four processors computes prefix sums on four numbers each. In step 2, prefix sums on the local sums is computed, and in step 3, the locally computed results are updated. Figure 13.3 illustrates these three steps. □

13.3.2 List Ranking

List ranking plays a vital role in the parallel solution of several graph problems. The input to the problem is a list given in the form of an array of nodes. A node consists of some data and a pointer to its right neighbor in the list. The nodes themselves need not occur in any order in the input.

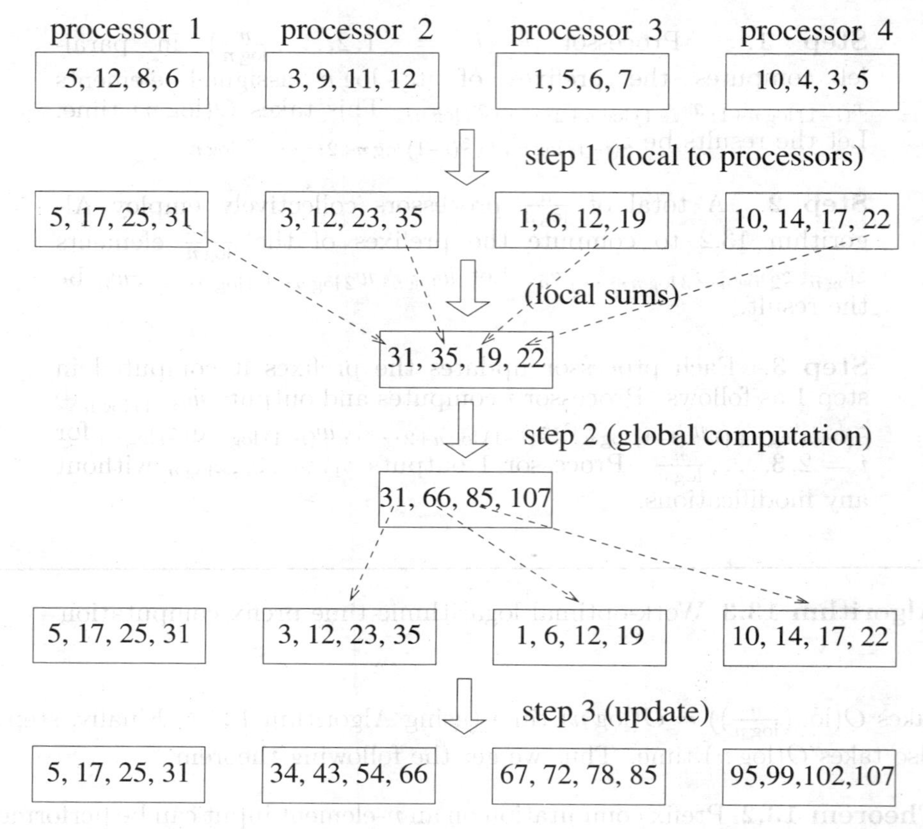

Figure 13.3 Prefix computation – an example

The problem is to compute for each node in the list the number of nodes to its right (also called the *rank of the node*). Since the data contained in any node is irrelevant to the list ranking problem, we assume that each node contains only a pointer to its right neighbor. The rightmost node's pointer field is zero.

Example 13.15 Consider the input $A[1:6]$ of Figure 13.4. The right neighbor of node $A[1]$ is $A[5]$. The right neighbor of node $A[2]$ is $A[4]$. And so on. Node $A[4]$ is the rightmost node; hence its rank is zero. Node $A[2]$ has rank 1 since the only node to its right is $A[4]$. Node $A[5]$ has rank 3 since the nodes $A[3]$, $A[2]$, and $A[4]$ are to its right. In this example, the left-to-right order of the list nodes is given by $A[6], A[1], A[5], A[3], A[2], A[4]$. □

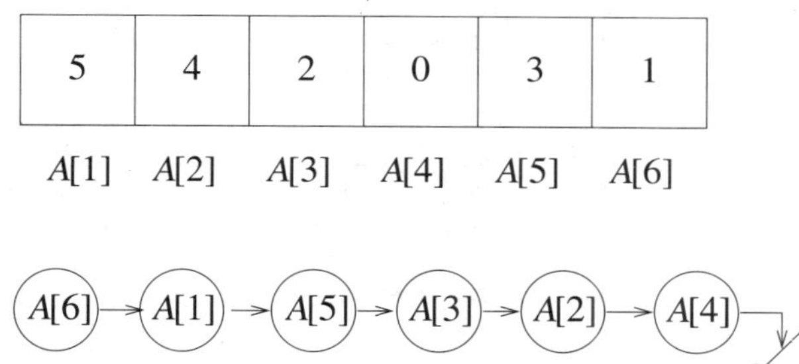

Figure 13.4 Input to the list ranking problem and the corresponding list

List ranking can be done sequentially in linear time. First, the list head is determined by examining $A[1:n]$ to identify the unique i, $1 \leq i \leq n$, such that $A[j] \neq i$, $1 \leq j \leq n$. Node $A[i]$ is the head. Next, a left-to-right scan of the list is made and nodes are assigned the ranks $n-1, n-2, \ldots, 0$ in this order. In this section, we develop two parallel algorithms for list ranking. The first is an n-processor $O(\log n)$ time EREW PRAM algorithm and the second is an $\frac{n}{\log n}$-processor $\widetilde{O}(\log n)$ time EREW PRAM algorithm. The speedups of both the algorithms are $\Theta(n/\log n)$. The efficiency of the first algorithm is $\frac{\Theta(n)}{\Theta(n \log n)} = \Theta(1/\log n)$, whereas the efficiency of the second algorithm is $\frac{\Theta(n)}{\Theta(n)} = \Theta(1)$. Thus the second algorithm is work-optimal but the first algorithm is not.

Deterministic list ranking

One of the crucial ideas behind these parallel algorithms is *pointer jumping.* To begin with, each node in the list points to its immediate right neighbor (see Figure 13.5(a)). In one step of pointer jumping, the right neighbor of every node is modified to be the right neighbor of its right neighbor (see Figure 13.5(b)). Note that if we have n processors (one processor per node), this can be done in $O(1)$ time. Now every node points to a node that was originally a distance of 2 away. In the next step of pointer jumping every node will point to a node that was originally a distance of 4 away. And so on. (See Figure 13.5(c) and (d).) Since the length of the list is n, within $\lceil \log n \rceil$ pointer jumping steps, every node will point to the end of the list.

In each step of pointer jumping a node also collects information as to how many nodes are between itself and the node it newly points to. This information is easy to accumulate as follows. To start with, set the rank field of each node to 1 except for the rightmost node whose rank

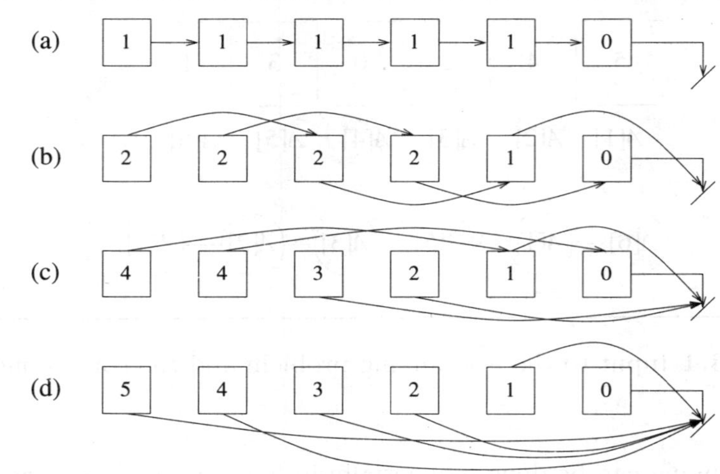

Figure 13.5 Pointer jumping applied to list ranking

field is zero. Let *Rank*$[i]$ and *Neighbor*$[i]$ stand for the rank field and the right neighbor of node i. At any step of pointer jumping, *Rank*$[i]$ is modified to *Rank*$[i]$ + *Rank*[*Neighbor*$[i]$], in parallel for all nodes other than those with *Neighbor*$[] = 0$. This is followed by making i point to *Neighbor*[*Neighbor*$[i]$]. The complete algorithm is given in Algorithm 13.4. Processor i is associated with the node $A[i]$, $1 \leq i \leq n$.

Example 13.16 For the input of Figure 13.4, Figure 13.6 walks through the steps of Algorithm 13.4. To begin with, every node has a rank of one except for node 4. When $q = 1$, for example, node 1's *Rank* field is changed to two, since its right neighbor (i.e., node 5) has a rank of one. Also, node 1's *Neighbor* field is changed to the neighbor of node 5, which is node 3. And so on. □

Definition 13.3 Let A be an array of nodes corresponding to a list. Also let node i have a real weight w_i associated with it and let $\oplus$ be any associative binary operation defined on the weights. The *list prefix computation* is the problem of computing, for each node in the list, $w_i \oplus w_{i_1} \oplus w_{i_2} \oplus \cdots \oplus w_{i_k}$. where $i_1, i_2, \ldots, i_k$ are the nodes to the right of i. □

Note that the list ranking problem corresponds to a list prefix sums computation, where each node has a weight of 1 except for the rightmost node whose weight is zero. Algorithm 13.4 can be easily modified to compute list prefixes without any change in the processor and time bounds.

```
for q := 1 to ⌈log n⌉ do
    Processor i (in parallel for 1 ≤ i ≤ n) does:
        if (Neighbor[i] ≠ 0) then
        {
            Rank[i] := Rank[i] + Rank[Neighbor[i]];
            Neighbor[i] := Neighbor[Neighbor[i]];
        }
```

Algorithm 13.4 An $O(n \log n)$ work list ranking algorithm

Neighbor						*Rank*						
5	4	2	0	3	1	1	1	1	0	1	1	to begin with
3	0	4	0	2	5	2	1	2	0	2	2	$q = 1$
4	0	0	0	0	2	4	1	2	0	3	4	$q = 2$
0	0	0	0	0	0	4	1	2	0	3	5	$q = 3$

Figure 13.6 Algorithm 13.4 working on the input of Figure 13.4

Randomized list ranking

Next we present a work-optimal randomized algorithm for list ranking. Each processor is in charge of computing the rank of $\log n$ nodes in the input. Processor i is assigned the nodes $A[(i-1)\log n + 1], A[(i-1)\log n + 2], \ldots, A[i \log n]$. The algorithm runs in stages. In any stage, a fraction of the existing nodes is selected and eliminated (or *spliced out*). When a node i is spliced out, the relevant information about this node is stored so that in the future its correct rank can be determined. When the number of remaining

---

Step 1. Doubly link the list. With n processors, this can be done in $O(1)$ time as follows. Processor i is associated with node $A[i]$ (for $1 \leq i \leq n$). In one step, processor i writes i in memory cell $Neighbor[i]$ so that in the next step the processor associated with the node $A[Neighbor[i]]$ will know its left neighbor. Using the slow-down lemma, this can also be done in $O(\log n)$ time using $\frac{n}{\log n}$ processors. Let $LNeighbor[i]$ and $RNeighbor[i]$ stand for the left and right neighbors of node $A[i]$. To begin with, the rank field of each node is as shown in Figure 13.5(a).

Step 2. while (the number of remaining nodes is > 2) **do**
{

> **Step a**. Processor q $(1 \leq q \leq \frac{n}{\log n})$ considers the next unspliced node (call it x) associated with it. It flips a two-sided coin. If the outcome is a *tail*, the processor becomes idle for the rest of the stage. In the next stage it again attempts to splice out x. On the other hand, if the coin flip results in a *head*, it checks whether the right neighbor of x is being considered by the corresponding processor. If the right neighbor of x is being considered and the coin flip of that processor is also a *head*, processor q gives up and is idle for the rest of the stage. If not, q decides to splice out x.
>
> **Step b**. When node x is spliced out, processor q stores in node x the stage number, the pointer $LNeighbor[x]$, and $Rank[LNeighbor[x]]$. $Rank[LNeighbor[x]]$ at this time is the number of nodes between $LNeighbor[x]$ and x. Processor q also sets $Rank[LNeighbor[x]] := Rank[LNeighbor[x]] + Rank[x]$;. Finally it sets $RNeighbor[LNeighbor[x]] := RNeighbor[x]$; and $LNeighbor\ [RNeighbor[x]] := LNeighbor[x]$;.

}

Algorithm 13.5 Splicing out nodes

nodes is two, the list ranking problem is solved trivially. From the next stage on, spliced-out nodes get inserted back (i.e., *spliced in*). When a node is spliced in, its correct rank will also be determined. Nodes are spliced in in the reverse order in which they were spliced out. The splicing-out process is depicted in Algorithm 13.5.

Node insertion is also done in stages. When a node x is spliced in, its correct rank can be determined as follows: If $LNeighbor[x]$ was the pointer stored when it was spliced out, the rank of x is the current rank

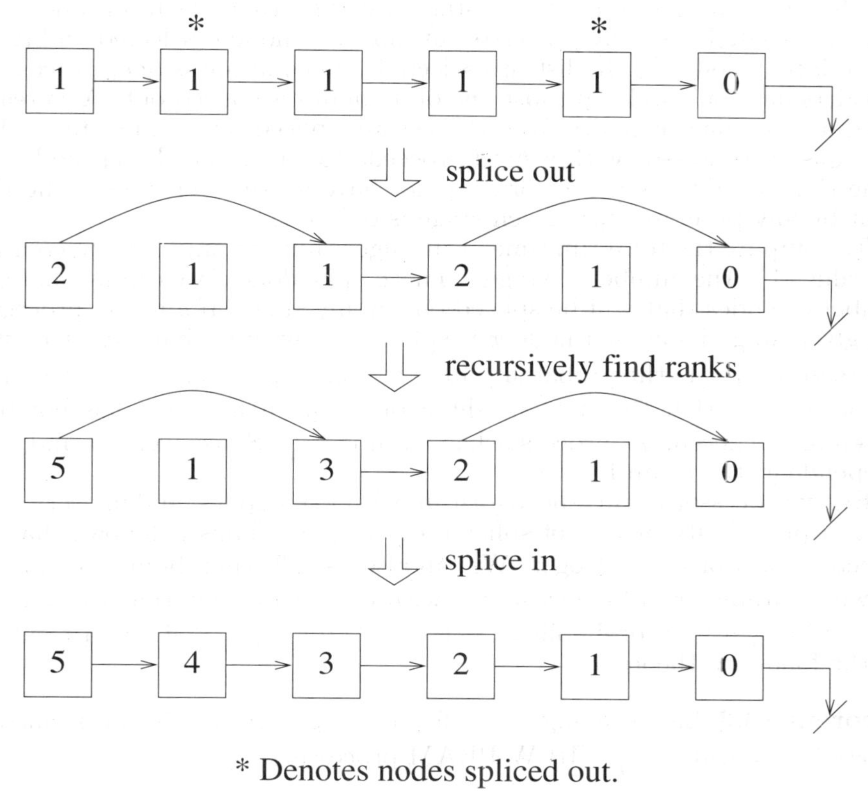

Figure 13.7 Splicing in and splicing out nodes. Only right links of nodes are shown.

of $LNeighbor[x]$ minus the rank that was stored when x was spliced out. Pointers are also adjusted to take into account the fact that now x has been inserted (see Figure 13.7).

We show that the total number s of stages of splicing-out is $\widetilde{O}(\log n)$. If a node gets spliced out in stage q, then it'll be spliced in in stage $2s - q + 1$. So the overall structure of the algorithm is as follows: In stages $1, 2, \ldots, s$, nodes are successively spliced out. Stage s is such that there are only two nodes left and one of them is spliced out. In stage $s + 1$, the node that was spliced out in stage s is spliced in. In stage $s + 2$, the nodes that were spliced out in stage $s - 1$ are spliced in. And so on. Following the last stage, we know the ranks of all the nodes in the original list.

The nodes spliced out in any stage are such that (1) from among the nodes associated with any processor, at most one node is selected and (2) no two adjacent nodes of the list are selected. Since in any stage, processor q considers only one node, at most one of its nodes is spliced out. Also realize that no two adjacent nodes from the list are spliced out in any stage. This is because a processor with a *head* proceeds to splice the chosen node only if the right neighbor's processor does not have a *head*. Therefore, the time spent by any processor in a given stage is only $O(1)$.

To compute the total run time of the algorithm, we only have to compute the value of s, the number of stages. This can be done if we can estimate the number of nodes that will be spliced out in any stage. If q is any processor, in a given stage its chosen node x is spliced out with probability at least $\frac{1}{4}$. The reasons are (1) the probability for q to come up with a *head* is $\frac{1}{2}$ and (2) the probability that the right neighbor of x (call it y) either has not been chosen or, if chosen, y's processor has a tail is $\geq \frac{1}{2}$. Since events 1 and 2 are independent, the claim follows.

Every processor begins the algorithm with $\log n$ nodes, and in every stage it has a probability of $\geq \frac{1}{4}$ of splicing out a node. Thus it follows that the expected value of s is $\leq 4 \log n$. We can also use Chernoff bounds (Equation 1.2 with parameters $12\alpha \log n$ and $\frac{1}{4}$ with $\epsilon = \frac{2}{3}$) to show that the value of s is $\leq 12\alpha \log n$ with probability $> (1 - n^{-\alpha})$ for any $\alpha \geq 1$. As a result we get the following theorem.

Theorem 13.3 List ranking on a list of length n can be performed in $\widetilde{O}(\log n)$ time using $\frac{n}{\log n}$ EREW PRAM processors.

EXERCISES

1. There is some data in cell M_1 of the global memory. The goal is to make copies of this data in cells $M_2, M_3, \ldots, M_n$. Show how you accomplish this in $O(\log n)$ time using n EREW PRAM processors.

2. Present an $O(\log n)$ time $\frac{n}{\log n}$ processor EREW PRAM algorithm for the problem of Exercise 1.

3. Show that Theorem 13.2 holds for the EREW PRAM also.

4. Let $f(x) = a_n x^n + a_{n-1} x^{n-1} + \cdots + a_1 x + a_0$. Present an $O(\log n)$ time $\frac{n}{\log n}$-processor CREW PRAM algorithm to evaluate the polynomial f at a given point y.

5. The *segmented prefix* problem is defined as follows: Array A has n elements from some domain Σ. Array $B[1:n]$ is a Boolean array with $B[1] = 1$. Define a *segment* of A to be $A[i:j]$, where $B[i] = 1, B[j] = 1$,

and $B[k] = 0,\ i < k < j$. As a convention assume that $B[n+1] = 1$. The problem is to perform several independent prefix computations on A, one for each segment. Show how to solve this problem in $O(\log n)$ time on a $\frac{n}{\log n}$-processor CREW PRAM.

6. If $k_1, k_2, \ldots, k_n$ are from Σ and $\oplus$ is a binary associative operator on Σ, the *suffix computation problem* is to output k_n, $k_{n-1} \oplus k_n$, $\ldots$, $k_1 \oplus k_2 \oplus \cdots \oplus k_n$. Show how you'll solve this problem in $O(\log n)$ time on an $\frac{n}{\log n}$-processor CREW PRAM as well as EREW PRAM.

7. The inputs are an array A of n elements and an element x. The goal is to rearrange the elements of A such that all the elements of A that are less than or equal to x appear first (in successive cells) followed by the rest of the elements. Give an $O(\log n)$-time $\frac{n}{\log n}$-processor CREW PRAM algorithm for this problem.

8. Array A is an array of n elements, where each element has a label of zero or one. The problem is to rearrange A so that all the elements with a zero label appear first, followed by all the others. Show how to perform this rearrangement in $O(\log n)$ time using $\frac{n}{\log n}$ CREW PRAM processors.

9. Let A be an array of n keys. The rank of a key x in A is defined to be one plus the number of elements in A that are less than x. Given A and an x, show how you compute the rank of x using $\frac{n}{\log n}$ CREW PRAM processors. Your algorithm should run in $O(\log n)$ time.

10. Show how you modify Algorithm 13.4 and the randomized list ranking algorithm so they solve the list prefix computation problem.

11. Array A is an array of nodes representing a list. Each node has a label of either zero or one. You are supposed to split the list in two, the first list containing all the elements with a zero label and the second list consisting of all the rest of the nodes. The original order of nodes should be preserved. For example, if x is a node with a zero label and the next right node with a zero label is z, then x should have z as its right neighbor in the first list created. Present an $\widetilde{O}(\log n)$ time algorithm for this problem. You can use up to $\frac{n}{\log n}$ CREW PRAM processors.

12. Present an $O(\log n)$ time $\frac{n^2}{\log n}$-processor CREW PRAM algorithm to multiply an $n \times n$ matrix with an $n \times 1$ column vector. How will you solve the same problem on an EREW PRAM? You can use $O(n^2)$ global memory. (*Hint:* See Exercise 1.)

13. Show how to multiply two $n \times n$ matrices using $\frac{n^3}{\log n}$ CREW PRAM processors and $O(\log n)$ time.

14. Strassen's algorithm for matrix multiplication was introduced in Section 3.8. Using the same technique, design a divide-and-conquer algorithm for matrix multiplication that uses only $n^{\log_2 7}$ CREW PRAM processors and runs in $O(\log n)$ time.

15. Prove that two $n \times n$ boolean matrices can be multiplied in $O(1)$ time on any of the CRCW PRAMs. What is the processor bound of your algorithm?

16. In Section 10.3, a divide-and-conquer algorithm was presented for inverting a triangular matrix. Parallelize this algorithm on the CREW PRAM to get a run time of $O(\log^2 n)$. What is the processor bound of your algorithm?

17. A *tridiagonal* matrix has nonzero elements only in the diagonal and its two neighboring diagonals (one below and one above). Present an $O(\log n)$ time $\frac{n}{\log n}$-processor CREW PRAM algorithm to solve the system of linear equations $Ax = b$, where A is an $n \times n$ tridiagonal matrix and x (unknown) and b are $n \times 1$ column vectors.

18. An optimal algorithm for FFT was given in Section 9.3. Present a work-optimal parallelization of this algorithm on the CREW PRAM. Your algorithm should run in $O(\log n)$ time.

19. Let X and Y be two sorted arrays with n elements each. Show how you merge these in $O(1)$ time on the common CRCW PRAM. How many processors do you use?

13.4 SELECTION

The problem of selection was introduced in Section 3.7. Recall that this problem takes as input a sequence of n keys and an integer i, $1 \leq i \leq n$, and outputs the ith smallest key from the sequence. Several algorithms were presented for this problem in Section 3.7. One of these algorithms (Algorithm 3.19) has a worst-case run time of $O(n)$ and hence is optimal. In this section we study the parallel complexity of selection. We start by presenting algorithms for many special cases. Finally, we give an $\widetilde{O}(\log n)$ time $\frac{n}{\log n}$-processor common CRCW PRAM algorithm. Since the work done in this algorithm is $\widetilde{O}(n)$, it is work-optimal.

Step 0. If $n = 1$, output the key.

Step 1. Processor p_{ij} (**for** each $1 \leq i, j \leq n$ **in parallel**) computes $x_{ij} = (k_i < k_j)$.

Step 2. The n^2 processors are grouped into n groups $G_1, G_2, \ldots, G_n$, where G_i ($1 \leq i \leq n$) consists of the processors $p_{i1}, p_{i2}, \ldots, p_{in}$. Each group G_i computes the boolean OR of $x_{i1}, x_{i2}, \ldots, x_{in}$.

Step 3. If G_i computes a zero in step 2, then processor p_{i1} outputs k_i as the answer.

Algorithm 13.6 Finding the maximum in $O(1)$ time

13.4.1 Maximal Selection with n^2 Processors

Here we consider the problem of selection for $i = n$; that is, we are interested in finding the maximum of n given numbers. This can be done in $O(1)$ time using an n^2-processor CRCW PRAM.

Let $k_1, k_2, \ldots, k_n$ be the input. The idea is to perform all pairs of comparisons in one step using n^2 processors. If we name the processors p_{ij} (for $1 \leq i, j \leq n$), processor p_{ij} computes $x_{ij} = (k_i < k_j)$. Without loss of generality assume that all the keys are distinct. Even if they are not, they can be made distinct by replacing key k_i with the tuple (k_i, i) (for $1 \leq i \leq n$); this amounts to appending each key with only a $(\log n)$-bit number. Of all the input keys, there is only one key k which when compared with every other key, would have yielded the same bit zero. This key can be identified using the boolean OR algorithm (Algorithm 13.1) and is the maximum of all. The resultant algorithm appears as Algorithm 13.6.

Steps 1 and 3 of this algorithm take one unit of time each. Step 2 takes $O(1)$ time (see Theorem 13.1). Thus the whole algorithm runs in $O(1)$ time; this implies the following theorem.

Theorem 13.4 The maximum of n keys can be computed in $O(1)$ time using n^2 common CRCW PRAM processors. □

Note that the speedup of Algorithm 13.6 is $\frac{\Theta(n)}{1} = \Theta(n)$. Total work done by this algorithm is $\Theta(n^2)$. Hence its efficiency is $\frac{\Theta(n)}{\Theta(n^2)} = \Theta(1/n)$. Clearly, this algorithm is not work-optimal!

13.4.2 Finding the Maximum Using n Processors

Now we show that maximal selection can be done in $O(\log\log n)$ time using n common CRCW PRAM processors. The technique to be employed is divide-and-conquer. To simplify the discussion, we assume n is a perfect square (when n is not a perfect square, replace $\sqrt{n}$ by $\lceil\sqrt{n}\rceil$ in the following discussion).

Let the input sequence be $k_1, k_2, \ldots, k_n$. We are interested in developing an algorithm that can find the maximum of n keys using n processors. Let $T(n)$ be the run time of this algorithm. We partition the input into $\sqrt{n}$ parts, where each part consists of $\sqrt{n}$ keys. Allocate $\sqrt{n}$ processors to each part so that the maximum of each part can be computed in parallel. Since the recursive maximal selection of each part involves $\sqrt{n}$ keys and an equal number of processors, this can be done in $T(\sqrt{n})$ time. Let $M_1, M_2, \ldots, M_{\sqrt{n}}$ be the group maxima. The answer we are supposed to output is the maximum of these maxima. Since now we only have $\sqrt{n}$ keys, we can find the maximum of these employing all the n processors (see Algorithm 13.7).

Step 1 of this algorithm takes $T(\sqrt{n})$ time and step 2 takes $O(1)$ time (c.f. Theorem 13.4). Thus $T(n)$ satisfies the recurrence

$$T(n) \;=\; T(\sqrt{n}) + O(1)$$

which solves to $T(n) = O(\log\log n)$. Therefore the following theorem arises.

Theorem 13.5 The maximum of n keys can be found in $O(\log\log n)$ time using n common CRCW PRAM processors. □

Total work done by Algorithm 13.7 is $\Theta(n\log\log n)$ and its efficiency is $\frac{\Theta(n)}{\Theta(n\log\log n)} = \Theta(1/\log\log n)$. Thus this algorithm is not work-optimal.

13.4.3 Maximal Selection Among Integers

Consider again the problem of finding the maximum of n given keys. If each one of these keys is a bit, then the problem of finding the maximum reduces to computing the boolean OR of n bits and hence can be done in $O(1)$ time using n common CRCW PRAM processors (see Algorithm 13.1). This raises the following question: What can be the maximum magnitude of each key if we desire a constant time algorithm for maximal selection using n processors? Answering this question in its full generality is beyond the scope of this book. Instead we show that if each key is an integer in the range $[0, n^c]$, where c is a constant, maximal selection can be done work-optimally in $O(1)$ time. Speedup of this algorithm is $\Theta(n)$ and its efficiency is $\Theta(1)$.

Since each key is of magnitude at most n^c, it follows that each key is a binary number with $\leq c\log n$ bits. Without loss of generality assume that

---

Step 0. If $n = 1$, return k_1.

Step 1. Partition the input keys into $\sqrt{n}$ parts $K_1, K_2, \ldots, K_{\sqrt{n}}$ where K_i consists of $k_{(i-1)\sqrt{n}+1}, k_{(i-1)\sqrt{n}+2}, \ldots, k_{i\sqrt{n}}$. Similarly partition the processors so that P_i $(1 \leq i \leq \sqrt{n})$ consists of the processors $p_{(i-1)\sqrt{n}+1}, p_{(i-1)\sqrt{n}+2}, \ldots, p_{i\sqrt{n}}$. Let P_i find the maximum of K_i recursively (for $1 \leq i \leq \sqrt{n}$).

Step 2. If $M_1, M_2, \ldots, M_{\sqrt{n}}$ are the group maxima, find and output the maximum of these maxima employing Algorithm 13.6.

Algorithm 13.7 Maximal selection in $O(\log \log n)$ time

every key is of length exactly equal to $c \log n$. (We can add leading zero bits to numbers with fewer bits.) Suppose we find the maximum of the n keys only with respect to their $\frac{\log n}{2}$ most significant bits (MSBs) (see Figure 13.8). Let M be the maximum value. Then, any key whose $\frac{\log n}{2}$ MSBs do not equal M can be dropped from future consideration since it cannot possibly be the maximum. After this step, many keys can potentially survive. Next we compute the maximum of the remaining keys with respect to their next $\frac{\log n}{2}$ MSBs and drop keys that cannot possibly be the maximum. We repeat this basic step $2c$ times (once for every $\frac{\log n}{2}$ bits in the input keys). One of the keys that survives the very last step can be output as the maximum. Refer to the $\frac{\log n}{2}$ MSBs of any key as its first part, the next most significant $\frac{\log n}{2}$ bits as its second part, and so on. There are $2c$ parts for each key. The $2c$th part may have less than $\frac{\log n}{2}$ bits. The algorithm is summarized in Algorithm 13.8. To begin with, all the keys are *alive.*

We now show that step 1 of Algorithm 13.8 can be completed in $O(1)$ time using n common CRCW PRAM processors. Note that if a key has at most $\frac{\log n}{2}$ bits, its maximum magnitude is $\sqrt{n} - 1$. Thus each step of Algorithm 13.8 is nothing but the task of finding the maximum of n keys, where each key is an integer in the range $[0, \sqrt{n}-1]$. Assign one processor to each key. Make use of $\sqrt{n}$ global memory cells (which are initialized to $-\infty$). Call these cells $M_0, M_1, \ldots, M_{\sqrt{n}-1}$. In one parallel write step, if processor i has a key k_i, then it tries to write k_i in M_{k_i}. For example, if processor i has a key valued 10, it will attempt to write 10 in M_{10}. After this write step, the problem of computing the maximum of the n keys reduces to computing

for $i := 1$ **to** $2c$ **do**
{

Step 1. Find the maximum of all the alive keys with respect to their ith parts. Let M be the maximum.

Step 2. Delete each alive key whose ith part is $< M$.

}

Output one of the alive keys.

Algorithm 13.8 Integer maximum

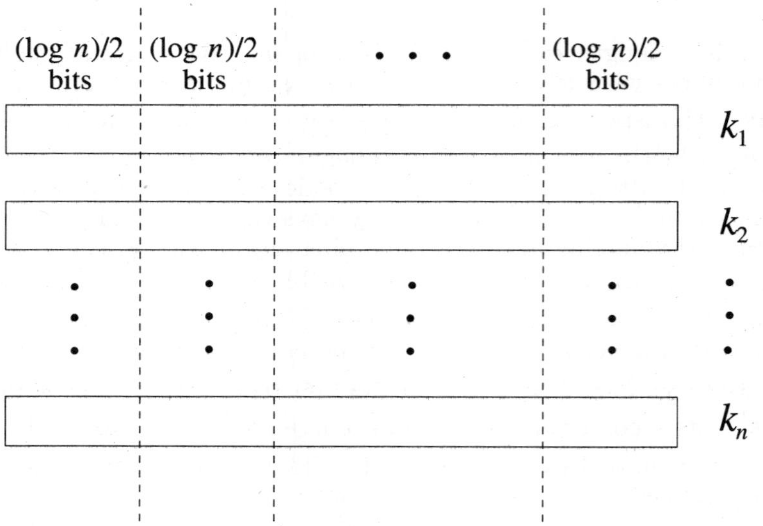

Figure 13.8 Finding the integer maximum

the maximum of the contents of $M_0, M_1, \ldots, M_{\sqrt{n}-1}$. Since these are only $\sqrt{n}$ numbers, their maximum can be found in $O(1)$ time using n processors (see Theorem 13.4). As a result we get the following theorem.

Theorem 13.6 The maximum of n keys can be found in $O(1)$ time using n CRCW PRAM processors provided the keys are integers in the range $[0, n^c]$ for any constant c. □

Example 13.17 Consider the problem of finding the maximum of the following four four-bit keys: $k_1 = 1010, k_2 = 1101, k_3 = 0110$, and $k_4 = 1100$. Here $n = 4$, $c = 2$, and $\log n = 2$. In the first basic step of Algorithm 13.8, the maximum of the four numbers with respect to their MSB is 1. Thus k_3 gets eliminated. In the second basic step, the maximum of k_1, k_2, and k_4 with respect to their second part (i.e., second MSB) is found. As a result, k_1 is dropped. In the third basic step, no key gets eliminated. Finally, in the fourth basic step, k_4 is deleted to output k_2 as the maximum. □

13.4.4 General Selection Using n^2 Processors

Let $X = k_1, k_2, \ldots, k_n$ be a given sequence of distinct keys and say we are interested in selecting the ith smallest key. The *rank* of any key x in X is defined to be one plus the number of keys of X that are less than x. If we have $\frac{n}{\log n}$ CREW PRAM processors, we can compute the rank of any given key x in $O(\log n)$ time (see Section 13.3, Exercise 9).

If we have $\frac{n^2}{\log n}$ processors, we can group them into $G_1, G_2, \ldots, G_n$ such that each G_j has $\frac{n}{\log n}$ processors. G_j computes the rank of k_j in X (for $1 \leq j \leq n$) using the algorithm of Section 13.3, Exercise 9. This will take $O(\log n)$ time. One of the processors in the group whose rank was i will output the answer. Thus we get the following theorem.

Theorem 13.7 Selection can be performed in $O(\log n)$ time using $\frac{n^2}{\log n}$ CREW PRAM processors. □

The algorithm of Theorem 13.7 has a speedup of $\frac{\Theta(n)}{\Theta(\log n)} = \Theta(n/\log n)$. Its efficiency is $\frac{\Theta(n)}{\Theta(n^2)} = \Theta(1/n)$; that is, the algorithm is not work-optimal!

13.4.5 A Work-Optimal Randomized Algorithm (*)

In this section we show that selection can be done in $\widetilde{O}(\log n)$ time using $\frac{n}{\log n}$ common CRCW PRAM processors. The randomized algorithm chooses a random sample (call it S) from X of size $n^{1-\epsilon}$ (for some suitable ϵ) and selects two elements of S as splitters. A choice of $\epsilon = 0.6$ suffices. Let l_1 and l_2 be the splitters. The keys l_1 and l_2 are such that the element to be selected has a value between l_1 and l_2 with high probability (abbreviated w.h.p.). In addition, the number of keys of X that have a value in the range $[l_1, l_2]$ is small, $\widetilde{O}(n^{(1+\epsilon)/2}\sqrt{\log n})$ to be specific.

Having chosen l_1 and l_2, we partition X into X_1, X_2, and X_3, where $X_1 = \{x \in X | x < l_1\}$, $X_2 = \{x \in X | l_1 \leq x \leq l_2\}$, and $X_3 = \{x \in X | x > l_2\}$. While performing this partitioning, we also count the size of each part. If $|X_1| < i \leq |X_1| + |X_2|$, the element to be selected lies in X_2. If this is the case, we proceed further. If not, we start all over again. We can show that the ith smallest element of X will indeed belong to X_2 with high probability and also that $|X_2| = N = \widetilde{O}(n^{(1+\epsilon)/2}\sqrt{\log n})$. The element to be selected will be the $(i - |X_1|)$th smallest element of X_2.

The preceding process of sampling and elimination is repeated until the number of remaining keys is $\leq n^{0.4}$. After this, we perform an appropriate selection from out of the remaining keys using the algorithm of Theorem 13.7. More details of the algorithm are given in Algorithm 13.9. To begin with, each input key is *alive*. There are $\frac{n}{\log n}$ processors and each processor gets $\log n$ keys. Concentration (in steps 3 and 7) refers to collecting the relevant keys and putting them in successive cells in global memory (see Section 13.3, Exercise 8).

Let a *stage* refer to one run of the **while** loop. The number of samples in any given stage is binomial with parameters N and $N^{-\epsilon}$. Thus the expected number of sample keys is $N^{1-\epsilon}$. Using Chernoff bounds, we can show that $|S|$ is $\widetilde{O}(N^{1-\epsilon})$.

Let S be a sample of s elements from a set X of n elements. Let $r_j = \text{rank}(\text{select}(j, S), X)$. Here $\text{rank}(x, X)$ is defined to be one plus the number of elements in X that are less than x, and $\text{select}(j, S)$ is defined to be the jth smallest element of S. The following lemma provides a high probability confidence interval for r_j.

Lemma 13.3 For every α, Prob. $\left(|r_j - j\frac{n}{s}| > \sqrt{3\alpha}\frac{n}{\sqrt{s}}\sqrt{\log n}\right) < n^{-\alpha}$. □

For a proof of this lemma, see the references supplied at the end of this chapter. Using this lemma, we can show that only $\widetilde{O}(N^{(1+\epsilon)/2}\sqrt{\log N})$ keys survive at the end of any stage, where N is the number of alive keys at the beginning of this stage. This in turn implies there are only $\widetilde{O}(1)$ stages in the algorithm.

Broadcasting in any parallel machine is the operation of sending a specific information to a specified set of processors. In the case of a CREW PRAM, broadcasting can be done in $O(1)$ time with a concurrent read operation. In Algorithm 13.9, steps 1 and 2 take $O(\log n)$ time each. In steps 3 and 6, concentration can be done using a prefix sums computation followed by a write. Thus step 3 takes $O(\log n)$ time. Also, the sample size in steps 3 and 6 is $\widetilde{O}(n^{0.4})$. Thus these keys can be sorted in $O(\log n)$ time using a simple algorithm (given in Section 13.6). Alternatively, the selections performed in steps 3 and 6 can be accomplished using the algorithm of Theorem 13.7. Two prefix sums computations are done in step 5 for a total of $O(\log n)$

$N := n$; // N at any time is the number of live keys
while $(N > n^{0.4})$ **do**
{

Step 1. Each live key is included in the random sample S with probability $\frac{1}{N^\epsilon}$. This step takes $\log n$ time and with high probability, $O(N^{1-\epsilon})$ keys (from among all the processors) are in the random sample.

Step 2. All processors perform a prefix sums operation to compute the number of keys in the sample. Let q be this number. Broadcast q to all the processors. If q is not in the range $[0.5N^{1-\epsilon}, 1.5N^{1-\epsilon}]$, go to step 1.

Step 3. Concentrate and sort the sample keys.

Step 4. Select keys l_1 and l_2 from S with ranks $\left\lceil \frac{iq}{N} \right\rceil - d\sqrt{q \log N}$ and $\left\lceil \frac{iq}{N} \right\rceil + d\sqrt{q \log N}$, respectively, d being a constant $> \sqrt{3\alpha}$. Broadcast l_1 and l_2 to all the processors. The key to be selected has a value in the range $[l_1, l_2]$ w.h.p.

Step 5. Count the number r of live keys that are in the range $[l_1, l_2]$. Also count the number of live keys that are $< l_1$. Let this count be t. Broadcast r and t to all the processors. If i is not in the interval $(t, t + r]$ or if r is $\neq O(N^{(1+\epsilon)/2}\sqrt{\log N})$, go to step 1; else kill (i.e., delete) all the live keys with a value $< l_1$ or $> l_2$ and set $i := i - t$ and $N := r$.

}

Step 6. Concentrate and sort the live keys. Identify and output the ith smallest key.

Algorithm 13.9 A work-optimal randomized selection algorithm

time. Therefore, each stage of the algorithm runs in $\widetilde{O}(\log n)$ time and the whole algorithm also terminates in time $\widetilde{O}(\log n)$; this implies the following theorem.

Theorem 13.8 Selection from out of n keys can be performed in $\widetilde{O}(\log n)$ time using $\frac{n}{\log n}$ CREW PRAM processors. □

EXERCISES

1. Present an $O(\log\log n)$ time algorithm for finding the maximum of n arbitrary numbers using $\frac{n}{\log\log n}$ common CRCW PRAM processors.

2. Show that prefix minima computation can be performed in $O(\log\log n)$ time using $\frac{n}{\log\log n}$ common CRCW PRAM processors.

3. Given an array A of n elements, we would like to find the largest i such that $A[i] = 1$. Give an $O(1)$ time algorithm for this problem on an n-processor common CRCW PRAM.

4. Algorithm 13.6 runs in time $O(1)$ using n^2 processors. Show how to modify this algorithm so that the maximum of n elements can be found in $O(1)$ time using $n^{1+\epsilon}$ processors for any fixed $\epsilon > 0$.

5. If k is any integer > 1, the kth quantiles of a sequence X of n numbers are defined to be those $k-1$ elements of X that evenly divide X. For example, if $k = 2$, there is only one quantile, namely, the median of X. Show that the kth quantiles of any given X can be computed in $\widetilde{O}(\log k \log n)$ time using $\frac{n}{\log n}$ CREW PRAM processors.

6. Present an $\widetilde{O}(1)$ time n-processor algorithm for finding the maximum of n given arbitrary numbers. (*Hint*: Employ random sampling along the same lines as in Algorithm 13.9.)

7. Given an array A of n elements, the problem is to find any element of A that is greater than or equal to the median. Present an $\widetilde{O}(1)$ time algorithm for this problem. You can use a maximum of $\log^2 n$ CRCW PRAM processors.

8. The distinct elements problem was posed in Section 13.2, Exercises 4 and 5. Assume that the elements are integers in the range $[0, n^c]$, where c is a constant. Show how to solve the distinct elements problem in $O(1)$ time using n CRCW PRAM processors. (*Hint*: You can use $O(n^c)$ global memory.)

9. Show how to reduce the space bound of the above algorithm to $O(n^{1+\epsilon})$ for any fixed $\epsilon > 0$. (*Hint*: Use the idea of radix reduction (see Figure 13.8).)

10. If X is a sorted array of elements and x is any element, we can make use of binary search to check whether $x \in X$ in $O(\log n)$ time sequentially. Assume that we have k processors, where $k > 1$. Can the search be done faster? One way of making use of all the k processors is to

partition X into k nearly equal parts. Each processor is assigned a part. A processor then compares x with the two endpoints of the part assigned to it to check whether x falls in its part. If no part has x, then the answer is immediate. If $x \in X$, only one part survives. In the next step, all the k processors can work on the surviving part in a similar manner. This is continued until the position of x is pinpointed.

The preceding algorithm is called a *k-ary search.* What is the run time of a k-ary search algorithm? Show that if there are n^ϵ CREW PRAM processors (for any fixed $\epsilon > 0$), we can check whether $x \in X$ in $O(1)$ time.

13.5 MERGING

The problem of merging is to take two sorted sequences as input and produce a sorted sequence of all the elements. This problem was studied in Chapter 3 and an $O(n)$ time algorithm (Algorithm 3.8) was presented. Merging is an important problem. For example, an efficient merging algorithm can lead to an efficient sorting algorithm (as we saw in Chapter 3). The same is true in parallel computing also. In this section we study the parallel complexity of merging.

13.5.1 A Logarithmic Time Algorithm

Let $X_1 = k_1, k_2, \ldots, k_m$ and $X_2 = k_{m+1}, k_{m+2}, \ldots, k_{2m}$ be the input sorted sequences to be merged. Assume without loss of generality that m is an integral power of 2 and that the keys are distinct. Note that the merging of X_1 and X_2 can be reduced to computing the rank of each key k in $X_1 \cup X_2$. If we know the rank of each key, then the keys can be merged by writing the key whose rank is i into global memory cell i. This writing will take only one time unit if we have $n = 2m$ processors.

For any key k, let its rank in X_1 (X_2) be denoted as r_k^1 (r_k^2). If $k = k_j \in X_1$, then note that $r_k^1 = j$. If we allocate a single processor π to k, π can perform a binary search (see Algorithms 3.2 and 3.3) on X_2 and figure out the number q of keys in X_2 that are less than k. Once q is known, π can compute k's rank in $X_1 \cup X_2$ as $j+q$. If k belongs to X_2, a similar procedure can be used to compute its rank in $X_1 \cup X_2$. In summary, if we have $2m$ processors (one processor per key), merging can be completed in $O(\log m)$ time.

Theorem 13.9 Merging of two sorted sequences each of length m can be completed in $O(\log m)$ time using m CREW PRAM processors. □

Since two sorted sequences of length m each can be sequentially merged in $\Theta(m)$ time, the speedup of the above algorithm is $\frac{\Theta(m)}{\Theta(\log m)} = \Theta(m/\log m)$; its efficiency is $\frac{\Theta(m)}{\Theta(m \log m)} = \Theta(1/\log m)$. This algorithm is not work-optimal!

13.5.2 Odd-Even Merge

Odd-even merge is a merging algorithm based on divide-and-conquer that yields itself to efficient parallelization. If $X_1 = k_1, k_2, \ldots, k_m$ and $X_2 = k_{m+1}, k_{m+2}, \ldots, k_{2m}$ (where m is an integral power of 2) are the two sorted sequences to be merged, then Algorithm 13.10 uses $2m$ processors.

Step 0. If $m = 1$, merge the sequences with one comparison.

Step 1. Partition X_1 and X_2 into their odd and even parts. That is, partition X_1 into $X_1^{odd} = k_1, k_3, \ldots, k_{m-1}$ and $X_1^{even} = k_2, k_4, \ldots, k_m$. Similarly, partition X_2 into X_2^{odd} and X_2^{even}.

Step 2. Recursively merge X_1^{odd} with X_2^{odd} using m processors. Let $L_1 = \ell_1, \ell_2, \ldots, \ell_m$ be the result. Note that $X_1^{odd}, X_1^{even}, X_2^{odd}$, and X_2^{even} are in sorted order. At the same time merge X_1^{even} with X_2^{even} using the other m processors to get $L_2 = \ell_{m+1}, \ell_{m+2}, \ldots, \ell_{2m}$.

Step 3. *Shuffle* L_1 and L_2; that is, form the sequence $L = \ell_1, \ell_{m+1}, \ell_2, \ell_{m+2}, \ldots, \ell_m, \ell_{2m}$. Compare every pair (ℓ_{m+i}, ℓ_{i+1}) and interchange them if they are out of order. That is, compare ℓ_{m+1} with ℓ_2 and interchange them if need be, compare ℓ_{m+2} with ℓ_3 and interchange them if need be, and so on. Output the resultant sequence.

Algorithm 13.10 Odd-even merge algorithm

Example 13.18 Let $X_1 = 2, 5, 8, 11, 13, 16, 21, 25$ and $X_2 =$ 4,9,12,18,23,27, 31,34. Figure 13.9 shows how the odd-even merge algorithm can be used to merge these two sorted sequences. □

Let $M(m)$ be the run time of Algorithm 13.10 on two sorted sequences of length m each using $2m$ processors. Then, step 1 takes $O(1)$ time. Step 2 takes $M(m/2)$ time. Step 3 takes $O(1)$ time. This yields the following recurrence relation: $M(m) = M(m/2) + O(1)$ which solves to $M(m) = O(\log m)$. Thus we arrive at the following theorem.

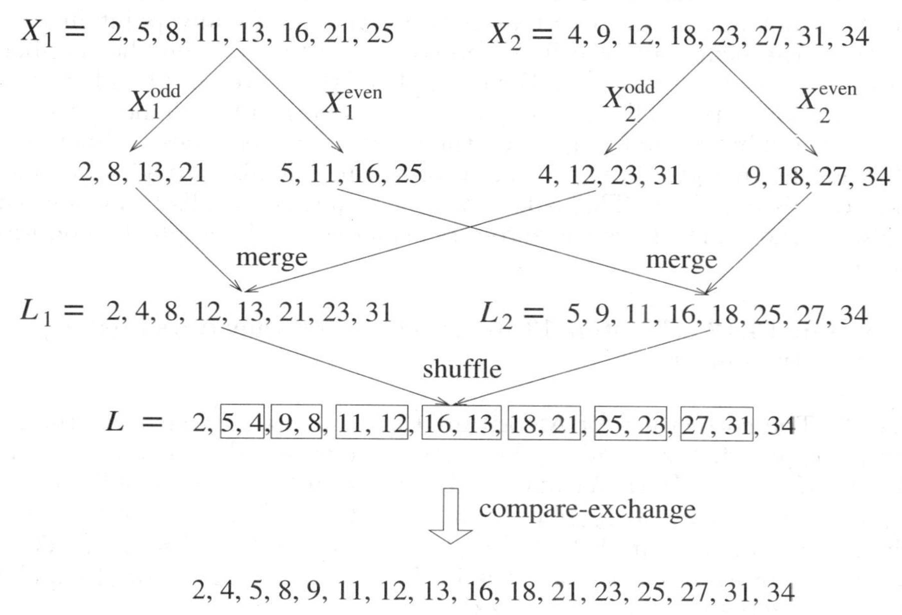

Figure 13.9 Odd-even merge – an example

Theorem 13.10 Two sorted sequences of length m each can be merged in $O(\log m)$ time using $2m$ EREW PRAM processors. □

The correctness of the merging algorithm can be established using the *zero-one principle.* The validity of this principle is not proved here.

Theorem 13.11 [Zero-one principle] If any *oblivious* comparison-based sorting algorithm sorts an arbitrary sequence of n zeros and ones correctly, then it will also sort any sequence of n arbitrary keys. □

A comparison-based sorting algorithm is said to be *oblivious* if the sequence of cells to be compared in the algorithm is prespecified. For example, the next pair of cells to be compared cannot depend on the outcome of comparisons made in the previous steps.

Example 13.19 Let $k_1, k_2, \ldots, k_n$ be a sequence of bits. One way of sorting this sequence is to count the number z of zeros in the sequence, followed by writing z zeros and $n - z$ ones in succession. The zero-one principle cannot be applied to this algorithm since the algorithm is not comparison based.

Also, the quicksort algorithm (Section 3.6), even though comparison based, is not oblivious. The reason is as follows. At any point in the algorithm, the next pair of cells to be compared depends on the number of keys in each of the two parts. For example, if there are only two keys in the first part, these two cells are compared next. On the other hand, if there are ten elements in the first part, then the comparison sequence is different.

Note that merging is a special case of sorting and also the odd-even merge algorithm is oblivious. This is because the sequence of cells to be compared is always the same. Thus the zero-one principle can be applied to odd-even merge. □

Theorem 13.12 Algorithm 13.10 correctly merges any two sorted sequences of arbitrary numbers.

Proof: The correctness of Algorithm 13.10 can be proved using the zero-one principle. Let X_1 and X_2 be sorted sequences of zeros and ones with $|X_1| = |X_2| = m$. Both X_1 and X_2 have a sequence of zeros followed by a sequence of ones. Let q_1 (q_2) be the number of zeros in X_1 (X_2, respectively). The number of zeros in X_1^{odd} is $\lceil q_1/2 \rceil$ and the number of zeros in X_1^{even} is $\lfloor q_1/2 \rfloor$. Thus the number of zeros in L_1 is $z_1 = \lceil q_1/2 \rceil + \lceil q_2/2 \rceil$ and the number of zeros in L_2 is $z_2 = \lfloor q_1/2 \rfloor + \lfloor q_2/2 \rfloor$.

The difference between z_1 and z_2 is at most 2. This difference is exactly two if and only if both q_1 and q_2 are odd. In all the other cases the difference is ≤ 1. Assume that $|z_1 - z_2| = 2$. The other cases are similar. L_1 has two more zeros than L_2. When these two are shuffled in step 3, L contains a sequence of zeros, followed by 10 and then by a sequence of ones. The only unsorted portion in L (also called the *dirty sequence*) will be 10. When the final comparison and interchange is performed in step 3, the dirty sequence and the whole sequence are sorted. □

13.5.3 A Work-Optimal Algorithm

In this section we show how to merge two sorted sequences with m elements each in logarithmic time using only $\frac{m}{\log m}$ processors. This algorithm reduces the original problem into $O(\frac{m}{\log m})$ subproblems, where each subproblem is that of merging two sorted sequences each of length $O(\log m)$. Each such subproblem can be solved using the sequential algorithm (Algorithm 3.8) of Chapter 3 in $O(\log m)$ time.

Thus the algorithm is complete if we describe how to reduce the original problem into $O(\frac{m}{\log m})$ subproblems. Let X_1 and X_2 be the sequences to be merged. Partition X_1 into $\frac{m}{\log m}$ parts, where there are $\log m$ keys in each part. Call these parts $A_1, A_2, \ldots, A_M$, where $M = \frac{m}{\log m}$. Let the largest key in A_i be ℓ_i (for $i = 1, 2, \ldots, M$). Assign a processor to each of these ℓ_i's.

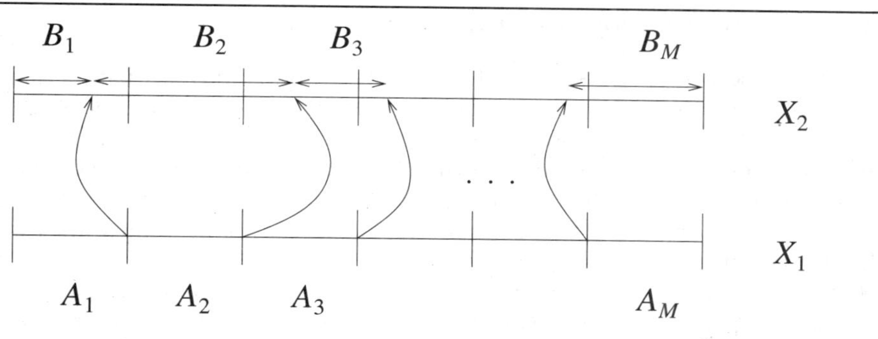

Figure 13.10 A work-optimal merging algorithm

The processor associated with ℓ_i performs a binary search on X_2 to find the correct (i.e., sorted) position of ℓ_i in X_2. This induces a partitioning of X_2 into M parts. Note that some of these parts could be empty (see Figure 13.10). Let the corresponding parts of X_2 be $B_1, B_2, \ldots, B_M$. Call B_i the *corresponding subset of* A_i *in* X_2.

Now, the merge of X_1 and X_2 is nothing but the merge of A_1 and B_1, followed by the merge of A_2 and B_2, and so on. That is, merging X_1 and X_2 reduces to merging A_i with B_i for $i = 1, 2, \ldots, M$. We know that the size of each A_i is $\log m$. But the sizes of the B_i's could be very large (or very small). How can we merge A_i with B_i? We can use the idea of partitioning one more time.

Let A_i and B_i be an arbitrary pair. If $|B_i| = O(\log m)$, they can be merged in $O(\log m)$ time using one processor. Consider the case when $|B_i|$ is $\omega(\log m)$. Partition B_i into $\lceil \frac{|B_i|}{\log m} \rceil$ parts, where each part has at most $\log m$ successive keys of B_i. Allocate one processor to each part so that the processor can find the corresponding subset of this part in A_i in $O(\log \log m)$ time. As a result, the problem of merging A_i and B_i has been reduced to $\lceil \frac{|B_i|}{\log m} \rceil$ subproblems, where each subproblem is that of merging two sequences of length $O(\log m)$.

The number of processors used is $\sum_{i=1}^{M} \lceil \frac{|B_i|}{\log m} \rceil$, which is $\leq 2M$. Thus we conclude the following.

Theorem 13.13 Two sorted sequences of length m each can be merged in $O(\log m)$ time using $\frac{2m}{\log m}$ CREW PRAM processors. □

13.5.4 An $O(\log\log m)$-Time Algorithm

Now we present a very fast algorithm for merging. This algorithm can merge two sorted sequences in $O(\log\log m)$ time, where m is the number of elements in each of the two sequences. The number of processors used is $2m$. The basic idea behind this algorithm is the same as the one used for the algorithm of Theorem 13.13. In addition we employ the divide-and-conquer technique.

X_1 and X_2 are the given sequences. Assume that the keys are distinct. The algorithm reduces the problem of merging X_1 and X_2 into $N \leq 2\sqrt{m}$ subproblems, where each subproblem is that of merging two sorted sequences of length $\leq \sqrt{m}$. This reduction is completed in $O(1)$ time using m processors. If $T(m)$ is the run time of the algorithm using $2m$ processors, then $T(m)$ satisfies the recurrence relation $T(m) = T(\sqrt{m}) + O(1)$ whose solution is $O(\log\log m)$. Details of the algorithm are given in Algorithm 13.11.

The correctness of Algorithm 13.11 is quite clear; we infer this theorem.

Theorem 13.14 Two sorted sequences of length m each can be merged in $O(\log\log m)$ time using $2m$ CREW PRAM processors. □

The above algorithm has a speedup of $\frac{\Theta(m)}{\Theta(\log\log m)} = \Theta(m/\log\log m)$ which is very close to m. Its efficiency is $\Theta(1/\log\log m)$, and hence the algorithm is not work-optimal!

EXERCISES

1. Modify Algorithm 13.11 so that it uses only $\frac{m}{\log\log m}$ CREW PRAM processors and merges X_1 and X_2 in $O(\log\log m)$ time.

2. A sequence $K = k_1, k_2, \ldots, k_n$ is said to be *bitonic* either (1) if there is a $1 \leq j \leq n$ such that $k_1 \leq k_2 \leq \cdots k_j \geq k_{j+1} \geq \cdots \geq k_n$ or (2) a cyclic shift of K satisfies 1. For example, $3, 8, 12, 17, 24, 15, 9, 6$ and $21, 35, 19, 16, 8, 5, 1, 15, 17$ are bitonic. If K is a bitonic sequence with n elements (for n even), let $a_i = \min\ \{k_i, k_{i+n/2}\}$ and $b_i = \max\ \{k_i, k_{i+n/2}\}$. Also let $L(K) = \min\ \{k_1, k_{1+n/2}\},\ \min\ \{k_2, k_{2+n/2}\}, \ldots, \min\ \{k_{n/2}, k_n\}$ and $H(K) = \max\ \{k_1, k_{1+n/2}\},\ \max\ \{k_2, k_{2+n/2}\}, \ldots \max\ \{k_{n/2}, k_n\}$. Show that:

   (a) $L(K)$ and $H(K)$ are both bitonic.

   (b) Every element of $L(K)$ is smaller than any element of $H(K)$. In other words, to sort K, it suffices to sort $L(K)$ and $H(K)$ separately and output one followed by the other.

Step 1. Partition X_1 into $\sqrt{m}$ parts with $\sqrt{m}$ elements each. Call these parts $A_1, A_2, \ldots, A_{\sqrt{m}}$. Let the largest key in A_i be ℓ_i (for $i = 1, 2, \ldots, \sqrt{m}$). Assign $\sqrt{m}$ processors to each of these ℓ_i's. The processors associated with ℓ_i perform a $\sqrt{m}$-ary search on X_2 to find the correct (i.e., sorted) position of ℓ_i in X_2 in $O(1)$ time (see Section 13.4, Exercise 10). This induces a partitioning of X_2 into $\sqrt{m}$ parts. Note that some of these parts could be empty (see Figure 13.10). Let the corresponding parts of X_2 be $B_1, B_2, \ldots, B_{\sqrt{m}}$. The subset B_i is the corresponding subset of A_i in X_2.

Step 2. Now, the merge of X_1 and X_2 is nothing but the merge of A_1 and B_1, followed by the merge of A_2 and B_2, and so on. That is, merging X_1 and X_2 reduces to merging A_i with B_i for $i = 1, 2, \ldots, \sqrt{m}$. We know that the size of each A_i is $\sqrt{m}$. But the sizes of the B_i's could be very large (or very small). To merge A_i with B_i, we can use the idea of partitioning one more time.

Let A_i and B_i be an arbitrary pair. If $|B_i| \leq \sqrt{m}$, we can merge them in $T(\sqrt{m})$ time. Consider the case when $|B_i|$ is $\omega(\sqrt{m})$. Partition B_i into $\lceil \frac{|B_i|}{\sqrt{m}} \rceil$ parts, where each part has at most $\sqrt{m}$ successive keys of B_i. Allocate $\sqrt{m}$ processors to each part so that the processors can find the corresponding subset of this part in A_i in $O(1)$ time. As a result the problem of merging A_i and B_i has been reduced to $\lceil \frac{|B_i|}{\sqrt{m}} \rceil$ subproblems, where each subproblem is that of merging two sequences of length $O(\sqrt{m})$.

The number of processors used is $\sum_{i=1}^{\sqrt{m}} \sqrt{m} \lceil \frac{|B_i|}{\sqrt{m}} \rceil$, which is $\leq 2m$.

Algorithm 13.11 Merging in $O(\log \log m)$ time

The above properties suggest a divide-and-conquer algorithm for sorting a given bitonic sequence. Present the details of this algorithm together with an analysis of the time and processor bounds. Show how to make use of the resultant sorting algorithm to merge two given sorted sequences. Such an algorithm is called the *bitonic merger*.

3. Given two sorted sequences of length n each. How will you merge them in $O(1)$ time using n^2 CREW PRAM processors?

13.6 SORTING

Given a sequence of n keys, recall that the problem of sorting is to rearrange this sequence into either ascending or descending order. In this section we study several algorithms for parallel sorting. If we have n^2 processors, the rank of each key can be computed in $O(\log n)$ time comparing, in parallel, all possible pairs (see the proof of Theorem 13.7). Once we know the rank of each key, in one parallel write step they can be written in sorted order (the key whose rank is i is written in cell i). Thus we have the following theorem.

Theorem 13.15 We can sort n keys in $O(\log n)$ time using n^2 CREW PRAM processors. □

The work done by the preceding algorithm is $O(n^2 \log n)$. On the other hand we have seen several sequential algorithms with run times of $O(n \log n)$ (Chapter 3) and have also proved a matching lower bound (Chapter 10). The preceding algorithm is not work-optimal.

13.6.1 Odd-Even Merge Sort

Odd-even merge sort employs the classical divide-and-conquer strategy. Assume for simplicity that n is an integral power of two and that the keys are distinct. If $X = k_1, k_2, \ldots, k_n$ is the given sequence of n keys, it is partitioned into two subsequences $X_1' = k_1, k_2, \ldots, k_{n/2}$ and $X_2' = k_{n/2+1}, k_{n/2+2}, \ldots, k_n$ of equal length. X_1' and X_2' are sorted recursively assigning $n/2$ processors to each. The two sorted subsequences (call them X_1 and X_2, respectively) are then finally merged.

The preceding description of the algorithm is exactly the same as that of merge sort. The difference between the two algorithms lies in how the two subsequences X_1 and X_2 are merged. In the merging algorithm used in Section 3.5, the minimum elements from the two sequences are compared and the minimum of these two is output. This step continues until the two sequences are merged. As is seen, this process seems to be inherently sequential in nature. Instead, we employ the odd-even merge algorithm (Algorithm 13.10) of Section 13.5.

Theorem 13.16 We can sort n arbitrary keys in $O(\log^2 n)$ time using n EREW PRAM processors.

Proof: The sorting algorithm is described in Algorithm 13.12. It uses n processors. Define $T(n)$ to be the time taken by this algorithm to sort n keys using n processors. Step 1 of this algorithm takes $O(1)$ time. Step 2 runs in $T(n/2)$ time. Finally, step 3 takes $O(\log n)$ time (c.f. Theorem 13.10). Therefore, $T(n)$ satisfies $T(n) = O(1) + T(n/2) + O(\log n) = T(n/2) + O(\log n)$, which solves to $T(n) = O(\log^2 n)$. □

Example 13.20 Consider the problem of sorting the 16 numbers $25, 21, 8, 5, 2, 13, 11, 16, 23, 31, 9, 4, 18, 12, 27, 34$ using 16 processors. In step 1 of Algorithm 13.12, the input is partitioned into two: $X_1' = 8, 21, 8, 5, 2, 13, 11, 16$, and $X_2' = 23, 31, 9, 4, 18, 12, 27, 34$. In step 2, processors 1 to 8 work on X_1', recursively sort it, and obtain $X_1 = 2, 5, 8, 11, 13, 16, 21, 25$. At the same time processors 9 to 16 work on X_2', sort it, and obtain $X_2 = 4, 9, 12, 18, 23, 27, 31, 34$. In step 3, X_1 and X_2 are merged as shown in Example 13.18 to get the final result: $2, 4, 5, 8, 9, 11, 12, 13, 16, 18, 21, 23, 25, 27, 31, 34$. □

The work done by Algorithm 13.12 is $\Theta(n \log^2 n)$. Therefore, its efficiency is $\Theta(1/\log n)$. It has a speedup of $\Theta(n/\log n)$.

Step 0. If $n \leq 1$, return X.

Step 1. Let $X = k_1, k_2, \ldots, k_n$ be the input. Partition the input into two: $X_1' = k_1, k_2, \ldots, k_{n/2}$ and $X_2' = k_{n/2+1}, k_{n/2+2}, \ldots, k_n$.

Step 2. Allocate $n/2$ processors to sort X_1' recursively. Let X_1 be the result. At the same time employ the other $n/2$ processors to sort X_2' recursively. Let X_2 be the result.

Step 3. Merge X_1 and X_2 using Algorithm 13.10 and $n = 2m$ processors.

Algorithm 13.12 Odd-even merge sort

13.6.2 An Alternative Randomized Algorithm

We can get the result of Theorem 13.16 using the randomized selection algorithm of Section 13.4. Theorem 13.8 states that selection from out of n keys can be performed in $\widetilde{O}(\log n)$ time using $\frac{n}{\log n}$ processors. Assume that there are n processors. The median k of the n given keys can be found in $\widetilde{O}(\log n)$ time. Having found the median, partition the input into two parts. The first part X_1' contains all the input keys $\leq k$ and the second part X_2' contains all the rest of the keys. The parts X_1' and X_2' are sorted recursively with $n/2$ processors each. The output is X_1' in sorted order followed by X_2' in sorted order. If $T(n)$ is the sorting time of n keys using n processors, we have $T(n) = T(n/2) + \widetilde{O}(\log n)$, which solves to $T(n) = \widetilde{O}(\log^2 n)$.

Step 0. If n is a small constant, sort the keys using any algorithm and quit.

Step 1. Partition the given n keys into $\log n$ parts, with $n/\log n$ keys in each part. Sort each part recursively and separately in parallel, assigning n processors to each part. Let $S_1, S_2, \ldots, S_{\log n}$ be the sorted sequences.

Step 2. Merge S_i with S_j for $1 \leq i, j \leq \log n$ in parallel. This can be done by allocating $n/\log n$ processors to each pair (i, j). That is, using $n \log n$ processors, this step can be accomplished in $O(\log \log n)$ time with Algorithm 13.11. As a by-product of this merging step, we have computed the rank of each key in each one of the S_i's $(1 \leq i \leq \log n)$.

Step 3. Allocate $\log n$ processors to compute the rank of each key in the original input. This is done in parallel for all the keys by adding the $\log n$ ranks computed (for each key) in step 2. This can be done in $O(\log \log n)$ time using the prefix computation algorithm (see Algorithm 13.3). Finally, the keys are written out in the order of their ranks.

Algorithm 13.13 Preparata's sorting algorithm

Theorem 13.17 Sorting n keys can be performed in $\widetilde{O}(\log^2 n)$ time using n CREW PRAM processors. □

13.6.3 Preparata's Algorithm

Preparata's algorithm runs in $O(\log n)$ time and uses $n \log n$ CREW PRAM processors. This is a recursive divide-and-conquer algorithm wherein the rank of each input key is computed and the keys are output according to their ranks (see the proof of Theorem 13.15). Let $k_1, k_2, \ldots, k_n$ be the input sequence. Preparata's algorithm partitions the input into $\log n$ parts $K_1, K_2, \ldots, K_{\log n}$, where there are $\frac{n}{\log n}$ keys in each part. If k is any key in the input, its rank in the input is computed as follows. First, the rank r_i of k in K_i is computed for each i, $1 \leq i \leq \log n$. Then, the total rank of k is computed as $\sum_{i=1}^{\log n} r_i$. One of the results that it makes use of is Theorem 13.14.

The details of Preparata's algorithm are given in Algorithm 13.13. Let

$T(n)$ be the run time of Preparata's algorithm using $n \log n$ processors. Clearly, step 1 takes $T(n/\log n)$ time and steps 2 and 3 together take $O(\log \log n)$ time. Thus we have

$$T(n) \;=\; T(n/\log n) \;+\; O(\log \log n)$$

which can be solved by repeated substitution to get $T(n) = O(\log n)$. Also, the number of processors used in each step is $n \log n$. We get the following.

Theorem 13.18 Any n arbitrary keys can be sorted in $O(\log n)$ time using $n \log n$ CREW PRAM processors. □

Applying the slow-down lemma (Lemma 13.2) to the above theorem, we infer a corollary.

Corollary 13.1 Any n general keys can be sorted in $O(t \log n)$ time using $n \log n/t$ CREW PRAM processors, for any $t \geq 1$. □

Preparata's algorithm does the same total work as the odd-even merge sort. But its speedup is $\Theta(n)$, which is better than that of the odd-even merge sort. Efficiency of both the algorithms is the same; i.e., $\Theta(1/\log n)$.

13.6.4 Reischuk's Randomized Algorithm (∗)

This algorithm uses n processors and runs in time $\widetilde{O}(\log n)$. Thus its efficiency is $\frac{\Theta(n \log n)}{\widetilde{\Theta}(n \log n)} = \widetilde{\Theta}(1)$; i.e., the algorithm is work-optimal with high probability! The basis for this algorithm is Preparata's sorting scheme and the following theorem. (For a proof see the references at the end of this chapter.)

Theorem 13.19 We can sort n keys, where each key is an integer in the range $[0, n(\log n)^c]$ (c is any constant) in $\widetilde{O}(\log n)$ time using $\frac{n}{\log n}$ CRCW PRAM processors. □

Reischuk's algorithm runs in the same time bound as Preparata's (with high probability) but uses only n processors. The idea is to randomly sample $N = \frac{n}{\log^4 n}$ keys from the input and sort these using a non-work-optimal algorithm like Preparata's. The sorted sample partitions the original problem into $N + 1$ independent subproblems of nearly equal size, and all these subproblems can be solved easily. These ideas are made concrete in Algorithm 13.14.

Step 2 of Algorithm 13.14 can be done using $N \log N \leq N \log n$ processors in $O(\log N) = O(\log n)$ time (c.f. Theorem 13.18). In step 3, the

Step 1. $N = n/(\log^4 n)$ processors randomly sample a key (each) from $X = k_1, k_2, \ldots, k_n$, the given input sequence.

Step 2. Sort the N keys sampled in step 1 using Preparata's algorithm. Let $l_1, l_2, \ldots, l_N$ be the sorted sequence.

Step 3. Let $K_1 = \{k \in X | k \leq l_1\}$; $K_i = \{k \in X | l_{i-1} < k \leq l_i\}$, $i = 2, 3, \ldots, N$; and $K_{N+1} = \{k \in X | k > l_N\}$. Partition the given input X into K_i's as defined. This is done by first finding the part each key belongs to (using binary search in parallel). Now partitioning the keys reduces to sorting the keys according to their part numbers.

Step 4. For $1 \leq i \leq N+1$ in parallel sort K_i using Preparata's algorithm.

Step 5. Output sorted(K_1), sorted(K_2), $\ldots$, sorted(K_{N+1}).

Algorithm 13.14 Work-optimal randomized algorithm for sorting

partitioning of X can be done using binary search and the integer sort algorithms (c.f. Theorem 13.19). If there is a processor associated with each key, the processor can perform a binary search in $l_1, l_2, \ldots, l_N$ to figure out the part number the key belongs to. Note that the part number of each key is an integer in the range $[1, N+1]$. Therefore the keys can be sorted according to their part numbers using Theorem 13.19.

Thus step 3 can be performed in $\widetilde{O}(\log n)$ time, using $\leq n$ processors. With high probability, there will be no more than $O(\log^5 n)$ keys in each of the K_i's ($1 \leq i \leq N$). The proof of this fact is left as an exercise. Within the same processor and time bounds, we can also count $|K_i|$ for each i. In step 4, each K_i can be sorted in $O(\log |K_i|)$ time using $|K_i| \log |K_i|$ processors. Also K_i can be sorted in $(\log |K_i|)^2$ time using $|K_i|$ processors (see Corollary 13.1). So step 4 can be completed in $(\max_i \log |K_i|)^2$ time using n processors. If $\max_i |K_i| = O(\log^5 n)$, step 4 takes $O((\log \log n)^2)$ time. Thus we have proved the following.

Theorem 13.20 We can sort n general keys using n CRCW PRAM processors in $\widetilde{O}(\log n)$ time. □

EXERCISES

1. In step 3 of Algorithm 13.12, we could employ the merging algorithm of Algorithm 13.11. If so, what would be the run time of Algorithm 13.12? What would be the processor bound?

2. If we have n numbers to sort and each number is a bit, one way of sorting X could be to make use of prefix computation algorithms as in Section 13.3, Exercise 8. This amounts to counting the number of zeros and the number of ones. If z is the number of zeros, we output z zeros followed by $n - z$ ones. Using this idea, design an $O(\log n)$ time algorithm to sort n numbers, where each number is an integer in the range $[0, \log n - 1]$. Your algorithm should run in $O(\log n)$ time using no more than $\frac{n}{\log n}$ CREW PRAM processors. Recall that n numbers in the range $[0, n^c]$ can be sequentially sorted in $O(n)$ time (the corresponding algorithm is known as the radix sort).

3. Make use of the algorithm designed in the previous problem together with the idea of radix sorting to show that n numbers in the range $[0, (\log n)^c]$ can be sorted in $O(\log n)$ time using $\frac{n}{\log n}$ CREW PRAM processors.

4. Given two sets A and B of size n each (in the form of arrays), the goal is to check whether the two sets are disjoint or not. Show how to solve this problem:

   (a) In $O(1)$ time using n^2 CRCW PRAM processors

   (b) In $\widetilde{O}(\log n)$ time using n CREW PRAM processors

5. Sets A and B are given such that $|A| = n$, $|B| = m$, and $n \geq m$. Show that we can determine whether A and B are disjoint in $\widetilde{O}((\log n)(\log m))$ time using $\frac{n}{\log n}$ CREW PRAM processors.

6. Show that if a set X of n keys is partitioned using a random sample of size s (as in Reischuk's algorithm), the size of each part is $\widetilde{O}\left(\frac{n}{s} \log n\right)$.

7. Array A is an almost sorted array of n elements. It is given that the position of each key is at most a distance of d from its final sorted position, where d is a constant. Give an $O(1)$ time n-processor EREW PRAM algorithm to sort A. Prove the correctness of your algorithm using the zero-one principle.

8. The original algorithm of Reischuk was recursive and had the following steps:

(a) Select a random sample of size $\sqrt{n}-1$ and sort it using Theorem 13.15.

(b) Partition the input into $\sqrt{n}$ parts making use of the sorted sample (similar to step 3 of Algorithm 13.14).

(c) Assign a linear number of processors to each part and recursively sort each part in parallel.

(d) Output the sorted parts in the correct order.

See if you can analyze the run time of this algorithm.

9. It is known that prefix sums computation can be done in time $O(\frac{\log n}{\log \log n})$ using $\frac{n \log \log n}{\log n}$ CRCW PRAM processors, provided the numbers are integers in the range $[0, n^c]$ for any constant c. Assuming this result, show that sorting can be done in time $O(\frac{\log n}{\log \log n})$ time using n^2 CRCW PRAM processors.

10. Adopt the algorithms of Exercise 7 and Section 13.4, Exercise 10, and the $O(\log n / \log \log n)$ time algorithm for integer prefix sums computation to show that n numbers can be sorted in $\widetilde{O}(\frac{\log n}{\log \log n})$ time using $n(\log n)^{\epsilon}$ CRCW PRAM processors (for any constant $\epsilon > 0$).

11. The *random access read (RAR)* operation in a parallel machine is defined as follows: Each processor wants to read a data item from some other processor. In the case of a PRAM, it is helpful to assume that each processor has an associated part of the global memory, and reading from a processor means reading from the corresponding part of shared memory. It may be the case that several processors want to read from the same processor. Note that on the CRCW PRAM or on the CREW PRAM, a RAR operation can be performed in one unit of time. Devise an efficient algorithm for RAR on the EREW PRAM. (*Hint:* If processor i wants to read from processor j, create a tuple (j, i) corresponding to this request. Sort all the tuples (j, i) in lexicographic order.)

12. We can define a *random access write (RAW)* operation similar to RAR as follows. Every processor has an item of data to be sent to some other processor (that is, an item of data to be written in the shared memory part of some other processor). Several processors might want to write in the same part and hence a resolution scheme (such as common, priority, etc.) is also supplied. On the CRCW PRAM (with the same resolution scheme), this can be done in one unit of time. Develop efficient algorithms for RAW on the CREW and EREW PRAMs. (*Hint:* Make use of sorting (see Exercise 11).)

13.7 GRAPH PROBLEMS

We consider the problems of transitive closure, connected components, minimum spanning tree, and all-pairs shortest paths in this section. Efficient sequential algorithms for these problems were studied in Chapters 6 and 10. We begin by introducing a general framework for solving these problems.

Definition 13.4 Let M be an $n \times n$ matrix with nonnegative integer coefficients. Let $\widetilde{M}$ be a matrix defined as follows:

$$\widetilde{M}(i,i) = 0 \qquad \text{for every } i$$

$$\widetilde{M}(i,j) = \min\ \{M_{i_0 i_1} + M_{i_1 i_2} + \cdots + M_{i_{k-1} i_k}\} \quad \text{for every } i \neq j$$

where $i_0 = i$, $i_k = j$, and the minimum is taken over all sequences $i_0, i_1, \ldots, i_k$ of elements from the set $\{1, 2, \ldots, n\}$. □

Example 13.21 Let $G(V, E)$ be a directed graph with $V = \{1, 2, \ldots, n\}$. Define M as $M(i,j) = 0$ if either $i = j$ or there is a directed edge from node i to node j in G, and $M(i,j) = 1$ otherwise. For this choice of M, it is easy to see that $\widetilde{M}(i,j) = 0$ if and only if there is a directed path from node i to node j in G.

In Figure 13.11, a directed graph is shown together with its M and $\widetilde{M}$. $\widetilde{M}(1,5)$ is zero since $M_{12} + M_{25} = 0$. Similarly, $\widetilde{M}(2,1)$ is zero since $M_{25} + M_{56} + M_{61} = 0$. On the other hand, $\widetilde{M}(3,1)$ is one since for every choice of $i_1, i_2, \ldots, i_{k-1}$, the sum $M_{i_0 i_1} + M_{i_1 i_2} + \cdots + M_{i_{k-1} i_k}$ is > 0. □

Theorem 13.21 $\widetilde{M}$ can be computed from an $n \times n$ matrix M in $O(\log n)$ time using $n^{3+\epsilon}$ common CRCW PRAM processors, for any fixed $\epsilon > 0$.

Proof: We make use of $O(n^3)$ global memory. In particular we use the variables $m[i,j]$ for $1 \leq i,j \leq n$ and $q[i,j,k]$ for $1 \leq i,j,k \leq n$. The algorithm to be employed is given in Algorithm 13.15.

Initializing $m[\ ]$ takes n^2 time. Step 1 of Algorithm 13.15 takes $O(1)$ time using n^3 processors. In step 2, n^2 different $m[i,j]$'s are computed. The computation of a single $m[i,j]$ involves computing the minimum of n numbers and hence can be completed in $O(1)$ time using n^2 CRCW PRAM processors (Theorem 13.4). In fact this minimum can also be computed in $O(1)$ time using $n^{1+\epsilon}$ processors for any fixed $\epsilon > 0$ (Section 13.4, Exercise 4). In summary, step 2 can be completed in $O(1)$ time using $n^{3+\epsilon}$ common CRCW PRAM processors. Thus the **for** loop runs in $O(\log n)$ time. The

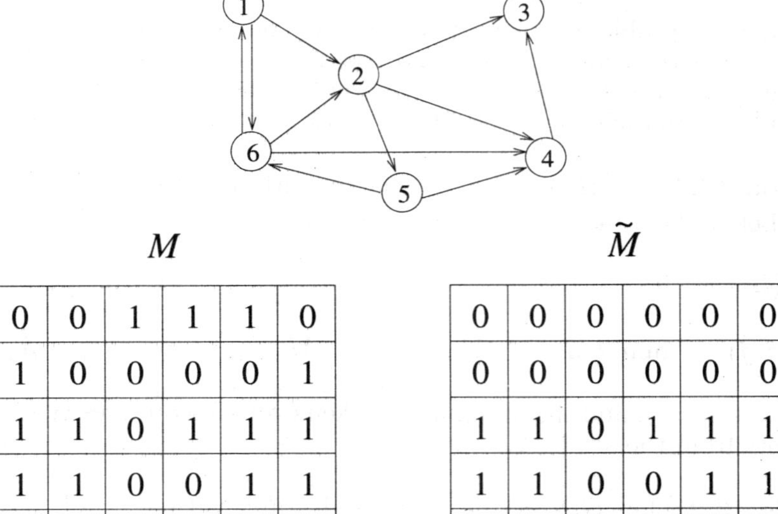

M

0	0	1	1	1	0
1	0	0	0	0	1
1	1	0	1	1	1
1	1	0	0	1	1
1	1	1	0	0	0
0	0	1	0	1	0

$\widetilde{M}$

0	0	0	0	0	0
0	0	0	0	0	0
1	1	0	1	1	1
1	1	0	0	1	1
0	0	0	0	0	0
0	0	0	0	0	0

Figure 13.11 An example graph and its M and $\widetilde{M}$

$m[i, j] := M[i, j]$ **for** $1 \leq i, j \leq n$ **in parallel;**
for $r := 1$ **to** $\log n$ **do**
{

Step 1. In parallel set $q[i, j, k] := m[i, j] + m[j, k]$ for $1 \leq i, j, k \leq n$.

Step 2. In parallel set $m[i, j] :=$ min $\{q[i, 1, j], q[i, 2, j], \ldots, q[i, n, j]\}$ for $1 \leq i, j \leq n$.

}

Put $\widetilde{M}(i)(i) := 0$ for all i and $\widetilde{M}(i)(j) := m[i, j]$ for $i \neq j$.

Algorithm 13.15 Computation of $\widetilde{M}$

final computation of $\widetilde{M}$ also can be done in $O(1)$ time using n^2 processors. □

The correctness of Algorithm 13.15 can be proven by induction on r. We can show that the value of $m[i, j]$ at the end of the rth iteration of the **for** loop is min $\{M_{i_0 i_1} + M_{i_1 i_2} + \cdots + M_{i_{k-1} i_k}\}$, where $i = i_0$, $j = i_k$, and the minimum is taken over all the sequences $i_0, i_1, \ldots, i_k$ of elements of $\{1, 2, \ldots, n\}$ such that $k \leq 2^r$. Algorithm 13.15 can be specialized to solve several problems including the transitive closure, connected components, minimum spanning tree, and so on.

Theorem 13.22 The transitive closure matrix of an n-vertex directed graph can be computed in $O(\log n)$ time using $n^{3+\epsilon}$ common CRCW PRAM processors.

Proof: If M is defined as in Example 13.21, the transitive closure of G can be easily obtained once $\widetilde{M}$ is computed. In accordance with Theorem 13.21, $\widetilde{M}$ can be computed within the stated resource bounds. □

Theorem 13.23 The connected components of an n-vertex graph can be determined in $O(\log n)$ time using $n^{3+\epsilon}$ common CRCW PRAM processors.

Proof: Define $M(i)(j)$ to be zero if either $i = j$ or i and j are connected by an edge; $M(i)(j)$ is one otherwise. Nodes i and j are in the same connected component if and only if $\widetilde{M}(i)(j) = 0$. □

Theorem 13.24 A minimum spanning tree for an n-vertex weighted graph $G(V, E)$ can be computed in $O(\log n)$ time using $n^{5+\epsilon}$ common CRCW PRAM processors.

Proof: The algorithm is a parallelization of Kruskal's sequential algorithm (see Section 4.6). In Kruskal's algorithm, the edges in the given graph G are sorted according to nondecreasing edge weights. A forest F of trees is maintained. To begin with, F consists of $|V|$ isolated nodes. The edges are processed from the smallest to the largest. An edge (u, v) gets included in F if and only if (u, v) connects two different trees in F.

In parallel, the edges can be sorted in $O(\log n)$ time using n^2 processors (Theorem 13.15). Let $e_1, e_2, \ldots, e_n$ be the edges of G. For each edge $e_i = (u, v)$, we can decide, in parallel, whether it will belong to the final tree as follows. Find the transitive closure of the graph G_i that has V as its node set and whose edges are $e_1, e_2, \ldots, e_{i-1}$. The e_i will get included in the final spanning tree if and only if u and v are not in the same connected component of G_i.

Thus, using Theorem 13.23, the test as to whether an edge belongs to the final answer can be performed in $O(\log n)$ time given $n^{3+\epsilon}$ processors. Since there are at most n^2 edges, the result follows. □

13.7.1 An Alternative Algorithm for Transitive Closure

Now we show how to compute the transitive closure of a given directed graph $G(V, E)$ in $O(\log^2 n)$ time using $\frac{n^3}{\log n}$ CREW PRAM processors. In Section 10.3 (Lemma 10.9) we showed that if A is the adjacency matrix of G, then the transitive closure matrix M is given by $M = I + A + A^2 + \cdots + A^{n-1}$. Along the same lines, we can also show that $M = (I + A)^n$. A proof by induction will establish that for any k, $1 \leq k \leq n$, $(I + A)^k(i)(j) = 1$ if and only if there is a directed path from node i to node j of length $\leq k$.

Thus M can be computed by evaluating $(I + A)^n$. $(I + A)^n$ can be rewritten as $(I + A)^{2^{\lceil \log n \rceil}}$. Therefore, computing M reduces to a sequence of $\lceil \log n \rceil$ matrix squarings (or multiplications). Since two matrices can be multiplied in $O(\log n)$ time using $\frac{n^3}{\log n}$ CREW PRAM processors (see Section 13.3, Exercise 12), we have the following theorem.

Theorem 13.25 The transitive closure of an n-node directed graph can be computed in $O(\log^2 n)$ time using $\frac{n^3}{\log n}$ CREW PRAM processors. □

13.7.2 All-Pairs Shortest Paths

An $O(n^3)$ time algorithm was developed in Section 5.3 for the problem of identifying the shortest path between every pair of vertices in a given weighted directed graph. The basic principle behind this algorithm was to define $A^k(i, j)$ to represent the length of a shortest path from i to j going through no vertex of index greater than k and then to infer that

$$A^k(i,j) = \min \{A^{k-1}(i,j),\ A^{k-1}(i,k) + A^{k-1}(k,j)\}, \quad k \geq 1.$$

The same paradigm can be used to design a parallel algorithm as well. The importance of the above relationship between A^k and A^{k-1} is that the computation of A^k from A^{k-1} corresponds to matrix multiplication, where min and addition take the place of addition and multiplication, respectively. Under this interpretation of matrix multiplication, the problem of all-pairs shortest paths reduces to computing $A^n = A^{2^{\lceil \log n \rceil}}$. We get this theorem.

Theorem 13.26 The all-pairs shortest-paths problem can be solved in $O(\log^2 n)$ time using $\frac{n^3}{\log n}$ CREW PRAM processors. □

EXERCISES

1. Compute the speedup, total work done, and efficiency for each of the algorithms given in this section.

2. Let $G(V, E)$ be a directed acyclic graph (dag). The *topological sort* of G is defined to be a linear ordering of the vertices of G such that if (u, v) is an edge of G, then u appears before v in the linear ordering. Show how to employ the general paradigm introduced in this section to obtain an $O(\log n)$ time algorithm for topological sort using $n^{3+\epsilon}$ common CRCW PRAM processors.

3. Present an efficient parallelization of Prim's algorithm for minimum spanning trees (see Section 4.6).

4. Present an efficient parallel algorithm to check whether a given undirected graph is acyclic. Analyze the processor and time bounds.

5. If G is any undirected graph, G^k is defined as follows: There will be an edge between nodes i and j in G^k if and only if there is a path of length k in G between i and j. Present an $O(\log n \log k)$ time algorithm to compute G^k from G. You can use a maximum of $\frac{n^3}{\log n}$ CREW PRAM processors.

6. Present an efficient parallel minimum spanning tree algorithm for the special case when the edge weights are zero and one.

7. Present an efficient parallelization of the Bellman and Ford algorithm (see Section 5.4).

13.8 COMPUTING THE CONVEX HULL

In this section we revisit the problem of constructing the convex hull of n points in 2D in clockwise order. The technique to be used is the same as the one we employed sequentially. The parallel algorithm will have a run time of $O(\log n)$ using n CREW PRAM processors. Note that in Chapter 10 we proved a lower bound of $\Omega(n \log n)$ for the convex hull problem and hence the parallel algorithm to be studied is work-optimal.

The sequential algorithm was based on divide-and-conquer (see Section 3.9.4). It computed the upper hull and the lower hull of the given point set separately. Thus let us restrict our discussion to the computation of the upper hull only. The given points were partitioned into two halves on the basis of their x-coordinate values. All points with an x-coordinate $\leq$ the median formed the first part. The rest of the points belonged to the second part. Upper hulls were recursively computed for the two halves. These two hulls were then merged by finding the line of tangent.

We adopt a similar technique in parallel. First, the points with the minimum and maximum x-coordinate values are identified. This can be done using the prefix computation algorithm in $O(\log n)$ time and $\frac{n}{\log n}$ processors. Let p_1 and p_2 be these points. All the points which are to the left of the line segment $\langle p_1, p_2 \rangle$ are separated from those which are to the right. This separation also can be done using a prefix computation. Points of the first (second) kind contribute to the upper (lower) hull. The computations of the upper hull and the lower hull are done independently. From here on we only consider the computation of the upper hull. By "input" we mean all the points that are to the left of $\langle p_1, p_2 \rangle$. We denote the number of such points by N.

Sort the input points according to their x-coordinate values. This can be done in $\widetilde{O}(\log N)$ time using N processors. In fact there are deterministic algorithms with the same time and processor bounds as well (see the references at the end of this chapter). This sorting is done only once in the computation of the upper hull. Let $q_1, q_2, \ldots, q_N$ be the sorted order of these points. The recursive algorithm for computing the upper hull is given in Algorithm 13.16. An upper hull is maintained in clockwise order as a list. We refer to the first element in the list as the leftmost point and the last element as the rightmost point.

Step 0. If $N \leq 2$, solve the problem directly.

Step 1. Partition the input into two halves with $q_1, q_2, \ldots, q_{N/2}$ in the first half and $q_{N/2+1}, q_{N/2+2}, \ldots, q_N$ in the second half.

Step 2. Compute the upper hull of each half (in clockwise order) recursively assigning $\frac{N}{2}$ processors to each half. Let H_1 and H_2 be the upper hulls.

Step 3. Find the line of tangent (see Figure 3.9) between the two upper hulls. Let $\langle u, v \rangle$ be the tangent.

Step 4. Drop all the points of H_1 that are to the right of u. Similarly, drop all the points to the left of v in H_2. The remaining part of H_1, the tangent, and the remaining part of H_2 form the upper hull of the given input set.

Algorithm 13.16 Parallel convex hull algorithm

We show that step 3 can be performed in $O(1)$ time using N processors. Step 4 also can be completed in $O(1)$ time. If $T(N)$ is the run time of Algorithm 13.16 for finding the upper hull on an input of N points using N

processors, then we have

$$T(N) = T(N/2) + O(1)$$

which solves to $T(N) = O(\log N)$. The number of processors used is N.

The only part of the algorithm that remains to be specified is how to find the tangent $\langle u, v \rangle$ in $O(1)$ time using N processors. First start from the middle point p of H_1. Here the middle point refers to the middle element of the corresponding list. Find the tangent of p with H_2. Let $\langle p, q \rangle$ be the tangent. Using $\langle p, q \rangle$, we can determine whether u is to the left of, equal to, or to the right of p in H_1. A k-ary search (for some suitable k) in this fashion on the points of H_1 will reveal u. Use the same procedure to isolate v.

Lemma 13.4 Let H_1 and H_2 be two upper hulls with at most m points each. If p is any point of H_1, its tangent q with H_2 can be found in $O(1)$ time using m^ϵ processors for any fixed $\epsilon > 0$.

Proof. If q' is any point in H_2, we can check whether q' is to the left of, equal to, or to the right of q in $O(1)$ time using a single processor (see Figure 3.10). If $\angle pq'x$ is a right turn and $\angle pq'y$ is a left turn, then q is to the right of q'; if $\angle pq'x$ and $\angle pq'y$ are both right turns, then, $q' = q$; otherwise q is to the left of q'. Thus if we have m processors, we can assign one processor to each point of H_2 and identify q in $O(1)$ time. The identification of q can also be done using an m^ϵ-ary search (see Section 13.4, Exercise 10) in $O(1)$ time and m^ϵ processors, for any fixed $\epsilon > 0$. □

Lemma 13.5 If H_1 and H_2 are two upper hulls with at most m points each, their common tangent can be computed in $O(1)$ time using m processors.

Proof. Let $u \in H_1$ and $v \in H_2$ be such that $\langle u, v \rangle$ is the line of tangent. Also let p be an arbitrary point of H_1 and let $q \in H_2$ be such that $\langle p, q \rangle$ is a tangent of H_2. Given p and q, we can check in $O(1)$ time whether u is to the left of, equal to, or to the right of p (see Figure 3.11). If $\langle p, q \rangle$ is also tangential to H_1, then $p = u$. If $\angle xpq$ is a left turn, then u is to the left of p; else u is to the right of p. This suggests an m^ϵ-ary search for u. For each point p of H_1 chosen, we have to determine the tangent from p to H_2 and then decide the relative positioning of p with respect to u. Thus indeed we need $m^\epsilon \times m^\epsilon$ processors to determine u in $O(1)$ time. If we choose $\epsilon = 1/2$, we can make use of all the m processors. □

The following theorem summarizes these findings.

Theorem 13.27 The convex hull of n points in the plane can be computed in $O(\log n)$ time using n CREW PRAM processors. □

Algorithm 13.16 has a speedup of $\Theta(n)$; its efficiency is $\Theta(1)$.

EXERCISES

1. Show that the vertices of the convex hull of n given points can be identified in $O(1)$ time using a common CRCW PRAM.

2. Present an $O(\frac{\log n}{\log \log n})$ time CRCW PRAM algorithm for the convex hull problem. How many processors does your algorithm use?

3. Present an $O(\log n)$ time n-processor CREW PRAM algorithm to compute the area of the convex hull of n given points in 2D.

4. Given a simple polygon and a point p, the problem is to check whether p is internal to the polygon. Present an $O(\log n)$ time $\frac{n}{\log n}$-processor CREW PRAM algorithm for this problem.

5. Present an $O(1)$ time algorithm to check whether any three of n given points are colinear. You can use up to n^3 CRCW PRAM processors. Can you decrease the processor bound further?

6. Assume that n points in 2D are given in sorted order with respect to the polar angle subtended at x, where x is the point with the lowest y-coordinate. Present an $O(\log n)$-time CREW PRAM algorithm for finding the convex hull. What is the processor bound of your algorithm?

7. Given two points $p = (x_1, y_1)$ and $q = (x_2, y_2)$ in the plane, p is said to *dominate* q if $x_1 \geq x_2$ and $y_1 \geq y_2$. The *dominance counting problem* is defined as follows. Given two sets $X = \{p_1, p_2, \ldots, p_m\}$ and $Y = \{q_1, q_2, \ldots, q_n\}$ of points in the plane, determine for each point p_i the number of points in Y that are dominated by p_i. Present an $O(\log(m+n))$ time algorithm for dominance counting. How many processors does your algorithm use?

13.9 LOWER BOUNDS

In this section we present some lower bounds on parallel computation related to comparison problems such as sorting, finding the maximum, merging, and so on. The parallel model assumed is called the *parallel comparison tree (PCT)*. This model can be thought of as the parallel analog of the comparison tree model introduced in Section 10.1.

A PCT with p processors is a tree wherein at each node, at most p pairs of comparisons are made (at most one pair per processor). Depending on the outcomes of all these comparisons, the computation proceeds to an appropriate child of the node. Whereas in the sequential comparison tree each node can have at most two children, in the PCT the number of children for any node can be more than two (depending on p). The external nodes of a PCT represent termination of the algorithm. Associated with every path from the root to an external node is a unique permutation. As there are $n!$ different possible permutations of n items and any one of these might be the correct answer for the given sorting problem, the PCT must have at least $n!$ external nodes. A typical computation for a given input on a PCT proceeds as follows. We start at the root and perform p pairs of comparisons. Depending on the outcomes of these comparisons (which in turn depend on the input), we branch to an appropriate child. At this child we perform p more pairs of comparisons. And so on. This continues until we reach an external node, at which point the algorithm terminates and the correct answer is obtained from the external node reached.

Example 13.22 Figure 13.12 shows a PCT with two processors that sorts three given numbers k_1, k_2, and k_3. Rectangular nodes are external nodes that give the final answers. At the root of this PCT, two comparisons are made and hence there are four possible outcomes. There is a child for the root corresponding to each of these outcomes. For example, if both of the comparisons made at the root yielded "yes," then clearly the sorted order of the keys is k_1, k_2, k_3. On the other hand if the root comparisons yielded "yes" and "no," respectively, then k_1 is compared with k_3, and depending on the outcome, the final permutation is obtained. The depth of this PCT and hence the worst-case run time of this parallel algorithm is two. □

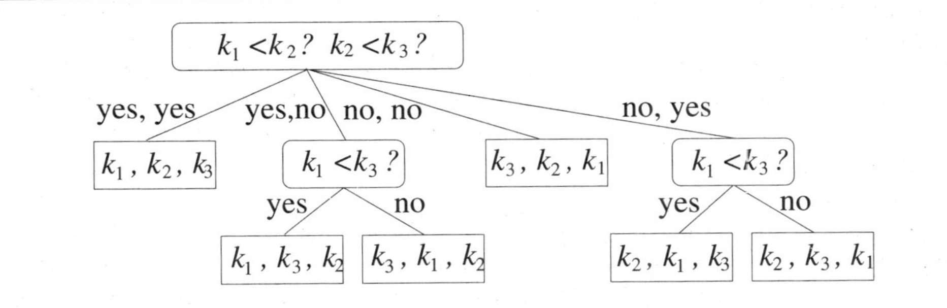

Figure 13.12 PCT with two processors that sorts three numbers

The *worst-case time* of any algorithm on a PCT is the maximum depth of any external node. The *average case time* is the average depth of an external node, all possible paths being equally likely. Note that in a PCT, while computing the time of any algorithm, we only take into account comparisons. Any other operation such as the addition of numbers, data movement, and so on, is assumed to be free. Also, at any node of the PCT, p pairs of comparisons are performed in one unit of time. As a consequence of these assumptions, any comparison problem can be solved in $O(1)$ time, given enough processors. Since a PCT is more powerful than any of the PRAMs, lower bounds derived for the PCT hold for the PRAMs as well.

Example 13.23 Suppose we are given n numbers from a linear order. There are only $\binom{n}{2}$ pairs of comparisons that can ever be made. Therefore, if $p = \binom{n}{2}$, all these comparisons can be made in one unit of time, and as a result we can solve the following problems in one unit of time: selection, sorting, and so on. (Note that a PCT charges only for the comparisons made.) □

13.9.1 A lower bound on average-case sorting

If $p \geq \binom{n}{2}$, sorting can be done in $O(1)$ time on a PCT (see Example 13.23). So assume that $p < \binom{n}{2}$. The lower bound follows from two lemmas.

The first lemma relates the average depth of an external node to the degree (i.e., the maximum number of children of any node) and the number of external nodes.

Lemma 13.6 [Shannon] A tree with degree d and ℓ external nodes has an average depth of at least $\frac{\log \ell}{\log d}$. □

We can apply the above lemma to obtain a lower bound for sorting, except that we don't know what d is. Clearly, ℓ has to be at least $n!$. Note that at each node of a PCT, we make p pairs of comparisons. So, there can be as many as 2^p possible outcomes. (The first pair of comparison can yield either "yes" or "no"; independently, the second comparison can yield "yes" or "no"; and so on.) If we substitute this value for d, Lemma 13.6 yields a lower bound of $\frac{n \log n}{p}$.

A better lower bound is achieved by noting that not all of the 2^p possible outcomes at any node of the PCT are feasible. As an example, take $p \geq 3$; the three comparisons made at a given node are $x : y$, $y : z$, and $x : z$. In this case, it is impossible for the three outcomes to be "yes," "yes," and "no."

To obtain a better estimate of d, we introduce a graph. This graph has n nodes, one node per input number. Such a graph G_v is conceived of for each node v in the PCT. For each pair $x : y$ of comparisons made at the PCT node v, we draw an edge between x and y. Thus G_v has p edges and is undirected. We can *orient* (i.e., give a direction to) each edge of G_v depending on the outcome of the corresponding comparison. Say we direct the edge from x to y if $x > y$. Note that the degree of the node v is the number of ways in which we can orient the p edges of G_v.

Since the input numbers are from a linear order, any orientation of the edges of G_v that introduces a directed cycle is impossible. The question then is how many such *acyclic orientations* are possible? This number will be a better estimate of d. U. Manber and M. Tompa have proved the following.

Lemma 13.7 [Manber and Tompa] A graph with n vertices and m edges has at most $\left(1+\frac{2m}{n}\right)^n$ acyclic orientations. □

Combining Lemmas 13.6 and 13.7, we get the following theorem.

Theorem 13.28 Any PCT with p processors needs an average case time of $\Omega\left(\frac{\log n}{\log(1+p/n)}\right)$ to sort n numbers.

Proof: Using Lemma 13.7, a better estimate for d is $\left(1+\frac{2p}{n}\right)^n$. Then, according to Lemma 13.6, the average case time for sorting is

$$\Omega\left(\frac{\log n!}{\log(1+2p/n)^n}\right) = \Omega\left(\frac{n\log n}{n\log(1+2p/n)}\right) = \Omega\left(\frac{\log n}{\log\left(1+\frac{p}{n}\right)}\right) \quad \square$$

13.9.2 Finding the maximum

Now we prove a lower bound on the problem of identifying the maximum of n given numbers. This problem can also be solved in $O(1)$ time if we have $p \geq \binom{n}{2}$.

Theorem 13.29 [Valiant] Given n unordered elements and $p = n$ PCT processors, if MAX(n) is a lower bound on the worst-case time needed to determine the maximum value in parallel time, then MAX(n) $\geq \log\log n - c$, where c is a constant.

Proof: Consider the information determined from the set of comparisons that can be made by time t for some parallel maximum finding algorithm. Some of the elements have been shown to be smaller than other elements, and so they have been eliminated. The others form a set S which contains the correct answer. If at time t two elements not in S are compared, then no progress is made in decreasing set S. If an element in set S and one not in S are compared and the larger element is in S, then again no improvement has been made. Assume that the worst case holds; this means that the only way to decrease the set S is to make comparisons between pairs of its elements.

Imagine a graph in which the nodes represent the values in the input and a directed edge from a to b implies that b is greater than a. A subset of the nodes is said to be *stable* if no pair from it is connected by an edge. (In Figure 13.13, the nodes e, b, g, and f form a stable set.) Then the size of S at time t can be expressed as

$$|S \text{ at time } t| \geq \min \{\max (h|G \text{ contains a stable set of size } h)| \\ G \text{ is a graph with } |S| \text{ nodes and } n \text{ edges}\}$$

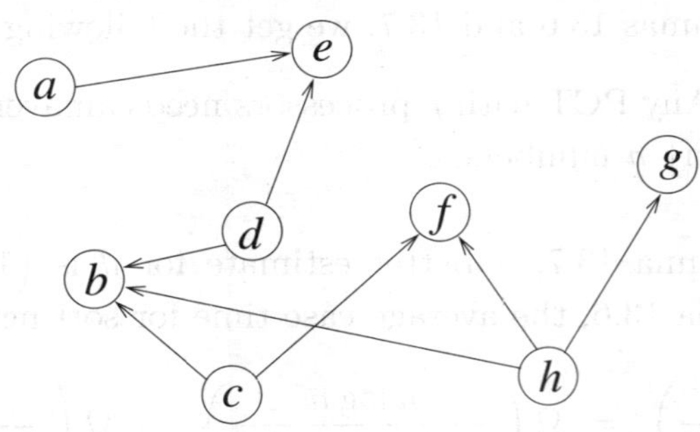

Figure 13.13 The set $\{e, f, b, g\}$ is stable.

It has been shown by Turan in *On the Theory of Graphs* (Colloq. Math., 1954) that the size of S at time t is $\geq$ the size of S at time $t-1$, squared and divided by $2p$ plus the size of S. We can solve this recurrence relation using the fact that initially the size of S equals n; this shows that the size of S will be greater than one so long as $t < \log \log n - c$. □

EXERCISES

1. [Valiant] Devise a parallel algorithm that produces the maximum of n unordered elements in $\log \log n + c$ parallel time, where c is a constant.

2. [Valiant] Devise a parallel sorting algorithm that takes a time of at most $2 \log n \log \log n + O(\log n)$.

3. **Theorem** Given n bits, any algorithm for computing the parity of these bits will need $\Omega(\frac{\log n}{\log \log n})$ time in the worst case if there are only a polynomial number of CRCW PRAM processors.

   Using this theorem prove that any algorithm for sorting n given numbers will need $\Omega(\frac{\log n}{\log \log n})$ time in the worst case, if the number of processors used is $n^{O(1)}$.

13.10 REFERENCES AND READINGS

A wide range of parallel computing models and algorithms for these models may be found in: *Handbook of Parallel Algorithms*, by S. Rajasekaran and J. Reif (editors), Chapman-Hall/CRC, 2008. Some excellent texts on parallel computing are:
Introduction to Parallel Computing, by A. Grama, A. Gupta, G. Karypis, and V. Kumar, Second Edition, Addison-Wesley, 2003.
Parallel Computation, by S. Akl, Prentice Hall, 1997.
Introduction to Parallel Algorithms and Architectures: Arrays-Trees-Hypercubes, by Tom Leighton, Morgan-Kaufmann, 1992.
Parallel Algorithms: Design and Analysis, by J. Já Já, Addison-Wesley, 1992.
Synthesis of Parallel Algorithms, edited by J. H. Reif, Morgan-Kaufmann, 1992.

For a definition of the PRAM and the metrics see:
"Parallel algorithmic techniques for combinatorial computation," by D. Eppstein and Z. Galil, *Annual Reviews in Computer Science* 3 (1988): 233–283.
"Performance metrics: keeping the focus on runtime," by S. Sahni and V. Thanvantri, *IEEE Parallel and Distributed Technology*, Spring 1996: 1–14.

Material on prefix computation and list ranking can be found in the texts mentioned above.

The work-optimal randomized selection algorithm is based on:
"Expected time bounds for selection," by R. W. Floyd and R. L. Rivest, *Communications of the ACM* 18, no. 3 (1975): 165–172.
"Derivation of randomized algorithms for sorting and selection," by S. Rajasekaran and J. H. Reif. in *Parallel Algorithm Derivation And Program Transformation*, edited by R. Paige, J. H. Reif, and R. Wachter, Kluwer, 1993, pp. 187–205.

For a survey of parallel sorting and selection algorithms see
"Sorting and selection on interconnection networks," by S. Rajasekaran, *DIMACS Series in Discrete Mathematics and Theoretical Computer Science* 21, 1995: 275–296.

Preparata's algorithm first appeared in "New parallel sorting schemes," by F. P. Preparata, *IEEE Transactions on Computers* C27, no. 7 (1978): 669–673. The original Reischuk's algorithm was recursive and appeared in "Probabilistic parallel algorithms for sorting and selection," by R. Reischuk, *SIAM Journal of Computing* 14, no. 2 (1985): 396–409. The version presented in this chapter is based on "Random sampling techniques and parallel algorithms design," by S. Rajasekaran and S. Sen, in *Synthesis of Parallel*

Algorithms, J. H. Reif, ed., Morgan-Kaufmann, 1993, pp. 411–451. A deterministic algorithm for sorting with a run time of $O(\log n)$ using n EREW PRAM processors can be found in "Parallel merge sort," by R. Cole, *SIAM Journal on Computing* 17, no. 4 (1988): 770–785.

For a proof of Theorem 13.19 see "Optimal and sub-logarithmic time randomized parallel sorting algorithms," by S. Rajasekaran and J. H. Reif, *SIAM Journal on Computing* 18, no.3 (1989): 594–607. Solutions to Exercises 2, 3, and 10 of Section 13.6 can be found in this paper.

The general paradigm for the solution of many graph problems is given in "Parallel computation and conflicts in memory access," by L. Kucera, *Information Processing Letters*, (1982): 93–96.

For more material on convex hull and related problems see the text by J. Já Já. For the lower bound proof for finding the maximum see "Parallelism in comparison problems," by L. Valiant, *SIAM Journal on Computing* 4, no. 3 (1975): 348–355.

Theorem 13.28 was first proved in "The average complexity of deterministic and randomized parallel comparison-sorting algorithms," by N. Alon and Y. Azar, *SIAM Journal on Computing* (1988): 1178–1192. The proof was greatly simplified in "The average-case parallel complexity of sorting," by R. B. Boppana, *Information Processing Letters* 33 (1989): 145–146. A proof of Lemma 13.7 can be found in "The effect of number of Hamiltonian paths on the complexity of a vertex coloring problem," by U. Manber and M. Tompa, *SIAM Journal on Computing* 13, (1984): 109–115. Lemma 13.6 was proved in "A mathematical theory of communication," by Shannon, *Bell System Technical Journal* 27 (1948): 379–423 and 623–56.

13.11 ADDITIONAL EXERCISES

1. Suppose you have a sorted list of n keys in common memory. Give an $O(\log n/(\log p))$ time algorithm that takes a key x as input and searches the list for x using p CREW PRAM processors.

2. A sequence of n keys $k_1, k_2, \ldots, k_n$ is input. The problem is to find the right neighbor of each key in sorted order. For instance if the input is $5.2, 7, 2, 11, 15, 13$, the output is $7, 11, 5.2, 13, \infty, 15$.

   (a) How will you solve this problem in $O(1)$ time using n^3 CRCW PRAM processors?

   (b) How will you solve the same problem using a Las Vegas algorithm in $\widetilde{O}(1)$ time employing n^2 CRCW PRAM processors?

3. The input is a sequence S of n arbitrary numbers with many duplications, such that the number of distinct numbers is $O(1)$. Present an $O(\log n)$ time algorithm to sort S using $\frac{n}{\log n}$ priority-CRCW PRAM processors.

4. A, B, and C are three sets of n numbers each, and ℓ is another number. Show how to check whether there are three elements, picked one each from the three sets, whose sum is equal to ℓ. Your algorithm should run in $\widetilde{O}(\log n)$ time using at most n^2 CRCW PRAM processors.

5. An array A of size n is input. The array can only be of one of the following three types:

   Type I: A has all zeros.
   Type II: A has all ones.
   Type III: A has $\frac{n}{4}$ ones and $\frac{3}{4}n$ zeros.

   How will you identify the type of A in $O(1)$ time using a Monte Carlo algorithm? You can use $\log n$ CRCW PRAM processors. Show that the probability of a correct answer will be $\geq 1 - n^{-\alpha}$ for any fixed $\alpha \geq 1$.

6. Input is an array A of n numbers. Any number in A occurs either only once or more than $n^{3/4}$ times. Elements that occur more than $n^{3/4}$ times each are called *significant* elements. Present a Monte Carlo algorithm with a run time of $O(n^{3/4} \log n)$ to identify all the significant elements of A. Prove that the output will be correct with high probability.

7. Let A be an array of size n such that each element is marked with a bucket number in the range $[1, 2, \ldots, m]$, where m divides n. The number of elements belonging to each bucket is exactly $\frac{n}{m}$. Develop a randomized parallel algorithm to rearrange the elements of A so that the elements in the first bucket appear first, followed by the elements of the second bucket, and so on. Your Las Vegas algorithm should run in $\widetilde{O}(\log n)$ time using $\frac{n}{\log n}$ CRCW PRAM processors. Prove the correctness and time bound of your algorithm.

8. Input are a directed graph $G(V, E)$ and two nodes $v, w \in V$. The problem is to determine whether there exists a directed path from v to w of length ≤ 3. How will you solve this problem in $O(1)$ time using $|V|^2$ CRCW PRAM processors? Assume that G is available in common memory in the form of an adjacency matrix.

9. Given is an undirected graph $G(V, E)$ in adjacency matrix form. We need to decide if G has a *triangle*, that is, three mutually adjacent vertices. Present an $O(\log n)$ time, $(n^3/\log n)$-processor CRCW PRAM algorithm to solve this problem.

Chapter 14

MESH ALGORITHMS

14.1 COMPUTATIONAL MODEL

A mesh is an $a \times b$ grid in which there is a processor at each grid point. The edges correspond to communication links and are bidirectional. Each processor of the mesh can be labeled with a tuple (i, j), where $1 \leq i \leq a$ and $1 \leq j \leq b$. Every processor of the mesh is a RAM with some local memory. Hence each processor can perform any of the basic operations such as addition, subtraction, multiplication, comparison, local memory access, and so on, in one unit of time. The computation is assumed to be *synchronous*; that is, there is a global clock and in every time unit each processor completes its intended task. In this chapter we consider only *square* meshes, that is, meshes for which $a = b$. A $\sqrt{p} \times \sqrt{p}$ mesh is shown in Figure 14.1(a).

A closely related model is the *linear array* (Figure 14.1(b)). A linear array consists of p processors (named $1, 2, \ldots, p$) connected as follows. Processor i is connected to the processors $i - 1$ and $i + 1$, for $2 \leq i \leq p - 1$; processor 1 is connected to processor 2 and processor p is connected to processor $p - 1$. Processors 1 and p are known as the *boundary processors*. Processor $i - 1$ $(i + 1)$ is called the *left neighbor* (*right neighbor*) of i. Processor 1 does not have a left neighbor and processor p does not have a right neighbor. Here also we assume that the links are bidirectional. A $\sqrt{p} \times \sqrt{p}$ mesh has several subgraphs that are $\sqrt{p}$-processor linear arrays. Often, the individual steps of mesh algorithms can be thought of as operations on linear arrays.

Interprocessor communication in any fixed connection machine occurs with the help of communication links. If two processors connected by an edge want to communicate, they can do so in one unit of time. If there is no edge connecting two given processors that desire to communicate, then communication is enabled using any of the paths connecting them and hence the time for communication depends on the path length (at least for small-sized messages). It is assumed that in one unit of time a processor can perform a local computation and/or communicate with all its up to four

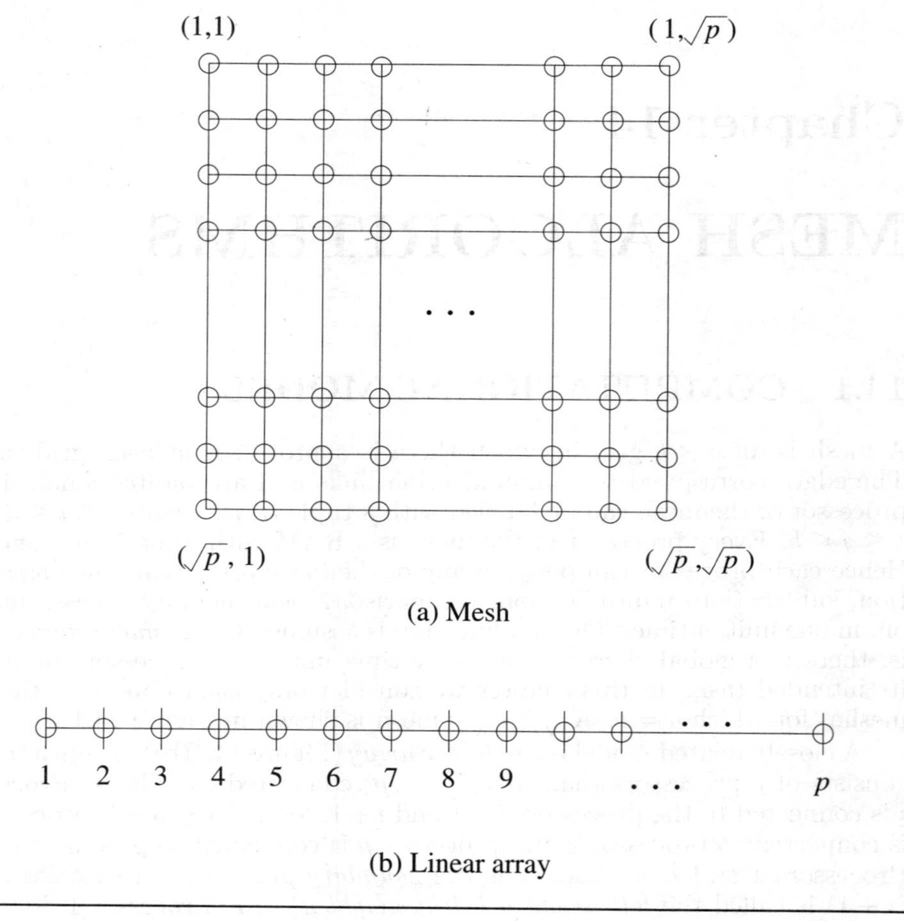

Figure 14.1 A mesh-connected computer and a linear array

neighbors.

In a mesh, all processors whose first (second) coordinates are the same form a *row* (*column*) of the mesh. For example, row i is made up of the processors $(i, 1), (i, 2), \ldots, (i, \sqrt{p})$. Each such row or column is a $\sqrt{p}$-processor linear array. Often, a mesh algorithm consists of steps that are local to individual rows or columns.

14.2 PACKET ROUTING

A single step of interprocessor communication in a fixed connection network can be thought of as the following task, called *packet routing*: Each processor in the network has a packet of information that has to be sent to some other processor. The task is to send all the packets to their correct destinations as quickly as possible so that at most one packet passes through any link at any time. Since the bandwidth of any communication channel is limited, it becomes necessary to impose the restriction that at most one packet pass through the channel at any time. It is possible that two or more packets arrive at some processor v at the same time and all of them want to use the same link going out of v. In this case, only one packet will be sent out in the next time unit and the rest of the packets will be *queued* at v for future transmission. We use a *priority scheme* to decide which packet is transmitted in such cases of link contentions. *Farthest destination first* (the packet whose destination is the furthest wins), farthest origin first (the packet whose origin is the farthest wins), first-in first-out (FIFO), and so on, are examples of priority schemes.

Partial permutation routing (PPR) is a special case of the routing problem. In PPR, each processor is the origin of at most one packet and each processor is the destination of no more than one packet. Note that on the EREW PRAM, PPR can be performed in one simultaneous write step. But in the case of any fixed connection network, PPR is achieved by sending and receiving packets along communication edges and is often a challenging task. Also, in any fixed connection network, typically, the input is given to processors in some order and the output is also expected to appear in a specified order. Just rearranging the data in the right order may involve several PPRs. Thus any nontrivial algorithm to be designed on a fixed connection network invariably requires PPRs. This is one of the crucial differences between network algorithms and PRAM algorithms.

A packet routing algorithm is judged by its *run time*, that is, the time taken by the last packet to reach its destination, and its *queue length*, the maximum number of packets any processor has to store during routing. Note that the queue length is lower bounded by the maximum number of packets destined for any node and the maximum number of packets originating from any node. We assume that a packet not only contains the message (from one processor to another) but also the origin and destination information of this packet. An algorithm for packet routing is specified by the path to be taken by each packet and a priority scheme. The time taken by any packet to reach its destination is dictated by the distance between the packet's origin and destination and the amount of time (referred to as the *delay*) the packet spends waiting in queues.

Example 14.1 Consider the packets $a, b, c,$ and d in Figure 14.2(a). Their final destinations are shown in Figure 14.2(g). Let us assume the FIFO priority scheme in which ties are broken arbitrarily. Also let each packet take the shortest path from its origin to its destination. At time step $t = 1$, every packet moves one edge closer to its destination. As a result, packets a and b reach the same node. So, at $t = 2$, one of a and b has to be queued. Since both a and b have reached this node at the same time, there is a tie. This can be broken arbitrarily. Assume that a has won. Also at $t = 2$, the packets c and d move one step closer to their final destinations and hence join b (see Figure 14.2(c)). At $t = 3$, packet b moves out since it has higher priority than c and d. At $t = 4$, packets c and d contend for the same edge. Since both of these have the same priority, the winner is chosen arbitrarily. Let d be the winner. It takes two more steps for c to reach its destination. By then every packet is at its destination.

The distance packet c has to travel is four. Its delay is two since it has been queued twice (once each because of the packets b and d). So, c has taken six steps in toto. Can the run time be improved using a different priority scheme? Say we use the farthest destination first scheme. Then, at $t = 4$, packet c will have a higher priority and hence will advance. Under this scheme, then, the run time will reduce to five! □

14.2.1 Packet Routing on a Linear Array

In a linear array, since the links are bidirectional, a processor can receive and send messages from each of its neighbors in one unit of time. This assumption implies that if there is a stream of packets going from left to right and another stream going from right to left, then these two streams do not affect each other; that is, they won't contend for the same link. In this section we show that PPR on a linear array can be done in $p - 1$ steps or less. Note that in the worst case, $p - 1$ steps are needed, since, for example, a packet from processor 1 may be destined for processor p. In addition to PPR, we also study some more general routing problems on a linear array.

Example 14.2 In Figure 14.3, packets going from left to right are marked with circles and those going from right to left are marked with ticks. For example, packets a and b have to cross the same edge at the first time step but in opposite directions. Since the edges are bidirectional, there is no contention; both can cross at the same time. Also, note that a packet that originates at node 1 and whose destination is p has to cross $p - 1$ edges and hence needs at least $p - 1$ steps. □

Problem 1 [One packet at each origin] On a p-processor linear array, assume that at most one packet originates from any processor and that the destinations of the packets are arbitrary. Route the packets. □

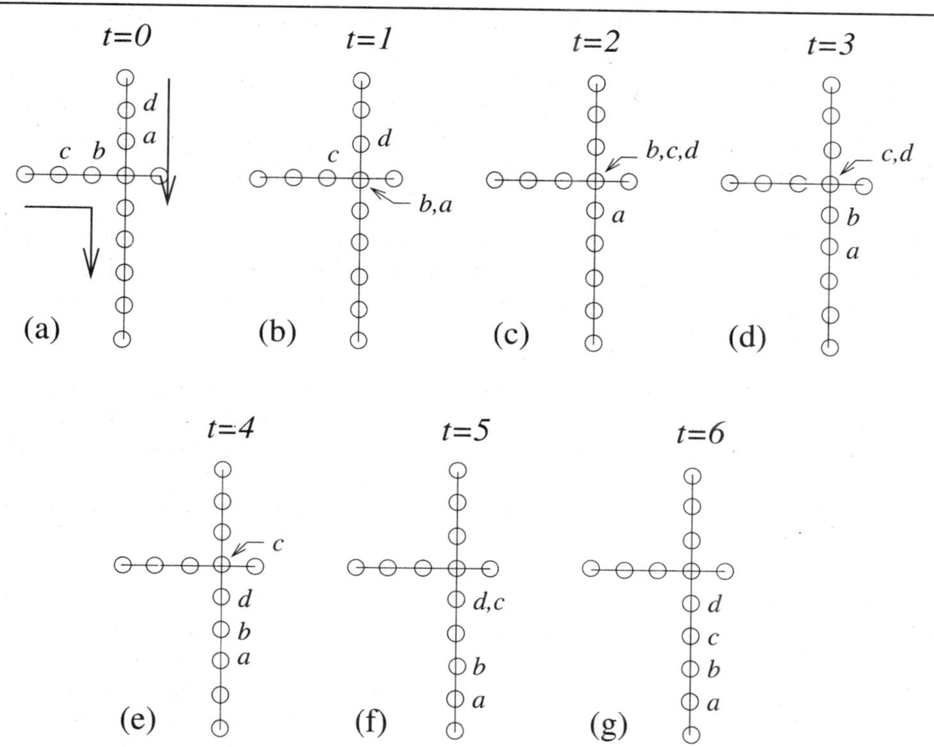

Figure 14.2 Packet routing - an example

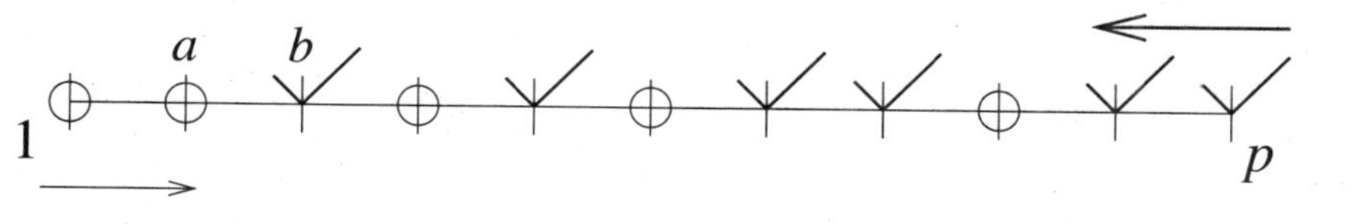

Figure 14.3 Left and right flows are independent!

Lemma 14.1 Problem 1 can be solved in $\leq p - 1$ steps.

Proof: Each packet q can be routed using the shortest path between its origin and destination. Consider only the packets that travel from left to right (since those that travel from right to left can be analyzed independently in the same manner). If q originates at processor i and is destined for processor j, then it needs only $j - i$ steps to reach its destination. Note that a packet can only travel one link at a time. There is no delay associated with q since it never gets to meet any other packet. The maximum of this time over all possible packets is $p - 1$. Also, the queue length of this algorithm is the maximum number of packets destined for any node. □

Problem 2 [At most one packet per destination] On a p-processor linear array, processor i has k_i ($1 \leq k_i \leq p$) packets initially (for $i = 1, 2, \ldots, p$) such that $\sum_{i=1}^{p} k_i = p$. Each processor is the destination for exactly one packet. Route the packets. □

Lemma 14.2 If the farthest destination first priority scheme is used, the time needed for a packet starting at processor i to reach its destination is no more than the distance between i and the boundary in the direction the packet is moving. That is, if the packet is moving from left to right, then this time is no more than $(p - i)$ and, if the packet is moving from right to left, this time is $\leq (i - 1)$.

Proof: Consider a packet q at processor i and destined for j. Assume without loss of generality that it is moving from left to right. Ignore the presence of packets that travel from right to left for reasons stated in Example 14.2. Let every packet traverse the shortest path connecting its origin and destination. Packet q can only be delayed by the packets that have destinations $> j$ and are to the left of their destinations. Let $k_1, k_2, \ldots, k_{j-1}$ be the number of such packets (at the beginning) at processors $1, 2, \ldots, j - 1$ respectively. (Notice that $\sum_{\ell=1}^{j-1} k_\ell \leq p - j$.)

Let m be such that $k_{m-1} > 1$ and $k_{m'} \leq 1$ for $m \leq m' \leq j - 1$. Call the sequence $k_m, k_{m+1}, \ldots, k_{j-1}$ the *free sequence*. Realize that a packet in the free sequence will not be delayed by any other packet in the future. Moreover, at every time step at least one new packet joins the free sequence. Figure 14.4 presents an example. In this figure, the numbers displayed denote the numbers of packets in the corresponding nodes. For example, there are three packets in node i at $t = 0$. At $t = 0$, $1, 0, 1, 1$ is a free sequence. Also note in this figure how the number of packets in the free sequence increases as time progresses. For example, at $t = 1$, one new packet joins the free sequence. At $t = 2$, four new packets join the free sequence!

Thus, after $p - j$ steps, all packets that can possibly delay q have joined the free sequence. Packet q needs only an additional $j - i$ steps, at most, to reach its destination (see Figure 14.5). The case when the packet moves from right to left is similar. □

Problem 3 [General packet routing] In a linear array with p processors assume that more than one packet can originate from any processor and more

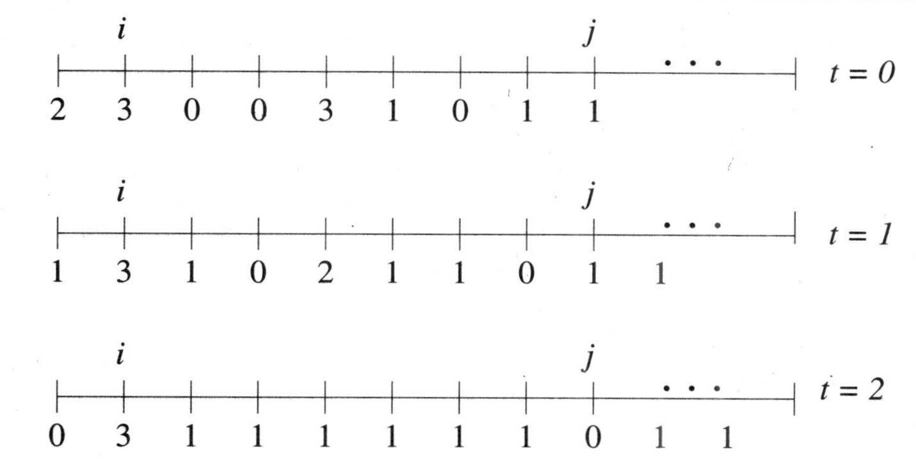

Figure 14.4 Free sequence

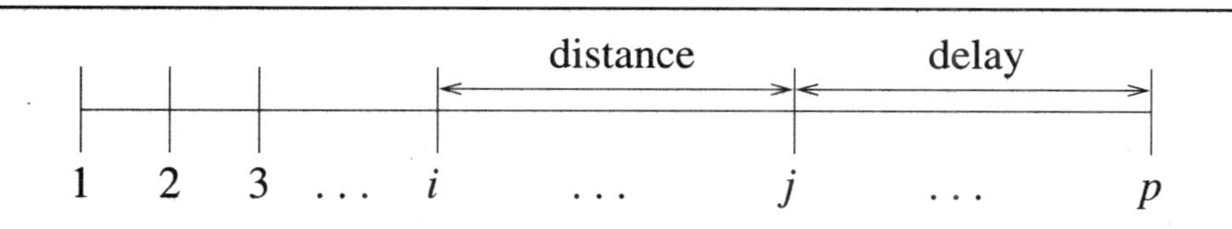

Figure 14.5 Proof of Lemma 14.2

than one packet can be destined for any processor. In addition, the number of packets originating from the processors $1, 2, \ldots, j$ is no more than $j + f(p)$ (for any j and some function f). Route the packets.

Lemma 14.3 Under the furthest origin first priority scheme, Problem 3 can be solved within $p + f(p)$ steps.

Proof: Let q be a packet originating at processor i and destined for processor j (to the right of i). Then q can potentially be delayed by at most $i + f(p)$ packets (since only these many packets can originate from the processors $1, 2, \ldots, i$ and hence have a higher priority than q). If q is delayed by each of these packets at most once, then it follows that the delay q suffers is $\leq i + f(p)$. Else, if a packet r with higher priority delays q twice (say), then it means that r has been delayed by another packet that has even higher priority and will never get to delay q. Therefore, the delay for q is $\leq i+f(p)$. Since q only needs an additional $j-i$ steps to reach its destination, the total time needed for q is $\leq j+f(p)$. The maximum of this time over all packets is $p+f(p)$. □

Example 14.3 Figure 14.6 illustrates the proof of Lemma 14.3. There are eight packets in this example: a, b, c, d, e, f, g, and h. Let g be the packet of our concern. Packet g can possibly be delayed only by the packets a, b, c, d, e, f, and h. Packet g reaches its destination at $t = 9$. The distance it travels is two and its delay is seven. In this figure, packets that have crossed node j are not displayed. □

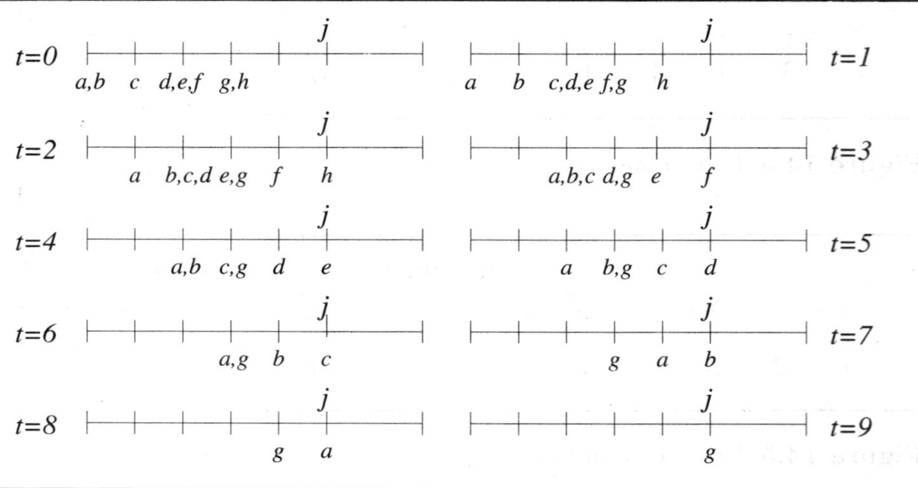

Figure 14.6 An example to illustrate Lemma 14.3

14.2.2 A Greedy Algorithm for PPR on a Mesh

For the PPR problem on a $\sqrt{p}\times\sqrt{p}$ mesh, we see that if a packet at processor $(1, 1)$ has $(\sqrt{p}, \sqrt{p})$ as its destination, then it has to travel a distance of $2(\sqrt{p}-1)$. Hence $2(\sqrt{p}-1)$ is a lower bound on the worst-case routing time of any packet routing algorithm.

A simple PPR algorithm that makes use of the packet routing algorithms we have seen for a linear array is the following. Let q be an arbitrary packet with (i, j) as its origin and (k, ℓ) as its destination. Packet q uses a two-phase algorithm. In phase 1 it travels along column j to row k along the shortest path. In phase 2 it traverses along row k to its correct destination again using the shortest path. A packet can start its phase 2 immediately on completion of its phase 1.

Phase 1 can be completed in $\sqrt{p} - 1$ steps or less since Lemma 14.1 applies. Phase 2 also takes $\leq \sqrt{p} - 1$ steps in accordance with Lemma 14.2. So, this algorithm takes at most $2(\sqrt{p} - 1)$ steps and is optimal.

But there is a severe drawback with this algorithm, namely, that the queue size needed is as large as $\frac{\sqrt{p}}{2}$. Let the partial permutation to be routed be such that all packets that originate from column 1 are destined for row $\frac{\sqrt{p}}{2}$. For this PPR problem, the processor $(\frac{\sqrt{p}}{2}, 1)$ gets two packets (one from above and one from below) at every time step. Since both of these want to use the same link, only one can be sent out and the other has to be queued. This continues until step $\frac{\sqrt{p}}{2}$ at which time there will be $\frac{\sqrt{p}}{2}$ packets in the queue of $(\frac{\sqrt{p}}{2}, 1)$ (see Figure 14.7).

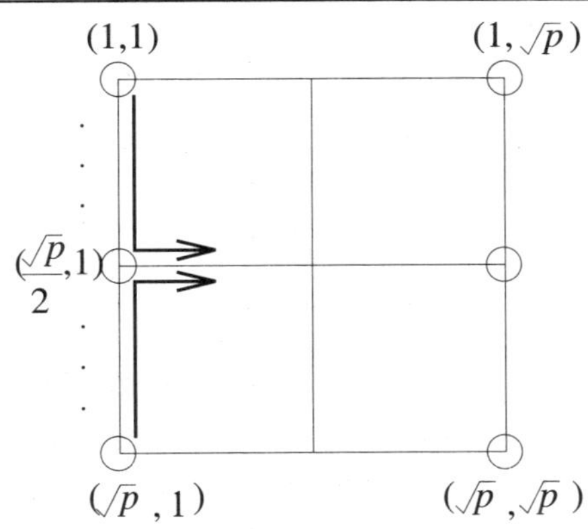

Figure 14.7 The greedy algorithm needs large queues

Ideally we would like to design algorithms that require a queue size that is $O(1)$ (or a slowly increasing function of p such as $O(\log p)$).

14.2.3 A Randomized Algorithm with Small Queues

The two-phase algorithm can be modified to ensure queues of size $\widetilde{O}(\log p)$ with the help of randomization. There are three phases in the new algorithm and the run time is $3\sqrt{p} + \widetilde{o}(\sqrt{p})$. Let q be any packet whose origin and destination are (i, j) and (k, ℓ), respectively. The algorithm employed by q is depicted in Algorithm 14.1. In this algorithm, the three phases are disjoint; that is, a packet can start its phase 2 only after all packets have

---

Phase 1. Packet q chooses a random processor (i', j) in the column of its origin and traverses to (i', j) using the shortest path.

Phase 2. Packet q traverses along row i' to (i', ℓ).

Phase 3. Finally, packet q travels along column ℓ to its correct destination.

Algorithm 14.1 A randomized packet routing algorithm

completed their phase 1, and it can start its phase 3 only after all packets have completed their phase 2. This constraint makes the analysis simpler.

Theorem 14.1 Algorithm 14.1 terminates in time $3\sqrt{p} + \widetilde{O}(p^{1/4} \log p)$.

Proof: Phase 1 takes $\sqrt{p}$ time or less applying Lemma 14.1, since no packet suffers any delays.

Consider a packet that starts phase 2 at (i', j). Without loss of generality assume that it is moving to the right. The number of packets starting this phase from processor (i', j) is a binomial distribution, $B(\sqrt{p}, \frac{1}{\sqrt{p}})$. This is because there are $\sqrt{p}$ packets in column j and each one can end up at the end of phase 1 at (i', j) with probability $\frac{1}{\sqrt{p}}$. In turn, the number of packets that start their phase 2 from $(i', 1), (i', 2), \ldots$, or (i', j) is a binomial distribution, $B(j\sqrt{p}, \frac{1}{\sqrt{p}})$. (We have made use of the fact that the sum of $B(n_1, x)$ and $B(n_2, x)$ is $B(n_1 + n_2, x)$.) The mean of this variable is j. Using Chernoff bounds (Equation 1.1), this number is no more than $j + 3\alpha p^{1/4} \log_e p$ with probability $\geq 1 - p^{-\alpha-1}$ for any $\alpha \geq 1$. Thus this number is $j + \widetilde{O}(p^{1/4} \log p)$. Now, applying Lemma 14.3, we see that phase 2 terminates in time $\sqrt{p} + \widetilde{O}(p^{1/4} \log p)$.

At the beginning of phase 3, there are $\leq \sqrt{p}$ packets starting from any column and each processor is the destination of at most one packet. Thus in accordance with Lemma 14.2, phase 3 takes $\leq \sqrt{p}$ steps. □

Note: In this analysis it was shown that for a specific packet there is a high probability that it will terminate within the stated time bounds. But for the algorithm to terminate within a specified amount of time, every packet should reach its destination within this time. If the probability that an individual packet takes more than time T (for some T) to reach its destination can be shown to be $\leq p^{-\alpha-1}$, then the probability that there is at least one packet that takes more than T time is $\leq p^{-\alpha-1}p = p^{-\alpha}$. That is, every packet will reach its destination within time T with probability $\geq 1 - p^{-\alpha}$.

The queue length of Algorithm 14.1 is $\widetilde{O}(\log p)$. During any phase of routing, note that the queue length at any processor is no more than the maximum of the number of packets at the beginning of the phase in this processor and the number of packets in this processor at the end of the phase. Consider any processor (i, j) in the mesh. During phase 1, only one packet starts from any processor and the number of packets that end up at this processor at the end of phase 1 is $B(\sqrt{p}, \frac{1}{\sqrt{p}})$. The mean of this binomial is 1. Using Chernoff bounds (Equation 1.1), this number can be shown to be $\widetilde{O}(\log p)$. During phase 2, $\widetilde{O}(\log p)$ packets start from any processor. Also, $\widetilde{O}(\log p)$ packets end up in any processor (the proof of this is left as an exercise). In phase 3, $\widetilde{O}(\log p)$ packets start from any processor and only one packet ends up in any processor. Therefore, the queue length of the whole algorithm is $\widetilde{O}(\log p)$. □

EXERCISES

1. In Example 14.1, compute the run times for the priority schemes farthest origin first and last-in first-out.

2. On a p-node linear array there are two packets at each node to begin with. Assume p is even. Packets at node 1 are destined for node $\frac{p}{2}+1$, packets at node 2 are destined for $\frac{p}{2}+2$, and so on. Let each packet take the shortest path from its origin to its destination. Compute the routing time for this problem under the following priority schemes: farthest origin first, farthest destination first, FIFO, and LIFO.

3. Do the above problem when the packets from node one are destined for node p, packets from node two are destined for $p-1$, and so on.

4. Partition a $\sqrt{p} \times \sqrt{p}$ mesh into four quadrants as shown in Figure 14.8. There is a packet at each node to start with. Packets in quadrant I are to be exchanged with packets in quadrant IV. Also, packets in quadrant II have to be exchanged with packets in quadrant III. The ordering of packets in individual quadrants should not change. Show how you route the packets in time $\leq \sqrt{p}$.

5. In the three-phase randomized algorithm prove that the number of packets that end up in any processor at the end of phase 2 is $\widetilde{O}(\log p)$.

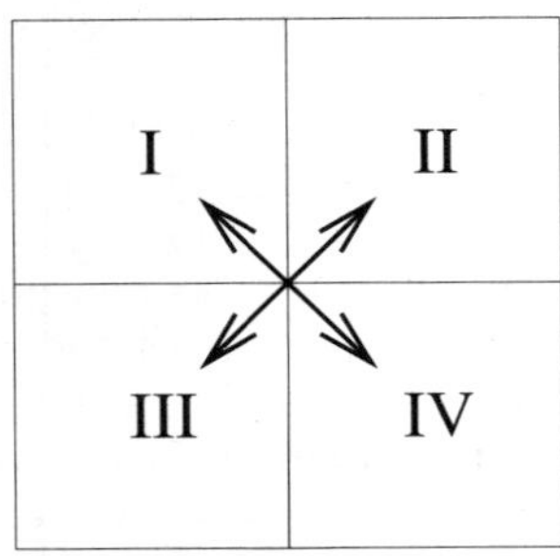

Figure 14.8 Figure for Exercise 4

6. The randomized mesh routing algorithm (Algorithm 14.1) of this section can be improved as follows. In phase 1, partition the mesh into slices so that each slice consists of $\frac{\sqrt{p}}{q}$ rows (for some integer $q > 1$). A packet q that starts from (i, j) chooses a random processor in the same column and slice as its origin and goes there using the shortest path. Phases 2 and 3 remain the same. Show that this algorithm runs in time $2\sqrt{p} + \widetilde{O}(\frac{\sqrt{p}}{q})$ and has a queue length $\widetilde{O}(q)$. Note that when $q = \log p$, the run time of this algorithm is $2\sqrt{p} + \widetilde{o}(\sqrt{p})$ and the queue length is $\widetilde{O}(\log p)$.

7. Suppose that in a p-processor linear array at most k packets originate from any processor and at most k packets are destined for any processor. Show how to perform this routing task in time $\frac{(k+1)p}{2}$ or less.

8. In a $\sqrt{p} \times \sqrt{p}$ mesh, assume that at most one packet originates from any processor and that the destination of each packet is chosen uniformly randomly to be any processor of the mesh. Prove that for this special case the greedy algorithm runs in time $2\sqrt{p} + \widetilde{o}(\sqrt{p})$ with a queue length of $\widetilde{O}(\log p)$.

9. Suppose that at most one packet originates from any processor of a $\sqrt{p} \times \sqrt{p}$ mesh and that the destination of any packet is no more than d distance away from its origin. Present an $\widetilde{O}(d)$ algorithm for routing this special case.

10. A p-processor *ring* is a p-processor linear array in which the processors 1 and p are connected by a link (this link is also known as the

wraparound connection). Show that the PPR problem can be solved on a p-processor ring in time $\frac{p}{2}$.

11. How fast can you solve Problem 2 on a ring (see Exercise 10)? How about Problem 3?

12. A $\sqrt{p} \times \sqrt{p}$ *torus* is a $\sqrt{p} \times \sqrt{p}$ mesh in which each row and each column has a wraparound connection. A 5×5 torus is shown in Figure 14.9. Present an implementation of the randomized three-phase algorithm (Algorithm 14.1) on a torus to achieve a run time of $1.5\sqrt{p} + \widetilde{o}(p)$.

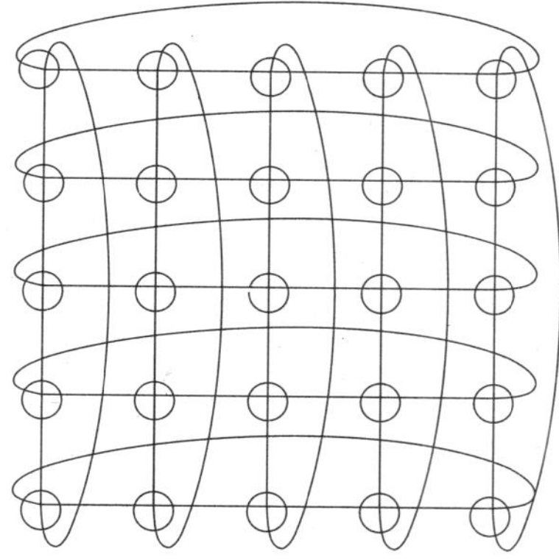

Figure 14.9 A 5×5 torus

13. A string $a_1 a_2 \cdots a_p$ from some alphabet Σ is called a *palindrome* if it is identical to $a_p a_{p-1} \cdots a_1$. A string of length p is input on a p-processor linear array. How can you test whether the string is a palindrome in $O(p)$ time?

14.3 FUNDAMENTAL ALGORITHMS

In this section we present mesh algorithms for some basic operations such as broadcasting, prefix sums computation, and data concentration. All these algorithms take $O(\sqrt{p})$ time on a $\sqrt{p} \times \sqrt{p}$ mesh. For many nontrivial problems including the preceding, sorting, convex hull, and so on, $2(\sqrt{p}-1)$ is a lower bound. This follows from the fact that a data item from one corner of the mesh needs $2(\sqrt{p}-1)$ time to reach an opposite corner. In the worst case, two processors in opposite corners have to communicate. The distance $2(\sqrt{p}-1)$ is the *diameter* of the mesh. (The diameter of any interconnection network is defined to be the maximum distance between any two processors in the network.) For any nontrivial problem to be solved on an interconnection network, the diameter is usually a lower bound on the run time.

The *bisection width* of a network can also be used to derive lower bounds. The bisection width of a network is the minimum number of links that have to be removed to partition the network into two identical halves. For example, consider a 4×4 mesh. If we remove the four links $((1,2),(1,3))$, $((2,2),(2,3))$, $((3,2),(3,3))$, and $((4,2),(4,3))$, two identical 4×2 submeshes arise. Here the bisection width is 4. In general, the bisection width of a $\sqrt{p} \times \sqrt{p}$ mesh can be seen to be $\sqrt{p}$.

The problem of $k - k$ routing is defined as follows. At most k packets originate from any processor and at most k packets are destined for any processor of the network. Route these packets. Let b be the bisection width of the network under concern. By definition, removal of b links results in an even partitioning of the network. If the routing problem is such that exactly k packets originate and are destined for any processor and that the packets from one half have to be exchanged with packets from the other half, this exchange can happen only through these b links. Thus any routing algorithm will need at least $\frac{\frac{kn}{2}}{b} = \frac{kn}{2b}$ time to perform this routing on an n-processor bisection b network. On a $\sqrt{p} \times \sqrt{p}$ mesh, this lower bound becomes $\frac{k\sqrt{p}}{2}$.

14.3.1 Broadcasting

The problem of broadcasting in an interconnection network is to send a copy of a message that originates from a particular processor to a specified subset of other processors. Unless otherwise specified, this subset is assumed to consist of every other processor. Broadcasting is a primitive form of interprocessor communication and is widely used in the design of several algorithms. Let $\mathcal{L}$ be a linear array with the processors $1, 2, \ldots, p$. Also let M be a message that originates from processor 1. Message M can be broadcast to every other processor as follows. Node 1 sends a copy of M to processor 2, which in turn forwards a copy to processor 3, and so on. This algorithm takes $p - 1$ steps and this run time is the best possible. If the processor of message origin is different from processor 1, a similar strategy could be employed. If processor i is the origin, i could start by making two copies of M and sending a copy in each direction.

In the case of a $\sqrt{p} \times \sqrt{p}$ mesh broadcasting can be done in two phases. If (i, j) is the processor of message origin, in phase 1, M could be broadcast to all processors in row i. In phase 2, broadcasting of M is done in each column. This algorithm takes $\leq 2(\sqrt{p} - 1)$ steps. This can be expressed in a theorem.

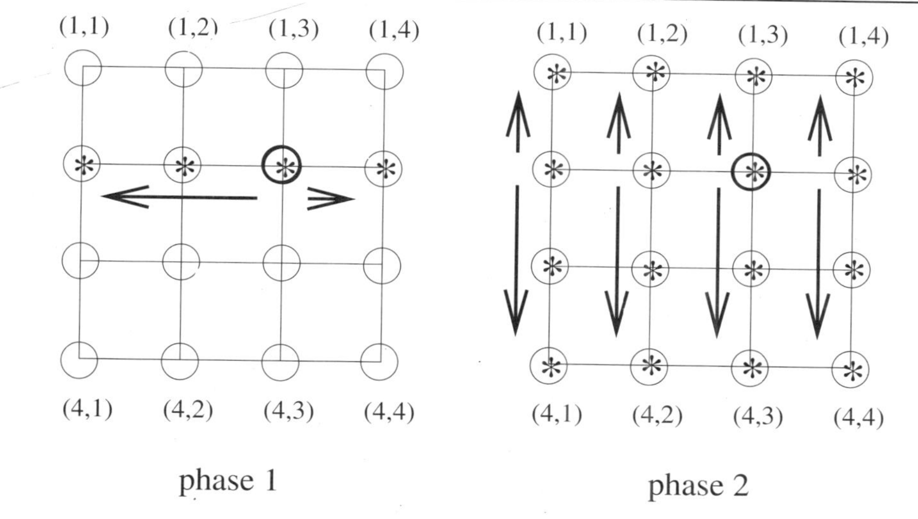

Figure 14.10 Broadcasting in a mesh

Theorem 14.2 Broadcasting on a p-processor linear array can be completed in p steps or less. On a $\sqrt{p} \times \sqrt{p}$ mesh the same can be performed in $\leq 2(\sqrt{p} - 1) = O(\sqrt{p})$ time. □

Example 14.4 On a 4×4 mesh, let the message to be broadcast originate at $(2, 3)$. In phase 1, this message is broadcast in row 2. The nodes $(2, 1), (2, 2), (2, 3)$, and $(2, 4)$ get the message at the end of phase 1. In phase 2, node $(2, 1)$ broadcasts in column 1; node $(2, 2)$ broadcasts in column 2; and nodes $(2, 3)$ and $(2, 4)$ broadcast in columns 3 and 4, respectively (see Figure 14.10). □

14.3.2 Prefix Computation

Let Σ be any domain in which the binary *associative* unit time computable operator $\oplus$ is defined (see Section 13.3.1). Recall that the prefix computation problem on Σ has as input n elements from Σ, say, $x_1, x_2, \ldots, x_n$. The problem is to compute the n elements $x_1, x_1 \oplus x_2, \ldots, x_1 \oplus x_2 \oplus x_3 \oplus \cdots \oplus x_n$. The output elements are often referred to as the *prefixes*. For simplicity, we refer to the operation $\oplus$ as addition.

In the case of a linear array with p processors, assume that there is an element x_i at processor i (for $i = 1, 2, \ldots, p$). We have to compute the

---

Processor i **(in parallel for** $1 \leq i \leq n$**) does:**

> if $(i = 1)$ processor 1 sends x_1 to the right in step 1; else
>
> if $(i = n)$ processor n receives an element (call it z_{n-1}) in step n from processor $n-1$, computes and stores $z_{n-1} \oplus x_n$; else
>
> processor i receives an element (call it z_{i-1}) in step i from processor $(i-1)$, computes and stores $z_i = z_{i-1} \oplus x_i$, and sends z_i to processor $i+1$;

Algorithm 14.2 Prefix computation on a linear array

prefixes of $x_1, x_2, \ldots, x_p$. After this computation, processor i should have the value $\sum_{j=1}^{i} x_j$. One way of performing this computation is as follows. In step 1, processor 1 sends x_1 to the right. In step 2, processor 2 computes $x_1 \oplus x_2$, stores this answer, and sends a copy to its right neighbor. In step 3, processor 3 receives $x_1 \oplus x_2$ from its left neighbor, computes $x_1 \oplus x_2 \oplus x_3$, stores this result, and also sends a copy to the right neighbor. And so on. In general in step i, processor i adds the element received from its left neighbor to x_i, stores the answer, and sends a copy to the right. This algorithm (Algorithm 14.2) then will take p steps to compute all prefixes. Thus we get the following lemma.

Lemma 14.4 Prefix computation on a p-processor linear array can be performed in p steps. □

A similar algorithm can be adopted on a mesh also. Consider a $\sqrt{p} \times \sqrt{p}$ mesh in which there is an element of Σ at each processor. Since the mesh is a two-dimensional structure, there is no natural linear ordering of the processors. We could come up with many possible orderings. Any such ordering of the processors is called an *indexing scheme*. Examples of indexing schemes are *row major*, *column major*, *snakelike row major*, *blockwise snakelike row major*, and so on (see Figure 14.11). In the row major indexing scheme, processors are ordered as $(1,1), (1,2), \ldots, (1,n), (2,1), (2,2), \ldots, (2,n), \ldots,$ (n,n). In the snakelike row major indexing scheme, they are ordered as $(1,1), (1,2), \ldots, (1,n), (2,n), (2,n-1), \ldots, (2,1), (3,1), (3,2), \ldots, (n,n)$; that is, it is the same as the row major ordering except that alternate rows reverse. In the blockwise snakelike row major indexing scheme, the mesh is partitioned into small blocks of appropriate size. Within each block the processors can be ordered in any fashion. The blocks themselves are ordered according to the snakelike row major scheme.

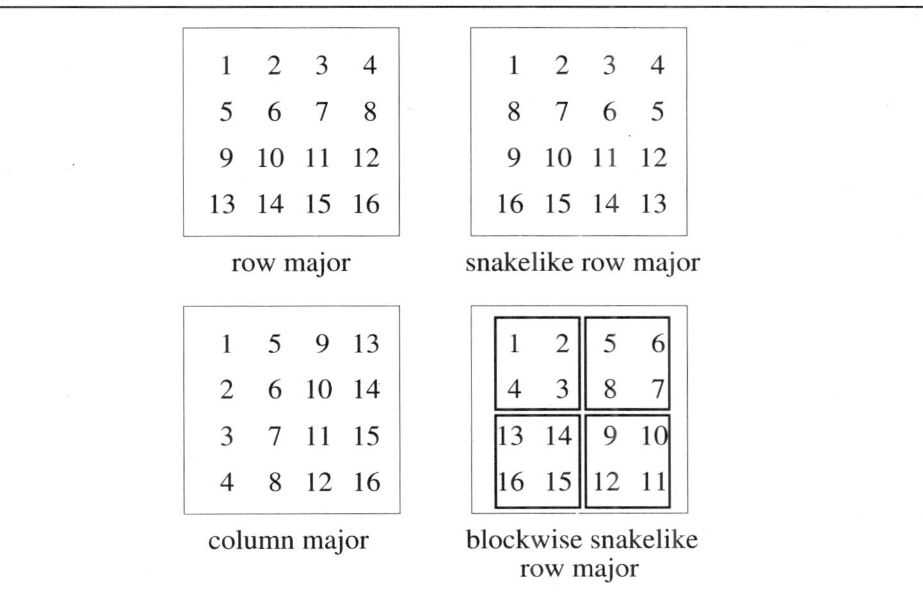

Figure 14.11 Examples of indexing schemes

The problem of computing prefix sums on the mesh can be reduced to three phases in each of which the computation is local to the individual rows or columns (Algorithm 14.3). This algorithm assumes the row major indexing scheme. The prefix computations in phases 1 and 2 take $\sqrt{p}$ steps each (c.f. Lemma 14.4), the shifting in phase 2 takes one step, and the broadcasting in phase 3 takes $\sqrt{p}$ steps. The final update of the answers needs an additional step.

Theorem 14.3 Prefix computation on a $\sqrt{p} \times \sqrt{p}$ mesh in row major order can be performed in $3\sqrt{p} + 2 = O(\sqrt{p})$ steps. □

Example 14.5 Consider the data on the 4×4 mesh of Figure 14.12(a) and the problem of prefix sums under the row major indexing scheme. In phase 1, each row computes its prefix sums (Figure 14.12(b)). In phase 2, prefix sums are computed only in the fourth column (Figure 14.12(c)). Finally, in phase 3, the prefix sums are updated (Figure 14.12(d)). □

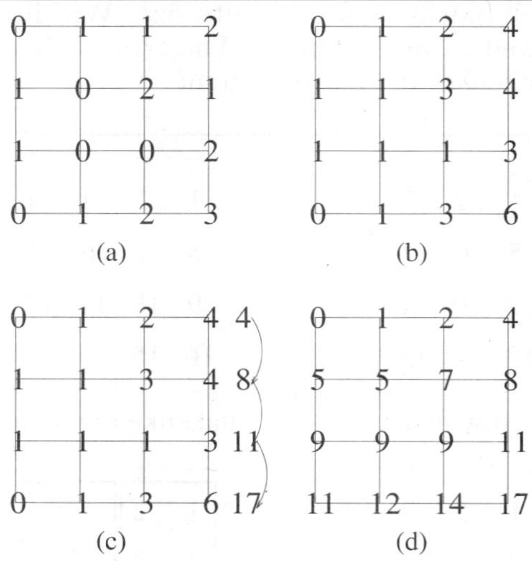

Figure 14.12 Prefix computation

Phase 1. Row i (for $i = 1, 2, \ldots, \sqrt{p}$) computes the prefixes of its $\sqrt{p}$ elements. At the end, the processor (i, j) has $y_{(i,j)} = \sum_{q=1}^{j} x_{(i,q)}$.

Phase 2. Only column $\sqrt{p}$ computes prefixes of sums computed in phase 1. Thus at the end, processor $(i, \sqrt{p})$ has $z_{(i,\sqrt{p})} = \sum_{q=1}^{i} y_{(q,\sqrt{p})}$. After the computation of prefixes shift them down by one processor; i.e., have processor $(i, \sqrt{p})$ send $z_{(i,\sqrt{p})}$ to processor $(i+1, \sqrt{p})$ (for $i = 1, 2, \ldots, \sqrt{p} - 1$).

Phase 3. Broadcast $z_{(i,\sqrt{p})}$ in row $i+1$ (for $i = 1, 2, \ldots, \sqrt{p}-1$). Node j in row $i+1$ finally updates its result to $z_{(i,\sqrt{p})} \oplus y_{(i+1,j)}$.

Algorithm 14.3 Prefix computation on a mesh

Prefix computations with respect to many other indexing schemes can also be performed in $O(\sqrt{p})$ time on a $\sqrt{p} \times \sqrt{p}$ mesh (see the exercises).

14.3.3 Data Concentration

In a p-processor interconnection network assume that there are $d < p$ data items distributed arbitrarily with at most one data item per processor. The problem of data concentration is to move the data into the first d processors of the network one data item per processor. This problem is also known as *packing*. In the case of a p-processor linear array, we have to move the data into the processors $1, 2, \ldots, d$. On a mesh, we might require the data items to move according to any indexing scheme of our choice. For example, the data could be moved into the first $\lceil \frac{d}{\sqrt{p}} \rceil$ rows.

Data concentration on any network is achieved by first performing a prefix computation to determine the destination of each packet and then routing the packets using an appropriate packet routing algorithm.

Let $\mathcal{L}$ be a p-processor linear array with d data items. To find the destination of each data item, we make use of a variable x. If processor i has a data item, then it sets $x_i = 1$; otherwise it sets $x_i = 0$. Let the prefixes of the sequence $x_1, x_2, \ldots, x_p$ be $y_1, y_2, \ldots, y_p$. If processor i has a data item, then the destination of this item is y_i. The destinations for the data items having been determined, they are routed. Prefix computation (Lemma 14.4) as well as packet routing on a linear array (Lemma 14.1) takes p time steps each. Thus the total run time is $2p$.

Example 14.6 Consider a six-processor linear array in which there is an item in processors 1, 3, 4, and 6. Then, $(x_1, x_2, x_3, x_4, x_5, x_6) = (1, 0, 1, 1, 0, 1)$ and $(y_1, y_2, y_3, y_4, y_5, y_6) = (1, 1, 2, 3, 3, 4)$. So, the items will be sent to the processors 1, 2, 3, and 4 as expected (see Figure 14.13). □

On a mesh too, the same strategy of computing prefixes followed by packet routing can be employed. Prefix computation takes $3\sqrt{p}+2$ steps (c.f. Theorem 14.3), whereas packet routing can be done in $3\sqrt{p} + \widetilde{O}(p^{1/4} \log p)$ steps (c.f. Theorem 14.1).

Example 14.7 Figure 14.14 shows a mesh in which there are six data items a, b, c, d, e, f, and g. The parallel variable x takes a value of one corresponding to any element and zero otherwise. Prefix sums are computed on $x_1, x_2, \ldots, x_{16}$, and finally the data items are routed to their destinations. We have assumed the row major indexing scheme. □

Theorem 14.4 Data concentration on a p-processor linear array takes $2p$ steps or less. On a $\sqrt{p} \times \sqrt{p}$ mesh, it takes $6\sqrt{p} + \widetilde{O}(p^{1/4} \log p)$ steps. □

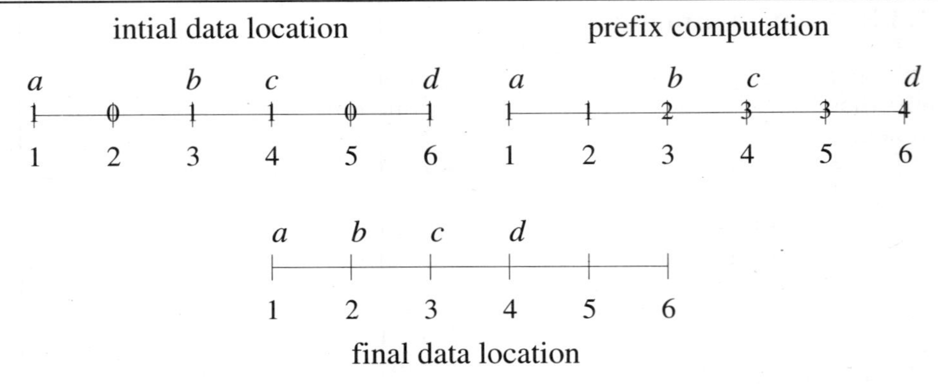

Figure 14.13 Data concentration on a linear array

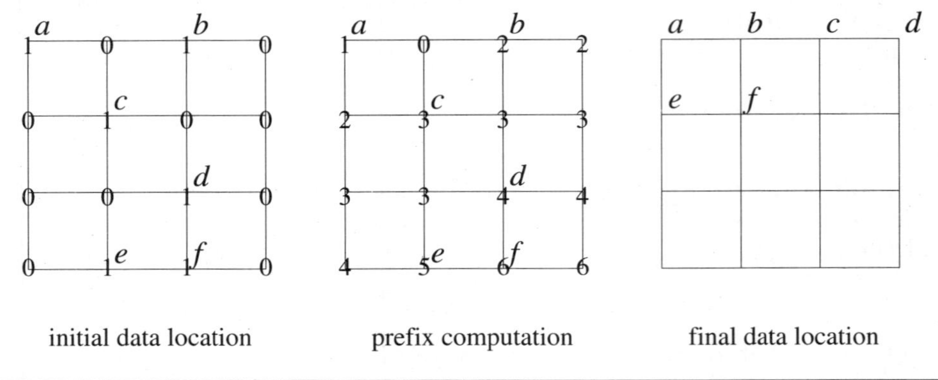

Figure 14.14 Data concentration on a 4×4 mesh

14.3.4 Sparse Enumeration Sort

An instance of sorting in which the number of keys to be sorted is much less than the network size is referred to as the *sparse enumeration sort.* If the network size is p, the number of keys to be sorted is typically assumed to be p^ϵ for some constant $\epsilon \leq \frac{1}{2}$. In the following discussion we assume that $\epsilon = \frac{1}{2}$. On the mesh, sparse enumeration sort can be done by computing the rank of each key and routing the key to its correct position in sorted order (see the proof of Theorem 13.15).

Let the sequence to be sorted be $X = k_1, k_2, \ldots, k_{\sqrt{p}}$. We need to sort

---

Step 1. In parallel, for $1 \leq j \leq \sqrt{p}$, broadcast k_j along column j.

Step 2. In parallel, for $1 \leq i \leq \sqrt{p}$, broadcast k_i along row i.

Step 3. In parallel, for $1 \leq i \leq \sqrt{p}$, compute the rank of k_i in row i using a prefix sums computation.

Step 4. In parallel, for $1 \leq j \leq \sqrt{p}$, send the rank of key k_j to $(1, j)$.

Step 5. In parallel, for $1 \leq r \leq \sqrt{p}$, route the key whose rank is r to the node $(1, r)$.

Algorithm 14.4 Sparse enumeration sort

X using a $\sqrt{p} \times \sqrt{p}$ mesh. Assume that the key k_j is input at the processor $(1, j)$ (for $j = 1, 2, \ldots, \sqrt{p}$). We also require the final output to appear in the first row of the mesh in nondecreasing order, one key per processor. To begin with, k_j is broadcast in column j so that each row has a copy of X. In row i compute the rank of k_i. This is done by broadcasting k_i to all processors in row i followed by a comparison of k_i with every key in the input and then by a prefix computation. The rank of k_j is sent to processor $(1, j)$. Finally, the keys are routed to their correct destinations in sorted order. In particular, the key whose rank is r is sent to the processor $(1, r)$. A formal description of this algorithm appears as Algorithm 14.4.

Algorithm 14.4 is a collection of operations local to the columns or the rows. The operations involved are prefix computation, broadcast, routing (see Exercise 10), and comparison each of which can be done in $O(\sqrt{p})$ time. Thus the whole algorithm runs in time $O(\sqrt{p})$.

Theorem 14.5 Sparse enumeration sort can be completed in $O(\sqrt{p})$ time on a $\sqrt{p} \times \sqrt{p}$ mesh when the number of keys to be sorted is at most $\sqrt{p}$. □

Example 14.8 Consider the problem of sorting the four keys $k_1, k_2, k_3, k_4 = 8, 5, 3, 7$ on a 4×4 mesh. Input to the mesh is given in the first row (Figure 14.15(a)) and the output should also appear in the same row (Figure 14.15(e)). In step 1 of the algorithm, keys are broadcast along columns (Figure 14.15(b)). In step 2, k_i is broadcast along row i (for $1 \leq i \leq 4$). At the end of step 4, the ranks of keys are available in the first row. Figure

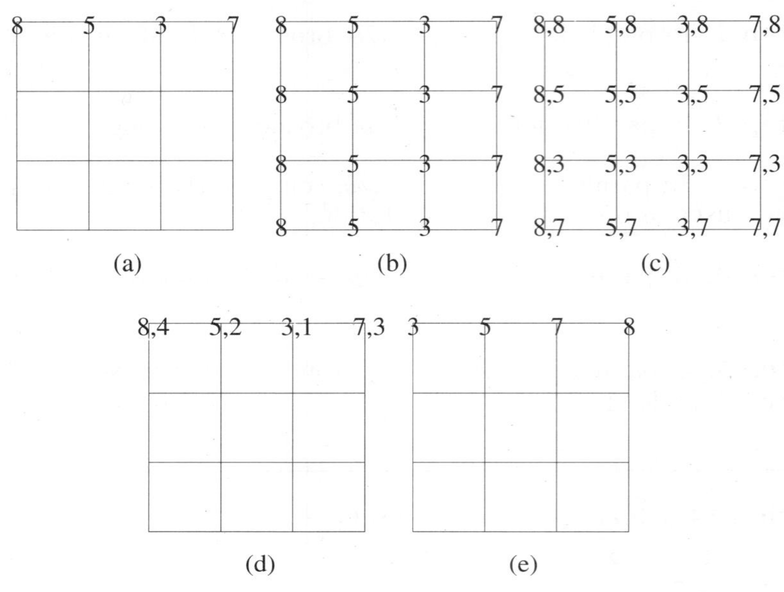

Figure 14.15 Sparse enumeration sort on a mesh

14.15(d) shows the keys and their ranks. Finally, in step 5, keys are routed according to their ranks (Figure 14.15(e)). □

EXERCISES

1. Let $x_1, x_2, \ldots, x_n$ be elements from Σ in which $\oplus$ is an associative unit time computable operator. The *suffix computation* problem is to compute $x_1 \oplus x_2 \oplus \cdots \oplus x_n, x_2 \oplus x_3 \oplus \cdots \oplus x_n, \ldots, x_{n-1} \oplus x_n, x_n$. Present an $O(p)$ time algorithm for the suffix computation problem on a p-node linear array.

2. Show how to solve the suffix computation problem on a $\sqrt{p} \times \sqrt{p}$ mesh in time $O(\sqrt{p})$.

3. Compute the prefix sums on the mesh of Figure 14.16 for the following indexing schemes: row major, snakelike row major, column major, and snakelike column major.

3	4	1	2
5	6	3	4
1	5	8	6
7	9	2	3

Figure 14.16 Figure for Exercise 3

4. Show that prefix computations with respect to the following indexing schemes can also be performed in $O(\sqrt{p})$ time on a $\sqrt{p} \times \sqrt{p}$ mesh: snakelike column major and blockwise row major (where the blocks are of size $p^{1/4} \times p^{1/4}$). Employ the row major indexing scheme within each block.

5. On a p-processor linear array there are p items per processor. Show how you compute the prefixes of these p^2 items in $O(p)$ time. The indexing scheme to be used is the following: all the items in processor 1 are ordered first, all items in processor 2 are ordered next, and so on.

6. On a $\sqrt{p} \times \sqrt{p}$ mesh there are $\sqrt{p}$ items per processor. Show how you compute the prefixes of these $p\sqrt{p}$ items in $O(\sqrt{p})$ time. Use the same indexing scheme as in Exercise 5.

7. Let $f(x) = a_n x^n + a_{n-1} x^{n-1} + \cdots + a_1 x + a_0$. Present linear array and mesh algorithms to evaluate the polynomial f at a given point y. What are the run times of your algorithms?

8. Present efficient linear array and mesh algorithms for the segmented prefix problem (see Section 13.3, Exercise 5) and analyze their time complexities.

9. You are given a sequence A of p elements and an element x. You are to rearrange the elements of A so that all elements of A that are $\leq x$ appear first (in successive processors) followed by the rest of the elements. Present an $O(p)$ time algorithm on a p-processor linear array and an $\widetilde{O}(\sqrt{p})$ time algorithm on a $\sqrt{p} \times \sqrt{p}$ mesh for this.

10. Present an $O(\sqrt{p})$ time deterministic algorithm for step 5 of Algorithm 14.4.

11. Let A be a sequence of p keys. Show how you compute the rank of a given key x in A on a p-processor linear array as well as on a $\sqrt{p} \times \sqrt{p}$ mesh. The run times should be $O(p)$ and $O(\sqrt{p})$, respectively.

12. Let $\mathcal{M}$ be a $\sqrt{p} \times \sqrt{p}$ mesh and let A be a $\sqrt{p} \times \sqrt{p}$ matrix stored in $\mathcal{M}$ in row major order, one element per processor. Consider the following recursive algorithm for transposing A.

    (a) Partition the matrix into four submatrices of size $\frac{\sqrt{p}}{2} \times \frac{\sqrt{p}}{2}$ each; let the partition be $\begin{bmatrix} A_{11} & A_{12} \\ A_{21} & A_{22} \end{bmatrix}$.

    (b) Interchange A_{12} with A_{21}.

    (c) Recursively transpose each submatrix.

    Show that this algorithm is correct and also determine the run time of this algorithm.

13. Matrices A and B are two $\sqrt{p} \times \sqrt{p}$ matrices stored in a $\sqrt{p} \times \sqrt{p}$ mesh in row major order. Show how to multiply them. What is the run time of your algorithm?

14. Show how to compute the FFT (see Section 9.3) of a vector of length p in $O(p)$ time on a p-processor linear array.

15. Implement the FFT algorithm of Section 9.3 on a $\sqrt{p} \times \sqrt{p}$ mesh. What is the run time of your algorithm?

14.4 SELECTION

Given a sequence of n keys and an integer i, $1 \leq i \leq n$, the problem of selection is to find the ith smallest key from the sequence. We have seen both sequential algorithms (Section 3.7) and PRAM algorithms (Section 13.4) for selection. We consider two different versions of selection on the mesh. In the first version we assume that $p = n$, p being the number of processors and n being the number of input keys. In the second version we assume that $n > p$. In the case of a PRAM, the slow-down lemma can be employed to derive an algorithm for the second case given an algorithm for the first case and preserve the work done. But no such general slow-down lemma exists for the mesh. Thus it becomes essential to handle the second version separately.

14.4.1 A Randomized Algorithm for $n = p$ (*)

The work-optimal algorithm of Section 13.4.5 can be adapted to run optimally on the mesh also. A summary of this algorithm follows. If $X = k_1, k_2, \ldots, k_n$ is the input, the algorithm chooses a random sample (call it S) from X and identifies two elements l_1 and l_2 from S. The elements chosen are such that they bracket the element to be selected with high probability and also the number of input keys that are in the range $[l_1, l_2]$ is small.

After choosing l_1 and l_2, we determine whether the element to be selected is in the range $[l_1, l_2]$. If this is the case, we proceed further and the element to be selected is the $(i - |X_1|)$th element of X_2. If the element to be selected is not in the range $[l_1, l_2]$, we start all over again.

The above process of sampling and elimination is repeated until the number of remaining keys is $\leq n^{0.4}$. After this, we perform an appropriate selection from out of the remaining keys using the sparse enumeration sort (Theorem 14.5). For more details, see Algorithm 13.9.

A *stage* refers to one run of the **while** loop. As shown in Section 13.4.5, there are only $\widetilde{O}(1)$ stages in the algorithm.

Step 1 of Algorithm 13.9 takes $O(1)$ time on the mesh. The prefix computations of steps 2 and 5 can be done in a total of $O(\sqrt{p})$ time (c.f. Theorem 14.3). Concentration of steps 3 and 6 takes $O(\sqrt{p})$ time each (see Theorem 14.4). Also, sparse enumeration sort takes the same time in steps 3 and 6 in accordance with Theorem 14.5. The selections of steps 4 and 6 take only $O(1)$ time each since these are selections from sorted sequences. The broadcasts of steps 2, 4, and 5 take $O(\sqrt{p})$ time each (c.f. Theorem 14.2). As a result we arrive at the following theorem.

Theorem 14.6 Selection from $n = p$ keys can be performed in $\widetilde{O}(\sqrt{p})$ time on a $\sqrt{p} \times \sqrt{p}$ mesh. □

14.4.2 Randomized Selection for $n > p$ (*)

Now we consider the problem of selection when the number of keys is larger than the network size. In particular, assume that $n = p^c$ for some constant $c > 1$. Algorithm 13.9 can be used for this case as well with some minor modifications. Each processor has $\frac{n}{p}$ keys to begin with. The condition for the **while** statement is changed to $(N > D)$ (where D is a constant). In step 1 a processor includes each of its keys with probability $\frac{1}{N^{1-(1/3c)}}$. So, this step now takes time $\frac{n}{p}$. The number of keys in the sample is $\widetilde{O}(N^{1/3c}) = \widetilde{o}(\sqrt{p})$. Step 2 remains the same and still takes $O(\sqrt{p})$ time. Since there are only $\widetilde{O}(N^{1/3c})$ sample keys, they can be concentrated and sorted in step 3 in time $O(\sqrt{p})$ (c.f. Theorems 14.4 and 14.5). Step 4 takes $O(\sqrt{p})$ time as do steps 5 and 6. So, each stage takes time $O(\frac{n}{p} + \sqrt{p})$.

Lemma 13.3 can be used to show that the number of keys that survive at the end of any stage is $\leq 2\sqrt{\alpha}N^{(1-(1/6c))}\sqrt{\log N} = \widetilde{O}(N^{(1-(1/6c))}\sqrt{\log N})$, where N is the number of alive keys at the beginning of this stage. This in turn implies there are only $\widetilde{O}(\log\log p)$ stages in the algorithm. In summary, we have the following theorem.

Theorem 14.7 If $n = p^c$ for some constant $c > 1$, selection from n keys can be performed on a $\sqrt{p} \times \sqrt{p}$ mesh in time $\widetilde{O}\left((\frac{n}{p} + \sqrt{p})\log\log p\right)$. □

14.4.3 A Deterministic Algorithm For $n > p$

In this section we present a deterministic algorithm for selection whose run time is $O(\frac{n}{p}\log\log p + \sqrt{p}\log n)$. The basic idea behind this algorithm is the same as the one employed in the sequential algorithm of Section 3.7. The sequential algorithm partitions the input into groups (of size, say, 5), finds the median of each group, and computes recursively the median (call it M) of these group medians. Then the rank r_M of M in the input is computed, and as a result, all elements from the input that are either $\leq M$ or $> M$ are dropped, depending on whether $i > r_M$ or $i \leq r_M$, respectively. Finally, an appropriate selection is performed from the remaining keys recursively. We showed that the run time of this algorithm was $O(n)$.

If one has to employ this algorithm on an interconnection network, one has to perform periodic load balancing (i.e., distributing the remaining keys uniformly among all the processors). Load balancing is a time-consuming operation and can be avoided as follows. To begin with, each processor has exactly $\frac{n}{p}$ keys. As the algorithm proceeds, keys get dropped from future consideration. There are always p groups (one group per processor). The remaining keys at each processor constitute its group. We identify the median of each group. Instead of picking the median of these medians as the splitter key M, we choose a *weighted median* of these medians. Each group median is *weighted* with the number of remaining keys in that processor.

Definition 14.1 Let $X = k_1, k_2, \ldots, k_n$ be a sequence of keys, where key k_i has an associated weight w_i, for $1 \leq i \leq n$. Also let $W = \sum_{i=1}^{n} w_i$. The weighted median of X is that $k_j \in X$ which satisfies $\sum_{k_l \in X, k_l \leq k_j} w_{k_l} \geq \frac{W}{2}$ and $\sum_{k_l \in X, k_l \geq k_j} w_{k_l} \geq \frac{W}{2}$. In other words, the total weight of all keys of X that are $\leq k_j$ should be $\geq \frac{W}{2}$ and the total weight of all keys that are $\geq k_j$ also should be $\geq \frac{W}{2}$. □

Example 14.9 Let $X = 9, 15, 12, 6, 5, 2, 21, 17$ and let the respective weights be $1, 2, 1, 2, 3, 1, 7, 5$. Here $W = 22$. The weighted median of X is 17. One way of identifying the weighted median is to sort X; let the sorted sequence be $k'_1, k'_2, \ldots, k'_n$; let the corresponding weight sequence be $w'_1, w'_2, \ldots, w'_n$; and compute the prefix sums $y_1, y_2, \ldots, y_n$ on this weight sequence. If y_j is the leftmost prefix sum that is $> \frac{W}{2}$, then k'_j is the weighted median.

For X, the sorted order is $2, 5, 6, 9, 12, 15, 17, 21$ and the corresponding weights are $1, 3, 2, 1, 1, 2, 5, 7$. The prefix sums of this weight sequence are $1, 4, 6, 7, 8, 10, 15, 22$. The leftmost prefix sum that exceeds 11 is 15 and hence the weighted median is 17. □

The deterministic selection algorithm makes use of the technique just described for finding the weighted median. To begin with, there are exactly $\frac{n}{p}$ keys at each processor. We need to find the ith smallest key. The detailed description of the algorithm appears as Algorithm 14.5. Here D is a constant.

Example 14.10 Consider a 3×3 mesh where there are three keys at each processor to begin with. Also let $i = 8$. Let the input be $11, 6, 3,\ 18, 2, 14,\ 10, 17, 5,\ 21, 26, 27,\ 12, 7, 25,\ 24, 4, 9,\ 19, 20, 23,\ 15, 8, 22,\ 1, 13, 6$. Figure 14.17 shows the steps in selecting the ith smallest key. It is assumed that parts are of size 1 in step 0 of Algorithm 14.5, to make the discussion simple.

The median of each processor is found in step 1. Since each processor has the same number of keys, the weighted median of these medians is nothing but the median of these. The weighted median M is found to be 14 in step 2. The rank r_M of this weighed median is 14. Since $i < r_M$, all the keys that are greater than or equal to 14 are deleted. The i remains the same. This completes one run of the **while** loop.

In the next run of the **while** loop, the weighted median is found by sorting the local medians. The local medians are $3, 2, 5, 7, 4, 8, 6$. Their corresponding weights are $2, 1, 2, 2, 2, 1, 3$. Sorted order of these medians is $2, 3, 4, 5, 6, 7, 8$, the respective weights being $1, 2, 2, 2, 3, 2, 1$. Thus the weighted median M is found to be 5. The rank r_M of M is 5. So, keys that are less than or equal to 5 get eliminated. The value of i becomes $8 - 5 = 3$.

In the third run of the **while** loop, there are eight keys to begin with. The weighted median is found to be 8, whose rank happens to be 3, which is the same as the value of i. Thus the algorithm terminates and 8 is output as the correct answer. □

In step 0, the partitioning of the elements into $\log p$ parts can be done in $\frac{n}{p} \log\log p$ time (see Section 13.4, Exercise 5). Sorting can be done in time $O(\frac{n}{p} \log \frac{n}{p})$. Thus step 0 takes time $\frac{n}{p} \min \{\log(n/p), \log\log p\}$. At the end of step 0, the keys in each processor have been partitioned into approximately $\log p$ approximately equal parts. Call each such part a *block*.

In step 1, we can find the median at any processor as follows. Determine first the block the median is in and then perform an appropriate selection in that block (using Algorithm 3.19). The total time is $O(\frac{n}{p \log p})$.

$N := n$;
Step 0. If $\log(n/p)$ is $\le \log\log p$, then sort the elements at each processor; else partition the keys at each processor into $\log p$ equal parts such that the keys in each part are $\le$ keys in the parts to the right.

while $(N > D)$ **do**
{

Step 1. In parallel find the median of keys at each processor. Let M_q be the median and N_q be the number of remaining keys at processor q, $1 \le q \le p$.

Step 2. Find and broadcast the weighted median of $M_1, M_2, \ldots, M_p$, where key M_q has a weight of N_q, $1 \le q \le p$. Let M be the weighted median.

Step 3. Count the rank r_M of M from out of all remaining keys and broadcast it.

Step 4. If $i \le r_M$, then eliminate all remaining keys that are $> M$; else eliminate all remaining keys that are $\le M$.

Step 5. Compute and broadcast E, the number of keys eliminated. If $i > r_M$, then $i := i - E$; $N := N - E$;

}

Output the ith smallest key from out of the remaining keys.

Algorithm 14.5 Deterministic selection on a $\sqrt{p} \times \sqrt{p}$ mesh

In step 2, we can sort the medians to identify the weighted median. If $M_1', M_2', \ldots, M_p'$ is the sorted order of the medians, then we need to identify j such that $\sum_{k=1}^{j} N_k' \ge \frac{N}{2}$ and $\sum_{k=1}^{j-1} N_k' < \frac{N}{2}$. Such a j can be computed with an additional prefix computation. Sorting can be done in $O(\sqrt{p})$ time (as we show in Section 14.6). The prefix computation takes $O(\sqrt{p})$ time as well (see Theorem 14.3). Thus M, the weighted median, can be identified in time $O(\sqrt{p})$.

In step 3, each processor can identify the number of remaining keys in its queue and then all processors can perform a prefix sums computation. Therefore, this step takes $O(\sqrt{p})$ time.

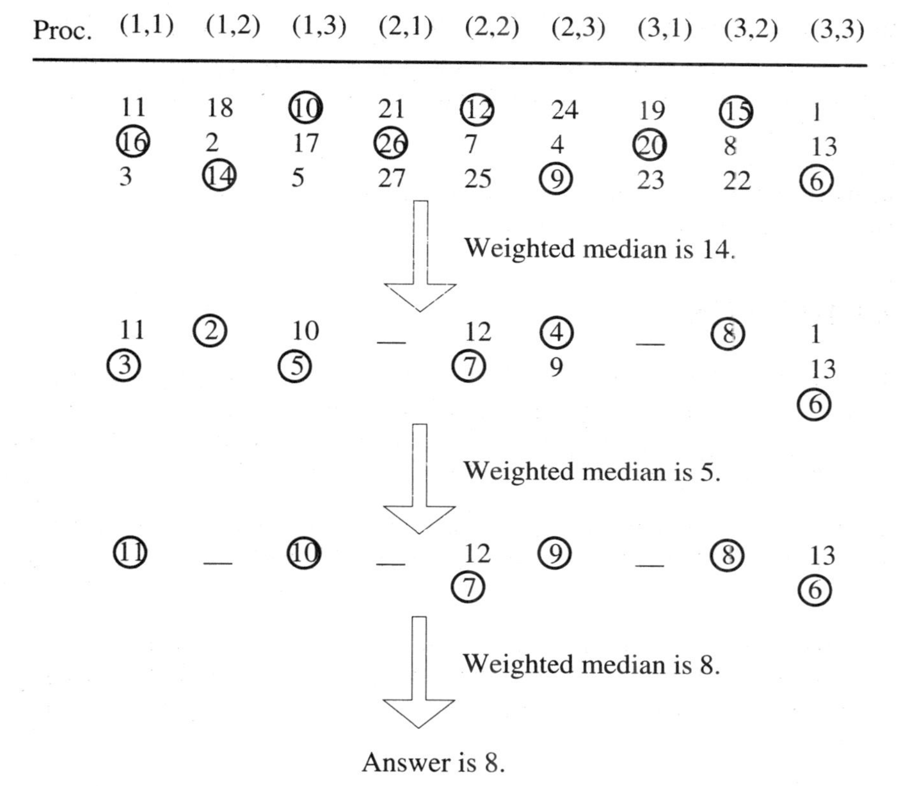

Figure 14.17 Deterministic selection when $n > p$

In step 4, the appropriate keys in any processor can be eliminated as follows. First identify the block B that M falls in. This can be done in $O(\log p)$ time. After this, we compare M with the elements of block B to determine the keys to be eliminated. If $i > r_M$ ($i \leq r_M$), of course all blocks to the left (right) of B are eliminated en masse. Total time needed is $O(\log p + \frac{n}{p \log p})$, which is $O(\frac{n}{p \log p})$ since $n = p^c$ for some constant c.

Step 5 takes $O(\sqrt{p})$ time, since it involves a prefix computation and a broadcast.

Broadcasting of steps 2, 3, and 4 takes $O(\sqrt{p})$ time each (c.f. Theorem 14.2). Thus each run of the **while** loop takes $O(\frac{n}{p \log p} + \sqrt{p})$ time.

How many keys are eliminated in each run of the **while** loop? Assume that $i \geq r_M$ in a given run. (The other case can be argued similarly.) The number of keys eliminated is at least $\sum_{k=1}^{j} \left\lceil \frac{N'_k}{2} \right\rceil$, which is $\geq \frac{N}{4}$. Therefore, it follows that the **while** loop is executed $O(\log n)$ times. Thus we get (assuming that $n = p^c$ and hence $\log n$ is asymptotically the same as $\log p$) the following theorem.

Theorem 14.8 Selection from n keys can be performed on a $\sqrt{p} \times \sqrt{p}$ mesh in time $O(\frac{n}{p} \log\log p + \sqrt{p} \log n)$. □

EXERCISES

1. Consider the selection problem on a $\sqrt{p} \times \sqrt{p}$ mesh, where $p = n$. Let $\mathcal{A}$ be a median finding algorithm that runs in time $T(\sqrt{p})$. How can you make use of $\mathcal{A}$ to solve an arbitrary instance of the selection problem and what is the resultant run time?

2. Present an efficient algorithm for finding the kth quantiles of any given sequence of n keys on a $\sqrt{p} \times \sqrt{p}$ mesh. Consider the cases $n = p$ and $n > p$.

3. Given an array A of n elements, present an algorithm to find any element of A that is greater than or equal to the median on a $\sqrt{p} \times \sqrt{p}$ mesh. Your algorithm should run in time $2\sqrt{p} + \tilde{o}(\sqrt{p})$. Assume that $p = n$.

4. Consider a $\sqrt{p} \times \sqrt{p}$ mesh in which there is a key at each node to begin with. Assume that the keys are integers in the range $[0, p^\epsilon - 1]$, where ϵ is a constant < 1. Design an efficient deterministic selection algorithm for this input. What is the run time of your algorithm?

5. Develop an efficient deterministic selection algorithm for the mesh when $n = p$. Also assume that i (the rank of the element to be selected) is either $\leq p^\epsilon$ or $\geq p - p^\epsilon$ for some fixed $\epsilon < 1$. What is the run time of your algorithm?

6. Design a deterministic algorithm for selection when $n = p$. Your algorithm should have a run time of $O(\sqrt{p})$ on a $\sqrt{p} \times \sqrt{p})$ mesh.

14.5 MERGING

The problem of merging is to take two sorted sequences as input and produce a sorted sequence of all elements. This problem was studied in Chapters 3 and 13.

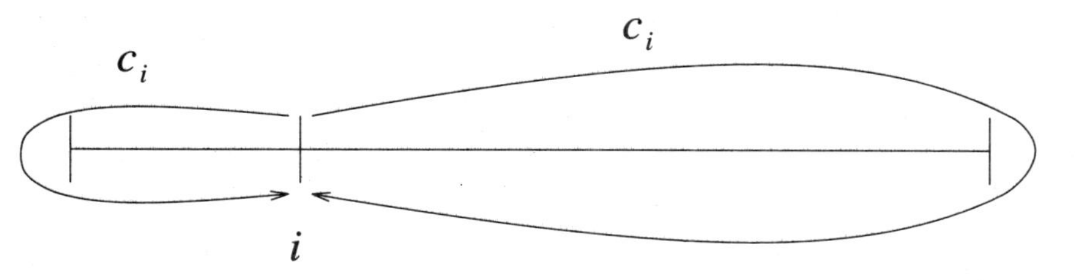

Figure 14.18 Computing the ranks of keys

14.5.1 Rank Merge on a Linear Array

The merge by ranking algorithm of Section 13.5.1 can be implemented to run in linear time on a linear array. Let $\mathcal{L}$ be a linear array with $p = m$ processors. The input sequences are $X_1 = k_1, k_2, \ldots, k_m$ and $X_2 = k_{m+1}, k_{m+2}, \ldots, k_{2m}$. To begin with, processor i has the keys k_i and k_{i+m}. Following the merge, the two smallest keys are in processor 1, the next two smallest keys are in processor 2, and so on. We show how to compute the rank of each key $k \in X_1$ and route it to its right place. An analogous algorithm can be applied for X_2 also. Processor i initiates a counter c_i with a value of 0. A packet containing c_i together with the value of k_i is sent along both directions. (If $i = 1$ or m, it is sent in only one direction.) The two copies of c_i travel all the way up to the two boundaries and come back to i (see Figure 14.18). Processor j on receipt of c_i increments c_i by one if $k_j < k_i$; otherwise it doesn't alter c_i. (This increment occurs only when c_i is in its forward journey.) In any case it forwards c_i to its neighbor. When the two copies of c_i return to processor i, the rank of k_i can be computed by summing the two copies and adding one. The time needed for rank computations is $2(p-1)$ or less. Once we know the ranks of the keys, they can be routed in time $O(p)$ using Lemma 14.1. In particular if r_i is the rank of k_i, this key is sent to processor $\lceil \frac{r_i}{2} \rceil$. None of the c_i's get queued since no two counters contend for the same link ever.

Lemma 14.5 Merging two sorted sequences each of length p can be completed in $O(p)$ time on a p-processor linear array. □

14.5.2 Odd-Even Merge on a Linear Array

The odd-even merge algorithm was described in Section 13.5.2 (Algorithm 13.10). On a $p = 2m$-processor linear array assume that X_1 is input in the first m processors and X_2 is input in the next m processors. In step 1 of Algorithm 13.10, X_1 and X_2 are separated into odd and even parts

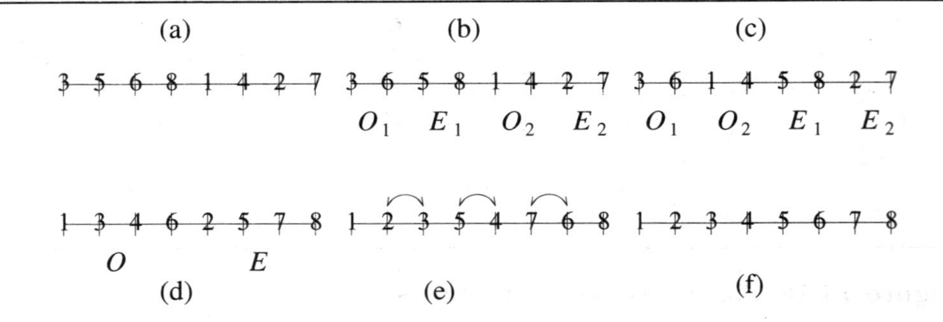

Figure 14.19 Odd-even merge on a linear array

O_1, E_1, O_2, and E_2. This takes $\frac{m}{2}$ steps of data movement. Next, E_1 and O_2 are interchanged. This also takes $\frac{m}{2}$ steps. In step 2, O_1 is merged recursively with O_2 to get O. At the same time E_1 is merged with E_2 to get E. In step 3, O and E are shuffled in a total of $\leq m$ data movement steps. Finally, adjacent elements are compared and interchanged if out of order. If $M(m)$ is the run time of this algorithm on two sequences of length m each, then we have $M(m) \leq M(m/2) + 2m + 1$ which solves to $M(m) = O(m)$.

Lemma 14.6 Two sorted sequences of length m each can be merged on a $2m$-processor linear array in $O(m)$ time. □

Example 14.11 Figure 14.19 shows the merging of two sorted sequences of length four each on an 8-node linear array. Separation of the sequences into their odd and even parts is shown in Figure 14.19(b). In Figure 14.19(c), O_2 and E_1 are interchanged. O_1 and O_2 as well as E_1 and E_2 are recursively merged to get O and E, respectively (Figure 14.19(d)). Next O and E are shuflled (Figure 14.19(e)). A comparison-exchange operation among neighbors is performed to arrive at the final sorted order (Figure 14.19(f)). □

14.5.3 Odd-Even Merge on a Mesh

Now we consider a $\sqrt{p} \times \sqrt{p}$ mesh. Assume that the two sequences to be merged are input in the first and second halves of the mesh in snakelike row major order (see Figure 14.20(a)). The X_1 and X_2 are snakes with $\frac{\sqrt{p}}{2}$ columns and $\sqrt{p}$ rows each. The final merge will be a snake of size $\sqrt{p} \times \sqrt{p}$ (as in Figure 14.20(f)). Assume that $\sqrt{p}$ is an integral power of 2. As the algorithm proceeds, more and more snakes are created all of which have the

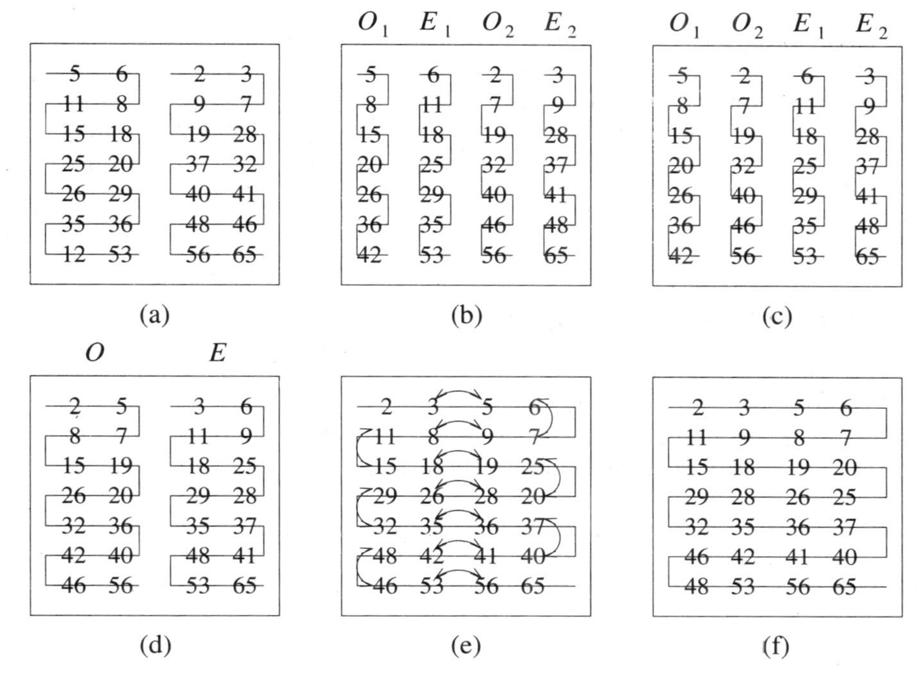

Figure 14.20 Odd-even merge on the mesh

same number of rows. Only the number ℓ of columns will diminish. The base case is when $\ell = 1$. A complete version of the algorithm is given in Algorithm 14.6. This algorithm merges two snakes with ℓ columns each.

Let $M(\ell)$ be the run time of Algorithm 14.6 on two sorted snakes with ℓ columns each.

In step 0, we have to merge two sorted columns. Note that the algorithm of Lemma 14.5 can be used since the data from one column can be moved to the other column in one step and then the algorithm of Lemma 14.5 applied. This takes $O(\sqrt{p})$ time.

Steps 1, 2, and 4 take $\leq \frac{\ell}{2}, \frac{\ell}{2}$, and ℓ steps of data movement, respectively. Step 3 takes $M(\frac{\ell}{2})$ time. Thus, $M(\ell)$ satisfies $M(\ell) \leq M(\frac{\ell}{2}) + 2\ell$, which on solution implies $M(\ell) \leq 4\ell + M(1)$; that is, $M(\sqrt{p}/2) = O(\sqrt{p})$.

Theorem 14.9 Two sorted snakes of size $\sqrt{p} \times \frac{\sqrt{p}}{2}$ each can be merged in time $O(\sqrt{p})$ on a $\sqrt{p} \times \sqrt{p}$ mesh. $\square$

Step 0. If $\ell = 1$, merge the two snakes using Lemma 14.5.

Step 1. Partition X_1 into its odd and even parts, O_1 and E_1, respectively. Similarly partition X_2 into O_2 and E_2. Parts O_1, E_1, O_2, and E_2 are snakes with $\frac{\ell}{2}$ columns each (see Figure 14.20(b)).

Step 2. Interchange O_2 with E_1 as in Figure 14.20(c).

Step 3. Recursively merge O_1 with O_2 to get the snake O. At the same time merge E_1 with E_2 to get the snake E. (See Figure 14.20(d)).

Step 4. Shuffle O with E (see Figure 14.20(e)). Compare adjacent elements and interchange them if they are out of order.

Algorithm 14.6 The odd-even merge algorithm on the mesh

14.6 SORTING

Given a sequence of n keys, recall that the problem of sorting is to rearrange this sequence in either ascending or descending order. In this section we study several algorithms for sorting on both a linear array and a mesh.

14.6.1 Sorting on a Linear Array

Rank sort

The first algorithm, we are going to study, rank sort, computes the rank of each key and then routes the keys to their correct positions. If there are p processors in the linear array with one key per processor, the ranks of all keys can be computed in $O(p)$ time using an algorithm similar to the one employed in the proof of Lemma 14.5. Following this, the key whose rank is r is routed to processor r. This routing also takes $O(p)$ time (Lemma 14.1). Thus we get the following lemma.

Lemma 14.7 A total of p keys can be sorted on a p-processor linear array in $O(p)$ time. □

---

for $i := 1$ **to** p **do**

> If i is odd, compare and exchange keys at processors $2j-1$ and $2j$ for $j = 1, 2, \ldots$; else compare and exchange keys at processors $2j$ and $2j+1$ for $j = 1, 2, \ldots$.

Algorithm 14.7 Odd-even transposition sort

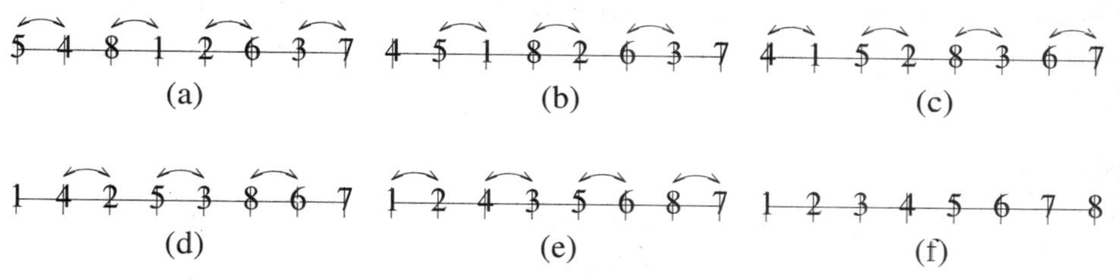

Figure 14.21 Odd-even transposition sort on a linear array

Odd-even transposition sort

An algorithm similar to bubble sort can also be used to sort a linear array in $O(p)$ time. This algorithm (Algorithm 14.7) is also known as the *odd-even transposition sort.* "Compare and exchange" refers to comparing two keys and interchanging them if they are out of order. Each iteration of the **for** loop takes only $O(1)$ time. Thus the whole algorithm terminates in $O(p)$ time steps. The correctness of this algorithm can be proved using the zero-one principle and is left as an exercise.

Lemma 14.8 The odd-even transposition sort runs in $O(p)$ time on a p-processor linear array. □

Example 14.12 Let $p = 8$ and let the keys to be sorted be $4, 5, 1, 8, 2, 6, 3, 7$. Figure 14.21 shows the steps of the odd-even transposition sort. □

Odd-even merge sort

The last algorithm we study on the linear array is based on merge sort; that is, it makes use of a known merging algorithm in order to sort. If there are p

keys on a p-processor linear array, we can recursively sort the first half and the second half at the same time. Once the results are ready, they can be merged using the odd-even merge algorithm (Lemma 14.6). The resultant odd-even merge sort has a run time $T(p) = T(p/2) + O(p)$, which solves to $T(p) = O(p)$.

Lemma 14.9 Odd-even merge sort runs in $O(p)$ time on a p-processor linear array. □

14.6.2 Sorting on a Mesh

We study two different algorithms for sorting on a mesh. The first is called *Shearsort* and takes $O(\sqrt{p}\log p)$ time to sort a $\sqrt{p} \times \sqrt{p}$ mesh. The second is an implementation of odd-even merge sort. This algorithm runs in $O(\sqrt{p})$ time and hence is asymptotically optimal.

Shearsort

This algorithm (Algorithm 14.8) works by alternately sorting the rows and columns. If there is a key at each processor of a $\sqrt{p} \times \sqrt{p}$ mesh, there are $\log p + 1$ phases in the algorithm. At the end, the mesh will be sorted in snakelike row major order. Since a linear array with $\sqrt{p}$ processors can be sorted in $O(\sqrt{p})$ time (c.f. Lemma 14.8), Algorithm 14.8 runs in a total of $O(\sqrt{p}(\log p + 1)) = O(\sqrt{p}\log p)$ time.

Example 14.13 Consider the keys on a 4×4 mesh of Figure 14.22(a). In phase 1, we sort the rows, sorting alternate rows in opposite orders. The result is Figure 14.22(b). The results of the next four phases are shown in Figure 14.22(c), (d), (e), and (f), respectively. At the end of the fifth phase, the mesh is sorted. □

Note that Algorithm 14.8 is comparison based and is also oblivious and hence the zero-one principle can be used to prove its correctness. Assume that the input consists of only zeros and ones. Define a row to be *dirty* if it has both ones and zeros, *clean* otherwise. Note that if the mesh is sorted, there will be only one dirty row and the rest of the rows will either have all ones or all zeros and hence will be clean. To begin with, there could be as many as $\sqrt{p}$ dirty rows; that is, each row could be dirty.

Call a *stage* of the algorithm to be sorting all rows followed by sorting all columns (i.e., a stage consists of two phases). We show that if N is the number of dirty rows at the beginning of any stage, then the number of dirty rows at the end of the stage is no more than $\frac{N}{2}$. This will then imply that after $\log(\sqrt{p})$ stages, there will be at most one dirty row left which can be sorted in an additional row sort. Thus there will be only $2\log(\sqrt{p}) + 1 = \log p + 1$ phases in the algorithm.

(a)

15	12	8	32
7	13	6	17
2	16	19	25
18	11	5	3

(b)

8	12	15	32
17	13	7	6
2	16	19	25
18	11	5	3

(c)

2	11	5	3
8	12	7	6
17	13	15	25
18	16	19	32

(d)

2	3	5	11
12	8	7	6
13	15	17	25
32	19	18	16

(e)

2	3	5	6
12	8	7	11
13	15	17	16
32	19	18	25

(f)

2	3	5	6
12	11	8	7
13	15	16	17
32	25	19	18

Figure 14.22 Shearsort – an example

for $i := 1$ **to** $\log p + 1$ **do**

> If i is even, sort the columns in increasing order from top to bottom; else sort the rows. The rows are sorted in such a way that alternate rows are sorted in reverse order. The first row is sorted in increasing order from left to right, the second row is sorted in decreasing order from left to right, and so on.

Algorithm 14.8 Shearsort

Look at two adjacent dirty rows at the beginning of any stage. There are three possibilities: (1) these two rows put together may have an equal number of ones and zeros, (2) the two rows may have more zeros than ones,

(a)	(b)	(c)
$0\ 0 \cdots 0\ 1\ 1 \cdots 1$	$0 \cdots 0 \cdots 0\ 1 \cdots 1$	$0 \cdots 0\ 1 \quad \cdots \quad 1$
$1\ 1 \cdots 1\ 0\ 0 \cdots 0$	$1 \cdots 1\ 0 \quad \cdots \quad 0$	$1 \cdots 1 \cdots 1\ 0 \cdots 0$

Figure 14.23 Proving the correctness of Algorithm 14.8

and (3) the two rows may have more ones than zeros. In the first phase of this stage the rows are sorted and in the second phase the columns are sorted. In case 1, when the rows are sorted, they will look like Figure 14.23(a). Then, when the columns are sorted, the two rows will contribute two clean rows (one with all ones and the other will all zeros). If case 2 is true, after the row sorting, the two rows will look like Figure 14.23(b). When the columns are sorted, the two rows will contribute one clean row consisting of all zeros. In case 3 also, a clean row (consisting of all ones) will be contributed. In summary, any two adjacent dirty rows will contribute at least one clean row. That is, the number of dirty rows will decrease in any phase by a factor of at least 2.

Theorem 14.10 The Shearsort algorithm (Algorithm 14.8) works correctly and runs in time $O(\sqrt{p}\log p)$ on a $\sqrt{p} \times \sqrt{p}$ mesh. □

Odd-even merge sort

Now we implement the odd-even merge sort method on the mesh. If $X = k_1, k_2, \ldots, k_n$ is the given sequence of n keys, odd-even merge sort partitions X into two subsequences $X_1' = k_1, k_2, \ldots, k_{n/2}$ and $X_2' = k_{n/2+1}, k_{n/2+2}, \ldots, k_n$ of equal length. Subsequences X_1' and X_2' are sorted recursively assigning $n/2$ processors to each. The two sorted subsequences (call them X_1 and X_2, respectively) are then finally merged using the odd-even merge algorithm.

We have already seen how the odd-even merge algorithm works on the mesh in $O(\sqrt{p})$ time (Algorithm 14.6). This algorithm can be used in the merging part. Given p keys distributed on a $\sqrt{p} \times \sqrt{p}$ mesh (one key per processor), we can partition them into four equal parts of size $\frac{\sqrt{p}}{2} \times \frac{\sqrt{p}}{2}$ each. Sort each part recursively into snakelike row major order. The result is shown in Figure 14.24(b). Now, merge the top two snakes using Algorithm 14.6. At the same time merge the bottom two snakes using the same algorithm. These mergings take time $O(\sqrt{p})$. After these mergings, the mesh looks like Figure

14.24(c). Finally merge these two snakes by properly modifying Algorithm 14.6. This merging also takes $O(\sqrt{p})$ time. After this merging, the whole mesh is in snakelike row major sorted order (as in Figure 14.24(d)).

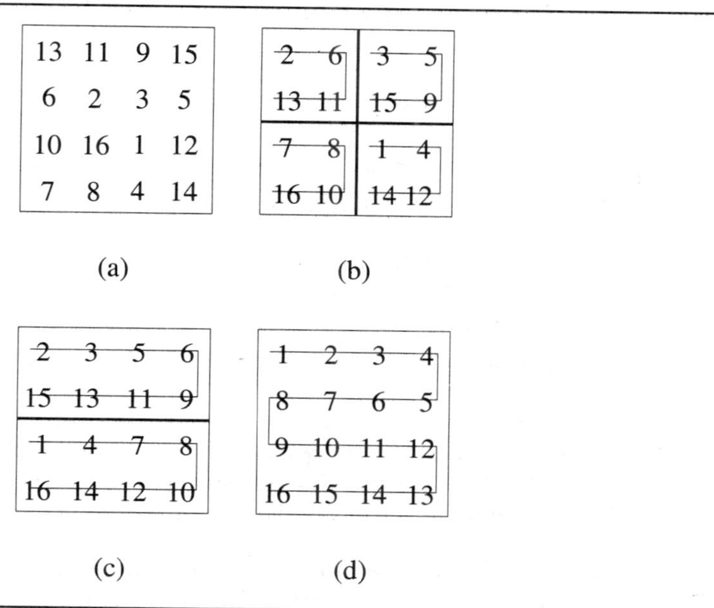

Figure 14.24 Odd-even merge sort on the mesh

If $S(\ell)$ is the time needed to sort an $\ell \times \ell$ mesh using the above divide-and-conquer algorithm, then we have

$$S(\ell) = S\left(\frac{\ell}{2}\right) + O(\ell)$$

which solves to $S(\ell) = O(\ell)$.

Theorem 14.11 We can sort p elements in $O(\sqrt{p})$ time on a $\sqrt{p} \times \sqrt{p}$ mesh into snakelike row major order. □

Example 14.14 Figure 14.24(a) shows a 4×4 mesh in which there is a key at each node to begin with. The mesh is partitioned into four quadrants and each quadrant is recursively sorted. The result is Figure 14.24(b). The top two quadrants as well as the bottom two quadrants are merged in parallel (Figure 14.24(c). The resultant two snakes are merged (Figure 14.24(d)). □

EXERCISES

1. Prove the correctness of Algorithm 14.7 using the zero-one principle.

2. Present an implementation of rank sort on a $\sqrt{p} \times \sqrt{p}$ mesh. What is the run time of your algorithm?

3. The randomized routing algorithm of Section 14.2 can be made deterministic with the help of sorting. The routing algorithm works as follows. Partition the mesh into blocks of size $\frac{\sqrt{p}}{q} \times \frac{\sqrt{p}}{q}$ each; sort each block in column major order according to the destination column of the packets (the advantage of such a sorting is that now packets in any block that have the same destination column will be found in successive processors according to column major order). From then on the packets use phases 2 and 3 of Algorithm 14.1. Prove that this algorithm has a run time of $2\sqrt{p} + O(\frac{\sqrt{p}}{q})$ with a queue size of $O(q)$.

4. Assume that each processor of a $\sqrt{p} \times \sqrt{p}$ mesh is the origin of exactly one packet and each processor is the destination of exactly one packet. Present an $O(\sqrt{p})$-time $O(1)$-queues deterministic algorithm for this routing problem. (*Hint:* Make use of sorting.)

5. Making use of the idea of Exercise 4, devise an $O(\sqrt{p})$-time $O(1)$-queue-length deterministic algorithm for the PPR problem (see Section 14.2).

6. The array A is an almost-sorted array of n elements. It is given that the position of each key is at most a distance d away from its final sorted position. Give an $O(d)$-time algorithm for sorting A on an n-processor linear array. Prove the correctness of your algorithm using the zero-one principle.

7. Let $\mathcal{L}$ be a linear array with $\log n$ processors. Each processor has $\frac{n}{\log n}$ keys to begin with. The goal is to sort the array. At the end, processor 1 should have the least $\frac{n}{\log n}$ keys. Node 2 should have the next bigger $\frac{n}{\log n}$ keys. And so on. Establish that this sorting can be accomplished in $O(n)$ time.

8. Prove that if in a $\sqrt{p} \times \sqrt{p}$ mesh the rows are sorted and then the columns, the rows remain sorted.

9. Consider the following algorithm for sorting a $\sqrt{p} \times \sqrt{p}$ mesh:

   (a) Partition the mesh into four quadrants of size $\frac{\sqrt{p}}{2} \times \frac{\sqrt{p}}{2}$ each.

   (b) Sort each quadrant recursively.

(c) Perform five stages of Algorithm 14.8 on the whole mesh.

Prove that this algorithm correctly sorts arbitrary numbers. What is the run time of this algorithm?

10. In this section we showed how to sort keys on a $\sqrt{p} \times \sqrt{p}$ mesh into snakelike row major order in $O(\sqrt{p})$ time. Prove that the mesh can be sorted into the following indexing schemes also in $O(\sqrt{p})$ time: column major and blockwise column major where the blocks are of size $p^{1/4} \times p^{1/4}$ (within each block employ the snakelike column major order).

11. Given is a sequence X of n keys $k_1, k_2, \ldots, k_n$. For each key k_i $(1 \leq i \leq n)$, its position in sorted order differs from i by at most d. Present an $O(n \log d)$-time sequential algorithm to sort X. Prove the correctness of your algorithm using the zero-one principle. Implement the same algorithm on a $\sqrt{n} \times \sqrt{n}$ mesh. What is the resultant run time?

14.7 GRAPH PROBLEMS

In Section 13.7, we introduced a general framework for solving the transitive closure, connected components, and all-pairs shortest-paths problems. We make use of this framework here also.

The matrix $\widetilde{M}$ (see Section 13.7) can be computed from M in $O(n \log n)$ time on an $n \times n \times n$ mesh. An $n \times n \times n$ mesh is a three-dimensional grid, in which each grid point corresponds to a processing element and each link corresponds to a bidirectional communication link. Each processor in an $n \times n \times n$ mesh can be denoted with a triple (i, j, k), where $1 \leq i, j, k \leq n$ (see Figure 14.25).

Definition 14.2 In an $n \times n \times n$ mesh, let $(i, *, *)$ stand for all processors whose first coordinate is i. This is indeed an $n \times n$ mesh. Similarly define $(*, j, *)$ and $(*, *, k)$. Also define $(i, j, *)$ to be all processors whose first coordinate is i and whose second coordinate is j. This is a linear array. Similarly define $(i, *, k)$ and $(*, j, k)$. □

Theorem 14.12 $\widetilde{M}$ can be computed from an $n \times n$ matrix M in $O(n \log n)$ time using an $n \times n \times n$ mesh.

Proof: The $n \times n \times n$ mesh algorithm is the same as the CRCW PRAM algorithm of Algorithm 13.15. We store the matrix $m[\,]$ in $(*, *, 1)$, which is initialized to M.

In step 1, to update $q[i, j, k]$, the corresponding processor has to access both $m[i, j]$ and $m[j, k]$. Each processor can access $m[i, j]$ by broadcasting

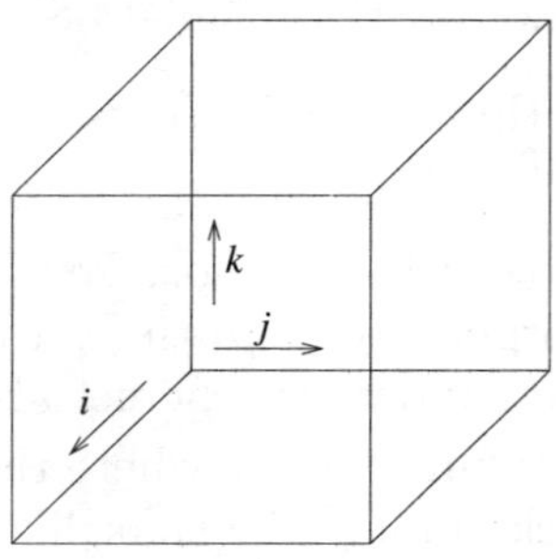

Figure 14.25 A 3D mesh

$m[i,j]$ along $(i,j,*)$. For processor (i,j,k) to get $m[j,k]$, we do the following: Transpose the matrix $m[\,]$ and store the transpose as $x[\,]$ in $(*,*,1)$. Now element $x[i,j]$ is broadcast along $(i,j,*)$. (Verifying that this ensures that each processor gets the correct data is left as an exercise.) Broadcasting can be done in $O(n)$ time each. Transposing the matrix can also be completed in $O(n)$ time (see Section 14.3, Exercise 12).

In step 2 of Algorithm 13.15, each $m[i,j]$ is updated to min $\{q[i,1,j], q[i,2,j], \ldots, q[i,n,j]\}$, for $1 \le i,j \le n$. This can be done as follows: Note that the n items of interest are local to the linear array $(i,*,j)$. Using this array, the updated value of $m[i,j]$ can be computed and stored in the processor $(i,1,j)$ in $O(n)$ time. These n^2 updated values of $m[\,]$ have to be moved to $(*,*,0)$. This transfer can be performed with two broadcast operations. First broadcast the updated $m[i,j]$ along the array $(i,*,j)$. Each linear array $(i,*,j)$ now has a copy of the updated $m[i,j]$. Second broadcast this $m[i,j]$ along the linear array $(i,j,*)$ so that the processor $(i,j,0)$ gets a copy of the updated $m[i,j]$. Now the updating of $m[i,j]$ can be done local to the linear array $(i,j,*)$ in $O(n)$ time.

Thus each run of the **for** loop takes $O(n)$ time. □

Consequently, the following theorems also hold.

Theorem 14.13 The transitive closure matrix of an n-vertex directed graph can be computed in $O(n \log n)$ time on an $n \times n \times n$ mesh. □

Theorem 14.14 The connected components of an n-vertex graph can be determined in $O(n \log n)$ time on an $n \times n \times n$ mesh. □

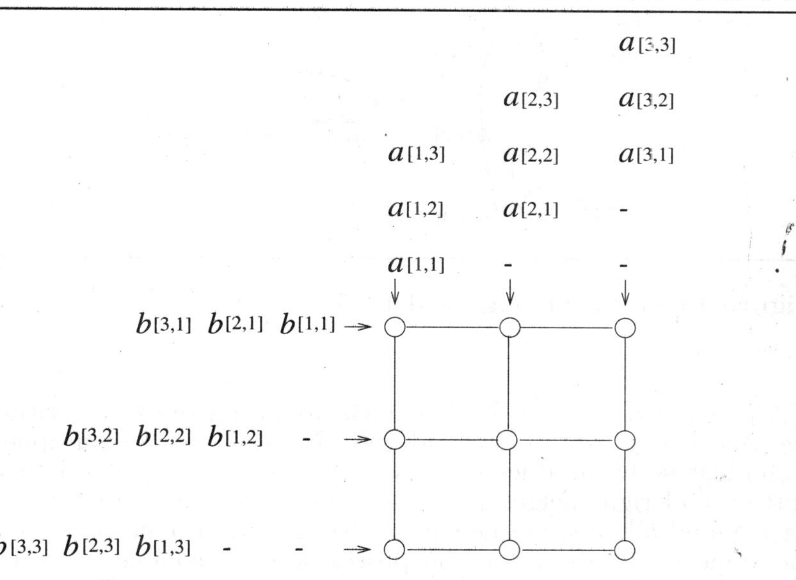

Figure 14.26 Multiplying two matrices

14.7.1 An $n \times n$ Mesh Algorithm for Transitive Closure

In Section 13.7.1 we saw that the transitive closure of an n-vertex graph could be computed by performing $\lceil \log n \rceil$ multiplications of an $n \times n$ matrix. In Theorem 14.15 we show that each of these multiplications can be done in $O(n)$ time on an $n \times n$ mesh.

Theorem 14.15 Two $n \times n$ matrices $A = a[i,j]$ and $B = b[i,j]$ can be multiplied in $O(n)$ time on an $n \times n$ mesh.

Proof: Let $C = c[i,j]$ be the product to be computed. Assume that the matrices can be input to the mesh as shown in Figure 14.26. In particular, the first column of A traverses through the first column of the mesh one item and one processor per time unit. That is, in the first time unit $a[1,1]$ reaches the processor $(1,1)$. In the second time unit $a[1,1]$ reaches the processor $(2,1)$ and at the same time $a[1,2]$ reaches the processor $(1,1)$. And so on. The second column of A traverses through the second column of the mesh starting from the second time unit (that is, $a[2,1]$ reaches the processor $(1,2)$ at time step 2, and so on).

In general, the processor (i,j) gets both $a[i,k]$ and $b[k,j]$ at time step $i+j+k-2$. Node (i,j) is in charge of computing $c[i,j]$. Note that $c[i,j] =$

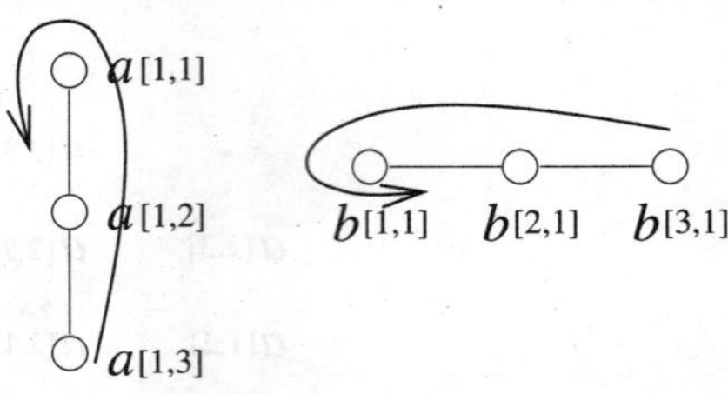

Figure 14.27 Simulating the data flow

$\sum_{k=1}^{n} a[i,k]b[k,j]$. Node (i,j) uses the following simple algorithm: If it gets two items (one from above and one from the left), it multiplies them and accumulates the product to $c[i,j]$. It then forwards the data items to its bottom and right neighbors respectively. Since it is guaranteed to get all $a[i,k]$'s and $b[k,j]$'s, at the end of the algorithm it has correctly computed the value of $c[i,j]$. Also, the processor (i,j) completes its task by step $(i+j+n-2)$ since there are only n possible values that k can take. Thus the whole algorithm terminates within $3n-2$ steps.

For this algorithm we have assumed that the right data item comes to the right place at the right time. What happens if the two matrices are already stored in the mesh? (In fact this is the case for the application of matrix multiplication in the solution of the transitive closure problem.) Let the two matrices be stored in the mesh in row major order to begin with. Transpose both the matrices in $O(n)$ time. Simulate the effect of data coming from above and the left as shown in Figure 14.27. In each row (column), there is a stream moving to the right (down) and another moving to the left (up). The stream corresponding to the ith row (jth column) should start at time step i (j). □

As a result, we also get the following theorem.

Theorem 14.16 The transitive closure matrix of a given undirected graph with n processors can be computed in $O(n \log n)$ time on an $n \times n$ mesh. □

14.7.2 All-Pairs Shortest Paths

In Section 13.7.2 we presented a PRAM algorithm for the all-pairs shortest-paths problem. The idea was to define $A^k(i,j)$ to represent the length of a shortest path from i to j going through no vertex of index greater than k, and then to infer that

$$A^k(i,j) = \min\ \{A^{k-1}(i,j),\ A^{k-1}(i,k) + A^{k-1}(k,j)\},\quad k \geq 1.$$

The importance of this relationship between A^k and A^{k-1} is that the computation of A^k from A^{k-1} corresponds to matrix multiplication, where min and addition take the place of addition and multiplication, respectively. Under this interpretation of matrix multiplication, the all-pairs shortest-paths problem reduces to computing $A^n = A^{2^{\lceil \log n \rceil}}$. We get this theorem.

Theorem 14.17 The all-pairs shortest-paths problem can be solved in $O(n \log n)$ time on an $n \times n$ mesh. $\square$

EXERCISES

1. Use the general paradigm of this section to design a mesh algorithm for finding a minimum spanning tree of a given weighted graph. You can use either a $k \times k$ mesh or an $l \times l \times l$ mesh (for an appropriate k or l). Analyze the time and processor bounds.
2. Present an efficient algorithm for topological sort on the mesh.
3. Give an efficient mesh algorithm to check whether a given undirected graph is acyclic. Analyze the processor and time bounds.
4. If G is any undirected graph, G^k is defined as follows: There is a link between processors i and j in G^k if and only if there is a path of length k in G between i and j. Present an $O(n \log k)$-time $n \times n$ mesh algorithm to compute G^k from G.
5. You are given a directed graph whose links have a weight of zero or one. Present an efficient minimum spanning tree algorithm for this special case on the mesh.
6. Present an efficient mesh implementation of the Bellman and Ford algorithm (see Section 5.4).
7. Show how to invert a triangular $\sqrt{p} \times \sqrt{p}$ matrix on a $\sqrt{p} \times \sqrt{p}$ mesh in $O(\sqrt{p})$ time.
8. Present an $O(\sqrt{p})$-time algorithm for inverting a $\sqrt{p} \times \sqrt{p}$ tridiagonal matrix on a $\sqrt{p} \times \sqrt{p}$ mesh.

14.8 COMPUTING THE CONVEX HULL

The convex hull of n points in the plane can be computed in $O(n)$ time on an n-processor linear array (the proof of this is left as an exercise). More interestingly, the same problem can be solved in $\widetilde{O}(\sqrt{n})$ time on a $\sqrt{n} \times \sqrt{n}$ mesh.

We begin by showing that a straightforward implementation of the algorithm of Sections 3.9.4 and 13.8 results in a run time of $O(\sqrt{n}\log^2 n)$. Later we show how to reduce this run time to $\widetilde{O}(\sqrt{n})$.

In the preprocessing step of Algorithm 13.16, the input points are sorted according to their x-coordinate values. The variable N is used to denote the number of points to the left of $\langle p_1, p_2\rangle$. This sorting can be done in $O(\sqrt{N})$ time on a $\sqrt{N} \times \sqrt{N}$ mesh. If $q_1, q_2, \ldots, q_N$ is the sorted order of these points, step 1 of Algorithm 13.16 can be done by partitioning the input into two parts with $q_1, q_2, \ldots, q_{N/2}$ in the first part and $q_{N/2+1}, q_{N/2+2}, \ldots, q_N$ in the second part. The first half is placed in the first half (i.e., the first $\frac{\sqrt{N}}{2}$ columns) of the mesh and the second part is kept in the second half of the mesh in snakelike row major order. In step 2, the upper hull of each half is recursively computed. Let the upper hulls be arranged in snakelike row major order (in successive processors). Let H_1 and H_2 be the upper hulls. Step 3 is completed in $O(\sqrt{N}\log N)$ time. Step 4 calls for data concentration and hence can be completed in $O(\sqrt{N})$ time.

Let $T(\ell)$ be the run time of the above recursive algorithm for the upper hull on an input of ℓ columns; then we have

$$T(\ell) \;=\; T(\ell/2) + O(\sqrt{N}\log N)$$

which solves to $T(\sqrt{N}) = O(\sqrt{N}\log^2 N) + T(1)$. Since the convex hull on a $\sqrt{N}$-processor linear array can be found in $O(\sqrt{N})$ time (see the exercises), we have $T(\sqrt{N}) = O(\sqrt{N}\log^2 N)$.

The only part of the algorithm that remains to be specified is how to find the tangent $\langle u, v\rangle$ in $O(\sqrt{N}\log N)$ time. The way to find the tangent is to start from the middle point, call it p, of H_1. Find the tangent of p with H_2. Let $\langle p, q\rangle$ be the tangent. Using $\langle p, q\rangle$, determine whether u is to the left of, equal to, or to the right of p in H_1. A binary search in this fashion on the points of H_1 reveals u. Use the same procedure to isolate v as well.

Lemma 14.10 Let H_1 and H_2 be two upper hulls with at most N points each. If p is any point of H_1, its tangent q with H_2 can be found in $O(\sqrt{N})$ time.

Proof. Broadcast p to all processors containing H_2 (i.e., the second half of the mesh). Consider an arbitrary processor in the second half. Let q' be the point this processor has. Also let x and y be the left and right neighbors of q' in the hull H_2. Each processor can access the left and right neighbors in $O(1)$ time (since the points are arranged in snakelike row major order). If $\angle pq'x$ and $\angle pq'y$ are both left turns, then q' is the point we are looking for (see Figure 3.10). The point q' is broadcast to the whole mesh. Each broadcast takes $O(\sqrt{N})$ time. □

Lemma 14.11 If H_1 and H_2 are two upper hulls with at most N points each, their common tangent can be computed in $O(\sqrt{N} \log N)$ time.

Proof: Similar to that of Lemma 13.5 (see Exercise 1). □

In summary, we have the following theorem.

Theorem 14.18 The convex hull of N points in the plane can be computed in $O(\sqrt{N} \log^2 N)$ time on a $\sqrt{N} \times \sqrt{N}$ mesh. □

The run time of the preceding algorithm can be reduced to $O(\sqrt{N} \log N)$ using the following strategy. In the preceding algorithm, at every level of recursion the number of rows remains the same. Even though the number of points decreases with increasing recursion level, there is no corresponding reduction in the merging time. At each level merging takes $O(\sqrt{N} \log N)$ time. This suggests that we should attempt to simultaneously decrease the number of rows as well as columns in any subproblem. One way of doing this is to partition the input into four equal parts like we did in the case of odd-even merge sort (see Figure 14.24). After partitioning, the convex hull of each quadrant is obtained in snakelike row major order. These four upper hulls are then merged as shown in Figure 14.24 (i.e., first merge the two upper quadrants and the two lower quadrants, and then merge the upper half with the lower half). Each merging can be done using the just-discussed merging technique in $O(\sqrt{N} \log N)$ time. If $T(\ell)$ is the run time of computing the convex hull of a $\sqrt{\ell} \times \sqrt{\ell}$ mesh, $T(\ell) = T(\ell/2) + O(\ell \log \ell)$; this solves to $T(\ell) = O(\ell \log \ell)$. Thus on a $\sqrt{N} \times \sqrt{N}$ mesh, the run time will be $O(\sqrt{N} \log N)$.

Example 14.15 Consider the problem in which $N = 16$ and $q_1, q_2, \ldots, q_{16}$ are (1, 1), (1.1, 4), (1.5, 3.5), (2, 6), (2.2, 4), (3, 4.5), (4, 7.5), (4.1, 6), (4.5, 5.5), (5, 5), (6, 8), (6.3, 7), (6.5, 5), (7, 6), (8, 7), (9,6). These points are organized on a 4×4 mesh as shown in Figure 14.28(a). Note that the q_i's have been partitioned into four and each quadrant of the mesh has a part. Within each quadrant the points are arranged in sorted order (of their x-coordinate values) using the snakelike row major indexing scheme. The upper hull of each quadrant is recursively computed. The results are shown in Figure 14.28(b). The upper hulls in the top two quadrants are merged. At the same time, the upper hulls in the bottom two quadrants are also merged (see Figure 14.28(c). Finally, the upper hull in the top half is merged with the upper hull of the bottom half. The result is (1, 1), (1.1, 4), (2, 6), (4, 7.5), (6, 8), (8, 7), (9, 6). □

We can reduce the run time further if we can find a faster way of merging the two upper hulls. We devise a recursive algorithm for merging two upper

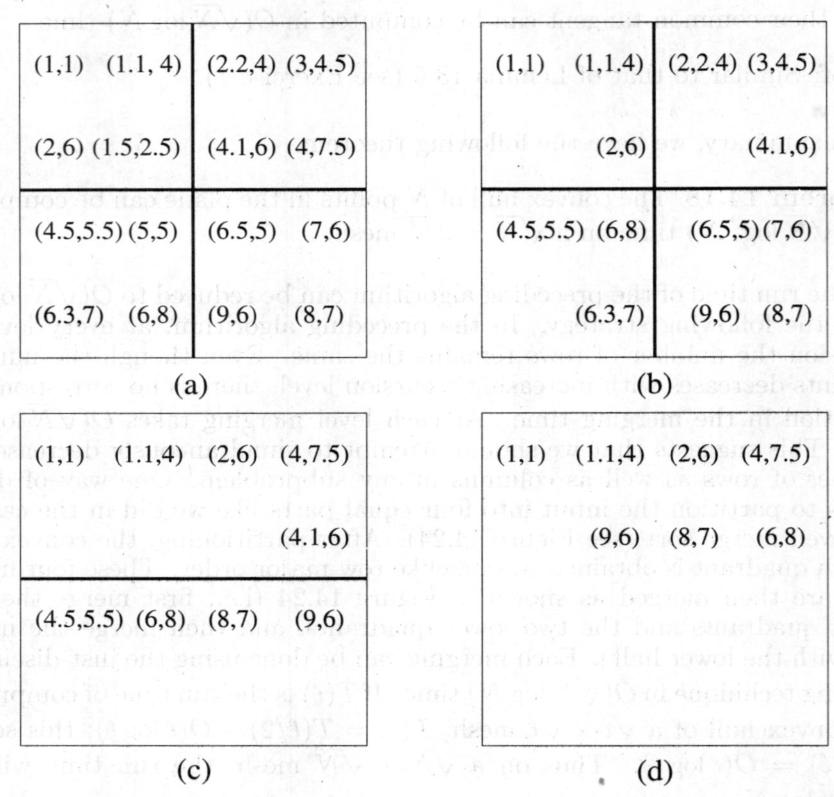

Figure 14.28 Upper-hull computation

hulls along the same lines as above. Consider the problem of merging H_1 and H_2 on an $\ell \times \ell$ mesh, where each hull is in snakelike row major order as shown in Figure 14.29. There are at most ℓ^2 points in all. Let $\langle u, v \rangle$ be the tangent. Algorithm 14.9 describes the algorithm in detail.

Let $M(\ell)$ be the run time of Algorithm 14.9. In step 1, elimination is done by broadcasting p so that processors that have a point to be eliminated will not participate in the future. Step 1 takes $O(\ell)$ time. So does step 2. Rearranging in step 3 can be done as follows. First perform a prefix sums operation to determine the address of each surviving point in the $\frac{\ell}{2} \times \frac{\ell}{2}$ submesh. Then route the points to their actual destinations. This routing and hence step 3 take $\widetilde{O}(\ell)$ time. Step 4 takes $M(\ell/2)$ time. In summary,

Step 0. If $\ell = 1$, u is the leftmost point and v is the rightmost point.

Step 1. Let p be the middle point of H_1. Find the point q of tangent of p with H_2 in $O(\ell)$ time. Now decide in $O(1)$ time whether u is to the left of, to the right of, or equal to p. As a result eliminate one half of H_1 that does not contain u. Similarly eliminate one half of H_2.

Step 2. Do step 2 one more time so that at the end only a quarter of each of H_1 and H_2 remains.

Step 3. Now rearrange the remaining points of H_1 and H_2 so they occupy a submesh of size $\frac{\ell}{2} \times \frac{\ell}{2}$ in the same order as in Figure 14.29.

Step 4. Recursively work on the submesh to determine u and v.

Algorithm 14.9 Merging two upper hulls in $\widetilde{O}(\ell)$ time

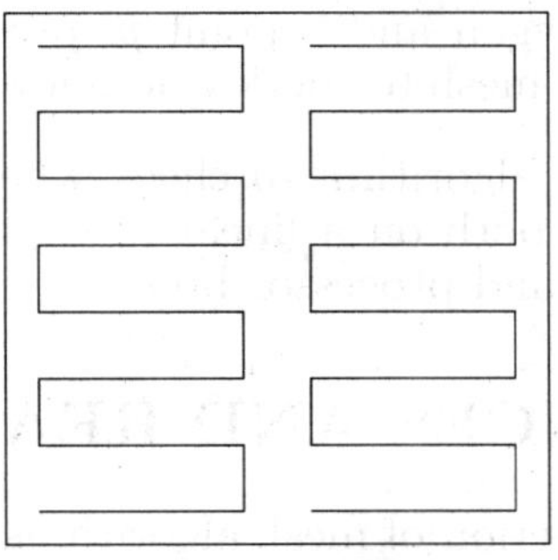

Figure 14.29 Merging two upper hulls

we have

$$M(\ell) = M\left(\frac{\ell}{2}\right) + \widetilde{O}(\ell)$$

whose solution is $M(\ell) = \widetilde{O}(\ell)$.

Lemma 14.12 Two upper hulls can be merged in $\widetilde{O}(\ell)$ time on an $\ell \times \ell$ mesh. □

As a corollary to Lemma 14.12, the recurrence relation for $T(\ell)$ (the time needed to find the convex hull on an $\ell \times \ell$ mesh) becomes

$$T(\ell) = T\left(\frac{\ell}{2}\right) + \widetilde{O}(\ell)$$

which also solves to $T(\ell) = \widetilde{O}(\ell)$.

Theorem 14.19 The convex hull of n points on a $\sqrt{n} \times \sqrt{n}$ mesh can be computed in $\widetilde{O}(\sqrt{n})$ time. □

EXERCISES

1. Prove Lemma 14.11.
2. Show that the convex hull of n given points can be determined in $O(n)$ time on an n-processor linear array.
3. Present an $\widetilde{O}(\sqrt{n})$-time algorithm to compute the area of the convex hull of n given points on a $\sqrt{n} \times \sqrt{n}$ mesh.
4. Given a simple polygon and a point p, present an $O(\sqrt{n})$-time algorithm on a $\sqrt{n} \times \sqrt{n}$ mesh to check whether p is internal to the polygon.
5. Present an efficient algorithm to check whether any three of n given points are colinear both on a linear array and on a $\sqrt{n} \times \sqrt{n}$ mesh. What are the time and processor bounds?

14.9 REFERENCES AND READINGS

For a comprehensive collection of mesh algorithms see *Introduction to Parallel Algorithms and Architectures: Arrays-Trees-Hypercubes*, by T. Leighton, Morgan-Kaufmann, 1992.

Handbook of Parallel Algorithms, by S. Rajasekaran and J. Reif (editors), Chapman-Hall/CRC, 2008.

The three-phase randomized packet routing algorithm is due to "Universal schemes for parallel communication," by L. Valiant and G. Brebner, *Proceedings of the 13th Annual ACM Symposium on Theory of Computing*, 1981, pp. 263–277. Related randomized packet routing algorithms can be found in:

"Optimal routing algorithms for mesh-connected processor arrays," by S. Rajasekaran and T. Tsantilas, *Algorithmica* 8 (1992): 21–38.
"Randomised algorithms for packet routing on the mesh," by S. Rajasekaran, in *Advances in Parallel Algorithms*, edited by L. Kronsjo and D. Shumsherud-din, Blackwell, 1992, pp. 277–301.

There exist optimal deterministic algorithms for packet routing on the mesh. See for example:
"Parallel permutation and sorting algorithms and a generalized interconnection network," by D. Nassimi and S. Sahni, *Journal of the ACM* 29, no. 3 (1982): 642–667.
"A $2n - 2$ step algorithm for routing in an $n \times n$ mesh," by T. Leighton, F. Makedon, and I. Tollis, *Proceedings of the ACM Symposium on Parallel Algorithms and Architectures*, 1989, pp. 328–335.
"Constant queue routing on a mesh," by S. Rajasekaran and R. Overholt, *Journal of Parallel and Distributed Computing* 15 (1992): 160–166.

Sparse enumeration sort was introduced by D. Nassimi and S. Sahni.

The randomized and deterministic selection algorithms presented in this chapter can be found in "Unifying themes for network selection," by S. Rajasekaran, W. Chen, and S. Yooseph, *Proceedings of the Fifth International Symposium on Algorithms and Computation*, August 1994.

For a comprehensive coverage of sorting and selection algorithms see "Sorting and selection on interconnection networks," by S. Rajasekaran, *DIMACS Series in Discrete Mathematics and Theoretical Computer Science* 21, 1995: 275–296.

The Shearsort algorithm was independently presented in:
"Some parallel sorts on a mesh-connected processor array and their time efficiency," by K. Sado and Y. Igarashi, *Journal of Parallel and Distributed Computing* 3 (1986): 398–410.
"Shear-sort: A true two-dimensional sorting technique for VLSI networks," by I. Scherson, S. Sen, and A. Shamir, *Proceedings of the International Conference on Parallel Processing*, 1986, pp. 903–908.

The odd-even merge sort on the mesh is based on "Sorting on a mesh-connected parallel computer," by C. Thompson and H. Kung. *Communications of the ACM* 20, no. 4 (1977): 263–271. For more on sorting algorithms on the mesh see:
"Randomized sorting and selection on mesh-connected processor arrays," by C. Kaklamanis, D. Krizanc, L. Narayanan, and T. Tsantilas, *Proceedings of the ACM Symposium on Parallel Algorithms and Architectures*, 1991.
"Block gossiping on grids and tori: Deterministic sorting and routing match the bisection bound," by M. Kunde, *Proceedings of the First Annual Euro-*

pean Symposium on Algorithms, 1993, pp. 272–283.
M. Kaufmann, J. Sibeyn, and T. Suel, "Derandomizing algorithms for routing and sorting on meshes," *Proceedings of the Symposium on Discrete Algorithms*, 1994, pp. 669–679.

Mesh algorithms for various graph problems can be found in:

"Solving tree problems on a mesh-connected processor array," by M. Atallah and S. Hambrusch, *Information and Computation* 69 (1986): 168–187.
"Graph problems on a mesh-connected processor array," by M. Atallah and S. Kosaraju, *Journal of the ACM* 31, no. 3 (1984): 649–667.

Optimal algorithms for convex hull and related problems can be seen in:

"Finding connected components and connected ones on a mesh-connected parallel computer," by D. Nassimi and S. Sahni, *SIAM Journal on Computing* 9, no. 4 (1980): 744–757.
"Mesh computer algorithms for computational geometry," by R. Miller and Q. Stout, *IEEE Transactions on Computers* 38, no. 3 (1989): 321–340.
"Parallel geometric algorithms on a mesh-connected computer," by C. Jeong and D. Lee, *Algorithmica* 5, no. 2 (1990): 155–177.
"Optimal mesh algorithms for the Voronoi diagram of line segments and motion planning in the plane," by S. Rajasekaran and S. Ramaswami, *Journal of Parallel and Distributed Computing* 26, no. 1 (1995): 99–115.

14.10 ADDITIONAL EXERCISES

1. A *binary tree of processors*, or simply a binary tree, is a complete binary tree in which there is a processor at each node and the links correspond to communication links. Figure 14.30 shows a 4-leaf binary tree. The inputs to the binary tree are usually at the leaves. An n-leaf binary tree has $2n - 1$ processors and is of height $\log n$. If there is a number at each leaf, we can compute the sum of these numbers as follows. Each leaf starts by sending its number to its parent. Every internal processor, on receipt of two numbers from below, adds them and sends the result to its parent. Using this simple strategy, the sum is at the root after $\log n$ steps.

   You are required to solve the prefix computation problem on an n-leaf binary tree. There is an element to begin with at each leaf processor. The prefixes should also be output from the leaves. Show how you perform this task in $O(\log n)$ time.

2. Assume that each leaf of an n-leaf binary tree (see Exercise 1) has $\log n$ elements to begin with. The problem is to compute the prefixes

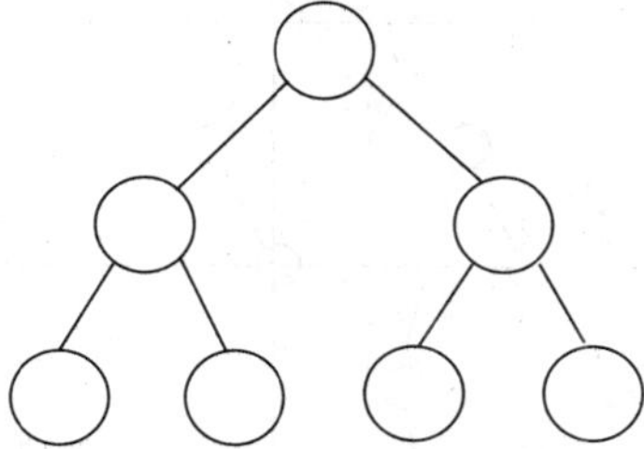

Figure 14.30 A binary tree of processors

of these $n \log n$ elements. Present an $O(\log n)$ time algorithm for this problem. Note that such an algorithm is work-optimal.

3. There are $\frac{n}{\log n}$ keys at each leaf of a $(\log n)$-leaf binary tree (see Exercise 1). Show how to sort these keys in $O(n)$ time. You can store $O(n)$ items at any processor.

4. There is a data item at each leaf of an n-leaf binary tree (see Exercise 1). The goal is to interchange the data items in the left half with those in the right half. Present an $O(n)$ time algorithm. Is it possible to devise a $o(n)$ time algorithm for this problem?

5. Present an efficient algorithm to sort an n-leaf binary tree (see Exercise 1), in which each leaf is input a single key.

6. A *mesh of trees* is a $\sqrt{p} \times \sqrt{p}$ mesh in which each row and each column has an associated binary tree. The row or column processors form the leaves of the corresponding binary trees. Figure 14.31 is a 4×4 mesh of trees in which only the column trees are shown. In a $\sqrt{p} \times \sqrt{p}$ mesh of trees, there are $\sqrt{p}$ data items in the first row. They have to be routed according to an arbitrary permutation π and the result stored in the same row. Present an $O(\log p)$ time algorithm for this problem.

7. There is a key at each processor in the first row of a $\sqrt{p} \times \sqrt{p}$ mesh of trees (see Exercise 6). Present an $O(\log p)$-time algorithm to sort these keys.

8. The first row of a $\sqrt{p} \times \sqrt{p}$ mesh of trees (see Exercise 6) has $\sqrt{p}$ points in the plane (one point per processor). Show how you compute the convex hull of these points in $O(\log p)$ time.

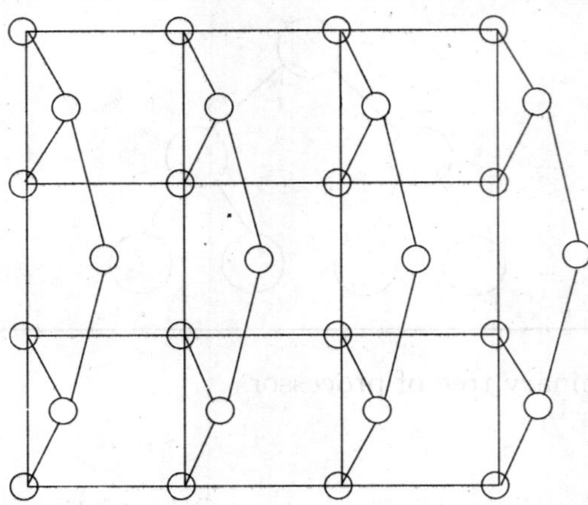

Figure 14.31 A mesh of trees (only column trees are shown)

9. Every processor of a $\sqrt{p} \times \sqrt{p}$ mesh of trees (see Exercise 6) has a data item. The goal is to perform a prefix computation on the whole mesh (in snakelike row major order). Show that this can be done in $O(\log p)$ time.

10. Show that the FFT (see Section 9.3) of a vector of length n can be computed in $O(\log n)$ time on an $n \times n$ mesh of trees (see Exercise 6).

11. Prove that an $n \times n$ matrix can be multiplied with an $n \times 1$ vector in $O(\log n)$ time on an $n \times n$ mesh of trees (see Exercise 6).

12. The problem of *one-dimensional convolution* takes as input two arrays $I[0:n-1]$ and $T[0:m-1]$. The output is another array $C[0:n-1]$, where $C[i] = \sum_{k=0}^{m-1} I[(i+k) \bmod n]T[k]$, for $0 \leq i < n$. Employ an n-processor mesh to solve this problem. Assume that each processor has $O(m)$ local memory. What is the run time of your algorithm?

13. Solve Exercise 12 on an n-processor mesh of trees (see Exercise 6).

14. Solve Exercise 12 on an n-leaf binary tree (see Exercise 1).

15. The problem of *template matching* takes as input two matrices $I[0:n-1, 0:n-1]$ and $T[0:m-1, 0:m-1]$. The output is a matrix $C[0:n-1, 0:n-1]$, where

$$C[i,j] = \sum_{k=0}^{m-1} \sum_{l=0}^{m-1} I[(i+k) \bmod n, (j+l) \bmod n]T[k,l]$$

for $0 \leq i, j < n$. Present an n^2-processor mesh algorithm for template matching. Assume that each processor has $O(m)$ memory. What is the time bound of your algorithm?

16. Solve Exercise 15 on an n^2-processor mesh of trees (see Exercise 6).

17. Solve Exercise 15 on an n^2-leaf binary tree (see Exercise 1).

Chapter 15

HYPERCUBE ALGORITHMS

15.1 COMPUTATIONAL MODEL

15.1.1 The Hypercube

A hypercube of dimension d, denoted $\mathcal{H}_d$, has $p = 2^d$ processors. Each processor in $\mathcal{H}_d$ can be labeled with a d-bit binary number. For example, the processors of $\mathcal{H}_3$ can be labeled with $000, 001, 010, 011, 100, 101, 110$, and 111 (see Figure 15.1). We use the same symbol to denote a processor and its label. If v is a d-bit binary number, then the *first bit* of v is the most significant bit of v. The *second bit* of v is the next-most significant bit. And so on. The *dth bit* of v is its least significant bit. Let $v^{(i)}$ stand for the binary number that differs from v only in the ith bit. For example, if v is 1011, then $v^{(3)}$ is 1001. A four-dimensional hypercube is shown in Figure 15.2.

Any processor v in $\mathcal{H}_d$ is connected only to the processors $v^{(i)}$ for $i = 1, 2, \ldots, d$. In $\mathcal{H}_3$, for instance, the processor 110 is connected to the processors $010, 100$, and 111 (see Figure 15.1). The link $(v, v^{(i)})$ is called a *level i link.* The link $(101, 001)$ is a level one link. Since each processor in $\mathcal{H}_d$ is connected to exactly d other processors, the degree of $\mathcal{H}_d$ is d. The Hamming distance between two binary numbers u and v is defined to be the number of bit positions in which they differ. For any two processors u and v in a hypercube, there is a path between them of length equal to the *Hamming distance* between u and v. For example, there is a path of length 4 between the processors 10110 and 01101 in a five-dimensional hypercube: 10110, 00110, 01110, 01100, 01101. In general if u and v are any two processors, a path between them (of length equal to their Hamming distance) can be determined in the following way. Let $i_1, i_2, \ldots, i_k$ be the bit positions (in increasing order) in which u and v differ. Then, the following path exists

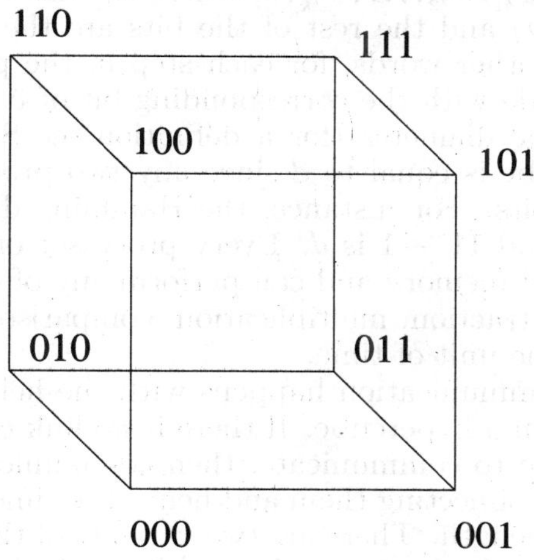

Figure 15.1 A three-dimensional hypercube

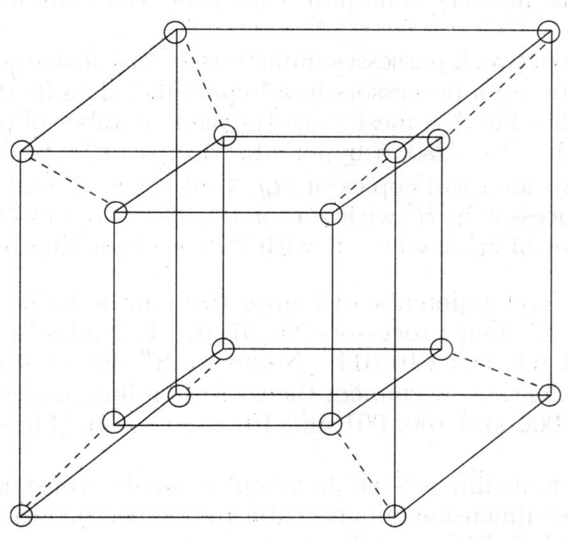

Figure 15.2 A hypercube of dimension four

between u and v: $u, w_{i_1}, w_{i_2}, \ldots, w_{i_k}, v$, where w_{i_j} has the same bits as v in positions 1 through i_j and the rest of the bits are the same as those of u (for $1 \leq j \leq k$). In other words, for each step in the path, one bit of u is "corrected" to coincide with the corresponding bit of v.

It follows that the diameter (for a definition see Section 14.3) of a d-dimensional hypercube is equal to d since any two processors u and v can differ in at most d bits. For instance, the Hamming distance between the processors $00\cdots 0$ and $11\cdots 1$ is d. Every processor of the hypercube is a RAM with some local memory and can perform any of the basic operations such as addition, subtraction, multiplication, comparison, local memory access, and so on, in one unit of time.

Interprocessor communication happens with the help of communication links (that is, links) in a hypercube. If there is no link connecting two given processors that desire to communicate, then communication is enabled using any of the paths connecting them and hence the time for communication depends on the path length. There are two variants of the hypercube. In the first version, known as the *sequential hypercube* or *single-port hypercube*, it is assumed that in one unit of time a processor can communicate with only one of its neighbors. In contrast, the second version, known as the *parallel hypercube* or *multiport hypercube*, assumes that in one unit of time a processor can communicate with all its d neighbors. In our discussion, we indicate the version used when needed. Both these versions assume synchronous computations; that is, in every time unit, each processor completes its intended task.

A hypercube network possesses numerous special features. One is its low diameter. If there are p processors in a hypercube, then its diameter is only $\log p$. On the other hand, a mesh with the same number of processors has a diameter of $2(\sqrt{p}-1)$. Also, a hypercube $\mathcal{H}_{d+1}$ can be built recursively as follows. Take two identical copies of $\mathcal{H}_d$. Call them $\mathcal{H}'$ and $\mathcal{H}''$. Prefix the label of each processor in $\mathcal{H}'$ with zero and prefix those of $\mathcal{H}''$ with ones. If v is any processor of $\mathcal{H}'$, connect it with its corresponding processor in $\mathcal{H}''$.

Example 15.1 The hypercube of Figure 15.1 can be built from two copies of $\mathcal{H}_2$. Each $\mathcal{H}_2$ has four processors, $00, 01, 10, 11$. Nodes in $\mathcal{H}'$ are prefixed with zero to get $000, 001, 010, 011$. Nodes in $\mathcal{H}''$ are prefixed with one to get $100, 101, 110, 111$. Now connect the corresponding processors with links; that is, connect 000 and 100, 001 and 101, and so on. The result is Figure 15.1.

Similarly, a four-dimensional hypercube can be constructed from two copies of a three-dimensional hypercube by connecting the corresponding nodes with links (see Figure 15.2). And so on. □

Likewise, $\mathcal{H}_d$ has two copies of $\mathcal{H}_{d-1}$ (for $d \geq 1$). For example, all the processors in $\mathcal{H}_d$ whose first bit is zero form a subcube $\mathcal{H}_{d-1}$ (ignoring all the other processors and links from them). Also, all the processors whose first bit is one form a $\mathcal{H}_{d-1}$. How about all the processors whose qth bit is zero (or one), for some $1 \leq q \leq d$? They also form a $\mathcal{H}_{d-1}$! Equivalently, if we remove all the level i links (for some $1 \leq i \leq d$), we end up with two copies of $\mathcal{H}_{d-1}$. In general if we fix some i bits and vary the remaining bits of a d-bit number, the corresponding processors form a subcube $\mathcal{H}_{d-i}$ in $\mathcal{H}_d$.

15.1.2 The Butterfly Network

The butterfly network is closely related to the hypercube. Algorithms designed for the butterfly can easily be adapted for the hypercube and vice versa. In fact, for several problems it is easier to develop algorithms for the butterfly and then adapt them to the hypercube.

A d-dimensional butterfly, denoted $\mathcal{B}_d$, has $p = (d+1)2^d$ processors and $d2^{d+1}$ links. Each processor in $\mathcal{B}_d$ can be represented as a tuple $\langle r, \ell \rangle$, where $0 \leq r \leq 2^d - 1$ and $0 \leq \ell \leq d$. The variable r is called the *row* of the processor and ℓ is called the *level* of the processor. A processor $u = \langle r, \ell \rangle$ in $\mathcal{B}_d$ is connected to two processors in level $\ell + 1$ (for $0 \leq \ell < d$). These two processors are $v = \langle r, \ell + 1 \rangle$ and $w = \langle r^{(\ell+1)}, \ell + 1 \rangle$. The row number of v is the same as that of u and the row number of w differs from r only in the $(\ell + 1)$th bit. Both v and w are in level $\ell + 1$. The link (u, v) is known as the *direct link* and the link (u, w) is known as the *cross link*. Both of these links are called *level* $(\ell + 1)$ *links*.

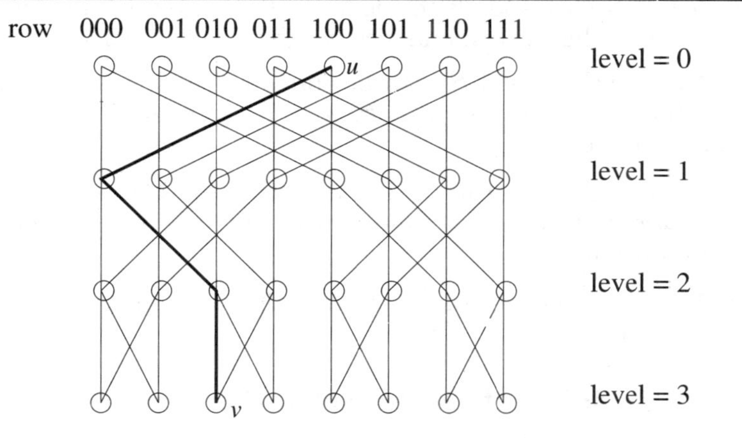

Figure 15.3 A three-dimensional butterfly

$\mathcal{B}_3$ is shown in Figure 15.3. In Figure 15.3, for example, the processor $\langle 011, 1 \rangle$ is connected to the processors $\langle 011, 2 \rangle$ and $\langle 001, 2 \rangle$. Since each processor is connected to at most four other processors, the degree of $\mathcal{B}_d$ (for any d) is four and hence is independent of the size (p) of the network. If u is any processor in level 0 and v is any processor in level d, there is a unique path between u and v of length d. Let $u = \langle r, 0 \rangle$ and $v = \langle r', d \rangle$. The unique path is $\langle r, 0 \rangle$, $\langle r_1, 1 \rangle$, $\langle r_2, 2 \rangle$, $\ldots$, $\langle r', d \rangle$, where r_1 has the same first bit as r', r_2 has the same first and second bits as r', and so on. Note that such a path exists by the definition of the butterfly links. We refer to such paths as *greedy paths.*

Example 15.2 In Figure 15.3, let $u = \langle 100, 0 \rangle$ and $v = \langle 010, 3 \rangle$. Then, the unique path between u and v is $\langle 100, 0 \rangle$, $\langle 000, 1 \rangle$, $\langle 010, 2 \rangle$, $\langle 010, 3 \rangle$. □

As a consequence, it follows that the distance between any two processors in $\mathcal{B}_d$ is $\leq 2d$. So, the diameter of $\mathcal{B}_d$ is $2d$. A butterfly also has a recursive structure like that of a hypercube. For example, if the level 0 processors and incident links are removed from $\mathcal{B}_d$, two copies of $\mathcal{B}_{d-1}$ result. In Figure 15.3, removal of level zero processors and links yields two copies of $\mathcal{B}_2$.

There is a close relationship between $\mathcal{H}_d$ and $\mathcal{B}_d$. If each row of a $\mathcal{B}_d$ is collapsed into a single processor preserving all the links, then the resultant graph is $\mathcal{H}_d$. In Figure 15.3, collapsing each row into a single processor, we get eight processors. These processors can simply be labeled with their row numbers. When this is done, the collapsed processor 110, for example, has links to the processors 010, 100, and 111, which are exactly the same as in a hypercube. Of course now there can be multiple links between any two processors; we keep only one copy. Also, the cross link from any processor $\langle r, \ell \rangle$ to level $\ell + 1$ corresponds to the level $(\ell + 1)$ link of r in the hypercube.

As a result of this correspondence, we get the following lemma.

Lemma 15.1 Each step of $\mathcal{B}_d$ can be simulated in one step on the parallel version of $\mathcal{H}_d$. Also each step of $\mathcal{B}_d$ can be simulated in d steps on the sequential version of $\mathcal{H}_d$. □

Definition 15.1 Any algorithm that runs on $\mathcal{B}_d$ is said to be a *normal butterfly algorithm* if at any given time, processors in only one level participate in the computation. □

Lemma 15.2 A single step of any normal algorithm on $\mathcal{B}_d$ can be simulated in one step on the sequential $\mathcal{H}_d$. □

15.1.3 Embedding of Other Networks

Many networks such as the ring, mesh, and binary tree can be shown to be subgraphs of a hypercube. A general mapping of one network into another is called an *embedding*. More precisely, if $G(V_1, E_1)$ and $H(V_2, E_2)$ are any two connected networks, an embedding of G into H is a mapping of V_1 into V_2. Embedding results are important, for instance, to simulate one network on another. Using an embedding of G into H, an algorithm designed for G can be simulated on H.

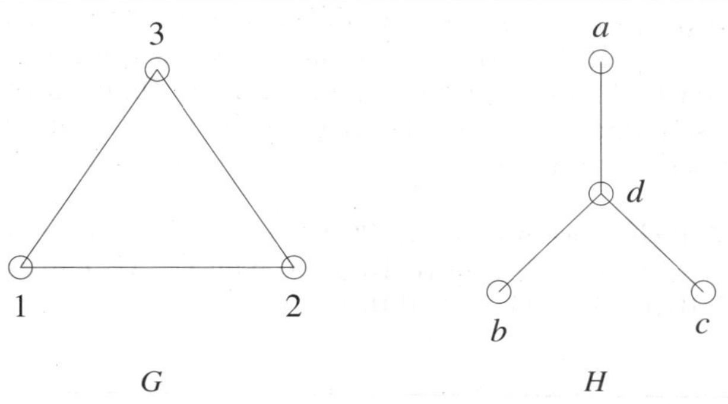

Figure 15.4 Embedding – an example

Example 15.3 Referring to Figure 15.4, one possible mapping of the vertices of G into those of H is $1 \rightarrow b$, $2 \rightarrow c$, and $3 \rightarrow a$. With this mapping, the link $(1, 2)$ is mapped to the path $(b, d), (d, c)$. Similarly $(1, 3)$ is mapped to $(b, d), (d, a)$. And so on. □

Definition 15.2 The *expansion* of an embedding is defined to be $\frac{|V_2|}{|V_1|}$. The length of the longest path that any link of G is mapped to is called the *dilation*. The *congestion* of any link of H is defined to be the number of paths (corresponding to the links of G) that it is on. The congestion of the embedding is defined to be the maximum congestion of any link in H. □

Example 15.4 For the graphs of Figure 15.4, the expansion is $\frac{4}{3}$. The dilation is 2, since every link of G is mapped to a path of length 2 in H. The congestion of the link (b, d) is 2 since it is on the paths for the links $(1, 2)$ and $(1, 3)$. The congestion of every other link of H can also seen to be 2. So the congestion of the embedding is 2. □

Embedding of a ring

In this section we show that a ring with 2^d processors can be embedded in $\mathcal{H}_d$. Recall that the processors of $\mathcal{H}_d$ are labeled with d-bit binary numbers. If $0, 1, \ldots, 2^d - 1$ are the processors of the ring, processor 0 is mapped to the processor $00 \cdots 0$ of $\mathcal{H}_d$. The mappings for the other processors are obtained using the Gray code.

Definition 15.3 The Gray code of order k, denoted $\mathcal{G}_k$, defines an ordering among all the k-bit binary numbers. The Gray code $\mathcal{G}_1$ is defined as $0, 1$.

The Gray code $\mathcal{G}_k$ (for any $k > 1$) is defined recursively in terms of $\mathcal{G}_{k-1}$ as $0[\mathcal{G}_{k-1}], 1[\mathcal{G}_{k-1}]^r$. Here $0[\mathcal{G}_{k-1}]$ stands for the sequence of elements in $\mathcal{G}_{k-1}$ such that each element is prefixed with a zero. The expression $1[\mathcal{G}_{k-1}]^r$ stands for the sequence of elements in $\mathcal{G}_{k-1}$ in reverse order, where each element is prefixed with a one. □

Example 15.5 $0[\mathcal{G}_1]$ corresponds to $00, 01$ and $1[\mathcal{G}_1]^r$ corresponds to $11, 10$. Thus $\mathcal{G}_2$ is $00, 01, 11, 10$ (see Figure 15.5). Given $\mathcal{G}_2$, $\mathcal{G}_3$ can now be derived as $000, 001, 011, 010,\ 110, 111, 101, 100$, etc. □

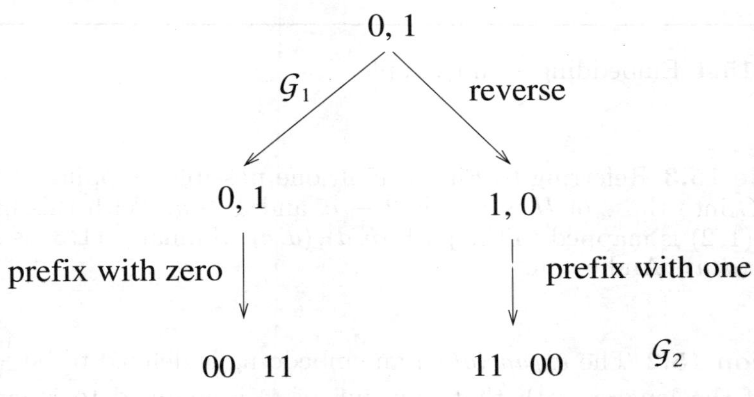

Figure 15.5 Construction of Gray codes – an example

One of the properties of $\mathcal{G}_k$ is that any two adjacent entries differ in only one bit. This means that $\mathcal{G}_d$ is an ordering of all the processors of $\mathcal{H}_d$ such that any two adjacent processors are connected by a link. Let $g(i, k)$ denote the ith element of $\mathcal{G}_k$. Then, map processor i $(0 \leq i \leq 2^d - 1)$ of the ring to processor $g(i, d)$ of $\mathcal{H}_d$. Such an embedding has an expansion, dilation, and congestion of one. For a ring of eight processors, the embedding of the ring into $\mathcal{H}_3$ is given by $0 \rightarrow 000$, $1 \rightarrow 001$, $2 \rightarrow 011$, $3 \rightarrow 010$, $4 \rightarrow 110$, $5 \rightarrow 111$, $6 \rightarrow 101$, and $7 \rightarrow 100$.

Lemma 15.3 A ring with 2^d processors can be embedded into $\mathcal{H}_d$ so as to have an expansion, dilation, and congestion of one. □

Embedding of a torus

Let $\mathcal{M}$ be a torus (for a definition see Section 14.2, Exercise 12) of size $2^r \times 2^c$. We show that there is an embedding of $\mathcal{M}$ into $\mathcal{H}_{r+c}$ whose expansion, dilation, and congestion are all one. This follows as a corollary to Lemma 15.3. There are 2^r rows and 2^c columns in $\mathcal{M}$. As has been mentioned before, if we fix any q bits of a d-bit number and vary the other bits, the resultant numbers describe processors of a subcube $\mathcal{H}_{d-q}$ of $\mathcal{H}_d$.

Therefore, if we fix the r most-significant bits (MSBs) of an $(r+c)$-bit binary number and vary the other bits, 2^c numbers arise which correspond to a subcube $\mathcal{H}_c$. In accordance with Lemma 15.3, this subcube has a ring embedded in it. For each possible choice for the r MSBs, there is a corresponding $\mathcal{H}_c$. A row of $\mathcal{M}$ gets mapped to one such $\mathcal{H}_c$. In particular, row i gets mapped to that subcube $\mathcal{H}_c$ all of whose processors have $g(i,r)$ for their r MSBs. This mapping of a ring into $\mathcal{H}_c$ is as described in the proof of Lemma 15.3. In other words, if (i,j) is any processor of $\mathcal{M}$, it is mapped to the processor $g(i,r)g(j,c)$.

Since all the processors in any given row of $\mathcal{M}$ are mapped into a $\mathcal{H}_c$, in accordance with Lemma 15.3, the mapped processors and links form a ring. Likewise, all the processors in any column of $\mathcal{M}$ get mapped to a $\mathcal{H}_r$, and hence the corresponding processors and links of $\mathcal{H}_r$ also form a ring. Therefore, this embedding results in an expansion, dilation, and congestion of one.

Lemma 15.4 A $2^r \times 2^c$ mesh can be embedded into $\mathcal{H}_{r+c}$ so that the expansion, dilation, and congestion are one. □

Example 15.6 Figure 15.6 shows an embedding of a 2×4 torus into $\mathcal{H}_3$. For the torus there are two rows, namely, row 0 and row 1. There are four columns: $0, 1, 2$, and 3. For instance, the node $(1,2)$ of the torus (Figure 15.6(a)) is mapped to the node $g(1,1)g(2,2) = 111$ of the hypercube (Figure 15.6(b)). In the figure both $(1,2)$ and 111 are labeled g. □

Embedding of a binary tree

There are many ways in which a binary tree can be embedded into a hypercube. Here we show that a p-leaf full binary tree $\mathcal{T}$ (where $p = 2^d$ for some integer d) can be embedded into $\mathcal{H}_d$. Note that a p-leaf full binary tree has a total of $2p-1$ processors. Hence the mapping cannot be one-to-one. More than one processor of $\mathcal{T}$ may have to be mapped into the same processor of $\mathcal{H}_d$. If the tree leaves are $0, 1, \ldots, p-1$, then leaf i is mapped to the ith processor of $\mathcal{H}_d$. Each internal processor of $\mathcal{T}$ is mapped to the same processor of $\mathcal{H}_d$ as its leftmost descendant leaf; also Figure 15.7 shows the embedding of an eight-leaf binary tree. The label adjacent to each processor is the hypercube processor that it is mapped to.

The embedding just discussed could be used to simulate tree algorithms efficiently on a sequential hypercube. If any step of computation involves only one level of the tree, then this step can be simulated in one step on the hypercube.

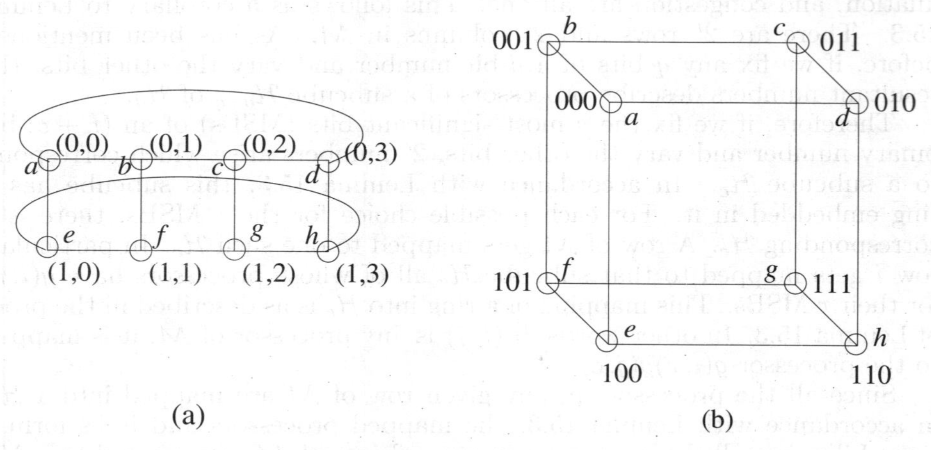

Figure 15.6 Embedding of a torus – an example

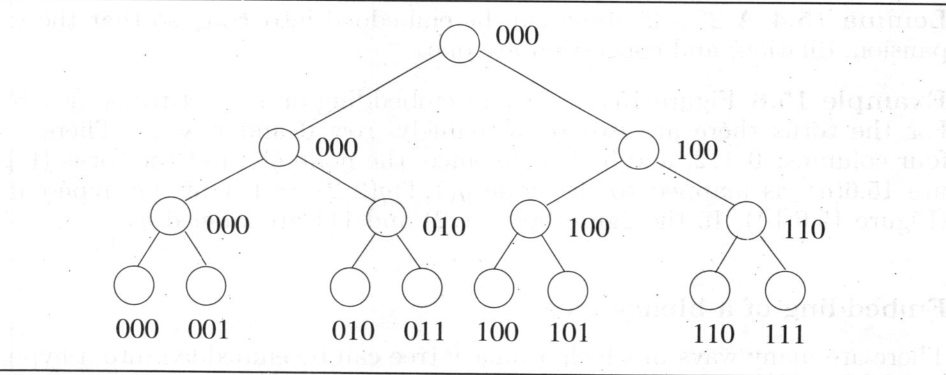

Figure 15.7 Embedding a binary tree into a hypercube

EXERCISES

1. How many links are there in $\mathcal{H}_d$?
2. What is the bisection width of $\mathcal{H}_d$?
3. Compute the bisection width of $\mathcal{B}_d$.
4. Derive the Gray codes $\mathcal{G}_4$ and $\mathcal{G}_5$.

15.2 PPR ROUTING

The problem of PPR was defined in Section 14.2 as: Each processor in the network is the origin of at most one packet and is the destination of at most one packet; send the packets to their destinations. In this section we develop PPR algorithms for $\mathcal{H}_d$.

15.2.1 A Greedy Algorithm

We consider the problem of routing on $\mathcal{B}_d$, where there is a packet at each processor of level 0. The destinations of the packets are in level d in such a way that the destination rows form a partial permutation of the origin rows. In $\mathcal{B}_3$, for instance, the origin rows could be all the rows and the destination rows could be $001, 000, 100, 111, 101, 010, 011, 110$. A greedy algorithm for routing any PPR is to let each packet use the greedy path between its origin and destination. The distance traveled by any packet is d using this algorithm. To analyze the run time of this algorithm, we only need to compute the maximum delay any packet suffers.

Let $u = \langle r, \ell \rangle$ be any processor in $\mathcal{B}_d$. Then there are $\leq 2^\ell$ packets that can potentially go through the processor u. This is because u has two neighbors in level $\ell - 1$, each one of which has two neighbors in level $\ell - 2$, and so on. As an example, the only packets that can go through the processor $\langle 011, 2 \rangle$ have origin rows $001, 011, 101$, and 111 (in Figure 15.3). Similarly, a packet that goes through u can reach only one of $2^{d-\ell}$ possible destinations. This implies that the maximum number of packets that can contend for any link in level ℓ is min $\{2^{\ell-1}, 2^{d-\ell}\}$. Let π be an arbitrary packet; π can only suffer a delay of $\leq$ min $\{2^{\ell-1}, 2^{d-\ell}\}$ in crossing a level ℓ link and has to cross a level ℓ link for $\ell = 1, 2, \ldots, d$. Thus the maximum delay the packet can suffer is $D = \sum_{\ell=1}^{d} \min \{2^{\ell-1}, 2^{d-\ell}\}$. Assume without loss of generality that d is even. Then, D can be rewritten as $D = \sum_{\ell=1}^{d/2} 2^{\ell-1} + \sum_{\ell=d/2+1}^{d} 2^{d-\ell}$ $= 2 * 2^{d/2} - 2 = O(2^{d/2})$. The value $O(2^{d/2})$ is also an upper bound on the queue length of the algorithm, since the number of packets going through any processor in level ℓ is $\leq$ min $\{2^\ell, 2^{d-\ell}\}$. The maximum of this number over all ℓ's is $2^{d/2}$.

Lemma 15.5 The greedy algorithm on $\mathcal{B}_d$ runs in $O(2^{d/2})$ time, the queue length being $O(2^{d/2})$. □

15.2.2 A Randomized Algorithm

We can improve the performance of the preceding greedy algorithm drastically using randomization. Recall that in the case of routing on the mesh, we were able to reduce the queue length of the greedy routing algorithm with the introduction of an additional phase where the packets are sent to random intermediate processors. The reason for sending packets to random processors is that with high probability a packet does not get to meet many other packets and hence the number of possible link contentions decreases. A similar strategy can be applied on the butterfly also.

The routing problem considered is the same as before; that is, there is a packet at each processor of level zero and the packets have destinations in level d. There are three phases in the algorithm. In the first phase each packet chooses a random intermediate destination in level d and goes there using the greedy path. In the second phase it goes to its actual destination row but in level zero. Finally, in the third phase, the packets go to their actual destinations in level d. In the third phase, each packet has to travel to level d using the direct link at each level. This takes d steps. Figure 15.8 illustrates these three phases. In this figure, r is a random node in level d. The variables u and v are the origin and destination of the packet under concern. The second phase is the reverse of phase 1, and hence it suffices to compute the run time of phase 1 to calculate the run time of the whole algorithm. The following lemma proves helpful in the analysis of phase 1.

Lemma 15.6 [Queueline lemma] Let $\mathcal{P}$ be the collection of paths to be taken by packets in a network. If the paths in $\mathcal{P}$ are *nonrepeating*, then the delay suffered by any packet π is no more than the number of distinct packets that *overlap* with π. A set of paths $\mathcal{P}$ is said to be *nonrepeating* if any two paths in $\mathcal{P}$ that meet, share some successive links, and diverge never meet again. For example, the greedy paths in $\mathcal{B}_d$ are nonrepeating. Two packets are said to *overlap* if they share at least one link in their paths.

Proof: Let π be an arbitrary packet. If π is delayed by each of the packets that overlap with π no more than once, the lemma is proven. Else, if a packet (call it q) overlapping with π delays π twice (say), then q has been delayed by another packet which also overlaps with π and which never gets to delay π. $\square$

Analysis of phase 1

Let π be an arbitrary packet. Also let e_i be the link that π traverses in level i, for $1 \leq i \leq d$. To compute the maximum delay that π can ever suffer, it suffices to compute the number of distinct packets that overlap with π (c.f. the queueline lemma). If n_i is the number of packets that have the link e_i in their paths, then $D = \sum_{i=1}^{d} n_i$ is an upper bound on the number of packets that overlap with π.

Consider the link e_i. The number of packets that can potentially go through this link is 2^{i-1} since there are only 2^{i-1} processors at level zero for which there are greedy paths through the link e_i. Each such packet has a probability of $\frac{1}{2^i}$ of going through e_i. This is because a packet starting at level zero can take either the direct link or the cross link, each with a

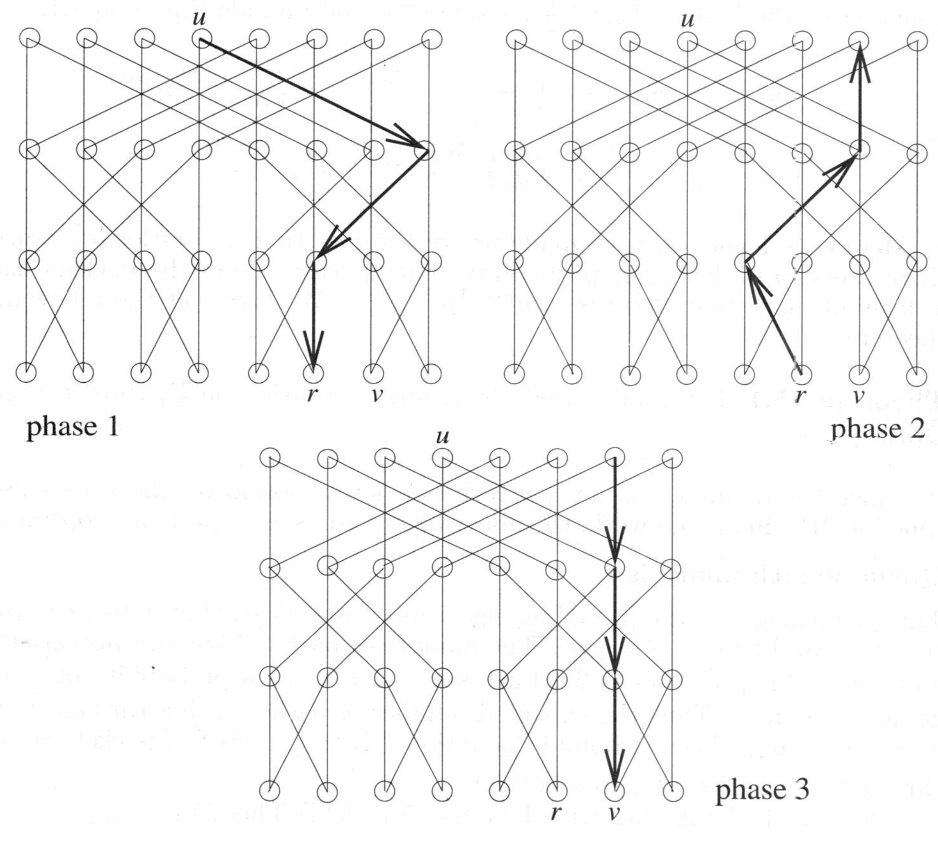

Figure 15.8 Three phases of randomized routing

probability of $\frac{1}{2}$. Once it reaches a processor at level one, it can again take either a cross link or a direct link with probability $\frac{1}{2}$. And so on. If the packet has to go through e_i, it should pick the right link at each level and there are i such links.

Therefore, the number n_i of packets that go though e_i is a binomial $B(2^{i-1}, \frac{1}{2^i})$. The expected value of this is $\frac{1}{2}$. Since the expectation of a sum is the sum of expectations, the expected value of $\sum_{i=1}^{d} n_i$ is $\frac{d}{2}$. Now we show that the total delay is $O(d)$ with high probability. The variable D is upper bounded by the binomial $B(d, \frac{1}{2})$. Using Chernoff bounds Equation 1.1,

$$\begin{aligned} \text{Prob.}[D > e\alpha d] &\leq \left(\frac{d/2}{e\alpha d}\right)^{e\alpha d} e^{e\alpha d - d/2} < \left(\frac{1}{2e\alpha}\right)^{e\alpha d} e^{e\alpha d} \\ &\leq \left(\frac{1}{2\alpha}\right)^{e\alpha d} < 2^{-e\alpha d} < p^{-\alpha-1} \end{aligned}$$

Here $\alpha \geq 1$ and we have made use of the fact that $d = \Theta(\log p)$. Since there are $< p$ packets, the probability that at least one of the packets has a delay of more than $2e\alpha d$ is $< p^{-\alpha-1}p = p^{-\alpha}$. We arrive at the following theorem.

Theorem 15.1 The randomized algorithm for routing on $\mathcal{B}_d$ runs in time $\widetilde{O}(d)$. □

Since the diameter of any network is a lower bound on the worst-case time for PPR in any network, the above algorithm is asymptotically optimal.

Queue length analysis

The queue length of the preceding algorithm is also $\widetilde{O}(d)$. Let v_i be any processor in level i (for $1 \leq i \leq d$). The number of packets that can potentially go though this processor is 2^i. Each such packet has a probability of $\frac{1}{2^i}$ of going through v_i. Thus the expected number of packets going through v_i is $2^i \frac{1}{2^i} = 1$. Using Chernoff bounds Equation 1.1, the number of packets going through v_i can be shown to be $\widetilde{O}(d)$.

Theorem 15.1 together with Lemma 15.1 yields Theorem 15.2.

Theorem 15.2 Any PPR can be routed on a parallel $\mathcal{H}_d$ in $\widetilde{O}(d)$ time, the queue length being $\widetilde{O}(d)$. □

EXERCISES

1. Lemma 15.5 proves an upper bound on the run time of the greedy algorithm on $\mathcal{B}_d$. Prove a matching lower bound. (*Hint:* Consider the bit reversal permutation. In this permutation if $b_1 b_2 \cdots b_d$ is the origin row of any packet, its destination row is $b_d b_{d-1} \cdots b_2 b_1$. For this permutation, compute the traffic through any level $\frac{d}{2}$ link.)

2. Assume that d packets originate from every processor of level zero in a $\mathcal{B}_d$. These packets are destined for level d with d packets per processor. Analyze the run time and queue length of the randomized routing algorithm on this problem.

3. If q packets originate from every processor of level zero and each packet has a random destination in level d of a $\mathcal{B}_d$, present a routing algorithm that runs in time $\widetilde{O}(q+d)$.

4. In a $\mathcal{B}_d$, at most one packet is destined for any processor in level d. The packet (if any) destined for processor i is at the beginning placed randomly in one of the processors of level zero (each such processor being equally likely). There are only a total of $(2^d)^\epsilon$ packets, for some constant $\epsilon > 0$. If the greedy algorithm is used to route, what is the worst-case run time? What is the queue length?

5. For the routing problem of Exercise 4, what is the run time and queue length if the randomized routing algorithm of Section 15.2.2 is employed?

15.3 FUNDAMENTAL ALGORITHMS

In this section we present hypercube algorithms for such basic operations as broadcasting, prefix sums computation, and data concentration. All these algorithms take $O(d)$ time on $\mathcal{H}_d$. Since the diameter is a lower bound on the solution time of any nontrivial problem in an interconnection network, these algorithms are asymptotically optimal.

15.3.1 Broadcasting

The problem of broadcasting in an interconnection network is to send a copy of a message that originates from a particular processor to a subset of other processors. Broadcasting is quite useful since it is widely used in the design of several algorithms. To perform broadcasting on $\mathcal{H}_d$, we employ the binary tree embedding (see Figure 15.7). Assume that the message M to be broadcast is at the root of the tree (i.e., at the processor $00\cdots0$). The root makes two copies of M and sends a copy to each of its two children in the tree. Each internal processor, on receipt of a message from its parent, makes two copies and sends a copy to each of its children. This proceeds until all the leaves have a copy of M. Note that the height of this tree is d. Thus in $O(d)$ steps, each leaf processor has a copy of M.

In this algorithm, computation happens only at one level of the tree at any given time. Thus each step of this algorithm can be run in one time unit on the sequential $\mathcal{H}_d$.

Lemma 15.7 Broadcasting of a message can be done on the sequential $\mathcal{H}_d$ in $\Theta(d)$ time. □

Example 15.7 Steps involved in broadcasting on a $\mathcal{H}_2$ are shown in Figure 15.9. The algorithm completes in two steps. □

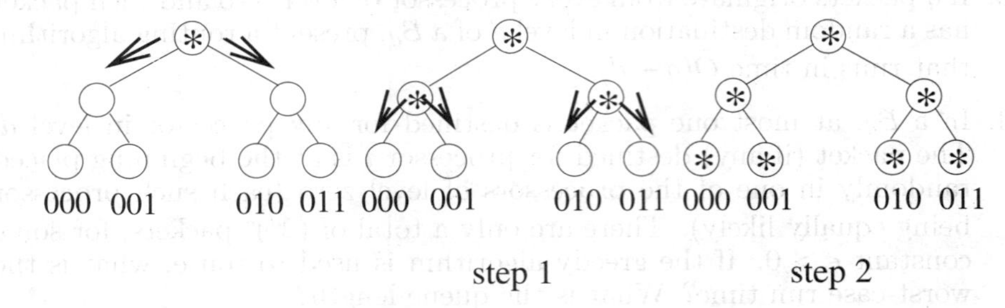

Figure 15.9 Broadcasting on a $\mathcal{H}_2$

15.3.2 Prefix Computation

We again make use of the binary tree embedding to perform prefix computation on $\mathcal{H}_d$. Let x_i be input at the ith leaf of a 2^d-leaf binary tree. There are two phases in the algorithm, namely, the *forward phase* and the *reverse phase*. In the forward (reverse) phase, data items flow from bottom to top (top to bottom). In each step of the algorithm only one level of the tree is active. Algorithm 15.1 gives the algorithm.

Example 15.8 Let Σ be the set of all integers and $\oplus$ be the usual addition. Consider a four-leaf binary tree with the following input: $5, 8, 1, 3$. Figure 15.10 shows the execution of every step of Algorithm 15.1. The datum inside each internal processor is its y-value. In step 1, the leaves send their data up (Figure 15.10(a)). In step 2, the internal processors send 13 and 4, respectively, storing 5 and 1 (Figure 15.10(b)) as their y-values. In step 3, the root sends 0 to the left and 13 to the right (Figure 15.10(c)). In the next step, the leftmost internal processor sends 0 to the left and 5 to the right. The rightmost internal processor sends 13 to the left and 14 to the right (Figure 15.10(d)). In step 5, the prefixes are computed at the leaves. □

In the forward phase of Algorithm 15.1, each internal processor computes the sum of all the data in its subtree. Let v be any internal processor and v' be the leftmost leaf in the subtree rooted at v. Then, in the reverse phase of the algorithm, the datum q received by v can be seen to be $\sum_{i=0}^{v'-1} x_i$. That is, q is the sum of all input data items to the left of v'. The correctness of the algorithm follows. Also both the forward phase and the reverse phase take d steps each. Moreover, at any given time unit, only one level of the tree is active. Thus each step of Algorithm 15.1 can be simulated in one step on $\mathcal{H}_d$.

Forward phase

> The leaves start by sending their data up to their parents. Each internal processor on receipt of two items (say y from its left child and z from its right child) computes $w = y \oplus z$, stores a copy of y and w, and sends w to its parent. At the end of d steps, each processor in the tree has stored in its memory the sum of all the data items in the subtree rooted at this processor. In particular, the root has the sum of all the elements in the tree.

Reverse phase

> The root starts by sending zero to its left child and its y to its right child. Each internal processor on receipt of a datum (say q) from its parent sends q to its left child and $q \oplus y$ to its right child. When the ith leaf gets a datum q from its parent, it computes $q \oplus x_i$ and stores it as the final result.

Algorithm 15.1 Prefix computation on a binary tree

Lemma 15.8 Prefix computation on a 2^d-leaf binary tree as well as $\mathcal{H}_d$ can be performed in $\Theta(d)$ time steps. □

Note: The problem of *data sum* is to compute $x_1 \oplus x_2 \oplus \cdots \oplus x_n$, given the x_i's. The forward phase of Algorithm 15.1 suffices to compute the data sum. Thus the time to compute the data sum is only one-half the time taken to compute all the prefixes.

15.3.3 Data Concentration

On $\mathcal{H}_d$ assume that there are $k < p$ data items distributed arbitrarily with at most one datum per processor. The problem of data concentration is to move the data into the processors $0, 1, \ldots, k-1$ of $\mathcal{H}_d$ one data item per processor. If we can compute the final destination address for each data item, then the randomized routing algorithm of Section 15.2 can be employed to route the packets in time $\widetilde{O}(d)$. Note that the randomized routing algorithm assumes the parallel hypercube.

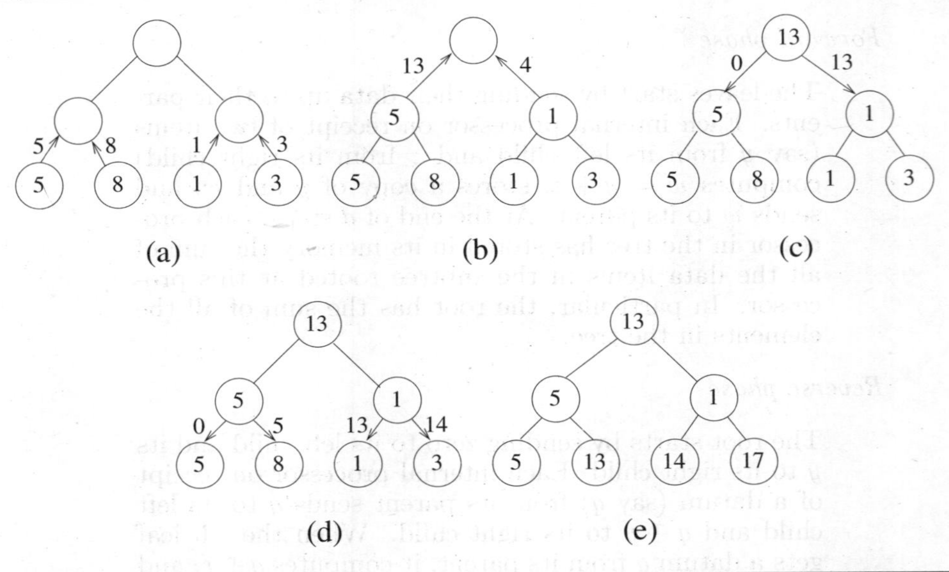

Figure 15.10 Prefix computation on a binary tree

There is a much simpler deterministic algorithm that runs in the same asymptotic time on the sequential hypercube. In fact we present a normal butterfly algorithm with the same run time and then invoke Lemma 15.2. We list some properties of the butterfly network that are needed in the analysis of the algorithm.

Property 1 If the level d processors and incident links are eliminated from $\mathcal{B}_d$, two copies of $\mathcal{B}_{d-1}$ result. As an example, in Figure 15.11, removal of level 3 processors and links results in two independent $\mathcal{B}_2$'s. One of these butterflies consists of only even rows (shown with thick lines) and the other consists of only odd rows. Call the former the even subbutterfly and the latter the odd subbutterfly.

Property 2 All processors at level d are connected by a full binary tree. For example, if we trace all the descendants of the processor $00 \cdots 0$ of level zero, the result is a full binary tree with the processors of level d as its leaves. In fact this is true for each processor at level zero.

Now we are ready to describe the algorithm for data concentration. Assume that the $k \leq 2^d$ data items are arbitrarily distributed in level d of $\mathcal{B}_d$.

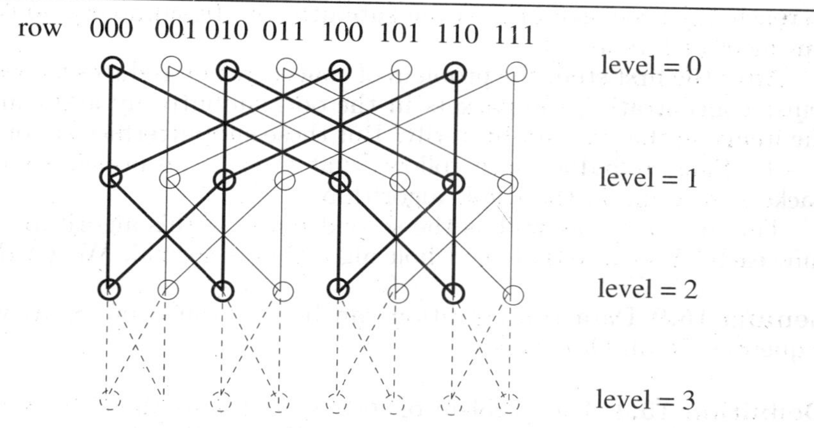

Figure 15.11 Removal of level d processors and links

At the end, these data items have to be moved to successive rows of level zero. For example, if there are five items in level 3 of $\mathcal{B}_3$, row 001 $\rightarrow a$ (this notation means that the processor $\langle 001, 3\rangle$ has the item a), row 010 $\rightarrow b$, row 100 $\rightarrow c$, row 101 $\rightarrow d$, and row 111 $\rightarrow e$, then at the end, these items will be at level zero and row 000 $\rightarrow a$, row 001 $\rightarrow b$, row 010 $\rightarrow c$, row 011 $\rightarrow d$, and row 100 $\rightarrow e$. There are two phases in the algorithm. In the first phase a prefix sums operation is performed to compute the destination address of each data item. In the second phase each packet is routed to its destination using the greedy path from its origin to its destination.

The prefix computation can be done using any of the trees mentioned in property 2 and Lemma 15.8. The prefix sums are computed on a sequence, $x_0, x_1, \ldots, x_{2^d-1}$, of zeros and ones. Leaf i sets x_i to one if it has a datum, otherwise to zero. In accordance with Lemma 15.8, this phase takes $O(d)$ time.

In the second phase packets are routed using the greedy paths. The claim is that no packet gets to meet any other and hence there is no possibility of link contentions. Consider the first step in which the packets travel from level d to level $d-1$. If two packets meet at level $d-1$, it could be only because they originated from two successive processors of level d. If two packets originate from two successive processors, then they are also destined for two successive processors. In particular, one has an odd row as its destination and the other has an even row. That is, one belongs to the odd subbutterfly and the other belongs to the even subbutterfly (see Figure 15.11). Without loss of generality assume that the packets that meet at level $d-1$ meet at a processor of the odd subbutterfly. Then it is impossible for one of these two to reach any processor of the even subbutterfly. In summary, no two packets can meet at level $d-1$.

After the first step, the problem of concentration reduces to two subproblems: concentrating the packets in the odd subbutterfly and concentrating the items on the even subbutterfly. But these subbutterflies are of dimension $d-1$. Thus by induction it follows that there is no possibility of any two packets' meeting in the whole algorithm.

The first phase as well as the second phase of this algorithm takes $\Theta(d)$ time each. Also note that the whole algorithm is normal. We get this lemma.

Lemma 15.9 Data concentration can be performed on $\mathcal{B}_d$ as well as the sequential $\mathcal{H}_d$ in $\Theta(d)$ time. □

Definition 15.4 The problem of *data spreading* is there are $k \leq 2^d$ items in successive processors at level zero of $\mathcal{B}_d$ (starting from row zero). The problem is to route them to some k specified processors at level d (one item per processor). The destinations can be arbitrary except that the order of the items must be preserved (that is, the packet originating from row zero must be the leftmost packet at level d, the packet originating from row one must be the next packet at level d, and so on). □

Definition 15.5 The problem of *monotone routing* is there are $k \leq 2^d$ packets arbitrarily distributed, at most one per processor, at level d of $\mathcal{B}_d$. They are destined for some k arbitrary processors at level zero such that the order of packets is preserved. □

Data spreading is just the reverse of data concentration. Also, monotone routing can be performed by performing a data concentration followed by a data spreading. Thus each can be done in time $\Theta(d)$.

Lemma 15.10 Data spreading as well as monotone routing takes $\Theta(d)$ time on $\mathcal{B}_d$ and the sequential $\mathcal{H}_d$. □

15.3.4 Sparse Enumeration Sort

The problem of sparse enumeration sort was introduced in Section 14.3.4. Let the sequence to be sorted on $\mathcal{H}_d$ be $X = k_0, k_2, \ldots, k_{\sqrt{p}-1}$, where $p = 2^d$. Without loss of generality assume that d is even. Let the input be given one key per processor in the subcube defined by fixing the first $\frac{d}{2}$ bits of a d-bit number to zeros (and varying the other bits). The sorted output also should appear in this subcube one key per processor.

Let v be any processor of $\mathcal{H}_d$. Its label is a d-bit binary number. The same label can be thought of as a tuple $\langle i, j\rangle$, where i is the first $\frac{d}{2}$ bits and j is the next $\frac{d}{2}$ bits. All processors whose first $\frac{d}{2}$ bits are the same and equal to i form a $\mathcal{H}_{d/2}$ (for each $0 \le i \le 2^{d/2} - 1$). Call this subcube row i. Also all processors of $\mathcal{H}_d$ whose last $\frac{d}{2}$ bits are the same and equal to j form a subcube $\mathcal{H}_{d/2}$. Call this subcube column j. The $\sqrt{p}$ numbers to be sorted are input in row zero. The output also should appear in row zero. To be specific, the key whose rank is r should be output at the processor $\langle 0, r-1 \rangle$ (for $1 \le r \le 2^{d/2}$).

To begin with, k_j is broadcast in column j (for $0 \le j \le \sqrt{p} - 1$) so that each row has a copy of X. In row i compute the rank of k_i. This is done by broadcasting k_i to all the processors in row i followed by a comparison of k_i with every key in the input and a data sum computation. The rank of k_i is broadcast to all the processors in row i. If the rank of k_i is r_i, then the processor $\langle i, r_i - 1 \rangle$ broadcasts k_i along the column $r_i - 1$ so that at the end of this broadcasting the processor $\langle 0, r_i - 1 \rangle$ gets the key that it is supposed to output.

The preceding algorithm is a collection of operations local to the columns or the rows. The operations involved are prefix computation, broadcast, and comparison each of which can be done in $O(d)$ time. Thus the whole algorithm runs in time $\Theta(d)$.

Lemma 15.11 Sparse enumeration sort can be completed in $\Theta(d)$ time on a sequential $\mathcal{H}_d$, where the number of keys to be sorted is at most $\sqrt{p}$. □

EXERCISES

1. The broadcasting algorithm of Section 15.3.1 assumes that the message originates from processor $00 \cdots 0$. How can you broadcast in $\Theta(d)$ time on $\mathcal{H}_d$ if the origin is an arbitrary processor?

2. Prove Lemma 15.10.

3. In a sequential $\mathcal{H}_d$, every processor has a packet to be sent to every other processor. Present an $O(pd)$ algorithm for this routing problem, where $p = 2^d$.

4. Present an $O(p)$-time algorithm for the problem of Exercise 3.

5. If we fix the first $d - k$ bits of a d-bit binary number and vary the last k bits, the corresponding processors form a subcube $\mathcal{H}_k$ in $\mathcal{H}_d$. There are 2^{d-k} such subcubes. There is a message in each of these subcubes. Present an algorithm for every subcube to broadcast its message locally (known as *window broadcast*). What is the run time of your algorithm?

6. The data concentration algorithm of Lemma 15.9 assumes that the data originate in level d. Present an $O(d)$ time algorithm for the case in which the data originate and are destined for level zero.

7. On a $\mathcal{B}_d$, there is a datum at each processor of level zero. The problem is to shift the data clockwise by i positions (for some given $1 \le i \le 2^d - 1$). For example, on a $\mathcal{B}_3$ let the distribution of data (starting from row zero) be $*, a, *, *, b, c, *, d$ ($*$ indicates the absence of a datum). If i is 3, the final distribution of data has to be $c, *, d, *, a, *, *, b$. Present an $O(d)$ algorithm for performing shifts.

8. The problem of *window shifts* is the same as shifts (see Exercise 7) except that window shifts are local to each subcube of size 2^k. Show how to perform window shifts in $O(k)$ time.

9. Give an $O(k)$ time algorithm for the *window prefix* computation problem, where prefix computation has to be done in each subcube $\mathcal{H}_k$.

10. On a $\mathcal{B}_d$, there are d items at each processor of level zero. Let the items at row i be $k_i^1, k_i^2, \ldots, k_i^d$. The problem is to compute d batches of prefixes. The first batch is on the sequence $k_0^1, k_1^1, \ldots, k_{2^d-1}^1$; the second batch is on the sequence $k_0^2, k_1^2, \ldots, k_{2^d-1}^2$; and so on. Show how to compute all these batch prefixes in $O(d)$ time. Is your algorithm normal?

11. Let $f(x) = a_{p-1}x^{p-1} + a_{p-2}x^{p-2} + \cdots + a_1 x + a_0$, where $p = 2^d$. Present an $O(d)$ time algorithm to evaluate the polynomial f at a given point y on $\mathcal{H}_d$. Assume that a_i is input at processor i.

12. Present $O(d)$-time algorithms for the segmented prefix problem (see Section 13.3, Exercise 5) on $\mathcal{H}_d$ and $\mathcal{B}_d$, where the input sequence is of length 2^d. On $\mathcal{B}_d$, data are input at level zero.

13. You are given a sequence A of $p = 2^d$ elements and an element x. The goal is to rearrange the elements of A so that all the elements of A that are $\le x$ appear first (in successive processors) followed by the rest of the elements. Present an $O(d)$ time algorithm on $\mathcal{H}_d$.

14. In a sequential $\mathcal{H}_d$, $2^{d/2}$ packets have to be routed. No more than one packet originates from any processor and no more than one packet is destined for any processor. Present an $O(d)$ time algorithm for this routing problem.

15. If T is the run time of any algorithm on an arbitrary 2^d-processor degree d network, show that the same algorithm can be simulated on $\mathcal{H}_d$ in time $O(Td)$.

15.4 SELECTION

Given a sequence of n keys and an integer i, $1 \leq i \leq n$, the problem of selection is to find the ith-smallest key from the sequence. We have seen sequential algorithms (Section 3.7), PRAM algorithms (Section 13.4), and mesh algorithms (Section 14.4) for selection. Like in the case of the mesh, we consider two different versions of selection on $\mathcal{H}_d$. In the first version we assume that $p = n$, p being the number of processors and n the number of input keys. In the second version we assume that $n > p$. It is necessary to handle the second version separately, since no general slow-down lemma (like the one for PRAMs) exists for $\mathcal{H}_d$.

15.4.1 A Randomized Algorithm for $n = p$ (*)

The work optimal algorithm (Algorithm 13.9) of Section 13.4.5 can be adapted to run optimally on $\mathcal{H}_d$ as well. There are $\widetilde{O}(1)$ stages in this algorithm. Step 1 of Algorithm 13.9 can be implemented on $\mathcal{H}_d$ in $O(1)$ time. In steps 2 and 5 prefix computations can be done in a total of $O(d)$ time (c.f. Lemma 15.8). Concentration in steps 3 and 6 takes $O(d)$ time each (see Lemma 15.9). Also, sparse enumeration sort takes the same time in steps 3 and 6 in accordance with Lemma 15.11. Selections in steps 4 and 6 take only $O(1)$ time each since these are selections from sorted sequences. Broadcasts in steps 2, 4, and 5 take $O(d)$ time each (c.f. Lemma 15.7). We arrive at this theorem.

Theorem 15.3 Selection from $n = p$ keys can be performed in $\widetilde{O}(d)$ time on $\mathcal{H}_d$. □

15.4.2 Randomized Selection for $n > p$ (*)

Now we consider the problem of selection when $n = p^c$ for some constant $c > 1$. Algorithm 13.9 can be used for this case as well with some modifications. The modifications are the same as the ones we did for the mesh (see Section 14.4.2). Each processor has $\frac{n}{p}$ keys to begin with. The condition for the **while** statement is changed to $(N > D)$ (where D is a constant). In step 1 a processor includes each one of its keys with probability $\frac{1}{N^{1-(1/3c)}}$. Thus this step now takes time $\frac{n}{p}$. Step 2 remains the same and still takes $O(d)$ time. The concentration and sparse enumeration sort of step 3 can be performed in time $O(d)$ (c.f. Lemmas 15.9 and 15.11). Step 4 takes $O(d)$ time and so do steps 5 and 6. Thus each stage takes time $O(\frac{n}{p} + d)$. There are only $\widetilde{O}(\log \log p)$ stages in the algorithm. The final result is this theorem.

Theorem 15.4 Selection from out of $n = p^c$ keys can be performed on $\mathcal{H}_d$ in time $\widetilde{O}\left((\frac{n}{p} + d) \log \log p\right)$. □

15.4.3 A Deterministic Algorithm for $n > p$

The deterministic mesh selection algorithm (Algorithm 14.5) can be adapted to a hypercube. The correctness of this algorithm has already been established in Section 14.4.3. We only have to compute the run time of this algorithm when implemented on a hypercube.

In step 0, the elements can be partitioned into $\log p$ parts in $\frac{n}{p} \log \log p$ time (see Section 13.4, Exercise 5) and the sorting can be done in time $O(\frac{n}{p} \log \frac{n}{p})$. Thus step 0 takes $\frac{n}{p}$ min $\{\log(n/p), \log\log p\}$ time. At the end of step 0, the keys in any processor have been partitioned into approximately $\log p$ nearly equal parts. Call each such part a block.

In step 1, we can find the median at any processor as follows. First determine the block the median is in and then perform an appropriate selection in that block (using Algorithm 3.19). The total time is $O(\frac{n}{p \log p})$.

In step 2, we can sort the medians to identify the weighted median. If $M'_1, M'_2, \ldots, M'_p$ is the sorted order of the medians, we need to identify j such that $\sum_{k=1}^{j} N'_k \geq \frac{N}{2}$ and $\sum_{k=1}^{j-1} N'_k < \frac{N}{2}$. Such a j can be computed with an additional prefix computation. Sorting can be done in $O(d^2)$ time (as is shown in Section 15.6). The prefix computation takes $O(d)$ time (see Lemma 15.8). Thus M, the weighted median, can be identified in $O(d^2)$ time.

In step 3, each processor can identify the number of remaining keys in its queue and then all the processors can perform a prefix sums computation. Therefore, this step takes $O(\frac{n}{p \log p} + d)$ time.

In step 4, the appropriate keys in any processor can be eliminated as follows. First identify the block B that M falls in. This can be done in $O(\log p)$ time. After this, compare M with the elements of block B to determine the keys to be eliminated. If $i > r_M$ $(i \leq r_M)$, all blocks to the left (right) of B are eliminated en masse. The total time needed is $O(\log p + \frac{n}{p \log p})$, which is $O(\frac{n}{p \log p})$ since $n = p^c$ for some constant $c > 1$.

Step 5 takes $O(d)$ time as it involves a prefix computation and a broadcast.

The broadcasting in steps 2, 3, and 4 takes $O(d)$ time each (c.f. Lemma 15.7). Thus each run of the **while** loop takes $O(\frac{n}{p \log p} + d^2)$ time. (Note that $d = \log p$.) The **while** loop is executed $O(\log n)$ times (see the proof of Theorem 14.8). Thus we get the following theorem (assuming that $n = p^c$ and hence $\log n$ is asymptotically the same as $\log p$).

Theorem 15.5 Selection on $\mathcal{H}_d$ can be performed in time $O(\frac{n}{p} \log \log p + d^2 \log n)$. □

Example 15.9 On a $\mathcal{H}_3$, let each processor have five keys to begin with. Consider the selection problem in which $i = 32$. The input keys are shown in Figure 15.12. For simplicity neglect step 0 of Algorithm 14.3; that is, assume that the parts are of size 1.

Processor	000	001	010	011	100	101	110	111
	5	20	18	35	63	21	62	11
	10	15	24	42	71	9	51	28
	6	7	12	3	1	36	45	17
	4	16	13	19	2	47	8	81
	27	23	32	22	55	26	30	25

Weighted median is 22.

Processor	000	001	010	011	100	101	110	111
	27	23	24	35	63	36	62	28
			32	42	71	47	51	81
					55	26	45	25
							30	

Weighted median is 36.

Processor	000	001	010	011	100	101	110	111
	—	—	—	42	63	47	62	81
					71		51	
					55		45	

Figure 15.12 Deterministic selection

In step 1, local medians are found. These medians are circled in the figure. The sorted order of these medians is $6, 16, 18, 22, 25, 26, 45, 55$. Since at the beginning each processor has the same number of keys, the weighted median is the same as the regular median. A median M of these medians is 22. In step 3, the rank of M is determined as 21. Since $i > 21$, all the keys that are less than or equal to 22 are eliminated. We update i to $32 - 21 = 11$. This completes one run of the **while** loop.

In the second run of the **while** loop, there are 19 keys to begin with. The local medians are $27, 23, 24, 35, 63, 36, 45, 28$ with corresponding weights of $1, 1, 2, 2, 3, 3, 4, 3$, respectively. The sorted order of these medians is $23, 24, 27, 28, 35, 36, 45, 63$ with corresponding weights of $1, 2, 1, 3, 2, 3, 4, 3$, respectively. The weighted median M is 36. Its rank is 10. Thus all the keys that are less than or equal to 36 are eliminated. We update i to $11 - 10 = 1$, and this completes the second run of the **while** loop.

The rest of the computation proceeds similarly to finally output 42 as the answer. □

EXERCISES

1. Complete Example 15.9.

2. Present an efficient algorithm for finding the kth quantiles of any given sequence of n keys on $\mathcal{H}_d$. Consider the cases $n = p$ and $n > p$.

3. Given an array A of n elements, the problem is to find any element of A that is greater than or equal to the median. Present a simple Monte Carlo algorithm for this problem on $\mathcal{H}_d$. You cannot use the selection algorithm of this section. Your algorithm should run in time $O(d)$. Show that the output of your algorithm is correct with high probability. Assume that $p = n$.

15.5 MERGING

The problem of merging is to take two sorted sequences as input and produce a sorted sequence of all the elements. This problem was studied in Chapters 3, 10, 13, and 14. If the two sequences to be merged are of length m each, they can be merged in $O(\log m)$ time using a hypercube with $O(m^2)$ processors (applying the sparse enumeration sort). In this section we are interested in merging on a hypercube with only $2m$ processors (assuming that m is an integral power of 2). The technique employed is the odd-even merge.

15.5.1 Odd-Even Merge

Let $X_1 = k_0, k_1, \ldots, k_{m-1}$ and $X_2 = k_m, k_{m+1}, \ldots, k_{2m-1}$ be the two sorted sequences to be merged, where $2m = 2^d$. We show that there exists a normal butterfly algorithm that can merge X_1 and X_2 in $O(d)$ time.

We use a slightly different version of the odd-even merge. First we separate the odd and even parts of X_1 and X_2. Let them be O_1, E_1, O_2, and E_2. Then we recursively merge E_1 with O_2 to obtain $A = a_0, a_1, \ldots, a_{m-1}$. Also we recursively merge O_1 with E_2 to obtain $B = b_0, b_1, \ldots, b_{m-1}$. After this, A and B are shuffled to form $C = a_0, b_0, a_1, b_1, \ldots, a_{m-1}, b_{m-1}$. Now we compare a_i with b_i (for $0 \leq i \leq m-1$) and interchange them if they are out of order. The resultant sequence is in sorted order. The correctness of this algorithm can be established using the zero-one principle and is left as an exercise.

Example 15.10 Let $X_1 = 8, 12, 25, 31$ and $X_2 = 3, 5, 28, 46$. For this case, $O_1 = 12, 31$ and $E_1 = 8, 25$. $O_2 = 5, 46$ and $E_2 = 3, 28$. Merging E_1 with O_2

we get $A = 5, 8, 25, 46$. Similarly we get $B = 3, 12, 28, 31$. Shuffling A with B gives $C = 5, 3, 8, 12, 25, 28, 46, 31$. Next we interchange 5 and 3, and 46 and 31 to get $3, 5, 8, 12, 25, 28, 31, 46$. □

It turns out that the modified algorithm is very easy to implement on $\mathcal{B}_d$. For example, partitioning X_1 and X_2 into their odd and even parts can be easily done in one step on a $\mathcal{B}_d$. The shuffling operation can also be performed easily on a $\mathcal{B}_d$. On a $\mathcal{B}_d$, assume that both X_1 and X_2 are input in level d. Let X_1 be input in the first m rows (i.e., rows $0, 1, 2, \ldots, m-1$) and X_2 in the next m rows. The first step of the algorithm is to separate X_1 and X_2 into their odd and even parts. After this, we recursively merge E_1 with O_2, and O_1 with E_2. To do this, route the keys in the first m rows using direct links and route the other keys using cross links (see Figure 15.13).

After this routing we have E_1 and O_2 in the even subbutterfly and O_1 and E_2 in the odd subbutterfly. In particular, E_1 is in the first half of the rows of the even subbutterfly, O_2 is in the second half of the rows of the even subbutterfly, and so on (see Figure 15.13(a)). The parts E_1 and O_2 are recursively merged in the even subbutterfly. At the same time, O_1 and E_2 are recursively merged in the odd subbutterfly. Once the recursive calls are over, A will be ready in the even subbutterfly (at level $d-1$) and B will be ready in the odd subbutterfly (see Figure 15.13(b)). What remains to be done is a shuffle and a compare-exchange. They can be done as follows. Each processor at level $d-1$ sends its result along the cross link as well as the direct link. When the processor in row i at level d receives two data from above, it keeps the minimum of the two if i is even; otherwise it keeps the maximum. For example, the processor $\langle 0, d\rangle$ keeps the minimum of a_0 and b_0. The processor $\langle 1, d\rangle$ keeps the maximum of a_0 and b_0. And so on.

If $T(\ell)$ is the run time of the above algorithm on a butterfly of dimension ℓ, then the time needed to partition X_1 and X_2 is $O(1)$. The time taken to recursively merge E_1 with O_2 and O_1 with E_2 is $T(\ell - 1)$ since these mergings happen in the even and odd subbutterflies which are of dimension one less than ℓ. Once the recursive merges are ready, shuffling A and B and performing the compare-exchange operation also take a total of $O(1)$ time. So, $T(\ell)$ satisfies $T(\ell) = T(\ell - 1) + O(1)$, which solves to $T(\ell) = O(\ell)$.

There are two phases in the overall algorithm. In the first phase data flow from bottom to top and in the second phase data flow from top to bottom. In the first phase, when any data item progresses toward level zero, it enters subbutterflies of smaller and smaller dimensions. In particular, if it is in level ℓ, it is in a $\mathcal{B}_\ell$. In the $\mathcal{B}_\ell$ the datum is in, if it is in the first half of the rows, it takes the direct link; otherwise it takes the cross link. When all the data reach level zero, the first phase is complete. In the second phase, data flow from top to bottom one level at a time. When the data are at level ℓ, each processor at level ℓ sends its datum both along the direct link and along the cross link. In the next time step, processors in level $\ell + 1$ keep either the minimum or the maximum of the two items received from above

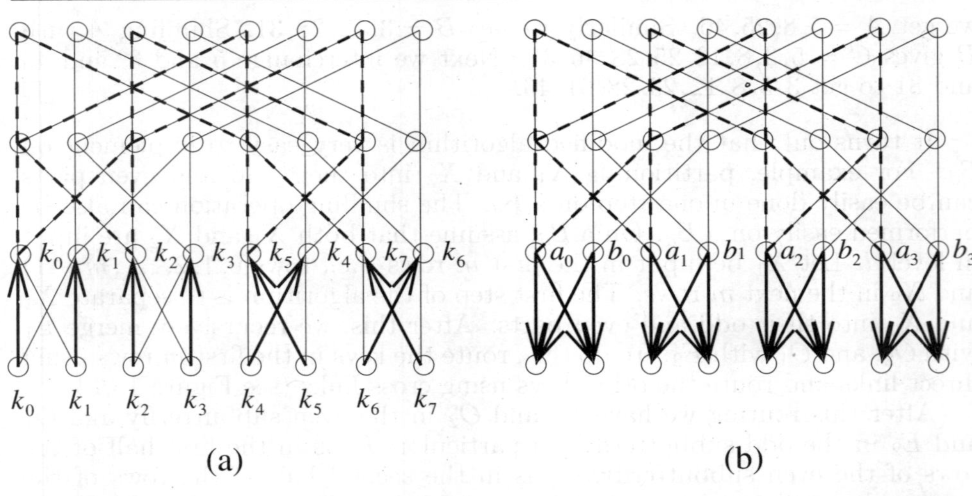

Figure 15.13 Odd-even merge on the butterfly

depending on whether the processor is in an even row or an odd row. When the data reach level d, the final result is computed. This also verifies that the algorithm takes only time $O(d)$ on any $\mathcal{B}_d$. Note also that this algorithm is indeed normal.

Theorem 15.6 Two sorted sequences of length m each can be merged on a $\mathcal{B}_d$ in $O(d)$ time, given that $2m = 2^d$. Using Lemma 15.2, merging can also be done on a sequential $\mathcal{H}_d$ in $O(d)$ time. □

15.5.2 Bitonic Merge

In Section 13.5, Exercise 2, the notion of a bitonic sequence was introduced. To recall, a sequence $K = k_0, k_1, \ldots, k_{n-1}$ is said to be *bitonic* either (1) if there is a $0 \leq j \leq n-1$ such that $k_0 \leq k_1 \leq \cdots \leq k_j \geq k_{j+1} \geq \cdots \geq k_{n-1}$ or (2) if a cyclic shift of K satisfies condition 1. If K is a bitonic sequence with n elements (for n even), let $a_i = \min\ \{k_i, k_{i+n/2}\}$ and $b_i = \max\ \{k_i, k_{i+n/2}\}$, $0 \leq i \leq n/2-1$. Also let $L(K) = a_0, a_1, \ldots, a_{n/2-1}$ and $H(K) = b_0, b_1, \ldots, b_{n/2-1}$. A bitonic sequence has the following properties (which you have already proved):

1. $L(K)$ and $H(K)$ are both bitonic.

2. Every element of $L(K)$ is smaller than any element of $H(K)$. In other

words, to sort K, it suffices to sort $L(K)$ and $H(K)$ separately and output one followed by the other.

Given two sorted sequences of m elements each, we can form a bitonic sequence out of them by following one by the other in reverse order. For example, if we have the sequences $5, 12, 16, 22$ and $6, 14, 18, 32$, the bitonic sequence $5, 12, 16, 22, 32, 18, 14, 6$ can be formed. If we have an algorithm that takes as input a bitonic sequence and sorts this sequence, then that algorithm can be used to merge two sorted sequences. The resultant algorithm is called *bitonic merge*.

We show how to sort a bitonic sequence on a butterfly using a normal algorithm. Let the bitonic sequence $X = k_0, k_1, \ldots, k_{n-1}$ with $n = 2^d$ be input at level zero of $\mathcal{B}_d$. We make use of the fact that if we remove all the zero level processors and incident links of a $\mathcal{B}_d$, then two copies of $\mathcal{B}_{d-1}$ result (see Figure 15.14). Call the subbutterfly with rows $0, 1, \ldots, 2^{d-1} - 1$ the *left subbutterfly* (shown with dotted thick lines in the figure) and the other subbutterfly the *right subbutterfly*.

In the first step, each level zero processor sends its key along the direct link and the cross link as shown in Figure 15.14. A level one processor, on receipt of two keys from above, keeps the minimum of the two if it is in the left subbutterfly. Otherwise it keeps the maximum. At the end of this step, the left subbutterfly has $L(K)$ and the right subbutterfly has $H(K)$. The $L(K)$ and $H(K)$ are recursively sorted in the left and right subbutterflies, respectively. Once the recursive calls are complete, the sorted sequence is at level d.

If $T(\ell)$ is the run time of this algorithm, we have $T(\ell) = T(\ell - 1) + O(1)$; that is, $T(\ell) = O(\ell)$.

Theorem 15.7 A bitonic sequence of length 2^d can be sorted on a $\mathcal{B}_d$ in $O(d)$ time. In accordance with Lemma 15.2, sorting can also be done on a sequential $\mathcal{H}_d$ in $O(d)$ time. □

EXERCISE

1. Prove the correctness of the modified version of odd-even merge using the zero-one principle.

15.6 SORTING

15.6.1 Odd-Even Merge Sort

The first algorithm is an implementation of the odd-even merge sort. If $X = k_0, k_1, \ldots, k_{n-1}$ is the given sequence of n keys, odd-even merge sort partitions X into two subsequences $X_1' = k_0, k_1, \ldots, k_{n/2-1}$ and $X_2' = k_{n/2}, k_{n/2+1},$

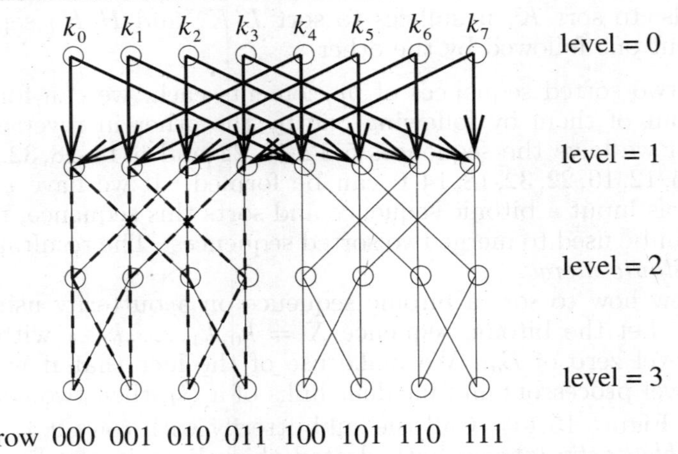

Figure 15.14 Bitonic merge on $\mathcal{B}_d$

$\ldots, k_{n-1}$ of equal length. The subsequences X_1' and X_2' are sorted recursively assigning $n/2$ processors to each. The two sorted subsequences (call them X_1 and X_2, respectively) are then finally merged using the odd-even merge algorithm.

Given 2^d keys on level d of $\mathcal{B}_d$ (one key per processor), we can partition them into two equal parts of which the first part is in rows $0, 1, \ldots, 2^{d-1} - 1$ and the second part is in the remaining rows. Sort each part recursively. Specifically, sort the first part using the left subbutterfly and at the same time sort the second part using the right subbutterfly. At the end of sorting, the sorted sequences appear in level d. Now merge them using the odd-even merge algorithm (Theorem 15.6).

If $S(\ell)$ is the time needed to sort on a $\mathcal{B}_\ell$ using the above divide-and-conquer algorithm, then we have

$$S(\ell) = S(\ell - 1) + O(\ell)$$

which solves to $S(\ell) = O(\ell^2)$.

Theorem 15.8 We can sort $p = 2^d$ elements in $O(d^2)$ time on a $\mathcal{B}_d$. As a consequence, the same can be done in $O(d^2)$ time on a sequential $\mathcal{H}_d$ as well (c.f. Lemma 15.2). □

15.6.2 Bitonic Sort

The idea of merge sort can also be applied in conjunction with the bitonic merge algorithm (Theorem 15.7). In this case, we have p numbers input at level zero of $\mathcal{B}_d$. We send the data to level $d-1$, so that the first half of the input is in the left subbutterfly and the next half is in the right subbutterfly. The left half of the input is sorted recursively using the left subbutterfly in increasing order. At the same time the right half of the input is sorted using the right subbutterfly in decreasing order. The sorted sequences are available at level $d-1$. They are now sent back to level d, so that at level d we have a bitonic sequence. This sequence is then sorted using the algorithm of Theorem 15.7.

Again, if $S(\ell)$ is the time needed to sort on a $\mathcal{B}_\ell$ using the above bitonic sort method, then we have

$$S(\ell) = S(\ell - 1) + O(\ell)$$

which solves to $S(\ell) = O(\ell^2)$.

Theorem 15.9 We can sort $p = 2^d$ elements in $O(d^2)$ time on a $\mathcal{B}_d$ using bitonic sort. As a result, applying Lemma 15.2, sorting can also be done in $O(d^2)$ time on a sequential $\mathcal{H}_d$ using bitonic sort. □

EXERCISES

1. Each processor of a sequential $\mathcal{H}_d$ is the origin of exactly one packet and each processor is the destination of exactly one packet. Present an $O(d^2)$ time $O(1)$-queue-sized deterministic algorithm for this routing problem.

2. Making use of the idea of Exercise 1, devise an $O(d^2)$ time $O(1)$-queue-length deterministic algorithm for the PPR problem.

3. You are given 2^d k-bit keys. Present an $O(kd)$ time algorithm to sort these keys on a $\mathcal{B}_d$.

4. Array A is an almost-sorted array of $p = 2^d$ elements. It is given that the position of each key is at most a distance q away from its final sorted position. How fast can you sort this sequence on the sequential $\mathcal{H}_d$ and the $\mathcal{B}_d$? Express the run time of your algorithm as a function of d and q. Prove the correctness of your algorithm using the zero-one principle.

15.7 GRAPH PROBLEMS

We use the general framework of Section 13.7 to solve graph problems such as transitive closure, connected components, and minimum spanning tree. We see how to implement Algorithm 13.15 on an n^3-processor hypercube so that its time complexity is $O(\log^2 n)$.

Let the elements of M be indexed as $M(i,j)$ for $0 \leq i,j \leq n-1$, as this will simplify the notation. Assume that $n = 2^\ell$ for some integer ℓ. We employ a $\mathcal{H}_{3\ell}$. Note that $H_{3\ell}$ has n^3 processors. Each processor of a $\mathcal{H}_{3\ell}$ can be labeled with a 3ℓ-bit binary number. View the label of any processor as a triple $\langle i,j,k\rangle$, where i is the first ℓ bits, j is the next ℓ bits, and k is the last ℓ bits.

Definition 15.6 On the hypercube $\mathcal{H}_{3\ell}$ let $(i,*,*)$ stand for all processors whose first ℓ bits equal the integer i, for $0 \leq i \leq 2^\ell - 1$. These processors form a $\mathcal{H}_{2\ell}$. Similarly define $(*,j,*)$ and $(*,*,k)$. Also define $(i,j,*)$ to be all the processors whose first ℓ bits equal i and whose second ℓ bits equal j. These processors form a $\mathcal{H}_\ell$. Similarly define $(i,*,k)$ and $(*,j,k)$. □

Theorem 15.10 Matrix $\widetilde{M}$ can be computed from an $n \times n$ matrix M in $O(\log^2 n)$ time using a $\mathcal{H}_{3\ell}$.

Proof: The proof parallels that of Theorem 14.12. In step 1, to update $q[i,j,k]$, the corresponding processor has to access both $m[i,j]$ and $m[j,k]$. Each processor can access $m[i,j]$ by broadcasting $m[i,j]$ in the subcube $(i,j,*)$. For processor $\langle i,j,k\rangle$ to get $m[j,k]$, transpose the matrix $m[\,]$ and store the transpose as $x[\,]$ in $(*,*,0)$. Now element $x[i,j]$ is broadcast in the subcube $(i,j,*)$. Broadcasting can be done in $O(\log n)$ time each. Transposing the matrix can also be completed in $O(\log n)$ time and the details are left as an exercise.

In step 2 of Algorithm 13.14, the updated value of $m[i,j]$ can be computed and stored in the processor $\langle i,0,j\rangle$ in $O(\log n)$ time using the prefix computation algorithm. The two broadcasts used in the mesh implementation to transfer the n^2 updated $m[\,]$ values to $(*,*,0)$ can be done in $O(\log n)$ time using the hypercube broadcast algorithm.

Thus each run of the **for** loop takes $O(\log n)$ time. So, the overall time of Algorithm 13.15 is $O(\log^2 n)$. □

The following theorems are implied as corollaries.

Theorem 15.11 The transitive closure matrix of an n-vertex directed graph can be computed in $O(\log^2 n)$ time on an n^3-processor hypercube. □

Theorem 15.12 The connected components of an n-vertex graph can be determined in $O(\log^2 n)$ time on an n^3-processor hypercube. □

All Pairs Shortest Paths

In Section 13.7.2, we noted that this problem can be solved by performing $\log n$ matrix multiplications. Two $n \times n$ matrices can be multiplied on an $\frac{n^3}{\log n}$-processor hypercube in $O(\log n)$ time (see Exercise 3), so we get this theorem.

Theorem 15.13 The all-pairs shortest paths problem can be solved in $O(\log^2 n)$ time on an $\frac{n^3}{\log n}$-processor hypercube.

EXERCISES

1. Show how to transpose an $n \times n$ matrix on an n^3-processor hypercube in $O(\log n)$ time. Assume that $n = 2^\ell$ for some integer ℓ.

2. Prove that two $n \times n$ matrices can be multiplied in $O(\log n)$ time on an n^3-processor hypercube. Assume that n is an integral power of two.

3. Show that two $n \times n$ matrices can be multiplied on an $\frac{n^3}{\log n}$-processor hypercube in $O(\log n)$ time.

4. Use the general paradigm of this section to design a hypercube algorithm for finding a minimum spanning tree of a given weighted graph. Analyze the time and processor bounds.

5. Present an efficient algorithm for topological sort on the hypercube.

6. Give an efficient hypercube algorithm to check whether a given undirected graph is acyclic. Analyze the processor and time bounds.

7. If G is any undirected graph, G^k is defined as follows: There will be a link between processors i and j in G^k if and only if there is a path of length k in G between i and j. Present an $O(\log n \log k)$ time n^3-processor hypercube algorithm to compute G^k from G. It is given that n is an integral power of two.

8. You are given a directed graph whose links have a weight of zero or one. Present an efficient minimum spanning tree algorithm for this special case on the hypercube.

9. Present an efficient hypercube implementation of the Bellman and Ford algorithm (see Section 5.4).

10. Show how to invert a triangular $n \times n$ matrix on an n^3-processor hypercube in $O(\log^2 n)$ time.

11. Present an $O(\log n)$ time algorithm for inverting an $n \times n$ tridiagonal matrix on an n^2-processor hypercube.

15.8 COMPUTING THE CONVEX HULL

Like the PRAM and mesh convex hull algorithms of Sections 13.8 and 14.8, the hypercube algorithm is based on the divide-and-conquer algorithm of Section 3.9.4. Assume that the n points are input on $\mathcal{H}_d$ (where $n = 2^d$) one point per processor. The final output is the clockwise sequence of points on the hull. We need to specify an indexing scheme for the processors. One possibility is to use the embedding of a ring on the hypercube; that is, the ordering among the processors is as specified by the embedding.

Referring to the preprocessing step of Algorithm 13.16, we can sort the N input points according to their x-coordinate values in $O(\log^2 N)$ time (Theorem 15.8). Let $q_0, q_1, \ldots, q_{N-1}$ be the sorted order of these points. In step 1, we partition the input into two equal parts with $q_0, q_1, \ldots, q_{N/2-1}$ in the first part and $q_{N/2}, q_{N/2+1}, \ldots, q_{N-1}$ in the second part. The first part is placed in the subcube (call it the first subcube) of processors that have zeros in their first bits. The second part is kept in the subcube (call it the second subcube) of processors that have ones in their first bits. In step 2, the upper hull of each half is recursively computed. Let H_1 and H_2 be the upper hulls. In step 3, we find the common tangent in $O(\log^2 N)$ time using the same procedures as used in the mesh implementation (see Lemmas 14.10 and 14.11). Let $\langle u, v\rangle$ be the common tangent. In step 4, all the points of H_1 that are to the right of u are dropped. Similarly, all the points of H_2 to the left of v are dropped. The remaining part of H_1, the common tangent, and the remaining part of H_2 is output.

If $T(\ell)$ is the run time of this recursive algorithm for the upper hull on an input of size 2^ℓ employing $\mathcal{H}_\ell$, then we have

$$T(\ell) \;=\; T(\ell-1) + O(\ell^2)$$

which solves to $T(\ell) = O(\ell^3)$.

We still have to indicate how to find the tangent $\langle u, v\rangle$ in $O(\log^2 N)$ time. The way to find the tangent is to start from the middle point, call it p, of H_1. Find the tangent of p with H_2. Let $\langle p, q\rangle$ be the tangent. Using $\langle p, q\rangle$, determine whether u is to the left of, equal to, or to the right of p in H_1. A binary search in this fashion on the points of H_1 reveals u. Use the same procedure to isolate v as well. Similar to Lemmas 14.10 and 14.11, the following lemmas can be proved.

Lemma 15.12 Let H_1 and H_2 be two upper hulls with at most N points each. If p is any point of H_1, its tangent with H_2 can be found in $O(\log N)$ time. □

Lemma 15.13 If H_1 and H_2 are two upper hulls with at most N points each, their common tangent can be computed in $O(\log^2 N)$ time. □

In summary, we have the following theorem.

Theorem 15.14 The convex hull of n points in the plane can be computed in $O(\log^3 n)$ time on a $\mathcal{H}_d$, where $n = 2^d$. □

EXERCISES

1. Prove Lemmas 15.12 and 15.13.
2. Present an $O(\log^3 n)$ time algorithm to compute the area of the convex hull of n given points in 2D on a $\mathcal{H}_d$ with $n = 2^d$.
3. Given a simple polygon and a point p, present an $O(\log n)$ time algorithm on a $\mathcal{H}_d$ (where $n = 2^d$) to check whether p is internal to the polygon.
4. Present an efficient algorithm to check whether any three of n given points are colinear. Use a hypercube with n processors. What is the time bound?

15.9 REFERENCES AND READINGS

For a comprehensive collection of hypercube algorithms see:

Introduction to Parallel Algorithms and Architectures: Arrays-Trees-Hypercubes, by Tom Leighton, Morgan-Kaufmann, 1992.

Handbook of Parallel Algorithms, by S. Rajasekaran and J. Reif (editors), Chapman-Hall/CRC, 2008.

Hypercube Algorithms with Applications to Image Processing and Pattern Recognition, by S. Ranka and S. Sahni, Springer-Verlag Bilkent University Lecture Series, 1990.

The randomized packet routing algorithm is due to "Universal schemes for parallel communication," by L. Valiant and G. Brebner, *Proceedings of the 13th Annual ACM Symposium on Theory of Computing*," 1981, pp. 263–277.

A more general sparse enumeration sort was given by D. Nassimi and S. Sahni. They showed that n keys can be sorted on an m-processor hypercube in time $O\left(\frac{\log n \log m}{\log(n/m)}\right)$. See "Parallel permutation and sorting algorithms and a new generalized connection network," *Journal of the ACM* 29, no. 3 (1982): 642–667.

The randomized selection algorithm can be found in "Randomized parallel selection." by S. Rajasekaran, *Proceedings of the Tenth Conference on Foundations of Software Technology and Theoretical Computer Science*, 1990, Springer-Verlag Lecture Notes in Computer Science 472, pp. 215–224.

The deterministic selection algorithm presented in this chapter is based on "Unifying themes for network selection," by S. Rajasekaran, W. Chen, and S. Yooseph, *Proceedings of the Fifth International Symposium on Algorithms and Computation*, August 1994.

For a comprehensive coverage of sorting and selection algorithms see "Sorting and selection on interconnection networks," by S. Rajasekaran, *DIMACS Series in Discrete Mathematics and Theoretical Computer Science* 21, 1995, pp. 275–296.

An $\widetilde{O}(\log n)$ time algorithm for sorting on an n-processor hypercube can be found in "A logarithmic time sort for linear size networks,' by J. H. Reif and L. Valiant in *Journal of the ACM* 34, no. 1 (1987): 60–76.

A fairly involved $O(\log n \log\log n)$ time deterministic sorting algorithm can be found in "Deterministic sorting in nearly logarithmic time on the hypercube and related computers," by R. Cypher and G. Plaxton, *Proceedings of the ACM Symposium on Theory of Computing*, 1990, pp. 193–203.

15.10 ADDITIONAL EXERCISES

1. Show how to compute the FFT (see Section 9.3) on an input vector of length 2^d in $O(d)$ time employing a $\mathcal{B}_d$.

2. Prove that two polynomials of degree 2^d can be multiplied in $O(d)$ time on a $\mathcal{B}_d$.

3. A d-dimensional *Cube Connected Cycles* network, or CCC, is a $\mathcal{H}_d$ in which each processor is replaced with a cycle of d processors (one for each dimension). A three-dimensional CCC is shown in Figure 15.15. There is a close connection between the CCC, butterfly, and hypercube networks. Compute the degree, diameter, and bisection width of a d-dimensional CCC.

4. Show how to perform prefix computations on a d-dimensional CCC (see Exercise 3) in $O(d)$ time. Assume that the 2^d data are given in the processors $(i, 1)$ $(0 \leq i \leq 2^d - 1)$.

5. Present an algorithm for sorting 2^d keys in $O(d^2)$ time on a d-dimensional CCC (see Exercise 3).

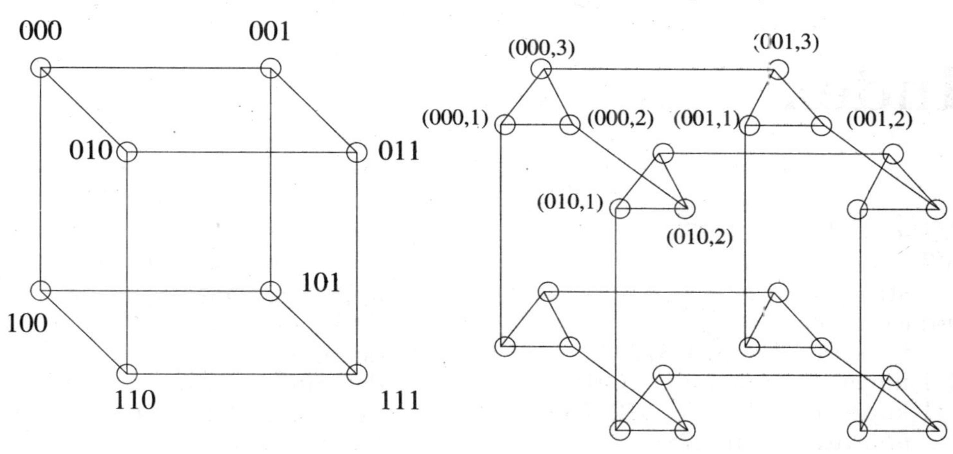

Figure 15.15 A 3D cube connected cycles network

6. The problem of *one-dimensional convolution* takes as input two arrays $I[0 : n-1]$ and $T[0 : m-1]$. The output is another array $C[0 : n-1]$, where $C[i] = \sum_{k=0}^{m-1} I[(i+k) \bmod n]T[k]$, for $0 \leq i < n$. Employ an n-processor hypercube to solve this problem. Assume that each processor has $O(m)$ local memory. What is the run time of your algorithm?

7. Solve Exercise 6 on an n-processor CCC (see Exercise 3).

8. The problem of *template matching* takes as input two matrices $I[0 : n-1, 0 : n-1]$ and $T[0 : m-1, 0 : m-1]$. The output is a matrix $C[0 : n-1, 0 : n-1]$, where

$$C[i,j] = \sum_{k=0}^{m-1} \sum_{l=0}^{m-1} I[(i+k) \bmod n, (j+l) \bmod n]T[k,l]$$

for $0 \leq i, j < n$. Present an n^2-processor hypercube algorithm for template matching. Assume that each processor has $O(m)$ memory. What is the time bound of your algorithm?

9. Solve Exercise 8 on an n^2-processor CCC (see Exercise 3).

Index